Contemporary
Literary Criticism

Guide to Gale Literary Criticism Series

For criticism on	Consult these Gale series
Authors now living or who died after December 31, 1959	*CONTEMPORARY LITERARY CRITICISM (CLC)*
Authors who died between 1900 and 1959	*TWENTIETH-CENTURY LITERARY CRITICISM (TCLC)*
Authors who died between 1800 and 1899	*NINETEENTH-CENTURY LITERATURE CRITICISM (NCLC)*
Authors who died between 1400 and 1799	*LITERATURE CRITICISM FROM 1400 TO 1800 (LC) SHAKESPEAREAN CRITICISM (SC)*
Authors who died before 1400	*CLASSICAL AND MEDIEVAL LITERATURE CRITICISM (CMLC)*
Black writers of the past two hundred years	*BLACK LITERATURE CRITICISM (BLC) AND BLACK LITERATURE CRITICISM SUPPLEMENT (BLCS)*
Authors of books for children and young adults	*CHILDREN'S LITERATURE REVIEW (CLR)*
Dramatists	*DRAMA CRITICISM (DC)*
Hispanic writers of the late nineteenth and twentieth centuries	*HISPANIC LITERATURE CRITICISM (HLC)*
Native North American writers and orators of the eighteenth, nineteenth, and twentieth centuries	*NATIVE NORTH AMERICAN LITERATURE (NNAL)*
Poets	*POETRY CRITICISM (PC)*
Short story writers	*SHORT STORY CRITICISM (SSC)*
Major authors from the Renaissance to the present	*WORLD LITERATURE CRITICISM, 1500 TO THE PRESENT (WLC)*
Major authors and works from the Bible to the present	*WORLD LITERATURE CRITICISM SUPPLEMENT (WLCS)*

ISSN 0091-3421

R

Volume 122

Contemporary Literary Criticism

Criticism of the Works
of Today's Novelists, Poets, Playwrights,
Short Story Writers, Scriptwriters, and
Other Creative Writers

Jeffrey W. Hunter
EDITOR

Justin Karr
Polly Vedder
Timothy J. White
ASSOCIATE EDITORS

Detroit
San Francisco
London
Boston
Woodbridge, CT

Library of Congress Catalog Card Number 76-46132
ISBN 0-7876-3197-3
ISSN 0091-3421

Printed in the United States of America
10 9 8 7 6 5 4 3 2 1

Contents

Preface vii

Acknowledgments xi

Preface

A Comprehensive Information Source
on Contemporary Literature

Named "one of the twenty-five most distinguished reference titles published during the past twenty-five years" by *Reference Quarterly,* the *Contemporary Literary Criticism (CLC)* series provides readers with critical commentary and general information on more than 2,000 authors now living or who died after December 31, 1959. Previous to the publication of the first volume of *CLC* in 1973, there was no ongoing digest monitoring scholarly and popular sources of critical opinion and explication of modern literature. *CLC,* therefore, has fulfilled an essential need, particularly since the complexity and variety of contemporary literature makes the function of criticism especially important to today's reader.

Scope of the Series

CLC presents significant passages from published criticism of works by creative writers. Since many of the authors covered by *CLC* inspire continual critical commentary, writers are often represented in more than one volume. There is, of course, no duplication of reprinted criticism.

Authors are selected for inclusion for a variety of reasons, among them the publication or dramatic production of a critically acclaimed new work, the reception of a major literary award, revival of interest in past writings, or the adaptation of a literary work to film or television.

Attention is also given to several other groups of writers—authors of considerable public interest—about whose work criticism is often difficult to locate. These include mystery and science fiction writers, literary and social critics, foreign writers, and authors who represent particular ethnic groups.

Format of the Book

Each *CLC* volume contains individual essays and reviews taken from hundreds of book review periodicals, general magazines, scholarly journals, monographs, and books. Entries include critical evaluations spanning from the beginning of an author's career to the most current commentary. Interviews, feature articles, and other published writings that offer insight into the author's works are also presented. Students, teachers, librarians, and researchers will find that the generous critical and biographical material in *CLC* provides them with vital information required to write a term paper, analyze a poem, or lead a book discussion group. In addition, complete bibliographical citations note the original source and all of the information necessary for a term paper footnote or bibliography.

Features

A *CLC* author entry consists of the following elements:

- The **Author Heading** cites the author's name in the form under which the author has most commonly published, followed by birth date, and death date when applicable. Uncertainty as to a birth or death date is indicated by a question mark.

- A **Portrait** of the author is included when available.

- A brief **Biographical and Critical Introduction** to the author and his or her work precedes the criticism. The first line of the introduction provides the author's full name, pseudonyms (if applicable), nationality, and a listing of genres in which the author has written. To provide users with easier access to information, the biographical and critical essay included in each author entry is divided into four categories: "Introduction," "Biographical Information," "Major Works," and "Critical Reception." The introductions to single-work entries—entries that focus on well known and frequently studied books, short stories, and poems—are similarly organized to quickly provide readers with information on the plot and major characters of the work being discussed, its major themes, and its critical reception. Previous volumes of *CLC* in which the author has been featured are also listed in the introduction.

- A list of **Principal Works** notes the most important writings by the author. When foreign-language works have been translated into English, the English-language version of the title follows in brackets.

- The **Criticism** represents various kinds of critical writing, ranging in form from the brief review to the scholarly exegesis. Essays are selected by the editors to reflect the spectrum of opinion about a specific work or about an author's literary career in general. The critical and biographical materials are presented chronologically, adding a useful perspective to the entry. All titles by the author featured in the entry are printed in boldface type, which enables the reader to easily identify the works being discussed. Publication information (such as publisher names and book prices) and parenthetical numerical references (such as footnotes or page and line references to specific editions of a work) have been deleted at the editor's discretion to provide smoother reading of the text.

- Critical essays are prefaced by **Explanatory Notes** as an additional aid to readers. These notes may provide several types of valuable information, including: the reputation of the critic, the importance of the work of criticism, the commentator's approach to the author's work, the purpose of the criticism, and changes in critical trends regarding the author.

- A complete **Bibliographical Citation** designed to help the user find the original essay or book precedes each critical piece.

- Whenever possible, a recent **Author Interview** accompanies each entry.

- A concise **Further Reading** section appears at the end of entries on authors for whom a significant amount of criticism exists in addition to the pieces reprinted in *CLC*. Each citation in this section is accompanied by a descriptive annotation describing the content of that article. Materials included in this section are grouped under various headings (e.g., Biography, Bibliography, Criticism, and Interviews) to aid users in their search for additional information. Cross-references to other useful sources published by The Gale Group in which the author has appeared are also included: *Authors in the News, Black Writers, Children's Literature Review, Contemporary Authors, Dictionary of Literary Biography, DISCovering Authors, Drama Criticism, Hispanic Literature Criticism, Hispanic Writers, Native North American Literature, Poetry Criticism, Something about the Author, Short Story Criticism, Contemporary Authors Autobiography Series,* and *Something about the Author Autobiography Series.*

Other Features

CLC also includes the following features:

■ An **Acknowledgments** section lists the copyright holders who have granted permission to reprint material in this volume of *CLC*. It does not, however, list every book or periodical reprinted or consulted during the preparation of the volume.

■ Each new volume of *CLC* includes a **Cumulative Topic Index,** which lists all literary topics treated in *CLC, NCLC, TCLC,* and *LC 1400-1800.*

■ A **Cumulative Author Index** lists all the authors who have appeared in the various literary criticism series published by The Gale Group, with cross-references to Gale's biographical and autobiographical series. A full listing of the series referenced there appears on the first page of the indexes of this volume. Readers will welcome this cumulated author index as a useful tool for locating an author within the various series. The index, which lists birth and death dates when available, will be particularly valuable for those authors who are identified with a certain period but whose death dates cause them to be placed in another, or for those authors whose careers span two periods. For example, Ernest Hemingway is found in *CLC,* yet F. Scott Fitzgerald, a writer often associated with him, is found in *Twentieth-Century Literary Criticism.*

■ A **Cumulative Nationality Index** alphabetically lists all authors featured in *CLC* by nationality, followed by numbers corresponding to the volumes in which the authors appear.

■ An alphabetical **Title Index** accompanies each volume of *CLC*. Listings are followed by the author's name and the corresponding page numbers where the titles are discussed. English translations of foreign titles and variations of titles are cross-referenced to the title under which a work was originally published. Titles of novels, novellas, dramas, films, record albums, and poetry, short story, and essay collections are printed in italics, while all individual poems, short stories, essays, and songs are printed in roman type within quotation marks; when published separately (e.g., T. S. Eliot's poem *The Waste Land),* the titles of long poems are printed in italics.

■ In response to numerous suggestions from librarians, Gale has also produced a **Special Paperbound Edition** of the *CLC* title index. This annual cumulation, which alphabetically lists all titles reviewed in the series, is available to all customers. Additional copies of the index are available upon request. Librarians and patrons will welcome this separate index: it saves shelf space, is easy to use, and is recyclable upon receipt of the next edition.

Citing *Contemporary Literary Criticism*

When writing papers, students who quote directly from any volume in the Literary Criticism Series may use the following general forms to footnote reprinted criticism. The first example pertains to material drawn from periodicals, the second to material reprinted in books:

[1]Alfred Cismaru, "Making the Best of It," *The New Republic,* 207, No. 24, (December 7, 1992), 30, 32; excerpted and reprinted in *Contemporary Literary Criticism,* Vol. 85, ed. Christopher Giroux (Detroit: Gale, 1995), pp. 73-4.

[2]Yvor Winters, *The Post-Symbolist Methods* (Allen Swallow, 1967); excerpted and reprinted in *Contemporary Literary Criticism,* Vol. 85, ed. Christopher Giroux (Detroit: Gale, 1995), pp. 223-26.

Suggestions Are Welcome

The editors hope that readers will find *CLC* a useful reference tool and welcome comments about the work. Send comments and suggestions to: Editors, *Contemporary Literary Criticism,* The Gale Group, 27500 Drake Rd., Farmington Hills, MI 48333-3535.

Acknowledgments

The editors wish to thank the copyright holders of the excerpted criticism included in this volume and the permissions managers of many book and magazine publishing companies for assisting us in securing reproduction rights. We are also grateful to the staffs of the Detroit Public Library, the Library of Congress, the University of Detroit Mercy Library, Wayne State University Purdy/Kresge Library Complex, and the University of Michigan Libraries for making their resources available to us. Following is a list of the copyright holders who have granted us permission to reproduce material in this volume of CLC. Every effort has been made to trace copyright, but if omissions have been made, please let us know.

COPYRIGHTED MATERIALS IN *CLC*, VOLUME 122, WERE REPRODUCED FROM THE FOLLOWING PERIODICALS:

African American Review, v. 26, Fall, 1992 for "Home: An Interview with John Edgar Wideman" by Jessica L. Lustig. Copyright © 1992 by the author. Reproduced by permission of the author.—*America*, v. 177, October, 1997. © 1997. All rights reserved. Reproduced with permission of America Press, Inc.,106 West 56th Street, New York, NY 10019.—*American Book Review*, v. 10, March-April, 1988. © 1988 by *The American Book Review*. Reproduced by permission.—*The Annals of the American Academy of Political and Social Science*, v. 476, November, 1984. Reproduced by permission.—*Armchair Detective*, v. 10, January, 1977; v. 19, Fall, 1986. Copyright © 1977, 1986 by *The Armchair Detective*. Both reproduced by permission.—*Belles Lettres*, v. 4, Fall, 1988; v. 4, Summer, 1989; v. 5, Spring, 1990; v. 7, Summer, 1992; v. 10, Spring, 1995. All reproduced by permission.—*Black American Literature Forum*, v. 20, Spring/Summer, 1986 for "The Shape of Memory in John Edgar Wideman's Sent for You Yesterday" by John Bennion. Copyright © 1986 by the author. Reproduced by permission of the publisher and the author.—*Book World--The Washington Post*, October, 1970 for "Tonto was an Uncle Tomahawk" by Cecil Eby; February, 1982 for a review of "Antarctic Traveller" by Joel Conarroe; August, 1992 for "Future Imperfect: Los Angeles 2052" by Wendy Smith; September, 1994 for "Defining the New Woman" by Maureen Corrigan; v. XXVI, February, 1996 for "Crazy in Manhattan" by Michael Parker; v. XXVI, September, 1996 for "Too Great a Sacrifice" by Paul West. © 1970, 1982, 1992, 1994, 1996 Washington Post Book World Service/Washington Post Writers Group. All reproduced by permission of the respective authors.—*Callaloo*, v. 8, Fall, 1985 for "'Beyond Discourse': The Unspoken Versus Words in the Fiction of John Edgar Wideman" by Jacqueline Berben. © 1985. Reproduced by permission of the author./ v.13, Winter, 1990. © 1990. Reproduced by permission of The Johns Hopkins University Press.—*Chicago Tribune Books*, March, 1991 for "A Girl's March away from Innocence" by Pinckney Benedict; March, 1992 for "Fay Weldon Delivers a Tale of Sexual Hijinks and Some Lively Stories" by Devon Jersild; August, 1992 for "Love finds a way in a sad, future L.A." by James Idema; March, 1994 for "Novelist Valerie Sayers' Feel for Life's Actual Daily Chaos" by Liz Rosenberg; June, 1997 for "Two Novels Look at Life in Northern Ireland" by Thomas McGonigle; July, 1997 for "Faith, Hope and Crisis" by Valerie Miner. © 1991, 1992, 1994, 1997 Tribune Media Services, Inc. All rights reserved. All reproduced by permission of the respective authors./ November, 1987. © 1987 Tribune Media Services, Inc. All rights reserved. Reproduced by permission of Knight Ridder/Tribune Information Services.—*Christian Science Monitor*, October, 1970. © 1970 The Christian Science Publishing Society. All rights reserved. Reproduced by permission from *The Christian Science Monitor*./ v. 86, October, 1994 for "Essays for Collecting and Dissecting" by Merle Rubin. © 1994 The Christian Science Publishing Society. All rights reserved. Reproduced by permission of the author.—*CLA Journal*, v. XXVII, March, 1985; v. XXXIII, March, 1990. Copyright, 1985, 1990 by The College Language Association. Both used by permission of The College Language Association.—*Clues: A Journal of Detection*, v. 3, Fall-Winter, 1982; v. 9, Fall-Winter, 1988. Copyright 1982, 1988 by Pat Browne. Both reproduced by permission.—*Commonweal*, v. CXXIII, June, 1996. Copyright © 1996 Commonweal Publishing Co., Inc. Reproduced by permission of Commonweal Foundation.—*Contemporary Literature*, v. XXXII, Fall, 1991. © 1991 by the Board of Regents of the University of Wisconsin. Reproduced by permission of The University of Wisconsin Press.—*Contemporary Sociology*, v. 16. March, 1987 for a review of American Indian Policy in the Twentieth Century, by Stephen Cornell. Copyright © 1987 American Sociological Association. Reproduced by permission of the publisher and the author.—*Critique*, v. XX, 1979; v. XXVII, Summer, 1987. Copyright © 1979, 1987 Helen Dwight Reid

Camilo José Cela

1916-

Spanish novelist, poet, dramatist, travel writer, and nonfiction writer.

The following entry presents an overview of Cela's career. For further information on his life and works, see *CLC*, Volumes 4, 13, and 59.

INTRODUCTION

Camilo José Cela is considered to be among the most important voices in Spanish letters since the Spanish Civil War. His work ranges from the psychological to the surreal, often mirroring the tragedy Spain has experienced with harsh realism and violence. Cela's prose style is experimental, frequently employing elements of fragmentation, repetition, and interior monologue within a shifting narrative perspective. Critics laud Cela's prose for its powerful characterization and effective dialogue.

Biographical Information

Cela was born on May 11, 1916, in Iria-Flavia in the province of Galicia, Spain. When he was 9, his family moved to Madrid where he attended various Catholic schools. In 1934, Cela began studying medicine, but he was diagnosed with tuberculosis and began an extended stay at a sanatorium during which he read extensively in Spanish literature. His illness initially prevented him from fighting in the Spanish Civil War, but in 1937 he was accepted into the Franco Nationalist army. He fought until he was wounded in 1938. Following the war, Cela held a variety of odd jobs, including movie actor, an apprentice bullfighter, and an advice columnist for a women's magazine. It was also during this time that Cela contributed to various fascist publications—and event which aroused suspicions about connections to the fascist party. In 1942, Cela published his first novel *La familia de Pascual Duarte* (*The Family of Pascual Duarte*, 1942). The novel upset General Francisco Franco's censors and helped quell some of the rumors concerning Cela's conservatism. Cela married in 1944 and had a son, Camilo, Jr., in 1946. He continued to write novels and several travel journals. In 1957, Cela was inducted into the Spanish Royal Academy, which he proceeded to offend by publishing *Diccionario secreto* (1968-70), a scholarly collection of obscene definitions left out of the Royal Academy's dictionary. In 1989, Cela won the Nobel Prize for literature.

Major Works

In Cela's first novel, *The Family of Pascual Duarte*, the title character, convicted of murder, composes his memoirs while awaiting his execution. A victim as well as a criminal, Pascual describes his squalid upbringing by an abusive, bitter mother whose other children turned to prostitution or proved mentally incompetent. Pascual also recounts his descent into violence, beginning with the death penalty for yet another homicide. Pascual refuses to blame society for his downfall and instead attributes his actions to fate and his own innate sinfulness. For *Pabellón de reposo* (*Rest Home;* 1943) Cela drew upon his own experience to examine the private anguish of tuberculosis patients confined to a sanatorium. Set in working-class Madrid immediately following World War II, *La colmena* (*The Hive;* 1951) chronicles three days in the lives of approximately 300 people who frequent a seedy café. *The Hive* has a highly experimental structure including techniques such as simultaneity of action, fragmentation, lack of chronological sequence, and a large number of characters. *Mrs. Caldwell habla con su hijo* (*Mrs. Caldwell Speaks to Her Son;* 1953) contains more than 200 short, unrelated chapters constructed around the rambling letters of an elderly Englishwoman to her dead son that reveal her incestuous love for him. In *San Camilo, 1936: Visperas, festividad y octava de San Camilo del ano 1936 en Madrid* (1969), Cela utilizes a stream-of-consciousness narrative style to examine the events leading up to the Spanish Civil War through the perspective of a young student. In addition to his novels, Cela also has written several travel sketches, including *Viaje a la Alcarria* (*Journey to Alcarria;* 1948), that recount his foot treks through Spain.

Critical Reception

Critics credit Cela with ushering in a new literary movement in Spain with *The Family of Pascual Duarte.* The movement, called "tremendismo," is characterized by an emphatic realism, the use of experimental techniques, and a new philosophical outlook. Some critics assert that tremendismo is not as much a literary movement as a trend. Other reviewers point out similarities between aspects of tremendismo and existentialism, but many dismiss it as a superficial connection. One of the overriding observations by critics is the tremendous pessimism in Cela's fiction. Robert Kirsner writes, "The course of Cela's writings has followed a determined path of misfortune, morbidity and mordacity." He further explains that "Cela's propensity toward the sordid and the shocking expresses a desire to experience all aspects of human existence." Some reviewers feel that Cela's writing declined throughout his career, and some complain that he did not deserve the Nobel Prize in 1989. Francis Donahue observes that "[o]ver the years, Cela's powers of novelistic invention have declined somewhat, but this has been offset by his growing mastery in the field of travel and local-color sketches." Cela's technical virtuosity, especially his unique approach to each project, is much discussed in criticism of his work. Sarah Kerr says, " . . . Cela, far from plagiarizing his own early success, has shown extraordinary technical resolve, creating a different shape and narrative technique and language for each project." Often, however, focus on the technical aspects of Cela's writing has prompted critics to neglect in-depth discussions concerning the themes of his novels. J. S. Bernstein asserts, "Too often, it seems to me, Cela's critics view him as an imperturbable virtuoso, a sort of literary prestidigitator whose remarkable successes are gained with no investment of self, and at little expenditure of talent and energy."

PRINCIPAL WORKS

La familia de Pascual Duarte [*The Family of Pascual Duarte*] (novel) 1942
Pabellón de reposo [*Rest Home*] (novel) 1943

Nuevas andanzas y desventuras de Lazarillo de Tormes (novel) 1944
Esas nubes que pasan (short stories) 1945
Viaje a la Alcarria [*Journey to Alcarria*] (travel essay) 1948
La colmena [*The Hive*] (novel) 1951
Mrs. Caldwell habla con su hijo [*Mrs. Caldwell Speaks to Her Son*] (novel) 1953
Historias de Venezuala: La catira (novel) 1955
Judios, moros y cristianos (travel essay) 1956
La cucana: memorias (memoirs) 1959; portion reprinted as *La rosa,* 1979
Gavilla de fabulas sin amor [illustrated by Pablo Picasso] (nonfiction) 1962
Izas, rabizas y colipoterras (short stories) 1964
Viaje al Pirineo de Lérida (travel essay) 1965
Diccionario secreto 2 vols. (nonfiction) 1968-70
San Camilo, 1936: Visperas, festividad y octava de San Camilo del ano 1936 en Madrid (novel) 1969
Oficio de tinieblas 5; o, novel de tesis escrita para ser cantada por un coro de enfermos (novel) 1973
Enciclopedia de erotismo (nonfiction) 1977
Cristo versus Arizona (novel) 1988

CRITICISM

Times Literary Supplement (review date 7 August 1953)

SOURCE: "The Hungry Present," in *Times Literary Supplement,* August 7, 1953, p. 505.

[*In the following review, the critic asserts, "As a social document* [The Hive] *is exceptional."*]

It is some indication of the remarkable quality of this novel [***The Hive***] by the most eminent young writer of General Franco's Spain that the most eminent refugee writer from the same Spain should have written 5,000 words introducing it to the British public: and it is some indication of the gulf which yawns between contemporary Madrid and contemporary London that every sentence of Señor Barea's introduction is needed to make this vivid, brutal and almost despairing work of art intelligible to a British reader.

Camilo José Cela fought for General Franco and holds a government position, which has made it possible for him to write this book apparently with impunity. His earlier novel, ***La familia de Pascual Duarte,*** even achieved publication in Spain. Señor Pío Baroja refused to write a prologue to it and advised him not to publish. "If you want them to put you in prison, go ahead." "I didn't go to prison,"

Señor Cela explained in the fourth edition to this novel which made him famous, "but the novel was withdrawn from circulation." *The Hive* has never been published in Spain, but on the dust-cover of the first—the Argentine—edition, Señor Cela himself explained his literary method and purpose:

> My novel *La Colmena,* the first book of the series *Caminos Inciertos* [*Uncertain Roads*], is nothing but a pale reflection, a humble shadow of the harsh, intimate, painful reality of every day. They lie who want to disguise life with the crazy mask of literature. The evil that corrodes the soul, the evil that has as many names as we choose to give it, cannot be fought with the poultices of conformism or the plasters of rhetorics and poetics. My novel sets out to be no more— yet no less either—than a slice of life presented without reticences, without external tragedies, without charity, exactly as life itself rambles on.

The slice of life is cut out of Madrid in the advancing winter of 1943, a segment filled mainly by Madrilenos of the middle class, their servants and their mistresses. Below this level of people haunted by the yearning for a cigarette, a solid meal, a cup of real coffee, there exists an even lower level, about whom the poet Martin Marco (with whom the author most closely identifies himself) at the conclusion declares: "These people are worse off than I am. It's appalling that such things can exist."

We are accustomed now to the literature of the concentration-camp, the prison recollections of those who have escaped the gas-chamber, the incredible bestiality and nobility of those living under the shadow of degrading death. *The Hive* is the only novel which sets out to depict that twilight world of a community living under open arrest, where no warders provide even the most inadequate meals, where the nagging enemy is hunger, not starvation, and the police State is corrupt and inefficient rather than ruthlessly oppressive. In such a country all is degraded to a level of meanness. The horrors of tyranny and the grandeurs of resistance are alike absent. The capital city is like a small parish, proliferating petty vices and indignities; a hive in which humanity is lost in a buzzing, useless busy-ness (except that the title may be said to be an insult to the bees).

As a social document this novel is exceptional. Throughout the reader is caught up, horrified, in war-time Madrid. No one who loved Spain and is curious to know how life proceeds behind the barrier of the Pyrenean censorship should fail to read it. At the same time, and in spite of the author's literary theories which confuse the reader with an enormous gallery of characters presented in very short passages, *The Hive* is a work of art of great power. The fragmentation of the narrative is as deliberate as the

fragmentation of Picasso's Woman of Guernica. Señor Cela's characters are not without souls; but the human spirit cannot flourish without food, warmth and a measure of security. The style of the novel reflects the agony of the artist, the traditionalist brought face to face with the horrors of a successful counter-revolution, yet still unconvinced of the righteousness of the cause against which he fought.

Pete Hamill (review date 10 January 1965)

SOURCE: "When the Castanets Stop Clicking," in *New York Herald Tribune Book Week,* January 10, 1965, pp. 3, 12.

[*In the following excerpt, Hamill complains that Cela's* Journey to the Alcarria *does not teach the reader anything about Spain or its author.*]

Ah, Spain. Her very name calls up the images: the swirl of skirts and hard white teeth and dark eyes of the women; the men with lined faces, quick eyes, calloused hands; all of them passing on dirt roads in the raw brown hills, with the tough masculine Sierras climbing away to the South Quaint trains, storks in the chimneys, mule carts and Hemingway. Those Spaniards are not like milk-veined Americans. They know about pride. They know about honor. They are not afraid to face up to death. They have bullfights there—not baseball. Bullfights. Only bullfighters live life all the way up.

In Spain, or at least, in this literary Spain, there is no sitting around drinking martinis in cocktail lounges with plastic-topped tables. Why, if you can't take your Fundador straight at a wooden table, you won't take it all. There are no gas stations in this Spain, nor deodorants, nor Wall Street Journals, nor PTAs, nor ranch houses with two-car garages, nor hamburgers, nor neon lights. Just clean, well-lighted places with grave waiters who know you are *simpatico* and call you Don. *Que tal, Don Ernesto? Que tal, hombre, que tal.* The only problem is the tourists. They're lousing up the country.

It is not Spain's fault, of course, that she has inspired some of the most arrant nonsense ever to reach the printed page. But somehow, this has always been true. Writers disintegrate before her; their prose smothers under a kind of purple rhetorical gas, made of one part naivete, and one part dishonesty. Setting off to write A Book on Spain, they make the country an article of belief; and believing in belief, they believe in nothing else. If they are like Robert Ruark, they make even the hated *Guardia Civil* into charming, polite human beings; if they are great writers like Hemingway, they turn out silly self-parodies like *The Dangerous Sum-*

mer, or chant their way through self-indulgent elegies like the last chapter of *Death in the Afternoon.* A moratorium on Books on Spain would probably advance the English language 25 years.

But the books continue to roll off the printing presses. Some are guide books, some are impressionistic love letters, some are fuzzy political tracts. Of these four books on Spain, all contain the best and the worst of the genre.

Strangely, the least satisfying is written by Spain's best novelist, Camilo Jose Cela (who also edits *Papeles de Son Armadans,* the most distinguished literary magazine in that censor-ridden country). Essentially a notebook based on a trip by foot through the country northeast of Madrid, Cela's book has none of the ferocious anger or bitter clarity of purpose that marked his novels, such as **The Hive** or **The Family of Pascual Duarte.** Instead, he has given us a neat bonbon of a book, reminding one in most ways of the lacy calligraphy on cigar boxes. The calligraphy is rather nice, but it does, after all, adorn a cigar box.

"The traveler," Cela writers early in the book," is full of good intentions; he intends to lay open the heart of the wayfarer, to look into the souls of other travelers, peering into their eyes as one peers over the edge of a well. He has a good memory, and he wants to rid himself of every evil thought as he leaves the city."

What follows, in careful, precise prose, is a kind of Spanish *Travels With Charley.* No hearts are laid open, no souls penetrated. Instead, we discover that once one leaves the evil city, and embraces the wide open spaces, there are no bad people in Spain. One meets, over and over again, the same people; helpful honest women washing clothes, charming children, an occasional idiot (who is of course anointed by God), and wise old men in berets. At the conclusion of the book we have learned no more about Spain, or Camelo Jose Cela, than we knew when we opened it, and we haven't been entertained much either.

Raymond Carr (review date 25 November 1965)

SOURCE: "The Spanish Tragedy," in *New York Review of Books,* Vol. V, No. 8, November 25, 1965, pp. 23-25.

[*In the following review, Carr describes Spain in the aftermath of the Spanish Civil War, as seen in Gabriel Jackson's* The Spanish Republic and the Civil War 1931-1939 *and Cela's* Journey to the Alcarria.]

The Spanish Civil War ended in 1939 and for a period Europe was engulfed in a larger tragedy. In retrospect the Spanish Civil War seemed what one of the Republican Ministers once called it—a paupers' war. The exiles, like the issues, were forgotten. They were embarrassing relics.

Why should the Spanish Civil War now compel an interest which goes beyond the usual curious concern for the past? Perhaps because of the symbolic overtones that gives Spanish history in general resonance and significance, making it a perpetual demonstration of the truth of Croce's dictum that all history is contemporary history. The continuing—and still bitter—controversy that rages around Las Cases and his "docile Indians" has a relevance beyond the history of the Spanish Colonial Empire; it was the first debate on the relationships between the developed West and the under-developed world. In the 1830s it seemed that the great European battle between liberal principles and reactionary government was being fought out in the mountains of Navarre and Aragon. Journalists, idealists and soldiers of fortune came to Spain. A hundred years later, in 1936, they came once more; once more Spain seemed part of a universal struggle between the ideologies that divided the Western World: Fascism and Democracy.

The price of symbolic significance and international resonance is distortion. The history of the Second Republic, its collapse and its defeat at the hands of Franco, were seen as an international occasion rather than as a domestic tragedy. No one would deny that the course of the Civil War became involved in, and its issue in a large measure dependent on, international power politics. Yet in its origins it was a Spanish affair, the outcome of secular stresses and the immediate tensions of domestic politics. As Mr. Jackson says, psychologically speaking, Spaniards felt, until the Spring of 1937, "that their fate was being resolved primarily by Spanish forces." It was only visiting intellectuals or professional propagandists who thought it was all a result of international plots.

The generals acted, not as agents of international Fascism, but in Spanish style, throwbacks to the era of *pronunciamientos.* They could not be certain of large-scale German and Italian support; indeed they did not think that they would need it. They did not contemplate a Crusade; they gambled on a nineteenth-century military takeover. Italy did not see that support of Franco in a long war would nearly destroy the Italian military machine; Ciano wanted, like Hitler, a useful ally on the cheap. A long war frayed tempers in the Nationalist camp. Germans considered Franco an old-fashioned clerical, a "slow" general unaware of the importance of tanks; Mussolini had doubts about the virility of the Spanish and the Spaniards doubted the utility of Italian ground troops.

The Second Republic committed many errors—a weak agrarian reform coupled with old-fashioned anti-clerical-ism; Mr. Jackson rightly calls their closing of church schools "a self-defeating sectarian policy." It rallied the right without strengthening the left. As a democratic concern, it fell because men of the left and of the right refused to accept the implications of democracy: the extreme left in 1934, the extreme right and the Anarchists throughout, and the more cautious army officers and middle classes after the victory of the Popular Front in February, 1936.

The men of moderation found the ground they sought to stand on eroded. This was the fate of Gil Robles and his political tight-rope walking and of the "bourgeois" socialist Prieto. Though I would place a heavier responsibility on the Socialist boycott of C.E.D.A. than does Mr. Jackson (the files of *El Debate* are as revealing as those of *El Socialista*), his account, here as everywhere else, is fair. He is perhaps correct in his view that Salazar Alonso, as Minister of the Interior in the Spring of 1934, made democracy difficult by regarding strikes, not as economic conflicts, but as steps in the Marxist-Leninist or Anarchist revolution. The Minister's view was perhaps not without some justification. More important, if Salazar Alonso saw the strikers as revolutionaries, they saw him as an exponent of Fascism. Neither position was true; yet as a result of such thinking, by the summer of 1936, the number of those who supported "humanist socialism" and democratic processes as conceived in 1931 was diminishing rapidly. The militants were taking over from the moderates; the forces of political life had become polarized at the extremes.

Why did the Republic lose the Civil War? The failure of the West to supply arms was no doubt decisive; Munich destroyed the last of a never very real hope. Yet would the Republic have triumphed had the domestic balance of forces been allowed to take their course? After all, the elections had already shown Spain split into two roughly equal camps.

Politically the problem of the Republic was to concentrate in an effective war government the spontaneous social revolution and the euphoria of July, 1936—the era so familiar in the photographs of militia men, marked trucks, and clenched fists. This task it achieved by taking the "Bohemian revolution" into the government with Largo Caballero's ministry. Even the Anarchist C.N.T., after denouncing all government as a bourgeois trick, jettisoned its principles and joined the Ministry because the leaders saw ("with tears" as Frederica Montseny once said) that there was no alternative. Yet by May 1937 political infighting and communist tactics had destroyed the revolutionary coalition. The Republican government lost its all-embracing cohesion; on the other side built-in loyalties and the army imposed unity on Nationalist dissidents. A feuding government was fighting a political monolith.

Nor did the Republic solve its military problem. The militias, through which the African Army had cut like a knife through butter until halted at Madrid, must be "militarized." The disorganized enthusiasm of the militia, presented as a great upsurge of the human spirit, was a nightmare to those planning a war with scarce resources. Yet, on a long and struggling front, the planning of the Republican general staff astonishingly enough twice achieved the strategical initiative: at Teruel and the Ebro. But, without fully trained armies, it proved one thing to break a weakly held front, another to follow up the breakthrough. All Republican offensives degenerated into a stubborn defense of two or three-day gains. This made Franco the Haig of the Civil War: the enemy could be bled to death.

Let me repeat that the arms issue was decisive: it was not so much that the Germans and Italians gave more, as that they gave continuously, while the Russians gave fitfully and in the end could, or would, give nothing at all. France and England failed altogether. My contention is only that the Republic failed to subordinate political intrigue to military necessity. One has only to read General Rojo's account of conditions on the Catalan front in order to realize how far the rot had gone.

Mr. Jackson's account of these events is altogether excellent [in his *The Spanish Republic and the Civil War 1931-1939*]. His book has balance and humanity. It paints fully in depth issues that have been hitherto brushed but lightly: the Republic's economic and financial policies; what he calls the "limits on suffering and destruction" in the war itself. It is a highly readable book which is at the same time a scholarly description of a great and grim historic tragedy.

The Spain that came out of this terrible conflict was a nineteenth-century concern: economic autarchy (in part enforced by the European war, in part a deliberate choice) was supported by intellectual isolation. In the Forties the world of Ferdinand and Isabella seemed more relevant than the world of modern totalitarianism. It was in this archaic ambiance that Camilo José Cela became a writer; no one will forget the shock in 1942 of his ***Pascual Duarte*** in a world so soaked in the banalities of official propaganda that creativity seemed inconceivable within it.

Journey to the Alcarria, written in 1948, describes Cela's travels on foot through a harsh countryside a few hours from Madrid: a region of poverty, bad roads, and small towns. A moral autobiography and a travel book at the same time, it veers from the picaresque to a Butor-like realism, from the style of a superior Baedeker to that of the poets of '98, from symbolism to flat topographical description reminiscent of the more prosaic eighteenth-century travelers.

The moral vision is there in the description of children and beggars, in the vignettes of violence: the rachitic boy, pinned to his chair, observing a verse-peddler "with an expression of envy, stupid and animal-like"; the bleeding idiot abused by a passing woman. Parallel to this generalized concern runs that search into the nature of Spain and Spanishness which obsesses and has perhaps rendered sterile so many Spanish writers. In Pastrana, the ruined palace of the Princess of Eboli, one room used by the Wheat Board and with its tiles in the process of destruction by peasants waiting to present their crop declarations, the dusty conventional museum with its collection of Philippine fauna, show an indifference to improvement and supply a "key to something that happens in Spain more frequently than is necessary." Past splendor overwhelms and in the end exhausts the peoples' will; golden memories retreat until they become a "benevolent and useless cultural residue."

The impact made by *Journey to Alcarria* on this reviewer is a curious contrast to the stronger impression made when it appeared in 1948. This is no fault of the translation, which is excellent. Images perhaps have become tarnished, its attitudes almost traditional, and the melancholy a little out of date. Thus according to the *Guide Bleu* the tapestries, whose absence in Madrid inspires a paragraph on the inhuman anti-order of great city museums, are back in Pastrana. But seven years after the Civil War, for the intelligent man, melancholy was the only retreat in a Spain that seemed hopelessly run-down.

Even so, *Journey to Alcarria* still exercises the magic of talented travel writing: one's next trip to Spain will include the Alcarria. In the modern age of car tourism such is the penalty inflicted on unspoilt regions by their poets.

Francis Donahue (essay date Autumn 1966)

SOURCE: "Cela and Spanish 'Tremendismo,'" in *Western Humanities Review*, Vol. XX, No. 4, Autumn, 1966, pp. 301-06.

[*In the following essay, Donahue describes how Cela's* The Family of Pascual Duarte *ushered in the Spanish literary movement "tremendismo."*]

In 1942 when twenty-six-year-old Camilo José Cela published a first novel in Madrid, *The Family of Pascual Duarte,* Spanish literature, strait-jacketed by the Civil War and its aftermath, began to take shape again.

Before *Pascual Duarte,* the literary shades had been tightly drawn in Spain. Readers were turning to the past—

to Benito Pérez Galdós' social realism of the nineteenth century, and to the works of the "Generation of 1898," keyed to an attempt to inventory Spain's values and defects, and to present impressionistically the country's inner essence. What new works did appear, between the end of the Civil War (1939) and 1942, were tentative, groping attempts at expression under the guns of a military dictatorship.

While *Pascual Duarte* did not tread on military toes, it did strike out boldly toward a new literary dimension for Spaniards. It was not an epic account of the Civil War. Nor was it a novel extolling the new regime. It was a taut, truculent novel which aspired to capture an emerging sensibility of post-war Spain.

The book was avidly read and debated. Although banned for a time, it soon ran through several Spanish editions. Translations followed—to Italian, Swedish, Dutch, German, Danish and English.

Within a short time, *Pascual Duarte* moved from the category of a controversial work by a practically unknown writer to a classic novel assuring Cela a permanent position among the titans of twentieth century Spanish literature.

Cela's novel, the supposed autobiography of a criminal awaiting execution, is filled with violence, cruelty, murder, even matricide. Pervading the work is a mood of anguish, carefully reined by the agent of these crimes, who seems driven to act as he does because of the harsh environment and his own violent nature. The crimes are carried out with a sense of compulsion yet without a sense of guilt. In the process, the protagonist is not hardened; he remains almost guileless.

The novel is, then, an account of man in his tragic human situation, set down in vernacular, unsentimental prose. Not sympathy but compassionate understanding—that is what the novel elicits.

Pascual Duarte taps roots deep in the national literary past. It recalls the picaresque tradition, a Spanish specialty dating back to *Lazarillo de Tormes* (1554) and running through Spanish letters ever since. Once again, a rogue anti-hero had appeared to lay bare the social sores of a Spanish society whose values were seriously out of joint.

The novel also reveals a typically Spanish fondness for grotesque deformation of reality, and a curious affection for the monstrous. A predilection for deformation and for the monstrous dates back to the super realistic writings of the sixteenth and seventeenth centuries. Spanish painting also bears witness to this spirit: Velázquez with his dwarfs and beggars, Goya and his "Caprichos," and many modern canvases of Picasso.

Growing out of this concern for deformation is Cela's brand of humor, latched to the grimmest aspects of life. With his cold and sardonic strain, Cela bizarrely lights up the grotesque unreality of his real characters.

At his best, Cela reveals a gift for repelling and attracting his reader at the same time. Instinctively, he knows how to evoke horror, passing often to a type of black humor, touching off a sudden unwanted laugh, one quickly shut off. When Pascual Duarte is in the act of stabbing one of his victims, the reader finds himself unwillingly breaking into a quick, sickening smile. Somehow, it recalls children laughing just at the moment that puppets kill one another in a Punch-and-Judy show. The reader, upon reflection, realizes that Cela has forced him to laugh, if only for a moment, at the lacerating fate of human beings, as if they were only puppets.

Yet the singularity of **Pascual Duarte** is not to be found in the grim humor nor in the carefully-wrought technique which allows Cela to relate the most extraordinary events with deceptive simplicity. It lies in the fact that Pascual is a good person whose tragedy is that he has no recourse but to be, time and again, a criminal. Under other circumstances, he could have been the most respected man in his village. It takes the reader some time to realize that Pascual is a better person than his victims, and that his criminal forays constitute a type of abstract, barbarous but undeniable justice, that of man-as-judge-and-enforcer of his own edicts on relatives and enemies alike.

Cela, in striving for absolute objectivity, tells us that the editor of the book is merely its "transcriber." The latter, after finding the manuscript in a store, spent long hours putting the pages in order. With that, "transcriber" Cela allows Pascual Duarte to unfold his story in his own words.

From the Death House, Pascual is jotting down his "black thoughts"—memories from the past—not necessarily in the order in which they occurred. His early life, as he recalls it, is of a piece with the picaresque. His father, a domineering alcoholic Portuguese, used to beat his mother with a belt. His illiterate mother was partial to her wine, often hidden under the bed. Pascual couldn't remember if she ever took a bath. When the inevitable storm broke at home, Pascual left his parents to their private warfare. He had learned that "the only way not to get wet is to stay out of the rain." His sister, toward who he had ambivalent feelings, was a prostitute practically from puberty.

Pascual's memories cluster around deaths in his family. When his father was bitten by a mad dog, he was locked up in a room for two days. After his agonizing screams died out, Pascual went in to find his father stretched out on the floor, eyes wildly open, his purpled tongue hanging ajar.

Pascual's younger brother Mario, an idiot child who never learned to walk or talk, had his ear almost chewed off by a pig. Later he was found floating dead in an oil vat:

> He was caught in the posture of a thieving owl tipped over by a gust of wind, turned up head over heels down into the vat, his nose stuck in the muck at the bottom. When we lifted him out, a thin trickle of oil poured from his mouth, like a gold thread being unwound from a spool in his belly. . . .
>
> We had to dry the little fellow off with strips of lint so · that he shouldn't appear all greasy and oily at the Last Judgment. . . .
>
> My mother didn't shed a tear over the death of her son . . . a woman who doesn't weep is like a fountain that doesn't flow, worthless.

Pascual's own son, although watched over with religious vigilance—to protect him against the hogs and the fevers—succumbed to pneumonia before he was eleven months old.

Now, Pascual recalls that his wife had once said, "Blood seems a kind of fertilizer in your life." It was true—he had often acted out of blood revenge. When a dog looked at him fixedly, Pascual killed the animal in a rage. When his wife Lola was thrown by a mare, suffering a miscarriage, Pascual had stabbed the mare to death.

After he learned that Lola had been violated by a procurer, with the connivance of his own mother, Pascual passed personal sentence on the attacker. At first he agreed not to kill the man, for Lola had begged him not to. Yet when the procurer, hearing of Lola's request, exulted, "So, she still loved me?" Pascual lost control. He stomped savagely on the procurer's chest. "The flesh of his chest made the same sound as a piece of meat on a spit." Blood flowed. The death sentence was consummated.

Finally, Pascual felt compelled to do away with his own mother, whom he hated for her connivance, ignorance, meddling and sluttishness. "There is no deeper hatred," he said, "than hatred for one's own blood." Late at night, he took knife in hand and moved into her room, hovering over the bed:

> I had to strike with my eyes wide open, all five senses alert. And I had to keep calm, and regain the self-control that seemed to be leaving me now at the sight of my mother's body. . . . After all, she was my mother,

the woman who had borne me . . . she didn't do me any favor, no favor at all, bringing me into this world. . . .

My mother shifted in her bed. . . . I threw myself upon her and held her down. She shrieked like a woman in Hell. It was the most awful struggle you can imagine. We roared like wild beasts. We frothed at the mouth . . . My clothes were torn, my chest bare. The damned witch was stronger than a devil. . . . She hit me and bit me. Suddenly her mouth found my nipple, my left nipple, and tore it away. That was the moment I sank the blade into her throat.

Her blood spurted all over my face. It was warm as a soft belly and tasted like the blood of a lamb. . . . I dropped her and ran, without stopping for a long time. . . . The countryside was fresh-smelling, cool, and a sensation of great peace welled in my veins.

I could breathe. . . .

In reflecting now and then on his confessions, Pascual lets the reader catch occasional gleanings of his psychological bleeding. Perhaps the closest he comes to direct statement is when he writes:

There is such a bitter taste in my throat that I think my heart must pump bile instead of blood. It mounts in my chest and leaves behind an acid taste under my tongue. It floods my mouth, but dries me up inside, as if it were a foul wind from a cemetery niche. . . .

I'm very near to crying. A self-respecting man cannot let himself be overcome by tears, as if he were a simple woman.

As the day of execution neared, Pascual stopped writing and sent off his memories to a friend. At this point, the "transcriber" intervenes to explain that he had learned of Pascual's last days in prison from letters written by a priest and a former prison official. After a period of resignation, Pascual broke down, spitting and stamping and struggling to hold onto life for a precious few minutes more. "When the depths of his soul were probed," writes the priest, "he was more like a poor tame lamb, terrified and cornered by life."

This seems to sum up Cela's own evaluation of his character.

Pascual Duarte ushered in the major Spanish literary movement of the post-Civil War period—"tremendismo." The term gained currency when a critic used the word "tremendo" (tremendous, dreadful) more than once to describe the effect caused by the novel.

"Tremendismo" has affected most Spanish writers of the post-1942 era, though not all follow its guidelines. Critics generally do not attribute to "tremendismo" the status of a literary generation as understood in German scholarship. They usually term the movement a trend, a tendency or a literary norm. Critics agree, however, that "tremendismo" has significantly shaped contemporary Spanish writing.

On close analysis, "tremendismo" seems to embrace three major ingredients: emphatic realism, experimental literary techniques, and a new philosophical orientation in the novel.

Emphatic realism is an attempt at securing an objective portrayal of life, mainly in its bitter, violent, negative, anguish-producing aspects. It is the natural outgrowth of a period of civil war, followed by great human dislocation, disillusion, fear and guilt, and the psychological gnawing of the memory of scenes of great brutality. "Many of those who are writing novels were only children during the Civil War," explains novelist Juan Goytisolo. "With the eyes of children they saw, calmly, atrocious things. They forgot them. But there was a moment in their lives, as they grew up, in which they suddenly remembered them again. And they remembered them more and more, as their bones grew harder and their blood richer."

From Joyce, Proust, Dos Passos, Camus and others, Cela and his fellow "tremendistas" adapted such experimental techniques as the concern for introspection, the interior monologue, the flashback, the concentration of the time element, and the scenario approach. The latter technique causes the writer to emphasize mental states and mood, and to devote less attention to physical locals or details.

The new philosophical orientation in these novels, while not clearly expressed, is related to existentialism. Critics differ on whether this orientation is derived from French literary existentialism. But this much is clear: twentieth century Spanish intellectuals were nurtured on the works of two early modern existentialists, Spaniards Miguel de Unamuno and José Ortega y Gasset. Unamuno stressed "The Tragic Sense of Life," the title of his most famous book, while Ortega emphasized his philosophical position that "I am myself and my circumstances."

"Tremendista" novels, while less philosophical and intellectual than French existentialist works, spotlight man in relation to specific circumstances or situations. And it is this metaphysical sensibility of the characters, reflecting the modern sense of anguish, which brings "tremendismo" into the mainstream of recent European literature.

Since setting the mold for "tremendismo," Camilo José

Cela has produced an appreciable body of work: novels, short stories and travel sketches.

In *The Hive* (1951), his second-best novel—some consider it his best—Cela charts the misdirected lives of more than 160 characters who inhabit Madrid's human beehive in 1942. Here are the procurers, waiters, prostitutes, chiselers, hangers-on, owners of shoddy businesses, the homosexuals and the mental defectives, all of whom pass through Doña Rosa's sleazy café. They are followed out of the café and into their personal lives, which often interact.

Somehow, the impression left is that of the author picking up handfuls of little ants, letting them run around meanly in his hand, while he observes them naked to the world, and then thrusting them back into their sordid habitats.

The book is in the tradition of the panoramic or Unanimiste novel, resembling somewhat John Dos Passos' *Manhattan Transfer.* It lacks a story-line. It offers only a steady parade of characters, no heroes or heroines. Sex and hunger are the driving passions. The tone is objective—and cynical. The time span is limited to three days.

The relentless accumulation of half-lives sketched against the background of the café or the brothel, the clawing for survival, and the lack of any moral sense—all flesh out this sprawling mural of a decadent section of Madrid. (This may explain why Cela chose to publish his novel outside of Spain—in Buenos Aires in 1951.)

The Hive, in the opinion of its author, is "but a pale reflection, a humble shadow of the harsh, intimate, painful reality of everyday life . . . my novel sets out to be no more—yet no less either—than a slice of life told step by step, without reticence, without external tragedies, without charity, exactly as life itself rambles on."

It is in this novel that Cela's style is seen at its sinewy best. It is, as critic Arturo Torres-Ríoseco has observed, "rich, abundant in slang, full of popular flavor, crude, vulgar, profane, but with a masculine charm, with that typically Spanish bravado called 'machismo.' I believe that from the time of Cervantes nobody has surpassed Cela in the mastery of the vernacular, in the unusual capacity for the linguistically grotesque, in the use of the picaresque expression, the savory adjective, and the humor with which he adorns his baroque descriptions."

Besides Cela, Spain has produced a number of other fine novelists in recent years, many of whom reflect the influence of "tremendismo," as well as the Civil War and its continuing impact on contemporary Spain. Standing today in the forefront of what some critics consider a renaissance in the novel are Carmen Laforet, Ignacio Aldecoa, Ana María Matute and Juan Goytisolo. Yet, thanks to *Pascual Duarte* and *The Hive,* Cela remains the finest living Spanish novelist. Since he is only 50, and continues to publish regularly, it may well be that his true masterpiece is, as the Spanish put it, "still in the inkwell."

David William Foster (essay date 1967)

SOURCE: "Social Criticism, Existentialism, and *Tremendismo* in Cela's *La familia de Pascual Duarte,*" in *Kentucky Foreign Language Quarterly,* Vol. XIII, 1967, pp. 25-33.

[*In the following essay, Foster provides an analysis of Cela's* La familia de Pascual Duarte *and its relationship to social criticism, existentialism, and tremendismo.*]

La familia de Pascual Duarte shocked the sensibilities of the Spanish reading public when it was published in the early '40's. Somehow, despite the cruel experiences of their Civil War, his countrymen were not prepared to receive graciously the repentant confessions of a man whose story relates in turn the killing of his hunting dog, the killing of his mare, the murder of the lover of his wife and sister, the murder of his wife, to culminate in the bloody scene of son murdering mother—all presented in a tone of meek apology and transmitted to us through a novelistic format which shields the source with lost manuscripts and detached letters of transmittal.

Pascual Duarte is a perplexing novel, yet it has now become one of the most widely read and discussed contemporary Spanish novels, although perhaps at times more for reasons of literary sociology than artistic merit. As a novel, it presents many technical problems arising from Cela's relative immaturity as a novelist at that time. For example, one is never certain whether to accept Pascual Duarte's confessions at face value and to lament accordingly Pascual's having been trapped by Fate and circumstance, or to suspect that Pascual's repentance is entirely sincere and the account of his nefarious deeds of violence are only further example of the perfidy of the human being. The structural design of Cela's novel offers little to support either contention. Furthermore, the two letters, the one contradicting the other, which report the circumstances of Pascual's execution at the close of the novel do little to clarify Pascual's motives. In the face of this structural ambivalence it is often difficult for the reader to reach a decision regarding the thematic intentions of the novel, and contradictory opinions abound. This paper attempts to deal with three areas of discussion impinging upon an interpretation of the novel: social criticism, existentialism and *tremendismo.*

One of the most important thematic considerations concerns the optimistic *versus* the pessimistic implications of the novel. Both Cela and innumerable reviewers and commentators have spoken at some length concerning the seeming condemnation of society and the adverse environmental pressures which are brought to bear upon Pascual in the course of the novel. Despite the fact that the usual option is for a critical statement underlining the tragedy of Pascual's life, there still remains the task of drawing conclusions in much broader and universal terms.

While one may easily say that it is society which is to blame for Pascual's dreary life and violent end, one must still decide whether it is a society seen in terms of those institutions which are not immutable, or a society seen in terms of the fundamental congress of mankind, which is immutable. A question which the reader might well ask himself is why the novel is set in Badajoz and not in Madrid. It is Madrid which provides the background for Pío Baroja's *La lucha por la vida* which is similar in many respects to **Pascual Duarte,** a fact which has spawned an over comparison between Baroja and Cela. However, Baroja's novel, in the picaresque-naturalistic tradition, attacks society as a system of particular institutions with which man finds himself in constant contact. For this reason Baroja would have need of the particular panorama of society offered by the capital. On the other hand, the institutions of society do not appear in Cela's work. Religion and the Church are present in the person of the benevolent priest, don Manuel, who is always spoken of by Pascual with respect and fondness. As such, don Manuel is an element in Duarte's favor and not the representative of an adverse institutionalized force. The same may be said of the prison priest, don Santiago, who encourages Pascual's writing of his confessions.

The penal institution appears twice in the narrative. First after the murder of El Estirao and, second, after the murder of don Jesús. But in neither case is it presented unfavorably. After his imprisonment for the death of El Estirao, Pascual's only comment is that they should have kept him a prisoner after his last incarceration, rather than releasing him after a token sentence. His treatment while awaiting execution for the death of don Jesús judged by his comments seems, good, and he acknowledges the justice of his imprisonment. The problem seems not to be the penal system per se, but the fact that society recognizes a problem in individuals like Pascual Duarte, and, not knowing what to do with them, imprisons them or even executes them. But it is only with this ultimate act dictated by a higher voice of society that the code of an organized society enters into the narrative. In short, society as a practice becomes important only *after* Pascual's character is irremediably formed.

It is thus the formation of his character and the circumstances of that formation which become significant. Growing up in Badajoz, then, as he tells us in his own words, society as a system of institutions does not exist. Society is rather a pattern of environment, the natural surroundings and human relations. It is on the basis of these elements that Pascual relates his downfall. **Pascual Duarte** is, after all, the story of a family in which that traditional fountain of virtue, the mother, is the most sinful and perverted member. In Catholic Spain where the cult of the Virgin Mary, the maternal prototype, has been developed to an extreme, such an arrangement on the author's part is calculated to arouse violent reactions. The point is made even more emphatically when we remember that the high point of the novel is the mother's assassination. Between Señora Duarte and El Estirao, the constant thorns in his side, Pascual is caught up in a web of degraded and amoral human relationships from which he can extricate himself only by the violent murder of his two tormentors. There would seem to be little doubt that Señora Duarte represents the decay of the familial relationship of man and the murder El Estirao the decay of the fraternal relationship. Both are isolated and insignificant human beings who act strictly in terms of other human beings, portraying only the basest of human emotions. Pascual stands in relief against their wickedness—perhaps too much in relief for plausibility. Why it is Pascual who is the one who is caught is, of course, explainable in terms of the novel's presence and the first person narrative. Pascual has the way clear to present himself as better than he may have been, in contrast to those whom he despises, in an attempt to justify his own behavior. And the novel *is* a justification of Pascual's uxorcide, the act toward which the narrative is directed. This need not detract from Pascual's basic honesty, but it is a facet of the novel which cannot be overlooked in any final analysis.

Just how transcendental Pascual's plight becomes, seen in these terms, cannot be measured by reference to the novel's structure and hence will not detain our interest at this point. This is something which each reader will have to consider for himself in terms of his appreciation of Cela's irony. Pascual himself is basically resigned to accepting his life as it has turned out, and any sense of tragedy must necessarily spring from the personal sensitivity of the reader. As far as Pascual is concerned, at the time of his letter of transmittal to Barrera, the slate has been washed clean and he has no argument with anyone:

> Noto cierto descanso después de haber relatado todo
> lo que pasé, y hay momentos en que hasta la
> conciencia quiere remorderme menos.
>
> Confío en que usted sabrá entender lo que mejor no
> le digo, porque mejor no sabría. Pesaroso estoy ahora
> de haber equivocado mi camino, pero ya ni pido
> perdón en esta vida. Para qué? Tal vez sea mejor que

hagan conmigo lo que está dispuesto, porque es más que probable que si no lo hicieran volviera a las andadas. No quiero pedir el indulto, porque es demasiado lo malo que la vida me enseñó y mucha mi flaqueza para resistir al instinto. Hágase lo que está escrito en el libro de los Cielos.

Along with *Pascual Duarte* the year 1942 saw the publication of *L'étranger.* Despite the fact that Arturo Torres-Rioseco has wanted to see a technical and philosophic link between the two novels, given Camus' intent to show man's essential lack of inherent commitment to morals and ethics as socially constituted codes and given conscience and remorse as the motives for Pascual's narrative, it is hard to see a concrete relationship between these two works. The structure of Camus' work is a simultaneous realization and comprehension of events, implying an intelligent awareness of his situation for *l'étranger* which Cela denies Pascual. Any comprehension or awareness granted Pascual comes much later, and its extent is certainly considerably limited. Camus' protagonist *knows* at each point what he is getting himself into and just does not care. Pascual is taken unawares (supposedly) and can only look back in remorse. In short, the structure of Camus' work, employing the diary format, may be profounder. Cela's work, built as an autobiography, has the advantage of irony and is subsequently more frightening in its message than the French work, which can only inspire despair. Both men are trapped, one resignedly and the other unwittingly. This is, very definitely, a profound distinction which must be recognized and treated accordingly.

Pascual Duarte is essentially a novel of an awakening. I say "of *an* awakening" rather than "of awakening," because the latter implies a gradual and cumulative process, whereas I want to insist upon the sudden awakening over a relatively limited and late span of time. Pascual's is not an awakening of the kind which bridges adolescence and adulthood, but one which exchanges irresponsible adulthood for sober maturity. Pascual's narrative does not cover his grasp of the meaning of life as it evolves out of his continuous experiencing of life, a typically existential approach. Instead, the story is the child of the moment put down at an established point in time and seen through relatively homogeneous eyes. It is a restricted and an incomplete awakening in the sense that it never matches the grasp of reality which Cela's irony demands of the reader.

There is a certain basic naivete on Pascual's part from which he is never fully able to escape and which constitutes the work's mordant irony. For this reason we cannot take too seriously as evidence of great insight Pascual's frequent mention of elements of predestination. On almost every page, he attributes the cause of his circumstances to forces beyond his comprehension: "Dios lo manda," "está escrito,"

"destinados," "Providencia" are all frequent and readily recognizable motifs. Yet, rather than pointing to a desire on Pascual's part to have us see how his fate has been irrevocably predestined by the malevolent forces of the universe, his words seem to reinforce his essential resignation to the world in which he has found himself. It must be remembered that it is a resignation in retrospect, and the pat little phrases are dropped too often and sound too much like proverbs to be taken as subtle attempts to form a tragic chorus of impending doom. Examined in the light of peasant stoicism in the face of familiar hardship, they become little more than the unconscious and stereotyped expressions with which Pascual's people have for centuries met hardship.

For these various reasons I reject the tag of "existentialistic" so often applied to Cela's novel. A desire to see *La familia de Pascual Duarte* as an example of Spanish existentialism motivates the comparison with *L'étranger.* Existentialism is a difficult concept with which to work. The absence of unanimity as to how it should be defined and the lack of any ground rules as to how such a philosophical attitude may be fruitfully applied to literature has occasioned an overuse of the term. Indeed, it has become fashionable to see almost any novel which even remotely deals with conflict and anguished despair as being essentially existentialistic. If existentialism is indeed the dominant characteristic of twentieth-century culture, then it need no more be singled out for discussion than the dominant note of Christianity characteristic of medieval literature. One should seek, it would seem, for demonstrable literary (and not philosophic) marks which would aid the poor bewildered critic who is not *engagé* in his often futile attempts to see why Christ and don Quijote are existential, much less all of the in-literature of our time. Perhaps a good beginning is to be found in distinguishing between authors who are existential and heroes (or anti-heroes, if you will) who are existential. If the principal characteristic of the existential man is his anguished awareness and his will to action and his desire to forge his own existence out of the chaotic rubble of the universe, Pascual Duarte would seem to be more a miserable and wasted soul than a checkmated Prometheus. I will beg the question here with regard to *L'étranger.*

Any discussion of *Pascual Duarte* must come to grips sooner or later with the problem of *tremendismo.* My treatment of it here will be brief, since I cannot believe it is valid as a critical concept. *Tremendismo* is usually defined as the neorealism which involves the concatenation of horrible and violent events presented amorally and without any obvious intent other than that of jarring the sensibilities of the reader. If this is so, the Spanish novel since the Civil War has no corner on this market, since the atrocities so presented can be found in abundance anywhere. I refer you to the more creatural portions of the picaresque novel. Nor can *tremendismo* be established on the basis of quantity, hardly a reliable index for a literary concept. But more important, the notion of *tremendismo* as it exists in the minds of the critic, seems to correspond to a desire to see a necessary link between the social and political upheavals of the Spanish Civil War and the contours of any culture following it. If anything, the War produced a feeling of guilt (as most wars do, especially civil wars) and a desire on the part of the younger generation to deal with certain problems which novelists tended conscientiously to overlook before. It is interesting to note that, as the Civil War fades into the past and the presence of Franco is accepted as normal, *tremendismo* seems to be spoken of less and less as being *the* characteristic of contemporary Spanish fiction. I have often speculated as to what the critics would have come up with if there had been no Civil War and Cela had published his novel just the same. A critical approach predicated on the belief in a cause and effect theory of the sociology of literature at best is an a posteriori activity having little validity beyond the moment at hand.

One notes also in passing that many examples of so-called *tremendismo* are attributable to motives explainable on the basis of contemporary psychology and psychiatry. Ana María Matute's *Los niños tontos* (1956) is reminiscent of the contemporary debunking of the Victorian belief in the innocence of children. Miss Matute's fiction in turn is aligned which other contemporary works on the same theme which have not the remotest connection with Spanish culture, to wit, the recent undergraduate best-seller, William Golding's *Lord of the Flies*.

With respect to *Pascual Duarte,* there are two basic observations to be made. In the first place, the events related by Pascual Duarte occur prior to the Civil War; Pascual is undisputedly executed during the War. Thus *tremendismo* must be discounted as a factor present here if we are assuming that it reflects the moral bankruptcy of the Spanish people following the hostilities. On the other hand, if we are going to ascribe to *tremendismo* Pascual's clinical narration of his violent acts, it would be at the expense of the note of helpless resignation and remorse with which Pascual Duarte seems to relate his life. By saying that Duarte is more amoral than neutrally resigned we obfuscate if not destroy the iron which gives the work its note of tragedy.

This short discussion in no way pretends to offer a unified interpretation of *La familia de Pascual Duarte.* Rather, I have attempted to grapple with a few of the recurring problems and controversies which attempts at interpretation have fostered. My wish is that Cela's novel be seen in terms broader than it has been to date. Undoubtedly many of the problems surrounding an understanding of the novel result

from its immediacy to us and to the fact that it is, one must admit, a bit of a potboiler. However, the work is here to stay, and it is decidedly not lacking in either artistic merit or thematic import. The disminuation of the desire to see *Pascual Duarte* as a social document narrowly reflecting a situation of the moment would bring with it a clearer understanding of the way in which Cela's novel is a work of literature and primarily to be valued as a human document of extensive proportions.

J. S. Bernstein (essay date Winter 1968)

SOURCE: "Pascual Duarte and Orestes," in *Symposium*, Vol. XXII, No. 4, Winter, 1968, pp. 301-18.

[*In the following essay, Bernstein presents parallels between Cela's* La familia de Pascual Duarte *and the myth of Orestes.*]

Classical mythology has continued to be a fruitful source of themes for the contemporary writer. Although no comprehensive survey exists of the presence of mythological material in modern European literature, several partial treatments have appeared. Classical mythology has also been a suggestive basis for studies in criticism and literary aesthetics. The modern writer often finds important stimuli in mythological motifs. A case in point is the Spaniard, Camilo José Cela, whose first novel, *La familia de Pascual Duarte,* appeared in 1942.

The diversity of critical estimation of this work bespeaks the presence in it of profound human issues and of several questions left unresolved by the author. We encounter in the novel a remarkable number of correspondences with the Orestes myth. Although to my knowledge no critical attention has been paid to these, J. van Praag Chantraine perhaps voices a hint of them when she says that the violence of *Pascual Duarte* "se acerca a los trágicos griegos por el 'fatum' que pesa sobre el protagonista." On the other hand, Gonzalo Torrente Ballester thinks the intention of the novel is clearly humorous. Juan Luis Alborg seeks to explain the work's impact as due to its expressive language and striking situation. Julian Palley doubts its verisimilitude. Sherman Eoff attributes Pascual's actions to an inferiority complex growing out of mistreatment in childhood. J. M. Castellet thinks *Pascual Duarte* is to Spanish literature what *L'Etranger* is to French. John J. Flasher concurs when he suggests a general existentialist quality in Cela. The violence and episodic character of the novel have been considered picaresque, hence "traditional" in Spanish literature. Yet, R. L. Predmore considers the violence a mark of the novel's "tremendismo" and a response to distinctly contemporary conditions. Jerónimo Mallo has discussed "tremendismo" in the modern Spanish novel with reference to Cela. In this study, I shall deal with the parallels between the novel and the Orestes tale.

La familia de Pascual Duarte purports to be the autobiography of a condemned murderer, written in prison while awaiting execution. His crimes include the murders of his wife's lover, his mother, and a wealthy landowner. He also performed other acts of a violent sort: shooting his pet dog, stabbing his mare, and wounding his friend, Zacarías, in a tavern fight. Pascual gives a full account of all his violent acts except the last one he commits, the murder of don Jesús, the one for which he is condemned to death. This event is shrouded in mystery, although it is precisely this one which costs Pascual his life.

The prime motive behind Orestes' matricide is the fact that he is the son and heir of Agamemnon; the revenge of Orestes, though it is carried out under divine injunction from Apollo, belies a strong identification between the hero and his father. Pascual's father, Esteban Duarte Diniz, was a strong man, given to violent fits of temper. There is an indication in his name of his marginal status in society; his two surnames are not Spanish but Portuguese. The family occupies a marginal status economically, due in part to Esteban's occupation as a smuggler. The family is marginal in a spatial sense as well, because they live in Extremadura, on the western edge of the country. Moreover, they do not even live in the "center" of this region—Badajoz, the capital of Badajoz province—but in Torremejía, a town some thirty miles east of the capital. Pascual says that the tried to stay out of his father's way, to avoid beatings, and that he soon learned not to intervene in the frequent quarrels between his parents. He says of his feelings toward his father, that "le tenía un gran respeto y no poco miedo." His father, but not his mother, could read, and often read the newspaper to the family. At his father's insistence, and over his mother's objections, Pascual was sent to school where he received a minimal education. When his father told him of the need for education "su voz en esos momentos me parecía mas velada y adquiría unos matices insospechados para mí ... [. . .] y acababa siempre por decirme, casi con cariño:—No hagas caso, muchacho. Ya voy para viejo!" This affection, rare enough in Pascual's experience, was very real, and formed part of the basis for the less critical attitude he shows toward his father than toward his mother.

Although Esteban died of rabies, and not at the hands of his wife and her lover, a reminiscence of Clytemnestra's hatred of Agamemnon can be seen in Esteban's wife's reaction to his demise: her laughter betrays a hostility similar to Clytemnestra's. Her callousness caused Pascual to stifle the tears he would have shed for his father. At Esteban's burial, Manuel, the parish priest, gave Pascual a sermon about honoring his father's memory, to which Pascual re-

plied that it would be better not to remember him. When Manuel then defended Esteban, Pascual was impressed with the priest's support of his father; his gratitude toward the priest for expressing support or affection for Esteban as he himself could not is seen in that, from the day of the burial on, "siempre que veía a don Manuel lo saludaba y le besaba la mano."

Pascual's relations with his father, while not full of unmixed affection, were characterized by a relatively strong identification. Pascual in fact had positive relationships with several men older than himself, among them Manuel, Conrado (the Prison warden), and Santiago (the prison priest). These relationships contrast strongly with the bitter hatred and hostility present in his relationships with his mother and first wife.

Esteban's death occurred two days after the birth of Pascual's half brother, Mario. The child's paternity was not certain; Pascual suspected that his mother had earlier taken Rafael as lover. Rafael, if not before Esteban's death then surely after, became Pascual's mother's lover: Rafael "en casa estaba porque, desde la muerte de mi padre, por ella entraba y salía como por terreno conquistado." Here is the note of adultery central to the Orestes myth. The adultery them was presented perhaps even earlier, although it is not stressed, when Pascual's sister was born. Esteban's only comment to his wife was to the effect that she was a *zorra*, 'slut.' Although Pascual did not actually kill Rafael he leaves no doubt that he would have, if he had had the chance. His hatred for Rafael almost defied the restraints imposed by Rafael's taboo status as his mother's lover. In response to an act of cruelty by Rafael against Mario, Pascual controlled his impulse to soothe Mario tenderly because he feared Rafael might criticize him; if he had, "por Dios que lo machaco delante de mi madre."

Pascual's relationship with his sister, Rosario, parallels Orestes' with Electra. Rosario's name means "rosary," and signifies the seemingly endless series of unfortunate situations in which she was involved: repeated sojourns in houses of prostitution, interrupted by respites at home to recover from illness. While it is true that Rosario bears a very common Spanish name, the fact is that she is called by *that* name and not some other. Rosario seemed beautiful to Pascual. He expresses their mutual love: "Yo la quería con ternura, con la misma ternura con la que ella me quería a mí." Rosario cared for him on his release from prison. Pascual defended his desire to continue his intimacy with her against Estirao's intention to take her away with him. The erotic undertones in their relations are apparent. Graves, commenting on Electra's significance in the myth, remarks: "In the revised account [given by the Attic dramatists], endogamy and partrilinear descent are taken for granted, and the Erinnyes are successfully defied. Electra, whose name, 'amber', suggests the paternal cult of Hyperborean Apollo, is favourably contrasted with Chrysothemis [Orestes' third sister], whose name is a reminder that the ancient concept of matriarchal law was still golden in most parts of Greece, and whose 'subservience' to her mother had hither to been regarded as pious and noble. Electra is 'all for the father', like the Zeus-born Athene." In a similar vein, H. D. F. Kitto mentions the "unaffected tenderness for each other that they display."

Just as Electra was "all for the father," Rosario had a special bond of affection with her father, Esteban. He used to sit by the side of her crib, "y mirando para la hija se le pasaban las horas, con una cara de enamorado." Their affection was mutual, as is shown by the fact that Rosario was the only one who wished to or was able to restrain Esteban's rages and violence by other than violent means: "Era a ella la única persona que escuchaba; bastaba una mirada de Rosario para calmar sus iras." Further, she seemed to have no relationship with their mother.

An additional point of contact with the Orestes myth lies in Pascual's relationship with Sebastián. A young gentleman, (he is called "el señorito Sebastián"), he is therefore from a relatively high social stratum; Pylades was the son of a king. Sebastián was Pascual's best man when the latter married Lola. He also was present during the fight between Pascual and Zacarías, and accompanied Pascual home afterwards. Though their relationship is surely not notable for its firmness—Sebastián appears on only three occasions—Sebastián's last appearance occurred after Pascual's return home from prison, and just before he murdered his mother. Finally, paralleling the marriage of Pylades and Electra, Sebastián took Rosario as mistress. Sebastián did not, as had Pylades, urge the matricide, nor bolster his friend's flagging resolve by recalling any divine injunction. There is a sense, however, in which Sebastián functioned as a facilitator of Pascual's murderous impulses and wrath. When Pascual was seeking Estirao after Lola's death, it was Sebastián who disclosed his whereabouts. This instance of Sebastián abetting and enabling is an echo of Pylades' function in the myth.

Another parallel with the myth occurs upon Pascual's return to Torremejía from prison. He had imagined a great reception at the railroad station; during the day and a half on the train Pascual visualized a hero's welcome. This is in a way absurd, for none of the townspeople knew that he was returning; he had been released after serving only three years of a twenty-eight year sentence for the murder of Estirao. The reality of his reception is quite the reverse of his phantasy. The station was deserted except for Gregorio, the station-master. He greeted Pascual indifferently and without great surprise. Like Orestes' return to Mycenae, Pascual's return was unheralded and almost unnoticed. The first place he passed on the way to his mother's house was the cemetery. Orestes' first act after his return was to visit Agamemnon's grave and offer suitable homage; the cemetery was naturally the resting place of Pascual's father. The cemetery has an additional function in the novel, for it was there that Pascual first possessed Lola.

After some indecision as to how best to gain entrance to the house, Pascual finally knocked at the door. His mother, not expecting him to be out of prison, and perhaps still drowsy, needed a few moments to realize who it was at the door. This recalls the fact that Clytemnestra did not recognize Orestes when he came to the palace, believing him to be a messenger bearing news of Orestes' death. The lack of recognition is repeated in the scene of the matricide; when his mother awoke, she demanded: "¿Quién anda ahí?"

Like Pascual, Orestes was married twice. Shortly after Pascual's return he married Esperanza, "hope," the niece of Engracia. She was very different from Lola: "De natural consentidor y algo tímida, . . . era muy religiosa y como dada a la mística." As her name seems to indicate, there appeared to be some hope that Pascual's life with her would be better than it had been with Lola. Lola's name is a shortening of Dolores, "pain, suffering," and pain seems indeed to have characterized her relationship with Pascual, for the brief happiness of their honeymoon soon deteriorated into mutual denigration and torment. Esperanza's mystical quality is probably an inheritance from her aunt, since Engracia was a quasimystical figure in the town, with power over life and death. Her name, "in grace," i.e., favored by God, and her function place her on the side of superhuman powers; Pascual says she was "nuestra providencia." She was an "especialista en duelos y partera, medio bruja y un tanto misteriosa."

An echo of the Orestes myth is present here also, although a distant one. Agamemnon returned from Troy with Cassandra, who had been endowed with the power to prophesy the truth, but cursed with the fate of never having anyone believe her prophesies. Cassandra correctly prophesied Agamemnon's imminent death. Similarly, Engracia appeared at the moment of Esteban's death, and uttered a prophesy. However, in this case, her words were believed and acted upon. She declared that since Esteban was rabid, one look from him would suffice to cause his wife to miscarry. Therefore, Esteban was locked in a closet where he died two days after the birth of Mario. In line with Esperanza's symbolic position as a person beyond human frailties, she is endowed with prophetic vision, for she has prescience of the matricide. She was present at the murder, holding a candle in her hand. After killing his mother, Pascual rushed from the house, jostling Esperanza and causing the candle (the beacon of hope) to go out.

Pascual's matricide comes as no surprise. As if the novel were, like the myth, the retelling of a story with which we are already familiar, the occurrence of the murder does not shock us. The shocking element, if any, lies in the method used. Pascual's mother was a repugnant creature who had the power of the evil eye, and was inadequate as a mother. She was incapable of sympathy, and had an adulterous affair with Rafael. Pascual deplores her complicity in Rafael's cruelty toward her son, Mario; nor did she cry when Mario died. Early in the novel, Pascual expressed his hatred for his mother. His recurring contacts with her serve to increase his hatred, which matured over the course of the book; many hints are provided which allow the reader to see the sinister outcome of his hatred. The reader knows that the murder will take place, furthermore, because Pascual carried out in phantasy the crime as it finally occurred, at a point well in advance of the actual event.

The murder is symbolically a sexual attack on his mother. He stabbed her in the throat; the blood which flowed is equated with the blood of a warm belly. As is true in Orestes's murder of Clytemnestra, the event took place at night, in the mother's bed. Clytemnestra "fights for her life, inch by inch of the way." Pascual's mother struggled also, but her fighting was physical rather than verbal. Another similarity is the great relief both murderers feel when the act is done; Pascual says: "Podía respirar. . . ." Finally, as in the Greek myth where no divine figure came forward to defend Clytemnestra or accuse Orestes, Pascual's mother—as is indeed true of his sister and Lola also—was very distant from religion and the Divinity. Pascual, on the other hand, had many contacts with priests and makes continual reference to God, and to God's forgiveness. Pascual had an affectionate bond with Manuel, was married in church, confessed often and fasted in prison; that is, a large measure of his spiritual sustenance derives, as is the case with Orestes, from religion. Though Pascual's references to God and religion may be thought conventional rather than deeply personal, the fact remains that he is associated with religion when his mother is not. This piece of irony—Pascual's piety—characterizes his last years in prison; clearly his piety, if he had any in earlier years, did not succeed in restraining his violent impulses.

Several subsidiary parallels with the Orestes myth may be pointed out. Early in the novel, Pascual tells us of killing his dog, Chispa. The event took place when Pascual sat on a favorite stone: "Una piedra redonda y achatada como una silla baja, de la que guardo tan grato recuerdo como de cualquier persona . . . [. . .] Cuando me marchaba, siempre, sin saber por qué, había de volver la cabeza hacia la piedra, como para despedirme, y hubo un día que debió parecerme tan triste por mi marcha, que no turve más suerte que volver mis pasos a sentarme de nuevo." When he returned to sit on the rock, Chispa sat down before him and looked at him

with "la mirada de los confesores, escrutadora y fría, como si no me hubiera visto nunca, como si fuese a culparme de algo de un momento a otro. . . ." Pascual became enraged and shot his dog. This act provided relief from the mounting tension he felt while the dog was looking at him.

Though it is true that the rock Pascual sits on functions as part of the setting for his action, Cela has made a great deal more of it than merely that. Thanks to the details used to describe the rock, it has become personified for Pascual. The personification of rocks and stones, and of nature generally, is a stylistic trait often encountered in Cela's writings. In his first work, we find this couplet: "Bien sabe Dios que yo siento doler las piedras; / Siento los huracanes heridos en el vientre." In *Pascual Duarte* an addition example is found in the stones of Pascual's kitchen floor which wounded the soles of his feet when he went, barefoot, to kill his mother. This is an instance of the congruence between an individual author's stylistic tendency or predilection, and the mythical account of the origin of the Delphic Oracle. For the rock Pascual sits on—which Cela personifies and describes in such detail—is the place where he gains relief from the accusation of Chispa; likewise, the stone of the Delphic Oracle, or one like it, is a prominent part of the myth.

Another thematic reminiscence centers on one version of Clytemnestra's dream. According to Aeschylus, on the eve of Orestes' return, his mother dreamed that she suckled a snake which bit her, drawing blood as well as milk. When Orestes learned of this dream he accepted the role of snake and promised to draw his mother's blood. The symbolism of the snake, be it in Eden, Mycenae, or Torremejía, is sufficiently well known. In *Pascual Duarte* the dream is present, but turned about. It is Pascual's mother who bit him on the nipple (actually tearing it off) and drew his blood. Since the bite signifies suckling as well, Pascual is symbolically cast in the role of the nurturing mother. Thus, just as his mother did not have milk enough to suckle Rosario, i.e., did not nurture her, Pascual does not nurture his mother at this moment. Rather he stabs her in the throat which, in addition to a symbol of the womb here, is part of the alimentary tract, the passage through which nurturing milk, which he could not and did not provide, would flow. At the moment Pascual stabs her and she bites him, their blood, flows together, and this blood union is patently a sign of incest.

If we prefer what Graves considers an earlier version of Orestes' death, then his execution as *pharmacos* (by having his throat slit) is the same as the method by which he actually puts his mother to death, and as that by which she had killed Agamemnon. Pascual is executed, through not for the matricide, by the garrote, this being the mode of execution of lowly criminals in Spain. His throat is also

penetrated by the band tightened by the screws of the garrote, as was his mother's by his knife.

The many similarities between the Orestes myth and
Pascual Duarte explored here for would not constitute
quite so remarkable a phenomenon if it were not for the
fact that analogous expression is given in *Pascual Duarte*
to the second aspect of the myth, the trial and acquittal of
Orestes with its attendant political and social meanings.
The trial (in Aeschylus'' and other versions) injects a deliberative element into the judgment of crimes. Normally,
Orestes would have been punished by death or exile, and
by confiscation of his property. Yet the hearings before the
Areopagus interrupt the automatic execution of the usual
penalties. At the point where Athene's defense of Orestes
was heeded the proceedings became a deliberative consideration of extenuating circumstances. Schlegel believed
that Aeschylus' "Principal object [. . .] was the recommend-
ing as essential to the welfare of Athens the Areopagus, an
uncorruptible yet mild tribunal, in which the white pebble
of Pallas [Athene] in favour of the accused does honor to
the humanity of the Athenians." In the struggle of social
ideologies Aeschylus produced a triumph for the patrilin-
ear system through dramatic action. Richard B. Sewall has
remarked that "Aeschylus, . . . was the first to subject the
idea of justice to the full dialectic of action." In addition,
he expressed in the *Oresteia* his partisanship of certain political factions in contention at the time. It would carry us
too far afield to detail these disputes; suffice it to point
out the existence of political overtones in the *Oresteia,* a
primary source of the myth.

Pascual's matricide was not the last murder he committed.
His punishment for it was not execution but imprisonment,
for a period not specified by Cela. The effect of this punishment, is similar to the outcome in Orestes' case. The
judgment is a blow against matriarchy and a vote for the
dominance of patriliny. This fact is bolstered by the lack
of mention of the mother's name. All the major characters
have names which may be read as symbolic of their personalities or circumstances; thus, they are limited, confined
within the restrictions of their novelistic personalities. The
mother is nameless. She is the generalized, pervasive, and
repulsive maternal principle which elicits a punitive,
exterminative impulse.

The fictional world of *Pascual Duarte* is in effect a matriarchy. While the major male characters, Esteban, Estirao,
Rafael, Jesús (strength through wealth), and Pascual are
strong, they are subdued by women or die by violence. The
secondary male characters, the priests and the warden, are
ineffectual and weak. The women in the novel, on the other
hand, are clearly dominant. The mother controls a good
deal of the action and is the person against whom Pascual
continually reacts. Engracia and Esperanza are assigned

powerful positions and endowed with extra-human powers.
Rosario is the one constant affectional tie for Pascual.
Lola, Pascual's first wife, is really not particularly feminine; she displays masculine aggressive characteristics,
which is perhaps why she meets an enigmatic death. Lola's
aggressiveness is seen in her continual taunting of Pascual.
At one point she enacted the function of Electra in the myth
by recalling Pascual's father to him; but in that case it was
to criticize his passively suffering his mother's nagging,
more than to urge him to her murder in a show of solidarity with him.

Lola, as did Rosario (who could calm their father's rages
with one look), and the mother (who was a basilisk when
angry), had the power of the evil eye. Edward S. Gifford
has written about the belief in the power of the evil eye as
a means of isolating a taboo (i.e., dangerous) person,
thereby insulating the believer against harm. Lola's death
is due to an apparent heart attack, after Pascual forced her
to reveal that the father of her unborn child was Estirao.

Naturally, the world of *Pascual Duarte* is not a matriarchy in strict anthropological terms; the novel is not a trea-
tise on kinship. However, in the main, that world is marked
by the three primary traits of matriarchy: female dominance, female kinship, and female inheritance. In the novel,
Pascual is dominated by the female characters. After the
death of his and Lola's son, Pascualillo, his wife and mother
unsettled him by their constant nagging. Many of his violent actions were stimulated by women or occurred in response to them. On at least two occasions his friendly and
humane impulses were stifled by women. His mother's
laughter when his father died prevented Pascual from expressing the mourning he felt. And it was Lola's taunting
about his masculinity that caused him to stop greeting the
priest and kissing his hand. He murdered Estirao because
the latter insulted his marital honor by referring to Lola's
love for him. He killed his mare because the animal threw
Lola, causing her to abort. In this regard, the matricide's
motivation is obvious. Further, Pascual tells us that he was
surrounded by "tries mujeres a las que por algún vínculo
estaba unido. . . ." He conceives of his relationships in
terms of his being related to the women, not their being
related to him. In addition, particularly in adulthood, Pascual
had no male friends or companions, save Sebastián whose
friendship was less than constant. The last mark of matriarchy is perhaps equivocal: although his mother inherited
the house upon Esteban's death, and Pascual returned there
to live instead of setting up a separate household with Lola
or Esperanza—that is, his world is matrilocal in part—Lola
and Esperanza do both live where he does, hence there are
also traces of patriliny.

Given the foregoing resemblances to the Orestes myth's
account of contending social orders, we can conclude that,

in a primitive way, **Pascual Duarte** constitutes a kind of destruction of the matriarchal principle, the defeat of *Mutterrecht,* and a vindication of patriarchy.

The last murder in Pascual's series of crimes, but the first one alluded to, in the epigraph to the novel, was the killing of don Jesús. Cela does not describe the event in the book, beyond calling it a killing off, or polishing off ("rematar"). From the vague details of chronology provided we can only conclude that the event took place during the Civil War. Don Jesús himself was a shadowy character, mentioned on only a few occasions. He was a wealthy aristocrat and Count of Torremejía. He owned the town's only two-story house, and owned property at the edge of which Pascual hunted partridges. Pascual's description of the town is meaningful for he mentions only three buildings, each of them representative of the "Establishment": the town hall, don Jesús' house, and the church. The church was "detrás de la plaza, y por la parte de la casa de don Jesús." That is, it was on the side of don Jesús. The State, the economically powerful, and the Church, are Pascual's points of reference in Torremejía. In the first pages of the novel we are already involved in the politics of the Spanish Civil War, but in a veiled way characteristic of the *literatura de evasión* which marks so much of Spanish literature of the last twenty-five or thirty years.

Each of the three buildings mentioned, moreover, was defective in some way. The town hall clock had stopped; it was only an ornament "como si el pueblo no necesitase de su servicio." The church was the scene of the first act of violence that Pascual tells us about in the novel proper; it was not Pascual's killing of his dog, Chispa, but rather the crippling fall of a stork, a life-bearer: "La cigüeña cojita, que aún aguantó dos inviernos, era del nido de la parroquial, de donde hubo de caerse, aún muy tierna, asustada por el gavilán." Don Jesús' house had the defect of vulnerability, as if subject to imminent attack: "Sobre el portal había unas piedras de escudo, de mucho valer, según dicen, terminadas en unas cabezas de guerreros de la antigüedad, con su cabezal y sus plumas, que miraban, una para el levante y otra para el poniente, como si quisieran representar que *estaban vigilando lo que de un lado o de otro podríales venir*" [my italics].

The alliance between the economic elite and the Church is seen also when Pascual attended Mass; having had little formal training in religion he was directed by the priest to follow Jesús' actions during the mass. Jesús is the model in religion—hence his name. The enigma surrounding Jesús' death involves the use of the verb "rematar." The novel's epigraph reads as follows: "A la memoria del insigne patricio don Jesús González de la Riva, Conde de Torremejía, quien al irlo a rematar el autor de este escrito, le llamó Pascualillo y sonreía." Though we might specu-

late on the circumstances of this killing—whether Pascual was part of a firing squad charged with administering the *coup de grâce,* whether he happened upon Jesús, already wounded, and merely "put him out of his misery"—two salient facts about it are clear. Jesús smiled at Pascual, and called him "Pascualillo," i.e., the same affectionate diminutive which Lola and Pascual apply to their beloved son. In evident contrast to the myth, Pascual is not, as was Orestes, the son of a king. He is, if anything, the opposite, given Esteban's marginal social status. However, it is not altogether surprising that Jesús, the only man in the novel who might conceivably embody kingly qualities and status, calls him by the "son" diminutive, "Pascualillo." Further, Pascual says he hopes Jesús will receive God's pardon in heaven, just as Jesús "a buen seguro" had pardoned him.

This killing, though not perfectly clear in detail, is the only one in the novel in which factors other than the purely personal are prominent. Pascual expresses no hatred toward Jesús; there is even doubt whether Jesús considered the killing a hostile or merciful act. Yet it is for this murder, not for the murder of his mother, that Pascual was condemned to death. The reason is not hard to discover; this is the only crime in the book with a political context. The murder may be seen as an attack by the proletariat upon a defective and ineffectual aristocracy which is already in decline.

Though Pascual's other killings were the result of his passion or intolerance of anxiety (Chispa), this one was devoid of any purely personal motivation; it was not vengeful. Therefore, as Treston says of Greek crimes of vengeance: "Once murder becomes a sin against the gods, or a crime against the State, the day of private vengeance has passed: that of State trial, State imprisonment, State execution takes its place." The political context of this crime is betrayed also by the fact that the novel closes with two letters, supposed to have been written respectively by the prison priest, Santiago (the Church), and Cesáreo Martín, a Civil Guardsman (the State). They describe Pascual's demeanor at his execution; that is, the Church and State preside over the execution of rigorous justice upon Pascual. This is to be contrasted with the clemency shown after the murder of Estirao: he was released from prison twenty-five years early. The then warden, don Conrado (the State), was a benign, almost jovial witness to and dispenser of leniency. Likewise, Pascual's punishment for the matricide was not death, but imprisonment.

Some light is shed on the problem of juridical severity by Ganivet: "En España, se prefiere tener un código muy rígido y anular después sus efectos por medio de la gracia. [. . .] Castigamos con solemnidad y con rigor para satisfacer nuestro deseo de justicia; y luego, sin ruido ni voces, indultamos a los condenados, para satisfacer nuestro deseo de perdón." The same severity exercised in punishing Pascual is at work in Pascual's own crimes. Marañón has commented that a "Duarte es mejor persona que sus víctimas y que sus arrebatos criminosos representan una suerte de abstracta y bárbara pero innegable justicia." The relative clemency shown Pascual in his earlier killings seems indeed to satisfy a Spanish "deseo de perdón," while Pascual's first two murders seem to respond to his "deseo de justicia."

In the murder of Jesús, the criminal deserves to be punished to the degree which fits the enormity of the crime. Cela's injection of the political question into the novel, in addition to providing a reminiscence of the political matters surrounding the *Oresteia,* is a way of impressing upon the reader the more serious nature of crimes against the State (i.e., against the regime and its supporters) than of crimes of personal vengeance.

Although the shift from private blood-vengeance to societal judgment of offenses in the Greek myth represents a shift from greater to lesser primitivism or brutality— Orestes' sentence is, after all, rather mild—in Cela, this shift is in the opposite direction. The ironic reversal centers on the contrast between the mercy and due consideration (of the "degree of punishment already suffered") shown him when he was paroled after three years' imprisonment for the murder of Estirao, and the merciless and perfunctory condemnation meted out for the killing of don Jesús. The movement here is from lesser to greater brutality, and constitutes an evasive commentary on contemporary political conditions. The perfunctory nature of Pascual's last punishment contrasts with the trial of Orestes before the Areopagus. There, Athene had intervened to insist upon "an examination into motives" and mitigating circumstances. Now, however, because of the vagueness surrounding the killing of don Jesús, the reader must conduct this "examination into motives" for himself; the reader is forced to assume the role of the twelve Athenians of the Areopagus, to become the judge of Pascual's behavior.

The relative severity of the sentence for his last murder reflects also the need felt by society to maintain an equilibrium between "indulgence and punishment. [. . .] Without it (so we dimly feel) the whole psychological and social structure on which morality depends is imperiled." Pascual is made the exemplary sufferer of this severity; he is singled out for punishment, in a sense as a scapegoat atoning for all the sins committed during the Civil War on both sides. Hence his name, 'Paschal,' the sacrificial lamb. We can see a displacement onto this last murder of the punishment which, following the outcome in Orestes' case (i.e., acquittal), could not be meted out to Pascual. Moreover, that aspect of the myth concerned with the persecution of Orestes by some still recalcitrant Furies, even after his ac-

quittal, is represented in *Pascual Duarte* by a contemporary analogue, the unremitting persecution of political criminals and dissenters. As Grant puts it: "Orestes is vindicated by an appeal to patriotic feeling." Pascual Duarte is condemned thanks to the same appeal.

The correspondences between *Pascual Duarte* and the Orestes myth do not bespeak a process of imitation on Cela's part, but rather an imaginative re-creation of the atmosphere and feeling surrounding the myth, together with an adaptation of various of its principal features. Cela shares with the writers of antiquity the artistic freedom to mold inherited mythic material, to accept or reject aspects according to their suitability for his purposes and particular genius. As I understand the relationship between the novel and the myth, *Pascual Duarte* exhibits a constellation of characters' relationships, personal motivations, and socio-political undertones remarkably in consonance with those of the myth. I would suggest that the myth is an expression of a certain nuclear problem, or set of potential actions, found in Western man's experience. When an author confronts that nuclear problem and writes about the human reality which had informed and animated the myth, the same human reality also informs his creation, producing echoes and parallels of other works of which he may have been ignorant. As I understand this aspect of *Pascual Duarte* then, the novel is animated by a similar *problemática vital* or constellation of life problems, as are the *Oresteia* and other versions of the Orestes myth (as well as, for example, Flaubert's *St. Julien* and Tarkington's *The Magnificent Ambersons*); thus, Pascual Duarte himself can be termed an Orestean hero.

David William Foster (essay date Spring 1969)

SOURCE: "Intrinsic and Extrinsic Pattern in Two New Novels by Camilo José Cela," in *Papers on Language and Literature,* Vol. V, No. 2, Spring, 1969, pp. 204-8.

[*In the following essay, Foster discusses how Cela uses pattern to structure the plots in his* Tobogán de hambrientos *and* La familia del héroe.]

The modern novel has undergone three major developments in the concept of plot structure: "total plot," "loose-ends plot," and pattern as a substitution for plot. Although the so-called "new" French novel—the third of these developments—has been principally a French phenomenon, it is possible to point to a few writers outside of France who have availed themselves of this form of the novel. In Spain, it is Camilo José Cela whose work best represents the concept of pattern in the novel. Camilo José Cela (1916-) has become the undisputed leader of the Post-Civil War novel in Spain with a series of audacious works beginning in 1942 with the publication of *La familia de Pascual Duarte,* the most widely read and discussed Spanish novel of its generation. Cela is a prolific writer whose works dominate the Spanish literary scene—even more so since his induction into the Spanish Royal Academy in 1957. It is possible to see the beginning of his interest in the new novel as early as *La colmena* (1951), the work generally considered to be his masterpiece. His subsequent works, *Mrs. Caldwell habla con su hijo* (1953), *La catira* (1955), *Tobogán de hambrientos* (1962), *Garito de hospicianos* (1963), *La familia del héroe* (1965), demonstrate in some ways the use of the major techniques of the new novel. Although *Mrs. Caldwell habla con su hijo* is apparently the first consistent example of the new novel in Spain, Cela's *Tobogán de hambrientos* and *La familia del héroe* will be concerned in the present discussion of Cela's reliance on pattern as a substitution for plot in the novel.

La familia del héroe represents Cela's use of what one may refer to as extrinsic pattern. In the novel, Evangelino Gadoupa Faquitrós, grandson of the hero, don Samuel Faquitrós, relates to a group of *contertulianos* the history of his illustrious family. The novel is divided into nine sections, each one occasioned by the vermouth which don Evangelino has ordered in the preceding chapter: "Primer vermú, Segundo vermú . . . Noveno y último vermú." Don Evangelino describes the grotesque descendants of his heroic grandfather in the form of a monologue which forms the bulk of the text. In terms of pattern, it is significant that Cela interrupts to describe don Evangelino in "Quinto vermú," the central segment of the work.

Cela adheres to another technique of the new novel, the eschewing of interiorization and the restriction of the subject matter to phenomena and reality which can be observed "objectively." When a listener interrupts the speaker to offer a possible explanation for the behavior of the latter's relatives, he is told: "Pues, mire usted, yo no le digo ni que sí ni que no: yo me limito a contarles a ustedes las cosas, tal como fueron." In another instance: ". . . les estoy contando a ustedes la historia de mi familia. El conjunto de las historias de todas las familias españolas, es la historia de España, la historia de la patria de nuestros mayores. La objectividad más absoluta es el mejor adorno del historiador."

It seems that Cela draws no relationship between the content of the novel and the formal expression which it assumes, given both the theme of his novel—the absurdity of the pretenses of civilized man—and its structure as outlined above. The pattern of the novel stands out as a separable structure, a framework or a design around which the slight narrative clings. Indeed, it would be possible to view the extrinsic pattern of *La familia del héroe* as the only

basis available to us for discussing the unity of the novel, a novel which, without the pattern, would be even more amorphous than it is. Cela's novel succeeds in advancing a particular vision of mankind that is given coherency and organization by means of the unity of the time and place of Gadoupa Faquitrós' story. This unity is substantiated or reinforced by the extrinsic pattern of the succession of the nine vermouths.

Tobogán de hambrientos, an earlier novel also dealing with the moral and original sin of mankind, likewise makes use of a formal pattern for purposes of esthetic unity. However, in this case it is possible to speak of a formal pattern which is in some intrinsic way related to the narrative theme as a whole.

Tobogán de hambrientos consists of two parts. Each part is divided into 100 numbered narrative units, each with a short identifying title. Part one (Primer Tiempo) is subtitled "Uno, Dos, Tres, Cuatro, Cinco . . ." Part Two (Segundo Tiempo) is called "Cinco, Cuatro, Tres, Dos, Uno." The first 100 narrative units characterize the personalities of a group of closely interrelated people who are presented in the order 1, 2, 3, 4, 5, . . . 100. There is no prescribed plan for progression from one individual to another. Everyone knows or is related to someone else, and the discussion of one person leads naturally into the discussion of another: his brother, his friend, his sweetheart, his father, his neighbor, all of whom in turn are linked to other members of the human complex. Following closely the new novel procedure of substituting pattern for plot, Cela's work is reminiscent of the conversation of a backward gossip who effortlessly moves from one person to another.

The second 100 narrative units present approximately the same group of individuals in reverse order, 100 . . . 5, 4, 3, 2, 1. Although a given individual may figure in several narrative units, two corresponding units in the two parts serve as a point of departure for tracing the complex relationship that an individual has with the rest of mankind. There is no time sequence in either part and no temporal relationship between the two separate parts. While incidents of cause-and-effect may be cited, the novel presents two separate and not necessarily related moments in the state of affairs of a given set of human correspondences. In this respect, *Tobogán de hambrientos* is similar in form to *La familia del héroe.* In *La familia del héroe,* however, the web of human relationships is not a consideration, and the formal elements are mechanistic and quite apparent. In *Tobogán de hambrientos* the multiplicity of individuals and the complexity of their mutual relations diminish the obviousness of the author's symmetrical pattern. There is no predicting the shape which a particular set of relationships will take even from one part to the next, and the formal structure of the novel functions as one means for defining the extent of the narrative. Since the novel ends with the same individual with whom it began, *Tobogán de hambrientos* constitutes a circular narrative. Cela's novel achieves the delineation of a segment of society which, if it were not for the external imposition of the form, would have an infinite extension. Cela justifies the formal elements of *Tobogán de hambrientos* on the following grounds:

> En estas páginas de hoy, el esqueleto que las sustenta es de culebra. No es mía la culpa de la afición que tengo (y que sí reconozco como mía) a coleccionar esqueletos dispares. Este *Tobogán de hambrientos* quizás no sea una novela para los legalistas de la preceptiva, aquellos que sueñan con matar a la literatura para ver si se está quieta de una buena vez y se deja estudiar con sosiego. A ellos quisiera rogar que inventaran un nuevo género (o una denominación, que lo anterior sería demasiado pedir) o que, alternativamente, se decidieran a sentenciar que este libro mío no tiene nada que ver con la literatura, supuesto tampoco probable.

> *Tobogán de hambrientos* pudiera clasificarse como cuento larguísimo, si admitiéramos que el substantivo y el adjectivo no se destruyen y neutralizan recíprocamente. La idea inicial de estas páginas brotó de mi pensamiento de que en esta vida todo está ligado y concatenado de forma que no queda jamás ni una sola pieza suelto; todas las cosas tienen un número—dijo, hace ya la mar de años, Filolao. El ejemplo de las cerezas es muy socorrido aunque, de paso, quizás ahora nos resulte también insuficiente: los hombres y sus acaeceres están mucho más ligados entre sí que las rabilargas y arracimadas cerezas del frutero.

The reader finds it difficult to keep in mind the 100 sets of intimate and intricate relationships of the characters. It is unnecessary that he do so, for little would be gained in the way of insight into the personalities of the characters and their doings. Rather, that the novel has any structure at all corresponds to what Cela feels to be the natural pattern of life. The elaborate structure of the novel is one reasonable way of reflecting the elaborate structure of the human relationships. As is true for the majority of the technical innovations in the novel, the presence of pattern corresponds, as Le Sage has pointed out in the study cited previously, to a particular metaphysical concept concerning the nature of reality and the novelist's means of knowing and portraying that reality. The meeting between the metaphysical concept and the actual elaboration of the work of art— the artist's attempt to give the illusion of truth to his concept of reality and his vision of mankind—results in the

particular structural format which the critic describes. Pattern as a substitute for plot mirrors the novelist's conviction that life is not plot, not adventure in the storyteller's sense of the word, but that it is, precisely, pattern. In addition to being a contrivance for purely esthetic purposes, pattern may then also become the novelist's means for coherent unity in the presence of chaotic life, or it may be his artistic attempt to reflect a particular pattern of existence of which his novel is a unique manifestation. And it is precisely Cela's novels which are excellent examples not only of art as pattern, but as well of the techniques of extrinsic and intrinsic pattern in so far as pattern reflects a particular segment of the theme. In addition, Cela's importance in the development of the contemporary Spanish novel derives in great part from his experimentation with the techniques of the new novel and from his commitment in his most recent works to that highly innovative mode of fiction.

Robert Kirsner (essay date 1970)

SOURCE: "Cela's Quest for a Tragic Sense of Life," in *Kentucky Romance Quarterly,* Vol. XVII, No. 3, 1970, pp. 259-64.

[*In the following essay, Kirsner explores the elements of tragedy in Cela's fiction.*]

From the very beginning of his literary career, even before the birth of that famous family of Pascual Duarte, Cela has sought to express a tragic sense of life. His first creation, *Pisando la dudosa luz del día,* composed presumably in the trenches of the Spanish Civil War in 1936, attempts to depict the waning of a doubtful light as life passes into the cavernous darkness of death. "Ven, Muerte, ven" cries out the youthful poet.

La familia de Pascual Duarte, published in 1942 but meaningfully dated 1937, strives to convey an atmosphere of impending doom. Conceived in the throes of imminent execution, the narration of Pascual Duarte aspires to capture the tragic essence of man's existence. Indeed, an air of decreed disaster pervades the milieu; yet, the aura of despair does not penetrate. The external account of the action shocks and dismays but the characters remain substantially aloof from the experience of tragedy. There is horror, but no pity. And without the assuasive element of compassion the terror that stalks the novel is without tension. As cruelty becomes a way of life, killing appears as a commonplace occurrence. The real drama lies in the author's groping for the portrayal of a tragic sense of life in a world that is inured and seemingly immune to violence and destruction.

The course of Cela's writings has followed a determined path of misfortune, morbidity and mordacity. His "strident voice in the desert" has been a lament, a cry of despair. Cela has been mourning over man's fate for more than thirty years. Whether in the role of novelist or critic, Cela's zealous search for tragedy does not abate. Even in the personal moments of his highly comfortable bourgeois existence in Palma de Mallorca, our author feels the need to remind his friends and himself of prevailing poverty in the mainland. As in his novels and books of travel a certain sadness invariably overtakes him.

Cela's quixotic credo is contained in this prologue to the first volume of his **Obra Completa:**

> Ha sonado en mi reloj de sangre la hora del difícil, del remordedor recuento: la triste hora del examen de conciencia, que siempre huele, querámoslo o no, a antesala de la muerte, a sosegada y venenosa y abdicadora antesala de la muerte.
>
> El hombre pierde siempre la permanente batalla que el tiempo le presenta, El hombre es la víctima propiciatoria que los dioses ofrecen, en sacrificio, al tiempo insaciable y jamás clemente. El tiempo, en su lucha con el hombre, juedga con él y, cuando se aburre, lo mata. O lo deja morir cortándole el chorro del tiempo. Pero en la pelea contra el tiempo, y aun sabiendo de antemano que seremos vencidos por él, a los hombres no nos cabe más postura que la de hacerle frente con decision, darle cara y, pase lo que pase, no huirle.

Here we have the expression of a posture that is *real* only in the sense that it expresses a wish fulfillment, a dream in the making. To be sure the struggle exists. In his every day life as in his literature, Cela battles with himself and his circumstances. But it is not a tragic joust. For try as he will, life emerges triumphant. The lugubrious appearance of the confrontation cannot conceal the joy of doing battle. In the works of Cela, even in the ones such as *Izas, Rabizas y Colipoterras* (1964), that depend on the visual degradation of human existence, there is an element of mirth, sardonic in substance and grotesque in its effect, but mirth nonetheless.

Cela's propensity toward the sordid and the shocking expresses a desire to experience all aspects of human existence. Of special concern to him is the awakening of his readers to all those *forbidden* thoughts that lurk in the minds of men. His mission is to bring the unconscious to the realm of the conscious, to give meaning and form to the shadowy substance of which our fears and inner desires are made. The examination of conscience may lead us to the antechamber of death, but the inexorable and irreducible reality of the antechamber is no less that of its ultimate destiny. It is here, in the antechamber, where we remain and where we experience the joys and agony of living. So it is with the literature of Camilo José Cela. It strives to bring to the reader a grim vision of utter destruction and void but the door to the apocalypse is hardly opened and subsequently the chamber of death is virtually forgotten. The odor of death is neither oppressive nor obstructive. There is a mere scent of sadness. And even that sometimes evaporates or is absorbed in the intense struggle for survival.

Cela's quest for the tragic has led him to undertake topics which are meant to be disturbing. In any form that he can, he will seek to explode feelings of complacency. If he cannot move the world by means of horror, he will do it by means of shame. Thus, his *Diccionario Secreto* (1968) aims to puncture the social halo of modestly and propriety which govern the linguistic inhibitions we practice in reference to our own bodies. The completion of the first volume of the Dictionary constitutes a learned venture. Indeed, the author amply demonstrates his erudition with copious references to etymology and literature. Unquestionably, it is a serious undertaking. So serious, in fact, that it attains an air of exaggerated immodesty. The contrast between subject matter and the scholarly approach inevitably a produces laughter or at least smiles. Rationally the words of Dámaso Alonso quoted at the beginning of the *Diccionario* are quite correct. ". . . (hay que) tratar abiertamente esta cuestión y sin remilgos de pudibundez. Imaginad qué pasaría en medicina si los médicos negaran atención a muchas inmundicias (físicas y morales) que tienen que considerar." The theory is above reproach. The application, nonetheless, brings about an incongruity between form and content. It would be naive to assume that the effect is not deliberate, Cela has always reveled in the creation of disparate imagery. His most meaningful symbol of expression has been the shockingly absurd. It is through horror and shame that he has created human situations. It is through horror and shame that he seeks to create a tragic vision of man.

In the early works horror resulted from the portrayal of man's inhumanity to man. Cruelty was the characteristic that constituted the key to man's heart. Hostility erupted in a volcanic fashion. Blood flowed freely. In *Nuevas Andanzas,* life was a slaughter house. Men even hung like sausage. "En el pueblo, cuando vino el señor juez con toda su corte de curialas y su rabo de Guardia civil, se procedió diligentemente a descolgar al padre, a la madrastra y a las dos criadas del Julián; y los vecinos, no sé si para festejar Dios sabrá qué rara figuración de la sangre o si solamente por espíritu de imitación, el caso es que también empezaron a descolgar de las campanas de sus chimeneas toda suerte de morcones, jamones, lomo en tripa, chorizos, salchichas, morecillas y demás embutidos, con lo que—si a la larga perdieron los que antes habían tenido—a la corta salimos todos gananciosos y bien alimentados." Still, the vision was execrable rather than tragic. The imagery was cannibalistic. There were no regrets, no conflict. In fact, for all its grotesqueness, the event was a happy one. The odor of death did not penetrate the banquet of the living. The awareness of hanging bodies could not compare, except in form, with the sight of hanging meats and sausages. Again, the instinct for survival reigned supreme.

Cela's first and most delightful book of travels, *Viaje a la Alcarria* (1948) also seeks to capture the tragic essence of human existence.

Unlike the early novels, *Viaje a la Alcarria* has a certain delicateness about it. The author reaches out for tragedy in a poetic manner. "Los misteriosos tranvías negros de la noche portan de un lado para otro su andamiaje sobre ruedas; van guiados por hombres sin uniforme, por hombres de boina, callados como muertos, que se tapan la cara con una bufanda . . ."

> Son buenas gentes que viven,
> laboran, pasan y sueñan,
> y en un día como tantos
> descansan bajo la tierra.

Yet, there is a note of serenity about life and death. Living and dying come together naturally, harmoniously. If in *Nuevas andanzas y desventuras de Lazarillo de Tormes* the spectacle of monstrous grotesqueness overstated the case for tragedy and produced laughter, here the transposition from toil to eternal rest flows much too smoothly to arouse pain or pity. There is a subdued note of sadness but the work does not dwell on laments. On the contrary, there is much rejoicing in *Viaje a la Alcarria.* The final words constitute a toast to life. "Empiezan a encenderse las luces eléctricas, y el altavoz de un bar suelta contra las piedras antiguas el ritmo de un bugui-bugui. Don Mónico, don Paco y el viajero se meten en el casino a tomarse un vermú con aceitunas con tripa de anchoas . . ."

In the 1940's Cela searched for the tragic meaning of life with a seriousness of purpose; he believed in the dignity of the quest. In the 1960's, however, it has been an undertaking tinted with despair. In the last decade Cela has struck mercilessly—at times even blindly—against the sacrosanct inhibitions of his society. His mission has always been to awaken his readers to the entombed realities of life, realities which give man a tragic quality. Nonetheless, the approach has varied greatly in recent years. His vengeance—and that is what Cela has called his writings—has been blunt. There are no literary characters from whom we can flee. No longer can the reader imagine himself different from those entities that have been created by a pen. For now Cela has directed his attack with words and pictures, in prose and in verse, against the prudery of his times. Thwarted in his attempt to create tragedy out of man's propensity toward destruction, Cela seeks to find such drama by means of uncovering social self deception.

In particular, the *Diccionario Secreto, Izas, Rabizas y Colipoterras* and *Viaje a U.S.A.* are examples of Cela's new cynicism. For all their scholarly and literary merits, they cannot conceal the very personal intent of the artist to ridicule society. Cela abandoned destruction for derision. And with his new weapon he has sought to create an image of man smitten by his own hypocrisy. The technique tends to be overwhelming. The desired effect is not achieved. What we have instead is a vision of man frolicking in the mire of human existence. The picture is not pretty, but neither is it tragic. In fact, there is less possibility for nobility in the works of the sixties than there was in the early ones. At least in the beginning of Cela's career blood as a leitmotif quite often served as an instrument of redemption. In the new writings there is no escape from the crudities of life. Perhaps Camilo José Cela spoke the inexorable truth about himself when he wrote in the 1960 preface to *Pisando La Dudosa Luz del Día,* also contained in the 1963 edition, "Dedico este libro a los muchachos que tienen ahora veinte años; los de entonces ya ni me importan. Al hombre, salvo luminosas y señaladas excepciones, lo prostituyen los años, la convivencia y la amarga lucha por la vida."

Brian Steel (essay date May 1972)

SOURCE: "Two Recurring Structures in Cela's *Prólogos*," in *Revista de Estudios Hispánicos,* Vol. VI, No. 2, May, 1972, pp. 249-64.

[*In the following essay, Steel analyzes Cela's use of parenthesis and apposition to draw conclusions about the author.*]

No one who has read any of Cela's *Prólogos* can have failed to notice the vigorous personal style in which they are written. In all but the more deliberately scholarly of these essays, the writer gives us a series of reflections on a variety of subjects and in a style which one would expect of a stimulating and provocative essayist or lecturer.

What contributes especially to this personal style in the *Prólogos* is Cela's very frequent use of two types of structures: parentheses and phrases in apposition. Because of the frequency with which the writer uses these structures, many of his sentences give the reader the same sort of dislocated effect which is heard in spoken conversation and especially in heated discussion when a speaker interrupts his sentences in order to fit in spontaneous comments prompted by something that he has just said or thought of. The effect, in speech or in writing, is that the listener or reader is given the impression that the speaker or writer is full of ideas, original associations and images and that he is impatient to share them with others. In written style, the effect of these frequent dislocations is to involve the reader more closely not only with what the writer has written but also with those aspects of the writer's personality which are revealed by these interpolations.

In Cela's **Prólogos** the net result of these essentially spoken (or oratorical) techniques is rather like a combination of the effects achieved by a witty after-dinner speaker and those achieved by an accomplished and imaginative writer. In other words, the two techniques in question may be seen as throwing light on two essential parts of Cela's literary personality: the fiercely independent writer and thinker and the serious artist.

Cela's self-assurance and "outrageous" pronouncements both in his writings and in his public life have been well publicised and they have led at least one Spanish critic, J. L. Alborg, to accuse Cela of being more concerned with building up and maintaining his public image as an *enfant terrible* than with the more worthy task of producing penetrating novels. Indeed, in an extremely hostile evaluation of Cela's work, Alborg comments:

> yo diría que la creación más afortunada que Cela ha conseguido a lo largo de sus escritos es la leyenda y la realidad de su propia persona: el único personaje verdadero trazado por su pluma es él.

Leaving to others the task of finding out whether Cela means all that he writes and says or whether he makes provocative or conceited statements merely to attract publicity, rather in the manner of a literary counterpart of Salvador Dali, we propose to examine in detail the two types of structures which are so constantly in evidence in the **Prólogos** written in the last twenty-five or so years that they cannot be mere accidents but must be considered as essential parts of Cela's essay style. However, in view of the personal nature of these structures, the examination should also reveal something about the writer himself.

Before examining examples of the more frequent of the two structures, parenthesis, it is necessary, for the sake of consistency, to define what we understand by parenthesis since Cela, like most of us, makes very liberal and arbitrary use of four punctuation signs (the comma, the dash, the colon and brackets) for a variety of purposes including those of signalling parentheses and phrases in apposition

and to detach any words which he wishes to stand out from the sentence (including non-restrictive relative clauses, prepositional phrases, etc.)

In order to compensate for the imprecise use of these punctuation signs, we propose to limit our study of parenthesis to those words, phrases, clauses or sentences which interrupt, or are appended to a sentence with which they have no structural link and of which they do not form a grammatical part (e.g. as subject, object, adverb, prepositional phrase, coordinate clause, etc.) In this way, the following would not qualify as containing examples of parenthesis because in spite of the punctuation the separated sections are structurally part of the sentence in which they occur:

> Mi novela—por razones particulares—sale en la República Argentina . . . and . . . su minúscula verdad (que, a veces, coincide con la minúscula y absoluta libertad exigible al hombre). (Both of these are from *Col.*)

In the following extracts, those parts which do not fulfil any grammatical role within the sentence in which they occur, are of the type which we intend to consider as parentheses:

> Los ciento sesenta personajes que bullen—no corren— por sus páginas . . . ; A la historia—y éste es un libro de historia, no una novela—le acontece que . . . ; Pienso que hoy no se puede novelar más—mejor o peor—que como yo lo hago. (All from *Col.*)

Although, according to our definition of parenthesis, phrases and larger units in apposition could be classified as parentheses, it seems more useful for our present purposes to regard them as separate structures or at least as a special type of parentheses because of their special and constant function as modifiers of a noun or noun group and because of their equivalence with relative clauses.

Having established a reliable way of identifying Cela's parentheses, we may now examine them in detail.

The most obviously spontaneous are those parentheses in the form of exclamations, which reveal, as in conversation, a variety of emotions and attitudes aroused in the writer (or speaker). Cela makes very extensive use of exclamatory parentheses and the following may be considered representative:

> ¡albricias!; ¡ay!; ¡cómo no!; ¡quién lo duda!; ¡quién lo sabe!; ¡oh, el instinto!; ¡qué ingenua soberbia!; ¡qué bella incertidumbre!; ¡qué momento amargo!

Even when considered out of context, many of these parentheses are quite clearly humorous in intent. Very of-ten—perhaps most often—the exclamatory parentheses are of an ironical (cf. most of the examples above) or mock-ing nature (e.g. mock indignation: *¡vaya por Dios!*, and *¡y yo sin saberlo!* or mockery of the attitudes of others, as in the sentence where Cela prefixes *¡qué descaro!*—as a typical "bourgeois" expression of disgust—to *el culo al aire*).

The effect of these parentheses on the reader is that as well as amusing him they leave him with the impression of Cela's strong personality. Indeed, if we except certain ex-planatory or functional parentheses like *aleccionaba Don Quijote a Sancho; se venía diciendo; sigo con Marañón,* etc. and conventional tags like *dicho sea de paso, la verdad sea dicha, el tiempo conmigo* (Cela avoids the more conventional Catholic phrase *Dios mediante*), most of Cela's parentheses can be seen as dogmatic pronounce-ments by a person quite convinced of the value of his own opinions (and exclamations).

In support of this theory that Cela reveals a dominant per-sonality in his parentheses, reference can be made to the other types of parentheses in his **Prólogos.** For instance, short parentheses like *creo yo, digo, repito, bien lo sé,* etc. (in which the first person element is quite clearly visible) are quite common whereas there are only very occasional examples of the more conventional and "humble" first per-son plural of the styles of essays and literary criticism (e.g. . . . *citemos al azar tres o cuatro ingredientes literarios*) and (*seamos humildes, inmensa y descaradamente humildes,* etc.) in which the form makes it quite clear that Cela is mocking the idea of being *humilde*).

In another group of parentheses, we find that Cela either corrects, defines, emphasizes or makes an observation on a word or phrase, once more in a peremptory and self-as-sured manner which leads us to understand that the writer will brook no argument on the matter:

> no se puede novelar más—mejor o peor—que como
> yo lo hago; extrañas cosas—tampoco demasiado
> extrañas—; ellos, que no yo; lenguas, que no hablas;
> virtud, que no vicio.

In yet another type of parenthesis, Cela emits an instant judgment or opinion of a term or idea just mentioned, as in:

> —todos lo son—; —ninguna lo es—; cosa poco
> probable; cosa ya dicha y tan evidente que ni la aludo.

Another way of indicating to his readers that Cela appears to discount the existence of any other point of view but his own, is his use of admonitions and reminders like *querámoslo o no; quiérase o no se quiera; tiña sus cueros como pueda hacerlo; recuérdese,* etc.

Although some of Cela's parentheses do not fit into any of the types so far identified, most of the ones which are not dogmatic are still indicative that the writer considers his spontaneous thoughts and reactions to be of vital interest to the reader, whereas they may well seem to us rather un-necessary and laboured as in the following extracts:

> en cuyos indices (iba a decir: en cuya estructuración,
> pero me contuve a tiempo); como quien lava (también
> se dice como quien mea, pero es más azaradora e
> imprecisa forma de señalar).

Usually, this great variety of "egocentric" parentheses does not lessen the reader's interest in the essays, but they do distract his intention and they may well cause him to won-der whether, in fact, Cela is not overdoing these spontane-ous "effects" and entertaining or brow-beating him in a rather facile or flippant manner instead of occupying him with more profound remarks.

In fact, it is not at all unlikely that the main reason for these displays of verbal and grammatical virtuosity is to assert Cela's belief in his right to think and say whatever he likes, especially if it is unconventional or provocative. In any case, the constant searching for effects can reduce the value of what is actually written.

Before turning to the second of the two recurring struc-tures in Cela's **Prólogos,** phrases in apposition, an impor-tant distinction must be made between three semantic types of apposition.

The most common and general use of apposition (in Span-ish and English alike) is to provide a concise description, identification, explanation or definition of the noun group to which the phrases are apposed. Thus in examples like *Sergio, su primo; Nixon, el presidente de los Estados Unidos; El jefe, don Jaime; Don Jaime, el jefe; El mes de octubre, estación de la vendimia,* the phrase in appo-sition merely states objectively a known fact about or char-acteristic of the noun or noun group to which it refers.

In the second semantic type of apposition, the apposed words give a definition or description which represents a more subjective opinion of the speaker or writer, an opin-ion which may also be a fact but which, because it is pre-sented in an original or unfamiliar way, needs more careful consideration before the reader decides whether it is true or not. Thus, to quote examples from Cela, the definitions contained in *el orden público—el pseudo orden de las gentes de orden—*or *los políticos (meros canalizadores* *de la inercia histórica)* are interesting but subjective evaluations which are not necessarily completely true. Similarly, in *los animales serios—el león, el asno, la cabra,* rather than an objectively factual statement we have a very subjective and unexpected identification, the purpose of which is simply to surprise or "shock" us.

This type of apposition, where the imagination and beliefs of the writer contribute to the presentation of an original view of the concept described, is a stylistic device of some importance. Because of the subjective nature of these definitions and also because some of them may present an objective truth in a subjective (original) manner, we should label them *artistic truths.*

The third—and, from the point of view of literary stylistics, the most interesting—type of apposition is one which displays both subjective judgment and artistic imagination. In her study of Cela's style, O. Prjevalinsky has pointed out Cela's predilection in his literary work also for this type of apposition which she describes as *metáforas asociativas* and which she defines as *dos imágenes yuxtapuestas: una que pertenece al plano real, y la otra, al figurado.* This definition may serve to distinguish *metáforas* from apposition of the second type although, in fact, it is not always easy to distinguish between these two subjective types of apposition. Prjevalinsky then gives as examples the following three *metáforas asociativas:*

> la memoria, esa quebradiza vena de la ilusión; la memoria, esa fuente de dolor; and la verdad, ese santo palo al que devora la implacable y veloz carcoma del chisme que anda en coplas.

Cela's predilection for apposition as a stylistic device in his **Prólogos** is quite clear. Further, as we would expect of a creative writer, he shows a distinct preference for the two subjective types, with which we shall deal shortly.

However, in order to give a full description of Cela's use of apposition, it is necessary to deal with all three types outlined above.

Cela uses the objective identification type where necessary (e.g. *Armando Mondéjar López, aquel niño que andaba con un dedo en la nariz, O.C.* Vol. II and *la ignara burguesía del país, aquella clase social que hizo grande a Francia, O.C.* I). Because this type is of no special stylistic interest and because it is objective, it merits little further comment here. However, on occasion, Cela uses this type of apposition with the specific purpose of being humorous, and, to do so, presents fiction as fact—which, in context, is not the same as practising deception:

> mi primer maestro, hoy representante de los

preservativos lavables Marie-Rose en las plazas de soberanía española del norte de Africa (*O.C.* II); el hispanista don Matthew G. Browning, alias Dante Gabriel Rossetti II, coronel de la RAF en situación de reserva y poeta lírico de musa retozona y llena de sentimiento (*PSA*).

Two further examples of this factual type of apposition may be of some interest because, although rather colorless from both the style and content points of view, they contain statements about Cela's own work:

> el naipe de mi obra dispersa, aquella que, de no haberla enchiquerado a tiempo en sus límites, se hubiera perdido sin remisión. (*Pág.*)

> su único camino necesario: el escribir sus páginas, una detrás de la otra, con calma y con aplicación, sin pausa, ni desfallecimiento, ni más respeto que el debido a la voluntad (o a la real gana) de sus títeres, sus héroes y sus contribuyentes. (*O.C.* IV)

Of the two subjective types of apposition, *artistic truths* and *metaphor,* the first is of interest because the examples that Cela uses tell us something of his ideas and attitudes towards people, institutions and other aspects of human activity. Particularly significant is the fact that, in almost every case, the apposed phrase or clause is negative in the sense that it reveals hostility, adverse criticism or contempt felt by the writer for the concept being defined or described. It is here that one finds more than one echo of Baroja's biting comments.

Here is a list of examples of appositions of this type used by Cela in his **Prólogos:**

People

> el hombre, ese pequeño miserable empeñado en entorpecer la generosa marcha de la naturaleza (*O.C.* III).

> los políticos (meros canalizadores de la inercia histórica) (*Col.*)

> las gentes oficialmente honradas: aquellas que están al corriente del pago de la contribución. (*PD*)

> los hombres llamados a gobernar el mundo—los escolares de hoy, y a quienes, a cambio de disciplina se les entrega, con el certificado de estudios, la patente de corso. (*VA*)

Spain

. . . la España contemporánea, país que, como ciertas familias, que no saben ser pobres, hace almoneda de la herencia, tabla rasa del recuerdo y sueldo de todos sus pudores. (*O.C.* IV, p. 521, in a letter to P. Polack)

. . . el Estado, aquello que sin ser precisamente el pueblo, ni los escritores, ni las Academias, a todos condiciona y constriñe. (*DS*)

Man's achievements

. . . la ley, esa entelequia . . . (*VA*)

. . . las guerras, [ni] los inventos mecánicos, [ni] la poesía romántica, esas tres calamidades. (*VA*)

. . . el orden público—el pseudo orden de las gentes de orden. (*PSA*)

Literary critics and their work (a favorite target of Cela's):

. . . los legalistas de la preceptiva, aquellos que sueñan con matar a la literatura para ver si se está quieta de una buena vez y se deja estudiar con sosiego. (*TH*)

. . . la preceptiva literaria, ciencia infusa buena para ejemplares discursos conmemorativos. (*O.C.* II)

Los poetas no son excepción; lo que les acontece es que tampoco son escritores más que para la exhausta e imprecisa nomenclatura al uso (falaz jerga inventada por académicos, profesores y subsecretarios) . . . (*O.C.* III)

Literature

el equipaje del escritor: ese macuto que ganaría en eficacia si acertara a tirar por la borda, uno tras otro, todos los atavismos que lo lastran. (Col.)

The third type of apposition, the *metáforas asociativas* referred to by Prjevalinsky, are of particular interest because they reveal Cela's artistic imagination at work. A pessimistic or melancholy attitude is clearly visible as the inspiration for most of them. In most cases the noun described is an abstract term:

la muerte, esa gran imprevisión. (*O.C.* I)

la suerte, dama esquiva. (*VA*)

la faz de los aconteceres—esa minucia historiable. (*PSA*)

la motivación del eufemismo—la asepsia de la expresión que alude a concepto considerado séptico— (*DS*)

la remordedora congoja; el orín que se ceba en el espíritu del sedentario habitado por los maíos pensamientos. (*O.C.* V)

In some of these appositions, the writer's basic inspiration seems to be an assumption that man is essentially an unjust creature:

la posteridad: ese gato calvorota y medio ronco que digiere pedradas, patadas y denuestos. (*O.C.* III)

el vagabundaje—ese oficio al que, ahogándole en su propia humildad, hasta se le niega sitio para su nombre en el diccionario. (*O.C.* V)

Some are more optimistic, or at least not completely pessimistic:

. . . las musas, esas sombras iluminadoras y huidizas que siempre comparecen al conjuro de la paciencia. (*O.C.* I)

la sonrisa, ese gesto sutil que vale para todo y que puede significarlo todo (*O.C.* I)

la memoria, esa ubre de bienaventuranzas jamás muida del todo. (*O.C.* IV)

In all the ***Prólogos*** examined, examples of apposition expressing an optimistic attitude or any emotion like lyrical joy or pleasure experienced by the writer were extremely rare. Nevertheless there are a few. Most optimistic or lyrical were:

la esperanza—el áncora misma de la vida. (*VA*)

la poesía: esa postrera esencia que vive en los demás y que el poeta despierta con su suave aliento. (*O.C.* II)

. . . las fragosidades del monte: la despeinada pelambrera del mundo donde habita la paz, esa caricia. (*O.C.* IV)

The following example of apposition, although negative in one sense (i.e. men are unable to relax and enjoy life), indicates Cela's own pleasure as he contemplates the joys of *vagabundaje*:

. . . (del) ocio, esa bendición que el hombre no suele saber gastar, deleitosamente, despaciosamente,

desconfiadamente, los lomos reclinados sobre el
chaparro de la cuneta, la bota al alcance de la mano,
el pitillo en la boca y la mente poblada de imprecisos
pájaros voladores, de inciertos y bien pintados pájaros
voladores. (*O.C.* V)

It must be repeated, however, that such "optimistic" examples of apposition are rare in the ***Prólogos,*** and that Cela's natural inclination seems to be to express feelings of resignation, melancholy and doubt. This inclination is perhaps what leads Cela to describe the writer's heart as:

. . . su corazón: ese avispero rodeado de flores de
piorno por entre las que corre un agua fresca y sin
nombre que, a lo que se va viendo, lo mismo le sirve
para un roto que para un cosido. (*O.C.* V)

What strikes the reader here is that, after creating a rather contrived image of the conflict in the writer's soul between worries and doubts on the one hand and tranquillity on the other, Cela feels obliged to shatter the peaceful part of the image by bringing the apposed phrase (and the reader) down to earth with a bump. This predilection for anticlimax is another feature of Cela's style.

In view of the dominant pessimism in Cela's use of apposition, we are forced to re-examine Cela's description of himself in the *Prologuillo* to ***Viaje a la Alcarria*** as

un hombre que pasa por la vida apoyado en las dos
angélicas muletas de la suerte y la esperanza. La suerte
sirve para mirar la vida con esperanza y la esperanza—
el áncora misma de la vida—vale para no temblar
aunque la suerte, dama esquiva, juegue a presentarse
y huir.

Before we dismiss this description as being obviously insincere, it is equally important to remember that the above portrait of the writer as an optimist is followed by lines which throw more light on his philosophy of life:

El protagonista de este libro de viajes—servidor de
ustedes—nada pide porque nada quiere ni necesita. La
paz es algo que los clementes dioses regalan a sus
elegidos. La paz, como el vagabundaje, tampoco es
un oficio sino una bendición.

We should like to suggest as a conclusion to this analysis that in his special use of apposition and parenthesis, Cela shows us that he firmly believes himself to be one of these *elegidos* and that he personally enjoys the peace and independence alluded to (which would explain why he feels optimism about his own personal situation) but also that he is not really interested in how the rest of his fellow beings are faring in life (although, since he is aware of their many inadequacies, he naturally feels pessimistic about them, their relationships and their institutions).

If these assumptions are correct, they would help to explain Cela's peculiar inability or unwillingness in his writing to go beyond quick, skilful sketches or caricatures of his characters and give, with compassion and understanding, penetrating portraits of human beings in their struggle with life's problems. This unwillingness to show characters in depth is possibly the most criticised feature of Cela's writing and has been succinctly described by Torrente Ballester:

Describe actos que pueden ser significativos, que
parecen abrirnos una puerta sobre una intimidad, sobre
un carácter, pero la puerta permanece cerrada, y el
novelista salta inmediatamente a otro personaje cuya
atractiva superficie le solicita . . . El lector pierde este
asidero por el que podría enterarse de una vida entera.
Tenemos de cada uno de ellos [i.e. Cela's characters]
preciosos datos: cómo hablan, cómo se mueven, cómo
visten y cómo viven, pero no sabemos cómo son.

If our interpretation of Cela's character, such as it is revealed in his use of parenthesis and appositions, were correct, it would also explain why Cela seems to have abandoned the novel (although at the moment the Hispanic world is eagerly awaiting Cela's promised ***San Camilo, 1936***) in favour of other forms of writing like his travel books and his *apuntes carpetovetónicos* which show off to their best advantage his fine gifts of observation and sketching and his stylistic brilliance.

Whether these assumptions and conclusions are correct or not, it is quite clear that in his constant use of the two personal grammatical structures of parenthesis and apposition, Cela provides us with material which invites us to form judgments of him as a person and as a writer. In spite of the danger that Cela may well be laying down a series of red herrings to deceive the literary critics whom he professes to despise so much, the two recurring structures described in this analysis must surely be considered when Cela's intellectual character and attitude to life are being described and evaluated.

David Henn (essay date October 1972)

SOURCE: "Theme and Structure in *La colmena*," in *Forum for Modern Language Studies*, Vol. VIII, No. 4, October, 1972, pp. 304-19.

[*In the following essay, Henn presents the themes Cela*

addresses in La colmena *and how the structure of the novel supports these themes.*]

Discussions of Camilo José Cela's fourth novel, **La colmena,** have too often been centered around the structure of the work whilst thematic aspects have usually been subordinated to this formalistic emphasis. The formal complexities of the novel, the cinematographic technique, simultaneity of action, fragmentation, lack of chronological sequence, the large number of characters appearing in such a short period of time, have all been examined to the relative neglect of the introduction and elaboration of themes. Whereas the structure of **La colmena** has been generally regarded as testimony to the author's architectural skill, his use and treatment of themes has, by and large, received all too little detailed consideration. The purpose of this study will be to examine themes and thematic phases or movements in the work and also to comment on the relation between theme and structure.

When **La colmena** first appeared in 1951 Cela stated, in what was subsequently termed the *Nota a la primera edición:* "Mi novela **La colmena,** primer libro de la serie *Caminos inciertos,* no es otra cosa que un pálido reflejo, que una humilde sombra de la cotidiana, áspera, entrañable y dolorosa realidad." Subsequently, critics have, for the most part, agreed upon the nature of the reality that the author displays in his novel. Eugenio de Nora mentions ". . . los aspectos más negativos de la vida (la ausencia de caridad, la promiscuidad y abyección de las relaciones sexuales, el mísero cálculo de los pobres seres obsesionados por la ganancia indispensable al sustento, la maldad gratuita, etc.), . . ." Paul Ilie indicates two fundamental themes of the novel and also suggests their cause: "Las condiciones económicas de Madrid revelan una gran desigualded en la distributión de la riqueza, de la cual nacen dos temas fundamentales en la novela: dinero y sexo." Alonso Zamora Vicente, whilst admitting economic hardship as a theme of **La colmena,** feels that the people portrayed have it in their own power to remedy the situation and suggests that it is their mediocrity and spiritual impoverishment that prevents them from doing so. The aimlessness of the existence of most of those seen in **La colmena,** and of Martín Marco in particular, is, in the opinion of D. W. Foster, a theme which the structure of the novel "is designed to emphasize." Finally, a theme stressed by José Ortega is the temporal aspect of the novel and, closely related to this, the repetitive nature of the lives of those encountered: "La temporalidad en **La colmena** es el elemento fundamental que envuelve y aprisiona a todos los personajes. . . . Esto, lo temporal y repetitivo de la existencia, es lo que Cela quiere mostrarnos con su 'maquinilla de fotógrafo'." The repetitive and monotonous existences of most of those seen in **La colmena** is, however, not necessarily the result of financial hardship and the

obvious limitations that this would impose. Indeed, in Chapter 1, where the clientele of doña Rosa's café is shown to be predominantly bourgeois, the atmosphere of both monotony and lethargy tends to suggest that the problem is spiritual rather than material. In the novel sex is seen to provide some relief for both wealthy and poor from a largely monotonous existence, although, as Nora points out, this relief takes two different forms: ". . . el sexo es, por una parte, la 'liberación' única al alcance de estos seres cercados por la miseria, en confluencia con el erotismo como diversión preferida y barata de los más o menos privilegiados. . . ."

Whilst the theme of monotony is particularly emphasized in the opening chapter of **La colmena** it also constitutes an important aspect of the rest of the novel. At times, Cela makes his own unequivocal statement:

> Detrás de los días vienen las noches, detrás de las noches vienen los días. El año tiene cuatro estaciones: primavera, verano, otoño, invierno. Hay verdades que se sienten dentro del cuerpo, como el hambre o las ganas de orinar.

Here, the inexorable march of time is suggested as a repetitive and monotonous process that manifests itself to man in terms of physical discomfort. The immediate problem for the hungry of **La colmena** is obviously that of survival; for those who are more financially secure it will be seen to be distraction. However, for both groups it could be argued that the basic challenge that has to be faced is that presented by the phenomenon of *time;* either time signalling the interval between a meal and subsequent hunger or, time as a vacuum to be filled by distractions in order to alleviate the monotony of a tedious existence, or both.

In the introduction to the first volume of his **Obra completa,** Cela states the following concerning the phenomenon of time:

> El hombre pierde siempre la permanent batalla que el tiempo le presenta. El hombre es la víctima propiciatoria que los dioses ofrecen, en sacrificio, al tiempo insaciable y jamás clemente. El tiempo, en su lucha con el hombre, juega con él y, cuando se aburre, lo mata, O lo deja morir cortándole el chorro del tiempo. Pero en la pelea contra el tiempo, y aun sabiendo de antemano que seremos venecidos por él, a los hombres no nos cabe más postura que la de hacerle frente con decisión, darle cara y, pase lo que pase, no huirle. A lo hecho, pecho. Es vieja ley que jamás falla, y el hombre debe morir matando o, al menos, defendiéndose. Al tiempo no lo maamos, cierto es, pero lo herimos. El tiempo, en su lidia con el

hombre, tampoco, aunque lleve la mejor parte, sale incólume y de rositas.

There is, of course, nothing new or startling in this observation on man's invincible adversary, time. Nor is there any attempt to make even a fleeting examination of the nature, subjective or objective, of the phenomenon. Cela's brief statement is concerned with *man* and time; expressing the belief that man should at least face the challenge that time presents and, presumably, regard the challenge as a stimulus.

The above statement is, then, primarily concerned with man's psychological attitude toward time rather than his ultimate physical impotence. Whilst death is inevitable, life or time does, at least, give man a certain potential. Obviously, physical or social limitations may, in many cases, impede or even prevent an exploration of the potential that time presents. Perhaps the most disturbing and striking characteristic of the society seen in **La colmena** is that most of these people, leading an aimless and stagnant existence, show little sign that they would wish to challenge or escape from their predicament. As Paul Ilie points out: "El pesimismo inherente a la novela brota no tanto de la situación de pobreza como de la incapacidad de las personas para mejorarla o para ayudarse a sí mismas psicológicamente."

The opening chapter of the novel, evening in doña Rosa's café, shows a section (predominantly lower middle-class) of post Civil War Madrid society. From the outset the author evokes an atmosphere of lethargy and stagnation, an atmosphere which is sustained throughout the chapter, although with a gradually decreasing emphasis. One of the most disturbing aspects of this stagnation is the attitude of apathy and resignation ascribed to these people: ". . . los clientes ven pasar a la dueña, casi sin mirarla ya, mientras piensan, vagamente, en ese mundo que, ¡ay!, no fue lo que pudo haber sido, en ese mundo en el que todo ha ido fallando poco a poco, sin que nadie se lo explicase, a lo mejor por una minucia insignificante" and, shortly afterwards: "Los clientes de los cafés son gentes que creen que las cosas pasan porque sí, que no merece la pena poner remedio a nada."

This suggested collective malaise, associated with the theme of the monotony of existence, is also examined on an individual basis. Jaime Arce is not untypical; he displays either an inability to think or, at best, exhibits a vague curiosity which apathy or lethargy or both prevent him from pursuing to any depth: "Don Jaime no solía pensar en su desdicha; en realidad, no solía pensar nunca en nada. Miraba para los espejos y se decía: ¿quién habrá inventado los espejos? . . . Don Jaime cambia de postura, se le estaba durmiendo una pierna. ¡Qué misterioso es esto! Tas, tas; tas,

tas; y así toda la vida, día y noche, invierno y verano: el corazón." Seoane, the café violinist, and therefore one of the few "creative" persons seen in **La colmena,** prefers not to think and instead spends the working day mentally anaesthetized: "Seoane mira vagamente para los clientes del café, y no piensa en nada. Seoane es un hombre que prefiere no pensar; lo que quiere es que el día pase corriendo, lo más de prisa posible, y a otra cosa." The torpor exhibited in Chapter 1 reflects a psychological or spiritual exhaustion in the people shown, a frightening submission to an apparently meaningless and monotonous existence: "Flota en el aire como un pesar que se va clavando en los corazones. Los corazones no duelen y pueden sufrir, hora tras hora, hasta toda un vida, sin que nadie sepamos nunca, demasiado a ciencia cierta, qué es lo que pasa." Thus, while doña Rosa assails and intimidates her employees, her clients have, for the most part, already been eroded to a state of quiescence and numbness by an intangible force that is omnipresent and has been frighteningly effective.

The thunder of doña Rosa's voice and her scathing comments do, at least, provide most of the brief intervals of diversion in the normally monotonous atmosphere of the café. From a technical point of view, her mobility and forthrightness stand in marked contrast to the generally static clients and their languid conversations. This contrast is facilitated by the author moving back and forth from doña Rosa to the clients and thus coupling a change of perspective with a change of tone. The clients rarely comment on her behaviour—a notable exception being Mauricio Segovia, who is not an *habitual* and therefore finds doña Rosa's tantrums, with which the regular customers are familiar, surprising. The main diversions for most of the clients are the novelties provided by Marco's ejection for failure to pay or the young poet who faints. These incidents are witnessed, commented upon, and then the languid conversations are resumed as the clients look wearily about them or at one another. Distraction is thus at a premium for the people of the café who apparently prefer the role of spectator to that of participant. An exception is provided by the two children playing at trains. They, at least, are making a conscious effort to relieve the boredom. Unfortunately, their efforts have become boring in themselves: "Son dos niños ordenancistas, consecuentes, dos niños que juegan al tren, aunque se aburren como ostras, porque se han propuesto divertirse y, para divertirse, se han propuesto, pase lo que pase, jugar al tren durante toda la tarde."

These two children illustrate, in this particular incident, a frustration that besets even the very young. However, and especially in the early part of Chapter 1, past and present frustrations of various clients provide a certain thematic unity: the fruitless business ventures of Leonardo Meléndez and Jaime Arce; Isabel Montes' loss of her young son; José Rodriguez de Madrid's lottery prize of a mere forty *pese-*

tas; Trinidad García Sobrino's thwarted ambition to become a *disputado;* and the prostitute Elvira's latest affair. Even doña Rosa gives the impression of being continually frustrated by her employees, whilst at the end of the chapter the reader learns that she, too, has probably suffered at the hands of an inclement fate:

> Suenan las nueve y media en el viejo reló de breves numeritos que brillan como si fueran de oro. El reló es un mueble casi suntuoso que se había traído de la exposición de París un marquesito tarambana y sin blanca que anduvo cortejando a doña Rosa, allá por el 905. El marquesito, que se llamaba Santiago y era grande de España, murió tísico en el Escorial, muy joven todavía, y el reló quedó posado sobre el mostrador del café, como para servir de recuerdo de unas horas que pasaron sin traer el hombre para doña Rosa y el comer caliente todos los días, para el muerto. ¡La vida!

The themes of monotony, apathy, frustration and lethargy dominate the opening chapter of *La colmena.* Despite the very beginning of the novel, where mention of the possible lesbianism of doña Rosa, her overriding interest in things financial and the considerable debt of Leonardo Meléndez might tend to suggest a different thematic direction for the chapter, sex and money (and hardship) are less in evidence than other themes. Sexual relationships, more extensively treated in later parts of the novel, are scarcely and obliquely mentioned here. The treatment is more in the form of background information dealing with, for example, the recent affair of Elvira and don Pablo, Consorcio López' past, or the present activities of doña Asunción's daughter. The only reference of any note to sexual morality occurs in the conversation between doña Pura and doña María, who believe that promiscuity was launched with the advent of the swimming-pool and is fostered by the cinemas.

Similarly, the problem of financial hardship is little in evidence. As has been mentioned previously, the clients of doña Rosa's café are predominantly bourgeois and, accordingly, both evidence and implication of hardship are seldom encountered in this early part of the novel. Elvira is one of the few examples of the more unfortunate seen in Chapter 1; she is currently having little success in her calling and lives "una vida perra, una vida que, bien mirado, ni merecería la pena vivirla." Toward the end of the chapter there occurs a sympathetic reminder of her indigence: "La señorita Elvira tiene un aire débil, enfermizo, casi vicioso. La pobre no come lo bastante para ser ni viciosa ni virtuosa." Apart from Eloy, impressed by Mario de la Vega's apparent affluence, and who needs a job (but fails really to show any enthusiasm for the idea), Martín Marco appears as the most obvious case of financial hardship. His ejection from the café provokes mixed reactions from some of those who notice the event, including Elvira, who understandably sympathizes with his plight.

Hardship, then, is a very minor theme in the opening chapter of *La colmena.* However, it is a theme that will be developed subsequently in the novel and particularly in Chapters 2, 4 and 6. The sexual theme is, likewise, little emphasized in this early part of the novel and will also be developed subsequently and particularly in Chapters 3, 4 and 5. Chapter 1 serves to stress the monotony and aimlessness of the lives of most of the café clientele and to introduce certain characters who will reappear later and illustrate many of the problems confronting and trying these people. Doña Rosa's café is, after the first chapter, seldom revisited by the author. In addition, approximately one third of the characters encountered in this chapter will not reappear in the novel (e.g. Leonardo Meléndez, Jaime Arce, Isabel Montes). Another third or so are seen perhaps two or three more times in the other chapters (e.g. don Pablo, Macario, doña Matilde) and the rest either appear infrequently but in important situations (e.g. Mario de la Vega, Consorcio López) or, with more regularity but without the pre-eminence enjoyed in Chapter 1 (e.g. doña Rosa, Elvira). There remains Martín Marco, unknown by name when first encountered and with apparently little more significance in Chapter 1 than the diversionary incident provided when he is ejected from the café. He is, however, central to the first two thirds of Chapter 2, reappears several times in Chapters 3 and 5, is again pre-eminent in Chapters 4 and 6 and dominates the short *Final.*

From a structural point of view, when Marco is followed away from the café at the very beginning of the second chapter the scope of the novel is about to be drastically enlarged, with the introduction of new places and new sets of characters. The tone is also modified. There begins a certain mobility (in marked contrast to the psychologically and physically static quality of Chapter I) which will bring with it an exploration at first hand of the problems facing that section of Madrid society portrayed in *La colmena.* The oppressive and stagnant atmosphere of the café is left behind and the reader is henceforward conducted into the streets, homes, bars, other cafés and *casas de citas* of the city. Technically, Marco initiates this outward movement in the novel. As a character, he is more often seen by the reader and more closely scrutinized by the author than any of the other forty or fifty people dealt with at length in the novel. His portrayal as the underfed and dissatisfied intellectual, expounding (often in a rather confused manner) the problems and grievances that he sees in his society, makes him the most fascinating and, at times, the most frustrating character of Cela's novel.

The external structure of *La colmena*—the lack of chronological sequence between and often within the chapters, fragmentation, cinematographic technique, simultaneity of action, etc.—has been discussed at length by Paul Ilie and D. W. Foster. Further points will be made concerning structure, but for the moment it is sufficient to mention the accepted chronological sequence of the chapters:—

1 2 4 6 3 5 *Final.*

The six chapters span a period of approximately two days and the *Final* is set three or four days later. Chapters 1, 2 and 4 cover five or six hours from mid-evening to midnight, or just after, of the first day. Chapter 6 sees the morning of the second day whilst 3 and 5 take place between early and late evening of that day. However, Chapters 1, 2 and 4 are not in strict chronological sequence. There is a certain overlapping between Chapters 1 and 2 evidenced by Marco's ejection from the café midway through the first chapter and his subsequent reappearance, talking to Pepe, at the beginning of the second. This overlapping also occurs within Chapter 2. Here, Marco's progress is followed from the time of his removal from the cafe (some time before 9:30 p.m.) until approximately 11 o'clock. He does not figure in the last third of the chapter which centres around the murder of doña Margot. The chapter is clearly divided into two distinct parts, the second part commencing with Leoncio Maestre who lives in the same building as doña Margot and who also provides a link between doña Rosa's café and the place of the crime. After seeing Maestre, the reader is then shown Suárez, the homosexual son of the deceased, arriving at the building by taxi. Suárez had last been seen leaving doña Rosa's café for a waiting taxi. Once again, this was prior to 9:30 p.m. and, assuming that this was the same cab ride (and not a particularly lengthy one), then the events described in the last part of Chapter 2 would commence at some time around 9:30 p.m. Suárez, of course, provides another link with doña Rosa's café. Similar links will occur when Mario de la Vega and Eloy come across a group of people outside the building where the crime has taken place and also when Mauricio Segovia and his brother see Suárez and his boy-friend in a bar. This chronological overlap within Chapter 2 and the times involved tend to refute D. W. Foster's suggestion of "a strong link" between Martín Marco and the murder of doña Margot. There also occurs an overlap between Chapters 2 and 4 with Roberto González' arrival home first mentioned in 2 and eventually seen in 4. The time, according to Filo's comment to her brother would be around 10.30 p.m. Thus Chapters 1, 2 and 4 are interlocking rather than strictly sequential and throughout the novel characters and situations are similarly linked or inter-connected, albeit tenuously at times and usually with only the reader aware of this fact.

As has been mentioned, when Marco is followed away from the café at the beginning of Chapter 2 not only does the narrative gain a certain mobility but the reader is introduced to a new environment and a new set of people. This new group (and Marco is, of course, one of them) serve to give a different perspective to the narration, with their own distinctive problems and attitudes. Marco is the dominant figure of most of the second chapter and it is through him that the themes of hardship and inequality are introduced and elaborated. Chapter 1 had, by and large, shown doña Rosa's everyday acquaintances, "her" people. Chapters 2, 4 and 6 will show Marco and many of "his" people. Marco's theorizing on prevalent social ills does not, by any token, convince the reader of the unfortunate plight of many of his fellows. This is rather displayed by the author, for although Marco does, via his thoughts and perorations, introduce the themes of hardship and inequality, his ideas are often so badly formulated or even nonsensical as to provoke an impatient or humorous reaction from the reader. Whereas his mental and physical activity stand in marked contrast to the people of the first chapter, his main problem is lack of a practical approach to the problems confronting him. Many of Marco's fellows have had the insight to see that the immediate problem of survival centres around the empty stomach or an essential medicine—in fact, money and its acquisition—he, on the other hand, does not seem to arrive at this conclusion until the *Final* and even at this point his sincerity is questionable.

As Marco is followed across the city and expounds his thoughts on social injustice and inequality it is apparent that his aims, although generally sound in principle, would require drastic or ludicrous means to be achieved: "—La vida—piensa—es esto. Con lo que unos se gastan para hacer sus necesidades a gusto, otros tendríamos para comer un año. ¡Está bueno! Las guerras deberían hacerse para que haya menos gentes que hagan sus necesidades a gusto y pueda comer el resto un poco mejor." This bellicose proposal is then followed by one equally fanciful but less draconian: "—Eso de que haya pobres y ricos—dice a veces—está mal; es mejor que seamos todos iguales, ni muy pobres ni muy ricos, todos un término medio. A la humanidad hay que reformarla. Debería nombrarse una comisión de sabios que se encargase de modificar la humanidad." Unfortunately, his utopian ideals do not keep Marco alive and, apart from his occasional work as a *francotirador,* he leads a largely parasitic existence.

Although hardship and the struggle for survival are the motifs of most of the second chapter, their presence is recurrent rather than continuous. There is, in fact, a strong contrast between the well-being of, for example, Pablo Alonso and Laurita and the precarious position of Filo and Roberto González. The former couple are able to enjoy luxuries available to only the wealthier in this society, whereas Filo and Roberto struggle to acquire the necessities of life: "Ella trabaja hasta caer rendida, con cinco niños pequeños y una criadita de dieciocho años para mirar por ellos, y él hace todas las horas extraordinarias que puede y donde se tercie." Roberto, with as many part-time jobs as he can manage, is thus patently aware of the reality of his situation and the responsibility that he has for his family. Similarly, the six-year-old *gitanito* who had stirred Roberto's conscience as another less fortunate than himself, maintains a precarious existence by dint of his own efforts. Marco, on the other hand, experiencing "una mala temporada," relies heavily on the generosity of others for his survival.

At times Cela emphasizes the contrasting fortunes of his characters by skilful juxtaposition of the short sections that constitute each chapter of **La colmena.** A striking example of this technique occurs with the reappearance of Elvira in Chapter 2. Firstly Marco and Filo are seen together, then Pablo and Laurita and, finally, Elvira and Leocadia:

. . . . . . Oye, ¿tienes dinero?

—No.

—Coge esas dos pesetas.

—No, ¿Para que? ¿Adónde voy yo con dos pesetas?

—También es verdad. Pero ya sabes, quien da lo que tiene . . .

—Ya sé.

—¿Te has encargado la ropa que te dije, Laurita?

—Sí, Pablo. El abrigo me queda muy bien, ya verás como te gusto.

Pablo Alonso sonríe con la sonrisa de buey benévolo del hombre que tiene las mujeres no por la cara, sino por la cartera.

. . . .
. . . . . . Ahora me tengo que cuidar mucho para que podamos ser muy felices. . . .

Pablo se deja querer.

—Quisiera ser la chica más guapa de Madrid para gustarte siempre. . . . ¡Tengo unos celos!

La castañera habla con una señorita. La señorita tiene las mejillas ajadas y los párpados enrojecidos, como de tenerlos enfermos.

—¡Qué frío hace!

—Sí, hace una noche de pedros. El mejor día me quedo pasmadita igual que un gorrión.

La señorita guarda en el bolso una peseta de castañas, la cena.

—Hasta mañana, señora Leocadia.

—Adiós, señorita Elvira, descansar.

Here, not only is the financial situation of Alonso and Marco contrasted, but also the opposing fortunes of Laurita and Elvira, where the prostitute's jaded appearance and meagre supper seem a world apart from the material well-being of Laurita and her desire to be "la chica más guapa de Madrid." Pablo Alonso is also clothing Marco—Filo's enquiry as to whether Martín is wearing "una camiseta mareada P.A." brings this fact to light. Both Pablo Alonso and the *tahonero* Ramón, are two of the "haves" in a society of "have nots" and yet both are aware of the problems of some of their acquaintances and respond with deeds. Even Celestino Ortiz is generous to Marco by allowing him credit, an idea which doña Rosa would no doubt find unpalatable. Indeed, it is noteworthy that her sole appearance in Chapter 2 merely shows her concern that Marco has been suitably dealt with for his default of payment.

Of the three people who are seen to leave doña Rosa's café in Chapter 1, Marco re-emerges at the beginning of the second chapter whilst the other two, Leoncio Maestre and Julián Suárez, reappear in the last part of the chapter and are subsequently detained in connection with the murder of doña Margot. The episode of the murder deals with the reactions of the deceased woman's neighbours and is largely situated in the building where the crime took place. There is no total unity of place since the author shifts his account back and forth from the scene of the crime to other parts of the city, but always using the building as the base of the narrative. By means of this technique, Cela allows the reader to keep Suárez and Figueras under surveillance, shows Mauricio Segovia and his brother commenting on the two homosexuals and also presents Mario de la Vega and Eloy at supper and then, later, coming across the crowd outside the building where the murder took place. In this way the murder episode is kept in perspective as one event in the life of a city and also, with Leoncio Maestre who discovered the body as he was about to return to the café and the reappearance of the other characters mentioned above, the café has been linked with the murder of the old lady. The author has carefully prepared this link for the reader whilst showing the characters concerned as oblivious of such a link. Therefore, up to the end of the second chapter, the author has presented three groups of people (the clients of the café, Marco's acquaintances and doña Margot's neighbours) located in different parts of the city and yet, in various ways, connected. Chapter 3 moves forward into the second day and marks a change of emphasis within the novel. Themes already developed are not abandoned, but temporarily submerged; Chapter 3 (and also Chapter 5) will deal in particular with the response of the wealthier to the problem of monotony. In these chapters will be seen an attempt to combat the phenomenon through diversion and this diversion will often be of an erotic nature.

Chapter 3, chronologically subsequent to Chapters 4 and 6, conducts the reader to the afternoon of the second day. The early part of the Chapter consists of a series of views of leisure time activities of some characters already encountered and some seen for the first time. In the first seven sections of the chapter the narrative moves from the "café de la calle de San Bernardo" to the "lechería de la calle de Fuencarral" to a "bar de lujo . . . detrás de la Gran Vía" to doña Rosa's café, from there to Celestino's bar and, finally, back to the "café de la calle de San Bernardo." In contrast to Chapter 1 there is no unity of place but instead, what might be termed a unity of "activity" or theme. Some familiar faces are seen in locations different to those of their first appearance. Don Pablo, señor Ramón and Martín Marco are in the café on San Bernardo; doña Matilde and doña Asunción in doña Ramona's *lecheria*; Pablo Alonso and Laurita in a *bar de lujo* and Petrita is seen in Celestino's bar. In this early part of the chapter, don Roque and Ventura Aguado appear for the first time. Both are unacquainted with each other and remain so throughout the novel. Aguado is introduced as a friend of Marco and subsequently Roque's daughter, Julita, is indicated as the *novia* of Aguado. Thus the trio which will dominate the fifth chapter is introduced quite casually to the reader.

With several notable exceptions such as Marco, Elvira and Petrita, the characters of Chapter 3 are, like those of Chapter 1, predominantly bourgeois. In consequence, the theme of hardship is rarely encountered here. Even Marco is temporarily wealthy, receiving money from Aguado and Nati Robles. The only real example of hardship and suffering in Chapter 3 is Victorita who, although employed, needs extra money in order to buy medicines for her consumptive *novio*. Therefore she is prepared to sell herself and is about to be introduced to Mario de la Vega by doña Ramona.

In general, however, there is little eroticism in Chapter 3 save mention of the occasional amorous escapade. The author, not for the first time, describes many of the potentially tenser situations with a certain levity. The murder of the night before is recalled with the scene at the *dirección general de seguridad* where the homosexuals Suárez and Figueras are detained and the tone here is far from serious. Similarly, the congregation of doña Margot's

neighbours, orchestrated by don Ibrahím, is given fairly frivolous treatment, the episode culminating in the revelation of Fernando Cazuela's find of the previous evening, during the search for the murderer: ". . . cuando todos los vecinos buscaban al criminal por orden de don Ibrahím se encontró con el amigo de su mujer, que estaba escondido, muy acurrucado, en la cesta de la ropa sucia." Even the scene showing Marujita Ranero's sinister telephone call to her former *novio* and father of her twins, Consorcio López, is terminated on a humorous note as López, in his excitement, sweeps over a shelf of bottles and, not surprisingly, incurs the wrath of the formidable doña Rosa. Finally, the only explicit erotic episode in the chapter occurs when Petrita gives herself to Celestino Ortiz as payment for Marco's debt to the bar owner. Her sacrifice is akin to that of Victorita. By contrast, however, Marco will presumably know nothing of her feelings toward him nor of her action on this occasion. Like Victorita, she is ennobled in the eyes of the reader and both girls, along with Filo and Roberto González, emerge as Cela's most sympathetic portrayals in **La colmena**.

Martín Marco appears only three times during the course of the third chapter, once in the company of Ventura Aguado and then with Nati Robles. Both are former colleagues of his and both represent a certain level of material achievement which Marco has failed to attain. It is perhaps not insignificant that the only exterior scene in the whole of Chapter 3 occurs with the meeting between Nati and Martín; after his encounter with Ventura in the café on San Bernardo, Marco has continued his odyssey and is next seen gazing into a shop-window, as at the beginning of the second chapter. This time it is a *joyería* as opposed to the rather more mundane *tienda de lavabos*. There is, of course, a simple explanation as to why Marco apparently spends so much of his time wandering the streets—Pablo Alonso's condition that he should leave his room by 9.30 a.m. and not return before 11 p.m. On this particular occasion, the sight of Marco wandering aimlessly serves as a prelude to Chapter 4, where he will be shown, especially in the latter part, moving at night in an increasingly frenzied manner through the near deserted streets. Whilst most are preparing for bed, the narrative shifts back and forth from bedrooms to the streets where Marco roams, reluctant to go "home." Thus, whereas Chapters 1 and 3 are composed almost totally of interior scenes, Chapters 2 and 4, with Marco dominating a large part of each chapter, display a continual alternation between interior and exterior events.

Chapter 4 marks the first major movement back in time, from the afternoon of the second day (Chapter 3) to the night of the first day. Accordingly, the new chapter might have been expected to continue and develop events narrated in Chapter 2. Yet, although the murder of doña Margot provided the hub of the last part of Chapter 2, there is but a single, indirect, reference to it in Chapter 4, and this comes from the author and not from one of the characters. With the notable exception of the *guardia,* Julio García Morrazo, and a few others of minor importance, the characters encountered in this chapter are already familiar. Victorita, briefly seen in Chapter 3, now emerges with García Morrazo, Marco and Roberto and Filo to dominate this nocturnal section of the novel.

García Morrazo, who serves as the external point of reference for most of the chapter, whilst presumably personally unacquainted with Marco, his structural counterpart of the latter part of the chapter, is linked with him through Celestino's bar and also Petrita who, it transpires, is the *guardia's* girl-friend. It is to Julio that Petrita goes upon completion of her chores in the González residence, thus achieving not only physical liberation from the day's work and environment but also the opportunity, for a brief while, to enjoy a certain solace and elevation as she makes love to her *guardia.* Similarly, Roberto and Filo, with the day's exertion over, are also able to escape for a while into the comfort and warmth of the physical expression of their love. The love play of Pirula and Javier is rather more stylized, yet not without tenderness, whereas Pablo Alonso, like Javier, able to see to the material needs of his woman, seems more detached in this situation. Pirula, at present living in style, had formerly worked with Victorita but now their ways of life are in complete contrast, a contrast which the author emphasizes by juxtaposing comments on their present situations:

> La señorita Pirula tiene un instinto conservador muy perspicaz, probablemente hará carrera. Desde luego, por ahora no puede quejarse: Javier la tiene como una reina, la quiere, la respeta. . . .

> Victorita no pedía tanto. Victorita no pedía más que comer y seguir queriendo a su novio, si llegaba a curarse alguna vez.

Victorita, determined not to forsake Paco and resolved to sell herself to obtain medicines for him, is the outstanding example of suffering (primarily emotional) in Chapter 4. Her situation also indicates how the less fortunate may be exploited and reminds the reader of the impotence of the "have nots" of this society in the face of exploitation by the "haves". In this case, the erotic designs of Mario de la Vega are engineered by doña Ramona and the reader is informed that Vega's new employee, Eloy, is the brother of Victorita's *novio.* Thus, another character link is presented and, later in the chapter, there is a further reminder of this link: "El hombre que iba a entrar cobrando dieciséis pesetas, no era cuñado de una muchacha que trabajaba de empaquetadora en la tipografía El porvenir, de la calle de

la Madera, porque a su hermano Paco le había agarrado la tisis con saña." The linking of groups or individuals, already a familiar technique, is, in this instance, tinged with irony. Vega, assuming his erotic pursuit materializes, will be helping both brothers; Eloy directly, as his employer, and Paco, indirectly, as an additional source of income for Victorita. As with many other situations in *La colmena,* the reader, granted omniscience and at times directly assisted by the author, is cognizant of the full extent of the Eloy—Vega—Victorita—Paco relationship, whereas the individuals concerned are not.

In a chapter where sexual relationships are the fundamental theme, the final irony occurs when Martín Marco, after wandering through the streets as others are going to bed, finally finds shelter for the night and, in the arms of the prostitute, Pura, refuses any sexual contact. The night enshrouds the city and provides its people with a brief respite before the new day brings the inevitable problems:

> La noche so cierra, al filo de la una y media o de las dos de la madrugada, sobre el extraño corazón de la ciudad.

> Miles de hombres se duermen abrazados a sus mujeres sin pensar en el duro, en el cruel día que quizás les espere, agazapado como un gato montés, dentro de tan pocas horas.

And yet, the "cruel día," when next seen (Chapter 5) is shown in terms of bourgeois diversion—away from the cafés and bars where these people had previously been encountered and instead in the *casa de citas* where they seek to alleviate the monotony of an uneventful existence. Marco, who appears only twice in the fifth chapter, was last seen seeking rest and shelter in doña Jesusa's *prostíbulo.* Chapter 5 will be primarily concerned with the affairs of Roque Moisés and his daughter Julita and their separate use of doña Celia's *casa de citas.*

Chapter 5 returns to the evening of "day 2" and is therefore subsequent to events of the afternoon of that day narrated in Chapter 3. In previous chapters of *La colmena* Cela has carefully linked characters personally unacquainted either by means of a third party, or often by showing them frequenting the same café or bar. In this way, the reader, acting as an observer rather than a mere recipient of information imparted by the author, is given access to the words and actions of the characters. At times the author has clearly signalled a relationship or connection and in this way aided the reader in his task of absorbing and relating the information contained in the narrative. As a result, in spite of the fragmentation, lack of chronological sequence and the large number of characters encountered in the novel, the reader is able, with the exercise of care and diligence, to appreciate the architecture of **La colmena** as well as the thematic content. Chapter 5 is, structurally, the most complex part of the whole novel and, technically, the most demanding on the reader.

The episode which completely dominates the fifth chapter—involving don Roque, his mistress Lola, Ventura, Julita and the photograph of don Obdulio—is centered around the use by father and mistress and daughter and *novio* of the same *casa de citas*. Up to the point at which the episode is related, each couple had been unaware of the other's use of the location. The coincidence involved here reiterates the idea of a group of people who, within a large city, appear able to move only in small, interlocking circles. Not for the first time in the novel, Cela is using a structural technique to emphasize a thematic quality—the confinement that these people suffer and to which they are largely oblivious. The lack of chronological sequence suggests a temporal confinement, the geographical and personal connections, a physical one.

Thematically, Chapter 5 is mainly dominated by the middle-classes seeking diversion. With the Moisés family it shows a not untypical section of this stratum engaged in erotic pursuits. As usual, it is the pursuit that is shown, rather than the actual activity. The episode involving members of the Moisés family lacks chronological sequence and, moreover, at least part of it must take place on a third day. Julita's meeting with her father at the *casa de citas* (mentioned p. 275 as a street meeting and witnessed p. 312) takes place during the evening of the second day. With the section commencing "Al día siguiente" which describes the arrival of the photograph of don Obdulio at the Moisés residence, the narrative has moved forward into "day 3". The section continues with the meeting between Ventura and Julita, where the latter states: "Ayer me encontré a mi padre en la escalera", and concludes with Ventura sending the photograph which Lola had originally sent to Julita, to don Roque.

Whilst Roque and his daughter's affairs dominate the fifth chapter, the sexual diversions of the middle-classes are by no means shown as being the sole prerogative of the Moisés family. Mario de la Vega reappears, this time in confrontation with Victorita and, most disturbing of all, is the scene toward the close of the chapter where the doctor, Francisco Robles, hands a thirteen-year-old girl over to doña Celia for his future enjoyment. This scene serves to anticipate Chapter 6—"La mañana"—where, against the background of the stirring city, the author gives biographical sketches of several of the girls of doña Jesusa's *prostíbulo*. The preceding chapter had dealt primarily with the sexual antics of the bourgeoisie; now there is a serious look at the histories of some girls who, through inclement circumstances, found themselves exploited and

abandoned. This final chapter ends the main body of the novel on a heavily pessimistic note. The city and its people awaken to the new day but there is, in the mind of the author, no room for hope of achievement or solace. Leading sterile and futile existences, these people have already been and will continue to be, relentlessly assailed and corroded by the apparently insurmountable problems facing them—the main problem being time or existence itself:

> La mañana sube, poco a poco, trepando como un gusano por los corazones de los hombres y de las mujeres de la ciudad; golpeando, casi con mimo, sobre los mirares recién despiertos, esos mirares que jamás descubren horizontes nuevos, paisajes nuevos, nuevas decoraciones.

> La mañana, esa mañana eternamente repetida, juega un poco, sin embargo, a cambiar la faz de la ciudad, ese sepulcro, esa cucaña, esa colmena . . .

> ¡Que Dios nos coja confesados!

Throughout the six chapters that constitute the main body of **La colmena** various themes have been introduced and developed. The inactivity of the opening chapter is succeeded by the activities of struggle and diversion, depending on the social stratum portrayed. Each chapter emphasizes particular themes. However, within these thematic phases different themes previously encountered do recur. The structure of the novel, the fragmentation of the narrative allow and facilitate this thematic flexibility. After the initial stages of the novel there is little need for the author to signal the reader of his thematic intentions; as the narrative progresses the reader is expected to see the reflection of a social or psychological problem in any situation being described. Accordingly, the author rarely addresses himself directly to the reader and instead prefers the depictive role.

Apart from the not infrequent moments of humour and irony, the tone of **La colmena** is strongly pessimistic. The problems of hardship, monotony, aimlessness and stagnation may often appear to have a short-term remedy, but the people involved seem generally incapable of finding a permanent solution. Even in the *Final*, as Martín Marco wanders away from the city centre and appears to display a welcome and overdue enlightenment one cannot but help suspect that his enthusiasm may be the product of a whim, his awakening a temporary matter. In any case, Marco has never been presented as representative of the society portrayed in **La colmena** and thus his new awareness, genuine or otherwise, is relatively unimportant within the context of the rest of the novel. For the vast majority, portrayed as either incapable of economic improvement or of appreciating their own bourgeois stagnation, there is precious little chance of material or spiritual salvation. They are trapped physically, socially or psychologically and the author gives no indication of any possible remedy.

Robert C. Spires (essay date December 1972)

SOURCE: "Cela's *La Colmena:* The Creative Process as Message," in *Hispania,* Vol. 55, No. 4, December, 1972, pp. 873-80.

[*In the following essay, Spires asserts that the theme of Cela's* La colmena *can only be understood by experiencing its form.*]

Camilo José Cela's **La colmena** has received almost universal acclaim as one of the most important post-Civil War Spanish novels largely on the basis of its interesting stylistic innovations and/or its social content, i.e., the social-moral atmosphere of Madrid immediately after the Spanish Civil War. Although these two aspects are of historical significance, to speak of the novel primarily in these terms tends to characterize it as a static document when in fact anyone who reads the work finds it to be first and foremost a dynamic, if perplexing, experience of discovery. The novel's dynamism can perhaps best be explained by studying the temporal and tonal paradoxes with which the reader is confronted, for it is in fact the reader's experience of and participation in the creative process of **La colmena** that reveals its thematic content and the revelation answers the charge that the novel lacks profundity.

Tonal paradox in the novel results form the narrator's fluctuating displays of cold detachment and anguished outrage. Temporal paradox is experienced by the reader as he is made to feel timelessness yet recognizes the existence of a governing temporal order. Since the first chapter serves as an excellent window on the novel, I shall focus my study of this latter phenomenon on the initial chapter. The obvious point of departure for studying this experience-through-paradox-process is the novel's structure.

The most obvious structural aspect of **La colmena** that the reader encounters is the fragmentation of episodes and the non-chronological development of action. For example, the narrator's point of focus may begin with a conversation in progress between two personages, leave them abruptly in the middle of their discourse of their discourse to pick up the conversations or thoughts of other characters, and then return to the original dialogue which is often resumed without any apparent temporal progression. The absence of a chronological order in presenting the fragments further complicates this technique. An episode whose fragments appear at the beginning of a chapter may be temporally si-

multaneous with another episode whose fragments appear in the middle or near the end of the chapter. Such a technique is in opposition to the traditional time-progression nature of the novel form since there is no necessary correlation between temporal simultaneity and juxtaposition. As a result of these devices, the reader experiences the sensation of arrested temporal progression. Also he has the illusion that each fragment exists independently of everything that precedes and follows it; consequently, each action and personage that appears within a fragment tends to assume an existence outside the temporal order of nature. The cruelty of the café proprietress, Doña Rosa, the plight of the aging prostitute, Elvira, the pathetic dreams of conquest of the cowardly bar owner, Celestino Ortiz, and the absurdity of Martín Marco's fluctuating sense of persecution and well-being, these and all other human traits portrayed in the novel become frozen in time as a result of the narrator's method of presentation. However, in addition to the sensation of timelessness apparent in the preceding examples, the careful reader cannot ignore the fact that there is an elaborate system of temporal associations that lies beneath the novel's apparent temporal chaos. The thematic significance of this temporal paradox can perhaps more clearly be understood in light of Henri Bergson's theory of duration.

Stated quite simply, Bergson rejected the common practice of equating time exclusively with space. In other words, true "time" is not restricted to the successive marks reached by the hands of a clock as they progress through space, but also includes the individual's personal experience of a given temporal span. The familiar statements, "time is standing still" and "time is flying" are popular expressions of this philosophical theory. Following this same line of reasoning, Bergson states that man's essential traits are timeless, a composite of his past and present existence. Duration, then, is this non-temporal aspect of an individual's being that may be revealed at any given moment through word or gesture. However—and here is the paradox—this non-temporal human essence present in every man is absolutely dependent upon the individual's temporal existence. Each man's non-temporal essence is peculiar to him and therefore ceases to exist with his death. Although duration superimposes itself on the separate ticks of a clock and in this sense is unaffected by temporal flow, in the final analysis it is dependent on the individual man, who cannot escape the tragic imprisonment of the temporal order of nature. **La colmena,** through its complex structure, in effect forces the reader to experience actively this abstract philosophical concept, even without benefit of critical analysis. As the reader observes Cela's techniques more carefully, he appreciates more completely the writer's creative process. In other words, he experiences to a greater extent the coming-into-being of the Bergsonian concept.

The time indicators that make the reader aware of the temporal structure of **La colmena** extend from very broad to extremely precise elements. First of all, there are frequent references to the progress of World War II that give the novel historical orientation. Also, the time span for the novel as a whole as well as for the individual chapters is specified and becomes obvious if one merely rearranges the order of the chapters to read: I, II, IV, VI, III, V, and the "Final." Such a rearrangement reveals that the action begins at the *merienda* hour of one day and ends at the *cena* hour of the next with the final chapter set two or three days later. Although there is some confusion occasioned by the overlapping of the time span of one chapter into the next, it does not require any extraordinary effort on the part of the reader to recognize that each series of episodes is enclosed within a temporal framework. Even within each framework the reader cannot ignore the existence of temporal associations that seem to specify the exact moment of some, if not all, the events presented. Unfortunately, this aspect of the novel's structure—with its thematic implications—has thus far been all but ignored by critics or, in at least one case, summarily and erroneously dismissed as unnecessary for an appreciation of the novel. On the contrary, a very fundamental thematic implication stems directly from the reader's appreciation of a dual effect: (1) the sensation of timelessness and (2) the awareness of a governing temporal order. The first chapter of **La colmena** is an excellent showcase for the techniques Cela uses throughout to create this paradoxical reality.

Doña Rosa is the chief point of focus in this chapter because she dominates the scene and also because she appears in fragments arranged in chronological order. The novel begins with a description of her as she lumbers through the maze of tables, apparently headed in the direction of the kitchen. At this point the narrator unceremoniously abandons Doña Rosa as he directs the reader's attention to several of the customers seated at the tables. Then, some twenty pages farther on, the reader's attention is once again directed to Doña Rosa as she shouts orders at the employees in the kitchen. In the midst of her verbal chastisement of one of the waiters, she suddenly turns to an unidentified employee and commands: "—Y tú, pasmado, ya estás yendo por el periódico." This apparently insignificant detail assumes considerable temporal significance when, near the end of the chapter, the narrator announces: "Alfonsito, el niño de los recados, vuelve de la calle con el periódico." In this way the reader is given the clue to the approximate time span for the chapter as the boy explains that his delay—which could not have been too excessive, considering Doña Rosa's comparatively mild challenge: "—Oye, rico, ¿dónde has ido por el papel?"—resulted from a line in front of the newsstand. However, these two passages are not easily connected because of the space between them and because of the appearance of so many new personages,

most of whom seemingly have no connection whatsoever with the other customers. Yet, in spite of the difficulty in pinpointing this association, even the casual reader must sense that the activities presented in this first chapter are governed by a fairly well-defined temporal framework in which Doña Rosa, with her constant movement, serves as the pendulum.

Nevertheless, Doña Rosa alone cannot temporally link the isolated activities of the more than twenty characters who appear in this first chapter. Supplementing her role as chronometer are some minor incidents whose impact briefly touches several of the customers, thereby allowing the reader to recognize the simultaneousness of these customers' activities with the incident in question. An episode in which a young poet faints offers an excellent example of the manner in which this device is employed.

The poet first appears in the ninth fragment of the chapter as he is lost in deep concentration, and the narrator comments briefly about his background. Then, some twenty-three pages farther on, the narrator returns to the poet, this time to explain that the deep concentration is due to the boy's efforts to find the proper word for his poem to rhyme with *río*. This effort apparently has been too intense for, as the narrator enters the personage's mind, one sees that the words are becoming jumbled. Two fragments farther on, another customer notes that a young man seated near him seems to be on the verge of fainting but is unable to reach the boy before he falls to the floor. This customer, a moneylender by the name of D. Trinidad, helps the youth to his feet and escorts him to the rest room and, upon returning to his own table after this altruistic gesture, engages in the following brief conversation with an unidentified person: "—¿Le ha pasado ya?—Sí, no era nada, un mareo." A few pages farther on, one of the musicians who has been talking with Doña Rosa during a break leans over to ask of a man at one of the tables: "—¿Y el mozo?" The unidentified man responds: "—Reponiéndose en el water, no era nada."

By shifting the point of view from which the reader sees this scene—and in so doing altering the details but not the essence of the conversation—the narrator has managed to make the reader experience the temporal paradox. Multiple reference to a single, identifiable instant creates a sense of timelessness. Nevertheless, there is enough happening to communicate a vague awareness of temporal order, of sequential cause and effect. Similarly, this same incident involving the poet can be connected to the lecture of a man by the name of Vega to a student seated beside him. This rather brief lecture, which is split between pages 33 and 58, is given time-sequence orientation by Vega's warning that young men who waste their time sitting in cafes "al final se caen un día desmayados, como ese niño litri que se han llevado para adentro." Finally, a man by the name of D. Jaime Arce breaks his habitual silence to deliver a very brief, if emotional, commentary on the world's financial problems. In spite of the brevity of these remarks, D. Jaime appears on pages 24, 45 (where we read his comments), and 63; in other words, the fragments devoted to him span almost the entire chapter. Yet, the reader can pinpoint his remarks to the final moments of the chapter by means of the narrator's observation that D. Jaime, upon drifting back into his normal state of silence after delivering his harangue, notices the young poet emerging from the rest room after recuperating.

The incident of the poet demonstrates the manner in which a given event serves to cut horizontally across the network of independent activities in order to impress upon the reader an awareness that these are governed by a common chronological point of reference. This device is also evident with the arrival of the newspapers which provide a mutual topic of conversation that draws the customers into a concluding temporal bond. In fact, sequential time may be the only common link in the lives of these basically self-centered people and, by analogy, Man in general.

One other technique that seemingly rejects the time-progression laws of nature is repetition of a scene with variations. One example is the short conversation between D. Trinidad and the musician concerning the welfare of the poet. An even more striking example is the occasion when Doña Rosa sends Alfonsito out for the evening papers. She orders one of the waiters, Pepe, to get back to his job. This moment is then continued five fragments farther on: "Pepe el camarero, se vuelve a su rincón sin decir una palabra." As he stands sulking over the replies he should have given to Doña Rosa, he notices two small boys playing train and so approaches them to say: "—Que os vais a ir a caer. . . ." The narrator then remarks: "Los niños le contestan 'no, señor,' y siguen jugando al tren. . . ." The repetition of this scene occurs some twenty-five pages on: "Los niños que juegan al tren se han parado de repente. Un señor les está diciendo que hay que tener más educación y más compostura, y ellos, sin saber qué hacer con las manos, lo míran con curiosidad. Uno, el mayor, que se llama Bernabé, está pensando en un vecino suyo, de su edad poco más o menos, que se llama Chús. El otro, el pequeño, que se llama Paquito, está pensando en que al señor le huele mal la boca." Technically speaking, there has been a shift in the point of view from which the narrator presents the scene. In the first excerpt he simply records the scene as a disinterested observer; while in the second the narrator actually enters the minds of the two boys to present the incident as experienced by them. This repetition device even transcends chapters. For example, after Doña Rosa has Martín Marco ejected from her café, we are given the following scene:

Pepe vuelve a entrar a los pocos momentos. La dueña, que tiene las manos en los bolsillos del mandril, los hombros echados para atrás y las piernas separadas, lo llama con una voz seca, cascada; con una voz que parece el chasquido de un timbre con la campanilla partida.

—Ven acá.

Pepe casi no se atreve a mirarla.

—Qué quiere?

—¿Le has arreado?

—Sí, señorita.

—¿Cuántas?

—Dos.

La dueña entorna los ojitos tras los cristales, saca las manos de los bolsillos y se las pasa por la cara, donde apuntan los cañotes de la barba, mal tapados por los polvos de arroz.

—¿Dónde se las has dado?

—Donde pude; en las piernas.

—Bien hecho. ¡Para que aprenda! ¡Asi otra vez no querrá robarles el dinero a las gentes honradas!

The repetition of this scene is presented in chapter two:

El camarero entra en el Café. Se siente, de golpe, calor en la cara; dan ganas de toser, más bien bajo, como para arrancar esa flema que posó en la garganta el frió de la calle. Después parece hasta que se habla mejor. Al entrar notó que le dolían un poco las sienes; notó también, o se lo figuró, que a doña Rosa le temblada un destellito de lascivia en el bigote.

—Oye, ven acá.

El camarcro se le acercó.

—¿Le has arreado?

—Sí, señorita.
¿Cuantas?

—Dos.
¿Donde?

—¡Donde pude, en las piernas,

—¡Bien hecho! ¡Por mangante!

Again the point of view has shifted. In the first of the two passages the narrator merely records the scene as he observes it while in the second the point of view originates within Pepe's mind and we see how he experiences the incident. Thus, by fragmenting these moments and then repeating them several pages or even chapters farther on, the narrator has given spatial extension to these few minutes. This horizontal extension of a given moment forces the reader to concentrate on the human essence that is portrayed, rather than become absorbed by some potentially dramatic element. However, in spite of the challenge such a technique poses to our ingrained concepts of time, the fact remains that these moments, as a result of the initial association with Doña Rosa, can also be pinpointed within the time-progression of the novel. Once again the structure of the novel suggests that in spite of man's timeless essence, his physical being cannot exist outside the temporal order of nature.

This paradox of the temporal and the non-temporal not only coexisting but being mutually dependent is given explicit expression by the narrator at the end of the first chapter as he describes the clock in Doña Rosa's café:

> Suenan las nueve y media en el viejo reló de breves numeritos que brillan como si fueran de oro. El reló es un mueble casi suntuoso que se había traído de la Exposición de París un marquesito tarambana y sin blanca que anduvo cortejando a doña Rosa, allá por el 905. El marquesito, que se llamaba Santiago y era grande de España, murió tísico en El Escorial, muy joven todavía, y el reló quedó posado sobre el mostrador del Café, como para servir de recuerdo de unas horas que pasaron sin traer el hombre para doña Rosa y el comer caliente todos los días, para el muerto, ¡La vida!

So again we see that temporal paradox constitutes one of the essential aspects of creation-in-process of *La colmena* that the reader experiences. He is made to feel—through fragmentation and nonchronological order—the timelessness of Man's essential traits, yet he also becomes a captive—through the network of time associations—of the temporal order of nature that imprisons all mankind.

The temporal paradox produces an appreciation of the circumstance in the *process* of becoming reality, rather than of a point fixed on the historical spectrum. This appreciation is further enhanced by a second phenomenon: tonal paradox. In fact, the two work in direct harmony since expressions of the narrator's emotional detachment correspond to representations of the timelessness of Man's nature, while his expressions of anguished outrage correspond to scenes demonstrating Man's imprisonment within the temporal order of nature.

The predominant tone encountered by the reader in *La colmena* is one of cold detachment and cynicism which is conveyed by the narrator's treatment of the various types of characters that appear in the novel. However, this cynical attitude is tempered by a paradoxical tone of anguish that appears from time to time throughout the work. Just as he has been drawn into the temporal structure, the reader is slowly pulled into the reality of this contradictory union of detachment and concern.

Perhaps the most obvious distancing device employed by the narrator is humor. According to Henri Bergson, laughter is dependent on an absence of emotional involvement between the observer and the object of ridicule. Therefore, by caricaturizing a personage in the novel, the narrator creates an emotional barrier between this personage and the reader. The portrait of a self-esteeming politician in the process of practicing a speech before the mirror is typical of the many humorous episodes in the novel:

> Don Ibrahim adelantó un pie hacia las candilejas y acarició, con un gesto elegante, las solapas de su batín, Bien: de su frac. Después sonrió.
>
> —Pues bien, señores académicos: así como para usar algo hay que poseerlo, para poseer algo hay que adquirirlo. Nada importa a título de qué; yo he dicho, tan sólo, que hay que adquirirlo, ya que nada, absolutamente nada, puede ser poseído sin una previa adquisición. (Quizás me interrumpan los aplausos. Conviene estar preparado.)
>
> La voz de don Ibrahim sonaba solemne como la de un fagot. Al otro lado del tabique de panderete, un marido, de vuelta de su trabajo, preguntaba a su mujer:
>
> —¿Ha hecho su caquita la nena?
>
> Don Ibrahim sintió algo de frío y se arregló un poco la bufanda. En el espejo se veía un lacito negro, el que se lleva en el frac por las tardes.

The reader's participation in the humor of this description begins with the narrator's self-correction in the first paragraph. This obvious mocking of D. Ibrahim's puerile insistence on imagining himself as actually standing in formal attire before his fellow senators conveys a condescending attitude. The impression is like that of an adult humoring a small child who insists on creating a make-believe world. This sense of superiority then paves the way for the comic climax which occurs when D. Ibrahim pauses to acknowledge the anticipated applause of his colleagues. The ensuing question of the neighbor that penetrates the thin walls, and D. Ibrahim's reaction to it—an insistence in maintaining his lofty fantasy in spite of the extremely earthy nature of the interruption—results in his almost total effacement. This example is typical of the manner in which humor is employed throughout the novel to help create the predominant tone of emotional detachment that the reader encounters.

There is a similar barrier created between the reader and the tragic figures of the novel. The following example concerning Elvira, an aging prostitute who has just been dropped by her lover, demonstrates a more subtle manner in which emotional detachment is achieved:

> La señorita Elvira sonríe. Doña Rosa entorna la mirada, llena de pesar.
>
> —¡Es que hay gente sin conciencia, hija!
>
> —¡Psché! ¿Qué mas da?
>
> Doña Rosa se le acerca, le habla casi al oído.
>
> —¿Por qué no se arregla con don Pablo?
>
> —Porque no quiero. Una también tiene su orgullo, doña Rosa,
>
> —¡Nos ha merengao! ¡Todas tenemos nuestras cosas! Pero lo que yo le digo a usted, Elvirita, y ya sabe que yo siempre quiero para usted lo mejor, es que con don Pablo bien le iba.
>
> —No tanto. Es un tío muy exigente. Y además un baboso. Al final ya lo aborrecía, ¡qué quiere usted!, ya me daba hasta repugnancia.
>
> Doña Rosa pone la dulce voz, la persuasiva voz de los consejos.
>
> —¡Hay que tener más paciencia, Elvirita! ¡Usted es aún muy niña!
>
> —¿Usted cree?
>
> La señorita Elvirita escupe debajo de la mesa y se seca la boca con la vuelta de un guante.

The episode develops on the basis of dialogue between two characters rather than on the basis of what the narrator says about them. In other words, the narrator appears to restrict his utterances to the function of "stage directions" that provide the platform on which the dialogue performs. Nevertheless, the subtle use of a morphological device affects the reader's emotional response. At the beginning of the passage the narrator factually reports the action, but at the end he uses the diminutive form just as Doña Rosa does. Her use of "Elvirita" rather than "Elvira" communicates emotional warmth—a degree of intimacy which would appear to be foreign to the detached narrator. Indeed, by using this device, he creates an ironic contrast between the endearing connotation of this diminutive form and the image of a hardened, if pathetic, prostitute spitting on the floor and wiping her mouth with the back of her glove. Elvira is indeed a pathetic figure, but her crudeness makes the diminutive seem sarcastic—not when it is used by Doña Rosa, but when it is used by the narrator who initiates the scene by reference to "Elvira" and ends it by reference to "Elvirita." The irony that results from this manipulation by the narrator, while obviously also directed at Doña Rosa and her hypocritical amiability, creates an emotional detachment from Elvira's pathetic state of existence. The contrast is further intensified by Doña Rosa's immediately preceding statement, "usted es aún muy niña." However, the first hint of a paradox in tone is also evident here for, in spite of the narrator's cynical treatment of Elvira, there is an irrepressible tendency to feel sympathy for this pathetic woman. The conflict here between the reader's instinctive feeling of compassion and the morphological change employed by the narrator is, as we have suggested, one of the first indications of the novel's paradoxical tone.

The conditions that elicited an emotional conflict within the reader in the example concerning Elvira are even more pronounced in the following concerning a small gypsy boy who sings in the streets to earn his sub-standard living:

> El niño no tiene cara de persona, tiene cara de animal doméstico, de sucia bestia, de pervertida bestia de corral. Son muy pocos sus años para que el dolor haya marcado aun el navajazo del cinismo—o de la resignación—en su cara, y su cara tiene una bella expresión de no entender nada de lo que pasa. Todo lo que pasa es un milagro para el gitanito, que nació de milagro, que come de milagro, que vive de milagro y que tiene fuerzas para cantar de puro milagro.
>
> Detrás de los días vienen las noches, detrás de las noches vienen los días. El año tiene cuatro estaciones; primavera, verano, otoño, invierno. Hay verdades que se sienten dentro del cuerpo, como el hambre o las ganas de orinar.

In spite of the pathetic aspects of this boy's life, the narrator's portrait of him seems to indicate that he chooses to reserve any display of personal emotion. The repetition of certain words sharpens the edges of the tonal paradox as it produces a sense of the narrator's detachment. First of all, the narrator emphasizes the boy's infrahuman characteristics—"de sucia bestia, de pervertida bestia de corral." Although the lack of cynicism in his expression distinguishes him from adults, it is the same innocent but stupid facial expression of a dumb animal. This animalistic image is also strengthened in the final paragraph as the narrator suggests that the boy's powers of logic and reason are limited to recognition of a change in the elements and of the physical demands of his body. Finally, all these bestial aspects are vivified by the narrator's use of present tense verb forms. Yet, in spite of the overt tone of cynicism in this description, a certain sense of compassion for the plight of this poor urchin is also evoked. The clue to this dichotomy of emotions can best be seen in the passage, "todo lo que pasa es un milagro para el gitanito, que nació de milagro, que come de milagro, que vive de milagro y que tiene fuerzas para cantar de puro milagro." The ironic use of the word "miracle" to explain the pathetic existence of this small boy is in violent opposition to the detached tone conveyed by the rest of the description. And so the narrator reveals two paradoxical attitudes: (1) cold aloofness and (2) a certain feeling of anguished outrage. The irony produced by the insistence on "miracle" veers toward sarcasm, but certainly it is not directed at the boy, but rather at some higher Being. This implicit expression of the narrator's underlying outrage, evoked here by the boy's misery, is given explicit expression at various points in the novel.

The first example of this explicit tone of anguish occurs in the initial chapter: "Acodados sobre el viejo, sobre el costroso mármol de los veladores, los clientes ven pasar a la dueña, casi sin mirarla ya, mientras piensan, vagamente, en ese mundo que, ¡ay! no fue lo que pudo haber sido, en ese mundo en el que todo ha ido fallando poco a poco, sin que nadie se lo explicase, a lo mejor por una minucia insignificante." The narrator seems to evoke a complete identification with these personages and their sense of hopelessness, an identification that is emphasized by the interjection "¡ay!" This same type of empathetic identification becomes even more evident a few pages farther on: "Flota en el aire como un pesar que se va clavando en los corazones. Los corazones no duelen y pueden sufrir, hora tras hora, hasta toda una vida, sin que nadie sepamos nunca, demasiado a ciencia cierta, qué es lo que pasa." The use of the first-person plural, "sepamos," explicitly associates the narrator with the plight of the café patrons and at the same time draws the reader into a similar emotional identification. These last two examples serve to underline the tonal paradox that characterizes this novel. Just as in the case of temporal paradox, this dichotomy in tone with which the reader is confronted is fundamental to the thematic implications of the work; in fact, the two paradoxes are directly related. For just as Man's essential traits are timeless, yet he as an individual is a prisoner of the temporal order of nature, so the tone of the novel fluctuates between cynical

aloofness in the face of this timeless human essence and lyrical expressions of anguish at the realization of mankind's imprisonment in the inexorable temporal order of nature:

> La mañana sube, poco a poco, trepando como un gusano por los corazones de los hombres y de las mujeres de la ciudad; golpeando, casi con mimo, sobre los mirares recién despiertos, esos mirares que jamás descubren horizontes nuevos, paisajes nuevos, nuevas decoraciones.
>
> La mañana, esa mañana eternamente repetida, juega un poco, sin embargo, a cambiar la faz de la ciudad, ese sepulcro, esa cucaña, esa colmena. . . .
>
> ¡Que Dios nos coja confesados!

As I noted at the beginning of this paper, it has been charged that *La colmena* fails as a novel because of its lack of profundity. Such a charge, I suspect, reflects an effort to locate its ideas explicitly stated. In *La colmena,* this cannot be done. Nowhere is the reader told that Man is both ludicrously timeless and tragically temporal; but this is exactly what we as readers are made to experience. So meaning, (i.e., theme or content) in this novel is in a very real sense the experience itself. To talk of stylistic innovations or social content as isolated facets not only fails to convey the dynamic nature of the novel, but in effect deprives it of its fundamental thematic message.

J. S. Bernstein (essay date 1974)

SOURCE: "Confession and Inaction in *San Camilo,*" in *Hispanofila,* 1974, pp. 47-63.

[*In the following essay, Bernstein outlines Cela's ideas about Spain and politics as expressed in his* San Camilo.]

In Cela's long-awaited novel about the Spanish Civil War we find as comprehensive and explicit a statement of his stance on political and social issues as any in his previous work. The novel's unnamed narrator delivers, in more than four hundred pages, a general confession of sins committed and imagined in which we hear a recital of details of the lives of historically prominent *madrileños*, and of the lives of some whose historical importance is negligible.

What concerns the serious reader of Cela's work is not so much having a clear picture of the sexual activities of a twenty-year-old student which, however shocking they may seem to a Spanish audience are almost literally as child's play when compared with what is to be found in Genet,

Burroughs, or any of a host of other contemporaries. What concerns him, particularly in an evidently autobiographical novel, is an approach to the political reality of that twenty-year-old. In **San Camilo** I think we have that approach, and can discover a great deal of what went into the formation of the mature Cela's thinking on politics and Spanish society.

In this study I shall review some of what Cela says and omits to say about his narrator. I will remark on some points of *desencuentro* between the author and the implied author, as well as some where the implied author seems to match quite well the author whose *tocayo* gives the novel its title. I will pay a certain amount of attention to the narrator's refusals to take action and will end with a summary of the single philosophical position expressed in the novel which Cela wholeheartedly endorses.

The bitterness, hopelessness, and black humor which have marked so much of Cela's work again make their appearance in this novel. Perhaps because this is his longest work, the depressing view of Spain and Madrid which Cela provides seems even bleaker than it did in his earlier prose. Another factor tending to increase the pessimism of tone may be what McPheeters has called the "crisis in his literary career." The longevity of the present regime also weighs distressingly upon a writer whose career began at the end of the Civil War. The reasons of this must be partly patriotic and partly personal. Cela's antipathy to and criticisms of the regime, of orthodox Spanish Catholicism, and of social and political conservatism are readily apparent in his work. His criticisms, while frequently dressed in literary symbolism (e.g., the upper-class world of Mrs. Caldwell reeks with decay and immorality), have not diminished with time; on the contrary, they have increased and become less and less veiled. The narrator's Uncle Jerome tells him: "Pese a todo hay que ser patriota, sobrino, fíjate que no digo nacionalista." Jerome goes on to distinguish between "fatherland" and "nation" in terms which refute the Nationalists' claim to be the sole recipients of God's grace; he says that God makes only *patrias* while it is men who make nations.

Cela's own career has coincided chronologically with the present regime in Spain. Some may see his continued residence in Spain rather than abroad as a proof of his conservatism, or worse, of his Fascism. The economic success of his writings, their many translations into foreign languages, his membership in the Academy provide enough targets for those who would disparage his achievement or his liberalism. If Cela had been undergoing a crisis in his career, with **San Camilo** he seems as vigorous and passionate as ever. The thirty years since the end of the war have wrought damage to the life of culture in the Peninsula, in particular because of the migration of intellectuals, and the

lengthy period during which their works, and even in some cases their names, could not be published in Spain. The long, censorship-ridden hiatus of literary freedom has not yet reached an end, although there are now and then some small and encouraging signs that censorship is subject to the attrition of peacetime. The critique of Fascism and of authoritarian orthodoxy which Cela offers in **San Camilo** is no less pointed for being at times balanced by a critique of anarchism, and of the inability of the socialists to govern. These critiques are the most thoroughgoing of any in Cela's work and refute, I think successfully, those who accuse him of regime sympathies.

The novel is an account of events in Madrid during eight days immediately preceding and following the outbreak of the Civil War. The narrator stands before his mirror and scrutinizes himself as he recounts what he knows about the war. His is an Apollonian awareness of condition and events in Madrid; he is present inside the Montaña barracks when it is under siege, and he is at the same time outside the barracks in the crowd besieging it. He has seen all the events on both sides of the battlelines, and informs the reader of the war plans of both sides. He also knows intimately the sympathies and activities of *madrileños* of the whole range of social status, from *diputados* and wealthy businessmen to whores and crippled cigaret vendors. The book is a witness, then, to the eruption of the Civil War. What I have previously called the "testimonial imperative" in Cela's work is a driving force behind this novel.

If his motive is testimony then his means is his mirror. In it he is able to see not only himself but all of Madrid. The use of the mirror as a literary device or symbol receives a characteristic deformation in Cela's hands; for in addition to the changes in geometric shape the mirror undergoes, the narrator acknowledges that he is no Narcissus. What he sees in his mirror is a twenty-year old student masturbating, making faces at the face he sees in the mirror, and being tempted to spit on his own image. Even though he is no Narcissus, his use of the mirror is structurally equivalent to Narcissus' use. The device permits him to deliver a 443 page account of *himself* in the role of witness, to scrutinize his own features, his sexual adventures, his lack of will, his role in the war, and to relate these same aspects in the other characters. And if unlike Narcissus he is not handsome or a hero, he nonetheless delights in the recital of his sins and those of others, the diseases and scabs which mark the populace, the rhetoric and hypocrisy which do not quite succeed in masking the motives of the war. The content is a lengthy absorption in self, relying on the apparently omniscient narrator's experience of the people and events presented.

The narrator would impress us with the value of memory. Memory is unavoidable, and even more important, unchanging and reliable: "la memoria cuando pasa el tiempo es como una fotografía a la que dieron con hiposulfito, que ya no se borra nunca o que tarda años y años, lo menos cincuenta años más, en medio borrarse." Though the novel purports to be an account of events which occurred thirty-three years ago, by his use of a term from physics, the half-life ("medio borrarse"), he attempts to reassure the reader that what the narrator gives us in the novel has not changed an inch from the truth as he lived it. The narrator's memory is also a formal device, for the confused and heterogeneous contents of his memory provided the formal continuity of the book; the reader is to think the novel essentially a linear account of what the author has remembered, a sort of stream of the narrator's consciousness. Whether in fact Cela wrote **San Camilo** straight out as it was published, or had recourse to any of a number of authorial methods of rearranging and shuffling sections of the prose, the narrator's memory links the events and the characters together, like the buckets on a water-wheel ("la noria de la memoria").

The trustworthiness and inviolability of memory is what sustains the reader's faith in the novel's accuracy and truth. But, the narrator obstructs the reader's trust because he says, "mírate en el espejo aunque sea con desconfianza, mírate en el espejo con un infinito recelo." What's worse is that he admits that he lies to himself and to us. The result is that the reader does not know when the narrator is lying and when he is telling the truth. One instance among many is the passage beginning: "Tú no has sido probablemente ninguno de los hombres que asesinaron a Calvo Sotelo pero pudiste serlo."

For the most part this does not matter greatly since in **San Camilo** not only are things not what they seem to be, but also things are not what they are. This is, I think, a sign of what Américo Castro has called the Spaniards' wish to "desandar lo andado," to disbelieve, with as much passion as that which invests their affirmative beliefs, that what is there is really there. Truth and memory, then, are as problematical in this novel as in real life. And if the novel's emblematic patron is St. Camillus, Confessor, the reader should not expect this general confession to be other than of an ordinary sort, that is, a blend of revelations of sin and disclaimers of sin, of contrition and concealment: "se conoce que no tiene tendecia a la confesión." Of the many things to which the narrator confesses, his "sinful" sexual acts and those of other characters are the most prominent and recurrent. For this very reason they are the least important items in his inventory of sins, and the ones he can confess with the least reticence and sense of guilt. In fact, he confesses them precisely because he knows they are considered sins. As for his other sins, the ones he *does* feel truly guilty about, these he mostly succeeds in concealing from us if not from himself.

The element of duplicity present in the narrator's testimony is impossible to gauge. Surely we can gauge it in regard to the external events, the real events of history which are mentioned frequently enough and give the reader an additional confidence in the narration's veracity. The reader can, by referring to almanacs and the like, check the dates of J. D. Rockefeller's ninety-seventh birthday, the fall of the Montaña Barracks, the arrival of the flight of Arnáiz and Calvo in Madrid, the standings of Spanish bicyclists in the Tour de France. These events external to the narrator's own conduct in the novel are presented in the language of newspaper items and radio bulletins. Where Cela's method differs from, e.g., Dos Passos' (in *U. S. A.*), is in the fact that Cela does not set the items off from the surrounding text typographically; they are run on with the narrator's descriptions of his own and other characters' experiences, thus appearing to be integrated into the narrator's personal experience.

But when it comes to the internal events of the novel, e.g., what the narrator claims he feels for Tránsito-Toisha, what mocking gesture he made to the cigaret vendor, where precisely he was when the Montaña Barracks fell, there is no way to gauge reliability. We have only the confidence the narrator inspires in us that he is telling the truth. His concealments, about which he warns us on occasion, are impenetrable; and his lies are unimpeachable. The reader is tempted to dismiss the problems resulting from this mingling of truth with falsehood, of external, real historical events with internal, fictional ones, by assuming that the narrator is Cela himself. On this assumption, the reader can appeal to the evidence found in the rest of Cela's work as a guide to estimating the narrator's lies and concealments in **San Camilo.** I think this assumption has certain clear dangers and may not be as productive as it might seem.

There are, to be sure, certain resemblances between the narrator and the author. Like Cela, the narrator was twenty when the war broke out. Like him he had been a sickly child, and suffered from tuberculosis. Like don Camilo, the narrator attended the University of Madrid and ostensibly studied for the customs service entrance examinations, while his real interests lay in other subjects. The narrator mentions Camilo José Cela twice by name, but it is not clear from these that he and Cela are different people. The narrator says: "dicen que los tuberculosos son líricos y liberales, a lo mejor es cierto," a remark which applies equally to both himself and to Cela.

Yet the narrator who purports to be the author of **San Camilo** is clearly different from the implied authors of Cela's other novels, though not every one of Cela's novels has had a distinct implied author. But it must be obvious that the implied author of, for example, **Mrs. Caldwell,** is a Cela much concerned with keeping up appearances, and where this becomes impossible rationalizing them away. One of Mrs. Caldwell's most singular traits is that she blames other for all her misfortunes. The narrator of *San Camilo,* on the contrary, is interested in demolishing facades and appearances; he voyeuristically strives to see behind the neat exteriors of people and events. The implied author of *Pascual Duarte* is a man who, whatever his motives and however justifiably, has killed three people. He is, moreover, intent on convincing the reader that he has repented of his crimes, and if given the chance, would not commit them again. The implied author of *San Camilo* not only is no criminal, but suffers from precisely the opposite affliction from *Pascual Duarte;* the latter could not refrain from acting in situations which provoked him, while the former finds no way to act in any of the provocative situations he finds himself in.

The implied author of *San Camilo* is a Cela different from the others who preceded him. It is a Cela of mature years who chooses to appear to the reader as a youth of twenty; in consequence, the narrator is wise beyond his years. His reluctance to take action is an inhibition brought on, in part, by his wisdom. Since his vision is Apollonian, he knows that within the rather restricted time-span of the novel his memory has retained everything that happened, everything worth telling. For the narrator the substance of the novel is past; it is entirely history. Knowing this he is like a god loath to interfere in the somewhat petty—however lethal—activities of his people. Since the substance is historical, preterite, the whole substance can be framed in a fairly neat, symmetrical structure: Parts I and III divided into four sub-parts each, Part II not subdivided and a epilog for a pedagogical *envoi.* Since everything is past, known by the narrator ahead of time, there can be no gratuitous acts, no "chance" occurrences, hence there is no need to provide for them by allowing a non-linear, and perhaps erratic, structure.

The narrator of *San Camilo* refuses to act in any way which might remotely induce a heroic stance in him. Heroism's natural culture is war; it is the condition in which it takes root and thrives. But the narrator debunks heroism continually. He belittles the heroes history calls great. And he shuns even the remotest suggestion that he himself could be capable of heroism. The narrator repeatedly denies that he is like a number of historical heroes. They are: Napoleon, St. Paul, Buffalo Bill, Roland, Viriatus, Caesar, the Cid, William Tell, and King Cyril of England. He claims to be just a common man, constitutionally unable to support a collective effort such as is demanded in wartime. He fosters his own rebelliousness toward the official claims upon his patriotism because he sees everything as ridiculous. His incessant disclaimers ("no, tú no eres San Pablo . . . tampoco eres el rey Cirilo de Inglaterra") are merely statements of fact, not of potentiality. For he says he might

have been a hero of one sort or another; his disclaimers recall those of Prufrock. The same Apollonian vision in Prufrock ("I have known them all already, known them all"), and the same desire to withdraw ("I should have been a pair of ragged claws"), are here in our narrator, even the marine image: "encónchate en ti mismo como el galápago, niégate a escuchar los cantos de la sirena." The Prufrockian echoes support my thinking the narrator wise beyond his years, for Prufrock's inhibitions are as much a function of habit and age ("I grow old . . . I grow old"), as they are of wisdom and the introspection of the confessional ("How should I begin / To spit out the butt-ends of my days and ways?"). There is in the narrator a greater overt emphasis on fear than there is in Prufrock since he is in a city at war.

The narrator makes no secret of his fear; quite the contrary, fear is one of the most repeated themes in the novel. It appears on the first page of the narration when the narrator says that perhaps his mirror reflects the astonished face of a dead man still hidden behind the mask of the fear of death, and that perhaps he is dead already but doesn't know it. The fear of death is a palpable, sensorial thing. The pungent taste of the copper, nickel, or silver coin on his palate is, like his other memories, unforgettable. It is a reality which inhibits action not only because it makes the narrator a coward, hence a man bent on self-preservation, but because fear leads to the murderous aggression against the feared person or object. Fear is a devil who is always with us; it is a negative feeling which makes people disbelievers.

There is nothing particularly remarkable about a twenty-year-old who fears death. Perhaps the degree of frankness with which the narrator confesses his fear is striking; but then again, this whole novel is a confession, a general examination of conscience. What is more remarkable is the narrator's implicit belief that the Civil War is a reflection of a national fear, equally as palpable and real as the narrator's individual fear. He implies that all Spain suffers from the fear of death. In what can be taken as the first steps toward a critique of *machismo* the narrator says that he could kill his brother for fear that the brother might think him afraid. The absurdity of this has its tragic consequence in the Civil War, despite the elaborate rhetoric employed by the combatants to mask their fear.

As the narrator's mirror is a device for his confession, the city of Madrid is a mirror of national conditions. Cela indicates that he wishes to see the Civil War as a conflict in which the participation of foreigners, on whichever side, was uncalled for. The novel's dedication specifically excludes "los aventureros foráneos, fascistas y marxistas, que se hartaron de matar españoles como conejos y a quienes nadie había dado vela en nuestro propio entierro." None of the characters in the novel is a foreigner, and when foreigners are mentioned they are either historical figures, or people in Madrid who do not meet the narrator face to face (e.g., the Phillipine aviators Arnáiz and Calvo). Those who leave the city during the time span of the novel do not go abroad, but to Segovia, Valencia, or San Sebastián. Those who come to Madrid during the novel do so for individual reasons as well as because of the war; e.g. Demetrio Hoyo Marín and his wife are in Madrid because her sister is taking the veil. The hordes of *desconocidos* who descend upon the city are in flight before the Franco forces who, of course, have Madrid as their target. The city thus is a replica in little of the national life and *problemática,* as it had been in **La colmena.** Now, however, events intensify the people's fear as the disruption and confusion of the early days of the war create city-wide pressures which involve every resident.

The wartime upheavals in city life have not yet, at this early point in the war, completely disrupted social and political life. The Church still functions, albeit with congregations numerically greatly reduced. The newspapers are still publishing, and an editor of one of them, Jesualdo Villegas of *El Heraldo,* appears frequently in different parts of the city, thus serving as a secular link between *madrileños* of opposing sympathies. The telephone is in constant use in the novel, another sign of the incomplete disruption of city and national life. Yet another link between all the people is the radio, over which at various points in the novel we hear the injunction: "¡españoles, mantened la conexión!" The injunction has a wider, symbolic meaning: it is a demand for the preservation of community and a call to secular communion.

But that communion is being shattered by the war. The fear of death has erupted into murderous civil aggression, and the normal life of the city has already begun to go haywire. Those activities and pursuits which are fullest of vitality and life are here criticized or deprecated by the narrator. The novel is full of them but they nowhere seem to be able to allay the fear of death and prove by their vital energy that life can go on. One of these activities is sports. They are present as external events of history; the reader is informed periodically of the standing of the Spanish entrants in the Tour de France at the end of each day's racing. Sports are also present as internal events in the narrator's own experience, e.g., his acquaintance with the female j'ai-alai players. Boxing, wrestling, hockey, and the bullfight are mentioned, but never with any hint that as sports they do anything for either the participants or the spectators but earn the former some money and distract the latter from their troubles.

The frantic activity of the city besieged may resemble the normal business of any large city; but the city is full of the smell of death and the narrator wonders why people don't notice it. Cela elaborates an olfactology of death in **San Camilo,** illustrating the degree to which the sense of smell is capable of refinement. He insists on distinguishing types of smells which people habitually confuse. With but very few exceptions the science of smells in the novel is a study of the obnoxious, the moribund, and the already decayed. Just as the olfactology here bespeaks a calculus of disease and decay, the numerous references to flies signal the narrator's efforts to distinguish between apparently identical sorts of crimes and to keep separate similar modes of dying.

The narrator's contemplation of the death throes of a fly in a coffee cup leads him to conclude that "si en un alma pone sus últimos huevos la mosca que va a morir mueren también todas las flores del contorno, . . . el crimen es bestia que se reproduce por partenogénesis y de un crimen puede brotar toda una barahúnda de crímenes." There are many, many kinds of flies and they are told apart by their surroundings: there are morgue flies and cemetery flies, mattress flies and urinal flies. Madrid is plagued by flies at this time of year, and some of the characters ask: "What the hell's going on with these flies?" What's going on is similar to what's happening in Sartre's *Les Mouches.* And by insisting on the immense number of varieties of flies and odors, Cela distinguishes the diseases and decay which surround and attract them. Cela's aim is, I think, to invite the reader to speculate on the immensity of the variety involved and thus find an antidote to his habitual indifference.

Just as the odors denote the various kinds of death in the novel, and flies the different sorts of decay, a prominent place is given in the novel to diseases of the characters. The embodiment of these diseases is the enormous variety of patent medicines, quack cures, medical treatments, and therapies mentioned in the novel. The characters are forever ingesting pills, tablets, syrups, and elixirs, applying lotions, ointments, and sprays, something which must gladden the hearts of the American, German, and Swiss managers of pharmaceutical houses in Spain, and confirm the direst fears of Servan-Schreiber. The remedies can be classed as cosmetic, patent, and medical. For removing facial wrinkles, there is Dorothy Gray's makeup, for increasing the bust, Pilules Orientales; there are underarm deodorants, Axilol, and vaginal douches, Cuprolina and Perleucuterol. The characters take Health Hyposulphates and Vitefosfor powder for poor appetite, and a tonic called Vial's Elixir; they kill bedbugs with Chinchicida Ducal, and intestinal worms with Catalá's caramels. Illnesses of the genito-urinary tract are thought to respond to Chaumel *al actiol,* while Erotyl is supposed to cure impotence, and Ladillol remove pubic crabs. In the midst of the fratricidal war whose terror and violence were universally traumatic in Spain, those not directly involved in military action or in the unorganized actions of street mobs suffer traumata of lesser significance: worms, crabs, poor appetite, flat-chestedness.

It is part of Cela's matter-of-fact attitude toward physical disability, deformity, and illness that these minor complaints assume no more than a minor role in characterization or motivation. And the widespread vision of illness which he presents helps to underline the matter-of-factness with which he mentions major injuries and deaths which *are* war-related. Because of their continual juxtaposition with trivial complaints, the major casualties of the war—death in combat, the suicides of besieged officers before capture by the enemy, and political assassinations—are reduced by a kind of suction to the trivial level of a case of bad breath.

Cela places no great hopes in the medical profession. No crusading doctors selflessly perform delicate operations to save lives. In fact, where doctors appear in the novel they are usually shown to be incompetent, civil-service hacks, serving their hours in a clinic or public hospital, and frequently taking a wry or perverse delight in the death throes of their patients, or the struggles against desperation of the patients' kin. Where an autopsy is performed on a colonel assassinated in the street, the doctors do not even agree about which side of the head the bullet entered.

The characters suffer from the minor complaints I have mentioned and attempt to treat them with nostrums, patent medicines, and folk remedies. Their habituation to these cures betrays a devotion which transcends reason; they persist in using them not because the remedies are effective, but because their faith in the medicines compels them to. Likewise, the omnipresence of these minor complaints contaminates those serious injuries and ailments which do occur, making them seem no more than minor annoyances. Those afflicted with major complaints find no more solace or solution to their problems than those with the minor ones. And as an "objective correlative" of the moral diseases besetting Spain at this period, the physical diseases persist: they do not go away by themselves, nor do they yield to the ordinary treatments. Likewise, all the claims presented by advertisers of those patent medicines, claims as fanciful as their acceptance is widespread, are the analogues of claims made for cures in the realm of moral diseases. The language of **San Camilo** is a literary Spanish liberally laced with street slang, newspapers, advertising prose, and political rhetoric. The strident propaganda of the Nationalists is debunked as severely as the claims of the Left Republicans. None of the many political analyses of the crisis stands unchallenged. Each of the many characters who advances an explanation of what is wrong with Spain is demolished in his reasoning or shown to be a fool, save for Uncle Jerome, about whom more in a moment.

Our attention is drawn to the illness and decay in the novel for another reason: the saint in the novel's title is the patron of the sick. St. Camillus of Lellis, Confessor, died in Rome in 1614. He is credited with establishing an Order of Clerks Regular for work in hospitals; he was proclaimed patron of hospitals (by Leo XIII) and of nuns who tend the sick (by Plus XI). The narrator places himself under the protection of St. Camillus because he sees Madrid as a sick city and Spain as a sick country and himself as minister to the sick. The disease is the fear of death and its symptoms are legion. The narrator ministers to all Spaniards, regardless of political affiliation or lack of it, not so much by washing their wounds or answering their complaints, as by witnessing their frenzied efforts to escape their disease. Thus his narrative witnesses the sports they engage in, the flies and smells which attend them, their erratic behavior on the outbreak of the war. By his witness he is present when the characters die, he abides with them in their dying, just as a nursing sister under the protection of St. Camillus.

Further, the narrator situates himself at the very center of a sphere of activity which is perhaps the most prevalent means the characters have of keeping the wolf of fear from their door: their sexual lives. A great many of the novel's episodes, especially in Part I, are set either in whorehouses, houses of assignation, or other locales suitable for pre- and extra-marital sexual activities. A very large number of the events of the novel involve prostitutes, mistresses, madams, retired bawds, and other women whose morals are in varying states of relaxation. The whores suffer no less from disease and physical ailments than the other characters, and they are no less under the patronage of St. Camillus.

The narrator spells out for the reader the differences between various sorts of accommodation for illicit sexual activities (e.g., 27), and takes pains in describing their décor, their personnel, their street addresses, and the social status of their various clienteles. He gives us the distilled folk wisdom concerning the ways one may treat whores of different races. Anyone who locates on a map of Madrid the addresses of brothels and houses of assignation provided by the narrator will mentally have taken quite a thorough tour of the city. If in addition he charts the different characters' meetings in those houses, linking together the men who frequent the various brothels with the different women who work in each of them, he will have gone a long way toward compiling a census of the characters in the novel. Further, he will realize that the brothels and similar locales provide the settings for meetings between characters who otherwise have nothing to do with each other, or even—in the case of León Rioja and his son, Dámaso—are too closely related for comfort.

As a fictional technique, this procedure seems no more artificial than Romero's in *La noria.* As a symbolic of action in the novel, the technique should be interpreted to mean that all or almost all of the *madrileños* are connected each with the other in their common pursuit of sex. They are all seeking feverishly to recover their national and collective communion with each other, in the midst of a war which even at its outset destroyed communion as only a civil war can. The whorehouses make up an authentic democracy; not only is the tissue of relationships among the characters woven in them, but also members of the highest and lowest classes are made equal by Cela's prose technique. Coupling the name of a prostitute with that of a general marries the two in what—given the omnipresence of the effects of the war—is a modern Dance of Death. The Dance recurs more explicitly when the narrator says: "los vivos y los muertos desfilan tumultuariamente y sin compás," and goes on to list the Dance's participants, from stillborn feti to Joan of Arc and Caupolicán IV.

It is in the exaltation of sex, the sex drive, and the healing and restorative powers of lust, that the narrator places his faith. If anything can preserve or restore the communion of Spain's people which was broken asunder as the war began it is sex: "acquí se jode poco y mal, si los españoles jodieran a gusto serían menos brutos y mesiánicos, habría menos héroes y menos mártires pero también habría menos asesinos y a lo mejor funcionaban las cosas, nadie quiere darse cuenta de que esto es así." The spokesman for sex is the narrator's uncle, Jerome. Amidst the cacophony of political claims from one and another quarter, above the din raised by hieratic pronouncements from partisans of the myriad of splinter groups, pronouncements which explode like bombs and splinter into shrapnel on every page of this war novel, there is one calm spokesman whose point of view is never contradicted by the narrator.

Uncle Jerome lives a simple existence, made possible by a small inheritance. He is not very much "in the world" of the novel, because he does not frequent whores or bars, the Parliament or the barracks, churches or sports events, as the other characters do. Though not in the world, he is very worldly and continually inquires of his nephew whether his sex life is satisfactory, whether he smokes too much, or drinks. He himself had lived with a mistress, Lieselotte Vonderhinten, at one time who was, like him, a philosophy student. He follows what to us today must seem a health faddist's diet: he eats only raw eggs, vegetables, milk, honey, and yogurt, tomatoes and [olive] oil. Though he does not work at a job, he does setting-up exercises which help him keep fit. He can afford to buy books from time to time and seems entirely a professorial type. Unlike some of the other characters of independent means (e.g., Cesáreo Murciego), he is not connected to the individual events of the novel and does not seem to have other than familial relationships. This is not to say he does not feel the events

of the war, the turmoil occurring throughout Madrid. As a *rentista* he is sufficiently fearful over the outbreak of the war as to move in, "for the duration," with his nephew's family, arriving in some agitation with his hair tousled.

Jerome is the spokesman for a philosophy which provides the backdrop, if not the justification, for the narrator's isolation and non-participation. He thinks human history is characterized by an inexorable march of nations toward freedom, and invokes—in what must be seen in the context of this novel as a Krausist point of view—the history of philosophy to bolster his opinion. He denounces violence as a solution to social or political problems, assigning equal blame to crimes of oppression committed by the Government in putting down uprisings as to crimes of aggression against the Government. The hope which lurks behind his opinion is that if Spain can only refrain from indulging in national outbreaks of violence long enough for some number of law professors and school teachers to be educated and employed, the nation's steps along the road to freedom can continue. These remarks remind us of those written by Galdós in 1881 (in the epigraph to *La desheredada*) to the effect that what Spain needs is arithmetic, logic, morality, and common sense. In 1936, there was still a great need in Spain for school teachers and professors of law; the Republic had made literacy and freer access to higher education one of its most important programs.

Uncle Jerome does not try to dispel what has been called the Black Legend of Spain. He takes it for granted that political and social edginess is contagious; "tu tío Jerónimo dice que los gobernantes son los culpables del nerviosismo de los gobernados . . . los nervios son tan contagiosos como la sarna y los gobernantes tienen la obligación de no toser ni escupir arañitas de la sarna sobre los gobernados, cuando los gobernantes están sarnosos acaba rascándose todo el país." Once ignited, political and military hysteria to which Spaniards are prone inflame the whole populace. He thinks that in Spain politics is the art of saving what can be saved, and ruling Spaniards so that they don't hunt each other down. For once the Spaniards' passions are unleashed, only destruction can result. Because Spain is a "liturgical country" within every Spaniard there lurks a "religious arsonist." What is essential is the control of the self-seeking revolutionary, Right or Left, whose only aim is to burn society down in order to get what he can personally.

Recourse to destruction is futile and self-seeking: "cada español está siempre a un paso de ser héroe de Cascorro, es como una fórmula mágica de arrepentimiento por tantos siglos de holganza y despropósito, eso es mala señal, el heroísmo, sobrino, el cascorrismo es tan contagioso como las viruela." The trick is in abstaining from incendiary revolutionism, for if one succeeds he has only gained a selfish end, and if he fails he loses his life. Jerome reminds us that in politics one never starts from scratch; political change has always to work with the givens of the situation. Hence, the dream of burning everything down and starting over again the proper way is but vanity.

The novel ends with an epilog, a twelve-page summation of Jerome's point of view. In what seems an anachronistic access of love for all men in a book which is set in 1936, Jerome says we must love each other, and let "the doors of our hearts open wide so love can come in." He tells his nephew to renounce violence, the "false wealth" of material possessions, and never to lose his appetite for sex. He knows that the Civil War will come to an end, life will continue, and the epilog's Aquarian tone is reinforced by the narrator's telling us of another of Jerome's mistresses, Cecilia. She is a Mother Earth figure whose daughter, Jerome thinks, will be a fit consort for his nephew. The narrator and Basilia will thus continue the chain of life.

I have drawn together some of the major themes of the novel in order to elicit what I take to be an intimately personal statement of Cela's. Despite the objectivism or neorealism of his prose and structure, Cela's is an impassioned denunciation of war and of violent political action, a denunciation which does not lose its point, though times and government may change. The narrator is paralyzed by his fear of death, so paralyzed that he does not even acknowledge any situations in which he *might* have acted. His own guilt at inaction is one with the collective guilt for the war: "la culpa es de todos." With the intimacy of the narrator's revelations goes a certain reticence which is reflected in the rather narrow time-span of the novel. What many readers would like to know from a narrator who closely resembles Cela in so many of his attitudes and reactions is what the circumstances were which led don Camilo to abandon inaction. One reason for the absence of any account of his military activities, and for choosing a temporal frame for the novel which would exclude them, is that the entire narration is a *critique* of action; as such, it can present only the actions of characters other than the narrator. The narrator's greatest sin is one of omission; it is the sin of inaction and his guilt stems from his paralysis.

Too often, it seems to me, Cela's critics view him as an imperturbable virtuoso, a sort of literary prestidigitator whose remarkable successes are gained with no investment of self, and at little expenditure of talent and energy. In this novel, however, I think he has produced a statement of suffering both personal and national whose anguish is almost tangible. His individual and patriotic, though not nationalistic, concern for the problematical qualities of Spain and Spaniards links him with the same concerns in Larra in the last century and in Unamuno in this.

Cedric Brusette (essay date January 1974)

SOURCE: "*La familia de Pascual Duarte* and the Prominence of Fate," in *Revista de Estudios Hispánicos*, Vol. VIII, No. 1, January, 1974, pp. 61-7.

[*In the following essay, Brusette asserts that the importance Cela places on fate in his* La familia de Pascual Duarte *causes the novel's pessimistic tone.*]

It is generally agreed that the tone of *La familia de Pascual Duarte* is one of extreme pessimism. The novel begins with the re-ordering of the events of the life of the protagonist, Pascual, starting with his childhood and ending with his execution. Since the form of the novel is largely first-person memoir, the vision of life of the protagonist-narrator is all the more important. The pessimism of the novel derives essentially from the vision of life of Pascual Duarte, a vision that becomes increasingly leaden with the shadow of fate spreading menacingly across its path. It is the purpose of this essay to examine the role assigned to fate in the development and texture of the novel. Several critics, notably Ilie, Zamora, and Mary Ann Beck allude to fate as part of Pascual's frame of reference but do not elaborate. Feldman sees the novel as existentialist and rejects the idea that Pascual is ". . . driven by inexorable 'fate'."

A careful reading of the novel identifies more than forty instances of the presence of fate in the vision of the narrative. Most examples reach us through the protagonist's philosophy of life, as he applies this philosophy to specific situations. Life was already set on the wrong course from the very beginning: ". . . el destino se complace en variarnos como si fuésemos de cera y destinarnos por sendas diferentes al mismo fin: la muerte." His life will simply conform to this general outlook. Even the highway leading to his town participates in his fate; it is of ". . . una lisura y una largura . . . de un condenado a muerte"; that is, leading essentially to death. To indicate the inescapable hold fate has on human life he compares it to the indelible marks of a tattoo: "Hay mucha diferencia entre adornarse las carnes con arrebol y colonia, y hacerlo con tatuajes que después nadie ha de borrar ya. . . ."

Man's purpose, and in particular Pascual's, is seen as the work of supernatural or cosmic forces: ". . . pero como no nos es dado escoger, sino que ya—y aún antes de nacer—estamos destinados unos a un lado y otros a otro, procuraba conformarme con lo que me había tocado." In this regard, the conception of Pascual Duarte resembles that of Unamuno's Octavio Robleda, who was born in the theater to an assigned role, that of perpetually undermining the character he portrayed and imposing his own. At times Pascual expresses his pessimism thus: "¡Quién sabe sino sería que estaba escrito en la divina memoria que la desgracia había de ser mi único camino, la única senda por la que mis tristes días habían de discurrir! . . ." and again, as the work of God: ". . . pero como Dios se conoce que no quiso que ninguno de nosotros nos distinguiésemos por las buenas inclinaciones . . ."; and at other times, it is the work of the devil: ". . . el viaje que tan feliz térimino le señalaba si el diablo . . . no se hubiera empeñado en hacer de las suyas en mi casa y en mi mujer durante mi ausencia," or the lasting impact of original sin: ". . . pero allí estaría . . . libre de toda culpa, si no es el pecado original."

Often, the presence of fate is seen in the foreboding, the dark machinations of elemental forces, and are expressed in imagery: the corpse of the unfortunate Mario (whose brief life, too, was dogged by fate) is viewed as ". . . una lechuza ladrona." Later, this figure will be repeated in combination with the "cypress," which Pascual now points out shortly after Mario's funeral: "El sol estaba cayendo; sus últimos rayos se iban a clavar sobre el triste ciprés, mi única compañía. . . ." As events begin to accelerate further beyond Pascual's control, the nocturnal scene presents its mysterious onlookers: "El ciprés parecía un fantasma, alto y seco, un centinela de los muertos. . . ," and in the tree ". . . una lechuza, un pájaro de mal agüero, dejaba oír su silbo misterioso." When he leaves the cemetery, disappointment awaits him at home, and so the image of the owl is found personified, in his very home: "La señora Engracia estaba a la puerta; hablaba con la *s,* como la lechuza del ciprés; a lo mejor tenía hasta la misma cara. . . ."

Sometimes fate is painted as a shadow falling across his path: ". . . la negra sombra"; ". . . un humor endiablado me acompañaba como una sombra donde-quiera que fuese"; and after the death of Pascualillo, ". . . temía la puesta del sol como al fuego o como a la rabia; . . . Todas las sombras me recordaban al hijo muerto." Later, when Lola has to tell him about her pregnancy by another man, her ". . . mirar era como un bosque de sombras." At other times, fate is a malevolent star: he was slowly forgetting the evil and disgrace of his life ". . . hasta que la mala estrella, esa mala estrella que parecía como empeñada en perseguirme, quiso resuscitarlos para mi mal," and the few times he tried to mitigate his bad conduct, ". . . esa fatalidad, esa mala estrella . . . parece como complacerse en acompañarme, torció y dispuso las cosas, de forma tal que la bondad no acabó para servir a mi alma para maldita la cosa." Fate, bringing him sorrow, concretizes his fear expressed as "Siempre tuve muy buen ojo para la desgracia . . . ," as a wicked wind: ". . . mueren los niños, los niños atravesados por algún mal aire traidor," and the wind grows in fierceness: ". . . chirría como si quisiera atravesarla algún mal aire . . ."; and his son, for whose life he fears, breathes heavily and ". . . el quejido del niño semejaba al llanto de las encinas pasadas por el viento." His son dies, and he remembers the night when "El mal aire traidor andaba aún por el campo." He also thinks that on that night "La lechuza estaría sobre el ciprés."

The figure of the witch also crosses his path. Not only is this figure present in his house as señora Engracia, but it impeded his forward progress even while he was on his honeymoon. His mare was frightened by a "pobre vieja," and so he accidentally knocked her down. Her smile seemed to be ". . . un presentimiento . . . de lo que habría de ocurrirle," and later, it is his mother, whose very existence would precipitate Pascual's ultimate damnation, who bewitches his path: he returns home from prison, and she "Abrió la puerta; a la luz del candil parecía una bruja."

Pascual's possibilities are also limited by social as well as natural inheritance. He describes the shortcomings of his parents early in the novel as ". . . defectos todos ellos que para mi desgracia hube de heredar." Lola, too, sees him as belonging to that brood of weaklings like his idiot brother, Mario: "¡Eres como tu hermano!" This simple sentence is an indictment of Pascual's putrid blood, exemplified in the death of his son, who could not resist the elements. It is not surprising, then, that Pascual exhibits qualities of resignation. He views his pending wedding with the following sentiments: ". . . lo mejor sería estarme quieto y dejar que los acontecimientos salieran por donde quisieran; los corderos quizás piensen lo mismo al verse llevados al degolladero. . . ." When unavoidable scandal occurred, he saw it as ". . . fatal como las enfermedades y los incendios, como los amaneceres y como la muerte, porque nadie era capaz de impedirlo."

The protagonist's possibilities in life are seen fatalistically in the gestures and manner of other people, in their perceptions and in the repeated situation. When Pascual returned from La Coruña to his wife, her ". . . cara daba miedo, un miedo horrible de que la desgracia llegara con mi retorno," and she tells him, sensing his murderous thoughts: "Es que la sangre parece como el abono de tu vida. . . ." The situation he is facing is the pregnancy of his wife by another man, an incident which duplicates what happened to his mother and father earlier in the case of his brother, Mario.

Pascual feels the obsessive need to kill his mother. He must remove from his path the last vestiges of the witch, of the figure of menacing death. In so doing, he will also be performing suicide on part of his inheritance. He views the murder of his mother as something that had to be, because of the nature of hate, which he experiences in his feelings towards her: "El odio tarda años en incubar, uno ya no es un niño y cuando el odio crezca y nos ahogue los pulsos, nuestra vida se irá. El corazón no albergará más hiel y ya estos brazos, sin fuerza, caerán. . . ." So he must go *forward* and do what *must* be done because ". . . uno piensa volver sobre sus pasos, desandar lo ya andado . . . No; no es posible." And so the relentless, neutral, forward progression continues in his life as it does in the life of Unamuno's Octavio Robleda in spite of all the efforts to reverse it; "No, no era posible cejar, había que continuar adelante, siempre adelante, hasta el fin."

Recognizing the unchanging, foreboding landscape, Pascual notes that ". . . estaba el cementerio . . . con su alto ciprés que en nada había mudado, con su lechuza silbadora entre las ramas . . . ," and its affinity with his very core, and tries to escape from himself: "La sombra de mi cuerpo iba siempre delante, larga, muy larga, tan larga como un fantasma . . . Corrí un poco; la sombra corrió también. Me paré; la sombra también paró." And filled with fear, "Cogí miedo, un miedo inexplicable; me imaginé a los muertos saliendo en esqueleto a mirarme pasar." He finally expresses the meaning of his flight from his own shadow: "Quería poner tierra entre mi sombra y yo, entre mi nombre y mi recuerdo y yo, entre mis mismos cueros y mí mismo."

Finally, Pascual capsules for us in biological terms the whole fatal character of his life, a life whose direction was determined very early, perhaps at the conception of life: "¡Nada hiede tanto ni tan mal como la lepra que lo malo pasado deja por la conciencia, como el dolor de no salir del mal pudriéndonos ese osario de esperanzas muertas, al poco de nacer, que—¡desde hace tanto tiempo ya!—nuestra triste vida es!" Pascual Duarte, then, as presented by his creator, Camilo José Cela, is traumatized, abused and cheated by life. He is, in the words of the prison chaplain: ". . . un manso cordero, acorralado y asustado por la vida," and the entire texture of the surrounding realities contributes to the general fatalistic ambience of his existence.

Lynette Hubbard Seator (essay date October 1975)

SOURCE: "The Antisocial Humanism of Cela and Hemingway," in *Revista de Estudios Hispánicos,* Vol. IX, No. 3, October, 1975, pp. 425-39.

[*In the following essay, Seator traces the parallels between the work of Cela and that of Ernest Hemingway, including their focus on the primacy of the individual, their affinity with the natural world, and their presentation of the restrictions of civilized society.*]

Ernest Hemingway's affinity for Spain is well-known. He was attracted by the Spanish character, and as proposed in a recent article, was perhaps influenced by the work of Pío Baroja. Whatever Hemingway may owe to the generation of 98 novelist, a comparison of him with the outstanding novelist of the succeeding generation, Camilo José Cela, intensifies what is perceived as Hemingway's Spanish *Weltanschauung.* Hemingway, unlike Baroja, depicts a confrontation with life in all of its dimensions and what Cleanth Brooks calls: "the struggle of man to be a human being in a world which increasingly seeks to reduce him to a mechanism, a mere thing." Cela's work presents a similar vigorous approach to life and concern with human dignity. Robert Kirsner writing on *Viaje a la Alcarria* observes that: "Here man does not surrender himself completely to external circumstances. He is not reduced to being a pawn of a material machination of 'cause and effect'."

Hemingway the writer so strongly reflects the vitality of his own life's involvements that the life of Hemingway the battle-scarred man of action has become something of a legend. In Cela too the living of life and knowing it through the senses is essential. Like Hemingway he has written poetry, been a soldier, a newspaperman, a novelist and a bull fighter. He and Hemingway have both been virile protagonists in the life they have so accurately observed, and so they are often protagonists in the literature they have created. Cela's accounts of his foot travels through the Spanish countryside in which he writes of what he has seen, smelled, heard, felt and done bear a resemblance to Hemingway's *The Green Hills of Africa.* A number of passages from *The Sun Also Rises* present the same feeling, as Hemingway in the identity of Jake Barnes travels, eats and sleeps in northern Spain. Here as in Cela's books of regional travel he is explicit as to the price of rooms and meals, the countryside and the customs. Neither Hemingway nor Cela, however, is intellectually or stylistically limited in these works to a terse account of the place and its people. There is attention to the subtleties of mood and atmosphere and often a lyric reflection on the nature of things.

> Las cosas están siempre mejor un poco revueltas, un poco en desorden; el frío orden administrativo de los museos, de los ficheros, de la estadística y de los cementerios, es un orden inhumano, un orden antinatural; es, en definitiva, un desorden. El orden es el de la naturaleza, que todavía no ha dado dos árboles o dos montes o dos caballos iguales. Haber sacado de Pastrana los tapices para traerlos a la capital ha sido, además, un error: es mucho más grato encontrarse las cosas como por casualidad, que ir a buscarlas ya a tiro hecho y sin posible riesgo de fraude.

Hemingway reflects a similar distaste for the changes wrought by a progressive society.

> A continent ages quickly once we come. The natives live in harmony with it. But the foreigner destroys, cuts down the trees, drains the water, so that the water sup-

ply is altered and in a short time the soil, once the sod is turned under, is cropped out and, next, it starts to blow away as it has blown away in every old country and as I had seen it start to blow in Canada. The earth gets tired of being exploited. A country wears out quickly unless man puts back in it all his residue and that of all his beasts. When he quits using beasts and uses machines, the earth defeats him quickly. The machine can't reproduce, nor does it fertilize the soil, and it eats what he cannot raise. A country was made to be as we found it. We are the intruders and after we are dead we may have ruined it but it will still be there and we don't know what the next changes are.

Along with the feeling of the presence of Hemingway as protagonist, in many of his works there is an interesting collection of primitive types. The characters satirized in *The Torrents of Spring* are particularly like the motley group who patronize Cela's *Café de artistas.* In these works Cela and Hemingway satirize the trite and false in writing as well as the oddities of human nature. Characters who people the bars, cafes, locker rooms, sick beds, camps and road sides of Cela and Hemingway tales tend to be pathetic in the crowded emptiness that is their lives. They are characterized in a variety of dialects, brogues, mixtures of languages and simple inarticulateness. A use of language which has greatly interested Hemingway critics is that of *For Whom the Bell Tolls* in which the Spanish mentality is portrayed through English which seems to be a direct translation from the Spanish.

> ". . . Perhaps it came from talking that foolishness about Valencia. And that failure of a man who has gone to look at his horses. I wounded him much with the story. Kill him, yes. Curse him, yes. But wound him, no."
>
> "How came you to be with him?"
>
> "How is one with any one? In the first days of the movement and before too, he was something. Something serious. But now he is finished. The plug has been drawn and the wine has all run out of the skin."

In *La Catira* Cela uses a dialect of Venezuela to characterize the people and their affinity to the land which holds and isolates them. ". . . Mía, mocho Clorindo, vale, pie a los santos que to baya a sali con bien. Un marrón te he e da pa toa la gente, vale. Yo no me muevo e el hato. . . ."

A look at Hemingway and Cela, each within his national context, reminds us of their respective roles as postwar novelist and the consternation caused by their first novels, *The Sun Also Rises* first published in 1926 and *La familia de Pascual Duarte* in 1942. After the First World War,

Americans were shocked to see themselves as part of a lost generation given to endless drinking and promiscuity. In Spain the aftermath of the revolution carried the same psychological devastation, alienation and dissolution of traditional values; and Cela horrified his countrymen with their presentation in his tremendistic novel. Pascual is a victim of circumstance, a primitive who can express his hostilities only through his violent acts, and so the final horror of his story lies in the truth of the words that begin it: "Yo, señor, no soy malo. . . ." As Pascual in his simplicity describes the circumstances leading up to his first bloody act, he tells how he turned back again to sit on his favorite rock because it looked so lonely at his leaving. The fixed look of his faithful dog seems to challenge Pascual for his softness, and so the man reacts with violence as spontaneously as he did out of pity.

> Un temblor recorrió todo mi cuerpo; parecía como una corriente que forzaba por salirme por los brazos. El pitillo se me había apagado; la escopeta, de un solo caño, se dejaba acariciar, lentamente, entre mis piernas. La perra seguía mirándome fija, como si no me hubiera visto nunca, como si fuese a culparme de algo de un momento a otro, y su mirada me calentaba la sangre de las venas de tal manera que se veía llegar el momento en que tuviese que entregarme; hacía calor, un calor espantoso, y mis ojos se entornaban dominados por el mirar, como un clavo, a del animal .
> . .
>
> Cogí la escopeta y disparé; volví a cargar y volví a disparar. La perra tenía una sangre oscura y pegajosa que se extendía poco a poco por la tierra.

Generally Hemingway protagonists represent more civilization and complexity, but under the skin they are driven by the same urges which are eventually but often less spontaneously fulfilled. When Agustín explains to Robert Jordan the impelling desire he had to kill the Fascist cavalrymen as they rode by within easy firing range, he characterizes his passion as being akin to the sexual drive.

> ". . . And when I saw those four there and thought that we must kill them I was like a mare in the corral waiting for the stallion. . . . The necessity was on me as it is on a mare in heat. You cannot know what it is if you have not felt it."
>
> "You sweated enough," Robert Jordan said. "I thought it was fear."
>
> "Fear, yes," Agustín said. "Fear and the other. And in this life there is no stronger thing than the other."

Agustín likens his instinctive desire to kill to the mating

instinct of an animal, and Pascual describes his visceral re-actions which also strongly suggest the description of sexual impulses: "un temblor," "todo mi cuerpo," "se dejaba acariciar," "me calentaba la sangre," "tuviese que entregarme." Jordan's intellectuality and civilization re-move his impulses from the superficial level of immediacy and cause him to abhor their manifestations in Agustín, but out of his own honesty he finds them to exist within him-self and to have an outlet acceptable within the social or-der.

> Yes, Robert Jordan thought. We do it coldly but they do not, nor ever have. It is their extra sacrament. Their old one that they had before the new religion came from the far end of the Mediterranean, the one they have never abandoned but only suppressed and hid-den to bring it out again in wars and inquisitions. . . . Stop making dubious literature about the Berbers and the old Iberians and admit that you have liked to kill as all who are soldiers by choice have enjoyed it at some time whether they lie about it or not.

Pascual Duarte, Agustín and Robert Jordan share the same primordial drives which are asserted in varying degrees. Of the three, Pascual is the most primitive and the most sen-sitive. It is when his tender feelings are bruised against the callousness of the human beings with whom he comes into contact that he is moved to commit a series of crimes which culminate in the murder of his own mother. Here the primitive urges that exist in man are not evil in themselves but become so when complicated and distorted by man's society. Pascual Duarte's situation was a product of the so-cial order which had created it but which remained indif-ferent. The comfortable houses in his town seemed to be so far removed from his own as to be part of another world. Only his priest recognized Pascual to be "una rosa en un estercolero" but could not transplant him to more favor-able terrain. Pascual in his dumb state of despair would not have been capable of articulating the words of Harry Mor-gan: "No matter how, a man alone ain't got no bloody chance." In *To Have and Have Not* Hemingway sees the individual as a victim of the social order but does not lose faith in his significance and dignity. Harry Morgan's vio-lent acts arising out of his economic necessity carry him along on an irrevocable tide as do Pascual's. Morgan acted with awareness rather than out of passion, but like Pascual he was presented with no alternative. In the case of Agustín and Robert Jordan they too finally are only victims of a so-cial product which is the war.

Although Hemingway found war to create a dramatic and real situation removed from the hypocrisy of a materialis-tic society, he abhorred it for its mass brutalization and de-struction. A soldier's act of cowardice or bravery might be of utmost importance in defining his character, but war it-self is never glorious or even expedient. National goals and ideals are lost; and out of the suffering, survival alone has significance. Hemingway's major war novels, *A Farewell to Arms* and *For Whom the Bell Tolls* point up the futility as well as the abject cruelty and ugliness of the war scene. Frederic Henry finds the war to be so purposeless and in-tolerable that he deserts, and Robert Jordan dies for a cause which no longer seems to exist. Many of the short stories among Hemingway's first collection, *In Our Time,* are ad-aptations of the articles that he did at the front, and in their careful selection of detail they reflect the horror that the young man felt at his early contacts with war. Seeing what the Greeks did to their pack animals must have created an indelible image in his mind since there are later references to the same incident.

> The Greeks were nice chaps too. When they evacu-ated they had all their baggage animals they couldn't take off with them so they just broke their forelegs and dumped them into the shallow water. All those mules with their forelegs broken pushed over into the shal-low water. It was all a pleasant business. My word yes a most pleasant business.

The only comment on the scene is the ironical use of the word "pleasant." Typical of Hemingway is the apparent sim-plicity and objectivity with which he presents this stark scene of outrageous cruelty. Cela is a master of the same technique with which he arouses feelings of disgust and an-ger in his reader while he stands aloof as an objective nar-rator.

> En la calle de Torrijos, un perro agoniza en el alcorque de un árbol. Lo atropelló un taxi por mitad de la barriga. Tiene los ojos suplicantes y la lengua fuera. Unos niños le hostigan con el pie . . .

> Unos basureros se acercan al grupo del can moribundo, cogen al perro de las patas de atrás y lo tiran dentro del carrito. El animal da un profundo, un desalentado aullido de dolor, cuando va por el aire.

A product of Cela's reaction to war itself is *El solitario* which grimly and sardonically paints the hideousness of the soldier's life with death. He writes: "La muerte causa menos dolor que la espera de la muerte." In another pas-sage he speaks of the loss of privacy and hence the loss of identity imposed by army life. "La guerra no es buen paisaje para la soledad. En la guerra, la soledad tiene demasiados atónitos espectadores. No quiero vivir, pero si quiero morir a solas: como he nacido. No hay causa noble fuera de la soledad del hombre y, en la batalla, la soledad del hombre se atropella por la mera presencia de los demás." Hemingway's Colonel expresses the same attitude toward a regimented life that denies a man his solitude: ". . . you go off to be alone, and think or not think, and pick a good piece of cover and there are two riflemen there already, or some boy asleep. There's no more privacy in the army than in a professional shit-house." In *La colmena* the aftermath of war is a mass struggle for existence that continues to rob human beings of their individuality. The undignified existence of the hungry and sickly café goers is like the swarming together of insects where there is an incessant stinging and buzzing but no exchange of affection or concern for one another. Nati wistfully remembers the innocent kisses she exchanged with Martin and how things were before their society had warped their lives: ". . . creí que las cosas eran así, como fueron entre tú y yo, y después vi que no, que no eran así . . . que eran de otra manera mucho peor. . . ." It is here in the crowded life of the city that Cela sees man at his worst, victimized and dehumanized by life in the postwar society of Madrid.

Conversely in the peaceful countryside, away from the swarming city, Cela finds beauty and dignity in life. His numerous narrations of his travels through the Spanish provinces reflect his love of the land and the people who live close to it. "Parece que no pero, en el campo, sentado al borde de un camino, se ve más claro que en la ciudad eso de que en el mundo, Dios ordena las cosas con bastante sentido." When Cela assumes the role of *vagabundo,* he expresses his feelings about the city. "Al vagabundo no le gustan las ciudades ni hace buenas migas con los ciudadanos." As Hemingway recounts his African travels, he reflects the same attitude. "I had loved country all my life; the country was always better than the people. I could only care about people a very few at a time." Over and over again Hemingway expresses his love for the natural world and the solitude he finds there. In hunting there is an escape from the world of people and an opportunity to find satisfaction in "killing cleanly." "Having killed . . . you feel a little quiet inside." The peace and quiet that Nick Adams found at the trout stream was one of its greatest attractions and was what took him back to it in his mind when as a young soldier he was afraid to sleep at night because his soul might leave his body as it had when he was hit. When Nick and Bill went out to the cabin during *The Big Three Day Blow,* Bill asked Nick: "Wouldn't it be hell to be in town?" In *Cross Country Snow* George is struck by the thought that: "Maybe we'll never go skiing again. . . ." Nick responds that they must because: "It isn't worth-while if you can't." Later, however, Hemingway found that hunting good snow wasn't worth-while because: "You saw too many people, ski-ing now."

Nuevas andanzas y desventuras de Lazarillo de Tormes

carries the same antisocial yet basically humanist attitudes as Cela's travel books. Paul Ilie observes that: "Al viajar, Cela cumple un acto social. Sus excursiones son prolongadas fugas del estado de sociabilidad al que el hombre se ve condenado . . . El viaje a la ventura apunta a una vida más primitiva que la del intelectual." Cela's Lazarillo suffers only abject cruelty at the hands of human beings until he leaves the towns and villages and finds the hermit, *El penitente Felipe,* who spends his time stargazing. His first question to Lazarillo is: "—¿Amas la Naturaleza y sus encantos?—Sí, señor; las dos cosas." Lazarillo found a happy life with *el penitente* while the natural world determined the rhythm of their lives. "Pasaron los días y las noches sobre nosotros; amaneció el Señor mañana a mañana encima de nuestras cabezas, ora risueño y soleado, ora un tanto lluvioso y como llorador. . . ." From his other masters Lazarillo received nothing but beatings, but looking back on those days he accepts them as an inevitable part of the order of things in the world. "Al andar de los años, cuando llegué a tener criado, hice lo mismo, y no creo que tampoco a éste le haya parecido mal; de momento a nadie gusta que le peguen un revés en el pescuezo o un punterazo en el trasero, pero a la larga, si uno es criado, acaba por reconocer que para eso está, y se aguanta." The social order is unjust and perpetuates itself and its acceptance. In a more complex way the Colonel of *Across the River and Into the Trees* detested his own unkindness to his driver, Jackson, but accepted it since he too in earlier days had experienced similar treatment. The Colonel is an innately sensitive person who is responsive to Renata's beauty and the beauty of the countryside, yet he must struggle against the corrupting ugliness of war and army life that have made him rough. "He sure is a mean son of a bitch, Jackson thought, and he can be so God-damn nice."

Both Hemingway and Cela project a frightful awareness of life being handed out in limited quantities and an urgent need to eat, drink and enjoy all that there is to be enjoyed as long as it is physically possible to do so. The Hemingway protagonist lives with a threat of imminent death from the war, a faulty heart, the forces of nature or the establishment, all of which at least give him some kind of a fighting chance which the aging process and its culmination do not. Hemingway, nevertheless, could not accept the "Life is real: life is earnest, and the grave is not its goal" philosophy which he attributes to "someone with English blood."

> And where did they bury him? and what became of the reality and the earnestness? The people of Castille have great common sense. They could not produce a poet who would write a line like that. They know death is the unescapable reality, the one thing any man may be sure of; the only security; that it transcends all modern comforts and that with it you do not need a bathtub in every American home, nor, when you have it, do you need the radio. They think a great deal about death and when they have a religion they have one which believes that life is much shorter than death.

A stark passage from *El solitario* asserts the horror of "the unescapable reality." "La vida es una brevísima tregua que hay que gozar de espaldas a los cementerios y sus puntuales gusanos devoradores de la carne que aun hubiera servido para dar felicidad a la carne." This biological aspect of death is frequently asserted. One of the patients of *Pabellón de reposo* objects to burial because to her it seems to be removal from the natural world.

> El recuerdo del 14 metido en una caja pintada de negro, con metro y medio o, dos metros de tierra encima, me sobrecoge.

> A los muertos no se les debiera enterrar: es cruel. Se les debiera dejar en los húmedos y verdes prados, a la orilla de los alegres riachuelos, recubiertos con un tul o con una gasa para que las mariposas no les molestasen. Sería, sin duda, más humano.

The Colonel finds on the other hand a certain satisfaction in identifying the final processes of death and burial with a return to life.

> For a long time he had been thinking about all the fine places he would like to be buried and what parts of the earth he would like to be a part of. The stinking, putrefying part doesn't last very long, really, he thought, and anyway you are just a sort of mulch, and even, the bones will be some use finally. I'd like to be buried way out at the edge of the grounds, but in sight of the old graceful house and the tall, great trees. I don't think it would be much of a nuisance to them. I could be a part of the ground where the children play in the evenings, and in the mornings, maybe, they would still be training jumping horses and their hoofs would make the thudding on the turf, and trout would rise in the pool when there was a hatch of fly.

Man's death is a counterpart of life to be understood in terms of life. Pascual Duarte and Agustín in their desire to give death respond as to the mating urge. When Robert Jodan and María make love they describe it as dying, and Pascual Duarte's first sexual experience is on the fresh grave of his brother Mario.

There is another form of death removed from that of the body that is antithetical to the love and awareness of life that is Hemingway's and Cela's. Characteristic of the mass existence that repels them is its unawareness and insensibility, its lack of commitment to living. "Vamos sintiéndonos vivir—en medio de un mundo que se siente, inexorablemente, morir—. . . ." "You just get dead like most people are most of the time." Nevertheless, the individual who asserts his humanity is finally as insignificant as those who comprise the unconsciousness of the social order.

> . . . and when, on the sea, you are alone with it and know that this Gulf Stream you are living with, knowing, learning about, and loving, has moved, as it moves, since before man, and that it has gone by the shoreline of that long, beautiful, unhappy island since before Columbus sighted it and that the things you find out about it, and those that have always lived in it are permanent and of value because that stream will flow, as it has flowed, after the Indians, after the Spaniards, after the British, after the Americans and after all the Cubans and all the systems of governments, the richness, the poverty, the martyrdom, the sacrifice and the venality and the cruelty are all gone . . .

Ultimately man must recognize his insignificance in a world that takes no notice of his arrival or his departure. This is the realization with which Pipía Sánchez is left after seeing the bodies of her son and two husbands given back to the land. "La tierra quea, negra . . . La tierra quea siempre . . . Manque los cielos lloren, durante días y días, y los ríos se agolpen . . . Manque los alzamientos ardan, güeno, y mueran abrasaos los hombres . . . Manque las mujeres se tornaran jorras, negra. . . ."

Cela and Hemingway each presented his country at a crucial moment with a new authenticity of expression and an awareness of the disparity between tradition and grim reality. When the values of their respective societies seemed to be in a state of disintegration, they affirmed the significance of the individual and his relationship to life itself. Their writings reflect a view of collective forms of civilized life as chaotic and degrading, in essence uncivilized, and a reverence for the "all abiding land" and things and people in their natural state. To find these Cela had only to set out for the provinces of Spain. Hemingway's destination was the same, but for him it was distant and exotic. He found Spain to be a country attractive for its primitivism and its freedom from the materialism that for him characterized the American way of life. Neither Cela nor Hemingway has written out of a social commitment but rather out of a commitment to life. They assert the reality of man's body and its passions as a component of his humanity which gives him the capacity to live briefly but completely. They share the view that to identify with the established order is to allow it to determine the shape of life and thus to accept a lifeless existence. Human relationships are meaningful at the personal level but are distorted by society so that finally in the worlds of Cela and Hemingway it is necessary to accept the notion that living like dying is an essentially lonely business.

Michael D. Thomas (essay date Summer 1977)

SOURCE: "Narrative Tension and Structural Unity in Cela's *La familia de Pascual Duarte*," in *Symposium*, Vol. XXXI, No. 2, Summer, 1977, pp. 165-78.

[*In the following essay, Thomas discusses the social and ontological questions in Cela's* La familia de Pascual Duarte.]

In past years, a fundamental difference of opinion has prevailed among critics of Cela's **La familia de Pascual Duarte** (1942). On the one hand, historians of Spanish post-Civil War fiction such as Gonzalo Sobejano, Pablo Gil-Casado, and Eugenio G. de Nora have presented a "social" interpretation of the novel. These scholars contend that Cela's first novelistic effort illustrates the decadent socio-economic condition of Spanish society surrounding the years of internal strife from 1936 to 1939. Robert Spires, Paul Ilie, and Robert Kirsner, on the other hand, have stressed the work's "ontological" focus, asserting that its pages represent an inward search for self-definition independent of societal considerations. A partial resolution to the problems this polemic presents can be found through analysis of the structure of Pascual Duarte's "memorias" and examination of the entire book's source of unity, that is, through a determination of the primary narrative tensions that draw the novel together and move it to a dramatic climax.

The ontological aspect dominates all others and unifies the work. While the social thrust does not lack importance, it is nonetheless subordinate if we speak of the novel as an emotive experience and not as a political document. The ontological conflict, in essence an inner one, is based on a psychological opposition between remorse—the guilty conscience of a criminal condemned to death—and a desire for self-justification. In terms of internal narrative organization, this conflict translates as a tonal vacillation between self-reproach and self-exculpation. Toward the novel's end, the intensified contrapuntal interplay of these two moral planes forms the basis for a climax in narrative structure. In his quest for authenticity of being, Pascual must answer for himself the crucial question, is he a despicable criminal, as so many persons would have him believe, or is he simply an unfortunate and wrongly-accused victim of circumstance? The novel's primary narrative tension, the reason why we as readers want to continue reading, rests in the response to this question.

The overall unity of the story goes beyond the apparent picaresque framework. Unity of experience, more readily definable, again, on a psychological level, lies in Pascual's gradual discovery of the chief reason for his emotive need to explore the past. His present moral distress originates in his having killed his mother. The irrational motive for this murder can be traced through his changing attitude toward her. We see Pascual express a wide range of feelings for his mother, from pity to resentment, from a desire to love to outright hatred. The four conflicting emotions, coupled with Pascual's moral torment, serve to draw together disparate parts of structure. Most of the novel reflects either his self-accusation or self-defense and the progressive hatred for his mother. Sections of the work that do not directly concern these factors are included to the extent that they relate to his mother complex. All are a part of Pascual's groping for meaning, of his wandering search for the spiritual relief he ultimately finds in the final chapter of the memoirs when he relates the matricide.

Any elucidation of Pascual's inner conflict presupposes a dual vision of his presence in the work: Pascual Duarte, protagonist of the action, as opposed to Pascual Duarte, narrator of the action. The internal conflict experienced by each Pascual may be outlined in the following form: the protagonist is consumed by hatred for his mother to the point that he feels an intense desire to murder her; the narrator, an old man waiting on death row, is mentally tortured by an internally motivated call to accountability because he may have slain his own mother without full justification. In order to facilitate study of how inner tension progresses, the book may be divided into three parts. Each corresponds to a separate stage in Pascual's fluctuating attitude toward his mother and demonstrates how, in varying degrees, self-reproach and self-exoneration control his emotional state. The first part encompasses the initial five chapters, up to and including the funeral of Mario, Pascual's idiot brother; the second, Chapters Six through Twelve, ends with the death of Pascualillo; and the final section, Chapters Thirteen to the matricide and the note from the individual who has transcribed the memoirs, completes the novel.

The first of these parts is prefaced by three documents: an introduction by the *transcriptor*, a cover letter written by Pascual to Don Joaquín, a wealthy friend of one of Duarte's victims, and a fragment of D. Joaquín's will detailing his wishes for the disposition of the manuscript after his death. Pascual recounts the early portion of his life, tells of his background and family, the killing of Chispa, his father's death, the birth of his sister Rosario, and the death of Mario. In accordance with the novel's tonal progression, Pascual-narrator, at the beginning of this section, is ambivalently apologetic. He quickly shifts to a self-justifying attitude toward his reader—D. Joaquín—and, in the quest for definition of the cause of his present anguish, ends the first stage of his search, remembering a virulent hatred for his mother and yet, almost paradoxically, feeling some guilt for his animosity.

The *transcriptor*, a hypocritical censor, begins the novel explaining that "el personaje [. . .] es un modelo de conductas; un modelo no para imitarlo, sino para huirlo; un modelo ante el cual toda actitud de duda sobra; un modelo ante el que no cabe sino decir:—¿Ves lo que hace? Pues hace lo contrario de lo que debiera." According to this self-appointed judge, we are faced with a didactic tale in which the distinction between good and evil is clear-cut. Pascual's letter appears to confirm the memoirs' moral-didactic function: "Usted me dispensará de que le envíe este largo relato en compañía de esta carta, también larga para lo que es, pero como resulta que de los amigos de don Jesús [. . .] es usted el único del que guardo memoria de las señas, a usted quiero dirigirlo por librarme de su compañía [. . .] para evitar el que lo tire en un momento de tristeza [. . .] y prive de esa manera a algunos de aprender lo que yo no he sabido hasta que ha sido ya demasiado tarde." Apparently, Pascual has taken stock of his errors and is feeling qualms of conscience: "quiero descargar, en lo que pueda, mi conciencia con esta pública confesión," and the desired "descargo" has been at least partially achieved: "Noto cierto descanso después de haber relatado todo lo que pasé, y hay momentos en que hasta la conciencia quiere remorderme menos." However, even at this early point, Pascual sees himself as a guiltless victim of a cruel fate: "Me atosigaba, al empezar a redactar lo que le envío [. . .] esa seguridad de que mis actos habían de ser, a la fuerza, trazados sobre surcos ya previstos." In Pascual's prefatory letter, then, we can discern the emotive oscillation that structures subsequent narration. Here, he seems to blame himself for his crimes and yet at the same time excuses himself. A first-time reader would know that something in Pascual's past is bothering him, but would assume from the limited information given so far that it has to do with Pascual's entire life or perhaps specifically with the murder of D. Jesús.

Pascual's wavering once established, the pendulum of conscience swings to the defensive in the first paragraph of the "memorias":

> Yo, señor, no soy malo, aunque no me faltarían motivos para serlo. Los mismos cueros tenemos todos los mortales al nacer y sin embargo, cuando vamos creciendo, el destino se complace en variarnos como si fuésemos de cera y en destinarnos por sendas diferentes al mismo fin: la muerte. Hay hombres a quienes se les ordena marchar por el camino de las flores, y hombres a quienes se les manda tirar por el camino de los cardos y de las chumberas. Aquéllos gozan del mirar sereno y al aroma de su felicidad sonríen con la cara del inocente; estos otros sufren del sol violento de la llanura y arrugan el ceño como las alimañas por defenderse. Hay mucha diferencia entre adornarse las carnes con arrebol y colonia, y hacerlo con tatuajes que después nadie ha de borrar ya.

Pascual's palliative attitude is sustained by a second allu-

sion to the possible role of fate in shaping the direction of each person's life. Pascual unknowingly modifies the moral dichotomy laid down by the *transcriptor*. He protests a single standard of justice such as that which has condemned him to death. Pascual perceives a binary opposition more comprehensively just than simply good against evil. Judged evil by society, he pleads the case of rich against poor, of pleasant environment as opposed to hostile surroundings. The rich, having had an easy life, impose their systems of morality on the poor, born in filth and raised in an unstable family background. The description of Jesús' house in this chapter indicates that Pascual is speaking of a specific rich-poor relationship: "había una de dos pisos, la de don Jesús, que daba gozo de verla con su recibidor todo lleno de azulejos y macetas [. . .] los geranios, y los heliotropos, y las palmas, y la yerbabuena."

But in this first chapter, Pascual abandons descriptive oppositions and turns to the least horrible of his killings, the slaughter of Chispa, which has significant ontological implications:

> La perra volvió a echarse frente a mí y volvió a mirarme; ahora me doy cuenta de que tenía la mirada de los confesores, escrutadora y fría, como dicen que es la de los linces [. . .] un temblor recorrió todo mi cuerpo [. . .]. La perra seguía mirándome fija, como si no me hubiera visto nunca, como si fuese a culparme de algo de un momento a otro, y su mirada me calentaba la sangre de las venas de tal manera que se veía llegar el momento en que tuviese que entregarme [. . .].

First, this passage is out of chronological sequence. Chispa's death probably occurs after Pascual kills his mother, since the dog is again mentioned—alive—just after Lola's abortion. In addition, we see the direct association of Chispa with the mother at the end of the first part. After Sr. Rafael has almost kicked the life out of Pascual's brother, Mario, his mother "le estuvo lamiendo la herida toda la noche, como una perra parida a los cachorros." Matricide is preying on his conscience and his guilt superimposes illogical feelings on the dog. In this sense, the chapter culminates not merely in the death of Chispa, but in a subconscious echo of Pascual's horrible crime of, the focus of his internal battle, matricide and in a violent reaction, as defensive as his opening paragraph, to all who would "accuse" him.

In Chapters Two through Four, Pascual shifts his attention more directly to the mother. Since he has not overtly relived his hatred for her in this section, his attitude advances from pity to mild resentment. Pascual first portrays his mother as a victim of his father's drunken wrath: "nos pegaba a mi madre y a mí las grandes palizas por cualquiera la cosa, palizas que mi madre procuraba devolverle por ver de corregirlo." Pascual and his mother are equally victimized and, in fact, the mother is seen in a positive light. In her own way, she is trying to "correct" the father, by fighting fire with fire. The narrator, however, does not hesitate to enumerate her many unsavory characteristics: "no tenía aspecto de buena salud, sino que, por el contrario, tenía la tez cetrina y las mejillas hondas y toda la presencia [. . .] de estar tísica [. . .] era también desabrida y violenta, tenía un humor que se daba a todos los diablos [. . .] en todos los años de su vida que yo conocí, no la vi lavarse más que en una ocasión." In spite of her repulsiveness, she is, in final analysis, a "desgraciada" more to be pitied than condemned. The same attitude prevails in certain comments which at this juncture show that Pascual's early feelings toward her are comparable to his own self-pity: first, "la *pobre* nunca fue modelo de virtudes" (italics is mine); and second, "llegué a pensar si no sería cierto que estaba endemoniada." He speculates that she is, like himself, a victim of an exterior metaphysical force, here, the devil, for him at least as powerful as the forces of fate.

The first true resentment becomes apparent when the mother is deficient not as a person, but in her maternal role: "Rosario se nos crió siempre debilucha y esmirriada—¡poca vida podía sacar de los vacíos pechos de mi madre!—" This relatively tame feeling is maintained through chapter four, re-surfacing when Pascual's father dies: "A mí me asustó un tanto que mi madre, en vez de llorar, como esperaba, se riese," and again after Sr. Rafael has kicked Mario: "La criatura se quedó tirada todo lo larga que era, y mi madre—le aseguro que me asusté en aquel momento que la vi tan ruin—no lo cogía y se reía haciéndole el coro al señor Rafael." Each time he remembers his mother's cruel laughter, Pascual uses the same verb, "asustar." On both occasions, he shows more "surprise" and "shock" than authentic malice.

Open hatred first appears just after Mario's death, an event which should have pained Pascual's mother more than he believes it actually did:

> Mi madre tampoco lloró la muerte de su hijo; secas debiera tener las entrañas una mujer con corazón tan duro que unas lágrimas no le quedaran siquiera para señalar la desgracia de la criatura [. . .] tal odio llegué a cobrar a mi madre, y tan deprisa había de crecerme, que llegué a tener miedo de mí mismo. ¡La mujer que no llora es como la fuente que no mana, que para nada sirve, o como el ave del cielo que no canta, a quien, si Dios quisiera, le caerían las alas, porque a las alimañas falta alguna les hacen!

In Pascual's eyes, his mother again fails to fulfill her maternal duty. Significantly, his negative emotions intensify

so quickly that they frighten even him, a point essential to our understanding of the narrator's behavior at the end of this section. Pascual gropes for a more precise definition of his feelings: "quería hacer un claro en la memoria que me dejase ver hacia qué tiempo dejó de ser una madre en mi corazón y hacia qué tiempo llegó después a convertírseme en un enemigo. En un enemigo rabioso, que no hay peor odio que el de la misma sangre," and then declares with confidence, "Odiarla, lo que se dice llegar a odiarla, tardé algún tiempo [. . .] y si apuntara hacia los días de la muerte de Mario pudiera ser que no errara en muchas fechas sobre su aparición."

There are two inherent ironies here which Pascual might himself perceive, suggesting to him that his reproach of his mother is unjust. In the first place, he cannot rightfully blame her for reacting like an "alimaña" since he himself used this comparison initially as a part of his own self-defense: "estos otros [. . .] arrugan el ceño como las alimañas por defenderse." In the second, his seduction of Lola at Mario's gravesite hardly demonstrates love or respect for the boy. At the end of this section, Pascual has come to a crucially important realization, that the animosity that once devoured him can be traced to his mother and that this feeling for her took recognizable form just after Mario's death. The intensity of his hatred is the dominant force here; possible guilt—the two ironies—is subjugated to the implicit level by open animosity. In this first section, then, Pascual's attitude toward his reader is predominantly defensive; this is reflected in his opening paragraph and his murder of Chispa. And his view of his mother changes dramatically, beginning as near indifference and ending on a strong note of hatred.

It is not surprising that the second part in our divisions begins with the narrator's first major return to the present, after not having written for two weeks. Each time he nears the point of re-living the hatred and the crime of matricide, he flees from his past, afraid to face it, "tal odio llegué a cobrar a mi madre, y tan deprisa había de crecerme, que llegué a tener miedo de mí mismo." In this second section, Pascual marries Lola, she aborts their first child when thrown from the *yegua*, Pascual loses his second son to an "evil wind" and his mother again begins to torment him. Whereas a defensive tone characterized the first section, conscience rules in the second, as Pascual delves further into his past.

Returned to the present, Pascual-narrator meditates lyrically on his surroundings in jail. As with the murder of Chispa, we witness a super-imposition of his feelings on external reality. His mother is still very much on his mind, as he gazes out his cell window: "Eran dos hombres, una mujer y un niño [. . .]. La mujer debía ser la madre, tenía la color morena, como todas, y una alegría en todo el cuerpo que mismo uno se sentía feliz al mirar para ella. Bien distinta era de mi madre, y sin embargo, ¿por qué sería que tanto me la recordaba? Usted me perdonará, pero no puedo seguir. Muy poco me falta para llorar." Though the scene has a profoundly emotional effect on Pascual, he admits that there is really no resemblance at all between the woman and his mother. His irrational guilt, plainly visible here, is combined with a longing for what might have been, perhaps, had he acted differently, or, perhaps, had his family circumstance been otherwise.

In an effort to avoid further painful discussion of his mother, Pascual turns to other incidents in his life: the abortion of his first child, the knife-murder of the *yegua,* and the death of his second son, Pascualillo. He himself confesses, despite his stabbing of the mare, that his greatest crime was yet to come: "el escándalo que sin embargo había de venir, fatal como las enfermedades y los incendios, como los amaneceres y como la muerte, porque nadie era capaz de impedirlo. Las más grandes tragedias de los hombres parecen llegar como sin pensarlas, con su paso de lobo cauteloso." This passage is a good example of how memory of killing his mother infuses unity into Pascual's story. He is constantly dealing with that memory, even when there is no explicit reference to the event and even when he is trying not to think about her. The "scandal" to which Pascual refers is by implication the matricide. This is evidenced in the image of the "paso de lobo," repeated directly in the final chapter with reference to the growing hatred for his mother: "La idea de la muerte llega siempre con paso de lobo, con andares de culebra."

After Pascualillo's death, Pascual's mother assails him with insults. He warns her:

—El fuego ha de quemarnos a los dos, madre.

—¿Qué fuego?

—Ese fuego con el que usted está jugando . . .

Pascual-narrator then approximates the death scene by means of an impersonal re-creation of what occurred. He is spiritually ready to relate it now and implicitly hopes that his mother's attack on him during his moment of weakness and personal tragedy is ample justification for his having killed her:

Se mata sin pensar, bien probado lo tengo; a veces, sin querer. Se odia, se odia intensamente, ferozmente, y se abre la navaja [. . .]. Uno se acerca cautelosamente; lo toca con la mano con cuidado. Está dormido bien dormido; ni se había de enterar . . .

Pero no se puede matar así; es de asesinos. Y uno

piensa volver sobre sus pasos, desandar lo ya andado . . . No; no es posible. Todo está muy pensado; es un instante, un corto instante y después . . .

Pero tampoco es posible volverse atrás. El día llegará y en el día no podríamos aguantar su mirada, esa mirada que en nosotros se clavará aún sin creerlo.

Habrá que huir [. . .].

In this passage, Pascual demonstrates the tonal fluctuation characteristic of his memoirs. Attempting to mitigate his act, he suggests that one kills without thinking or without even wanting to do so. He recounts the matricide, removing his direct and active participation—"se"—and without naming his victim—"el enemigo"—thus burying his guilt. The sententious statement, "es de asesinos," reflects his emotional distance from the crime at this point, but he then adds "no podríamos aguantar su mirada," reminding us of the sequence that led to the murder of Chispa and emphasizing inevitability in both events. While killing his mother may have been unavoidable, in Pascual's eyes, he is unable to re-live the actual murder. He battles within himself, but at the crucial moment cannot confront this horrible memory from his past, and we see that, in the second part, remorse is the implied victor in Pascual's psyche.

As in the case of Chapter Six, the intensity of hatred and a heavy conscience are conflicting forces. At the end of part two, the latter is the more powerful. It precipitates the protagonist's decision to flee his mother's presence, "habrá que huir," and the narrator's second major return to the present, yet another temporal flight from culpability. The third section begins here. Pascual-narrator has interrupted his writing for an even longer period, this time, "cerca de un mes entero he estado sin escribir." This part contains a pre-execution confession, Pascual's flight from his town, the death of Lola, the murder of El Estirao, and Pascual's return from Chinchilla where he served three years for the crime. It ends with the matricide and the transcriber's final note. If in the first part we saw a defensive tone and hatred, and in the second we observed guilt win over hatred, in the final section, we are left with an ambiguous suggestion about the resolution of the three conflicting elements—hatred, guilt, and personal vindication—in Pascual's mental and emotional make-up, along with an implicit statement on the nature of morality in modern society.

As Pascual returns from prison, his thoughts are again on his mother, "volvería a encontrar [. . .] a mi madre que en tres años a lo mejor Dios había querido suavizar." But she receives him with despicable indifference. At this point, his emotional state again becomes agitated and unstable. He knocks on the door of his house:

—¡Quién!

—¡Soy yo!

—¿Quién?

Era la voz mi madre. Sentí alegría al oírla, para qué mentir.

—Yo, Pascual.

—¿Pascual?

—Sí, madre, ¡Pascual!

Abrió la puerta; a la luz del candil parecía una bruja.

—¿Qué quieres?

—¿Que qué quiero? [. . .]

Estaba extraña. ¿Por qué me trataría así?

Pascual tries to be civil and is naively surprised at his mother's reaction. He feels happy to hear her voice, but, because of her coldness, "los odios de otros tiempos parecían como querer volver a hacer presa en mí." Still fighting with his conscience, he adds in the next sentence, "Yo trataba de ahuyentarlos, de echarlos a un lado."

In narrative structure, the final chapter represents the novel's climax, but does not resolve the inner conflict permanently, at least not in light of other evidence presented by the *transcriptor.* The organization of the chapter may be easily divided into five parts, each showing the ambivalence that previously characterized larger sections of the novel, but also focusing more than ever on the true reason for the narrator's present existential anguish. The chapter opens with a sharp tone of growing hatred: "Me quemaba la sangre con su ademán, siempre huraño y como despegado, con su conversación hiriente y siempre intencionada, con el tonillo de voz que usaba para hablarme, en falsete y tan fingido como toda ella." The shift to a second sub-section is almost immediate. Pascual considers a permanent move from the area: "Muchas vueltas me dio en la cabeza la idea de la emigración: pensaba en La Coruña, o en Madrid, o bien más cerca, hacia la capital, pero el caso es que—¡quién sabe si por cobardía, por falta de decisión!—la cosa la fui aplazando." As he begins to see the truth, he realizes he cannot flee, either spatially (the protagonist) or temporally (the narrator), as before: "La tierra . . . no fue bastante grande para huir de mi culpa . . . La tierra . . . no tuvo largura ni anchura suficiente para hacerse la muda ante el clamor de mi propia conciencia." Pascual has finally brought the two conflicting elements

together. His guilty conscience is now out in the open. Seeing this, Pascual-narrator philosophizes on what he probably should have done: "Hay ocasiones en las que más vale borrarse como un muerto, desaparecer de repente como tragado por la tierra."

In the third sub-section, Pascual begins to develop an elaborate justification for his crime: "Pero un día el mal crece, como los árboles, y engorda, y ya no saludamos a la gente; y vuelven a sentirnos como raros y como enamorados. Vamos enflaqueciendo, enflaqueciendo [. . .]. Empezamos a sentir el odio que nos mata; ya no aguantamos el mirar; nos duele la conciencia, pero ¡no importa!, ¡más vale que duela!" In these lines, Pascual-narrator arrives at a firm resolution. When he equates the hatred with self-preservation, "el odio que nos mata," suggesting self-defense, he judges that it is better to live with a guilty conscience than not to live at all. In spite of this realization, the power of conscience is still quite strong. In the fourth sub-section, the idea of "madre" continues to cause reluctance and torments Pascual as he stands before his sleeping mother: "No me atrevía; después de todo era mi madre, la mujer que me había parido, y a quien sólo por eso había que perdonar . . . No; no podía perdonarla porque me hubiera parido. Con echarme al mundo no me hizo ningún favor, absolutamente ninguno." In the final sub-section, he decides to leave the room and flee once more: "Pensé huir" and "di la vuelta para marchar. El suelo crujía. Mi madre se revolvió en la cama." Pascual jumps on her and, after a brutal struggle, slashes her throat. He does run away now, but seems to have found a spiritual exoneration and relief: "El campo estaba fresco y una sensación como de alivio me corrió las venas. Podía respirar. . . ."

Whether or not we sympathize with Pascual at this point is irrelevant. He has found a temporary resolution to his interior conflict, one directly related to an ontological crisis. It would appear that self-justification has been in this instance superior to remorse. The killing was, in Pascual's mind, inevitable. And each struggle with conscience proved to him the futility of seeing it otherwise. However, the *transcriptor*'s final note casts a strong shadow of doubt on the finality of the emotional catharsis. The transcriber tells us that the cover letter and Chapters Twelve and Thirteen were written in purple ink, evidently at the same time. He concludes from this that Pascual is neither as forgetful nor as confused as he would have us believe. Though we have no way of verifying the presence of purple ink on the original manuscript, the suggestion does add an ambiguous but important dimension to the novel. Chapter Twelve deals with Pascualillo's death and the impersonal narration of the events leading up to the matricide, which Pascual is unable to re-live; and in Thirteen, Pascual confesses to Father Lurueña. Although his confession may not be sincere, he does admit to himself: "En este largo mes que dediqué a pensar, todo pasó por mí: la pena y la alegría, el gozo y la tristeza, la fe y la desazón y la desesperanza [. . .]. Son muchos treinta días seguidos dedicado a pensar en una sola cosa, dedicado a criar los más profundos remordimientos, solamente preocupado por la idea de que todo lo malo pasado ha de conducirnos al infierno. . . ."

From the *transcriptor*'s point of view, the ink should prove to the reader that Pascual is more intelligent than he seems, that he may therefore be held accountable for his actions, and that, because of Pascual's cleverness, any suggestion of remorse on his part is no more than a sly trick not to be trusted. If this part of the manuscript was written in purple ink, it would imply—apart from the *transcriptor*'s conclusions—that Pascual's period of relief was all too short, since the small section, replete with self-reproach and hesitation, would have been the last one written. If there was indeed no purple ink, this would suggest that Pascual was able to live with himself until his death (a possibility that would be distasteful to the *transcriptor*). No factual conclusion can be drawn from this "evidence" presented us, but one thing does seem certain, that a hypocritical and closed-minded moral conscience was the eventual victor over Pascual, purple ink or no purple ink. His last frustrated statement, "¡Hágase la voluntad del Señor!" is a rightful appeal to divine justice, since the justice of man and society has failed him: "este pobre yo, este desgraciado derrotado que tan poca compasión en usted y en la sociedad es capaz de provocar."

The novel's thematic message surfaces clearly in this final series of problems. As we review our lives, formally or informally, each of us is caught in a conflict between feeling remorseful about past errors and seeing justifications for our mistakes as victims of forces and circumstances beyond our control. Whether or not we personally experience relief in our confrontation with the past, there are those about us—the *transcriptor*, D. Joaquín, the guard at the prison—always ready to condemn us without mercy or a full understanding of our situation. While this type of condemnation is certainly characteristic of post-war Spain, it may also be considered the novel's archetypal code. Pascual's quest for his "being," for a definition of self, and to clear his conscience are undertaken in more a psychological than social medium and conclude on a plane of human emotions not limited to a specific historical epoch.

Certain correlations do in fact exist between ontological and social considerations. In the novel, we are made to feel patterns of intensifying hatred that culminate in intra-family murder, as in the 1930s in Spain. We see the opposition of moral systems lead eventually to violence and tragic death. In such situations, justice is often based not on truth or compassion, but on arrogance and a lack of information—for example, the suppressed passages of the manuscript. Pascual's crisis is implicitly provoked by a system of justice which perpetuates social inferiority and, without pity, executes the authentic products of that inferiority. For Pascual-narrator, however, the social experience is less important than the personal one. The "pena y alegría, gozo y tristeza" to which he refers are all related to the private ordeal with the memory of his mother and not to any type of public apology. In a dynamic but unified structure, he passes through a complex maze of emotions and tensions fighting to resolve an internal conflict essentially ontological in nature.

Sarah Kerr (essay date 8 October 1992)

SOURCE: "Shock Treatment," in *New York Review of Books,* Vol. XXXIX, No. 16, October 8, 1992, pp. 35-9.

[*In the following essay, Kerr presents an overview of Cela's life and major works, and traces his relationship to the political and cultural climate in Spain.*]

After the death of General Franco, King Juan Carlos appointed the novelist Camilo José Cela to Spain's Parliament and asked him to help oversee the literary style of the new democratic constitution. Cela remembers a Senate vote in which he managed to avoid taking a position with the same steadfast, principled evasion that has been a theme in his fiction: "President Fontan said, 'Senator Cela, you vote neither yes nor no, and you don't abstain?' I stood and said respectfully, 'No, Mr. President, I am absent.'"

Cela was in his sixties at the time, just beginning to be recognized as an old statesman of Spanish letters. His companion reputation, as a clowning, sometimes combative literary stuntman, had matured years earlier: since he published his first novel in 1942, Cela has known that being "absent" draws attention. He has turned noncommitment into a weird form of advocacy, defying the regular views of propriety and objecting to narrow officialism in Spain's governing and religious bureaucracies even as he occasionally has held positions of some power. When he was in his twenties he fought for Franco in the Civil War and worked for him as a censor, criticizing the Republicans who lost and left the country; then he wrote violent and depressing novels that made him, briefly, Spanish censorship's most public victim. In the Fifties and Sixties, he sought and gained entry into the conservative Royal Academy, and terrified it by putting out a book of sexual expressions barred from the academy's official dictionary. At many points in his career, including the speech he gave accepting the Nobel Prize for Literature in 1989, he has argued for the writer's independence. Other times he has appeared to argue that the independent writer has nothing to say.

Cela's great talent for savaging everyone else's hypocrisies while guarding his own privacy often seems more defense than offense, a strategy learned, perhaps, in the early years of Franco's muffling dictatorship. A writer then needed huge resources of self-preservation, for in the period following the Civil War Spain supplied little monetary or mental nourishment to feed a literary career. With the final victory of the Nationalists in 1939, the best-known intellectuals and artists, the philosopher Ortega y Gasset and the historian Americo Castro, the film director Luis Buñuel and the cellist Pablo Casals, had moved elsewhere in Europe or gone to Mexico, Argentina, or the United States. The new cultural bureaucracy in Spain seemed unlikely to produce figures rivaling the exiles' reputation internationally; in their book *Spain: Dictatorship to Democracy*, the historians Raymond Carr and Juan Pablo Fusi have described how universities began teaching that the Enlightenment and modern philosophy were "anti-Spanish." Journalists reported on Franco's happy family life or rehearsed Spain's old glories, the wealth of its sixteenth-century empire and lost "unity" under the Catholic Counter-Reformation. A population dragged back by war to nineteenth-century income levels was entertained by literature about triumphing Christians; new editions of *Ben Hur* and *Quo Vadis* became best sellers.

With open complaint risky, the most ambitious writing might at least try to record Spain's trauma. Cela's first novel, *The Family of Pascual Duarte* (1942), was sophisticated in design but close in purpose to sheer documentary reporting. The inner life of the title character, a murderous peasant, was of less consequence than the concrete details of his training in crime and aggression. The book had a tone of deadpan observation; ideas and feelings were alluded to but overwhelmed by wit and irony.

The novel's cynicism shocked and became extremely influential; a fact inevitably repeated about Cela is that the first creation is, after *Don Quixote*, the most widely read of all Spanish novels. Yet it may not be called typical of his style because Cela, far from plagiarizing his own early success, has shown extraordinary technical resolve, creating a different shape and narrative technique and language for each project. Some of his novels are plotless, extremely self-conscious and aggressive literary performances; in a parallel career as a journalist and essayist, he has produced hundreds of tentative essays on literature and diffident, wry newspaper columns on Spanish politics.

The five books available in English, a small portion of Cela's published work (over eighty volumes in Spanish), have a wide enough span of both chronology and form to give the non-Spanish reader a sense of his stylistic dexterity: after *Pascual Duarte,* there are *Journey to the Alcarria* (1948), a small travel sketch; *The Hive* (1951),

a bitter experimental novel of Madrid with several hundred characters; *Mrs. Caldwell Speaks to Her Son* (1953), the casual, aphoristic notebook of a senile English widow; and *San Camilo, 1936* (1969), which uses real and invented historical figures and events, and scant punctuation, to describe the first days of civil war.

The characters in Cela's fiction, by contrast, have been consistently humble and confined. His favorite types are prostitutes, criminals, and mental defectives with poor odds for changing their lives. Frequently, too, there is a country-city opposition—Cela thinks the "big cities are responsible for the downfall of humanity"—but the main difference seems to be the quality of misery each environment produces, the city offering clutter and depravity, the country a purer, more epic defeat. Cela writes in a prologue to *The Hive:* "I wanted to develop the idea that the healthy man has no ideas. I sometimes think that religious, moral, social, and political ideas are nothing but manifestations of an imbalance in the nervous system." The remark sounds the same joking hostility that appears behind some of his outrageous public episodes—his attempt once to draw water up his rump on a television talk show—but it is more than a throw-away line written to upset. Cela's novels imagine a world restricted to coarse biological demands, one in which, as we read in *The Hive,* "There are truths one feels in one's body, such as hunger or the need to make water." He writes constantly, but not from any belief in literature's edifying potential: he loves to say in interviews that, had Shakespeare and Dante and Cervantes never lived, the world still would have turned.

Cela was born May 11, 1916, in Iria-Flavia, a village in the isolated province of Galicia in northwest Spain. His father, Camilo José Cela y Fernández, was a conservative customs official and part-time journalist, a student of esperanto and reader of Nietzsche and Schopenhauer. His mother, Camila Enmanuela Trulock y Bertorini, was the daughter of an English manager of the West Galicia Railway; her Italian grandfather, the Bertorini side, was the engineer who designed it. According to the memoirs of his childhood, the mother had a more "aesthetic understanding of life" than her husband, and an "almost pathological tenderness" that made her seem like a Tolstoy heroine. From her chaotic, intuitive character Cela learned to think of images gliding among the five senses: "this rose smells like the silhouette of that bridge; velvet is soft to the touch like Beethoven's *Fur Elise*."

Cela has said he wishes he had never grown past five or six, but he describes himself in his memoirs as a depressive child, slow to read and write and prone to he in bed and cry without provocation. Much joy seems to have come from stories of odd relatives such as Uncle Claudio, who lived with eighteen children by marriage and thirty or forty illegitimate ones in the same house, and Aunt Ana, who left her large fortune to the town druggist so he could put cats to sleep without their feeling any pain. His foreign heritage also did him good:

> Feeling oneself connected to various geographies doesn't seem to me any disadvantage, not least for the writer. Some bloods polish the roughness of others and the mix of them all lets one see things with a certain aplomb, with the necessary coldness and with sufficient perspective.

The pirates from Cornwall, and all of Cela's other English and Italian forebears, served two purposes. By mixing up his ancestry, they saved him from thinking too much about pure Spanishness, a recurring national worry since the expulsion of Jews and Moors in 1492. They also gave him an early appreciation of detachment.

In Madrid, where the family moved when he was nine, Cela was the apathetic charge of various Catholic institutions, which he slyly says had no effect on his life-long skepticism and only pushed him to educate himself by walking around the city. Already when he was eighteen and preparing to be a doctor he felt more attracted to literature, particularly to Nietzsche as his father had been, and to lectures by the poet Pedro Salinas, who noticed and encouraged him. He published some poems (he had little experience writing prose), which came out in Argentina owing to connections he had there.

In 1934, as he began studying medicine, Cela was diagnosed with tuberculosis. It was just one of the several severe physical problems to bother him. (He was frequently sick and survived a bad fall as a child, and he was shot in the thigh in the Civil War. When he was already well known someone in a nightclub brawl stabbed him in the buttocks: the wound occasionally has intruded on the sedentary writing life and, according to Cela's son, forced him to seek relief in some twenty operations.) But the illness led to a stay in the sanatorium, the setting of an early novel, *Pabellón de Reposo* (*Rest Home*), and during recovery to a thorough reading of a seventy-volume collection of Spanish writers. Most of his literary tastes formed during this one intense period of study, which yielded the discovery, among others, of the vitriolic satirist Francisco de Quevedo (1580-1645), whom Cela calls "the most astonishing writer the Spanish language has ever had." Prolonged sickness must also have contributed to the resigned, static feeling of Cela's novels, though it does not appear to have driven him to introspection.

Tuberculosis at first kept him from fighting in the Civil War, but Cela reapplied and was accepted into Franco's Nationalist army in 1937, and served until he was wounded in early 1938. Here begins the part of his career that later saw charges, coming mostly from younger novelists writing in the 1980s, of comfortable, even happy cooperation with the fascists. There is a famous letter of March 1938, in which Cela, discharged because of his injury, applies to the Madrid office of Franco's "Investigation and Vigilance" forces and offers "facts about the conduct of certain people which could be useful" to the Glorious National Movement. After the war he contributed to fascist publications, including a piece saluting the campaign of a Nationalist army captain, and had a ludicrous assignment with the government censoring harmless newsletters: *New Pharmacy, Messenger from the Heart of Jesus,* and the *Bulletin of the School for Railroad Orphans.* (Cela was always short of money, since acceptance by the new government did not necessarily pay well; at different points he tried movie-acting and apprentice bullfighting, and, right after the war, writing an advice column for a women's magazine.)

Cela has declined to outline his allegiances during this period, and he has appeared rude, calling the war a scuffle between equally idiotic extremes, and in one glib interview, a "rugby game." But the intellectuals he associated with may give a truer sense of his inclinations. He was close to a group, among them the ethnographer Julio Caro Baroja and the historian Gregorio Marañon, who wrote for Falangist journals but tried to keep open to writers from before the war who were now banished from the lists of approved reading; Curr and Fusi describe how several in the group were punished by their government for their soft attempts at liberal-mindedness and quietly "deserted" the regime. Cela's defense of those years is abrupt: "It's good military and political strategy to keep from dying when you can't yet kill the enemy."

The publication of **The Family of Pascual Duarte** in 1942 while he was studying law did much to rescue Cela from further accusations of conformity. The novel, his fastest and most entertaining, is told in the form of the confession of Pascual Duarte, a bumpkin from the poorest part of Spain who has killed several of his family and acquaintance. He describes shooting his beloved dog, stabbing a horse to death, and raping a woman in a cemetery ("I bit her until blood came, until she was worn out and docile as a young mare"), and remembers the hideous departures of his retarded younger brother, found bobbing in a tub of oil (this after the boy's ears were earlier chewed off by a hog), and of his father, locked frothing in a cupboard to die from rabies. Cela playfully appends "testimonials" verifying Pascual's confession and execution in which two myopic witnesses, a priest and a guard, quibble over his character. Was he a hyena or a "poor tamed lamb," deranged or serene and repentant at the end? Both condemner and pardoner are poor judges, but so is Pascual, who admits to the noblest and the basest feelings and constantly apologizes for his narrative's disorder.

The novel appalled Franco's censors, who quickly held up the second edition and rather comically continued to worry years later that reading this "abnormal" writer might induce an "inexplicable physical malaise." (They rarely put the threat in political terms.) The reaction seemed to confirm Cela's parody of the pathetic vulnerability of honest writing under Franco: in fact the fictional transcriber who claims to have found the criminal's manuscript and scraped off its more "repugnant intimacies" is less squeamish than the real censors were, since he thinks its publication valuable as a "model to be shunned."

Despite the ban, copies printed in a garage in the city of Burgos sold out, and Cela was told by critics that he had started a new protest literature, *tremendismo,* that criticized Spain's general decay using descriptions of highly concentrated decay. Arguments for the novel's political message point out that Pascual confesses in the early days of Civil War, and his last victim, killed before the novel opens, is a rich landlord; speaking for the Swedish Academy, Knut Ahnlund said that "the story of this matricide can be read as an allegory, as a saga of the tremendous misfortunes and discords of this country." Cela himself vaguely agrees that Pascual is hateful to society's "burghers, institutionalists, and god-fearers" (enemies broad enough to be found on either side of Spain's political divide), and is executed because "keeping him alive was too inconvenient; the truth is that we didn't know what to do with him."

But he is right to remind readers who call him "tremendous" that Spanish writers have a long-established habit of describing all the possible pleasures and deformations of the human body, practiced as vividly by moralizing authors as it was in picaresque adventure stories. In the *Little the Sermons on Sin* (1438), the Archpriest of Talavera fights wickedness with outrageous misogyny, insults, and threats of gross physical punishment that excite more than they persuade. His advice to a woman stupid enough to marry someone younger: "Let her take comfort in her evil senility, her tanned old hide, her wrinkled belly, her stinking mouth and rotten teeth! For a youth a pretty girl, and burn the rancid hag!" Later there is Cervantes, whom we might expect to be more wild than a priest. But it is still surprising how hard one must look for the sweetness that made *Don Quixote* seem suitable for adaptation to Broadway; the Impossible Dream is lost among scenes in which the hero is thrashed cartoonishly flat, or comic episodes based on someone's trying to contain a bowel movement.

If Cela contributed a new kind of shock to the Spanish novel, it was his juxtaposition of drollery and artifice with

an enormous sense of resignation, all appearing in the opening paragraph of *Pascual Duarte:*

> I am not, sir, a bad person, though in all truth I am not lacking in reasons for being one. We are all born naked, and yet, as we begin to grow up, it pleases Destiny to vary us, as if we were made of wax. Then, we are all sent down various paths to the same end: death. Some men are ordered down a path lined with flowers, others are asked to advance along a road sown with prickly pears. They first gaze about serenely and in the aroma of their joyfulness they smile the smile of the innocent while the latter writhe under the violent sun of the plain and knit their brows like varmints at bay. There is a world of difference between adorning one's flesh with rouge and eau-de-cologne and doing it with tattoos that later will never wear off . . .

The clean, informal prose describing such an inflexible bitterness is as important as the murders are in setting up the novel's brutal atmosphere.

Because the stories are similar, **The Family of Pascual Duarte** is sometimes compared with Camus's *The Stranger,* which came out in France a few months earlier, as an example of Spanish existentialism. But Cela finds documenting the filth in this world more important than the giddy intellectual questioning of Camus. It might make more sense to compare him, as the novel's translator Anthony Kerrigan has, to the foul-mouthed nihilism practiced by Celine. Pascual's problem cannot be put abstractly. His rage is set off like "a nest of vipers" and soothed by the smell of his own dirty pants.

In 1944, after he had published **Pabellón de Reposo** and his third novel, **Nuevas andanzas y desventuras de Lazarillo de Tormes (New Adventures and Misfortunes of Lazarillo dc Tormes)** about a twentieth-century *picaro,* Cela married. In 1946 he had a son, Camilo, Jr., and in the summer of that year began the first of several books about his walking trips through Spain. Since, outside of the accounts of writers who were Republican sympathizers during the Spanish Civil War (Spender, Orwell, Hemingway, and others), modern Spain has been seen in England and America mostly as a brilliant travel itinerary, it is worth comparing Cela's approach with the famous travel books written by English hispanophiles. One has merely to look at the titles to see how far he is from the more reflective and sentimental English examples. Cela doesn't seek a personal, historical interpretation of the kind found in V. S. Pritchett's *The Spanish Temper.* He doesn't follow Somerset Maugham's *Don Fernando* in calling up an emblematic figure to try to "explain" Spain, nor does he stay any place long enough for the patient anthropology of

Gerald Brenan's diary of the Alpujarras region, *South of Granada.*

His *Journey to the Alcarria* (1948) is about moving through places and not understanding them; it contains a whole philosophy of being "on foot." In the first chapter we see Cela in Madrid studying maps of the region he is preparing to visit, a dry, honey-producing backwater northeast of Madrid. The solitude of planning in the middle of the night and the distractions of the dirty city exhaust him—he "gets tired all at once, like a wounded bird"—and as he falls asleep he decides to skip dry research and make the trip "a bit haphazardly, rather like a fire on a threshing floor."

Cela's trip follows the effort of Spanish writers at the start of the century, the essayist Miguel de Unamuno, the poet, Antonio de Machado, Ortega y Gassett, and others, to find some of Spain's residual greatness in the countryside. But he prefers strictly recording the present to reflecting on more cosmic matters; the "quarrel between reason and faith, between the European consciousness and the medieval soul" that Pritchett describes in Unamuno shrinks here to a fight between the hungry traveler and a vendor who won't sell him her raw tomatoes. Conversations are ritualistic back-and-forths about the weather or the direction a road is taking, and much time is absorbed by naps and looking for water. Exposition is omitted; Cela describes scenes that are already underway and leaves off before they finish, always smothering the impulse to interpret:

> An old light-colored ox with long horns and a sharp thin face like a knight of Toledo is drinking from the basin of a brimming fountain beside the washing place, barely dipping his grizzled muzzle into the water. When he has finished drinking he lifts his head and passes behind the women, humble and wise. He seems like a loyal eunuch, bored and discreet, who guards a harem as turbulent as the break of day. The traveler follows the animal's slow, resigned progress with perplexed eyes. Sometimes the traveler feels transfixed by things he cannot possibly explain.

The traveler is drawn to pitiful people, lonely children and deformed idiots whose external tics he relates rather than their intimacies; his reassurances to a serious little boy that he too loves picking his nose is the book's most personal exchange. He enjoys their customary repressed banality and interferes only in private, with casual ironies in the commentary. Usually, too, whenever the war comes up he tries to divert the talk:

> The traveler walks down a few narrow streets and smokes a cigarette with an old man at the door of the house.

"This seems like a fine town."

"It's not bad. But you should have seen it before the war, when the airplanes came."

The people of Brihuega talk about before and after the airplanes the way Christians talk about before and after the Flood.

"Now it's not even a shadow of what it was before."

The old man feels contemplative and mournful. The traveler looks down at the pebbles on the street and lets his words fall slowly and almost at random.

"Good-looking girls too, from what I've seen."

Discomfort at the sight of his own emotion is the sour side of Cela's motto that "all things are to be found in the vineyard of the Lord," a phrase that can sound either exceptionally tolerant or pessimistic. The obsession with external things seems motivated by an almost complete blockage of interior feeling, a small version, perhaps, of the entire country's inability to discuss the war except in muddled symbols. Cela states the problem in his compressed manner when he writes that "the traveler is a man whose life is criss-crossed with renunciations." On a train he feels "as though he were walking through an immense warehouse full of coffins, peopled with souls in torment bearing the double baggage of their sins and their works of charity"; in a romantic garden he forbids himself indulging in "delicate, unhealthy lines from Shelley." This sense of his hopelessness and restraint, and of Spain's, is responsible for the book's deep melancholy.

But Cela regulates his prose so perfectly that his reticence seems both real and a literary device made up for the book. The contradictions in the impossible title of "the traveler," one who belongs neither in the city nor with the peasants, recall the joke of one of Cela's favorite novelists, the Basque Pío Baroja (1879-1956), who wrote in a guestbook for his title and profession "a humble man and a wanderer" but remarked later that the tag was "literary fantasy"—he might as easily be called "a proud and sedentary person." A few years ago, Cela appeared to spoof the element of put-on in the improvised simplicity of his old role: he recently starred in a Spanish television series that recreated the trip, this time going flamboyantly in a Rolls Royce, with a beautiful black model, Oteliña, for his chauffeur.

Since the early 1940s Cela had been taking notes on his own life and on the hostile atmosphere in Madrid after the Civil War. He drew on them to write *The Hive* (1951), a novel of three hundred characters stunned to complete apathy by the poverty and lingering suspicions of the postwar period. Cela complained later that young Spanish imitators usurped his "objective objectivism," a technique fitting together small, plotless sketches to accumulate what he called a whole "slice of life, drawn without charity," and used it to write corrupted political literature. But censors saw some form of protest in his version of a city walked by zombies, thieves, and hypocrites. The novel had to find a publisher in Argentina, and even there suffered some slight revision from Perón's fault finders.

The lack of a unified point of view in **The Hive** has drawn comparisons with Dos Passos's swarming picture of New York in *Manhattan Transfer* and with the mobile camera techniques of some neorealist films. We follow types— prostitutes and businessmen, fake poets and vindictive matrons—over forty-eight hours in 1942, three years after the Civil War finished; violence is common, but less spectacular than it was in **Pascual Duarte** because people have absorbed and accepted it. A boy singing flamenco in the street learns to deflect a drunk woman's kick with an ingenious failure of comprehension:

> The boy has the face, not of a person, but of a domestic animal, of a poor dirty beast, a powerful farmyard beast. He is too young in years for cynicism—or resignation—to have slashed its mark across his face, and therefore it has a beautiful, candid stupidity, the expression of one who understands nothing of anything that happens.

Tallying a schedule for any of the characters is difficult since chapters switch between morning and evening of both days and rereport incidents according to different witnesses. As the novel "progresses" every few pages see a new but identically sweet, duped prostitute or girlfriend, and it becomes hard to tell people, especially women, apart. Hints of a traditional plot appear with the murder of an old woman, but come to nothing. Instead, we get to overhear dull speeches on logic by the victim's academician neighbor and talk next door of a little girl's constipation. The case is never solved.

A foolish "political" poet, Martin Marco, who contributes to right-wing journals but still hopes the authorities will "pull down the big cities and build them up again, all alike, with perfectly straight streets and central heating in every building," connects tangentially to the lives of several other characters; his generous sister and her husband are among the handful of likable creations in the novel. But he is inflated to only slightly more than two-dimensionality, enough to contain both Cela's sad shame for the insecure writer and a near satire of intellectual pretense. A street sign commemorating two dead playwrights confuses him:

> "Damn it all, they must have done something to be so

famous. Only—oh, well—who's the bright lad who dares say it?"

Like fluttering moths, unruly chips of conscious thought drift through his mind.

> "Yes: an era of the Spanish stage . . . a cycle which they undertook to complete and succeeded in completing . . . theater faithfully mirroring the healthy customs of Andalusia. . . . It all smacks of charity to me, it belongs with suburban flag days and all that. What can one do about it? Anyway, nobody will budge them now. Here they are, and not God Almighty Himself can budge them."

It perturbs Martin that there exists no strict classification of intellectual values, no tidy list of brains.

Martin's fate seems likely to be as blandly depressing as the rest: in an epilogue a few days later he wanders stupidly through Madrid unaware that he is sought by the police, whether for the widow's murder or for old political associations, we are not sure.

With action broken into the smallest possible units for study, **The Hive** collects so many details that it threatens to become an abstraction. Cela remarks in the prologue that the properly impartial observation of people and situations, while concentrating on the present, is based on something eternal and immovable, perhaps on laws from biology:

> History, unfailing history, goes against the grain of ideas. Or to the margin of them. . . . History is like the circulation of blood or the digestion of food. The arteries and the stomach, through which the historic substance runs and is digested, are of hard and cold flint.

The idea that history has no meaning suggests the influence of Unamuno's theory about Spain, developed over several essays, of *intrahistoria,* the real, organic experience of the people running underneath the political record, which is a distraction. People are helpless, failed by politicians and books and gods. Yet Cela's study and arrangement of that life gives him a domineering authority over the entire novel. When he appears on occasion disguised as a wry, omniscient narrative voice to remind us that "we none of us ever understand with full clarity what it is that happens to us," he is like a scientist evaluating his diseased lab sample; at times the novel has the detached and assured tone of a clinical report.

Cela's next novel concentrates on a single delusion. **Mrs. Caldwell Speaks to Her Son** is supposed to be the notebook of an English woman gone crazy since her son drowned in the Aegean Sea. (In a preface Cela pretends to have met the woman on the trip to the Alcarria). The diary is less the unfolding of a life over time than it is the grouping, under 213 headings, of witty, completely illogical thoughts and incestuous tributes to the dead son. Sometimes we are asked to remember a fact, the son's old girlfriend or where he used to live, but the chapters build on one another only as the later entries, written as Mrs. Caldwell becomes further unbalanced, are woollier than the early ones.

Each section is a busy collision of the general motto announced at the beginning with the peculiar associations that flow from it. Here is Chapter 52. "The Skin, That Seismograph":

> When the human race manages not to feel too vile, it will use the skin, that great invention, for a seismograph.
>
> For my part, my son, I can tell you that I feel very happy when a shiver runs up my spine, or when the light hair on my arms stands on end, or when I notice a chill and somewhat rough skin brushing across my temples.
>
> Then I understand that a tiny, blind fish comes out of your eyes.

It is not Cela's goal to speculate on the universal mother-son relationship, or to propose, by the novel's close, a theory of mental illness. Madness is felt, not understood, by the disconnection of reading so many hermetic prose poems as a novel.

After he wrote *Mrs. Caldwell* Cela slowly confirmed his place among Spain's literary elite, in part by way of another notorious episode. His son writes that in 1953 Cela arrived broke in Venezuela just as the dictator there, Marcos Pérez Jiménez, decided to sponsor a nationalist novel. He got the commission. (Venezuela's minister of the interior apparently had considered asking Camus or Hemingway.) The Venezuelans were disappointed when he produced *La Catira* (*The Blond,* 1955), a sadistic story about a runaway bride called Primitiva Sanchez, set in the Venezuelan plains and told in dialect, but the giant sum Cela was paid made him rich. He bought a house in Majorca and in 1956 started a journal there, *Papeles de Son Armadans,* that extended some courageous openings to writers ignored by Franco, resisted the regime's centralizing insistence on Castilian Spanish with poems printed in Galician and Catalan, and published solid literary criticism, especially on poetry. In Majorca he also arranged for a constant round of readings and concerts to take place in his house and organized important literary conferences. (Understandably, these contributions, which he called "exactly the opposite" of

combative, were later counted as important in the Nobel committee's decision to honor him.)

Through the magazine Cela published several sketches and essays, a collaboration with doodles by Picasso, whom he visited for the first time when the painter was eighty, and a dramatic poem, *María Sabina* (1967). He also continued writing travel books and finished another novel, *Tabogán de Hambrientos* (*Toboggan of Hungry People*). He won his campaign to enter the conservative Royal Spanish Academy in 1957, and appeased doubting cynics by having reporters photograph him nude in the shower on the morning of his initiation.

In 1968 Cela issued through his own publishing house the two-volume *Diccionario Secreto,* an insanely thorough and erudite collection of obscene definitions ignored by the dictionary of the Royal Academy. The first part lists hundreds of ways to say "testicles" drawn from obscure tropes by writers from Spain's Golden Age, lexicons of regional Spanish and Latin American variants, commonly understood equivalents such as eggs and the number two, and relevant slang phrases like *nadar sin calabazas,* literally "swimming without your pumpkins." The second book uses the same method for a longer study of urine and the penis.

Despite its glee at shocking Spain's prudes, the dictionary might be Cela's most earnest attempt to convince his readers of something: he used the ideas from the introduction for his speech accepting the Nobel Prize in 1989. From the Greeks, he writes, have come two theories of language. One says that people's choice of words is fluid, always subject to new agreements; the other, which he supports, sees a necessary relationship between things and their names. Spain is rich in this second, natural language, but the government's inhibiting bureaucracy and timid writers have favored the first view and created an unnatural "acceptable" speech, based on euphemism, that "looks for cleanliness not in what is said but in how it is said."

This corruption is not a problem just of nationality—it is to be found as well in Americans' embarrassed substitution of "rooster" and "donkey" for rougher terms—but the challenge of the book seems meant particularly for censors in Spain who at that time had only recently begun loosening their views. Although censorship there was mostly Catholic-controlled, Cela has a vague theory attributing the origins of Spain's facility for euphemism to the Jews who stayed in Spain after 1492 and had to convert to Catholicism. Compared with the rowdy medieval poets and priests, he writes, the *conversos* were "virtuous in their conduct and prudent in their writing and their speech, making show of a reserve not so much calculated as it was deeply felt, adequate to their mentality, and as useful to their conscience as it was effective for their ends." In a different essay Cela argues that intolerance beginning under Ferdinand and Isabella was due not to Spain's cultural deprivation after 1492 but to the deformation of Catholicism by nonbelievers who stayed: "The identification of Church and State is an oriental concept—Moorish or Jewish, never Christian." The theory is probably more cranky than anti-Semitic: in his childhood memoirs Cela writes that "the Jews have all my sympathy, and the state of Israel is one of history's most curious and plausible historical experiments." And among other things it does not appear to allow for evidence that Fernando de Rojas, author of a dialogue novel, *La Celestina* (1499), which is one of the memorably bawdy books in Spanish literature and which Cela himself adapted to modern Spanish, was a *converso*.

The reasons Cela gives for his extreme hatred of official-sounding language (among the changes he proposed in the 1978 constitution was removing the phrase "political pluralism" because he "didn't like it") reveal the hesitating nature of his rebellion, which denies the authority of people but remains loyal to a powerfully static order that he imagines organizing the material world. Cela's ambivalence is not that of the Anglo-American liberal wondering how to preserve the best parts of tradition or puzzling over the intellectual traps of different ideologies. Those worries for him are histrionics: free, unpolluted expression accurately "calls things by their names." His son recalls walking in the forest with Cela when he was a boy and watching him quiz strangers on their songs and sayings and the names of local creeks and boulders, which he then repeated reverently. Cela himself has written that he rarely begins work on the theme or plot of a book until he finds its perfect, natural title.

His preference for the colloquial also makes some of his stunts more plausible as serious gestures. Perhaps his extravagant appearances on Spanish television and the flip exchanges in the Senate are intended partly as attacks on the lazy misuse of language. Not surprisingly for one so attuned to the danger of words used badly, in a crisis Cela frequently has resorted to the argumentative force of mute actions: as a boy he went on hunger strikes when feeling peevish, as an adolescent he tried running away, and as a young man he got into frequent fights from which he still carries scars. The adult Cela's attacks usually have been verbal, but he still has been ruthless in punishing the boring as well as the dishonest: Cela's son describes him at a party enduring a socialite's thoughtless chatter as long as he could and then vengefully attributing to her his own huge fart.

San Camilo, 1936 (1969) continues the contest between humility and exhibitionism, setting an archive full of details about the beginning of the Civil War amid the broken thoughts of a twenty-year-old poet in Madrid. (The poet's medical studies, illness, and middle-class feelings suggest Cela's own life at the outset of the war, even though another minor character is named Camilo José Cela.) Events triggering the war are described: we see the murder and burial of the monarchist martyr Calvo Sotelo that precipitated Franco's rebellion in Morocco, the outbreak of "Glorious National Uprising" on July 18, 1936 (coincidentally the feast day in honor of Cela's patron Saint Camillus, also the patron of hospitals), and the first skirmishes. Cela plugs in period trivia that he spent years compiling, droning radio coverage of Spanish competitors in the Tour de France that year and advertisements for beauty aids.

Once introduced these facts are swiftly embalmed. Politicians appear meanly assembled in brothels (Republicans and Republican-sympathizing journalists are seen as especially depraved), and partisans left and right get reduced to sordid equivalence ("I murder or am murdered you murder or are murdered he murders or is murdered, it doesn't matter much"). Most often the novel has the narrator masturbating and mumbling rank fantasies into a mirror:

> . . . no, don't kill her, hit her on the mouth but don't kill her. . . . Magdalena has no tattoos but she does have scars, sores, and bruises, scars from two Caesareans and various boils, rose-colored sores with greenish flecks, bruises from the bites of whoregobblers, the point is to be able to recognize corpses easily, they ought to tattoo a number on people's backs so they could never get away . . .

The witty, monotonous, abusive voice in the narrator's monologue is the same one Cela uses to describe the Communist leader La Pasionaria whipping up a Republican crowd, the same one quoting a newspaper account of two lovers electrocuted that summer in New York, the same one tracking dozens of made-up side characters. Some of these, like the narrator's girlfriend Transito/Toisha, change names; others, such as Matiítas, a homosexual clerk in a condom shop, die suddenly in violent assaults or accidents (he is sitting ecstatically on a rifle when it goes off) but continue to be present as rotten corpses. One is never sure who is talking, thinking, or doing, which is the point, since

> . . . we Spaniards are all guilty, the living, the dead, and those of us who are going to die, do not disguise your pain as anger or as fear, no, not as fear either, anger and fear are stronger than you they will grip you without your going to look for them, without your watering them with your wild rabbit's tears, spit words out of your mouth, strip yourself of words, wash yourself of words, which all mean the same thing blood and stupidity, insomnia, hatred and tedium . . .

The battering style produces a rich musical hysteria belonging neither to the narrator nor to collective Madrid. But the novel's evaluation of Spain's problems sometimes sounds naively gloomy. "Man is an avaricious and needy beast," and war is an infection the beast catches. If responsible government means that "rulers have the obligation not to cough or spit little spiders of mange on the ruled," Cela accuses the country's rulers of having coughed.

In an epilogue a thoughtful uncle explains that the fight between the fascists and the left is, like the Inquisition, one of Spain's periodic, purging epidemics in which honor is attained only by self-preservation and by believing in something "other than history, that great fallacy." After the novel's earlier, rather square equation of the disarray in pre-war Spain with excessive sex, he tells the narrator to ignore it, and sleep with as many girls as he can manage.

Cela continues to publish new books, including, recently, *Mazurca para dos muertos* (*Mazurka for Two Dead Men*) (1983), another Civil War novel set in his home province of Galicia, and *Cristo versus Arizona* (1988), a novel set around the OK Corral, which one Tucson reviewer, writing in Spanish, called "a violation." But his reputation, the literary one, anyway, rests mostly on works written in the Forties and Fifties, especially on *Pascual Duarte* and *The Hive.*

When Cela won the Nobel Prize in 1989, *The New York Times* called his selection "the symbol of a changing, modernizing Spain." An American professor, carried away, perhaps, about the new prominence of his field, wrote in a Spanish magazine that now that "Spain is news all over the world and there is an impulse to celebrate its spirit of democracy and reconciliation after years of fighting and dictatorship, it is perfectly logical to select a figure who embraces the whole period."

It seems curious that such pessimistic books should be taken as a bridge to democracy—there must be some reconciling element in Cela's willingness to shock. Perhaps it is that his bile is impartial and splatters evenly, blaming and forgiving all. For if Cela's obsession with the precise details of aggression can be ugly and demanding, it is also soothingly abstract, cynical rather than tragic. His novels revisit the Civil War but seem to counsel oblivion; his record of defiance scolds, but sometimes appears to suggest that little could have been done differently.

Roberto Gonzalez Echevarria (review date 29 November 1992)

SOURCE: "Death and Revenge in Spain's Backwoods," in *New York Times,* November 29, 1992, pp. 15-7.

[*In the following review, Echevarria praises Cela's* Mazurka for Two Dead Men *as "a powerful book."*]

Through the bus window, the change in landscape from Castile to Galicia is abrupt. The colors change suddenly from ocher to green. The harsh rhythm of crags and arid flatlands is replaced by lush hills with sensuous curves, shrouded in mists or crowned by shockingly low clouds. The air is cool and humid, and a pungent smell of grass and dung fills the air. The winding road curves around small dairy farms and through tiny hamlets with incongruous signs advertising local and national products. The signs are in Spanish but the names of streets and stores betray that not just a geographic border has been crossed, but a cultural one as well. At a stop, a barmaid breaks off her chatter in Galician to take my order in Spanish. She converses without annoyance, but with an effort. Her hair is honey-colored and her eyes a soft blue. I feel foreign.

Galicia is tucked into the northwest corner of Spain, against a coast of dramatic beauty, and its great moments in history occurred in the Middle Ages. Santiago de Compostela, its spiritual center, drew thousands of pilgrims from all over Europe. They brought Gothic architecture to Spain and French words that made their way into Spanish. Earlier, the Visigoths, pushed northward by the Arab invasion of the eighth century, had formed in Galicia the last bastion of Christian Spain. Spain's national mythology has it that it was in Galicia that the Reconquest, which culminated 500 years ago in Granada, began.

The political efficacy of this mythic background, combining religious zeal and military glory, was not lost on one of Galicia's most notorious sons, Francisco Franco. And the cultural efficacy of Galicia has left a powerful mark on Camilo Jose Cela, who was given the Nobel Prize in Literature in 1989 and whose powerful novel, *Mazurka for Two Dead Men,* evokes his homeland through the first four decades of this century, including the time of the Spanish Civil War.

Galician culture is known to be characterized by sensitivity and love, as well as by a certain melancholy. Some of the earliest European lyrics were composed in Galician, a language closer to Portuguese than to Spanish. They are about—what else?—unrequited love, or grief for a lover gone to war. "Love's Reason," composed in the Middle Ages, is perhaps the first and one of the best of Europe's long love poems. In the 19th century, the region saw the birth of Rosalia de Castro, who wrote in both Galician and Spanish and who was the best poet born in the Iberian Peninsula in the years between the Golden Age (the time of the playwrights Lope de Vega and Calderon, and the poets Luis de Gongora and Francisco Gomez de Quevedo) and Federico Garcia Lorca.

Recent Galician history is much less apt to be romanticized. Other regions of Spain, notably Castile, either set the pace of history or felt its weight, while Galicia remained isolated, backward and often desperately poor. Its sons and daughters left by the thousands to become servants, small merchants and menial laborers elsewhere in Spain, or in Latin America. They were regarded as prototypical rubes, mocked for their coarseness and poor Spanish. As a young man in Havana I found it difficult to imagine the beauty of the country the *gallegos* had left behind, and their famous longing for it (their *morrina,* or homesickness) seemed a mannerism. Like immigrants elsewhere, however, they were industrious, frugal and determined to gain respectability by accumulating wealth and power. By the first generation many had both, among them the family of Fidel Castro.

Camilo Jose Cela was born in 1916 in the town of Iria Flavia in the Galician province of Coruna. ***Mazurka for Two Dead Men,*** published in Spain in 1983 and now available in an English translation, delves into the Galicia of his youth and early manhood. He emphasizes the clear autobiographical side to his novel by calling one of his characters Don Camilo, and telling parts of the history of a family named Cela. But this book is far from being a nostalgic or Proustian evocation of time past, and it is certainly not a pastoral.

Instead, as is characteristic of Mr. Cela, ***Mazurka for Two Dead Men*** is an account of the brutality of life in the rural towns of Spain, a brutality of which the Civil War, when it comes, seems to be but a mere continuation in a larger scale. Told through the voice of various narrators, it has the rare virtue of making interesting, even poetic, the tawdry lives of people whose horizons are so severely limited.

The novel is told from inside the beliefs and superstitions of what is essentially a peasant community that has barely changed since the Middle Ages. Like the Irish, with whom they share a Celtic background, Galicians are known for their rich lore and superstitions. *Cruceiros,* stone monuments in the form of tall crosses erected to ward off witches and other apparitions, still dot the landscape, particularly at crossroads. There is no ironic distance in Mr. Cela's portrayal of the people of Galicia, no high or modern culture to interpret or pass judgment on what the characters say or do. He achieves in this novel a style in which the pompous, the general, the rhetorical, are rigorously absent; and if any opinions or interpretations creep in that are not in the language of the characters, they are rudely dismissed.

On each of the few occasions that one of the narrators— the one writing a novel that may or may not be the one we are reading—philosophizes, he offers an apology. By the way, this concession to modernist technique, or "metafiction," is tucked away inside so many other voices, and the voice of this narrator is so much like those of his potential characters, that it is totally unobtrusive. The tone of the discourse is uniformly vulgar, but never obscene or pornographic. Obscenity or pornography would have infused it with a self-consciousness that does not exist here.

Vulgar speech names without analyzing, seemingly from within the perimeter of lives led according to the most brutal human needs and desires. Murder, child abuse, adultery, bestiality, rape, onanism—all occur regularly, but they are never called by such terms or by any others remotely like them. These acts are given the names they have in the language peasants and small-town people use with one another. Mr. Cela portrays a seamless world, with little or no distinction between human life and nature. There is an artlessness in him that is effective in this novel because it does not appear to be deliberate. This is his highest achievement in this novel. In some other works and in his personal pronouncements, his vulgarity and bluntness are often his downfall, for they become affectations.

The Galicia of the 1920's, 30's and 40's appears here as a peasant society in which people and animals coexist in violence. The struggle for survival knows no boundaries between man and beast; both live within the same material and cultural orbit, the same system of exchange. Lolina is crushed by an ox; Policarpo has several fingers bitten off by a horse; Rosicler likes to masturbate Miss Ramona's monkey, while other women are said to have sex with dogs. At the end, an inescapable vengeance is carried out by trained dogs, not directly by human hands. The revenge of a peasant named Adega, who is one of the principal narrators, makes literal this symbiotic relationship between animals and humans. She disinters the body of the man who killed her husband, feeds it to a pig, and then not only eats the animal but with gruesome neighborliness gives away some of the meat and sausages.

Several deaths frame the action of the novel. One is that of Lazaro Codesal, a young man from the region shot in the back by Moors in the Melilla campaign, during Spain's war in Morocco in the 1920's, while he masturbated under a tree. The other is that of Afouto, called Lionheart in the translation, who is treacherously murdered by Fabian Minguela (known as Moucho) during the Civil War. Codesal's death causes the line that divides the area where these people live from the mountains to disappear, according to the narrator. Gaudencio, a blind man who is the accordionist at Sprat's brothel and the brother of Adega, plays a mazurka called "Petite Marianne" twice, first when Afouto is killed in 1936, and again in 1940, when Moucho, his murderer, is killed.

The disappearance of the line that had divided hills from

homeland, and a steady rain, contribute to the sense of isolation; and the repetition of stories, such as the one about Codesal's death, begins to lift language from mere gossip to lore. In fact, the basic stories in the novel are told and retold in monotonous declarative sentences that acquire an almost liturgical cadence. This repetition endows them with an aura of truth, or at least the sort of truth by which the society lives. The same tone is used to give recipes for sausages, dietary restrictions and various prescriptions to cure wounds or other ailments. Eating, cooking tips, healing, telling stories about murder and vengeance, gossiping, expostulating about the fatality of violence in the natural world and in human society, are the prevailing themes of the novel's discourse.

That Codesal was killed while peacefully masturbating (a fact told with some outrage by the narrators) adds to the sense of self-enclosure. It is as if self-reflection and death were the true boundaries of this society, one in which most families are related. Incest lurks in the background, as the product of an evil desire that binds the people together in violent promiscuity and guilt.

Masturbation becomes an emblem of this world of self-reflection, a world ruled by cruelty and peopled by bodies scarred or deformed by other humans or by animals. Death, on the other hand, has an active role in the narrative, not only because violence and disease are so prevalent, but also because, since the stories are told in a present removed from the action by some years, the narrators refer to some of the actors as dead people, as in "the dead man who killed my old man." The recurrence of such turns of phrase begins to give the world of *Mazurka for Two Dead Men* a ghostly air, as if everything happened in a region of the dead, or as if death, or the death instinct, ruled the region of the living.

Novels often deal with crime and punishment because they recall their origin in picaresque fiction, which, when it began, deliberately mimicked the language of the law. *Mazurka for Two Dead Men* is no exception. Mr. Cela emphasizes this by frequently incorporating legal documents in the text. The narrator-novelist has managed to get his hands on the forensic report of the autopsy performed on the murderer. This report closes the novel, creating a huge irony. Despite, or perhaps because of, its scientific and legal jargon, the report reaches a patently wrong conclusion about the man's death. It determines that death was accidental, inflicted by two or more wolves. But nothing is accidental in this novel. The whole action is moved by the sense that if you kill someone, sooner or later you will pay, that an imbalance created by one transgression will eventually be rectified, because things just cannot stay as they are.

This is, of course, the stuff of tragedy more than of the novel, as is Adega's brutal revenge. In consuming the murderer and having the community partake of his body, she is not only restoring a lost material balance but also reintegrating the murderers into the ruthless moral economy of the region. Tragedy escapes the language of the law, or perhaps precedes it, and the grandeur of *Mazurka for Two Dead Men* lies precisely in its blurring of the line between the written language of novels, which recalls the law, and the aural, poetic speech of tragedy.

In recent years, the Spanish novel has been marginalized or shocked into slavish imitation by the success of Latin American writers of the stature of Gabriel Garcia Marquez, Carlos Fuentes and Mario Vargas Llosa. Mr. Cela, characteristically, went his own way; that meant, in my view, a courageous eclipse, from which only the Nobel Prize (a reward to democratic Spain) saved him. But now the Spanish novel seems to have found a new voice in the works of writers like Eduardo Mendoza and Antonio Munoz Molina, among others. Though this novel is not part of that renewal, the excellence of *Mazurka for Two Dead Men* should at least serve as a reminder that among the many Spanish-speaking countries, Spain is still a source of powerful literature.

Patricia Haugaard, the translator, commits a few blatant mistranslations. But on the whole she manages to capture Mr. Cela's poetic crudeness and the sense of isolation in which his Galicia lives. *Mazurka for Two Dead Men* is a powerful book that should find a wide readership in English.

Javier Escudero (review date Winter 1996)

SOURCE: A review of *El asesinato del perdedor*, in *World Literature Today*, Vol. 70, No. 1, Winter, 1996, pp. 165-66.

[*In the following review, Escudero complains that Cela's* "El asesinato del perdedor *is terribly boring and difficult to read from the very first pages.*"]

Camilo José Cela, the author of such famous novels as *La familia de Pascual Duarte* (1942), *La colmena* (1951), and *San Camilo 1936* (1969), received the 1989 Nobel Prize in Literature in recognition of his valuable literary work. His novels, especially those published before 1975, are characterized by innovative narrative recourses and preferential attention paid to social and existential problems. In later years the writer has abandoned his social orientation to continue both with his formal and thematic experiments, as seen in *Mazurca para dos muertos* (1983) and *Cristo versus Arizona* (1988). These later novels, which are harder to comprehend, are not read as much as his earlier ones.

The release of *El asesinato del perdedor,* the first novel published by Cela after receiving the Nobel Prize, confirms the writer's desire to continue investigating the same narrative thread of the past few years. In the story, which contains no divisions into chapters or scenes, it is possible to identify two parts. In the first, a narrative voice relates certain events regarding the life of the protagonist, Mateo Ruecas, whose story, Cela informs us, is based on an actual event. The author nevertheless reelaborates the motives that push Mateo to his suicide after he is accused of a public scandal and put in prison. In the second part the author incorporates an innumerable series of voices. Their discourse, which is both disconcerting and hallucinatory—for they jump through time and space without paying attention to any type of logic—has no thematic relation to the story of Mateo Ruecas. There are also numerous existential references, especially to the theme of death, which are presented in a humorous form. However, the aspect that unites all the conversations is the abundance of allusions to sexual intercourse, sodomy, prostitution, masturbation, and bestiality, all viewed from a masculine perspective.

El asesinato del perdedor is terribly boring and difficult to read from the very first pages. The plot holds no interest, there is no thematic unity, and Cela uses to excess a comical tone as well as repetitive obscenities. The writer sketches an unhappy reflection on the human condition while joking about all the established morals. In this continuing wish to innovate, Cela has arrived at a point where

he is alienating his readers more and more and converting his literary work into a pure art of gesticulation.

FURTHER READING

Criticism

Cela, Camilo José. "Nobel Lecture: In Praise of Storytelling." *PMLA* 106, No. 1 (January 1991): 10-17.

Praises the importance of storytelling to the history of humanity upon his acceptance of the 1989 Nobel Prize.

Dougherty, Dru. "Form and Structure in *La colmena:* From Alienation to Community." *Anales de la Novela de Posguerra* 1 (1976): 7-23.

Discusses how the structure of Cela's *La colmena* leads to the restoration of social harmony and community at the end of the novel.

"Snapshots of Madrid." *Time* 62, No. 14 (5 October 1953): 114.

Complains that in Cela's *The Hive,* the author "spreads himself too thinly over too many characters, and his vignettes, taken together, lack the sharpness that they have separately."

Seamus Deane

1940-

(Full name Seamus Francis Deane) Northern Irish critic, poet, and novelist.

The following entry presents criticism of Deane's career through 1997.

INTRODUCTION

Regarded as one of Ireland's leading commentators on Irish literature and culture, Deane has analyzed and interpreted "the matter of Ireland," or what constitutes "Irishness," in numerous essays and books that challenge traditional notions of the people and civilization of Ireland. Besides several volumes of poetry and a novel, Deane has produced a far-reaching body of scholarship and criticism on a variety of past and contemporary Irish writers, ranging from Jonathan Swift, W. B. Yeats, and James Joyce to Samuel Beckett, Brian Friel, and Seamus Heaney, as well as such English authors as Francis Godwin, Thomas Hardy, and Joseph Conrad. In both prose and verse he has addressed diverse themes, including Irish history and politics, the political philosophies of Edmund Burke, Charles Parnell, Montesquieu, and Voltaire, the influence of the Irish Revival and "the troubles" on Irish literature and culture, and, above all, the character of Irish identity. Deane also served as general editor of the critically acclaimed, three-volume *Field Day Anthology of Irish Writing* (1991), which both reflects his vast knowledge of Irish literature and represents a keystone for Irish literary studies.

Biographical Information

Born the son of an electrician in Derry, (short for Londonderry), Northern Ireland, Deane received his secondary education at St. Columb's College. He took his bachelor's degree in 1961 and his master's degree in 1963 from Queen's University in Belfast and his finished his doctoral work from Cambridge University in 1966. Upon completing his studies, Deane taught English literature for two years in the United States at Reed College in Portland, Oregon, and at the University of California in Berkeley. He returned to Ireland just before "the troubles" erupted in October, 1968, and lectured at University College in Dublin from 1968 to 1980, when he became a professor of modern English and American literature there. In 1972, Deane published his first poetry collection, *Gradual Wars,* which won the A. E. Memorial Prize for Poetry. Following the publication of his next volume of verse, *Rumours* (1975), he taught again at American universities during the late

1970s. In 1980, Deane helped convene Field Day, a loosely organized group of Northern Irish writers and actors, mostly from his hometown, who staged new plays across Ireland and independently published pamphlets on Irish cultural themes, including his own *Civilians and Barbarians* (1983) and *Heroic Styles* (1984). After his third collection of poems, *History Lessons,* appeared in 1985, Deane focused his writing on scholarly interests, publishing the essay collections *Celtic Revivals* (1985) and *A Short History of Irish Literature* (1986) and the sociopolitical study *The French Revolution and Enlightenment in England* (1988). During the early 1990s he edited the *Field Day Anthology of Irish Writing* (1991) as well as a six-volume edition of Joyce's works for the Penguin Twentieth Century Classics series. Since 1993, when he left University College, Deane has taught Irish studies at the University of Notre Dame in the United States and published his first novel, *Reading in the Dark* (1995), which was nominated for the Booker Prize in England. Deane also has compiled a series of lectures delivered in 1995 in *Strange Country* (1997).

Major Works

Reflecting his circumstances and experiences in strife-torn Derry, Deane's lyric poetry concerns the historical sources and often bloody consequences of violence and investigates the ways that memory and tradition both pervert and rejuvenate communal values. The poems of *Gradual Wars* dramatize the effects of sectarian violence, tracing how divisive cultural attitudes shape personal identity and impede social expressions of emotion. *Rumours* contains reminiscences about the poet's childhood, his relationship with his father, and his wartime and vocational experiences, most notably in the poems "Scholar I" and "Scholar II," which focus on the relation between life and literature. Expanding the themes of his earlier verse, *History Lessons* articulates the pursuit of relief from the burden of history and its attendant bloodshed, drawing connections between personal memories of violence, the situation in contemporary Northern Ireland, and the shadowy forces that influence the history of humanity. Deane's prose works comprise the bulk of his writings. Evincing revisionist perspectives, his numerous scholarly essays frequently examine traditional and stereotypical literary representations of Irish cultural history and national identity, suggesting the significance of Ireland's status as a colonized nation. In such early pieces as "The Literary Myths of the Revival" (1977; reprinted in *Celtic Revivals*), *Civilians and Bar-*

barians, and *Heroic Styles,* Deane traced the origins of these preconceptions to the attitudes espoused by both English colonizers and the natives themselves toward "the matter of Ireland." The essays collected in *Celtic Revivals* and *A Short History of Irish Lierature,* as well as the selections and prefatory essays of the *Field Day Anthology of Irish Literature,* stress a relationship between Irish political history and the evolution of its literature in terms of Ireland's colonial status, often rewriting customary views of Irish writers and myths. *The French Enlightenment and Revolution in England* and *Strange Country* extend Deane's revisionism toward political events that more generally affected continental Europe than Ireland, including such developments as the rise of nationalism and imperialism as well as the ideology of progressive modernism. *Reading in the Dark* is an Irish *Bildungsroman* set in Derry in the 1940s and 1950s. Loosely autobiographical, Deane's only novel follows the maturation of an unnamed boy as he unravels a mysterious secret that haunts his mother, gradually learning of his grandfather's role in the rumored disappearance of his uncle in 1922.

Critical Reception

Although Deane's poetic skills have elicited a generally favorable response from commentators, his critical acumen has earned him the respect of fellow critics and scholars. As Eamon Hughes says: "Deane, it goes without saying, is a powerful and shrewd critic with whom it is at times a pleasure to agree, and an equal pleasure to disagree when in the face of his persuasive power one is forced to rethink." Despite a few detractors, many critics value Deane's cultural criticism for attempting to clarify the attributes of Irish national identity. Most critics, though not entirely in agreement with his choices, point to his editorial efforts in compiling the *Field Day Anthology* as his most accomplished achievement. John Byrne asserts that the collection "is clearly destined to become the standard text for all Irish Literature courses in American colleges for years to come." However, Deane's fiction also has attracted considerable interest, particularly for the way the specific characters, themes, and events of his novel evoke the universal conditions of life in Northern Ireland, yet at the same time resonate with qualities that define Ireland in general. "Deane is persuaded that being Irish is a very specific way of being human, one that permits the determined to have the last laugh, no matter who the joke is on," states Edward Conlon. "For him the question is less whether Ireland will ever be free than whether the Irish will be free of Ireland, with its violent hopes and seductive griefs."

PRINCIPAL WORKS

Gradual Wars (poetry) 1972

Rumours (poetry) 1975
Civilian and Barbarians (essay) 1983
Heroic Styles: The Tradition of an Idea (essay) 1984
History Lessons (poetry) 1985
Celtic Revivals: Essays in Modern Irish Literature (criticism) 1985
A Short History of Irish Literature, 1580-1980 (criticism) 1986
Selected Poems (poetry) 1988
The French Revolution and Enlightenment in England, 1789-1832 (criticism) 1988
The Field Day Anthology of Irish Writing 3 vols. [editor] (poetry and prose) 1991
Reading in the Dark (novel) 1995
Strange Country: Modernity and Nationhood in Irish Writing since 1790 (lectures) 1997

CRITICISM

Douglas Dunn (review date December 1973)

SOURCE: "The Specked Hill, The Plover's Shore," in *Encounter,* Vol. XLI, No. 6, December, 1973, pp. 70-76.

[*In the following excerpt, Dunn identifies the consequences of violence as the principal theme of* Gradual Wars, *noting the effect of the collection's artificial tone on its themes.*]

Seamus Deane avoids superficial negations [in *Gradual Wars*], either in favour of the kind of specifics Simmons finds "boring"—

> The unemployment in our bones
> Erupting on our hands in stones

or, more rewardingly, in favour of complex ironies and ambiguities. He frequently toys with lush and sophisticated styles, as if pointing out their uselessness at the same time as implying he would prefer to write more like Wallace Stevens than himself, faced as he is with the subject of Derry, where he comes from. Literacy and intelligence are embarrassments in killing times, and in **"The Thirtieth Lie"** he out shovels the slogans and intellectual props which he had "spat out, for years, like pap," reducing himself to an identity.

Deane writes of being "snared" by the past. He steps off a train at Derry and,

> Once more I turn to greet
> Ground that flees from my feet.

The place rejects him; he is not alienated by will. This imaginative idea, however, is as vague as Montague's mystified History, or Longley's "something." Elsewhere he writes of "the ghost that comes by the wall," a spectre of the past that marauds for vengeance. This is surprising in Deane's case, because the main drift in his poems is towards a hard-headed ambivalence about real issues. He is not afraid of feeling, but he wants to be accurate; at the same time, he is not afraid of intellect, but doesn't want it to get in the way: head guides heart. The excellence of his writing can be seen in these lines:

> Now unless I feel
> Attrition as our strategy,
> I cannot edge nearer you.
> Violence denatures
> What once was fidelity.
> Nor need this be wrong.
> Look! The razors
> Of the perception are now
> So honed they cut
> The lying throat of song.

Important as it is that a man should continue to write well while the society he comes from erupts, Deane's poems are particularly interesting in that they are about what violence does to people. His most powerful theme is the intrusion of violence on love, while there are frequent suggestions that violence is itself created by a lack of love, by loneliness, as well as public repression. Much of his writing is still more literary than it need be, which could also be said of Longley. Literary artifice does seem in this context like a haven from realism—although on such difficult subjects realism is often the haunt of mediocrity.

Gavin Ewart (review date 25 November 1977)

SOURCE: "Accepting the Inevitable," in *Times Literary Supplement*, No. 3948, November 25, 1977, p. 1381.

[*In the following excerpt, Ewart assesses the themes, poetic diction, and imagery of* Rumours.]

Rumours is Seamus Deane's second book. The simplicity of the equivalents invoked (Governmental kindness=school milk=cold, inhuman) marks it as not very sophisticated—though none the worse for that. He uses the unrhymed lyric mostly but also, not quite so successful, the spasmodically rhyming lyric. Poems about his relationship with his father (**"The Birthday Gift"** for example) are some of the best. The language is apt but sometimes on the edge of rhetoric ("Little phoenix. The cold ash / Of your feathers holds no spark / On which I may breathe") and sometimes almost

over the edge ("And came into the light their grooms / Blood-stained from their honeymoons"). Potent images are within his grasp—"The steeple of slamming iron let fall / Delicate ikons of tinkling glass" (church bells); but sometimes he may be writing more wisely and more glibly than his experience entitles him to ("Piety and rage / Change their ratios with age") and sometimes the rhymes force archaic words on him (ruth/truth). Poetic diction still lurks in the background ("Their world was as a cloud"). **"A Fable",** about Belfast's sectarian violence, is a tale confused in the telling—the dead body of what could have been a good poem.

These are faults, but there are some faultless poems, within their limits highly satisfying: **"The Brethren"** (rhymed memories of childhood), **"Shelter"** (wartime reminiscence), **"Scholar I", "Scholar II"** (life and lit), **"Signals"** (a love poem), and **"Watching. It Come"** (life and love, an excellent stoical rhymed lyric). The book, as a whole hints at even better poems on the way.

J. T. Keefe (review date Autumn 1984)

SOURCE: A review of *History Lessons*, in *World Literature Today*, Vol. 58, No. 4, Autumn, 1984, p. 608.

[*In the following review, Keefe focuses on the emergence of a distinct persona in the poems of* History Lessons.]

Seamus Deane is a distinguished member of a literary movement that has emerged from the North of Ireland and has the "Troubles" of the last few decades as its mainspring. His third book of poems, *History Lessons,* continues the poet's quest for an answer to the intolerable burden of history and the bloody explosions it fuels. The poems are wrought with tension and a nervosity that in the personal lyrics occasionally tend to overwhelm that fragile form. In **"Breaking Wood,"** however, there is an autumnal resignation as the poem moves serenely and surely to a memorable conclusion.

Two poems in an assured and commanding voice stand out as examples of a direction Deane is creatively pursuing. The dramatic content of both hints at a dramatic persona the poet has hitherto not allowed full play. **"Christmas at Beaconsfield"** is an impressive and clever dramatic evocation needing only, perhaps, the actual presence of the poet himself—as a character, ghost, observer—rather than a distancing of himself with "imagining . . ." and "almost certainly. . . ." Dramatic command is at the center of the poetic force of **"Directions."** In these poems we can detect the poet discarding tentativeness for a firm intention of moving to center stage.

Conor Cruise O'Brien (review date 18 August 1985)

SOURCE: "Cult of Blood," in *The Observer Review,* August 18, 1985, p. 18.

[*In the following review, O'Brien addresses certain nuances of Irish politics, nationalism, and revisionism examined in* Celtic Revivals.]

The modern writers examined in these essays [*Celtic Revivals*] are Joyce, Yeats, Synge, O'Casey, Patrick Pearse, Samuel Beckett, Thomas Kinsella, John Montague, Brian Friel, Derek Mahon and Seamus Heaney.

At his best, and especially when contemporary politics don't come into play, Mr Deane is a very good critic. Most of his essays are illuminating in one way or another—though sometimes verging on the precious or the pompous, and sometimes going over the verge. Some pages are brilliant; some are profound; some are both (and a few are neither).

The essay on **'Joyce and Nationalism'** is, I believe, the best thing that has been written on this subject. Mr Deane shows that what is often called 'Joyce's repudiation of Irish nationalism' is something considerably more complex than a repudiation. The essay ends with the words:

> Ireland as an entity, cultural or political, was incorporated in all its mutations within Joyce's work as a model of the world and, more importantly, as a model of the fictive. In revealing the essentially fictive nature of political imagining, Joyce did not repudiate Irish nationalism. Instead he understood it as a potent example of a rhetoric which imagined as true structures that did not and were never to exist outside language. Thus, as a model, it served him as it served Yeats and others. It enabled them to apprehend the nature of fiction, the process whereby the imagination is brought to bear upon the reality which it creates.

The essay on Patrick Pearse is also I believe the best on that subject; though this is a less impressive feat, since the critical literature on Pearse's writings is neither abundant nor impressive. Mr Deane is good on Pearse's relationship to the British imperialist ideology which dominated these islands, and a lot of other places, in Pearse's day:

> In Ireland, the only mythology which could compete with this imperial one was the nationalist ideal. They were, in some respects, remarkably similar. Each lived in the conviction that there was a sleeping giant, liable to be raised to life again by the spectacle of the Hun at the Gate or by the Fenian Dead.

Mr Deane is also interesting on Yeats, who comes into several of his essays. There is a pretty phrase on the Celtic Twilight: 'an idea of tradition and continuity so vague as Ireland's needed all the dimness it could get.' (The use of the rather moth-eaten word 'Celtic' in the title contains, I take it, various shades of irony. These may well elude some Anglo-Saxon readers.)

As the jacket of *Celtic Revivals* says, these essays 'examine the close connection between literature and politics in Ireland,' and that examination does produce some good insights. But the reader is likely to be confused—and may well feel some disquiet—about the political angle from which the examination is being conducted. At times Mr Deane may sound like some kind of Marxist. Thus he writes that 'separation from socialism left Irish nationalism ideologically invertebrate.' So you might think, when he comes to compare the socialist Sean O'Casey with Yeats—whose 'sympathy for fascism' and 'support to the philosophy of fascism' Mr Deane acknowledges—that O'Casey's politics would be found more acceptable than those of Yeats.

Quite the reverse; for Mr Deane's basic political criterion is nationalist not Marxist. It is in Yeats's plays, he says, not O'Casey's, that we find 'a search for the new form of feeling which would renovate our national consciousness. . . .' Poor O'Casey, on the other hand, is no more than 'a provincial writer whose moment has come again in the present wave of revisionist Irish history, itself a provincial phenomenon.'

Brief note on 'revisionism,' as used in Ireland: An 'Irish revisionist' is not a deviant Marxist, a Hibernian disciple of the late Eduard Bernstein. An Irish revisionist is one who, like me, believes that the cult of Patrick Pearse and of blood-sacrifice has helped the emergence of the Provisional IRA, is in other ways unhealthy, and ought to be challenged. O'Casey's sin, in the eyes of anti-revisionists like Mr Deane, is to have written plays—'Juno and the Paycock' especially—that depict manic nationalism, and its consequences, in an unfavourable light. Yeats, on the other hand, was generally pretty sound on subjects like blood-sacrifice, as anti-revisionists see these matters. 'The script calls for freshly severed human heads.'

Another good example of the anti-revisionist approach is contained in the essay on Seamus Heaney. Mr Deane quotes the following lines from the poem 'Punishment' in Heaney's collection, *North:*

> I who have stood dumb
> when your betraying sisters,
> cauled in tar,
> wept by the railings,
>
> who would connive

in civilized outrage
yet understand the exact
and tribal, intimate revenge.

The reference is to girls tarred and chained to chapel railings by the IRA in Catholic areas of Northern Ireland. Mr.
Deane comments (in part): 'Heaney is asking himself the
hard question here—to which is his loyalty given: the outrage or the revenge? The answer would seem to be that
imaginatively, he is with the revenge, morally, with the outrage.'

That antithesis seems to me a sight too neat. 'Morality' and
'imagination' cannot really be segregated like that. The
poet's imaginative reaction is not free from moral concerns
and contradictions: it clearly contains pity and horror and
guilt, *as well as* an acknowledged complicity—through 'understanding'—with the punishers. To classify the poet as
being 'imaginatively . . . with the revenge' is to do him
much less than justice. But the critic's phrase is illuminating, as to the role of the imagination in the 'renovated national consciousness' to which the anti-revisionists aspire.

I believe that the present political orientation of this distinguished but uneven critic is regrettable, both in itself and
as now affecting his critical work. His impulsion towards
manic nationalism may have helped him with the understanding of certain aspects of modern Irish literature, but
it obscures or distorts others. His future progress as a
critic seems to depend on getting that Old Man of the Irish
Sea off his back. The essay **'Joyce and Nationalism'** could
perhaps be the beginning of that dislodgement.

Patricia Craig (review date 5 September 1985)

SOURCE: "Valorising Valentine Brown," in *London Review of Books,* Vol. 7, No. 15, September 5, 1985, pp. 10-
11.

[*In the following review, Craig favorably compares* Celtic
Revivals *to contemporaneous cultural critiques of literary constructions of "Anglo-Irishness."*]

In a recent *Times* article, Philip Howard pounced on the deplorable word 'valorisation' which seems to be trying to
edge its way into the English language. 'To enhance the
price, value or status of by organised . . . action' is one of
the meanings he quotes for it. Here is an example of one
such usage: 'the literary critics' valorisation of tradition'.
This phrase occurs towards the end of W. J. McCormack's
dissection of Anglo-Irishness as a literary and historical
concept, *Ascendancy and Tradition*. 'Valorise', indeed, is
a verb much favoured in this book, along with others like

'energise' and 'traumatise'. There's a word that might be
applied to this style of writing: unstylish. At one point we
catch the author of *Ascendancy and Tradition* considering the way in which Joyce and Yeats 'as a binary and mutually dependent cultural production confront the totality
of history'. There the two unfortunate literary figures stand,
symbiosis thrust upon them. At another moment, the history of Ireland is called 'bifurcated', which makes it sound
like a pair of trousers. It is very provoking of W. J.
McCormack to write in this benighted way. The less he has
to say, the more fussy and fustian his manner becomes. On
the poem 'Nineteen Hundred and Nineteen', we get this:

> The title employs words, not numerals, but it employs
> one of several possible verbal formulations. It prevents
> us from particularising the year as One Thousand, Nine
> Hundred and Nineteen; it prevents us from slurring it
> to a loose Nineteen Nineteen. Thus, the element Nine-
> teen is repeated but not emptily so, for we are directed
> to the middle term, indicating the completed nineteenth
> century and its nineteen year excess. The post scrip-
> tum date, on the other hand, is unpronounceable or at
> best variously pronounceable.

Close scrutiny, you might say, is one thing; obsessive and
fruitless scrutiny another.

McCormack's main contention seems to be that 'ascendancy' and 'tradition' alike are figments of the imagination
of W. B. Yeats. It's well-known, of course, that the Protestant Ascendancy of the 18th century (a term not current,
in fact, as McCormack reminds us, before 1792) didn't actually embody all the qualities Yeats attributed to it—cour-
tesy and decency; a high-minded approach to political
matters and an aristocratic lineage. As far as the last is concerned—well, there's the hidden Ireland uncovered by
Daniel Corkery in 1928 (his study of 18th-century
Munster appeared under that title), inhabited by people who
took a very poor view indeed of the new English-speaking
aristocracy that had ousted the old Irish-speaking one. 'Valentine Brown', as these purists saw it, was the sort of ludicrous name an arriviste landowner might call
himself—someone who'd installed himself in a demesne
of the great McCarthys, now dead or dispersed. In this
world, the speaker of 'cunning English' quickly got himself condemned for opportunism, everything English being
associated with the kind of baseness Yeats decried. Still, it
was quite another Ireland the poet had in mind when he
singled out the 18th century, labelling it 'the one Irish century that escaped from darkness and confusion'. Swift, Berkeley, Burke, Goldsmith and Sheridan: all these stood for
clarity of thought, while Dublin gaiety, Belfast liberalism,
and the sense of national consequence acquired at
Dungannon, all contributed something to the Yeatsian image of a mellow era. That this particular form of Irishness

was conceived in opposition to an unsatisfactory present— 'Man is in love and loves what vanishes'—and (as Louis MacNeice has it) 'in defiance of the Gaelic League' and all it stood for, doesn't in the least detract from its efficacy.

As for 'tradition' and the literary critics' 'valorisation' of it—McCormack advises us to bear in mind the original legal meaning of the word ('handing over'), and to ponder on the 'distinction between the handing over of an object or a property, and the handing over of ownership or rights to such an object or property'. Doesn't this smack somewhat of obfuscation? McCormack (who has written far more cogently on tradition elsewhere) goes on to specify the social and cultural dynamics of the process of handing down—whatever these are—as the crucial factor in the business, but he doesn't uncover them in any individual case, or tell how, once enumerated, they can enlarge our understanding of what isn't, after all, a concept especially difficult to grasp. Such assertions can only arouse in the reader an urge to stick up for 'tradition' and the way in which it's commonly interpreted. The search for a precise terminology resulting in convolution and imprecision: that is one of the things that's gone wrong with the book.

Still, the book has much to recommend it. Its consideration of Edmund Burke is exhaustive. Burke, one of the 18th-century figures whose apotheosis was ordained by Yeats, has lately been attracting the attention of academics like McCormack and Seamus Deane, both of whom have written about him in *The Crane Bag.* Burke's social observations are worth repeating: Irish cabins, he said, were 'scarcely distinguishable from the Dunghill' and the furniture they contained 'much fitter to be lamented than described'. The food eaten in these places wasn't up to much: potatoes and sour milk, and even worse in times of famine, when many people were driven back on boiled weeds and blood stolen from cows. 'Pain, destruction, downfall, sorrow and loss'—in the words of the poet Aoghan O Rathaille—doesn't seem too strong a term to apply to the condition of the penalised Irish. From Burke, opponent of anarchy and advocate of Catholic emancipation, came a formula for British liberalism in the 19th-century, as Seamus Deane points out in an article on **'Arnold, Burke and the Celts',** reprinted in *Celtic Revivals.* McCormack, in a *Crane Bag* essay, has linked Burke's writings, and especially the *Reflections,* to the body of Anglo-Irish fiction which began with Maria Edgeworth. (In this essay, he sensibly remarks that, 'though there are difficulties attaching to the term "Anglo-Irish literature", it is too late to purge it from our critical vocabulary'—an attitude one wishes he'd displayed more often in *Ascendancy and Tradition.*) The *Reflections,* as he now asserts, uses the 'big house' as a dominant metaphor, and moreover shows it getting into a familiar state of ruin. From Maria Edgeworth's 'the wind

through the broken windows . . . and the rain coming through the roof' to Caroline Blackwood's Dunmartin Hall (in *Great Granny Webster*), with puddles in the corridors and warped doors, the Anglo-Irish house has characteristically fallen a victim to disrepair. There are, of course, a good many symbolic points to be adduced from this.

McCormack goes to some lengths to show that Castle Rackrent was only 'a house of the middle size', not great at all by the standard of English houses, and he jots down the probable cost (between £1,000 and £1,100), with the number of bedrooms, living-rooms and so on that a typical 'squire's house' might contain. However, as he says, Castle Rackrent shrinks or expands at the author's whim, just as the events of Le Fanu's *Uncle Silas* are cast in a perpetual autumnal haze (as Elizabeth Bowen noted), in defiance of the usual arrangement of the seasons. Anglo-Irish disdain for the tedious requirements of naturalism? Certainly a moral pattern takes precedence over verisimilitude, in Irish fiction of the last century, and it's usually to do with some form of reconciliation—typically the interdenominational marriage. You also find—as the effect of Burke's ideas worked its way further and further down the literary scale—a lot of aristocratic heroes who believe in a strong form of government tempered with kindness to the governed.

In his effort to let none of the latent meanings of a text escape him, McCormack sometimes pounces on a particle of import that isn't there, like a demented lepidopterist making an assault on a shaft of sunlight. Take the Joyce story 'Eveline'. The most satisfying account of this story that I have read comes in Hugh Kenner's *The Pound Era,* and is properly mindful of Joyce's Dublin knowingness. 'Eveline' opens with a perfectly felicitous and unobtrusive metaphor: 'She sat at the window watching the evening invade the avenue.' McCormack gets his teeth into 'invade' and won't let go of it until he's forced a connection between it and the 'soldiers with brown baggages' alluded to in part two of the story. Next, we're told that 'behind both nominal heroines' (the Countess Cathleen is hitched to Eveline here) 'lies the personification of Ireland as Patient Woman, *an tsean bhean bhocht*'. Leaving aside the fact that *an tsean bhean bhocht* can only be translated as 'the poor old woman', not a tag applicable to either the Joyce or the Yeats figure—leaving that aside, isn't the grafting on to Joyce's story of another, nationalist story a bit gratuitous? When McCormack goes on to wonder if Eveline—poor, romantic Eveline—opts for 'some domestic form of Home Rule in North Richmond Street', or 'alternatively', if she can be termed 'an abstensionist', he is being either fatuous or facetious.

The book covers roughly the same ground as "'The Protestant Strain'" (playfully subtitled 'A Short History of

Anglo-Irish Literature from S. T. Coleridge to Thomas Mann')—McCormack's contribution to *Across a Roaring Hill,* a collection of essays on 'the Protestant imagination in modern Ireland'. In both these undertakings, the short and the long one, McCormack shows a salutary urge to acknowledge all the complexities, social, ideological or whatever, underlying the term 'Anglo-Irishness', and affecting its outlets in literature. However—through a fear of what he calls 'isolationist aesthetics', meaning, I think, an insular approach—he draws altogether too much into the vicinity of his subject: economics, Nazism, authoritarianism and all.

It's McCormack who quotes Louis MacNeice on the benefits of being Irish, with the sense of belonging to 'a world that never was' among them: but it is Seamus Dean who incisively enumerates the sources of the various transformations—heroic, chivalrous, folklorish and so on—to which the idea of Irishness was subjected. Deane quotes Joyce on Ireland's 'one belief—a belief in the incurable ignobility of the forces that have overcome her'—and goes on to consider the ways in which the concomitant notion of Irish integrity was enshrined in literature. In 1903, when Joyce made this remark, it was customary to differentiate between the adulterated and the 'real' Ireland, though not between the real and the chimerical. The West of Ireland was the place in which the country's strongest substance was thought to reside (as McCormack points out). It was through his contact with the West that Padraig Pearse devised his prescription for a nation (as he put it) 'not only Gaelic, but free as well; not only free, but Gaelic as well'. Synge, however, believed that the essence of the Gaelic West—bursting with colour and vitality—could be rendered in English, though an English not current in any locality before or since, if we leave aside the haunts of those play-actors observed by Miles na gCopaleen, who 'talk and dress like that, and damn the drink they'll swally but the mug of porter in the long nights after Samhain'. Synge's Irish-English, true enough, achieves its narcotic effects at the expense of both Irish dryness and English wryness of tone.

Seamus Deane has included in his collection a couple of good essays on Pearse and Synge; nothing is missing from the latter but a touch of mockery at the succulent Irishness portrayed by the author of *The Playboy.* On Pearse, Deane remarks that the 'former apotheosis of the martyr has now given way to an equally extreme denunciation of the pathological elements involved' (you can see a comparable process, considerably speeded up, taking place in the literature of the First World War). Pearse's programme for national regeneration certainly contained elements not in keeping with the properties of the present. 'His nationalism tottered on the brink of racism,' Hubert Butler noted in 1968, in one of the pieces assembled in *Escape from the Anthill.* Deane doesn't go as far as this in his appraisal of the ar-

chitect of 1916: but he does, astutely, connect Pearse's Gaelic revivalism with 'what used to be called "muscular Christianity"'. Going into the fight 'white', indeed, was a concept Pearse would have cherished.

Deane and Hubert Butler are both authoritative commentators on the depleted condition of Irish letters during the middle part of the present century—'once the major excitements of the Revival were over', as Deane has it, and when a pair of gauche states, one north and one south, were struggling to find their feet. The atmosphere prevailing in both parts of the country, at this time, would greatly have discomfited the fosterers of Irish spirituality. Butler, in a *Bell* article deploring the unruly literary views of Patrick Kavanagh, distinguished between the parochialism of 1901, which contained the potential for enlargement of outlook, and that of 1951, which didn't. He likens the mind of the Mucker poet, when it's not engaged with poetry or fiction, to 'a monkey house at feeding time'. It was in the same year, 1951, Deane tells us, that John Montague, also writing in *The Bell,* called for an end to the apathy which seemed the predominant feeling about cultural matters, and at the same time 'demanded of his generation that it reflect Catholicism as a living force in Irish life'. His implication, like Kavanagh's contention, was that the Anglo-Irish Protestant impulse in literature had run its course—as indeed, by 1951, it had. However, for some time before this, and in the wake of the major achievements of the Revival, writers like Sean O'Faolain and Frank O'Connor had been reflecting Catholicism like billy-o, as a force to be repudiated or encouraged, or just in acknowledgement of its inescapability. Hadn't the time arrived to dispense with sectional assertion in any interests whatever? Or perhaps it couldn't be done, given the tendency of every social group to claim exclusive access to certain tracts of the national consciousness. Thus we have Patrick Kavanagh (as Butler says) light-heartedly arguing that 'you cannot be Irish if you are not Catholic,' and Butler himself insisting that to be Irish and Catholic debars you from possessing any insight at all into the mentality of Anglo-Ireland.

Hubert Butler—born in 1900, and Anglo-Irish to the bone—goes in for amiable castigation of the bumptious or unenlightened, and for discursiveness and frankness of manner. He also has an aptitude for the diverting comparison: 'Her intellect, like a barrage balloon that has lost its moorings, hovers uncertainly between Fishguard and Rosslare.' He has a thing or two to say about Catholic Ireland, especially in its odder, less Christian manifestations: for instance, we have the case of a man who, in 1895, roasted his wife in full view of relations and neighbours, having convinced himself—or so it appeared—that he was trouncing a changeling. Butler reminds us of the interest in fairy lore which prevailed at the time in scholarly circles. The colourful business at Ballyvadlea—fairy rath, herb doctor and all—shows the obduracy of superstition in the face of priestly admonitions. A more orthodox variety of rancid Catholicism asserted itself in a Wexford village, in the late 1950s. A Protestant mother, married to a Catholic, chose to enrol her six-year-old daughter at a local non-Catholic school. The outrage aroused by this act was such that a boycott was organised against every Protestant in the district. A bishop congratulated the people concerned on their 'peaceful and moderate' protest. In the third of his articles considering the peculiarities of Catholic life as they get reported in newspapers, Butler recounts the tussle which occurred in 1955 between Honor Tracy and the *Sunday Times*. A 'graceful sketch of an Irish village', complete with ironical aspersions on its frantic fund-raising operations when a new house was wanted by the canon, appeared in that newspaper. Its author was Honor Tracy. The paper's staff had taken the village to be imaginary. However, once the sketch was published, an angry canon from Doneraile in Co. Cork promptly surfaced clamouring for restitution. The *Sunday Times* capitulated. Miss Tracy, who read into its apology to the canon a criticism of her conduct as a journalist, turned on the paper. A court case ensued. The author of the article was awarded costs and damages. At this juncture, the inhabitants of Doneraile, on whose behalf Miss Tracy had thought she was campaigning, took up the cudgels for the canon. A demonstration in support of him and his new house was organised, with the parish choir, the Gaelic League and the Children of Mary out in force. Such exhibitions of Catholic fervour aren't uncommon. We're reminded of an episode in Peadar O'Donnell's novel of 1934, *On the Edge of the Stream,* when a similar crowd assembles to repudiate in public the message of a socialist agitator. O'Donnell views this outbreak of Catholicism with mock amazement: 'grown-up men and women,' he assures us, stood there singing in unison 'I am a Little Catholic'. It's not unusual either to hear heated voices raised in Ireland against the avarice of clerics. However, Hubert Butler isn't writing to endorse any such emphatic view. He isn't on anyone's side in the Doneraile dispute. Miss Tracy, not an Irishwoman, is taken to task for implying that she had got the measure of the natives. So are those who attribute the whole thing to Irish dottiness. The spectacle of Catholic solidarity, and its implications for moderation in Ireland, can hardly have pleased Hubert Butler, any more than anyone else, and neither can he have relished public debate on the messy business of possible self-interest in priests. Yet, as he says, it is no very comfortable matter for an Irish Protestant to criticise any instance of priestly greed, even if it should exist, when the countryside has so many half-empty rectories, deaneries and episcopal palaces, 'for whose maintenance Catholics and Nonconformists once paid tithes'. There is scarcely one of them, he mentions, into which the Doneraile canon's 'little house would not fit several times over'. It is this fair-minded attitude, as well as his perceptiveness about the achievements and the

charm of the Anglo-Irish, that makes Hubert Butler's essays so agreeable.

Patrick Parrinder (review date 24 July 1986)

SOURCE: "Celtic Revisionism," in *London Review of Books,* Vol. 8, No. 13, July 24, 1986, pp. 16-17.

[*In the following excerpt, Parrinder delineates Irish cultural history as defined in* A Short History of Literature, *deconstructing Deane's bias against Irish national mythology.*]

[What] today can we mean by 'English' literature? Seamus Deane begins his *Short History of Irish Literature* by asserting that the term 'Anglo-Irish' for the body of writing with which he is concerned is now anachronistic. Deane here is lending powerful support to the modern tendency to appeal to national divisions, rather than language divisions, in defining a literature. Such a tendency will not be confined, I believe, to the other side of the Irish Sea. In future, we may need to distinguish Modern English literature, a Romantic offshoot of the same type and vintage as Irish, Scottish and American literature, from an older English literature as well as from the generic subject of Literature in English. In other words, the 'English literature' which began with Shakespeare and Spenser may be seen to have started to splinter irrecoverably during the lifetime of Samuel Johnson. If English imperialism, beginning with the Tudors, had allowed English to become one of the great literatures of the world, it also hastened its eventual disintegration into the separate national components of Literature in English. Modern English literature can then be read as an affair of (native or naturalised) English writers, expressing a complex but initially local English identity.

Before too many readers protest, let it be said that the foregoing paragraph is an experiment in taking an 'Irish' view, looking at English literature to see if it will conform to an Irish (or Scottish or American) model. The new books by Seamus Deane [*A Short History of Irish Literature*] and Liam de Paor [*The Peoples of Ireland* and *Portrait of Ireland*] are judicious and informative in their own right, but they have the added interest of embodying two influential and competing conceptions of cultural identity from an Irish perspective. De Paor is closest to the traditional Romantic outlook. His writing is sometimes reminiscent of Sean O'Faolain's vigorous study of *The Irish* (1947), a book which its author described in the uncomplicated idiom of forty years ago as a 'creative history of the growth of a racial mind'. Seamus Deane, by contrast, offers a political reading of cultural nationalism, bringing a steely scepticism to bear on the Romantic tribal mentality.

Of de Paor's two books, *The Peoples of Ireland* is straight history, while *Portrait of Ireland* is a personal (though scholarly) essay which the publishers have unfortunately tried to transform into a coffee-table book by the addition of a job-lot of tourist-board photographs. Both works reflect the historiographical advances and changed political perspectives of the last four decades. Nevertheless, de Paor's very readable summaries of Irish history, literature and topography in *Portrait of Ireland* are the prelude to a chapter, 'Time out of Time', in which (like O'Faolain) he seeks to define permanent features of, or at least permanent influences on, the Irish character and temperament. In this chapter de Paor's training as an archaeologist, which is a strength in both books, is very much in evidence. Much as Wordsworth turned to Stonehenge, the author of *Portrait of Ireland* turns to the Book of Kells and the Tara brooch for intimations of what is truly Irish. These masterpieces of ancient Celtic art share a grotesque and fantastic profusion of ornament, 'following a kind of mad logic through bewildering convolutions'—a pedantic intricacy similar, it has often been argued, to the fiction of Joyce and Jonathan Swift. Joyce himself was a firm believer in such 'Celtic' qualities, and they offer an obvious context for his own art. Do we have here—as Vivian Mercier, for one, has implied—an unbroken tradition of genuinely Irish expression reflecting the national character? De Paor, for all his appealing mixture of archaeological enthusiasm and scholarly caution, seems to me to imply that we do. Seamus Deane would almost certainly disagree.

As a Northern Catholic, Deane has the best of reasons for being suspicious of Romantic cultural nationalism. 'Reference after reference was made to Edward Carson, the Relief of Derry, William the Third, the British Empire and the Battle of the Boyne,' runs the newspaper report of a recent Ulster rally. Once the past is accepted as a legitimate guarantee of contemporary identity, the Book of Kells and the Tara brooch are not necessarily any better than the Battle of the Boyne. It is the fervour of the belief, not the beauty and antiquity of its symbols and totems, which seems to matter. Both in his *Short History* and in his distinguished recent collection of essays, *Celtic Revivals,* Deane mounts a fierce and even-handed attack on the pieties of Irish national mythology. From his revisionist viewpoint Yeats's championship of the Protestant Ascendancy and Patrick Pearse's sentimentalisation of the Spirit of the Gael are equally deplorable. Instead of a continuous national tradition, Deane's sense of Ireland's cultural history is of a series of discontinuous, and heavily ideological, historical revivals. Historical assertion in Ireland, he implies, has been one of the prime vehicles of false consciousness.

As a scholar and critic, Seamus Deane seems to have little interest in the long perspectives: his chapter on 'The Gaelic background' is much the shortest in his *Short History.* What unifies Irish literature, for him, is principally its status as the literature of a colony given to outbursts of historical revivalism. As a colonial literature, it has no proper beginnings, no founding epic (the first substantial work analysed at any length in the *Short History* is [Swift's] *A Tale of a Tub*), and no settled relationship to the Irish people or their language. It strengths lie in its interrogation of forms and the wariness of its language. The unspoken parallel history of Modern English literature is needed to put the tradition that Deane surveys in its literary context. This 'colonial' reading of Irish literature is forceful and candid, and much of its impact comes from its pithy and penetrating assessments of individual writers. The book is generous in its use of quotation, and contains some memorable epigrammatic judgments. Deane's bias may, however, be questioned in two respects. First, his hostility to Romantic cultural nationalism perhaps leads to a few forced readings. Secondly, my suspicion is that cultural nationalism is too formidable an adversary to be slain by any individual critic. A state of complete detachment from nationality and of imperviousness to its myths is unattainable in the contemporary world. To attack one set of cultural-nationalist presuppositions may be an effective way of endorsing another set.

Deane's impatience with Romantic antiquarianism can be sensed in the *Short History* when he comments on John Montague's poem about a group of old country neighbours: 'Like dolmens round my childhood, the old people.' These old people, who inspire mixed feelings of tenderness and repugnance, are compared by the poet to a 'standing circle of stones'. For Deane this is a 'petrifying inheritance', and he credits the old people with a 'Gorgon stare' which is in danger of distracting Montague from 'the appeal of the sensual, the sexual, the living landscape'. Though Deane has few rivals as a commentator on contemporary Irish poetry, the misjudgment here is doubly ironic. It is ironic that Deane misses Montague's Wordsworthian reverence for the dolmens, which by no means belong to a 'dead' landscape (whatever that might be), and ironic too that he expresses his distaste for these monuments of Irish prehistory by means of a metaphor derived from ancient Greek mythology. Above all, what Deane has missed is the subtle sensitivity and tact of Montague's evocation of old age and its impact on the young.

Part of the general vocabulary which Deane brings to bear on Irish literary history consists of terms like 'culture', 'community', 'solidarity' and 'dispossession', which seem to be indebted to Raymond Williams. Following the implicit direction of some of Williams's work, one senses that Deane might have written a short history of Irish *literacy*— a cultural history, that is, of the practice of writing and reading in Ireland—rather than sticking to a chronological account of the literary canon. Many of his comments on language, on the deliberate construction of a nationalist heritage and on Irish writers' perceptions of (and failures to perceive) their country's colonial status seem to point this way. Such comments cannot be followed up within the conventional literary-historical textbook format. The result is something of a compromise.

One sign of the compromise is that prominence is given to a number of confessedly very bad books, on the grounds of the historical significance that is claimed for them. The myth that the **Short History** endorses (though it cannot altogether sustain it) is, I believe, that of an ultimately seamless relationship—almost a profound congruity—between a country's political history and the development of its literature. The literature is stunted by the politics, but it also in some way completes the politics. The one is a distorted and often inverted, but still recognisable, reflection of the other. Seamus Deane's Irish literature is political in origin (its birth being effectively marked by the assertion of a non-English identity within English literature), and it is still political today. This means that in the **Short History** a political and a literary-critical vocabulary exist side by side; neither subsumes the other, and each is tacitly supposed to have renounced its hegemonic claims. The results are often highly persuasive, even if a doubt remains about the method. 'Irish literature sometimes reads like a series of studies in dying cultures; the moment of political death is the dawn of cultural life,' remarks Deane at one point. Contemporary writers, he adds, have been intent on finding a way out of this labyrinth of 'Irishness'.

The achievement of Samuel Beckett, whose 80th birthday we are currently celebrating, does not directly challenge this Caudwellian view of Irish literature, though it may make us wonder about its relevance. Beckett surely stands as the archetype of the kind of modern writer who has tried to put his work beyond the reach of any political thesis. In Deane's words, Ireland functions in his work as a 'mode of absence': but Beckett is now being reclaimed by the Irish. (Shades of Stephen Dedalus—is Beckett important because he belongs to Ireland, or is Ireland important because it functions as a mode of absence in Beckett?) *The Beckett Country* records a photographic exhibition, including superb pictures by David Davison and Nevill Johnson, of locations mentioned in Beckett's writings. These have been devotedly traced—and in a few cases tactfully invented—by Eoin O'Neill.

Cultural tourism, as Deane observes in **Celtic Revivals,** found its most influential Irish apologist in J. M. Synge. Yeats added his considerable support—notably in 'Under Ben Bulben', when he ordered his epitaph in Drumcliff churchyard (citing a clerical ancestor of whom remarkably little had been heard until the poet needed an Irish burial-place). The 'Beckett country' around Foxrock and the

Dublin mountains, though attractive enough, can hardly match the resonance of the Yeats Country and the Aran Islands. And though Beckett's father was an Anglo-Irish Protestant, there is little of the aura of cultural death about this prosperous Dublin commuter and his family.

Tom Halpin (review date Fall 1989)

SOURCE: "The Razors of Perception," in *Irish Literary Supplement,* Vol. 8, No. 2, Fall, 1989, p. 20.

[*In the following review, Halpin provides an overview of* Selected Poems, *outlining the general characteristics of Deane's poetry.*]

In the course of an interview several years ago, Thomas Kinsella was challenged to assert the value of the artistic act, conditioned as it is both by the inevitable limitations of the artist as a human being and by the apparently unrestructurable nature of reality itself, its random disorder and dispiriting contingency. Kinsella's reply was clear: "If an artistic response is called into existence, that itself modifies the situation. It's a positive response even if we never solve anything. It colours reality in a way that makes it more acceptable." This is not the only way of understanding poetry and its relation to the material of the writer's experience, but for certain temperaments, particularly when the realities they are challenged by are of an exceptionally heart-rending and intractable nature, it is frequently all that can be envisaged in coping with the brute facts of life. If there is a fruitful way of responding to the poetry of Seamus Deane, it seems to me to be in some such terms as these.

Deane's *Selected Poems* is garnered from his three published collections of the last seventeen years, *Gradual Wars* (1972), *Rumours* (1977), and *History Lessons* (1983), together with a number of new poems and translations. One implication of a selection like this is that the writer is taking critical stock of the work he has already done, that he feels he has reached a point in his development where he can indicate its main lines, and, however unconsciously, suggest something of the way in which he wishes to be read.

Deane's poetry reflects his life from his childhood in Derry City in the 1940s and 1950s (remembered in **"Counting"** as "a radio / Childhood, lived in the backwaters of reception"), through marriage, parenthood, a vocation in scholarship and teaching, journeys to the United States and the Soviet Union—a widening front of experience and possibility shadowed, however, by the memory of an inheritance of hurt and depression (recalled in **"A**

World Without a Name" as "always a street / Hissing with rain, a ditch running / Svelte with fifth, mouths crabbed / With rancour and wrong, the smooth Almond of speech burnt"), and then overshadowed by the irruption of the violence which had always simmered never far beneath the surface of his world. The matter of Ulster, both in its more overtly abrasive as well as its more implicit manifestations—"The unemployment in our bones / Erupting on our hands in stones" (**"Derry"**)—has been the inescapable and intensely painful catalyst of Deane's imaginative and critical processes. At the same time, he is nervously aware that what has happened and is happening at home is essentially a manifestation of a more general malaise: traveling across the United States to teach for a time in California (in **"Hummingbirds"**) he is forced to note how "The times work like a virus"—"We have driven from Atlantic to Pacific / Time, through zoned cities where / Local rapists force the Israelis / Off the front page." All around, "crimes / are created afresh in the young": violence is generic and universal, reality is menacing and sinister everywhere. The awareness towards which one is forced by experience is as forbidding as experience itself is ineradicably tainted:

> Pollution entered everything and made it
> Fierce. Real life was so impure
> We savoured its poisons as forbidden
> Fruit and, desolate with knowledge,
> Grew beyond redemption. Teachers
> Washed their hands of us.
> Innocent of any specific crime,
> We were beaten for a general guilt.
> (**"Guerillas"**)

What emerges everywhere in Deane's poetry is the extent to which the natural human aspiration towards alliance with a place or a person is felt to be vitiated from the outset by impending or actual misalliance. Early in the selection, in a poem significantly subtitled "After Derry, 30 January 1972," we read that where one's place had been concern, "The Peace/ Had been a delicately flawed / Honeymoon signalling / The fearful marriage to come." Near the end, one of the new poems, **"Homer Nods,"** begins by broaching more nakedly personal apprehensions: "Were the seas the surge beneath / The marriage-bed? Was this unbelonging / Man escaping over the wine / Of water the fate of having / To belong?" This continuous awareness of apparently foredoomed abrasion is reflected in turn by the persistent struggle, at the level of the actual writing, to find forms and structures adequate to the material: the problem is one of how to integrate, as a poem, and without falsification or evasion, that which is of its very nature subject, apparently, only to disintegration. Insofar as the problem is a formal one, it is also a moral one, for what is the point of artistic performance if disintegration and disorder are ultimately the only meaning of what the imagination engages? The pos-

sibility that there might be another, imaginatively healing or enhancing dimension of meaning to be elicited from apparently random disorder through the very exercise of an artistic response, is made all the more difficult when the temperament or outlook in question is Deane's. His faith in the possibility of an even provisionally satisfying artistic response is marked by a deep, almost paralyzing scepticism: "The razors / Of perception are now / So honed they cut / The lying throat of song" (**"Fourteen Elegies: Eleven"**).

Admittedly, these lines—registering the extent to which the forms of understanding forced upon us by historical experience make the consolations traditionally associated with art seem anachronistic and hollow—come from early in Deane's first collection, *Gradual Wars,* which is painfully scored by the shock and terror of newly-awakened violence. But the same can be said, in some degree or other, of *Rumours* ("History is your wall of pain. / Garrison, the planter's warp / In the rebel climate's grain") and *History Lessons* ("History is personal; the age, courage."). The present selection ends, significantly, with the fine recent **"Reading *Paradise Lost* in Protestant Ulster, 1984,"** a powerful but desolate cry in the face of what seems predestined and irreparable in his inheritance ("ah, whence arose / This dark damnation, this hot unrainbowed rain?"). And yet what remains as an undeniable aftertaste from reading this volume is a sense of the increasing triumph of the poetry itself, even if it never solves anything, and perhaps most of all when it accepts this limitation as inseparable from the mysterious ambiguities and satisfactions of the poetic enterprise and thereby releases other energies to play.

Probably the most insistent characteristic of a poem by Deane is its unremitting intensity of concentration upon the subject, a quality often inseparable from an embattled sense of the difficulty of clarification. There is a recurring impression, particularly in his earliest work, of something close to anguish as the dominant emotion informing, indeed determining, the taut, nervous, sharply-cut movement of the lines. Equally often, though, even miraculously, the subject seems to arrange itself in such a way as to most clearly disclose its inner meaning, as if in answer to the desperate insistence of the imagination in the face of equally powerful knots and tangles of resistance. Memorable explosions of imagery signal the imagination's triumphant, if provisional, penetration and containment of the intractable matter in question—"And the red startled sopranos / Of the sirens settle / To a blue yap. Whatever you call it / Night after night we consume / The noise as an alcoholic / Drinks glass after glass until his voice / Is hurled like a flaw / Into his numbed palate." A moment like that, from the beginning of *Gradual Wars,* is representative, as is this focal passage from the collection's title poem:

"Darkness / Is pierced by it, it / Has the blind focus / Of a nail shuddering / In the quiet wood / Which is going to / Split as pipes / Choked in ice do." The matter shows itself capable of yielding to a language and a music, however tense and spikey, which is now part of our understanding of the matter itself. By disclosing its accessibility to transmission in terms of significant verbal from, the hard facts of brutality and horror have been permanently colored by Deane's artistic response. But it has been a close-run and hard-won performance: the pressures of the reality upon which the art has encroached are evidenced in the recurring intensities of image and rhythm.

By the time we reach the poems culled from *History Lessons,* there is a markedly deeper trust revealed in the form of the poem itself as the measure of its authenticity and completion. Without any slackening in concentration or in characteristic verbal brilliance—passages and images that impact upon the ear "as though / A small shrapnel of birds scattered"—there is less overt reliance upon the single arresting image as the focus of a poem's meaning, and more confidence in the sustained singing quality of the voice in tune with the more elaborately organizing imagination. Poems which dramatize the tensions between the poignancies of personal feeling and the more implacable determinants of history and politics, like **"Osip Mandelstam"** (with its lovely singing lines on the self-delighting poetic act: "the gold light / The goldfinch carries into the air / Like a tang of crushed almonds"), **"History Lessons," "Send War in Our Time, O Lord," "Hummingbirds,"** as well as poems which are more exclusively private and self-communing, like **"Daystar," "The Party Givers," "Breaking Wood,"** reveal a voice which is more at home with itself over longer stretches, relishing its capacity to stay with its subjects until they have, as it were, told themselves. A more varied blend of lyrical possibilities is also explored within these poems—the tone of the voice speaking is more confidently flexible and supple, by turns passionate, reflective, sensuous, muscular, plangent—and this development in turn signals an exploration of his characteristic concern with vulnerability and contingency in terms that are different in degree from those connected with the attrition of the individual reality by the terrorizing force of contemporary historical experience. The latter element, of course, is still pervasive: **"Send War in Our Time, O Lord,"** a moving enactment of the fall from innocence to experience, sets the individual finally in the context of a maelstrom in which his own reality is marginal, where "The history boys are on the rampage, / The famous noise in the street / Where a jaguar camouflage / Ripples on armoured cars / In a skin of symbols." But experience in *History Lessons* is felt more frequently now in other, more interior ways than heretofore, as in **"The Party Givers,"** for example, at the end of which the couple, having played the perfect hosts throughout a long evening and seen the last guests on their

way, find themselves standing momentarily stunned at the edge of an unwonted and chilling self-recognition as "Morning knifes in":

> The window wanes
> Into rainlight, you cup your
> Face in your hands, and drink
> Abandon. Is such weariness the price
> For being so wonderfully at home
> To others? Or is the party simply over
> And we familiars in a foreign life?

Experience in this sense, something painful but potentially at least the condition of emotional clarification and renewal, is the theme of the exquisitely delicate **"Daystar"** ("I sensed / The sheer transparency of spring / In which the kitchen shines. / The night fever convalesces.") and the strong and moving **"Breaking Wood"** ("Soon / the fume of wood upon the air / Will take my feeling to the night").

That poems such as these may, in some measure, represent Deane's truest, most authentic voice coming into its own is reinforced by the fact that, for me at least, some of the best things in the book are his presumably recent translations from the Italians Zanzotto and Luzi, and the German Rilke. I am not qualified to say to what degree they are actually "translations," but they have a remarkably first-hand feel about them and read as work in which Deane's imaginative temperament has found memorable release. The results fuse a haunting sensuousness and delicacy of detail ("Like a vowel / In the valley's mouth, the hours / Of moonlight speak my strange / Life with the connivance / Of the hedgerow's leaves") with a challenging richness and density of implication.

One can quibble, of course, with this or that in the volume as a whole. The omission of the short sequence "Scholar" (from *Rumours*) is a loss. The elaborate legal conceit at the heart of **"Summer Letter"** (from the same collection) seems to me to have been overdone; the poem suffers rather badly when compared to the freer flow of a later poem like **"Daystar."** The Kafkaesque and/or early Auden echoes in **"Directions"** are distracting. That the volume is brought to an end with **"Reading *Paradise Lost* in Protestant Ulster, 1984"** (immediately preceded by **"The Churchyard at Creggan,"** Deane's translation of "Úr-Chill a' Chreagáin" by Art MacCumhaigh) could be interpreted as betraying a needlessly programmatic impulse; frankly, I can't make up my mind whether it does or not. But these are quibbles. What we have here, overwhelmingly, is a body of work which compels recognition as a memorable, muscular, courageous testament to the imagination's resistance and resilience in the face of circumstances that threaten to usurp and immure its essentially self-delighting energies. Again and again, and with an increasing sense of the inward satisfactions to be derived from the exercise of the artistic response, "The kerosene flash of his music / Leaps from the black earth" (**"Osip Mandelstam"**). Deane, in the process of facing unflinchingly into the storm of contemporary disruption and breakage that is his inheritance, has made his poems earn their keep in what has frequently been the hardest way possible. In the thinnest and most fragile of margins between desolation and hope, paralysis and possibility, the poems have, somehow, come into being. Yet their very existence represents the supervention of something positive, though never equivocally hopeful, upon the situation; they constitute a strengthening and a clarification of the thin margin in which they have come into being, and their incapacity to resolve anything other than the question of their own right to exist is both a definition and a guarantee of their artistic integrity and authenticity. Poetry, in Auden's famous phrase, may "make nothing happen," but the imagination that has made these poems happen is one without which our consciousness would be even more incomplete than it is.

Alan Ryan (review date 9 November 1989)

SOURCE: "Effervescence," in *London Review of Books,* Vol. 11, No. 21, November 9, 1989, pp. 10-11.

[*In the following excerpt, Ryan examines the main arguments of* The French Revolution and Enlightenment in England, *emphasizing the ways in which British writers explored the British political character through their preoccupation with the French national character at the turn of the eighteenth century.*]

The view expressed by Monied Interest in Dickens's story 'The Flight' might have made an epigraph for Seamus Deane's *The French Revolution and Enlightenment in England.* It was Monied Interest who declared that it was 'quite enough for him that the French are revolutionary—"and always at it".' The eight essays that make up what Froude would have described as 'a short study on a great subject' cover both more and less than the title of Professor Deane's book implies. The Revolution itself looms large and obtrudes less continuously than one might expect, while the Enlightenment looms rather larger. But what really holds the book together is an idea that is at once illuminating and obscure: the idea that in responding to the Revolution and to the Enlightenment which had produced it, British writers were engrossed with its Frenchness.

In tackling this theme, Seamus Deane covers a period of some fifty years, ranging back to Condillac, Helvétius and Holbach, and carrying the story on to the 1820s. 1789 is anything but salient. Burke's *Reflections* were an early re-

sponse to the early hopes of the revolutionaries and Deane is mostly concerned with later reactions: Coleridge came to terms with Rousseau between 1799 and 1809, British responses to the politics of the French émigrés were affected by Napoleon's seizure of power in 1799 and by the Peace of Amiens in 1803, while Hazlitt was carrying on his Jacobin campaign against English conservatism and Benthamite radicalism down to the 1820s. The central issue around which everything rotates is the French national character, and whether there was something in it that caused the Revolution, and doomed the Revolution; and if so, what that was.

It was not merely that 1789 had turned out to be something wilder, more violent and altogether less intelligible than the Glorious Revolution of 1688. That was certainly true, but it was only a part of the truth. What was more important to those who thought in these terms was to discover what it was that caused the French to take up ideas that were the common stock of advanced European thought and to make them the pretext for regicide and terror; and whatever that was, it could emerge clearly only in the light of a contrast with the British character. Though Professor Deane has a lot else to say, his distinctive theme is the various ways in which British thinkers explored the British political character in their obsessive exploration of the French.

That this is the way to read a good deal of Burke, we probably take for granted. Burke's *Reflections* were provoked by Richard Price, an English Dissenting minister, and addressed to an anonymous French gentleman, but when Burke says 'you' he is apostrophising the French nation at large, and when he says 'we' he claims to speak for the whole British people—or at any rate for all those among them who were politically active. What is more surprising is that Burke's categories of analysis and polemic recur in Sir James Mackintosh, permeate Coleridge's ruminations on Rousseau, and provide an unexpected link between Carlyle and Southey. On Hazlitt, Deane puts forward the startling but in the end persuasive hypothesis that Hazlitt thought Jacobinism had been defeated both in England and in Europe less by British Toryism than by the essentially French philosophy of self-love put forward by Condillac and Helvétius and naturalised into England by Adam Smith and Bentham. Hazlitt raged against reaction and tyranny in England, but the intellectual roots of what he raged against were French, not English.

Even the group which welcomed 1789 most warmly, the politically active ministers of the Dissenting Churches, felt the same doubts about French tendencies. French sexual mores were too lax; the Philosophes had gone too far in broadening a justified attack on the superstitions and despotic affinities of Catholicism into a general assault on Christianity as such. Since most Dissenters had only wanted their own legal and political disabilities removed, it took very little to persuade them that 1789 was not 1688, and that the French had, as was to be expected, gone too far.

Professor Deane is properly anxious to point out that not everyone went down the same xenophobic track. Godwin, for one, switched from rationalism to the philosophy of moral sentiment between editions of *Political Justice,* but retained a lofty cosmopolitan perspective from which one nationality was scarcely distinguishable from another. Bentham and James Mill thought the subject of national character would have a place in a rational science of legislation, but agreed that as things stood appeals to national character were largely an aspect of political abuse—a view spelled out in one of John Stuart Mill's earliest essays in the *Westminster Review* and defended all his life.

Professor Deane is equally scrupulous about distinguishing one antipathy and its objects from another. In the early stages of the Revolution, émigré priests were made much of, since it was the Revolution's attack on the Church that caught the eye: but it was not to be expected that British political opinion would remain attached to a vengeful and reactionary group that looked forward to the restoration of just the kind of Catholic absolutism the British had rid themselves of a hundred years before. After 1799, a more lasting affection lighted on Mme de Staël and constitutionalists like Mallet de Pan, who admired the constitutional compromises of the British system of government and were sworn enemies of Napoleon. The British propensity to congratulate themselves on the unique perfection of the British constitution was quite consistent with a hunger for congratulation from other sources too.

Seamus Deane begins, as we all begin, with Burke. It has long been fashionable to find in Burke a divided consciousness, less unequivocally anti-revolutionary than he liked to think. His acute consciousness of the fact that his career had been built entirely upon his own merit must often have made him wonder whether the Ancien Régime deserved the devoted service that men like him had given it. His *Letter to a Noble Lord,* written in 1797 after the death of his only son, gives vent to a deep bitterness at the contrast between his concern for the welfare of aristocratic England and aristocratic flirtation with revolutionary ideas that would bring down the whole edifice. The delicate balance between his sense of his own abilities and his belief in the virtues of aristocratic government must always have taken some preserving, especially when the estate he purchased at Beaconsfield did so much more to wreck his finances than to elevate his social standing.

Many commentators have argued that his Irish background, and his awareness of the grievances of the Catholics in his home country, must have made him more sympathetic to the siren songs of the revolutionaries than his ferocious assaults on them would suggest. Seamus Deane extracts a neater and more persuasive analogy. In his unpublished *Tracts Relative to the Laws against Popery in Ireland,* written in 1765, Burke took issue with the English historians who depicted the Irish as naturally rebellious. He denied that nature had anything to do with it: it was oppression that made the Irish rebellious, not a flaw in their nature. Burke drew the obvious analogy between Irish Catholics fleeing Ireland and the persecuted Protestants fleeing France: both were an indictment of the policies that drove them from their homeland. Whenever he considered the Protestant Ascendancy, Burke attacked it as a monster of bigotry and injustice, fuelled by no religious feeling and expressing only a passion for persecution. During the 1790s, the full moral lesson could be drawn. The Protestant Ascendancy was an abomination because Irish Protestants formed a plebeian oligarchy, and in Burke's opinion, 'a plebeian oligarchy is a monster.' This was Burke striking at all his enemies—the other two plebeian oligarchies on his mind were Warren Hastings's East India Company, and the Jacobins.

What the English did in Ireland was what the Jacobins did at home by proscribing their enemies in the name of a fictional national interest. The policies of the English in Ireland looked all the more wicked because they were so much at odds with the character of English politics at its best. At its best, English politics relied on a chain of affection and duty, stretching from the humblest to the greatest, and based on the love for place and family celebrated in Burke's emphasis on the 'little platoons'. As Seamus Deane puts it, 'France was a threat, Ireland a dire warning, England the ideal middle term between the two.'

Hugh Kenner (review date 26 January 1992)

SOURCE: "There's Music in the Ould Sod Yet," in *The New York Times Book Review,* January 26, 1992, pp. 3, 23.

[*In the following review, Kenner outlines the contents of the* Field Day Anthology of Irish Writing, *assessing its strengths and weaknesses.*]

At four times the word count of the King James Bible, the new three-volume *Field Day Anthology of Irish Writing* makes an Irish Statement: We've been here from Time's Beginning, and we're silver-tongued. What else it states is harder to paraphrase, so tangled has been the long Irish story of co-opting some past to serve some present end.

Cu Chulainn for instance, a noted skull-basher; the way a

scribe wrote the story down in Irish maybe a millennium ago, this hero, attacked by such a dog as needed to be held by nine men, simply "put one hand on the apple of the hound's throat and the other at the back of his head, and dashed him against the pillar-stone . . . so that all the hound's limbs sprang apart."

An unlikely role model, you'd think, for W. B. Yeats, who could resemble a hearthrug ornament. But Yeats during his long life would devote five plays to Cuchulain, who in a time of windbags could seem Homeric; who moreover, mortally wounded, arranged that he'd be killed swinging his sword while tied upright to a stake. He became the very incarnation of Heroic Defeat, something Yeats's Ireland cherished with part of its mind. Patrick Pearse, who led the 1916 rebellion and died before a firing squad's volley— Pearse "summoned" (wrote Yeats) "Cuchulain to his side." The Dublin Post Office lobby, where Pearse's men held out for many hours, offers a bronze statue of Cuchulain bound to that stake.

Cu Chulainn? Cuchulain? That difference is part of the story. As Yeats used a legendary time, so a later age is using his, and one way of distancing the Age of Yeats has been to hint that its scholarship was amateurish, its revival of the old language merely enthusiastic. Still, however it's spelled, say "coo-HULL'n." Then reflect that uncertainty over what sounds to make remains one way to fence out aliens. Nowhere does this huge anthology offer a mite of help with the likes of "Eibhlin Ni Chonaill" (say Evelyn O'Connell) or "medhbh" (say, as Yeats did, "Maeve.") It's a great help just to know that "bh" everywhere makes shift for "v."

Such a sequence—era after era redefining preceding eras for present use—has called forth a big anthology indeed, since what's being framed is less a sequence of texts than a sequence of redefinitions, notably the one whose pages we're now turning. Thus a hundred pages of the chapter "Anglo-Irish Verse, 1675-1825" help make the point that, despite modern scholars' inattention, there were versifiers then about besides Swift. One is Nahum Tate, whose "While Shepherds Watched Their Flocks by Night" is retrieved from English hymnbooks to enforce a continuing theme, that many "English" writers were really Irish, including such diverse figures as Oliver Goldsmith, Edmund Burke, Thomas Sheridan, Oscar Wilde and Joyce Cary. (Tate's "seraph," by the way, gets footnoted "angel," though generations of hymn singers haven't been baffled; who needs help with what is a topic the editors don't address with any system.)

Volume One takes us to 1850; Volume Two, which includes Synge, Joyce and Yeats, to 1945; Volume Three, which includes Ronan Sheehan's story "Paradise," here published for the first time, to 1991. (The set was first published by Field Day Publications in Ireland.) The 1850-1945 range

is especially interesting. Readers of Yeats and Joyce have long been aware of a foretime when a Great Past was being somewhat clumsily revived. Young Ireland (Thomas Davis) has been heard of, also Sir Samuel Ferguson; little else. But now the first half of Volume Two, some 550 pages, prepares us for the Abbey Theater period (1904 onward) with much that's been scarcely accessible, so unlikely would seem the rewards of dredging it up.

Thus we've 111 pages of "Poetry and Song 1800-1890," headed by Seamus Deane's tart observation that "some of the best-known poems are, to present-day taste, among the worst." That was because "incoherence of purpose was disguised in the language of utopian possibility," a likely outcome when Catholics, Protestants, Gaelic fanatics, Temperance zealots, others, were vying to identify an essential Irishness that might surge toward rebellion, or revolution, or separation from Britain, or independence under the crown, or an orgy of head-bashing, or just the threat of it, or any combination (or none) of the above. Utopian possibility, everyone was agreed on that; all agreed too that Literature should bespeak the soul of the people. Hence—O Lord—hence

> Why leave I not this busy broil,
> For mine own clime, for mine own soil,
> My calm, dear, humble, native soil!
> There to lay me down at peace
> In my own first nothingness.

—which is George Darley in 1835, pretending in London that he longs to be back in dear Ireland, where all is serene, composed. (Hah. Why did he linger in London?)

Or here's Thomas Furlong (1829, two years posthumously) identifying Irish Song with the simply natural:

> Fling, fling the forms of art aside—
> Dull is the ear that these forms enthrall;
> Let the simple songs of our sires be tried—
> They go to the heart, and the heart is all.

What's being flung aside would include Campion, Mozart, Schubert. . . . But, ah, Irish Eyes Are (artlessly) Smiling. (That song, by the way, the one "Irish" song everyone knows, stems not from the Ould Sod but from New York, where its intent was to nudge exiled Irish lads toward smiling-eyed Irish lasses. Racial purity, yes.)

Or here, in another section, is (amazingly) Fred Higgins, who in 1940 feigned he'd been given some bones of Queen Jezebel's:

> And as once her dancing body
> Made star-lit princes sweat,

So I'll just clack: though her ghost lacks a back
There's music in the old bones yet.

Though Yeats in his final phase made that possible, in no incarnation could Yeats have written it. It's remembering "Archy and Mehitabel." Assimilations were nothing if not eclectic.

Volume Three though, 1945 to now; and look, where's Desmond Egan? The first Irish poet who hasn't had to find ways to sound Irish? Yes, he's absent. Totally. Not a mention. In a clique-ridden land, he may have got on someone's nerves. Or some schema or other doesn't accommodate him, the way it seemingly accommodates . . . oh, look for yourself.

But if "Contemporary Irish Poetry" (120 pages) disappoints, Volume Three can offer riches aplenty elsewhere, notably the best short introduction to Beckett ever printed (it's by J. C. C. Mays); a wondrous selection of "Political Writings and Speeches: 1900-1988" gathered by Mr. Deane, the general editor of the anthology and a professor at University College, Dublin; or a "Revisionism" section, where you find Sean O'Faolain asserting (in 1944) that a slogan like "Not merely free but Gaelic as well, not merely Gaelic but free as well" could set mouths a-watering Pavlovlike. That's still true after half a century.

One could wish throughout for better proofreading, also for some sense of what doesn't need annotating, also for a scheme of cross-references that would tell us how the Irish original for this in Volume Two is available in Volume One. Still, if you're interested at all in Ireland, forgo two meals on the town and buy the set.

Anne Devlin (review date 25 August 1996)

SOURCE: "Growing Up in Ireland's Shadowlands," in *The Observer Review,* August 25, 1996, p. 17.

[*In the following review, Devlin evaluates the narrative structure and style of* Reading in the Dark, *indicating the relation between stories and reality.*]

From the moment on the opening page of ***Reading in the Dark*** when the boy is stopped on the stairs by his mother, because a shadow has fallen between them, I was disarmed, though I had to wait 134 pages until the shadow surfaced again in its original context, in the tale 'Mother', before I understood that it was never possible to go straight at this thing that has fallen between them.

I am of the opinion that women and men have different strat-egies when it comes to telling stories—as with everything else. My favourite book of a haunting is Toni Morrison's *Beloved*—but not for Seamus Deane is Morrison's confrontational opening: '124 was spiteful.' Morrison says she does it so the ones who won't like it leave immediately. Deane lays out his book like a collection of folktales—and though I started after his shadow on the landing, I was soon halted by the next tale on people with green eyes.

Reading in the Dark is built like a labyrinth—a labyrinth of separate passages which in the end turns into one at the centre. The father tells the story of the field of the disappeared because he is unable to tell the actual story of his brother's disappearance. The boy hears the story of Larry's silence—he has had sex with a she-devil—only later to hear another story that on the same night Larry executed an informer.

The visionary stories and folk-tales are invented to disguise something more dangerous to the community's sanity. And trapped at the centre is the heartbreaking tale, 'Mother'—where the family watch the woman go mad from a knowledge she cannot share.

> I wanted to run into the maw of the sobbing, to throw my arms wide, to receive it, to shout at it, to make it come at me in words, words, words,—no more of this ceaseless noise, is animality, its broken inflections of my mother.

The boy is bewildered by the fact that his father is burdened by a secret which his mother knows is a lie; but if the secret lie only burdens his father, the revealed truth would kill him.

In 'Accident', the boy sees Rory Hannaway killed under a reversing truck, but feels nothing for Rory's mother or the driver when they see the crushed child. Yet when a policeman arrives and is sick, the boy suspends his fear despite his family's persistent persecution by the police and loathing of the traditional enemy, and feels only sympathy for the man. His sense of treachery is only abated when he accepts a lie from another boy who tells him that it was a police car which killed Rory. Only then can he experience true sorrow for the legitimate sufferers—Rory's mother and the driver who will never work again. In other words, the lie—the distorted narrative—becomes an antidote when the sensibility has become impaired or traumatised through fear or shock; this must be, if not the cultural function of narrative, at least the psychological function.

Art comes out of distortions: the distortions also make us ill. They make us ill because no one else accepts them.

When the boy translates all he has gleaned about the family secret into Irish and reads it to his uncomprehending father while his mother listens, it is an impulse to end the isolation imposed on him by knowing too much. Other languages do seem to provide a safer zone than the mother tongue for certain kinds of experience. Deane aptly demonstrates this in the marvellous encounter where the priestly master attempts to explain the facts of life to the boy in a series of Latin terms: '*Emittere,* to send out. The seed is sent out . . . ' Finally, the boy is forced to ask himself: 'Do you have to have Latin to do this?'

We are in the territory of the power of the word. No more so than when his mother finally finds words to articulate her grief and she says: 'Paradise was not far away when I died.' I found myself holding my breath here. This is the language of shock.

Paradise is very close to catastrophe; this is the nature of opposites. The boy does give us a glimpse of what this paradise might be in a vision of the druids' herbal spells and the gorse-tainted air around the old fort at Grianan in Donegal—the home of the sleeping and legendary warriors and where too the sounds of the druid women's watery voices can be heard murmuring with sexual pleasure: 'Yes-ess. Yes-ess.'

The location of Paradise is on Lough Foyle, and the catastrophic feud farm is on the opposite bank, Lough Swilly with Derry between and everything to be fought for.

But that paradise has been violated and catastrophe is the norm. The whole family tragedy has been set in motion by a lie perpetrated by a policeman. Burke, in an act of revenge against the boy's grandfather. Knowing the truth doesn't help: we have to know how to deflect grief enough to let love flow undiminished and undisturbed on its true course, if paradise is ever to become anything more than an elusive longing for a past that never existed and a future—a day—that will never come.

A law has been broken—a taboo older than the laws of consanguinity. It is this that the boy knows and the father does not. So the boy must go away to allow the mother to love the father without his eyes on her.

It is contact with reality that is killing, not the magical shadow worlds we create to combat it. That is why we need our stories. I have nowhere read a portrait of a woman going mad with grief as shattering as the portrait of the mother in this tale nor anywhere a sense so achingly described as that of the boy's distress at losing her, through having too much access to her history.

Terry Eagleton (review date 30 August 1996)

SOURCE: "The Bogside Bard," in *New Statesman,* Vol. 125, No. 4299, August 30, 1996, p. 46.

[*In the following review, Eagleton concentrates on the public appeal of Deane's fictional rendering of personal memories in* Reading in the Dark.]

A colonial culture is a culture of secrecy. Seamus Deane's superb first novel [*Reading in the Dark*], set in the Derry Bogside of the 1940s and 1950s, is all about who knows what in a place awash with rumours, hauntings, metamorphoses and misinformation. People and things materialise and evaporate, mysteriously change shape or sex, cocoon themselves and others in ever thicker layers of deception. It is a world as materialist as Balzac's, splashed with scents, tastes and patterns of light, yet spectral as Henry James', as the certitudes of the present are infiltrated by the ghostly fictions of the past.

Set in an actual border region, *Reading in the Dark* also occupies some transitional zone between fiction and autobiography. In doing so it acts out the crossings of fact and fable over which the narrative broods. Its youthful protagonist, a kind of cross between Lawrence's Paul Morel [in *Son and Lovers*] and James Joyce's Stephen Dedalus [in *A Portrait of the Artist as a Young Man*], grows up in a postwar Northern Ireland of rural beauty and state brutality, son of a Catholic Republican family with a shattering secret at its heart.

In a venerable Irish tradition, the secret turns out to involve betrayal, and locks the mother into a paralytic, untranslatable sorrow: one of the most poignant aspects of a story rich in emotional subtlety. At the core of this dazzlingly eloquent narrative is something muffled and labyrinthine that beggars speech. This is a domestic tragedy, to be sure, but, in the complex interlacings of public and private histories of a colonial society, it also becomes an allegory of a people's grief.

In this parochial, lovingly rendered world, it is no longer possible to disentangle family feuds, hauntings and buried terrors from a wider politics that blights and shrivels lives. The scent of rain or earth or hair in this atmospheric book is threaded with the smell of injustice. It is a working-class, Republican version of Irish Gothic, which is similarly full of domestic violence, festering secrets, the return of the repressed. Like such Gothic tales, this novel is on the cusp between past and present, aware that a past which has poisoned the present might also, suitably reconstructed, help to repair it.

How salvageable that past actually is, or how likely it is to fragment into fantasy, is one of Deane's most pressing preoccupations—both here and in his attempt, as general editor of the *Field Day Anthology of Irish Writing,* to coax some coherence from the ruptured traditions of his country's literature.

Of all genres, autobiography seems the most confident that the past can be recuperated; but that form is crossed here with a fiction that threatens to undermine its self-assurance. And if myth and history interbreed here, they do so with a vengeance in the Northern Ireland that is the book's subject.

It is part of Deane's artistic triumph that *Reading in the Dark* is at once an act of loving fidelity to the social landscapes of his childhood and a hard-headed refusal to idealise them. Its sombre depth is laced with a wry humour.

The book is least successful in its cuffing of autobiographical material into fictional shape: we don't see the political betrayals at stake, we don't know the characters involved, so that for the hero's grandfather to have arranged the execution of his uncle is a more gripping matter for him than it is for us. The past that determines the tale is too notional, as autobiography gets the edge over imaginative recreation.

Yet the past, after all, is what we are made of; and in the Derry and Donegal of this book it is literally coeval with the present, strewing the contemporary landscape in the form of ruins. Seamus Deane, perhaps Ireland's finest literary critic, is also a well-known socialist Republican, and reading this novel one can already hear the grinding of the literary Unionist knives. Isn't this just the sort of nostalgic, superstitious, violence-ridden stuff one would expect from a Bogside bard?

In fact, *Reading in the Dark* takes the hackneyed mode of childhood remembrance and wrings from it a literary masterpiece, couching its story in a prose at once serviceable and beautifully poetic. A work of adroit artistry, it is also the kind of story one can imagine the plain people of Derry eagerly devouring. A work with the sophistication of a John Banville might thus have the potential readership of a Maeve Binchy.

Julia O'Faolain (review date 27 September 1996)

SOURCE: "The Boy Who Wanted to Know," in *Times Literary Supplement,* No. 4878, September 27, 1996, p. 22.

[*In the following review, O'Faolain identifies the narrative value of folktales in* Reading in the Dark *as compromising the novel's realism.*]

This first novel by the poet Seamus Deane has the focused

compression of poetry. Short sections—lots of white paper here—present carefully chosen incidents whose meanings expand into complexity as the narrative gathers momentum.

Reading in the Dark is, on one level, an optimistic tale. As an Irish *Bildungsroman,* confronting familiar hurdles, it follows a Catholic Derry boy through his childhood in the 1940s to the great day when he can tell his family that he's got his degree: "a First". It is a first for the family, too, and the father, an electrician's mate who "would have loved to have been educated", waits hours for his son to come boozily in the door with the news. Remorse at seeing his father's face makes the boy relinquish a teasing plan to pretend failure. He says at once, "I got it." His father smiles, and the bitter-sweet moment could be the climax of a simpler novel. But this family's emotional life is strangled.

The hidden side of their story emerges slowly, as what starts out like a classic account of a bright working-class boy's growing to consciousness, joining the middle class and being detribalized, reveals a darker dimension. Political treachery has leached into private experience, and the boy's relations with his mother have been damaged, for, far from being the wan, positive but passive mother-figure so familiar in Irish fiction, she turns out to be an Eve who carries and transmits a taint.

This is not the only reversal of expectancy. But then, reversals are normal in a place where a teacher's pep talk warns pupils that each year is bringing them "closer to entering a world of wrong, insult, injury, unemployment, a world where the unjust hold power and the ignorant rule". Small wonder in such a context—Catholic Derry, 1948—that the boy who wants to know more than his siblings finds himself reaping rue. Knowledge does not empower, and, with or without a dark family secret, life for Deane's unnamed hero was never going to be easy. Frustration has half-deranged his community, including the priests who teach him and the policemen who have him and his mates always in their bad books. Two chilling sequences feature bullies from these corps. Running their gauntlet clearly took the sort of resourcefulness which turns woodcutters' sons into ogre-killers.

The first incident shows a priest setting traps for his pupils, while allocating numbers of canestrokes for all likely contingencies. "Every morning, at nine o'clock sharp, he came rushing into the room his soutane swishing, his face reddened as if in anger, his features oddly calm." Soon he claims to "owe" one boy eighty-four strokes.

This is realism. Pedagogic sadism was widespread in the Catholic Ireland of those years. I know this because my father wrote about it in a Dublin paper, and the seething letters he received from all over the country included some about boys being hospitalized. Priests and those they appointed were untouchable then.

So the "black uniforms", as one character calls them, were indeed ogres. But the encounter with Police Sergeant Burke is pleasing, because our hero gets the better of him. Burke, knowing the family shame—a relative was a police informer—forces the boy to ride in the police car, so that people will think him too an informer. The boy is then ostracized by all, until, in desperation, he turns to the bishop. He is sincerely eager, he claims, to beg Burke's pardon for throwing a stone at his car. But how can he? If he's seen entering the police station, people will think he's informing. The bishop sends a priest with him to see Burke. This manoeuvre is observed and, later, the boy tells his mates that the priest was scolding Burke for "his lies about me. I think Burke's going to be excommunicated. . . ." The boy is welcomed back to the community. The occasion is a rite of passage.

What shows through this incident like a watermark is its use of folk-tale elements, both formal and thematic. The past may be "blood under the bridge", but its after-effects need neutralizing if you belong to a family with a blight on it. This wisdom, like the two tricks—Burke's and the boy's—belong to the mental world of the yarns which Deane's characters enjoy telling each other. His novel is pod-full of these, and it is clear that their use is therapeutic in the stricken Derry community where few things can be said clearly. Ghost and fairy lore is a useful source of metaphor when you need to tell children why one man was struck dumb, others disappeared, and their own mother is unhinged. The outcome of score-settling and murder is falsified memory.

So the folk-tale works credibly here. By contrast, there is some Yeatsian hokum in the invocation of the saga heroes who might rise "from their thousand-year sleep to make final war on the English". As though registering this, the prose cringes into cliché when Deane's nameless—universal?—protagonist looks out from the old heroes' fort to "where cottage lights twinkled, as distant as stars".

Throughout, the novel counterpoints old and new. Even on its last page, armoured trucks are followed past the house by a gypsy boy riding his horse bareback out of an almost lost past. This and the substitution in the "haunted" mother's mind of her old obsession by thoughts of her newly dead husband, provide a resolution which would probably work better in a poem. The effect here, though seductive, diminishes the vigour of the realism which becomes doubly distanced by being seen both through the lens of memory and those of a writer as manipulative as Seamus Deane. There are, as I hope I have indicated, beautifully told passages in

this intelligent book. Its realism is impeccable, but our collusion with the story is interrupted a little too often by authorial nudges, inviting us to savour yet another artful effect.

Derek Hand (review date Spring 1997)

SOURCE: "The Endless Possibilities of Ordinary Life," in *Irish Literary Supplement*, Vol. 16, No. 1, Spring, 1997, pp. 19-20.

[*In the following review, Hand connects the narrative perspective of* Reading in the Dark *to aspects of Deane's critical career.*]

It is inevitable that a first novel by an author with a well established academic and critical career will be approached—certainly by other critics and academics—with the lumbering baggage of various expectations and preconceptions of what will be found there. This is very much so with Seamus Deane's **Reading in the Dark**. One reason for this is that the novel has been a long time coming—in a biographical note in **The Field Day Anthology of Irish Writing** published in 1991, **Reading in the Dark** was listed as having been published the previous year.

Whatever the explanation for such a delay—and six years is a long time—these preconceptions and expectations cannot be said to be based solely on a casual curiosity engendered by an overly long gestation period. Rather they are bound up with a knowledge of Deane's own substantial critical output as one of Ireland's foremost commentator on Irish literature and culture. And, at a time when that culture and literature are being subjected to various conflicting readings and interpretations in an ongoing act of definition and redefinition of Ireland and Irishness, it is understandable why there should be so much interest in this first novel.

It is as a part of this wider quarrel that the very minor controversy surrounding **Reading in the Dark** when it is was short-listed for the 1996 Booker Prize can best be appreciated. Some commentators protested that a work so autobiographical could not be, and should not be, allowed into a competition for fiction. It was, and is, a spurious argument. **Reading in the Dark** is a novel; in terms of structure, plot and characterization it reads like a novel and therefore should be treated accordingly. And, anyway, autobiography is not so much about past fact and reality as about an act of creating the self in the present. It too, then, is fiction and it is naive to think otherwise.

Basically some people do not agree with Seamus Deane's

interpretation and analysis of the "matter of Ireland." One needs only to think of the barrage of criticism which met the publication of *The Field Day Anthology of Irish Writing* of which Deane was General Editor. Some of the criticism, while actually being fair, was used as a means of diverting attention away from the very real achievements of the project. It was a situation, as they say, where an attempt was made to throw the baby out with the bath water. Sadly, it was an attempt that for all intents and purposes succeeded.

Similarly with *Reading in the Dark,* and the spurious argument about the different claims of fiction and autobiography: rather than do the difficult thing and deal with the book as it is and not as one expected it to be, the easy option is preferred and diversionary tactics employed. Happily, in this instance, these begrudging commentators were in the minority and, though the novel did not win the Booker Prize, it has been well received critically and commercially.

Happily, too, *Reading in the Dark* confounds any such presumptions and presuppositions we may have had of it being merely a continuation in fictional terms of Deane's critical stance and viewpoint. Deane does not intentionally attempt to tell the "big" story of Ireland or the north of Ireland; rather he focuses on a "small" story through which larger issues may be viewed. At this point it is worth saying that the novel is not an overtly self-reflexive, highly self-conscious and knowing fiction that others, like John Banville for example, might engage in. This work does not bend character and situation to some abstract idea or end; instead it foregrounds the story it has to tell, thus allowing the reader to engage in an act of interpretation.

Reading in the Dark tells the story of how the young unnamed narrator growing up in Derry in the 1940s and 1950s pieces together a mysterious secret that quite literally haunts his family. But this secret—this story—is not the only story that the young boy meets with: the world presented in this book is made up of stories, each one vying for the boy's attention. Early on he learns a valuable lesson about stories and their worth. The first novel he reads is *The Shan Van Vocht* and it thrills him with its love affairs and rebellions and deeds of daring do:

> I'd ... lie there ... re-imagining all I had read, the various ways the plot might unravel, the novel opening into endless possibilities in the dark.

However, in school his teacher reads out a classmate's essay which describes in detail a typical evening at home: the mother laying out the dinner things, the sound of the kettle and the ticking of the clock.

This is a revelation for our narrator, and he is embarrassed because his own work had been full of big dictionary words that allowed him to tell of places found only in his novel: "I'd never thought such stuff was worth writing about. It was ordinary life." Now it is the ordinary and the everyday—his own life and his family's story—which possesses endless possibilities.

In recent times there have been a number of books dealing with childhood: Patrick McCabe's *The Butcher Boy* and Roddy Doyle's *Paddy Clarke Ha Ha Ha* for instance. Deane's work is different from these in that the narrator's perspective is that of looking back from the vantage point of the present, thus permitting a certain depth and substance that is lacking in Roddy Doyle's book, for example. It is this aspect of the novel that allows a connection to be made between this work and Deane's critical career. For, in a way, what we are presented with is "A Portrait of the Critic as a Young Man" or "A Portrait of the Critic as a Young Reader."

The world is full of signs and wonders—stories—to be read and interpreted. Be it the world around him, the ordinary world, or the world of myth and legend and song: all need to be made sense of. An ardent desire for knowledge drives the young narrator in his search for the key that will unlock the family secret. It is desire common to all critics and scholars and, indeed, Deane in his poem, **"Scholar I"** admits: "Is there a book that I / Would not burn for the truth?"

The problem is that real life and the ordinary world are fraught with many difficulties, not least of which is that in the real world real people feel real pain. Deane shows that an act of criticism and/or interpretation never exists in a vacuum, that there are very serious and real consequences to engaging in such acts. In short, the story he tells highlights the human dimension to critical acts.

Of course, this does not mean that such knowledge should not be striven for; it must be, but the human cost must be acknowledged also. One presumes that is a lesson the author himself has learnt, and it is one we can all learn from in a time when the stakes are very high indeed in terms of Irish literary and cultural criticism.

Though this family secret, unspoken yet frighteningly palpable, permeates everything and impacts upon everyone in the novel, it does not follow that *Reading in the Dark* is a bleak book. There are many wonderful scenes of growing up in Derry, playing in Grianan Fort, going to the pictures, the facts of life. There is a chapter, "Maths Class," which is perfectly executed and possesses an underlying rhythm that reads like music. Another chapter, "Roses," captures beautifully the frustration of youth and the tragic excesses youth will go to in an effort to express that frustration.

It is the central plot of a slowly unraveling mystery, however, which gives the novel a certain edge, allowing an at times humorous "coming to consciousness" tale combined successfully with a story of deadly seriousness.

It is certainly a magnificent first novel, assured and confident and well worth a wait of six years. It being so personal a story, though, one wonders if Seamus Deane has the ability or the inclination to craft another novel. One hopes that he has.

Josephine Humphreys (review date 4 May 1997)

SOURCE: "Ghosts," in *The New York Times Book Review,* Vol. 102, May 4, 1997, p. 6.

[*In the following review, Humphreys summarizes the theme and plot of* Reading in the Dark, *praising the characterizations and "animated" descriptions of inanimate objects.*]

Two memories rise, ominous as thunder on a clear day, in the opening pages of this first novel by the poet Seamus Deane. The narrator, an unnamed young man looking back on his childhood in Northern Ireland, remembers climbing the stair when he was 5. His mother had just started down, and they were about to meet on the landing when suddenly she said. "Don't move." He could see nothing between them except the window, where the Derry cathedral seemed to hang against the sky. But she saw more. "There's somebody there. Somebody unhappy. Go back down the stairs, son." And although later she reassured him there had been no ghost, "Just your old mother with her nerves," he found her crying near the kitchen stove. The child was left excited and shaken, alert to every tick and glimmer in the house—and to the mystery of his mother. "We were haunted!" he realized.

In language strikingly lucid and scenes fired by a spare, aching passion, **Reading in the Dark** combines the intimacy of a memoir with the suspense of a detective story. Mother has a secret; but so do Father, Grandfather, Aunt Kate, Crazy Joe the local oddball and almost everyone else in the squalid, rubble-strewn town of Derry. A priest tells a cryptic tale of murder, a policeman hints at untold intrigue. Even something as innocent as a circus, the boy's second early memory, suggests how hard it is going to be for a child like this one, with a great capacity for trust and love, to recognize in the world around him exactly what is lovable and trustable.

At the circus with his brother Liam, he's dazzled by Mr. Bamboozelem, the magician in high boots and red satin coattails who pulls rabbits and rings from thin air only to make them vanish again. "When everything had stopped disappearing, he smiled at us behind his great mustache, swelled his candystripe belly, tipped his top hat, flicked his coat of flame and disappeared in a cloud of smoke and a bang that made us jump a foot in the air." Only the magician's mustache remains, hanging for an instant in the darkness before it, too, fades away. Liam scoffs; it's a trapdoor trick, he says, and the clown who seems to be wiping away a real tear is only part of the act. But the boy is unconvinced. "Was Mr. Bamboozelem all right?" he worries. "Everyone was laughing and clapping but I felt uneasy. How could they all be so sure?"

As the title implies, this novel is about ways of knowing. How can truth be apprehended under conditions of little light? This particular boy, unlike his tough brother, needs a clear picture of how things really are. Carefully he watches not only his parents but the world at large for hints and clues. But clarity is rare in Northern Ireland in the 1940's and 50's. Truth is no more likely to come from mother and father than from priest and policeman. A chum may be an informer. People disappear. Derry itself is a hellish town where wild bonfires are a relief from the cold gray landscape, and the major entertainment is an organized massacre of rats at the bomb shelter ruins. Landmarks are the slaughterhouse, with its sound of squealing hogs, and the burned distillery where in 1922 the boy's uncle, an Irish Republican Army gunman, was last seen on the parapet moments before the place blew up, casting Uncle Eddie, it is said, into "that rosy glow of exploding whisky."

Little hope is offered by church or school; one priest teaches by ridicule while another prefers insult. And always there is the danger of the police. At 8 the boy is beaten by a sergeant; four years later the same sergeant frames him as an informer. When friends and family turn away from him, life becomes a daily torture. In desperation he concocts a scheme to pit the clergy against the police and reclaim his reputation. Clever deception becomes his own device, and he learns to survive the way his father, a boxer turned electrician's assistant, did before him.

Amazingly, however, given the bleak poverty and violence of Derry, **Reading in the Dark** is a novel suffused with magical loveliness. Beyond the town is a green zone of countryside into which children may escape, wander through an ancient fort, look down on the seacoast. Even richer is the web of Irish legend and folklore woven through every aspect of daily life, transforming the mundane into something spine-tingling and enigmatic, sometimes grotesque but never dull. At night in bed, the boy reads of shadowy romantic figures, wind and fire, heroes of the Irish rebellion. He hears stories of children who change sex, and of a beautiful woman who seduces a young man on the eve of his wedding, then suddenly vanishes from his arms, leaving him with a smoking crotch and no language.

One day in school a teacher reads aloud the essay of a classmate, a simple description of a country supper: blue-and-white jug, slab of butter with the shape of a swan pressed into it. "It was ordinary life—no rebellions or love affairs or dangerous flights across the hills at night. And yet I kept remembering that mother and son waiting in the Dutch interior of that essay, with the jug of milk and the butter on the table, while behind and above them were those wispy, shawly figures from the rebellion, sibilant above the great fire and below the aching, high wind." To accurately read life, to know, must require a combination of two visions, the plain-seeing with the imaginative. If there is truth to be found in myth, there is also magic in real things.

And it's the specificity of real things that most enchants him—a candle "stubby in its thick drapery of wax," the linoleum pattern "polished away to the point where it had the look of a faint memory," "a long, chill pistol, blue-black and heavy." In fact, there seem to be no inanimate objects; everything is charged with energy and significance. This is the real "haunting" of the novel: an inspirited, animated reality. A boiler bursts, angry and hissing; a pond has the look of "sexual velveteen." Chimneys breathe, shadows watch, ice snores. Odors have a powerful exactness, from the acrid smell of diphtheria and the whiff of soap on his dead sister's pillow to "the police smell" that sometimes wakes him from sleep, leaving him breathless and panicky.

Increasingly, the boy becomes obsessed with uncovering the truth about his uncle's disappearance, and the more he learns, the more tangled the mystery grows. If the novel has a weakness, it is in the management of this intricate plot of betrayal and error and secrecy; yet the very cumbersomeness of truth is one of the lessons of **Reading in the Dark**. The question of Uncle Eddie's fate is incidental, anyway, to a more crucial question: how does a boy preserve his own innocence?

Answers come in bits and pieces, from unexpected quarters—from the very sources of deception. **Reading in the Dark** suggests that while there are deep flaws in the church, the law and the family, all have, a core of reliability. So when Father Regan reminds his class that "our transient life, no matter how scarred, how broken, how miserable it may be, is also God's miracle and gift," he delivers a nugget of truth. With a hand raised in blessing over the boys who will soon enter "a world where the unjust hold power and the ignorant rule," the priest assures them of an inner peace that everyone can find, "Hold to that; it is what your childish innocence once was and what your adult

maturity must become. Hold to that, I bless you all." It is a genuine blessing, trustable.

"Hauntings are, in their way, very specific. Everything has to be exact, even the vaguenesses," the boy says when he has finally hunted down all the specifics to reveal the exact truth at last. The revelation brings him no bursting dawn, only an attenuated half-light. Gunfire will erupt again in the streets of Derry and the Troubles will return. In the end the cathedral will still hang in the window, the mother will descend the stairs and truths arduously unearthed will slowly begin to be reburied. But, for Seamus Deane's readers, life has been illuminated, washed in an elegiac, graceful and forgiving light.

Richard Eder (review date 11 May 1997)

SOURCE: "Ghost Story," in *Los Angeles Times*, May 11, 1997, p. 2.

[*In the following review, Eder comments on the function of family secrets in* Reading in the Dark, *highlighting the thematic significance of pivotal scenes.*]

It begins, puzzlingly, with a series of disconnected childhood memories from the 1940s in Derry, in Northern Ireland. The little boy's mother senses an invisible presence on the stair's landing and sobs inconsolably. An aunt tells a terribly frightening ghost story of a brother and a sister who drive their nanny mad by exchanging features—hair, eyes, smile, even gender—with each other.

The kindly, mournful father, a shipyard worker, takes the boy and his brother for a seaside walk and points out a patch of turf overhanging the cliff's edge that the birds seem to avoid. It is, he says, "the land of the disappeared."

Less mistily, there is his glimpse of a neighbor run over by a van, a policeman vomiting while getting the body out and, later, the inevitable neighborhood rumor that it was the police who were driving the van. There is a violent stand-off between the police and the Catholics on St. Patrick's Day, and fireworks and booming drums on the Protestant marching days.

There is the rough interrogation of the family after the boy sneaks a pistol out of his father's bureau and shows it to a friend. There is the mystery of why the father, whose long-vanished brother fought in the IRA, was not arrested for possessing the weapon.

These scenes and others make an initial blur, but it is the blur of a film developing. Gradually it takes on a fearful, unforgettable clarity. Northern Irish poet Seamus Deane devises as a fictional memoir **Reading in the Dark,** the web of legend, secrecy and obsession with betrayal that choked and still chokes the history of his country.

It is the story of a Catholic family and its beleaguered community. It looks back to the 1920s and the beginning of Irish partition and leads up into the 1970s. In a larger sense, it is a story of the intractability of civil division, the crippling, ineradicable energies of defeat and the twin curse of too much remembering and too much silence.

These are devastations, but **Reading in the Dark** evokes them not as rhetoric but as the moth holes and rotted-out pieces in the fabric of one family's life. We would not be so enthralled and moved if Deane had not evoked the life itself with so much humanity, delicacy and fierce wit. Yeats' "terrible beauty," a cliché by now, could have been waiting for this near-magical book to arrive.

The darkest devastation in the family is its secrets. The book begins with ghosts and mysteries as a 6- or 7-year-old might apprehend them. It continues with an obstinate search for answers when the same boy achieves the fearsome lucidity and utter lack of caution of a 12-year-old. The search takes him up to 19 and 20, when, knowing the answers, he begins to know the moral and intellectual ambiguity to which all answers lead.

The family secrets are interlocked. First is that Eddie, the father's brother, was executed by his IRA companions as an informer back in 1922. The second is that it was the wife's father—the boy's grandfather—who ordered the execution. The third is that Eddie was the wrong man; the fourth is the identity of the real informer. The grandfather, dying, blurts these things out as the boy sits with him.

There is a fifth secret and a sixth. But this is enough disclosure, considering the choking urgency a reader shares with the boy as he pieces together other scraps and clues over the next few years.

The damage that half-destroys the mother, a brave and loyal woman, and the father, a man of simplicity and kindness, is not so much the secrets themselves as the fact that he knows only the first of them and she comes to know them all. She cannot bring herself to tell him about the tragic error, her father's role or the rest of it, out of dread that it will destroy their marriage.

Her compunction condemns her husband to think of his brother as a traitor. Silence is the killer. It sends her into a two-year breakdown from which she never entirely recovers; in him, it nurtures a perpetual, leaching pain. The tragedy is both personal and historical—it leaves us wondering what other reading in the dark is being done at this moment by some 12-year-old in Bosnia, for instance.

The beauty of Deane's lament—as is true of Frank McCourt's Irish childhood memoir, *Angela's Ashes,* a lovely but smaller work—is that it is not told as such. The narrator speaks with all the vitality, the appetite for life and discovery and the pleasurable distractibility of his age. Those news shots of children playing soccer in some bombed-out ruin may spell tragedy, but the thunk of each kick is young nature's irrepressible high spirits.

Some of the book's high spirits go to depicting the classes at the boy's school, taught by priests. They are arrogant and sarcastic; they use wit, wordplay and the unconditional authority they possessed back in the 1950s to prevail over their charges. It is a familiar kind of scene by now, going back at least to the whiplash classroom thundering in Joyce's *Portrait of the Artist as a Young Man* and reworked by Catholic writers ever since.

There is a difference here. For one thing, the boys are not cowed. They stand their ground and score, an occasional point—one, for example, in a wonderfully kinked duel in algebra class and another in religion. It is as if they were enduring tennis instruction from a vastly superior player, victims of verbal smash-shots but growing in their own proficiency. For another thing, the priests are presented with complexity as well as wit.

There is a comic and touching scene in which the director of spiritual studies gives the boy his customary one-on-one sex talk. It is no penitential warning; the lesson is mild, in fact, and expounded in valiantly conscientious detail. The boy, about to meet a girlfriend for a real-life smooch, submits with patronizing glee and skips out as soon as he can. Yet:

> As I ran, I imagined Father Nugent hesitantly closing his door and looking at the armchairs on either side of the fire, now mute and emptied of all confidences in the whitened light of his lamp and the tall windows.

Deane gives a nuanced portrait, in fact, of the Catholic Church in Northern Ireland at mid-century. Belligerent and constricted, it played a role in both holding together and restraining the minority community. In the book's most complex and ingenious scene, in fact, the local bishop comes to the rescue of the boy who, through a mischance and the malice of the local police, finds himself labeled as a neighborhood informer. It is a brilliant upending of the police sergeant who engineers the rumor.

Bishop aside, the episode is pivotal. For a week or so, the boy is a pariah, not only among the neighbors but within his own family. The shock sets him on the long path of re-placing ghosts and mysteries with truth. It is more than the moment when a child begins to grow up. It is the moment in history when primal myth gives way to the clarity of tragedy.

Over the next half-dozen years, the boy achieves his tragic truth. As he does, there is one more pivot, one that elevates *Reading in the Dark* beyond brilliance. Looking at his mother and father grown old, he realizes that the truth that would ease them would also destroy them. From deliverer of secrets he grows up to become their guardian.

Robert Boyers (review date 19 May 1997)

SOURCE: "Identity and Diffidence," in *The New Republic*, Vol. 216, No. 20, May 19, 1997, pp. 33-6.

[*In the following review, Boyers traces the development of betrayal as the central theme of* Reading in the Dark, *explicating narrative implications about the political character of Northern Ireland.*]

Irish history is bad history. So says one character in Seamus Deane's first novel [*Reading in the Dark*], and no other character in the novel seems much inclined to deny it. In a land of "small places," as it is described here, people have too often made "big mistakes." They lie to themselves and to one another. They rely on old certainties when they might better have abandoned them. They carry around "stale" secrets and bitter resentments. Their courage is too often merely a willingness to absorb meaningless defeats and inflict pointless damage. For all their eloquence and their gift for storytelling, they are not, typically, much good at distinguishing truth from fiction, the past from the present. The language of feud and retribution, of shame and fatedness, is on every tongue.

Of course, clear-sighted Irish men and women can also see plenty to be proud of in their past, but all agree that the history of Northern Ireland contains every kind of motive for resentment, rage, and hopelessness. "The whole situation makes men evil," says one of Deane's priests, and "evil men make the whole situation." To live in a place like Derry in the 1940s and '50s, when Deane's novel is set, is to remember failed rebellions and to confront, day after day, British policemen whom one has learned to regard as intolerable, in their casual brutalities and in their unwelcome efforts at commiseration and intimacy. Most of what goes on in such a place has nothing to do with politics, as it happens, but always there is a sense of "the whole situation," and persons who might well have looked to themselves as the source of present difficulties are embittered and coarsened

by the long sense of injustice that they have had to bear. The priests speak, when they can, of "an inner peace nothing can reach" and "no insult can violate," but the Irish refuse to forget the "cruel birth" of their country, and they suffer their history like a perpetual humiliation.

Deane's novel is no polemic. It presents no case for or against his countrymen, no brief for a particular reading of Irish history. It is mainly the story of a boy's coming of age, and it is told mostly in very brief chapters with titles such as "Maths Class," "Crazy Joe," "The Facts of Life" and "Sergeant Burke." The chapters mostly cover minor events: the boy encounters and engages with family members and strangers, with schoolmates, priests, and teachers. He goes to classes, gets in and out of trouble, and generally behaves very much in the way we might expect of a boy in such a time and place. The sequence is strictly chronological, and incidents are often "necessary" only in the sense that they convey the flavor of the narrator's experience.

The novel is haunted by the story of a series of betrayals, a story revealed in bits and pieces picked out of fragmentary confessions and intimations. The betrayals are personal and political, and, though they have the power to corrupt lives in Deane's little world, they never take control of the narrative. The boy at the center of the novel makes what he can of the fragments, understanding dimly, then more clearly, that members of his own family are implicated in the various betrayals. At times he is angry and confused, at other times he is overwhelmed by pity and tenderness. Alert to the deceptions of priests, policemen, and politicians, he is properly skeptical of traditions and myths, but he entertains no serious possibility of reversing deep-rooted customs or assumptions. Blindness, like love or hate, is a condition that persists, no matter the inducements to see or to change.

A reader who comes to Deane's novel without substantial understanding of "the troubles" of Northern Ireland will learn little from the narrative. It refers, vaguely, to early struggles and uprisings, but it offers no hard information, and its ideas are rudimentary. Dramatic encounters are briefly recalled. People refer, occasionally, to protests "at the founding of the new state" or to retaliation for a particular injustice, but the encounters as recalled are not especially important in themselves. The IRA gunmen on a roof are no more comprehensible than the policemen who surround them. Riots are just events that happen, like the death of a child or the infidelity of a husband. If people sometimes behave in particular ways for particular reasons, they are rarely good reasons, and acknowledging them leads nowhere. "There was a belief" in this thing or that, in this cause or that dark necessity, but it does no one any good, apparently, to persist in the belief or to abandon it.

Deane tells the stories of people's lives with a crisp lyricism, though it is not always easy for a reader to remain interested in characters who have few thoughts and little inclination to open themselves to sharp sensory experiences. People are said to live in silence, to feel hopelessly separated from one another, "trapped," desiring routinely "to be free of the immediate pressures." The regret for missed opportunities darkens every consciousness. My Father? "He would have loved. . . ." My Grandfather? He "realized for sure the mistake he had made. . . ." My own life? "Rehearsing conversations I would never have." To make something of lives so committed to the desultory and unconsummated is a challenge, and Deane is not always up to it.

Lacking the will to analyze and the appetite for metaphysics or morals, Deane is content to set things down as if they spoke for themselves. But often they do not say much more than "failure" and "regret." Deane's people are so inured to the facts of their lives that they are almost constitutionally averse to development. To his credit, Deane resists the temptation to claim for these characters qualities that they do not possess, but too often we feel that they are important to him for reasons that he does not know how to share. The work sometimes reads more like a memoir than a novel, in that people and events matter only because they were actually a part of the narrator's experience.

As if alert to the prospect that Deane's book will seem to many readers thin, lacking in ideas and development, Seamus Heaney has praised it as "sudden" and compares it to Isaac Babel. But Deane's book is not "sudden" like a Babel story, and it is without many of the virtues that make a Babel story distinctive. Deane's irony, only occasionally in evidence, is broad, more an irony of circumstance than of voice. We do not find in Deane the internal conflict—as between the physical and spiritual—that seethes everywhere just beneath the surface in Babel. Deane knows and accepts his people and his place as they are; he does not allow what he knows to raise in him the self-doubt that gives such edge to Babel's laconic fictions.

In Deane's book, we have the material for moral inquiry, but the inquiry is not pursued. Still, there are passages of exceptional vitality. The boy sits through a memorable "facts of life" session with the school's spiritual director and is confounded by unfamiliar words and concepts. ("Ask him, you stupid shit, ask him, that's what you're here for, but I couldn't do anything except stare at him.") The mother suffers a breakdown and begins to communicate long-buried thoughts in a language strangely suggestive and obscure. ("Paradise was not far away when I died.") The voluble police sergeant confesses that he has beaten suspects he knew to be innocent, since not to have done so "would have looked strange." Throughout the novel, often in unlikely

places, things come suddenly to life. We remember that these people are more than the sum of their refusals and resignations. The mother, who absorbs several varieties of humiliation, is eloquent in repudiating the "dirty politics" of the British and the routine admonitions directed at those who struggle and resist. The father, hardworking and forlorn, is stubbornly faithful and resilient, and his aversion to posturing is so powerful that he chastises his young sons, on their knees in prayer, for making "a meal of it" and "trying to look like little saints."

Though **Reading in the Dark** is a first novel, Deane has been a literary presence since 1972, when he published the first of several volumes of poems. More recently he attracted attention as the general editor of **The Field Day Anthology of Irish Writing, 550-1990,** a massive three-volume compendium that presents not only an extraordinary range of literary voices but an abundance of "texts," from incendiary pamphlets to political speeches and historical accounts of public events. The controlling idea of the anthology appears to be that it is futile and misleading, at least in the case of the Irish, to isolate literature from politics. And Irish writers have been more or less unanimous in affirming this sense of their work. Yeats wrote that Irish writers were necessarily "maimed" by the "great hatred" that they carried around with them, and that his own meeting with the Fenian leader John O'Leary was singularly important in bringing "the poet in [to] the presence of his theme." Even those who did not choose to dwell on political themes, such as Joyce, were deeply absorbed with questions of marginality and identity. Deane himself has said that "the dominant public experience of my career has been the political crisis in Northern Ireland."

What is most remarkable about Deane's novel, then, is its refusal to permit the lives of its characters to be wholly swallowed by politics. Desultory their lives may be, but the presumptive causes are more various than any single-minded obsession with "the situation." And, of course, the novelist who, like Deane, immerses himself in various lives is always likely to discover occasions for verbal extravagance and merriment. Examples abound in this book. A classroom instructor in mathematics leaves an indelible picture of manic aggression and wit, unleashing a relentless verbal assault on the "brain dead" and "memory-less" among his charges. Is this a reflection of an inveterate Irish inferiority complex that can issue also in physical brutality and torture? Deane does not instruct us to read it that way. Does the instructor's emphasis on "corruption," and on the "evolutionary cul-de-sac" represented by especially recalcitrant students, not produce in them a resentment and defensiveness that can be fed and turned to violence by skillful demagogues? Deane charts no such consequence. His chapter on "Maths Class" offers, in place of diagnosis, the marvelous and the unaccountable, an expression of verbal playfulness that, in spite of his punitive sarcasm, requires neither justification nor relevance.

Where the political does take center stage in Deane's novel, moreover, it may well seem indistinguishable from the dissemination of propaganda. In 1956, an Anglican priest in British army uniform visits the boy's school as a part of the "battle for the hearts and minds of men" against the specter of world communism. The battle is represented by the genial priest as "a battle of faithlessness against faith; a battle of subtle wiles against manly freedom; a battle of cold atheism against the genial warmth of that Christian faith that has lit so many Irish hearts down the centuries." In the face of this battle, the disputes that divide Irish men and women are said to be "no more than family quarrels." A "traditional" society, whatever its internal dissensions, will wish to uphold "the eternal verities, says the priest; its people will know what is truly important to its survival and what is, in the long term, incidental.

The boys, of course, are mostly deaf to these appeals. Accustomed to hearing things that they know to be untrue, they rarely pay much attention to the particulars of the case presented to them. What they are likely to hear in the way of political discourse can be readily dismissed. It is encouraging to note how little susceptible to the priest's calculated pieties are the Irish schoolboys. Yet neither are these children on their way to anything approaching a mature grasp of political issues. At least Deane makes no such claim for them.

The best that can be said for the political intelligence of the adults in Deane's world is that occasionally they feel sorry for the troubles of others and reflect, in a spirit of resigned incomprehension, on the way that events elude their grasp. "It's a strange world," says the boy's father, moved by his own encounter with the father of a British soldier shot dead by an IRA sniper in the course of a street search. "I feel for him. Even if his son was one of those," the father says. No more comes from him on this score, no more is to be expected. His reality does not demand complexity of him, or a sustained reconsideration of old positions. The facts are what matter: the curfews, the street barricades, the armored trucks, "the avocado battle-dress of the soldiers," the intermittent gunshots, the routine humiliations of search, suspicion and seizure.

Does it matter that the story of these people is told from the perspective of a working-class boy? Deane wrings from the tale very little of the easy charm and naivete of the usual first-person child's narrative. No effort is made to simulate the familiar headlong rush of infant volubility, the childish locutions or fragmentary reticences intended to evoke innocence or embarrassment. Even where there is an immediacy in the language, in the contrivance of a retro-

spective present tense, the language belongs to an adult voice: "She would come down with me," he writes of his mother, "her heart jackhammering, and her breath quick . . . her face in a rictus of crying, but without tears."

Just so, where sequences are organized to make a point, we feel that it is a point elected by the adult novelist, who is at once inside the experience he narrates and well past it. "Was that house really a brothel?" the boy wonders, retreating from an open door and the painted face of "a young woman with tousled hair . . . What would it be like with her?" he wonders further, later whispering to himself the chastening words of St. Ignatius on the subject of mortal sin. But we stand always a little outside of this confusion, kept deliberately out by the poetic cadence and elevation of the writing, as in the following conclusion to the chapter called "Brothel":

> And still the vision of that young woman drifted there, vague one moment, the next vivid, reaching for me, unloosing the clasp of her skirt that rustled down as I leapt back and came forward, blurring inwardly, making my election.

More important than the boy's perspective is his working-class background, however little Deane wishes to make it an issue. There are, in this world, few places to hide from the indignities that the boy comes to expect. The occasional beatings or taunts administered by local policemen are matched by the assaults of street gangs and the bruising insults of others alert to every prospect of inflicting abuse. Growing up among unsophisticated persons nursing their own memories of want and hurt, the boy has little chance of escaping the vindictive parochialism of his community. Sometimes, in Deane's world, it seems that the worst thing a decent person can do is to talk to a policeman, as if to do so were to sell one's soul to the devil.

As in other Irish works focused on betrayal, the central term in the lexicon of abuse here is "informer." To inform is to forfeit any semblance of self-respect and to sever irreparably one's ties to the community. Forgivable in principle, the informer is in practice regarded as grotesque and out of bounds. When the father utters, about a member of his own family, the words "he was an informer," the son can only beg him to unsay them. "Say nothing," he repeats to himself. "Never say. Never say." Members of families thought to have contained an informer are tainted, carry a curse and may expect at any time to be punished for the unhappiness that has befallen them. To marry into such a family is not only ill-advised, it is a breaking of "sacred laws."

Like everything else in Deane's world, his people may regret certain attitudes and practices regarding informers, but the attitudes are too deeply rooted to deplore or to reform. When the boy finds himself suspected of informing on a few street toughs who had intended to rough him up, he finds no support, even within his own family. Never mind that he gave no information to the policemen who questioned him. Never mind that no movement or organization was at stake, no oath violated. "Have you no self-respect, no pride?" screams his mother.

> "Thank God my father's too ill to hear about this— the shame alone would finish him. A grandson of his going to the police!"

> "I didn't go to the police. I threw a stone at them."

> "Same thing in the circumstances. . . ."

Nor is the usually more generous father more understanding. "Why didn't I take a few punches . . .? Didn't I know what sort of people the police were? Had I no guts, no sense, no savvy, no shame?" Tempted to mark up the entire demand system of the community to "stupidity," the boy concludes that his father and all the others are "right" but "wrong too." To live in such a place, it seems, is to accept that wisdom consists in learning to tolerate what in any case will not change. If it is stupid to be battered for no good reason, and stupid to regard as "informing" what is no such thing, and stupid to live perpetually in fear of disapproval by persons who are ignorant and malicious, it is also stupid to pretend that one can get along in such a place without making substantial concessions to the reigning shibboleths and expectations.

Of course, **Reading in the Dark** is a novel. What would seem contradiction in another genre is here variousness and complexity. Deane need not tell us that he disapproves of much that passes for the facts of life in Derry for us to grasp their awfulness and their sometimes terrible vitality. And, for all the stubborn blindness in many of Deane's characters, there is a tenacity that can seem almost wonderful. The situation of Northern Ireland, discernible here only in fragments, allows for a complicated communal life, however crippling its myths. Deane's novel is driven by an impressive power of remembrance, and by a conviction that the proper business of the novelist is to make ordinary lives in their own way eventful, so that possibility exists even where fatality reigns.

Thomas McGonigle (review date 8 June 1997)

SOURCE: "Two Novels Look at Life in Northern Ireland," in *Chicago Tribune Books,* June 8, 1997, p. 8.

[*In the following review, McGonigle commends the narration of* Reading in the Dark.]

The North, Northern Ireland, Ulster, The Six Counties. How you name that part of Ireland that is part of the United Kingdom reveals your politics, religion and attitude toward what has been going on there since 1968 and, of course, how you think about the 800-year entanglement of Ireland and England.

There is no neutrality when it comes to this situation, and if I write about Seamus Deane's autobiographically driven novel, **Reading in the Dark,** as being a tremendously moving depiction of a sensitive Catholic boy's growing up in Derry, I have already given myself over to the Nationalist Republican side of the argument, because no Protestant, no Loyalist would ever refer to the city of Derry as anything but Londonderry. Such scrupulosity on my part might seem excessive, but it echoes that of Deane, one of those Irish writers who is engaged in the long project of trying to precisely and coldly define what it means to be Irish, thus freeing Irish men and women from the encrusting sentimentality that attaches itself to every aspect of Irish life.

Lois Gould's novel *No Brakes,* while outwardly a worldly wise and hip romp of a mock thriller set during a three day vintage car rally in Northern Ireland within the last few years of The Troubles is actually of a much older tradition in Irish life: A foreign writer goes to Ireland and by opportunistically setting a novel there is able to carry on about how the Irish are peculiar and picaresque, the very notion contemporary Irish writers such as Aldan Higgins, Nuala Ni Dhomhnaill, Francis Stuart and Deane himself have been trying to dispel.

A terrible family secret—one that is both public and private and that involves the Irish Republican Army—is at the heart of **Reading in the Dark.** Despite the skill with which Deane constructs the unfolding of the secret, the reader is far more impressed by the mind of the unnamed narrator, which remains as an exemplar of measured reflection and admirable reticence.

Tracing what it was like to be an intelligent boy in Derry from 1945 until the late 1950s, Deane avoids every cliche of what is often presented as Irish life. There is a complexity to the family life and an acceptance of the ordinary pain that that entails—agonizing illness, death and the slow, sure withering of age.

Like an alcoholic who never forgets his first drink, the bookish narrator has not forgotten the experience and consequences of reading, in the dark, his first novel, *The Shan Van Vocht,* a highly romantic story set during the rebellion of 1798. Later in school, the narrator's English teacher reads a simple, descriptive, model essay about ordinary country life, and the narrator remembers:

> I felt embarrassed because my own essay had been full of long and strange words I had found in the dictionary—'cerulean,' 'azure,' 'phantasm' and 'implacable'—all of them describing skies and seas I had seen only with the Ann of the novel. I'd never thought such stuff was worth writing about. It was ordinary life— no rebellions or love affairs or dangerous flights across the hills at night. And yet I kept remembering that mother and son waiting in the Dutch interior of that essay, with the jug of milk and the butter on the table, while behind and above them were those wispy, shawly figures from the rebellion, sibilant above the great fire and below the aching, high wind.

. . . ***Reading in the Dark*** is proof that it is still possible to find words to precisely language ordinary human life, a heroic act in this degraded moment of human history.

Edward Conlon (review date 8 September 1997)

SOURCE: "Violent Griefs and Seductive Hopes," in *The New Leader,* Vol. LXXX, No. 14, September 8, 1997, pp. 16-17 .

[*In the following review, Conlon compares the autobiographical elements of* Reading in the Dark *to those of Frank McCourt's* Angela's Ashes, *finding Deane's novel representative of a more general Irish identity than McCourt's.*]

The word "mystery" derives from a Greek term for someone who kept his mouth shut: an initiate into the sacred rites and transcendent experiences of the ancient world. To outsiders, such individuals were distinguished by their refusal to speak of their secrets. So a mystery became what we don't understand, whether in the secular realm or the holy. Both are explored in ***Reading in the Dark*** a first novel about an Irish childhood by the eminent scholar and critic Seamus Deane.

As with many first novels, generous helpings of autobiographical material not only lend an emotional warmth and weight to Deane's book but invite speculation concerning its degree of factual content. This being the case, it may be read as a kind of fraternal twin to Frank McCourt's *Angela's Ashes,* a memoir, for all its awful and hilarious candor, related with the somewhat suspect panache of the raconteur. The two authors have had long careers as teachers. Their successes with the general reader have been late (Dean is almost 60 years old, and McCourt is over 60) and

sudden: *Angela's Ashes* is a bestseller; ***Reading in the Dark*** was shortlisted for Britain's Booker Prize. And the stories have obvious commonalities beginning with their hoarily familiar backdrops (church and pub in one, church and the Irish Republican Army in the other). In each, the shapeliness of fiction and the rude force of fact combine to potent effect.

Yet McCourt's memoir about the viciously circular odyssey of his early life in the slums of Brooklyn and Limerick has the feel of singularity. His family was dysfunctional in a way that goes beyond jargon (it could not even feed its children). His chronicle is about the exceptional, about failure and misfortune and survival that are extraordinary, and largely self-wrought. Its terrors and delights have the consoling remoteness of legend. A progressive might argue that the lack of condoms, penicillin and Alcoholics Anonymous is all that stood between the McCourts and stability, but the book exhibits a surpassing conviction that character and fate were the true agents of destiny for them. *Angela's Ashes* is bardic and vaudevillian, stage Irish in both senses, recalling Brendan Behan and J. P. Donleavy as much as Peter O'Toole and Richard Harris.

Deane's nameless narrator on the other hand, is the transparently ordinary every child of literature, a watcher and listener, self-revealing primarily through and against his revelations of others. His is the story of stories: of history, of ghosts and of family secrets. It covers the public epic of the Irish struggle, with its slogans and rebel songs, and the profoundly articulate silences of a family whose martyrs and traitors evade easy judgment. The tales are not so much what you tell, or what you do; they define who you are.

Deane was born in Derry in 1940, a period of orderly oppression between the civil wars of his parents' generation and the continuing Troubles. His narrator's coming of age is ironically undercut by the recognition that progress, personal or national, is both an honorable ambition and a fool's desire. The forward march of time brings less the liberation of adulthood than a deepening immersion into a "haunted forever." The border between past and present and between good people and bad, seems as arbitrary and penetrable as that between the Irish Republic and the North. What happened to the McCourts happened only to the McCourts but what happens to the characters in Deane's book happens to everyone in the neighborhood, and keeps on happening

Reading in the Dark gathers little episodes as if they were tiles in a mosaic to create an image of a child's life in a family and a country where division is the norm. But for Deane the opposition of Catholic and Protestant is less significant, and less interesting, than the tensions between forgiveness and forgetting, memory and myth. The narrator's family is working class, Catholic, large and loving, a sturdy vessel seemingly able to withstand the upsets and losses they encounter.

The disappearance of two uncles—his father's brother, his mother's sister's husband—adds a note of color and mystery to family conversations, but to him as a child the vanished uncles are quaintly folkloric figures. The similarity of their supposed exits (both are suspected of having gone to Chicago) foreshadows a link between their fates, as well as a failure of the imagination on his parents' part, and perhaps the failure of stories themselves as a power to explain and protect, tame and pay tribute to an unruly past. Something has to face the past, and since it can't be the family, the stories must try. As Deane has written of Seamus Heaney, "writing has itself become a form of guilt and a form of expiation from it."

The narrator learns as he grows older not only what his parents sought to keep from him but what they kept from each other, out of kindness and guilt, and the potency and terrible burden of secrets that travel through generations like a curse. Deane describes their toll on his mother with heartbreaking tact: "She cried for weeks, then months. A summer passed in a nausea of light, and we took turns at the cooking and shopping. . . ." His mother observes, when she later recovers, that "people in small places make big mistakes. Not bigger than the mistakes of other people. But there is less room for big mistakes in small places."

There are wonderful set pieces of familiar scenes, like the narrator's sit-down with a priest to learn the facts of life. It begins with the metaphysical preamble ("First, the life-is-a-mystery bit . . . ") and moves on to the anatomical particulars, leaving him to wonder: "Do you have to know Latin to do this? Does He say to Her, 'Here you are. This is from the Latin for throw or send.'" Typical boy and archetypal moment are rendered with an unforced freshness that rescues the scene from cliché: "What I had heard was certainly improbable. It sounded like a feat of precision engineering, one which I couldn't associate with what the church called lust, which seemed wild, fierce, devil-may-care, like eating and drinking together while dancing to music on the top of the table." The book has many similar moments of quiet comedy and casual poetry that heighten and relieve the dark drama of historical reckoning.

They are also essential because the mystery in the plot, although highly satisfying, is unpacked a little too soon and a little too neatly; the narrator still has to tug at loose ends after the curtain has already been torn open. Eventually, it becomes clear that for the author the mystery of what happened is secondary, subsumed by the mystery of why it did. We never get more than a partial explanation, but this must

suffice: It allows the truthful stories and the useful, protective ones to compete in shaping a past that has a defining grasp on the present.

Deane is persuaded that being Irish is a very specific way of being human, one that permits the determined to have the last laugh, no matter who the joke is on. For him the question is less whether Ireland will ever be free than whether the Irish will be free of Ireland, with its violent hopes and seductive griefs. *Reading in the Dark*'s answer, in its confession of sins, betrayal of secrets and outpouring of songs, is—not so sadly—that no one can say yet.

Eamon Hughes (review date Fall 1997)

SOURCE: "Tradition and Modernity," in *Irish Literary Supplement,* Vol. 16, No. 2, Fall, 1997, p. 21.

[*In the following review, Hughes addresses the ambiguities he finds in Deane's definition of modernity in* Strange Country.]

Taking Burke's *Reflections on the Revolution in France* as his "foundational text," Seamus Deane examines the "contrast and contest between tradition and modernity" which extends through and beyond the Irish nineteenth century. This discourse appears in a number of oppositional pairings—culture and economics, the national and the rational, speech and print, Ireland and England—and issues in the nineteenth century in "a narrative of strangeness" about Ireland because Ireland cannot be absorbed into a normalising narrative of progress and economic development.

Moving from Burke to Flann O'Brien, Deane's concern is with the way in which writers have negotiated between oppositions with the aim of destabilizing stereotypical ascriptions. The theoretical co-ordinates of *Strange Country* are, then, broadly deconstructive with a Foucaultian sense of discourse as a series of negotiations rather than a stable position. Thus Burke's defence of tradition is part of the anti-revolutionary thrust of his work, and yet, with regard to Ireland, that defence of tradition becomes revolutionary. Thus, Ireland's "strangeness" is both a cause and an effect of the way in which it is treated by Britain and can then be taken as both a sign of dependency by the English and as a sign of independence by the Irish nationalist. Either way it remains discursively locked in.

Deane pursues his argument through a variety of authors, texts and topics stretching from Edgeworth to Flann O'Brien and taking in *inter alia* Mangan, Mitchel, Yeats's "The Second Coming," Synge's *Playboy,* Irish typefaces and revisionism. Deane, it goes without saying, is a powerful and shrewd critic with whom it is at times a pleasure to agree, and an equal pleasure to disagree when in the face of his persuasive power one is forced to rethink. His readings, to take just a few examples, of Mangan, of Yeats's "The Second Coming" and of Flann O'Brien are therefore all to be recommended.

Of the questions that the book raises, Deane's own position is probably the most important, partly because the broadly deconstructive force of the book is destabilizing of position and partly because of its lack of acknowledgement that it participates in the very discourses which it addresses. As a lecture series the book emerges from speech into print. Deane is in the position of the rational intellectual translating the strangeness of Ireland to an English audience; and finally he is just as much subject to his question about whether an impartial spectator position is available as the revisionist historians he attacks in the final pages.

Now, I am not asking for Deane to have produced a set of lectures which took their own form and occasion as their subject matter but this absence of self-reflexivity is of a piece with the absence of definitions of the key terms of the book. To understand Deane's position we need to understand how he defines tradition and modernity. In regard to the former, Deane seems to accept Burke's sense of tradition, especially as his definition of a "foundational text" ("one that allows . . . for a reading of a national literature in such a manner that even chronologically prior texts can be annexed by it into a narrative that will ascribe to them a preparatory role in the ultimate completion of that narrative's plot") is so reminiscent of T. S. Eliot's definition of "tradition." But if Deane accepts Burkean "tradition," there is a curious lack of definition of "modernity."

Deane is right that we need to be wary of accepting modernity uncritically, but that wariness needs to be informed. "Modernity" for Deane is associated with global capital and distinct from modernism and modernization, but these implicit definitions beg numerous questions. Is nationalism to be seen (as has traditionally been the case) as anti-modern, or as itself part of modernity; Benedict Anderson's association of nationalism with the technologies of print and time defines nationalism as a phenomenon of modernity which asserts a claim to be traditional. Does "modernity" have an aesthetic aspect; if so then what Deane has to say about the difficulties of representing Ireland may be better understood not as difficulties with existing representational modes but as modern forms of representation.

Alternatively, modernity may take in issues such as migration and urbanization about which Deane has only passing comments to make. Then again modernity may be under-

stood in its industrial, scientific and technological aspects, about which Deane is again silent. 1916 provides a moment at which these various aspects of modernity all occur. This is the year of book publication of *A Portrait*; the year of both the Easter Rising and the Somme; and the year in which Ireland adopted Greenwich Mean Time partly, at least, for the convenience of modern transport systems. At the end of reading **Strange Country** I know that I am to be wary of modernity, but which of its aspects I should be particularly wary of I am not sure.

I cannot therefore escape the sense that at some level Deane is himself a Burkean, concerned to maintain tradition as both concept and practice, in the face of a modernity which he still (however much he protests and deconstructs it) sees as somehow English. Certainly this would explain the puzzling absence of Shaw's *John Bull's Other Island* which explores exactly the same range of issues, stereotypes and ambiguities which make up Deane's discursive archive. Similarly, Deane's reading of Synge's *Playboy* is traditionalist; his sympathies are clearly with Christy whose "language of heroic solitude" he reads the play as celebrating.

Pegeen is then an anachronism confined to the zone of the sexual; but isn't hers the true language of heroic solitude within the play? Aren't her final grief-stricken words only an acknowledgement of the consequences of her opening words, spoken as she writes them in a letter, thereby connecting herself to the modern world of print and postal systems? She is the modern hero who having lost the traditional past must face into an unknowable future.

For all of its power in addressing the ambiguities of Ireland and in deconstructing stereotypes **Strange Country** is an oddly stifling book, buried under the weight of collapsing polarities with no way out. Modernity is not only about losing the past; it is also about losing any secure sense of the future. Traditional societies have a firm idea of what the future will hold because the future is for them always already prefigured within the past. Robbed of tradition by progress such societies now have no such prefigured future but rather must face the condition of futurity. This can be contrasted with Deane's interesting passages on boredom which relate back to his Foucaultian and deconstructive models in which everything always already is; futurity as promised by the modern is the sense that something else will be. He approaches this in his reading of Yeats's "The Second Coming," but seems to me to fail to realise that Yeats's desire for apocalypse is tempered by a sense that the future is unpredictable that it is the future which is the truly strange country.

Tom Deignan (review date 11 October 1997)

SOURCE: A review of *Reading in the Dark*, in *America*, Vol. 177, No. 10, October 11, 1997, p. 28.

[*In the following review, Deignan considers the thematic relations of the title of* Reading in the Dark, *noting the influence of Deane's poetic skills on his narrative technique.*]

Set in post-World War II Northern Ireland, Seamus Deane's debut novel, **Reading in the Dark** is a panoramic story of—what else?—family ties and political trauma. But more unusual than the novel's subject matter is the talent Deane, a Notre Dame professor and Derry native, brings to his task. Narrated by a nameless boy-turned-man, **Reading in the Dark** moves seamlessly from 1945 to 1971 through a series of highly poetic vignettes, stories and memories, introducing along the way a mysterious uncle who may have informed on his I.R.A.-connected relatives, a dying grandfather who may have ordered the uncle's execution and a tortured mother and father torn between illusion and reality, neither of which provides comfort or stability.

Following a youth spent learning to pronounce the names of the diseases that regularly befall family and friends, Deane's narrator grows up near Lorne Moor Road in Derry, a "city of bonfires." Without once mentioning his age, Deane portrays his narrator's maturation skillfully, his slow but sure comprehension of the myriad complexities and blunt truths of Catholic family life in Northern Ireland—the mythic landscape, the borderline poverty and the personalized politics. While mastering the unwritten codes that govern public life in the North for a Catholic "marked family," the narrator also begins to grasp the more intimate problems under his own roof. "So broken was my father's family," he comments, "that it felt to me like a catastrophe you could live with only if you kept it quiet, let it die down of its own accord like a dangerous fire."

Deane also hints at a (likely autobiographical) burgeoning interest in books and ideas. "For Christ's sake," the narrator's brother yells one night, "put off that light. You're not even reading, you blank gom." Of course, the narrator was reading, but of course he must also put out the light, "and lie there, the book still open, re-imagining all that I had read, the various ways the plot might unravel, the novel opening into endless possibilities in the dark." This is the strongest allusion Deane makes to the novel's title, but it is only one of many. Early on, Deane firmly establishes the themes and imagery that are the sturdy spine of this novel: darkness and light, illumination and ignorance, the dual nature of heat and fire, which can comfort but also burn and kill. The book's title, in this sense, becomes a metaphor for growing up and groping for certainty in this troubled, opaque landscape.

Deane also dips deeply into the timeless pool of Irish folklore, which also mystifies and unnerves his narrator. In one quiet, charged scene, the narrator and his brother are shown the "Field of the Disappeared" by their father, where "the souls of all those from the area who had disappeared, or had never had a Christian burial . . . collected three or four times a year—on St. Brigid's Day, on the festival of Samhain, on Christmas Day—to cry like birds and look down on the fields where they had been born. Any human who entered the field would suffer the same fate."

The narrator cannot resist approaching the field, drawing a stern warning from his father. "I don't believe all that," the narrator counters. But the daunting landscape is clearly as intimidating as it is alluring to him, as is evident in Deane's evocative prose.

This also reflects a larger theme pursued by Deane—the dual nature of existence. The life experience that comes with age is coveted, but also feared, since revelations can scar a life forever. In this sense, **Reading in the Dark** is a human detective story, as Deane's narrator stitches together hints and clues on his way to constructing some sort of tattered personal history. Learning what lies in the far reaches of one's family—as with one's country—is a necessity, but a frightening one, a process approached with equal doses of restlessness and regret.

Deane, who has written three short works of literary criticism (including the valuable **A Short History of Irish Literature**), has also published four books of poetry, a fact evident in his lush prose and sharp descriptions—there is "exploding whiskey," and the narrator's sister, coughing up blood, sounds like a "fox barking." That Deane can use such a fractured, poetic form to tell a story so lucidly, is a testament to the fact that **Reading in the Dark** marks the arrival of yet another talented Irish writer of fiction.

Thomas Flanagan (review date 23 October 1997)

SOURCE: "Family Secrets," in *The New York Review of Books*, Vol. XLIV, No. 16, October 23, 1997, pp. 54-5.

[*In the following review, Flanagan establishes the literary and cultural contexts of* Reading in the Dark, *comparing the novel to James Joyce's* A Portrait of the Artist as a Young Man *and providing a historical background to Derry and its environs.*]

On the stairs, there was a clear, plain silence.

It was a short staircase, fourteen steps in all, covered in lino from which the original pattern had been polished away to the point where it had the look of a faint memory. Eleven steps took you to the turn of the stairs where the cathedral and the sky always hung in the window frame. Three more steps took you on to the landing, about six feet long.

"Don't move," my mother said from the landing. "Don't cross that window."

I was on the tenth step, she was on the landing. I could have touched her. "There's something between us. A shadow. Don't move."

I had no intention. I was enthralled. But I could see no shadow.

"There's somebody there. Somebody unhappy. Go back down the stairs, son."

I retreated one step. "How'll you get down?"

"I'll stay a while and it will go away."

The opening page of Seamus Deane's *Reading in the Dark* suggests, in its deliberate spareness, qualities which in the unfolding will more fully reveal themselves. It is a childhood experience, but the voice speaking across the years is poised and literary—"a plain silence," "the look of a faint memory." We learn that it is a working-class house—the staircase brief, the lino pattern rubbed away. It is a house across which shadows fall that may be supernatural visitants. This is a culture, we soon learn, in which spirits are given a half-credulous, half-skeptical acceptance. "People with green eyes were close to the fairies, we were told; they were just there for a little while, looking for a human child they could take away."

The novel's short, crisp chapters, carefully dated and intricately linked by image, carry the narrator from childhood, in 1945, to the beginning phases, in 1968, of Northern Ireland's most recent troubles. By then, what had earlier seemed emanations from another world have resolved themselves—perhaps too neatly—into occurrences of another kind, natural but just as sinister as menacing to the minds of the living. Near the novel's close, brusquely and almost as afterthought, the "Troubles" as we have known them from headlines and television enter the story: "We choked on CS gas fired by the army, saw or heard the explosions, the gunfire, the riots moving in close with their scrambled noises of glass breaking, flashing petrol-bombs, isolated shouts turning to a prolonged baying and the drilled smashing of batons on riot shields." But it is not afterthought. *Reading in the Dark,* as might have been expected of its author, is a book centrally and subtly historical and

political, and offers evidence that, at least in Northern Ireland, the political and the private are bound together.

This is his first novel, but Seamus Deane, who was a schoolmate in Derry City of Seamus Heaney and Brian Friel, has long been established as one of Ireland's most challenging literary critics. His criticism, whether of literature or of public life, is acerb, shrewd, independent, and enlivened by a brisk and not always genial wit. In Ireland's always-lively culture wars, a significant event was the publication, in 1977, of **"Literary Myths of the Revival,"** his sardonic demythologizing of the movement led by Lady Gregory, Synge, and, first and foremost, Yeats: "Yeats had demonstrated throughout his long career that the conversion of politics and history into aesthetics carries with it the obligation to despise the modern world and seek refuge from it." His harsh strictures are not entirely palliated by his deep responsiveness to the beauty of Yeats's verse. Deane himself is an exact and probing poet, angular and lean. *Reading in the Dark* has been long in gestation and execution, and bears the marks of this: it is polished, adroit, and deeply disturbing.

For one thing, it deliberately subverts two modes of fiction. One is formed by the novels—so numerous as almost to constitute a genre—that have sought to express the atmosphere and terrors, the emotional scars, the crippled lives, which constitute a portion of life in present-day Northern Ireland. Deane's novel, set in the decades before the present troubles and convincingly displayed as their inevitable prelude, quietly establishes a historical perspective lacking in most of those novels. And Deane stands apart from these writers in a second way: his identification with his nationalist community is guarded from sentimentality by the formal severities of his structure and language.

The other mode, the *Bildungsroman,* has as its great Irish instance Joyce's *Portrait of the Artist as a Young Man.* It is a central text for modern Irish literature, and Deane plays off it, sometimes for comic purposes, and at other times to mark the distance between Stephen Dedalus and his own unnamed narrator. (Almost nameless: by detective work one discovers that he is named Seamus Greene.)

Three of Deane's chapters ("The Facts of Life," "Retreat," "Religious Knowledge") deliberately and almost jokingly echo Joyce's in setting and even in imagery. Deane's narrator is in a Christian Brothers school in Derry, and Stephen far to the south, first at an elite Jesuit boarding school and then in the clerically dominated Royal University, but they have similar encounters with the clergy. Stephen is summoned to the room of the Dean of Studies, who is having trouble with his fire; Deane's narrator is summoned to the room of his Spiritual Director, who has a fire blazing even though it is a warm day. In each novel, the fire is given a little useful life of its own. Deane's encounters, though, allowing for the element of parody, itself a Joycean technique, possess a warm-blooded humor far removed from Stephen's Byronism and Joyce's icy distance from his protagonist.

A *Portrait,* with its suavities and ambiguities, expresses the progressively more severe separation of Stephen Dedalus from his culture. "When the soul of a man is born in this country," Stephen tells his nationalist friend Davin, "there are nets flung at it to hold it back from flight. You talk to me of nationality, language, religion. I shall try to fly by those nets." As Deane has written elsewhere, Stephen supplants the language of the tribe with his own, so that the subject of the book becomes its author.

> In that light, the novel is a series of carefully orchestrated quotations, through which we see a young mind coming to grips with his world through an increasing mastery of language. Further, we recognize that this is a moral not merely a formal achievement.

In one of the diary entries, theatrical and faintly ambiguous, which bring the *Portrait* to its close, Stephen writes: "Mother is putting my new second-hand clothes in order. She prays now, she says, that I may learn in my own life and away from home and friends what the heart is and what it feels."

The mother's prayers in Deane's novel arise from her perception of a guilt which cannot be lifted. His is a close, warm family, despite crippling strains that are nursed in bitter silence, in partial truths and half-revelations, in multiple misunderstandings of what lies in the past.

> I felt it was almost a mercy when my mother suffered a stroke and lost the power of speech, just as the Troubles came in October 1968. I would look at her, sealed in her silence, and now she would smile slightly at me and very gently, almost imperceptibly, shake her head. I was to seal it all in too. Now we could love each other, at last, I imagined.

It is a family that is close even as it shatters.

For the mother, the shadow at the window has several identities, but chiefly it is that of her husband's brother Eddie, who disappeared in the April of 1922, after a big shoot-out at a local distillery between the IRA and the police. By some accounts, he fell into one of the exploding vats of whiskey when the burning roof collapsed. But rumors have placed him abroad, in Chicago or in Melbourne. One winter's day, the boy overhears the matter discussed as his father and his mother's brothers repair the boiler in his small house. Eddie's story blends in with other tales of disappearances, returns from the dead, exorcisms.

We are given no direct historical information, and are expected to know that 1922 was a crucial time in the history of Northern Ireland—was in fact the time that marked its creation as a political entity. The Black-and-Tan war against England had ended in a treaty, of which the most disastrous consequence was the partition of the island, with Ulster's Catholics hived off into what would in short order become a police state, in which they were bullied and severely discriminated against by an armed Protestant majority. The conflict had dark, tangled roots stretching back into earlier centuries, but now it was to bear poisonous fruit. The new statelet, memorably described by one of its prime ministers as "a Protestant state for a Protestant people," kept a vigilant control over its minority, within which a few— the IRA—attempted from time to time a futile armed resistance. The others kept their sullen, sardonic distance from a state whose very reason for existence would have made ineffective and humiliating any vow of allegiance.

The economy bore down heavily upon Catholics. The narrator's father is an electrician's helper who, when times are good, works at the British naval base: "going out foreign," it is called. His Aunt Katie works in the shirt factory, the traditional women's job, from which the women stream home, "arms linked, so much more brightly dressed, so much more talkative than the men, most of whom stood at the street corners." The neighborhood police informer, Fogey McKeever, is "a young, open-faced man of twenty or so with a bright smile and wide-spaced, rounded eyes." It is Fogey whose information sends into the narrator's house the RUC men who beat up the father and his sons. And he is far from being the novel's only informer: this is a police culture in which informers thrive.

For the Catholics, there are two spiritual resources—the Catholic Church and the neighboring county of Donegal. The city of Derry (which British cartographers insist on calling Londonderry) is separated from the rest of its county by the River Foyle, which empties into a great lough and thence into the Atlantic. It is embedded into the flank of County Donegal, which politically is not part of Northern Ireland at all but rather is the northernmost part of the Republic of Ireland (or, as it is known in the north, the Free State). It is a great, mountainous, sea-girt reservoir of what remains of Ireland's Gaelic life. Both sides of the narrator's family came into Derry City from Donegal, carrying with them songs, folk beliefs, tales of fairies and revenants, music, the memory of dark, unspoken betrayals. Donegal is a repository, also, of the Irish language, of which the parents can recall only school-learned rudiments. Later, when the narrator thinks he knows the family's secrets, he writes them out, for his own satisfaction, in Irish. The parents cannot understand this account of their own secrets when he reads it out to them.

Near a lost farmhouse in Donegal lies "the field of the disappeared," where the souls of those who never had Christian burial return on Saint Brigid's day and on the festival of Samhain, "to cry like birds and look down on the fields where they had been born." On a high hill commanding both Fough Foyle and Lough Swilly stands the Grianan of Aileach, an ancient and enormous stone fort, built, tradition holds, by the ancient gods, but more likely in some early Christian century. The Fianna, Ireland's heroic warriors, lie sleeping below, waiting for the special person who will rouse them to make final war on the English. All this lies a day's walk from Derry City, behind its border. It has always offered easy refuge for rebels on the run. Early on in the novel, alone or on visits to his ancestral Donegal with friends, the narrator encounters them all—the ruined farm, the field of the disappeared, the fortress. By the close of the novel, he has unriddled their meanings in the life of his family. They have held, for the narrator at least, the unwinding and ironical mysteries of what happened to Eddie, the IRA uncle, in 1922.

The Catholic Church plays a pervasive and deeply ambiguous part within this subjugated Derry culture. It shares with its people a sense of injustice and a conviction that beyond the borders of the United Kingdom it is recognized as the true church. But the priests, negotiating with the governing power, are complicitous with it. Brother Regan, delivering the Christmas address in primary school, counsels the boys in acceptance and inner peace as they prepare for a world of "wrong, injury, insult and unemployment, a world where the unjust hold power and the ignorant rule." Sergeant Burke of the Lecky Road barracks of the Royal Ulster Constabulary, brutal by profession and an associate of the policemen who beat up the narrator and his father, is himself a Catholic. When he dies in bed, his priest-sons concelebrate the Requiem Mass. It is attended by the Bishop. "'How dare he do that,' hissed my mother." But it is received wisdom that "the police and the priests were always in cahoots," a knowledge that cohabits easily with a deeply held Catholic faith.

In 1957, at the height of the cold war, the boys at secondary school are addressed by a priest, a chaplain in British army uniform, who has been sent by the government's Ministry of Education. He reminds them that Derry, a naval port, is "part of the Western world's preparations for the defeat of the international Communist threat, . . . a battle of cold atheism against the genial warmth of that Christian faith that has lit so many Irish hearts down the centuries. Our internal disputes are no more than family quarrels, local troubles, transient divisions." This inspired chain of cold war platitudes runs on through long paragraphs, reminding

us, and perhaps by Deane's intention, of the famous sermons on Hell in *A Portrait.*

Next day, in history class, Father McAuley reveals to the boys that this was no true Catholic priest, but a class of English heretic called Anglo-Catholic. Nevertheless McAuley is at one with him, sharing a global vision which looks beyond troubles in "our little streets toward the approaching world conflict." Outside the classroom, the narrator's tough chum, Irwin, clarifies matters as seen from those streets: "Propaganda. That's all that is. First, it's the Germans. Then it's the Russians. Always, it's the IRA. What have the Germans or Russians to do with us? It's the British who are the problem for us. McAuley's a moron."

The British officer concealed in priestly robes is an old theme, running from the rebel ballad of 1798 to the pyrotechnic of *Ulysses.* Ben Dolland, in *Ulysses,* sings the ballad: "The false priest rustling soldier from his cassock. A yeoman captain." And Bloom reflects: "They know it all by heart. The thrill they itch for." But of all the traditional themes which this novel touches upon, one dominates over all the others, and sets the key for both the theme and the music.

A pair of contrasting icons can be used in a rough-and-ready way to separate out two shaping motifs of the Irish novel—the Ruined Big House and the Informer. Deane himself has written of the former: "The Big House surrounded by the unruly tenantry. Culture besieged by barbarity, a refined aristocracy beset by a vulgar middle class—all of these are recurrent images in twentieth-century Irish fiction, which draws heavily upon Yeats's poetry for them." In fact, this specifically Anglo-Irish tradition stretches back far beyond Yeats to the very first novel of Irish life, Maria Edgeworth's *Castle Rackrent* in 1800. The Protestant Ascendancy, in a move that would have won Faulkner's admiration, began to mourn its own passing when it was at the very height of its political, economic, and cultural power. And thus forward through the Victorian Charles Lever and the Edwardian Somerville and Ross into our own times, with the derelict gardens and gates, the burned-out big houses of Elizabeth Bowen and Jennifer Johnston.

The Informer, who betrays to the conqueror the secrets of a submerged people is the theme that runs through the songs, legends, history, art, even the folk beliefs of that "other" Ireland from which Deane comes. The hulking shadow of a drunken and remorseful Victor McLaglen, flung across rain-glistening Dublin slum walls, falls from John Ford's *The Informer* into the dark bog of the Irish past. "The indispensible informer," so the incorrigible Stephen Dedalus calls the breed.

Reading in the Dark dramatizes the shattering consequences for a family of informing, suspicions of informing, constructions of the past by which a supposed informer's face, pressed against window glass, carries to the generations of a family the conviction of tangled sins against the heart of a community. Near the beginning of the book, the narrator discovers that Eddie may not have died in the 1922 shoot-out, or vanished into Chicago or Melbourne. More probably, he was killed as an informer, and upon orders of the narrator's grandfather, an old Republican stalwart. But only a part of this is true: truth, the narrator discovers as he grows up and goes off to the university, is complex and twists back upon itself. Just possibly, it may at last become fully known, but it can never be fully communicated.

One can only read Deane's fine novel with admiration. It has much to say about families, about a beleaguered but tenacious culture, about a compulsion to unravel the riddles and misheard language of the past and the pain which this can engender. And it does so with a skillfulness which never diminishes its emotional power. One's only reservation has to do with its very skillfulness. Everything in the book, everything, is put to work as symbol, from a cathedral framed by a window to a Chekhovian German pistol to the tinted darkness of a church interior. But this may be what happens when poets write novels. And it is this heavy structuring by images that allows the book its triumph, which is to impose order and the loveliness of meaning upon disorder and violence.

FURTHER READING

Criticism

Byrne, John. Review of *The Field Day Anthology of Irish Writing,* edited by Seamus Deane. *Agenda* 33, Nos. 3-4 (Autumn-Winter 1996): 272-82.
    Details the contents of the anthology with respect to the aims of its editors, singling out Deane who "deserves tremendous credit for his personal contribution."

Kilfeather, Siobhan. "The Whole Bustle." *London Review of Books* 14, No. 1 (9 January 1992): 20-1.
    Reviews *The Field Day Anthology of Irish Writing,* emphasizing the politics of its compilation.

Quinlan, Kieran. "Under Northern Lights: Re-visioning Yeats and the Revival." In *Yeats and Postmodernism,* edited by Leonard Orr, pp. 64-79. Syracuse, NY: Syracuse University Press, 1991.
    Examines Yeats and the Irish Revival in terms of new historicism thought espoused by Deane and others of the Field Day group.

Westendorp, Tjebbe A. "Songs of Battle: Some Contemporary Irish Poems and the Troubles." In *The Clash of Ireland: Literary Contrasts and Connections,* edited by C. C. Barfoot and Theo D'haen, pp. 223-33. Amsterdam: Rodopi, 1989.
    Identifies the range of attitudes towards "the troubles" in contemporary Irish poetry, summarizing Deane's as "Brits Out."

Additional coverage of Deane's life and career is contained in the following sources published by Gale: *Contemporary Authors,* Vol. 118; and *Contemporary Authors New Revision Series,* Vol. 42.

Vine Deloria, Jr.
1933-

(Full name Vine Victor Deloria, Jr.) Sioux nonfiction writer and editor.

The following entry presents an overview of Deloria's career. For further information on his life and works, see *CLC,* Volume 21.

INTRODUCTION

Vine Deloria is representative of the well-educated politically active sector of American Indians. Deloria is especially concerned about the plight of Indians forced to live in a white man's system. In his writings, Deloria argues for the return of sacred Indian grounds and an isolationist policy that would enable his people to function as a separate nation within the United States.

Biographical Information

Deloria was born on March 26, 1933, in South Dakota to an Episcopal minister and his wife. Deloria is a Standing Rock Sioux who was raised on a reservation. In 1958 he received his Bachelor of Science degree from Iowa State University. Following in the footsteps of his father and grandfather, Deloria trained for a career as a minister. After receiving his degree in divinity from the Lutheran School of Theology in 1963, however, he realized a more effective means of serving the Indian's cause was through the legal system. Consequently he earned a law degree from the University of Colorado in 1970. Deloria became involved in Indian affairs as executive director of the National Congress of American Indians in Washington, D. C. During his leadership, from 1964 to 1967, Deloria turned the nearly defunct organization into a forceful voice for Indian tribes. Deloria also has been active in the Council on Indian Affairs, the Institute for the Development of Indian Law, and the Indian Rights Association. In addition to his involvement in these organizations, Deloria has written and edited several books on Indian affairs and taught political science at several universities.

Major Works

Deloria has stated that his exposure to Western culture has served to reaffirm his childhood commitment to the traditional Indian way of life. The main premise of his writings focuses on the need for an Indian cultural nationalism, as opposed to the intellectual assimilation of minorities advocated by the white establishment. Deloria approaches the

issues from a religious and legal standpoint. In *Custer Died for Your Sins* (1969), Deloria satirizes the way in which anthropologists and churches have historically perpetuated stereotypes and misconceptions of Indians. In *God Is Red* (1973), Deloria proposes that Christianity is no longer practical; that its promise of heaven is too remote from everyday life in an industrial society; and that the naturalism of Indian religion is the only hope for Western civilization. In *Behind the Trail of Broken Treaties* (1974); *The Indian Affair* (1974); and *American Indians, American Justice* (1983), Deloria examines the history of Indian-white relations, especially the role of the government. In these books he criticizes federal policy toward Indians and their institutions as being ethnocentric and destructive. Deloria also proposes that the United States government should honor its treaty obligations to Indians concerning their lands. Despite the seriousness of his subjects, Deloria's writing is informal and often wryly humorous, making it accessible to any reader interested in the modern American Indian.

Critical Reception

Most reviewers comment on the lack of bitterness present in Deloria's work. Critics praise his use of humor and his scholarly approach to the sometimes very emotional question of Indian rights. Edward Abbey stated, "Despite the sense of injustice and frustration which he and most Indians must surely feel, Mr. Deloria presents his case without the deep bitterness we might expect." Although many people do not agree with his ideas, Deloria is nevertheless respected for the sincerity and integrity of his works. Wilcomb E. Washburn asserts, "The secret of Deloria's success in becoming the preeminent Indian spokesman is his inexhaustible energy, his wry good humor, his not inconsiderable scholarly gifts, and his diplomatic skill."

PRINCIPAL WORKS

Custer Died for Your Sins: An Indian Manifesto (nonfiction) 1969

We Talk, You Listen: New Tribes, New Turf (nonfiction) 1970

Of Utmost Good Faith [editor] (nonfiction) 1971

The Red Man in the New World Drama: A Politico-Legal Study with a Pageantry of American History [editor and author of introduction] (nonfiction) 1971

God Is Red (nonfiction) 1973; republished as *God Is Red: A Native View of Religion,* 1992

Behind the Trail of Broken Treaties: An Indian Declaration of Independence (nonfiction) 1974

The Indian Affair (nonfiction) 1974

A Better Day for Indians (nonfiction) 1976

Indians of the Pacific Northwest: From the Coming of the White Man to Present Day (nonfiction) 1977

The Metaphysics of Modern Existence (nonfiction) 1979

American Indians, American Justice [with Clifford M. Lytle] (nonfiction) 1983

The Aggressions of Civilization: Federal Indian Policy Since the 1880s [editor with Sandra L. Cadwalader] (nonfiction) 1984

The Nations Within: The Past and Future of American Indian Sovereignty [with Lytle] (nonfiction) 1984

A Sender of Words: Essays in Memory of John G. Neihardt [editor] (nonfiction) 1984

American Indian Policy in the Twentieth Century [editor] (nonfiction) 1985

Frank Waters: Man and Mystic [editor] (nonfiction) 1993

CRITICISM

Edward Abbey (review date 9 November 1969)

SOURCE: A review of *Custer Died For Your Sins,* in *New York Times Book Review,* November 9, 1969, p. 46.

[*In the following review, Abbey asserts that in* Custer Died For Your Sins, *Deloria "writes with much humor and even sympathy for what he believes to be the white Americans' pathetic inability to feel and understand the true nature of the situation we are living in."*]

Even our Indians are turning against us now. Red Power. All the chickens coming home to roost. In ***Custer Died For Your Sins*** the author reminds us—and Vine Deloria, former executive director of the National Congress of American Indians, is himself an Indian—that America was discovered not by Columbus, not by Leif Ericson, but by the Indians—over 20,000 years ago. This simple fact has somehow eluded the rest of us, perhaps because the original discoverers of this continent were regarded by the English settlers not as people or human beings but simply as part of the wild life, i.e., as animals.

"They used to shoot us for our feathers," Mr. Deloria complains, going on to point out that the practice of scalping, for instance, was invented in New England by white men. Why? For the same reason that mountain-lion trappers in Arizona nowadays remove the scalps of their victims, as proof of kill, in order to collect the bounty.

Details such as these were never mentioned in our public-school history classes. Why not? The word "genocide" is used a little too easily and carelessly these days (it flows trippingly on the tongue); but in the case of the American Indians, particularly those unfortunate enough to find themselves in the path of our Pilgrim and Puritan forefathers, the term may not be inapplicable. How many Indians are left in New England? Along the Eastern seaboard?

The many parallels between the war in Vietnam and the war against the American Indian have not escaped the American Indian. In his chapter on Indian humor Vine Deloria reports the results of an opinion poll taken among Indians on the question of Vietnam: 15 per cent replied that the United States should get out of Vietnam; 85 per cent that the United States should get out of America.

In filling in the many little gaps in school textbooks on American history, Mr. Deloria accuses the United States Government of ignoring or violating some 400 treaties made with Indian tribes, and contrasts this record with the alleged reason for our "presence" in Vietnam. "History may well record," he writes, "that while the United States was squandering some one hundred billion dollars in Vietnam while justifying this bloody orgy as commitment—keeping, it was also busy breaking the oldest Indian treaty, that between the United States and the Seneca tribe of the Iroquois Nation." He refers here to the Pickering Treaty of 1794, which was signed by, among others, one G. Washington, Pres., and illegally broken in the early 1960's by the construction of the Kinzua Dam on the Allegheny River, which flooded the Senecas out of their ancestral homeland.

Mr. Deloria recounts the long history of Indian grievances in blunt language but without exaggeration or melodrama. He writes also of more contemporary afflictions which the Indians must endure, such as anthropologists, missionaries, the bullet-headed bureaucrats of the B. I. A. (Bureau of Indian Affairs) and other Government agencies, and of such potentially disastrous policies as "termination," by which the Government would have eliminated medical and educational services, and "relocation," an ingenious scheme thought up by someone in Washington whereby surplus reservation Indians are transferred to big-city slums where it is hoped they will sort of fade away and be forgotten. All in the name of "economy," of course.

Despite the sense of injustice and frustration which he and most Indians must surely feel, Mr. Deloria presents his case without the deep bitterness we might expect. Indeed he writes with much humor and even sympathy for what he believes to be the white Americans' pathetic inability to feel and understand the true nature of the situation we are living in. He makes constructive suggestions. He is even hopeful. Not very hopeful, but hopeful.

As for us, what should be our response? It is not enough to indulge in racial self-hatred, as I have seen some of my white brothers and sisters doing lately. Nor can we all go back to Europe; they don't want us either. The only solution, I am afraid, is a dose of justice. Even if it hurts.

As for Mr. Deloria, he has written a good book, not only about Indians and their troubles but about us and our troubles. The two are the same, which is one of the things he is trying to tell us. *Custer Died For Your Sins* is even better than its title.

Christian Science Monitor (review date 2 April 1970)

SOURCE: "A Sophisticated Indian Looks at the Savage Whites," in *Christian Science Monitor*, April 2, 1970, p. 7.

[*In the following review, the critic praises Deloria's humor and hopefulness in his presentation of the American government's broken promises to the Indians in* Custer Died for Your Sins.]

All of Vine Deloria's stylistic limitations, all the lifeless passages which smack of going through the motions in order to get a book-length manuscript, cannot defeat the subject matter of this angry polemic [entitled *Custer Died for Your Sins*].

The condition of the American Indians is, for the most part, intolerable. In the names of manifest destiny, economic growth, expanding the frontier, laissez-faire capitalism and cultural homogeneity, the original inhabitants of America have been slaughtered, uprooted, swindled, chastised, excluded, and despised.

Mr. Deloria, a Sioux himself, sums it all up unsparingly.

The brutality shown by earlier generations of white Americans was, he suggests, frank at least. In our own day the Indians have been deprived of guaranteed government assistance, subjected to cultural fragmentation, and double-crossed by the United States Government.

Despite the fact that many people think so, the Indian treaties are not quaint historical jokes. Every time the government violates an Indian treaty, which it does, Mr. Deloria points out, with deadening regularity, a little more of its credibility is killed off. While 40,000 GIs die in Vietnam in defense of Washington's treaty obligations, the United States goes on breaking some of the most solemn and oldest treaties in its national history.

Mr. Deloria assumes that the true spirit of a powerful nation can only be observed in its dealings with lesser powers. When the country first undertook to contain the Indians, the national argument was the need for space in which to grow. Isn't that called lebensraum?

Somehow in all this Mr. Deloria manages to retain both a biting sense of humor and a hope for the future; that the grace of the Indian under pressure may be the example to leaven the American whole.

Cecil Eby (review date 4 October 1970)

SOURCE: "Tonto was an Uncle Tomahawk," in *Washington Post Book World*, October 4, 1970, p. 4.

[*In the following review, Eby discusses the commercial relationship between white America and its use of land versus the Indians' veneration of nature as presented by Deloria in* We Talk, You Listen.]

Adding to the already formidable list of "problems" bedeviling white America is the rise, in recent years, of Red Power. Armed not with tomahawks but with briefcases chock-full of broken promises and treaty violations, the Indian has joined other minority groups in demanding his due.

Once upon a time white America could count on a docile Indian population content to subsist on mission charity and Congressional dole, with a repast now and then at the tourist trough as a reward for good behavior. Today this eleemosynary epoch seems about to end. The Indian has become militant and aggressive, and the paleface finds few weapons at hand to combat this new Red Menace. It would be a trifle ridiculous for an investigating committee to denounce the Indian as "Un-American," and the U.S. Cavalry—that trusty arbiter of Indian affairs in times past—is engrossed in activities elsewhere.

Perhaps the first stirrings of the "New Indian" were felt in the middle-Fifties when a band of Cherokees put to rout a North Carolina conference of the Ku Klux Klan, ripping off sheets and exposing frightened white faces underneath. More recently the Penobscots have stopped traffic in Maine to extract toll from summer tourists crossing territory claimed by the tribe. Others have pressed suits in federal courts for restoration of stolen land, which just about takes in the entire North American continent. And in their most dramatic venture to date, Indians have occupied Alcatraz and held the whites at bay, inverting the classic confrontation at the beleaguered wagon train. This "New Indian" does not tread respectfully in the American pantheon. He has doubts about Jim Thorp, he dismisses Tonto as an "Uncle Tomahawk," and he labels General George Custer "the Adolf Eichmann of the nineteenth century."

In two books, *Custer Died for Your Sins* (1969) and *We Talk, You Listen,* Vine DeLoria Jr. describes the thrust of the Red-Power movement without anointing himself as its oracle or its official spokesman. No one, not even a former executive director of the National Congress of American Indians, could legitimately speak for half a million Indians represented by more than three hundred tribes, many of them as jealous of one another as outraged at the Great White Father. There is no monolithic organization or unified set of objectives that all tribes have agreed on, unless it be the demand that whites abide by contracts which they (not Indians) have written. DeLoria brings into focus the moods and habitat of the contemporary Indian as seen by a Standing Rock Sioux, not by a research anthropologist or a jobber in the basketry trades. He peels away layers of tinsel and feathers heaped upon the Indian by misinformed whites (beginning with Columbus), and he reveals an uncanny ability for impaling them on the fine points of their own illogic.

Whites are so guilty of stereotyping, says DeLoria, that they lump together all "minority problems" as the struggle of each oppressed minority to enter into the shining world of the affluent majority. The problem of the blacks, for example, has been to wrest an economic base from whites unwilling to surrender what they have. Blacks are trying to

forge a weapon which can open doors closed to them in the past. With the Indians it is just the opposite. Since originally they controlled all the land, their historical battle has been to keep the whites from appropriating it. The blacks struggle to obtain what they have never had before; the Indians, to retain possession of that portion of the land not yet taken from them—some fifty-four million acres valued at three billion dollars. (DeLoria seems not to take seriously the demands voiced by some Indian extremists for the return of all of North America to its original owners.) The red man is no landless redneck. His holdings are enormous. What he has to do is to slave off encroachments of slippery whites who argue that Indians fail to "use" their land and who doubtless calculate how productive this land would be if it were put in the soil bank. What the Indian wants are guarantees that existing treaties will be honored, along with a minimum of meddling from bureaucrats, missionaries, and sociologists. The white man, says DeLoria, has given the Indian little more than "poverty and disease." No wonder, then, that in a recent poll only 15 per cent of Indians sampled wanted the United States to get out of Vietnam, while over 80 per cent wanted it to get out of America!

Custer Died for Your Sins contains more information about Indian affairs than does DeLoria's new book, which moves into an area of broader humanistic concerns. *We Talk, You Listen* is apocalyptical and ecological. It attacks the corporate patterns of American life—which he sees as analogous to feudalism—and defends the tribal variables found in minority cultures, whether Indian, black, or Amish. Already great numbers of Americans have "gone Indian" rather than endure megasystems and superstructures alien to the human spirit. They have adopted pre-Columbian mannerisms and garb, found refuge in tribal communes, and championed causes presumed to be inimical to traditional Western culture. DeLoria finds in these manifestations a desire to return to the Indian concept of land as an entity to be lived with rather than exploited and to the Indian notion of the tribe as a communal family in which objects are shared rather than owned. The ultimate irony of white progress is that its machines and their by-products may succeed in eradicating all human life on this planet. On the day before the world ends, the Indians' veneration of small animals would not seem irrelevant.

For DeLoria the answer seems to lie in returning to simpler frameworks of human existence like those developed by Indians. Yet the simplest course often proves the most difficult one to plot. The message conveyed by slogans like "God is Red" and "Better Red than Dead" makes ecological sense. As poetic utterances they are eloquent and seductive—but they cannot be programmed by a computer. The peculiar tragedy of white America at the present time is that it knows what ought to be done but knows not how to do it. Even if briefly allied together on a last doomsday march, it is likely that the Indian and the white man would bear different drummers.

Rosemary Radford Ruether (review date 5-12 January 1974)

SOURCE: A review of *God Is Red*, in *New Republic*, Vol. 170, Nos. 3078-3079, January 5-12, 1974, pp. 25-6.

[*Ruether is an American educator and theologian. In the following review, she highlights the contrasts between Christianity and Native American religions that Deloria presents in* God Is Red.]

Vine Deloria, spokesman for the rise of "red consciousness," is the son of an Indian Episcopalian clergyman. Himself seminary-trained, Deloria's criticism of the white man's relation to Indian society has increasingly focused on the character of Christianity. Deloria believes that the white man's destruction-relationships with other people and with the earth have been inculcated and justified to a large extent by his religion. In this new book [*God Is Red*] Deloria contrasts critical aspects of Christianity with the spirit of Indian religion.

The source of white imperialism lies in the Christocentric view of history. Christians see themselves as God's sole elect people who have been commissioned to conquer all other nations in Christ's name. Other nations appear on the Christian historical horizon only when Christians are about to conquer them. Preaching to all nations translates into seizing the lands of other peoples and annihilating their cultural identities. To deny the truth of other people's religion is to deny to them the right to exist autonomously.

By contrast, Indian religion affirms diversity and particularity. Peoplehood, land and religion form a single covenantal relationship that gives each community unique character. Each people, in their own context, is a "chosen people" with their own "promised land" where they are to find their destiny. Religion is a function of peoplehood. The Hebrew religion understood this unique relation of peoplehood, land and covenantal relation with God. But this understanding was distorted into abstract spiritualizing when Christianity severed its roots with Judaism. This is why the Jews have always, correctly, rejected the Christian claim to Israel's election and messianic hope.

Christianity also developed an antagonistic view of the relation of man and nature that translated into ecocide. Nature is regarded as an enemy to be subjugated and repressed. For the Indian nature is a subject, not an object.

God is not made in the image of man. God is the great spirit of all things. Christianity boasts of the "brotherhood of man," meaning by this the subjugation of all other identities other than the Christian one. The Indian speaks rather of the "brotherhood of life," accepting each people and each living being's right to possess their own unique nature. Man must find his place within the ecosystem. He must stand within, not against or outside of, the great web of life.

The religion of sacred history must give way to the religion of sacred space. In sacred history one people alone dominates the central axis of history. In religions of sacred space each people has its own space, its own land and identity. Christianity makes creation a pseudohistorical event of the distant past and salvation a historical event of the distant future. For the red man, creation is now and revelation takes place in the present. God still speaks to the prophets, and each person is called to his own "vision quest."

The white man's religion promises immortality, but creates an obsession with and fear of death. The Indian is fearless toward death, because he lives, not as an atomic individual, but in the collective soul of the tribe. Ancestors do not depart for a distant heaven, but live here on earth in communion with the living members. Bones of the forefathers and mothers go down into the earth to provide the seeds from which the crop of living humanity springs up in each new season. Christianity sees death as unnatural; the red man sees death as the natural completion of his life, a transformation point in the continuous flow of life that goes down into and is reborn from the mother earth. When the white man roots up the bones of Indian dead to make them artifacts in his museums, he shows his inability to understand the Indian spirit. For in so doing he pulls up the roots of the ongoing life of the tribe.

Lacking a sense of social solidarity, the white man's religion abstracts the self out of its social context into an isolated confrontation with an "angry" God. The salvation he receives does not flow back into a renewed social life. A gap opens up between "moral man" and the immoral society which is the actual reality of Christian history. Individualism characterizes a religion that cannot close the gap between its high personal ideals and its disastrous social reality. Indian religion, however, is intrinsically socialistic. The tribe provides each member with an equal right to exist. Its social ethics coincide with its social laws and customs. This is illustrated in the contrast between the white and the red man's view of crime. The white man believes the criminal should be "punished"; Indian tradition exacts compensation, not punishment. This rehabilitates the criminal into society and restores the injured ones.

Deloria sees Christian power as a destructive episode on

an earth that once belonged, and must in the future belong, to the Indian. He recognizes the difficulty of translating the customs of a pre-technological society into the relation these values must assume in a post-technological era. If Christianity is to learn these values, it must radically change its historical character. The white man may be the political owner of the land, but the red man is still its spiritual owner. America can survive only if the white man becomes an Indian, learns to revere the sacred spaces of this land and put his bones into the earth so they become his roots. The treaty of red and white man must be a covenant with nature as well. Only then can they sign a treaty which will not be broken; which shall stand "as long as the grass shall grow and the rivers flow."

James R. Kerr (review date November 1984)

SOURCE: A review of *American Indians, American Justice,* in *The Annals of the American Academy of Political and Social Science,* Vol. 476, November, 1984, pp. 186-87.

[*In the following review, Kerr praises* American Indians, American Justice *as a highly readable examination of the United States federal government's policies concerning American Indians and their effects on Native American governmental and judicial institutions.*]

This admirable book [*American Indians, American Justice*] analyzes the roots of Indian tribal government and justice and how they have been modified by the American legal system. It asks the important question, How much of Indian self-government and traditional Indian culture and values can survive, given the pressure toward adapting Indian institutions to the values of contemporary American society?

Both authors are lawyer-political scientists and their principal interest is studying the pervasive influence of the white man's political system on the Indian tribes. The federal government has greatly affected tribal institutions; significant Supreme Court rulings provided the basis for the government's absolute power over Indians. Congress has pursued vacillating policies ranging from the treaty-making period through removal and relocation, allotment and assimilation, to reorganization and finally self-determination. Executive branch and paternalistic bureaucratic wardship have weakened tribal institutions.

The story is told in a direct, nonpolemical, but profoundly convincing manner that leads one to the conclusion that federal policy has often been guided by the ethnocentric belief that Indians should be encouraged to adopt the val-

ues and civic ethic of white America and that similarity, not diversity, characterizes Indian tribal institutions and values. Federal intrusion into tribal governance has had the effect of rendering tribal self-government dormant, weakening tribal courts, and eroding adherence to tribal customs and religious rituals. In the area of tribal criminal justice, federal preemption of serious crimes has stripped tribes of the authority to deal with much criminal conduct.

Because reservation Indians are subject not only to tribal, state, and federal governments but also to shifting congressional policy and the legalistic maze created by treaties, federal laws, court opinions, and tribal constitutions, the task of rendering complexity to an acceptable level of simplicity and clarity is a major challenge. Deloria and [and his coauthor Clifford M.] Lytle have succeeded. Subjects such as the concepts of Indian country, tribal criminal and civil justice, and self-government are splendidly described. It is argued that the concepts of tribal sovereignty and Indian country are now merely backdrops against which federal preemption, constitutional rights of Indians, and other policy issues are examined.

Deloria and Lytle not only examine contemporary Indian judicial institutions; they also evaluate their strengths and weaknesses. Other topics dealt with include legal representation and defense of Indian rights, Indian legal interest groups, and current issues regarding voting, criminal defendants' rights, religious freedom, and entitlement to basic educational and social services.

In sum, Deloria and Lytle have compellingly presented a strong case that the weakening of tribal self-government and traditional customs and values has been fostered by the insensitivity and lack of understanding underlying federal policy with respect to tribal governance. Federal policy since 1961 has been somewhat more enlightened. The success of this book is that it untangles the complexities of the evolution of the Indian judicial system in a manner that lay and professional readers will find engrossing.

Wilcomb E. Washburn (essay date January 1985)

SOURCE: "Toward Indian Nationhood," in *Natural History,* Vol. 94, January, 1985, pp. 76, 78-9.

[*In the following essay, Washburn asserts that in* The Nations Within, *"When all is said and done, Deloria and Lytle, while not providing a practical solution to the Indian future, have laid the basis for a more mature consideration of that future by Indian tribal leaders."*]

Vine Deloria, Jr.! The name—to some contemporary white

Americans—conjures up emotions similar to those raised in the nineteenth century by the names Geronimo and Red Cloud. For many years Deloria, with his pen (and now with his word processor), has struck terror in the hearts of snooping anthropologists, guilt-laden editorial writers, obtuse historians, and others who grapple with the contemporary or historical Indian, whether as an economic "problem," a literary symbol, or a political force.

The secret of Deloria's success in becoming the preeminent Indian spokesman is his inexhaustible energy, his wry good humor, his not inconsiderable scholarly gifts, and his diplomatic skill. Deloria has his detractors among Indians and whites, but his critics have had amazingly little success at shaking his self-confidence or denting his reputation. In the present volume, [*The Nations Within: The Past and Future of American Indian Sovereignty,*] as in the earlier *American Indians, American Justice,* Deloria shares author credit with Clifford M. Lytle, his colleague in the Department of Political Science at the University of Arizona. The partnership, unequal though it may be, is fruitful. Lytle's participation seems to have added depth and responsibility to the sparkling, cynical, but often careless approach that characterized some of Deloria's earlier works, such as *Custer Died for Your Sins.*

There are two books here. One, sober and scholarly, deals with the Indian past; the other, imaginative and speculative, deals with the Indian future. The first "book" is a detailed consideration of the Indian Reorganization Act of 1934; the second deals with the recent and as yet not fully defined Indian struggle for a new identity. The two sections are appropriately joined under the felicitously chosen title *The Nations Within,* which signifies both the achievement of self-government under the Indian Reorganization Act and the current movement toward a national (and international) Indian identity.

The first part—a well-researched, general study of the bill that, under the guidance of Commissioner of Indian Affairs John Collier, completely reoriented the federal government's conduct of Indian affairs fifty years ago—does not seek to match the scholarly detail of earlier studies of Collier and the Indian Reorganization Act by such scholars as Kenneth Philp, Lawrence Kelly, and Graham Taylor. But while *The Nations Within* is popular and readable, it is not unscholarly except where the reader is asked to accept on faith the authors' attribution of motives. For example, the authors allege that Sen. Sam Ervin attached the Indian Civil Rights Bill to a fair housing bill in 1968 in order to kill the housing bill—a strategy that, if it did exist, was unsuccessful. This speculation is presented without any citation of authority or tangible proof. Some will accept the authority of Deloria on such matters because of the prominent role he played as executive director of the

National Congress of American Indians from 1964 to 1967 and because of his influential role and continuing access to both Indian and white political leaders before and after his tenure as head of this organization. But such personal reminiscences are unreliable guides to the past; they smack too much of the journalist's shaky sources, which may be the raw material but not the substance of history.

In contemporary America the journalist's role is often that of advocate, and Deloria and Lytle have too openly assumed this role. This is particularly true when they move on to consideration of a "movement toward nationality" on the part of Indian tribes.

Because special interest, sympathy, and guilt are inextricably mixed in all considerations of the American Indian, it is difficult to obtain an unemotional, realistic, and impartial assessment of such a volatile subject as Indian sovereignty. Despite their sophistication, the authors fall into the trap of judging John Collier's achievement (in getting Congress to pass the Indian Reorganization Act, which established the legitimacy and defined the powers of Indian self-government as an integral part of the law of the land) by an ideal, rather than a practical, standard. Collier is judged, not by what he wrested for the Indians from a sometimes uncomprehending, sometimes skeptical Congress, but by what he failed to obtain, such as a formal declaration of Indian political sovereignty. Neither Deloria nor other critics of Collier consider the probable fate that Collier averted: the total destruction of Indian tribal identity and sovereignty. To say that Collier's legislative struggle "in most respects represented a solid defeat" because the final version differed radically from the original proposal is to miss the forest for the trees.

The publisher claims that, in addition to their analysis of the Indian Reorganization Act,

> Deloria and Lytle trace the rise of Indian militancy and the decline of tribal government into near welfare-agency status, and show the political effects of Reagan's crippling budget cuts. They conclude with a set of sound proposals that take into account current economic realities while suggesting how traditional institutions can be used to resurrect sovereignty today.

Alas, if only publishers' blurbs would correspond to objective truth! Deloria and Lytle give a too-sympathetic account of the militant activities of the American Indian Movement (AIM) radicals at Wounded Knee and elsewhere, but fail to demonstrate that these actions have advanced the cause of Indian nationhood and sovereignty. The authors ignore the "work" of Leonard Peltier (about whom Peter Matthiessen wrote an entire book, *In the Spirit of Crazy Horse,* in 1983), the AIM activist currently in prison for shooting two FBI agents at Wounded Knee in 1973. Peltier has virtually become a patron saint of AIM, and his plight has been cited by the Soviet Union to blunt Western criticism of Soviet treatment of Andrei Sakharov.

Neither do the authors of **The Nations Within** do more than allude to the radicals' indictment of the United States for alleged crimes against humanity, such as genocide and sterilization of Indian women, before the Russell International Tribunal. Deloria is too honest a scholar and too sophisticated a politician to defend the radical Indian positions on such issues, which have little or no merit. Yet he makes use of the radical rhetoric to express the vague hope of Indian leaders such as himself for an evolution of Indian self-government into full Indian "nationhood."

Deloria is equally vague as to the practical steps that must be taken before Indian nationhood is achieved. He wistfully alludes to the "famous Twenty Points" (of which he was a principal author) presented to White House officials Leonard Garment and Bradley Patterson during the 1972 election-week March on Washington. These points, which included restoration of constitutional treaty-making authority and the provision that all Indians be governed by treaty relations, were so totally out of touch with reality that they had no chance of influencing the debate on Indian policy. After trashing the Bureau of Indian Affairs (which now, as a cautionary measure, no longer exists as a separate, identifiable entity in Washington), the 1972 protesters and looters were provided tickets, at taxpayer expense, to return home. Had Collier not erected such a powerful protective shield around Indian tribes by engineering the passage of the Indian Reorganization Act, the white backlash that followed this ill-conceived "protest" would probably have eliminated whatever remnants of tribal self-government had continued to exist.

Equally futile were the 206 recommendations issued in 1977 by the American Indian Policy Review Commission—staffed almost exclusively by American Indians—whose principal recommendation, as Deloria wryly notes, was for "more money." It seems never to have occurred to the Indian leadership—such as it was and is—that recommendations designed to wring power, money, and support from the non-Indian majority of the country must have some relationship to political reality.

Deloria and Lytle fail to provide specific recommendations for smoothing the route from self-government to nationhood. The authors call for retention of Indian cultural values, reconciliation of factional elements within Indian communities, and so on, but leave largely unspecified the nature of the Indian identity, economic system, and political character that is expected to emerge. Recommendations are phrased in party convention language, to encompass ev-

erything, please everyone, and offend no one. Thus Deloria and Lytle assert that "relations between the tribe and the federal and state governments must be stabilized, and mutual respect and parity in political rights must be established." Yet the authors are belittling in their references to the "government-to-government relationship" that underlies President Reagan's Indian policy. The authors assert incorrectly that "the ideology generally adopted by Republican administrations . . . makes Indians wards of the government. . . ."

Deloria and Lytle also seem to think that by calling something by a different name, one creates a different reality. Calling a tribal council a national council does not maximize tribal sovereignty (even if one expands the membership) or cause it to be exercised "in a more comprehensive manner." Calling policemen peace officers does not constitute a "structural recasting of the police function." Resolving the real differences between "traditional" and modern Indian tribal governments cannot be accomplished with pious platitudes or easy criticism of elected tribal officials. Most curiously, the authors do not seem to have a substitute for elective government by majority rule, the bête noire of the traditionals and radicals.

Indian claims against the U.S. government, adjudicated by the Indian Claims Commission, Court of Claims, and the U.S. Supreme Court, constitute particularly sensitive issues among Indian leaders. Of all the land claims, the Sioux claim is the most famous. The Sioux are still divided on the question of whether to accept the 1980 Supreme Court decision replacing a series of earlier judicial determinations of the amount of compensation the United States owes the Sioux for the taking of the Black Hills over a century ago. Deloria, a Sioux, does not tell us where he stands on the issue, preferring instead to straddle it. As he notes, "Claims are both satisfying in terms of fulfilling ancient promises and disruptive in that they take an inordinate amount of time and energy away from other reservation activities that would be more profitable in the long run."

When all is said and done, Deloria and Lytle, while not providing a practical solution to the Indian future, have laid the basis for a more mature consideration of that future by Indian tribal leaders. They have done this, first of all, by providing a well-written and basically accurate consideration of the Indian Reorganization Act. They grudgingly give John Collier credit for what he did accomplish, even while chiding him for not doing more. Secondly, they recognize that the act is the fundamental and indispensable foundation on which the movement toward Indian nationhood, if it is ever to occur, must be built. Thirdly, they point out that a successful movement toward nationhood for all Indian tribes must be sustained by rhetoric that is pro-Indian rather than anti-white. "Self-determination involves having a responsible group that has pride in itself but does not generate this pride by pointing out the shortcomings of other groups."

The Nations Within takes a significant step toward creating this responsible approach. Whether the Indian nations will achieve the full extent of the sovereignty that the authors visualize is, however, doubtful.

Southwest Review (review date Autumn 1985)

SOURCE: A review of *American Indian Policy in the Twentieth Century,* in *Southwest Review,* Vol. 70, No. 4, Autumn, 1985, pp. 550-51.

[*In the following excerpt, the critic states that the essays contained in Deloria's* American Indian Policy in the Twentieth Century *"contain valuable information of interest to scholars and general readers alike."*]

American Indian Policy in the Twentieth Century, edited by Vine Deloria, Jr., presents eleven essays that examine several often ignored areas in Indian history. Tom Holm, for example, in "The Crisis in Tribal Government," suggests that Wounded Knee II was not a "typical" inner city riot, but instead was an attempt to reinstate traditional Sioux values in that tribe's complicated political system. In an entirely different vein, Mary Wallace's "The Supreme Court and Indian Water Rights" shows how the Court's recent decisions have moved away from the long-standing *Winters* doctrine, which implicitly reserved Indian water rights, toward allowing state courts to adjudicate federal reserved water rights. General readers will be most interested in Daniel McCool's "Indian Voting." As McCool points out, the Fourteenth Amendment of the U.S. Constitution extended citizenship to "all persons born or naturalized in the United States, and subject to the jurisdiction thereof." But a federal district court ruled in 1871 that this did not apply to Indians! As a result, Indians were effectively prohibited from voting. By 1924, however, a maze of laws granted citizenship to nearly three-fourths of all Indians, and this process was completed in that same year by the Citizenship Act. Nevertheless, many states still refused to recognize Indians as citizens of the states in which they resided, arguing that reservations were not part of the state (Utah did not relent until the 1950s). World War II proved to be the catalyst in the Indians' struggle to vote, since so many Indians served with distinction in the armed forces. Still, the states erected barriers to full citizenship with such devices as gerrymandering, literacy tests, and lack of facilities. Only the various civil rights acts of the 1960s and 1970s finally settled the issue. Since then, despite their small numbers, Indians have had considerable impact on

elections in western states, especially in close races. As McCool notes, the Indian vote has been decisive in five recent Senate races, but it is not always an easily predictable vote. In Arizona, for example, the Papago are strongly Democratic, the Hopi Republican, and the Navajo have changed from Republican to Democratic.

Although many of the essays are seriously marred by a deadening abundance of jargon, all contain valuable information of interest to scholars and general readers alike.

Thomas Burnell Colbert (review date February 1987)

SOURCE: A review of *American Indian Policy in the Twentieth Century,* in *The Historian,* Vol. XLIX, No. 2, February, 1987, pp. 287-88.

[*In the following review, Colbert asserts that the essays in Deloria's* American Indian Policy in the Twentieth Century *are educational and informative.*]

Native American studies programs at colleges and universities have increased in number and size over the last twenty years. Likewise, the amount of scholarly activity focusing on Indian life and history has proliferated. However, much of the endeavor, especially within the discipline of history, has centered on Indian-white relations in the years before the twentieth century. Consequently, even a specialist on Native American history might, for example, be uncomfortable and uniformed when discussing Nixon's self-determination policy. And that circumstance, as well as other considerations, enhances the benefits to be derived from this collection of eleven essays[, ***American Indian Policy in the Twentieth Century***]—edited by Vine Deloria, Jr., a noted Native American spokesmen, writer and teacher— which is intended to add some perspective on present-day Indian policies of the federal government. The approach is topical, not chronological, with a wide range of subjects: human rights, Indian voting, tribal governments, water rights and the influence of the Bureau of Indian Affairs—to list a few.

Within this mixed bag of articles, a common thread in almost all is the importance of federal law and legal decisions. Indeed, Joyotpaul Chaudhuri in the lead essay, "American Indian Policy: An Overview," tends to set the tone for the others by asserting that "the law reflects, more intensely than is the case for other minorities, the shifts in attitudes and American politics" affecting Indians. The next nine contributions, in turn, deal with specific areas of concern in contemporary Indian affairs. The final essay in the book, **"The Evolution of Federal Indian Policy Mak-**

ing" by Deloria, not only complements the preceding pieces but also offers insightful commentary on the meandering course of Indian Policy from the early days of the United States to today. In particular, Deloria states that an "easily defined federal policy designed specifically for American Indians" has not "existed since Congress adopted termination as a reachable goal in 1954." He furthermore concludes that the longtime problems involving the legal status of Indians as members of tribes within the political domain of the United States has been replaced by concerns associated with their roles as members of a minority group and that differences between Indians and whites "seems finally to have evolved into a social problem area and may finally be resolved as other such problems have been resolved."

In all, the authors contributing to this collection have handled effectively their respective topics and thus produced very informative, clearly written and well-documented essays. At the same time, the diversity of research interests represented exemplifies the variety of pertinent issues of Indian policy meriting examination. And for the historian either with general curiosity or with expertise in Indian policy, *American Indian Policy in the Twentieth Century* offers useful, thought-provoking reading.

Stephen Cornell (review date March 1987)

SOURCE: A review of *American Indian Policy in the Twentieth Century,* in *Contemporary Sociology,* Vol. 16, No. 2, March, 1987, pp. 157-59.

[*In the following review, Cornell traces the policy issues addressed in Deloria's* American Indian in the Twentieth Century.]

Vine Deloria introduces this valuable new collection[, *American Indian Policy in the Twentieth Century,*] with the observation that the last few decades in Indian affairs have seen substantial progress. This progress, he argues, has been in the formulation of Indian policy, where Indian input is greater than it has ever been. Whether or not policy *outcomes* actually have improved remains, as these papers indicate, a complicated question.

Indian-white relations generally have been viewed as just that: relations between two more or less monolithic groups in which the interesting events happen where the two meet head-on, as they continually do. It is the strength of this book that it often abandons this traditional, dyadic conception and examines instead the array of actors and interests, both Indian and non-Indian, which in fact are involved. On the Indian side this includes not only tribes but tribal bu-

reaucracies, traditional communities, economic interest groups, nonreservation Indians, and others, each often with their own agendas. The non-Indian world is no less diverse, including the national Indian affairs bureaucracy, local bureaucrats, state governments, corporations, distant policy makers such as Congress, and an assortment of publics both friendly and unfriendly to Indian concerns. These actors sometimes work with each other, sometimes against each other. Only occasionally or at an abstract level can one think simply in Indian-white terms.

That we have tended to think in just such terms in the past is probably less an indicator of how much more complex has become the array of actors than of how much less lopsided has become the distribution of power. As Indian-white relations have become more negotiated and less imposed, the various interests and agendas on the Indian side in particular have become more apparent. Where there is power there is conflict, and there is power in Indian hands these days. It is by no means ultimate power. As Sharon O'Brien effectively points out in her chapter on Indian policy and human rights, Congress' plenary power in Indian affairs inevitably pulls the teeth from "self-determination," the catchword and idea which supposedly describes Indian policy today. But Deloria's point remains, and it is precisely because of this enlarged Indian role in policy formation that the complexities of the Indian world have become so important.

The most compelling chapters in this book are sensitive to this new political landscape. For example, the chapters by Tom Holm on factional conflict in tribal government, by Fred Ragsdale on the complexity of jurisdictional issues and the legal powers of tribes, and by Daniel McCool on Indian voting give some sense of the ways in which these interests and actors aggregate and disaggregate in various contexts, both within and across intergroup boundaries.

The chapters by Ragsdale and McCool speak also to questions of how Indians pursue these interests. McCool's is one of the few systematic studies of Indian voting we have. Deloria finds support in it for Indian voting power; I found it less encouraging. There aren't many Indians in this country, and in only a few places are they numerous and concentrated enough to put substantial pressure on the electoral system (though they have done so on occasion with decisive effect). But even there, as McCool points out, it requires close races and a disciplined electorate to accomplish very much.

As Ragsdale observes, Indians have had more clout in the courts, which on the whole have been friendlier to Indian interests than have the other branches of government. But Ragsdale advises caution. *How* Indians use the courts has consequences. As tribes act more and more like non-Indian corporate actors, and demand similar standing, they may find themselves increasingly subject also to the limitations and obligations attached to such standing. Defining and preserving tribal sovereignty is a tricky business.

It is made trickier by the inconsistency of the judiciary. Mary Wallace provides a critique of recent court decisions on water rights which should be read in conjunction with Ragsdale. She is especially concerned with recent court decisions which favored adjudication of water rights in state as opposed to federal courts. Taken together these two papers document advancing erosion in the crucial separation of state and tribal rights and jurisdictions.

Of course increased Indian participation raises a host of control issues which are resolved in ways other than litigation. If Indians are to be involved in policy making, how can the interests of non-Indians continue to be served? Robert Nelson and Joseph Sheley offer an intriguing analysis of how the Bureau of Indian Affairs maintains control of tribal actions at the local level while paying lip service to self-determination. And Michael Lacy applies the concept of co-optation to a number of policy-related events to understand how the federal government has tried either to give legitimacy to its own interests within Indian communities, or to channel Indian opposition into institutionalized patterns of politics where outcomes can be more easily controlled.

The area where the clash of diverse interests is most apparent is reservation economic development. David Vinje argues that the fundamental issue is the nature of the bottom line: is the point to develop viable economies or to preserve distinct cultural communities? His three case studies suggest the two need not be in conflict, but that too often tribes "view the economic sector as culturally neutral," and fail to consider ways to develop which build on, rather than ignore, cultural traditions. His chapter also supports Deloria's argument that what we need is not so much broad national policies as more focused, small-scale programs designed to meet the particular needs—and take advantage of the distinctive strengths—of discrete Indian communities.

Six of the book's eleven papers appeared in *The Social Science Journal*, Vol. 19 (July 1982); the others are published here for the first time. As a thematic collection it has some holes: there is no discussion of urban Indians, victims of a kind of default mode in Indian policy; none of Indian education; and none of Indian health services. All present difficult and important policy issues. But one cannot have everything. What we have here is very welcome indeed, and recommended not only to specialists in Indian affairs, but to political sociologists and others as well.

James Biser Whisker (review date 1989)

SOURCE: A review of *A Sender of Words: Essays in Memory of John G. Neihardt*, in *Reprint Bulletin*, Vol. XXXIV, No. 1, 1989, p. 16.

[*In the following review, Whisker asserts that the essays in* A Sender of Words *are in honor of John G. Neihardt and his importance to Amerindian studies, rather than a critique of his work.*]

The title of the work comes from a letter of 1931 from a visionary Sioux Indian named Black Elk to the subject of these essays, John G. Neihardt. Black Elk was the subject of Neihardt's most significant work, *Black Elk Speaks*. Few, if any, Americans better understood the Americans culture, at least as its remnants existed into the first half of the 20th century. This collection of essays on the contribution, thought and meaning of Neihardt appears just after the one hundredth anniversary of Neihardt's birth.

The contributors are a veritable who's who among Amerindian apologists and spokespersons of our time. This is not a set of essays which seek to critique the subject; rather, these essays are in honor of Neihardt. The authors universally pay tribute to the man and his work. The editor of this book, and a major contributor to it, is Vine Deloria, Jr., author of **Custer Died for Your Sins**. Dee Brown (*Bury My Heart at Wounded Knee*) is a major contributor. The essays do cover every aspect of Neihardt's writings, and in this, the book stands far above many other sympathetic anthologies of essays.

To the reader who does not already know, Neihardt's position in Amerindian studies grows steadily. There is an influential Neihardt Foundation; and a Neihardt Day (held on the first Sunday in August); and the historical society of Nebraska makes great efforts at recognizing his work. Neihardt was a talented poet and keen observer of the western Amerindian scene.

The book certainly belongs in academic libraries and any library with holdings in western Americana and on the Amerindian. The book represents a very good value in today's market; it has been put together in an attractive and durable fashion.

Tod D. Swanson (review date January 1995)

SOURCE: A review of *God Is Red: A Native View of Religion*, in *Journal of Religion*, Vol. 75, No. 1, January, 1995, pp. 161-62.

[In following review, Swanson lauds how Deloria has updated his God Is Red *for the 1990s.]*

The second edition of **God Is Red** is a badly needed updating of a groundbreaking book. Before it was first published in 1973, scholars tended to portray Native traditions either as though they were frozen in a timeless past or as though they were precarious survivals of premodern times. By contrast, Vine Deloria presented the Native religions as a viable alternative for modern Indian people. Just as Jewish theologians had started with the holocaust, Deloria started with the religion of contemporary Indian people as they had emerged from the nineteenth-century massacres, from the twentieth-century policies of termination, and finally from the Indian renaissance of the early 1970s.

The book was also groundbreaking in the way it treated Christianity as a contrasting field. Deloria is well aware of the diversity between the Native traditions, but when they are contrasted with Christianity, strong family resemblances between them emerge. While Christianity is a religion of universal history (which for Deloria translates into manifest destiny), the Native religions begin and end with specific places. "Tribal religions," he writes "are actually complexes of attitudes, beliefs, and practices fine-tuned to harmonize with the lands on which the people live." Differences between tribal traditions are largely attributable to differences in the lands which the ceremonies engage. Secular scholars had often portrayed the Indian religions as though Christian contact had not happened. Christian scholars portrayed them either as inferior to, as preparation for, or as compatible with Christianity. Deloria's approach is fundamentally different. Chapter by chapter he contrasted the most basic Native assumptions about the world to those of Christianity from the perspective of their encounter. Deloria's comparisons are not, of course, neutral (the book is an apologia for Native religion), but they are thought-provoking.

Twenty years later **God is Red** has not been surpassed in any of these regards. But because Deloria took his starting point from the contemporary reservation life of the early 1970s, the book had become outdated. The second edition is a thorough rewriting of the book from the perspective of the 1990s. Important political and religious developments that have affected the reservations during the twenty-year interval are taken into account. In its rewritten form **God Is Red** can be used as a textbook without continual reference to the twenty-year gap. Because many American college students are of Christian background, Deloria's stark contrasts make good classroom discussion material either for broader courses on comparative religion or for more specific courses on Native American religions.

Perhaps the most controversial section in the first edition was Deloria's use of Immanuel Velikovsky's theories on the extraterrestrial origins of Native religion. For many readers this one section tended to throw the credibility of the whole book into question. Undoubtedly, many of Deloria's fans hoped that he would drop this section from the new edition, but he did not. I think the reasons go deeper than simple loyalty to an old mentor; perhaps it is that Deloria is a believer who takes Native origin myths seriously: messengers from the spirit world did indeed bring tobacco, the pipe, the ceremonies, and so on. This naturally raises the question of where the spirit messengers come from. As an answer to this question, extraterrestrial theories are appealing. Deloria is of course aware of the Eliadian and other nonliteralist approaches to the study of myth, but from a native perspective all of these can appear to be secularized Christian approaches. Hence, Deloria sticks with his extraterrestrial theories. For those who do not wish to read or assign them, the sections on extraterrestrial origins are confined to discrete chapters, and the rest of the book reads well without them.

FURTHER READING

Criticism

Wild, Peter. Review of *A Sender of Words*. *Western American Literature* XX, No. 1 (Spring 1985): 79-80.
 Discusses the insights *A Sender of Words,* edited by Deloria, provides readers concerning the work of John G. Neihardt.

Additional coverage of Deloria's life and career is contained in the following sources published by Gale: *Contemporary Authors,* Vol. 53-56; *Contemporary Authors New Revision Series,* Vols. 5, 20, 48; *Dictionary of Literary Biography,* Vol. 175; *DISCovering Authors Modules: Multicultural; Major Twentieth Century Writers,* Vol. 1; *Native North American Literature;* **and** *Something About the Author,* Vol. 21.

P. D. James

1920-

(Full name Phyllis Dorothy James White) English novelist, short story writer, nonfiction writer, essayist, and critic.

The following entry presents an overview of James's life and career. For further information about her life and works, see *CLC,* Volumes 18 and 46.

INTRODUCTION

James is a respected crime and mystery writer who is credited with expanding the scope of the mystery genre. Although she makes use of elements of traditional detective fiction, James is particularly concerned with establishing the psychological motivations of her characters. James is also noted for her sophisticated prose style, highlighted by literary allusions and quotations, and her vivid, realistic characters and settings.

Biographical Information

James was born in Oxford, England, in 1920. Her father was an Inland Revenue officer, and the family of five did not have much money. James had the opportunity to attend Cambridge Girls High School, but she ended her education when she left the school at the age of 16. Two years after the start of World War II, James married Dr. Connor Bantry White, who served during the war in the Royal Army Medical Corps. Her husband returned from the war suffering from extreme mental illness for which he had to be hospitalized. In order to support her two young daughters and herself, James took night classes in hospital administration and became an administrator working for the National Health Service. Her experience in the health field helped in the writing of *Shroud for a Nightingale* (1971) and *The Black Tower* (1975), which are both set in hospitals. James had always dreamed of becoming a writer and when she finally decided to try her hand at writing, she thought a mystery novel would be good practice for her. The novel, *Cover Her Face* (1962), was accepted by the first publisher to which she sent it. James decided that she liked the discipline of the detective genre, and continued to employ it in all but a few of her future novels. After her husband died in 1968, she transferred to the Department of Home Affairs, roughly equivalent to the United States Department of Justice. Her experience at this job helped with her to write knowledgeably about forensic science and police investigation. James eventually retired from civil service and became a local magistrate, in addition to continuing her writing career.

Major Works

One of James's goals as a writer of detective fiction is to fulfill the elements of the genre and still employ the tools which make "serious fiction" satisfying. Her early novels, including *Cover Her Face, A Mind to Murder* (1963), *Unnatural Causes* (1967), and *Shroud for a Nightingale*, evidence her interest in realism. Although structured in traditional "whodunnit" fashion, these works rely on rounded credible characterizations that separate her work from that of the traditional "country house mystery" of traditional British detective fiction, in which static characters exist only to advance the plot of the mystery. Scotland Yard detective Adam Dalgliesh is the protagonist in each of these novels, as well as several of James's later books. A published poet as well as a police inspector, Dalgliesh is portrayed as a detached and devoted professional who is acutely sensitive to the emotions and motivations of the individuals he encounters in his work. The developments in Dalgliesh's private and professional life are engrossing subplots to the novels in which he is featured. In *Devices and Desires* (1989), Dalgliesh gets pulled into the investigation of a serial killer while vacationing on the Norfolk coast and resolving his late aunt's affairs. James focused less on Dalgliesh and his personal life in *A Certain Justice* (1997). In this novel, a barrister is murdered and her arrogance and cut-throat career climbing leaves a string of suspects. In *An Unsuitable Job for a Woman* (1972), James introduces the character of Cordelia Grey, a female protagonist who is considerably different from Dalgliesh. Grey is a young, inexperienced private investigator who cannot rely on the resources of the police department. *An Unsuitable Job for a Woman* chronicles Grey's first investigation, in which she uncovers a murder originally believed to be a suicide. James departed from the detective genre in two novels. First in *Innocent Blood* (1980), a woman who was adopted as a child locates her real parents and discovers that her father was a rapist and her mother was a murderer. In *The Children of Men* (1992), James chronicles the extinction of the human race and the baby that may be its salvation.

Critical Reception

Critics have conflicting views about James's proliferation of details in her novels. Some reviewers have praised her evocation of place through the use of description; others have found it a distraction to the action of the plot. Christopher Lehmann-Haupt complained that "so much of her scene-setting serves no other purpose than to create impenetrable atmosphere." Reviewers have noted that she effectively conveys the specifics of forensics and police investigation. Critics have consistently lauded James for giving readers more psychological depth than the average detective story. Commentators often note that James provides the motivation and larger human questions underlying the crimes in her novels, instead of simply presenting a neatly solved puzzle. Walter Wangerin, Jr. stated, "Plot, under Miss James's hand, is never merely external action. Always she explores character, the complexities of motive and thought and emotion; and always she wonders about the nature of humankind in general—this baffling admixture of good and evil, faith and failure, love and a murderous self-sufficiency." One aspect of her work often noted is the juxtaposition of the regular, ordered world presented in her novels and the disordered chaos wrought by the introduction of the crime. Ben Macintyre noted that "it is precisely the contrast between such external fastidiousness and the complex, sometimes depraved internal lives of James's characters that gives her books such emotive power." Some critics laud James for her feminist departure from the typical male detective through the character of Cordelia Grey. Many critics assert that James's work transcends the mystery genre because it contains the elements one looks for in a literary novel. However, a few have disagreed, contending that James represents the best of her genre because of what she has accomplished within the confinements of the

detective story. Joyce Carol Oates concluded, "P. D. James does not 'transcend' genre; she refines, deepens, and amplifies it."

PRINCIPAL WORKS

Cover Her Face (novel) 1962

A Mind to Murder (novel) 1963

Unnatural Causes (novel) 1967

The Maul and the Pear Tree: The Ratcliffe Highway Murders, 1811 [with Thomas A. Critchley] (nonfiction) 1971

Shroud for a Nightingale (novel) 1971

An Unsuitable Job for a Woman (novel) 1972

The Black Tower (novel) 1975

Death of an Expert Witness (novel) 1977

Innocent Blood (novel) 1980

The Skull Beneath the Skin (novel) 1982

A Private Treason (play) 1985

A Taste for Death (novel) 1986

Devices and Desires (novel) 1989

The Children of Men (novel) 1992

Original Sin (novel) 1994

A Certain Justice (novel) 1997

CRITICISM

P. D. James with Jane S. Bakerman (interview date January 1977)

SOURCE: "Interview with P. D. James," in *Armchair Detective,* Vol. 10, No. 1, January, 1977, pp. 55-7, 92.

[*In the following interview, James discusses her approach to crafting a mystery, her view on feminism, and how she wants to be remembered.*]

P. D. James is a unique person in a number of ways, not the least of which is the fact that she has never had a rejection slip from an editor! With a typical touch of humor and a broad smile, she reported that as she prepared her first novel for submission, her children cautioned her that "All good writers can paper their walls with their rejection slips!" And then, when the book, **Cover Her Face,** was accepted by Faber and Faber, the first publisher to whom it was offered, the children's "confidence in the book was somewhat shaken. They felt good novels ought to be rejected!"

But the confidence of James's fans remains unshaken. Her six novels, **Cover Her Face,** 1962; **A Mind to Murder,** 1963; **Unnatural Causes,** 1967; **Shroud for a Nightin-**

gale, 1971; *An Unsuitable Job for a Woman,* 1972; and *The Black Tower,* 1975, along with her short stories (two of which have won Ellery Queen prizes) have earned her a wide following among American as well as British readers of mystery-detective fiction. Her solid reputation as a careful crafts person, clever creator of plots, and shrewd commentator on human psychology is underscored not only by her work but also by her attitude toward it.

P. D. James, mystery novelist, is also Phyllis White, civil servant and mother. The mother of two grown daughters and the grandmother of four—two girls and two boys—James took a job in the civil service after World War II, when her husband returned from the military service permanently disabled. She began working for the National Health Service as an administrator, primarily doing mental health work. In 1968, after her husband's death, she transferred to the Home Office, "the Department of Home Affairs; it's a mixture, really, of the Department of Law and the Department of the Interior, concerned with law and order."

This juggling of two very demanding professions has several effects on her work. First, it provides her with a "certain amount of information." Time spent working in the Police Department taught her a good deal about police procedure, organization and crime investigation, and, through her work, she's also met forensic scientists, pathologists, who are a source of information. These sources, along with the careful library research she does, help guarantee the accuracy about forensic pathology the author considers absolutely necessary in crime fiction. But the main value of the job, perhaps any job, she feels, is that it keeps her in touch with a wide range of people, with the working world.

A second effect of the full time job is that her writing has to be done in her "spare" time, and that time consists primarily of the hours between 6:30 and 8:30 A.M. and the weekends. This kind of schedule, which also sometimes incorporates some hours of revision in the evenings, demands a good deal of self-discipline. Juggling this routine requires that the writer not bring her office responsibilities home with her, but James makes clear that she values both her careers:

> I regard the writing as more important. The office is a way of earning a living; it is very safe and carries a pension at the end of it and is at the same time a demanding and very interesting job. Government *is* interesting; it brings me, though I'm not a *very* senior civil servant, in touch with Ministers of the Crown. It gives me an entree into the House of Commons and into the House of Lords during debates, and I see how policy is made. All this is fascinating to a writer. I think I'd been the poorer without it, but I like to think of myself as a writer who is also a civil servant.

The same sort of self-control which enables James to balance two exacting careers is reflected in her comments about the objectivity a writer must obtain in order to achieve a stance from which she can observe, interpret, and comment:

> I think writers can always stand outside and observe, particularly novelists, whether they're observing culture or whether they're observing the interaction of human beings. One stands outside one's own experience even. One is able, even at moments of tragedy, to be watching it—to be suffering, even. I think this is essential to a writer. One is *in* society, as we all area, but at the same time detached and watching.

The emphasis on this tight schedule and the self-discipline and self-control it demands must not, however, overshadow the personal impression James gives. She is cheerful, open, communicative, and very well informed. Her laughter is warm and comes quickly to the surface, and though she says she's very like her central character, Inspector Adam Dalgliesh, he does not display her ready wit and humor.

As one might expect, James's personality is reflected in her quarters. The living room of her London apartment is enlarged by high, white walls and the use of a wall-size mirror on the inner wall. Fronting on Dorset Square, the room, which incorporates a dining area, is very full, but uncrowded—a kind of symbol, perhaps, for James's life. The furniture is contemporary; the many feet of shelf space are filled with books (Trollope is a favorite) and bric-a-brac, some acquired at street markets. The walls carry pictures which combine family pieces and some "just collected because I liked them." The overall effect is pleasant and comfortable.

Just as the room is a place for thinking as well as a place for living and working, James is, as her readers well know, a thoughtful person. This contemplativeness was reflected in her comments when I asked her why the crime novel seems to be such a good metaphor for contemporary society. She began by revising the question:

> Is it because, really, crime is such an individual act, a breaking out of convention? Really, we all walk some kind of psychological tightrope, and this is a stepping into space—

> The fiction is the imposing of a moral order, where, apparently, there is none. But really, even if one feels impotent in the face of violence and tragedy and injustice in this world, somehow the pattern at the end of the novels does come right. Also, there's a completion; the circle is joined.

I think possibly, you know, its psychologically reassuring in the sense that it is a purging of guilt. That basically, when saying "Who done it?" that one can say, at least in this case, "Not I."

This awareness of humanity's common sense of guilt is reflected in the character Dalgliesh, who in **Shroud for a Nightingale,** for example, feels he ought to say to the murderer that he knows her because he knows himself. James agrees that we are all guilty of something, though perhaps not murder—of "deceptions, of meannesses, of failures in human relationships," and thus we can understand failings—even very terrible ones—in others. But the author draws a clear line between understanding and condoning wrongdoing. "I think there's a difference between the acknowledgment of a common humanity and a sentimentality about crime, which I don't personally share. I don't like sentimentality and hope my hero isn't sentimental!"

Dalgliesh is not sentimental, nor is he, like some fictitious detectives, infallible, but he is sensitive and he "reflects many of my views and attitudes to life, and I have a sympathy for him," James says, pointing out that one wouldn't go on writing "about a man if one didn't quite admire him or at least sympathize with him." She perceives him as

> a very detached man, essentially a very lonely man in a lonely profession, one which brings him into contact with tragedy, with *evil.* At the same time, he has the sensitivity of a poet, which I think makes him a complex character and the reconciliation of these two very different facets of his character is interesting.

Beginning with this view of the human condition and with this concept of her central character, James then projects him, in each novel, into a closed society, which not only produces a clearly defined locale, but which also generates interest:

> I think the interaction of human beings in a closed society is absolutely fascinating: the power struggles, the attempt to establish and retain one's own identity, the way in which people group defensive or offensive alliances, particularly against strangers. And I think, too, that there's a certain dramatic element in the detective coming *into* this society, penetrating it, seeing it with fresh eyes—and the whole society reacting to him. Of course, it's also convenient in that if you have a closed society, then you have a closed circle of suspects!

Although Dalgliesh is the penetrator of the closed society, he is not its only observer in the novels; James uses the third person and shifts the point of view from observer to observer within each book; this variety lends complexity and richness, in her view, and also allows her to describe scenes to which the detective is not privy. She gives one particularly good example:

> There's far more richness in a novel where one is able to enter into different human beings and particularly to see the *same* event through their different eyes. A small example of that is in **A Mind to Murder,** when the body is discovered, and because it's a nervous reaction that he has, the consulting psychiatrist, Dr. Steiner, has to turn away because he finds he's giggling. And it's purely nothing he can control. To the other person there, he seems to be weeping, and to her it's extraordinary that he should be so distressed over the death of someone he didn't in fact like. I think this is useful; it adds psychological tone. . . .

Steiner is a good example of the kind of people about whom James likes to write—able and intelligent. "They may be rather wicked people, but on the whole, I find that intelligent people are more interesting." Sometimes these characters trigger an idea for a scene or a story, but essentially, James believes that she doesn't write directly from life. However, she frequently comes across "scraps of conversation," houses, or places which stimulate her imagination.

> I remember seeing the river in a certain light, the Thames at low tide, the birds clustering at the end of a wharf and the water looking like oil . . . these sorts of scenes, one sees them and observes them, and will probably record them, and if the current book or the next book is going to deal with this sort of place—

the details are ready to hand. She feels that she must "get into the book, in a sense, enter into the world of the book," and to do so, she not only needs to work regularly, every day, but also spends a great deal of time on very, very careful planning and plotting. Not only are the individual characters fairly complete in her mind before she actually begins writing, but so are the individual scenes:

> Exactly who will be present, the time of day, the look of the place—and the room, the smell of the room—the whole atmosphere is there before I start.

> I have charts and a synopsis and pages where the time sequence is set out in great detail so that I know what each of my characters is doing, certainly on the more important days, possibly over a matter of weeks. And, details of the characters. Of course, the characters soon become so real, one doesn't need to refer to this. But when plotting, it's important: names and physical appearance are important.

This immersion in the world of the book coupled with the careful planning account, very likely, not only for her absorption in it ("I think I'm writing, in a sense, for myself or to express something I need to express"), but also for the success of her method.

> I don't write the book starting at the beginning and going right through to the end at all. I write it in scenes. Yes, I think that's the word, in dramatic scenes. I think, "I will now do the episode in the cottage between A and B," and this can then be put on one side and I'll go back to it later. But this method does mean that I can work on a part of the novel which, at that particular moment, I feel I could do best.

While she recognizes the excitement and thrill that come with a passage which goes well the first time and the delight generated by finding that a piece of material which stimulated her imagination fits beautifully into a work, James regards the creative process as primarily a matter of self-discipline.

> I think a writer does need a very great deal of discipline. I think any prospective writer who feels that this is a matter of inspiration, primarily, and not a matter of discipline, is due for some very unpleasant surprises. It seems to me that as a craft, even if one puts it no higher, it is a highly disciplined art form . . .

> There can be passages, I think, either because one's in the mood or because one particularly wants to write it (sometimes they're the best passages) which are right the first time. They are spontaneous, and too often one spoils them by altering them. But I think these are very rare passages. And that for most of the work, the rewriting is tremendously important; I don't think I've known of a writer who didn't feel this.

James, herself, usually does about two full revisions, first writing out a very rough draft by hand and then putting it on tape. It's typed from the tape and she does another major revision on that version, occasionally even supplying some final changes in the second typed draft. This careful reworking, along with her detailed planning and tight work schedule, require that a novel take about eighteen months minimum to complete, "usually it takes rather longer."

While this process is going on, the author does not find herself talking about the book in progress; in fact, "on the whole, I don't relish talking at length about my work, really." Readers will be glad to know, however, that there *is* a new book in progress, now plotted and in the writing stages; it will probably be complete by the end of 1976 if the schedule goes as planned; thus far, it has no set title, though a number of possibilities are being considered.

Though P. D. James doesn't discuss her works as they are

being written, she says she might, when the book is finished, talk over a technical difficulty and her method of handling it with a fellow writer. She does belong to the International Crime Writers Association and enjoys the fellowship, though her time for active membership is limited. One of the most enjoyable facets of the group, she thinks, is its freedom from professional jealousy. "It certainly doesn't happen with crime writers, who are very friendly. Perhaps we sublimate our worst emotions in our books!"

Another group of agreeable people is her followers, many of whom write to her. Usually, they tell her about the pleasure the books have afforded them, but sometimes they ask technical questions or request advice. Despite the fact that she must limit her letter-writing time in order to meet her writing schedule, James does try to answer the letters. "It seems only courteous when they've taken the trouble to write . . ."

Because one of the delights to these readers is the game of trying to guess the culprit in any crime story, I asked James if she considered the guessing-game factor central to her works and if she, for instance, made a list, checking if off to be sure she'd given all the clues.

> Sometimes I make a list, but certainly, yes, I do try to be punctilious over the detective part of it. I give all the clues; I hope I give them fairly. It should be possible to reason out the solution. I do consider the readers; it *is* a detective story, and they have a right to expect that it'll be fair.

> But at the same time the solution must be psychologically right. It's just no good if it merely fits neatly because these are the facts and this is the timetable and that's what the clock said and so on—Psychologically, the crime *must* arise from human nature.

> How much the readers really bother, I think, is another point. I know when I read them, I'm obviously, in the back of my mind, thinking, "Aha!"—but I think far more frequently, "Aha! That's a clever clue and I'm meant to be taken in by this but I won't!" rather than that I'm listing them in my mind.

Because she is an English woman and a mystery writer, the comparison between P. D. James and Agatha Christie is, probably, inevitable. Certainly, her American publishers identify her as an heir of the late detective writer. Like many readers in the genre, James finds Christie's puzzle-making "remarkable, a sort of sleight of hand! She brings it off practically every time!" But she also comments,

> I think we're fairly different writers. I think it's just a way the publishers have of saying that they hope I get

as well known. I have an admiration for her, but I'm a very different writer.

When asked why so many women writers like herself and Christie have been successful in the mystery-detection field, James replied:

> I think because we're careful about detail, and this is important. I think women like writing about human beings and their reaction to each other, and detective novels are about human beings and their reaction to extreme stress. I think that we often write about a fairly domestic situation; the contrast between this and the horror of the actual murder is very effective. This is true particularly of English detective fiction, less true, perhaps, with American, but we are far more intrigued by the body in the library, as it were, or the body in the cottage than we are by half a dozen slain bodies down the mean streets. It is the domestic murder which interests us, and women are good at that.

Among female readers and critics, James is often considered a feminist. I asked her how she felt about that, and her response was immediate and vigorous!

> Yes, I am a feminist in the sense that I like and admire women very much. I'm not in sympathy with the more extreme factions of Women's Lib because I suppose what I believe is that women are as intelligent as men and in many ways as able, but women have got other qualities as well.

> These are qualities of sympathy and of understanding (an instinctive wish to look after people who are weaker than themselves) and of less aggression. This is what the world *wants*! It would be a great pity if we start emulating men and emulating the qualities of men which are their least attractive qualities.

> But I'm a tremendous feminist and I think that women should have absolutely equal opportunity. I think that all over the world their abilities are very wasted. I certainly feel very strongly about unfairness—sexual unfairness, legal unfairness. I hate to see discrimination of any kind. It makes me very cross. But I like men. I have men friends. I dislike the kind of, I suppose, anti-man Women's Lib.

> Yes, I am very much a feminist, very much. Certainly when I was a girl, it seemed to me deplorable how girls were automatically expected to take inferior roles. Even in a family where there were very clever girls and stupid boys, the education would be for the boys and not for the girls. And I think, thank God, we've moved very

far from that; I think we have a far more equal role. But we mustn't, I think, be ruthless about it.

Like her writing, this comment reflects her concern for the individual and for the kind of freedom for the individual which allows him or her to be himself, to make the contribution he or she is best able *to* make. This same concern is also apparent in her response to the worn but important question, "What advice would you give to the beginning writer?"

> I would say to keep on . . . to learn all you can from other writers, from *good* writers, to be original, to be yourself, not to copy other people . . . to try and look at the world always with fresh eyes and to put things down honestly: what you think and what you feel.

> It seems somewhat contradictory to say, "Study the classics, study the people who are good writers," and at the same time, "Be yourself," but it isn't really contradictory. There's a tremendous lot to be learned from people who've *known* how to do it and do it well; but at the same time, one has to bring an individual voice to it.

Late in the interview, I turned to yet another old but useful question and asked P. D. James how she would like to be remembered.

> As a human being, I should like to be remembered as a one who enhanced the pleasure in life for other people. I don't mean I *am* that sort of human being, but that people, when they looked back at me, would want to smile or to laugh. And that my children would want to look back at me and feel that they had been the happier because I'd been their mother.

> I think as a writer, I would like to be remembered as an honest and original craftsman, who was able to give pleasure, and entertainment, and release from the anxieties of our violent world to a large number of people—and to have troubled to try and do it well.

She does trouble to do it well, and the time and effort she invests are well spent, indeed. The books are sound, insightful, and bring delight to their readers, largely because their author "takes the trouble" to put down honestly what she has observed with fresh and compassionate—but never sentimental!—eyes.

Erlene Hubly (essay date Fall-Winter 1982)

SOURCE: "Adam Dalgliesh: Byronic Hero," in *Clues: A*

Journal of Detection, Vol. 3, No. 2, Fall-Winter, 1982, pp. 40-46.

[In the following essay, Hubly analyzes the character of Adam Dalgliesh as a Byronic hero.]

Various readers of P. D. James' novels have attempted to understand the character of her detective, Adam Dalgliesh, by discussing him in terms of classic detective fiction. Francis Wyndham, for example, writing in the *London Times* Literary Supplement, has placed Adam in the tradition of "the gentleman detective" as developed by Dorothy Sayers and Ngaio Marsh. As such he is "a suitably romantic sleuth," attracted to women, able to carry on "stylish courtships" of them, fond of music and good literature (Jane Austen is his favorite writer), sensitive and yet ruthless enough to be able to perform his sometimes distasteful duties. Norma Siebenheller, in her book on James, discusses Adam in terms of this same tradition. Like the earlier English mystery writers—Dorothy Sayers, Ngaio Marsh, Margery Allingham and others—James writes "literature tightly constructed and civilized" novels in which inventive characterizations, psychological insights and detailed descriptions replace violence, physical conflict and rough-and-tumble action. And yet, Siebenheller argues, James also departs from that tradition in significant ways. Rather than write books in which the puzzle is all important, as did Agatha Christie and to a lesser extent Sayers, Marsh and Allingham, in which an element of make-believe pervades throughout, James has chosen to portray a more realistic world, one peopled with characters whose actions are carefully motivated and whose reactions are true to their complex personalities.

It is in this tradition—that of realistic popular fiction, rather than that of classic detective fiction—that Siebenheller places both James and her detective Adam Dalgliesh. "A far cry from the almost comical characters who served Christie and Sayers as sleuths," Adam is a real detective, a professional policeman who solves crimes using standard police procedures rather than sudden and capricious insights or revelations. In addition, Adam is a far more complex character than either Christie's or Sayers' protagonists, a man who, because of early emotional traumas, has built a protective wall around himself which no one can penetrate, a man whose most marked characteristic is his detachment, his fierce desire for privacy.

While both Wyndham's and Siebenheller's observations about Adam are useful, Wyndham placing him in the tradition of classic detective fiction, Siebenheller seeing him as a departure from that tradition, they do not fully account for either the man Adam Dalgliesh or the fascination he has had for readers. In order to do that we must go to an even

earlier literary tradition than that of "the gentleman detective"—to the tradition of the Byronic hero.

The Byronic hero, as developed by Byron in such poems and dramatic works as *Childe Harold's Pilgrimage, Lara* and *Manfred,* is, among other things, a rebel against society, a man who, for a number of reasons, finds it impossible to adjust to or accept society. Peter Thorslev, in discussing the figure in his book *The Byronic Hero,* has noted that these heroes are solitaries, men who either because of the acuteness of their minds and sensibilities or because of some conscious moral choice have placed themselves outside the rules that govern others, rebelling at first against society only, then against the natural universe, and finally against God himself. This is, of course, a description that does not apply to Adam Dalgliesh, who is, above all else, a policeman, a man committed to defending and upholding the laws of society. In this respect he differs greatly from the Byronic hero, from Manfred, for example, who, by self-admission, belongs to "the brotherhood of Cain," a man who has sought after forbidden things, a man who, by loving his sister Astarte incestuously, has broken the social code.

Adam's insistence upon upholding society's laws springs, in part, from personal fears. Although somewhat cavalier in his answers when asked why he became a policeman— "I like the job"; "it's one I can do reasonably well; it allows me to indulge a curiosity about people and, for most of the time anyway, I'm not bored with it."—Adam's real reason for becoming a policeman is far more imperative. Mary Taylor, the matron of the nurses' training school in **Shroud for a Nightingale,** comes closer to the reason Adam became a detective when she, after having observed Adam for a number of days and intuiting much about him, notes: "What would a man like you be without his job, this particular job? Vulnerable like the rest of us?"

In citing Adam's vulnerability Mary Taylor has hit upon one of his most distinguishing characteristics and certainly one of the reasons he became a detective. For at the core of Adam's being is a fear of chaos. It is a fear that goes back to Adam's childhood, when as a fourteen year old boy he experienced what was to him "a horror eclipsing all subsequent horrors"—the murder, by her brother, of a young girl Adam was just beginning to imagine himself in love with. It is a fear that culminates eight years later in another even more traumatic death—that of Adam's wife soon after childbirth, a death which cuts across Adam's life, forming his vision of the world.

Death, then, that which can suddenly and inexplicably destroy one's world, death becomes the enemy. Against such a reality Adam develops a number of defenses, chief among which is his job. If Adam's father, an Anglican minister, tried to fight death on a theological level, by denying its power, Adam, the inheritor of a secular world, fights it on another. Constantly encountering death in the murder cases he investigates, he tries to bring order out of chaos: if he cannot stop death he can at least catch and punish those who inflict it on others. His, then, is an endeavor which offers reassurance, which seems to restore order to an otherwise disorderly world.

Adam, then, is a fierce defender of the social code, feeling that rules, in a world of flux and chaos, are man's only hope. He is, then, in this respect, the antithesis of the Byronic hero, who glorifies in disorder, who views the rules as something inapplicable to him and thus as something that can be broken. And yet Adam does have other qualities that place him squarely in the Byronic tradition, qualities which we would now like to explore.

Based on the persona of Byron, who upon the death of his great-uncle inherited the title of Lord, the Byronic hero is an aristocrat, either by birth or sensibility, the capacity for feeling, in this tradition, an indication of the depth of one's soul. Adam Dalgliesh, although not an aristocrat by birth, is one in sensibility, having developed early a great capacity both to feel and to suffer. Like Byron, Adam is a poet, and the title of one of his books of poems, *Invisible Scars,* indicates both the nature and the degree of his suffering: he has been wounded and his wounds have left lasting scars; internal, these scars cannot be seen by others, but only felt by their bearer. His life early defined by loss—the murder, when he was fourteen, of a young girl he was just beginning to love—the death of his wife and infant son when he was in his mid-twenties—Adam's growth has been marked by pain, a pain so intense that it has defined his life.

Central to the Byronic hero is an overwhelming grief for a lost love whose death the hero somehow feels responsible for. Manfred, Byron's darkest hero, seeks forgetfulness from a past he cannot escape, from the memory of an incestuous relationship with his sister Astarte, who in apparent remorse at such forbidden love, killed herself. Manfred, left alone to suffer for them both, blames himself for her death: "My embrace was fatal"; "I loved her, and destroy'd her." Wandering over the earth after Astarte's death, continually searching for love, Manfred has never been able to find her likeness or equal, and thus imprisoned in the past, seeks release through the only means left: his own death.

Unlike Manfred, Dalgliesh's love was not incestuous, and yet he was implicated in his wife's death, for she died a few hours after childbirth. Adam's embrace, then, like Manfred's, was fatal: in impregnating his wife he also insured her death. Like Manfred, Adam has never been able to forget his lost love, and once a year, on the anniversary of his wife's death, goes to a Catholic church, where in "this most private action of his detached and secretive life," he lights a candle to her memory. Believing that all emotional involvements are painful, he has carefully insulated himself from others, engaging only in casual love affairs, committing himself to no one. Only in his poetry does Adam reveal himself, protected by the very private act of writing.

There are, of course, several women who do break through, temporarily at least, Adam's defenses. Deborah Riscoe is the most important of these. Meeting her in one of his early cases, she the daughter of the woman Adam exposes as the murderer in *Cover Her Face,* Adam finds himself, when they meet again several years later, "to be on the brink of love." By the time of his third case, that reported in *Unnatural Causes,* Adam's feelings for Deborah have progressed to the point that he is thinking of marrying her. Taking a holiday in order to decide the issue, Adam visits his aunt Jane; becoming involved, however, in a case, Adam does not, until the end of his holiday, turn his thoughts to Deborah. By then it is too late, for Deborah, sensing Adam's indecision, has taken matters into her own hands and broken off their relationship. It is a decision Adam seems to agree with, for he does not try to see her again, and Deborah Riscoe passes from his life.

From time to time readers of James' novels, James herself, have speculated on whether or not Adam will ever marry again. We would suggest that he will not, for Adam, a prisoner of his past, can love only himself. Early traumatized by death, believing that all emotional attachments lead to loss, Adam cannot escape himself; all his loves are but versions of himself. Like the Byronic hero who seeks himself in others like himself, Manfred for example, in his sister Astarte, whose eyes, hair, features, even the tone of her voice are like his, Adam's loves are narcissistic, reflections of himself. For although Adam goes through the motions of loving Deborah Riscoe, it is two other women, his aunt Jane and Mary Taylor, we would argue, who really claim his attentions, and both are reflections of himself.

Aunt Jane is, of course, closely related to Adam through family ties: her brother was Adam's father. They also share other histories: both lost a loved one early in life, Aunt Jane her fiancé, killed in the First World War; Adam, his wife dying soon after childbirth. Both have sought solace by immersing themselves in solitary pursuits, Aunt Jane in birdwatching, Adam in writing poetry. Temperamentally they are also alike: the adjectives used to describe Aunt Jane, "sensitive, uncommunicative and rather difficult," could apply to Adam as well. Like Adam Aunt Jane is a solitary and detached figure, one who does not express her feelings to others. Her most distinguishing feature, her rock-like self-sufficiency, is the quality that Adam most admires in her, and it is the quality that he has spent his life developing in himself. Adam's identification with his aunt is so strong that, near the end of the book in which she appears, **Unnatural Causes,** when his aunt withdraws from her living room in apparent indifference after hearing the murderer's confession, Adam is suddenly frightened at her lack of involvement: "Never before had his aunt's uninvolvement struck him so forcibly; never before had it seemed so frightening." His fear, of course, is not for his aunt alone, but for himself as well. For just the night before Adam had withdrawn from the same room and the same people in order to be alone, to try and decide whether or not to marry Deborah Riscoe. It was a decision he could not make, and his inability to involve himself with Deborah has left him as alone as his aunt. Thus his fear for his aunt the next day; thus his fear for himself.

Aunt Jane serves as a foil to Deborah Riscoe throughout the book, for certainly Aunt Jane's presence makes it difficult for Adam to envision loving any other woman. In a scene early in the book, while sitting before the living room fire with his aunt, who is silently knitting, Adam finds himself openly comparing the two women—his aunt with her strong character, her self-sufficient ways, her solitary and yet appealing life at Pentlands, her home in the country—to Deborah, whose easy sophistication, whose preference for the city—its restaurants, theaters and pubs—seem to exclude her from Pentlands, and thus from Adam's heart.

For it is Aunt Jane whose presence dominates the book in which she appears. Adam, ostensibly on a holiday in order to decide whether or not to marry Deborah Riscoe, does not think much about Deborah but is constantly impressed with his aunt, whom he is visiting. During the course of the book it becomes obvious that she is the woman Adam most admires; she is the woman he most looks forward to seeing. His visits to her, twice a year, restore him in ways no other activity can, their walks together on the beach, he carrying her sketching paraphernalia, she pointing out various birds to him, their closeness, felt but not spoken, enabling him to return to London at the end of his holiday "with a sense of relief." And she, undemanding, asking nothing of him, not even affection, understood because so like himself, is finally "the only woman in the world with whom he was completely at peace." It is a high compliment, indeed, from a man who values, above all else, peace and tranquillity; no other woman among Adam's acquaintances offers him such satisfaction.

If Aunt Jane's attraction is, in part, because she is so like Adam, Mary Taylor, the Matron of the Nightingale Training School for Nurses, appeals to Adam for the same reason. Again the attraction is narcissistic, the similarities between the two striking: both are imposing figures, tall, slender and impressive on the first meeting. Each has distinguished himself in his career, Mary as an administrator

of a nurses' training school, Adam as a detective at Scotland Yard. Each is a prisoner of his past, each having suffered early a traumatic experience involving death: Mary, at the age of eighteen accused, wrongly, of having taken part in the killings of thirty-one Jewish workers in a Nazi slave camp; Adam at the age of twenty-six having lost his wife and infant son in childbed. Each is a solitary figure, happiest when alone; each views the love or concern of another as a burden best discarded. Each sees himself as superior to the average, a superiority whose rewards, an increased sense of awareness, is also its greatest liability, resulting also in an increased sense of vulnerability. And finally each, feeling that chaos lies just below the surface of reality, has sought refuge in rules and regulations, building his life around them as if they might prevent disaster.

Adam's meeting, then, with Mary Taylor involves a shock of recognition, for in getting to know Mary, Adam begins to see himself. His attraction to her is immediate and clear: upon seeing her for the first time he is impressed by her "casual elegance and a confidence that was almost palpable." Adam's involvement with Mary deepens at their first meeting alone in her flat: appraising her features, noting her face with its distinctive bone structure, Adam suddenly thinks that "she was one of the most beautiful women he had ever met." Engaging her in conversation, he is impressed by her intelligence, her facility with words, and thinks, after one of her clever repartees, that their conversation was becoming "a verbal pavane," one which, if he were not careful, he would "begin to enjoy."

During the course of the case he becomes increasingly interested in Mary Taylor. As if jealous of anyone else in Mary's life, he seems obsessed with her friendship with Ethel Brumfett, wondering what Mary Taylor could see in such an "essentially stupid and dull woman," wondering finally, with horror, if they might be lovers. And in a scene near the end of the book, after Adam has been hit on the head with a golf club and must have the wound sutured, his feelings for Mary finally emerge. For the things Adam notes about her here are the things a lover, about to make love, would notice: her cool and steady hands upon his head, her hands as they undress him, taking off his tie, removing his jacket, unbuttoning his shirt, the sheen of her dressing-gown and the long plait of hair falling over her left shoulder, the feel of her body as she draws his head against her breast, steadying him as his wound is sutured by Dr. Courtney-Briggs. Characteristically, Adam fights this attraction; refusing to admit his need for her, her strength, her cool hands, her supporting body, he refuses to take anesthesia as his wound is stitched. And as if to prove his independence from her, he, as she helps him stand after the stitching is finished, pushes her away.

Theirs is, however, a bond that Adam cannot so easily dismiss, as he himself later recognizes. For he finally knows Mary Taylor because he knows himself, can read her mind because he knows his own. "How can you possibly know how I felt about Ethel Brumfett and her intolerable devotion to me?" Mary Taylor asks Adam. "Because I know myself," he answers her, silently to himself. Theirs is a bond Mary Taylor later openly acknowledges for both of them, when noting how they both have tried to hide their fears and doubts about life behind a belief in rules and regulations, she observes: "You and I are not so different after all, Adam Dalgliesh."

Indeed they are not, and later when Mary Taylor kills Ethel Brumfett, her action threatens Adam in a most personal way. Not only does it undermine his belief in his ability to judge people—how could he have been so attracted to a woman capable of murder—but it also threatens his whole concept of himself. For if he is like Mary Taylor, then he too could be capable of murder. Mary Taylor is the dark side of Adam, and his anger at her betrayal of them both, at his own fears that he, too, could murder, causes him to hunt her down with a vengeance, pursuing "the case as if it were a personal vendetta, hating himself and her."

Adam's involvement with Mary Taylor, then, serves to reveal several of his Byronic characteristics: his narcissism, his independent and solitary nature, his own murderous impulses. It reveals yet another of these characteristics: his basic agnosticism. For like Mary Taylor, Adam, while on the surface reassuring and comforting to those who serve under him, holds a private credo that is stark, almost nihilistic. Although Mary, early in the book *Shroud for a Nightingale* expresses this credo for herself, it could belong to Adam as well:

> She could imagine the blank incomprehension, the resentment with which they would greet her private credo.

> "I haven't anything to offer. There isn't any help. We are all alone, all of us from the moment of birth until we die. Our past is our present and our future. We have to live with ourselves until there isn't any more time left. If you want salvation look to yourself. There's nowhere else to look."

For Adam, like his Byronic predecessors, has inherited a world in which God is dead, in which religion has lost its power, in which death triumphs over all. Man stands utterly alone, armed only with his intelligence. Heaven and hell have been secularized, internalized, the mind itself the sole creator of good and evil. Byron's hero, Manfred, addressing the Spirits who come to take him away at the end of the poem, expresses best this new faith in the powers of the human mind, which alone is immortal and which makes of all things "its own place and time": "The Mind which is

immortal makes itself / Requital for its good or evil thoughts,— / Is its own origin of ill and end— / And its own place and time." In such a world man becomes his own point of reference; in such a world there is little appeal to things other than the self. In *The Black Tower* we learn that Adam, as a boy, had tried to visualize what "the spiritual life" was like, and had often asked his father's curate, Father Baddeley, to explain it to him:

> Was it lived at the same time as the ordinary regulated life of getting up, meal times, school, holidays; or was it an existence on some other plane to which he and the uninitiated had no access but into which Father Baddeley could retreat at will?

Although Father Baddeley had tried to explain it to Adam, Adam had not understood. And it is a question that Adam, as a man, still does not know the answer to.

For the church, in James' novels, is an ineffectual force, and serves only as a setting for ominous events. James' is a world in which science has replaced religion, a world in which the best of men, such as Adam, turn to science rather than to religion to solve the riddles of mankind. There is no place for religion, always an intangible; the problems are too insistent, too real, too ever-present. It is a world in which men go to church regularly and yet end up killing their neighbors, a world in which chapels are places where lovers meet to carry on illicit affairs, couples making love on the altars where men once worshipped, a world in which religious pilgrimages to Lourdes are nothing more than covers for smuggling drugs into England, a world in which murderers wear monks' habits while killing their victims.

Amidst all this chaos Adam moves, armed only with his job, his poetry, his human intelligence. There seems to be no other help. Men are strangers to one another and to God, and the passage in the *Book of Common Prayer* that Adam comes across near the end of one of his cases, *Death of an Expert Witness,* could apply to Adam as well as to all men:

> For I am a stranger with thee, and a sojourner, as all my fathers were. O spare me a little, that I may recover my strength: before I go hence, and be no more seen.

P. D. James with Rosemary Herbert (interview date Fall 1986)

SOURCE: "A Mind to Write," in *Armchair Detective,* Vol. 19, No. 4, Fall, 1986, pp. 340-48.

[*In the following interview, James discusses how her novels differ from those of the traditional detective genre, and the inspiration behind her characters and plots.*]

"The extraordinary thing" is a phrase used often by British detective novelist P. D. James. There are many extraordinary things to be said about this vibrant woman whose ageless, wrinkle-free face and warm personality belie the fact that she has in her life faced great personal tragedy and in her writing has explored convincingly the psychological motivations for murder.

In her publicity photographs, James appears to be serious, pensive, perhaps even a touch reserved or severe. Many interviews in the past focus on the difficulty she faced when her husband, a doctor, returned from World War II to remain seriously mentally ill throughout the remainder of his life. Before meeting her, it is easy to picture a determined, perhaps rather silent woman, working away for years as a high-level British civil servant, efficiently balancing a demanding career in criminal law with bringing up two daughters, while earnestly tapping away on her typewriter in the early mornings, turning out detective novels hailed without exception by critics as masterpieces in the genre. But a face-to-face meeting with this woman obliterates this impression almost entirely, and certainly immediately.

I have met James several times over a period of five years, both in her London home and in various parts of the United States. Whether she was serving cucumber sandwiches and tea in London or cheering for Yale at a Harvard—Yale football game, James is a woman of great warmth and casual grace. She was born in Oxford, England, in 1920 and educated at Cambridge Girls High School. Her principal career was as a civil servant in administration at London's Home Office, work that was necessary to support her family. She has two daughters. In recent years, she has served as a magistrate in London and devotes the rest of her work time to writing and occasionally teaching. She resides in London in a Regency house that is bright and welcoming and well-ordered, much like her own personality.

In this interview, James tells us a bit about the child who always knew she would become a writer. She also tells us about her detective novels featuring Adam Dalgleish and Cordelia Gray, as well as her work that departs from the detective story format: her thriller, her play, and her non-fiction study of a series of nineteenth-century crimes, ***The Maul and The Pear Tree: The Ratcliffe Highway Murders 1811.*** Written in collaboration with T. A. Critchley, the British police historian, this latest volume is published by The Mysterious Press and Warner Books in its first American edition. It was first published in England in 1971.

[*Herbert:*] *You have said that you knew from a very early age that you wanted to be a writer.*

[James:] Yes, I think from an early age I was aware that I had what I suppose in common parlance is "a gift." I knew I had been granted a talent. I don't think I ever doubted that I could write. I mean, obviously, one *does* learn. One learns techniques. One develops—or hopes to develop. But I think I was aware that this was something I *could* do and the problem was going to be to make myself do it!

Do you have an image of yourself that would tell us what you were like as a girl?

Well, I think I had a very strong fantasy world from a very early age. I had numerous totally imaginary people who were very real to me to whom I talked and with whom I communicated. This was almost from early childhood. I told stories at a very early age; I used to tell them at night. We had one large nursery when we were very young, and I used to tell the stories at night to my sister and brother.

Were they mystery stories?

No, They were adventure stories.

Do you recall what you were like in terms of personality?

I seem to have been a curious mixture because I think I was popular and gregarious at school and yet at the same time very private.

That's an unusual balance to strike.

I think it is. My mother was a very warm woman, a very emotional sort of person, entirely different from my father, and I can see in myself the traits that I've taken from each. My father was very intelligent but I think rather cold emotionally. But he had a sense of humor and a tremendous independence, and as I got older I valued more and more these qualities in him. I had a very close relationship with him.

Did you always see yourself as writing in the detective area?

No. But, by the time I came to settle down to write the first book, there was no particular internal discussion about what sort of book it would be. I knew I was going to attempt a detective story for my first novel.

Did this arise out of a love of detective fiction?

Well, I certainly read it for pleasure. And Dorothy L. Sayers was certainly a very potent influence upon my youth. I love construction of course in novels, and I wanted to write a well-constructed novel. And I also thought that a detective novel would have the best chance of being accepted for publication!

Of course, I later discovered that within the detective form I could write a novel that has a moral ambiguity and psychological subtlety like a serious novel. Writing within the constraints isn't in fact inhibiting; it's positively liberating! This is why I carry on.

What do you think is the value of detective fiction for today's reader?

I wouldn't in a very difficult world underestimate the element of relaxation and escape. This is not in any way to be disparaged. I think detective novels do provide vicarious excitement, and they do help to purge irrational guilt and fears, I think. They do distance the terrors of death in rather a paradoxical way; they provide the reassurance that there can be a solution and that solution can be arrived at by *human* ingenuity and *human* intelligence and *human* courage.

Detective fiction usually centers around death. Do you see yourself as a person who has always been sensitive to the fragility of life?

Yes. I think this is so. I think I was born with this sense of the extraordinary fragility of life and that every moment is lived really not under the shadow of death but in the *knowledge* that this is how it is going to *end*. So that death is in a sense an ever-present thought. It sounds a little morbid, but I don't see it at all as morbid because I think I'm really rather a happy person who was always aware of this. I think for some people detective fiction does help to exorcise this fear. It distances death, really. It almost takes its horror, part of it anyway, and throws it out the window. The reader knows that order will be restored out of disorder.

The world of the murder story is a paradoxically safe world. This was particularly true of the old cozies. They still have their charm. Theirs was an ordered world with everyone moving according to hierarchy, with people knowing where they stand in the scheme of things and no one powerless, no one anonymous, everyone known, recognized, and valued.

Although your novels are far from cozy, they do show how very important individuals are to one another and the strong impact that people have on one another's lives.

Yes. The characters and their motivation are the most important part of the book to me. But I *do* think that it's important that the plot should stand out, that the clues should

be fair. The clues should be presented with cunning but also with essential fairness.

I'm interested in the question of guilt in the detective novel. Obviously, the cozy sought to establish the fact of guilt, the answer to the question "Whodunit?" But the cozy didn't pursue and develop the effects of guilt on the criminal or on anyone connected with the criminal. In much detective fiction today, the psychology of guilt is better explored. In writing your novels, what kind of thought do you give to the question of guilt?

I think I give it quite a lot of thought. My new novel is *about* guilt. I think guilt is a fascinating subject altogether, because to be human is to be guilty, whether the guilt is rational or not. I think perhaps the difference between the cozy detective story and the modern detective story—which may also be called the crime novel—is that the latter does turn its attention to this question of guilt. And of course in the crime novel you may not have much detection, you may *know* who the guilty person is, and your novel really is *about* the effect of that deed on the person and on his society. This also bears on the thinking of W. H. Auden, who saw the detective story as a kind of morality play.

Yes, the dialectic of guilt.

And of course in the cozies we had the satisfaction, I suppose, of feeling that whatever else we may be guilty about, we're not guilty of having slipped the dagger under Sir Gaspar's ribs in the library! I am sure that the attitude of the writer to guilt distinguishes the true crime novel from mere entertainment.

I think one could also say that the crime novel at its best is concerned with the limits of free will, because in this kind of novel you really feel in the end, "Well, how much choice do these people have?" This is the fascinating thing, that you are *trying* to work to an extent within the old-fashioned conventions but at the same time you are trying to write a book which has some claims to be regarded as a novel because it is psychologically true.

In the detective novel that Auden was writing about, an idyllic society was shattered by an appalling crime—usually murder—but eventually complete order is restored. This doesn't seem to be possible—or indeed desirable—in a novel like **Death of An Expert Witness.**

Oh, yes. The days of getting everybody together in the library at the end are no more. You must have the solution to the mystery, but I think in the modern detective story, although we discover who did it and why and how and when and so forth, the effects of the crime are a great deal more disruptive than they were in the older mystery. It is *not* just a nice return to Eden. The modern detective story shows exactly how disruptive and contaminating murder can be and how no life in that society surrounding it is untouched by it.

What do you see as the chief difference between American and British detective fiction?

I think we're much more interested in the emotions that give rise to murder. It's malice domestic largely with us. I agree with Auden that the single body on the drawing-room floor is more horrifying and powerful than hundreds of bodies riddled with bullets down the mean streets. Strong emotion rather than strong action. That's basically the difference.

And yet you have never shied away from showing a graphic scene of death in fiction or in nonfiction.

Yes. Absolutely. But it is generally an individual death.

Your latest book, **The Maul and the Pear Tree: The Ratcliffe Highway Murders 1811,** *is a work of nonfiction and a collaboration. It was published in 1971 after you had established yourself as a fiction writer. How did you and T. A. Critchley decide to write this story together?*

We wrote it about sixteen years ago. I was then working in the Home Office, which as you know is the British equivalent of your Department of Justice, basically. Tom Critchley was my boss. We were both working in the police department.

I had been reading, I think in the London Library, the Newgate Calendar, which of course is a description of notorious and horrible crimes, and there was a chapter on the Ratcliffe Highway crimes, with a picture of poor John Williams's body being paraded around Wapping after he had presumably committed suicide. I read the account, and it seemed to me that there was a great deal of doubt about this whole crime. And so I mentioned this to Tom Critchley, and he said, "Did you realize that this was the crime which De Quincey wrote about in his famous essay 'Murder Considered as a Fine Art'?" "No, I didn't," I said. So I read that essay and said to him, "Well, it was an extraordinary account that De Quincey's written, but it seems to me that he's not got the facts right. There's a lot more behind this than one knows." So Critchley said, "Well, let's send for the Home Office files. Let's see what we can find out."

Then it became absolutely fascinating, and we decided that we would write up the case and make a book of it. It really was a very interesting book to write. I think as a bit of social history it is interesting, and it certainly shows what a

murder investigation was like in London in 1811, and also what policing was like.

The case was notable in part because of the population's reaction to it. It involved brutal murders that were pinned on a man who committed suicide before he could be brought to justice.

Of course, what was *so* extraordinary is that the murders had such an effect on public opinion that when Williams was found dead of course they paraded his body around the streets. What an *incredible* thing that was to do as late as 1811. I don't know another case in which this happened. It's a *certain* indication of how appalled the populace were.

I think we have a feeling that the East End of London was such a violent place in 1811 and murders were happening all the time. But obviously they were *not*. They were *not*! There was a great deal, no doubt, of mob violence, a great deal of thieving and a great deal of criminal behavior of one kind or another. But atrocious murder of this kind *was*, really, *rare*. And one can see this in the effect the crime had on the populace.

The book indicates that the spectacle of the crowd parading the body of the alleged murderer around the streets was even discussed in Parliament.

Yes, even Sheridan, the playwright, made a marvelous speech.

I was interested to learn that it was felt that capital punishment was a deterrent to serious crime, and it was believed that the more people who could view a hanging the better. The example was supposed to be made public both to deter people from committing crimes and to serve as a public retribution. Therefore, if a criminal succeeded in committing suicide he was cheating the public of its revenge.

Oh, Yes. *And* of course suicide was regarded as a very great crime in itself. It was regarded as self-murder, and there were very strong theological objections to it in those days. So there were the two things: the man was a self-murderer, which made him wicked anyway, and he had cheated justice. He should have been publicly hanged to *mark* people's *abhorrence.*

This notion is very interesting in the light of just why the murder story—true or fictional—is so fascinating. Murder is of course the essential crime against society in the sense that the victim can no longer get retribution; so therefore society must do so for him.

Yes, absolutely. It's a crime for which you can *never, ever* make retribution to your victim. And with this particular crime people felt it was particularly abhorrent and dreadful because of the very nature of the victims. Here was poor Timothy Marr, a decent, hard-working little man with his wife and child, *brutally* done to death, not even safe in their own house. And over and over again there was the sense that there must be something absolutely rotten at the heart of the nation where such things could happen.

In studying this case, you learned about the poor state of forensic knowledge, the disorganized force of night watchmen who were the only law-enforcement people in the neighborhoods, the inefficient approach to investigation of a crime. What was it like to be a historical sleuth?

I found it was very interesting. It was surprising how much information we were able to get.

Did your own work in the police department give you any particular knowledge that helped you to investigate this historical crime that an average researcher might not have?

I don't think so, really. In the police department we weren't concerned with the investigation of crime. That's all done by the police themselves. We were really concerned with the administration of the police force. I think the fact that I'm a detective writer was very helpful, because I looked at the case from the point of view of the human side of the story. I looked at the personalities. I looked at the clues. I think I contributed mostly that and a lot of the more descriptive writing. Tom Critchley was probably the prime collector of information, the prime researcher.

I wondered if as a collaborator Mr. Critchley was a kindred spirit or if he had complementary differences.

I think complementary differences. He's much more a researcher and an academic writer. He writes very good prose indeed, and his book is the definitive history of the police in England and Wales. As a historian of the police he was very much at home with some of the problems of policing at that time.

Did you learn a lot about parts of London which you had previously rarely visited?

Yes. Yes. This part of London has changed almost more than any other part. The area was all dependent on what I think we called "that dark bloodstream of a river."

How did writing nonfiction seem similar to writing your novels?

It is a different kind of writing, but there are some things that are similar. I think it's terribly important in the detective story to create an atmosphere, tension, and mood. And of course, setting influences plot, and it even influences character. So the description of setting is vital in a novel, but it's also vital in a work like this.

I am interested to know why you decided to have the book reissued now and how it came about that The Mysterious Press is publishing it in conjunction with Warner?

I had felt up till now that it really was such an English story that it might not have much appeal to American readers. But Warner's asked for it, and as they are my paperback publishers I thought why not? It's been very well produced. And it's wonderful for my fellow writer to have a chance of publication in the States.

I understand that your next novel will be published by Knopf in the autumn. This represents a change of publishers.

Yes. Scribner's continues to have my backlist. The new novel is set in London and features Adam Dalgleish. It's called *A Taste of Death.* They're very, very enthusiastic at Knopf. I just feel hopeful that the book will repay their confidence in it!

How do you decide which detective, Cordelia or Adam, will appear in each book?

It depends on what sort of plot comes to mind—whether it's suitable for her or whether it's suitable for a professional detective.

Whether or not it's a suitable job for a woman!

(Laughs)

One might think that if you had a plot idea, any detective writer could use it and apply his detective to it; but actually there are more subtleties to it than that, are there not?

Yes. I suppose that there's something in what you say in that if you get a good idea for perhaps an original form of murder you could say, "Well that's the central idea of the book, this original way of disposing of someone, and the detective is of secondary importance." But when you have a detective who's an amateur and one who's professional there are certain crimes that an amateur is less likely to be called into.

That's true.

And with Cordelia's work it's nearly always a crime that the police haven't recognized as such, or a situation in which the police wouldn't normally be involved. In the first [book featuring Cordelia] the police thought it was a suicide and she was called in by the boy's father to find out why. And then in the second one, Cordelia was guarding this actress on the island. So Cordelia got involved in crimes in which it was logical for an amateur to be called in.

It did not matter in the old cozy days. Of course, with Peter Wimsey, he worked closely with the police. In fact, he used them just as his helots to do all the dull work! (*She smiles.*) But of course nowadays the readers are more sophisticated; they know that isn't so.

I think that in America the private eye has a bigger part to play. There are more of them and they're licensed and people probably use them more, for fairly serious crimes, but it doesn't happen here. I can't see private eyes getting much involved in murder here. So that's a constraint on it. There's immense scope for private eyes, but if you do have an obviously murdered body then the police are going to do the professional police work.

Have you ever considered using another sleuth besides Cordelia or Adam?

No, never.

Innocent Blood *was a departure from the detective novels featuring Adam and Cordelia. How was the inspiration for it different for you?*

With most of the Dalgleish and Cordelia books I think the original inspiration that would spark off the novel has been a place and then has come the characters and the detective and the plot. And although place was tremendously important in **Innocent Blood** because it's set in London and London is in a sense integral to the story, it wasn't a for question of "I want to set a book in London," as it was for instance with **An Unsuitable Job for a Woman** that "I wanted to set a book in Cambridge." Instead, the inspiration for **Innocent Blood** derived from a combination of a piece of legislation and a real-life murder case. The Legislation for Children Act in 1975 gave eighteen-year-old adopted children in England and Wales the right to set out on the journey of exploring who their real parents were by having access to their birth certificates. And the murder was a case called The Raven case. It was a long time ago, about 25 years ago. There was a young man who had been to visit his newborn child in hospital and had murdered his parents-in-law on the way home. And at the time, all these years ago, when he was hanged, I thought, "What about the newborn baby? How on earth and at what age do you tell a child that the reason why he has not got any grandparents and hasn't got a father is that the father was executed for their

murder? Do you change your name? Or do you even go so far as to have him adopted?" So when the Children Act was passed, those two ideas came together. And I thought, "Suppose somebody began this journey of exploration who had fantasized a very satisfactory background and then discovered something as horrific as that?" So that was an entirely different inspiration from visiting a place and feeling, "I want to set a book here."

In what ways was this book similar to your other work?

I think it shows the influence of the detective story in that it is a book which does in fact have clues—clues to personality, clues to events that have happened.

Another departure from detective fiction is your play.

Yes. It is called **A Private Treason.** It's very difficult to describe what's in a play because there are so many complex interactions. But basically it is about a 36-year-old *very* intelligent woman who's got a senior job in the civil service and falls in love with a very much younger man. It's concerned with the conflict between somebody who has always lived by the mind and somebody who lives totally by the emotions.

I think it was a somewhat over-literary play. It was probably an unfashionable play (*She smiles*) in that everyone spoke literate English. It was a well-crafted play. And I think it was a novelist's play.

But the theatre was filled every night.

Oh, yes. It ran for five weeks in Watford in April 1985. This is a place just north of London where plays are tried out. It had Susanna York in the lead role.

Is the play a mystery story?

No, but there is a crime within it, although it is not a mystery story as such.

Will the play be performed in the foreseeable future on the London stage or elsewhere?

There are no plans to produce it. I would wish to polish it more, first, but I'm not certain I will take the time to do so.

To bring us back to you as a person and a writer, I would like to ask: having lived a life that, as it turned out, was at times a difficult one, would you have wished to have had an easy life?

Well, it's dishonest to say "no" because I think we all live our lives trying to minimize our pain and maximize our happiness. But I think as a writer it's better to face a degree of trauma. Someone said if you want to be a writer you should have as much trauma in your early years as you can bear without breaking. I think something in me believes that, yes.

Do you feel that the goodness in people ultimately prevails over the inevitable rougher sides of human nature?

I hope it can. I like to think it can. I suppose we all need to believe that love is stronger than death, that the human spirit is indestructible, can surmount almost anything that fate can throw against it. But part of me believes that personal tragedy and in particular physical pain can break anybody. There is, I suppose, in my own personality a dichotomy between the optimism which is part of my nature—probably just a physical thing—and this knowledge of just how dark and dreadful life can be for many people.

Many of my books are—well, they're to do with death—but they're also to do with love, different aspects of human love.

Julian Symons (essay date 5 October 1986)

SOURCE: "The Queen of Crime: P. D. James," in *New York Times Magazine,* October 5, 1986, pp. 48-50, 54, 58, 60, 70.

[*In the following essay, Symons discusses James's new book,* A Taste for Death, *and talks to the author about her life and writing in the detective genre.*]

> The bodies were discovered at eight forty-five on the morning of Wednesday 18 September by Miss Emily Wharton, a sixty-five-year-old spinster of the parish of St Matthew's in Paddington, London, and Darren Wilkes, aged ten.

These are the opening lines of P. D. James's new book, *A Taste for Death,* and they are typical of her work in their factual exactness, their brisk presentation of what we need to know about two characters who are there not just to discover corpses. The bodies, of a tramp and a Minister of Parliament, are in the Little Vestry of the church. The scene is horrific, the room a shambles, blood everywhere. And it is all garishly lit by the long fluorescent tube that disfigures the Little Vestry's ceiling. Brightening the blood, making the figures seem unreal, the ghastly light is the particular P. D. James touch that makes the reader shudder a little.

A Taste for Death is the longest, most ambitious and the best of Phyllis James's 10 novels. Her first, *Cover Her Face,* was written 25 years ago under the influence of the work of Dorothy L. Sayers, and for a while James stayed in the gentlemanly (or lady-like) tradition of the British detective story. She broke away from it decisively in 1980 with *Innocent Blood,* which contains no puzzle element at all. And now, in the new book, she has blended a whodunit and a fully-realized modern novel. In Britain it has been given the long, respectful reviews generally accorded only a major novelist. In the United States, Alfred A. Knopf will publish it on Nov. 1, and it is already a main Book-of-the-Month Club selection, and has been sold to Warner Books for mass-market reprint for a sum said to be in the high six figures.

The Queen of Crime—a title awarded by publishers, which she would never dream of claiming for herself—lives in an elegant flat-fronted house in London's Holland Park. There, in a partly covered patio garden, we talked about her books, her life, her feelings about detective stories, and about Adam Dalgliesh, the central character in most of her novels. Dalgliesh, who began as a detective chief-inspector, and by her sixth novel, *The Black Tower,* had risen through the ranks to commander, appears once again in *A Taste for Death.* He is a dedicated professional policeman, supremely efficient, sensitive but with reticence verging on coldness in personal matters. In James's first book, we are told that Dalgliesh's wife died in childbirth, his infant son shortly thereafter. His withdrawal from any subsequent emotional commitment has been almost total. Throughout another book, *Unnatural Causes,* he is unable to bring himself to propose marriage to a woman he loves, and when at last he does so, it is too late. She has already written a letter saying no. Dalgliesh is also a respected poet, which substantiates the complexity that makes him unique among the professional detectives of crime fiction.

I wondered how much of all this P. D. James had initially conceived. Had Dalgliesh been based on anybody she knew?

"Absolutely not," she says. "Except for the surname, which was that of my English mistress at school. An odd spelling, isn't it? People often get it wrong. I used him in my first book, and I was chiefly concerned then with creating a detective quite unlike the Lord Peter Wimsey kind of gentlemanly amateur, though I admire Dorothy Sayers. I didn't imagine that years later people would be asking questions about his origin and his background. But I knew I wanted a real professional. And Dalgliesh, no doubt about it, is a good cop."

About his remoteness, she says, "I wanted him to be something more than just a policeman, you see, a complex and sensitive human being. Perhaps that's partly why I also made him a well-known poet, though I've only dared to quote a few lines he wrote, and that was in an early book. What else? I wanted him to be quite obviously very intelligent. I hope I'm not any kind of snob, but if I am—and I suppose we're all snobbish about something or other—I'm an intellectual snob. I do like clever people, and I admire intellect."

Reminded that she had said once that nothing seems to her more sexually attractive than intelligence and talent, she gives her hearty laugh. "Yes," she says. "I'd stick to that. I could never have fallen in love with a man who was handsome but stupid. Perhaps Adam Dalgliesh is an idealized version of what I'd have liked to be if I'd been born a man."

If one were creating a character sketch of Phyllis Dorothy James purely from a reading of her books, it would be of a cool, collected figure, friendly enough, but probably difficult to know and talk to. But that is not the person who opens the door when you go up the steps and ring the bell of her house. She smiles, arms outstretched in greeting, and says, "How lovely to see you, dear." Fellow crime writers, asked for a word or phrase to describe her, said "hospitable," "unpretentious," "marvelously extrovert," "wonderfully friendly," all of which are on the mark. Yet they do not convey her utter lack of affectation and pretension, or the way she radiates good nature and pleasure in whatever she is doing, whether it is cooking for a large party ("I'm a good plain cook, emphasis on the plain"), talking to fans at a book signing or discussing intricate points of criminal detail at a conference of mystery writers.

She is little under average height, with a high color, mobile features, observant eyes. A ready and excellent conversationalist, she is inclined to call friends and even acquaintances, like myself, "dear." She is the kind of person any friend would consult in trouble, with the certainty that she would offer practical, sensible, emotionally sympathetic advice and help. If that makes her seem an unlikely creator of Adam Dalgliesh, one can imagine her having a strong fellow-feeling for her second-string detective, the private investigator Cordelia Gray, a courageous but vulnerable-seeming young woman who appears in two previous books.

A Taste for Death introduces the prickly but likable Inspector Kate Miskin, who seems destined to have a part in a future novel. In James's books, women of very different ages and social class are treated with understanding and in considerable depth.

The London house is sizable, with four bedrooms, a handsome drawing room housing her considerable collection of "Famous Trials"—all taken from courtroom transcripts—and a pleasant kitchen leading out to the patio garden. The author lives in the house alone, except for two recently ac-

quired Burmese kittens. Her emotional life is strongly linked to her two daughters and their families—she has five grandchildren—who often come to stay.

"It suits me to live alone," she says. "I sometimes think of turning the top floor into a self-contained flat and having a lodger, but I'm not sure I'd want somebody coming in and out. I really don't like anybody about when I'm working."

Her habits, like those of many writers, are slightly obsessive. If she is writing, she gets up at 7, makes a pot of tea, settles down to work until midday. Then she shops, goes for an hour's walk, perhaps has a friend to lunch. If her grandchildren are visiting, she plays canasta with them in the evening; if not, she watches television.

Does this portrait of her seem altogether like the work of those Victorian painters who made any subject appear to be a picture in a stained-glass window? Certainly there is another P. D. James, the woman whose imagination sparks off some of the most memorable scenes in the literature of crime.

In her 1971 novel *Shroud for a Nightingale,* for example, the death of a student nurse during a demonstration of intragastric feeding provides one of the most effectively chilling scenes in any crime story. It had occurred to her as a possible method for murder when she witnessed just such a demonstration.

"That was an exception," she says. "My books hardly ever start with an ingenious method of murder. That's not the kind of thing that particularly interests me. Almost always the idea for a book comes to me as a reaction to a particular place and setting. Sometimes it's East Anglia, where I love the wide skies, the marshes, the estuaries, the little villages. Not pretty, but full of character. I like to create in books some kind of opposition between places and characters. *Death of an Expert Witness* was set at a forensic science laboratory in East Anglia, and I got great pleasure out of placing a crime in that strongly institutional setting, and contrasting the discipline of the institution with the undisciplined—anarchic, if you like—nature of murder, and showing how it affected the people."

She says that, as a result, her books are often long in the preparation. It has been four years since her most-previous book, *The Skull Beneath the Skin,* was published. Before sitting down to write, she spends considerable time going around with a note-book. The length of her research varies, but "I always seem to know," she says, when the time comes to begin writing, which she does partly by hand, partly on the typewriter, and finally by dictating the whole thing onto a recording machine for a typist.

She writes and speaks with much affection about East

Anglia and has a cottage there, in the charming small town of Southwold, but still spends most of her time in London.

She says: "I love Southwold, but I'm an urban person. I'm at home in London, though of course there are things I dislike." She gestures at the bars on the windows in her basement dining room. "Those, for instance. Unfortunately, they're necessary, and so is the burglar alarm. I hate that, and I hate the fact that I can't walk up Notting Hill, five minutes away, in the evenings without the likelihood of being accosted. I dislike violence, I'm frightened of it, and life in this country has become much more violent in recent years. There's an underlying unrest, and it's no longer rational."

Rationality, the desire for order and reason, is something she values very highly, in small and large things equally. One woman interviewer watched in surprise as Phyllis James, after giving her coffee in the kitchen, briskly put on rubber gives and washed up the coffee cups. She has no car. ("Where would I put it? This house doesn't have a garage. I wouldn't want to leave it in the street.") Normally, she travels by train and arrives much too early at the station. The forensic and other details in her books are accurate, and a feeling for rationality and common sense is behind several of her public activities. She tends to play down the importance of these, but she is, at present, chairman of the management committee that runs the British Society of Authors, and is also a justice of the peace, which in England is a local magistrate. These are time-consuming activities.

Asked if she enjoys them, she says: "I don't think 'enjoy' is quite the word. Perhaps I enjoy the Society of Authors. One meets interesting people. But much of the time spent on the bench is incredibly dull. I regard that as a public service and think I'm quite good at it. I hope I'm not prejudiced, and I believe I'm compassionate. I'm in favor of the greatest possible intellectual freedom in our lives, but I do also very much believe in the rule of law. The two things are not contradictory. In spite of the support the state gives the poor, I'm afraid we're individually less compassionate than we were in my youth. I don't want to romanticize the past. Don't think that. When I was a child, at Ludlow in Shropshire, I saw children going to school without coats or shoes. There was real poverty in a lot of homes. Nobody would want to go back to that. And yet, you know, I'm sure people were kinder to each other then."

Are her feelings political? A laugh. "I don't think so. In my time I've voted for all three political parties, Conservative, Labor and Liberal."

Her love of the rational extends to literature. Her favorite novelist is Jane Austen, whom she rereads, every year, and she names Trollope and George Eliot among others who appeal. She has recently become immersed in Henry James. It is no surprise, perhaps, that she doesn't much care for Dickens: "I suppose I'm a classicist, not a romantic. I don't really like the caricatures he makes of characters."

Among modern novelists: "I like Penelope Lively, Margaret Drabble, Anita Brookner. I think C. P. Snow's *The Masters* is a fine novel, and I respect the whole achievement of the *Strangers and Brothers* books. And I admire Graham Greene and Evelyn Waugh, admiration rather than enjoyment, although I think Waugh was a wonderful stylist." Joyce and his followers, modern American novelists? No. Her taste is for literal realism, not caricatural exaggeration or modernist experiments.

An Anglican, not a Roman Catholic, she has referred to herself on occasion as "quite a religious person." She goes to church not every Sunday, but sometimes.

Usually, she talks briskly, with very few hesitations or qualifications, but asked exactly what does she believe in, she answers slowly and carefully:

"I think a religious sense is like an esthetic sense. You're born with it or you aren't, and I don't mean that those born without it are less good people. I can only speak for myself. I have a need for the assurance that some beneficial power exists. I do believe in that."

Does she believe in an afterlife?

"I don't know. I'm not sure that I do."

And the existence of a personal God?

"That's a different question too." A pause. "What I will say is that I have had in my own life personal experience of the love of God."

Would that have been in difficult times?

"Yes. In difficult times."

The difficult times are now a long way back. She is in her middle 60's, and says with typical cheerful common sense that she has at most four more books left to write. Her immense success has come in the last decade, with the publication in 1977 of **Death of an Expert Witness,** followed three years later by **Innocent Blood,** which was a bestseller in America. Before that she sold well enough, but not in such numbers that she felt ready to give up her demanding and enjoyable job as a principal in the criminal policy department of the Home Office. That job was a triumphant culmination to a life that had contained more pain, unhappiness and struggle than most. When she says some things in it were "rather appalling," the words are spoken matter-of-factly, without self-pity.

P. D. James was born in 1920, the eldest of three children in a family that was, she says, not very close. She recalls her early years as not particularly happy. Her father was an Inland Revenue officer, a restless man of whom she was sometimes frightened, although in retrospect she admires his courage and independence. And she remembers with pleasure summer holidays when he put up his old Army bell tent on the cliffs outside the East Anglian fishing port of Lowestoft, and parents and children explored the area by bus and on foot. There was not much money, and although Phyllis was sent to the excellent Cambridge High School for Girls, she left at 16, and that was the end of her education.

Phyllis James was 19 when World War II began, and not quite 21 when she married Dr. Connor Bantry White, who served during the war in the Royal Army Medical Corps. She looked after their two daughters, born in 1942 and 1944, and waited for her husband to come home.

But Dr. White returned from army service a mentally sick man, suffering from what was eventually diagnosed as schizophrenia. Until his death in 1964, he was in and out of mental hospitals, from which he sometimes discharged himself and then had to be compulsorily readmitted. Like many other schizophrenics, at times he was violent.

When his widow speaks of him, it is with affection, even tenderness. A man who was obviously temperamentally very different from his wife—his favorite novelist was Dickens, his favorite book *Ulysses*—he lived long enough to see her first two books published, and was delighted by them and proud of her. But the later 1940's are a period she doesn't like to talk about. Her husband received no war pension, and the family was extremely poor. She went to evening classes and studied hospital administration, and she got a job as a £300-a-year clerk, which still left the family close to poverty. Her daughters, age 5 and 3, were sent to boarding school. For a time she lived with her in-laws, and in summer they looked after the children. It must have been a hard and bitter time. She once said that success had come to her 30 years too late.

Yet she enjoyed her professional life, and her intelligence and determination took her upward through Britain's Civil Service. In 1968, already the author of three novels, she took an examination to become a principal in the Home Office.

Asked how high on the Civil Service scale a principle is, she says, "Above an assistant principal and below a deputy secretary, dear. Are you any wiser? I was a bureaucrat. Or, if you're being polite, an administrator." Hearty laughter.

Bureaucrat or administrator, her work was important, and it has been immensely useful to her as a crime writer. She was responsible for the appointment of scientists and pathologists to all of England's forensic research laboratories—a role that put her in touch with police authorities throughout the country—an adviser to ministers on the intricate legal problems relating to juvenile crime.

This successful career, though, was never all that she wanted. She started to write in the early 1960's, when the stringencies of making a living had eased a little, beginning with a crime story because she thought it would be useful practice for the novel she would begin the next year. But in 1962, ***Cover Her Face*** was accepted by the first publisher who read it, and by the time she had written two more mysteries, she had come to think that the detective story's restrictions (the necessity of a plot, a puzzle, a solution) were really a useful discipline.

The first books are well told and enjoyable but, to use her own term, they are formula writing. With the fourth, ***Shroud for a Nightingale,*** she had the confidence to make full use of her background and the kind of people she knew well. The scene is a general hospital in the National Health Service, and she set out to create real characters with genuine motives for the way they behaved. She indulged also her intense interest in the appearance and history of buildings through her account of the hospital, "an immense Victorian edifice of red brick, castellated and ornate to the point of fancy, and crowned with four immense turrets."

In ***A Taste for Death,*** she has invented two buildings: the church in which the bodies are found, which has "an extraordinary Romanesque basilica" designed by the Victorian architect Sir Arthur Blomfield; and a house, designed by the great Sir John Soane, in which several of the principal characters live.

"The church, anyway the exterior, is St. Barnabas in Oxford, and some of the interior comes from a church near Marble Arch," she says. "The house is based on the marvelous Soane Museum, in Lincoln's Inn Fields. I just transferred church and house to the part of London where my story was set."

Where people live is important to her in the creation of her characters, more important, she says, than what they wear: "I'm interested in the clothes of my women characters, less so in those of the men. I believe you can describe people, and understand them through the houses or apartments they live in, the furniture they choose to buy, the way they decorate rooms. However humble or ordinary the place may be, there are still distinctions between what people do. Do they put wallpaper or emulsion paint on the walls? What's the design on the paper or the color of the paint? What sort of pictures are on the walls? All these things tell you something."

A Taste for Death is her best book in part because she has imagined in detail the settings in which she has placed even the minor characters. One lives in a dismally ordinary block of modern flats, brought to life for us by the observation of twin flower beds outside, filled with variously colored dahlias that "glare upwards like a bloodshot eye" at the inhabitants. When Dalgliesh visits a private clinic to interview a suspect, he looks at a painting by the Victorian Sir William Frith, admiring the meticulousness with which the painter shows military heroes returning from some colonial adventure, and their mantled ladies and pantalooned daughters waiting to greet them.

The concern with religion, apparent in her comments and exhibited in some earlier books, is treated boldly in the new novel. Did Sir Paul Berowne, one of the victims found in the vestry, have a religious experience a day or two before his death that would have changed him? Dalgliesh is skeptical, but the possibility adds the element of seriousness about death that James is intent on bringing to her crime stories. Looking down at the bodies, Dalgliesh thinks "We can vulgarize everything, but not this," then reflects that even so, this corpse will quickly cease to be a man and become "an exhibit, tagged, documented, dehumanised."

Although James hopes her own books will be treated as more than light entertainment, she is quite undogmatic about whether a crime story should be serious or frivolous.

"I don't think there's any one thing it *should* be. If it's to satisfy readers it must be excellent of its kind, and there are several kinds. I very much enjoy Edmund Crispin, who's extremely frivolous, with a marvelous comic sense. I like Sayers in spite of her social snobbery. She wrote very well. Agatha Christie wrote badly, but I respect her ingenuity. I take a lot of pleasure in Dick Francis. I *don't* like Patricia Highsmith's books about Tom Ripley, a psychopath who is made the hero. I think a crime story should be in favor of rationality. That's what the form is all about."

Among Americans, she admires Raymond Chandler, Ross Macdonald and particularly Dashiell Hammett, who, "at his best was a very fine novelist," she says. "I haven't read Elmore Leonard. And of course I couldn't write like an American, or like any of the others, for that matter. But I don't think that's the way to put it. Our books are an expression of our personalities. I write detective stories. I hope they're novels, too, and I don't see any contradiction

in that. But if I felt there *was* a contradiction, if the detective element got in the way of the novel and I had to sacrifice one or the other, then the detective element would have to go. I hope and believe I shan't have to make such a choice. I believe you write as you need to write, and you do the best you can with your particular talent. You're lucky enough to have been born with a gift, and you should be grateful for it."

James F. Maxfield (essay date Summer 1987)

SOURCE: "The Unfinished Detective: The Work of P. D. James," in *Critique*, Vol. XXVIII, No. 4, Summer, 1987, pp. 211-23.

[*In the following essay, Maxfield analyzes the character of Cordelia Gray and asserts that at the end of* An Unsuitable Job for a Woman, *there is still room for growth of the character.*]

> The adult's ego . . . continues to defend itself against dangers which no longer exist in reality; indeed, it finds itself compelled to seek out those situations in reality which can serve as an approximate substitute for the original danger, so as to be able to justify, in relation to them, its maintaining its habitual modes of reaction. (Sigmund Freud)

> My father was not disposed to educate girls. (P. D. James)

P. D. James's *An Unsuitable Job for a Woman* is probably the best known of her nine mystery novels because of its unusual conception of the detective protagonist. First published in 1972, *An Unsuitable Job* appeared to many of its early readers to be a feminist breakthrough. The heroine, Cordelia Gray, follows a profession hitherto reserved almost exclusively to males: lone-wolf, private detective. The prevailing critical interpretation of the novel seems to hold that Cordelia triumphantly demonstrates her ability to function successfully at a job not previously deemed suitable to women. Carolyn Heilbrun characterizes Cordelia as "independent, autonomous, self-supporting, and intelligent." But in truth, although Cordelia does in large measure possess the qualities Heilbrun attributes to her, she is by no means an exemplary feminist heroine.

The obviously ironic title of the novel and its first five chapters lead the reader to think the central theme of *An Unsuitable Job* is going to be that at least this woman, Cordelia Gray, is quite capable of being a private detective. The title is alluded to on three separate occasions in the first half of the book; interestingly, in all three cases the speaker is a woman. Immediately after the death by suicide of Bernie Pryde, Cordelia's older partner in the detective agency, the barmaid in the pub formerly frequented by Bernie addresses Cordelia: "You'll be looking for a new job, I suppose? After all, you can hardly keep the agency going on your own. It isn't a suitable job for a woman." The barmaid's job, the server of a predominantly male clientele, is of course deemed entirely suitable for a female. The same criticism of Cordelia's choice of a profession is later made by Isabelle de Lasterie, a young French woman whose only "job" in life appears to be to look beautiful and attract male admirers. Cordelia's commitment to her profession is merely confirmed by the criticisms of women whose chosen styles of life she regards with contempt. The third reference to the title phrase is offered by Cordelia herself to complete a sentence begun by a Cambridge history tutor: "I should have thought the job was—." The tutor, Edward Horsfall, then goes on to reject Cordelia's completion in terms not wholly complimentary to either her or her sex: "Entirely suitable I should have thought, requiring, I imagine, infinite curiosity, infinite pains and a penchant for interfering with other people." Whatever the qualities that aid her in the pursuit of the truth, Cordelia functions quite effectively as a detective for the first three-quarters of the novel. No reader well versed in detective fiction would have the slightest reason up to this point to believe that any male investigator could have done a better job.

Cordelia has been hired by Sir Ronald Callender, the eminent director of a science research laboratory, ostensibly to find out why his son Mark dropped out of Cambridge in the spring term of his final year, took a job as a gardener at a country house, then hanged himself less than three weeks later. Cordelia eventually concludes that Mark had discovered that he couldn't have been the biological son of both his supposed parents (his blood type being different from either of theirs) and that therefore the inheritance that came to his mother twenty-one years before (and the one that would come to him in four years at the age of twenty-five) had been obtained under false pretenses. She also learns that when Mark's body had originally been discovered, he had been clad only in female underwear, his face smeared with lipstick, several pornographic pictures of women on a table beside him. Being told of the circumstances of Mark's death, two of his college friends, Hugo Tilling and Davie Stevens, visited the death scene with the intention of cleaning up the body so that it would present a more respectable appearance. But when they got to Mark's cottage, they found someone else had already accomplished this task—removed the female undies, the lipstick (except for a trace later noted by the police), the pornographic pictures (except for one dropped outside the cottage and later picked up by Cordelia), and covered the lower half of the body with a pair of jeans. When Cordelia confronts Sir Ronald Callender in chapter six, she hypothesizes that he

strangled his son, fearing the young man would expose the fraud surrounding his birth and thus raise a scandal that would prevent Sir Ronald's laboratories from getting a grant from the Wolvington Trust. He then set up appearances to make it "look like accidental death during sexual experiment." Cordelia further surmises that Sir Ronald hired her primarily to discover who had altered the appearance of the corpse. Sir Ronald's failure to deny her charges leads both Cordelia and the reader to conclude that she has correctly solved the mystery of Mark Callender's death.

Cordelia not only exhibits the ability to ferret out and interpret evidence that we associate with the master detective, she also displays some of the raw physical courage that is the stock-in-trade of the hard-boiled private eye. When the novel's secondary villain, Sir Ronald's lab assistant, Chris Lunn, hurls Cordelia down a well, she laboriously and painfully inches her way up to the top by moving her feet and upper back alternately against the opposite walls. When Lunn returns to make sure she is dead, Cordelia confronts him with the pistol she has inherited from her deceased partner; and after Lunn flees from her, she pursues him in a high speed automobile chase.

The end of the chase—the death of Lunn in the collision of his van with a gasoline transporter—marks a turning point in the novel for Cordelia. From this moment on, she is by no means as masterful as she was before. Just prior to confronting the murderer, she passively allows her pistol to be taken away from her by his mistress-secretary Miss Leaming; she has no reply when Sir Ronald tells her that she will never be able to prove her charges against him and that if she tries, he will "ruin" her by making her "unemployable"; she stands idly by as Miss Leaming shoots her lover-employer in the head with Cordelia's own pistol. After so conspicuously failing to act decisively, Cordelia now hurls herself into a flurry of largely inappropriate activity. She attempts to disguise Sir Ronald's murder as suicide, even though Miss Leaming seems entirely ready to accept the consequences of her act. This cover-up almost results in Cordelia's being arrested as an accessory after the fact, and it doesn't save Miss Leaming who dies in an automobile accident (which may actually have been a suicide—a self-punishment for her crime). Although Cordelia survives her confrontations with both Sir Ronald and Superintendent Dalgliesh, it is through fortuitous disasters befalling others (Sir Ronald, Miss Leaming), not through clearly thought out, purposeful action of her own. Instead, she is driven to both action and inaction by psychological compulsions she scarcely understands.

Cordelia does realize that she is covering up for Miss Leaming not out of concern for the woman herself, but simply because she is Mark's mother: "I was thinking of Mark, not of you." But even when she thinks of Mark, she is thinking less of the real young man who died shortly after his twenty-first birthday than she is of a sort of male projection of herself. At one point in the story, she becomes consciously aware that her whole interpretation of what happened to Mark Callender is influenced by (if not created lock, stock, and barrel out of) her identification with him:

> She believed Mark Callender had been murdered because she wanted to believe it. She had identified with him, with his solitariness, his self-sufficiency, his alienation from his father, his lonely childhood. She had even—most dangerous presumption of all—come to see herself as his avenger.

To be the avenger of a person with whom one identifies is, needless to say, to be symbolically involved in avenging oneself. Much of Cordelia's ineffectual and even misguided behavior in the last two chapters of the novel derives from her subconscious tendency to identify Mark Callender with herself, Sir Ronald with her father, and Miss Leaming with the mother she never knew.

Early in the book, we are told that Cordelia's was "a childhood of deprivation." As she tells the barmaid, "I only had a mother for the first hour of my life." She likes to believe her mother loved her intensely during that hour, and even as an adult, she occasionally holds fantasized conversations with an idealized mother she imagines to be completely supportive of her goals and ambitions: "It was just as she expected: her mother thought being a detective an entirely suitable job a for a woman." But in her actual childhood, she was abandoned by her father to a series of largely unsatisfactory surrogate mothers whose central lesson for her was the necessity of concealing her true emotions:

> All her foster parents, kindly and well-meaning in their different ways, had demanded one thing of her—that she should be happy. She had quickly learned that to show unhappiness was to risk loss of love. Compared with this early discipline of concealment, all subsequent deceits had been easy.

Since the "love" one gains by means of concealing true emotion is of doubtful authenticity, it seems certain that the deprivation of Cordelia's childhood was less material than emotional.

Her life, however, took an upswing when at the age of ten she was sent by mistake to a Catholic convent. There she was taken under the wing of Sister Perpetua who encouraged her to use her mind and apply herself to her studies. When Cordelia was fifteen, Sister Perpetua led her to believe she would have a strong chance to go to Cambridge in "two years' time." But then her father spoiled Cordelia's plans by summoning her to join him: "There were no 'A' levels and no scholarship and at sixteen Cordelia finished her formal education and began her life as cook, nurse, messenger, and general camp follower to Daddy and the comrades."

Cordelia describes her father to Miss Leaming as "an itinerant Marxist poet and amateur revolutionary." He was obviously a man to whom the cause was all important and personal relationships—including the one with his daughter—insignificant. The two references to his death in the novel suggest little grief on Cordelia's part. To Miss Leaming she merely says, "'He died in Rome last May after a heart attack and I came home.'" In doing so, she obviously left all involvement with the comrades, the Party—her father's values—behind her. When she touches the corpse of her partner Bernie, she thinks, "This was death; this was how Daddy felt. As with him the gesture of pity was meaningless and irrelevant. There was no more communication in death than there had been in life." Cordelia is named after a famous literary character who was banished by her father, but there are considerable differences between the situations of Lear's daughter and her namesake. P. D. James's Cordelia is banished at a very early age, apparently shortly after birth; she has no memory of having once been loved to console her in her banishment. And although she physically rejoins her father, it is clear that no true reconciliation ever takes place.

When Cordelia first interviews Sir Ronald Callender, the similarities between her life and Mark's must immediately strike her. He too lost his mother at an extremely early age: "she died when Mark was nine months old." (The fact that Evie Callender was not his true biological mother—something Mark didn't learn until he was twenty-one—is irrelevant to the sense of loss he would have felt when he was young.) He too was sent away by his father, "to a pre-prep school when he was five and to a prep school subsequently." Just as working for the Revolution was Cordelia's father's first interest, personal relationships being at best a very distant second, Sir Ronald Callender had dedicated his life to scientific research and will not maintain a relationship with anyone who might interfere with his cherished projects. That was why young Mark had to be sent off: "I couldn't have a child here running unsupervised in and out of the laboratory."

Cordelia thus begins her investigation of the supposed suicide of Mark Callender with a sense of the deceased young man being in several significant respects her male counterpart. Her identification with Mark makes her susceptible to do exactly the thing that Miss Markland (the elderly sister of the owner of the estate on which Mark worked as gardener) warns her against: "It's unwise to become too personally involved with another human being. When that human being is dead, it can be dangerous as well as unwise." It is likely, however, that Cordelia has succumbed to this danger even before the advice is given. A couple of pages later when she discovers a pornographic photo of a female nude crumpled in the weeds outside the cottage where Mark had been staying, her reaction to this possible bit of evidence is not detached and analytical but personal and emotional: "she felt contaminated and depressed."

When Isabelle de Lasterie eventually tells Cordelia how Mark's body looked when she found it—and Hugo sententiously explains how the death was merely the result of "bad luck," a matter of the belt buckle slipping during the performance "of one of the more innocuous of sexual deviations"—Cordelia flatly responds, "I don't believe it." Although she has by now discovered what Mark had—that he could not have been the child of both of his presumptive parents—she has not yet found any clear motive for why another person would wish to murder him. And although she has learned some admirable things about Mark—e.g., his willingness to care for the autistic child Gary Webber and the senile Dr. Gladwin—none of these things is absolutely incompatible with a preference for an "innocuous sexual deviation." (Indeed, given the fact that Mark has grown up without a mother, it might not be so unusual for him to seek to know the feminine through the experiment of dressing in female clothes and wearing lipstick—and to identify further with the deceased mother by feigning his own death by hanging.) Cordelia is unwilling to believe Hugo's interpretation of Mark's death simply because she identifies so strongly with the dead man that she can't conceive of him engaging in such a sexual deviation. (Or perhaps subconsciously, the image of Mark in female undies and lipstick uncomfortably suggests to her that she is involved in a parallel set of perverse actions in playing the role of private eye and carrying a .38 semiautomatic.) Cordelia's rejection of Hugo's theory turns out to be correct, but it is based much more on emotion than reason.

The following day Cordelia examines the will of Mark's grandfather and finds that no one—except several "highly respectable charities"—stood to benefit from the young man's death. This final piece of information leads Cordelia to the conclusion that Mark could only have been killed by someone wishing to conceal the fraud perpetrated twenty-one years earlier: the obtaining of a substantial inheritance by Evelyn Callender from her industrialist father by duping him into thinking she had produced a grandson for him. But before Cordelia can go to confront Sir Ronald with her inferences, she has to undergo a highly significant ordeal. Chris Lunn, Sir Ronald's "absolutely sinister" lab assistant flings her down a well, then clamps the cover back on leaving her to drown.

In realistic terms, Lunn's action is unaccountable. He has no way of knowing how threatening Cordelia's discoveries are to his employer. Sir Ronald later claims he has not instructed Lunn to do any more than "keep an eye on" Cordelia. Why then does the young man choose to "exceed his instructions" by trying to kill her? If Lunn knows enough to perceive Cordelia as a threat to Sir Ronald, he would surely also know why his employer hired her—to find out who altered the appearance of Mark's body. Why would Lunn attempt to kill Cordelia before she could provide Sir Ronald with the information he desired?

In the last analysis, one must conclude that Lunn acts not on the basis of realistic motivations but for essentially symbolic reasons. What does Lunn himself symbolize? For one thing, he is Ronald Callender's "true son," the son who functions as a mere extension of the father's personality. Like Sir Ronald, Chris Lunn is devoted to scientific research, whereas Mark, the biological son, although "he could very well have read one of the sciences," chose instead "to read history," to assert himself as a separate person with different interests from his father. Like Sir Ronald, Lunn is prepared to be totally ruthless to further the goals of the Callender Research Laboratory, willing even to resort to murder, while Mark's commitments were to the welfare of other people and to his conscience ("My son was a self-righteous prig," says Sir Ronald). Lunn is so completely an extension of Sir Ronald that he beds the older man's mistress Miss Leaming. Even if Lunn is technically exceeding his "instructions" when he tries to kill Cordelia, he is essentially acting as his employer's double. He is trying to kill Cordelia for exactly the same kind of reasons for which Sir Ronald killed his son.

If Lunn represents Sir Ronald in the murder attempt on Cordelia, she, because of her identification with Mark, represents the victimized and utterly rejected child. The setting chosen for the murderous attack reinforces these ideas. When Cordelia last sees the well as she is taking her final leave from Mark's cottage, she is shocked to see that Miss Markland has planted flowers about the rim: "Thus strangely celebrated, the well itself looked obscene, a wooden breast topped by a monstrous nipple." If the top of the well is thus associated with one part of the female anatomy, it is not so farfetched to associate the interior with another portion. When Cordelia is hurtling down toward the water at the bottom, the experience is strangely familiar to her: "The fall was a confusion of old nightmares, unbelievable seconds of childhood terrors recalled." The terrors of childhood are many, but surely one of the most fundamental is the terror of parental rejection—the fear that one or both parents wish the child had never been born. Such fears would come readily in early years to a child like Cordelia who would know that her birth caused her mother's death and that her father abandoned her to the care of others. For Cordelia, therefore, the psychological experience of being thrown into the well is that of being thrust back into the womb—a manifestation of her fear, or perhaps even sense, that her father would have preferred her never to have been conceived. But treading water at the bottom of the well, Cordelia does not succumb to despair; she affirms to herself her right to exist: "She had always been a survivor. She would survive." She braces herself against the opposing walls of the well and slowly, arduously inches her way upward, a process she at one point consciously identifies with a struggle to be born: "It seemed she had been climbing for hours, moving in a parody of a difficult labor towards some desperate birth."

It is significant, though, that Cordelia cannot be born again without the aid of two other people. One is the dead Mark Callender, whose belt—the one with which he was hanged—Cordelia wrapped twice around her waist earlier that morning. When she is exhausted from the climb, her strength nearly gone, she loops the belt over the ladder just out of reach above her and pulls herself up to the top of the well. The belt that caused Mark's death thus becomes a means to preserve her life. But Cordelia's climb, to the top of the well does not of itself save her; she is not physically able to remove the heavy wooden cover of the well, and she presently realizes that the murderer will be returning before sunrise to make sure she has drowned. Only the fortuitous arrival of Miss Markland, who removes the well cover before Lunn returns, saves Cordelia from being flung back down the well a second time.

The significance of Miss Markland's role in the novel will be examined below; for now, it is sufficient to note that instead of lavishing gratitude on her savior, Cordelia briskly dismisses the older woman and prepares to confront her attacker. She makes two significant preparations for this encounter: she puts on one of Mark's jumpers and gets and loads the pistol she inherited from Bernie. Wearing the jumper like wearing the belt affirms her solidarity with Mark as she anticipates facing the person who, at this moment, she must assume to be his killer. The pistol is a more complexly symbolic object. If being a private detective is not conventionally regarded as a suitable job for a woman, Cordelia's possession of the .38 is not merely unsuitable but illegal. Throughout the first three-quarters of the novel, this illegal weapon is Cordelia's prized possession, a source of security and confidence to her:

> Bernie had meant her to have the gun and she wasn't going to give it up easily.

> It was a heavy object to carry with her all the time but she felt unhappy about parting with it, even temporarily.

> . . . she longed for the reassurance of the hard cold metal in her hand.

> She . . . could see . . . the crooked, comforting outline of the pistol. . . .

> I'm perfectly safe. Besides I have a gun.

But when Cordelia confronts (and recognizes) Chris Lunn, she realizes "she wouldn't fire" even though "in that moment, she knew what it was that could make a man kill." And in the following chapter she passively yields the pistol to Miss Leaming, for Cordelia now believes "she could never defend herself with it, never kill a man." The pistol ultimately becomes to her (although she wouldn't put it in these terms) a symbol of phallic aggression, of a ruthless destructiveness she perceives as distinctly male in character. This does not mean that a woman *cannot* use a pistol in a violent aggressive manner (Miss Leaming does so only a few pages later), but that Cordelia has chosen to define herself as a woman for whom such an action would be . . . unsuitable.

After the death of Ronald Callender, Cordelia goes so far as to claim "she hadn't wanted him to die," but it seems highly probable that the real reason she covers up for Miss Leaming is simply because the older woman has done exactly the thing she herself wished to do. Sir Ronald is the heightened image of her own rejecting father. Miss Goddard (the former Nanny Pilbeam, nursemaid to Mark's presumed mother and briefly to the boy himself) speaks of how Mr. Bottley "never really cared for [his daughter] Miss Evie," perhaps because his wife died when the child was born. Miss Goddard, however, considers this "just an excuse for not taking to the child." Thinking of her own background, Cordelia replies, "Yes, I knew a father who made it an excuse too. But it isn't their fault. We can't make ourselves love someone just because we want to." Strangely, much the same argument is put forth by Ronald Callender when he is justifying to Cordelia his decision to kill his son: ". . . if [a parent] doesn't love, there's no power on earth which can stimulate or compel him. And when there's no love, there can be none of the obligations of love." Sir Ronald, of course, is a little more extreme in his denial of the "obligations of love": he literally murdered his son where Cordelia's father merely destroyed the life she wanted, the one she would have led if allowed to attend Cambridge. Nevertheless, Cordelia obviously perceives Mark's victimization as a mirror of her own.

Cordelia allows the pistol to be taken from her, because she knows she will not be able to use it against Ronald Callender. One reason is her shock at witnessing the violent death of Chris Lunn, but another surely is her identification of Sir Ronald with her father. No matter how evil the scientist is, how deserving of punishment, for Cordelia to shoot him would symbolically be an act of parricide. After he has been killed by Miss Leaming, Cordelia denies that she had "wanted him to die" because to admit this desire would be tantamount to acknowledging she wished for her own father's death—something it is highly probable that she did wish for since his death released her from a form of slavery and allowed her to seek an independent life. And Cordelia's behavior at the event indicates that the death of Sir Ronald was also desired by her. When she sees Miss Leaming approaching with "the gun held closely against her breast" (signifying that this killing will be an act of the heart, motivated by maternal love, in contrast to Sir Ronald's coldly rational of murder), Cordelia knows "exactly what [is] going to happen," because it is what she has subconsciously wished for. Although she feels as if there is time for her to intervene, "to leap forward and wrench the gun from that steady hand," she makes no move—not even when Sir Ronald "[turns] his head toward Cordelia as if in supplication." The use of the world "supplication" suggest Ronald Callender is begging Cordelia, not Miss Leaming, for mercy—as if the younger woman has passed sentence on him and the older is merely the executioner who carries it out. Cordelia may merely be imagining the supplication she sees on the man's face, but she clearly chooses not to respond to it—she allows the execution to proceed.

If Ronald Callender is associated in Cordelia's mind with her father, it stands to reason that Miss Leaming, the true mother of Cordelia's counterpart Mark, should symbolically be associated with her mother. Early in the novel, we are told that Cordelia likes to fantasize about her dead mother, imagine her as someone warmly supportive of her daughter's goals in life. The only surrogate mother Cordelia has ever had who did play such a role in her life was Sister Perpetua who encouraged her to "try for Cambridge." When Cordelia is struggling to climb out of the well, she partially loses consciousness and has a brief dream vision in which Sister Perpetua oddly turns into Miss Leaming:

> Sister Perpetua was there. But why wasn't she looking at Cordelia? Why had she turned away? Cordelia called her and the figure turned slowly and smiled at her. But it wasn't Sister after all. It was Miss Leaming, the lean pale face sardonic under the white veil.

This dream may indicate Cordelia's subconscious realization that what she needs or desires at this particular point in her life is not the teacher, Sister Perpetua, but the avenger, Miss Leaming. Although Elizabeth Leaming has been subservient to Ronald Callender for much of her adult life (her role being only a slightly glorified version of the one Cordelia played for her father), she is nevertheless more on a level of equality with him than the youthful Cordelia—and as Mark's real mother she has a greater right to avenge his death. Mark's mother taking revenge on his cruel and heartless father symbolically represents

Cordelia's mother exacting retribution on her daughter's heartless (if not quite so cruel) father. Although Cordelia and Miss Leaming "don't even like each other," they are nevertheless allies against the evil father.

The novel, however, contains another mother figure for Cordelia. This is Miss Markland, who by removing the cover of the well insures that Cordelia's "difficult labor" does culminate in (re)birth. Miss Markland's role might at first seem to be more that of the midwife than the mother, but a couple of pages after the rescue, she makes clear that she at least regards Cordelia as a surrogate child. Years before, "her son, the four-year-old child of herself and her lover" had drowned in the very same well. By saving Cordelia's life, she has partially redeemed herself for her neglect or carelessness that led to the death of the child. Listening with appalled fascination to the story, Cordelia realizes, "What to her [Cordelia] had been a horror, to Miss Markland had been a release. A life for a life."

Cordelia, though, is reluctant to accept the relationship that she feels Miss Markland has thrust upon her. She almost brutally drives the older woman out of the cottage: "You've saved my life and I'm grateful. But I can't bear to listen. I don't want you here. For God's sake go!" Jane S. Bakerman interprets this action as a sign of Cordelia's maturity: she chooses to behave "coldly—but professionally" instead of acceding to Miss Markland's "demand" for "attention, support, daughterliness, comfort." But it seems to me that Cordelia's rejection of Miss Markland is neither cold nor professional. Certainly there would have been nothing "unprofessional" about seeking Miss Markland's practical assistance—asking her to call the police, for example. In truth Cordelia drives Miss Markland away not for rational reasons but emotional ones. She wants to avenge herself directly and personally on her attacker. She is also terrified by the story of the drowned child: ". . . it was horrible and unthinkable and she could not bear to hear it." She cannot bear this story, because it is once again *her* story. An illegitimate and perhaps unwanted child is left to wander about on his own and tumbles to his death in cold suffocating, water. The same thing could easily have happened to Cordelia in her early years—and perhaps in an emotional-psychological sense it did happen. Cordelia's ability to respond openly to other people, to reveal her innermost feelings, perhaps even to herself, perished in the cold, suffocating water of the well of loneliness that was her childhood.

Because of Cordelia's deeply ingrained sense of the harm that has been done to her in her childhood, she cannot respond maturely to Miss Markland's display of her own grief. When she is told the story of the child's drowning, Cordelia tells herself Miss Markland "must be mad." Later she has a similar response after seeing how Miss Markland has planted flowers about the well: "She was suddenly terrified of meeting Miss Markland, of seeing the incipient madness in her eyes." But Miss Markland is not mad. Rather she has wisely given expression in her outburst to Cordelia to grief and guilt she has (unwisely) kept pent up for years. Similarly, her planting of the flowers around the well, converting it into a shrine for her dead son, seems a fundamentally healthy action. She is no longer going to repress the memory of her son and his death but instead pay tribute to his memory—just as Mrs. Goddard does in faithfully tending the grave of her husband. Identifying only with the suffering of the neglected child, Cordelia either cannot or refuses to empathize with the sufferings of the remorseful negligent parent. Were she to understand and forgive Miss Markland, Cordelia might also have to forgive her father and the "succession of foster mothers." The utterly evil Ronald Callender, on the other hand, in no way disturbs Cordelia's self-righteousness.

An Unsuitable Job does not contain an unlimited number of parent figures, but it does offer quite a few. Two additional father figures deserve some comment. Bernie Pryde has been Cordelia's mentor in the detective business; in a sense he has almost adopted her in that he has given her a bedsitting room in his house. But Bernie, although as senior partner in the firm he is in a position of nominal authority over her and is definitely old enough to be her father, is regarded by Cordelia as essentially another child. His childlike quality is evidenced in his "boyishly naive obsession" with the .38 semi-automatic and his psychological dependency on *his* father figure, Superintendent Adam Dalgliesh, who is the source of all of Bernie's wisdom concerning criminal investigative processes. In this sense, Bernie like Cordelia is an abandoned child, for Dalgliesh got him fired from the police force.

When Cordelia is interrogated by Dalgliesh, Bernie's father figure easily becomes her own. As with the other fathers in her life, Cordelia instinctively mistrusts him: "He sounded gentle and kind, which was cunning since she knew that he was dangerous and cruel. . . ." Dalgliesh exerts pressure on Cordelia to confess her part in the cover-up of Ronald Callender's murder, and she resolutely sticks to her story even though she is increasingly tempted not to "confess" but to "confide" the truth to the Superintendent. To an extent, she is yearning for a reconciliation with the father, for the establishment of genuine communication with him. This communication occurs in a different way after Dalgliesh announces Miss Leaming's death and tells Cordelia she need not return for further questioning. At that moment, Cordelia's defenses suddenly crumble, and she expresses her emotions totally and openly. Her dramatic and uncontrollable crying is basically for herself (she is still, I think, not mature or empathetic enough to cry for Miss Leaming); but when she expresses "her pent-up mis-

ery and anger" in words to Dalgliesh, "strangely enough" her grievances are focused on Bernie. This displacement of her own self-pity onto Bernie is in actuality not so strange at all. Bernie is the "child" who has been cast off by Dalgliesh just as Cordelia was cast off by her father. Although he does not acknowledge any sense of wrong doing for firing Bernie, Dalgliesh does apologize for having forgotten the man's existence and in a sort of backhand compliment to Pryde's junior partner tells Cordelia, "I'm beginning to wonder if I didn't underestimate him." Dalgliesh's concessions may seem slight, but appear to be greater than any ever made to Cordelia by her own father. The interview with Dalgliesh, although it doesn't seem strictly necessary to the mystery plot of the novel—which is adequately resolved by the information Cordelia receives from Miss Leaming in their final conversation—is important to Cordelia's psychological development, because it suggests that some degree of true reconciliation with the father is possible.

When asked why she has chosen to write mystery novels, P. D. James once replied:

> I think there may have been in my very early life some emotional trauma or insecurity, and this [writing murder mysteries] is some way of trying to construct a world in which there is an ultimate answer to problems that may otherwise seem unacceptable seem unacceptable or insolvable.

I would suspect that in Cordelia Gray, James, is portraying this "early trauma or insecurity" more directly than in her other novels (with the possible exception of *Innocent Blood*) and that the author's identification with her protagonist's plight creates a characterization of far greater depth and complexity than is the norm for mystery fiction. But the "trauma or insecurity" may also give rise to the most obvious flaw of the book. Chris Lunn and Sir Ronald Callender are so utterly villainous that they belong more to the realm of myth or fairy tale (the evil sorcerer and his faithful troll) than to that of realistic fiction. In essence these characters are merely projections of Cordelia's worst fears concerning parental authority. Killing them off, therefore, is, as James says, a way of providing in her fiction "an ultimate answer" (total destruction of representatives of the trauma's source) to a problem that in real life can never be completely solved or removed. But even though the novel disposes of its villains rather patly, the treatment of the heroine is completely realistic: we know at the end of the book that Cordelia Gray not only needs to but will continue to grow and that her battles with the past as she moves into the future will by no means all be lost.

Betty Richardson (essay date Fall-Winter 1988)

SOURCE: "'Sweet Thames, Run Softly': P. D. James's *Waste Land* in *A Taste for Death*," in *Clues: A Journal of Detection,* Vol. 9, No. 2, Fall-Winter, 1988, pp. 105-18.

[In the following essay, Richardson delineates the common symbolism and imagery between T. S. Eliot's The Waste Land *and James's* A Taste for Death *and asserts that work is still meaningful to readers who do not recognize the influence.]*

The considerable popular success of P. D. James's *A Taste for Death* defies current conventions of detective and suspense publishing. *A Taste for Death* is 459 pages in hardcover edition at a time when detective novels more often are between 170 and 230 pages. The writing is literate, and it is literary: the novel teems with allusions to literature and other arts. Of violence there is little and of explicit sex, none.

The reader sees the slaughtered bodies of Sir Paul Berowne and tramp Harry Mack but sees them distanced through the shocked eyes of an aging spinster; at the end of the novel, an old woman's death is graphically shown. Thwarted personality development, including sexual development, leads to the multiple murders, but the reader must figure that out for herself or himself. And that is all. How, then, does James produce a work that for many weeks appeared on the *New York Times* list of best sellers, that is sold in supermarkets and discount stores, and that appeals to relatively unsophisticated undergraduates in college detective fiction courses?

In part, James succeeds because her writing is firmly based on myths and symbols that are commonplaces of modern culture as well as conspicuous features of well known literary works. Her writing, then, is accessible to the reader who can recognize the literary references, but it is equally accessible, if not as meaningful, to the reader who merely responds with emotion to symbols familiar from film, song, and television. For example, in *A Taste for Death,* James calls upon many of the symbols and images seen in the writings of T. S. Eliot, especially *The Waste Land,* but these devices—among them, water, rats, abortion, isolation—would have an emotional impact upon readers completely unfamiliar with Eliot's work.

The plot of *A Taste for Death* is itself unexceptional and would not seem to justify the lengthy text. Miss Emily Wharton, age sixty-five, routinely goes to arrange flowers in the church of St. Matthew's in Paddington, London. On this occasion, she is accompanied by her self-appointed guardian, 10-year-old streetwise urchin Darren Wilkes, who pities the lonely, naive woman. In the Little Vestry of the church, they find the bodies of Berowne, who has undergone a religious experience there and has asked to stay

there again on the night of his death, and of Mack, who habitually dosses there for lack of better ideas. Their throats have been cut.

Commander Adam Dalgliesh, a James series detective, is called into the case, if, indeed, there is one. Previously acquainted with and sympathetic to Berowne, Dalgliesh insists this is double murder, although Berowne's death might conveniently be dismissed as suicide, while of unsound mind, following the meaningless murder of Mack. Assisted by Chief Inspector John Massingham and Inspector Kate Miskin, both personally plagued by problems involving aging relatives, Dalgliesh interviews Lady Ursula Berowne, the victim's mother; Barbara Berowne, his widow; Stephen Lampart, Barbara's cousin and lover; Dominic Swayne, Barbara's brother, and a number of minor characters including Berowne servant Evelyn Matlock (Mattie), Berowne mistress Carole Washburn, and unsuccessful romantic novelist Millicent Gentle. Through the latter, Dalgliesh traces the last hours of Berowne's life, makes a case for murder, and identifies Dominic Swayne as the killer. On the run, Swayne wounds Father Barnes, priest of St. Matthew's, almost murders young Darren, and does kill Kate Miskin's grandmother after taking Miskin and the older woman as hostages. Captured, Swayne maintains he will soon be free again, and, for all the reader knows, he is right.

This plot line, however, is fleshed out by James's symbols, most importantly water. The Thames, "London's dark blood stream," is central to this novel in much the same way as the Thames is vital to Eliot's *Waste Land* and the Mississippi to *Huckleberry Finn* and *Show Boat.* Of symbolic value, also, is the filthy, stagnant canal with littered banks (a contrast with the flow of the great river) along which much of the action occurs.

Such usage is typical of James. In her *Unnatural Causes,* the scene is the seacoast; the flickering lights in the homes along the shore, tiny and fragile against the sea's turbulence, would suggest loneliness even to a reader unacquainted with Matthew Arnold's "Dover Beach." The climax of this novel is clearly symbolic action: Dalgliesh builds a frail human bridge across raging waters. That bridge is destroyed by the murderer, just as murder, in the abstract, destroys the sense of community that, in James's work, is essential to a fully human existence. In *The Black Tower,* the sterility of life in a nursing home is measured by the patients' desire to see the ocean and their inability to do so. The setting of *The Skull Beneath the Skin* is an island, haunted by present and past violence perpetrated by those who ignore John Donne's "overworked aphorism" and gratify their own selfish desires at the expense of the larger human community of which they deny they are a part. In several novels, as in *A Taste for Death,* storms occur at moments of revelation; in much the same way, Eliot placed "What the Thunder

Said" as the concluding section of *The Waste Land.* For both writers, the storm's great message seems to be Eliot's "Datta. Dayadhvam. Damyata" ("Give, sympathize, control").

In *A Taste for Death,* as in Eliot's poem, the Thames unifies past and present. (An entirely different article might be written about how it links problems of the aging, or the past, with problems of abortion, or the future.) As F. O. Matthiessen remarks of *The Waste Land,* "this glimpse of present life along the river, depressingly sordid as it is, being human cannot be wholly different from human life in the past." To make this point, Eliot calls upon images of the first Queen Elizabeth; James evokes images of the England of Webster, Shakespeare, Dylan Thomas, and many more. While visiting Berowne's constituency, for instance, Dalgliesh, confronting the problems of power politics, sits at the table where Benjamin Disraeli once dined and gazes out over the river as that great Victorian statesman must once have gazed.

The questers for truth in this novel live near the river. Dalgliesh lives in a high place overlooking the Thames. Kate Miskin, an apprentice quester, looks forward to having a similar place. The archetypal Wise Woman of this tale, Millicent Gentle, lives in a "large white shack on stilts" almost in the water. From her "wide sitting room windows it was possible to imagine oneself on a ship with nothing in view but the white veranda rail and the sheen of the river." Gentle is the Aphrodite described by psychologist Christine Downing as "a connecting, not a dissolving, consciousness" in whose waters "we do not drown, but discover reflections which add depth to our experience." Berowne draws serenity from her during the final days of his life. From her, Kate Miskin learns a new and positive view of life. Walking along the river near Gentle's shack, Dalgliesh experiences a moment of inexplicable, transcendent joy.

Most characters' lives, though, are represented by the foul canal, not the flowing river. In Eliot's *Waste Land,* "A rat crept softly through the vegetation / Dragging its slimy belly on the bank / While I was fishing in the dull canal. . . ." Swayne stalks Darren along just such a canal. As he prepares to kill the child, they see a dead rat, looking "curiously human in death, with its glazed eye and the small paws raised as if in a last despairing supplication." This image of the vile, but in this case poignant, outcast and predator, a familiar figure in contemporary film and television, represents both Swayne and Darren, although Darren will be given a new life at the novel's end. Both are predators upon life, but they are also victims of the foul backwaters of life. They exist as animals. Likewise, the rubbish on these banks is familiar, not only from film but from Eliot who, in *The Waste Land,* sees the "testimony of summer nights" as an array of "empty bottles, sandwich paper, / Silk handker-

chiefs, cardboard boxes, cigarette ends. . . ." James uses trash to represent spiritual desolation in other of her novels. The beach is strewn with debris in *The Black Tower; Innocent Blood* in part takes place in an "industrial wasteland"; an innocent young man is sacrificed to science in *An Unsuitable Job for a Woman* near a lovely copse that secretly harbors junk.

If trash represents the spiritual state of the community, individual despair is represented, again as in *The Waste Land* (and in popular culture since the best sellers of Charles Dickens, if not before) by incongruous dwelling places. Whatever James's characters have in common, writes Danial Dix, they share "the sense of being out of place in their very homes." This, too, is characteristic of James's writings in which, with conspicuous regularity, stately homes are chopped up into cells. For instance, in *A Mind to Murder,* cells for psychiatric treatment have been hewn from a Georgian house, while sociologists and oriental scholars are crammed into a late eighteenth-century building in *Innocent Blood.* In *Shroud for a Nightingale* and *The Black Tower,* old buildings have been carved up for similarly utilitarian medical purposes. In *A Taste for Death,* Emily Wharton, discoverer of the bodies, lives in a room in a seedy boarding house where she is bullied by the neighbors and ashamed to reveal that she must use the toilet or empty a chamberpot. (Without realizing the implications for her own life, she decides she could not keep a cat in such confinement.) Darren Wilkes shares squalid rooms with a drunken slut of a mother; he pathetically decorates his own space, as best he can, with the products of his thievery. Father Barnes, failed priest, lives in the one decent flat in a tacky building that has replaced an old rectory; there he is bullied by his housekeeper. Carole Washburn lives in an anonymous cell in "an apartment house of the dead." Even Kate Miskin, until late in the novel, isolates herself, trying to cut herself off from her grandmother and her miserable childhood in an urban housing project. She wants rigidly separate compartments for her past, her career, her painting, and her sex life.

These are victims of "a crowded world where noninvolvement" is "practically a social necessity." More spiritually desolate are those who possess economic and intellectual resources but who nonetheless live fragmented lives cut off from the larger human community. Members of the Berowne family are among them. Sir Paul Berowne has lived a "separate cabined" life in an historic house. He reserves space in other places for the various pieces of his life: intimacy, political duties, and the rest. These shards are not allowed to overlap. Examining the study in Berowne's home, Dalgliesh feels that he is in a museum, that Berowne must have "sat in this richly ornamented cell like a stranger." Elsewhere in the house, Lady Ursula lives in her own museum, one celebrating a world that died in

1914, its mood qualified only by the invalid equipment that emphasizes her own isolation. Belowstairs lives Mattie, given sanctuary by the family and then exploited and emotionally abandoned.

More ominous are the lovers, Barbara Berowne and Stephen Lampart. Barbara is the elegant lady of *The Waste Land's* "A Game of Chess," encapsulated by her own beauty and by terminal ennui. When Barbara recalls her parents' heartless conversations about her and her brother Swayne, it is clear that both are the victims of complete emotional impoverishment. Barbara simply does not know that she exists unless men desire her. She "likes to feel that attention is being paid to her," Lampart tells Lady Ursula. "You have to admit that about the sexual act. Attention, specific and intense, is certainly being paid." Fixed forever in the emotional crises of an unloved childhood, Barbara, like any other emotional infant, enjoys seeing pain inflicted on the world that has caused her own agony, and so she is sexually excited by watching Lampart perform cesarean sections on other women in what is a kind of scientific parody of the black mass. Dalgliesh wonders if Lampart and Barbara copulate on the operating table after the surgery.

Lampart, too, makes a kind of cult of pain and death. An aggressive social climber without a fixed place in the world, he has become an obstetrician who "dislikes children intensely," does not much like women, and has had himself sterilized. His "elegant Edwardian villa" has been carved into a nursing home where wealthy mothers-to-be can indulge themselves in luxury, only to be "outraged" when labor starts and they realize "that there are some humiliations and discomforts that even dear Stephen can't do much about." But, just as the luxury is a thin veneer over the harsh realities of childbirth, so the nursing home itself is a facade covering a grimmer reality. Lampart also runs an abortion clinic there. After amniocentesis, women can choose to abort if they do not like the sex of the embryo, providing they can pay Lampart's fees. As has the killer of his son in **An Unsuitable Job for a Woman,** Lampart has substituted the cult of science and self for a more humane creed and is a zealot in defense of his religion of death. With Lampart's "fanaticism," Dalgliesh thinks, he might have been "a seventeenth-century religious mercenary."

Then there are the utterly homeless, whose rootlessness makes them victims or killers. One of these, of course, is Harry Mack, but in this novel, as in *The Waste Land,* there are "nymphs" who are also "departed." Theresa Nolan was bred in a country cottage where her room "held a green luminosity as if it were underwater," but she has come to the city, wandered from job to job, been impregnated by Swayne and abandoned, had an abortion, been overwhelmed with guilt, and sought out a green park glade in which to kill herself. If she is a spirit of the woods, Diana Travers is the spirit of the water. A woman of many disguises, Diana is either killed by Swayne or allowed to drown because she mocked him. Her death occurs after she dives naked into the Thames. She is pulled from the water with "weeds wrapped around her neck like a green scarf." Mattie is another such victim. She is the unstable daughter of a man who, perhaps through Berowne's carelessness, has been convicted of murder and died in prison. Her fragile sanity shattered, she has been institutionalized and taken in by Berowne after her release. So lonely is she that she provides Swayne with an alibi for the brutal murders rather than give up the illusion of love, although what Swayne offers her is merely the mechanical sex of Eliot's "young man carbuncular." Sex, as Lampart remarks, is one way of getting attention.

Rootlessness and emotional and intellectual impoverishment, carried to an extreme, result in Dominic Swayne. His nickname, "Dicco," suggests the dickens, euphemism for the devil, but his last name suggests Eliot's Apeneck Sweeney. In his person, he resembles Sweeney with his broad shoulders, long arms, and "simian strength." His grotesque appearance, in fact, has caused his father to question his legitimacy, as Barbara remembers in recalling their childhood. Rejected by parents, without Barbara's protective beauty, Swayne steals bits of life wherever he finds them. He stays with a reluctant acquaintance and borrows cars and even bathwater from Barbara Berowne. Swayne does not want to be exiled from the human community; even at the end, a multiple killer, he brags that it is through him that Darren's leukemia has been diagnosed and the child given another chance. But, even more than his sister, Swayne is emotionally an infant, and he knows no other way to relate to people except through destruction. When he kills Kate's grandmother, he boasts that he is doing Kate a favor in relieving her of a burden; he cannot rejoin his mother because he has destroyed a stepfather's prized painting. His destructive relationship with Paul Berowne is violently Oedipal, with Barbara as its object, and he believes Barbara, who is incapable of love, will love him when she learns he has killed the husband who threatened to leave her. He might, he says, have spared Berowne had the latter begged for mercy (that is acknowledged Swayne's power), but Berowne did not and so was destroyed, in Freud's words, as god, as father, and as "totem-animal-sacrifice" to Swayne's rapacious emotional hunger. For Swayne, as for Sweeney in Eliot's "Sweeney Agonistes" and for the villains in a thousand movies, "Life is death." Yet, while a predator, Swayne is also the inevitable product of a rootless society, which is why the reader is apt to believe him when he claims he will soon be loose again. If not this Swayne, society will spawn many others like him.

Opposed to these characters are those who seek truth, primarily Sir Paul Berowne and Adam Dalgliesh. Berowne is the Fisher King, the Maimed King, described by Jessie L. Weston in *From Ritual to Romance* and used by Eliot in *The Waste Land,* although he is portrayed so that he might be any basically decent martyred leader from popular culture or real life. Mythically, in Cleanth Brook's words concerning Eliot, the plight of the desolate land "is summed up by, and connected with, the plight of the lord of the land, the Fisher King, who has been rendered impotent by maiming or sickness." Eliot's poem, Brooks continues, is based upon contrast "between two kinds of life and two kinds of death. Life devoid of meaning is death; sacrifice, even the sacrificial death, may be life-giving, an awakening to life." But the Fisher King's experiences are meaningless unless a knight—in this story, Dalgliesh—can remove the curse by asking "the meanings of the various symbols that are displayed to him in the castle."

Berowne, whose first name suggests the Paul of the Bible, is a "Minister of the Crown," a leader of his country. He is also a fundamentally decent man whose life is a mess. One observer says that his "critical faculty" was suborned by Barbara's beauty, that he mistook her, probably, for the "Holy Grail." In an earlier meeting, while they sat in a railroad compartment as if they were "two penitents in a private confessional," Berowne had told Dalgliesh that "Most of the things I expected to value in life have come to me through death." His title came by way of the death of his older brother in northern Ireland. So did Barbara, who had been engaged to this brother, but Berowne still could not have married Barbara had not his first wife died in an auto accident. No one, including Berowne, is sure how much responsibility he bears for that accident.

All these prizes are hollow. Barbara is shallow. While she is pregnant by him at the time of his death, he finds intimacy not with her but with Carole Washburn. His daughter is alienated by the events leading to his marriage to Barbara and has run away. In his spiritual illness, he is spectacularly insensitive to the needs of others—Mattie is one, but not the only one. He can do nothing for the plights of his constituents but lecture them on his powerlessness. Having lost touch with, or trivialized, the potentially most meaningful relationships, he becomes fixed in the blind rituals of his caste and position, much as Lampart makes a creed of his science, as social workers form a "new priesthood" in *Innocent Blood,* as a scientist sacrifices his son to his cult of science in *An Unsuitable Job for a Woman.* Berowne is different, though, in that he does not believe in what he is doing.

His life is transformed by an undefined religious experience in the Little Vestry. He astounds those around him with his plans to change his life; only Lady Ursula is prepared to cope, taking steps to guarantee the life and inheritance of his unborn son. Berowne returns to the vestry, having

found peace during his last hours with Millicent Gentle. Indeed, Swayne says that, when Berowne realizes he is to die at Swayne's hands, he is acquiescent. "He knew I was coming," says Swayne. "He was expecting me." Instead of pleading for his life, Berowne simply says, "So it's you. How strange that it has to be you." Swayne later complains that it was "As if I had no choice. Just an instrument. Mindless." The vestry, then, is the Perilous Chapel of which Weston writes when she describes "*the story of an initiation* (or perhaps it would be more correct to say the test of fitness for an initiation) *carried out on the astral plane, and reacting with fatal results upon the physical.*" With Berowne in death is the novel's ultimate rootless victim, Harry Mack, who looks, the next morning, as if he were wearing a "breastplate of blood," a phrase suggesting the chivalric images that haunt this novel.

As the knight who is to interpret, Dalgliesh comes to the case with some prior knowledge based on previous meetings with Berowne. His attitude toward Berowne's religious conversion is ambiguous, although he impulsively lights a candle to the victim's memory, just as, in *A Mind to Murder,* he recalls lighting a candle on the day his own wife and infant son died. A blocked poet, Dalgliesh perceives Berowne as a kind of alter ego and even their physical resemblance is marked. Dalgliesh's function in the novel is, indeed, to question and try to understand. He is a less active figure here than in the other novels in which he appears, remaining strangely in the background even in the search for Swayne.

His passivity, though, is typical. In this novel, characters are caught up in inexorable events that lead to other events, just as Swayne believes himself to be a mindless instrument in Berowne's death. That death sets other events in motion; as Eliot writes in *Murder in the Cathedral,* the "small folk" are "drawn into the pattern of fate." Emily Wharton is one such person. Another is Father Barnes who, after Swayne is identified as the killer, encounters him in the church. Swayne later calls Barnes a "priest with a taste for martyrdom," a phrase evocative of Eliot's Thomas Becket; like Becket, Barnes rises to a kind of spiritual courage that his previous behavior had only hinted at. Barnes challenges Swayne, addressing him as "My son" and correctly naming the evidence for which Swayne is searching. Swayne shoots him. Lying bleeding in the church nave, Barnes faces death with courage and without self-pity. Unlike Becket, however, Barnes survives on into comic anticlimax, exploiting the sensational events in the church to increase his congregation and collection.

Kate Miskin is drawn in and renewed. At the novel's beginning, she is bitter and aloof, defending her fragile identity by inventing tidy compartments for various aspects of her life. Yet she has chosen the career of detective or seeker of truth. In following Dalgliesh, she encounters Millicent Gentle, from whom she learns spiritual wholeness and the acceptance of life. That same point about wholeness is made again when Kate's life is saved by her lover, Alan Scully. A literate and religious man, Scully does not allow himself to be compartmentalized. A literary reference concerning Berowne's last name brings Kate's danger to his attention, and his dogged insistence brings the police to her rescue. Had he been content to be one of Kate's compartments, she would have died.

Held hostage and waiting for death, Kate is moved to tenderness, for the first time, by her grandmother's vulnerability. Where once she found the aging flesh repulsive, now she helps the old woman to the toilet, shielding her grandmother from Swayne with her own body. In doing so, she learns for the first time of her own parentage and of her dead mother's love for her, knowledge that she needs but had previously rebuffed.

Unlikely as it may seem, a vital moment of communion occurs at that moment in the bathroom, but the water of the toilet is part of the general water imagery of the novel. Just as Miss Emily should not need to conceal her chamberpot or be shamed by her flushing of the toilet and Swayne should not have had to steal his bathwater from Berowne, so Kate should not have been repelled by the facts of animal existence that all humans share. Her acceptance of the basic facts of existence is an essential part of her growth. There are other such moments of communion in the novel. At the beginning, Emily and Darren share tomato soup and fish fingers in "a ritual communion." Father Barnes and his bullying housekeeper are finally united by their common awareness of the "gushing" waterpipes at the church, a "blood-stained gurgle" that carries off the mixed blood of Berowne and Mack, of lord and tramp.

In *A Taste for Death,* this kind of communion is the one victory that humans can attain. Most of the time—Scully's case is one exception—intentions count for very little. Despite his destructiveness, Swayne is the instrument by which Darren is given another chance. Kate, at the moment of her grandmother's death, for the first time wants her grandmother to live. Barbara Berowne's childhood deprivation causes her to torment Mattie until Mattie betrays Swayne, Barbara's brother. Emily trying to help Darren, becomes the instrument by which Swayne traces the child and attempts to kill him, but she herself could not have found Darren had not Kate betrayed his whereabouts because of her own childhood hatred of social workers. Dalgliesh traces Berowne's final hours, but it's a chance question from Kate that leads to Millicent Gentle's crucial revelations. More often than not, humans are instruments in some pattern greater than they, or the reader, can comprehend.

Central to that pattern is the church. *A Taste for Death* ends, as it begins, with Emily Wharton in church. She, too, has suffered and changed. She has seen horror. She has loved Darren, and he has been taken away from her. The routine flower arrangements of the opening chapter have given way to a search for truth, one that necessarily begins in doubt. At the novel's end, she kneels, gripping the grille (a kind of cage that appears often in the novel), and prays because she once heard a priest say, "If you find that you no longer believe, act as if you still do. If you feel that you can't pray, go on saying the words." She asks God to speak to her. He does not, because James does not provide easy or sentimental answers. But, like Dalgliesh and the other seekers, Emily is beginning to ask the right questions. The novel does reward—spiritually and emotionally, not economically or physically—those who do that.

That James is a reader of Eliot is obvious, since, among other things, a passage from his "Whispers of Immortality" introduces *The Skull Beneath the Skin.* Her appreciation of this literature, however, far transcends the use of prefatory poetry. Eliot's lore, images, and symbols are intrinsic to *A Taste for Death.* Yet her artistry is such that the work can be read meaningfully by those entirely unaware of these intellectual underpinnings. As detective stories go, then, this is a work of unusual richness and complexity. As writing goes, it is the kind praised by Eliot himself in "The Use of Poetry": "The most useful poetry, socially, would be one which could cut across all the present stratifications of public taste—stratifications which are perhaps a sign of social disintegration." In *A Taste for Death,* James has stretched the detective story far beyond that genre's conventionally narrow boundaries.

Christine Wick Sizemore (essay date 1989)

SOURCE: "The City as Mosaic: P. D. James," in *A Female Vision of the City: London in the Novels of Five British Women,* University of Tennessee Press, 1989, pp. 152-87.

[*In the following essay, Sizemore analyzes the role of London, with its mosaic of villages and people, in James's fiction, especially* A Taste for Death *and* Innocent Blood.]

A strong sub-genre of urban fiction is the detective novel. Throughout the twentieth century, women writers have infiltrated this seemingly "masculine" genre. Among contemporary writers, P. D. James, in particular, presents a complex portrait of the city as a mosaic in her detective stories and her novel *Innocent Blood.* The city in these works is an intricate picture built up out of many small pieces. But the mosaic is not only an image of the city in these works; it is also the method of a detective or mystery novel. From the point of view of the detective, it is not just a question of putting together pieces of a puzzle, because the picture has not yet been created. The detective must create it by fitting together the small pieces available. The pieces which P. D. James' detectives must use to create their picture of the city are London's "villages," all the districts of London that must be connected together to form a coherent whole.

The concept of London as a collection of villages echoes throughout P. D. James' works. In *Unnatural Causes* (1967), the male detective Adam Dalgleish refers to the district of Soho as "a cosmopolitan village tucked away behind Piccadilly with its own mysterious village life." In *Skull Beneath the Skin* (1982), a character who is a drama critic explains: "No one has all the London gossip. London, as you very well know, is a collection of villages, socially, occupationally, as well as geographically." In *Innocent Blood* (1980) Norman Scase, who is tracking the heroine, thinks of London as a place, "which asked no questions, kept its secrets, provided in its hundred urban villages the varied needs of ten million people." In her most recent work, *A Taste for Death* (1986), it is a female detective, Kate Miskin, who sees the mosaic of city, the linking of all the villages into an overall pattern. As she looks from the balcony of her Lansdowne Road flat, she thinks to herself:

> The world stretched out below her was one she was at home in, part of that dense, exciting conglomerate of urban villages which made up the Metropolitan Police district. She pictured it stretching away over Notting Hill Gate, over Hyde Park and the curve of the river, past the towers of Westminster and Big Ben.

Kate Miskin not only sees the individual villages and landmarks, she also sees the pattern that links them:

> This was how she saw the capital, patterned in police areas, districts, divisions and sub-divisions. And immediately below her lay Notting Hill, that tough, diverse, richly cosmopolitan village.

The image of the connectedness of the urban villages belongs to P. D. James' female characters, and it reflects their ability to connect to other people. Kate Miskin, unlike the traditional detective, is willing to get involved with others, and it is she who has the vision of London as a pattern, a mosaic. This is an image of London which Philippa Palfrey in *Innocent Blood* learns to see when she learns to connect with other people. Furthermore, it is the female characters, Kate Miskin, Philippa Palfrey and Cordelia Gray, another untraditional detective, who recognize the beauty of the city and celebrate it. There is nonetheless a hint in

A Taste for Death that Adam Dalgleish, in the earlier works a typical uninvolved male detective, may start to see the beauty of the city as he gets to know Cordelia Gray.

The Tradition of the Detective Novel

The urban mystery or detective story began to appear in England in the late nineteenth century. Raymond Williams notes that it emerged as a "predominant image of the darkness and poverty of the city . . . became quite central in literature and social thought." If the image of the city is that of darkness, then the urban hero becomes the one who can penetrate that darkness and make sense of the city. Williams explains:

> the urban detective, prefigured in a minor way in Dickens and Wilkie Collins, now begins to emerge as a significant and ratifying figure: the man who can find his way through the fog, who can penetrate the intricacies of the streets. The opaque complexity of modern city life is represented by crime; the explorer of society is reduced to the discoverer of single causes. . . . [Sherlock Holmes' London is] : the fog, the gaslight, the hansom cabs, the street urchins, and through them all, this eccentric sharp mind, this almost disembodied but locally furnished intelligence, which can unravel complexity, . . . the clear abstract system beyond all the bustle and fog.

The tradition of the detective novel clearly deals with the questions and darkness of the city, but from Williams' description, it seems to do so in a particularly masculine way: the rational abstract intelligence, elevated and separated from others, which isolates and differentiates until it identifies a single cause.

Feminist critic Carolyn Heilbrun, however, finds that the British tradition of detective novels is not as strictly masculine as it first appears. She points out that British detective novels contain autonomous and well-developed female characters and sympathetic male characters. Even if Sherlock Holmes is the "quintessential male" in his excessive ratiocination, his female clients and antagonists are strong and resourceful women. Heilbrun also sees a clear difference between the violent, gory "tough-guy" tradition with limited roles for women that evolved in American detective novels and the British tradition of "effete," "charming," and "tender" male detectives: "Manliness . . . was left for the Watsons in the outfit. The British in their detective fiction from Holmes on, were the first, and perhaps the last, to equate manliness with stupidity." Although ratiocination remains a prominent trait in British male detective heroes, the macho quality admired in American fiction does not appear. Heilbrun links the tradition of sympathetic male detective heroes to the success of many of the women writers who took over the British detective story in the 1920s and 1930s; furthermore Heilbrun notes a "special phenomenon" in these British women mystery writers. They start out with a charming, gentlemanly male detective, but then they bring in a woman character who begins to take over whole books: Sayers' Harriet Vane, Marsh's Agatha Troy, and Christie's Miss Marple.

Heilbrun hails P. D. James as the inheritor of this tradition. After creating a successful male police detective in Adam Dalgleish, James wrote *An Unsuitable Job for a Woman* (1972) and created private detective Cordelia Gray, to whom she returned in *Skull Beneath the Skin* (1982). In *A Taste for Death* Cordelia Gray appears briefly, and the female police officer Kate Miskin is introduced. In 1980, Heilbrun praised James as the best detective novelist of the tradition of Sayers and They in the past two decades: "The best of P. D. James' detective novels raise the genre to new heights. . . . [They] preserve all the glories of the earlier detective fiction while adding a modernity of detail and setting, and a concern with contemporary problems that does more than resurrect a past genre: it both recreates and strengthens it." Furthermore, P. D. James' works portray a city as not just a place of darkness. The dark alleys and corners are there, especially in the early Adam Dalgleish novels, but Cordelia Gray and Kate Miskin see light and change in the city as well as darkness.

P. D. James' portrayal of contemporary problems reveals a woman's viewpoint, particularly in the Cordelia Gray and Kate Miskin novels and in *Innocent Blood.* Although P. D. James creates the traditional uninvolved, rational male detective in Adam Dalgleish, she creates female detectives in Cordelia Gray and Kate Miskin who are not only autonomous and strong, but also exhibit some of the qualities of involvement with and concern for other people that the psychologists Carol Gilligan and Jessica Benjamin particularly associate with women. P. D. James too identifies these qualities as female. In a 1977 interview James said: "I believe . . . that women are as intelligent as men and in many ways as able, but women have got other qualities as well. These are qualities of sympathy and of understanding (an instinctive wish to look after people who are weaker than themselves) and of less aggression. This is what the world *wants*!" SueEllen Campbell even thinks that the women characters cause a "generic shift" in these detective novels which, like Sayers' *Gaudy Night,* have a "thematic richness" that is "at least partly a response to the presence of a heroine . . . for whom there is no established formula." This shift created by the focus on female characters and female concerns becomes even more pronounced in P. D. James' *Innocent Blood,* with its young, developing heroine.

The Early Detective Novels: Adam Dalgleish and Cordelia Gray

P. D. James' awareness of the differences in qualities associated with men and women is evident in her portrayal of her male and female detectives. Adam Dalgleish is a typical British male detective: although he is a published poet, he is still analytical and non-involved whether he is observing the streets or interrogating people. Yet even in an early novel, *A Mind to Murder* (1963), he feels guilty about this detachment:

> His job, in which he could deceive himself that non-involvement was a duty, had given him glimpses into the secret lives of men and women whom he might never see again except as half-recognized faces in a London crowd. Sometimes he despised his private image, the patient, uninvolved, uncensorious inquisitor of other people's misery and guilt. How long could you stay detached he wondered, before you lost your own soul?

In *Unnatural Causes* one of the suspects sums up Dalgleish's professional detachment, saying, "Doesn't being a policeman protect your privacy? You have a professional excuse for remaining uninvolved. . . . I think you are a man who values his privacy." Although this sense of privacy and uninvolved rationality places Dalgleish in the tradition of male detective heroes, P. D. James makes clear the cost of his non-involvement. All his personal relationships are sacrificed to this stance. In some period before the series began, he had a wife, but she and their baby died in childbirth. Another woman is in love with him, but at the end of *Unnatural Causes* she leaves to take a job in New York because she can "no longer bear to loiter about on the periphery of his life." P. D. James said in a recent interview with Dale Salwak that she is conscious of these qualities in Adam Dalgleish. She did not want to create a character so perfect that he would be boring: "I do have to remind myself there are things about his character which I don't admire. He's so almost completely detached at times, even a little cold, and I wouldn't have thought easy to work for at all." Only his writing poetry, like Holmes' playing the violin, shows his potential for sensitivity.

Cordelia Gray does not have to feel guilty about detachment because although she is strong and autonomous, she does allow herself to get involved. At the beginning of *An Unsuitable Job for a Woman,* her openness to involvement almost undermines her professionalism. Cordelia Gray is faced with keeping a detective agency open all by herself after the suicide of her partner, who had cancer. Her first case, the seeming suicide of Mark Callender, takes her to Cambridge, where she almost succumbs to the undergraduates' offer of camaraderie. She had not been to the university herself; her mother died at birth, and her father, a revolutionary, took her out of convent school at sixteen so she could join him on the continent. When the Cambridge undergraduates take her for a picnic and a ride in a punt, she is almost lulled into giving up her case and agreeing that Mark Callender's death is suicide. Cordelia Gray, however, is more independent and plucky than the undergraduates, and she perseveres, enduring threats and even an attempt on her life. Finally, she does get involved after she has solved the mystery of Mark's death. When Miss Leaming, Ronald Callender's secretary, kills him upon learning that he grotesquely murdered their son, Cordelia protects the woman, not really for her own sake, but because Miss Leaming is Mark's mother and Cordelia grew to respect Mark during her investigation. She also hated Ronald Callender for desecrating Mark's body and setting Mark up as an object of contempt. Cordelia carefully helps Miss Leaming to make it look as if Sir Ronald committed suicide. She manages to stick to her story even under Adam Dalgleish's questioning, although she knows he suspects the truth. In spite of the supposed detachment required of a detective, Cordelia is not afraid of sympathy for and involvement with people. She was genuinely fond of her partner, Bernie Pryde, and at the end of her questioning by Dalgleish, she bursts into tears, partly of relief, but mostly for Bernie, whom Adam had fired even though Bernie idealized him. She lashes out at Adam, "after you'd sacked him, you never enquired how he got on. You didn't even come to the funeral."

In both *An Unsuitable Job for a Woman* and *Skull Beneath the Skin,* it is Cordelia, with her acceptance of involvement and connection, who walks around London. Even though both novels in which she appears are set primarily outside London, they both open with Cordelia walking down Kingly Street, just past Oxford Circus, to her office. She has kept Pryde's detective agency solvent by taking cases searching for lost cats and dogs. She has even trained her inefficient elderly secretary, Miss Maudsley, to help look for cats: Miss Maudsley "managed to conquer her timidity when in pursuit of cat thieves and on Saturday mornings walked purposely through the rowdy exuberance and half-submerged terrors of London's street markets as if under divine protection, which no doubt she felt herself to be." Also in *Skull Beneath the Skin* she gets involved even at risk of her own life by trying to save the young murderer, who is terrified into trying to drown himself. In response to the monstrous selfishness of the real villain, Ambrose Gorringe, Cordelia cries in anger, "You killed him [the young murderer], and you tried to kill me. . . . Not even in self-defense. Not even out of hatred. My life counted for less than your comfort, your possessions." After dealing with Ambrose, Cordelia finds it reassuring to get a call from Miss Maudsley, who urges her home to find a Siamese cat because it belongs to a girl who is just out of the hospital after a leukemia treatment. The city has room for detectives with compassion.

In P. D. James' early detective novels, her male detective,

Adam Dalgleish, does not see the city as a positive place where missing cats can be found. When Dalgleish walks through Soho in *Unnatural Causes,* he correctly identifies it as a village, but it fills him with disgust:

> It was difficult to believe that he had once enjoyed walking through this shoddy gulch. . . . It was largely a matter of mood, no doubt, for the district is all things to all men, catering comprehensively for those needs which money can buy. You see it as you wish. An agreeable place to dine; a cosmopolitan village tucked away behind Piccadilly with its own mysterious village life, one of the best shopping centres for food in London, the nastiest and most sordid nursery of crime in Europe. . . . Passing the strip clubs, the grubby basement stairs, the silhouettes of bored girls against the upstairs window blinds, Dalgleish thought that a daily walk through these ugly streets could drive any man into a monastery.

Some of the same aspects of the city are portrayed in *Innocent Blood.* The city is seen as reflecting an observer's mood. Although a district is vividly portrayed as a "village" within the city, here, from a male point of view, it is a grim district with no redeeming qualities. The same disgust is present in *Shroud for a Nightingale,* when the male Sergeant Masterson goes into London to interview an informant and ends up at a macabre dance contest at the Athenaeum Hall. The urban districts are there, but are not yet seen as part of the glittering tiles of a mosaic.

The same difference is evident in male and female observation of architectural change and renovation. Bernard Benstock, writing primarily about the Dalgleish novels, notes that almost "every important building that serves as the central stage of her tragic dramas has been converted from something else, and each is either in the process or in potential danger of being reconverted or abandoned or torn down in turn." This awareness of architectural change is especially vivid in the city where the male observers, as in Dickens, are disgusted by the change, but the female observers, as in Lessing, can delight in it. In *Unnatural Causes,* Adam Dalgleish goes to London to search for a suspect and walks through a mews which has just been renovated:

> The cobbled entrance was uninviting, ill-lit and smelt strongly of urine. Dalgleish . . . passed under the archway into a wide yard lit only by a solitary and unshaded bulb over one of a double row of garages. The premises had apparently once been the headquarters of a driving school. . . . But they were dedicated now to a nobler purpose, the improvement of London's chronic housing shortage. More accurately, they were being converted into dark, under-sized and over-priced cot-

tages soon, no doubt, to be advertised as "bijou town residences" to tenants or owners prepared to tolerate any expense or inconvenience for the status of a London address and the taste for contemporary chi-chi.

The darkness of the houses and the snob appeal of the district recall Dickens' description of the Barnacle house in *Little Dorrit,* an ill-smelling, cramped house located on the fringes of a fashionable neighborhood:

> Mews Street, Grosvenor Square, was not absolutely Grosvenor Square itself, but it was very near it. It was a hideous little street of dead wall, stables, and dung-hills, with lofts over coachhouses inhabited by coachmen's families, who had a passion for drying clothes and decorating their window-sills with miniature turnpikegates. . . . Yet there were two or three small airless houses at the entrance end of Mews Street, which went at enormous rents on account of their being abject hangers-on to a fashionable situation.

In *Shroud for a Nightingale,* the renovations Dalgleish encounters in North Kensington are less chic and even grimmer than those in *Unnatural Causes:*

> Number 49 Millington Square, W.10, was a large dilapidated Italianate house fronted with crumbling stucco. There was nothing remarkable about it. It was typical of hundreds in this part of London. It was obviously divided into bed-sitting rooms since every window showed a different set of curtains, or none, and it exuded that curious atmosphere of secretive and lonely over-occupation which hung over the whole district.

In *Skull Beneath the Skin,* however, the renovation of Cordelia Gray's flat off Thames Street is seen in a positive light:

> as she moved from the single large sitting room to her bedroom she could see spread below her the glittering streets, the dark alleyways, the towers and steeples of the city, could glimpse beyond them the necklace of light slung along the Embankment and the smooth, light-dazzled curve of the river. The view, in daylight or after dark, was a continual marvel to her, the flat itself a source of astonished delight. . . . No building society had been interested in a sixth-floor apartment at the top of a Victorian warehouse with no lift and the barest amenities. . . . But her bank manager, apparently to his surprise as much as hers, had been sympathetic and had authorized a five-year loan.

The buildings Adam Dalgleish sees throughout London have been thoughtlessly chopped up into small bedsitters or carelessly renovated with a false attempt at chic. Cordelia, who has done some of the renovation herself, is rewarded by a glorious view of London that sustains her after her sorties out into the countryside to solves murders. Although both detectives go into the city of London in the course of these early novels, it is Cordelia Gray who is portrayed as the lover of London.

Not only Cordelia but even one of the female murderers has a more positive view of the city than Adam Dalgleish. *A Mind to Murder* is set in London in a psychiatric clinic located in a Georgian Terrace house on an imaginary London square with a mews to the rear. Occasionally the story follows characters to their London residences, such as Nurse Bolam's flat in a narrow terraced house at 17 Rettinger Street N.W.1. The ground floor smells of "frying fat, furniture polish and stale urine," but in summer evenings she could "watch the sun setting behind a castellation of sloping roofs and twisting chimneys with, in the distance, the turrets of St. Pancras Station darkening against a flaming sky." In P. D. James' early detective novels, it is only the women, whether they be detectives or murderers, who see the beauty of London.

A Taste for Death

In James' most recent detective novel, *A Taste for Death* (1986), which is set entirely in London, there is some hint that Dalgleish can change. A friend mentions that Dalgleish was seen dining with Cordelia Gray; perhaps he is beginning to learn from her. In *A Taste for Death,* the victim is for the first time someone Dalgleish knew, however briefly, Sir Paul Berowne, a government minister, and Dalgleish worries whether he is too involved. Dalgleish is less sure of himself in this novel. He is no longer writing poetry and is somewhat "disillusioned" with police work. He asks himself: "And if I tell myself that enough is enough, twenty years of using people's weakness against them, twenty years of careful non-involvement, if I resign, what then?" This time, though, he recognizes that he is involved. After a difficult interview in which he tries to get information from the Special Branch, Dalgleish thinks:

> what depressed him most and left him with a sour taste of self-disgust, was how close he had come to losing his control. He realized how important it had become to him, his reputation for coolness, detachment, uninvolvement. Well, he was involved now. Perhaps they were right. You shouldn't take on a case if you knew the victim. But how could he claim to have known Berowne . . . a three-hour train journey, a brief ten-minute spell in his office, an interrupted walk in St. James's Park? And yet he knew that he had never felt so great an empathy with any other victim.

In spite of feeling empathy for Berowne, Dalgleish still remains a rational man. Upon hearing a priest suggest that he thought he saw the stigmata on Berowne's hands shortly before the minister was killed, Dalgleish is shocked and even feels "revulsion" towards "the bizarre intrusion of irrationality into a job so firmly rooted in the search for evidence . . . demonstrable, real." When two assistants discuss Dalgleish, one says to the other, "AD likes life to be rational. Odd for a poet, but there it is." Even if Dalgleish remains rational and is depressed by his involvement, he nonetheless has a vision of London in this novel similar to those experienced by female characters in P. D. James' other novels. While an Assistant Commissioner looks into a file, Dalgleish looks out over the city of London and contrasts Manhattan, whose "spectacular soaring beauty always seemed . . . precarious," with the gentler panorama of his own city:

> London, laid out beneath him under a low ceiling of silver-grey cloud, looked eternal, rooted, domestic. He saw the panorama, of which he never tired, in terms of painting. Sometimes it had the softness and immediacy of watercolour; sometimes, in high summer, when the park burgeoned with greenness, it had the rich texture of oil. This morning it was a steel engraving, hard-edged, grey, one-dimensional.

Here Dalgleish actually stops to observe the city below him and draws an analogy between the variety of London and styles of painting.

P. D. James introduces a new female character, Police Inspector Kate Miskin, in *A Taste for Death.* Kate, an illegitimate child whose mother died in childbirth, was brought up by her grandmother in a "meanly proportioned, dirty, noisy flat . . . of a post-war tower block" and attended a multi-racial state school, Ancroft Comprehensive. Kate has no nostalgia for her childhood. She is delighted with her new job and her flat in an old Victorian building near the corner of Lansdowne and Ladbroke Roads because it allows her to escape the past: "She had little feeling for the past; all her life had been a striving to struggle free of it." When asked why she chose police work, Kate thinks to herself: "I thought I could do the job. I was ambitious. I prefer order and hierarchy to muddle." Kate says she prefers order and hierarchy and freedom from the past, but she naturally involves herself with people, and during her first case, she comes to terms with her past. When she and Adam Dalgleish go to visit Berowne's mistress, Carole Washburn, the male detective admires Kate's feminine ease with people:

> It was typical of her, thought Dalgleish, this unsentimental, practical response to people and their immediate concerns. Without hectoring or presumption, she

could reduce the most embarrassing situation to something approaching normality. It was one of her strengths. Now, above the tinkle of kettle lid and crockery, he could hear their voices, conversational, almost ordinary.

Listening to them, Dalgleish suddenly feels, that they "would both get on better without his male, destructive presence."

When Carole Washburn has some information to give the police, it is Kate she asks to see. She and Kate meet in Holland Park, and she tells Kate about a letter Berowne received from a girl who committed suicide. As Kate talks to Carole about Berowne's wife, Carole bursts into tears. Kate's first impulse is to invite Carole back to her flat for coffee. Kate at first checks herself, then submits to her own feelings of sympathy:

> suppose Carole were required to give evidence in court, then any suggestion of friendship, of an understanding between them could be prejudicial to the prosecution. And more than to the prosecution; it could be prejudicial to her own career. It was the kind of sentimental error of judgement which wouldn't exactly displease Massingham if he came to hear of it. And then she heard herself saying:

> "My flat is very close, just across the avenue. Come and have coffee before you go."

Kate knows she should be careful not to be "sentimental" and become involved with people while investigating a case, but she does anyway. She met her lover, a theology librarian, when she went to investigate a stolen book. This time, when she sees how distraught Carole is, her sympathy for people and, as P. D. James says of women in general, her "instinctive wish to look after people who are weaker" than she is, take precedence over her "better" judgment.

In this novel Kate also comes to terms with her past in the person of her aging grandmother. Kate doesn't want her grandmother to move in with her because she cherishes her freedom and is committed to her job. Nonetheless, when her grandmother is mugged, Kate takes her in and realizes that personal relationships are even more important than her job:

> Nothing is more important to me than my job. But I can't make the law the basis of my personal morality. There has to be something more if I'm to live at ease with myself. And it seemed to her that she had made a discovery about herself and about her job which was of immense importance, and she smiled that it should have happened while she was hesitating between two

brands of tinned pears in a Notting Hill Gate super-
market.

Kate Miskin comes to terms with her past, and it is not surprising that someone who can come to terms with her own
past and who values involvement with other people above
the law can, like Maureen Duffy's characters, see the past
in the city and recognize that nature is part of the city. Like
Dalgleish, Kate too can see the panorama of the city; from
the balcony of her flat, she looks out over London past "the
great limes [lindens] lining Holland Park Avenue":

> To the south the trees of Holland Park were a black
> curdle against the sky, and ahead the spire of St. John's
> church gleamed like some distant mirage. . . . Far be-
> low to her right under the high arc lights the avenue
> ran due west, greasy as a molten river, bearing its un-
> ending cargo of cars, trucks and red buses. This, she
> knew, had once been the old Roman road leading
> westward straight out of Londinium; its constant grind-
> ing roar came to her only faintly like the surge of a dis-
> tant sea.

Kate meets witnesses in Holland Park, and every night she
looks out at the lime trees and the plane trees that line the
great rivers of avenues. She learns to deal with her own past,
and she can connect London and Londinium. She can see
the mosaic of the city.

Innocent Blood

P. D. James' most vivid portrayal of London is not in one
of her detective novels, although ***A Taste for Death*** comes
close, but in ***Innocent Blood*** (1980). Several reviewers call
Innocent Blood a "straight" novel, but Nancy Joyner points
out that it still includes many elements of the traditional
mystery form: two violent deaths described in detail; two
amateur detectives, Philippa Palfrey and Norman Scase;
clues that lead up to a final revelation, and the London setting. It is in this novel, as Philippa Palfrey tries to put together the pieces of her past to find her identity, that
London and its many districts and neighborhoods are presented in great detail and that the image of London as mosaic emerges most strongly. It is particularly important
because it is reflected in the novel's detective structures
as well as its theme.

Philippa Palfrey is younger than the protagonists of
Lessing's, Drabble's, and Murdoch's novels and her task is
the establishment of identity and the development of the
ability to love. Unlike most teenagers, who break with their
past or at least strain against it to find their identity, she is
an adopted child who must discover her past and connect
with it. Philippa is like Cordelia Gray and Kate Miskin in
being intelligent and independent, but unlike them she has

not yet learned to be concerned for others. Although she
has achieved for her adoptive parents, she has no real love
for them nor does she think they really love her. Maurice
Palfrey, and his second wife Hilda, had adopted Philippa
after Maurice's first wife and son were killed in an automobile accident. Philippa has almost no memory of her
first eight years before she was adopted. Her fantasy, aided
by Hilda, has been that she is the daughter of a lord and his
serving maid because she has a memory of the rose garden and the library of Pennington, a country manor house.
Now she must let her fantasies evaporate and slowly, piece
by piece, build up her real past. She does this by moving
around London, where each district is like a small village
or piece of mosaic tile that, put together, is the larger reality of London.

The city cannot create an identity for Philippa; like the small
glittering tiles of a mosaic or the mirrors that Philippa and
Norman Scase look into, the city can only reflect back what
is before it. When Philippa goes out to find an apartment
for herself and her natural mother, she sees the city as a
mirror for the observer's mood:

> She came to know a different London and she saw it
> through different eyes. The city was all things to all
> men. It reflected and deepened mood; it did not cre-
> ate it. Here the miserable were more miserable, the
> lonely more bereft, while the prosperous and happy
> saw reflected in her river and glittering life the confir-
> mation of their deserved success.

Ultimately the city can only reflect, but that quality offers
Philippa two things, a reminder of physical reality and the
freedom of anonymity. When Philippa first discovers her
parents' names, she takes the train from Liverpool Station
out "through the urban sprawl of the eastern suburbs; rows
of drab houses with blackened bricks and patched roofs."
The train passed "wastelands rank with weeds" and finally
arrived at Seven Kings Station near Bancroft Gardens
where her parents lived. There in the "leafy privacy and
cosy domesticity" of Church Lane with its "identical semi-
detached houses . . . architecturally undistinguished, but at
least . . . on a human scale," she learns from neighbors that
Martin and Mary Ducton were the rapist and murderess of
twelve-year-old Julie Scase, and that her father died in
prison. Her earlier fantasy about her past bursts like an iri-
descent soap bubble and she feels faint and sick.

Philippa regains her sense of self by concentrating on a
piece of shiny paving stone that evokes the image of a mosaic tile: "she opened her eyes and made herself concentrate on the things she could touch and feel. She ran her
fingers over the roughness of the wall." After Philippa
grounds herself in reality by feeling the texture of the wall,
she is able to see the paving stone:

It was pricked with light, set with infinitesimal specks, bright as diamonds. Pollen from the gardens had blown over it and there was a single flattened rose petal like a drop of blood. How extraordinary that a paving stone should be so varied, should reveal under the intensity of her gaze such gleaming wonders. These things at least were real, and she was real—more vulnerable, less durable than bricks and stones, but still present, visible, an identity.

Physical reality isn't much of an identity; Philippa has much to learn, including the meaning of the rose petal, red as blood, but at least she starts with one piece of identity, her physical existence. The paving stone glittering with bits of reflected light is itself a piece of mosaic revealing wonder and variety. It foreshadows the many villages that make up London and the pieces of the picture Philippa must put together of her past. Philippa pulls herself together enough to take the train back into London, but she spends "the rest of the day walking in the City." The city reflects her mood in the grey rainy sky, and even the "pavement stones were as tacky as if . . . [rain] had fallen heavily all day, and a few shallow puddles had collected in the gutter into which occasional dollops dropped with heavy portentousness from a sky as thick and gray as curdled milk." This time the paving stones reflect no gleam of light. Philippa will have to discover that on her own.

The city also offers Philippa the freedom and anonymity in which to get to know her natural mother, Mary Ducton, whom she brings to London after her mother's release from prison. By moving out of her adopted parents' house and renting a flat in another district, Philippa achieves anonymity for herself and her mother. They glory in it as Martha Quest did in *The Four-Gated City:*

> Their freedom did, indeed, seem to be limitless, stretching out in concentric waves from those three small rooms above Monty's Fruit and Veg to embrace the whole of London. The freedom of the city—of the lumpy grass under the elms of St. James's Park, where they would search for a spare length of grass . . . and lie on their backs, staring up through a dazzle of shivering green and silver and listening to the midday band concert.

The city offers Philippa and her mother the anonymity of the crowd, but it does not offer escape from their own past. As Hilary Burde discovered in Iris Murdoch's *A Word Child,* the past can find them in the city even if they come to the city to try to escape it. Norman Scase recognizes the opportunity that London offers but he, in his vow to avenge the death of his daughter, represents the past that haunts Mary Ducton. Norman Scase loses Philippa and Mary Ducton when they first get off the train from the

prison in York, but he knows he can find them in spite of the city's anonymity:

> He didn't believe for one moment they were in the country. It was in the vast anonymity of the capital that the hunted felt most secure. London, which asked no questions, kept its secrets, provided in its hundred urban villages the varied needs of ten million people. And the girl was no provincial. Only a Londoner would have stridden with such confidence through the complexities of King's Cross Underground Station.

London may be secretive, but Norman Scase has a map, and like a good detective he can fit the pieces of a puzzle together and discover which urban village Philippa has chosen.

These villages, or districts, are described in even greater detail in *Innocent Blood* then in P. D. James' other novels. When Maurice Palfrey, Philippa's adoptive father, thinks back to his first wife and their selection of a house, he remembers that they tried to decide which district had the character they wanted: "All districts of London were apparently impossible for her. Hampstead was too trendy, Mayfair too expensive, Bayswater vulgar, Belgravia too smart." Finally they find Caldecote Terrace in Pimlico. After the death of his first wife and her son Orlando, Maurice marries his dowdy secretary Hilda, not really because he loves her, but because she weeps for Orlando. Hilda is not a society woman like his first wife; she prefers to keep house and cook. Pimlico becomes Hilda's village, and when Norman Scase loses Philippa and Mary Ducton on the subway, he finds the Palfreys' address, Caldecote Terrace, which "lay on the fringes of Pimlico, southeast of Victoria and Ecclestone Bridge." When Norman goes there he discovers "a cul-de-sac of converted but unspoiled late eighteenth-century terraced houses which lay off the wider and busier Caldecote Road." Although he feels "like an interloper entering a private precinct of orderliness, culture, and comfortable prosperity," he is on his mission as a detective and has trained himself to observe carefully. At first he imagines what the district is like:

> They would, he imagined, affect to despise the smartness of Belgravia; would enthuse about the advantages of a socially mixed society, even if the mixing didn't actually extend to sending their children to local schools; would patronize as a duty the small shopkeepers in Caldecote Road.

He soon gives up his reverie and starts to observe the area carefully:

> The street had an impressive uniformity; the houses were identical except for variations in the patterns of

the fanlights and in the wrought-iron tracery of the first-floor balconies. The front railings guarding the basements were spiked and ornamented at the ends with pineapples. The doors, flanked with columns, were thoroughly intimidating; the brass letter boxes and knockers gleamed.

Kevin Lynch notes in *The Image of the City* that a "city district in its simplest sense is an area of homogeneous character, recognized by clues which are continuous throughout the district. . . . The homogeneity may be of spatial characteristics . . . of building type . . . of style or of topography. It may be a typical building feature. . . . Where physical homogeneity coincides with use and status, the effect is unmistakable. In Pimlico, as P. D. James describes it, the eighteenth-century terraced houses have an "impressive uniformity," varying only in the shapes of fanlights and the patterns of wrought-iron tracery. Although Maurice Palfrey is the professional sociologist, Norman Scase's intent focus on detection and eye for details give him accurate "preconceptions" of the upper-middle-class liberal inhabitants of this district. The physical boundaries of the district are reinforced by its visual characteristics, and together they clearly delineate the "urban village."

Pimlico is a well-defined district with clearly differentiated public and private paths. Norman Scase knows that he cannot watch the Palfreys' house from Caldecote Terrace because he would be noticed. In Caldecote Road, the public area, however, he is safe:

> The road was in marked contrast to the terrace, a disorderly muddle of shops, cafes, pubs, and the occasional office, typical of an inner London commercial street from which any glory had long departed. It was a bus route, and small, disconsolate groups of shoppers, laden with their baskets and trolleys, waited at the stops. . . . Here, if not in Caldecote Terrace, he could loiter in safety.

Although Norman at first mistakes the plain, unassuming Hilda for a maid, he finally identifies her and trails her, hoping for a lead to Philippa:

> Pimlico was her [Hilda's] village, and it became his, bounded by Victoria Street and Vauxhall Bridge Road, two flowing thoroughfares like unnavigable rivers over which she never ventured to pass.

Pimlico's clearly marked public and private paths and the unmistakable boundaries of the two thoroughfares define the district. Within it are not only housing and shopping facilities but even recreational areas. It has its own park, Embankment Gardens, with a view of the Thames. Hilda goes there to eat lunch on summer days and to lean on the parapet, staring "at the gritty fringes of the Thames, plumed with gulls, at the great barges as they grunted upstream, slapping the tide against the embankment wall." The Thames functions not only as an edge for the district, but also as a link with the rest of London, as the barges go upstream. In spite of the specific boundaries, Hilda is content to stay within the confines of Pimlico because she already knows other parts of London; she grew up as the only child of working-class parents "in a small terraced house in the poorer part of Ruislip." Philippa, however, feels that Pimlico is part of the "charade" of a fabricated past. She thinks her reflection in the mirror of her room in Caldecote Terrace is inaccurate and unreal. She "had half expected the image to fudge and quiver like a reflection seen in a distorting mirror." The district of Pimlico alone, no matter how well defined in and of itself, cannot reflect back to Philippa a complete identity. To get that she must go out into the city of London and get to know other districts.

To discover her past, Philippa needs to see the other districts of London anew. As she looks for her own apartment in the city, she gains a new perspective:

> Once, from the security of Caldecote Terrace she would have seen the meaner streets of north Paddington, Kilburn, and Earls Court as fascinating outposts of an alien culture, part of the variety and color of any capital city.

> Now with disenchanted and prejudiced eyes she saw only fifth and deformity; the bursting bags of uncollected rubbish, the litter which choked the gutters . . . the walls defaced by the scribbled hate of extremists of the left and right.

Philippa also feels uncomfortable with the people of the district:

> The alien shrouded bodies crouching on the curbside, watching from the open doors, threatened her with their strangeness; the prevailing smells of curry, of herded bodies, of scented women's hair, emphasized the sense of exclusion, of being unwanted in her own city.

Philippa learns to accept strangeness and finally even to be concerned for others when she moves into her apartment on Delaney Street with her mother.

P. D. James describes Delaney Street as being "at the Lisson Grove end of Mell Street" near Praed Street and Edgware Road, but Delaney Street is a made-up name, as are Mell Street and Caldecote Terrace. Although P. D. James uses real main streets like Praed Street and Edgware Road, Victoria Street and Vauxhall Bridge Road, she often makes up street names for residences in her novels. Frequently these names are very close to real street names. For instance, there is a Caldecot Road (without the final *e*) in another part of London. There is no Delaney Street, but there is a Delancey Street. Mell Street, as Nancy Joyner notes, is "clearly modelled on London's Bell Street." In **A Taste for Death,** the most urban of all her traditional detective novels, James adds an author's note when she uses real street names for residences: "My apologies are due to the inhabitants of Camden Hill Square for my temerity in erecting a Sir John Soane house to disrupt the symmetry of their terraces and to the Diocese of London for providing, surplus to pastoral requirements, a Sir Arthur Blomfield basilica and its campanile on the banks of the Grand Union Canal."

Delaney Street first gives Philippa the anonymity that she needs to put together her past. Safe in her newfound anonymity, she can get to know the district. Delaney Street becomes her new "village":

> the core of their joint life lay in Delaney Street and Mell Street. Philippa told herself that she couldn't have found a better part of London in which to be anonymous. The district had a life of its own, but it was one in which the sense of community was fostered by seeing the same familiar faces, not by inquiring into their business. Delaney Street was a quiet cul-de-sac inhabited chiefly by the middle-aged or elderly living above their small family shops. It had something of the atmosphere of a self-sufficient, ancient, and sleepy village, a sluggish backwater between the great surging rivers of the Marylebone Road and the Edgware Road.

Like Pimlico, Delaney Street has clearly defined boundaries and identifiable, homogeneous physical features. It fits Jane Jacobs' definition of an ideal city neighborhood in that it offers privacy and yet some degree of community and contact. Philippa and her mother have the anonymity they need. Although they deliberately do not drink at their local pub, the Blind Beggar, in order to maintain their privacy, still "they felt accepted in the street." No longer "unwanted in her own city," Philippa can relax and begin to learn from the district.

Philippa begins to celebrate the variety and festive quality of the district as she and her mother go out into the crowds of Mell Street on marketing day:

> It was a small, intimate, bustling market, cosmopolitan but at the same time very English. . . . Early in the morning the seller of second-hand rugs and carpets wheeled up his great wooden barrow and patterned the road with his wares. . . . The tarmac itself became festive. Later the market took on something of the atmosphere of an eastern souk when the brass seller arrived to set

out his jangling pots, and a Pakistani who sold cheap jewelry hung across his stall a swinging curtain of wooden beads.

The shops also set the tone of the district:

> Behind the stalls were the small shops: the old—fashioned draper where one could still buy woolen combinations and sleeved vests . . . the Greek delicatessen smelling of syrup and sharp Mediterranean wine; the small general store, clean, sweet-smelling, perpetually dark . . . the half-dozen junk shops.

No longer does Philippa feel threatened by strangeness and difference. She can perceive the festivity of market day and enjoy the variety of shops and people.

Having come to know the "village" of Delaney Street, Philippa can branch out to get to know some of the people of various classes that make up the city. Previously she knew only her private school friends and her adoptive father's academically and socially distinguished acquaintances. Now Philippa learns to get along with some lower-class women when she and her mother take jobs as waitresses at Sid's Place, a fish-and-chip shop off Kilburn High Road. There they share waiting on tables and washing up with Black Shirl, who knifed her mother when she was twelve; with Marlene, who has bright orange spiked hair and tattoos on her arm; and with waif-like, pale Debbie. When Debbie holds a knife to Marlene's throat, Philippa is not as calm as her mother, who, "undisturbed, by the irrational explosions of violence," merely persuades the girl to give her the knife. The incident makes Philippa, however, aware of the economic injustice of the city:

> Two vivid and contrasting mental pictures came frequently into her mind: Gabriel calling for her . . . swinging himself out of his Lagonda, running up the steps of number 68, his cashmere sweater slung from his shoulders; Black Shirl humping to a corner of the kitchen the great bag of washing for her five children which she would wheel in a pram to the launderette on her way home. Perhaps Maurice's [Palfrey, her adoptive father] mind was patterned with equally vivid images, contrasts which had made him a Socialist.

Philippa has still not developed as much of a concern for others as her mother, who feels guilty that she and Philippa talk about the three women "as if they're objects, interesting specimens." Philippa says that it doesn't matter as long as they do not know, but Mary Ducton replies, "Perhaps not to them. It might to us." Philippa still regards others objectively, from the outside, filing people away in her subconscious to use someday when she becomes a writer, but at least as she gets to know a greater variety of people, she becomes more aware of economic injustice. She starts to connect Pimlico and Delaney Street.

It is the connection of districts that for Lynch makes a mosaic of the city. When "regions are close enough together and sufficiently well joined . . . [they] make a continuous mosaic of distinctive districts." Lynch explains that the districts can be connected in different ways: "District may join to district, by juxtaposition, intervisibility, relation to a line, or by some link such as a mediating node." In **Innocent Blood** the links that connect the "villages" and make them into a city are not only in the mind of Philippa, but also physically present in the forms of the underground and the trains, which function as the mediating nodes. Lynch defines a node as a place of "junction" and "convergence of paths." The underground and the trains represent "junction" not only in themselves, but as they connect the various districts. It is also by means of the underground that the various characters connect with each other. All the characters use the trains and the underground; there are numerous references to Liverpool Street Station, King's Cross Station, Piccadilly Circus, and the stops on the Circle Line. Even though both the "villages," Pimlico and Delaney Street, have strong boundaries in the heavily-traveled thoroughfares, these boundaries can be crossed. They function as "seams" rather than as "barriers," to use Lynch's terms, and the districts are connected into a mosaic. It is via the underground that Norman Scase first tracks Hilda and then Philippa and her mother. Although Pimlico is Hilda's "village," she leaves it once a fortnight to serve as a juvenile magistrate, a job she takes to please Maurice. Norman Scase trails her from Victoria Station, to her change at Oxford Circus to the Bakerloo line, and out at Marylebone Station. It is on this trip that Hilda leads him to nearby Delaney Street, where she stops on her way home. Once Norman Scase has found Philippa and her mother, it "was simple enough to trail them on the underground. They usually went from Marylebone, the nearest station." If Norman Scase doesn't know districts, he doesn't worry. The underground and his map of London connect the city for him: "On his larger map he traced the route of the Circle line. Bloomsbury, Marylebone, Bayswater, Kensington. The districts were unfamiliar to him, but he would get to know them." Norman's approach to the city differs from Philippa's. Although an observant detective and able to use the connecting underground system, he still needs his map to get to know the city. She, however, goes into the districts of the city, lives there, and comes to understand the people of the city. Her ability to connect becomes more powerful than that of the purely rational detective because it eventually becomes an ability to connect emotionally and value other people. She is the one who will see the mosaic.

Philippa is comfortable riding the underground, and she begins to think about connection between districts and economic policies, but before she can connect fully and learn to love others, she must come to terms with her past. At first she thinks she can get rid of the past that is merely a blur in her memory. After Philippa and her mother first get to London, she takes her mother to Knightsbridge to buy some expensive new clothes. Then they pack up everything that her mother had brought with her from prison into an old battered case and throw it into the Grand Union Canal. As the case submerges under the "greasy surface" of the canal,

> Philippa felt an almost physical relief, as if she had flung away something of herself, of her past—not the past which she knew and recognized, but the formless weight of unremembered years, of childhood miseries which were not less acute because they lurked beyond the frontier of memory. They were gone now, gone forever, sinking slowly into the mud.

In her relationship with her mother, Philippa tells herself that "L. P. Hartley was right; the past was another country and they could choose whether to visit there." Philippa, who often thinks in literary allusions, is comfortable with an intellectual past, but not a personal and emotional one. When she thinks back to life with the Palfreys, and Maurice bringing her morning tea, an allusion flits through her mind, slightly misquoted from Marlowe's *Jew of Malta:* "But that was in another country and, besides, that wench was dead." The "wench" that she was with Maurice and Hilda Palfrey, however, is no more dead than the first eight years of her life with her mother. The only "wench" who is dead is Julie Scase, and even she lives on in her father's determination for revenge.

Philippa also attempts to ignore the past when she watches TV. On their days off from Sid's fish-and-chip shop, Philippa and her mother watch a family drama, and Philippa thinks that the "convenient ability to live for the moment with its subliminal message that the past could literally be put behind one had much to recommend it." But even that innocuous TV show intersects with the past when they turn on the TV early and see Maurice Palfrey, supposedly an atheist, debate with a bishop. As they listen to the show, Mary Ducton reveals that she understands both her past and the nature of belief. She observes of Maurice: "Your father knows and hates what he knows. I believe, but I can't love anymore. He and I are the unlucky ones." Mary Ducton explains that she cannot love because she has to feel contrition for the murder of Julie Scase in order to receive God's forgiveness, but contrition is now impossible because she has spent her time in prison convincing herself that she wasn't responsible. The crying child reminded her of her little brother who was often beaten by their father; she had to quiet it lest more beatings occur. She says to Philippa:

I can't spend ten years explaining to myself that I wasn't responsible, that I couldn't have prevented myself doing what I did, and then when I'm free . . . decide that it would be pleasant to have God's forgiveness as well.

Mary Ducton understands that she must accept the past. This conversation leads to Philippa's questions about baptism, and she learns that she was christened "Rose."

Behind the name "Rose" and Philippa's relationship to it lie a series of references to roses throughout the novel. They all relate to the idea of human connection and compassion. As the novel opens, Philippa looks at a bowl of roses in the social worker's office, not "scentless, thornless . . . florist's" roses, but garden roses. Philippa thinks of her fantasy of a lord and maid meeting in the rose garden at Pennington. The social worker urges that Philippa trace her father through an intermediary, warning: "We all need our fantasies in order to live. Sometimes relinquishing them can be extraordinarily painful, not a rebirth into something exciting and new, but a kind of death." Relinquishing her fantasies will lead to a death for Philippa, not her own, but her mother's. Still Philippa will learn from relinquishing her fantasies even though the social worker's warning exhibited valid human concern and compassion. Other roses occur throughout the novel. There are small pink rosebuds on the curtain surrounding the hospital deathbed of Norman Scase's wife. Norman Scase does not really love his wife anymore; she had given up everything to grief and a desire for revenge, but he does sit at her deathbed and hold her hand. The punk waitress Marlene has a tattoo of hearts and roses on her arm. When Hilda, sitting on the juvenile magistrate's bench, looks down at a young girl whose baby has been taken from her for fear she or her husband beat the child, she notices a metal brooch in the shape of a rose dragging on the young mother's flimsy cotton top: "She yearned to lean over the bench and stretch out her hands to the girl, to get out from her seat and fold the rigid body in her arms." And it is when he sees Hilda clumsily trying to arrange a bowl of roses that Maurice Palfrey blurts out that he is the one who is infertile, not she: "Because of a bowl of ruined roses, because of a moment of futile compassion, he had blurted it out. Not the whole truth . . . but a part of the truth, the essential truth. A secret he had kept for twelve years." Although such compassion seems futile to Maurice, it lifts a burden from Hilda and makes her realize that she "needn't spend her life making up to him for a deprivation which was nothing to do with her." She can resign from the juvenile magistrate bench where she cannot help anyone; she can fulfill her long-held wish for a dog. Reacting against the fragility and messiness of real roses, Maurice decides suddenly that he doesn't like them anymore:

> They were an overpraised flower, soon blowzy, their

beauty dependent on scent and poetic association. One perfect bloom in a specimen vase placed against a plain wall could be a marvel of color and form, but flowers ought to be judged by how they grew. A rose garden always looked messy, spiky, recalcitrant bushes bearing mean leaves. And the roses grew untidily, had such a brief moment of beauty before the petals bleached and peeled in the wind, littering the soil.

Richard Gidez points out that Maurice and Hilda are really talking about Philippa in their comments on roses. Maurice had thought that he could take Philippa out of the messy, spiky garden of ordinary life and rear her as a perfect specimen, but now Philippa has gone back to ordinary life. Suddenly it occurs to Maurice that the roses parallel the human condition. People, like roses, cannot be judged in isolation, but rather must be perceived as growing in a garden. The messiness, the thorns, the briefness of the beauty, and the disintegration are all a part of the real human condition.

This cluster of images is tied to the city and to the central action of the novel when Philippa, who is with her mother, sees Norman Scase on an outing in Regent's Park with the blind clerk from his hotel, Violet Tetley. All the roses are in bloom: "In Queen Mary's rose garden the roses, plumped by the rain, held the last drops between delicate streaked petals: pink Harriny, bright yellow Summer Sunshine, Ena Harkness, and Peace." For Philippa, Queen Mary's Rose Garden brings back memories:

> There was one rose garden which she could remember, but that had been at Pennington and her imagined father had been there. . . . Odd that so clear a memory, scent, warmth, and mellow afternoon light, recalled with such peculiar intensity, almost with pain, should be nothing but a childish fantasy. But this garden, this park were real enough, and Maurice was right about architecture. Nature needed the contrast, the discipline of brick and stone. The colonnades and pediments of John Nash's terraces, the eccentric outline of the zoo, even the technical phallus of the Post Office Tower soaring above the hedges, contributed to the park's beauty, defined it, and set its limits.

Nature and the rose garden are not some idyllic place away from human life and the city, but rather need the city, and not only the old colonnades, but even the new Post Office Tower. Philippa, thinking back to Maurice, connects the city and the rose garden. Like the architectural critics Jacobs and Lynch, James presents nature and the city not as contrasting elements, but as parts of a coherent whole. Even when Norman Scase climbs out the lavatory window of the pub into the "wasteland" of junk and backyards on Delaney Street, there are flowers on the waist-high weeds: "They looked so fragile with their small, pink flowers, yet they had forced their way through this impacted earth, in places splitting the concrete." Plane trees (sycamores) grow all over London, not only in Bancroft Gardens and Caldecote Terrace, but even in Delaney Street. Backyards have beautiful weeds and plane trees and the city has public rose gardens. It is in the rose garden that Philippa unwittingly makes contact with her mother's past as she smiles at Norman Scase and Violet Tetly.

Philippa had thought that she could ignore her own past life as Rose Ducton, and even as Philippa Rose Palfrey, but she cannot. Mary Ducton's past intersects with Philippa Palfrey's when they meet Gabriel Lomas at an exhibit of Victorian paintings at the Royal Academy. With some underhanded lies to Hilda, Gabriel learns of Philippa and Mary Ducton's apartment and sends a reporter there. Philippa manages to intimidate the reporter, but she and her mother decide to leave London for the Isle of Wight. Philippa even suggests that her mother change her name. Mary Ducton replies, "I couldn't do that. That would be defeat. I have to know who I am." Although Mary Ducton wants to avoid contaminating Philippa's past with her own, she does not deny her past. Philippa decides to take some of Maurice's antique silver and pawn it to finance their trip. It is at this moment that Mary Ducton for the first time calls Philippa by the name Rose: "Suddenly her mother called her back. She said, 'Rose! You won't take anything that isn't yours?'"

When Philippa arrives at Caldecote Terrace, she finds Maurice in bed with one of his graduate students. After the graduate student is dismissed, Maurice and Philippa talk, feeling an intensity between them. Philippa says that she will give up going to Cambridge and just live with her mother. Maurice finally says to her, "it's time you stopped living in a fantasy world and faced reality." He reveals the significance of her name, Rose Ducton. He points out that Philippa assumed that she was adopted after the murder, but in fact she was adopted before the murder because her mother had abused her. Her mother had been unable to stand the screaming, unloving child who had inherited her violent temper. Her mother herself had put Philippa in a foster home, and both her natural parents consented to her adoption. Philippa goes back to Delaney Street in a daze and confronts her mother angrily. Mary Ducton finally asks, "Is what I did to you so much more difficult to forgive than what I did to that child?" Philippa responds, "I don't want to see you ever again. I wish they'd hanged you nine years ago. I wish you were dead," and she flees out of the apartment into the city streets.

As Philippa runs through the city, experiencing the death of the last of her fantasies, the city reflects her anguish. Earlier, Maurice says to her that if his adoption order "lacks the emotional charge of the blood tie, hasn't your family

had enough of blood?" Being Rose Ducton had meant abuse from the mother who had fractured her skull and drawn her blood. The city reflects her mood: "The city was streaked with light, bleeding with light. The head lamps of the cars dazzled on the road and the crimson pools of the traffic lights lay on the surface like blood. The rain was falling in a solid wall of water." Philippa runs away from the Warwick Avenue Underground station, along a "wide road, lined with Italianate houses and stuccoed villas," to the Grand Union Canal and there takes off the sweater her mother just knit her and throws it into the canal, trying one last time to jettison her past. She walks until she is completely exhausted and looks for a place to rest when suddenly a gang of youths start to chase her. She only barely escapes by ducking behind a gate and going into a "dark, evil-smelling area, almost colliding with three battered dustbins." As she sits in this cramped, stinking space,

> [t]here came to her in the darkness no blinding revelation, no healing of the spirit, only a measure of painful self-knowledge. From the moment of her counseling she had thought of no one but herself. Not of Hilda, who had so little to give but asked so little in return and needed that little so much. . . . Not of Maurice, as arrogant and self-deceiving as herself, but who had done his best for her, had given with generosity even if he couldn't give with love, had somehow found the kindness to shield her from the worst knowledge. Not of her mother.

The thought of her mother makes Rose aware of her true feelings:

> She knew, too, that what bound her to her mother was stronger than hate or disappointment or the pain of rejection. Surely this need to see her again, to be comforted by her, was the beginning of love; and how could she have expected that there could be love without pain?

Sitting in the alleyway, Philippa at last, though painfully, learns to accept her past and think of others. The city reflects her pain: "In her mind the city seemed to stretch forever, a silent half-derelict immensity, palely illuminated by the recurrent moon. It was a dead city, plague-ridden and abandoned, from which all life had fled except for that band of scavenging louts." Just then the city reveals that it is not dead and abandoned; across the street she sees an elegant young woman in an evening dress. Philippa crosses over to her to ask directions. She tells Philippa that she is in Moxford Square and explains to her how to get home. Philippa hurries home to Delaney Street, which was "sleeping as quietly as a village street . . . [while the] rain-washed air smelled of the sea" to tell her mother that she loves her. But she is too late for her mother; Mary Ducton has already committed suicide. Philippa can still save Norman Scase, however, who has crept into the apartment and stuck his knife into the corpse. Philippa finds Norman sitting there, saying over and over to himself, "she won't bleed." Although Philippa reads the note from her mother which says "I can die happy because you are alive and I love You," she does not spend her time on the dead. She turns to Norman saying, "[the] dead don't bleed. I got to her before you." Philippa acknowledges her past and her deed, then forgets her focus on self and exhibits concern for others by helping Norman escape. She holds his head as he vomits into the sink, dismisses him, and puts her fingerprints on the knife.

After saving Norman, she calls Maurice, realizing that she too needs human connection and help. Maurice, for whom all the graduate students had been only a substitute for Philippa, arrives quickly and embraces her with "a clasp of possession, not a gesture of comfort." He takes care of the details with the police, takes her home to Caldecote Terrace, and tucks her into her own bed. Philippa learned to love her natural mother; she also needs to come to terms with her relationship to her adopted father. At the beginning of the novel, Philippa thinks she is searching for her real father whom she supposes is an earl at Pennington. She learns early that her natural father is dead and later that he was a weak man unable to protect her from her mother. After her mother's death, Philippa turns to Maurice, her adoptive father. All through the novel, even when with her mother, Philippa thinks of Maurice. She remembers how he taught her to appreciate good wine; she quotes to herself his opinion on architecture and buildings; she thinks about why he became a socialist; and she even recalls how he used to bring her tea in the mornings. When she goes back to Caldecote Terrace and finds him in bed with his student, Philippa wants to hear him say that he has missed her, but he doesn't say it. After he tells her how her real mother had abused her, she angrily asks him what motive he had for adopting her. Maurice finally responds, "Perhaps what I hoped for was love." As he thinks back to when he first saw Philippa, he reveals that her memory of the rose garden at Pennington was real, but that it was not an earl or any natural father whom she met there as a child, but Maurice.

In the epilogue Philippa reveals that she has a new relationship with Maurice. At Cambridge, she meets Norman Scase as she comes out of church. She reassures him that she will not reveal his past to his new wife, the blind Violet Tetley, but what she does not say echoes in her mind, "I used my mother to avenge myself on my adoptive father." Those feelings, however, are forgiven as Philippa and her father re-establish their relationship. Philippa explains to Norman:

> "My adoptive father arranged everything; he's a great fixer. Afterward he took me on a long holiday to Italy. We went to see the mosaics at Ravenna."

She didn't add, "And in Ravenna I went to bed with him." . . . What, she wondered, had it meant exactly, that gentle, tender, surprisingly uncomplicated coupling; an affirmation, a curiosity satisfied, a test successfully passed, an obstacle ceremoniously moved out of the way so that they could again take up their roles of father and daughter, the excitement of incest without its legal prohibition, without any more guilt than they already carried? That single night together . . . had been necessary, inevitable, but it was no longer important.

Having accepted her past, gotten to know her mother, and reestablished connection with Maurice, Philippa has put together the mosaic of her past. Watching Norman Scase go down the path, Philippa hopes that in marrying the blind Violet Tetley, "he would find his patch of rose garden. . . . If it is only through learning to love that we find identity, then he had found his. She hoped one day to find hers. She wished him well. And perhaps to be able to wish him well with all that she could recognize of her unpracticed heart, to say a short, untutored prayer for him and his Violet, was in itself a small accession of grace." Philippa now understands the meaning of her name, "Rose," although she doesn't use it because it "didn't suit" her. She does not think she has completely learned to love yet, but she recognizes what it is and values the grace that allows her a prayer for Norman's happiness.

The references to the mosaics at Ravenna bring to an end a pattern that has run throughout the novel. Wherever mosaics or similar images have appeared, they have been associated with churches and with characters who have learned how to love. Hilda goes to Westminster Cathedral, passing through Lady Chapel, "gleaming with gold mosaics"; Mary Ducton's request to go to church raises in Philippa's mind images of London churches including "Margaret Street, in a dazzle of mosaics, gilded saints, and stained glass." Philippa discusses several times the possibility of going to Ravenna to see the mosaics, but she only goes after she has learned to love her mother and to reconnect with Maurice. The mosaics stand for the value of human connection, given only perhaps by grace as their association with the churches implies. They are like Philippa's closing spontaneous prayer for Norman Scase. As Philippa's peace of mind and awareness of grace illustrate, she has been able to put together the pieces of her life. It is a similar knowledge that has allowed her to put together the mosaic of the city and see the connections that link the urban villages.

Michael Wood (review date 7 December 1989)

SOURCE: "Hanging Out With Higgins," in *London Review of Books,* Vol. 11, No. 23, December 7, 1989, pp. 18-9.

[*In the following excerpt, Wood asserts that James's Devices and Desires "is a thriller and a detective novel."*]

P. D. James's new novel[, ***Devices and Desires,***] seems to return us straight to Auden's theology [as set out is his essay 'The Guilty Vicarage' in which he asserts that thrillers are more serious than detective fiction]. It is set in rural East Anglia, and takes its title from the Anglican prayer book: 'We have erred and strayed from thy ways like lost sheep, we have followed too much the devices and desires of our own hearts.' A psychopath called the Whistler is on the loose, killing young women. Then the haughty and handsome female administrator of a nuclear power station is murdered. Has the Whistler struck again, or has he found a disciple? Suspects include several scientists at the power station, a retired schoolmistress, a writer of cookery books, a protester against the use of nuclear energy, a secretary who has secretly joined an international terrorist organisation, and, marginally, Adam Dalgliesh, James's poet-detective, who has just inherited an old mill in the area, and is awkwardly close to several of these people. The book ends in a brilliant train of misdeductions and evasions, and an explicit contrast with the work of H. R. F. Keating, standing in perhaps for all detective fiction of the old school, where 'problems could be solved, evil overcome, justice vindicated, and death itself only a mystery which would be solved in the final chapter'. This book itself of course belongs to the old school, and does solve its central mystery at last: but it also signals with unusual clarity what the school is up to.

Dalgliesh, reflecting on his work, is also, necessarily, musing on the sort of fiction he is in: 'Perhaps this was part of the attraction of his job, that the process of detection dignified the individual death . . . mirroring in its excessive interest in clues and motives man's perennial fascination with the mystery of his mortality, providing, too, a comforting illusion of a moral universe in which innocence could be avenged, right vindicated, order restored. But nothing was restored, certainly not life, and the only justice vindicated was the uncertain justice of men.' 'Excessive interest' hints at the same reservation as Macdonald's image of Los Angeles; the rest of the passage confirms Auden's diagnosis, but denies his conclusion. An escape which so thoroughly knows it is an escape is a form of realism and asks to be judged like any other form of activity. James doesn't write quite as well as is often claimed—she is too keen on ripe old prose of the 'mystic-thicket-woven-from-thin-shafts-of-light' variety—and her characters cling a little too cosily to their stereotypes: but her ability to embed searching questions in a strong and complicated narrative is really impressive.

The novel emphatically argues, for instance, that death is not 'only a mystery'. An interesting conflict is remembered, in which a policeman calls a rotting female corpse a thing and is severely rebuked by Dalgliesh:

> Sergeant, the word is 'body'. Or, if you prefer, there's 'cadaver', 'corpse', 'victim', even 'deceased' . . . What you are looking at was a woman. She was not a thing when she was alive and she is not a thing now.

This is just, but a little preacherly, and Dalgliesh has his own later encounter with what was a person and now feels like a thing. The question, I take it, is not a matter of words but of how we feel about endings, the abrupt crossing from life into death, the sudden absence of human identity. This is not an excuse for detection: it is what stalks detection itself, the story behind the stories, the reason, one might guess, for all the whimsical titles, those would-be jaunty whistlings in the dark: *Bodies in a Bookshop,* or *Dead on the Level,* or *Death on the Rocks* or *Murder among Friends* (all of these titles are mentioned by Binyon). ***Devices and Desires*** is a thriller *and* a detective novel.

Judith Crist (review date 28 January 1990)

SOURCE: "A Detective in Spite of Himself," in *New York Times Book Review,* January 28, 1990, pp. 1, 31.

[*In the following review, Crist lauds James's vivid characters, evocation of place, and risk-taking in* Devices and Desires.]

Her newest mystery, ***Devices and Desires,*** is P. D. James at better than her best.

That this British writer has long transcended classification as a writer of books of mystery and detection goes without saying. That she is a first-class novelist has come clear over some 30 years and is reaffirmed by her 11th work. What "gives any mystery writer the claim to be regarded as a serious novelist," she wrote in 1983, is "the power to create [a] sense of place and to make it as real to the reader as his own living room—and then to people it with characters who are suffering men and women, not stereotypes to be knocked down like dummies in the final chapter." By hewing to this standard with literary flair and an eye as perceptive as her heart, she has established primacy in her field.

P. D. James has placed herself in the tradition of Wilkie Collins, Dorothy L. Sayers and Margery Allingham, but my own thought is that if Anthony Trollope or George Eliot or Miss James's own beloved Jane Austen had turned a hand to murder or mystery, she would have her heredity. She offers her readers the satisfactions of an artfully constructed, beautifully written story of flesh-and-blood individuals in a time and place we get to know as well as its inhabitants. Not, mind you, that she ignores the conventions of the mystery story: the crime, the clues, the suspects and the puzzlement are there, but so absorbing a read does she offer that final revelations seem almost a bonus. And this time out, with the revelations and resolution, Miss James has taken a risk—and taken it successfully.

Devices and Desires—the title, borrowed from the general confession in the Book of Common Prayer, was also used as a section heading in her last work, *A Taste for Death* (1986)—brings back Adam Dalgliesh, one of her unique creations, a detective neither accented, eccentric nor renegade, now the head of a special squad at New Scotland Yard, a renowned policemen and an acclaimed poet. But in the course of this new outing and its risky resolution, Dalgliesh is destined to feel "the frustrating involvement with a case which would never be his yet from which it was impossible to distance himself."

The hook—that Jamesian opening sentence—is there, too: "The Whistler's fourth victim was his youngest, Valerie Mitchell, aged fifteen years, eight months and four days, and she died because she missed the 9.40 bus from Easthaven to Cobb's Marsh." Thus we are introduced to the first of the "suffering men and women"—and children—who will concern us. The Whistler's purlieu is Norfolk, and four days later Dalgliesh is drawn into the story when he takes off from London for a two-week vacation on the Norfolk coast. His destination is the remote (and fictional) headland of Larksoken, where he will settle the affairs of his recently deceased Aunt Jane, his last living relative, who has left him a historic windmill and house there and £750,000.

Dalgliesh, a sensitive and compassionate observer, is initially our key to the Larksoken community, its inhabitants as varied as their scattered dwellings (which date from a restored 16th-century martyr's cottage to a tacky trailer), its skyline marked by the ruins of an abbey and dominated by the Larksoken Nuclear Power Station, its rhythms underlined by the sea and the wind and the chill of a serial killer at large.

Through Dalgliesh and on our own we encounter a fascinating mix of people: an enigmatic cooking writer and her scientist brother, who is the chief of the power station; a muddled antinuclear activist and the voluptuous young unmarried mother who shares his trailer; power-station executives and underlings with ambitions and aberrations of their own; a widow whose teaching career has been destroyed by the "fashionable orthodoxies" of race relations

(must a *black*board be called a *chalk*board?); an icy beauty involved with an "unprepossessing wimp"; an alcoholic painter and his four motherless children. Sibling relationships with figurative as well as literal blood ties, a variety of sexual relationships, the pros and cons of nuclear power, religion and religiosity are explored and exposed.

Dalgliesh serves too as our link to Terry Rickards, a long-ago London colleague, now head of the Norfolk homicide branch, who seeks him out as a sounding board. He is, in Dalgliesh's view, a "conscientious and incorruptible detective of limited imagination and somewhat greater intelligence," and their relationship is both territorial and prickly when the Whistler strikes again and closer to home, his fifth victim a power-station secretary. And when still another victim, a power-station administrator, is killed in what may or may not be a copycat murder, Dalgliesh, discovering the body, qualifies as both witness and suspect.

Preoccupied with the detritus of his beloved aunt's life; bemused by the childhood memories it evokes and pondering his own future as an independently wealthy man, Dalgliesh is indeed part poet. But he is in larger part policeman, a seasoned investigator who, on another's turf, can still recognize a major clue, know how to deal with intelligence operatives in two more deaths, gain insight into a power-station scientist's suicide, perform heroic physical feats in a crisis and finally make an informed "guess" at the solutions even when the cases are officially given "open verdicts."

But his is only a guess. The risk that P. D. James has taken here is in letting readers see with their own, rather than the detective's, eyes and know more than Dalgliesh, Rickards or the intelligence agents can know or learn. We and the author share the terror of an innocent running "smiling towards the horror of her death," the irony of a schemer with time only to say "I'm sorry. I'm sorry" as the end comes, the suspense of "the silent watcher waiting" for a victim, the ice of a murderer's summing up: "I did what I had to do, and it was worth it." We share a knowledge with Miss James of secrets that are kept, of virtue and principle, of hatred on the face and evil in the heart.

While it has the richness of a classical novel, this topical tale is told in a taut time framework and unfolds in the near cinematic scenes that are Miss James's style. This is why her work translates so well to film. (*A Taste for Death,* her fifth novel to be televised here on public television, will come to "Mystery!" in March.)

If there is a minor flaw in *Devices and Desires,* it is that for the whodunit fan there is small question of who in Larksoken is marked for murder, though the identity of the murderer, albeit impeccably clued for us, comes as a shocker. But, as always with P. D. James, the whodunit element is the lagniappe, so interesting are her characters, so absorbing her depiction of time and place, so rich the texture of the tale she tells. She has not failed us, and she has exceeded herself.

Hilary Mantel (review date 26 April 1990)

SOURCE: "Crime and Puzzlement," in *New York Review of Books,* Vol. XXXVII, No. 7, April 26, 1990, pp. 35-7.

[*In the following review, Mantel complains that the detective genre is too confining for James's talent.*]

February 1990: the literary editor of a British newspaper writes to *The Spectator,* protesting about what he sees as an elitist stranglehold on literary prizes. "Booker judges have ignored the merits of authors like William Boyd, Graham Greene, P. D. James." The reader who does not keep up with the politics of the review columns might well be puzzled. Doesn't P. D. James write best-selling detective stories? What is she doing in the company of Greene? When did the categories of fiction become so confused?

Those commentators who would elevate James's books to the status of literary novels point to her painstakingly constructed characters, her elaborate settings, her sense of place, and her love of abstractions: notions about morality and duty, pain and pleasure, are never far from the lips of her policemen, victims, and murderers. Others find her pretentious and tiresome; an inverted snobbery accuses her of abandoning the time-honored conventions of the genre in favor of fancy up-market stuff. Writing in *The Spectator* (October 7, 1989) Harriet Waugh wants P. D. James to get on with "the more taxing business of laying a tricky trail and then fooling the reader"; Philip Oakes in *The Literary Review* groans, "Could we please proceed with the business of clapping the darbies on the killer?" (October 1989). Wherever P. D. James's books are discussed there is a tendency, on the one hand, to exaggerate her merits; on the other, to punish a genre writer who is getting above herself. A feature of the debate is that familiar, false opposition between different kinds of fiction—the belief that pleasurable books are somehow slightly shameful, and that a book is not literature unless it is a tiny bit dull.

Phyllis Dorothy James should not really be a contentious figure; she is, as profile writers love to point out, a grandmother. Born in Oxford in 1920, she is a former civil servant, and she has been a magistrate and a governor of the BBC. In *A Taste for Death,* the fat, ambitious, and messy novel that precedes the present one, she contrives to provide a self-portrait. One of her characters, a photographer,

is commissioned to take pictures of writers; in an uncharacteristically sly and witty passage, James sets before the camera "a buxom grandmother, noted for her detective stories, who gazed mournfully at the camera as if deploring either the bloodiness of her craft or the size of her advance."

In *An Unsuitable Job for a Woman* (1972) and *The Skull Beneath the Skin* (1982) James gave brief play to a young, detective called Cordelia Gray, but her chief creation is Commander Adam Dalgliesh of Scotland Yard. Although he is a thorough professional, Dalgliesh is also, like most detectives dreamed up by Englishwomen, a thorough gentleman. Urbane, elegant, and brave, he has a parallel career as a published poet, and garnishes his speech with references biblical and literary. The only son of elderly parents, he had a lonely upbringing in a country rectory; his mother died when he was fifteen. He has lost his own wife and newborn son; they were the victims of a "chance in a million" medical accident. Sometimes Dalgliesh seems too perfect to live, and too finely spiritual to care much about dying. At the beginning of *The Black Tower* (1975) he has been falsely diagnosed as terminally ill:

> It was embarrassing now to recall with what little regret he had let slip his pleasures and preoccupations, the imminence of loss revealing them for what they were, at best only a solace, at worst a trivial squandering of time and energy.

In *A Taste for Death* he is hardly less enervated:

> The poet who no longer writes poetry. The lover who substitutes technique for commitment. The policeman disillusioned with policing.

P. D. James's new book is set on the Norfolk coast, in that windswept and lightly populated area of England remarkable for its fine but frequently neglected churches. Its title comes from the Book of Common Prayer: "We have erred and strayed from thy ways like lost sheep. We have followed too much the devices and desires of our own heart." James's preoccupation with religion softens the harsh realities in which her books deal. To perversion and blood lust, to carnage and cut throats, she brings the sensibility of the communicant Anglican. If there is no justice in this life—and in a P. D. James novel, there sometimes isn't— it is a comforting thought that there will be justice in the next.

The book's first sentence has the Jamesian mark. It is precise, direct, and opens beneath the reader a chasm of malign coincidence:

> The Whistler's fourth victim was his youngest, Valerie

Mitchell, aged fifteen years, eight months and four days, and she died because she missed the 9.40. bus from Easthaven to Cobb's Marsh.

The Whistler is a serial killer with a grisly line in postmortem handiwork; and what he whistles, as he leaves the scene of the crime, is a few bars of an obscure hymn. He operates in the area of the Larksoken nuclear power station, a concrete monolith that shares a lonely headland with the ruins of a Benedictine abbey.

As it happens, Dalgliesh has just inherited property in the neighborhood, An elderly aunt, his only remaining relative, has left him a converted windmill and a sum of money—enough money to allow him to quit the Yard, if he wishes, and devote himself full time to poetry. He is a happier man than the brooding and exhausted creature we left at the end of *A Taste For Death.* Burton's *Anatomy of Melancholy* still supplies his casual reading, but there are hints that he might be falling in love—perhaps with his young colleague Inspector Kate Miskin—and he has broken his creative silence with a collection of poems called *A Case to Answer.*

Dalgliesh is published by Herne & Illingworth, a plausible and familiar outfit who have offices in Bedford Square; and at a plausible and familiar publishing party, their cookbook editor asks him to deliver a set of proofs to Alice Mair, an author living in Norfolk. "I wouldn't really wish to trust these proofs to the post," she says; and whereas in real life an author would reply, "Norfolk is large; send them by a courier service," Dalgliesh takes possession of the precious papers, and is led by this thin and shameless plot device to the persons at the heart of the drama.

Dalgliesh is invited to dinner by Alice Mair; among others, he meets her brother Alex, who is the director of the power station, and Larksoken's acting administrator, an abrasive young woman called Hilary Robarts. A place at table is kept for another Larksoken employee, who bursts in at a late hour to announce that he has found the Whistler's latest victim; shocked, and later drunk, he reveals more than is tasteful about the killer's *modus operandi.* So when in due course Dalgliesh is taking a walk on the beach and comes across a corpse, the people at the dinner party—in addition to a local teen-ager acting as a waitress—are suspects. For the new death is that of Hilary Robarts herself, and although her murder has all the Whistler's trademarks, the serial killer cannot possibly be responsible; he has committed suicide in a seaside hotel some hours earlier.

Hilary Robarts's enemies extend beyond the dinner party. There is Ryan Blaney, a drunken artist and widower who lives with his four children in a ramshackle cottage that Robarts owns. She is trying to evict him: motive enough

there, perhaps? Also on the scene are Caroline Amphlett, Alex's personal assistant, an ice-cool blonde who has started an unlikely love affair with a boring, blotchy young scientist; an antinuclear campaigner whom Robarts is suing for libel; a waif called Amy, who lives with the protester in his caravan, who sometimes receives old postcards from London, and who has no job, no welfare entitlement, yet a small but mysterious income.

P. D. James's handling of the nuclear power issue is knowledgeable and cautious. Larksoken dominates the Norfolk landscape as its churches once did, but Alex Mair thinks it transitory, "both the science and the symbol." Yet while it lasts, it purveys a message

> both simple and expedient, that man, by his own intelligence and his own efforts, could understand and master his world, could make his transitory life more agreeable, more comfortable, more free of pain.

We may assume James to be in broad agreement with Alex, since she frequently uses her characters as mouthpieces; but in this novel nuclear power is a device rather than a desire. In inventing Larksoken James has created only a modern version of the closed society—the island, the country house—in which to entrap her large and diverse cast. The headland itself is a closed world, its inhabitants able to monitor one another's comings and goings; all of it can be overseen by the godlike Dalgliesh, from the top story of his windmill. But within this world the power station is a smaller world still, enclosed by its security systems and the demands that it places on its personnel, isolated as they are by arcane, dangerous knowledge.

Devices and Desires is a leisurely and confident book, a considerable feat of organization. It is a much better book than its predecessor, for it does not have the monotony of tone of *A Taste for Death* that makes it hard to read more than fifty pages at a time; and it is much more successful in keeping the reader in suspense, for in the last book the guilty party was set up early on as a highly unpleasant sociopath. There is some strikingly good writing in *Devices and Desires,* and a great deal of competent unmemorable workaday prose. P. D. James has cultivated a style that seldom teases or questions the reader, and does not question itself. Her descriptive writing leaves nothing unsaid; she has not mastered the art of the judicious omission. Certainly her digressions are part of the pleasure of her books, and give them dignity and weight. The patinas and aromas of a country kitchen, the wineglass pulpit in the church at Salle, all receive more loving attention than does the plot itself, and from time to time an image that is both felicitous and congruous, embedded in an otherwise unremarkable passage, will surprise:

> Before them, at the edge of the cliff, crumbling against

the skyline like a child's sand castle rendered amorphous by the advancing tide, was the ruined Benedictine abbey. He could just make out the great empty arch of the east window and beyond it the shimmer of the North Sea, while above, seeming to move through and over it like a censer, swung the smudged yellow disc of the moon.

Her dialogue, on the other hand, is weak. Speakers are hardly differentiated, and all of them are too fluent, given to speechifying, articulate in an unlikely way about their deepest emotions, their most troubling and troublesome thoughts. When the Whistler is still on the loose, Meg Dennison describes her feelings thus:

> When night falls and we're sitting there by the fire, I can imagine him out there in the darkness, watching and waiting. It's that sense of the unseen, unknowable menace which is so disquieting. It's rather like the feeling I get from the power station, that there's a dangerous unpredictable power out on the headland which I can't control or even begin to understand.

The characters are always ready with an obliging label for their own feelings. The discoverer of a corpse says, a few hours after the event, "Looking back, my emotions were complicated, a mixture of horror, disbelief and, well, shame."

This stilted stuff is the work of a writer who has never, found her characters' voices, and who has not thought it necessary to distinguish their observations and sentiments from her own. But set against that, there is the immense trouble she takes to provide the most minor character with a detailed *curriculum vitae*. Sometimes the digressions are carried to irritating lengths; when a pathologist turns up to examine Hilary Robarts's mutilated body, we are given a quick rundown on his tastes in music and women, when all we want to know from him is how long she's been dead. Here, the accumulation of detail does little but hold up the action.

Yet the crablike excursions around and behind the characters can also be felicitous. Jonathan Reeves, the colorless young scientist who has been taken up by Alex Mair's assistant, is a marginal character, but P. D. James subjects his cramped and stifled childhood to her detailed scrutiny:

> His father had worked for fifty years in the carpet department of a large store in Clapham. . . . The firm let him have carpets at less than cost price; the off-cuts . . . he got for nothing. . . . Sometimes it seemed that their thick-pile wool and nylon had absorbed and deadened not only their footsteps. His mother's calm response to any event was either "Very nice," equally

appropriate in an enjoyable dinner, a royal engagement or birth or a spectacular sunrise, or "Terrible, terrible, isn't it? You wonder sometimes what the world's coming to," which covered events as diverse as Kennedy's assassination, a particularly gruesome murder, children abused or violated or an IRA bomb. But she didn't wonder what the world was coming to. Wonder was an emotion long since stifled by Axminster, mohair, underfelt.

So there you have the post-1945 lower-middle classes of England: their interior decor, their phiiistinism, their peculiar self-contained fortitude. It seems ungrateful to ask if there is something extravagant and unnecessary in the character building, when it is so convincingly done; James has a keen eye for the little social markers the British employ and enjoy. P. D. James's ability to distill and bottle the essence of Britishness—or what seems to be the essence of Britishness—must surely be a factor in her popularity in the US; and in a nation increasingly self-conscious about its "heritage" and national character, it may well be a source of happiness to her readers at home.

Of course, detective fiction in Britain has always been class-conscious. A murder in a slum is not an object of remark; but a murder in a country house is worth a book. If we assume—and it's the traditional assumption—that the affluent middle classes lead well-conducted, orderly lives, murder has great shock value; and well-bred persons with everything to lose, persons of position and wealth, are likely targets for blackmailers, and are more likely to indulge in complicating, face-saving cover-ups. Besides, when we stumble across the body in the library, find Lady Bountiful slashed and clobbered beside her objets d'art, we can console ourselves that wealth did not bring her happiness. Useless to convict the classic detective story of coziness; it was meant to make us feel better, and coziness was its heart.

P. D. James does not give us the bloodless corpses of a more genteel age—her images are graphic, though never gloating—and she aims to run the gamut of society, from the lord to the tramp. She is most comfortable among the middle classes, and is not good with the lower orders. She uses her working-class characters to provide humor—of which, otherwise, there's not much in her books.

Yet in every matter—emotional, social—Dalgliesh is the arbiter of taste. Idealized and idolized by his creator in the most old-fashioned way, just as Dorothy L. Sayers idolized Lord Peter Wimsey, Dalgliesh is everything a woman would wish a man to be. He will rush into a burning room to save someone with whom he has slight acquaintance; but he can also cook up a comforting cassoulet. He is reserved, self-contained, needs nobody—but he is sensitive to the feelings of others. Another policeman in the novel, Rickards, is less attractive and more fallible than Dalgliesh. Rickards is in charge of the local police investigation. He lacks both Dalgliesh's probing intellect and his social savoir-faire; his young wife has a "dressing table, kidney-shaped, . . . trimmed with pink-and-white flowered voile, the pretty matching set of ring-stand and tray . . . neatly in place."

One takes the point: here's more of the lower middle-class's prissiness and tackiness. Yet in real life you would have to go back a few years to find a dressing table like that. P. D. James takes immense trouble to put her characters in their contexts, to convey to us the mundane details of their lives, but it is a qualified sort of social realism she employs. Sometimes the text is abuzz with current concerns. A neighbor of Alice Mair's, for instance, is a former London schoolteacher, who was driven from her job by a ferocious race-relations lobby after she refused to call a blackboard a "chalkboard." Elsewhere, one feels social changes have passed the author by: does any young woman these days give up work in *anticipation* of becoming pregnant?

In one important respect, however, James, is against coziness. Throughout *Devices and Desires* she seems to be engaged in a conscious rebellion against the neatness of detective fiction. When the ex-schoolteacher seeks spiritual counsel from the elderly clergyman for whom she keeps house, she finds him absorbed in one of the Inspector Ghote stories of H. R. F. Keating; and the priest is impatient to be done with her difficult questions and get back to the gentler, more certain world that the book offers him. Ghote, says P. D. James,

> would get there in the end, because this was fiction: problems could be solved, evil overcome, justice vindicated and death itself only a mystery which would be solved in the final chapter.

A P. D. James book does not leave its readers with any similar comfort. The mere solution of the crime will not put the world to rights. Any solution will in itself contain areas of ambiguity, and guilt will be well distributed between murderer, victim, and bystanders. In this latest book, the crime itself seems less important than the effect it has on those left alive; it brings out their interesting vulnerabilities and perplexities, and causes them to engage in pages of moral debate. Murder, as James remarks in *A Taste For Death,* is "the first destroyer of privacy"; and in the wake of murder, the people left alive lay bare their souls. "At the heart of the universe there is love," says one character; another counters, "At the heart of the universe there is cruelty."

James is so absorbed in this debate that she wraps up her plot in a way that some readers may find unsatisfactory. Caroline Amphlett proves to be a member of a terrorist group operating from Germany; the witless waif Amy, an animal liberationist, has been drawn into a plot to take over power stations throughout Europe. This subplot is worked in late, proves to be only a diversion from the identity of the real murderer, and does not in itself convince. In *A Taste for Death* James gave a young female character a set of left-wing, vaguely subversive views, perhaps reasoning that such a device adds another layer of menace; here she repeats the trick, on a bigger scale but in a similar unsophisticated way. The reader finds that motives he had taken to be personal were in fact ideological, and may justifiably grumble that he has no way of keeping up with the ploys of an author who is prepared to toss in the notion of an international terrorist ring without some little advance warning.

When the story is at its most domestic it is at its most plausible, and the true murderer does have personal motives. Disappointingly, they are motives the reader has already begun to guess at, but no doubt the author does not care about that; the revelation of bloody deeds and who did them is secondary to the revelation of the murderer's selfish, irreligious, amoral view of life, and her "intellectual and spiritual arrogance." Throughout the book the reader knows more than the police, for he is privy to the secrets of the murderer's childhood and the details of her relationship with her brother. The reader certainly knows more than Dalgliesh; Adam is not part of the local force, is not officially attached to the investigation, and he is kept on the sidelines by his own sense of propriety and by the antagonism of Rickards. The identity of the murderer is revealed to the reader in a conversation between Alice and another character, in which Dalgliesh plays no part; so it is impossible to see how he arrives at the truth, and one can only attribute it to the free-floating intuition with which his creator has so thoughtfully provided him.

The truth may be that it is not the specifics of detection that interest P. D. James at this stage of her career; it is the nature of the detective's job. On the scene of the crime, the police watch and listen as others express their shock and grief—they share in other people's lives, but at the same time stand back and observe them, ready, with the notebook. Dalgliesh's misgivings about his profession are misgivings he shares with his author. Policemen, like novelists, have to find the shape and form in random and meaningless events; like policemen, novelists rebuke themselves for coldness of heart. As a tool for getting at the truth, police work has its dissatisfactions and limitations; so does crime fiction.

> By the end you know everything, or think you do. Where, when, who, how. You might even know why

if you're lucky. And yet, essentially, you know nothing. All that wickedness, and you don't have to explain it or understand it or do a bloody thing about it except put a stop to it.

The detective closes his file; the author closes her book; both are exhausted, both dissatisfied. Where does this dissatisfaction lead?

The same Philip Oakes who takes P. D. James to task for her indirect methods agrees that she is justifiably praised for her "ability to flower within the discipline of a genre." But this discipline is now a constraint. In *Devices and Desires* signs of strain are evident. The murderer is a character whom James has brought us to respect, but whom she—and we—in the end must find morally repulsive. Subtleties are on offer—too many subtleties to be contained within the format of murder investigation-solution; and within the adipose mass of this novel is a thinner, sharper, wiser book trying to fight its way out.

Some years ago, James wrote an interesting novel called *Innocent Blood,* a psychological thriller with no Adam Dalgliesh, no Cordelia Gray. Her admirers will wonder if she will now provide another such book, a book not subject to the stultifying rules of detective fiction. It seems almost an insult to apply the label "promising" to an author who is in her seventieth year and who has written eleven novels; but her books constantly promise what they do not perform. Once the rules of a chosen genre cramp creative thought, there seems no reason why an able and interesting writer should accept them. It is fashionable, though reprehensible, for writers to prescribe for other writers. But perhaps the time has come for P. D. James to slide out of her handcuffs, kick off her concrete boots, and stride onto the territory of the mainstream novel.

Kathryn Hughes (review date 25 September 1992)

SOURCE: "Barren Earth," in *New Statesman & Society,* Vol. 5, No. 221, September 25, 1992, p. 55.

[*In the following review, Hughes praises the first part of James's* The Children of Men *as "fascinating stuff," but complains that the narrative of the second section "begins to droop."*]

The Children of Men is P. D. James' first attempt to move outside the detective novel, a literary form that she has done so much to rehabilitate over the past ten years. It's interesting, therefore, that for this most significant of forays she chose another well-defined genre in which to work.

The whole point about a dystopia is that it presents us with a nightmare vision of the future in order to warn about disturbing trends in the present. This is where *The Children of Men* succeeds magnificently. The year is 2021. In a clever reversal of the usual Malthusian armageddon, the population is drastically on the decline. No children have been born for 25 years and, despite the three-monthly compulsory sperm and gynae checks, it seems unlikely that any ever will.

To fill the aching void, kittens and dolls are fussed over, baptised and snatched from their prams by would-be "mothers". Meanwhile, an ever-increasing number of old people keep their heads down in a desperate hope of dodging the Quietus: the state-organised mass suicide whose benign rituals fail to offer comfort or meaning.

This terrible tale is told by Theo Farren, an Oxford history don. But what an Oxford this is. With no undergraduates left to teach, Farren is reduced to taking souped-up evening classes on Victorian Life and Times for 50 year-old women who should, in a better world, be occupied with their grandchildren. In this era of state-supported narcissism, he reports every week to the city's massage centre, aka Lady Margaret Hall, for a "carefully measured hour of sensual pampering".

While his brain is as sharp as ever, Farren has surrendered his moral and ethical self to the ethics of "protection, comfort and pleasure", which just about hold the rage and darkness in check. Whereas once he had a post of influence as adviser to the ruling Council, these days Farren spends his time in resigned anomie, pottering around the Ashmoleum. The roots of his paralysis soon become clear: 25 years ago he committed the greatest crime of all, accidentally killing his baby daughter during one of the last fertile years on the planet.

Like most dystopias, the first part of *The Children of Men* is fascinating stuff, painting a future that has just that right blend of familiarity and strangeness. Above all, it is fun to insert ourselves in James' imaginary historical trajectory: the 1990s, it emerges, were a time of mass emigration, religious and tribal war. The playing out of our own demographic "hiccough", the ageing population, is done with particular skill. James' prose is as lucid as ever, devoid of pretension and utterly compelling.

The problem comes in the second part of the book. The moment Farren chooses action and engagement, the narrative begins to droop. Approached at Magdalen Evensong—rituals such as these now seem strangely desolate—he finds himself drawn to a group of five dissidents. One of them, the oddly named Julian, is pregnant, and the group decides to go on the run in order to protect this most miraculous of births from state interference. From here the story degenerates into the how-much-petrol-have-we-got-left? variety. Even the scary bits—somebody gets lynched, someone else gets garrotted—fail to raise the required shock.

As these rather obvious parallels with the nativity story suggest, James works into her narrative a story of Christian redemption. Despite his attendance at Evensong, Farren has resigned himself to a wearied and wearying agnosticism, regarding the group's Christianity as just one more sloppy delusion of the New Age. However, his love for Julian and his awe at her ability to create life pull him back to the heart of belief. In the end, he breaks the paralysis of so many years by making the sign of the cross on the child "with a thumb wet with his own tears and stained with her blood". A better world, it seems, is on its way.

Walter Wangerin, Jr. (review date 28 March 1993)

SOURCE: "O Brave New World, That Has No People In't!" in *New York Times Book Review,* March 28, 1993, p. 23.

[*In the following review, Wangerin discusses the two adventures in James's* The Children of Men.]

On New Year's Day, 2021, "the last human being to be born on earth was killed in a pub brawl." He was 25. It has been 25 years since a global disease rendered all human sperm infertile, 25 years, therefore, since *any* baby has been born to bear the future of humankind. The same day marks the 50th birthday of Theodore Faron, doctor of philosophy. On this day he begins to keep a journal as a "small additional defense against personal accidie."

With such swift strokes P. D. James establishes the central premise of her new novel, ***The Children of Men.*** There follow two worthy adventures for Miss James, for her protagonist and for the thoughtful reader:

The first concerns final efforts at saving this race, the people, us. The first adventure exemplifies what has always made Miss James's detective fiction structured and strong: story. But Theodore Faron's real *story*—the sequence of events that drives toward a conclusion that must succeed, or else all fails—is slow to start. Not till Chapter Six does Faron meet the woman, Julian, who will involve him and us in plots. And even then things unfold slowly. Faron is not easily persuaded to crack his self-containment for the sake of others. It's not in his character. (He notes his "terror of taking responsibility for other people's lives or happiness.") Nor is it in the times. ("But those who lived gave way to the almost universal negativism, what the French

named *ennui universel.*") In fact, the novel's Book One, "Omega," acts much as a set-up for the story that does not dominate until Book Two, "Alpha."

But it doesn't matter. The reader can certainly wait for action since the second adventure of the book—perhaps the more fascinating one—is the meditation that its premise encourages. In a recent interview, Miss James said, "I thought, if there was no future, how would we behave?" No future, not because it has been canceled suddenly, as by nuclear war, but because it has been cut off at the source: no babies, no next generation. Those alive are thus granted their fullness of years but their deaths are made dreadfully significant. When they die, all die. Contemplating *that,* in Book One, is the more terrible adventure. For look what becomes of us when *we* are the end, the point of it all:

Love is lavished on the inanimate. "Doll-making was the only section of the toy industry which . . . flourished; it had produced dolls for the whole range of frustrated maternal desire." And when Faron sees one woman dash the doll of another against a stone wall, its "mother" screams "the scream of the tortured, the bereaved, the terrified."

The last-born men and women, that final generation whom society calls "our Omegas," are strikingly handsome and talented but, as far as others are concerned, cold and incurious. Faron writes, "If from infancy you treat children as gods they are liable in adulthood to act as devils."

Fatalism, boredom, crime and religious hysteria increase. The Isle of Man is turned into a penal colony where thieves are dumped to survive or to die murdering one another.

The people hoard against a time when the state will fail. But, careless of anybody save themselves, they permit a dictator to rule England absolutely, serving his own power rather than their welfare. By his decree the old are herded onto a ship for a seeming mass suicide, a ritual called the Quietus. But these people are in fact not suicides but victims—drugged and set adrift to drown. And Theodore Faron, trying to save one woman from the Quietus, is beaten senseless by a soldier of the state.

That, for him, is the crucial event. Pity cracks his solitude. He begins to heed Julian, the woman who believes she holds in herself the potential for a future. Since the dictator of England is Faron's cousin, Julian has begged him to reason with the man before she and her group begin subversive activity. After the Quietus Faron agrees and speaks with his cousin. But the dictator remains immovable, and Faron makes a commitment to others in spite of himself. And so begins the action of the book.

Plot, under Miss James's hand, is never merely external

action. Always she explores character, the complexities of motive and thought and emotion; and always she wonders about the nature of humankind in general—this baffling admixture of good and evil, faith and failure, love and a murderous self-sufficiency. In her other novels, the author's attention is upon the plot and these concerns appear only indirectly. But here Miss James makes these contemplations the very business of her book, and her view is Olympian.

From the premise of this novel, death takes on tremendous dimension. And as Faron grows to love Julian, love is purged of personal return. In the time of endings, choices are reduced to the most basic, for self or for others, and those who choose selflessness choose genuine sacrifice, dying for Julian—who believes she is pregnant—and for the sake of the future.

And birth—for this must be the *real* plot, the *real* rebellion, the *real* potency and salvation of humankind—the birth of a single child becomes a thing of ineffable glory.

If there is a baby, there is a future, there is redemption. From this, Miss James's book draws—but not heavily—a mythic breath.

And she herself signals the source of its title and perhaps of its hope. During a makeshift funeral for one who sacrificed his life for Julian and the future, Faron reads from an old prayer book this psalm: "Lord, thou hast been our refuge: from one generation to another. . . . Thou turnest man to destruction: again thou sayest, Come again, ye children of men."

James Sallis (review date 4 April 1993)

SOURCE: "The Decline and Fall of the Human Race," in *Los Angeles Times Book Review*, April 4, 1993, p. 12.

[*In the following review, Sallis argues that James fails in her intentions in* The Children of Men.]

There is but one liberty: to come to terms with death, Camus wrote, after which all things are possible.

It is not individual death that James confronts in her new novel[, **The Children of Men,**] but the potential death of the human race itself. Suddenly, mysteriously, humankind has stopped bearing children. Values have collapsed. Apathy blankets what activity remains.

There is, of course, no art; museums and all our grand ambitions stand unattended; government-sponsored porn shops attempt to flog what sexual, creative drive lies dormant. "Human mules deprived of posterity," men and women endure the rag ends of their lives. Women push dolls in elaborate prams about the streets; men preserve what empty social forms they can. In a few the sense of despair is so great that they ally themselves to horrendously doomed causes.

The stage is set, then; we are prepared for a sweeping, perhaps ultimately poetic evocation of mankind's twilight, something in the vein of Stapledon, or of George Stewart's *Earth Abides.*

What would society be like, what might it become, or unbecome, under absolute sentence of death? Able to pass nothing on, unable to reproduce itself even symbolically, without social structures to place and hold us in place, what reasons could humankind find for going on?

Unfortunately, P. D. James fails to follow through on the implications of her theme and instead elects to let it all down into a curious meld of melodrama and religious symbolism. The impending birth of a child—immaculate, one might say, since no explanation for this reversal of mankind's barrenness is offered—brings on a flurry of religious referents: the manger-like shed where the birth takes place, the ritual killing of the father, the pursuit by authorities, the personal sacrifices and martyrdom of those close, even the betrayal by one "disciple."

Something beyond mere habit draws readers to genres such as the mystery or science-fiction. With the latter sometimes called a literature of ideas, the attraction is often the genre's potential for concept, and all too often this has led to a fiction in which characters are carried off on the runaway horse of plot.

When writers veer toward science-fiction, as mystery novelist James does here, it's precisely this idea that beckons, and however fine these writers are, because they have little idea of what has been and is being done in the genre, because they're overwhelmed by the sheer amplitude of what they are essaying, the results are often disappointing.

Writing of dystopias casts these difficulties into further relief. Few non-genre writers even recognize the need to imagine, truly imagine, an alternative society; fewer still have the imaginative power and discipline to do so. Because of this, virtually all mainstream dystopias (along with most genre ones, I rush to emphasize) come down simply to some thwarting of individualism and, with its re-trumpeting, restoration of an order remarkably like the one we've got. Thesis, antithesis, status quo.

Squarely in the British tradition, James is a master of character and contributing incident, her novel from first to last exceedingly well-wrought. Its primary pleasures are those of craft: a deft interleafing of lives, the reflective interaction of first-person and omniscient point of view, the sure voice and pace, the seamless narrative.

Children of Men, is, too, an elaborately figured novel. There is, first, the religious undertow. An ongoing, almost programmatic political discourse winds its way throughout. A man's killing of his own daughter flows into the murder of one woman's doll by another jealous woman on the street, and this in turn on to the birth of the new child. The novel's early elegiac tone is quite beautiful: equal measures of celebration and sorrow, a sadness for all things unsaid, undone, forever unredeemed.

It's at the very point this tone shifts that the novel falters, exposing a hollowness more distressing than its decline into melodrama and conventional territory.

Since useful works of art rarely are about what they seem to be about, then we must wonder; finally, whether *The Children of Men* may not be at its deepest level a kind of eulogy for Britain and for a way of life that James recognizes is gone. Her metaphor of a world from which the life force has departed, her portrait of a final, declining generation, even the novel's polite, dissembling language, suggest this.

To every appearance, James set out to provide a cosmic poem; considered for a while folding in the makings of a political novel; decided somewhere along the way to interpolate a religious fable; and ended up with a book that's none of these, but a kind of sympathy card for her own time and class. Relics of empire thick on the tea cozy, as one poet put it . . . however beautiful the relics, however fine and bracing the tea.

P. D. James with Kate Kellaway (interview date 16 October 1994)

SOURCE: "On the Case of the Baroness," in *Observer Review,* October 16, 1994, p. 19.

[*In the following interview, Kellaway discusses with James setting, the enjoyment of detective fiction, and research.*]

In P D James's outstanding new novel, *Original Sin,* set in London, she writes about buildings with detailed attention, as if they were suspects. Her imagination is a zealous architect. *Original Sin* is dominated by a stupendous, white pseudo-Venetian edifice by the Thames, occupied by a pub-

lishing company and called, with stark irony, Innocent House. She says: 'Houses betray character so clearly, they really do.'

Her house in Holland Park, built in 1830, is grand and green with white slatted shutters, a square, reliable face with a faded burglar alarm on the wall. Baroness James of Holland Park is small, vigorously intelligent and benign (she addresses me soothingly as 'dear').

We settle in her sitting room on a sofa, upholstered in linen, in a leafy beige-and-green William Morris design. In the infrequent pauses in the conversation, I try to apply P D James's own methods to her sitting room—an autumnal room full of antiques. I scribble particulars: a red-and-gold mirror, imitation primroses popping cheekily out of a box, a solitaire board with plain glass marbles; two Staffordshire dogs on the mantelpiece, noses sniffily held high.

It's a comfortable, conservative room and in this, it reflects its owner (she's right-wing, C of E, a Vice-President of the Prayer Book Society). It is only after leaving that I realise the room reminds me of something else. The dogs, the primroses, the sofa are all in the novel, in the flat of mediocre, elderly crime writer, Esmé Carling. She's a grotesque alter-ego for P D James, sacked by her firm after 30 years, then bumped off.

P D James (born in 1920) has also been writing for over 30 years. Her novels are Victorian in their spaciousness, exciting but leisurely. These are books to escape into, delighting in the sense that you are in safe hands, no matter how unsafe the subject. Her last book, *The Children of Men,* was an enjoyable sortie into futuristic fiction but with *Original Sin* she has, triumphantly, reverted to original form.

There is a nice line in the book: 'what people believed about themselves seldom bore resemblance to how they behaved in reality.' Did P D James think this true of herself? 'We produce for the world and for our protection a carapace,' she says fluently, 'I probably come over as self-confident but I wonder if I am. I'm even-tempered, I have to say, but I'm sure I'm capable of considerable violence and aggression.' As she speaks, a little white cat, on the edge of sleep, presses its head adoringly under her hand.

'I wonder if the personality is fixed or fluid, whether it is a rock or a moving river. One is never able to point and say: that's the place where it really resides.' In *Original Sin,* most characters lead over-furnished, under-fulfilled lives. Murder comes almost like fresh air blowing into stuffy rooms. P D James says that W H Auden thought 'good' settings (English villages) necessary to crime novels. She does not feel that the setting need be virtuous but agrees that order must be overtaken by 'disorder that can't be put right'.

Is it not shameful that the violence, the disorder, should be so enjoyable to read about? She argues that, within a detective novel, violence 'reinforces a reader's sense of safety, offers a controllable level of violence. There's sort of catharsis of horror'. Her books take months to plot: 'The process is mysterious, it feels as if the characters exist in limbo and I am getting in touch with them. It's revelation rather than creation. My writing is visual, I write as if I were shooting film.'

How would she feel if her detective Adam Dalgleish were to materialise on her doorstep? 'If I met him I would say "I did enjoy your last book of verse" and I wonder if he would then look at me very coolly . . . Dalgleish is a spectator. C P Snow, not and author you think of quoting that often, said "there's great dignity in the role of spectator but if you do it for long enough you lose your soul".'

She writes at her kitchen table with a pot of coffee at hand (the novel runs on caffeine too, after each corpse, there's a call for coffee). Does writing come effortlessly? 'On the whole it is enthralling—I think that is the word to use.'

She finds research enthralling, too. While studying the history of the Thames and the wreck of a palace steamer called the Princess Alice in 1778, a friend gave her a memo book of the period. She was amazed to read: 'My son James was Drowned in the Princess Alice which sank the Poor Fellow was found on the evening 7th Sept 78 and Buried at St Thomas Church on the Evening, 9th Sept 78.'

P D James shows me the battered book. The handwriting is flourishing, the writer's name forgotten. P D James discovers a recipe for ginger beer, involving bruised ginger, loaf sugar, yeast, which she reads aloud. It is much longer than the report of the son's death. P D James studies the book, rapt, sympathetic, calm. She is, by nature, a detective herself.

Nicci Gerrard (essay date 23 October 1994)

SOURCE: "The Fast River and the Tranquil Lake," in *Observer Review,* October 23, 1994, p. 20.

[*In the following essay, Gerrard contrasts the work of P. D. James and Walter Mosley, focusing on her* Original Sin *and his* Black Betty.]

Baroness P D James writes novels that are like reservoirs: pleasant, contained, uninfested, damned up, with the occasional controlled trickle of water releasing pressure. Walter Mosley writes novels that are like fast rivers: out of control, dirty with the discharges of human lives, flooding and

parching with the seasons, rushing to a polluted sea. In P D James's fiction, bodies are fished out of the water, which then resumes its customary tranquillity. In Walter Mosley's, corpses are tugged past on swollen rapids, irrecoverable and part of the tide in the affairs of men.

She's white, English, Conservative and conservative. He's black, American, radical and with the dubious blessing of being President Clinton's favourite living writer. She writes old-fashioned detective stories of order disrupted then restored, which are essentially and wonderfully reassuring. He writes ragged thrillers in which domestic violence and political corruption are the norms.

She uses the language of the *Prayer Book* and Palgrave's *Golden Treasury.* He turns to the language of the street, sing-song patois of despair. Her settings are vaulty churches, the plainsong of mudflats and curlews, elegant drawing rooms. His are seedy bars, shacks, alleyways where men fight, dirt tracks. She's a melancholy, calm optimist; he is a rhapsodic, sexy pessimist. They face each other across a gulf of cultures and values: the jig saw and the ice pick.

In James's most recent novel, *Original Sin,* all the virtues and faults of the old practitioner are laid out. In a gleaming, mock-Venetian palace on the Thames, which houses the literary publisher, Peverell Press, a murderer is at large: killing the new and thrusting director, playing grotesque practical jokes, filling the conventional lives of the editors, secretaries and accountants with dread. Almost all of the players had motive and opportunity: who could it be?

Well, I'm not telling you. But Adam Dalgliesh and his team are back, after James's brief excursion into futuristic mode with *The Children of Men,* and they examine the clues with their customary satisfying precision. Not so satisfying is the editing: there are careless and intrusive repetitions throughout the book (on page 387 we read: 'He turned the pages with some interest. There were thin red lines down each margin and the middle of the page. He knew little of the Anglican Prayer Book but he turned the stiff brown pages with some interest'—this is first draft stuff).

Some of the characters do not develop beyond working-notes: Mandy Price, perky working-class secretary with an urchin's quickness; Miss Blackett (Blackie), the dowdy and dutiful PA who adored the old boss and loathes the new order; Frances Peverell, gentle, lovely and deprived . . .

In one sense, James's conventional woodenness hardly matters; it's even part of her enduring appeal and pleasure, for she makes every episode and each character in *Original Sin* significant to the plot. How can we expect her, labouring as she is under the bulk of her satisfying formula, to write about the mess, randomness and insoluble hopelessness of human lives? How can she hope to write well when she has to write. predictably? How can she be complicated when in the end everything reduces to one answer and no questions?

With Mosley's *Black Betty* nothing reduces. The novel—Mosley's fourth Easy Rawlins thriller—opens with an epigraph which is entitled 'Ghetto Pedagogy' ('Dad?' 'Yes.' 'Why do black men always kill each other?' Long pause, 'Practising'). It continues on a long note of vivid despair. Kennedy is in the White House, Martin Luther King in the news, but for Easy Rawlins, times are getting tougher: there's no money; Easy's best friends, the dapper and murderous psychopath Mouse, is looking for very rough rough justice; Easy's woman has left him for another man; his children need more than his brand of patch-together tenderness. Then he's asked to track down Black Betty, and he leaves his problems behind him, only to blunder into new ones.

In Mosley's fictional world, there's no such thing as innocence. There's hope (which Mosley calls naivete), and anger (which Mosley calls sense). There's law (white law), cops (the real criminals) and justice (which exists only in a heaven he doesn't believe in). There's love (which he calls heartache), and trying (failure), and then, of course, there's trouble ('The first thing that a black man and a poor man learns is that trouble is all he's got so that's what he has to work with').

Mosley's novel carries the opposite message from James's Easy Rawlins solves one crime but unleashes several more. As soon as he acts, he betrays and is betrayed. The book—written in language that is quick, witty and soulful—is about the lack of control that ordinary black people have over their lives. Not a whodunnit or whydunnit but a we've-dunnit again.

Harriet Waugh (review date 29 October 1994)

SOURCE: "Look, No Handcuffs," in *Spectator,* October 29, 1994, pp. 39, 41.

[*In the following review, Waugh lauds James for "deliver[ing] a tightly woven plot, with no unnecessary digressions" in* Original Sin.]

What a relief! The mooning poet, uninterested in murder, of *Devices and Desires,* is hardly glimpsed in P. D. James' new novel, *Original Sin.* Instead she delivers a tightly woven plot, with no unnecessary digressions.

Chief Inspector Adam Dalgleish and his team are called in to investigate the death of Gerard Etienne, the good-looking, hard-nosed chairman of the old-fashioned, privately owned publishing house, Peverell Press. It is not initially clear (except to the reader who can see it coming) whether Gerard's death is murder or accident, although Dalgleish does know that the firm is already contending with the suicide of one of its editors and a malicious practical joker out to embarrass the company and make it look incompetent. To temporary secretary Mandy Price (who is the unlucky discoverer of two of the four bodies that punctuate the narrative), her fellow employees seemed an odd bunch right from the start. The Peverell Press, founded in 1792, is housed in Innocent House, a mock Venetian palace on the Thames at Wapping. The chairman, Henry Peverell, has just died and his partner, a reclusive hero of the French Resistance, Jean-Philippe Etienne, has retired to the marshes leaving the firm in the able hands of his son Gerard who, to save it from bankruptcy, is embarking on brutally enforced changes, Innocent House is to be sold and few jobs are safe.

Frances Peverell, the pretty, retiring daughter of the previous chairman, who is one of the partners and has always lived at Innocent House, hates Gerard both for his intention of selling her family heritage and because he coolly seduced and discarded her. The youngest partner of the firm, James de Witt, is in love with her and has real cause to know that Gerard is an evil man. Gerard's brittle sister Claudia, who would take over as chairman in the event of his death, wishes to free some of her money from the company to buy her toy-boy antique-dealer lover a shop. Then there is Blackie, Henry Peverell's devoted secretary, who is humiliated and denigrated by Gerard; Gabriel Dauntsey, an old man, once a promising poet, who has written nothing since the war but is in charge of the poetry list; and Mrs Carling, a boozy detective novelist who is being dropped by the firm and is unlikely to find another publisher.

So when Gerard is discovered one morning, shirtless, with Blackie's cloth snake wound round his neck and stuffed in his mouth in the archive room at the top of the building the reader is hardly surprised. There are plenty of suspects and, as it turns out, secrets for Dalgleish to absorb into his amoeba-like mind, especially as the murderer does not stop at Gerard.

Original Sin, unlike P. D. James' last two detective novels, is truly plot-driven. The characters and the past gradually divulge their secrets. Lies are exposed that shock the reader, and, most importantly of all, there is no melodramatic sub-plot tacked on with a view to a subsequent television series. The novel is greatly influenced to good effect by Mamet's flawed film *Homicide,* giving the final double twist at the end a kick like a mule. As has become usual with contemporary detective fiction, handcuffs play no part in the denouement.

It is difficult not to feel sorry for the police heroes of these tales as they arrive too late to do anything but give a valedictory glance at the outcome of murder and mayhem. Their deductive ability is set at naught. Instead, the passions of man bring about their own inevitable retribution. There is, I think, a natural conservatism at the heart of the detective-fiction writer that resents the anti-climax inherent in a life sentence which often means the murderer doing time for as little as ten years. It has led to the emasculation of the police inspector. At least the American private eye shoots the murderer.

Christopher Lehmann-Haupt (review date 2 February 1995)

SOURCE: "Death and Dire Doings?: Time to Call Dalgliesh," in *New York Times Book Review,* February 2, 1995, p. C17.

[*In the following review, Lehmann-Haupt complains that James's* Original Sin *contains too much clutter and irrelevant descriptions.*]

The touch of symbolism is not gentle in *Original Sin,* P. D. James's latest mystery featuring Comdr. Adam Dalgliesh of New Scotland Yard. At the story's opening, Mandy Price, a young temporary typist, rides her motorbike to work at The Peverell Press, a venerable London publishing firm situated in a mock-Venetian palace on the Thames called Innocent House.

When Mandy arrives, she is taken upstairs by Claudia Etienne, a senior executive, to fetch a tape recording that needs transcribing. Miss Etienne pushes open the door to the archive room. As the text then reads:

> The stink rolled out to meet out to meet them like an evil wraith, the familiar smell of vomit, not strong but so unexpected that Mandy instinctively recoiled. Over Miss Etienne's shoulder her eyes took in at once a small room with an uncarpeted wooden floor, a square table to the right of the door and a single high window. Under the window was a narrow divan bed and on the bed sprawled a woman.

> It had needed no smell to tell Mandy that she was looking at death.

Catapulted by this strong opening, the reader races ahead to learn that the woman on the bed has committed suicide, in part because she has been sacked by the house's new head, Gerard Etienne, Claudia's brother, a brusquely forceful man who wants to modernize Peverell Press. In the process he will make many enemies, and apparently for this reason he will soon be discovered in the same archive room dead of carbon monoxide poisoning. Wrapped around his neck with its head stuffed in his mouth will be found a toy snake made of striped green velvet and "intended to be laid along the bottom of doors to exclude draughts, or wound round the handles to keep the door ajar."

In a novel called *Original Sin,* a snake has been wrapped around a corpse in a place called Innocent House. Beside the building flows the River Thames, described portentously enough in the novel to suggest the river of life.

Yet however heavily such symbolism may weigh, Miss James for a change actually develops its meaning here instead of squandering it as she has done so often in her previous fiction. As the plot of *Original Sin* develops, the apparent frivolousness of representing evil with a button-eyed toy snake seems more and more appropriate considering its irrelevance to the real guilt that hands over Innocent House.

And as the reason for Etienne's murder is revealed, we are confronted with deep issues of sin and retribution, one of the most perplexing of which engages Inspector Daniel Aaron, a subordinate of Dalgliesh's who asks of his Jewish heritage: "Why must I define myself by the wrongs others have done to my race? The guilt was bad enough; do I have to carry the burden of innocence also? I'm a Jew, isn't that enough? Do I have to represent to myself and others the evil of mankind?"

The real trouble with *Original Sin,* as so often with Miss James's fiction, is the disturbing clutter of its narrative. For all its philosophical questing, the story remains at heart a whodunit, and much of its energy goes to pumping up plausible suspects who are either not thematically relevant or not particularly interesting. Among these is Esme Carling, a mystery writer about whom her agent remarks after she is murdered: "She wasn't that bad. I mean, she could write literate prose, and that's rare enough nowadays. Peverell Press wouldn't have published her otherwise. She wasn't consistent. Just when you thought: God, I can't go on with this boring drivel, she'd produce a really good passage and the book would suddenly come alive."

One has to bite one's tongue.

And then there is Miss James's insistence on describing absolutely everything. She does write literate prose that creates a variety of moods. But so much of her scene-setting serves no other purpose than to create impenetrable atmosphere. For instance, pages are devoted to describing in loving detail the locale of a lunch that Dalgliesh eats with a friend, the Cadaver Club, "not among the most prestigious of London's private clubs but its coterie of members find it among the most convenient." And yet the story never returns there.

A character can't enter a room without being lost in its furnishings. A result is the loss of all sense of pace. When the story reaches its climax and details become important to what's happening, the narrative has no reserves to draw upon.

You also have to wonder sometimes about Miss James's awareness of her effects. Surely, given the novel's symbolic threads, an incident in which a character returns home to find her garden vandalized by motor bikers is intended to be a play on her central theme of paradise lost. But why, having introduced a woman with two children who, during World War II, was betrayed and sent to Auschwitz, does she insist on naming her Sophie? Is this by choice? Then what is the point? Some sort of obscure homage to William Styron? Or is it simply inadvertent?

Like so much else in *Original Sin,* this detail leaves you wondering if the story is far more subtle than you are giving it credit for being or if there is simply less here than meets the eye.

Michael Malone (review date 2 April 1995)

SOURCE: "The Snake in the Archives," in *New York Times Book Review,* April 2, 1995, p. 11.

[*In the following review, Malone praises James's* Original Sin *as a well-written mystery novel.*]

The latest novel from P. D. James, *Original Sin,* is a portrait of Peverell Press, a venerable London publisher situated in Innocent House, a mock Venetian palace on the bank of the Thames. It is a complex, compelling novel with a murder investigation for a plot. Those who admire the book are likely to say it is "more than a mystery," but this fine novel needs no such excuses. How useful can our definition of the murder mystery be if every well-written instance must be praised by saying it "transcends the genre"? It is a porous form indeed if it can stretch from Charlie Chan to *Crime and Punishment,* and can include among its practitioners authors as various as Mickey Spillane and the stately Baroness James of Holland Park.

Original Sin does not zip by (the first murder is not revealed until a hundred pages into the story), but flows along in 19th-century style, wide, deep, magisterial, like the Thames that so atmospherically fills its pages. Indeed, as in Dickens's *Our Mutual Friend,* the Thames becomes a powerful character in this novel. It serves not only to transport the players, hide the bodies and expose the secrets, but to place this narrative quite consciously within a literary tradition and a national history symbolized by the immemorial traffic of the Thames "bearing on its strong tide the whole history of England," from the Vikings and Romans to the great port of sailing ships and smoky Victorian bustle.

It is typical of Lady James to use a single setting (often a city business, rather than the weekend manor house of the Golden Age mystery) as a way to cluster her characters. In *A Mind to Murder* it was an upscale psychiatric clinic. Here it is an old-fashioned "gentlemen's" publishing company near bankruptcy. Innocent House (on the site of a walk that once led defendants found innocent from magistrate's court to freedom) is a beautiful Georgian building, four stories of glowing marble and a grand hall with a painted ceiling depicting "the curving river plumed with the sails of high-masted ships and small cherubs with pouted lips blowing prosperous breezes in small bursts like steam from a kettle." But it is anything but innocent, and never has been. Lady Peverell, the builder's wife, allegedly threw herself from the balcony, and her ghost still walks the blood-stained courtyard.

After a long first section in which we explore the private lives of all the major characters at the press, murder strikes. Gerard Etienne, the new head of the company, a ruthless bottom-liner (he's climbed the Matterhorn, and listens to Wagner), is determined to hurry the press into the modern age by getting rid of excess baggage. He starts firing superfluous or out-of-date staff (the first to go promptly commits suicide), and cutting form the list unprofitable writers who don't give readers the cheap romances and thrillers they presumably want. Even worse, Etienne plans to sell Innocent House Itself and move to a modern building. Is It any wonder he's found gassed to death in a carefully vacuumed archives room, with a cloth snake (the company mascot, called Hissing Sid) around his neck, the head stuck in his mouth?

Who did it? Claudia, Gerald's sleek and smart sister, who urgently needs £350,000 to buy an antiques store for her greedy, irresponsible, shallow and sexy boyfriend? Frances, Gerald's cast-off mistress, last of the Peverells, a lovely, gentle, pious woman, now passionately angry about his betrayal and fiercely determined to keep Innocent House in the family? Blackie, Etienne's faithful, eminently sensible secretary, now mocked and demoted to the periphery of power? Or another in the roundup of the usual suspects?

No one is better than Lady James at describing the particulars of police inspecting a crime scene, questioning the witnesses and analyzing the evidence to identify a killer. In this five-act mystery, it is fitting that the evidence should be *literary:* manuscripts, letters, diaries, contracts, archives. After a second and a third murder, the plot tumbles quickly into the open, even to a highway chase. It's appropriate, too, that the solution to the murders lies hidden in past events, and is uncovered by meticulous historical research. These crimes descend from the original sins of the fathers. And from brooding on old injustices, old betrayals, unforgotten, unrepented. "If God is eternal, then His justice is eternal. And so is His injustice," an Anglican nun tells Commander Adam Dalgliesh, the exceptional detective who has served as the protagonist of most of Lady James' mysteries. In *Original Sin,* murder is long in the hatching. "The tragedy of loss is not that we grieve," an editor at the press reflects following a funeral, "but that we cease to grieve, and then perhaps the dead are dead at last."

Lady James, a novelist of broad gifts and great skill, here is writing in full mastery of her craft and in full indulgence of her predilections. The staples to which we have become accustomed are all present in force, including the textually rich details of architecture and furnishings that at times work in support of the story, and at other times seem to emerge from the author's compulsion to describe all that her eye has seen, whether that is an Anglo-Celtic church on Blackwater estuary or the cool bare lines of a modern flat in the Barbican. As ever, Lady James, the grande dame of fictional forensic pathology, vividly renders the ugly reality of violent death: the smell of a corpse, the look of an autopsy in a sterile post-mortem room, the random residue of lives abruptly stopped.

Our point of view is beautifully initiated by the author's use of an "innocent" observer to lead us into the evils of Peverell Press. We arrive there with a young, sharp-eyed temporary typist, Mandy, and it is she who discovers two of the three murder victims. This "What Mandy Knew" view of Innocent House finds another Jamesian echo in the pivotal testimony of a Maisie-like, preternaturally wise child called Daisy. Allusions and symbols like this abound, and at times treated rather heavily through the plot.

Dalgliesh is back in charge, as dazzling as a movie star, but curiously passive. Far more active are his two juniors, who are sexually attracted to each other, fiercely competitive and convinced that they suffer the disadvantages of their minority status. Detective Inspector Kate Miskin, working-class, bright, hard-working and single, has sacrificed love to ambition. Inspector Daniel Aaron has sacrificed familial duty. His mother wails that "you'd rather be mixed up in murder than be with your parents." We hear a lot about Aaron's views on atheism, Jewish guilt ("You feel the need

to keep explaining to God why you can't believe in him," he says) and Jewish suffering. His ruminations are not gratuitous, because it turns out that the history of the Holocaust is central to the plot of *Original Sin.*

In addition to the police, we are re-introduced to some character types we've met in earlier novels. Among others, there is a suicidal spinster and a garrulous, gossipy cleaning lady. There is, as well, some grousing about civilizations decline (shoddy partitions are ruining the proportions of classical rooms) and a conservative *cri de coeur* about current social ills and bleak prospects for the future. An earl's youthful daughter is as affectless as a mannequin and amoral as a cat. Adolescent vandals on motorbikes destroy the cottage garden of a minister's elderly widow. "My God," she cries, "what sort of generation have we bred?" Indeed, most of the young people in the novel seem to symbolize a callous modernity, devoid of loyalty, manners or traditions, that leaves in its noisy wake a number of broken victims.

The most dramatic example of such a castoff in *Original Sin* is an aging female mystery writer, who, after having provided Peverell House for decades with successful, if increasingly quaint, mysteries, is summarily cast aside by the ruthless new regime. "REJECTED—AND AFTER 30 YEARS!!!" Esmé Carling scrawls in futile outrage on her last manuscript *Death on Paradise Island.* When her body is found floating in the Thames just below Peverell House, it is easy for her former publishers to believe she killed herself; after all, she'd lived for the work they just rejected. But in fact the writer was murdered (an exploitable fact her trendy agent plans to turn to profit) because she had stumbled upon a real mystery far more dangerous than the fictions she'd created. Lady James treats this vain, hard-working woman with gentle comedy and compassion. "She had at least respected the English language and used it as well as lay in her power," Dalgliesh muses. "In an age rapidly becoming illiterate that was something." In the case of P. D. James, a far better mystery writer than her hapless Mrs. Carling, that is something indeed.

Robert Ward (review date 9 April 1995)

SOURCE: "Publish *and* Perish," in *Los Angeles Times Book Review,* April 9, 1995, p. 13.

[*In the following review, Ward compares the publishing world portrayed by James in* Original Sin *to that portrayed by Zev Chavets in* The Bookmakers, *and discusses how the two books work as narratives.*]

As we travel dazed, anxious and weary-eyed in our air-bagged, steel-reinforced luxury cars down the blurry Information Superhighway, authors continue to do their less than fashionable job of measuring what will be lost in the new age of the megabyte and sound bite. Writers remain, thank old outdated God, exasperatingly human. They are going to have their own idiosyncratic emotions about the new age, and they are going to be stubborn and old-fashioned enough to actually write (the fools!) about all this. Some scribes are going to deal with it all head on, like the Cyberpunk gang (see William Gibson or my own favorite, Neal Stevenson), but others, like the two writers we consider here, will see the historical opportunity to write about the lost world of literature and the death of publishing as a moral force in the world . . . in the popular form of the crime novel.

Neither the English writer P. D. James nor the American Zev Chavets is being drawn gently into this particular good night. Though *Original Sin* and *The Bookmakers* couldn't be any more different stylistically, they both show writers doing what they do best: saying "No."

Perhaps not exactly "no" with thunder. The crime novel, for all its promise of mystery and dark secrets and hair-raising fright, is too cozy a form to ever really upset anybody. Neither of these writers is out to offend anyone. They are simple entertainers, looking for an audience, but even so, both of them end up dealing with the moral bilge that comes leaking like a radioactive canister from the glamworld of big-stakes publishing.

Of the two, Chavets is from the laughing-boy school. *The Bookmakers* is clever, filled with farcical Westlakian plot twists, and even features a lovable midget hit man named Afterbirth. It's that kind of book, a cross between literature, "Saturday Night Live," and a Road Runner cartoon.

The setup, however, suggests a darker strain that runs just beneath all the manic activity. Chavets' hero, Mack Green, is a washed-up novelist. Though he has scored both critically and commercially with his first two books, his next two are utter failures and, as our story begins, he's practically suicidal. One night as he staggers home, he's held up by a mugger at gunpoint; it occurs to him that he doesn't care if the kid kills him or not. The mugger too is confused by Mack's attitude and loses his leverage. Seconds later Mack has disarmed him.

As he lets the kid go, an idea is born. He'll salvage his career by writing a novel about a novelist who takes a huge advance for a novel that he'll write in one year, the last year of his life—for once he's finished the book, he'll kill himself. Mack sees his big idea as a way to score, because "everybody wonders what he'd do if he only had a year to live. And suicide books are big these days. It can't miss."

Mack tells the idea to his agent, Tommy Russo, who thinks it's swell too, and together they approach Mack's editor, Stealth Wolfowitz. Wolfowitz loves the idea, gives Mack a healthy advance, and Mack heads back to his old hometown, Oriole, Mich., to gather up the proper You Can't Go Home Again details that will give the book the desired presuicide poignancy.

Alas, what Mack doesn't know is that editor Wolfowitz hates his guts, and is the sole reason that Mack's last two novels failed. The editor's fury stems from the fact that long ago, when he and Mack were best friends, Wolfowitz found out that sloppy but lovable Mack was occasionally sleeping with his wife, Louise. To repay him, Wolfowitz deliberately sabotaged Mack's chances by publishing his second book at the same time John Updike's and Norman Mailer's new novels were coming out, thus assuring Mack less shelf space and third-tier reviews.

Now, Wolfowitz sees an even better chance to deliver the real death blow to Mack's career. He'll hire a hit man (the aforementioned midget) and have Mack murdered. Then he'll sell Mack's new "novel" as nonfiction—the last, broken-hearted letter to an uncaring world by a beaten and desperate author. What could be better? Wolfowitz gets his bestseller and gets to off the writer.

The rest of the novel is Mack's comic rescue. What's interesting about the book is that Mack finds strength in the world he left behind. Each of the people Mack meets or rediscovers provides him with part of the answer to his problem, and not only the problem with Wolfowitz. In the end Mack has become a complete man, having found a real community—as opposed to the totally mercantile community of the New York publishing world.

There's no use making too much of *The Bookmakers*. Like Chavets' last book, the funny *Inherit The Mob*, it's a bonbon of a novel, but it's a tasty one, and though I doubt that going back to the old neighborhood would work in the end (isn't the old neighborhood itself being mentally paved over by the Info Superhighway?), it is a fantasy that most of my Los Angeles contemporaries revisit about once a day.

If Chavets' book is a pleasant snack of a novel, P. D. James' is a full-course meal. Unfortunately, it's the kind I try to avoid due to excessive calories and fat content. Somewhere in this long, dull novel there is a really interesting story trying to get out, but it's lost under tons of superfluous characters, and a plot that has the narrative drive of an elephant on Ativan.

As the novel begins we learn that the venerable publishing house, The Peverell Press, is under siege. Henry Peverell, the gentlemanly publisher, dies of a heart attack, and his position is taken by ruthless and ambitious Gerard Etienne. At the partners' meeting, Etienne announces that the company will have to be sold to a financier named Hector Skolling and that they will be forced for financial reasons to move from the mock Venetian Palace on the Thames that has been the company's home for over 100 years. Etienne is brutal and sarcastic and announces that he's going to clean house. The old reliable but dull accountant Sydney Bartrum will have to go, as will the handyman Fred, George the switchboard operator, and any novelist who isn't making money. One of these, an old fashioned mystery writer named Esme Carling has already been told of her fate and she's furious enough to kill. If that's not enough, Etienne has also offended Frances Peverell, the former publisher's daughter, by bedding, then dumping her. . . .

And so on, and on and on and on. There are many suspects in *Original Sin,* any one or combination of whom might have reason to kill the odious Etienne. Eventually one of them does, and with him dies the real interest of the book, for Etienne is the novel's one really juicy character. Etienne is emblematic of all that is wrong with the current publishing scene. He doesn't care a whit about literature, conveniently labels anything that isn't immediately profitable "elitist" and is anxious to move into the corporate Big Time.

When Etienne talks to the other partners in the firm, all of whom long for the finer world in which publishers actually revered and felt a moral duty to publish good books, it's telling that not one of them can muster an argument against him. They don't like his crude thuggish tactics but are too enfeebled physically and mentally to offer any resistance.

It is exactly this failure to offer a debate that explains the entropy in James's novel. If you wish to make a mystery novel more than a puzzle, as it is painfully obvious James wishes to do, then you must create a dramatic tension between the villain's point of view and everyone else's. What if James had given us suspects with their own smart views of how publishing might move ahead, and still retain some of its older virtues? In other words, what if Etienne had run into a real adversary?

Both James and Chavets offer not so much a view of what's happening in the world of publishing as they do an emotional reaction to a very real spiritual crisis. James's tone is elegiac. She knows what is being lost: subtlety, real beauty, clarity. The dominant tone in *Original Sin* is that of an exhausted, barely flickering humanism. Chavets's view of the same spiritual breakdown is schoolboy-nihilism-meets-1930s-populism. In the aptly named *Bookmakers* everything is for sale, including book reviews, agents, editors and publishers. It's all one big fast shuck, and the best

way to fight it is to go home again and hook up with some real people who haven't yet been infected with the virus of the age.

Of the two views, James' is closer to my own. Chavets is both too cynical and too sentimental. But art, even popular art such as both these books aspire to be, is a high-maintenance mistress. In the end, your political and social opinions only matter if your book works as a narrative. Chavets' attitudes may be Capra-corny, but his book isn't dull. James is mature, responsible, a finer writer with a first-rate intelligence. But in *Original Sin,* she forgets that narrative has to move forward and that even great villains need worthy adversaries. In the end she bores us, and that's one sin that you can't blame on the Brave New World of the flashy, empty publisher.

Geoffrey Robertson (review date 5 October 1997)

SOURCE: "The Psychos Are Nicer Than the Lawyers. So It's True to Life on that Score," in *Observer Review,* October 5, 1997, p. 16.

[*In the following review, Robertson asserts that James's fans will not be disappointed with* A Certain Justice.]

'Come off it, Piers! Oxford degree in theology? You're not a typical copper.' 'Do I have to be? Do you have to be?' Not in a P. D. James novel, you don't. This is the place where all our policeman are wonderful. [In *A Certain Justice,*] Inspector Piers the theologian and the deeply sensitive Constable Kate (who missed her vocation as a Jungian analyst) are helping our published poet Commander Dalgleish, the Yard's philosopher-in-residence, to crack a murder in the Temple. It is coppers like these (and Morse, of course) who make English detective novels so inherently unbelievable. But they read well, nonetheless. Since P. D. James is such a fine writer, does reality matter?

In this book more than most, perhaps it does. The plot is set so concretely in the legal profession—the Chambers rather than the Firm—that it invites comparison with Grisham and Turow and the American realist school of crime fiction, where gritty storytelling holds attention precisely because it does have the ring of truth (whatever it lacks in literary quality). Sadly, this novel's allegedly contemporary lawyers are set in a time-warp, somewhere between the *Notable Trials* series and an early episode of *Rumpole of the Bailey.*

Venetia Aldridge QC is a clever, cold-blooded careerist who 'gets her kicks defending people she thinks are guilty'. So it would serve her right if the underachieving daughter she dislikes does marry the murderer for whom Venetia has skilfully arranged a wrongful acquittal. But one night in the Middle Temple, just before she is likely to achieve the prize of becoming head of chambers, someone skills the QC with a single stab, and someone else puts a full-length wig on the corpse and splatters it with blood.

The problem for our police—a trio the Yard could field to win *University Challenge*—is that Venetia has so many colleagues with a motive to kill her. There is the QC rival for the position of head of chambers. There is a senior clerk, worried that Venetia will replace him with a practice manager. There is the attractive female pupil much admired by the men, whom Venetia will veto for a seat in chambers. There is the ambitious barrister who fears she will report him for professional misconduct and so delay his accession to silk, and there is his wife's favourite uncle (providentially, a barrister in the same chambers) who just might have helped the family fortunes by dispatching this sharp-tongued Assistant Recorder.

I know fiction is stranger than truth, but this is all too much. (The notion that anyone would kill to become head of chambers is especially risible.) Some of the law is a little shaky as well: the book opens with a trial meant to be a cliff-hanger, but since the prosecution pivots on a 'fleeting glance' identification the judge would, in real-time, have withdrawn it from the jury.

This matters only if we take crime fiction seriously. As fiction *simpliciter,* the book is further evidence that P. D. James is one of the most spine-chilling writers around. No other writer (except Ian McEwan) brings out the terror of nondescript places where bad things happen, be they suburban homes or courtrooms or building sites or the coastal reed-beds where *A Certain Justice* has its gripping denouement.

Much of the writing's impact comes from its bleak pessimism—what Enoch Powell identifies as the true Tory approach to human nature. 'All human seeking after the good, the harmonious life . . . is illusory,' thinks one character, identifying the book's theme. Its psychopaths are more sympathetic than its barristers, consumed by mean-minded rivalry and obsessive selfishness. These characters are too unbelievably horrid, but the capped tooth of middle-class English malice has seldom been better described.

The plot ebbs rather than flows, however, with an unconvincing character introduced towards the end to unveil its key events through the stilted device of a long letter to a priest, which takes up 22 pages in the book. If P. D. James really wishes to explore the ethically interesting notion of a barrister taking responsibility for the consequences of her professional actions, we need to have those actions described directly and through Venetia's own mind, not as a retrospective penned by an occasional observer.

Still, *A Certain Justice* will not disappoint P. D. James fans. *This Life* it is not (there is no sex), and it is no less accurate than that television programme about life in chambers circa 1997—by which, I mean, not very accurate at all. At least barristers are more appealing on the box than in the book.

Harriet Waugh (review date 18 October 1997)

SOURCE: "Who Caused the Deaths and What the Deaths Caused," in *Spectator,* Vol. 279, No. 8829, October 18, 1997, p. 48.

[*In the following excerpt, Waugh praises James's* A Certain Justice.]

P. D. James was an eminent civil servant during much of her writing life. I do not know whether it was on retirement from her job that a secret rebellion took place against the way the system works here, but it is odd that since she wrote *A Taste for Death,* published in 1986, no murderer of hers has had to face a jury of his peers in a criminal court or sweat it out behind bars. This could, of course, come out of a belief in good civil service economy. It is the taxpayer, after all, who finances the criminal justice system. So, instead, she dispenses with all that, and has her murderers die rather melodramatically. Oddly, this seems to give their deaths a sameness. Occasionally murderers remain unpunished:

> Console yourself with the thought that all human justice is necessarily imperfect and that it is better for a useful man to continue to be useful than spend years in gaol,

one of them, who is not a danger to society, says to Dalgliesh. Could he be speaking for the author? Personally, I am shocked by the amoral pragmatism shown by Mrs James about the fates she bestows on her law-breakers. Despite this, admirers of her novels (amongst whom I count myself) will not be disappointed by *A Certain Justice.*

It has to be said that Venetia Aldridge QC is not a sympathetic victim. Despite being beautiful and clever, she has no friends. Although sex is taken care of by occasional meetings with a married politician, her life is entirely work-driven. She is irritable, chilly and acid-tongued. She has many enemies. Among them is her unhappy, boorish teenage daughter, who announces that she is marrying a young, clever, dangerous psychopath whom Venetia has recently got off on a charge of murdering his aunt. Even though this perverse pair of babes in the wood are at the emotional centre of the novel (the other characters are not nearly as strongly delineated), they are not the prime suspects when Venetia is discovered in chambers, sitting at her desk, stabbed through the heart, the barrister's wig on her head dripping blood. They have a very good alibi, having dined together under the unfriendly eye of Venetia's housekeeper. It turns out that every member of the chamber, with the exception of its head, Hubert Langton, has reason to wish Venetia ill, and since he has no memory of where he was during the crucial hours when the deed was done, he morbidly fears the worst.

How Venetia came to be such a disagreeable person is part of the twisted tale. Her father was a mildly sadistic headmaster and owner of a prep school, who terrorised his wife and daughter and caused the death of one of his pupils. Venetia's outlet from misery at home was a secretive but innocent friendship with a lonely, physically unattractive master at the school who instilled in her his obsessive passion for the legal niceties and intricacies of murder trials. Although this friendship ends devastatingly badly, the legacy of it is her brilliant career as a criminal barrister. What Dalgliesh and his team have to work out is whether it is her work as a barrister, her professionally uncompromising attitude to the failures of her fellow workers, or her emotional deficiencies that has led to her death. Then there is a second murder and the plot begins its ineluctable unravelling, leading at the very end to what I felt to be a certain injustice. . . .

Ben Macintyre (review date 7 December 1997)

SOURCE: "Going Postal," in *New York Times Book Review,* December 7, 1997, p. 26.

[*In the following review, Macintyre states that James resolves the plot in* A Certain Justice, *but ends the novel with moral and emotional questions left unanswered.*]

For her latest murderous *mise en scene,* [*A Certain Justice,*] P. D. James takes us to a set of lawyers' chambers in London's Middle Temple, the heart of the English legal establishment, a closed and comfortable world encrusted with centuries of respectability, precedent and reasoned argument. There we find Venetia Aldridge, a celebrated and widely detested barrister, propped at her desk with a neat hole in her heart left by a letter opener, a sharpened replica of the sword of justice; on her head is a judge's horsehair wig dripping with fresh blood that, it swiftly becomes

apparent, does not come from the veins of the late and unlamented Venetia Aldridge.

This macabre montage is vintage James: the language of ancient place and tradition—temples, chambers, oak paneling, afternoon tea—colliding with a grisly modern murder, inexplicably staged and defying logic. Here are intimations of desecration, of calm outward lives torn apart by inner violence: the genteel juxtaposed with the gruesome.

There are few more English writers than Baroness James of Holland Park. "The English . . . obviously regarded praying much as they did a necessary physical function, something best done in private," she writes. "A necessary physical function" sounds like the sort of euphemism one would find in the rule book of an English boarding school circa 1930, but it is precisely the contrast between such external fastidiousness and the complex, sometimes depraved internal lives of James's characters that gives her books such emotive power.

We know what is coming to Venetia Aldridge, Queen's Counsel, from the third sentence of *A Certain Justice,* when the author notes that the lawyer has "four weeks, four hours and fifty minutes left of life." Over those four weeks, James assembles the composing elements of her doomed character, the childhood and profession that have made her so successful—and so repellent. Aldridge is single-minded, arrogant, callous and utterly determined to further her career. She exploits the weakness of others with glinting disdain, seeing the law not as a mechanism of equity but as a test of intellectual cunning and dramatic talent.

Under English law, a barrister need not be convinced of a client's innocence and must withdraw only if certain of his or her guilt. For Aldridge, the distinction appears moot, for the more compelling the evidence of evildoing, the greater the challenge to introduce reasonable doubt in the jury's mind, and the higher the professional rewards of success. This is, James writes, "a lucrative game according to complicated rules . . . a game that was sometimes won at the cost of a human life."

Aldridge shows no evidence that she cares whether Garry Ashe, an intelligent young psychopath as adept at the game as she, murdered his prostitute aunt in a gritty and condemned council house. She minds only that she gets him off, and so, with a typically virtuoso courtroom performance, she does.

The moral conundrum at the heart of James's tale lies in the double-entendre of its title. Is justice certain in the sense of exact or immutable, or is it only a certain measure of fairness, qualified and incomplete?

"Most of us have to live with the results of what we do. Actions have consequences. . . . She won her victories and that, for her, was the end; others have had to live with the consequences, others have paid the price," one of her "victims" notes after discovering that the better the lawyer, the greater the capacity to perpetrate an injustice by enabling the guilty to go free.

Aldridge begins to wonder about the cost (if never the legal principle) of defending a man she knows is not innocent only when the acquitted Ashe takes up with her unhappy, unattractive and unloved daughter, Octavia, and thus becomes the first among a host of potential suspects when the barrister ends up on the wrong end of her own sword of justice, bewigged and soaked in another's gore.

In the best whodunit tradition, there are at least a dozen possible candidates for her murderer, each with motive, means and malice: her fellow barristers, the office cleaner, the sleazy Member of Parliament who wants to break off their mutually cynical affair, the schoolmaster who inspired the victim's taste for the law and keeps an obsessive scrapbook of her cases.

In less subtle hands these might lapse into cliché or caricature, but instead James leaves the lingering sense that each life is a separate embryonic novel, possibly irrelevant to "the case" but individually real. She sketches each with a few deft brushstrokes: Harold Naughton, the elderly and respectful clerk with his uncertain future and cauterized emotions—"When the children were at home, Harold got on well with them both. He had never found it difficult to get on well with strangers." Or Drysdale Laud, the bachelor barrister whose path to head of chambers is blocked by his female rival—"He and his mother had an affection for each other which was based on a respect for the other's essential selfishness." Or Hubert Langton, retiring head of chambers and once-great lawyer, losing his memory and control with age and bossed into increasing irrelevance by a daughter "in whom a certain sensitivity, acquired rather than innate, was at war with a natural authoritarianism."

James's people are wounded, compromised, familiar souls, whose quotidian frailties are exposed through an eye that is more sharp than generous, often witty but seldom funny. Around her central drama, James creates these smaller worlds with forensic precision, using incredible and melodramatic death to illustrate credible and movingly recognizable lives.

The one exception in *A Certain Justice* may be Adam Dalgliesh himself, the poet-detective well known to admirers of the James canon. Dalgliesh was always a feline and exacting figure, but here he comes close to being a token presence, appearing about a third of the way into the book

and oddly distant and preoccupied thereafter. On the way to visit a suspect, Commander Dalgliesh (being an intellectual) is "struck by an imperative need to glimpse the sea," and once there experiences, somewhat bizarrely, "a tingling happiness, almost frightening in its physicality, that soul-possessing joy which is so seldom felt once youth has passed."

One suspects that the author is a touch tired of her veteran sleuth and may be preparing to put him out to grass: most likely a book-lined retirement, with a nice cup of Earl Grey and a consultative role in future mysteries.

In obedience to the classic crime-writing genre, James finally offers up the guilty party, resolving a complicated plot with impeccable logic. But there the symmetry ends, for the moral and emotional questions she asks do not admit of such neatness. "Human justice is necessarily imperfect," and in James's world there is no guiding hand of fairness to bring the criminal to the dock, the innocent to safety, the lost to redemption.

Langton, the old-fashioned lawyer with the addled mind trying to cling to a flawed system to which he has devoted a devoted life, still does not want to know who killed Venetia Aldridge, and finally he shuffles away from Dalgliesh, representative of some higher but still imperfect code. "Dalgliesh thought: He doesn't want to speak. He doesn't even want to see me." The two men are "carefully distanced" as they trudge off.

The image of a humbled law shutting out reality to preserve its rules and equanimity closes a book in which revenge is not quite sated and deserts are not always just. That may not be the most satisfying conclusion, but it contains a certain truth.

Joyce Carol Oates (review date 5 February 1998)

SOURCE: "Inside the Locked Room," in *New York Review of Books*, February 5, 1998, pp. 19-21.

[*In the following review, Oates traces several of James's novels and praises her* A Certain Justice.]

So it is here at last, the distinguished thing!

—Henry James, on his deathbed

Henry James's famous final words might be the epigraph for the literary genre we call mystery/detective. In these usually tightly plotted, formulaic novels a corpse is often discovered as soon as the reader opens the book:

The corpse without hands lay in the bottom of a small sailing dinghy drifting just within sight of the Suffolk coast. It was the body of a middle-aged man, a dapper little cadaver, its shroud a dark pin-striped suit which fitted the narrow body as elegantly in death as it had in life. . . . He had dressed with careful orthodoxy for the town, this hapless voyager; not for this lonely sea; nor for this death.

—P. D. James, *Unnatural Causes* (1967)

On the morning of Bernie Pryde's death—or it may have been the morning after, since Bernie died at his own convenience, nor did he think the estimated time of his departure worth recording—Cordelia was caught in a breakdown of the Bakerloo Line outside Lambeth North and was half an hour late at the office.

—P. D. James, *An Unsuitable Job for a Woman* (1972)

The bodies were discovered at eight forty-five on the morning of Wednesday 18 September by Miss Emily Wharton, a sixty-five-year-old spinster of the parish of St. Matthew's in Paddington, London, and Darren Wilkes, aged ten, of no particular parish as far as he knew or cared.

—P. D. James, *A Taste for Death* (1986)

The Whistler's fourth victim was his youngest, Valerie Mitchell, aged fifteen years, eight months and four days, and she died because she missed the 9:40 bus from Easthaven to Cobb's Marsh.

—P. D. James, *Devices and Desires* (1989)

In *A Certain Justice,* P. D. James's new, fourteenth novel, the opening is given a stylish aerial perspective that suggests something of the novel's sophisticated variant on the old form:

> Murderers do not usually give their victims notice. This is one death which, however terrible that last second of appalled realization, comes mercifully unburdened with anticipatory terror. When, on the afternoon of Wednesday, 11 September, Venetia Aldridge stood up to cross-examine the prosecution's chief witness in the case of *Regina v. Ashe,* she had four weeks, four hours and fifty minutes left of life.

In this essentially conservative and conventional genre, form always mirrors content, and the principle of equilibrium that has been violated at the outset of the novel must

be restored, at least to the reader's satisfaction; that is, mystery must be "solved"—or dissolved. The chaos and general messiness of actual life with which the traditional novel contends can't be the subject of mystery/detective fiction, for its premise is that mystery, the mysterious, that-which-is-not-known, can be caused to be known and its malevolent power dissolved. Of course, in superior examples of the genre, which would include most of P. D. James's novels, there are ironic qualifications: murderers may be disclosed, for instance, yet not officially identified, and not punished (as in *An Unsuitable Job for a Woman,* as well as in the present novel, *A Certain Justice*). Often in P. D. James the morally reprehensible and the despicable, frequently accessories to crime, may prevail, to be capable of inflicting further damage upon their fellows.

P. D. James is expert at suggesting the complexity, often bureaucratic, that qualifies justice or renders it impotent. Born in 1920 in Oxford, she was an administrator for the National Health Service from 1949 to 1968 and from 1968 to 1979 she worked consecutively in the forensic science and criminal policy services of the Police Department. There's mordant zest in her presentation of bureaucratic claustrophobia and petty, and not-so-petty, hatreds among colleagues. Thematically, her novels are *cris de coeur* from solitary persons like the young private detective Cordelia Gray and the older, melancholic widower Commander Adam Dalgliesh of New Scotland Yard, who find themselves immersed in narratives that resist satisfactory closure; for identifying the solution to murder isn't the same thing as having enough evidence to prove murder. One can recognize evil but lack the power to stop it.

P. D. James's novels are known for their verbal density and near-static narrative movement, yet there are moments here and there of passionate lyricism in which the author herself seems to speak, as in this outburst at the conclusion of *The Skull Beneath the Skin* (1982):

> Suddenly [Cordelia Gray] felt an immense and overpowering anger, almost cosmic in its intensity as if one fragile female body could hold all the concentrated outrage of the world's pitiable victims robbed of their unvalued lives.

The more disillusioned Adam Dalgliesh, learning he's been misdiagnosed as suffering from a fatal leukemia when in fact he has a nonfatal mononucleosis, in the opening pages of *The Black Tower* (1975) thinks pettishly that he'd reconciled himself to dying and surrendering the "trivial" concerns of his life, which include police detection. And now,

> He wasn't sure that he could reconcile himself to his job. Resigned as he had become to the role of spectator—and soon not even to be that—he felt ill-

equipped to return to the noisy playground of the world and, if it had to be, was minded to find for himself a less violent corner of it. . . . The time had come to change direction. Judges' Rules, rigor mortis, interrogation, the contemplation of decomposing flesh and smashed bone, the whole bloody business of man-hunting, he was finished with it.

(For "man-hunting" one might substitute "crime novel-writing.")

Less convincingly, Adam Dalgliesh, tall, dark, austere, saturnine, is meant to be a poet of enigmatic verse, a superlunary figure in the eyes of such female admirers as Cordelia Gray and his romantic-minded colleague Detective Inspector Kate Miskin, yet he is strangely lacking in spirit, intuition, and the sort of verbal virtuosity one might reasonably expect of a protagonist set up as, not an ordinary policeman, but a literary man with a modicum of popular success. P. D. James wisely refrains from offering us samples of Dalgliesh's work:

> He didn't overestimate his talent. . . . The poems, which reflected his detached, ironic and fundamentally restless spirit, had happened to catch a public mood. He did not believe that more than half a dozen would live even in his own affections.

Like any veteran professional, Dalgliesh has anesthetized himself to shocks and has become in the process, as his creator surely can't have intended, something of a dour, condescending prig.

Tweedy Dalgliesh may be P. D. James's fantasy detective, but it's her female characters with whom she most clearly identifies and in whom the spark of exhilaration resides. In *An Unsuitable Job for a Woman* young Cordelia Gray on her first case dares to commit perjury in order to protect a middle-aged murderess with whom she sympathizes—an extraordinary violation of law on the part of one whose profession is so involved with matters of guilt and innocence. Yet Cordelia gets away with it, clearly with P. D. James's blessing. Detective Kate Miskin, who has made her way up from a stifling, impoverished background, is both a competitive policewoman who takes pride in bettering her male colleagues at the shooting range and a covert admirer of sexually attractive officers; she's energetic, adventurous, and willing to acknowledge the complicity of detective and murderer. While her superior officer, Dalgliesh, broods, Kate thinks.

> They were on their way to a new job. As always she felt, along the veins, that fizz of exhilaration that came with every new case. She thought, as she often did, how fortunate she was. She had a job which she en-joyed and knew she did well, a boss [Dalgliesh] she liked and admired. And now there was this murder with all it promised of excitement, human interest, the challenge of the investigation, the satisfaction of ultimate success. Someone had to die before she could feel like this. And that . . . wasn't a comfortable thought.

This is the complicity, too, of the mystery writer and her subject: someone has to die before she can execute her art.

It has been remarked that the genre of mystery/detective is as formal, or formulaic, as the sonnet, yet there's a crucial distinction among types of sonnets (Shakespearean, or English; Petrarchan, or Italian; Spenserian) and yet more distinction among individual, often idiosyncratic sonneteers. No American literary genre is more commercially profitable than the mystery, of which millions of hard-cover novels are sold annually, and yet more millions in soft-cover, in flourishing sections in bookstores and in 180 independent "mystery" stores, yet the genre itself contains subgenres of immense importance to practitioners and readers: if you're an admirer of American hard-boiled mystery (Raymond Chandler, Dashiell Hammett, James M. Cain, Jim Thompson, Ross Macdonald, James Ellroy, Robert Parker, James Lee Burke, Michael Connelly) you probably won't like American soft-boiled mystery (Ellery Queen, Rex Stout, Lawrence Block, Mary Higgins Clark, Sue Grafton, Margaret Truman, Lilian Jackson Braun and her cat-sleuth series); if you favor espionage (Robert Ludlum, John Le Carré, Len Deighton, John Gardner) chances are you won't like historical mystery (Ellis Peters, Michael Clynes, Peter Ackroyd, Caleb Carr, Anne Perry, Joan Smith); though if you like legal thrillers (Erle Stanley Gardner, Melville Davisson Post, John Grisham, Richard North Patterson) you may well like police "procedurals" (P. D. James, Ed McBain, Ruth Rendell, Elizabeth George, Patricia Cornwell, Peter Turnbull, Thomas Harris).

Overlapping with these subgenres are novels of suspense, or thrillers, a vast category that includes writers as diverse as Cornell Woolrich, Barbara Vine (pseudonym of Ruth Rendell), Robin Cook, Michael Crichton, Elmore Leonard, Dick Francis, Donald E. Westlake, Walter Mosley, Edna Buchanan, James Crumley, Michael Malone, S. J. Rozan, among others. In a separate category is Sherlock Holmes, the original sixty tales by A. Conan Doyle Plus "sequels" by other writers and commentary on the career and private life of this most famous of all private detectives. In an ancillary and increasingly quaint category is the traditional British mystery as practiced by Agatha Christie, Dorothy Sayers, Martha Grimes, Julian Symons, Margaret Yorke, R. D. Wingfield, et al., characterized by genteel country-house settings, affably amateur detection, bloodless corpses, and tea. (The much-repeated query throughout P. D. James's novels, "Will you have some tea?," suggests the author's affinity with this tradition.)

As in a scientific experiment, the mystery/detective novel advances a number of plausible theories which are investigated by the agent of detection (in P. D. James this agent is a professional policeman, never an amateur), who discards them one by one as fresh disclosures come to light until, by the novel's end, yet ideally before the reader has caught on, only one solution remains. This solution should seem both inevitable and surprising—a daunting combination—though in actual fact, and this is true for P. D. James as well as her less celebrated colleagues, the murderer's identity is often anticlimactic, and as Edmund Wilson wrote in his classic grouse "Who Cares Who Killed Roger Ackroyd?," it isn't uncommon for even devoted readers of the genre to finish a novel without absorbing its ending or even remembering much of it shortly afterward. No literary genre (excepting perhaps women's romance) so lends itself to brainless addiction, for the reason that, while engrossing as it proceeds, at least in theory, the mystery/detective novel dissolves immediately at its conclusion. As Robert Frost said of the lyric poem, though the trope is more applicable to mystery/detective fiction than to most lyric poems, it rides on its own melting "like ice on a hot stove."

The classic structure of mystery/detective fiction is an artfully, sometimes a maddeningly withheld conclusion. The investigation proceeds by carefully plotted chapters, not directly toward its goal but horizontally and laterally, as in a maze. The chaotic open forms of Romanticism would be inappropriate for morality tales in which a principle of disequilibrium is always specific and identifiable. There's an inevitable airlessness to the genre, an atmosphere of confinement most clearly represented by the locked-room mystery (for which P. D. James's most characteristic novels, including *A Certain Justice,* exhibit an unfortunate predilection). In these mysteries a murder or murders are committed in a very finite space, during a very finite period of time; there are X number of suspects, introduced to us at the start, whose comings and goings and alibis must be minutely calculated. This is the novel as crossword puzzle, hardly as simulated life.

At its most excessive in the fussily choreographed Ellery Queen mysteries of the 1930s and 1940s, the locked-room mystery approaches self-parody. (See, for instance, *The Chinese Orange Mystery* (1934), in which every detail of a stagey murder scene is "reversed"—to disguise the fact, which only sharp-eyed Ellery Queen notices, that the victim was a priest whose collar was "reversed.") Yet even in P. D. James's skilled hands, the conventions of the form can become unintentionally comic:

Dalgliesh said: "So, if we're thinking at present of those

people who had keys to Chambers, were there on Wednesday and knew where to lay hands on the wig and the blood, it brings us down to the Senior Clerk, Harold Naughton; the cleaner, Janet Carpenter; and four of the barristers: the Head of Chambers, Hubert St John Langton; Drysdale Laud, Simon Costello and Desmond Ulrick. Your priority tomorrow is to check more closely on their movements after seven-thirty. And you'd better check what time the Savoy has its interval, how long it lasts and whether Drysdale Laud could get to Chambers, kill Aldridge and be back in his seat before the play started again. . . .

In actual police work, abrupt confessions and informers play an enormous part in the solving of crimes; in fiction, rarely. The informer has no role in the storytelling process, for the object of the story is not to resolve the mystery but to forestall the resolution for some two hundred and fifty or more pages. Obviously, the mystery writer's ingenuity determines the degree to which false leads seem natural to the reader and not transparently concocted. P. D. James is shrewd enough to both cook her data and appear rueful about it after the fact, by way of her hero Commander Dalgliesh. As when an associate remarks, at the conclusion of *A Mind to Murder,* a version of the locked-room mystery set in a psychiatric outpatient clinic in London, that the case which has been made to seem bafflingly complex as a result of numerous "likely" suspects was after all perfectly straightforward: the most obvious suspect, the most obvious motive.

> "Too obvious for me, apparently," said Dalgliesh bitterly. "If this case doesn't cure me of conceit, nothing will. If I'd paid more attention to the obvious I might have questioned why [the murderer] didn't get back to Rettinger Street until after eleven. . . ."

Dalgliesh can't tell us that, if he'd pursued the obvious, *A Mind to Murder* would have been tidily wrapped up in twenty pages.

In *A Certain Justice,* a variant of locked-room mystery set in a minutely described Chambers (lawyers' quarters in London close by the Bailey), P. D. James is so backed into a corner that she must resort to the narrative cliché of having the murderer boastfully confess to Dalgliesh ("What a pity for you that it is unprovable. There isn't a single piece of forensic evidence to link [me] with the crime"), knowing that Dalgliesh can't arrest him, and the novel ends with startling abruptness on the next page, as if both Dalgliesh and P. D. James were exhausted. This unsatisfactory ending tends to blur Dalgliesh's professionalism as a police officer and makes us question James's motive in so presenting him, at this stage in his career, as lacking the energies of his younger colleagues, particularly Kate Miskin.

Unlike the sympathetic murderess of *An Unsuitable Job for a Woman,* who has killed the man responsible for her son's death and whom Cordelia Gray manages to get off, the murderer of the clever defense lawyer Venetia Aldridge is a professional rival.

The art of mystery/detective fiction isn't an art of conclusions, however, but of suspension, and suspense. What appeals to readers in P. D. James's work is the balance between the pursuit of mystery (in fact, a fairly actionless pursuit by detectives among articulate and sharply drawn suspects) and what might be called her (P. D.) Jamesian sensibility, an introspective prose that creates a powerful interior world at odds with the exterior world that is presumably the focus of investigative mystery. Dalgliesh and certain of his colleagues perceive the world through the lens of a discriminating, often skeptical intelligence; these are cultured police officers with often impressive vocabularies. Even the cleaning women, as in *A Certain Justice,* may reveal themselves as sharp-eyed observers of the scene, and the psychopathic killer Garry Asche, who has killed his aunt, a prostitute, and whom, in a brilliant display of her talents, Venetia gets off even while she is convinced of his guilt, possesses "an I.Q. well above the normal" and a sensibility to match.

P. D. James is wonderfully skilled at evoking atmosphere, especially a mood of nostalgic melancholy, particularly in the many scenes that take place in historic old churches. P. D. James is also an indefatigable descriptive artist, sharing with her contemporary Iris Murdoch a passion for Balzacian inventory, whether of cityscapes and landscapes, the London Underground, artworks, architecture, interiors, clothing, or people. But her great gift is for the presentation of information in vividly rendered detail, as with the meticulous description of the inner workings of a psychiatric clinic, or of a nuclear power station, or, as in *A Certain Justice,* London's competitive Middle Temple. One feels, reading P. D. James, that a hidden world exists complete and mysterious before the eruption of a crime exposes it to outsiders' eyes; this is often not the case in mystery/detective fiction, in which sets may have an air of being perfunctorily assembled, as characters may be hardly more than names on the page, mere puppets in the novelist's hands.

In *An Unsuitable Job for a Woman,* an early novel, twenty-two-year-old Cordelia Gray undergoes a rite of passage as she begins to fall in love with the young man whose death, and whose desecrated corpse, she's been hired to investigate, while living in what had been his residence, a rural cottage not far from Oxford. P. D. James doesn't merely trace the progress of Cordelia's emotional involvement, but allows the reader to participate in it, this "atmosphere of healing tranquility" so at odds with Cordelia's urban (London) life. In *Death of an Expert Witness* (1977) we're brought into the intricate, feuding hierarchy of a forensic science laboratory in Chevisham. The setting of *A Mind to Murder* is the Steen Clinic for psychiatric outpatients; in *The Skull Beneath the Skin* it's a rich man's estate on an island off the Dorset shore where an amateur production of Webster's *The Duchess of Malfi* is to be performed.

> [Courcy Castle] made [Cordelia Gray] catch her breath with wonder. It stood on the edge of the sea, almost as if it had risen from the waves, a castle of rose-red brick, its only stonework the pale flush lines and the tall curved windows which now coruscated in the sun. To the west soared a slender round tower topped with a cupola, solid yet ethereal. Every detail of the mat-surfaced walls, the patterned buttresses, and the battlements was distinct, unfussy, confident. The whole was compact, even massive, yet the high, sloping roofs and the slender tower gave an impression of lightness and repose which she hadn't associated with High Victorian architecture. . . . The proportions of the castle seemed to her exactly right for its site. Larger and it would have looked pretentious; smaller and there would have been a suggestion of facile charm. But this building, compromise though it may be between castle and family house, seemed to her brilliantly successful. She almost laughed aloud at the pleasure of it.

In *Original Sin* (1994), the most blackly comic, most Murdochian, among P. D. James's novels, we learn more than we might wish to know of Britain's oldest, most distinguished publishing firm, the Peverell Press, founded 1792 with quarters in Innocent House—a Venetian-inspired Georgian building on the Thames, "four storeys of coloured marble and golden stone which, as the light changed, seemed subtly to alter colour."

The new novel, *A Certain Justice,* is set primarily in lawyers' chambers in London's Middle Temple. Here the unsparing focus is upon high-rank London lawyers in their public and private lives and the possibly "just" fate of an aggressive female criminal lawyer who has made a lucrative career out of successfully defending guilty clients. Who could be a more deserving victim than a coolly beautiful careerist feminist who's also a negligent mother to a troubled teenaged girl, a demanding lover of a married politician, an abrasive colleague—and an unscrupulous defense lawyer to boot? Venetia Aldridge, fated soon to die as a consequence of her very success, is typically unflinching in assessing herself:

> . . . It was only for the convicted clients that she felt even a trace of affection or pity. In her more analytical moments she wondered whether she might not be harbouring a subconscious guilt which after a victory,

and particularly a victory against the odds, transferred itself into resentment of the client. The thought interested but did not worry her. Other counsel might see it as part of their job to encourage, to support, to console. She saw her own in less ambiguous terms; it was simply to win.

Yet Venetia is thrilled by her own brilliantly manipulating theatrical performances in court, all the more satisfying to her when she's successfully defending the sadistic young murderer Garry Asche, whose guilt she takes for granted.

Like the predecessor corpses in *An Unsuitable Job for a Woman, A Mind to Murder,* and *Original Sin,* Venetia Aldrige's corpse is found luridly "desecrated," as an expression of someone's sadistic loathing: she's found dead at her desk in Chambers, stabbed through the heart with a letter opener yet doused in blood not her own, a judge's horsehair wig placed mockingly on her head. The last, intended, irony is that Venetia has been ambitious to become a judge, to the dismay of certain of her rivalrous colleagues.

For all the blame-the-victim subtext to *A Certain Justice,* Venetia is presented by P. D. James not only with irony but with sympathy. Her passion for the law, her work-obsessed personality, her mordant intelligence identify her as a soulmate of Commander Dalgliesh (whom she never meets) and of perhaps, P. D. James herself. A woman who (like Kate Miskin) has largely invented herself out of a loveless, deprived background (her father was a boys' school headmaster whose sadistic "disciplining" once drove a young boy to suicide), Venetia broods upon the past she should have left behind, not knowing, as the reader won't know unless he or she cares to read the expertly plotted novel a second time, how this ignoble past, in no way Venetia's fault, will doom her both to a brutal death and to the mocking desecration of her corpse by one who wanted "for her just once to pay the price of victory."

Venetia is thought-tormented, yet she often shows a lyrical sensibility. In one of her reveries Venetia thinks how "memory [is] like a film of sharply focused images, the set arranged and brightly lit, the characters formally disposed, the dialogue learnt and unchangeable, but with no linking passages." Yet like her murderer, she's in thrall to memory.

It's Venetia Aldridge, too, who recalls Henry James's admonition, "Never believe that you know the last thing about any human heart."

> But he was a novelist. It was his job to find complexities, anomalies, unsuspected subtleties in all human nature. To [her], as she grew into middle age, it seemed that the men and women she defended, the colleagues she worked with became more, not less, predictable.

Only rarely was she surprised by an action totally out of character. It was as if the instrument, the key, the melody were settled in the early years of life, and however ingenious and varied the subsequent cadenzas, the theme remained unalterably the same.

But Venetia is fatally complacent about knowing the characters of her own colleagues.

Leaving aside the somewhat perfunctory ending, *A Certain Justice* is, in its economy, its relative swiftness of pace, and the complexity of its characters, one of P. D. James's most accomplished recent novels; it even includes, a rarity in this cerebral writer's work, several chapters of thriller-type suspense. (There's a subplot involving Venetia's rebellious daughter, who has been seduced by the calculating killer Garry Asche, in a romantically wild setting on the North Sea coast.) If the primary—and primal—function of the mystery/detective novel is to suggest a restoration of equilibrium after murder's violent assault upon it, this fourteenth novel of P. D. James succeeds admirably. P. D. James does not "transcend" genre; she refines, deepens, and amplifies it.

FURTHER READING

Bibliography

Gidez, Richard B. "Selected Bibliography." In his *P. D. James,* pp. 148-51. Boston: Twayne Publishers, 1986.
> Contains a listing of sources by and about P. D. James.

Siebenheller, Norma. "Bibliography." In her *P. D. James,* pp. 145-49. New York: Frederick Ungar Publishing Co., 1981.
> Contains a listing of sources by and about P. D. James.

Criticism

Campbell, Sue Ellen. "The Detective Heroine and the Death of Her Hero: From Dorothy Sayers to P. D. James." *Modern Fiction Studies* 29, No. 3 (Autumn 1983): 497-510.
> Discusses the development of the detective heroine in the work of P. D. James and Dorothy Sayers.

Cooper-Clark, Diana. "Interview with P. D. James." *Designs of Darkness.*
> Discusses with P. D. James the genre of detective fiction, the themes in her work, and her approach to writing.

D'Erasmo, Stacey. Review of *Devices and Desires. Village Voice Literary Supplement,* No. 84 (April 1990): 10.

Presents the main questions James presents in *Devices and Desires.*

Ericson, Carl E. Review of *A Taste for Death. Theology Today* XLIV, No. 4 (January 1988): 550, 552, 554-55.

Asserts that P. D. James's *A Taste for Death* addresses theological issues about faith and experiencing God.

Finn, Molly. "Not Tonight, We Have a Headache." *Commonweal* CXX, No. 8 (23 April 1993): 26-7.

Complains that "The framework of [*The Children of Men*], all too plain to see, is never richly clothed; the numerous characters wander over a skillfully depicted landscape like so many sticks."

Foster, Catherine. "Taut and Terrifying Mystery." *Christian Science Monitor* (26 February 1990): 12.

Praises James's *Devices and Desires* as "a taut and sometimes terrifying good read."

Gidez, Richard B. "P. D. James and the English Classic Mystery." In his *P. D. James,* pp. 1-14. Boston: Twayne Publishers, 1986.

Provides an overview of James's life and career.

Heffner, Carla. "Tea and Perfidy." *Washington Post* (30 April 1980): E1, E13.

Asserts that James's *Innocent Blood* moves away from the detective novels for which James is known.

Joyner, Nancy Carol. "P. D. James." In *10 Women of Mystery,* edited by Earl F. Bargainnier, pp. 106-23. Bowling Green, OH: Bowling Green State University Press, 1981.

Analyzes the setting, themes, and characterization present in James's work.

Phillips, Barbara. "Uneasy Mix of Style, Suspense." *Christian Science Monitor* (25 June 1980): 17.

Asserts that James's attempt at "serious fiction" with *Innocent Blood* is not successful due to its intrusive descriptive passages and static characters.

Porter, Dennis. "Detection and Ethics: The Case of P. D. James." In *The Sleuth and the Scholar: Origins, Evolu-tion, and Current Trends in Detective Fiction,* edited by Barbara A. Rader and Howard G. Zettler, pp. 11-18. New York: Greenwood Press, 1988.

States that James's "tales of violence and murder are nothing if not didactic; P. D. James has morally improving designs on her public."

Reading, Peter. "Terminal Themes." *Times Literary Supplement,* No. 4669 (25 September 1992): 26.

Lauds James's *The Children of Men* for exhibiting the same well-paced plot and convincing depiction of character and setting which make her crime stories exciting.

Ross, Michele. "Dalgliesh Takes on a Publishing House." *Christian Science Monitor* (23 February 1995): B3.

Praises James's characterization and clarity of writing in *Original Sin.*

Rubin, Merle. "The Harsh and Somber World of P. D. James." *Christian Science Monitor* (31 October 1986): 23-4.

Calls James "a kind of 19th-century realist, committed to the painstaking representation of the texture of daily life and the peculiarity and uniqueness of each individual character."

Rye, Marilyn. "P. D. James." *Great Women Mystery Writers: Classic to Contemporary,* edited by Kathleen Gregory Klein, pp. 167-70. Westport, CT: Greenwood Press, 1994.

Presents a brief overview of James's life and work.

Salwak, Dale. "An Interview with P. D. James." *Clues: A Journal of Detection* 6, No. 1 (Spring-Summer 1985): 31-50.

Discusses with P. D James her writing, the crime genre, and influences on her work.

Wood, Ralph C. "Rapidly Rises the Morning Tide: An Essay on P. D. James's *The Children of Men." Theology Today* 51, No. 2 (July 1994): 277-88.

Discusses the Christian vision of James's *The Children of Men* and calls it "the most provocative novel I have read in many years."

Additional coverage of James's life and career is contained in the following sources published by Gale Research: *Bestsellers,* **Vol. 90:2;** *Concise Dictionary of British Literary Biography: 1960 to Present; Contemporary Authors,* **Vol. 21-24R;** *Contemporary Authors New Revision Series,* **Vols. 17, 43, 65;** *Dictionary of Literary Biography,* **Vol. 87;** *Dictionary of Literary Biography Documentary Series,* **Vol. 17;** *DISCovering Authors Modules: Popular Fiction and Genre Authors;* **and** *Major Twentieth-Century Writers,* **Vol. 1.**

Cynthia Kadohata

1956-

American novelist.

The following entry presents criticism of Kadohata's work through 1994. For further information on her life and career, see CLC, Volume 59.

INTRODUCTION

Cynthia Kadohata, an award-winning American writer of Japanese ancestry has published a number of short stories in prestigious literary journals as well as two novels about the coming of age experiences of young women of Japanese American heritage. *The Floating World* (1989) appeared to critical acclaim and was followed three years later by the somewhat less well received *In the Heart of the Valley of Love* (1992). Kadohata is frequently hailed as a significant new literary spokesperson for Asian Americans. It is a position about which she is ambivalent, declaring in a 1992 interview with Lisa See in *Publishers Weekly* that it is impossible for either her work or that of Amy Tan and Maxine Hong Kingston to stand for all Asians: ". . . there's so much variety among Asian American writers that you can't say what an Asian American writer is." Both of Kadohata's novels contain many clearly autobiographical features and have frequently been lauded for their striking imagery and their hauntingly lyrical narrative. Kadohata's writing has been compared to that of such writers as Raymond Carver, Bobbie Ann Mason, Mark Twain, and J. D. Salinger.

Biographical Information

Cynthia Kadohata was born July 2, 1956 in Chicago, Illinois into a working-class Japanese American family. Her childhood was peripatetic as her family moved often, to Georgia, Arkansas, Michigan, California, in search of work. This wandering existence is strongly reflected in her first novel *The Floating World*. After high school Kadohata worked in a department store and in a restaurant before enrolling in Los Angeles City College. From there she transferred to the University of Southern California where she earned a degree in journalism in 1977. After an automobile jumped the curb and severely injured her arm, Kadohata moved to Boston where she concentrated on her writing career. In 1986, after 25 rejections *The New Yorker* published one of her stories. Her work has also appeared in other literary journals, such as *Grand Street* and the *Pennsylvania Review*. After a short spell studying in the graduate writing program of the University of Pittsburgh,

Kadohata transferred to Columbia University's writing program. However, when *The Floating World* received warm critical reviews, she abandoned her program at Columbia. In 1991 Kadohata received a national Endowment for the Arts grant and won a prestigious Whiting Writers' Award. Her second novel, *In the Heart of the Valley of Love*, appeared in 1992. In the same year Kadohata married.

Major Works

Kadohata's first novel, *The Floating World*, narrated by twelve-year old Olivia Ann tells the story of her extended Japanese American family, the Osakas, traveling throughout 1950s America from state to state and job to job seeking both economic and emotional well being. The "floating world" of the title is the ever-changing, frequently unfriendly, physical and personal environment through which the Osakas pass, "the gas station attendants, restaurants, and jobs we depended on, the motel towns floating in the middle of fields and mountains." However, the family itself is "stable, traveling through an unstable world while my father looked for jobs." The family members are original, strongly individualistic, characters owing little to stereotypical fictional representations of Asian Americans: Obasan, the eccentric and abusive grandmother who had three husbands and seven lovers; Olivia's stepfather, Charlie O, a cheerful and likable yet feckless character who constantly searches for meaning amidst the chaos of his world; and Olivia's refined mother whose great love was a married man with whom she had an affair and who fathered Olivia. While an important theme of the novel is the discrimination encountered by this Japanese American family in their nomadic existence throughout middle America, a much broader theme is the overall immigrant experience of this ethnic group set against the conflicting forces of the preservation of cultural identity and that of assimilation. Particularly interesting is the depiction of the exploited economic rural subculture of the strange yet expert profession of chicken-sexing in which the Osakas work. On another level *The Floating World* impressively and convincingly portrays Olivia's coming of age. She develops from the thoughtful child narrator of her family's physical and metaphorical peregrinations and her parents' unhappy marital life to a teenager who falls in love, leaves her family for a new job in Los Angeles and the "real world" and finds another boyfriend. Kadohata's second novel, *In the Heart of the Valley of Love*, published in 1992, is a science fiction work set in 2052 Los Angeles. The world depicted is one where law and order have largely broken down and where violent class conflict exists between the haves who live in "richtowns" and the have-nots. Corruption, pollution, disease, and crime pervade society. Much of the novel centers about the coming of age of the protagonist, Francie, a street smart young woman of mixed Asian and American descent who, just as *The Floating World*'s Olivia, clearly owes much to Kadohata's own life. Though the LA society represented is frightening and cruel, all is not despair. There is hope in Francie's life, especially in her love for Mark, the student she meets at community college, and in the frequent goodwill and selflessness found in a society on the brink of extinction. The novel's strongest feature is the evocation of atmosphere, a skill Kadohata also displayed with great effect in *The Floating World*. However, as a number of critics have pointed out, her defective plotting and lack of a coherent story detracts from *In the Heart of the Valley of Love*.

Critical Reception

Kadohata has been widely extolled as an important new Asian American writer. Her reviews for *The Floating World* were overwhelmingly favorable. Shirley Geok-lin Lim called the novel "a fine contribution to the growing body of Asian-American women's writing." In particular, critics praised the originality of the atmosphere, the stark simplicity of the settings, and the strength and versatility of the writing. Many also acclaimed Kadohata's ability to draw

strong, genuine characters who seem to understand painful reality. Critical assessment of *In the Heart of the Valley of Love*, though on the whole favorable, has been more mixed. Reviews ranged from the declaration in *Kirkus Reviews* that it was "A beautifully crafted novel that warns and hurts and delights" to Barbara Quick's appraisal that the narrative "seems haphazardly constructed out of Francie's deadpan stream-of consciousness observations, which read like a bad translation of Camus. The result is like listening to someone describe a long and pointless dream." Much of the negative criticism of this work focused on the implausible story, the inadequacies of the plot, and the unconvincing characterization. Nevertheless, while Michiko Kakutani castigated the novel as "an uncomfortable hybrid: a pallid piece of futuristic writing and an unconvincing tale of coming of age," she also commended the writing as "lucid and finely honed, often lyrical and occasionally magical." Such praise for Kadohata's writing style is shared by many critics.

PRINCIPAL WORKS

The Floating World (novel) 1989
In the Heart of the Valley of Love (novel) 1992

CRITICISM

Valerie Matsumoto (review date November 1989)

SOURCE: "Pearls and rocks," in *The Women's Review of Books*, Vol. VII, No. 2, November, 1989, p. 5.

[*In the following review, Matsumoto praises* The Floating World *emphasizing the novel's Japanese American elements.*]

There is a book I have been hoping to find for years, every time I walked past a rack of new releases. It would be, I felt, a novel in the voice of a Japanese American woman of my generation (third, or Sansei) who came of age after World War Two. In her writing I would catch glimpses of Sansei children playing games like jan-kenpo (paper-scissors-rock) and lugging sacks of rice into the kitchen. They and their Nisei (second-generation) parents would be making their way in postwar America, seeking to escape the shadows of the concentration camps. What I was looking for was a kindred experience in print, a literary cousin.

When ***The Floating World*** appeared, I pounced on it, delighted. What I did not expect was that this riveting book would explode the freight of assumptions my vision carried. My comfortable notions about Japanese American regionalism and family receded as I was drawn into the floating world of the Osakas, traveling from job to job across the Pacific Northwest and to the Midwest.

The Osakas emerged, a quirky, complex and quite original middle American family that enthralled and threw me off balance from the first sentences: "My grandmother was my tormenter. My mother said she'd been a young woman of spirit; but she was an old woman of fire." The complicated influence of this grandmother, addressed formally as "Obaasan" and never affectionately as "Obaachan," permeates the book. Strong, short-tempered and a feared boxer of ears, she takes pride in having had three husbands and seven lovers. She predicts ghastly futures for her grandchildren, but is pugnaciously ready to defend them from outsiders. Driven to plant her history in the minds of her family, she relentlessly bombards them with her stories, "a string of pearls and rocks."

It is she who describes their traveling environment as "ukiyo," the floating world of "the gas station attendants, restaurants, and jobs we depended on, the motel towns floating in the middle of fields and mountains." In Japanese, "ukiyo" has two meanings: the demimonde of the geisha and entertainers, and also, in the Buddhist sense, transience and change. For the Osaka family, "ukiyo" refers to the unstable world through which they journey, a small tribe venturing through uncertain, sometimes hostile, territory.

The guide to this world is twelve-year-old Olivia, a fearless talker eager to exercise her prowess, insatiably curious, alternately awed and insightful. Through her eyes we see the loudly cheerful stepfather Charlie O, hapless and determined, who calls her "honey-dog" and pins his hopes of success on ownership of a garage. Laura, the beautiful wife he adores but will not allow to take a paid job, is "pensive, graceful, moody and intellectual," busying herself with church and library in her thirst to learn. There are no stock characters here, simply people we come to know and care about.

Cynthia Kadohata, born in Chicago in 1957, has led a life as peripatetic as that of her characters. She and her family moved from Georgia to Arkansas—twice—as her father took different chicken-sexing jobs. After a few years' sojourn in California as a teenager, she has since lived in Boston, Pittsburgh and New York. Her background has enabled her to give readers a rare perspective on working-class, racial minority people in the Midwest. For those who know something about West Coast Asian American communities, *The Floating World* is a salutary eye-opener.

While the Osakas are reluctant to settle in a town where they would be the first Japanese, and are "very quiet in public," there is a sense that interracial relations are less rigid in Arkansas, which doesn't have the historic precedent of California's anti-Asian movements. This fluidity becomes apparent when the family attends a local novelist's birthday party at which the guests, Japanese American and white, end up exuberantly chasing farm animals in the fields.

All of these characters defy stereotyping. Laura, no Nisei Donna Reed, wavers over relinquishing her lover, Shane (formerly Taro Nagosaki). Not simply a staid businessman, Charlie O is an enthusiastic, untalented painter who dances wild war dances with his friend, Mr. Tanizaki, to entertain their families. Even the minor characters are indelibly drawn, from Toshi, the only female chicken-sexer, to Olivia's birth father, encountered as a ghost.

The impact of the larger events of American history and the Japanese American immigrant experience is evident in the texture and shape of these people's lives. The unspoken but real legacies of discrimination surface when Olivia talks with white outsiders, trying both to impress and taunt them: "See, I can talk like you, I was trying to say, it's not so hard." Her embittered grandmother says, "Smile at them. Hakujin [white people] don't know when a smile is an insult." What she tries to teach Olivia is that

> if you hated white people, they would just hate you
> back, and nothing would change in the world; and if
> you didn't hate them after the way they treated you,
> you would end up hating yourself... So it was no good
> to hate them, and it was no good not to hate them.
> (p.9)

The importance of the support networks upon which the Japanese Americans have relied is embodied in the families with which the Osakas join up periodically in their journeying and in the tightly bound community of the chicken-sexers. To the hatchery workers who sort chicks in 17-hour shifts, teamwork is crucial, since they are hired as crews and one person's inefficiency can jeopardize the jobs of all. The sexers are so attuned to one another that "if one stood, or even just yawned, the others seemed to know. Once Toshi straightened her back and a man, without looking up, said, 'Getting tired, Toshi?'" When Mr. Tanizaki is fired by his group he goes deaf with shock at being severed from the close-knit work culture.

Contrary to her parents' dreams of college-buttressed security, when Olivia leaves Arkansas for California, ostensibly to study, her "disorderly life" continues, "simply because I didn't yet realize that there were other ways of living." With perceptive humor Kadohata sketches Olivia's experiences in "the entertainment-industry culture of failure" in Los Angeles, ranging from her job in a Beverly Hills lamp shop to the exploits of her Chinese American boy-friend who wrecks cars for a living.

Kadohata is a writer of great strength and range. She captures with equal facility the tense rhythms of the chicken hatchery work and Olivia's first sexual experience (after which she and Tan devour everything in his family's refrigerator). A few telling details convey the whole world of a moment, as the pencil marks on a doorjamb where children have been measured disclose the lost domesticity of a Nisei gambler. This story flows like a clear stream, revealing at every eddy unexpected depths and the startling beauty of examined lives.

Those who seek exotica will not find it here. Instead, in the shifting light of truck-stops, small-town porches and seedy Hollywood apartments, Kadohata depicts the struggles of three generations coming to terms with their history. Their search for grace illuminates our own pathways through the floating world.

Shirley Geok-lin Lim (review date Spring 1990)

SOURCE: A review of *The Floating World*, in *Belles Lettres*, Vol. 5, No. 3, Spring 1990, p. 20.

[*In the following review, Lim discusses the regional and ethnic specificity of* The Floating World *and hails the novel's depictions of working-class life.*]

The Floating World, Cynthia Kadohata's first novel, appears with bona fide credentials from mainstream America. In fact, chapters had previously appeared in *The New Yorker*. Unsurprisingly, her strong prose style is reminiscent of *The New Yorker*'s influence on contemporary American fiction in its plangent syntactic economy of effect.

Although the book is called a novel, it is more precisely a series of eighteen linked stories forming a loose configuration of intersecting moments amounting to a *bildungsroman* of sorts. What distinguishes it from other first novels on growing up in America is its regional and ethnic specificity.

Olivia Ann, the narrator/protagonist, is a young girl in an extended Japanese-American family unique in American fiction. For one thing, the point of view is clearly that of a *Sansei* (third-generation Japanese-American). While the stories begin with Obasan, the first-generation Japanese-American grandmother, there is little of the sentimentality associated with stereotypical American portrayals of the Asian family. The eccentric immigrant ancestress abuses

and frightens the children so deeply that Olivia Ann refuses to wake her family when she finds Obasan dying on the bathroom floor, and none of the children cry at her funeral.

The stories reveal a world that in its intergenerational conflicts, sexual tensions, and economic instabilities is not much different from the contemporary America of Raymond Carver and Bobbie Ann Mason. What gives Kadohata's stories a brittle and poignant edge is that these familiar, ill-matched characters drifting through a featureless terrain of motels and makeshift rented homes are given cultural significance in a Japanese-American subculture. As the children move from foster parent to their own family and from state to state (in a peculiarly American rendition of the Japanese concept of *ukiyo*, (the floating world of artists, geishas, and bohemians), they remain within a stable community of relatives and other Japanese-Americans.

Some of the best passages in the novel are the depictions of economic activity among these landless, unsettled people. Working in the hatcheries in the South as sexers separating male from female chicks, they form an exploited but proud class of expert rural workers. Paradoxically, the floating world of migrant Japanese-Americans is solidly grounded in these fine particularities of a working class milieu, portrayed through a woman's sensibility. Kadohata's novel is a fine contribution to the growing body of Asian-American women's writing.

Barbara Flottmeier (review date April 1990)

SOURCE: A review of *The Floating World*, in *VOYA*, April, 1990, p. 30.

[*In the following review, Flottmeier provides a very brief synopsis of* The Floating World *and discusses its suitability for young adults.*]

Olivia and her family are Japanese Americans living in the 1950s, moving from home to home, job to job, struggling for part of the American dream and trying to maintain some part of their own heritage. From the vantage point of an adult, Olivia remembers those itinerant days in "a floating world," usually in the family car: various motels, roadside fruitstands, and different jobs for her stepfather. This is a world in which the family is the stabilizing force and the world outside is flexible and changing. With the clarity, simplicity, and directness of a child of about 12, she records everyday events of the family's life without rancor, self-pity, or prejudicial commentary. She brings to life her family members' individuality, especially her hot-tempered, irascible grandmother who passes on heritage and superstition alike. Her stepfather's struggle to find normalcy for his family dovetails tellingly with his love for Olivia when he temporarily leaves his only permanent job to help her run a vending machine route across the Southwest when she grows older.

This is a wonderful book about culture identity, outlining simple events that Olivia finds memorable in the life of her family. *Children of the River* by Linda Crew (*VOYA*, June 1989) is another book about culture identity and assimilation, which will work well with **The Floating World** as part of units about the emigrant and refugee experience. Because the cover art is rather unattractive and the story line more suitable to adults, this book, while beautifully written, will have to be booktalked with intensity before young adults will pick it up on their own.

Kirkus Reviews (review date 15 May 1992)

SOURCE: A review of *In the Heart of the Valley of Love*, in *Kirkus Reviews*, Vol. LX, No. 10, May 15, 1992, pp. 629-630.

[*The following laudatory review of* In the Heart of the Valley of Love *also provides a brief plot synopsis.*]

In an acutely moving second novel, Kadohata (**The Floating World**, 1989) again records the spin of worlds—of pain or maybe love. Some of it makes sense; some of it does not. ("Is the world as wiggly for you as it is for me?") The time is 2052 in L.A., decaying in a disintegrating landscape where the stars have faded behind pollution, disease is common, raw violence is on the rise, and the gap between castes, government, police and people turning feral is unbridgeable. A 19-year-old Japanese-American woman hopes to survive.

Narrator Francie leaves her aunt after the aunt's boyfriend has been arrested. She enjoyed observing their love, but "with people dying or getting arrested . . . you hated to love people." Francie decides on college for something to do and works on the college paper. Here are her first friends in L.A. Besides Mark, soon to be her lover, there are: a former gang member, a misfit, a slapdash version of an investigative reporter, a minor celebrity who may or may not be a murderer, and Jewel, the chief editor, dying of cancer, who at first can't shake loose from an abusive lover. With Mark, Francie visits elders and a tattoo artist (tattooing is a proud matter like "challenging God"), notes death and dyings, travels about, bribes with gas and water "creds," while here and there Francie finds things to admire—a bead, lovemaking, an infrequent blue sky. At the last Francie and Mark will pay tribute to people dead, and with the last rays of sunlight hustle away from a gathering mob.

Kadohata's 2052 L.A. is a strangely familiar worst scenario of environmental and political doomsayers, and it's darkly illuminated here by grandly scary to theatrical conceits. But Kadohata locates within the "melancholy, fatigue and disappointment" the tender heart of love—buried deep. A beautifully crafted novel that warns and hurts and delights.

Michiko Kakutani (review date 28 July 1992)

SOURCE: "Past Imperfect, and Future Even Worse," in *The New York Times*, July 28, 1992, Sec. C, p. 15.

[*In the following review, Kakutani criticizes the inadequate plot structure of* In the Heart of the Valley of Love *while praising Kadohata's "obvious talent" as a writer.*]

In her luminous first novel, **The Floating World** (1989), Cynthia Kadohata gave readers a meticulously observed portrait of a Japanese immigrant family's experiences during the 1950's. In her latest book, she makes a fast-forward leap into the future, abandoning the emotional intimacy of that earlier book to create an apocalyptic picture of America on the brink of civil disorder and social collapse.

The year is 2052, and Los Angeles has become a frightening, frightened city, ceaselessly patrolled by police helicopters and squad cars. Water and gas are rationed, and nonsynthetic food is hard to find. People are randomly arrested and jailed; some disappear completely. Cancer rates have soared, and strange new diseases—one of which causes the skin to break out in small, black pearls—afflict the old and young. Historians are saying "the Dark Century" has arrived.

"I didn't think conflagration was coming," says Francie, the novel's narrator. "Conflagration was destined to fall. Collapse was coming. The city had been deteriorating for a long time, and it was just that the rate of deterioration seemed to be increasing"

Like much recent futuristic fiction, **In the Heart of the Valley of Love** doesn't offer a radical, sci-fi vision of a brave new world; it simply delivers an imaginative extrapolation of contemporary reality. Beverly Hills and Brentwood (referred to as Richtown) are still the enclaves of the wealthy; East and Central Los Angeles are still menaced by gangs. Deconstruction is still fashionable at colleges, and Disneyland is still a popular tourist attraction. Drive-by shootings have increased, and so have riots and arson.

Ms. Kadohata's heroine, Francie, a 19-year-old Japanese-American, is a child of her times: edgy, street-smart and detached. Her parents died when she was young, and she notes that "people became sick and died so abruptly that you hated to love anyone." Francie is superstitious, self-reliant and very literal-minded. "When people told jokes," she says, "I never got the punch line because I was too busy thinking. But how did this rabbit learn to talk? Or, Why can't something as powerful as a genie manage to get out of a bottle?" She spends her free time taking care of her plants, and talking to a pair of rocks she refers to as her parents. She isn't a whole lot of fun.

Since her parents' death, Francie has lived with her Aunt Annie and her aunt's boyfriend, Rohn: two enormously fat people who love teasing Francie and each other. After Rohn mysteriously disappears and Francie is hit by a car, Francie decides to go back to school. She enrolls in a community college and begins working for the school newspaper. There, she meets Mark: a sarcastic entrepreneur, who will become her boyfriend; his best friend, Lucas, a former gang member who always wears a necktie, and Jewel, a wisecracking woman who is constantly breaking up with her abusive lover.

The remainder of **In the Heart of the Valley of Love** is made up of disjointed episodes in which Francie and her friends have assorted adventures. They use the newspaper to champion the cause of a student they believe has been falsely accused of murder. They desultorily investigate a school administrator who has allegedly been sleeping with students in exchange for passing grades.

Mark and Francie campaign to get Jewel away from her violent boyfriend. They spend a strained evening with Jewel's parents. They drive to the desert to look for Rohn. They get tattoos.

None of these incidents really add up to a story: none of them really illuminate Francie's state of mind. In fact, the intuitive sympathy Ms. Kadohata demonstrated for her characters in **The Floating World** is almost completely lacking in this volume. She seems uninterested in exploring the inner lives of the people in "Heart of the Valley," uninterested in describing the complex emotional geometry that connects them to one another. Instead, she seems intent on using their adventures as a kind of loose armature on which to drape assorted observations and descriptions of the world in 2052.

Unfortunately, Ms. Kadohata's vision of the future is not sufficiently original or compelling—the way, say, Denis Johnson's was in *Fiskadoro*–to sustain this sort of approach. As a result, "Heart of the Valley" is an uncomfortable hybrid: a pallid piece of futuristic writing and an unconvincing tale of coming of age.

If **Heart of the Valley** feels like a misconceived project,

however, it should not detract attention from Ms. Kadohata's obvious talent. The writing in this volume is lucid and finely honed, often lyrical and occasionally magical. One looks forward to—and expects better things of—her next novel.

Lisa See (essay date 3 August 1992)

SOURCE: "Cynthia Kadohata," in *Publishers Weekly*, August 3, 1992, pp. 48-49.

[*In the following summary of her interview with Kadohata, See provides details of the novelist's life, reports on her ambivalence towards being hailed as a new voice on the Asian American literary scene, and relates her approach to the writing process.*]

On the lanai of her Hollywood bungalow, Cynthia Kadohata sits with her legs curled under her body, periodically brushing her black hair away from her face. As she shyly responds to *PW*'s questions about her work, her answers are like interior monologues—exploratory, self-searching, provisional and at times uncertain. Surely she should feel little hesitation over her career—at age 36 she has produced two novels, received a prestigious Whiting Award and an NEA grant, and earned comparisons to Mark Twain, Jack Kerouac, Raymond Carver and William Faulkner.

In 1989 Kadohata received glowing reviews for **The Floating World** (Viking), an apparently autobiographical novel about a Japanese American family traversing the country—a mundane yet magical world of backwater towns, gas stations and truck stops—with a cranky grandmother in tow. In her new novel, **In the Heart of the Valley of Love**, out this month from Viking (Fiction Forecasts, June 1), Kadohata has used her sparse prose to paint a picture of Los Angeles in the year 2052. It is a world where the haves live in "richtowns" and the have-nots contend with frequent riots, corruption and the black market. Until recently, this vision might have seemed more appropriate to the realm of science fiction, but the Rodney King riots in Los Angeles have proved—if nothing else—how open Kadohata's eyes, ears and heart are to the world around her.

Readers of **The Floating World** will already have formed a sense of Kadohata's early life, much of it spent on the road with her family. She was born in Chicago, then moved to Arkansas, Georgia, Michigan, back to Chicago and, finally, at age 15, to Los Angeles, where she attended but dropped out of Hollywood High School. "I had gone to an alternative high school in Chicago, and Hollywood High wouldn't accept a lot of my credits," she explains, pausing to add, "But I also didn't fit in. I became intensely shy. It got to the point that going to the grocery store and talking to the cashier really made me nervous." She clerked in a department store and she served up hamburgers at a fast-food restaurant. When she was 18, she gained admission to Los Angeles City College. She later transferred to USC, where she graduated from the school of journalism.

Then, in 1977, while Kadohata was walking down a street in L.A.'s affluent Hancock Park, a car jumped the curb and smashed into her, breaking her collarbone and mangling her right arm. She didn't realize the extent of her injuries until her doctor told her that had she not had prompt attention, she'd be looking at a "sure amputation." She was 21, and the accident made her realize that anything could happen. "Life is unpredictable," she observes.

At loose ends and still recovering from her accident, Kadohata moved to Boston, where her sister was living, and discovered the city's great bookstores. "I started looking at short stories," she remembers. "I had always thought that nonfiction represented the 'truth.' Fiction seemed like something that people had done a long time ago, and [like something that] wasn't very profound. But in these short stories I saw that people were writing *now*, and that the work was very alive. I realized that you could say things with fiction that you couldn't say any other way."

Supporting herself with temp work and the money from her insurance settlement, she set herself the goal of writing a story a month, submitting her work to the *Atlantic* and the *New Yorker*. In 1986, after 25 rejections, the *New Yorker* bought a piece called "Charlie O"; later it took two more; *Grand Street* and the *Pennsylvania Review* also published her tales. All would end up as chapters in **The Floating World**. (The *Atlantic*, she notes wryly, has yet to buy her work.) After a stint in the University of Pittsburgh's graduate writing program, she decided to enter Columbia University's graduate writing course as a way of "segueing into New York."

She still feels torn between traditional education and the education of the road. "It's always a battle in my head: 'Oh, I've got to be reading. I feel so guilty.' On the other hand, I feel if I don't go out there and do wacky things, like traveling, it will make my writing dry. Besides, you can't help admiring people who never went to school, travel around and are incredible writers. There's something romantic about that."

Despite her commitment to writing, Kadohata dropped out of Columbia, too. There were several factors this time: the tuition was expensive and life on the road continued to beckon but, most important, she sold **The Floating World**. On a plane during the winter break of '87-'88, she had read an article about super-agent Andrew Wylie. "I thought,

'Now this is a scary person,'" she says now. Coincidentally enough, when she got back to New York, she found two letters from Wylie in her mailbox: he had read her story **"Jack's Girl"** in the *New Yorker* and wanted to see more. "I called a friend and said, 'That scary man wrote to me.' She said, 'Cynthia, you call [him] *right now*.'" When she finally met Wylie, she found him to be "very smart, very kind."

Even after Wylie sold **The Floating World** to Dawn Seferian at Viking in the spring of 1988, Kadohata still found the prospect of being a writer intimidating. "I would go into bookstores and browse through all those how-to-write books. It still doesn't feel totally natural to say that I'm a writer. I'm still really drawn to that section in a bookstore, and it's still discouraging. It's sort of like picking at a scab." She shrugs off her good notices for **The Floating World**. "Reviews feel arbitrary."

After the release of **The Floating World**, many critics suggested that Kadohata was a new voice on the Asian American scene—a Japanese Amy Tan, as it were. "For the first time in my life, I saw that there could be expectations of me not only as a writer but as an Asian American writer," she says. "On the one hand, I felt like, 'Leave me alone.' On the other hand, I thought, 'This is a way I can assert my Asianness.' I wrote the book, and I'm Asian, and I'm the only person who could have written it."

But within the Asian American community, especially on the West Coast, the politics of writing about the Asian American experience can be demanding and internecine. To take one example, literary feuding between Maxine Hong Kingston and playwright Frank Chin has been memorably bitter. No less so was the furor among Asian Americans over Ronald Takaki's nonfiction account of Asian immigration to the U.S., *Strangers from a Distant Shore*. Some readers of *Amerasia Journal* challenged Takaki's footnotes; others complained that he had not included enough women and that he was pandering to commercial tastes (often, it seems, a sin in Asian American circles). Even in college writing classes, Asian American students have been known to dismiss Amy Tan's work, insisting, "That's not the way it happened in *my family*."

Kadohata has not been able to sidestep these artistic controversies and conundrums. They are impossible to resolve, she believes, for she could not write what was true to her if she had to make that story "historically correct" for the entire Japanese American experience. For instance, "My grandparents were already married when they came to this country," she says. "Well, I've been told my book wasn't historically correct because most Japanese weren't married when they came here. One Japanese interviewer accused me of being socially irresponsible. He asked me if in **The**

Floating World I was saying that all Japanese grandmothers are abusive and in conflict with themselves. Of course not! Obasan [the grandmother] was a character in a novel—not a person representing all Japanese grandmothers. He said that Amy Tan and Maxine Hong Kingston were catering to white people, but I think they and other Asian American writers are just writing from their hearts. Why should their work or my work stand for all Asians? That's impossible."

She describes a panel on Asian American writers sponsored by the Academy of American Poets in which she participated: "Those of us on the panel kept saying that we were writers, trying to play down the Asian part. But I must admit that it did feel safe for all of us to be up there together. The next day, someone complained that the organizers hadn't found a Filipino writer. It's all very category-oriented. But you see, there's so much variety among Asian American writers that you can't say what an Asian American writer is."

While the protagonist of *In the Heart of the Valley of Love* is a young woman of mixed Asian and American background, theme and setting are far different from those of her first novel. Arriving at them was not easy. Kadohata's Viking contract stipulated that she submit the first half of the novel upon completion. When she reached that point, the narrative was still located in the present. "I wanted to move it into the future, but I kept thinking it was too nutty, too ridiculous. Finally I said to myself, 'Oh just forget it. Just do it.' Before I made that decision, the writing had been hard work, but once it was set in the future, it made sense to me as a book. It changed the mood for me. It made everything seem more eerie. I had the freedom to do anything."

Although the book takes place in 2052, it is very much grounded in the present. Kadohata's world is not exactly "futuristic" but rather more like Los Angeles on a bad day. Speaking of which, Kadohata notes, "My boyfriend and I used to go to a bakery, and it always seemed peaceful, except that every five minutes, someone homeless or crazy walked by. When you see, day after day, that more and more communities are enclosing themselves, you realize that inevitably it can't work. It seemed to me that there was going to come a time when there would be riots [in L.A.], but I was as amazed as anyone when they came. I guess I should have set the book just three years ahead."

Although Kadohata says that she doesn't write according to a schedule, her friends call her a "pitiless writing machine." She is bewildered by the comment. "I just do it and don't complain about it," she says. She wanted the writing in *In the Heart of the Valley of Love* to have a dreamlike quality, which came more easily once the book was set in

the future. "I've always had paranoid dreams that have cataclysmic changes in them. And they've always ended with my having to do something violent to survive or to help someone I love survive. I think the book ends on a hopeful note. Yes, this can happen and everything will be okay. Writing the book may have purged my fears."

It also became a way of dealing with her accident. Francie, the book's 19-year-old protagonist, is pinned against a wall when a car jumps a curb; her arm is crushed. "I thought this was a way for me to come out of the closet, in a sense," she says. "I have friends who have never seen my arm. Sometimes I catch people, especially women, staring at it. Sometimes I have to turn away, because I don't want them to see that I know they're looking." But for Kadohata, writing about events in her life has sometimes blurred the line between what is real and fictitious. "Sometimes I can't remember if something has happened to me or to my character. My memories become their memories, and their memories become mine."

She's begun working on her next book, which she coyly describes as "a pile of writing that's not even close to being shown to anyone yet." What she will say is that she has been interviewing people in their 70s, 80s and 90s. "I guess the book will be about the friendship between two women as they go over their lives together and separately. My first two books were written in the first person, and I'm sick of writing the word 'I.' I'd like to write from a different point of view, and right now I'm compelled to be with older people."

But always there's the lure of the road as an inspiration. "I remember once I was crossing the country by bus," Kadohata says dreamily. "I don't remember where I was going or where I was coming from, except that I was in a slightly seedy bus station at three in the morning in the middle of nowhere. I had this feeling of 'I am really happy at this moment.'" Kadohata may not always be at ease with her career, but there is no hesitation as she speaks about the sources of her art.

Wendy Smith (review date 16 August 1992)

SOURCE: "Future Imperfect: Los Angeles 2052," in *Washington-Post,* Aug 16, 1992, Sec. BW, p. 5.

[*In the following review, Smith praises the skillfully evoked atmosphere and the "finely wrought prose" of* In the Heart of the Valley of Love.]

Readers of Cynthia Kadohata's first novel, *The Floating World*, will recognize in her second the deadpan, slightly ironic voice of a female protagonist who describes her adventures in a strange, unpredictable environment with lyrical images that create the magical atmosphere—and the cool emotional distance—of a fairy tale. *In the Heart of the Valley of Love*'s Francie is 19, while Olivia was 12 at the beginning of *The Floating World*, but the older selves who look back in the two books to examine their youth from some unspecified future date sound very much the same.

The pasts they consider, however, are radically different. Olivia and her family roamed across Arkansas and the Pacific Northwest in the 1950s driven by prejudice and the imperatives of her parents' troubled marriage from one self-contained Japanese-American community to the next. Francie scrambles to eke out an existence in and around Los Angeles in the year 2052, when the only meaningful social distinction is the gulf between the inhabitants of the "richtowns" that exist in every American city, who attend universities and go into business as though nothing had changed in 100 years, and everyone else: the "non-whites and poor whites [who] made up sixty-four percent of the population but made only twenty percent of the legal purchases," a population in which half the adults can't read and all have been excluded from the nation's economy.

In this nastily plausible near-future, riots and brownouts are everyday occurrences, the privatized mail delivery hardly functions, gas and water credits are more valuable than cash, the remains of unfinished highways arch over the plains "like half of concrete rainbows," a pollution-induced skin disease raises "black pearls" under almost everyone's skin and most people avoid the 12 ½ percent sales tax by buying on the black market. The legal order bears so little relation to reality that "just about everybody broke laws all the time. . . There was probably nobody in the entire country, except a few. . . , who couldn't be arrested for *something*. Occasionally, the police arrested a randomly chosen person, and if you went searching for him or her, they might arrest you too."

As in *The Floating World*, atmosphere is Kadohata's strong point. She skillfully evokes a dangerous, capricious world in which "with people dying or getting arrested or all the time leaving each other, you hated to love people, you really did." Francie's narration has the authentic, burned-out sound of a shell-shocked survivor, still open to experience—her descriptions of the creepy 21st-century landscape are the best things in the novel—but wary of emotional involvement. Her attitude towards sex is chillingly matter-of-fact (AIDS has apparently been eliminated, or at least is never mentioned), and although she frequently claims to love Mark, the student she meets when she enrolls at a local two-year college, the relationship she shows us seems compounded more of physical proximity than any

real closeness. Seldom has a novel's title been more at odds with its essence.

Kadohata's point may be that the nature of intimacy has changed in a time when getting through the day is a top priority, but this doesn't make for a very compelling story. The reader quickly comes to share Francie's detached attitude towards the rest of the characters, none of whom is as intriguing or as strongly sketched as the iron willed grandmother, sexually restless mother and gentle father in *The Floating World*. The author's lack of interest in plotting, already apparent in her first book, becomes more problematic here: Olivia's narrative, although diffuse, gained some momentum and direction from the simple fact that it showed her growing up and moving away from her family; Francie acquires an apartment and a boyfriend, but there's no sense of her learning or changing over the course of the novel.

Despite its coldness and lack of storytelling drive, *In The Heart of the Valley of Love* offers much to admire. Kadohata's scathing social commentary has as much to say about America today as in the year 2052; if our politicians read novels and had any sense of shame, it would make them squirm with its vision of a nation that has abandoned all pretense of including everyone in the social contract. Her finely wrought prose creates haunting pictures that linger long after her flatly conceived characters have faded from memory. When this talented writer decides to tell a story and people it with three-dimensional figures, her gift for images and ideas will have a truly powerful fictional outlet.

Barbara Quick (review date 30 August 1992)

SOURCE: A review of *In the Heart of the Valley of Love*, in *New York Times*, August 30, 1992, Sec. 7, p. 14.

[*In the following review, Quick writes that the narrative of* In the Heart of the Valley of Love *is lacking in focus and is poorly constructed.*]

In her second novel, Cynthia Kadohata has tried something extremely difficult: to take a story of the disaffected 1990's and project it 60 years ahead in time. What makes futuristic fiction work is an accretion of telling detail so convincing that the reader suspends disbelief. Unfortunately, **In the Heart of the Valley of Love** has lots of detail but very little conviction. The setting is Los Angeles in 2052, but the author seems not to have exercised her imagination: this is the smog-filled and crime-ridden city of 1992, with just a few differences (water and gas rationing; odd, unexplained skin diseases). Apart from some specific biographical details, the book's narrator, a 19-year-old named Francie, bears a remarkable resemblance to the slightly younger Japanese-American narrator of Ms. Kadohata's first novel, **The Floating World**. Though supposedly generations apart, these two adolescents seem very much the same person: alienated, opaque and drawn to angst-filled speculation about the absurdity of existence. The plot concerns Francie's involvement with her college newspaper, the handful of other students who work there and the aunt and surrogate father who have raised her from the time she was 13. But the narrative lacks focus; it seems haphazardly constructed out of Francie's deadpan stream-of-consciousness observations, which read like a bad translation of Camus. The result is like listening to someone describe a long and pointless dream.

James Idema (review date 30 August 1992)

SOURCE: "Love finds a way in a sad, future L.A.," in *Chicago Tribune*, August 30, 1992, Sec 14, p. 7.

[*In the following review, Idema writes that Kadohata's depiction of a disintegrating 2052 Los Angeles in her novel* In the Heart of the Valley of Love *is convincing and likens the main protagonist Francie to Holden Caulfield.*]

Contrary to George Orwell's vision 35 years previous, 1984 turned out to be not such a bad year. Upon reading **In the Heart of the Valley of Love**, one hopes that novelist Cynthia Kadohata is even less prescient about 2052 and the world as it is observed that year by her heroine, a 19-year-old Japanese-American orphan living in Los Angeles. But don't count on it. Kadohata's projection of an exhausted planet is all too convincing.

Here is Francie recalling the scene in Chicago, where she lived when she was 12 and she and her friends "were very afraid of growing up":

> "There were a lot of expressionless people walking around, especially in big cities. They'd learned it in childhood. There was a long time when it seemed to me that . . . everyone I knew or had known had been beaten or was being beaten or was dying or had witnessed death. Everyone I knew understood the particular mix of fear and numbness that only repeated and intense physical suffering can inspire."

That was Chicago. She has moved to Los Angeles with her parents and, after their deaths, lives with her aunt and her aunt's boyfriend, who traffic in black market goods, a more or less acceptable occupation in a society where virtually everybody cheats to stay alive.

Francie packs a Mace gun because of the random violence. Fans at a baseball game are killed for rooting for the opposing team. People are rioting not for change but for destruction. Prolonged drought has led people to use the word "dry" in conversation to indicate something bad. The sun is hazy, the stars faded by pollution. Breathing is often difficult, and new diseases await identification. Windmills and solar panels mark the landscape, as do the "concrete rainbows" of an unfinished highway network.

Against this baleful background, Kadohata manages with lean, uncomplicated prose to tell a remarkable story of love and redemption, with characters who are credible and sympathetic. Francie, who tells her own story, is particularly endearing because of her unaffected response to her situation. "I was nothing if not adaptable," she observes. "That's me, Queen of the Adapts."

One is reminded of Holden Caulfield, another wise child, when Francie seems to address the reader directly. "The way it was today," she says in the beginning, "with people dying or getting arrested or all the time leaving each other, you hated to love people, you really did."

But she loves her Auntie Annie and Auntie's roguish friend, Rohn, and especially, Carl, a tattoo artist and philosopher, who possesses yoyu, a Japanese word that Francie's mother once told her means "something left over" and indicates "a spiritual excess that allowed some people to be generous."

The idea that generosity, friendship and love, as well as good humor, could bloom among people who obviously live near the edge of extinction seems incredible, but this novelist, through her resilient, resourceful heroine, makes us believers.

"Auntie said Christmas used to be the biggest holiday of the year, but later it became New Year's, which was a mildly apocalyptic holiday, and Thanksgiving, because the fact that there was less and less to be thankful for made one all the more thankful for what there was."

In the Heart of the Valley of Love is Cynthia Kadohata's second novel. Her first, **The Floating World**, portrayed a Japanese-American family in the California of the '50s, drifting from one low paying job to another. The humanity that illuminated that story is abundant in this one as well.

A. Robert Lee (essay date 1994)

SOURCE: "Eat a Bowl of Tea: Asian America in the Novels of Ghish Jen, Cynthia Kadohata, Kim Ronyoung, Jessica Hagedorn, and Tran Van Dinh," in *The Yearbook of*

English Studies, edited by Andrew Gurr, Modern Humanities Research Association, 1994, pp. 263-280.

[*In the following excerpt, Lee, after analyzing aspects of America's "obsession" with Asia and strains of anti-Asian sentiment pervading American society, discusses the Asian-American literary renaissance and its resultant controversies, and then provides a plot summary of Kadohata's* A Floating World, *focusing in particular on its Asian American elements.*]

Cynthia Kadohata's **The Floating World** gives a new turn to American picaresque. Set in the 1950s, and told in the precocious, Holden Caulfieldish voice of Olivia Ann, *sansei* teenager, it offers a kind of inspired 'road' drama. The odyssey it chronicles, that of a migrant, three-generation Japanese-American family's search for work through the rural and small-town Pacific Northwest in the wake of the 'relocation' trauma, could not be more full of quirks and niches—not least (and with *Huckleberry Finn* alongside *The Catcher in The Rye* as a reference-book) 'travelling' as itself a kind of full-time American home. The America it unveils, Asian and non-Asian, involves a double angle of vision, that of Olivia herself, and that of an American Japaneseness with its own *gestalt*, its own uniquely presiding laws of motion and gravity.

Like Jen in *Typical American*, Kadohata begins with names. First she has Olivia invoke her grandparents and Japan's nineteenth-century granting of patronymics to its commoners. After emigration to Hawaii, and with World War II, the family changes *nisei* names, Satoru, Yukiko, Mariko, Haruko, and Sadamu, to Roger, Lily, Laura, Ann, and Roy, in order to enrol the children at school. Finally, on the mainland, a whole generation undergoes American naming ('My brothers and I all have American names: Benjamin Todd, Walker Roy, Peter Edward, and me, Olivia Ann'). Looking back, Olivia acknowledges the distance between her forebears and herself: 'Today their Japanese names are just shadows following them'.

That, however, is to reckon without her waspish, three-times married *obasan* ('My father wanted us to call her Grandma—more American'). The old lady literally carries Japan into America, full of lore, rites, memories of her husbands, sayings, and story-telling. Olivia, whom she harries and pinches when not in her own way loving her, even hears her dreaming in Japanese. When she 'surprises' the family, albeit it in her eighties, by dying—where more appropriately as a marker than in a California motel?—she has

already taught the family to perceive the world of the *hajukin*, the white people of America, through a screen of Japaneseness:

My grandmother liked to tell us about herself during evenings while we all sat talking in front of the motels or houses we stayed at. We were traveling in what she called ukiyo, the floating world. The floating world was the gas station attendants, restaurants, and jobs we depended on, the motel towns floating in the middle of fields and mountains. [. . .] *We* were stable, traveling through an unstable world while my father looked for jobs. (pp. 2-3)

This makes perfect grist for Olivia, her contrary, unravelling string of encounters met with, and narrated, in a matchingly contrary style, Western substance yet also Eastern shadow.

Her opening brush with a quietly crazed ex-professor points the way. Only her grandmother's smiling, Japanese guile saves Olivia from likely murder ('Hajukin don't know when a smile is an insult' she tells the girl). Fostered out to Isamu, a lonely Nebraska-Japanese farmer whose daughter has spurned him, Olivia helps him write out his entire world in a phone-book containing only seven names. En route to Gibson, Arkansas she summons up her childhood as more motion than stillness ('pictures of one world fading as another took its place'). In Gibson, too, she translates her Grandmother's diaries ('I liked the two languages, Japanese and English, how each contained thoughts you couldn't express exactly in the other' (p. 91)). She also finds love with the Southern-accented, *nisei* David Tanizaki, a relationship which has its own oblique correlation in her job as a put-upon factory chicken-sexer.

From there she steps south to west, to Los Angeles, fantasizing a conversation with her own long dead father ('I'd never met a ghost before, but I figured the thing to do was communicate') and, as his heir, finds a still newer life as vending-machine owner and repairwoman. Unbraiding these, and each further recess in the histories of her *obasan* and parents, gives **The Floating World** its very real singularity. Native-born, and a would-be American 'baton-twirler' and 'shortstop' as may be, Olivia observes of the 'floating world' which from childhood has opened before her in so 'easternly' a manner: 'Someone was always seeing a ghost or having a hunch or hearing a rumor. No idea had definite form; every fact could dissolve into fiction' (p. 32). This, on her part, and behind her on Kadohata's, is to put America under new auspices, nothing less than its own 'Japanese' magic realism.

Additional coverage of Kadohata's life and career is contained in the following source published by Gale: *Contemporary Authors: Vol. 140.*

Katha Pollitt
1949-

American poet and essayist.

The following entry presents an overview of Pollitt's career through 1999. For further information on her life and works, see *CLC*, Volume 28.

INTRODUCTION

Pollitt is considered a foremost feminist poet and essayist. She has earned praise for her collection of essays, *Reasonable Creatures* (1994), in which she advocates revisionist thinking about modern gender ideology. In addition, Pollitt is a well-respected poet whose first collection, *Antarctic Traveller* (1982) won the National Book Critics Circle Award in 1983.

Biographical Information

Pollitt was born in New York City on October 14, 1949. Her father, a lawyer who championed liberal causes, and her mother, a real estate agent, were prolific readers. When their daughter became interested in poetry writing during her middle years, they encouraged her. Pollitt attended Radcliffe College, earning a BA in 1972 before completing an MFA in Creative Writing at Columbia University in 1975. She began publishing her poetry in *The New Yorker* and *Atlantic Monthly* in the mid-1970s and earned critical attention. In 1982, she published a collection of poetry, *Antarctic Traveller*, which solidified her reputation as a noted poet. She served as Poet-in-Residence and taught creative writing at Barnard College. After working as a copy editor and proofreader at *Esquire* and *The New Yorker* and publishing numerous book reviews, Pollitt began her career with *The Nation* in 1982. In 1986, she became a contributing editor and was promoted to associate editor in 1992. She writes a biweekly column on feminist topics entitled "Subject to Debate" for *The Nation* magazine. In 1994 Pollitt published a collection of these essays entitled *Reasonable Creatures*. She has earned grants from the New York Foundation of the Arts in 1987, the National Endowment for the Arts in 1984, a Fulbright in 1985, and was named a Guggenheim Fellow in 1987. She is divorced with one daughter and continues to live and work in New York City.

Major Works
Known equally for her poetry and her feminist essays, Pollitt stated in an interview with Ruth Conniff that her career has followed two exclusive and separate paths. Her

1982 poetry collection *Antarctic Traveller* garnered wide acclaim; and her essyas in Reasonable Creatures earned Pollitt a reputation as a provocatice feminist writer. In these poems she skillfully employs visual imagery as a means of exploring human thought and emotion. Likened to Wallace Stevens, she contrasts art and life, maintaining a distance between the subject of her poem and the observer. In works such as "Five Poems on Japanese Paintings", which serves as the lynchpin of the collection, she contrasts romance and disillusionment. In the segment entitled "Moon and Flowering Plum," for example, Pollitt employs a brief description of nature as a means for subtly addressing the implications of indecisiveness and commitment. In addition to her visual works, Pollitt also writes pastoral pieces, with a strong Japanese influence, and applies her imagination to reinterpret familiar domestic scenes. For instance, in "Vegetable Poems," she captures the personality of the eggplant, onion and tomato. She is noted for her use of the "blurred you" in which the pronoun "you" may refer to either the audience or the author, thus establishing a relationship of shared experience between writer and reader. In her collection of essays *Rea-*

sonable Creatures, Pollitt advocates that society should view women as no different from men. She rejects the idea that women are more nurturing than men, and are thus more suited for care giving roles, arguing that by defining themselves as different, women will limit their choices as well as alienate themselves from power and each other. In her book, she addresses controversial political and social events such as the "Baby M" surrogate mother case, the William Kennedy Smith rape trial, and former Vice-President Dan Quayle's reaction to the television program *Murphy Brown*. Weaving events from her own life into analysis of current gender ideology, Pollitt promotes clear and rigorous thinking about current events and the issues behind them. She attacks both political conservatives and liberals in her essays, and debates the viewpoints of other feminist writers such as Germaine Greer, Carol Gilligan and Deborah Tannen.

Critical Reception

Critics acclaim Pollitt's first collection of poetry, praising her poise, skillful use of language, mature ear for rhythm, and her intellectual and cerebral interpretations. Roberta Berke writes: "Pollitt combines awareness of contraries and her intelligence with a vivid imagination. . . ." Reviewers credit her with unusual maturity as a poet, praising her ability to contrast romance with disillusionment and her skill at maintaining an objective distance from her subjects. Some readers have noted excesses in her poetry: an overreliance on the "blurred you" device, too tightly controlled emotions, and an overindulgence in rich vocabulary and imagery which threatens to swamp her poems. However, reviewers agree that in her best works such as "Blue Window" and "Moon and Flowering Plum" she is impressive. While Pollitt's essays have earned more controversy than her poetry, she is considered one of the most thought-provoking and insightful feminist writers. Critics praise her writing style, which they characterize as witty and engaging, as well as her practical and well reasoned interpretations of modern events. Reviewers such as Rickie Solinger argue that Pollitt is successful because she demands that her readers grapple with new and complex ideas, which she presents in understandable and accessible ways. Scholars note that she has redefined feminist thinking, pushing society to reconsider the tenets of feminist ideology, and she is unafraid of both liberal and conservative opponents. Reviewers note that she advocates clear-thinking and solid scholarship, and laud her for attacking the unsophisticated arguments of other political commentators. However, Kirsty Milne faults Pollitt for failing to provide positive male role models in her essays. Other readers claim that Pollitt promotes a personal agenda and often favors the interests of women over children. Suzanne Rhodenbaugh and Christine Stansell argue that the essays in *Reasonable Creatures* are built so heavily upon specific events of the

1980s and 1990s that the commentary is inaccessible to younger readers. Despite the criticisms, most scholars agree that Pollitt has played a significant and important role in defining gender ideology. Boyd Zenner remarks that Pollitt is " . . . one of the most incisive, principled, and articulate cultural critics writing today."

PRINCIPAL WORKS

Antarctic Traveller (poetry) 1982
Reasonable Creatures: Essays on Women and Feminism (essays) 1994

CRITICISM

Joel Conarroe (review date 21 February 1982)

SOURCE: A review of *Antarctic Traveller*, in *Washington Post Book World*, Vol. XII, No. 8, February 21, 1982, pp. 5, 13.

[*In the excerpt below, Conarroe, editor of* PMLA *and executive director of the Modern Language Association, praises Pollitt's use of sound and rhythm in her poetry.*]

It is notoriously difficult for a poet to get a first manuscript accepted (more Americans write verse than read it) and virtually impossible unless he or she has already been published in the better periodicals. Katha Pollitt, not quite 10 years out of Radcliffe, has been appearing regularly in such visible places as *Poetry* and *The New Yorker*, but until the arrival of her first book I had only a scattered sense of how consistently striking and accomplished she is. ***Antarctic Traveller*** is a stunning collection. One that I recommend to anyone who is discouraged about the state of American letters.

Pollitt herself is not an Antarctic traveler; she is an armchair explorer, an interior voyager. The actual traveler of the title poem returns "full of adventures, anecdotes of penguins," but will never again quite fit in, will "never be wholly ours." The poet, by contrast, is wholly at home in her urban world of taxis, night-mirrored windows, feverish writing in five notebooks at once, and evenings at the ballet.

"Our real poems are already in us and all we can do is dig." Jonathan Galassi's words serve as an epigraph to her poem **"Archaeology,"** and even though Pollitt does not really believe them (or so she said at a recent reading in New York), she clearly does not have to search very far for her own material. At the end of this poem, in fact, we find an image that puts her sources in perspective.

> Now come the passionate midnights in the museum
> basement
> when out of that random rubble you'll invent
> the dusty market smelling of sheep and spices,
> streets, palmy gardens, courtyards set with wells
> to which, in the blue of evening, one by one
> come strong veiled women, bearing their perfect jars.

From the random rubble of her experience, whether it be watching Baryshnikov, enduring a 30th birthday, responding to Eliot's snobbery, reading Wittgenstein, or "dreaming in the dusk in an ecstasy of longing," she invents her carefully formed, passionate poems.

Pollitt speaks to all our senses, but she manipulates sound, fuses manner and matter, in particularly remarkable ways. Since art is long, reviews short, I choose just two examples. From a memorable series of **"Vegetable Poems,"** a resonant aria to an eggplant—yes, an eggplant:

> Like a dark foghorn in the yellow kitchen
> we imagine the eggplant's
> melancholy bass
> booming its pompous operatic sorrows
> a prince down on his luck. . . .

"Booming its pompous operatic sorrows"—what a wonderful line. And equally appealing, in its ponderous gracefulness, is the description of seals that dive and surface, "then lumber with heavy grace back up to their mates."

Like many young writers Pollitt does not do justice, in her public readings, to the subtle rhythms and sound patterns of her lines but rushes through the poems as if they were prose. Had we met I would have told her at the reading I attended that if **"Seal Rock"** or **"Chinese Finches"** were my poems I would say them slowly, lovingly. Then I would have greeted her at the beginning of a brilliant career.

The Virginia Quarterly Review (review date Summer 1982)

SOURCE: A review of *Antarctic Traveller*, in *The Virginia Quarterly Review*, Vol. 58, No. 3, Summer, 1982, p. 92.

[*In the review below, the critic describes* Antarctic Traveller *as a well crafted debut.*]

These poems convey the quotidian and the unfamiliar equally well with dazzling imagery and careful craftsman-

ship. For instance, in a series of **"Vegetable Poems"** the everyday potato is seen with "softened, mealy flesh / rotting into the earth . . . but still flinging up roots and occasional leaves / white as fish in caves," and the unfamiliar **"A Turkish Story"** tells of a rug weaver who kept his daughters at home, unmarried, while he worked on a rug that would have no errors. When he died, his daughters married husbands "strong as the sea. / They danced on the rug and its errors blazed like stars." *Antarctic Traveller* is a young poet's first book, and it's a good one.

Robert B. Shaw (review date December 1982)

SOURCE: A review of *Antarctic Traveller* in *Poetry*, Vol. CXLI, No. 3, December, 1982, pp. 178-79.

[*In the following excerpt, Shaw argues that Pollitt is most insightful when she remains detached from her subjects.*]

At the center of Katha Pollitt's *Antarctic Traveller*, her first book, are **"Five Poems from Japanese Paintings."** Even without these one would have noted in her writing those qualities which for the Japanese, as she says, encompass "the virtues of the noble man: / reticence, calm, clarity of mind." Whether inspired by paintings or daily surroundings, Pollitt's poems are marked by a beautiful economy of line, a selective cherishing of detail. The Orient's respect for nuance underlies her similes: on the Hudson "a sailboat quivers like a white leaf in the wind:; on a Japanese screen "Prince Genji, the great lover, / sails in triumph from bedroom to bedroom: in each / a woman flutters like a tiny jeweled fan." If the style of these poems recalls ancient Japanese masters, the mood they evoke is more that of a modern Western painter such as Edward Hopper, in whose stark interiors light is the most eloquent inhabitant. We see rooms or landscapes in which anticipation or regret linger as distilled presences, the human actors having left a moment ago or having not yet arrived. The poet draws intensity from life's interstices. When she is most introspective she maintains an austere, appraising distance, deliberately estranged from the self so as to be capable of judgement. In **"Blue Window"** she explores "that longing you have to be invisible, / transparent as glass, thin air," and concludes:

> It is your other, solitary self
> that calls you to the window where you stand
> dreaming in the dusk in an ecstasy of longing
> while your white apartment full of plants and pictures
> grows strange with shadows, as though under water
> And in another moment
> you would stream out the window and into the sky
> like a breath—

but it is almost too dark to see. In the next apartment
a door is flung open. Someone speaks someone's
name.

Such detachment takes on an ironic trenchancy at the end
of **"Turning Thirty"**:

Oh, what were you doing, why weren't you paying
attention
that piercingly blue day, not a cloud in the sky,
when suddenly "choices"
ceased to mean "infinite possibilities"
and became instead "deciding what to do without"?
No wonder you're happiest now
riding on trains from one lover to the next.
In those black, night-mirrored windows
a wild white face, operatic, still enthralls you:
a romantic heroine,
suspended between lives, suspended between
destinations.

The pun suggested by the last image is irresistible: this poet
has a gift for reflection. What is uncommon is for this capacity to be joined with a delicately acute vision of the
world outside the self, a world where "at three o'clock in
the morning / the Staten Island ferry sails for pure joy," and
where, in a January thaw, "on the pond the round ice floats
free: / a moon / gone black in black water." This book has
many triumphs and no blunders. It makes one impatient for
more.

William Logan (review date Spring-Summer 1983)

SOURCE: "First Books, Fellow Travelers," in *Parnassus:
Poetry in Review*, Vol. 11, No. 1, Spring-Summer, 1983,
pp. 216-22.

[*In the following excerpt, Logan reviews* Antarctic Traveller, *finding fault with Pollitt's tightly controlled, emotionally distant poems, but praising her use of
imagination.*]

Olds rudely enjambs her headlong style; Katha Pollitt has
better manners. She is respectful of line breaks, her
teleutons, almost always nouns or verbs at phrase-end, revealing a desire for solidity and completeness, to have in
every line an anchor. Such a style is soothing, like the slow
rocking of a ship in tranquil latitudes:

That longing you have to be invisible,
transparent as glass, thin air—
that is what moves you certain times to tears

watching the evening fill with city lights
and the long dusty summer avenues
rise weightless through the air
and tremble like constellations in a sky
so deep and clear you are your one desire,
Oh, let me be that blue . . .

("Blue Window")

The self-addressed and banal phrases wash up against their
breakwaters—air, tears, lights, avenues—and soon the apartment "grows strange with shadows, as though under water."
Beyond herself, outside herself, "It is your other, solitary
self / that calls you to the window where you stand / dreaming in the dusk in an ecstasy of longing. . . . " The central
tension in this shrewdly titled first book is between what
Pollitt so obviously is and what she cannot (or should not?)
be. The landscapes she dreams on are obviously composed;
only rarely does she suffer so violent a longing as actually
to place herself within them. Hers are tentative motions;
the shy poet, back at her desk, reveals not just by the matter but the manner of her desires how far she is willing to
go—only as far as, say, the library.

Though she is unwilling, or unable, to give herself wholly
over to fantasy, Pollitt travels furthest—or as far as she
can—by traveling at home:

What does the sea want, my clothes, my keys, my
face?
This is the mind's Sargasso,
expansive as Kansas flatlands, the big dead place.

The weeds stir, they make promises. I'm light as a
shell.
Immobile, the sea bottom
glints at my emptiness with ship's tackle, jewels,
railway tickets, photographs. . . .

("In Horse Latitudes")

The strange is utterly domesticated here, as if the sea bottom had become a messy dresser drawer. This is indeed "the
mind's Sargasso," a seascape not seen but imagined, as having a scholarly footnote explain the derivation of "horse
latitudes" makes clear. This sea is not entered but entertained.

When Pollitt goes so far as to give herself over to persona—and a mind entranced by images of history must be
so tempted, despite its diffidence—she manages this breakdown of decorum by removing dangers to recollection (**"Of
the Scythians"**), thus distancing them beyond fear, or by
anachronistically taming them (**"Penelope Writes"**). The
raid of the Scythians can be recalled by no one but the

poem's aged narrator, for whom horror has been reduced to a dotty feeling of superiority. Penelope, on the other hand, is a repressed and angry housewife: "For years / I've sat at the window, those men at the kitchen table." What a homely, modern scene for Odysseus to return to!

The countervailing tendency in Pollitt's work is to estrange the domestic. Some of her most luxuriant poems, which may owe as much to Erica Jong as to Neruda or Wilbur, are paeans to vegetables: the potato, the tomato, the onion, the eggplant:

> Like a dark foghorn in the yellow kitchen
> we imagine the eggplant's
> melancholy bass
> booming its pompous operatic sorrows
> a prince down on his luck
> preserving among peasants
> an air of dignified, impenetrable gloom
> or Boris, dying,
> booming, *I still am Tsar.*

("**Eggplant**")

Such exuberant invention almost distracts from the dangling modifier the poem begins with. This restlessness, this constant desire for metamorphosis and yet suspicion of it, can only come from someone committed to a fantasy world not superior or inferior but equal to the real one. Pollitt has that love of visual art (the central section of her book meditates on five Japanese paintings) that enforces the distance between observer and observed, real and ideal. She is almost too level-headed, but some of her best effects derive from her modesty.

Unlike Olds, who ruthlessly usurps the role of survivor, Pollitt approaches survival obliquely, through the "you" that, in poetry, is often the "I," especially in a poet of such self-reflective capacity, for whom the only "you" may be the one addressed in the mirror.

> Outside your window
> ailanthus trees, bringing you an important message
> about the nutritive properties of garbage,
> wave their arms for attention, third-world raiders,
> scrawny, tough, your future if you're lucky.

That typical uncertainty ("if you're lucky") makes Pollitt's voice more attractive than Olds's. Titling such a poem **"Failure"** is also her distinctive mark.

Pollitt often succumbs—in compensation?—to romantic overstatement. To the degree she understates herself she overstates her fictions, so that, in a poem about a rugweaver and his daughters, "When he died each married a husband

strong as the sea. / They danced on the rug and its errors blazed like stars." That romantic inflation is reminiscent of the fiction writer Mark Helprin's fabulistic simplifications. In poem after poem Pollitt seems too easy on herself, failing to question her romances (with images, not people—of lovers we hear almost nothing at all), allowing the most errant fable to pass for poetic truth. Her vocabulary is rich with color, and even overstuffed: some of her poems waddle about like force-fed geese. There is something relentlessly cheery about her; she can be as exhausting as an energetic hostess ushering her guests through immaculate parlors. If Pollitt were all glitter and no gravity, however, she would not be worth attention.

When the poet admits her image-making, the conscious distances she imposes between herself and her object, her art is of a higher order altogether—*not* because she is suddenly aware of some post-structuralist theory of language as evasion, but because the resulting poem admits to herself her evasions. Such self-revelation in so cool and canny a poet is always filled with pathos:

> Well, what's wrong with that? Nothing, except
> really you don't believe wrinkles mean character
> and know it's an ominous note
> that the Indian skirts flapping on the sidewalk racks
> last summer looked so gay you wanted them all
> but now are marked clearer than price tags: not for
> you.
> Oh, what were you doing, why weren't you paying
> attention
> that piercingly blue day, not a cloud in the sky,
> when suddenly "choices"
> ceased to mean "infinite possibilities"
> and became instead "deciding what to do without"?

("**Turning Thirty**")

This suffers from her telltale inflation; but the early lines, especially, exude a joyous self-mockery not so artfully employed since Elizabeth Bishop, a self-mockery that contains, despite its insouciance, a note of resignation and despair.

Excluding Marilyn Hacker, Pollitt is more aware of contemporary social life than any of her peers—in the pages of *Antarctic Traveller* appear Roland Barthes, Design Research pillows, Baryshnikov, and the walnut tortes of Manhattan restaurants. In the best poems, however, she dips below that glossy social surface and brings up rhyme both elegant and true.

> Let love go down to disarray,
> they sipped their water peaceably
> and nibbled the seed in their spoonsize manger
>
> for all the world small citizens

still of that practical, prosperous land
where the towns sleep safe in the Emperor's hand
and fields yield fruit and women sons
and red means wealth and never danger
and even the thief hung up by his thumbs
bares black snaggle teeth with a sort of pride
to demonstrate for the watching crowd
to what swift grief all folly comes.

                                        (**"Chinese Finches"**)

One might rail against the neatness and self-possession of that resolution—it is not entirely demanded by the rhyme—but Pollitt is a poet who *believes* that folly comes to grief. Forget about the suffering of the thief. The qualities she finds virtuous, it may be inferred from **"Wild Orchids,"** are "reticence, calm, clarity of mind." These may not be strange virtues for someone so taken by the visual, made vertiginous by vegetables. Her reticence is her most attractive asset, most available in rhymes she has yet to exploit fully:

Those speckled trout we glimpsed in a pool last year
you'd take for an image of love: it too should be
graceful, elusive, tacit, moving surely
among half-lights of mingled dim and clear,
forced to no course, of no fixed residence,
its only end its own swift elegance.
What would you say
if you saw what I saw the other day:
that pool heat-choked and fevered where sick blue
bubbled green scum and blistered water lily?
A white like a rolled-back eye or fish's belly
I thought I saw far out—but doubtless you
prefer to think our trout had left together
to seek a place with less inclement weather.

                                        (**"Two Fish"**)

Rhyme controls, perhaps a little too easily, that horror of vision, the eye that suddenly sees too much. The war between reserve and fantasy drives Pollitt to splendid contrivances, even for a poet who trusts in invention ("when out of that random rubble you'll invent / the dusty market smelling of sheep and spices, / streets, palmy gardens, courtyards set with wells / to which, in the blue of evening, one by one / come strong veiled women, bearing their perfect jars").

The final poem, **"To an Antarctic Traveller,"** shrugs off constraint—a frenzy of concoction, it balances image after image like plates spinning on poles:

Down there, No was final,
it had a glamor: so Pavlova turns,
narcissus-pale and utterly self-consumed,
from the claque, the hothouse roses; so the ice

perfects its own reflection, cold Versailles,
and does not want you, does not want even Scott,
grinding him out of his grave—Splash! off he goes,
into the ocean, comical, Edwardian,
a valentine thrown out. Afternoons
in the pastry shop, coffee and macaroons,
gossip's two-part intricate inventions
meshed in the sugary air like the Down and Across
of an endless Sunday puzzle. . . .

It is still someone else's adventure (Merrill's, perhaps), someone else's journey; but there is a loosening of imagination here that promises a sort of poem different from her elegant composures, her "reticence, calm, clarity of mind." She might yet yield to the emotions frozen in constructing her ice palaces. If those controlled emotions ever did break out, there would be a different picture altogether— "the ego glinting at the heart of things."

Kirkus Reviews (review date 15 June 1994)

SOURCE: A review of *Reasonable Creatures: Essays on Women and Feminism,* in *Kirkus Reviews,* June 15, 1994, pp. 828-29.

[*In the following review, the critic praises Pollitt for asking new questions from a feminist perspective.*]

Most of the essays collected here (and previously published in *The Nation, The New Yorker,* and elsewhere) bring an important critical, often feminist, perspective to controversial issues: sex and sexuality, children and families, abortion and motherhood.

Debates about the literary canon, according to poet Pollitt (***Antarctic Traveller,*** not reviewed), rest on the assumption that the only books that students will read are those lucky enough to make "the list." Maybe, she suggests, since there's so little reading going on at all, the list is really not so important. She imagines a country of "real readers" who read voluntarily, actively, and self-determinedly, exploring all kinds of literature in all kinds of settings; but she doesn't see this happening as long as the debate is about which books to force down readers' throats, in which case one book is as bad as another. In an examination of politics and family-values rhetoric, Pollitt analytically separates "the family" and "family values," claiming that the conflation of these two terms obscures "two distinct social phenomena that in reality have not very much to do with one another." This distinction allows Pollitt to question the ways in which these terms are used by pundits and others, on both the left and the right, to evade more pertinent issues, such as economic inequality. In a cutting indictment of Katie Roiphe,

Pollitt challenges the notion that current rape statistics are based on feminist manipulation of definitions and a reinterpretation of "bad sex" the morning after. Although others have critiqued Roiphe on the same points, Pollitt asks new questions about sexuality and sexual responsibility.

This could be a good resource for women's studies and young feminists, though despite its acuity, it won't provide much new information to those readers already up-to-date on feminist politics.

Maureen Corrigan (review date 25 September 1994)

SOURCE: "Defining the New Woman," in *Washington Post Book World*, Vol. XXIV, No. 39, September 25, 1994, p. 10.

[*In the following review of* Reasonable Creatures, *Corrigan, a literature instructor at Georgetown University, praises Pollitt's skillful definition of feminist issues and her sharp logic.*]

It seems an odd thing to say about a social critic so engaged with her historical moment, but Katha Pollitt is a woman seriously out of joint with her time. Pollitt is really a daughter of the Enlightenment, a fan of that 18th-century cant-buster, Dr. Samuel Johnson. Against our culture's predilection for feelgood thinking and lazy sentimentality masquerading as morality, Pollitt pits the neoclassical virtues of reason and wit. To read the 19 essays and reviews dating from 1985 to the present collected in *Reasonable Creatures* is to be bombarded, gloriously, by the force of Pollitt's contempt for intellectual sloppiness. For instance, in an essay entitled **"Naming and Blaming: The Media Goes Wilding in Palm Beach,"** Pollitt dissects the specious reasoning by which the media, in the William Kennedy Smith case, decided that naming rape victims was an issue up for grabs:

"And so," she sighs, "we are having one of those endless, muddled, two-sides-to-every-question debates that, by ignoring as many facts as possible and by weighing all arguments equally, gives us that warm American feeling that truth must lie somewhere in the middle."

Or, as another great American writer once tersely said, "Isn't it pretty to think so?"

Hemingway and Pollitt, of course, part company once the conversation turns from cerebral performance to sexual politics. The title of Pollitt's book comes from another of her 18th-century idols, Mary Wollstonecraft, who authored the ground-breaking feminist polemic *A Vindication of the Rights of Women* ("I wish to see women neither heroines nor brutes," Wollstonecraft wrote, "but reasonable creatures."). The essays here address what our culture usually mislabels as "women's issues": the battle over abortion, domestic violence, surrogate motherhood, the erratic quality of reproductive and gynecological health care, and the appalling state of children's entertainment. It's a natural question to ask if any of these topical essays, culled from periodicals like the *Nation* and the *New Yorker,* are dated. The good news—and the bad news—is no.

I'm not clear on how Pollitt justified wedging **"Why We Read: Canon to the Right of Me . . ."** into this thematic collection, but I'm glad she did. This 1991 essay stands as the single smartest commentary I've read on the still-sputtering debate over the literary canon. It opens in quintessential Pollitt fashion, not with a thesis but with a dilemma: Pollitt finds she agrees with all sides in the controversy. She then ushers us into the process of energetically thinking through the issue, appraising the pros and cons of both the liberal and the conservative sides. (The only group she witheringly dismisses is the alleged radicals, people who really give that honorable word a bad name: "How foolish to argue that Chekhov has nothing to say to a black woman—or, for that matter, to me . . . The notion that one reads to increase one's self-esteem sounds to me like more snake oil. Literature is not an aerobics class or a session at the therapist's.")

Finally, Pollitt spots a more serious issue that's being ignored: the dismal state of reading in our country. The canon debate is so crucial, Pollitt realizes, because so many Americans read so few books of any kind. She says: "While we have been arguing so fiercely about which books make the best medicine, the patient has been slipping deeper and deeper into a coma." This and so many other of Pollitt's essays seem to be structured along the lines of Edgar Allen Poe's great detective story "The Purloined Letter" (starring another champion of "ratiocinative methods," C. Auguste Dupin). Pollitt prowls around familiar ideological precincts and then, at last, pounces on the "purloined letter"—the obvious but disruptive idea—that everyone else overlooks.

Another masterpiece of argumentation is **"Marooned on Gilligan's Island: Are Women Morally Superior to Men?"**, in which Pollitt criticizes the "intellectual-flabbiness" of "difference feminists" like Carol Gilligan and Nancy Chodorow, who universalize features of male and female development rather than credit them to the different economic and social positions men and women hold. In a brilliant aphoristic flourish, Pollitt contends that "difference feminism" is: "a rationale for the status quo, which is why men like it, and a burst of grateful applause, which is why women like it. Men keep the power, but since power is so bad, so much the worse for them."

Pollitt is one of those all-too-rare symbol analysts who always take economics, class, and the legacy of the past into account in their criticism of ideas and social trends. Thus, in an essay entitled **"Hot Flash,"** she wonders whether the current media fascination with menopause isn't a backlash against middle-class women who, buoyed up by feminism, thought they could compete with men and stay desirable. ("No one," Pollitt observes, "is interested in the hot flashes of cleaning ladies. . . . ") And, in this collection's guiltiest pleasure, Pollitt eviscerates *The Morning After,* Katie Roiphe's first-hand look at sexual politics on campus. Pollitt faults Roiphe for, among other things, her distorted characterization of the history of the Women's Movement. Poor-Roiphe. Watching Pollitt train all the force of her intellect on her is like watching a brilliant Professor dissect the posturings of, well, a graduate student.

Susan Shapiro (review date 9 October 1994)

SOURCE: A review of *Reasonable Creatures: Essays on Women and Feminism,* in *New York Times Book Review,* Vol. 99, October 9, 1994, p. 22.

[*In the following review of* Reasonable Creatures, *Shapiro questions Pollitt's use of statistics, but praises the collection.*]

Whether the subject is breast implants, Lorena Bobbitt or bad sex, Katha Pollitt has a strong opinion about it. *Reasonable Creatures* collects 19 funny and furious essays, previously published in *The New York Times, The Nation* and *The New Yorker.* In which Ms. Pollitt takes on the most compelling issues of our day concerning the sexes and turns them upside down. Along with her razor-sharp wit and her impatience with sound-bite solutions, what sets Ms Pollitt apart from other feminist writers is her concern for social justice. For example, she takes the psychologist Carol Gilligan to task for basing a theory of gendered ethics on "interviews with a handful of Harvard-Radcliffe undergraduates." Although she criticizes others for shoddy data, Ms Pollitt's own statistics are not carefully annotated and at times seem questionable. Still, this is a small oversight in an otherwise cunning and complex collection.

Merle Rubin (review date 25 October 1994)

SOURCE: "Essays for Collecting and Dissecting," in *Christian Science Monitor,* Vol. 86, No. 232, October 25, 1994, p. 13.

[*In the following excerpt, Rubin praises Pollitt's ability to cut to the heart of issues in her collection of essays* Reasonable Creatures.]

. . . .Of a more consistent quality are the 19 timely pieces by poet and journalist Katha Pollitt in *Reasonable Creatures: Essays on Women and Feminism.*

They are, indeed, about women's issues, but Pollitt, a true descendent of large-visioned, feminists like Mary Wollstonecraft, effectively demonstrates why these issues are relevant to everyone.

These essays from *The Nation, The New Yorker,* and the *New York Times* were written in response to a variety of current events and news stories, from the "Baby M" surrogacy case to the William Kennedy Smith rape trial. They share a recurrent theme: Pollitt's belief that women should be treated like "reasonable creatures" (Wollstonecraft's phrase) with the freedom and responsibility to make choices for themselves; rather than being viewed as mere "instruments" put on this planet first and foremost for the convenience of others.

A pungent stylist with a powerful ability to cut through cant, Pollitt is also a sharp-eyed media critic, not only of conscious or unconscious gender bias (as one might expect), but also of self-serving behavior among her fellow journalists.

Claiming that the public, under the First Amendment, has a "right to know," whether it's the names of rape victims or secrets withheld for reasons of national security, members of this same profession have willingly gone to jail rather than reveal the names of their sources. The public's right to know, in this instance, took a back seat to professional self-protection. . . .

Katha Pollitt with Ruth Conniff (interview date December 1994)

SOURCE: An interview, in *The Progressive,* Vol. 58, No. 12, December, 1994, pp. 34-40.

[*In the following interview, Pollitt discusses her political views and the differences between her poetry and prose.*]

"Although feminism came out of the Left and naturally belongs on the Left, sometimes you wouldn't know it.'

Like Broadway, the novel, and God, feminism has been declared dead many times," Katha Pollitt writes in the introduction to her new book, *Reasonable Creatures: Essays on Women and Feminism*, published in September by Knopf. Pollitt herself is one of feminism's liveliest writers, tackling, in her delightfully witty prose, such diverse issues as family values, breast implants, male Muppets, and the notion that women are somehow more special than men. Her book is comprised of the essays and regular columns she writes for *The Nation*, as well as pieces that first appeared in *The New Yorker* and *The New York Times*. Besides being one of America's best political essayists, Pollitt is an accomplished poet. She has won numerous awards for her poetry, including a National Book Critics Circle Award for *Antarctic Traveler*, published in 1983.

Katha Pollitt grew up in Brooklyn, graduated from Radcliffe, and earned an M.F.A. in poetry at Columbia University. For several years she was poet-in-residence at Barnard College, where she has also taught writing. She worked as a copy editor and proofreader at *Esquire* and *The New Yorker*, and wrote free-lance book reviews, before becoming first Literary Editor and then an associate editor of *The Nation*.

I visited her in the cheerful, cluttered apartment she shares with her seven-year-old daughter, Sophie, and her partner, Paul Mattick, on the Upper West Side of Manhattan. When I arrived, she was attempting to make coffee. Mattick intervened, averting a near disaster with the grounds and boiling water. "Women don't belong in the kitchen," they said simultaneously, laughing.

In person, Pollitt comes across the same way she does in her writing—funny and personable, extremely sharp—taking aim at stereotypes and fuzzy thinking.

As we talked, her four cats wandered in and out of her study, walking all over her desk and sitting on her lap. We were interrupted several times by phone calls and faxes from people who wanted to tell her about the rave reviews for her book.

[*Conniff*]: *Why did you pick the title* Reasonable Creatures?

[Pollitt]: It's part of a quotation from Mary Wollstonecraft, the founding mother of modern feminism. She was the first woman to write a full-dress argument for the emancipation of women, and I'm a big fan of hers.

The quotation was, "I wish for women to be neither angels nor brutes but reasonable creatures." And what she meant was that women should be neither placed on a pedestal nor considered to be of a lower nature than men, but treated as human beings. I think it's truly amazing that 200 years later this is still a controversial statement. You still have to make an argument that women should have the same rights and responsibilities as men, beginning with the right to control your own body and what goes on inside it. So I think it's pretty timely.

I also chose the title because I think it points up my difference with what I call "difference feminists"—like Carol Gilligan, for example—who see women as being so differently formed from men that they make decisions according to a whole other set of criteria. Miraculously, it turns out that what this difference is is exactly the sexist stereotype, with a positive spin put on it: Women are more loving, more sharing, more caring, more intuitive, less hierarchical, "lateral thinkers," and all this. I wanted to set myself squarely against that style of feminism.

Do you think that you are one of a few people who believes women and men are the same kind of creature?

No. Lots of people think it. But the other strand of feminism is also quite strong. And it's much more fashionable. And the reason is that it explains the world we see without resorting to the concept of sexism. What it says is that women don't have power because they don't want power. For example, Suzanne Gordon, in her book, *Prisoners of Men's Dreams*, thinks women go into low-paid jobs in the helping professions because they are more helpful people. This is a very silly idea. I'm saying that it doesn't have to do with the personal gender-characteristics of the people involved. It has to do with the economy, which is organized along gender lines, and with the way you're socialized.

What do you think about Emily's List—an organization that gives money specifically to women candidates?

Well, I'm glad you're asking me this question. I have a very complicated relationship to Emily's List, which is this: I belong to Emily's List. I send money to people on their list. But at the same time that I am writing out my little checks, I am wondering, why am I doing this? These politicians quite often are not particularly enlightened or feminist or liberal.

I think that people in American politics are always looking for short-cuts. For example, if we elect women, will they automatically on the whole, on average, defend the interests of women, and be less warlike, and be more honest and altruistic and all this kind of thing? I think that, yeah, if you elect a feminist she's going to do that. But just being a Democratic woman is not going to do that. How many of these women are going to stand up and say that the Clinton welfare-reform program is going to devastate the poor and that it's sexist. And that in fact all women with small children ought to receive more benefits than they do? There are a few. Lynn Woolsey, for example, was on welfare, so she's a wonderful person to have in Congress. But some of the others, they're just as big on trimming the budget and "we all have to carry our weight" as the guys are. There's an illusion that women have only women's interests at heart. Women have all the interests of their class, just like men do.

Nonetheless, given identical politics, I'd rather have a woman than a man in office, because I think there's a value in gender-equity for its own sake. There are all kinds of issues where men and women do see things differently, not because women are lateral thinkers and men are hierarchical, but because women have a different life experience, and so they have different fears and different hopes as well.

But these kinds of small and marginal and subtle differences—you can't make a political movement out of them. You have to make a political movement out of politics. It can't be made out of voting for a this-colored person or a this-gendered person as if they'd almost unconsciously carry out your goals.

What do you think about the prospects for organized left-wing politics in this country?

I guess I would have to say at the risk of startling or bothering some of your readers, I don't think there is a Left in this country. There are liberals in this country. But I don't know of any movement, really, that mounts any kind of fundamental challenge to capitalism, and to the basic way this country is organized. The way things are set up I think there is very little space to enact even liberal politics. You see this every time Clinton has some kind of vague, liberal notion that flits through his mind, like, "Let's vaccinate all the children." It immediately becomes immensely complicated and difficult and he's attacked on every front and then he drops it. Now, maybe some of that is a facet of his personality and some of it is a facet of Congress. But if there was a great, big organized movement saying, "Vaccinate the children! Vaccinate the children!" they'd figure out a way to do it. What I think is amazing is the way the left-er end of the spectrum has collapsed into Clintonism. You saw this with health care. And you see it with the crime bill. This is going to be the major achievement of the Clinton Administration—this insane punitive mess. You didn't see "the Left" out there on this issue. And I think the reason for that is the same reason you don't see Marian Wright Edelman out there on the hustings saying Clinton's welfare ideas will hurt children and poor people. It's the whole lesser-of-two-evils, this-is-our-last-best-hope, we-have-to-go-along-to-get-along mentality. Instead of trying to create some sort of independent basis for social change you piggy-back on the conservative wing of the Democratic Party.

And so I feel that when we speak about the Left we're speaking about three people.

Surely more than three. I think of you as part of the Left, and The Nation *as well as* The Progressive.

Well, sure. You're one person, I'm another. I'm not saying there's nobody. What I'm saying is there isn't a social basis for this politics. There isn't an organization. What is the left-wing organization? *The Nation* Associates?

There are little things, there's this brush fire over here and these workers over there. But there isn't anything like an organized political movement. And the minute one develops, it collapses back into the Democratic Party again.

In your book, you take a couple of shots at the American point of view that the truth lies in the middle, and you seem to take a shot at Anna Quindlen for this attitude. Is that true?

Well, it's funny. Anna Quindlen is always the first person I read on the op-ed page of *The New York Times,* and often the only person I read on the op-ed page. And since I myself have started writing a column, I have an enormous amount of respect for her. Twice a week, for eight years or so, she has managed to turn out a piece of writing that is pretty lively and energetic and that has something to say, and that I almost always agree with. And I think there are issues on which she is very, very good. She is really good about abortion. And she's a good reporter and writer. I'm really sorry that she's leaving.

She wrote a piece about a basic civil-liberties question, which was whether or not to identify child-molesters to their neighbors after they've been released from prison. She talked about how she had two points of view; as a columnist, she could make a case against the law, but as a mother she would want to know. It seemed like one of those truth-lies-in-the-middle treatments. What did you think about that?

About the issue or the column?

Both.

I would share her perplexity. It's not an issue that I've thought through very deeply, and I would certainly want to ask: If sex offenders are tagged through life with their crime, what about other people? Should they be tagged through life, too? You can make a case that there are lots of areas where there is recidivism, not just this. But certainly, as a parent, I am more bothered by the idea that unbeknownst to me, a neighbor of mine might be preparing to kidnap and murder my daughter.

Ultimately, we need to think in a larger sense about crime, including sex crimes. The discussion is one about how long do you put them away and what do you do when they get out. It's much less about what happens while they're in there, and what I would like to see happening is that we would all ask ourselves, "How come our society produces so much violent crime and so much sexual crime?" That's a hard conversation to have. I'm not sure myself what the answers would be, although I'm sure football is in there somewhere.

Do you find yourself a feminist among civil libertarians and a civil libertarian among feminists?

Although there are certainly particular issues where you might find your wish to see women safe and cheerful conflict with your civil-libertarian outlook, basically I see these as having much more in common than opposed. The media have played a destructive role here in that when these two movements are discussed together, they are always discussed in opposition. So, for example, the major role played by the civil libertarians in reproductive-freedom issues is mentioned much less than the fact that some feminists would like to use the law to attack pornography, and all civil libertarians think that's an infringement on the First Amendment. But mostly, I see these two movements as friends.

You wrote a letter to the editor of The Nation *right before you started your column—what was that all about?*

Well, Carlin Romano wrote a review of Catharine MacKinnon's book *Only Words* which was published in our magazine, in which Carlin pretends to fantasize about raping Catharine MacKinnon and someone else does rape Catharine MacKinnon. It was to say to Catharine MacKinnon, you think there's no difference between words and deeds? I'll show you the difference. And we got a tremendous amount of flak for this. It was one of a number of pieces that we published that, although you could defend each of them in some abstract and complicated way, the bottom line was that the magazine was not attuned to the frivolousness of making this sort of joke. So I wrote a letter saying, "What's going on? I take a leave of absence and look what you do." You know, *The Nation* is often criticized for having male-oriented politics and publishing mostly men, and I think the criticisms have some validity.

So did that have anything to do with you starting your column?

No, no. Victor Navasky and I had discussed my doing the column for a long time. I will say, though, that there is always a space on the "Left" to be against feminism—in a way that there's not a space to be a racist. And although

feminism came out of the Left and naturally belongs on the Left, sometimes you wouldn't know it. You wouldn't know it if you looked at what Andrea Dworkin likes to call the male Left. I think she draws much too harsh a portrait, but I don't think you could find a person publishing in a progressive magazine who would, say, support capital punishment. But you can certainly find pro-lifers. You can certainly find people who think that mothers should be home with their children. You can certainly find people who have bought the media caricature, which is that a feminist is a banker in a power suit.

What do you think of declarations of post-feminism, that many women say they are not feminists?

The idea that you need other people to make common cause with in order to achieve a goal feels to many people like failure. That's why you have a lot of working-class people who anathematize unions. I get letters from women like this who say, "I'm a Republican, I have an MBA, and everyone tells me I can't make it but I know I will. Because I'm determined and I'm the best, you see."

The American ideology is, "If you're the best you don't need anybody." So that makes it very hard for joining a political movement based on solidarity not to seem like weakness and a confession of your own inability to succeed by your own efforts. Now what people in America have a hard time getting through their heads is that, first of all, nobody succeeds entirely by their own efforts, but also, not that many people succeed. Capitalism is like a card game: Every time somebody wins, somebody else has to lose. We think that if everybody were equally hard-working and well prepared and determined, we would all make money. But no.

Now we have the anti-feminist feminists, as I call them—Christina Hoff Sommers, for example, who says women don't need feminism anymore. What that movement is about is saying to professional women, "You don't have to concern yourself with these problems of women who are poorer than yourself, and you don't have to concern yourself with some battered wife, or some bedraggled rape victim. You know, you're doing fine. So let those women go. Because you can compete successfully in the world of men."

I was talking the other day with a high-school coach who said he won't pat girls on the back, or be in a room alone with them, because he's afraid of being accused of sexual harassment. It's the same thing Nat Hentoff writes about at universities, that sexual-harassment suits have had a chilling effect, and male teachers are now going to treat female students like they have the plague. What do you think about all that?

Well, I don't think the price that women should pay for access to their teachers should be that every now and then one of them is going to be assaulted. I think that's a very short-sighted response to this problem—keep them at arm's length.

I think Nat Hentoff likes to portray these issues as, "Here are these wacko Women out there with their absurd sensitivities and as a result of that, a relationship that was very good and valuable is being destroyed." But I don't think that's the picture. I think you could say as a result of there being a couple of truly vile men out there who have been protected by administrations for a long time, and about whom no action has been taken, we end up with this situation. Why frame it as these women are spoiling it for everybody? Why not say these men are spoiling it for everybody? The anger is always directed at the women.

What do you think about that part of Catharine MacKinnon's work—the idea of the hostile work environment?

I agree with Nadine Strossen of the ACLU, that you don't want it to be that someone puts up a *Playboy* pin-up, or somebody reads *Playboy* in their own lunchtime, and because there is a woman in the office all of a sudden that is illegal. But there is a lot of hostility to women in the workplace. That's definitely true. And I don't think it should have to be true that in order to go to work and earn a salary women should have to put up with being constantly insulted and demeaned. And I think that there's some middle ground here that, if we were all people of good will, would not be all that hard to arrive at.

How does one go about trying to achieve that?

Men and women need to talk to each other. One thing about speech codes is the way that, because lawyers are so important in these discussions, it immediately turns to damages, to throwing people out of school and firing people. What I would rather see is a free and open discussion about sexism, about racism, about prejudice, about class privilege. That's the discussion you don't get to have once you start with all this speech-code stuff. And that's the discussion I think people don't want to have. If one student calls another a nigger or some other horrible epithet, what if you said, "Why do you say that?" What if you had a discussion about racism?

Take Charles Murray, for example. Now this is very interesting, because Charles Murray [in his book *The Bell Curve*] is saying something that large numbers of white people believe. They don't say it, but many, many white people at some level of their being think that the seemingly intractable situation of the black underclass indicates that black people are genetically inferior. It's very hard to get people

to admit that they have this idea. But how do you get them not to have this idea if they always say, "I don't think that. No, look, black, white, purple, polkadot, it's all fine with me." Then you don't get to have a discussion where you examine what it means to think these things. Maybe there are other reasons that explain what seems to you to be evidence of this biological inferiority theory. You can have a discussion about this idea even though it's reprehensible. But that's a discussion that you don't get to have if you just call someone a racist and kick the person out of school.

So do you think Charles Murray is doing a service?

No, absolutely not. Because that discussion is not going to happen because of this book. What he's doing is he's making it acceptable to say this, but not as part of a discussion with black people. His main interest is to de-fund the welfare state. He just wants to say "Oh, don't spend all this money on remedial education, they're too stupid."

So you don't think it's good that someone is saying it out loud, because that's what it sounded like you were saying.

No. I don't think it's good. I mean I guess you could say yes, and it was good that Hitler voiced all that anti-Semitism, too, because now we can have a conversation about it. But no, Charles Murray is not like a student. Charles Murray is not some eighteen-year-old who was brought up to be a racist, and now he's in college and thinks maybe he shouldn't say it, you know, because it's rude. Charles Murray is a major political actor with certain policy goals that he wants very much to achieve. That's a very different sort of thing. I'm not saying that he doesn't have a right to say what he wants, but I think it's very important to combat his ideas most vigorously.

What do you think of the debate about pornography?

I have a lot of sympathy for a very deep critique of heterosexuality. But what I don't have a lot of sympathy for is spending enormous amounts of political energy on the futile attempt to get rid of certain kinds of images.

People like to argue about pornography because it's about sex. And it relates to certain academic feminist interests having to do with representation. But as politics, it is a true waste of time.

And it's worse than a waste of time, because not only does it use up energy that could be better devoted to something else, it places feminism in the camp of those who think that women are less sexual than men, that women's sexuality is less diverse and perverse than men's.

I think that it's very interesting that the women's movement in thirty years has not been able to get paid parental leave, something that many other countries have, something that's very modest, but actually would help people a lot. It has not been able to get a national system of day care—something else that exists in many countries. But it has been able to inject into the public discourse the views of Andrea Dworkin and Catharine MacKinnon on pornography.

I think it's been able to do this because it's hitching a ride on a feeling that is already very deep, which is Puritanism: Sex is bad, looking at it is bad, thinking about it is bad, and masturbation isn't very good either, and it's just all bad. So people are ready for this argument.

You don't find anybody defending pornography as pornography, except for Alan Dershowitz and women—Sallie Tisdale wrote an article, and now a whole book about it. She's really interested in pornography. Pornography is a multi-multi-million-dollar industry. But when is the last time someone made a case for pornography and said, you know, I like it? It's a pleasure. It's harmless. I don't beat and rape women. But I enjoy watching dirty movies. This is a case that is very, very rarely made, because people are ashamed of it. At the same time, they want to do it. And I think the shame and the wanting to do it are related.

That's how Puritanism works. It's a two-part system.

What do you think of Camille Paglia, who also sees violence and sex as inseparable?

I think she is very much like Andrea Dworkin and Catharine MacKinnon. The media have constructed feminism as a cat fight between Katie Roiphe and Camille Paglia on the one hand and Catharine MacKinnon and Andrea Dworkin on the other. But you'll notice that all these people agree that sex is a kind of violence, that it's exploitative. Except Paglia thinks that's good, or that's nature. Whereas, I think at some point Andrea Dworkin and Catharine MacKinnon would want to say it's culture, but it just happens to be that way as far back as you can go.

Paglia is sort of the Charles Murray of sex. You know, "There's nothing you can do about it."

But take your garden-variety act of sex; they all agree that what is going on here is essentially sadomasochism, really. And that's its central feature. None of them have much use for the idea that sex is amusing, that it can be light, that it can involve affection or friendship, that people can laugh while they have sex, that it can really be rather sweet. This is the point of view that Katie Roiphe—all of twenty-six years old—would dismiss from her vast experience as utopian.

Well, I don't think it is. I think the kind of sex I have de-

scribed is the kind of sex that lots and lots of people have. And it is one of the things that people like about having sex.

I come away from reading about this debate thinking, it's all so grim. Is sex really all that grim? You know, especially when you consider, if you believe these sexual surveys, women are having more pleasure in bed than they've had since they started trying to figure out women's sexual experience in some kind of a pseudoscientific way. And yet when you read all this you just think, it's all so grim and hateful, why would anybody bother?

They just have no sense of the subtlety of it all—that sex can be used to express a lot of different feelings. So you see, I'm still a romantic. I still believe in love.

Do you think that having a lighter or friendlier view of sex is part of having a left-wing political perspective?

No. I guess I think it's more individual than that. I've been very struck, as I go through life, to see how people's personal lives, while not immune to change for political reasons, come from a deeper place. If you look at the fathers that are involved with their children, I don't think you can say it's the Democrats, and not the Republicans. It's much more complicated. I think people's behavior has much less to do with their professed beliefs than is usually acknowledged.

But there's a great desire to preserve what we call traditional gender relations. And in their different ways, both the Camille Paglia-ites and the anti-pornography feminists do that. In each of these scenarios, men and women act in stereotypical fashion, don't they?

In the media, you see the women fighting about whether, as Mim Udovich quips, all sex is rape or all rape is sex, and then the man, the moderator, gets to come in and say, "But I love my wife." He gets to be the reasonable creature. It's a way of portraying feminism as a battle between competing mad notions.

Speaking of media portrayals of women, I especially liked your piece about the all-male Muppets.

Yes, it's amazing to think that it took twenty-five years for Sesame Street to have the idea that they should develop a female Muppet.

Who was the little girl who was in such despair when she found out Big Bird was a boy?

That was the daughter of a dear friend of mine—the same one who thought that her mother, who is a doctor, had to be a nurse.

One thing that is underarticulated about women in this country is that women are sexist, too. So you look at the credits on Sesame Street—there are women writers, the psychologist who advises them is a woman, the producer is a woman, too. A lot of sexism is unconscious; one thing that men and women have in common is that they hate women.

Do you think that aside from problems like the male Muppets, your daughter has escaped seeing herself as a lesser person because she's a girl?

Girls at her age are quite female-chauvinist, actually, I don't know how new that is. Just the way boys are—boys are very into being boys, and girls are very into being girls. But I have found that the kids in Sophie's class have an expectation of fairness between the genders that wasn't there before. So she'll say, "Do you love me?" And I'll say, "Of course I love you, all mothers love their daughters."And she'll say "and their sons." I didn't mean all mothers love their female children. But she will immediately pick that up and want it to be universal. And she's not the only kid like that. These kids also—they'll say that something's sexist. I've heard Sophie say, "Men, they all have to think they're so important." And it may surprise your readers, but I don't talk like that!

Where does she get it?

I have no idea. This is one of the things you discover when you have a child. They will come out with things and you have no idea where they came from. Often they have quite specific sources—something a friend said, something they heard on television, a story they read. But you don't know what that origin is. And suddenly it's like this little person is a radio station through which the culture is beaming itself.

What were your influences when you were growing up? Do you come from a family of writers?

No. My father was a lawyer, my mother sold real estate. My mother had wanted to be a writer, and I think because of that she was particularly encouraging. She was always finding poems and sending me poems when I was in summer camp, encouraging me to read, and sharing books with me and reading what I wrote with great interest. Both my parents were very encouraging. I was very lucky that way.

Did you start writing when you were very young?

Well, I started being interested in poetry when I was in about sixth grade. I always loved to write. And I used to come home from school and go up to my room and sit on my bed and write my poems. And I was writing angry letters to the newspaper.

Even when you were a kid?

Well, I recently came across a letter I had written when I was twelve years old to *The New York Times*. It was about some complicated legal case involving someone who was accused of being a spy, but I have absolutely no memory of writing this letter or what this case was. It was actually like something I would write today. I thought, oh my God, have I been doing this for that long?

So if it was someone accused of being a communist spy— was that partly your parents' concern with that case?

Oh, I'm sure it was. I was a child of the McCarthy era. These issues were very much in the air at our house.

What did your parents do during that time?

Well, I don't think they did anything very interesting, but I still feel uncomfortable talking about their politics. I will say that my father worked for the electrical workers' union—the more militant of the two electrical workers' unions—for a while. He had a number of dissident union cases, and cases related to the Smith Act, which in effect made it illegal to be a member of the Communist Party. And it was a very different world then. Victor Navasky's book *Naming Names* is a very good account of that era from the side of people who did give testimony and turn their friends in and all that. You come to understand how in a way that is not the case today, people felt that their lives, their identities, and their ability to exist depended on filling very narrow social roles.

Did you look at The Nation *when you were a kid?*

Yeah. My entire life has had *The Nation* in it. I can see those old issues with a few headlines in fat black type, sitting on my parents' dining-room table.

Do you feel like you are part of the same world that your parents were part of then?

No. I have a very different life from them. They had, for example, a very jolly group of friends, and politics were part of their social life in a way that is not true for me. And their politics brought them much more in contact with people from different social classes, whereas I tend to stay in my study. You know, it's funny because everyone has nothing but bad to say about the 1950s. But I think actually people had a lot more fun then. There were more parties. My friends and I are always wondering, why are there so few parties? I think people work harder now. And I think people lead more isolated lives than they did then.

Is your life the way you imagined it would be when you were a little girl?

That's an interesting question. In some ways, yes. I thought my life would be more exotic and exciting. I thought that more would be required. I imagined a life full of starker choices.

What do you mean by stark choices?

Well, if you grew up in the McCarthy era, one of the things that you would be constantly thinking about is, what would I do? Would I turn my friends in? Would I give in? You grow up and you learn no one is interested. Nobody's asking. And that's where the true irrelevance of politics becomes clear. I guess I shouldn't say that, because there are certainly a lot of people who have got in a lot of trouble with the Government for their politics. But I think that the one good idea that Herbert Marcuse had was the idea of repressive tolerance. American society has a very great capacity for absorbing protest and dissent. The Clinton Administration is a good example of that. The academy is another.

Your poetry is not political. I'm interested in those two parts of your life. Did you start out as a poet, and then how did you get sucked into the political writing?

Well, I always was a two-track writer. I always wrote poetry and prose. And the prose I started out writing was book reviews. I wrote many, many, many book reviews, storing up an enormous amount of bad karma for myself when I came out with a book. I did think, oh God, the knives will be sharpening all over America. So I reviewed books and I made a good portion of my living by doing this for all different kinds of magazines at all different levels of seriousness. But at a certain point I became tired of reviewing books. George Orwell said the really hard part of being a book reviewer is thinking of something to say about this very ordinary, not-that-interesting, run-of-the-mill book. At a certain point I was more interested in what I had to say than in the book I was reviewing. I started more and more using book reviews—as a kind of jumping-off place for my own reflections. And then at a certain point the book dropped out. And I started writing on my own.

How are your poetry and your politics related?

I have to say that I see poetry and political writing as rather different endeavors. What I want in a poem—one that I read or one that I write—is not an argument, it's not a statement, it has to do with language. I'm looking for a kind of energized, fresh, alive perception. The politics of the writer

seem to me—well, we can talk about it, but it's not what I care about most. I would say my favorite modern poet is Philip Larkin. You can't get much more conservative than that. But if you look beyond, okay, he loves Margaret Thatcher, what you get from him—besides amazing, memorable, alive language and the revitalization of traditional forms—is a picture of what it is like to live in England now that is quite moving and true. He puts a different political slant on it than I would. But to me it's much more interesting to read that than to read a poem with whose politics I would agree, but that doesn't have a lot of depth of language and imagination to it. There isn't that much political poetry that I find I even want to read once, and almost none that I would want to read again. A lot of it is aural poetry, too. I like the written form. I like the several layers of meaning on each other. I think that's much harder to do with aural poetry.

So the poetry you read and write is not best read aloud?

Oh, well, best for what? I love to hear poetry read out loud. And I always write with the ear in mind. But not just the ear. I don't write a poem in order to speak it out loud. I think poetry-readings have had the effect of encouraging poets to make their poems simpler—more like a little anecdote, more like a story that you would tell around the dinner table. Well, that's okay. I don't want to be too judgmental about this. But I think it has its limits. And I have the experience constantly of going to poetry readings, and I'll have the impression that this is really interesting. I like it. It's funny, it's good. Then when I find the book, the poem is just dead on the page. It's just not an interesting piece of writing. There is nothing going on. It is all put there by the performance, by the voice, by the story that the poem is telling. But nothing would have been lost had that poem been told as a little 300-word op-ed piece, or a paragraph in a letter. And for me, what I like about poetry is the verbal concentration and levels of meaning. A poem with only one level of meaning is not a very interesting poem.

Did your parents read a lot?

Oh, yes. They did. There were a lot of books at our house. But here's the thing, you know, my parents read poetry. They didn't read poetry like scholars. But they read Dylan Thomas and Shakespeare's sonnets and Keats and e. e. cummings. It was just there. They enjoyed it. Poetry has never been really popular, compared to, say, the novel. But I think the idea that you would just never approach it, that you would write it off completely because it was too difficult or refined, I think that is a new thing among the class of people who would read other serious books.

You wrote a column about being interviewed about Richard Nixon, in which you noted that you're almost al-

ways asked to comment on women's issues. Do you plan to continue to write about women or not?

Yes, I kind of left that open. These issues are very much on my mind. I believe that if I keep writing my column, eventually I will have written about every single facet of feminism since time began. No—I did enjoy writing about Nixon, the last real President. But, you know, at *The Nation* I have the only regular potential space for a feminist column. I am the only columnist who is at all interested in these subjects or even favors them strongly—well, that's a little too strong, but let's not forget Christopher Hitchens's pro-life column, which must always be mentioned. So I feel, well, this is my brief in life. If I don't do this, then that's that much less representation of feminism.

Kirsty Milne (review date 3 March 1995)

SOURCE: "Logical Liberator," in *New Statesman and Society*, Vol. 8, No. 342, March 3, 1995, pp. 37-8.

[*In the following review of* Reasonable Creatures, *Milne argues that Pollitt's essays about American political events have resonance for a British audience.*]

Call me insular or even truculent. But I've had enough of photogenic young US feminists disinventing date rape and rediscovering the tyranny of body image. So it's a comfort to meet Katha Pollitt, who wasn't born yesterday, who's read her Mary Wollstonecraft and her Germaine Greer, who knows that class exists as well as gender.

These essays, written for the *Nation,* the *New Yorker* and the *New York Times,* are cheeringly argumentative and heart-eningly accessible. No jargon, no ghastly Germanic abstractions: just funny, questioning comment on topics that even a benighted British audience can recognise. Lorena Bobbitt makes an appearance, and there's a stout defence of Hillary Clinton. Pollitt takes a *cause célèbre*—like the William Kennedy Smith rape trial or the Baby M surrogate mother case—and unpacks the trunk of assumptions that comes with it. She is living proof that journalism needn't be glib and feminism needn't be dull.

Of course there are cultural chasms. America's obsession with abortion means that Pollitt expends a lot of energy fending off the pro-life movement: one of her least successful pieces records attempts to converse with a man picketing a clinic near her office. But other topics that might seem alien to us have the chill of imminence about them.

"Foetal rights, Women's Wrongs" tracks the growing tendency to hold a pregnant woman responsible for damaging her baby with drugs or drink. In New York, signs warn expectant mothers off alcohol, and strangers tell pregnant women: "Don't you know you're poisoning your baby?" Pollitt cites the case of Jennifer Johnson, a Florida woman arrested after her baby tested positive for cocaine, and then charged with delivering drugs to a minor.

To Pollitt, this "focus on maternal behaviour" is just another way of blaming women. "How," she asks, "have we come to see women as the major threat to their newborns, and the womb as the most dangerous place a child will ever inhabit?" Blaming mothers, she argues, lets society off the hook (Jennifer Johnson sought help at a drug treatment programme, but was turned away). And fetishising foetuses conceals a lack of concern for real live children. Not to mention—she's brave enough to say it—real live women.

Pollitt is equally suspicious of paid "surrogate" motherhood, which she regards as "reproductive Reaganomics", degrading to the woman whose body is rented and to the child whose life is sold. "Contract maternity is not a way for infertile women to get children," she argues. "It is a way for men to get children." Surely this is confusing the power of men with the power of money. The danger is not so much that men will exploit women, but rather, as Pollitt suggests in a later essay, that the rich childless couple will exploit the single mother on welfare?

In general, Pollitt resists the temptation to paint women as victims—or as angels. She attacks what she terms "difference feminism" (the idea that women are inherently nicer, more peaceful and cooperative than men) and traces it back to Victorian notions of "separate spheres", and the comfort of moral superiority as a substitute for practical power.

And where are the men in this collection? They're here all right, in the guise of murdering husbands, absent fathers, sexist columnists, and patriarchal judges. Not as good guys, not as sons or brothers, not as the father and grandfather to whom Pollitt dedicates her book. It's a bit worrying when such a commonsense, articulate feminist has nothing to say about improving diplomatic relations with the other half of the human race.

Rickie Solinger (review date April 1995)

SOURCE: "First-Class Citizen," in *The Women's Review of Books*, Vol. XII, No. 7, April, 1995, pp. 1, 3.

[*In the following review of* Reasonable Creatures, *Solinger argues that Pollitt's strengths are her wide ranging knowledge and practical arguments.*]

In recent days I've had occasion to talk on the phone to a couple of women whom I've never met, an English professor in Pittsburgh and a newspaper reporter in Indianapolis. Even though the professor's work focuses on women and she's a regular reader of this review, and the journalist writes about women's issues, neither of them had heard of Katha Pollitt. I tried to take the news quietly in both cases, but I was shocked. And depressed.

It's no fun collecting proof of how difficult it is for the most brilliantly accessible and keenly perceptive feminist writer around to break into mass culture—of even feminist culture—in this country. Maybe it's that the essays of Katha Pollitt (who is also a distinguished poet) appear in venues that are too progressive (*The Nation,* where she writes a biweekly column, "Subject to Debate"), or too elitist (*The New Yorker*), or too provincial (*The New York Times!*), for most folks to come across them. If that's the case, then the publication of a collection of these essays is an event the old New York theatre critics would have called an occasion for shouting from the rooftops.

Katha Pollitt is simply a treasure and a beacon in beleaguered times, in part because her style draws so richly from camps that usually turn their backs on each other. She is, for example, a literary intellectual who is also a journalist—a "two-track" writer, she calls herself. Her lawyer-like method of argumentation sits harmoniously on the page with the poet's sharp sense of detail and language and wit. This arsenal is brought into the service of a feminist politics that is more optimistic and practical than visionary and revolutionary. In the essays collected in *Reasonable Creatures*, Pollitt argues that women in the United States are still not accorded full citizenship rights—economically, sexually, parentally, for example. Still, despite pervasive and entrenched misogyny, she makes the case that we shouldn't give up. The cause of gender equality can be furthered by honest, clear-sighted discussion and alliance-building, if these efforts are grounded in civil rights and civil libertarian values.

Pollitt begins with a severely stripped-down version of a feminist as "a person who answers 'yes' to the question, 'Are women human?'" Feminism, she goes on,

> is not about whether women are better than, worse than or identical with men. And it's certainly not about trading personal liberty—abortion, divorce, sexual self-expression—for social protection as wives and mothers, as pro-life feminists propose. It's about justice, fairness and access to the broad range of human experience. It's about women consulting their own well-being and being judged as individuals rather than as members of a class with one personality, one social function, one road to happiness. It's about women hav-

ing intrinsic value as persons rather than contingent value as a means to an end for others: fetuses, children, the "family," men.

Clearly, Pollitt is the kind of feminist who thinks essentialism has nothing to offer women and plenty to offer those who prefer their females nurturing, if second-class, citizens.

Most of the nineteen essays in *Reasonable Creatures* first appeared in *The Nation,* where Pollitt's charge is to write about what she terms "so-called women's issues." Coursing across such timely topics as menopause, male violence against women, affirmative action, the right-to-life movement—as well as explaining why Germaine Greer is not now and never was the feminist she's cracked up to be—Pollitt tests public policies and public discussion about these issues against her humane notions of feminism. And in the process she appears to imagine that her reader is both an ordinary person and a thinking person. Whether she's plumbing the misogyny of "family values" talk, or considering what's wrong with excusing some men for slapping their wives around occasionally while branding the more sensational perpetrators monsters, Pollitt counts on readers to be able to hold a couple of ideas in their minds at one time, stand up to a paradox, look a vulgar contradiction straight in the eye but refuse to look a gift horse in the mouth, and follow a sound analogy wherever it may lead.

One particularly rich and shapely essay in the collection, **"Why I Hate Family Values,"** was written in 1992, not long after Murphy Brown gave birth and Dan Quayle had a fit about it. Pollitt uses the surreal outburst of our most sit-com-like Veep to plumb the agenda of "family values" proponents in order to show how those folks cloak their reactionary fears and frustrations in pious moralisms, then set out to condemn and punish the ones they've labelled immoral and dangerous transgressors—chiefly poor women.

Pollitt often places herself at her young daughter's birthday party, or at the day-care center, or in the basement laundry room of her Upper West Side New York apartment building as she begins to dig into the weighty cultural and political issues of our times. We can identify, right off the bat: you don't have to be a policy wonk to see what's happening out there. This time, Katha is driven to the TV and parturient Murphy Brown out of sheer exhaustion from having read her little daughter umpteen volumes of the Berenstain Bears (the most moralistic series of contemporary books for tots, as it happens).

It doesn't take Pollitt long to move from TV-land to the heart of the matter—that in the days after the infamous episode, Quayle wasn't really expressing concern about women like Murphy Brown (or Brown "herself," alas!). He was, as Pollitt puts it, railing about "inner-city women who will be encouraged to produce out-of-wedlock babies by Murph's example—the trickle-down theory of values." But even this expression, Pollitt shows, is a cover for a deeper anxiety and preoccupation: that is, the enormous hostility festering in the culture toward changing social relations in the late twentieth century, in the US and elsewhere. "Family values" flag-wavers express their unhappiness about high rates of teen sexuality, single motherhood, open homosexuality, non-marital cohabitation, divorce and abortion (and the ungodly individuals creating these trends) as a simple, all-American matter of morality, immorality and righteous punishment, but that, too, is a cover. What they really can't stand is the assault on patriarchal traditions these trends represent.

Pollitt offers a number of alternative explanations for the behaviors "family values" proponents love to hate, explanations that have nothing to do with immorality and a lot to do with rationality, demographics and feminism—including one for a "behavior" that she is personally familiar with, divorce. Despite some shoddy but high-profile studies of the effects of divorce on children, Pollitt argues that divorce is a good idea when marriage turns bad, *especially* for children, who, common-sense tells us, do not flourish in loveless, joyless, sometimes violent family settings. The "family values" folks don't want to hear any of this. Instead they persist in "trying to put the new wine of modern personal relations in the old bottles of the sexual double standard and lifelong miserable marriage."

Along the way, Pollitt does what she does best. She makes her argument without reluctance to criticize moralizers of all political stripes, Right, Left and center. Nor is she reluctant to get personal with the material on hand. As a conscientious and principled and divorced mother of a young child, she personally does not appreciate the moralistic preachments of politicians, psychiatrists, or liberal columnists, targeting and besmirching her and her kind.

And speaking of her kind, Pollitt is clear about that, too. She regularly makes appropriate distinctions that few other media commentators bother with—like class distinctions. In this same essay, she draws attention to the perniciousness and stupidity of using Murphy Brown to stand for unwed mothers:

> The handful of forty something professionals like Murphy Brown who elect to have a child without a male partner have little in common with the millions of middle-and working-class divorced mothers who find themselves in desperate financial straits because their husbands fail to pay court-awarded child support. And

neither category has much in common with inner-city girls like those a teacher friend of mine told me about the other day . . . impregnated by boyfriends twice their age and determined to keep their babies . . . to have someone to love who loves them in return.

Here as elsewhere, Pollitt uses her resources to great effect, quoting Samuel Johnson as easily and aptly as she refers to Christopher Lasch, a whole raft of social scientists, or the Berenstain Bears.

In the end, Pollitt is perfectly clear about what she calls this "confusion of moral preachments with practical solutions to social problems." Getting as practical as one can, she points out that what ails the family in contemporary America has very little to do with values at all, and a lot to do with money—too little of it to sustain stable households in too many cases. In her most characteristic no-nonsense fashion, she concludes with a prescription: "Instead of moaning about 'family values' we should be thinking about how to provide the poor with decent jobs and social services, and about how to insure economic justice for working women. And let marriage take care of itself."

I particularly like the piece called **"Lorena's Army,"** which begins, "I didn't watch much of Lorena Bobbitt's trial. I was too busy trying to locate the hordes of feminists who, according to the media, were calling her a heroine and touting penis removal as a revolutionary act. Where were these people?" I am also very fond of the way Pollitt, a mom who has vowed never to lift a hand to her own daughter, delivers a much-deserved spanking to little Miss Katie Roiphe for "careless and irresponsible" behavior, due to the fact that "she has not done her homework" on the subject of sexual violence. These two essays and others are sharply critical of the insidious absurdities involved in the quite common impulse in our culture to pity, for example, small-breasted, or unmarried, women, as losers and victims, out to decry the use of the victim label when it's applied to women who have been grossly underpaid or denied job promotions, or raped or beaten or murdered by their male mates.

Only one pair of essays left me wondering what Katha Pollitt really thinks: **"Why We Read: Canon to the Right of Me . . . "** and **"The Smurfette Principle."** In the first, Pollitt reviews the opposing briefs of the Great Books mavens and the multiculturalists, and concludes:

> Something is being overlooked: the state of reading, and books, and literature in our country at this time. Why, ask yourself, is everyone so hot under the collar about what to put on the required-reading shelf? It is because while we have been arguing so fiercely about

which books make the best medicine, the patient has been slipping deeper and deeper into a coma.

The trajectory and the effect of literature is not, she argues, essentially political. So college reading lists should be made up without undue reference to the gender or race of authors, but with primary reference to "the subtle, delicate, wayward and individual, not to say private" way that books affect us. And college students will be better off.

My relation to literature may be less protoplasmic than Pollitt's. Still, I can grant her its subtle and delicate effects. But why, I must ask, does she see "the text" as so much more authoritative and so much more potentially destructive for the preschool set she writes about in **"The Smurfette Principle"** than for their post-secondary sisters and brothers clawing their way, in the wilderness, toward personhood? I agree that parents of young children need reminding that "sexism in preschool culture deforms both boys and girls." But I'm pretty sure that it functions that way for big boys and girls, too.

In the churlish tradition of saving the best for last and then withholding its full pleasures, I will tease readers who haven't feasted on Pollitt's work in *The Nation* by hinting that the juiciest piece in this collection is the Virginia Woolf-inspired essay, **"Marooned on Gilligan's Island: Are Women Morally Superior to Men?"** As I recall, this essay sparked quite a lot of barbed debate in the letters column of *The Nation,* and I imagine it would do the same among readers of these pages. Read it and exult—or gnash your teeth!

I love Katha Pollitt's essays partly because I just about always agree with her. Even more important, I can depend on her to sharpen my thinking and beef up my own arguments. But even if I don't have a functional use for a given essay, each one of them, and the collection altogether, are like gold, because Pollitt consistently pulls off this amazing feat—making essay after essay out of arguments as pointed as they are smart, elegantly shaped, good-humored and zestful. Here's hoping that all the feminists in Pittsburgh and Indianapolis, Atlanta and Topeka, from California to the New York island, buy this book, read it, and pass it on.

Boyd Zenner (review date Spring 1995)

SOURCE: "A Female Opinionmeister," in *Belles Lettres*, Vol. 10, No. 2, Spring, 1995, pp. 19, 26.

[*In the following review, Zenner, an editor at the University Press of Virginia, provides an overview of the topics addressed in* Reasonable Creatures.]

Not too long ago, Katha Pollitt devoted one of her semi-monthly *Nation* columns to a somewhat rueful consideration of why women commentators are so seldom asked to provide analysis on nongender-specific topics. "Am I being too cynical in arguing that female opinionmeisters specialize in women's issues partly as cultural adaptation?" she wondered. I can only say, hooray for cultural adaptation if that is what it took to steer Pollitt into the roiling waters of feminist social criticism. We certainly need her.

Both for those already familiar with Pollitt's work and for those coming to it for the first time, *Reasonable Creatures: Essays on Women and Feminism* will confirm her standing as one of the most incisive, principled, and articulate cultural critics writing today. The 19 essays collected here—all written over the course of the last decade, in response to a variety of contemporary provocations—investigate not only sexism, but also racism and class bias, slipshod research techniques, and the media complicity, all of which lie at the root of many of the skewed images of female "reality" that confront us every day.

The book gets off to a running start with **"*That* Survey: Being Wedded is Not Always Bliss."** Surely you remember "that survey": the one purporting to show, as Pollitt tells us, "that as single women grow older their 'chances' of marrying descend as precipitously as the tracks of the Man Who Skied Down Mount Everest." Dispensing with the survey itself as an exercise in outmoded demographics (recognizing, for example, only the categories of "married" and "single," and based solely on census findings), Pollitt focuses her attention on the haste with which the media snapped up the study, decided to interpret its findings as a sinister new trend (when, in fact, as Pollitt convincingly shows, they indicate nothing of the sort), and crafted from them a full-scale condemnation of the "failure" of feminism.

The critique of journalistic ethics continues in a strong piece on "media wilding" over the William Kennedy Smith rape trial. "I drink, I swear, I flirt, I tell dirty jokes," Pollitt announces in the opening paragraph. She continues:

> *I have also, at various times, watched pornographic videos, had premarital sex, and sunbathed topless in violation of local ordinances. . . .There are other things, too, and if I should ever bring rape charges against a rich, famous, powerful politician's relative,* The New York Times *will probably tell you all about them—along with, perhaps, my name. Suitably adorned with anonymous quotes, these revelations will enable you, the public, to form your own opinion: Was I asking for trouble, or did I just make the whole thing up?*

Pollitt rejects the specious rationale put forward for revealing the Palm Beach woman's name: anonymous charges are "un-American," everyone already knew who the woman was anyway, naming the victim will eliminate the "stigma" of rape. Apparently, she points out, these compelling arguments are nullified when the victim is an upper-middle-class white woman and the attackers a band of lower-income black youths, as in the Central Park jogger case:

> *That anonymity is held to be essential to the public good in a wide variety of cases but is damned in the Palm Beach case shows that what the media is concerned with is not the free flow of information or the public good. . . . What is at stake is the media's status, power, and ability to define and control information in accordance with the views of those who run the media. . . . The jogger could have been the daughter of the men who kept her name out of the news. But William Kennedy Smith could have been their son.*

Disgust over race- and class-based inequities also suffuses Pollitt's discussion of procreation-for-hire arrangements, such as those revealed in the Baby M and Baby Boy Johnson cases, which are examined in separate chapters here. For low-income women, Pollitt contends, surrogacy fees can offer an incentive so powerful that it supersedes good judgment, leaving them open to exploitation as geese capable of laying golden eggs.

The same economic disparity that makes such arrangements possible works against the surrogate in custody cases—particularly those involving principals of different races. Why do childless couples elect surrogacy when adoption is infinitely less problematic? Pollitt speculates that it may be because

> *. . . genetic determinism is having one of its periods of scientific fashion [no kidding!], fueling the fear that an adopted baby will never 'really' be yours. At the same time, hardening class distinctions make the poor, who provide most adoptive babies, seem scary and doomed: What if junior took after his birth parents?*

It is clear that for Pollitt being a feminist critic means criticizing feminists along with everyone else.

She rebukes middle-class professional women who, identifying themselves as feminists, rush to disavow images of passivity, helplessness, and irrationality, forgetting that many working-class and poor women are trapped in economic circumstances that rob them of agency. The insistence upon seeing themselves as possessors of complete free will and self-determination, Pollitt believes, may also

invite women to embrace the "intellectually flabby" arguments of difference feminism. In **"Marooned on Gilligan's Island,"** she chides difference feminism proponents Carol Gilligan and Deborah Tannen for faulty research methodology, and scoffs at the notion of women as the only true repositories of nurturing and nonviolence. While representing itself as something new, she argues, difference feminism is nothing more than a return to the hoary Victorian separate-spheres concept, and in the end pits women against women: "nurturers" versus "traitors."

The volume's concluding chapter, **"Fetal Rights, Women's Wrongs,"** is a passionate condemnation of women-as-walking-wombs concept upon which both public policy and private belief are too often founded. Touching on issues ranging from legally enforced (and sometimes fatal) pregnancy to the Johnson Controls fetal-protection policy case, Pollitt issues a stern reprimand to those who would infantilize or objectify women, or place their concerns in artificial opposition to their children's—even, in the case of Johnson Controls, to their theoretical children's. The argument interweaves several of Pollitt's recurrent themes: the public repercussions of racism and class antagonism, the pathologizing of women's biological functions, and the media sexism that helps to disseminate negative stereotypes. It is one of the best essays in the book.

There is neither time nor space enough here to enumerate all the many merits of *Reasonable Creatures*. Pollitt's graceful style and frequent flashes of real wit are reason enough for rejoicing, but even more impressive is the fact that they never obscure the power and urgency of what she has to say. But do not take my word for it: Get hold of this book and see for yourself.

Christine Stansell (review date Spring 1995)

SOURCE: "An Opinionated Woman," in *Dissent*, Vol. 42, No. 2, Spring, 1995, pp. 280-83.

[*In the following review of* Reasonable Creatures, *Stansell discusses Pollitt's unique contributions to feminist writing.*]

Holding opinions is a treacherous business for a woman. Shrill! Silly! Imprecations and accusations lurk at the edges of life and female psychology, fueling prejudices and women's own self-censorship. Feminist writer Naomi Wolf recently called attention to how little women's opinions figure in our op-ed pages, journals, public affairs shows, and columns, all "strikingly immune to the general agitation for female access." Gender socialization, suggests Wolf—both what men expect of women and what women expect of themselves—undermines the boldness and self-assertion necessary to a strong public voice.

Opinionated women, it is true, too often still register as in over their heads, presumptuous in proportion to how far they venture outside their proven expertise in matters of personal life. Reading any of the tiny number of female opinion journalists who have succeeded, you sense their difficulties in claiming full authority, the temptation to take refuge in a more palatable domestic identity. In Anna Quindlen, the most successful of the circle, the tendency to evoke the accouterments of conventional femininity is chronic: the kids, the husband, the concern for the needy, the note of girlish pleading. But even in a tough, funny writer like Barbara Ehrenreich, the domestic voice has intruded over the years, the evocation of children's foibles and a comic domestic chaos, as if Jean Kerr were a ghost that couldn't be quite banished.

Katha Pollitt's gift has been an ability to move beyond these limitations and, in doing so, to create a newly imagined space for opinionated women. Both the charming girl and the wacky mom are absent from Pollitt's self-presentation. What emerges rhetorically is rather a fierce female intellectual, unapologetically feminist and utterly intrepid. Pollitt never pulls her punches: as you may note after a moment's reflection, that is rare among women in life as well as in print. As she notes in an aside in an essay reprinted in the collection *Reasonable Creatures,* "[w]e are in a transition period, in which many women were raised with modest expectations and much emphasis on the need to please others." In her columns in the *Nation,* she reminds readers how much more women might reasonably expect for themselves. She also shows how much fun a woman can have when she jettisons, at least literarily, the need to please.

A book composed of columns constitutes something of a contradiction. These pieces derive their energy from their immediacy; they are not expository or reflective but rather served as fuel for fires burning at the time. Fresh from your argument, you read a Pollitt column and, still sizzling with what you might have said, appropriate her thoughts as ammunition for your next encounter. Ferocious, canny, Pollitt is both inspiration and reinforcement for the mundane, bumbling argumentative self. It is this imaginative relationship between writer and reader that led Wolf, after Pollitt's devastating attack on some current piece of antifeminist palaver, to call her a national treasure.

But by the same token, the essays do not always fare well over time. Passions of the moment fade and the specifics of the controversies become blurry. What was the Baby M case all about? What, exactly, was all the fuss about middle-aged single women not finding husbands? Who was Hedda

Nussbaum? In preparing the columns for publication. Pollitt took care to choose those involving issues that resonate beyond the moment—antifeminism, reproductive ethics, sexual abuse. But inevitably her treatment of these deeper concerns is limited by tying them to events that, given the dizzying pace of the news, can seem passé and even, to younger readers, incomprehensible. *Reasonable Creatures* does develop certain lines of argument—Pollitt's concern with an emergent rhetoric of fetal rights, her ongoing broadside against media scandalizing about women, a militant assertion of the value of women's sexual and economic independence. Readers who know little about feminism, however, will not necessarily find an entree here, since there is no systematic exposition of feminist politics.

What does unify the essays is a luminous voice inflected with a distinct generational sensibility. Politically, Pollitt carries on a line of feminist thinking intermeshed with the democratic left, a long tradition revivified by that wing of the women's liberation movement that came out of the 1960s with its ties to the New Left frayed but unbroken. A hallmark of this democratic feminism has been, since the nineteenth century, its resistance to moralistic notions about the supposedly distinct, higher nature of women and their essential differences from men. Pollitt gives a sound drubbing to updated versions of the nobility of Woman rendered by thinkers like Carol Gilligan as a universal ethic of female care giving and pacific inclinations. Always Pollitt insists on the sexes' shared nature as "reasonable creatures"—the phrase of Mary Wollstonecraft that gives the collection its title. What Wollstonecraft described as a determination "to see women neither heroines nor brutes" sets Pollitt's brand of militance aside from other strains of feminism. It inoculates her both to the special pleading for women which can mark a liberal like Anna Quindlen and to the melodramatizing of female innocence perpetrated by radicals like Catherine Mackinnon.

But neither does Pollitt give any quarter to the wishful thinking, now fashionable among neoliberals, that confuses sexual egalitarianism as a political goal with a description of life as we know it, if only feminist demagogues would cease to brainwash women. *Reasonable Creatures* is imbued with an awareness of all the structural constraints that militate against women's claiming a full humanity, an understanding of how sexual inequality gets tangled up with economics and class. Traces of a dialogue with Marxism are apparent, not in any ideological language but in an edginess to Pollitt's interest in how the class system breeds a misogyny that eventually bears down on all women. The pieces on surrogate motherhood are a fine instance of how Pollitt can fuse an argument about the exploitation of working-class women with one about the travails of their more privileged sisters. Surrogacy—"checkbook motherhood" is Pollitt's term, rendered with characteristic tartness—is one outcome of an economic system that makes many women so financially hard-pressed that the pittance they are paid for bearing a child seems attractive. "Like all domestic labor performed for pay," Pollitt concludes bitingly, "house-cleaning, baby-sitting, prostitution—childbearing in the marketplace becomes disreputable work performed by suspect marginal people. The priceless task [of pregnancy] turns out to have a price after all: about $1.50 an hour." But what about the infertile women whom these gestational mothers help? Pollitt follows out this objection to the end and reminds us, damningly, that the contracting parties in surrogacy arrangements are not a pregnant woman and an adoptive mother but a pregnant woman and a monied man, the sperm donor, who uses her to preserve his genetic inheritance. "Contract maternity is not a way for infertile women to get children . . . it is a way for men to get children."

At the heart of Pollitt's thought is a critique of the family, developed by the old politics of women's liberation and elaborated by twenty-five years of subsequent left-wing feminism. This view, bolstered and expanded by the very best of feminist history and social science, has been under attack for the duration, subjected to calumnies so intense that even the most militant are prone, at times, to advertise our own domestic successes as protection against the assumption that anyone who adheres to "that" kind of feminism must despise children and detest men. One of the thrills of reading Pollitt is her refusal to trim her sails with these winds. **"Why I Hate Family Values"** is a memorable contribution on this score. Here she makes the *au courant* gesture toward her own cozy nest—the essay begins with her reading her daughter a bedtime story—but charmingly subverts it by informing readers that she has recently separated from her husband. No *angst* for the newly single mother. "The family-value advocates would doubtless say that my husband and I made a selfish choice. . . . But I am still waiting for someone to explain why it would be better for my daughter to grow up in a joyless household." She goes on to connect the wave of middle-class breast-beating over divorce and single-parent families with a politics that, on the bottom line, is about the perfidies of vulnerable women. "Family values and the cult of the nuclear family is, at bottom, just another way to bash women, especially poor women. If only they would get married and stay married, society's ills would vanish."

Pollitt's forte is to use this understanding of sexual politics to slash through some controversy shrouded in liberal piety and obfuscation. It is perhaps her proximity to literary and publishing circles in New York City, where she lives, that makes her so shrewd about the eagerness of an enlightened media to sponsor old misogynist myths repackaged as modern sexual *realpolitik*. She has almost a second sense about the wiles of a culture that dishes out equality

with a vengeance, formally acknowledging feminist goals yet reproducing social inequalities of gender in ever more duplicitous ways. A delightful piece on the *New York Times*'s decision to publish the name of the victim in the Palm Beach rape trial of William Kennedy Smith is a good example. Why *not* name the woman? she inquires rhetorically and proceeds to lay out the arguments for "fair play" and dismantle them piece by piece. Would not naming rape victims remove the stigma from rape? She crowns her investigation of this particular instance of equality-with-a-vengeance with a dead-on, baleful gaze at the male narcissism and cant that inform it. "One also has to wonder," she muses, "about the urgency with which . . . male proponents of the antistigma theory, with no history of public concern for women, declare themselves the best judge of women's interests and advocate a policy of which they themselves will never have to bear the consequences."

For all that Pollitt is very much a woman of her generation, it is one of her virtues never to look back. Years of conservative reaction have made her feisty and smart rather than morose and maundering. She has created a persona of a middle-aged feminist as beguiling, dashing and cheerful—quite a feat amid a climate so hostile to such personages. The writer drops enough hints about herself to allow readers to sketch in more: an adoring mother of a treasured daughter, unembarrassed user of Clairol to wash out the gray hairs, passionate feminist who counts both men and women as friends.

Pollitt is also a fine poet, too little heard from lately. Years ago she asked in a poem, "What if a woman / is not the moon or the sea?" *Reasonable Creatures* is an exploration of the territory outside metaphor and myth where the value of a woman's life is its own measure.

Suzanne Rhodenbaugh (review date Spring-Summer 1995)

SOURCE: "Opinion Pieces, The Third Sex, and Feminism's Tent," in *Salmagundi*, Nos. 106-7, Spring-Summer, 1995, pp. 288-96.

[*In the following review of* Reasonable Creatures, *Rhodenbaugh considers Pollitt's feminist rhetoric, claiming that Pollitt favors the rights of women over the needs of children.*]

Katha Pollitt's *Reasonable Creatures: Essays on Women and Feminism* is not a book of essays, but a collection of opinion pieces. Its nineteen inclusions, thirteen of which first appeared in *The Nation*, with the balance in *The New York Times* or *The New Yorker*, read like op-ed takes on issues such as abortion, surrogate motherhood, rape and menopause, particularly as those issues have come to the forefront in recent news stories, court cases, books and articles.

Pollitt is not the first commentator and will not be the last to collect editorials and call them essays: that's neither here nor there. Nor is topicality necessarily a limitation. A current topic may be the provocation for an essay, but not constitute the bounds of what is explored or discovered. Temporality is at issue, though, for these commentaries mean to win arguments on specific contemporary questions. Had I read them in daily newspapers or weekly magazines—the contexts in which they were first published—they would have served for interrupting the flux of information and helping me make meaning of news. That's the nature of opinion pieces: they contribute to the stream of ideas and perspectives out of which we come to at least qualified or provisional understandings. I enjoy and value them, but almost never save them to re-read, just as I relish Mark Shields' weekly political commentary on the MacNeil-Lehrer Newshour on public television, but have never heard anything so memorable as to cause me to order a videotape of the program.

From essays, I want more. I want language I can savor, insights which leap the bounds of their purported topics, all in all a reading experience to which I'd want to return. I want, in short, some measure of timelessness.

The only one of these commentaries to which I'd return is **"Why We Read: Canon to the Right of Me . . . ,"** where Pollitt eschews all extremes in the debate over literary canon, and points out the irony of the debate itself, given that we are less and less a nation of readers, and that the canon war treats literature as a medicinal, good primarily for forming whatever character any given advocate prefers. It's a commonsensical piece of writing, and an interesting one, and it seems no accident that it also happens to be the only one in this book where she's not writing from any ism. I hear in **"Why We Read"** the poet who wrote *Antarctic Traveller*, I wish I'd heard her more often.

For the reader for whom the distinction between essay and opinion piece is less important, a second broad reaction to *Reasonable Creatures* may be to ask, what is it to be a feminist? As I understand the term, it is to be not only committed to equity for women, but also to analyze events, situations, trends, issues, ideas and artistic expressions in terms of their effects on, and assumptions about, the one-half of the human race which is female. Feminism came out of the consciousness that half the human race was missing or greatly diminished in the world's reckonings.

Feminism can thus be both a corrective and an enlarger of vision. It brings to visibility, and therefore puts within the bounds of caring, those aspects of life significantly affected by gender as it is played out in the economic-social-political matrix. Like the civil rights movement, which brought to consciousness the racial concomitants of experience, feminism changed our calculations: it required consideration of how women affect and are affected.

Like any perspective identifiably delimited by a condition or class less inclusive than human, it keeps its focus on its affected class of persons, its constituency. This is its strength as a basis for organizing and legal gains, and to the extent feminism is a social and political movement, it cannot do otherwise. As a stance or mode of analysis, however, feminism's focus is also its limitation. Because it makes primary *effect on women,* it necessarily makes secondary other classes and conditions of humanness.

This makes particularly problematic what appears to be Pollitt's project in *Reasonable Creatures*. She says she wants women to be seen as "human beings . . . no more, no less," wants them to be seen, in the language of Mary Wollstonecraft from which she draws her title, as "neither heroines nor brutes, but reasonable creatures"; but she wants to do this via commentary on matters often painted as "women's issues," and from a vantage point where effect on women is the primary concern. The project seems internally contradictory or oxymoronic, for the book doesn't instance or ask for a gender-neutral or supra-gender—a merely human—response to events and issues. Rather, it insistently asks that we make effect on women the overwhelmingly important consideration across a range of human dilemmas.

Here, those dilemmas arise most painfully with respect to what we might call the third sex: children. They cannot be posed as foil for women, as men sometimes are; they cannot be posed as negator or oppressor, because they are the least culpable of the three sexes; yet because their potential being or actual being can negate or oppress women, they intersect with, even constitute, the crucible or crux of the hardest dilemmas.

That men are equal partners in conceiving children, and should be equal partners in raising them, and that societal conditions bear disproportionately on women, does not change the facts that only women bear children; that the "disposition" of a born child is also disproportionately in a woman's province, because the male partner may or may not be present; and that therefore a sexually active heterosexual female is faced, a large part of her lifespan, with decisions and conditions which greatly affect her own freedom, *and* affect fetuses, babies, and children. This is not fair, but it's the biological ground it seems must be acknowledged, if feminism's tent is to be raised on it. This acknowledgment, in turn, would seem to require granting the acuteness of the moral and psychic pain in the choices women must make, their heavier responsibility for those choices, and the inevitable effects on the third sex.

Pollitt seems to downplay the pain, the responsibility, and the effects on the third sex. I feel this to be so even though I agree in large part with her on the implications for the legal status of women and public policy. Her emphases, and the routes she takes to her conclusions, are what I find off-putting, and to the extent they represent a feminist analysis, I think they may help explain why many women are outside feminism's tent.

In **"Children of Choice,"** for example, Pollitt asks, "If the fetus is a person, how can its life be less important than a woman's liberty and pursuit of happiness?" and answers, "The fact is, when your back is against the wall of unwanted pregnancy, it doesn't matter whether or not you think the fetus is a person." Her answer rings true to me experientially, and yet it closes the book on the moral question without ever having engaged it. Abortion may be the toughest, least answerable human dilemma, and I can't fault anyone for wanting to avoid it and/or give the pragmatist's or relativist's answer, but I would point out that abortion is not about *either* "women's bodies, family planning and sexual freedom," in Pollitt's formulation, *or* "babies' lives": it's about both. That's the very reason it's such a wrenching issue. And when the moral dilemma it presents is ignored or downplayed as inconsequential, those who feel the dilemma acutely may be shut out of the field of respect and concern. What's more, the commentator is left preaching to the converted.

In fact Pollitt goes beyond not granting the fullness of the dilemma: she also uses reductionist language and ad hominem argument, most notably in the throw-away journalism of **"Our Right-to-Lifer: The Mind of an Antiabortionist,"** where she makes a "not very intelligent" "religious fanatic," a picket outside a New York abortion clinic, the stand-in cipher for marginalizing those opposed to abortion.

The overriding importance to Pollitt of the effect on women is not at all limited to the abortion debate, however. It holds true as well in circumstances where fetuses are now admittedly "babies," as in **"Fetal Rights, Women's Wrongs,"** where she argues against legal and economic penalties against women who endanger their babies during gestation, as by alcohol and drug abuse. Here again I find myself agreeing with the legal implications of her argument, yet put off, even appalled, at the route and thrust of that argument.

She ably points out the impossibility of determining the exact antecedents to a baby's health, noting that the father's behavior during and after conception, and environmental impacts, affect the baby as well as the mother's behavior. Yet it seems a mistake to call maternal behavior during pregnancy "a relatively small piece of the total picture," going so far as to say prenatal care is "much more important."

In the face of horrific effects on children born addicted to crack or heroin or damaged by fetal alcohol syndrome, and the consequent destruction of whole communities, Pollitt's focus on women is too narrow:

> . . . what fetal rights is really about—controlling women. It's a reaction to legalized abortion and contraception, which has given women, for the first time in history, real reproductive power.

She also poses a false choice here: concern for women and other members of a community, such as those on Indian reservations devastated not only by alcoholism, but also by violence, poverty and other social ills, *versus* the "fetal rights" of those who will be born into such communities. In taking to task Michael Dorris, who wrote in *The Broken Cord* of the damage done his adopted son Adam by fetal alcohol syndrome, she asks:

> Why is it so hard for us to see that the tragedy of Adam Dorris is inextricable from the tragedy of his mother? Why is her loss—to society, to herself—so easy to dismiss?

I don't believe the people most closely involved in addressing poverty and related social ills *do* dismiss an Adam Dorris' birthmother, or fail to see that the tragedies are inextricable. Black community leaders and Indian tribal leaders are fully aware of the depth and complexity of those tragedies, and their interrelatedness; their frustration is in trying to devise interventions that could lead to change.

But possible solutions are not in Pollitt's bailiwick. She operates more like a lawyer, carving out areas of legal protection and entitlement for women, and deflecting responsibility for solutions to a distant "society" or "the government." In **"Fetal Rights, Women's Wrongs"** she's so compelling on the logical and practical impossibilities of codifying sanctions against women for behaviors during pregnancy, that we almost lose sight of the problems which engendered the discussion in the first place. We almost forget to ask, i.e., what *about* those addicted babies, those alcohol-damaged babies, some of whom are also HIV positive?

Pollitt doesn't address them, having "won," through persuasion, what seems a logical if pyrrhic victory for their mothers: the right not to be punished for, or constricted from, the heavy drinking and drug use which damage their babies—and themselves.

In commentaries on two surrogate motherhood cases, the primacy Pollitt puts on *effect on women,* as opposed to children, is most strikingly developed. In **"Contracts and Apple Pie: the Strange Case of Baby M,"** she argues against surrogate motherhood (which she rightly points out should be called "contract motherhood" in this case, since Mary Beth Whitehead was indisputably the biological mother of Baby M). Her rhetorical strategy is to answer ten "blatantly foolish things being said in support" of contract motherhood. Under the ninth of these answers, on parts of the sixteenth and seventeenth pages of this eighteen page commentary, she finally gets around to effects on children—the contract mother's other children, and the message they get when their mother bears a child for pay, and, at last, the child born of such an arrangement:

> And, of course, there is the contract baby. To be sure, there are worse ways of coming into the world, but not many, and none that are elaborately prearranged by sane people. Much is made of the so-called trauma of adoption, but adoption is a piece of cake compared with contracting.

I happen to agree with Pollitt in her opposition to contract motherhood, and I also think there was a case to be made for both sides of this custody dispute: for Mary Beth Whitehead, and for the biological father and his wife, William and Elizabeth Stern. But it also seems to me the welfare of the living child should have been the preeminent concern. Yet by Pollitt's strategy of argument, the child is treated as the offproduct of a dispute significant foremost for its effect on women. It apparently seemed reasonable to her to discuss effect on women first, and the baby more as afterthought. What's more, she never addresses the welfare of Baby M, never tackles whether Mary Beth Whitehead *should* have gotten full custody.

In **"Checkbook Maternity: When is a Mother Not a Mother?"** Pollitt comments on a case wherein a child was conceived in vitro by his biological parents, and transplanted into a "gestational surrogate" for gestation and birth. The judge denied Anna Johnson, the gestational surrogate, visitation rights. While opposing the legality of surrogacy, Pollitt nevertheless favors Johnson's visitation rights:

> Recent court decisions (not to mention social customs like open adoption, blended families and gay and lesbian parenting) have tended to respect a widening circle of adult relationships with children. . . . Given the increasing number of children living outside the classic

nuclear-family arrangement, and the equanimity with which courts divide them up among competing adults, it seems rather late in the day to get all stuffy about Anna Johnson.

But Pollitt by her argument seems to share in that equanimity. Never mind that the young child might be confused or hurt, to understate the matter, by a court-ordered relationship with a woman who rented herself for his gestation and birth, but whom he otherwise did not know. Pollitt not only ignores the psychological import for this child, she even manages to twist Johnson's wish for visitation rights into an imperative for the child: "The children of surrogates—even nongenetic surrogates like Anna Johnson—have the right to know the women through whose body and through whose efforts they came into the world."

In the next-to-last paragraph of this commentary Pollitt does get around, if not to this particular child, then to effect on children-in-the-abstract: surrogacy "degrades children by commercializing their creation." She also notes that harm may be done the surrogate's other children. But her primary concern remains, as elsewhere, effect on women:

> The most important and distressing aspect of Judge Parslow's decision . . . is that it defines, or redefines, maternity in a way that is thoroughly degrading to women.

It does so, she argues, by treating the gestational surrogate as a mere womb, a mere environment, and ignoring the mother-child ties she simply asserts are inevitably created when a woman carries a child to term. The very thing Johnson decided to do: rent her womb, Pollitt objects to being characterized as renting her womb. She also makes much of Johnson's status as a low-income black woman, and the potential for victimization of the already-victimized by surrogacy arrangements.

Yet her focus on how maternity is "defined" seems to spin off very far from the reaches of the real, and finally to have little to do with either Anna Johnson's life or this child's life. It's a very abstract, perhaps identifiably "feminist" kind of concern, this "how maternity is defined." A reasonable person might contend that the judge in this case did not invent or promote gestational surrogacy, or wish to define or redefine maternity, but *was* faced with a decision about a particular real child's best interests, and made his ruling based on that concern. For reasons I cannot fathom, that is apparently anathema to Pollitt.

Her real claim to "reasonableness" in *Reasonable Creatures* may reside, all said and done, not in her views on human dilemmas, but in her willingness to take on others in the feminist loop: she's game for critiquing other feminists, and some of the strains or trends she identifies in feminist thinking. In **"The Romantic Climacteric,"** for example, she strongly criticizes Germaine Greer's *The Change: Women, Aging and the Menopause,* and in **"Not Just Bad Sex"** she takes aim at Katie Roiphe's *The Morning After: Sex, Fear and Feminism.* In **"Marooned on Gilligan's Island: Are Women Morally Superior to Men?"** she takes on "difference feminism," pointing to fallacies in proclaiming women inherently more peaceful, more empathic, etc., and warning of unintended negative consequences for women by such arguments.

In the arguments she has within feminism's tent, she demonstrates she's no knee-jerk apotheosizer of women, no polemicist in a hazy swoon of a sisterhood which might try to accommodate or validate any analysis written or spoken by a woman, at least a woman who's liberal or radical.

That this may make her more "reasonable" than some feminists, and some anti-feminist female commentators, the reader will probably grant. Faced with a Suzanne Fields to the right, a Catharine MacKinnon to the left, and a Camille Paglia (below, above and beyond?), the reader might indeed feel blessed for the offerings of someone so reasonable as Katha Pollitt. But it's something else again to feel that

Pollitt has done all she can to respond to the dilemmas she addresses.

Charles Solomon (review date 26 November 1995)

SOURCE: A review of *Reasonable Creatures: Essays on Women and Feminism,* in *Los Angeles Times Book Review,* November 26, 1995, p. 15.

[*In the following review of* Reasonable Creatures, *Solomon argues that Pollitt's essays will interest readers even if they disagree with her views.*]

In well-crafted essays, Pollitt, an editor at *The Nation,* discusses such topics as rape, abortion, domestic violence, sexism and surrogate motherhood. She argues that as our complex social and economic system "comes under stress-from the transition to a global economy, the back-to-the-home agenda of the Christian right, the dismantling of the safety net by the Gingrich conservatives and the exhaustion of liberalism—the issues that feminism raises will become not less important, but more so." Pollitt's incisive prose remains interesting, even when the reader disagrees with her position.

Additional coverage of Pollitt's life and career is contained in the following sources published by Gale: *Contemporary Authors,* **Vols. 120, 122;** *Contemporary Authors New Revision Series,* **Vol. 66; and** *Major Twentieth-Century Writers.*

Valerie Sayers
1952-

American novelist.

The following entry presents an overview of Sayers's career. For further information on her life and works, see *CLC,* Volume 50.

INTRODUCTION

Sayers is one of a generation of writers who ushered in a period of "new regionalism" in American literature. Focusing her work on a single geographic area—the fictional town of Due East, South Carolina—Sayers at once paid homage to southern American writers such as William Faulkner, Eudora Welty, and Flannery O'Connor, and advanced the genre by dealing with specifically contemporary issues, particularly loss of religious faith, mental illness, and the chasm between the genders. Critics have praised Sayers for her realistic and sympathetic portrayals of family life, her compact, resonant prose, and her scrupulous attention to detail.

Biographical Information

Sayers was born and raised in Beaufort, South Carolina, to a Roman Catholic family, a background that figures prominently in her fiction. At seventeen she left the South to attend Fordham University in New York City, earning her undergraduate degree in 1973. Following her graduation, Sayers returned to Beaufort to teach a writing course at the Technical University of the Low-Country. At that time she began to seriously entertain the idea of writing professionally. In 1974 she married Christian Jara, and the couple moved back to New York, where Sayers enrolled in the master of fine arts program at Columbia University. Her thesis was a collection of short stories. She took a teaching position at a branch of the City University of New York and began writing her first novel, which was never published. In 1983 she finished work on her second novel, which was published as *Due East* in 1987. Sayers followed the success of *Due East* with four more novels and much critical acclaim. In 1994 she was appointed Director of Creative Writing at Notre Dame University in South Bend, Indiana.

Major Works

Mary Faith Rapple, the heroine of *Due East,* is fifteen, unmarried, and pregnant. An unusually bright and spirited young woman, she becomes a defiant loner in her small town, maintaining that her pregnancy is a virgin conception.

The novel explores the tentative relationship between Mary Faith and her father, Jesse, in the trying months of her pregnancy—a relationship suffused with a shared but unspoken grief for Mary Faith's mother, who died of cancer three years earlier. Sayers's next novel, *How I Got Him Back,* picks up Mary Faith's story four years later and introduces other characters who recur in her subsequent works, including Tim Rooney. In *How I Got Him Back* three women—Mary Faith, Marygail Dugan, and Becky Perdue—struggle to maintain relationships with the men in their lives in an atmosphere intolerant to spiritual peace and mental stability. In *Who Do You Love* Sayers tells the story of a single day in the Rooney family: November 21, 1963—the day before President John F. Kennedy was assassinated. Dolores Rooney is a New Yorker, transplanted through marriage to the town of Due East, who has never adjusted to life in the South. Dolores's infidelity, her husband Bill's impending bankruptcy, and their precocious eleven-year-old daughter Kate's sexual curiosity form the basis for most of the action in the novel. In *The Distance Between Us* Sayers for the first time moved away from the South and her recurring characters. Although Franny Starkey and Steward

Morehouse grow up together in Due East, they go to New York, where the sexually promiscuous Franny meets Michael Burke, a militant Irish alcoholic and drug abuser, with whom she travels to Ireland. The three characters' lives are hopelessly entwined, with each trying to find salvation through his or her artistic ambitions. In *Brain Fever* Sayers returned to more familiar characters; this time Tim Rooney, now married to Mary Faith Rapple but in search of his first wife, Bernadette, in New York. On the brink of mental collapse, Tim meets several people on his journey who guide him through his search and his breakdown; ultimately, his religious faith is restored, although he does not recover completely from madness.

Critical Reception

Sayers has been roundly praised by critics, who find her probing of contemporary religious issues and the apparent chaos of modern daily life humourous, moving, and provoking. Her focus on the American South in particular has earned her much acclaim for its intimate portrait of the culture. While some critics have found her use of multiple narrators distracting, others agree that this technique allows the reader greater access to the thoughts and feelings of individual characters. Jonathan Yardley has written of Sayers: "She's smart and irreverent, but she's also kind and compassionate; she gives us imperfect people and makes us like and care about them, an essential task for any novelist but one accomplished by surprisingly few."

PRINCIPAL WORKS

Due East (novel) 1987
How I Got Him Back; or, Under the Cold Moon's Shine (novel) 1989
Who Do You Love (novel) 1991
The Distance Between Us (novel) 1994
Brain Fever (novel) 1996

CRITICISM

Alfred Corn (review date 29 January 1989)

SOURCE: "Trouble in the Form of a Redhead," in *New York Times Book Review*, January 29, 1989, p. 7.

[*In the following review, Corn asserts that in* How I Got Him Back, *Sayers shows great promise as a novelist. Corn also compares her work to that of other celebrated southern writers.*]

Southerners are sexy, but that is only part of the problem. Yankees who saw the movie *The Big Chill*, shot in Beaufort, S.C., were made aware by the setting and some of the characters that there is a New South, populated by a restive generation that has survived the upheavals of the 1960's and is now more or less resigned to assimilation into Middle America. Valerie Sayers, who grew up in Beaufort and has published one earlier novel, *Due East,* gives a fair sample of the new breed in her second book [*How I Got Him Back*]. This story is also set in the fictional town of Due East, S. C., which bears a strong resemblance to Beaufort, with its old white-columned houses and newer suburban homes, the closeness of salt marshes and the sea and a staunch little congregation of Roman Catholics in the parish of Our Lady of Perpetual Help.

Nearly all the characters in *How I Got Him Back* are Catholic, and at least two of them are concerned with the problems mentioned in the title. Becky Perdue refuses to believe that her husband, Jack, really means to leave her for a common redhead with no education named Judi. Marygail Dugan hopes despite everything that she has not lost her husband, Stephen, to a young unmarried mother named Mary Faith Rapple. Life in Due East is anything but placid.

One of the ladies of the church's Altar Guild, who serve in this novel as a sort of deploring Greek chorus, asks, "You suppose the whole world is living in sin?" and receives the reply, based on recent Due East gossip: "You better believe it." They probably don't even know that Tim Rooney, a sort of Berriganish avant-garde Catholic, is having an affair with Eileen Connelly, the plain dish of ordinary sex improved by the salsa of exhibitionism and bondage. Spiritual leadership in the parish is no doubt flagging. Father Berkeley, a whisky priest with a good heart but declining powers, does what he can but is often indisposed. In fact, drink adds to Becky Perdue's difficulties as well, alienating her from all but one of her four children and giving Jack Perdue grounds for a custody suit. Madness never seems far away from the women involved in the marital tug-of-war, and eventually it overtakes Marygail on Easter weekend just before her baptism into that church outside of which there is no salvation.

Ms. Sayers has a complicated story, and she uses a number of methods to tell it—first- and third-person narration, letters, interior reverie, even a suite of rankly amateur poems written by Marygail. Tim, Becky and Stephen are the intellectuals, able to bring perspectives from Pascal, Donne, Blake and Graham Greene to bear on the stuff of their lives. (Father Berkeley, too, with his chronic doubt and his afternoon brandy, has certainly fictionalized himself with Greene's help.) The whole novel has a definite Christian-symbolic substructure, beginning in the season of Epiphany and moving toward Passiontide, when all the plot threads suddenly knot up together in a way that hints at divine intervention. This mixture of soap-opera plot, sacred story, sitcom humor, sex and analysis makes for heady reading. Ms. Sayers's first novel was praised for its passion and this one is equally vehement, filled with sharp confrontations, broad gestures and recklessly driven cars.

These characters are memorable and believable, however much they startle with excursions into the abnormal. Ms. Sayers has a gift for voice and the honest, gritty commentary about human behavior in stressful circumstances. She writes clearly and forcefully, with her own version of the humor that Southern writers from Eudora Welty to Flannery O'Connor to Reynolds Price use so tellingly. Her asides and filling in of the characters' past histories are marked by unusual powers of observation and fresh angles on ordinary experience. A writer with as much talent as Valerie Sayers will be almost certain in future books to take more trouble with narrative sequence, to dispense with melodramatic flourishes, to write more concisely and to make her conclusions more plausible. Better than getting spouses back is simply never to lose them in the first place. Ms. Sayers has the basic equipment to enthrall quite a wide and faithful readership.

Deanna D'Errico (review date Summer 1989)

SOURCE: "Two Timers," in *Belles Lettres*, Vol. 4, No. 4, Summer 1989, p. 7.

[*In the following review, D'Errico praises Sayers's evocative portrayal of people and places in* How I Got Him Back, *calling her "a virtuoso of portraiture."*]

Mary Faith Rapple, unwed mother and heroine of Valerie Sayers's outstanding first novel, **Due East,** has been "crazy in love" with Stephen Dugan since she bared her pregnant body to him at age fifteen. Now, in **How I Got Him Back,** she is almost twenty-one; he has promised to leave his wife and marry her. But as she sits in the park, waiting to feed Stephen a bag of cold crab omelets that she made from a recipe in that morning's newspaper, she reflects "with a chill that becomes less and less pronounced as she grew used to its presence . . . that [he] had become very fond of her and her boy. Fond. Once he had been passionate. . . . She had to think of a way to make him want her so badly that he wouldn't mention custody and marriage." Will Mary Faith get Stephen back?

Marygail Dugan was nineteen when she met husband-to-be Stephen: "nut-brown, horse-faced, horse-toothed, skinny, angular, all elbows and knees. She wore micro-miniskirts and pink tank tops made of spun sugar: she looked just fine

and she knew it, too." For years she has ignored Stephen and occupied herself instead with drugs, the Due East Little Theater, and sleeping with Marines. But now Stephen has sold a screenplay, and she is afraid that "he is going to be rich and try to take Maureen away from me and I'll have to go back to Columbia and live with Momma and Daddy and go to the country club every afternoon and play tennis with *lawyers'* wives. Oh god. OhgodOhgodOhgodOhgod." Will Marygail get Stephen back?

Becky Perdue's husband, Jack, has left her after some twenty years of marriage for Judi with an *i*, a dyed redhead who paints hearts on her fingernails. She has felt nothing but contempt for him for years; she had never forgiven him for being an Izod-clad real estate agent instead of an intellectual. But now that he is gone, Becky has fallen into a "black hole." She has gotten drunk in the middle of the day on nips of Rebel Yell she has found in her son's closet and is unable even to clean the cereal bowls off the kitchen island that, along with acres of beige carpet, she loathes. "I grew up in Due East, and as far as I'm concerned, islands were made to take boats to. Islands were made to leave you with sunburns and chiggers and ticks. They were not made to be in the middle of my kitchen." Jack finds Becky in this state, and Becky finds herself thinking "he was wearing a yellow alligator shirt and his belly pressed it out in a roll over the top of his pants. His belly looked like a lump of dough and I couldn't believe that after all these years of having Jack's stomach revolt me I suddenly wanted to take this lump of pale dough and knead it." Will Becky get Jack back?

The novel itself is a bit of little theater in which the plot is propelled by numerous questions. Will Tim Rooney, the unemployed philosopher who distinguished himself to the town by taking a whiz in the front pew of Our Lady of Perpetual Help on Christmas Day ever win Mary Faith's love? Will the tired and aging Father Berkeley stop drinking long enough to find a new site for the church, and does he have enough faith left to shepherd the faithless back into the fold? Will the ladies of the Altar Guild ever stop fighting over what flowers to put at Mary's feet, and will they heed May's prediction that Marygail will choose Easter for her nervous breakdown? Will the rain let up enough for Stephen's made-for-TV movie to be filmed on location in Due East? Will Becky or Mary Faith ever forget the image of Eileen Connelly, naked and bound, standing in Tim Rooney's bedroom window?

Who gets whom back and other questions, titillating as they are, are beside the point. The ample pleasure of reading this novel lies in getting to know its fascinating cast of characters intimately and in glimpsing how their lives intersect. Sayers is a virtuoso of portraiture. This group portrait develops detail by detail through the multiple third-person points of view like particles of light that, when absorbed through Sayers's lens, bring into clear outline another angle of a character's personality.

The occasional shift to first person is somewhat jarring—as if a character suddenly steps forward and speaks out loud in your ear. But Sayers pulls it off, and when you read Stephen's confession, you are likely to nod your head in agreement and then forgive him, and Sayers, for reaching out from the page and grabbing your lapel.

> I have never been comfortable in the first person, any more than I've been comfortable in this marriage or in this affair. For years I have written a hokey weekly column and daily drivel for the *Courier* without resorting to the first person. For years I have churned out I-less poems and sent them off to obscure literary quarterlies which had never before published poems not written in the first person. A dissertation, two unpublished novels, a made-for-TV movie script so bad it's *good,* so bad it scares me: pages, folders, cartons of work, all without resorting to the voice of choice in the 1980s.

Sayers's characters are so three-dimensional that readers may find themselves both liking and disliking them, hoping that they will succeed and that they will not. The second visit to Due East is even better than the first, and I hope that Sayers will allow us to come again.

Pinckney Benedict (review date 10 March 1991)

SOURCE: "A Girl's March away from Innocence," in *Chicago Tribune Books,* March 10, 1991, pp. 6-7.

[*In the following review, Benedict finds the ending of* Who Do You Love *somewhat unsatisfying but asserts that the novel overall "fulfills its mission."*]

The action of Valerie Sayers's new novel, **Who Do You Love,** takes place during the fateful month of November 1963 in the small South Carolina coastal town of Due East. At the center of the book stands the Rooney family, Catholics living in "a place where the other kids called you mackerel snapper and asked you were the nuns bald under those habits."

That's the way Bill Rooney, the failing pater familias of **Who Do You Love,** describes his home town, which also is the setting for Sayers's two previous novels, **Due East** and **How I Got Him Back.** Bill is a Southerner, raised not far from Due East, who moved to New York City to be a jazz piano player and then returned to his home ground with his young bride.

Dolores Rooney is that bride, 15 years and three children

later. A transplanted Yankee, still uncomfortable in the South, she has a penchant for condescending imitations of her Southern acquaintances ("We *might* could get there in time for the little old sun to set") and for saying things like, "Oh Lord, I guess I've been down South too long. I'm getting so native." It's little wonder that she manages to set on edge the teeth of virtually every Southerner around her.

Bill and Dolores' three children are Andy, Tim and 11-year-old Kate, who is the youngest and a "boiling pot," as her mother describes her. The chief concern of **Who Do You Love** is Kate's resolute march from innocence into knowledge, and much of the narrative is built around her various misadventures. These are presented in Kate's precocious, sometimes precious vocabulary (she firmly asserts that the Rooneys were "the very last the penultimate family" in Due East to buy a television), which is one of the chief charms of the book.

The primary dramatic episode arises from Kate's failure to distinguish drunken seduction from murder and mayhem. When she trails a threatening local figure known as the Snake Man to his trailer, she believes she's witnessing a kidnaping and killing. Her confusion about what is actually a sexual encounter lasts too long to be entirely credible, but the episode is well-realized:

> The Snake Man was *kissing* the Victim. The Snake Man had paused in front of her hiding place to *kiss* that poor girl who was so lost in her own terror that she could not support herself to stand up straight. Kate considered showing herself at just that instant: she could climb the bank and cry out like a banshee.

Occasionally, however, Kate's language gets away from Sayers. When Kate can't keep her thoughts from returning to a salacious image, Sayers writes that "the girl in the red nightie's thigh reappeared." When Kate feels tension, we learn that "her lips were streaked with little white surges of panic." Somewhat more diverting is Sayers's fondness for rendering her characters' inarticulate noises. One man says, "Awhhh. Pfff," Bill Rooney utters the classic comic book groan, "Argh," and a kiss is represented as follows: "Chhhhchhhhhchhhhh-smmmooochch." I would love to hear Sayers read that passage aloud.

Another of the book's charms is its ability to move from one character's mind into another's. Kate and Dolores provide the dominant narrative threads, but Bill's point of view occasionally takes over. And each of these characters has a unique voice and vision.

While Kate spends much of her time in jittery contemplation of the mystery of her sexuality, Dolores is convinced that the girl is independently knowledgeable and secure.

Kate is ashamed that she doesn't yet own a bra, that she is "the only sixth-grader who would never have a boy come along and thwang! pull the back strap of her Maidenform."

Still, Kate believes that she cannot ask her preoccupied mother about such an intimate subject. Dolores, on the other hand, assumes that her daughter chooses proudly to exhibit her blossoming adulthood "without a brassiere and without apology."

Bill Rooney has his own misconceptions. He imagines that his pregnant wife is a listless romantic, given to daydreams and brief flirtations. In fact, she is a woman of vast, often misdirected passion, who engaged in incest with a cousin as a teenager, who had an affair with a wealthy young neighbor during her first pregnancy and who now feels herself being drawn inexorably into another affair, this time with a visiting reporter from the *New York Times*.

But if Dolores' yearnings push her into doomed sexual relationships, her conscience, trained by Catholic notions of guilt and mortal sin, pricks her constantly.

The novel's chief plot lines—Dolores' advancing affair, Bill's approaching bankruptcy, Kate's discovery of sex and of her mother's infidelity—are bound together rather loosely. And the book's final episode, in which the Rooney family and all of Due East react to the news that President Kennedy has been assassinated, doesn't really resolve the various storylines.

The Kennedy denouement is telegraphed on the first page, where the month and year are prominently proclaimed; and the sense that the shooting will be pivotal is reinforced by the frequent references the characters make to Kennedy. By the time Kate's teacher says to her class, "I'd like you all to prepare yourselves for an announcement," the reader has been waiting for that particular shoe to drop for some 300 pages. Nor is Kennedy's death presented as the epiphany one might expect; instead it is just another episode in a novel made of episodes.

But despite its shortcomings, *Who Do You Love* deals fairly and entertainingly with all of its interesting principal players, giving each of them their due time on stage. Determinedly amiable, it is a novel that fulfills its mission.

Howard Frank Mosher (review date 7 April 1991)

SOURCE: "24 Hours in Due East, S. C.," in *New York Times Book Review*, Vol. 96, pp. 3, 29.

[*In the following review, Mosher finds* Who Do You Love *a satisfying, likeable, and well-written novel.*]

Over the past decade or so, a number of America's finest younger novelists have staked out fictional claims on out-of-the-way corners of the country. Sometimes referred to by critics as the "new regionalism," this fiction is, in fact, neither especially new nor, in any limiting or quaint sense of the word, regional. One thinks, for example, of the dark and decaying New England mill towns of Ernest Hebert and Russell Banks, of Cathie Pelletier's remote Canadian border terrain with its idiosyncratic clans of French and Yankee backwoodsmen, and of Ivan Doig's high Western plains, rich in historical lore.

Who Do You Love, Valerie Sayers's third book set, like her previous novels *Due East* and *How I Got Him Back,* in the appealingly named coastal town of Due East, S. C., is a book written in just this tradition. Perched on an off-the-beaten-track fringe of the Atlantic seaboard, Due East is a community of stately white houses with wide yards shaded by live oak and pecan trees, long-established family businesses catering mainly to the nearby Parris Island Marine base, and attractive beaches guarded by vast wetlands and scrub woods unspoiled enough to hold wildcats—not to mention rattlesnakes. With its lovely late-afternoon sunlight and seaside vistas and easygoing pace—the main topic of conversation downtown on an unseasonably warm fall day seems to be whether to turn on the air conditioners—it's a place you could fall in love with at first sight and settle down in for life.

Dolores Rooney, a wide-eyed young college student from New York, did exactly that back in 1946; and even now, 17 years older and only too well aware of Due East's grimy underside and moral shortcomings, Dolores is still full of affection for her adopted home. "Never mind the trailer lots on the way out of town, or the lucky cheap gas stations on the highway; never mind, just for the moment, the mean little plumbingless shacks on the Islands, where they painted the doors and window frames blue to ward off evil spirits, never mind the rednecks five miles up the road. At just this dreamy moment Due East was so sublime that it was almost a spiritual, not a physical, place: even the brown marsh grass, squatting in brown mud at low tide, was beautiful."

Not that Dolores doesn't have her own share of midlife problems. The novel opens in November 1963, on the eve of President John F. Kennedy's assassination, with Dolores, 37 years old and pregnant with her fifth child, full of concern about her family. Kate, her precocious 11-year-old, is preoccupied with doubts about sex; for weeks now, she's spent hours a day conducting covert (and very funny) dictionary word searches, with maddeningly redundant results "She'd found *intercourse: intercourse* meant *copu-*

lation and *copulation* meant *coitus* and *coitus* meant *intercourse*." Dolores's older daughter is off at college, with two brothers soon to follow. Bill, Dolores's well-meaning but feckless husband, is at his wit's end to keep his failing little real estate business afloat. Moreover, as liberals and practicing Roman Catholics in a predominantly conservative, Protestant community—where businessmen drift into one another's shops to tell the latest racist jokes, and the respected local druggist has had his soda fountain yanked out in order to outwit the impending integration laws—the Rooneys frequently find themselves out of step with their neighbours.

Although Dolores appears to be entirely in control of her life, she's haunted by guilt dating back to two events in her past: a sexual liaison, when she was 13, with a cousin who went on to become a priest and a brief affair with a graduate student soon after she was married. As a result, Dolores's entire adult life has been one long, unsuccessful act of atonement—from her feverish volunteer work on church and community projects to her self-mortifying choice of reading material, including St. Thomas Aquinas's more misogynistic pronouncements and St. Teresa of Avila's "Way of Perfection." The sad fact is that Dolores McGillicudhy Rooney can hardly walk down the street without being overcome by remorse.

Structurally, Ms. Sayers's latest, and best, fictional exploration of Due East unfolds almost entirely within a 24-hour period culminating in President Kennedy's assassination, with numerous reminiscences filling in the Rooney family background. On a few occasions in the early chapters, the pace flags briefly with the introduction of overly long personal histories. But the novel quickly picks up with the sudden development of a whirlwind romantic attachment between Dolores and a young *New York Times* reporter named Tom Prince, who is in town to cover a court-martial at Parris Island.

From her first chance encounter with Tom Prince, Dolores is amused by his youthful and ingratiating manner, by her own infatuation and by the awkwardness, comic and otherwise, of their situation. After giving Tom a guided tour of the town, Dolores invites him home for dinner with Bill and the kids. Wine and talk flow freely, so much so that the meal ends with a Rooney family donny-brook over, typically enough, religion and politics. Later, Dolores seeks Tom out at his motel to apologize, and the ensuing scene is sexy and funny in about equal parts.

Throughout the novel, Ms. Sayers's unsparing yet unfailingly good-natured sense of humor sets the tone for her skillful handling of a wealth of material. Nothing, is sacred—from boozing old Bill's secret (and hilarious) sexual fantasies, to the most intimate disclosures of the confessional booth, to Mrs. Always-a-Lady Lovelace's sixth-grade classroom's first response to the news of J. F. K.'s death. "This mean they won't integrate the high school next year?"

Humor and irony, family history, an unusual and fascinating setting, affecting characters—**Who Do You Love** has them all, along with a racy, light-handed prose style that's never less than entertaining. In the end, you have the satisfied sense of having spent much longer than a mere 24 hours in Due East. And Dolores? Without spoiling the novel's wonderfully affirmative ending, it's fair to say that she manages to achieve at last, in a single crowded day, a remarkably wise insight into herself and her relationship with her big, squabbling, funny, smart, problem-ridden and immensely likable family.

Brewster M. Robertson with Valerie Sayers (interview date 7 February 1994)

SOURCE: An interview with Valerie Sayers, in *Publishers Weekly,* Vol. 241, No. 6, February 7, 1994, p. 66.

[*In the following interview, Sayers discusses her career and influences, as well as major themes in her novels.*]

Both geographically and culturally, the moss-bearded live oaks and white-columned antebellum mansions fronting the waterfront on Bay Street in idyllic Beaufort, S. C., seem far removed from the labeled Golden Dome crowning the Administration Building at Notre Dame University. But for novelist Valerie Sayers, newly appointed Director of Creative Writing at the South Bend, Ind., university, homegrown Beaufort is the connecting link to her literary roots.

Sayers's road from Beaufort to South Bend includes a 20-year detour by way of New York, where she began her writing career. Her fourth novel, **The Distance Between Us**, is out this month from Doubleday in a 100,000-copy first printing, and Sayers has embarked on a 12-city, coast-to-coast reading tour. An appearance in nearby Charleston has allowed an overnight sidetrip to visit her mother and two sisters, who still live in the picturesque community that cinema-goers would recognize as the setting for the films *The Big Chill* and *The Prince of Tides*.

Sayers readily acknowledges Beaufort as the model for the fictional town of Due East, which gave her first published novel its title and has since become the wellspring for her work. The town may well figure in a movie version; Propaganda Films is holding options on both **Due East** and Sayers's second novel, **How I Got Him Back.**

Walking along the sun-dappled Beaufort dockside in

sweatshirt and jeans, the 41-year-old Sayers looks more like a freckle-faced coed than a professor. Time has not diminished her affection for her native city, which she recalls as a magical place in which to grow up. Going off to Fordham in New York City at age 17 was "like Alice falling down the rabbit hole," she says. "I always assumed I'd come back here to live, but it just hasn't been in the cards."

In *The Distance Between Us* Sayers traces a collection of flower-children through the rebellious '60s, uprooting a pair of socioeconomically antithetical soulmates from their rural Southern backwater and scattering them to the four winds. Brassy antiheroine Frances Starkey is one of nine offspring of an Irish-Catholic high school principal in the largely Protestant town. Searching for a "bed of her own," she becomes compulsively promiscuous, a trait that blights her romance with Steward Morehouse, grandson of the town's wealthiest citizen.

Grieving over her father's untimely death, artistic Franny enrolls in a Catholic university near Washington, D.C., where she is confronted with a collection of hard-drinking, hash-smoking Jesuit priests who wink at their own random womanizing and espouse a sensualistic version of social-protest Catholicism. There she meets and eventually marries alcoholic Michael Burke, an aspiring writer.

The middle section of the book is a surreal fiction-within-a-fiction screenplay, in which Michael romanticizes the couple's honeymoon in Ireland as an ill-fated gunrunning adventure for the IRA. Sayers had never attempted screenwriting before, and she says she was "terrified" that readers would put down the book at that point. She emphasizes that her goal was not simply to do something offbeat; the idea developed organically from the plot. As it turned out, the screenplay, with its surprising denouement, is one of the most effective parts of the narrative.

When asked about possible autobiographical content in her early novels, Sayers dances coquettishly around the issue. In *The Distance Between Us,* however, such content is hard to miss. Like heroine Franny, Sayers recalls working summers at the tomato-packing sheds out near the airport on Lady's Island. "Everybody I ran around with worked there . . . it was the social event of the year," Sayers says. And, like daddy's-girl Franny, Sayers adored her father and went north to attend his alma mater. Sayers was devastated when he died of a heart attack while she was a sophomore at Fordham. "My father was wonderful, funny and unflappable. He was my inspiration," she says.

The fourth of seven children of damn-Yankee Irish-Catholic parents, Sayers was born after the family moved to Beaufort, where her father was employed as a civilian psychologist at the Parris Island Marine Recruit Depot. Along with to-

mato farming and the shrimping industry, the local Marine and Naval installations remain today the economic lifeblood of the area.

As an undergrad at Fordham, Sayers met Christian Jara, who was studying to become a filmmaker, as does Steward Moorhouse in the novel. Sayers is quick to point out that Christian is nothing like Franny's husband, alcoholic Michael Burke. She admits, however, that she knew "roguish priests. I don't remember ever going to a party without someone trying to con me for IRA gunrunning money." Then as now, her seemingly ingenuous, upbeat manner can be deceiving. "A drama teacher once told me it was obvious I had no firsthand experience with four-letter words," she recalls. "I didn't bother to tell him what a trash-mouth I really was. I suppose that outwardly I might convey an air of innocence, but as a writer my job is to tell the truth."

Following graduation in 1973, Sayers returned to Beaufort to teach at the Technical College of the Low-country for a year. She recalls afternoons spent reading Dickens, Eliot and Faulkner in her favorite sanctuary: the huge, embracing limb of a live oak. She also felt a strong sympathy with Flannery O'Connor, who grew up in Savannah, less than an hour down the road.

The writing course Sayers taught at Tech reawakened her own interest in the craft. Her family had always encouraged her to write, she says, and in high school she had produced the teen column for the *Beaufort Gazette*. "But the idea of writing as a career seemed too intimidating, on the one hand, and not very glamorous on the other. In college I tried poetry, but I wasn't very good. It was that year teaching at Tech when I became interested in writing fiction."

At that point, however, Jara came down to Beaufort to sweep Sayers off to the altar. The couple returned to Manhattan, where Jara pursued opportunities as a filmmaker and where Sayers enrolled in the M.F.A. program in creative writing at Columbia. Her thesis was a collection of stories. "At that stage, the idea of something on the magnitude of a novel seemed impossible," she says.

Her next teaching job, at an arm of CUNY, generated serious commitment to her own work. By the time her son, Christian, was born in 1978, she was immersed in rewriting her first novel. "Most likely, Chris will tell you that Christian's first word was, 'typewriter,'" she laughs.

Now gathering dust in her South Bend basement, that first effort was titled *My Sister Has Left Me*. Sayers says wryly, "That title should tell you something about the level of my prose at that stage."

The book was good enough to win the attention of her first

agent, however. (Sayers does not wish to disclose the agent's name, since their parting was not amicable. Southern good manners seem to underlie her reluctance.) Although no publisher bought that initial effort, Sayers was undaunted by rejection slips and began writing another book. "Having an agent provided all the validation I needed to move ahead," she observes.

About the time her son Raul was born in 1983, Sayers had finished that second book, which became *Due East.* Its heroine is teenager Mary Faith Rapple, brought up Baptist, who proclaims herself an atheist and insists that the baby she conceives is the product of a virgin birth. "That book is about faith and the hope of redemption," Sayers says. The manuscript, originally titled "After My Mother Died," made the rounds for two years. She had "about given up" when editor Lisa Wager read the book and bought it for Doubleday late in 1985. It was at Wager's suggestion that Sayers used the name of the seacoast town as the title.

Sayers was distressed when Wager, having edited about half of *How I Got Him Back,* left for Putnam. The manuscript was turned over to Casey Fuetsch. "I've been twice blessed," Sayers says. "Casey makes me better than I know how to be."

How I Got Him Back (1989) tells of three women who lose their men and decide to do something about it. While writing *Who Do You Love,* Sayers became aware of "increasing philosophical differences" with her agent, and she deliberately kept herself uncommitted on the new manuscript. Although she says she will always feel deeply grateful for that agent's efforts on her behalf, she felt it was time for a change. Accepting ICM's Esther Newberg's offer to represent the new manuscript was, says Sayers, "the best decision of my career."

A Catholic woman pregnant with her fifth child is the protagonist of *Who Do You Love.* Trapped in a disheartening marriage, she is contemplating an adulterous affair. Sayers invests the situation with emotional complexity and historical resonance by setting the story during the evening before, and in the morning of, November 22, 1963, the day JFK was assassinated.

Asked about her preoccupation with Catholicism, Sayers quickly points out that her first heroine, Mary Faith Rapple, was a Baptist. She concedes that early on she may have been subconsciously using the Baptist religion as a metaphorical catchall to camouflage her need to write about faith and the Catholic experience. She says, however, that at that stage it never occurred to her that Catholicism would play such a large part in her later work.

Sayers's storylines are always complicated by eddies of re-

ligious ambivalence. While sin and hope of redemption are the reassuring themes, an underlying sense of dissatisfaction with the Church always renders her epiphanies slightly bittersweet. She explains the obscure tripartite wordplay in the title, *How I Got Him Back*: "Recapture of the errant male; Revenge for his transgression; and Redemption. HIM meaning GOD!"

Asked to describe herself in a single word, Sayers laughingly replies: "Radical!" Fellow novelist and friend Lois Battle—a transplanted Australian schooled under the strict hands of the nuns, who now makes her home in Beaufort—agrees. "Valerie is an intellectual and a free spirit, but you have to understand, she's Catholic to the core," Battle says. "You can translate that as complicated!"

Sayers agrees with that assessment. "I'm definitely Catholic—and that comes with a lot of guilt-ridden baggage. But make no mistake, while I'm rebellious and while sometimes I get very put out with the Church's rigidity, the unyielding hierarchy, the antiquated structure, I have never had a moment's crisis of personal faith."

And things do seem to work out for her. She is enchanted with her teaching assignment at Notre Dame, a job she found via the prosaic route of an advertisement in the MLA job list. Characteristically, she announces, "We're truly blessed. Chris can produce videos from almost anywhere, and the university allows me complete freedom to write and travel to do publicity for my books."

She reads other contemporary novelists with enjoyment. High on her list is Maureen Howard's *Natural History,* "for the density and richness of its language." She also admires Ron Hansen's *Mariette in Ecstasy* "for his startling prose style." It should not be surprising that both novels have Catholic themes.

Sayers's next novel, *Brain Fever,* reintroduces Tim Rooney, a character from an earlier book. "The last Catholic existentialist in the South," Rooney has denied his faith and is having a nervous breakdown. But this time the *Due East* setting may give her trouble, observes Sayers, tongue in cheek. She and *PW* are driving across the Lady's Island drawbridge after a trip out to Hunting Island, where she has pointed out the location of Aunt Blinky's cabin, the remote setting for the final scene of *The Distance Between Us.* Waving her hand at the seabirds circling lazily above the church-steepled skyline, she asks, "Can you imagine someone actually having a nervous breakdown in a place like this?"

Jill McCorkle (review date 20 February 1994)

SOURCE: "One Good, One Bad, One Angry," in *New York Times Book Review,* Vol. 99, February 20, 1994, p. 23.

[*In the following review, McCorkle finds* The Distance Between Us *skillfully written and thematically realistic.*]

Valerie Sayers's fourth novel, **The Distance Between Us,** explores some 40 years in the lives of Steward Morehouse and Franny Starkey, an unlikely couple devoted to a relationship that for the most part exists and thrives on what might have been. Raised by his wealthy paternal grandparents and his exotic mother, to whom Franny bears a striking resemblance, Steward is a young Southern gentleman with a healthy trust fund. The daughter of a high school principal, Franny is the town "bad" girl, a green-eyed Scarlett O'Hara gone to seed. What they ultimately have in common, other than roots in Due East, S. C., and a strong physical attraction to each other, is the loss of their fathers.

It is this same loss that first links Franny to Michael Burke, her future husband and the third point of the novel's romantic triangle. He is an "angry young man" whose Irish features are used to telegraph his temperament. Michael is bitter toward his father, who died of alcoholism, yet he indulges in the very cycle that produced his resentment, drinking heavily and taking any drug available. Franny's weakness lies in her decision to stay with Michael, even as her sexual desires are driven by her sense of loss. Steward also bounces between relationships (including an affair with Franny's sister). Salvation for each depends in many ways on artistic ambition (Franny paints, Michael writes, Steward makes films); here they vent and reinvent their lives.

While these characters are often unsympathetic, Ms. Sayers's skillful plotting still provides enough tension to hold the reader's interest and drive the novel forward. From South Carolina to Ireland to New York, she stirs up endless possibilities, turns where you least expect them. And her ability to skip large periods of time gracefully, only to loop back and fill in the blanks, creates the sort of distance between episodes that allows us to see Franny, Michael and Steward mirroring reality in their art. Among Franny's paintings, for example, we notice a most revealing Last Supper, in which the faces and bodies are those of all her past lovers. Meanwhile, Steward attempts to balance his silver-spoon roots by making a documentary about the woman who kept house for his grandparents.

Many of the minor characters are colorful and endearing. Gloria, the housekeeper, Michael's mother, who is in a rest home in her later years; Franny's brain-damaged brother, Walter, who sings a constant chorus of "Harrigan"; Franny's college roommate Peggy, who in the late 1960's "could have been poster girl for the Catholic College Women's Association, circa 1955"; and Michael's longtime friend Kevin, who proves to be a disturbing misfit. They represent the solid realities within the lives of the three central characters, and their presence serves to illuminate this somewhat jarring triangle. In addition, the subplots that spin out from the experiences of Ms. Sayers's supporting cast provide some of the novel's most moving scenes.

The stability offered by its fringe characters is vital to **The Distance Between Us,** since Steward, Franny and Michael tend to be somewhat chameleon-like. Michael goes from political organizer to computer-magazine editor to boyish-looking screenwriter and novelist. His beard comes and goes, depending on his mood. Franny starts out attractively wild and winds up a hardened, jaded mother of four. Steward ventures from Due East to Hollywood.

At one point, Steward talks about the manuscripts that are submitted to him, mentioning that he even received one novel with a screenplay right in the middle. Here Ms. Sayers allows his eye to direct us toward her own work; in the middle of **The Distance Between Us** we find Michael's first screenplay, *The Gunrunners,* in which he features characters named Franny and Michael Burke, dramatizing their lives in a way that paints both truthful and distorted visions of their future paths. This digression, though important in establishing Michael's character, sometimes strains the reader's patience.

Despite such lapses, Ms. Sayers (whose previous novels include **Due East** and **How I Got Him Back**) is a first-rate writer, her prose rich with memorable descriptions that bring her landscapes, particularly the Southern ones, into sharp focus. If at times her story feels weighted down, this derives less from her very appealing style than from the occasional awkwardnesses of following the internal conflicts of three dissatisfied individuals for whom life is a constant, sometimes tedious struggle.

Liz Rosenberg (review date 20 March 1994)

SOURCE: "Novelist Valerie Sayers's Feel for Life's Actual Daily Chaos," in *Chicago Tribune Books,* March 20, 1994, p. 6.

[*In the following review, Rosenberg praises Sayers's ability to capture life "in all its messy glory."*]

To say that Valerie Sayers is a natural-born writer wildly underestimates the facts. She has published four novels in the past seven years, all of them set in the fictional town of Due East, modeled on Sayers's own hometown, Beaufort, S. C.:

> The road was dark with moss: above him the old oaks formed an arch to welcome him home, and in the first light the birds were dark, too, and raucous. Men passed in pickup trucks, their gun racks heavy. . . .

She has carved out for herself a corner of the South as clearly delineated as Faulkner's famous Yoknapatawpha County, a sense of the importance and holiness of place that calls to mind Eudora Welty's writing on the subject. And her new novel, *The Distance Between Us,* describes a geography both literal—Due East, New Orleans, Brooklyn, Ireland—and metaphorical.

Sayers has written repeatedly not only about the same place but often the same characters, seen now from one angle, now another. In her third novel, *Who Do You Love,* the action focused on a young woman named Kate Rooney. Now, in *The Distance Between Us,* Kate's best girlhood buddy, the skinny, stubborn Franny Starkey, takes center stage, while Kate plays a relatively minor role.

There is a kinship among Sayers's best female characters: They are tough, fiery, given to self-destruction and self-redemption, throwing themselves into crises with a vigor so pure it's nearly spiritual. Franny's first crisis is her first "grand passion" with a wealthy fellow Due Easter named Steward Morehouse.

Steward is as bedimmed as Franny is alive, as restrained as she is impulsive—in short, the "grand passion," such as it is, is a disaster. Franny can't be good, try as she might, and her "badness" is the germ of the novel, driving her to marry a charming, hard-drinking, working-class Irishman named Michael Burke, driving Steward Morehouse to despair and Franny herself from one precipice to the next.

Plot is not Sayers's great strength, and looked at in a certain light, nothing much happens in *The Distance Between Us.* It resembles history as someone once defined it: "one damned thing after another." The whole novel has a helter-skelter effect.

But apparently it is life's sloppiness that interests Sayers—the marriages, affairs, children, jobs—and not its meaning. She does not ask large questions, and therefore her characters don't loom large.

But Sayers has a feel for the tumult of daily life, and her particular brand of realism—slightly wild, slightly distorted—can be enormously gripping. Few novelists can create a world as absorbing as that of Due East:

> The Starkeys rode Hurricane Gracie out in Pat Starkey's junior high, where the gym roof collapsed and Doris made her children say all fifteen verses of the rosary, Joyful, then Sorrowful, then Glorious. They drove back through town that night past houses peeled open, one family's complete set of Tupperware still piled on the kitchen counter.

And few can create heroines as lively as Franny Starkey, seen first as a child through the already bitter love of little Steward Morehouse's eyes:

> Her nose was always sunburned, but the rest of her skin was as white as his. Her black eyebrows could have been drawn on with a big smooth Magic Marker. She always had on summer clown suits that billowed out around her fanny.

Sayers does make some genuine mistakes in *The Distance Between Us.* Franny's husband, the usually drunk or drugged-out Michael Burke, is nearly too unlikeable to bear for these 500-plus pages. His awful screenplay, much of it very bad writing about the IRA, is reproduced in full for more than 100 pages.

There are writers one reads for wisdom, and writers, like Sayers, to whom one turns for something more like a recreation of life's actual chaos. It is not what she knows that makes her work compelling but what she vividly sees and hears—the South seen at night from a train window, "only watery flashes in the night, only the shadows of furrows and rows, a neat geometric memory of tobacco and corn and mustard and collards"; the scraps of a lover's pleas, "and in between the speeding cars he was saying: 'You . . . ever . . . with . . . so . . . you can't . . . anymore.'"

The best moments in *The Distance Between Us* are scenes like these, with their sense of life in all its messy glory.

Michael J. Farrell (essay date 27 May 1994)

SOURCE: "Sayers's Folks Stagger toward Redemption," in *National Catholic Reporter,* Vol. 30, No. 30, May 27, 1994, p. 17.

[*In the following review, Farrell examines elements of Catholicism in Sayers's novels.*]

If you are one of seven kids, you have to be resourceful to stand out. If you're from the uptight town of Due East, you can stand out by being the school slut. If you are also a Catholic, it takes creativity to be good at the same time. If, furthermore, you plan to be a painter in Paris and you wear your father's ties because it is 1965 and they are doing it in London—if so, you presumably would want to leave town at the first opportunity.

No harm to the Jesuits, but you wouldn't want to go to the Jesuit University of America, even if it existed.

It does exist in Valerie Sayers's fourth novel, *The Distance Between Us* and that's where Franny Starkey goes.

"You'd better say you a rosary the first night and every night after or you'll never remember where you came from," her mother tells Franny as she boards the bus for JUA. Instead, Franny finds solace in reciting a litany of the Due East swains loved and left in her wake: "Tony Rivers. Beanie Boatright, just once. Gordy Nichols, De Vrau Frank, Bill Frank, Johnny Bewley, Amen."

And up ahead at the Jesuit University of America, Michael Burke lies in wait, with a devilish halo of red hair, a really loud Irish lad from Brooklyn whom no mother in her right mind would want her daughter messing with.

But messing is precisely what Franny is soon doing with Burke, amid amazing ropes of talk and unpredictable goings-on.

"Michael came out of the Safeway looking like a circus clown, a dozen cans of tuna fish in his pockets and a sirloin steak tucked in the back of his jeans, the scarlet blood running down the backs of his legs." He's just "liberating stuff," he tells Franny. For practice. For the upcoming revolution. Half a block away, he donates the purloined groceries to a startled old woman. Michael Burke's option for the poor. Son of Playboy of the Western World, "the sheer variety of drugs he consumed was appalling, even to her. You couldn't possibly ingest as many drugs as he did and be celibate as long as he claimed."

But no longer. And then, after a frisky afternoon in the sack, when Franny proposes returning to her own chaster bed, Michael reminds her, "Joe and Simon are cooking for us tonight. They're all psyched."

Joe and Simon are circa-1970s Jesuits, good guys sort of letting it all, or most of it, hang out around campus, whom Michael visits every Friday night "for poker or politics." But tonight was special. "He was taking the girlfriend home to meet the priests."

"What's the spiritual catch?" she asks.

"Fran, they're Jesuits, which means they're crafty. . . ."

Home to Notre Dame

For anyone interested in exploring the quixotic relationship between Catholicism, Catholic universities, art and creativity, Valerie Sayers is a most appropriate place to

start. Since last fall she has been director of the creative writing department at Notre Dame University. She is a native of Beaufort, S. C. (the Due East that is home for all her four novels), married to filmmaker Christian Jara, and the mother of two sons. Notre Dame seems the Byzantium toward which she has long been sailing: "My own work is concerned, among other things, with what it means to be a Catholic, what belonging to the institutional church means as well as what religious faith means. Those are important questions for me. Notre Dame is a kind of coming home: a place where the questions my own work raises will be taken for granted."

While Notre Dame's reputation for creative writing does not yet match its renown for either theology or football, Sayers insists that "everyone wants to write fiction"; even business students, she adds with wonder. Asked what she tells young hopefuls for motivation and inspiration, she explains to *NCR* on the phone, "I don't tell them what to do. I let them cut loose with whatever intrigues them at the moment . . . and ideas seem to explode from them."

This reticence to pontificate is a hint to look at her work to find out who Sayers is.

The Distance Between Us will be a major nostalgia trip for people of a certain age, veterans of the tumultuous days when the '60s peaked, and hedonism and idealism held for one more moment before breaking like a spent wave on the shore of the less exotic '70s. Burke is a writer (a high percentage of Sayers's characters are artists, screenwriters and kindred creators) working on unbegun masterpieces as he downs great quantities of booze and drugs. But the Jesuits, crafty or hopeful, insist on seeing a silk purse in this rambunctious sow's ear. They con him into doing street theater at a big demonstration in New York. Afterward, Michael drags Franny home to Brooklyn, where the Burkes and their kin are plentiful as rabbits and noisy as Babel.

"We're a strange tribe," Michael explains. "Breeding like that. I think it's out of panic." There is continuous, surreptitious talk about the Irish Republican Army and gunrunning.

Franny, who is supposed to be studying painting, soon gets pregnant instead. Panic of a different hue. She loses the baby. They get married. If it all made sense, how could it be 1971?

Sayers, who, unlike Franny, was, she insists, a good little girl, went off at 17 to Fordham University. While the novel is not autobiographical ("I never try to portray anybody I know. The interesting thing is that people see themselves in the most peculiar characters"), she concedes that life sometimes did imitate the art that would come later. Some Jesuits, for example, were indeed "experimenting with the kinds of things that everybody else in the wider culture was experimenting with." But she expresses minor consternation that a *Publishers Weekly* profile attributed to her the unlikely scenario that the Jesuits were running guns for the IRA: "On the contrary, they were always thinking of these wacky, creative, nonviolent solutions that didn't have a prayer."

THE FIGHTING IRISH

But gunrunning there is. In what must be a first in the history of the world, an entire screenplay is incorporated within the framework of the novel. In this helter-skelter script (Irish film noir), Michael and Franny find themselves on an Irish honeymoon, which takes them to the legendary Puck Fair in Killorglin, Kerry, a pagan festival at which a goat is crowned king amid monumental drinking. But some cagey characters in what they themselves choose to call the fight for Irish freedom stay sober long enough to con the "Yanks" in several directions.

While Michael makes a run for the border with weapons of war destined for Belfast, he loses Franny, who, not knowing the entire score, indeed scarcely any of the score, allows herself an early act of unfaithfulness to her new and by now endangered husband.

This, although it eventually turns scary, will probably be seen by many as a lighthearted paean to Irishness by a writer part of whose ancestry came from the real Killorglin.

As the Kerry bombs are being made, the woman of the house embarks on a lethal tirade when she finds herself under the same roof as a fistful of condoms. "It's not the bomb she objects to," says the bomb man. "It's using birth control to make the bomb."

This is not *In the Name of the Father*. But considering the author's current whereabouts, a more apt title for it than *Gunrunners* might have been *The Fighting Irish*.

VIRGIN BIRTH IN DUE EAST

"I'm interested in pursuing people in trouble; I'm not just interested in looking at perky, well-adjusted people," Sayers told *NCR*. In her first novel, **Due East,** spunky 16-year-old heroine Mary Faith is in real trouble from page one. Her mother dead, she lives alone with her decent but distracted father. She's pregnant and keeps waiting for her father to notice, which he never does, until eventually she imagines that "somehow I'd get through nine months and a delivery, and one night he'd say, 'How did that baby get to the supper table?'"

Eventually she has to tell him. It will be a virgin birth, she

explains. Her father is understandably skeptical. He has already told his friends that Mary Faith is a bit crazy anyway. She gets convoluted consolation from this: It should make the virgin birth story easier to swallow.

Her father suggests an abortion, but Mary Faith won't hear of it. Her father drives off into the night, leaving Mary Faith disconsolate. She is imbued with a rich imaginative life. Though a Baptist herself, if only nominally, and "even if I didn't believe in God, I was always fond of Mary, and I always thought the idea of a virgin birth was something fine. Fine and wicked, too, the way it made it seem as if Jesus Christ was too good for the love of a man and a woman."

Besides, she ponders dolefully, "how my baby was conceived was close to a virgin birth anyway." The would-be father was an eccentric, shy, guilty high school senior who carried around *The Brothers Karamazov* and wanted to save the world in a leftist sort of way until he took 30 Quaaludes and died after a week. "He hadn't even known I was pregnant, and I was glad he hadn't had *that* to be guilty over, too." She ponders whether she ought, in due time, to tell the child what happened. She decides on an evasive scenario: "I would have thought up a real good father for her, a priest who couldn't leave his church or a married man who couldn't leave his six other children."

A significant feature of Sayers's writing is its candor. If the love is lusty, she says so. She doesn't flinch from calling things by their names, does not beat around any bush. Her people's stomachs sometimes growl. They occasionally think the unthinkable or disgusting as well as the poignant or sublime.

To her students, she told *NCR*, "what I go on about most is honesty, pushing as deeply as you can for honesty, and that there's a connection between honesty of content and honesty of form." And later she takes this a step further: "My view of fiction has always been a moral view in the deepest sense of that word." She does not, she concedes, find this moral sensibility more finely honed within the Catholic confines of Notre Dame than in the allegedly more heathen ambience of New York where she spent the previous 20 years.

Writers frequently resent being tagged a "Catholic novelist." "I don't think I'm pinned yet as a Catholic writer," says Sayers. She considers the term "potentially limiting in the sense that 'feminist novelist' can be limiting," but concedes: "I'm a Catholic novelist in the sense that I'm a Catholic in everything I do. My religious beliefs inform my view."

The natural ease and frankness with which she writes about sex and other forbidden fruit may seem at odds with an institutional church that practically hyperventilates at any mention of the flesh. This brings her back to the honesty angle. And, she adds, whenever the church tries to sweep the unmentionable under the ecclesiastical carpet, "those dust balls have a way of accumulating at the edges and being found out." Moreover, she rejects the image that all clergy match the institutional stereotype of the church, and her conversation affirms she has met many priests she holds in high esteem.

The Catholic Thing

To the suggestion that her stories might be primarily concerned with the surface manifestations of cultural Catholicism, she responds with vigor: "I think it's much deeper than that. . . . Franny is promiscuous. She certainly doesn't seem to be a model Catholic. And yet she has a very deep and unshakable faith. There's one little passage where she's thinking about the Eucharist and the notion that you would die if you went without it. The sacraments are so basic a part of her life that she cannot imagine life without them. . . . Throughout the novel she becomes more and more aware of her faith, and her husband starts to berate her, that she's trying to be a saint or something, and she has in fact decided to be some kind of saint, and that of course goes all wrong."

While the contentious issues that rack the church do not constitute themes of her novels, Sayers insists she does not duck them. Abortion, for example, becomes a real issue Mary Faith must grapple with in *Due East,* as must Franny in *The Distance Between Us.*

But above and beyond individual theological spasms there is the faith as a given, incontrovertible as the ground beneath and sky above. On the very first page of Sayers's third novel, *Who Do You Love,* Dolores Rooney is described, on the day, as "a Mary, not a Martha," a reference that might fly right over uninitiated heads.

And, 165 pages later, Dolores' husband, Bill, is in the confessional and wrestling with real Catholicism as he tells Fr. Sweeney that, no, he hasn't committed adultery, "it's just that my wife's pregnant and all I can think about is other women—you know, impurely." And we are treated to a rare instance of the tables turned: Bill Rooney falling over himself to admit sin, as if the validity of his lurid imaginings were a test of his masculinity, while the priest is equally adamant that Rooney hasn't committed anything worth confessing.

In *Due East,* secular and sacred, the intransigent world and incomprehensible church, are the ongoing horns of Mary Faith's dilemma during her pregnancy. Determined not to have an abortion, she can't think where to turn except to the Catholic church. But, being Baptist and all, she knows no Catholics and is skeptical about the local priest, Fr. Berkeley, although he has "kind, light eyes," but she fears he would soon be calling her "sweetheart" and "sugar" and asking her to address the Due East Right to Life Committee, "and his heart would break if I told him I didn't believe in God and didn't mind who else had an abortion."

Reviewers of all Sayers's books have repeatedly commented on their authenticity of voice: The words are not so much imaginative fabrications as recognizable echoes of real life, untidy and uncertain, shreds and patches scavenged in pursuit of the aforementioned honesty.

Mary Faith ruminates: "No, what I wanted was nuns, some tough cookies with a maternity center for girls who weren't praying when they said 'Jesus Christ.' The sisters would talk to me about religion, but they'd know beforehand I wasn't going to buy it, and they'd see I had good books to read and they'd make all the mothers-to-be turn out the lights at 10 o'clock."

Reminiscent of Kaye Gibbons' feisty females (*Ellen Foster,* for example), Mary Faith is a very smart kid, otherwise she could never be expected to conceptualize or articulate the immense baggage of her little life, the hopes and heartbreaks and people dying on her.

She visits the hospital where her father is very ill. He can't hear her, but she talks on compulsively anyway: "The baby is coming and I'm just going to care for it. And you're just going to care for me. If you mean to make anything of your life, you're not going to desert me now. You hear, Daddy? You turned your back on me when she [her mother] died, and you turned your back on me when I got pregnant, but you're not going to turn your back on me and die. . . . I'm sick of you all dying when I need you. So don't you die, hear? Don't you die."

Life Seamy but Salvageable

Sayers's second novel, *How I Got Him Back,* is also set in Due East, four and a half years after Mary Faith's baby is born, a son, Jesse, to whom she now happily refers as a "holy terror." The slings and arrows and infidelities of marriage and family are dragged into the foreground.

The erosion of old dreams and promises is beautifully condensed by one of many disillusioned characters: "That night, when we collapsed in our hotel rooms, I found my rosary beads in my makeup bag. I couldn't make out why they were there—I stopped saying rosaries the day I signed my mother into the state hospital—but there they were, black beads covered with a fine mist of lavender eye shadow. So I said the sorrowful mysteries, almost in a trance, and, still not believing, asked the Blessed Virgin first to give me more patience with my children and second to stop making me feel this way about my husband and third to make me stop falling in love with big men I saw in grocery stores."

Mary Faith, meanwhile, is taking religious-instruction classes, while insisting she has no intention of ever becoming a Catholic, though here and there she seems to protest too much. A lot of people are drinking or drunks, including Fr. Berkeley. Yet people like Catherine of Siena and Teresa of Avila drop in on the narrative all the time, while the world and the flesh are giving the devil a run for his money, and Mary Faith's new beau is being driven crazy by sexual temptations (naturally) while vaguely planning to be a monk.

"I'm interested in pursuing people in trouble," Sayers had said, and most of her people are. In *The Distance Between Us,* Franny marries Michael and they have three kids in four years, and that's trouble. Glorious youth, when they could combine saving the world with endless pleasure, gives way to making inane ends meet. And there's more. Complex characters are seldom without a past that comes creeping back creating havoc. In Franny's past, long before Michael, there was a rich kid, Steward, pseudo-aristocratic but quaint, who made an indelible mark. Steward turns up again just when he can do most harm. There's a triangle. It's eternal.

But so is redemption, insists Sayers: "Grace comes to your rescue in the end. I am very aware of that after the fact, but in the composition, as I approach the ending, it often seems to me that I'm approaching cataclysm and that there's no way to go but down. And it's as if I am rescued at the last moment by this impulse." She does concede that this recent novel took the more pleasant low road: "There was a certain joyfulness in indulging that sort of cinematic ending with all the strings tied up." In this case it may be too easy—redemption too neat and nifty—but Sayers creates no characters who do not, sooner or later, pay their dues. She is surprised at the number of mainline reviewers who are dismayed at what "downers" her story endings are, "but I see them as tremendously hopeful," she says. "Maybe it's only people of Irish background who can see those little glimmers of possibility as optimistic." Often, it's heavier than optimism; it's a call, and the author looking the reader in the eye with a saucy challenge. As Mary Faith waits in the hospital to have her baby, her roommate talks on: "My momma dreamed God came down and said wouldn't she please take over for him. God said he was so tired, he couldn't take being God no more. And my momma in the dream said no, God, I don't know nothing about being God. That's too scary for me. And God said please, you got to take over for me."

But Mary Faith is a tough nut to crack, telling how her own mother, too, dreamed: that Jesus wouldn't let her die. Then: "My mother died of cancer. I believe in cancer cells."

But then she throws hopelessness to the wind and goes on and has a baby and the lurid description is thoroughly earthy Sayers: The doctor "held up a cheesy blue baby turning red by degrees, head wet with goo, while the nurses wrapped a white cloth around him. He didn't look like anything, not like a person. A rat. I didn't want him. I wanted to die."

But of course she doesn't die. She goes on, like life.

Michael Parker (review date 25 February 1996)

SOURCE: "Crazy in Manhattan," in *Washington Post Book World,* Vol. XXVI, No. 8, February 25, 1996, p. 7.

[*In the following review, Parker praises Sayers's honest portrayal in* Brain Fever *of mental illness and the universal search for faith despite adversity.*]

Valerie Sayers's newest novel, and her first to take place predominantly outside fictional Due East, S. C., opens with this quote from Kierkegaard: "To have faith is precisely to lose one's mind so as to win God." Faith, or the loss of it, drives Tim Rooney to renounce his financee Mary Faith Rapple just weeks before their wedding and light out for Manhattan. As the story forges northward, both protagonist and author trade familiar territory for the woolly risks of what seems another planet from Due East.

For a writer as brash and supple as Sayers, whose previous novels have shown her to be strongest in creating a world at once mysterious and credible, another planet would not seem to pose a problem. Especially if it is inhabited by people; Sayers has that species down, particularly those people who talk crazy sense while holding themselves barely above the fray. Yet while there are copious pleasures strewn along the shoulder of this road, the results of the trip are mixed.

No doubt New York City is the right place for Tim to lose his mind and find his faith. He misspent his youth as an undergraduate at Columbia, and it is in part the memory of those outlaw years, of "our mass insanity, our shared hallucinations, our concurrent demands for peace and the right to blow up the Bank of America" that incites him to leave Mary Faith and her 9-year-old son Jesse in search of his long lost wife Bernadette. Tim and Bernadette's marriage lasted only six nights, until Tim, dosed on LSD, asked to tie her up before sex. "That's all I wanted to do: get a whiff of Bernadette, a reminder of who I'd been when I married young," says Tim. But the trip becomes quickly and comically complicated. Before he even leaves South Carolina, Tim picks up a spunky hitchhiker named Angela, refugee from old-money Charleston who has also fled the altar and who has friends—rich, southern, faux-boho-with-a-loft-in-Soho friends—who don't seem to mind, or be able to recognize, a sponge.

Guilt-ridden over wretched family history and past crackups, Tim turns out to be more sieve than sponge, and several minor characters are required to plug his many leaks. Aside from Mary Faith, Jesse, Angela and the loft-dwellers, there is gold-toothed, dread-locked G. B. Brights, a former student from Tim's days of academic temp work who follows him to Manhattan after seeing him withdraw 15 grand from a Due East bank and stuff it into his socks. G. B. shadows Tim as he runs around the city in search of ghosts until his cash-cushioned soles bleed like the barbwired feet of another hellbent Southerner in search of his lost faith, Flannery O'Connor's Hazel Motes.

The lost-and-found faith part of this story is as old as storytelling itself, but Sayers works hard to make it new. Other, less successful parts of the story focus on what's new in New York. Sayers lingers on details of Manhattan life—the pretentious furnishings of Soho lofts, downtown nightclubs filled with "black lights, drug-crazed faces"—that detract from the story of Tim's unraveling. Too often the cityscape is rendered straight on, in details that seem more in keeping with a bemused columnist than a failed philosophy professor battling life-threatening demons.

Just as Tim's take is dead-on in places, so is his voice, and the way he shapes his story. The most successful fictional portraits of breakdowns utilize style and structure; one thinks of the overripe and sibilant lyricism of Conrad Aiken's "Silent Snow, Secret Snow," which suggests the dislocation of the psyche through a harrowing accretion of image. Though the details of Tim's breakdown are often vivid, the lucid manner in which they are recalled leads to questions about the seriousness of his illness. Similarly, Tim's voice, which tends toward trenchant one-liners, only intermittently sounds like a man who hits bottom when standing in the middle of Union Square dressed in black pajamas, attempting to lead the crowd in a chant of "BOSNIA BOSNIA BOSNIA" modeled on Al Pacino's "ATTICA" mantra in *Dog Day Afternoon.* Obviously Tim has recovered enough to tell his story with clarity and wit, yet in order to be convinced of his mania, I found myself in need of more evidence in the telling aside from the occasional run-on sentence and the few gaps in time Sayers supplies.

The most satisfying source of tension in this novel is not whether Tim will find Bernadette and recover the religion he decides he has been slowly losing all those years in

"picture book" Due East, or whether he will be rescued by those he left behind. What kept me interested was not plot but psychology. I spent much of the book trying to find out what exactly was wrong with Tim Rooney, and even after Tim was safely back on his Haldol, and it was clear that his breakdown was real, I sensed he had been suffering as well from less pathological (and more common) maladies: guilt, fear of commitment, and an inability to love, which stem from a narcissism that is as much cultural as personal.

"To be able to recognize a freak, you have to have some conception of the whole man, and in the South the general conception of man is still, in the main, theological," Flannery O'Connor wrote in her famous essay on the grotesque. Sayers may have moved her characters northward, but her conception of our freakishness remains rooted in the Christ-haunted South. In *Brain Fever,* she is able to conceive not only the whole man but the society that forms him, and even though this tale of maladjustment is too well-adjusted in the telling, it is graced by a tenacious and generous vision.

Elizabeth Benedict (review date 17 March 1996)

SOURCE: "Descent into SoHo," in *New York Times Book Review,* March 17, 1996, p. 8.

[*In the following review, Benedict admits to some flaws in Sayers's character development in* Brain Fever *but overall admires the novel's psychological depth.*]

The kingdom of madness is a destination we never visit voluntarily, and such are its shifting borders and evanescent landmarks that those who make the journey are often not sure where they are headed or when they have arrived.

For Gogol's madman, the St. Petersburg insane asylum to which he is committed is Spain, he is its king and the earth is about to land on the moon. For Tim Rooney [in *Brain Fever*], the unwitting trip he takes while narrating Valerie Sayers's immensely rich, readable fifth novel is a reprise of an earlier descent that led to his sister's suicide, a failed search for a monastery that would welcome "a recovering madman" and a prescription for Thorazine.

At 16, with an acceptance letter from Columbia University, Tim thought himself "a young Wittgenstein." At 45, he is a failed academic with a 27-year-old fiancée, a history of breakdowns and a highly charged, deeply ambivalent relationship with the Roman Catholic Church. He lives, like most of Ms. Sayers's characters to date, in novels that include *How I Got Him Back, Who Do You Love* and *Due East,* in the once sleepy seaside South Carolina town of

Due East (modeled on the author's hometown of Beaufort), a town "where even the poverty is picturesque."

In this novel Ms. Sayers plays with so many notions of sanity and insanity, and of tenderness and mercy, that this 40-day-long diary of a madman, with echoes of Christ's 40 days in the desert, is as much a case study as a lesson in faith through the eyes of an on-again, off-again Catholic and those of his jilted fiancée (an atheist, former Baptist and unwed mother). Both have appeared before in Ms. Sayers's work, as have these themes of fidelity, apostasy and salvation. Tim is attracted to Mary Faith Rapple in part because she is "the daughter of four fundamentalists, unwavering in her disbelief," while she admits to admiring the "fierceness of his religion. . . . If he were a Presbyterian or a Methodist, I don't believe I would have troubled myself."

Having been described at different times as schizophrenic, neurotic, manic-depressive and alcoholic, Tim is off his latest medication at the start of **Brain Fever** and begins losing touch with his fragile sanity on Holy Thursday. He's ignited by Mary Faith's declaration that she will join him in church on Easter Sunday. Suddenly, she wants them to marry in the church whose strictures she knows have caused him torment akin to madness: "She didn't say sexual torments, but she didn't need to."

Before long, carried off by tiny waves of paranoia and manic delusion, he decides to become a man of action instead of an unemployable philosophy professor. He abandons Mary Faith, her 11-year-old son, whom he is about to adopt, and Due East, and drives to New York City. He's got $15,000 stuffed into his socks and the cockeyed intention of settling a score with the wife who left him after six days of marriage in the early 1970's, when they were both practicing Catholics "and no one was in the church anymore, no one but us." Those few days were also part of an "hour of mass insanity," a time when "we all went crazy together" and "my hallucinations were exclusively chemical and always intended." Are you crazy if you are just keeping up with the *Zeitgeist,* Ms. Sayers wants us to wonder, or might madness have immutable properties, so many parts oxygen, hydrogen and carbon?

Outside Charleston, Tim picks up Angela Bliss, a young female hitchhiker—another fugitive from her own upcoming wedding—who is also bound for New York, where some rich South Carolina friends have a SoHo loft; conveniently there is an extra room for Tim, who tells them he is an actor about to audition with Sidney Lumet. From Spring Street he sets off every morning to Washington Square Park to look for his former wife, now an esteemed professor at N.Y.U., and to discover that some of his paranoia has nothing to do with brain fever; a former student, an African-American called G. B. Brights, spotted him in South

Carolina on his own drive north and takes a sycophant's interest in him, inviting him to meet his aunt in Brooklyn. These two households become the antipodes of Tim's increasingly unstable universe, as he bounces from one to the other in search of solace, safety and sometimes sex.

In the meantime, aging Father Berkeley in Due East, another fixture in Ms. Sayers's earlier books, tries to corral Mary Faith into setting off to find Tim, whereabouts unknown, though she is smarting mightily from having been left, very nearly, at the altar. "He hasn't left you," he implores her. "He's left his senses."

This chapter, one of eight narrated by Mary Faith, is the most moving in the novel. It is Ms. Sayers at her very best: Mary Faith, the wounded lover, atheist and Hester Prynne of Due East, being pressed into service and self-sacrifice by a fragile old priest who smells of "mothballs and nicotine" and from whom she expects religious platitudes—"*But God will give you strength* or *Let us call on Him for courage*"—but who offers instead his almost steady hand on her head as she weeps.

"I was weeping," she tells us, "over priests sitting there on your father's old lounger and asking you to believe that this really is a woman's lot: to nurse men and to wait on them, to send them off to their crazy adventures and then, when they've made it too dangerous for themselves, to go fetch them and forgive them and be steady and faithful."

Mary Faith's occasional and very same "Reports" are a wonderful counterpoint to Tim's often manic narratives. But what also makes hers so compelling is that they are tightly focused on the mission she undertakes with Father Berkeley. By contrast, Tim's entries, especially once he gets to New York, tend to be busy and hyperactive, as he is, full of destinations, new characters, paranoid fantasies and what were not long ago delusions of grandeur about bringing peace to Bosnia. In a way she could not have intended when she wrote the novel, Ms. Sayers has managed to suggest that madness can be a chemical imbalance and perhaps a species of prophecy too.

The principal weakness of **Brain Fever** is that the assortment of characters Tim moves among for most of it—the hitchhiker, her SoHo friends and G. B. Brights—are an aimless lot, not clearly motivated by much of anything except a tendency to commiserate about their heartache and troubled histories. They are there, it seems, to give Tim a setting and a support group in which to lose his mind. But this is a small quarrel about a novel of such large ambition, compassion and psychological depth, not to mention the pleasures of Valerie Sayers's graceful prose.

Alice McDermott (review date 1 June 1996)

SOURCE: "Crazed Protagonist Deranges Novel," in *Commonweal*, Vol. CXXIII, No. 11, June 1, 1996, pp. 20-21.

[In the following review, McDermott praises Sayers's writing style in Brain Fever *but finds her portrayal of mental illness oversimplified.]*

The problem at the heart of this witty, energetic fifth novel by the author of ***Due East*** and ***The Distance Between Us*** is not that its narrator, Tim Rooney, is a madman: bug-eyed geniuses giving diabolically brilliant accounts of themselves are not unknown in literature. The problem is that Tim Rooney ("middle-aged failed academic, failed musician, failed husband") is mentally ill—a far less romantic assessment, and one more likely to be associated in the contemporary reader's mind with emotional pain and ruined lives. Those associations belie the wit and energy and exuberance of Rooney's careening account, in an endearing Southern drawl, of a horrendous mental breakdown.

Tim Rooney has broken down before. Seven years ago he returned to his father's house in Due East, South Carolina—site of the author's four previous novels—to "have a crackup." "I took a whiz in the front row of Our Lady of Perpetual Help at the midnight Mass. I made various claims to be the Christ child and Blaise Pascal and Bobby What's-his-name, the sympathetic one on *Dallas*." He has lived through "the Clozapine years, the lithium years, the Prozac years" and, as the novel begins, has "reentered sanity." He plans to marry Mary Faith Rapple, the lovely young girl next door and to adopt her eleven-year-old son, Jesse, whom he adores.

But then Mary Faith arrives at his house on Holy Thursday evening in a new Easter outfit and asks that he bring her to church Easter morning. She is an atheist. He is, if not a good Catholic, a tenacious one. Suddenly, the shadow of his illness descends: the hallucinations, the buzzing sound, the chill. Brain fever.

He calls off the wedding ("I cannot be responsible for a false conversion"), and then loses his own faith on Holy Saturday when he wakes in his sister Dottie's bed—Dottie, the youngest of the Rooney offspring, who drowned herself at twenty-one. On Easter Monday morning, he stuffs $15,000 into his socks and heads for New York City. "With a new clarity, sharper even than the Drixoral variety," he knows he must find Bernadette, his wife from a six-day marriage that ended twenty years ago.

It is not surprising that religion should be a catalyst for Rooney's breakdown. His father was a musician prone to violence, but his mother was an activist Catholic. "She lined her children up at the kitchen table to write appeals to her congressman for civil rights and human rights and poverty rights and the right to be as right about the moral issues of the day as she always happened to be." Rooney himself believed a statue of the Blessed Mother smiled at him as a child.

Leaving Due East, Rooney is followed by a black man in a black truck—a guardian angel? In Charleston he picks up Angela Bliss, a beautiful hitchhiker running away from her own wedding. Angela is remarkably nonplussed by Rooney, even as he nearly drowns them both, even as he grows more and more paranoid about being followed. When they reach New York, she brings him, blacked-out and raving, to a loft in Soho owned by two more Southerners, Velma and Fred. In the morning, Rooney explains away his deranged behavior by telling them he is an actor testing a role, and Velma and Fred, in what is either incredible naiveté or unsurpassed Southern hospitality, invite him to stay on.

In the course of his forty-day descent into insanity, Rooney has bouts of clarity, bouts of memory, bouts of joy and panic and lust and regret. Sayers is remarkably skillful in seamlessly moving him back and forth, from one state to the other, in delineating his transformation from charming eccentric—he reminds everyone of Kramer from *Seinfeld*—to deranged street creature or, as he would have it, outlaw.

Rooney soon discovers that his guardian angel is G. B. Bright, his former student, and that Bright has been asked by Father Berkeley, Rooney's pastor in Due East, to keep an eye on him. G. B. does more than that, he rescues Rooney from the street, drinks with him, feeds him as he deteriorates, bathes and changes him when he becomes incontinent, even, with a wisdom that mysteriously eludes all the other characters, attempts to get him to a doctor.

Meanwhile, back in Due East, Father Berkeley has enlisted Mary Faith in a quest to rescue Rooney, telling her, "You have the chance to make a choice now. You can chose not to take on the nursing of a man who will have these . . . incidents all his life." She and Jesse head for New York with the old priest, who is certain that on the fortieth day of his madness, Rooney will take his own life.

Instead, there is a reunion. Having found Bernadette, Rooney has moved on to confront larger reasons for guilt: his sister's suicide, his mother's loss of faith, Bosnia. Ensconced in Washington Square Park, clothes in tatters, feet bleeding, feverish, he engages the crowds in a mad chant: Bosnia Bosnia—"so many souls to save,"—and that's where Mary Faith and Jesse find him.

As in her previous novels, Sayers's voice is so engaging, so precise and funny and strong, that it is unfortunate here to find her subject undermining it. It is not that the author lacks sympathy for her character's situation—Mary Faith acknowledges and embodies the pain Rooney's illness can cause—or that her story needs more pathos, more seriousness. It is rather that she, like Angela and Velma, seems slow to recognize that this loquacious Southern eccentric is in the throes of a serious illness, and that our understanding of mental illness, like our knowledge of tuberculosis and cancer, has changed forever its usefulness as a literary device.

Valerie Miner (review date 6 July 1997)

SOURCE: "Faith, Hope and Crisis," in *Chicago Tribune Books*, July 6, 1997, Sec. 14, p. 2.

[*In the following review, Miner lauds* Brain Fever *as "rewarding for that large population of us who have been both Catholic and crazy."*]

Valerie Sayers's fifth book, *Brain Fever,* is a brilliantly agile road novel whose characters career from small-town South Carolina to the wilderness of New York City. This witty, picaresque story is also a skillful, philosophical allegory about the lines between faith and madness.

Brain Fever opens on Holy Thursday as Tim Rooney, 45-year-old adjunct philosophy professor, medicated schizophrenic and practicing Catholic, is confronting a crisis of faith:

> See here: I was never one who had to make a leap of faith—I sucked it in, with my mother's milk. When I was a boy I built shrines to Mary and never doubted that she smelled every wildflower I picked her and would shield me from the taunts of children who found flower picking unseemly. . . . I believed all through adolescence, all through the first sordid pokings of desire. I believed all through my secular philosophy studies, all through those loose days of the sixties, when we believers hooted at the Church's hilarious sexual pronouncements and thought the hierarchy had been invented for our amusement. . . . I was an anarchist Catholic junkie, O! I was an iconoclast *pro* religion in an age of disbelief. I believed as I went mad. . . . I still believed when I reentered sanity. . . .

By the day after Easter, Tim has decided not only to abandon his church, but to dump his beloved fiancé, Mary Faith, and her young son, Jesse. He rejects Catholicism; Due East, S. C.; all family and friends. That fateful Monday, Tim gets up, shines his shoes, packs his bag, withdraws $15,000 from the bank, stuffs the bills into his socks, then drives slowly toward New York, scene of his student success at Columbia University and of happy—if conveniently reconstructed—memories.

Eccentric but credible characterization is the key to Sayers's success. Tim's manic, first-person narrative is rendered in the utterly genuine and sympathetic voice of a middle-age, failed academic with a generous heart who is losing his grip (once again) on sanity, perhaps on his very life. While Sayers conveys the pain Tim's dislocation, his story is oddly cheerful. Tim's messianic delusions—a cross between Don Quixote and Jesus Christ—are tempered with a wry consciousness about his often-ludicrous self-presentation. The story stays afloat on Tim's humor, intelligence and reckless optimism.

Driving north through Charleston, Tim spies an angel in the dark. The nocturnal hitchhiker is Angela Bliss, who is running away from an elaborate Southern wedding and the staid married life that will follow. Of course, she is heading to New York City. Meanwhile, back in Due East Mary Faith is beside herself with bitter worry. Father Berkeley, Tim's family priest, forms a search party with Mary Faith and Jesse. Through a series of reminiscences and flashbacks, readers learn the madcap and tragic history of the Rooney clan and, by extension, the quirky cultural lore of Due East.

Tim is one of five children of a radical Catholic activist mother with a conscience the size of the Atlantic Ocean. His father is violent and financially inept. One of his sisters commits suicide. Always troubled by mental illness, Tim's life has alternated between misadventures and pharmacological remedies. "[T]hat was my job, losing my mind. My mother couldn't go to a secular school, so I went. My mother couldn't love my father, so I did, when I could. My mother couldn't go crazy, so . . . They designate one of us in every family. I was the sacrificial son."

While Tim drives north with the young, lusty Angela, Mary Faith, Jesse and Father Berkeley form a very different kind of road troupe. Their journey transforms each of the bickering Samaritans. Particularly moving is Mary Faith's realization of why she loves the mad philosopher, and Jesse's progress from anxiety to anger to regained affection for Tim. Father Berkeley is convinced that in true Christian metaphor, Tim has subjected himself to exile in the wilderness (the uncivilized New York) and that they must find him within the proverbial 40 days or disaster will ensue.

Sayers humorously exposes the parochialisms and idiosyncrasies of both Due East and New York. Due East is a superficially cordial village, a town where Mary Faith lives her whole life next door to the Rooneys without feeling free to greet Tim's sister in the back yard. The New York scenes tellingly juxtapose surreal and stereotype: Tim's car is stolen the first night; he cowers from a bat flying around his subway compartment; he grooves at a cross-gender bar called Intergalactica; he gives away all his money to people sleeping in a park.

In some ways, *Brain Fever* is a wildly utopian novel, for Tim narrowly escapes through one net of grace to another. So nimbly does he evade death and assault that you begin to wonder if there is something holy about his innocence. Women always come to Tim's rescue: Angela finds him a New York sanctuary; he is nursed by a rich, white, Southern transplant in a grand SoHo loft; he's provided temporary haven by a tough-minded black school-teacher in a modest Brooklyn apartment. And, of course, there is Mary Faith, racing across the country to save him. The most engaging member of Tim's supporting cast is G. B. Brights, a young black man with dreadlocks and a worried face. G. B., a former student of Tim's from South Carolina whom he has forgotten about, just happens to be in New York, and he appears on the brink of several Rooney disasters to act as Tim's guardian angel.

One of Sayers's virtuoso moments is the scene in which a filthy, ragged, pajama-clad Tim lectures a tough crowd in Washington Square. What begins as a passionate homily about relieving Bosnian suffering gets twisted in Tim's mind as he invokes the spirits of actors Al Pacino and Florence Henderson. His listeners are drawn into rapt solidarity until his cock-eyed crusade is interrupted by the intercession of yet another set of angels:

> "BOSNIA!" I would have gone on, I would have continued, I would have chanted FREE TIBET! and MOZAMBIQUE! and TIANANMEN SQUARE! So many souls to save.

The finish line of this geocultural romp is provocatively left undrawn—relegating Tim's romantic and professional future to readers' imaginations. The connections between his childhood apparition of the Virgin Mary and his more recent hallucinations about Florence Henderson remain tantalizingly opaque. In the end, faith—all kinds of faith (in humanity, in love, in God, in New York, in Due East)—saves the day, and Tim comes to understand that despair is the only state from which one can't be redeemed. *Brain Fever* is a novel with wide appeal and is particularly rewarding for that large population of us who have been both Catholic and crazy in our doubting lives.

Additional coverage of Sayers's life and career is available in the following sources published by Gale: *Contemporary Authors*, **Vol. 134,** *Contemporary Authors New Revision Series;* **Vol. 61.**

Fay Weldon

1931-

English novelist, short story writer, dramatist, and scriptwriter.

The following entry presents an overview of Weldon's career. For further information on her life and works, see *CLC*, Volumes 6, 9, 11, 19, 36, and 59.

INTRODUCTION

Considered by many to be one of the finest contemporary English satirists, Weldon has focused in her novels and short stories on the state of women's lives in modern culture. Weldon finds the prescribed positions of women in social institutions oppressive, and skewers not only institutions, but both male and female behavior within them.

Biographical Information

Weldon was born in Alvechurch, Worcestershire, England, and spent her early childhood in New Zealand. She returned to England to attend Hampstead Girls' High School in London. Weldon then went to the University of St. Andrews, earning her master's degree in economics and psychology in 1952; in 1988 she received a Ph.D. in literature from the University of Bath and a subsequent doctoral degree in literature from the University of St. Andrews in 1992. In the late 1950s she worked as a writer for the Foreign Office and the *Daily Mirror* in London before moving on to work as an advertising copywriter. In 1960 she married Ron Weldon, an antiques dealer; the couple divorced in 1994. In addition to novels and short stories, Weldon is an accomplished playwright, scriptwriter, and writer of children's stories. Her awards include a Writers Guild award, a Giles Cooper award, a Society of Authors traveling scholarship, and a *Los Angeles Times* award for fiction.

Major Works

Weldon is known for infusing her works of social commentary with biting wit and grotesque imagery. But while she usually presents a dark picture of the female condition and the state of gender relations, she also frequently ends her books on a hopeful note. Esther, the heroine of her first novel *The Fat Woman's Joke* (1967) regains her self-respect and her husband's appreciation during a separation from him in which she succumbs to an eating disorder. In *Down among the Women* (1972) Weldon portrayed three generations of oppressed women; but rebellion and hope for independence are embodied in the third generation, rep-

resented by the protagonist's illegitimate daughter. Although she depicts women as oppressed and exploited, Weldon analyzes the ways in which they are responsible for their own problems and the unfortunate situations of other women. Women betraying each other is one of her major themes. In *The Life and Loves of a She-Devil* (1983) a large, unattractive woman named Ruth, disillusioned by romance novels, is rejected by her husband in favor of a beautiful romance writer. Ruth exacts revenge by transforming herself through plastic surgery into the exact double of the writer, destroying both her husband and his mistress but also losing her entire identity. In many of Weldon's works both male and female infidelity are responsible for the dissolution of marriages. In *The Cloning of Joanna May* (1989), an examination of the nature versus nurture question, Joanna's husband Carl has her cloned, then divorces her for having an affair. Thirty years later Joanna and the clones—none characterized as sympathetic or successful people—meet, and Carl and his new mistress end up falling into a nuclear reactor. In *Life Force* (1992) the lives of four women are disrupted when the man they all have slept with returns after a twenty-year absence; all four of them fall into self-destruction and chaos because of their obsession with the man's enormous phallus—the "life force" of the title. In *Trouble* (1994; published as *Affliction* in England) Weldon took on modern psychotherapy, as two new-age therapists seem to deliberately ruin the marriage of a man who seeks their help to deal with his massive insecurities about his wife's sudden success. *Wicked Women* (1995), a collection of short stories written since 1972, features a cast of characters who all, male and female, come off poorly, despite the title. *Worst Fears* (1996) concerns a woman dealing with unexpected revelations after her husband's sudden death. Believing she had the perfect marriage, Alexandra Ludd discovers that her husband has been sleeping with her best friends for years, and after his death she is snubbed by everyone including the family dog.

Critical Reception

Critics find Weldon's satires on gender relations and contemporary issues, such as cloning and nuclear terror, witty and scathing. Some reviewers have commented on the increasing bitterness of her later works, finding them too hopeless and grim to offer any kind of satisfying resolution to readers; others believe her characterizations of men are shallow and overly negative. Still, Weldon's astute social observations and outrageously inventive plots have earned her both critical praise and a loyal popular readership.

PRINCIPAL WORKS

The Fat Woman's Joke (novel) 1967
Down among the Women (novel) 1971
Female Friends (novel) 1975
Remember Me (novel) 1976
Words of Advice (novel) 1977
Praxis (novel) 1978
Puffball (novel) 1980
Watching Me, Watching You (short stories) 1981
The President's Child (novel) 1983
The Life and Loves of a She-Devil (novel) 1983
Polaris and Other Stories (short stories) 1985
The Shrapnel Academy (novel) 1986
The Heart of the Country (novel) 1987
The Hearts and Lives of Men (novel) 1987
Leader of the Band (novel) 1988
The Cloning of Joanna May (novel) 1989
Darcy's Utopia (novel) 1990
Moon over Minneapolis (short stories) 1991
Life Force (novel) 1992
Trouble (novel) 1994
Splitting (novel) 1994
Wicked Women (short stories) 1995

Worst Fears (novel) 1996

CRITICISM

Susannah Clapp (review date 24 February 1978)

SOURCE: "Soft Machines," in *New Statesman and Society,* Vol. 95, No. 2449, February 24, 1978, p. 258.

[*In the following review, Clapp calls* Little Sisters *"glittering" and "witty."*]

Fay Weldon's latest novel [*Little Sisters*] is by turns hectoring, funny, astute and artificial. Full of dreadful warnings relating to the 'black pool of desire and destiny' awash in women, it delivers its moral messages with a depersonalised urgency, variously shrinking or swelling its characters into embodiments of fairy-tale oppositions: they are chiefly distinguished by being either old or young, rich or poor, barren or fertile; all use sex for the 'sharing out of privilege'.

The interest of *Little Sisters* lies not in its components but in the cleverness with which these are manouvered. An exotically grisly account of Sixties London kookery, in which men wore toupees woven from pubic hair, manufacture navel gems and send ugly sisters hurtling from windows, is pitted against a supposedly authentic, non-fantastic story in which a shriveled millionaire (whose fortune comes from plastic flowerpots) and his crippled wife entertain a balding antique dealer and his luscious young girl friend—planning, amid an abundance of bad taste, to impregnate the girl and acquire an heir.

The first of these tales is presented as a fictional unweaving of the past: a cautionary tale told to the voluptuously nodding young girl who 'blushes and grinds her tiny teeth' while patronised. Its force as moral fable, urging the girl's escape to (presumably) her very own fecundity, is dubious; and since both narratives interweave the mundane and the bizarre in almost equal proportions, the distinction which labels only the first as fantasy is made (perhaps intentionally) to seem arbitrary. Nevertheless, by providing an alternative version of what in retrospect seems inevitable it makes future escape appear more possible—and this makes the interjections of worldly wisdom, delivered throughout in admonitory present-tense gasps, more palatable because less definitive. Faced with the basically inert ingredients of the main narrative, the exuberant inventiveness of the fantasy becomes a requirement; in using it, Fay Weldon has manufactured a glittering, witty piece of machinery without a center.

Agate Nesaule Krouse (essay date 1979)

SOURCE: "Feminism and Art in Fay Weldon's Novels," in *Critique,* Vol. XX, No. 2, 1979, pp. 5-20.

[*In the following essay, Krouse contends that Weldon's novels contain both artistic value and a feminist consciousness without resorting to didacticism.*]

Recent interest in women writers and women's experience has helped establish some literary reputations and revive others. While many women writers are being ignored, several have gained prominence because they seem to speak for authentic female experience. Certainly a healthy curiosity about women's lives—too often falsified or ignored in contemporary fiction—has been responsible for the popular success and only somewhat guarded critical approval of such flawed novels as Alix Shulman's *Memories of an Ex-Prom Queen,* Erica Jong's *Fear of Flying,* Susan Schaeffer's *Anya,* and Lisa Alther's *Kinflicks.* A more important result of such curiosity is the increasingly serious attention paid to writers like Lessing, Drabble, and Atwood, who have revealed the lives of women in major contemporary novels.

Because fears persist that a writer deeply committed to exploring the problems of women will produce fiction "contaminated" by sociology, political rhetoric, self-pity, or autobiography, one must show that while a new writer may be a feminist she is also an artist, and that while she understands and sympathizes with women, she also writes novels whose structure, style, point of view, irony, or other formal elements recommend them to repeated consideration after curiosity is satisfied. Such a writer is British novelist Fay Weldon, author of *The Fat Woman's Joke* (1967)—the American title is *. . . And the Wife Ran Away* (1968), *Down Among the Women* (1972), *Female Friends* (1974), and *Remember Me* (1976).

If one is curious about the lives of women, one can do no better than read Weldon. Her major subject is the experience of women: sexual initiation, marriage, infidelity, divorce, contraception, abortion, motherhood, housework, and thwarted careers—all receive consideration. But she is not tedious about the rich texture of everyday female existence she creates. Unlike the vivid fictional worlds of Oates and Lessing, which often depend on exhaustive detail and lengthy description, Weldon's exists because she most often selects the telling and the funny, the absurd and the horrifying. Her short descriptive passages also serve many purposes. For example, a few lines about contraception indicate not only the experience of numerous individual characters but also reveal the helplessness and hopefulness of a whole generation of women, suggest so-

cial attitudes, sketch life in London in the 1950's, treat a subject often ignored, and provide humor:

> It is the days before the pill. Babies are part of sex. Rumors abound. Diaphragms give you cancer. The Catholics have agents in condom factories—they prick one in every fifty rubbers with a pin with the Pope's head on it. You don't get pregnant if you do it standing up. Or you can take your temperature every morning, and when it rises that's ovulation and danger day. Other days are all right. Marie Stopes says soak a piece of sponge in vinegar and shove it up.

Such brief descriptive passages are only part of Weldon's extremely effective rendering of female lives. Instead of relying on a single minutely analyzed protagonist, she creates numerous vividly individualized women within the same work whose lives intertwine. Weldon's fiction often mirrors the insights of feminist theorists about the nature and situation of women: love does not last, marriage is not happy, motherhood is not serene. Her multiple female characters function particularly well to make convincing a fictional world which indirectly questions many traditional assumptions. The experiences of her characters complement each other and, therefore, validate each other as well. Nine of Weldon's most important characters in ***Down Among the Women*** find marriage or other extended relationships with men unhappy and impossible to sustain—too large a number to dismiss, especially since these characters are clearly differentiated. If unconventional Wanda and too conventional Susan cannot be happy with the same man, retaining an optimistic view of male-female relationships is harder than it would be if a single protagonist or only one type of woman found men difficult.

Yet Weldon does not heavy-handedly use her female characters to hammer out a simplistic thesis about nasty men and victimized women. Through point of view and tone, her vision of women's relationships with men is more satisfyingly complex. True, her women suffer intensely; she writes, "Down here among the women you don't get to hear about man maltreated; what you hear about is man seducer, man betrayer, man deserter, man the monster." But she describes how her characters—who live "down among the women" rather than in some ideal world where gender is irrelevant—perceive and discuss men. Furthermore, the above sentence occurs close to one of several reminders that the reader is not in the midst of an unremittingly realistic novel, convincing though the scenes and characters may be: "There will now be a short intermission. Sales staff will visit all parts of the theatre." The reader is witnessing a performance, an artistic creation shaped by an intelligence which does not oversimplify. For after several anecdotes about male selfishness, which follow the statement about "man the monster," the narrator sympathetically observes, "Man seems not so much wicked as frail, unable to face pain, trouble and growing old." Likewise, incidents demonstrating the basic pattern—that relationships with men are very difficult—are highly inventive and varied, but not all incidents fit the pattern. Several happy relationships are achieved at the end of the novel, because women themselves have changed and grown.

One thematic pattern emerges with few minor incidents to contradict it. Weldon's women are not by nature monogamous, irrevocably attached to the one man who makes them suffer. If they are—as Helen and Y. in *Down Among the Women* or Midge in *Female Friends,* they eventually die at their own hand. Victims of an obsession that life without a particular man is impossible, these characters suggest symbolically that such obsession is self-destructive. Perhaps since the whole stereotypical pattern of monogamous women and polygamous men is very much alive in contemporary fiction in spite of feminist theory and biological fact to the contrary, Weldon does not undercut her own radical insight by varied incidents suggesting a different minor pattern. The theme of women's capacity for more relationships than the double standard would allow, made convincing by her multiple characters, is not insisted upon by rhetoric nor repetition. Rather, it emerges as one possible underlying pattern.

Weldon's multiple characters are also part of her most modern and most profoundly feminist theme: the significance of women's friendships. Virginia Woolf wrote of "how immense a change" is evident in a novel by one of her contemporaries who had chosen to describe friendship between two women: the "relationships between women . . . in the splendid gallery of fictitious women, are too simple. So much has been left out, unattempted." In earlier literature, Woolf observes, "almost without exception they [women] are shown in their relation to men . . . And how small a part of a woman's life is that"; the writer who knows how to portray friendships between women "will light a torch in that vast chamber where nobody has yet been." For Woolf, female friendships are the key to fully human and complex characters as well as signs of a strikingly modern work. Although we have some notable exceptions—Mary McCarthy, Doris Lessing, and Marge Piercy, few contemporary novelists have treated the subject successfully.

Weldon treats women's friendships in all her novels, which her multiple characters give her plenty of opportunity to do, and they are her major subject in *Female Friends.* By recounting the lives of three women who in their childhood have been thrown together by the Second World War, she suggests, that the reasons for women's friendships are extremely complex. Majorie, Chloe, and Grace have all at some point slept with Patrick Bates, and two of them have even had a child by him. He is, however, mostly irrelevant to their continuing commitment to each other; the three have been young together, have had figuratively the same mother, and have seen each other's suffering. While they may disapprove of each other's behavior in the bitingly direct things they say, they nevertheless sympathize with each other and do not break off friendship for something as cruel and abstract as failure to "behave well." Chloe, the most maternal, cares for Grace's children because she understands that Grace's punitive ex-husband "battered the maternal instinct out of her"; she also keeps in touch with unloved and exploited Marjorie. Men come and go, but the relationships between women endure. Male friendships do not last and are based on money, drink, or promiscuous sexuality.

Weldon is not sentimental about undying loyalty among women, who hurt each other as often as men hurt them: "So you [Madeleine] were wronged; so were a million, million others, dead and gone on their way. You were wronged by women as much as men; you know you were. By your mother; by your friends; by your especial sisters." In a possible allusion to Lessing, Chloe reflects:

> Our loyalties are to men, not to each other.

> We marry murderers and think well of them. Marry thieves, and visit them in prison. We comfort generals, sleep with torturers, and not content with such passivity, torment the wives of married men, quite knowingly.

> Well, morality is for the rich, and always was. We women, we beggars, we scrubbers and dusters, we do the best we can for us and ours. We are divided amongst ourselves. We have to be, for survival's sake. (*Female Friends*)

Unlike Lessing, however, who explains women's primary loyalty to men as unalterably rooted in psychology and biology, Weldon has a much clearer feminist perception of the social causes—the very fact that her women can be friends or make amends to each other is hopeful. Nor do Weldon's women brood like Lessing's that their deepest needs can be satisfied only by one man or that their friendships may be lesbian. Weldon's work is not marred, as a critic has argued that Lessing's is, by "alienation from the authentic female perspective, a perspective which is clearly sketched in and then smeared by the censor in Lessing."

Marjorie, at the deathbed of her mother, has the most significant vision of women's friendships, which seems to be shared by Weldon. Recalling Midge, the wife whom Patrick Bates has driven to suicide, Marjorie says, "We should interfere more in each other's lives, and not just pick up pieces. . . . We just stood back and let her die" (*Female*

Friends). She gives her houses to Chloe, so the latter can leave Oliver, the husband whose monstrous selfishness and hypocrisy provide some of the funniest moments in the novel. Her act is responsible for the happy ending of a novel filled with the suffering of women. Weldon has shown throughout that women are at the hands of chance—"And wham, bam, so our lives are ordered," death, men, and even each other, but she singles out friendship and motherhood as two forces that can mitigate inescapable pain: "Maternal warmth . . . seeps down through the generations, fertilising the ground, preparing it for more kindness." Active friendship between women allows one to live and rejoice: "As for me, Chloe, I no longer wait to die. I put my house, Marjorie's house, in order, and not before time. The children help. Oliver says, 'But you can't leave me with Francoise,' and I reply, I can, I can, and I do."

Weldon's interest in the experience of women, her perceptions about their sexuality and friendship, her intelligent view that women's lives are of necessity different from men's, her successful rendering of what to live "down among the women" means make her a most valuable contemporary novelist for the committed feminist and for the general reader who is curious about women. But Weldon's novels are appealing even if one does not share her feminist insights. Their structure, narrative techniques, point of view, style, and humor place them among the finest achievements in recent fiction by women.

Weldon's first novel, **The Fat Woman's Joke,** is an apprentice work showing strengths only fully realized in the later novels. It portrays a crisis in the life of middle-aged, overweight Esther, who has discovered the exploitation inherent in a married woman's lot. Having gone on a diet, Esther and her husband, Alan, have faced each other across the void left by elaborately discussed and lovingly prepared meals. Stomachs have growled and tempers flared. Violence and adultery have proved irresistible to the half-starved Alan. Esther has moved to a squalid flat, where she gorges as she divulges her story in barbed language to visitors. Flashbacks and parallel scenes flesh out a situation more suitable for a short story, a symbolic joke that happy marriage is based on consuming.

Down Among the Women is far more ambitious. The lives of three generations of women are presented. Weldon has achieved coherence in a novel with so many characters and with incidents spanning twenty years by focusing on one family of women to whom all other characters have some link. The story begins in 1950, as radical, unconventional Wanda is preparing for a Divorcees Anonymous meeting, an unusual group in Post-War London. Her unwed daughter, Scarlet, whom she has named after the blood of political martyrs, is monstrously pregnant with Byzantia, representative of the third generation. Scarlet's friends, their lovers and husbands, Wanda's ex-husband and his new wife, as well as a few more distantly related characters people the novel.

The point of view also provides coherence. An unidentified first-person narrator is introduced in the first chapter. Watching her children play, she sits in the park, "a woman's place," where Scarlet occasionally joins her. The narrator—who may be either one of Scarlet's friends or a persona for the author—is referred to at the beginning of four of the fourteen chapters. Other chapters begin with observations about what "we" who are "down among the women" believe or experience; some chapters omit such formal introduction and plunge directly into the characters' lives. Incidents are presented repeatedly from a third-person omniscient point of view. Occasionally, however, the narrator tells us to "listen now" as Wanda sings or to take a short intermission. Only in the conclusion, "Down Among the Women," which follows Chapter 14, is the narrator's identity revealed: "My name is Jocelyn. I sit in the park and consider the past, and what became of us all, and how little the present accords with our expectations of it." Jocelyn is a specific character, accident-prone and repressed, who eventually comes to terms with her sexuality and motherhood. She is no more fully developed than Scarlet's other friends.

The point of view gives **Down Among the Women** a clean and unified shape. The first-person narrator provides a frame for the incidents presented since all of them seem available to a central intelligence. Weldon does not, however, limit the scenes to those at which Jocelyn is present. Rather, knowing the general drift of her friends' lives, Jocelyn has imaginatively fleshed them out with specific incident and dialogue. Since, in one sense, the whole narrative is a meditation Jocelyn has on the park bench, the events form a unified whole. The complex chronology, which includes changes in society and in individual lives from 1950 to 1970, is thus contained by a woman thinking. In addition, Weldon develops some of her most poignant effects by having Jocelyn range freely between past and present. For instance, we know from the beginning that the beautiful Helen is doomed to die, which makes us regard her single-minded, manipulative pursuit of the artist X. more charitably. At the bleakest moments in Scarlet's marriage to impotent, rigid Edwin, we know that "spring is coming" for her. The point of view and the resulting complex but unified chronology, then, are responsible for many of Weldon's best ironic and comic scenes.

The point of view is also an indication of the profundity of Weldon's feminism. To create individual incidents or characters who will exemplify some feminist tenet is probably less difficult than to create a work whose very structure is feminist. Weldon may be unique among the new feminist novelists in developing such a structure. **Down Among the**

Women demonstrates that women's experience, though varied, has many common elements. The whole novel could profitably be analyzed as a definition of womanhood: passages describing how one has to live "down among the women" contrast with anecdotes of male behavior; characters leave the girls and join the women. Weldon is an essential writer for anyone who agrees with feminist theoreticians that women's culture has not been fully explored, and her decision to leave the narrator unnamed until the next-to-last page is one of her most brilliant strokes, unifying content and form perfectly.

When we learn the narrator's identity, the way we regard individual scenes does not significantly change. Jocelyn is neither more perceptive nor artistic than the other characters. The reader senses that any average woman could feel intensely and express movingly the joy and anguish of many women. Fay Weldon, whose intelligence and sympathy clearly shape the novel, does not claim exclusive authorial credit for its creation. To leave the "I" unassigned so that it could be an authorial voice must have been tempting. Instead, Jocelyn, the author, the women characters, and all women merge. The point of view underlines the theme that the experience of women is, in the best sense, communal. While feminist theory richly informs the novel, the structure itself elevates *Down Among the Women* far above a thesis-ridden book.

Weldon is also a superb comic writer, who can be enjoyed largely for her wit and humor. She is primarily a witty writer, who sees incongruities, uses skillful phraseology, surprising contrasts, epigrams, and comparisons. At the same time, she also has a large sympathy for human foibles, so that her work is incisive without the cold brittleness of a writer like Mary McCarthy. Her comic effects are rich and varied: visual descriptions, inverted commonplaces, slang, and verbal assaults by one character on another. She is not above including jokes and songs. Wanda tells Scarlet, who is in a sanctimonious mood about motherhood, the story of the randy milkman; impotent Edwin sings "an awful warning, / Never do it in the morning." She uses progressive repetition to suggest that the funny may also be the terrifying: Jocelyn accidentally freezes her parrot, gasses her cat, sets fire to her flat, and scalds her small son. The laughter increases, then dies. Coincidence provides many of the funniest moments: Scarlet has her baby in her new stepmother Susan's bed, who is then forced to have her son in the hospital, where she is put in isolation because she has post-puerperal fever:

> Doctors come and stare at her, and ask her how she's feeling. "Fine," she says, and they look bemused, and at each other, as they inspect, tap, and medicate. They don't understand it, and why should they? They have their test-tubes mixed.

In the ward another young woman drifts slowly off towards death, unnoticed.

Susan rallies enough to turn her equally young stepdaughter out of bed. Such blending of the terrible and the ridiculous is one of the major reasons why a novel filled with the pain endured by women—lack of love, abandonment, violence, and death account for three-fourths of the events—is neither painfully depressing nor cheerfully sentimental. It also places Weldon in the mainstream of contemporary fiction.

Female Friends is also a very funny novel. In addition to using most of the comic devices mentioned above, Weldon, who has also written for *Upstairs, Downstairs* relies a great deal on dialogue. The narrative is interspersed with innumerable passages written in the style of a play with the characters' names set off on the left, followed by their words and sometimes brief stage directions indicating tone. Many conversations are startling. Like Ivy Compton-Burnett's characters, Weldon's are often terrifyingly direct, though more specific about physical facts. "Do they make you watch?" asks Grace as soon as it has been confirmed that Chloe's husband and the au pair girl are sleeping together. "And how was Marjorie's moustache? Or does she shave, these days?" asks Grace, as she tries to pack, in a scene that is visually comic: "she will lift a jersey or bra to her nose and sniff, and if she finds it offensive she will either throw it into the wastebin, if she considers it too far gone, or spray lavishly with cologne before returning it to its pile. Chloe is half admiring, half shocked."

The point of view in *Female Friends* has some similarity to that of *Down Among the Women.* Chapters including the first-person point of view of Chloe alternate with chapters told entirely from the third-person point of view. Chapters with the first-person narrator are again not restricted to events at which Chloe is present. Although the reliance on dialogue gives the impression that Weldon is using primarily the objective or dramatic point of view, the narrative as a whole is actually omniscient: it moves easily from the past to the present and includes reflections and incidents realistically available only to characters other than Chloe. Again, Weldon allows one of her women characters to speak for the experience of other women, to give imaginative shape and emotional weight to events she could only know about in general terms.

Introducing Chloe as a central intelligence at the very beginning of the novel has effects different from those achieved in *Down Among the Women*. Weldon is once more working with a complex chronology, but now the present of her first-person narrator, Chloe, is more definite than Jocelyn's musings on a park-bench. Two days and nights constitute her present: Chloe, isolated in the country because her husband insists on ecology as long as it is no inconvenience to him, visits her friends Majorie and Grace in London, then returns to the home she shares with her own and with her friends' Children, as well as to her husband, Oliver, whom she is forced to share with Francoise, the au pair girl. That night Oliver demands greater tolerance from Chloe than he has before. He insists that she make love with Francoise, only to accuse her of revealing her true lesbian nature. The next day Chloe meets her two female friends at the deathbed of Marjorie's mother, and Marjorie comes to her insight about the need for active friendship among women. As a result, Chloe can move into her house and leave Oliver.

The vivid two days of Chloe's present alternate with incidents from the past in the lives of the three friends. The numerous scenes are unified because Weldon chooses to focus on a character to whom all others have a direct relationship: besides being Marjorie's and Grace's friend, Chloe makes a home for her own children as well as those of Grace and of Midge (the dead wife of Patrick Bates, former lover of all three friends)—a fact that allows the tangled affairs of the adults to emerge naturally. In addition, Chloe thinks of herself as being "in the mainstream of female action and reaction": she, therefore, parallels other women from earlier generations—her own gentle mother. Gwynneth, and her surrogate mother, Esther, who, like Chloe, cared for other women's children and gave them security and a common past. Numerous other contrasts and parallels provide further unity.

The point of view of *Female Friends,* assigned extensively to a more specific central intelligence and situation, gives the novel complexity, unity, irony, and humor. In *Down Among the Women,* Weldon presents many women suffering as a result of their sex, yet she is ultimately optimistic about the fate of women. One of the central insights in the novels is an imaginative rendering of changes in attitude from generation to generation. By living without a husband, Wanda has preserved her integrity, but she has also paid for it. Her daughter's friends seek happiness through men, but her granddaughter, Byzantia, echoes Wanda's independence and foreshadows a new kind of woman:

> "You amaze me," says Byzantia. "Fancy seeing success in terms of men. How trivial, with the world in the state it's in".

> "Merely as a symbol of success," pleads Scarlet, "I don't mean to offer it as the cause."

> "A symptom more like," says Byzantia, "of a fearful disease from which you all suffered. One of you even died on the way. I think the mortality rate is too high."

When asked to define the disease, Byzantia cannot. Definitions, she says, are in any case no part of her business. It is enough to tear the old order down.

Byzantia, like her grandmother Wanda, is a destroyer, not a builder. But where Wanda struggled against the tide and gave up, exhausted, Byzantia has it behind her, full and strong.

Down among the women.

We are the last of the women.

In *Female Friends,* however, Weldon shows significant dramatic development in one woman. Chloe has been taught by her mother, whose heart-rending loyalty to her beloved employer has caused her to be exploited financially and emotionally, to "understand and forgive," a phrase that becomes one of the motifs against which to measure Chloe's change. Weldon begins with "the day Chloe's life is to change—in the way that lives of calm people do change, through some alteration to attitude rather than of conduct." Chloe has found living according to her mother's precept exhausting. "I could do with some anger to energise me, and bring me back to life again. But where can I find the anger? Who is to help me? My friends? I have been understanding and forgiving my friends, my female friends, for as long as I can remember." Although the expectation is set up that Chloe's revitalizing anger will be turned against her friends, her understanding of them and other women, regardless of how they might be judged according to any exacting standard, remains Chloe's most attractive characteristic.

Instead, Chloe has to cease to "understand and forgive" Oliver's selfishness, infidelity, and hypocrisy in order to free herself from a marriage that is joyless and humiliating. She recognizes her mother's meekness in the face of terrible injustice as "a miserable, crawling, snivelling way to go, the worn-out slippers neatly placed beneath the bed, careful not to give offence." She eventually finds herself laughing at Oliver, "really quite lightly and merrily . . . and in this she is, at last, in tune with the universe." Grace has been saying that Chloe is "too dangerous a martyr," that "bad behavior is very animating." Chloe, supported by her friends in her change of attitude toward Oliver, rejects her mother's lesson: better to be alive to rejoice, to enjoy the present. Even Marjorie's and Grace's lives seem to take a turn for the better once Chloe has rejected the notion that women have to suffer, forgive, and endure.

By suggesting in *Down Among the Women* that hope for an easier life lies in future generations, Weldon seems to have set herself the task of showing that even for an individual, middle-aged, submissively conditioned woman a better life is possible if she can change and if she has female friends. Such a theme is only sketched in: the richness of the novel forbids a simple statement to stand for it. The mingling of the two days in Chloe's present and the varied incidents of the past are brought together into a complex whole through the interplay of the first- and third-person points of view, which merge when Chloe, ironically echoing the marriage ceremony, says about leaving Oliver, "I can, I can, and I do." In addition to the complex but carefully unified structure, *Female Friends* has many of Weldon's other strengths: vivid imagery, a strong sense of time and place, memorable dialogue, complex events, and multiple characters that are neither confusing nor superficially observed—a rich rendering of life with brevity and wit.

Remember Me shares the above strengths. Once again it reveals a complex chronology—a few days in the present are superimposed over past events—through it no longer uses the first-person narrator. *Remember Me* also shows Weldon's willingness to re-examine previous thematic concerns and her ability to adapt or invent new narrative techniques. The middle-aged wife displaced by a younger woman promising greater domestic serenity and renewed sexual vigor to a man all too aware of his age has appeared in all three previous novels. Here Weldon faces honestly the full implications of the rage such a woman may feel if she has no prospects for a better future, if her situation is different from Chloe's in *Female Friends.* Divorced, poor, and depressed, Madeleine lives in a squalid basement flat with her lumpy, hopeless daughter, Hilary, while ex-husband Jarvis shares the pleasures of his elegantly refurbished house and bed with his selfish, beautiful, new wife, Lily. Madeleine presents herself as the victim she unquestionably is, "elbowing and stamping to achieve a yet more ragged pair of jeans, a yet more matted jersey by way of illustration" of what Jarvis has done to her. "All Madeleine can do for Hilary, all she knows how to do, is despise Jarvis and Lily—and what kind of help is that to Hilary?" Weldon not only presents but also authorially comments on the costs of such hate to both mother and daughter. Madeleine's one ineffectual moment of hopefulness for a new future—another man, the pathetic Mr. Quincey from Dial-a-Date, rather than the serene life without men espoused by the lesbian Renee—is ironically a causes of her death in a car accident.

Madeleine, the angry victim, has not been able to affect others significantly while alive, but in death she becomes a powerful motivating force for re-examination, recognition, change, and growth in others. When Madeleine's leg is severed and the steering wheel driven into her chest, her spirit passes into the plump, kindly, compliant Margot, the doctor's wife who has always served her husband and children without questioning the loss of self in marriage and motherhood. As Madeleine is dying, the dinner at ex-husband Jarvis' house is disrupted: Margot experiences a searing pain in her leg and shortness of breath; windows bang, children wake, the clock stops. The next morning Margot's previously serene family is disconcerted by her sudden expressions of grim anger, resentment, hate, and regrets for her lost self. The "convulsive tumult of discontent and resentment" also produces positive results: selfish Lily recognizes some of her faults and feels intensely maternal love and pain, Jarvis rediscovers the ability to feel as he grieves for Madeleine, Margot recognizes that Madeleine is part of herself and makes amends to her by taking in the orphaned Hilary. Like Addie in *As I Lay Dying,* Madeleine motivates others to act after her death, but instead of bringing out heroism in her sons, she awakens a sense of human solidarity in characters of both sexes.

In spite of the sharply observed details of interior decoration, dress, food, and conversation, patterns and themes are more important in *Remember Me* than the conventions of realism. Supernatural elements are used to underline the power of women's resentment against injustice. Madeleine is a most active corpse. In the morgue, her eyes keep opening, her body seems warm, she looks beautiful rather than haggard as she was in life, the shrouds repeatedly fall on the floor in disarray. The ambulance carrying her to the mortuary has an accident, so that the corpse, falling out with eyes open, has a lasting effect on those passing by. The morgue attendants sense she is lively and hear murmurs.

The supernatural elements are appropriate since the resentment felt by women is powerful and authentic, yet not always scrupulously fair or rational. As "the focal point of some kind of group energy," "the focus of womanly discontent," Madeleine expresses anger recognized as valid and commonplace by those hearing the whispers:

> How can I manage on the money you give me? How can I cope with a growing boy with you out at work all day? Of course the place is untidy; I'm at my wits' end coping with the mess you make. If you'd ever played football with the lad, his hair wouldn't be the length it is . . . How you ill-treat me, monster! Villain! Going off to war with two legs, coming back with one, and not hurrying home either. Beast!

> Why are you going into that dark vale, why are you leaving me here all alone? What is your male death to my female misery? Devil! Monster! Deserter!

The sense of being misunderstood and mistreated is also evident in the lives and thoughts of both female and male characters.

The plot violates the conventions of realism in its extreme

reliance on coincidence. The multiple characters from six families are shown to belong neatly within the same narrative by two paired sexual liaisons on the night of Jarvis' twenty-ninth birthday party sixteen years before. Staid, nice Margot, now the doctor's wife, had made love with Jarvis that night on his wife Madeleine's bed. Margot's son, always unquestioningly regarded as the doctor's, is probably Jarvis' son. When Margot takes in the orphaned Hilary, she notes the resemblance between the two children. Her husband had probably made love with the betrayed Madeleine on the same night. Scores of other coincidences, carefully enumerated in Chapter 10, emphasize the theme that chance, misunderstanding, and necessarily limited knowledge play a significant part in human life.

The dominant symbol and character is a corpse. Blisters, twisted ankles, vomit, blood-poisoning, abortion, post-abortion infection, menstruation, blows, slaps, pimples, burns, fat, sweat, hair, false teeth, operations, mutilations, drowning, paralysis, cancer, senility, and death are recurrent images underscoring human mortality. In the hands of a naturalistic novelist such details would be close to unbearable. Weldon's skillful handling of tone and her playfulness with narrative techniques, however, distance many of the horrors, make them comically absurd, and hence either funny or at least endurable for both characters and readers. What else can one do about past blows but laugh, as Madeleine used to about her mother's walking into an aircraft propeller, if one is not to be corroded by bitterness and grief? How else can one deal with mortality but defy it, as old Alice did, chomping with her dead husband's false teeth, two people speaking out of the same mouth, and clattering her necklace of polished gallstones?

Numerous techniques distance the horrifying, present a complex vision in a very brief space, and emphasize artifice rather than realism. The most important of these are refrains, riddles, interior monologues, incisive but tentative character analyses, and authorial comments. Refrains provide easy movement within individual chapters from one character or family to another, from the present to the past, from the trivial to the traumatic. Refrains such as "Good morning!" "Unfair!" or "Ordinary life!" allow for comic or poignant juxtaposition and give unity to individual chapters. The complexities of family life and characters' underlying motives are sometimes made explicit by passages Weldon calls "riddles." She reports an ordinary conversation about cereal, lost shoes, or a friend's visit in dialogue with each line numbered; a translation with correspondingly numbered lines follows. The riddles are delightful not only because Weldon has the good sense not to use them too often but also because the translations do not follow any consistent, predictable pattern. Ordinary words do not necessarily mean the opposite, the nastiest, the most self-revealing, nor the most universal. Sometimes a cigar is just a cigar, and

at other times Weldon sees meanings that would astound Freud.

Interior monologues in which the characters define themselves and explain their motives and insights are interspersed in the narrative. The monologues are stylized and rational statements rather than attempts to render tentative inner emotions, flux of sensations, and pre-speech levels so familiar in stream-of-consciousness novels. In simple declarative sentences characters define themselves first in terms of their relationships: they are wives, daughters, and mothers as well as sons and husbands, since here Weldon develops several male characters more fully and sympathetically than she had previously. The monologues are similar in style, regardless of the individual character's psyche as revealed in action and dialogue. They are artistically shaped summaries clearly different from the psychological realist's attempt to capture in language the complexity of an individual's inner life. Nevertheless, they increase our sympathy for the speaker and contribute significantly to the incongruities, comedy, and complexity of the novel. In addition, they also further several themes: the strong influence of mothers (rather than fathers) on children; the difficulties of modern marriage; the understandable individual motive unfairly judged by others; the kindness, guilt, and ability to feel in persons who, nevertheless, deal terrible blows to others; and the tension between being one's self and the inescapable truth that we are all part of one another.

Weldon is incisive in seeing the subtle, cruel motive lurking beneath surface kindness as well as the opposite. She allows the complexity of human motives to stand rather than making final neat judgments about her characters. Moreover, she does not resolve all questions about facts as a realistic novelist would: did Lily drown her inconvenient baby sister? did Jarvis deeply love Madeleine in the past or is the intense unhappiness of his first marriage a rewriting of history during his second one? does he love or dislike his second wife, Lily? are the fathers of the two children really reversed, as Margot decides after sixteen years of never questioning their paternity?

Although death and rage are in the foreground, *Remember Me* is a very funny novel, the result of narrative techniques as well as strengths in dialogue, description, and comic devices similar to those found in Weldon's earlier work. Undeniably, her vision is darker. Feminist insights into injustices suffered by women are too numerous to list, yet Weldon also understands and sympathizes with men. The war between the sexes in unavoidable because women do suffer, and their rage is a powerful force transcending individual life. While such anger is destructive, it cannot be dismissed. It can pass from one woman into another, and it can even bring out compassion and gentleness in both women and men after it has been recognized and expressed. After the upheavals caused by Madeleine's angry spirit, an equilibrium is re-established:

> "Oh, my sisters," whispers the memory of Madeleine to the still troubled air, "and my brothers too, soon you will be dead. Is this the way you want to live?"

> Which at least seemed to create some kind of concensus, for or against, because after that there was nothing but the wind to ruffle the grasses and disturb the little gay pots of dried flowers on the more recent graves, and whatever trouble there was dispersed, and there was peace.

Weldon's numerous authorial comments foreshadow and reinforce the conclusion. They are tentative enough to avoid sentimentality and oversimplification, but they suggest positive values in human life and reveal a cautious optimism in the face of forcefully delineated suffering. Such comments, yet another departure from realism, also provide unity and justify the reliance on coincidence in the plot.

> As we grow older we sense more and more that human beings make connections in much the same manner as the basic materials of matter. . . . The linkages are unexpected; they can be of objects, plants, places, events, anything. It is perhaps why we should take good care to polish furniture, water plants, telephone friends with whom we apparently have nothing in common, pay attention to coincidence, and in general help the linkages along instead of opposing them—as sometimes, in our panic at our very un-aloneness, we are moved to do.

> All things have meaning. Almost nothing is wasted. Old friends encountered by chance; old enemies, reunited to hate again; old emotions, made sense of and transmuted into energy; old loves reappearing; all the material flotsam washed up by the storms of our experience—all these have implication, and all lead us to the comforting notion that almost nothing in this world goes unnoticed; more, that almost nothing is unplanned.

Fay Weldon is important because she has succeeded in uniting the negative feminism, necessarily evident in novels portraying the problems of women, with a positive feminism, evident in the belief that change or equilibrium is possible. She has also succeeded in writing feminist comedy, demonstrating that feminism is neither humorless nor impossible to assimilate into a work of art. Experimentation with narrative techniques, careful structure, complex vision, and artistic maturity place *Down Among the Women, Female Friends,* and *Remember Me* among the significant achievements in recent fiction.

Benjamin DeMott (review date 27 December 1981)

SOURCE: "Stories and a Novel," in *New York Times Book Review,* December 27, 1981, pp. 8-9.

[*In the following review, DeMott offers praise for Weldon's collection of short stories in* Watching Me, Watching You, *but notes her evolution from overly depressing subjects in her first novel,* The Fat Woman's Joke, *to less bleak resolutions in later works.*]

American admirers of Fay Weldon, the English playwright, novelist and short story writer, will especially welcome *Watching Me, Watching You* because it contains, in addition to 11 short stories, a reissue of her out-of-print first book, a novel that appears under its original English title *The Fat Woman's Joke.* Here and there in the short stories Miss Weldon offers wry versions of yesterday's feelings. (During the Battle of Britain, a wife remembers, "quite a lot of women claimed that air-raids were preferable to their husbands' attentions.") In one or two pieces ghosts walk, breaking china in trendy vicarages. Mostly, though, the writer concentrates on hard-eyed, mushy-headed specimens collected from the contemporary media world—and they're a grotesque lot on the whole.

In **"Christmas Tree"** we meet Brian, a money-making, working-class TV dramatist retreating from Hollywood to Devon in hopelessly self-deceived pursuit of an honest rural mate. **"Holy Stones"** is about a fortyish atheistical newspaper columnist named Adam who's miserable on his honeymoon in Israel because he is unable to shake the religious faith of his 23-year-old Jesus-loving bride. **"Spirit of the House"** shows us a pair of publicity-mad peers whose home world includes a Disneyland, a zoo and a youngster who, having taken a first-class honors degrees in math at Oxford, sits all day at a computer terminal in the Great House library working out "efficient mathematical formulae for the winning of the pools." Elsewhere, we follow a parade of idle fornicators, 60's heroines, (owners of fading boutiques) lusting after lost glory, family groups fighting holiday tedium with endless games of Monopoly.

Our times. Harmonies abound between the stories and that first novel. *The Fat Woman's Joke* concerns Esther and Phyllis in their 30's, Susan and Brenda 10 years younger—Londoners who chat away to each other, chapterlessly, in sentences often reminiscent of Ivy Compton-Burnett. Esther has recently fled her unfaithful adman husband—and the tortuous discipline of a diet—for basement digs in Earls

Court, where she's eating herself into defiant obesity and ruminating on the wretchedness of married woman-kind and of the general human lot as well. Phyllis listens partly because she's bent on persuading Esther to return home to husband and son, partly because she feels guilty (Phyllis has had her bosom lifted and has allowed herself to be seduced by Esther's husband), partly because she's fascinated by the ghastly portrait of her own future as a middle-aged wife upon which Esther's despairing honesty lifts a curtain.

As for Susan and Brenda: the former is a painter and part-time stenographer, immensely assured on such subjects as sex, clothes, diet and married men, and the latter aspires to comparable confidence on exactly the same matters. The link between Susan/Brenda and Esther/Phyllis is that Susan is involved in concurrent affairs with Esther's husband and Esther's teen-age son. The novel's narrative path traverses Susan's and Phyllis's various treacheries toward a climax at which Esther's husband, fed up with casual bed partners and poor meals, appears on Esther's Earls Court doorstep, pressing her to come home.

There's one splendid comic sequence in *The Fat Woman's Joke* featuring a non-English-speaking Indian gentleman whom Brenda picks up in a pub, brings home to Susan's apartment, admires aloud for the spirituality of his mien and copulates with on Susan's rug. The two women discuss the gentleman at length afterward as he sits on Susan's couch, and the gentleman never speaks; he does, however, place two one-pound notes in Brenda's hand on departing, making a telling moment. There's also considerable force and wit in Esther's sermons on the desperate hatefulness of women's lives. And the echoes of Compton-Burnett—the sound of poised and icy candor—aren't by any means unwelcome. (Esther's husband to Phyllis: "You are gentle and docile and slim and pretty and neat, like a doll. You endure. You are not in the least clever and you never say anything devastating. I should have married you.")

But in a Compton-Burnett book you don't just get chilling candor and rich syntax: you get non-schlock period furnishings, the occasional faithful servant (the day helper in *The Fat Woman's Joke* is exceedingly stony) and no obsession whatever with diets. I'm saying, in a word, that Fay Weldon's first novel (like most of the 11 stories) strikes me as a shade depressing—too icy and astringent, too relentlessly knowing. Miss Weldon has produced more that one dark book in her past—I think particularly of her *Down Among the Women* (1972). But she also has a cheerier side—witness the sunny ending of last year's lively "**Puffball.**" I'm glad to know, at last, where this writer started, but what's really pleasing is her direction at the moment as a novelist. It's a lot less blackish mood than that in which she began, a dozen years ago, with *The Fat Woman's Joke*.

Anita Brookner (review date 7-20 October 1982)

SOURCE: "Passion," in *London Review of Books*, October 7-20, 1982, p. 11.

[*In the following review, Brookner finds* The President's Child *more compassionate and less heavy-handed ideologically than Weldon's earlier works.*]

The President's Child works, effortlessly, on many levels. First, it is a political thriller. Isabel Rust, a television producer and former hack reporter, once had an affair with a man who is supposedly being groomed as Democratic candidate for the Presidency of the United States. Her apparently spotless marriage was hastily contrived by her to provide a home for herself and the child of that previous union. On the surface, all is middle-class respectability in Camden Town. But as news coverage of the Primaries increase, people begin to notice the resemblance between Isabel's son and his real father: Isabel herself is seen by the candidate's campaign managers as a potential menace, and various moves, entirely credible, are made to dispose of her.

On this level, the invention is powerful and sustained. But it is not at this level that the gravity of the book is made manifest. Mrs Weldon has in the past been a devastating but partial protagonist in the familiar argument of man's inhumanity to woman. Here she breaks free of her own propaganda, and in one of the most lyrical passages written by a woman for many years, she acknowledges the primacy, the absolute necessity of passion, the centrality and totality of physical love, and the difference between this and whatever other arrangements may have to be made. Mrs Weldon's celebration of this discovery is not only fervent: it is worshipful. The spiky ladies who populated her earlier novels now fade into the background, while the foreground is dominated by a woman and her lover, and what passes between them is not scornfully reduced but restored to its rightful place. At a time when many women novelists are content to launch chronicles of sexual consumerism, it comes as an agreeable surprise to find Mrs Weldon calmly pushing these back onto the sidelines where they belong, and writing with complete conviction and with an edge of amorous sadness about a love affair marked off from all others. And, as always, she concentrates her meaning in a single phrase: 'He made me what my mother could not—he made me whole.'

And there is an even deeper level on which this novel is serious, for it deals with cause and effect, with right and wrong, with authenticity and bad faith. Bright facades reveal tragedies and delinquencies which one is somehow not surprised to discover. The snappy infighting of her previous novels is abandoned for a more sombre realisation of what life may be about, and in the course of this process perspectives undergo a change. 'Feminism is a luxury,' pronounces the narrator. 'The world is graded into fit and unfit, not male and female.' There are fewer possibilities than were once assumed to be available. Perhaps duty is inescapable. Perhaps even God exists. The moral burden is resumed with some dignity and is used to structure an already excellent fiction.

Art Seidenbaum (review date 19 April 1987)

SOURCE: A review of *The Shrapnel Academy,* in *Los Angeles Times Book Review,* April 19, 1987, pp. 2, 8.

[*In the following review, Seidenbaum offers reserved praise for* The Shrapnel Academy, *noting that because of the novel's extreme violence and cynicism it is for those with "strong stomachs."*]

This [*The Shrapnel Academy*] is an explosive little novel, to English drawing room comedy what the Hindenburg was to zeppelin flight.

Shrapnel Academy, a well-endowed mythic military school named after the man who invented the exploding cannonball, gathers a sort of numskulls' Noah's Ark for the annual Eve-of-Waterloo dinner. Gen. Leo Makeshift, oafish but agreeable, will deliver the Wellington lecture; Bella Morthampton, his secretary in title but his mistress in fact, will devour the tough caribou patties from a 1794 Canadian recipe; Mew Whittaker will be mistaken for a *Times* of London correspondent when, in reality, she represents the ferociously feminist *Women's Times.* Fold in, among others, an idiot savant who makes his living selling deadly weapons, an overage secret agent, a dithering married couple and two frightened faculty members—a human sampler of the old Empire in accelerated decline.

Imagine Alastair Sim, Joyce Grenfell, Joan Greenwood, Ian Carmichael, Terry-Thomas and Sir Alec Guinness at one table; discover they have hidden alliances and watch them savage each other.

Joan Lumb runs this foolish academy, a lady with an exquisite sense of putting people in place and putting classes in descending orders of status. "So important," according to Lumb, "to get the seating arrangements right. A dinner party's like a cocktail—no matter how good the ingredients, if you don't stir properly, everything's wasted." Male, white managers are at the top of her social hierarchy; male,

black managers rank ahead of female, white servants in the middle; female, black servants are at the bottom.

And at the literal bottom of the academy are uncounted hundreds of servants of all colors—plus their spouses, friends and fellow runaways from Nicaragua, Sri Lanka, Cuba, Soweto—all those impolite places where bigotry or battle make life dangerous. Lumb, like any colonial officer, doesn't know what malice lurks among the lower lives. She doesn't even have a census of the oppressed population.

Upstairs, the relics clutching to title and tiara. Downstairs, the refugees holding to life and limb. Boom.

That doesn't seem so funny, does it? More like a Marxist struggle knotted in old school ties? Well, Fay Weldon isn't any kinder to the huddled masses than the gross gourmands. She caricatures the grotesqueries of polite and impolite society, drums up a murderous little conflict within the building and uses the absurd academy as a microcosm for making a bloody mockery of all wars. Before she has finished clearing the banquet table: A servant has died in childbirth—from inattention; a dog has been slaughtered and served to the guests—as a mousse in finger sandwiches—and a nuclear explosion levels both class distinctions and the structure.

If that still doesn't seem so funny, Weldon interlards her story with asides to the reader and scraps of narrative from historic battles. Little shards, like shrapnel itself, can be devastating: "Peace may look good to governments," says the satiric authorial voice, "but it is only the quiet time an army needs to recover from the last war and prepare for the next. . . . Peace is good for agriculture, but bad for the economy, bad for love and bad for civilian morale. Civil unrest, blasphemy, discontent and crime flourish in times of peace."

Other scraps seem merely precious: "Gentle Reader! What have I said! You are no more gentle than I am. I apologize for insulting you. You are as ferocious as anyone else. The notion that the reader is gentle is very bad for both readers and writers, and the latter do tend to encourage the former in this belief." If readers were indeed gentle, goes the logic, then we wouldn't be blowing each other to smithereens.

Fay Weldon has worked her way through feminism and fantasy and plain fatness in nearly one dozen earlier novels. She has written for the stage and the screen. She carries a long, shiny needle, the better to puncture what passes for acceptable behavior. Here, as before, she knows the fatuity of people in highest places: "It is hard to imagine how barbarous the language of our leaders is, in private, how simple and emotive their judgments, how their love of money and power and vengeance rises to the surface like the white crust on boiling strawberry jam."

The cruelty also rises. Truly gentle readers may be appalled at the gore and violence flying around this farce. Truly cynical readers may be delighted by a comedy of manners in which everyone's manners are most atrocious. This reader was sometimes appalled, often amused—and generally disconcerted by the asides, wondering whether they were designed as playfulness, punctuation or simple padding. A belly laugh for strong stomachs.

Alan Bell (review date 10 April 1988)

SOURCE: "Love-Child Conquers All," in *Los Angeles Times Book Review,* April 10, 1988, p. 6.

[*In the following review, Bell finds* The Hearts and Minds of Men *somewhat heavy-handed initially but adds that the novel is redeemed in its second half.*]

Little Nell, in this grown-up fairy tale [*The Hearts and Minds of Men*], is a love child in the genuine sense of the word, conceived at the first glance exchanged by her parents at a party in 1960s London. As the prompt result of a blissful consummation, she preserves, through the ups and (more usually) downs of her parents' marriage, something of the radiant happiness of their first moments of mutual discovery. Nearly aborted by a panicking mother, she survives to become a Christmas Day baby, attended by astrological omens that give her an uncanny ability to attract dangerous events and nasty people into her benevolent orbit, but from infancy, she shines like a good deed in a naughty world.

Her mother, Helen, is a nice, sensible, pretty young thing, whose apparently fey character grows well in strength throughout the book, triumphing over the adversity of some unfortunate marriages, until years later, she blossoms as a prominent dress designer, hardened by the early experience of divorce from Nell's father, Clifford.

From the outset, Clifford is destined to be a celebrity, a London art dealer rapidly on the rise, not yet quite famous for being famous but fully aware of the advantages of a high profile in the art-schmart world of international dealing. Undoubtedly skilled both in commerce and connoisseurship, he is also a user, discarder, and wounder of women. Clifford's doubtful achievements bring with them the punishment of having to marry his mistress, than which few worse fates could be devised.

The mistress, Angie, belongs to a rather stagy cast of vil-lains who represent the massed forces of Evil. She is rich beyond her deserving, with a few South African gold mines to keep her in mink and outbid any wool-clad opponents. Angie can well afford to make up for her inferior looks by buying whatever she wants in life, whether it is culture or revenge. Art galleries rise and fall to her manipulations, and this Queen-of-the-Night character has ample means to bide her time before she decides she can start "to upset a few people."

The forces of good and evil are not allowed to play out their match without interference. They are pursued by the author's voice intruding a commentary which is as unwelcome as a neighbor whispering throughout a movie. Fay Weldon has used this technique in earlier novels but never quite so insistently. It is a very feminine voice she writes in, as one would expect of so delicate a portrayer of pregnancy and childbirth, and the commentary is an odd mixture of triteness and shrewdness. "I am sorry to say . . ." too frequently introduces the author's remarks on yet another moral lapse in her characters. There is too often a conflict between Weldon's pity for her creations and her manipulation of them.

Is it too masculine to see her as overindulgent to the swinish Clifford, when she feels his overblown jealousy should be forgiven because he has deviously been given reasonable grounds for suspicion? Weldon is certainly too kind to Helen's father, a boorish, bullying artist of growing fame, who feeds his genius by his ill-treatment of his submissive wife. The father's slaughterhouse and torture paintings may be the finest artistic flower of their generation, but the domestic background in which they were nurtured is far from admirable. Too much is forgiven this half-mad genius because of a celebrity that turns out to have been partly engineered by the deft manipulations of Clifford's gallery. The temperamental license of the creative artist is allowed to go well beyond the point of patient endurance.

"Wait, dear reader," as our author would say. "Do not let yourself be put off by this glib, knowing commentator." Halfway through the book, the chattering Chorus becomes less annoying, and it is a measure of the author's skill that by the end the "dear reader" has come almost to welcome the commentary of the worldly wise lady in the next cinema seat. Instead of hushing her, we start agreeing and debating, perhaps with this view of marital discord:

> Into the great bubbling caldron of distress we call jealousy goes dollop after dollop of every humiliation we have ever endured, every insecurity suffered, every loss we have known and feared; in goes our sense of doubt, futility; in goes the prescience of decay, death, finality. And floating to the top, like scum on jam, the knowledge that all is lost: in particular the hope that some-

day, somehow, we can properly love and trust and be properly loved and trusted in our turn.

Such ruminations should not give the impression of overwhelming seriousness in a novel with a strong vein of fairy-tale fantasy. Nell becomes a tug-of-love child, finds herself kidnapped, then in rapid succession is miraculously saved from an air crash and is bought by a rather endearing pair of elderly French black magicians who adopt her as part of a program of rejuvenation therapy. Spirited away from their mildly Satanic clutches, she casts up, traumatized but resilient, in an English home for "disturbed" children, but is soon off with the Gypsies to a hippie commune in remote rural Wales, kept buoyant by sheer niceness, however nasty her surroundings.

Even when mistakenly classed as mentally retarded, educationally sub-normal, even with her head shaved because of suspected head lice and hunted by dogs when she escapes from the mental hospital, Nell is a smiler and a survivor. Throughout her adventures, she has secretly carried a locket containing a precious jewel which is not only an amulet for her safety but eventually leads her back to her parents. Needless to say, it is she who reconciles them.

The embers of their marriage have never gone entirely cold. Helen's love for Clifford has been kept alive by the belief that her daughter never really died in the air disaster. Nell proves this by reappearing as a self-possessed, artistic young woman with her redeeming happiness intact. The novel, which goes somewhat deeper than its mere story-line would suggest, ends with the message: "Reader, to the happy, all things come. Happiness can even bring the dead back to life."

Regina Barreca (review date Fall 1988)

SOURCE: "At Last, Laughs," in *Belles Lettres*, Vol. 4, No. 1, Fall 1988, p. 2.

[*In the following review, Barreca finds the comic elements and happy endings of* The Hearts and Lives of Men *and* The Heart of the Country *a welcome change from Weldon's earlier novels, noting that Weldon does not compromise her artistry to effect a positive outcome for her characters.*]

When Fay Weldon was asked what she thought about the magnificent public response to *The Hearts and Lives of Men,* the first of her novels truly to capture the attention of the American reading (and critical) audience, she said, "It's all very nice, but it's for the wrong book." I think Weldon was referring to the fact that *Hearts and Lives*

originally appeared in the British weekly magazine *Woman* and that it was written piece by piece for serial publication. Perhaps she believed it less "literary" than some of her other works. Perhaps she was concerned that new readers would find her too frivolous, too glib. When asked why she decided to write a serial novel, she answered that *Woman* had approached her agent to see whether she would write a short story for them. "Being an agent," Weldon continued, "he said 'why not one a week?' and that's how it started."

Fortunately, *Hearts and Lives* does not suffer from the problems of disjointedness or frivolity that worried Weldon: It is a quintessentially and wonderfully Weldonesque novel. One of the best things about Weldon is that she has created a new category for simile. We can safely say, in response to the question "How are things going?" that life is like a Fay Weldon novel. This answer is all encompassing. Our lives become Weldonesque when the following elements can no longer be denied: that there is no such thing as coincidence; that justice—haphazard as it appears—is swift, satisfying, and ultimately inescapable; that we are none of us safe, however secure we feel; and that "to the happy all things come: happiness can even bring the dead back to life, it is our resentments, our dreariness, our hate and envy, unrecognized by us, which keep us miserable. Yet these things are in our heads, not out of our hands; we own them; we can throw them out if we choose."

The Hearts and Lives of Men can safely be called a comedy. The novel begins by telling us in the second paragraph, "There! You already know this story is to have a happy ending . . . Why not?" Has Weldon turned traditional? Hardly. She creates a comedy that depends on the inversion and subversion of traditional, masculinist comedy. She overturns convention in much the same way as the artist in her novel, John Lally, paints "the Rape not of the Sabine Women, but by the Sabine Women. It was they who were falling upon helpless Roman soldiers."

It is a story of love at first sight and of divorce, of black and white magic, of airplane crashes and near misses, of children abandoned and reclaimed. Helen and Clifford, the lovers whose catalytic romance prompts much of the tale's adventure, fall into one another's arms in the early sixties when people "wanted everything and thought they could have it. . . . Dinner, in other words, and no washing up." Their relationship continues through marriages to various people, including one another on occasion, over twenty years or so. They have "as good a chance as any" of "getting away with" a happy ending, but of course they might not deserve it. Who of us does deserve happiness? After reading this novel, such questions no longer seem rhetorical.

After reading *The Heart of the Country,* we realize that there is no such thing as a rhetorical question in a Weldon novel. Ask a question and (by God or the Devil) you will get an answer. *The Heart of the Country* is marginally a better book than *The Hearts and Lives of Men.* Weldon is in more familiar, more mythical territory where judgments are not weighed with caution and where we are not asked to have sympathy for the despicable characters, as we are in *Hearts and Lives.* Instead of opening with love at first sight, this novel (written before *Hearts and Lives* and already successfully adapted as a British miniseries) opens with the exclamation "Oh! The wages of sin! Natalie Harris sinned, and her husband Harry left for work one fine morning and didn't come back."

Natalie commits the usual sins of lust, pride, and envy, but she is cursed finally for the "special sin of splashing the poor." This is a modern sin, Weldon's first-person/third-person narrator, Sonia, explains. Sonia, instructed by her psychiatrist, is attempting to step outside of herself and look at herself as others see her ("that is to say in the third person") when she enters into Natalie's story. She describes the way that Natalie, driving her two elegant children to their private school in her Volvo station wagon, splashes unemployed, unhappy Sonia as she is walking her three children to the state school they hate. "'God rot her,' said Sonia aloud . . . she could deliver a curse or two effectively. God heard. God sent his punishment on Natalie. Or was it the Devil? He forgave her other sins, but got her for this one. Natalie committed the sin of carelessly splashing Sonia. Sonia cursed her. Misfortune fell on Natalie. Cause and effect?" Words have power in Weldon's reality. "One must be careful with words," she wrote back in *The Fat Woman's Joke,* her first novel. "Words turn probabilities into facts and by sheer force of definition translate tendencies into habits." Nothing is more powerful than language. Language is the stuff of love and, equally, the stuff of politics.

The Heart of the Country is an explicitly political novel, as is any novel dealing with getting benefits from the state (Natalie must get "tutorials on the Welfare State" from Sonia, among others.) Women shifted to the margin by society become political because they do not follow "the advice given to economically dependent female spouses since the beginning of time—wait for her husband to cease his wanderings, and be as loving as lovable in the meantime." Not unlike Ruth in *Life and Loves of a She-Devil,* the women get their own back. It happens during carnival. Carnival is comedy, right? But this is a women's comedy, and so there must be a sacrifice and not a ritual one either. "That was the purpose of the event. Burn a virgin, fire a barn, drown a witch. Clear old scores and start afresh! What do you think the carnival is about? Fun and games? Oh, no."

As for comedy, well, this book has one of the happiest endings of any I have read, acknowledging as it does that chal-

lenge, not stasis, is what makes for happiness; that comedy for women depends often on what was always misread as her pain, "that it is up to women to fight back, because the men have lost their nerve"; that, in fact, through the guise of dependence and sentiment "she had been laughing at him all the time." Weldon maps the territory where comedy and terror meet, consume one another, and create an altogether new landscape.

Patricia Craig (review date 12-18 May 1989)

SOURCE: "All Our Dog Days," in *Time Literary Supplement,* No. 4493, May 12-18, 1989, p. 518.

[*In the following review, Craig considers* The Cloning of Joanna May *not up to Weldon's usual high standards.*]

Fay Weldon's current practice is to take some exorbitant facet of modern life—political intrigue, television stardom, plastic surgery—and incorporate it into one of her colourful little analyses of the drive towards misbehaviour and the clashing interests of men and women. In *The Cloning of Joanna May,* her fourteenth novel, it is genetic engineering that set things going. "Fiddling around with women's eggs", as a character puts it, is one of the enormities open to enterprising operators. The story is this: Joanna May's husband Carl May, without her knowledge and with the co-operation of a Dr Holly, has imposed a novel means of reproduction on his thirty-year-old wife. An egg is removed from her womb, split into four and implanted elsewhere, and with the resulting births new versions of the original are obtained. This outrageous multiplication is supposed to have taken place in the 1950s, and it's thirty years before the prototype gets to hear about the copies. In the meantime, Carl May has divorced her for infidelity with an Egyptologist, relegated her to a house on the banks of the Thames, near Maidenhead, and dealt with the man, the culprit, by having him run over.

Carl May, a power in the land as the blurb describes him, has risen not only from sordid but from unspeakable beginnings. His mother kept him chained in a dog kennel. Weldon often lumbers her characters with some egregious ancestry, as if in deference to a tabloid view of the world, or at least in acknowledgement of all the awfulness that exists and gets reported in newspapers. Her fiction tends to be sensational in content, to underscore her aversion to this or that social abuse, but very much toned down in manner: she is famous for being both audacious and sardonic in her approach. She sets out to make the preposterous plausible (more or less), as in *Life and Loves of a She-Devil,* as well as indicating the universal significance in all the little individual plots and predicaments she creates. All her characters come complete with striking life histories and sociological implications, neatly summarized. The new novel considers (among other things) the question of identity, and whether this is strengthened or diluted by replication; the effect of environment comes into it too. The book's peculiar premise enables it to demonstrate what becomes of an individual in varying circumstances: the May clones are, respectively, a journalist, a fashion model, a childless suburban housewife and a knocked-about mother-of-three.

As well as the topical decoration we expect from Fay Weldon—child abuse, genetic gimmickry and nuclear alarms—the narrative accommodates some not very pointed punning ("If the I offend thee pluck it out") and some over-insistent patterning, as, for example, with the paired-off systems of nuclear physics and Egyptology, technology and the Tarot pack, self-determination and divination. It is all too much, like Carl May's posited power over life and death, which leads to the notion that it is possible to get yourself re-created as your ex-wife's quasi-grandchild. Fay Weldon would seem to be upholding the life-instinct, in however distorted a form it manifests itself; with this novel, however, she has got herself into something of a muddle through mucking about with the universe.

As Weldon's concerns get larger, her style seems to go to pot. Instead of the usual sharpness we find banality ("Where did clouds come from?" wonders one of the characters in a woolly moment, while another thinks with affection of "his wife, sharer of his chips"). Overwriting and tiresomeness come into the picture too—"how could she, being female, give birth to something male?" Exchanges of the utmost childishness take place between the Chairman of Britnuc and his repudiated wife: "You have made me bad, Joanna May . . ."; "You have destroyed me", she says to him. Worst of all is the clumsiness that has overtaken Fay Weldon's prose. The following sentence isn't untypical:

> Without the assault of these passionate saving graces she would have aged slowly and gracefully, developed a touch of arthritis here, a backache there: Oliver would have drifted off . . . and her fate would have indeed been that of the elderly woman who has never been employed, has no husband, no children, no former colleagues or particular interests, a handful of friends still around, with any luck (though their particular loyalties stretched by distance, exhaustion, their own problems) but who is fortunate enough to have a lot of money.

The plot keeps coming back to Carl May, his "bimbo", Bethany (brought up in a brothel), his spectacular progress from dog house to executive suite, and his vengefulness; but it only becomes gripping, in the customary Weldon manner, when we got to the clones and their eventual meet-

ing. What this leads to is an assertion of feminine, or sisterly, solidarity: all very fine and inspiriting, but not quite sufficient to quell our unease with ingredients such as rebirth, rottenness and a kennel upbringing—presented, by and large, without the deftness we associate with this author. Still, what with man-made disasters, like Chernobyl, and those coming out of the blue, like the great wind of the autumn before last, Fay Weldon perhaps has a point in envisaging all our days as dogdays.

Robert Ward (review date 4 June 1989)

SOURCE: Review of *Polaris and Other Stories* and *Leader of the Band,* in *New York Times Book Review,* June 4, 1989, pp. 1, 26.

[*In the following review, Ward offers praise for* Polaris and Other Stories *but finds* Leader of the Band *unsatisfying.*]

Fay Weldon, a risky, engaged writer, is an ardent feminist, a novelist of characters and ideas. In an age where much fiction is cut-rate minimalist, or cocaine chic, Ms. Weldon shows us another path. She is complex, smart and political without cheating us on esthetics. And she is profoundly funny. Her **Life and Loves of a She-Devil** is a small masterpiece of invective, the ultimate feminist revenge novel, but one so truly amusing and consistently intelligent that even a guilt-ridden male chauvinist can't resist it.

The publication of even one Weldon book is a cause for celebration; this time out we are fortunate to have two, **Polaris and Other Stories** and **Leader of the Band,** a quirky, jazzy novel. Both books show us an artist who is attempting to deepen her talent, who is taking serious artistic risks.

The 12 stories that make up **Polaris** are widely varied in tone, ranging from lyrical, straight-ahead dramatic to almost Gothic horror. All of Ms. Weldon's familiar concerns—sex, sexual politics, the joys and agonies of family and adultery and an obsession with the horrors of gynecology—are evident. (Indeed, this medical obsession reminds me of William S. Burroughs's Dr. Benway, who stabbed patients with his scalpel in order to save them with last-minute, operating table heroics.) Most of the stories have a dead-on surety of tone, a maturity that tells us there is indeed a second act in Ms. Weldon's career.

The title tale is a love story about a Navy submariner, Timmy, and his new wife, Meg. The plot is simple: they meet, fall in love unexpectedly (in Weldon as in Lawrence, love is the great unknown, the wild ride that hurtles the lovers toward disastrous ends even as it carries them away in glory). They marry, Timmy goes away on duty in the submarine, and all too soon events conspire to ruin their perfect happiness.

When Timmy goes to sea, Meg visits Zelda, the wife of another submariner, Jim. (Unbeknown to Meg, Timmy has already had an affair with Zelda.) The two women begin talking about their husbands, and Meg gets a very nasty shock:

> "If the Navy chooses to put him on Polaris, that's their responsibility. He's still just a navigator," Meg persisted. "A kind of timeless person." And indeed, she saw Timmy as one of the heroes on Odysseus's boat, underneath a starry Grecian sky, steering between Scylla and Charybdis.

But a few minutes later, Zelda sets her straight:

> "Darling, your husband is one of the Attack Team. There are three of them on Polaris. The captain, the first officer and the navigator. With a little help from the captain, your husband and mine could finish off the world. Didn't he ever tell you?"

> "They wouldn't want to finish off the world," said Meg, presently, taken aback. Timmy had never told her this.

It's the last line, of course, that's devastating. Timmy and Meg are so close they may even share ESP. He can practically communicate with her from under the North Sea, yet he never bothers to tell her what he really does. In the end, it is not simply the isolation from one another that causes the rent in their relationship but their failure as political people, a failure of both intellect and nerve. At one point in the story, Ms. Weldon writes of Meg:

> She was like a child: she would not ask more, for fear of finding out more than she cared to know: of having to do what she ought, not what she wanted. A little girl who would not look down at her shoes before school, in case they needed cleaning.

Meg is not the only character created by Ms. Weldon to fit this description. Bitterness, a deep disappointment and concurrent anger are often starting points for her fiction. In **"Delights of France or Horrors of the Road,"** the narrator talks to her psychiatrist about her sudden unexplained paralysis and about her wonderful husband, the particle physicist, Piers. Piers is a success, Piers is a Nobel Prize candidate, Piers loves to hike in the wild, Piers knows wine and so on. In the end, the pathetic narrator says: "Talking will get us nowhere. I do love my husband." She would rather be paralyzed than admit to her own rage, her fury at her condescending, domineering bully of a husband.

Love, in Ms. Weldon's world, is mystical, blinding; but also fearsome and savage. In this she also reminds me of Lawrence and his romantic dreams of a perfect union of blood. In **"Who?,"** Howard, a 38-year-old area sales manager (with a wife, Alice, and three children) goes to the doctor to check on his recurrent headaches and falls in love at first sight with Elaine, the doctor's wife and secretary. Ms. Weldon tells us that "Elaine was bending over the T-Z section of the filling cabinet when Howard came up to the desk." Then, "It was as if, they told each other later, they recognized each other. That is to say, they knew in advance what was to come: how they were to move into the light, leaving others in the shadows."

Their affair takes a radical course; they leave their spouses, lose their jobs and end up penniless. Worse, when Elaine telephones Howard one day, he doesn't know who she is.

> "Darling!" she said. "Who's that?" he asked.

> "Elaine, of course," she replied.

> "Who did you say?" "Elaine." There was a silence. Then—

> "Oh, sorry, darling. I was dreaming."

The story could end here, but Ms. Weldon goes on to nail it down, with a final paragraph:

> Nevertheless it had been said, and was the beginning of the end. He knew that she knew, and she knew that he knew, and so forth, that although love flowed out of him, freely and passionately, it was the love itself that mattered, and not the object of the love. They were both, when it came to it, strangers to each other.

A nicely written moral, as morals go, but unnecessary. If Ms. Weldon's writing has one serious flaw, it is her lack of confidence in her readers; too often she steps in and adds these little messages.

In her best stories, no moralizing is needed. Indeed, there is one story—a gynecological horror tale called **"And Then Turn Out the Light"**—which is quite simply one of the most ghastly stories I've ever read: a small masterpiece of evil involving a woman, her surgeon and their "love." There's not a word wasted in it, and it shows us what brilliance Ms. Weldon is capable of when she fully trusts her art.

Leader of the Band, her new novel, reprises all of the familiar themes. A picaresque romp, it tells us the story of Starlady Sandra, a brilliant and witty astronomer (discoverer of the planet Athena) who also happens to be a television star. Married to a boring barrister, Sandra meets Mad Jack, the trumpet player in a Dixieland band called the Citronella Jumpers. She is swept away by a tide of passion, and runs off with him on tour. Of course, many feminist novels (from Kate Chopin's *Awakening* to Sue Kaufman's *Diary of a Mad Housewife*) have mined this territory before, but few feminist heroines have been this liberated from the outset. Sandra is not a guilt-racked liberal, worried about the life she left behind. Rather, she is a brilliant, feisty woman who loves sex and her own opinions in equal amounts. Here is Sandra on fame:

> Fame in a man is for a woman a great aphrodisiac: fame in a woman appeals to the man who likes public [sex]. Pity.

These are cool and witty comments, but therein lies the book's problem: Sandra's intellect and wit dominate every scene. We never really get to know Jack at all. Again and again, Sandra says, "Jack . . . oh, Mad Jack," as if, by repeating this incantation, she can will the character into existence. But will is no substitute for artistic invention. We learn too little about Jack, too little about the other band members and their groupies to even care about them. Instead we are borne back into the narcissistic and hyped-up voice of Starlady Sandra herself. This isn't all bad; she is funny, charming and brilliant, but one begins to grow weary of her endless self-absorption, as one does of an after-dinner monologuist who is still droning on long after the port has been drunk and the cigars have burned down to ash.

There are also forays into the author's obsession with gynecology. We learn, shockingly, that Sandra's father was a Nazi, that he "became medical officer in one of those camps where non-desirable races—those most closely aligned to the monkeys—that is to say gypsies and Jews and others recognisable from the shape of their skulls as being very like chimps, and lagging behind in the evolutionary race—were used as work-horses."

This is of course a bombshell, and a strange one to drop in a comic novel. Naturally, the lines above, and later ones concerning her "pride" in her father's work, are meant ironically. Sandra admits that thinking of what her father did in the camps "doubles me up with pain once a month." But the problem with introducing loaded material of this sort is that it begs to be fully dramatized. An entire novel could be written about the daughter of a German medical officer, but we get here only wisecracks, irony and a smidgen of pain, then move on to other matters.

A friend once said, "Novelists have to be smart, but not too smart," and I believe this to be true. Fay Weldon's wit, her intellect, her love of play—usually so effective—get in the way in *Leader of the Band*. There is ice where there should

be warmth, opinions where there should be flesh and blood. Yet even a minor Weldon novel is welcome. She is a rare writer—impassioned, angry, quirky and brilliant, and even her failures are interesting and instructive. *Leader of the Band* will undoubtedly land her somewhere else, a better place. Meanwhile, we have *Polaris,* as fine a group of stories as we are likely to get this year.

Judith Dunford (review date 20-27 August 1990)

SOURCE: "Losing to Despair," in *New Republic,* Vol. 203, Nos. 8-9, August 20-27, 1990, pp. 40-42.

[*In the following review, Dunford contends that Weldon's trademark anger has become tired and mechanical in* The Cloning of Joanna May *and* Leader of the Band.]

The twentieth century has made it easy for writers to see humans as nothing but poor creatures in a disordered universe. Fay Weldon has produced a line of witty, ironic books out of her prevailing sense of how unfairly the odds are stacked and how little can be done to redress the balance. Her characters dangle on strings held by some mad marioneteer, their lives pulled this way and that by cosmic spite, coincidence, the mandates of biology, the darker demands of society.

Weldon is like a hornet, buzzing angrily with topics, ready to be politically shrill about almost anything that comes up in the chaos of contemporary events. The more she writes, it seems, the more she wants to write. Her last two novels have come out in less than a year. In the most recent, *The Cloning of Joanna May,* Weldon takes up the ancient question of nature and nurture. Her villain is Carl May, who has risen, through his own talents, from a horrifying childhood—his parents kept him chained around the neck in a dog's kennel—to become head of the British nuclear power industry and a member of the Board of Directors of practically everything else. He is a nasty piece of goods, the coldest, most manipulative man of science, all the human juices squeezed out.

The one love in his life was his wife, Joanna, a beauty of good, middle-class family, who, like Desdemona, married him because of the pity and terror she felt at his story. He wants her exclusively for himself, so he rules out children and keeps her like an ice queen in the abundance allowed the wife of the CEO. When, at age thirty, the restless Joanna thinks she is pregnant (wrongly—she is merely hysterical), he insists that she have an abortion, and without telling her has the head of the abortion clinic clone one of her eggs four times. The results are donated for implantation to four applicant-mothers. For Carl, the self-made man making self-made women, it is a peculiar mixture of love and spitefulness to reproduce his wife at the height of her beauty, a height from which she can only descend—and not tell her about it.

When the novel opens it is thirty years later, the time of the Chernobyl disaster, when the air over England and all of Europe is malignant and no one knows what to do. We learn that a few years earlier Joanna May had grown restless and frustrated with her life as her husband's most treasured acquisition, and had taken a lover. When they are discovered *in flagrante*, Carl has the lover killed and throws Joanna out, this time imprisoning her in the sterile comforts of alimony in a house on an island in the Thames. In the meantime the clones have grown up in their various homes, unaware of one another and of Joanna, further illustrations of The Influence of Early Home Life on Behavior (not on Character, though: they all have more or less the same character, more or less the same looks) and Weldon's view of modern women's options.

One is child-ridden and worn; her husband beats her. The others are childless. One is a bored suburban housewife in a perfect house whose husband is always off on another business trip. One is a self-absorbed photographer's model, one a university graduate, a reader for HBO who refuses to give up her independence to live with her sometime boyfriend. None is happy or attached to any man worth the attachment. When their men are not brutal, they are whiny, selfish, petulant, or vague one-night stands.

To Weldon's credit, the women are not much better; Weldon's ideology is never quite so primitive. Joanna and her clones are cranky, weak-kneed, unfocused, boring co-conspirators in the narrowing of their choices. They all meet very late in the novel when, in what seems to be a burst of impatience to get to the end, Weldon puts them through a quick series of coincidences dubious even in one of her elaborate fantasies, and has them determine to make better sense of their lives. Still, she takes the time to kill off Carl with poetic justice. As a public relations gesture meant to reassure a public anxious over Chernobyl, Carl and his mistress (Weldon's version of the tart-with-a-heart) jump into a nuclear reactor cooling pond to demonstrate the harmlessness of atomic energy. He dies of radiation poisoning.

Leader of the Band, which Weldon published last year, is the story of Sandra Harris, Starlady Sandra of a popular science program on television, forty-two years old, a first-rate astronomer, next in line for Royal Astronomer, one of the lucky few to have discovered a new planet. Astronomer, or no, Sandra has more than the usual sense of rattling around in an uncozy Creation. Like Carl May, she has a horrifying family history. Her mother, now in a madhouse, was the

dusky issue of the coupling in a hedgerow of an Anglican bishop's daughter and a passing gypsy.

Because of her swarthy good looks, she had been selected at fifteen to be impregnated by a Sylvia Plath fantasy de luxe, a Mengele-type Nazi doctor who conducted genetic experiments with his own sperm. (People do get born in complicated ways in Weldon novels.) Mengele-daddy was shot (not hanged) after the Nuremberg trials and never saw his perfect, blond Master Race replica, Sandra. Mother eventually married, gave birth to a son more entirely in her own image, madness included, who reached manhood just in time to throw himself under a train. Sandra is worried that she, too, may be off the rails.

Her reaction is to retreat into an outer tightness and control, a pure selfishness. Determined not to pass along any of her complicated genes, to stay childless, she is lured into a yuppie marriage with a chubby little achiever, divorced, who installs her in the well-equipped house of her predecessor. Good housekeeping is Weldon's nightmare. Here, too, the poor thing is kept as a prisoner of her husband's ambitions, serving as his cook and hostess; she, too, escapes into adultery. One day, at a party at the Greenwich Observatory, she and a member of the band lock eyes. Suddenly we are in the middle of a Gothic romance. Sandra all but swoons into his arms, he peels back her white satin dress (in the foliage, like her grandmother), and she leaves bed and board, tiled bathroom, chic wardrobe, and all her medical records to move into his camper. Gypsy blood will out!

Weldon can make good use of exorbitant plots like these when she can make them work as metaphors for the accidental nature of existence, for the liberty it gives individuals to be successful by being unscrupulous. She writes about the claims of nature, which are always outrageous (often thanks to the meddlings of man), and the constraints of nurture (which are always nightmarish, certainly for women). But the fantastic twist of her fantastic plots is a triumph over imprisonment, a celebration of free will that exposes the inequities of social life. Despite Weldon's weakness for rhetoric, the spirit behind the exposé is less fiery radicalism than fairy-tale optimism, all-lived-happily-ever-after.

They are flimflam, of course, but pulled together with wit and verve. What makes her distinctive is her mad vitality, the always interesting way she tends to rush about in her own mind. When Weldon flies high, she is entertaining, even enlightening about the pretenses, absurdities, cruelties of life, gender, and society. As a storyteller she uses her satiric, mocking plots not only to tell us that the world is a tangled place but to draw us in—often in the same manner, the same voice—as any tale of once upon a time. In Weldon's novels, things *happen,* there are beginnings and endings. They may not satisfy the characters, but they can satisfy us.

The world, Weldon is always saying, just pulls the rug out from under you. Still, the good at heart may make their way to a steady corner, given time. A basic Weldon theme is that children, new lives, the old-fashioned nuclear family, for all its shares and pitfalls, for all its conversations spoken with forked tongue, may still be the best—the only—shot we have. Weldon has described herself as a feminist who washes her sons' socks, and she is careful to note her wifehood and motherhood on her books' jackets.

Weldon's mind is a furious one, but always for the obvious cause. She is against meanness, exploitation, and cruelty, and for the generous impulse. She wishes in the usual way that the world were a decent place, that something could be done. When her writing is zippy, what comes through, along with her more than usual indignation, is her quirky quarter-turn away from the absolutely pat and predictable position. For example, she resists making women into long-suffering, noble, patience-on-a-monument types. At her best, Weldon is sharp and witty, gets the twitches, impulses, mannerisms exactly right. Her point of view allows you to be contentedly irate; she peoples the landscape with characters you can like, dislike, or even fear. As her following has recognized in the easy succession of "Weldons," she is another British pro.

Leader of the Band and *The Cloning of Joanna May* have a family resemblance to the earlier books. (There are fourteen previous novels and short-story collections.) They have the regular jumble of characters leading lives that we recognize as modern by their snarled netting of impulse, incoherence, and battering by uncontrollable forces. They are lightly spiced with Weldon's beloved metaphor, magic, without which her readers would feel they had not gotten the genuine article. Her wrath is everywhere in evidence, her ideas skitter and glitter in every direction.

But in these recent books, something has happened to her writing. It's as though Weldon, who like the rest of us must feel the despair-a-day that comes with the morning paper, has finally been overwhelmed. The crush of all that anger, all that desperation, appears to have squeezed out of these novels what Weldon, as a novelist, does best. Both books sound as though they were written from the top down. So many topics tackled—heavy topics, too: feminism (especially as it applies to women inching into middle age), heredity, power, ambition, love and marriage, sexual mores, free will, the hollowness of the middle class, the absurd social order, the wickedness of unbridled science, the sins and futility of war, and more. In *The Cloning of Joanna May* there is a lot of wheel-spinning over what constitutes

the self, many paragraphs on the "eye" that sees and the "I" that is. Some topics come packed in little essay-ettes:

> Those who have rows are more alive than those who don't: make better friends, more interesting companions. They may wreak havoc but they understand their imperfections—witness how they project them upon others—they cry to heaven for justice. They believe in it.—*Cloning*

> Love, honor, obey and support, as long as we both shall live. Been to India, lately; seen the men *sitting*, while the women building workers heave and shovel: been to Africa, where the men smoke ganja and the women hoe the brick-hard soil: been out to dinner and counted the number of times your hostess *gets up*? No wonder the men feel bad about it.—*Starlady*

A lot of angry chatter. But meanwhile the characters have becomes dangerously thin and standoffish, the absurdity of the plots no longer entertainingly pointing to something more serious. In *The Cloning of Joanna May,* in which the writing takes on a peculiarly dispirited quality, all the people are, fittingly enough, as flat as cards. Starlady Sandra is a wan creation whom we do not especially like, whom we are not meant especially to like, who hardly likes herself:

> I had had affairs, even fallen in love, with various men: most wanted children: those who did I did not like. Sad. To prefer a Porsche and a peaceful annual holiday to the creation of children may seem sensible, but it is not likable.

When Weldon stops carrying us along in the rush of events, when her characters have no vitality, then we are forced to confront her less as a novelist who is engaged and more as a pure idea-monger. And then we are in trouble. Of course we recognize that she still stands on the side of the angels. But now the ideas have the ring of boilerplate bombast, the writing sounds choked-up and deadened, or pumped up into "cute" or simply soap-box-shrill.

In *Leader of the Band,* Weldon is still able, here and there, to cut some of the minor characters loose from all this message-bearing and pneumatic prose-mongering, and they can be vivid. There is Mad Jack the trumpeter's unhappy teenaged daughter, confused and wretched over her father's taking a mistress, a situation she is barely old enough to understand. There is Matthew, Sandra's pretentious twit of a husband, for whom we genuinely suffer when Sandra deserts him at the party.

There is a fine moment when Sandra, like many another Weldon heroine, learns that she is pregnant (Weldon likes to resolve things with a new life when she can. In *The Cloning of Joanna May,* she does it by producing a new clone, one that Joanna can raise herself—the right way):

> I went to the doctor's surgery, just up the road from the Crédit Lyonnais, and sat only briefly in a small white room among posters of poisonous snakes and mushrooms. . . . Doctor Tarval was, or so I thought at first, a not very bright young man in his middle twenties, with an owl face, cropped hair, and perfect French manners. Language was a slight problem, but the vocabulary of pain can be mimed.

When Weldon can bring herself to resist the temptation to write tracts, she is once again the Weldon we remember. Otherwise, there is a sense that she is too obviously miming her own pain, not her characters', that the gestures have grown too frantic, or, finally, too exhausted.

Robert Houston (review date 25 May 1990)

SOURCE: "Her Sisters, Herself," in *New York Times Book Review,* Vol. 95, March 25, 1990, p. 7.

[*In the following review, Houston praises Weldon's "quirky" humor in* The Cloning of Joanna May.]

In a recent interview about the filming of her novel *The Life and Loves of a She-Devil,* Fay Weldon said, "My idea of morality isn't about women becoming strong and forceful, competent or whatever: it's about having a good time." And so, in fact, is the idea of *The Cloning of Joanna May.* In her latest novel, Ms. Weldon manages to boot the archenemy, boredom, out of her characters' lives as handily as she does from her readers', and it's a reasonable bet that she's had a good time it. Her book is part satire, part social commentary, part comedy of manners, part fantasy, but its true charm is that it ultimately refuses to be anything but itself—which is surely welcome relief to readers who might have begun to fear that dreary minimalist clones would lurk behind every book jacket forever.

Throughout most of *The Cloning of Joanna May,* the fallout from Chernobyl is being blown over England. But it is emotional fallout that immediately concerns Ms. Weldon's heroine. Joanna May is the childless, sixtyish, spurned former wife of Carl May, an old-style baron of a new-style industry, nuclear power, a man who had the misfortune to spend a good deal of his childhood chained in a dog kennel. While she's recovering from the divorce, Joanna discovers that, as an experiment in another kind of power, Carl secretly had her cloned 30 years before. Somewhere she has four unknown sisters/daughters/twins.

At first, Joanna reacts angrily, "I want my life back," she demands. Carl has used up her youth and kept her from having children, but "he shan't have the clones. I want them. I need them. They're mine." However, as she searches for them, she calms down a bit and discovers that "I wanted to see what I would be, born into a newer, more understanding, world; one which allowed women choice, freedom and success. . . . How very *interesting* to see how it all turned out. What fun it would be—that rare commodity."

Eventually, Joanna and her four younger clones find one another, as clones will. All have been in unsatisfactory relationships with men, all have been bored or in despair. Lysistrata style, they band together to readjust their lives and their men, share what children they have and begin at last to have a good time, while Carl goes down in his own private, ego-triggered Chernobyl.

Seeing the novel in such simplistic plot terms, of course, makes it appear thematically simplistic: male power bad and life-destroying, female power good and life-giving. While the book suggests that its author has no serious argument with this premise, to stop there would terribly misrepresent the very rich complex of character, theme and form that Ms. Weldon has built.

In good 18th-century manner, for example, her omniscient narrator often uses the events of the novel as occasions for mini-essays on society, civilization, relations between the sexes and humankind in general. In equally good 20th-century style, she switches with impunity between that narrator and Joanna May's first-person account. And the plot starts, backs up, interrupts itself; the story grows by accretion and indirection, the way modernism has taught us to tell stories. What counts is what works.

Likewise, Ms. Weldon's characters obey no ordinary rules of fiction. Sometimes, as is the case with Joanna and her clones, they behave generally like quite credible contemporary people with quite credible problems, clonehood notwithstanding. At other times, as with a rock group that Carl hires to do his dirty work, they are delightfully sinister burlesques, as if the Monty Python troupe and Anthony Burgess had collaborated to produce them. At yet other times—and here Ms. Weldon is least successful—the characters are less people than creations that stand for people, grab bags of attitudes and ignorance and idiosyncrasies who wander somewhere between real people and burlesques and never quite cohere as either. Carl himself, despite wonderful moments, is one of these, as are his young mistress, Bethany, and the doddering half-mad scientist, Dr. Holly, who has done the cloning at Carl's behest.

However, it is the book's energy, its wit, its intelligence, its humor that win through. If the targets of all these writerly virtues are a bit easy and shopworn by now—television, nuclear energy, soulless science, big business, male power, clinging or frivolous women—the joy of watching Ms. Weldon's quirky talent at work on them isn't at all diminished. What must be said in the end is that if a reader wants breakthroughs in feminist theory, wants a realistic novel of character. wants heart over head, political correctness over delight in contradiction and maverick vision, she or he had best look elsewhere. Every page of **The Cloning of Joanna May** makes it clear that this is Fay Weldon's fiction; she'll tell her story just the way she wants to. Try to stuff it into anyone else's pigeonhole and it won't fit. Classifiers, it proclaims, simply need not apply.

Gary Krist (review date 3 March 1991)

SOURCE: "The Fuzzy Vision of a True Believer," in *New York Times,* March 3, 1991, p. 9.

[*In the following review, Krist calls* Darcy's Utopia *one of Weldon's "most ambitious books," noting that she achieves even her unlikely conclusion "with aplomb."*]

Some writers chronicle the War Between Men and Women. Fay Weldon, a subtler observer by half, reports on a more elusive conflict—the War *Among* Men and Women. She understands that the battle lines of this other war seldom run along gender boundaries, but rather cut across the sexes to pit spouses against lovers, first wives against second wives, children against the parents who abandon or torment them. And in more than a score of novels, story collections and plays, she has never let us forget the ruinous consequences of this war—the state of perpetual heartache we call Modern Life.

In her latest novel, **Darcy's Utopia,** Ms. Weldon introduces us to a character with a plan to end the hostilities, or at least to lessen the carnage. Eleanor Darcy, a strong-willed woman with a flair for provocation (both sexual and intellectual), finds herself an instant media sensation in England after her second husband, a high Government adviser, is jailed for misappropriation of public funds. Taking advantage of her celebrity, she consents to a series of interviews to set forth her vision of the future—the utopia of the book's title, a theoretical society, in which "all men will believe in God and all men will be capable of love." While Eleanor is understandably a little fuzzy on specifics, the details that do emerge—the abolition of money, the requirement that all procreation be approved in advance by the community—are iconoclastic, to say the least. Like most ideological visions, however, Eleanor Darcy's has a seductive internal logic that can easily blind the unwary to its practical inadequacies.

It's this blindness, this intoxication with the closed world of the utopia, that Ms. Weldon makes the target of her satire. The novel is full of utopias of every stripe—social, political, erotic. Primary among them, of course, is Eleanor's experimental society, outlined in conversations with two journalists—Hugo Vansitart, who is interviewing Eleanor for a highbrow intellectual journal, and Valerie Jones, who is working on a profile for a woman's magazine called *Aura*. But there are also the various failed utopias of Eleanor's past lives—the smug Roman Catholicism and self-important Marxism of her first husband, for instance, and the radical economics of her second (his attempt to erase poverty by distributing cash wholesale to the British public is what landed him in jail). Finally, there is the romantic utopia of Hugo and Valerie themselves, who in the course of their assignments become so infatuated with each other that they decide to leave spouses and children behind and set up a love nest together in an expensive Holiday Inn in central London.

Jumping from interview transcripts to sections of the *Aura* profile-in-progress to bits and pieces of Valerie's own internal monologue, Ms. Weldon displays her usual glee in knocking her characters about. Few writers are as merciless as she in doling out misfortunes and hard times. But there is a certain wistfulness to her satire here. Ms. Weldon has never been overly generous with her sympathies, but she depicts several of the people in this book—Valerie in particular—with uncharacteristic fondness.

Perhaps that shouldn't be so surprising. Blind passions, for all their impracticality, do possess a kind of grace; those who succumb to them have as much of God in their eyes as the Devil. And one senses in Ms. Weldon's kinder mockery an element of nostalgia for the certainty of the true believer—whether the creed be an all-consuming romance of the kind promised in magazines like *Aura* or the economic dogma of, say, a Margaret Thatcher (to whose ideological fervor Eleanor Darcy's has more than a passing resemblance).

But, of course, nonbelievers can always console themselves with the fact that events tend to prove their cynicism right. The bill at the Holiday Inn, after all, must eventually be paid; the children cannot stay with a sitter forever, and society's poor cannot be made to disappear permanently in the creative bookkeeping of supply-side economics. Hugo and Valerie, like the lovers at the end of *A Midsummer Night's Dream,* do finally awaken from their moral slumber.

Darcy's utopia, however, doesn't die so easily. Eleanor continues her crusade, attracting converts, causing more casualties than she prevents in the War Among Men and Women. By novel's end, she has become the patron saint of the Darcian Movement, a new and growing religion complete with its own hymns and clergy. While the book's last twist of plot may tax the credulity of even the most indulgent readers, Ms. Weldon tosses it off with such aplomb that we find ourselves accepting it. Credibility, after all, has never been one of this author's priorities. She's more interested in telling the truth than in making it believable. And in this, one of her most ambitious books, she tells it without flinching, reminding us that as long as there are mortals on this earth, the supply of fools will never run out.

> My advice to everyone is to change their name at once if they're the least unhappy with their lives. In Darcy's Utopia everyone will choose a new name at seven, at eleven, at sixteen and at twenty-four. And naturally women at forty-five, or when the last child has grown up and left home, whichever is the earliest. . . . Then life will be seen to start over, not finish. It is a perfectly legal thing to do. . . . So long as there is no intent to defraud. . . . But so many of us, either feeling our identities to be fragile, or out of misplaced loyalty to our parents, feel we must stick with the names we start out with. The given name is a dead giveaway of our parents' ambition for us—whether to diminish or enhance, ignore us as much as possible or control us forever. . . . No, it will not do. It will have to change.

Devon Jersild (review date 8 March 1992)

SOURCE: "Fay Weldon Delivers a Tale of Sexual Hijinks and Some Lively Stories," in *Chicago Tribune Books*, March 8, 1992, pp. 4-5.

[*In the following review, Jersild calls Weldon's writing in* Life Force *and* Moon over Minneapolis *"intimate . . . passionate, and funny."*]

Fay Weldon's 19th work of fiction is as loopy as one might hope for, and as funny and satirical as one has come to expect from this irreverent, energetic British writer. Narrated by Nora, whose job at Accord Realtors leaves her plenty of time to "get on with writing this unpublishable work" (it's 1991, and there's a recession), *Life Force* has the gossip and intrigue of a good soap opera, the sexual adventure of *True Confessions* and the far-fetched but somehow satisfying coincidence of a novel by Charles Dickens.

Realistic as its surface tends to be, *Life Force* is hardly an old-fashioned novel. Weldon's comic, self-reflective, postmodern perspective turns the whole melange into subversive social commentary.

Nora tells the story of four female friends whose lives are turned upside down by the return of their lover-in-common, Leslie Beck, now a widower whose vigor, after 20 years, is undiminished. He possesses the Life Force of the title, being endowed with astonishing sexual prowess, though his energy is "not so much of sexual desire as of sexual discontent: the urge to find someone better out in the world, and thereby something better in the self; the one energy working against the other, creating a fine and animating friction."

Nora, Susan, Rosalie and even Marion "the spinster" worship the phallus in the person of Leslie (for whom they have epithets unprintable here); one by one, back in the 1970s, each of them succumbed to his appeal, cheating on their husbands, bearing his children, betraying each other and his wives. Yet for the most part all has gone along quite evenly—at least on the surface—in this safe, chaste suburb of London. Until now, that is, when Leslie comes back on the scene, and the consequences of all that misbehavior fly home to roost.

The wonderful fun of this novel is in Nora's voice. Alert to every movement in the mating dance, she comes to terms with her own marriage by writing about her friends. On Rosalie and her husband, she comments, "I think Wallace treated sex with Rosalie as he treated mountains: something to be attacked with energy, but not too often; surmounted, finished, a flag planted to automatic applause, and then a nice long rest." And here she is exploring her ambivalence toward marriage by writing in the voice of Marion: "Marriage is easier when the man is noticeably taller than the woman: it makes the balance of power, usually in the man's favor, seem a more natural state of affairs."

As Nora's tale unfolds and the facts become too dreary for her to relate with glee, she turns from "autobiography" to "fiction"—and is quite pleased by her efforts when events take more and more startling turns. Yet as her marriage unravels, the grim reality of Nora's life can be felt beneath all the fun. At one point, quickly picking up a cigarette after thinking she might give them up, she comments, "Self-destruction is the natural state; anything else is an effort." The life force is also the death force, and in Weldon, to resist it is to live a half-life, to be paralyzed; to go with it is be hurtled in to chaos, to speed through mishaps and miseries and ecstacy, stolen pleasures and rewards.

Weldon's attitude toward all of this is distinctly un-American; she never tries to fix anything; indeed, she actively enjoys the absurdity of life. There is no self-improving impulse lurking beneath these pages; no morals or maxims to take to heart. Life is learned not by sitting back and taking stock but by plunging into it—and messing up, like everybody else.

According to Nora, there's not much use in fighting the current anyway. She is not the only Weldon character to voice the following belief, but perhaps she says it best: "The way it goes when you're a child, that way it continues . . . We play the cards of life a certain way, albeit unconsciously; we can acquire skill in handling them, of course we can, but mostly it just comes naturally, and the most important factor is the hand we are originally dealt: it is our fate pattern, like it or not."

Such a perspective is sharply at odds with our current therapy culture, wherein we are encouraged to reshape ourselves and start anew. And Weldon takes sly pleasure in her characters' retrograde philosophies. Nora, turning conventional wisdom on its head, remarks on the danger of contemplating her life: "If only the recession would end, and the property market look up again . . . there'd be no time to so much as consider the state of my navel, out of which, like scarves from some magician's very deep and personal hat, I seem able to draw events and memories, like bloody entrails. . . . My fear is this: Supposing I were to draw out too many, or they started spilling out of their own accord, uncontrolled; how could I continue to digest? I might just die from loss of undisclosed material."

Interestingly, the last four stories in Weldon's new collection, *Moon Over Minneapolis,* are in the voice of women speaking to their silent pyschoanalyst. Several others show characters revealing themselves in the form of a monologue—in **"The Year of the Green Pudding,"** a copy editor confides her guilty secret to her personnel manager; in **"Down the Clinical Disco,"** a woman just released from an insane asylum tells her story to another woman at a pub. Certainly Weldon knows a good deal about the nooks and crannies of repression and denial and the roundabout ways that people make decisions.

On the other hand, her voice is so intimate, so passionate and funny, that one comes away from her fiction with the sense of having made contact with the author's fully present, forceful self. It is hard to read Weldon's work without thinking of her—and not Leslie Beck—as the embodiment of the Life Force.

Michael Malone (review date 26 April 1992)

SOURCE: "The Life Force Has a Headache," in *New York Times,* April 26, 1992, p. 11.

[*In the following review, Malone favorably evaluates* Life Force *and* Moon over Minneapolis.]

Fay Weldon is a satirist who casts a kind eye on the human

comedy as she passes by. And she passes by at a brisk pace. In a distinguished body of work (16 novels, as well as short-story collections, plays, television dramas and several volumes of nonfiction), she has proved to be a shrewd spectator of manners and mores, both upstairs and downstairs (she wrote episodes of the *Masterpiece Theater* series). In her fiction, the cast of characters moves easily between public and private stages, from posh gatherings and day-care centers to the intimacies of bedrooms. Like so many of her fellow ironists—Evelyn Waugh and Muriel Spark come to mind—Ms. Weldon can lay waste the pretensions of a decade in the sketch of a single dinner party. And, like her greatest predecessor, Jane Austen, she specializes in that particularly risible comedy of errors that exists between those incompatible creatures, men and women.

In this battle, Ms. Weldon stands, as the title of one of her novels has it, **Down Among the Women.** Hers is a fictional world populated by women of all ages and classes: women with their lovers and babies, their friends and enemies; women who experience a full range of fears, jealousies and unabashed lusts. Look at the titles: **The Fat Woman's Joke, Female Friends, Little Sisters, The Life and Loves of a She-Devil.** But if Ms. Weldon fires her cannon from the female vantage point, this feminist student of sexual politics has a tolerant heart for most of the men in her books, even for the womanizers, even for the bounders—even for Leslie Beck, the "hero" of her deft and vibrant new novel, **Life Force.**

In this account of roughly 20 years in the lives of some upper-middle-class Londoners, Leslie Beck, a politically, morally and esthetically incorrect businessman, represents the life force—or, rather, his penis does. In fact, for the women in lustful, flame-haired Leslie's world, this penis symbolizes creation itself, a 10-inch organ that is one-seventh his entire height and that has earned him the nickname "The Magnificent."

To the four central female characters of Ms. Weldon's novel, the size of Leslie's "life force" is far from a matter of indifference. Indeed, one look at it and they are hooked for decades. Nora (the book editor's wife), Rosalie (the mountaineer's wife), Susan (the writer's wife) and Marion (the unmarried art gallery owner) have all slept with Leslie, and greatly enjoyed it. And all but one have been impregnated by him—in some cases after a one-night stand. Leslie is nothing if not potent. (Indeed, he is exactly that: aside from his sexual vitality, he is an utter loss.)

In the early 1970's, in a handsomely refurbished Victorian house, Leslie Beck and his first wife sat at the center of a circle of married friends. Almost 20 years later, as the novel opens, he suddenly re-enters their lives with news of the death of his second wife, a painter whose canvases portray the settings of her faithless spouse's affairs. *Life Force* is a series of flashbacks about how Leslie's infidelities with each of these four women began and ended—and how they changed everything in the intervening years.

"Nothing happens, and nothing happens, and then everything happens," observes Nora. Indeed, during the Beck-less years, these women find that "life dribbles away"—feeding their cats, raising their children, planning vacations, watching nature documentaries on television and worrying about their decreasing property values. For this novel is also a wonderful social commentary about how a certain class of couples evolved from the liberal idealists and artists of the 70's into the affluent, health-conscious professionals of the 80's, and then declined into the politically constricted, sexually defeated men and women of the financially fretful 90's. Now middle-aged, they can no longer afford to squander their talents and their money and their sexuality. Their profligacy has led, or so at times they fear, to the political backlash and the recession and the AIDS epidemic. Even the fecund Leslie the Magnificent has become old and shriveled up, shorter in every way.

It is Nora, now a secretary at Accord Realtors, wife to a mild-mannered editor and former mistress to Leslie, who tells the story of the affairs, the story of these women's long-finished, and still nostalgically remembered, entanglements with the life force. Nora has time to set down this account because of Britain's economic slump: the real estate market is so puny that no customers interrupt her at the office. This economic reality for "real-tors" (a pun?) allows time for Nora to write non-reality (fiction), just as the times allow Susan's husband finally to start his philosophical book on "reality" when he leaves Susan for Nora, after Nora's husband leaves her for Susan. Or do they leave at all? Does Rosalie's husband (long thought dead in a mountaineering accident) really return, a victim of amnesia?

All these tidy knots, which Nora ties at the end of her "autobiography," may be (she warns us) not true at all, but make-believe, chosen because fiction makes life more fun. Nora is, in the end, more than a recorder; she's a creator, making herself the collective voice of the women, and so she is their authority, their author, just as Leslie Beck is the author (the progenitor) of the illegitimate children he fathers.

In this way, for all its social barbs and dry humor, *Life Force* is less a comedy of manners than it is a parable about the act of creativity itself. As Nora says, "The novel you read and the life you live are not distinguishable. Leslie Beck's Life Force is the energy not so much of sexual desire as of sexual discontent: the urge to find someone better out in the world, and thereby something better in the self." To create that something better in the self is the province of art as well as fornication.

Significantly, three acts of infidelity with Leslie take place in primordial, elemental sites. One in air (high-rise scaffolding), one in earth (a cave), one by water (at the seashore as the tide comes in), while the paintings of these sex acts are destroyed in a fire. Also significant is the fact that only unwed Marion, who—at Leslie's request—sold her baby (to a South African industrialist, no less), gives birth to a male. And that male is an artist. Marion only sells art, she doesn't create it. Leslie's life force is male, but it is females who in the marvelous art of Fay Weldon's novel take that force and with it create life. Or fictions.

Fay Weldon's **Moon over Minneapolis** is a collection of fast-paced stories about contemporary life. Many of these 19 tales (never previously published in book form) describe women in painful, circumscribed or exploitative relationships, but the tone is satiric and the effect comic. Ambitious, overbearing and unfeeling mothers and their gullible, passive daughters appear in a number of guises, from the rigidly feminist Liz and her airline stewardess daughter, Romula, in **"I Do What I Can and I Am What I Am"** to avaricious, elegant Marion and her ungainly offspring, Erin and Elspeth, in **"A Visit From Johannesburg: Or Mr. Shaving's Wives"** to sexually promiscuous Greta and naive, earnest Bente in **"Au Pair."** Other stories describe delusive affairs, tormented loves or burned-out marriages. A 25-year-old graduate student on vacation with her professor-lover abruptly ends the affair in **"Ind Aff: Or Out of Love in Sarajevo."** ("Ind Aff" is their private abbreviation for "inordinate affection," which, despite her earlier avowals of passion, is precisely what the narrator discovers she does not feel for her lover.) Although their plots can be absurd and thin, these stories are enlivened by Ms. Weldon's caustic wit. Occasionally harsh in her judgments, she is typically perspicacious, consistently clever and always entertaining.

Regina Barreca (review date Summer 1992)

SOURCE: "Wise Wickedness," in *Belles Lettres,* Vol. 7, No. 4, Summer 1992, p. 18.

[*In the following review, Barreca asserts that both* Life Force *and* Moon over Minneapolis *will add significantly to Weldon's canon of feminist literature.*]

When Fay Weldon was finishing the manuscript of **Life Force,** she felt, paradoxically, at a loss for words.

"When the critics ask what the new book is about, what can

I say?" she wondered. "I can't very well tell them it's about a man with a ten-inch dong, can I?" I suggested that she remind them that they always complained that she never fleshed out her male characters, and that here she does so with a vengeance.

The book does indeed deal with Leslie Beck "The Magnificent," as he is usually known, who is a catalyst in much the same way that Ruth from *Lives and Loves of a She-Devil* was. "Things happen because of Leslie and his sense of energy; he is slightly unholy, lower-class, ready to take on challenges in order to mount/surmount his destiny." Leslie is remarkable because "he likes women. And women never forgot him." Weldon had described a character from an earlier novel as someone who did not "regard women as sex objects, but thought of himself as one," and the same applies to this hero. The most seductive thing he says to women is "Tell me about why you are unhappy", and this is what draws them. The community of women at the heart of the book are all Leslie's past, present, and future lovers, bound to one another by love and betrayal, with Leslie simply an emblem of their connectedness.

Yet, as in all Weldon's works, the central questions here concern women's lives and choices. "Forget Leslie Beck," says one of the two narrators, "Were we good women or bad?" With her characteristic wit and her brilliant detailing of the everyday, even as she moves from the realistic to the fabular, Weldon has provided us with a book that is bound to become another classic feminist novel.

In the brief, cautionary tales in *Moon Over Minneapolis,* Weldon also questions the nature of fate and individual will, desire and imagination, as well as the relationship between the political and the personal. In a particularly effective tale titled **"Ind Aff,"** the narrator falls in love with her older thesis director (married and the father of three children). She confuses "mere passing academic ambition with love," believing this man's assessment that she has "a good mind but not a first class mind." The narrator wishes to believe that this is "not just any old professor/student romance," but since Peter Piper likes to "luxuriate in guilt and indecision," and has taken her with him on a holiday to see whether they are "really, truly suited," we are certain that Weldon is indeed presenting the quintessential student/teacher relationship.

Desperately drawn to her teacher because he represents much more than he offers, the narrator must overlook his stinginess, his whining, and his "thinning hair" because he seems powerful and authoritative (speaking in "quasi-Serbo-Croatian"). She loves him with "Inordinate Affection," she claims. "Your Ind Aff is my wife's sorrow" Peter moans, blaming a girl who was born the first year of his marriage for his wife's unhappiness, absolving himself from blame.

Yet when they are waiting to be served wild boar in a private restaurant, she notices a waiter her own age, and, looking at this virile, handsome man, she feels "quite violently, an associated . . . pang." Having associated love with a sensation of the heart or the head, she describes this desire as the "true, the real pain of Ind Aff!" The waiter has no authority but does possess "luxuriant black hair, [and a] sensuous mouth." She asks herself in a moment of clear vision "What was I doing with this man with thinning hair?" Weldon, as forgiving as she is ruthless, concludes that sometimes we "come to [our] senses. People do, sometimes quite quickly." With her blessing, and informed by her wise wickedness, we are permitted to review, revise, and go on with our own lives renewed.

Deirdre Neilen (review date Autumn 1992)

SOURCE: Review of *Life Force,* in *World Literature Today,* Vol. 66, No. 4, Autumn 1992, p. 723.

[*In the following review, Neilen states that Weldon's satire in* Life Force *"leaves us laughing through our tears."*]

Fay Weldon's latest novel, **Life Force,** announces its intention pictorially on the jacket; a photo of part of Michelangelo's *David* meets the reader's gaze. However, unlike most of the partial depictions of the work which concentrate on the torso, this one concentrates on the phallus. The publishers seem as squeamish as Victorians, since they provide a paper wrapper to hide the offending part until presumably the reader gets the book home. Weldon no doubt is laughing at this cat-and-mouse game. Her novel, after all, wants to shed light on this symbol of male power and female desire. She intends not to cover up any of the myths surrounding it, and she has a great deal of fun puncturing society's presumptions about it.

The novel follows the lives of four middle-class couples about twenty years after all four of the women had sex with Leslie Beck. Leslie has one claim to fame, his "10-inch dong," which all the women find magnificent and irresistible. As Nora, the narrator, says, "Women are too kind to men . . . Forever telling them that size makes no difference." Without this size, Leslie would be the sum of all his other parts, and the women recognize him as sleazy, cruel, and vulgar. He is not someone for whom one should risk home and husband and child, yet Rosalie, Nora, Marion, and Susan do exactly this.

Life Force begins when Leslie's second wife dies and he attempts to sell her paintings to Marion's gallery. The women discover that Anita Beck has somehow painted all the rooms and places where her husband was unfaithful. Her studio seems a bewitched place, and Nora eventually burns it down so as to stop the chain of events Leslie's reappearance in their lives has caused. He has fathered some of the women's daughters, and now the wives have to be careful whose sons their daughters date. He has fathered one son and sold him in order to make money for his failing businesses. He had his first wife committed to a mental institution so he could marry his secretary and thus gain access to her father's money. In short, he is a thoroughly unlikable man, and it is a tribute to Weldon's writing that she somehow makes Beck and his forays among the women amusing and sometimes even touching.

As usual with Weldon, the novel also examines friendship between women. The news is not good. These women say they are friends, but they really see no life or meaning with one another beyond comparing notes about husbands and lovers. They have sex with the other husbands and then blame the women for these transgressions more than the men. This is not to say that Weldon's women admire men more; they do not. In fact, they seem resigned to knowing that the men are inferior beings, yet they can't imagine living without them.

This then is Weldon's legacy. She writes satirically about a particular class in England located "somewhere between the street protestors and the bourgeoisie establishment." We laugh at their pretensions and perhaps pity their aspirations, but Weldon implies there is nowhere else to go and no other game to play. Like most satire, *Life Force* leaves us laughing through our tears.

Patricia Juliana Smith (essay date Summer 1993)

SOURCE: "Weldon's *The Life and Loves of a She-Devil*," in *The Explicator,* Vol. 51, No. 4, Summer 1993, pp. 255-57.

[*In the following essay, Smith examines the "self-defeating and self-erasing strategy" of the character Ruth in her attempt to free herself from the illusory expectations offered to women by the romance novel genre.*]

The conclusion of Fay Weldon's *The Life and Loves of a She-Devil* presents what a grammarian more concerned with form than content might perceive as a problematic tense shift:

I am a lady of six foot two, who had tucks taken in her legs. A comic turn, turned serious.

Why would Ruth Patchett, the eponymous protagonist, say, "I am a lady of six foot two," when she had already "had tucks taken in her legs" and was therefore only five foot eight? Grammatically speaking, we could read the subject complement "a lady of six foot two" and the dependent phrase that follows as a unit indicating that Ruth's final state is, unquestionably, an altered one. Yet I would also suggest that Weldon's use of "I am" in her protagonist's closing statement is indicative of the ontological problem the text requires the reader to confront: Exactly who, by the end of her narrative, is Ruth Patchett?

The Life and Loves of a She-Devil chronicles the process by which the ugly duckling Ruth achieves high-tech revenge against her faithless husband Bobbo and his mistress Mary Fisher, a writer of popular romances who is "small and pretty and delicately formed, prone to fainting and weeping and sleeping with men while pretending that she doesn't." Through an elaborate scheme involving constantly changing identities and egregious acts of computer fraud, Ruth brings about Bobbo's financial ruin and subsequent imprisonment for embezzlement, while she personally acquires wealth and success through her more legitimate business endeavors. Her ultimate revenge against the guilty pair, however, is her *becoming* Mary Fisher by means of plastic surgery. Ironically, by doing so she becomes, both literally and figuratively, her own worst enemy.

Weldon's concluding fragment employs the figure of chiasmus to indicate the constantly evolving, and devolving, nature of Ruth's identity as she changes not only names but also the conventional character types that she enacts through the course of the narrative. She is first presented as a tragicomic variant of the pharmakos, masochistically accepting blame and victimization from her husband, her children, and, ultimately, her idol Mary Fisher.

Yet while Northrop Frye dictates that ironic comedy requires "driving out the pharmakos from the point of view from society," Weldon's woebegone scapegoat turns the table on her persecutors. As Bobbo abandons her, she experiences a moment of enlightenment and embraces as her new identity the diabolical character he attributes to her: "Self-knowledge and reason run through my veins: the cold slow blood of the she-devil." This shift in Ruth's subject position, together with her new, secret self-consciousness, marks her evolution into the eiron. In this comic figure, she is empowered as she accumulates worldly experience, material wealth, and self-esteem through her adventures as she avenges herself on the self-deceived Bobbo and Mary. Although she achieves enviable material and personal successes, Ruth is nevertheless unwilling or unable to accept the ironic adage that living well is the best revenge, and she embarks on an inevitably self-defeating and self-erasing strategy, that of becoming the very object of her own wrath.

As she is externally transformed through plastic surgery into the physical image of Mary Fisher, she is simultaneously transformed mentally as she unconsciously assumes the romance writer's self-deceptive world view. The final chapter serves as Ruth's apologia, in which she triumphantly boasts of all she has accomplished, the usurpation not only of the now-dead Mary's outward form but also her wealth, her social contacts, and her lovers, including the broken Bobbo. In her smug superiority, however, Ruth reveals her own self-deception. In the strangest of comic turns, the eiron has subsumed the alazon and thus has turned ridiculously—and even pathetically—serious.

The Life and Loves of a She-Devil would seem to validate the argument of *The Anatomy of Criticism* that irony is the polar opposite of romance. Weldon's novel is not, however, merely a clever deployment of Frye's flow charts of modes and mythoi. Rather, through this examination of the complex and overlapping relationship between the female eiron and the female alazon, Weldon anatomizes the self-deception afflicting women who relentlessly internalize not only the falsehoods presented by the purveyors of romantic fiction but also the limited and limiting gender roles that the genre supports and attempts to reify. Through Ruth's eiron phase, her ability to form community with other women, although motivated, ironically, by nothing more recondite than her obsessive desire for revenge, nevertheless allows her to escape her initial abjection and results in personal and economic gain for herself and for the women around her. But although Ruth is aware that "Mary Fisher did a wicked thing" in offering false hopes and dreams to her readers, she is herself unable to eschew such chimera. Subsequently, she rejects what she perceives to be "the muddy flood of purgatory wastes" of cooperation with other women in order to pursue illusionary glamors "flickering and dangerous with hell-fire."

Late in the novel Ruth surreptitiously observes the daughter that she abandoned long before. Noting that Nicola lives and works with, rather than against, other women, she assesses her with disdain: "She will never make a she-devil." Ruth fails to see that Nicola, having found an alternative to the deceptions of romance fiction, has no need to be a "she-devil." For readers who read Weldon's multifaceted irony clearly, it is apparent that Ruth has chosen the wrong plot upon which to structure her metafiction.

Tama Janowitz (review date 17 October 1993)

SOURCE: "The Cure of the Married Therapists," in *New York Times,* October 17, 1993, p. 14.

[*In the following review, Janowitz finds* Trouble *a unique mix of humor and painful examinations of the unraveling of a marriage.*]

Not a great deal of really humorous fiction has been written in the latter half of the 20th century. Humorous or satirical fiction by men often involves the reader's identification with a bad boy—a drunkard, a lout, a glutton, a womanizer. *The Ginger Man, Portnoy's Complaint, A Confederacy of Dunces* most quickly come to mind. Of course there are exceptions, as there are to the generalization that humorous books by women often involve the reader's identification with the heroine as victim. *After Claude, Fear of Flying, Kinflicks, The Dud Avocado*—in these books, women are seduced and abandoned by various men, kicked out of hearth and home, and so forth.

Fay Weldon's latest novel, ***Trouble,*** is not only funny but extremely painful; the pain is like the pleasure to be found in scratching a mosquito bite. Perhaps her humor can be categorized as women's humor: certainly among various women acquaintances of mine many are fans, yet I have not found a man who picks up her novels for entertainment. And ***Trouble*** is entertaining, in a way that is not—at least by me—to be found in most novels that slice open and dissect the intricate patterns of human interactions. Such novels can be pompous or dry, yet Ms. Weldon manages not only to be witty but to keep the reader engrossed, tearing along to find out what happens next.

The scene is London. Annette is married, happily, she thinks, to Spicer, who after 10 years of marriage abruptly turns out to be a real rat. Or perhaps he was all along: it is only when Annette becomes pregnant and Spicer begins seeing a New Age therapist that his various injustices and manipulatory patterns become clear to her.

Early on, after an argument, Annette attempts to heal the rift by preparing a special dinner for two, sending their two children (one from her earlier marriage, one from his) out to the movies, putting on perfume (which previously Spicer always requested and which, as of late, she realizes she has forgotten to wear) and opening a particularly good bottle of wine (Spicer is a wine merchant).

Still in a rage when he comes home, he manages to thwart her attempt at reconciliation, exclaiming: "You're wearing scent, so I know that in your calculating way you have sex with me planned for tonight. . . . You open a bottle of St.-Estephe '85 without consulting me—you are so competitive it extends even into the world of wine! . . . You must have me all to yourself, so you send the poor kids off to the cinema, regardless of what they want, let alone the fact that I might want to see them. You cook beef although you know perfectly well the only protein I can eat these days is white meat—chicken or a little fish—and you overcook the mange-tout in a way that can only be deliberate. . . ."

At this point, one recognizes an event that perhaps all women—and possibly men as well—have experienced: at attempt to do something good that is seemingly deliberately misinterpreted. Ms. Weldon is a master at exposing anguished moments: the moment when, on coming home from a cocktail party, your spouse accuses you of acting foolish; the moments in life when one's soft spots of insecurity are probed. Reality, as one sees it, rewritten by someone else.

Annette confides in her best—her only—friend, Gilda, about her deteriorating sex life with Spicer; naturally Gilda instantly relays these intimacies to her husband, Stephen, who naturally repeats these confidences to Spicer, who sees this as another treachery on Annette's part.

As Annette's pregnancy progresses, Spicer's behavior grows worse. (It doesn't help that she has a novel about to be published and has been invited to appear on *Oprah Winfrey*.) It seems he's been quite the cockatrice all along, having affairs, secretly extracting funds from his company. Yet his behavior is not accounted for by Annette's pregnancy, or her novel, but rather by his extensive sessions with the New Ager-Jungian-Astrologist-Therapist, Dr. Rhea Marks.

Spicer forces Annette to see Rhea Marks's husband, another therapist, Dr. Herman Marks. Dr. Herman very nearly rapes her under the guise of attempting to help her with her sex problems. This molestation is rewritten by the doctor and later held up as an example of Annette's paranoia. And eventually the therapists are responsible for the denouement.

Of course such things happen: there are plenty of corrupt and manipulative therapists. But Ms. Weldon can portray the most ordinary interactions in scenes from a marriage, the ritualized behavior of men and women together, in so bitterly funny and accurate a way that it is almost a shame to lay the trouble in this marriage on two therapists whose canon involves the magical powers of some mysterious underworld of archetypes, Saturn and Medusa and Lilith. The premise grows awfully close to the world drawn in *Rosemary's Baby*. Ms. Weldon's uniqueness is her insight into motivations of modern types, a capability so honed that there must be moments of truth for every reader. She exaggerates what would ordinarily be boring—the mundane exchanges between people—so that we recognize and laugh at ourselves. This enlivens a good deal of the bleakness in the commonplace world and inflates our roles in it.

To objectify human existence is to remove our shame at being ourselves, and for this we must praise and thank Ms. Weldon and her wicked pen. (Or word processor.)

Daniel Harris (review date 28 November 1993)

SOURCE: "The Weldon Manifesto," in *Los Angeles Times Book Review*, November 28, 1993, pp. 2, 9.

[*In the following review, Harris offers a negative assessment of* Trouble, *noting that the novel fails to live up to Weldon's usual standards.*]

What differentiates the ferocious satires of British author Fay Weldon from the typical bed-hopping, feminist sex comedy is their harsh determinism. For most of her female characters, holy matrimony, far from being full of connubial bliss and the attendant pleasure of the pitter-patter of little feet, is about as consensual as being clubbed by a cave man and dragged back to a cul-de-sac in the suburbs. Weldon's women are swept up in a sort of marital Darwinism, a brutal process of natural selection in which secretaries continually usurp their boss's wives, who, in turn, often retaliate with creative forms of psychological torture. The vindictive heroine of her masterpiece *The Life and Loves of a She-Devil,* for instance, systematically sabotages her husband's newfound happiness with a writer of treacly romances by transforming herself through plastic surgery from a sexless frump into a voluptuous centerfold. In such bitingly satiric cautionary tales, divorce frequently proves to be an unexpected boon for the forsaken wife, who experiences both romantic and economic rebirth after being summarily dumped, as in the short story **"Redundant! or the Wife's Revenge,"** in which a humdrum piece of domestic chattel blossoms into a liberated woman when her husband leaves her for their daughter's lesbian lover.

Weldon takes the hackneyed scenario of sentimental betrothals followed by inevitable midlife adulteries and infuses it with the gleeful malice of one of the most reductive examinations of the human body in all of contemporary fiction. She describes sex as a kind of genetic battlefield, a desperate effort on the part of that abstract entity, the human race, to create the perfect specimen; marriage is just the fig leaf with which we camouflage this imperative to procreate, a flimsy disguise that Weldon delights in snatching off—exposing to her readers again and again the fierce physiological dramas that we sublimate in this duplicitous institution.

Central to many of her plots is the rise of the Nietzschean

superwoman, an embodiment of naked ambition who, like Becky Sharp in Thackeray's *Vanity Fair,* manages to escape from her proletarian upbringing to become the Machiavellian consort of a prosperous spouse or even an entrepreneur in her own right, like Marion in Weldon's last novel, **Life Force,** who finances her art gallery by auctioning off her baby to a South African millionaire. It is tempting to interpret these self-made heroines as an extravagant burlesque of Weldon's own meteoric rise to fame, which occurred after a decade of relative poverty during which she scrambled to make a living as a temp, a profession that takes pride of place in her fiction as the spawning ground of her most ingenious and diabolical she-devils.

The paradox of her fiction, however, is that, while Weldon admires the chutzpah with which many of her characters trample over the wives and children who stand between them and the men they use as the vehicle of their ambitions, she ultimately despises the state of complacent affluence that these greedy materialists aspire to achieve. No sooner do the conniving temps of these embittered fairy tales ensnare a successful corporate executive than they are cast aside, like the wife they replaced, and deposed by yet another Becky Sharp. These women emerge out of the seething multitudes of hungry romantic careerists just waiting for their chance to advance up a hierarchical power structure that Weldon describes as the equivalent among women of a food chain. It is the much compromised feminism of this unending round of musical chairs, in which the relentless exuberance of her scheming Lady Macbeth is at once celebrated and reviled, that gives her fiction its distinctive note of scathing cynicism.

While Annette, the downtrodden protagonist of Weldon's new novel, **Trouble,** is certainly no superwoman, she fits to a T the classic profile of the usurper. She is the second wife of a gullible chauvinist, Spicer Horrocks, who turns against her when she inadvertently challenges his self-esteem by publishing a successful novel. Their relationship abruptly deteriorates when Spicer falls under the spell of a manipulative pair of "healers" who, preaching a unique blend of psychobabble and astrology, succeed in convincing him that Annette is the incarnation of the "Inner Enemy" conspiring to molest his Child Within. At once a tirade against the unconscionable scam of quack psychotherapy and a wicked broadside of the whole institution of marriage, the book ends apocalyptically when Annette miscarries in her final month of pregnancy and is then booted out of her own house, which Spicer, now the glassy-eyed disciple of these two unscrupulous Charlatans, converts into an institute for the Assn. of Astrological Psychotherapists.

This catastrophe leads Annette to deliver a series of delirious monologues about the disappointments of marriage, a raving manifesto of Weldon's own sexual nihilism. Her con-

cluding speeches are really the only saving grace of this otherwise capricious novel, which, regrettably, bears the hallmarks of a hasty piece of contract work dashed off to satisfy a publisher's implacable demand for this most gifted of author's annual pound of flesh.

The major problem with **Trouble** is not only the absurdity of its basic premise—about bodysnatching astrologers poisoning a once uxorious man's mind against his pregnant wife—but also its form. The novel consists almost entirely of interminable gab sessions in which Annette and her best friend Gilda rattle on over the telephone about Spacer's increasingly icy indifference, as well as his escalating tendency to spout meaningless shibboleths about "internalized negative figures" and "anti-synchronicity." In choosing to keep the book's third-person narration down to a bare minimum, Weldon has deprived her readers of one of the most interesting aspects of her incomparable style as a storyteller, an idiosyncrasy that can perhaps best be defined by the typographic convention that distinguishes many of her short stories and novels: the extra space with which she sets her paragraphs off by themselves so that any given page looks like a heap of disjointed fragments, a mosaic of sententious proclamations, each of which has its own internal unity.

The effect of this fragmentation is extraordinary. What Weldon essentially does in her best work is to strip her stories of the transitions between individual scenes and distill the lives of her characters down to discontinuous moments, emblematic episodes that are often separated from each other, not only by blank spaces, but by huge leaps of time. By drastically foreshortening the period that elapses between an action and its consequences, a crime and its punishments, she heightens the impression her books make of being instructive fables that show men and women making bad decisions in one paragraph and then reaping their just rewards in the next. In this way, she creates the atmosphere of a parable, a folk tale, the sort of story that does not attempt to give you full-blooded, naturalistic characters in real situations but animated cartoons. Rumplestiltskins and Rip Van Winkles who move quickly through the decades, as if their lives had been speeded up through time-lapsed photography. Weldon is most comfortable with these capsulized abridgments and is far less successful with an experiment such as **Trouble,** in which the reader will miss the unusual style of Britain's preeminent laughing tragedian who guffaws with such irresistible cruelty at her characters' sexual adversities.

Anita Brookner (review date 12 February 1994)

SOURCE: "My Husband Became a Zombie," in *The Spectator,* Vol. 272, No. 8640, February 12, 1994, pp. 29-30.

[*In the following review, Brookner finds* Affliction—*published as* Trouble *in the United States—topical but less than satisfying.*]

To lose one's husband to another woman is bad, to lose one's husband to another man may be slightly worse, but to lose one's husband to a pair of therapists, one of each sex, is arguably the worst blow of all. Of course the husband in question has to be singularly disturbed for this to happen, and therefore axiomatically in need of a therapist. So the unsupervised practice continues. Something of this fate seems to have been visited upon Fay Weldon, one of the most independent and vigorous writers of contemporary fiction, and her new novel [*Affliction*] chronicles the sinister takeover that wrested an amiable but credulous man from the bosom of his family and turned him into a zombie, spouting idiot-speak, and eventually into a criminal who despoils his wife and children and who is prevented from feeling a scintilla of remorse by the gurus who control his life, his property, and what remains of his brain.

But revenge is a dish best served cold, as is novel writing. In a book composed largely of dialogue and fairly bristling with rage, Fay Weldon contrives to be both brutal and indelicate, in ways which do her argument no favour. Her argument, I take it, is that unauthorised intrusion into the psyche is a dangerous malpractice, and it makes little difference whether the therapist is qualified or not, for, as the author is justified in pointing out, fictions are best kept on the page.

The interpretations which Dr Rhea Marks erects on the ruins of her patients' minds are in fact debased fictions, all the more reprehensible for being untalented. Dr Rhea Marks, I hasten to add, is the therapist consulted by Spicer, the male protagonist in this *marivaudage* from Hell. He is, or was, married to Annette, who is pregnant and unhappy, and who thought she was pregnant and happy until Spicer started mystifying her with star signs and sextiles and Iron John platitudes. Invited, together with Spicer, to Dr Rhea Marks's Hampstead consulting room, Annette learns that her negativity is putting obstacles in her husband's way, and that it would be better if they parted, at least for a while. It should be added that, acting on the suggestion of friends, Annette has already been seeing Dr Herman Marks, who just happens to be the husband and partner of Dr Rhea. Dr Herman's interest seems to lie in the area of sexual molestation, of which he is also a glib practitioner. Any protest, of course, is merely a reaction from the past, and from the all-registering subsconscious. Thus it is not Dr Herman who is at fault, but Annette's father.

This delusional system, which is at last being revealed for what it is, at least in the States, where it first became popular, is grimly dealt with by Fay Weldon, but her readers will have to struggle with a rising tide of exasperation, not only because of the nature of the material but because her treatment of it lacks deftness and is totally without irony. Both her main characters, Annette and Spicer, are unsympathetic, and although it is Spicer who goes off the rails, his victim wife is merely hesitant and irritating. Despite the nonsense Spicer talks he is far from being mystical or other-worldly; he likes his wife to be compliant, and the couple's sex life is tiresomely explicit. Nor does Annette appear to have many resources. She has a job as a television researcher, but spends most of her time in bed. And on the strength of a first novel, not yet published, she is invited onto the *Oprah Winfrey* show. This detail, like so many others (but in fact there are rather few) fails to convince.

It is inevitable that Annette's fate is to go from bad to worse. Once she has collapsed in a taxi and been taken to hospital she falls into the net of bereavement counsellors, holistic healers, and hypnotherapists. Apparently this saves money on the drugs bill. Peter, the hypnotherapist, does not have much success, but his sales pitch is persuasive. By this stage Annette is talking into a tape recorder, but Spicer puts paid to what could for once have been a genuinely therapeutic exercise and orders her to leave the hospital. At home the Doctors Marks are waiting for her. They have moved in. This is very convenient, as the lease on their Hampstead house has expired. Naturally it is Annette who leaves. In this contest of three against one she was always outnumbered. The gain to the therapists, apart from money, has been self-justification. But the gain to the patient, in this case Spicer, is also self-justification. The beauty of the whole nefarious process is self-evident.

I admire Fay Weldon. She has collapsed the confessional novel into something amusing and effective, and formally she deserves her place in the history of fiction. And it may well be that she has produced a tract for our times—she has always been unnervingly topical. But the greater thrust of this book is contained in soliloquies (the tape recorder, the telephone) and it seems as if she has abandoned her usual method and gone back to the confessional. 'Never mind', says Annette finally, I can put it all into a novel.' Whether it was this novel, and whether one would care to read it a second time is open to doubt. But if *Affliction*—even the title is significant—opens avenues for discussion it will be seen to have done this work at least with no little acumen.

Anne Chisholm (review date 13 May 1995)

SOURCE: "One Woman at One Time Plays Many Parts," in *The Spectator,* Vol. 274, No. 8705, May 13, 1995, pp. 39-40.

[In the following review, Chisholm describes Splitting *as somewhat flimsy, but "vintage Weldon."]*

Fay Weldon's novels, including this one [*Splitting*], are not as weird as they at first appear. For some time now—this is her 28th book—she has been taking the ordinary events of women's lives, the small change of marriage, adultery, motherhood, friendship and betrayal and, with the skills of an alchemist or an amiable witch, transforming the dull, familiar stuff into something rich and strange. Her fiction is not for the literal-minded; she never writes proper stories with plots and resolution at the end, and her characters seldom behave like real people. However, for all the tricks she plays, her books are well grounded in her own hard-earned wisdom and her sad, shrewd observation of the ways of the world.

Her new novel concerns a contemporary commonplace, an impending divorce. A woman is living alone in a London hotel while she struggles to come to terms with the fact that her husband wants to marry someone else. Lady Rice, before she married into the landed gentry, was a pop star, Angelica, rich and famous on account of a song entitled 'Kinky Virgin'. She gave away her success and her money for love; now, as her marriage disintegrates, her personality also fragments. Rejected by her husband, she hardly knows who she is any more. Out of the splintering woodwork come assorted alternative or repressed personalities; from time to time they take her over and act on her behalf. Thus Lady Rice becomes Jelly White, the neat and calculating secretary to her husband's lawyer, and able to derail his plans; at times she is also the delinquent Angel, openly craving sex with strange men. It is Angel who comes closest to explaining what is going on in *Splitting:* 'Women tend to be more than one person,' she remarks, 'at the best of times. Men just get to be the one.'

As is usual in a Weldon novel, men do not come too well out of *Splitting:* they are all weak, dull, lecherous or crooked. Not that she lets women off lightly either; she remains beady-eyed about their capacity for self-delusion, dependence and self-pity. 'How can he possibly prefer her to me?', wails Lady Rice, as she schemes, in her secretarial guise, for all the alimony she can get. But then we all know, as Weldon reminds us, that victims are seldom nice, and that 'a woman scorned is thrust into hell and must work her way up out of it'. Behind all the antics and the transformation scenes lurks real pain at the cost, emotional as well as financial, of broken marriages. Divorce, she tells us, is 'war against the self, and there can be no real victory in it on either side.'

At the same time, Fay Weldon remains determined, as a writer, not to let her readers settle down. Lady Rice turns out to be related to a dotty old couple living in a vast gothic house on the river in Chelsea; suddenly the novel is full of ghosts and hallucinations and guest appearances from Aleister Crowley and Nina Hamnett. For her next trick, she switches narrators to a male voice, Ajax, 'the purifier, the scourer of thought; the hero of old; the banisher of the bath ring of guilt.' In this voice she proceeds to tell the story of Angelica's marriage, entitled, clearly with malice aforethought, Ajax's Aga Saga. A series of ludicrously confused village affairs ensues, as Susan, the 'Great Adultress', devours other women's husbands, Weldon is clever enough to get away with this, but only just. Her prose sparkles distractingly with wit, allusions and puns.

The end of the novel is weak. A bang on the head banishes the alter egos, and produces normal, well-integrated Angela, who takes up with nice ordinary Humphrey. Sexy Angel is still about, so anything can happen, but it hardly matters any more. This is not a novel to analyse or to take too seriously, but admirers will find it vintage Weldon, not a smooth ride but a wild, daft, exhilarating read.

Bertha Harris (review date 11 June 1995)

SOURCE: "A Woman Scorned," in *New York Times,* June 11, 1995, p. 48.

[In the following review, Harris applauds Weldon's ability to "unsentimentally" further the cause of "oppressed" heroines.]

Fay Weldon's latest beleaguered heroine hears voices in her head. Over the years since the publication of her first novel, *The Fat Woman's Joke,* in 1967, Ms. Weldon has given her abandoned, impoverished wives some extraordinary weapons to employ against the husbands who have left them for someone nicer, younger, prettier or more suitable. To be effective, all of these weapons (which have included witchcraft and chocolate cake) have required brains, imagination and a single-minded, self-serving capacity for revenge and vindication. None have ever been so exotic or so marvelously contrived as the multiple personality with which Ms. Weldon has endowed Angelica White in her 20th novel, *Splitting.*

At 17 years of age, the lovely Angelica is about to become compliant, docile, passive: she wants to be a wife, married to Sir Edwin Rice. Angelica used to be a rock-and-roll star, Kinky Virgin. Hence, she is rich, not the least of her attractions, because young Sir Edwin, who is fat and lazy and does drugs, is not. Edwin's mother died a raving drunk, but appears as a ghost at her son's wedding, still raving drunk:

his mad father passes the time by knocking his own front teeth out with a rusty cleaver, and despises Edwin for his obesity. The Kinky Virgin band also disapproves of Edwin; their kindest, least obscene assessment of his character is "snobby twerp, nerd . . . from the posh end of yuppie-dom." The ceilings of Edwin's yuppie-dom, Rice Court and its surrounding acres of countryside, are literally and figuratively falling in when he decides that he loves Angelica. "Who these days could win a virgin bride?" he wonders.

Angelica is in a bit of a collapse herself. She is still reeling from the shock of catching her mother wearing a miniskirt and living with a lover—transgressing against youth by posing as the daughter. "Widows are meant to fade away," Angelica protests. Consequently, she loses her "appetite for excess," removes the rings from her nose and colors her hair a respectable brown. "The exhilarations of the rock stadium" are replaced by the new, docile sensation of becoming helpmeet to "Edwin's woes."

In effect, Angelica's troubles begin when she resolves that it's "time to give up and grow up." With marriage, the splitting of Angelica begins: Angelica White, former rock star, is now Lady Rice, wife and hostess. The voices in her head start giving her some hardheaded advice: "Who, lately married, ever anticipates divorce?"—which Lady Rice ignores. "I'm not interested in money," she declares, "I'm not one bit materialistic," and promptly forks over nearly all of her 800,000 Kinky Virgin pounds to the Rice estate. Edwin's conniving land agent (upper class by osmosis—he's in love with Edwin) has reasoned that the money "was the tax Angelica had to pay because she had no presentable family and no social status." A tidy bit of legal skulduggery committed behind her back insures that "in case of future litigation," Lady Rice will have no claim on her own money.

Eleven years pass, during which Edwin's father starts taking Prozac and, six weeks later, marries a "blond and leather-booted woman" who believes that Angelica isn't classy enough to be Lady Rice. More traitors to their sex— the classic floozies, bimbos and home wreckers that populate every Fay Weldon novel—arrive on the scene, all bent on furthering their own wicked designs at Lady Rice's expense. The sensible voices in Angelica's head begin (to Lady Rice's surprise) to speak up for her when she would rather go on believing the best about men and women. But her hardheaded alter egos, no matter how protective of their hostess, are no defense against Anthea Box, the forceful, weatherbeaten Empress of Home Wreckers, who carries a "riding crop from force of habit."

Thanks especially to Anthea, Edwin turns conclusively against Lady Rice (he'll be sorry!) and drags her by the hair out of Rice Court and locks her out. His expensive solicitor is already in place, waiting to file a divorce action

against Lady Rice that includes charges of adultery, bad cooking, lesbianism and bestiality ("her kissing of the family dogs" is "a major matrimonial offense"). Edwin can afford the most expensive lawyer—with Kinky Virgin's money, the Rice family's properties have been restored and are making money hand over fist as an English heritage tourist trap.

Edwin believes he has thrown Lady Rice into the world destitute and alone: "He was vanishing her." And she deserves no less; although his charges against her are claptrap, she did once remark, "Flop and wobble," while in bed with him. Lady Rice was only musing about a dreadful jelly her mother used to make, but Edwin chooses to believe that she has unforgivably committed "verbal assault."

Lady Rice agrees with Edwin: she is lost. But not so. Like avenging guardian angels, her alternate personalities emerge to snap her out of the doldrums. The most practical one, Jelly, has absorbed the computer skills Lady Rice acquired while helping out in the Rice Court Offices; in no time, Jelly has stolen the Rice Court credit cards and sets up Lady Rice (and herself) in luxury at the Claremont. Jelly also takes a secretarial job in which she deftly sabotages Edwin's divorce solicitor. With Jelly, verbal assault against Edwin is the least of it.

When Angel, who dresses similarly to Kinky Virgin, emerges, she insists that the "four-fold entity"—Lady Rice, Angelica, Jelly, Angel—enjoy some super sex with a chauffeur (he has a heart of gold and his name is Ram) in the back of a limousine.

Ultimately, the heroine of *Splitting*—all four faces of her—triumphs. Resourcefulness, cunning, aggressive sexuality, secretarial skills, plus the gift for unexpected music that she makes with delightful and also musical Ram—she has always had it, all of it, in her. And Fay Weldon's fiction, all brilliantly complex and hilarious as it is, is forever and unsentimentally also on the side of the oppressed—especially if they listen to the voices in their heads that tell them to snap out of it and get a real job.

Susan Crosland (review date 9 December 1995)

SOURCE: "So Witty or So Wise," in *The Spectator,* December 9, 1995, p. 41.

[*In the following review, Crosland praises some stories in* Wicked Women, *but finds fault with what she considers Weldon's reliance on static, "cartoon" characters.*]

Don't worry. When the seesaw swings up, Fay Weldon is

on form: sparkling, sharply observing, insights delivered with a light touch that puts us in a good mood, however dark the comedy. And one of the great things about short stories is you can pick and choose. Most of these [in *Wicked Women*] have appeared over the past four years in publications as various as the *Literary Review* and *Cosmopolitan*, or been written for well-intended bodies from the British Council to Teenage Trust.

The selection opens with far the longest tale, a new offering, '**End of the Line**'. It concerns a redundant nuclear scientist, married of course, assailed (not unwillingly) by a beautiful New Age journalist called Weena. I shall get it out of the way and then move on to the wonderful upswings that follow and justify having this book on your bedside table. The faults of this main offering—and they are pretty relentless—are imposed, I think, on Weldon-the-writer by a massive wound she has suffered.

In order to air it yet again, she has a cast of static cartoons—even the odious Weena unseriously odious because she is a cut-out. We don't require character development in a short story, but we do need to care a teensy bit about one or two participants. Otherwise, there's no tension.

Moments of redemption occur when the author empowers ruthless-young-Weena with gifts of observation and unlaboured jokes. When told, 'There's a dozen Vegan girls out there already lining up for your job,' Weena replies, 'Let 'em line,' confident that 'she was safe enough. She blow-jobbed the editor on Friday afternoons, and not many Vegan girls would do that these days, not even for the sake of employment.' But too soon we are dispirited again by buzz word predictability.

And then, lo! '**Run and Ask Daddy If He Has Any More Money**', first published in the *Radio Times*, races from the starting-gate and tears around the course. Lovely observations: 'In Milly's view a man was only working if you could see him working, and who can see a man thinking?' Or: 'He used to be a mere lecturer but his Polytechnic turned into a University and voila! there he was, Professor Frood, a pillar of society: looked up to and trusted: a family man.'

Weldon first became the Feminist's Guru in the Seventies when solemn women wrote earnestly about oppression of the superior sex. She drove the same points home entertainingly—thus with far more effect—by wrapping them up in irony and scintillating humour. Her stories were peppered with insights, literary allusions thrown in as a bonus that teaches you something irrelevant along the way. She became the Wise Woman.

Yet 'Guru' and 'Wise Woman' are heavy burdens for a creative writer to bear: more becomes expected of her.

Weldon had resonance with her flip-canny observations that we recognised. Now readers, notably those under 30 who still imagine everlasting heaven on earth exists if only someone will show them the way to it, feel let down when the Wise Woman doesn't give them a map.

This occasional disappointment is compounded by the span of Weldon's illimitable energies: the prolific writer adorns liberal platforms on every subject under the sun. The spin-off from the public persona has, I think, weakened some of her writing, impelling her to start off with an opinion and use her characters as vehicles for that opinion: instead of personalities that can expand, she presents social/political cartoons. When she puts these back in a drawer until the next public platform, then Weldon-the-writer captivates afresh.

Take '**Wasted Lives**', written for the *New Yorker*. Poignant, witty, it is about a middle-aged Western man and the Eastern European woman who is his lover on his business trips to what I take to be post-Wall Prague. 'I was fond of her but did not love her, or only in the throes of the sexual excitement she was so good at summoning out of me.' Here Weldon abandons stereotypes and sex-war to deal perceptively with colluding, ultimately conflicting techniques used by a good-natured man and an aspiring young woman in the bigger battle of survival. Read it.

Karen Karbo (review date 9 June 1996)

SOURCE: "Love Fails Again," in *New York Times Book Review*, Vol. 101, June 9, 1996, p. 19.

[*In the following review, Karbo finds in* Worst Fears *an unexpected compassion, which, she writes, "makes it one of her best novels yet."*]

If you want the truth about the man-woman thing, forget all those cloying self-help books and read Fay Weldon. Her 20 novels,—*Worst Fears* is her 21st—are the literary equivalent of a stiff drink, a dip in the Atlantic in January, a pep talk by a mildly sadistic coach.

Ms. Weldon's work will never inspire a compact disk of love songs or a cookbook filled with goopy treats. The author of the diabolical best seller *The Life and Loves of a She-Devil* calls it as she sees it—not a popular approach when dealing with our most cherished state of self-delusion, romantic love.

Alexandra Ludd is a minor actress who lives happily in the West Country of England in a historic hovel called the Cottage, along with her husband. Ned, an Ibsen scholar, their 4 year-old son, Sascha; and Diamond, an ill-tempered Labrador retriever. *Worst Fears* opens with the untimely death of Ned, at 49, of an apparent heart attack, suffered while Alexandra was up in London starring as Nora in A Doll's House and Ned was home alone watching a tape of *Casablanca.* Also apparently.

What follows is a snappy whodunit of the heart. The plot unfurls to reveal that Ned was not, in fact, alone when he died, and, on the heels of this, the more complicated and profound revelations that the marriage of Ned and Alexandra was something of a sham, Ned was a cad, Alexandra was a dunce and the women who called themselves Alexandra's friends were duplicitous in just about every way imaginable. In short, Alexandra's worst fears turn out to be true.

One of the pleasures of Ms. Weldon's novel lies in the way the tables are turned on Alexandra. Midway through *Worst Fears,* all the sympathy she would naturally receive as the grieving widow are accorded instead to Ned's mistress. "It's hard for women when their married lovers die," says her brother-in-law, Hamish, piously. "Rightly or wrongly, the widow has the sympathy of the world: surely you could afford to spare a little for her?"

Alexandra is abandoned by her friends, browbeaten by her own mother, sold out by the producer of her play. Even the dog snubs her.

Ned's mistress is Jenny Linden, a gnomish set designer and every contemporary woman's worst fear. She has a puckered face; short, dirty hair; double chins and, the ultimate horror, flab. But, during the course of the novel, Alexandra realizes that Jenny possesses a "stubborn, sexy helplessness in the face of her own passions, which men found so attractive." That Jenny—initially absurd to the point of caricature—grows into a convincing and even touching love object is a testimony to Ms. Weldon's knack for writing about desire and the unexpected power of the weak.

Ms. Weldon's earlier books are hysterical, fierce and gleefully mean in a way that only British novelists seem to be able to get away with. Yet *Worst Fears* also possesses a few uncharacteristically quiet moments, the sort that betray an unvarnished kindness that's part of genuine understanding.

> In the belief that a woman had to be beautiful, and sensuous, and witty, and wonderful, in order to trigger real love, erotic love, the kind of emotional drama that ran through to the heart of the universe, the hot line to the source of life itself, the in-love kind, Alexandra had been wrong. More, she had shown herself to be vain, and foolish, and shallow, and Ned had noticed. Not that his noticing had anything to do with it. You did not

love necessarily where you were admired or cease to love when admiration failed. Love came and went; it was there or it wasn't. The blessing of the gods, and their curse.

I can't imagine that Fay Weldon has suddenly gone kinder and gentler on us; she's the quintessential anti-romance novelist and always will be. But she's filed down a few sharp edges in *Worst Fears,* and that makes it one of her best novels yet.

Jane Gardam (review date 2 November 1996)

SOURCE: "More Lecherous than Loamshire," in *The Spectator,* Vol. 277, No. 8780, November 2, 1996, pp. 45-46.

[*In the following review, Gardam discusses Weldon's humorous examination of sin and evil in* Worst Fears.]

As usual, Fay Weldon has written a very moral book [*Worst Fears*]; that is to say a book that takes a good look at sin and then satirises the moraliser along with everybody else. 'Look,' she says, 'how excited we get about our immorality, how we enjoy judging and deploring each other's vices. How deluded we are if we don't analyse what passes for fidelity and success and love and friendship and loyalty.' 'Is it not better,' she asks, 'to be on the watch against the illusions of these things rather than to swan along smiling and imagining that we are happy?'

It's a stringent, almost puritan, almost Old Testament code. 'When the moment of reckoning comes,' she says, 'beware'! Only Job's comforters will come knocking at the door and if you happen to be someone like Job, someone in the public eye, beware even more, for there will be no comforters at all, only a photographer from the *Sun* lurking in the vegetable patch.

Then must the poor widow barricade herself inside her lovely country house alone and brood on why the corpse of her marvellous husband ('She will never see his like again') was not found in bed, why her best friends were present at the time of his death, 5.30 am, and why his bedsheets had already been laundered by breakfast time.

It is Agatha Christie country, in a way, though Weldon's concern with evil is more lively than ruminative Miss Marple's and her characters are not from Loamshire but from 1990s Metroland-in-Wessex. All are classless, pagan, pragmatic and sexually obsessed. In fact there's nobody in the book you'd want to spend five minutes with except the cat and kittens, and the cat, a dismal object who's always walking away—maybe he's got sense—is only worth six.

No, this rustic place is much worse than Loamshire, for in Loamshire there is comfort—rooted communities and mealtimes and manners and minimal fornication. Metroland-in-Wessex is a sink.

But for some folks a very attractive sink, I suppose, a fat white porcelain one, repro. Vic. c.1880 (all the antiques in this novel are carefully dated), shiny and clean. A 'Belfast' of course, with perma-polished taps and a preserving pan of home-made jam standing on its teak draining-board. Above it hangs a bunch of local herbs of the meadow, for even the doctor in M-in-W prescribes lime tea instead of sleeping pills, and nearby hangs a kingly mirror, mercury-based, c.1790, before which the heroine, actress Alexandra, would stand beside her golden, theatre-critic husband and hear him say, 'What a divine couple!'

Now these things might lull a hard-working actress slogging away with Ibsen on the London stage in order to bring in the only money that is around; might cause her to believe that she can't be living in a tainted village with a multiple adulterer who has secretly disinherited her of her estate, disclaimed their child, is selling her house over her pretty, unobservant head and has begun secret proceedings for divorce and remarriage. Well, you wouldn't believe it, would you? Especially when you have been totally faithful to him. Well, sort of.

Nor would you suspect that when the grim reaper came to gather in this energetic man he would be wearing only a black and scarlet satin suspender belt and would confront him in your marital bed in the arms of another of your friends, who is dressed more or less in wellingtons.

Now Alexandra is not noticeably a very good woman but she's better than the rest and the only one who's not a hater. She understands fast that she has not been an adequate lover and has not been loved herself by anyone. But instead of collapsing she gets on the phone and with the openess of a nice old-fashioned schoolgirl, as it might be in *What Katie Did,* asks everybody whatever has been going on. All the friends reply with lies, then with half-lies, then with terrible truths and basilisk glares—the wellingtoned one and the really dangerous slutty one and the criminal's wife up at the Big House who has plastic breasts and a creepy peasant mother whom nobody minds but asks only to lunch and not to dinner.

And everybody else turns on her. Her hyperactive three-year-old doesn't need her. The undertaker disapproves of her for being late visiting the body. The village shop and the solicitor dislike her, and even the dog takes to snarling at her and wagging its tail when weeping mistress number one comes to take him for a walk at half-hourly intervals. And then there's a terrible woman, the first wife, who in-

stalls herself in the London flat and says it's hers and please will Alexandra clear off as she's counting the crockery. And there's the pally lot in the theatre all saying, 'But, darling, surely you knew?' And there is her mother who was at Cheltenham Ladies' College and proffers pedantry and philosophy and says that now she will be bringing up her grandson.

So now this wronged woman goes crashing through her world like a demon. She breaks and she enters, she burgles and she steals, she smashes up cars and rampages and flings people about. No Mrs Job, she. Away she goes with her knife and her axe as soon as look at you and when you're stirring your boiling home-made jam on the draining-board she causes you to pour it over your feet. The only enemy Alexandra ignores is the nastiest, the nanny, the seeming sycophant, a gargantuan woman bred in pig slurry in a refurbished hovel that turns out to be full of Alexandra's lost possessions ('Everything not plastic is nicked') She hears this creature's true opinion of her with what in another book might be called patrician unconcern. But she is by then maybe just tired. And so Alexandra comes at last to deal the lot of them a gloriously avenging blow that frees her from them for ever and leaves them reeling. And as she strikes—what is this? The heavens open and another force joins in what in yet another book might be called the hand of God. But no—of course not. Not God in M-in-W. Retribution anyway—and glorious. I only wish I could be bothered to like Alexandra a bit more and I might cheer louder. But then, if Alexandra had a bit more to her she'd be more clued up about her friends and there'd be no story. I was quite glad about the happy ending though, and she'll be fine in Hollywood.

What tosh it all sounds. And yet evil and slander do spawn and snowball and destroy. Unlikely worlds—Swift's, Voltaire's—are real enough to be wonderful settings for satire. Weldon's world may not be yours or mine but it's clear she's been there herself and seen suffering in it. And she's one of the few women novelists who can make our idiot, sinful lives look funny. '

Kirkus Reviews (review date 15 March 1997)

SOURCE: A review of *Wicked Women,* in *Kirkus Reviews,* March 15, 1997, p. 417.

[*In the following review, the anonymous critic offers praise for* Wicked Women.]

The antagonists who populate these 20 stories [in *Wicked Women*] are indeed very wicked (no surprise to readers of Weldon's 21 novels, including *Worst Fears,* 1996), but they're not always women. Both sexes and all ages come in for some merry tweaking by this master of sexual satire—making this outing a familiar pleasure for old fans and a thoroughly satisfying introduction for newcomers.

When Defoe Desmond's middle-aged wife confronts him about his affair in **"End of the Line,"** she's covered with white ash (she happens to be cleaning the fireplace), and when she kisses him she leaves the ashy mark of death on his cheek. What better indicator that it's time for Defoe to bail out with the fiendishly seductive Weena Dodds, a *New Age Times* journalist itching to move into the manor house? Weena is certainly evil (she specializes in married men, taking pleasure in ruining their lives and leaving them begging as she moves on to greener pastures), but there comes a day when even the cleverest siren racks up one too many enemies. On the other hand, it's sometimes the man who turns out to be cold-blooded, as in **"Wasted Lives,"** whose film-executive narrator casually dumps his Eastern European mistress the moment he learns that she's pregnant with his child. In **"Valediction,"** an aging couple's children show their true colors by trying to push said parents out of the family home. And in **"Through a Dustbin, Darkly,"** a ghost works her vengeance by pushing her former husband's young second wife to burn down the house they live in. Every kind of evil that lurks in the heart is gleefully explored in all its permutations here, and somehow it all ends up very cheering—wherein lies Weldon's tremendous talent.

Though the stories date from as far back as 1972, and in one or two cases their age shows, there are far more hits than misses in this unsentimental education in the war between the sexes.

Deborah Mason (review date 29 June 1997)

SOURCE: "Divine Justice," in *New York Times Book Review,* June 29, 1997, p. 29.

[*In the following review, Mason calls Weldon "one of the most cunning moral satirists of our time."*]

Fay Weldon has never been content merely to play God with her characters: she would rather be the avenging Yahweh. Her justice is unblinking, her wrath is boundless—most often directed against faithless husbands and their scheming lovers—and her punishments are indecently satisfying. She is a Yahweh with a profound appreciation of irony. Weldon, after all, is the creator of the wronged and lumpish wife in **The Life and Loves of a She-Devil** who inflicts a fiendishly comic, years-long revenge on her accountant husband

and his romance-novelist lover by turning their own conceits against them. Exploiting the husband's financial arrogance and his mistress's fantasy of the invincibility of love, Weldon's heroine siphons off their bank accounts, their fizzy champagne romance and, finally, their sanity.

With 21 novels and three story collections, Weldon has reigned as the champion of the discarded wife, the embryonic woman who grows up by default and becomes shrewd by suffering. Her genius is to portray all this heroic self discovery not with sermonizing but with deft satire.

In **Wicked Women,** Weldon's bristling new collection of stories, she broadens her targets. Attuned to the deeper currents of family and sexual unrest, this satire is so stinging that reading it is like seeing someone stripped of clothing in a public place. Yes, Weldon's heroines still deal with cheating spouses and struggle to protect the family nest. But now they also use a bit of wickedness to contend with insecure househusbands who punish their wives for surpassing them, self-absorbed adult children who can't see beyond their own muddled lives, and the culture's communal hand wringing over sexual identity.

Throughout the book there is a sense that apocalyptic winds are gathering force all over Weldon's England: shadowy "market forces" are leveling picturesque villages to build "development complexes" infested with social dry rot; woozy New Age shrinks and astrologers are subverting the national discourse; rumors are swirling about a potion called Red Mercury that has shadowy origins in the Russian Mafia and the potential to polish off the world.

Weldon is a worthy adversary for these post-modern devils. Delivering a knockout blow to those old punching bags, touchy-feely therapists, she blames them for the casual shattering of marriages and for the delusive idea that family loyalties and relationships can be paved over or efficiently rerouted like England's M1 highway. In **"Santa Claus's New Clothes,"** the children and the grandchildren have their first Christmas dinner with Dr. Hetty Grainger, their father's former therapist and new wife, who "murmured rather than spoke." Hetty hadn't thought twice about taking over Mum's house; she paused only in the master bedroom to "perform some kind of ceremony with candles and incense which would, she said, deconsecrate the bed" and "free the material object from its person-past." Her mistake is to murmur over dinner about the "civilized" way the divorce and remarriage have proceeded. The remark elicits from her new 9-year-old stepson the fatal question, "What's civilized?" Hetty's fatuous answer opens up a hilariously deadpan inquisition by the other children that peels away her soothing earth-mother disguise to reveal the baby-eater underneath.

In the riotous and startlingly timely **"Not Even a Blood Relation,"** Weldon draws on some frisky revisionist science to help her protagonist defend hearth and home. Beverley Cowarth, 61, is the widow of Hughie, a recently deceased and bankrupt earl, and the mother of three angry adult daughters. And no wonder: the oldest, Edwina, was meant to be Edwin, the Cowarth male heir, and when she arrived, her parents "just added on an 'a' and ignored her thereafter"—as they did with her sisters, Thomasina and Davida. Now the three plan to sell the ancestral home out from under their mother, who, in terms of the Cowarth family line, is "not even a blood relation"—and far too old to produce a male heir, even if Hughie were still alive. But by enlisting the help of a much younger, adoring Australian fiancé and the services of a very good Roman synecologist, Beverley outwits them all—making for a few delectable twists best left for Weldon fans to gloat over.

Other stories end in devastation, lost humanity and profound sadness. The graceful **"In The Great War (II)"** tells of a careless love triangle that exacts the suicide of two women and the death of a 6-year-old child. **"Web Central,"** one of the few heavy-handed stories here, takes on the terrors of futuristic isolation. It pictures a society whose privileged classes are sealed in solitary rooms, their moods regulated by drip feeds and their intercourse with the world conducted entirely on computer screens. And the powerful **"Heat Haze"** annihilates the idea that a child's agony over her parents' messy life can be managed and explained away like a nasty case of flu, with no one taking any blame. Deciding that someone must pay for the fallout from her father's admission of homosexuality and her mother's subsequent death, a young ballet dancer offers herself up—refusing food and intimacy, and bartering her body—to protect the remnants of family she has left.

With the year 2000 and its tidy string of zeroes reawakening our external longing for conclusive endings, Weldon's wrap-ups are eloquent and absolute. They are born of her belief in the dogged persistence of genetic bonds and in an uncompromising universe of clear rights and wrongs with their own inevitable consequences. With *Wicked Women,* Weldon has become one of the most cunning moral satirists of our time. In her rueful stories, justice is done—whether we like it or not.

Ann Treneman with Fay Weldon (interview date 4 July 1997)

SOURCE: "After the Devil—A Little Horror," in *Times Educational Supplement,* No. 4227, July 4, 1997, p. 7.

[*In the following review, Weldon and Treneman discuss Weldon's children's book,* Nobody Likes Me!]

Everything has a colour in **Nobody Likes Me!,** Fay Weldon's book for children. Sleep is brown and red and purple round the edges, a cry is pale blue, a roar black, a yelp white. I wonder, as the author sits on the green and gold sofa at her home in Hampstead, north London, what colour this conversation might be.

She is wearing a black dress and gold slippers and her voice is high and light. At first it seems hard to believe this is the same woman whose nearly 30 books include *The Life and Loves of a She-Devil.* And then her glance falls on the lighthouse on the back of her new book. "That really is very phallic," she murmurs, and laughs. It was the first of many small shocks.

Her book tells the story of a small boy called Rex, who has temper tantrums and rips up his yellow and mauve party invitation. He crawls into the black under his bed and pretends to be a bear. In his fantastical dreams he is always the odd one out. But he awakes to his mother's new-found attentions and promises that the party will be fine. The language is poetic and the storyline as finely drawn as Claudio Munoz's illustrations.

The title seems not to fit, though. "Nick, my husband picked it. It's terribly rash to call a book something like this," she says, happily. "It's sort of a turn-off, isn't it?"

She wrote the book 15 years ago because she was asked to. But, having made the request, the publisher then rejected the work. A previous version was eventually published in 1989, but sank without trace. This edition will not suffer the same fate.

The story is improved and, as Weldon notes, the illustrations are beautiful. It is also truly a child's-eye tale. "Writing for children is slightly like writing advertising copy in that every word counts," she says. "The relationship between sentences has to work exactly."

Fay Weldon's women are always noteworthy, and Rex's mum does seem rather glamorous in her "clickety-clack silver sandals" and lovely red dress. Weldon disagrees. "Again, it is a child's-eye view of clothing. She is wearing her best red dress and she's been to the dentist, so her teeth are terribly white. She is ever so slightly horrific, because mothers are. It's all quite terrifying."

So where is father? "Oh, he's at work." Does the mother work too? "Oh no. She's a very frivolous mum. She can't stand the little boy. This is the difficulty. The little girl is very pretty but the little boy stamps in puddles and tears up invitations and is just a boy. And his trousers are too tight." This is said with a flourish. "The whole thing is about being inappropriately clothed, or mothers not loving you enough or mothers loving your sister, who wears a pink coat and is perfect."

But the mother does make the boy a costume. Surely that was nice? "Yes, she does, but that may have been my editor, who insisted she show some of her good side."

She suddenly asks if there are cannibals in the book. There are girls in pink gingham, an eagle in a greeny-white egg and an old-fashioned party with golden forks, but no cannibals. There were cannibals in a former version, she says. "Rex is left on a desert island and the cannibal asks him to tea. But then Rex realises he is going to be the tea. My editor talked me out of putting that one in."

She leans forward. "Really, the dream is just an anxiety dream." This is worrying, in that Fay Weldon's aversion to therapy (her first husband left her during his) is well-known. She adds: "This is a sort of therapy book. It's a self-help book that works subliminally. The child has these dreams and they make him angry. So if you write about them and explain them and solve them, it can help.

"Just because I don't go to a therapist doesn't mean I am against emotional literacy."

There the lesson ended. And the colour? Gold streaked with bolts from the blue.

FURTHER READING

Criticism

Buckley, Christopher. "Misery Loves Company." *Washington Post Book World* XXIII, No. 46, (November 14, 1993): 2.

> A review in which Buckley appreciates Weldon's wit and intelligence in *Trouble,* but ultimately finds the book overwhelmingly depressing.

Cumming, Laura. A review of *Wicked Women. The Observer* 10651 (December 10, 1995): 16.

> A review of *Wicked Women* in which Cumming finds the novel to be didactic and journalistic, with little human interest or character development.

Maddocks, Melvin. "Mothers and Masochists." *Time* (February 26, 1973): 91.

> A review in which Maddocks discusses feminist elements in *Down among the Women.*

Skow, John. "Elsa Undone." *Time* 110, No. 8, (August 22, 1977): 72-3.

> A review in which Skow finds *Words of Advice* superficial but a worthy summer read.

Additional coverage of Weldon's life and career is contained in the following sources published by Gale: *Contemporary Authors,* **Vol. 21-24R;** *Contemporary Authors New Revision Series,* **Vols. 16, 46, 63;** *Contemporary Dictionary of British Literary Biography, 1960 to the Present; DISCovering Authors Modules: Popular Fiction and Genre Authors; Dictionary of Literary Biography,* **Vol. 14, 194; and** *Major Twentieth-Century Writers.*

John Edgar Wideman

1941-

American novelist, short story writer, nonfiction writer, and critic.

The following entry presents an overview of Wideman's career through 1997. For further information on Wideman's life and career, see *CLC*, Volumes 5, 34, 36, and 67.

INTRODUCTION

Wideman, whom critic Don Strachen called "the black Faulkner, the softcover Shakespeare," is best known for novels and short stories that trace the lives of several generations of families in and around Homewood, a black ghetto district of Pittsburgh where he lived until he was twelve years old. His major theme involves the individual's quest for self-understanding amidst personal memories and African-American experiences. Kermit Frazier commented: "The characters in Wideman's fiction can escape neither collective nor personal history and memory, so they are forced to deal with them in some way—be it successfully or ineffectually." Although Wideman deemphasized specifically black issues early in his career, his later works evidence his interest in "bringing to the fore black cultural material, history, archetypes, myths, the language itself, . . . and trying to connect that with the so-called mainstream." Many critics concur that Wideman's blend of Western and black literary traditions constitutes a distinctive voice in American literature.

Biographical Information

Wideman attended the University of Pennsylvania before being selected as the first black Rhodes scholar since Alain Locke in 1905. In England, Wideman studied eighteenth-century literature and the early development of the novel. His first two novels, *A Glance Away* (1967) and *Hurry Home* (1969), reflect this formal training as well as his own experiments with narrative technique. Wideman later accepted a fellowship at the prestigious University of Iowa Writers' Workshop. Yet he began his college career not as a writer, but as a basketball star. Wideman once remarked: "I always wanted to play pro basketball—ever since I saw a ball and learned you could make money at it." He was recruited as a player by the University of Pennsylvania and began studying psychology, hoping to gain what he called "mystical insight." Ultimately the study of psychology failed to provide him with the type of wisdom he sought, and Wideman changed his major to English. His main con-

cern continued to be basketball, and although he played well enough to be named to the Philadelphia Big Five Basketball Hall of Fame, his basketball career ended in college. Wideman began to focus on writing instead of basketball, and within one year after graduating from Oxford in 1966, Wideman's first novel was published. During the late 1960s and early 1970s, Wideman was an assistant basketball coach, professor of English, and founder and director of the Afro-American studies program at the University of Pennsylvania; he has also served as a professor of English at the universities of Wyoming and Massachusetts. In addition to these duties, he has been a curriculum consultant to secondary schools nationwide since 1968.

Major Works

A Glance Away and *Hurry Home* involve a search for self by protagonists who are confused and dominated by their pasts. In *A Glance Away*, a rehabilitated drug addict returns to his home, where he renews family and social ties while trying to avoid a relapse; in *Hurry Home,* a black law school graduate seeks cultural communion with white so-

284

ciety by traveling to Europe, then reaffirms his black heritage in Africa. In *The Lynchers* (1973), Wideman focuses upon racial conflict in the United States during the 1960s. In *The Homewood Trilogy,* which comprises the short story collection *Damballah* (1981) and the novels *Hiding Place* (1981) and *Sent for You Yesterday* (1983), Wideman uses deviating time frames, black dialect, and rhythmic language to transform Homewood into what Alan Cheuse described as "a magical location infused with poetry and pathos." The interrelated stories of *Damballah* feature several characters who reappear in the novels and relate tales of the descendants of Wideman's ancestor, Sybela Owens. *Hiding Place* concerns a boy's strong ties to his family and his involvement in a petty robbery that results in an accidental killing. In his nonfiction work, *Brothers and Keepers* (1984), Wideman comments upon his brother's involvement in a murder similar to that described in his novel *Hiding Place. Sent for You Yesterday* won the 1984 PEN/Faulkner Award for fiction. Through the characters of Doot, the primary narrator, and Albert Wilkes, an outspoken blues pianist, Wideman asserts that creativity and imagination are important means to transcend despair and strengthen the common bonds of race, culture, and class. The eponymous narrator of *Reuben* (1987) is an ambiguous and enigmatic figure who provides inexpensive legal aid to residents of Homewood. Among his clients are Kwansa, a young black woman whose brutal ex-husband, a recovering drug addict, seeks custody of their illegitimate child as revenge against her, and Wally, an assistant basketball coach at a local university who comes to Reuben because he fears he will be blamed for the illegal recruiting practices of his department. Wally, who may have actually murdered a white man, is possessed by an ingrained hatred that leads him to fantasize of violence against middle-aged white males. Race-related strife, violence, and suffering are also prominent themes in *Fever: Twelve Stories* (1989). In the collection's title story, Wideman juxtaposes present-day racism in Philadelphia, a city once offering freedom for slaves through the Underground Railroad, with a narrative set during the yellow fever epidemic of 1793. In the novel *Philadelphia Fire* (1990), Wideman combines fact and fiction to elaborate on an actual incident involving MOVE, a militant, heavily armed black commune that refused police orders to vacate a Philadelphia slum house in 1985. With the approval of W. Wilson Goode, the city's black mayor, police bombed the house from a helicopter, killing eleven commune members—including five children—but creating a fire that destroyed approximately fifty-three houses. The book's narrator, Cudjoe, a writer and former Rhodes scholar living in self-imposed exile on a Greek island, returns to his native city upon hearing about the incident to search for a young boy who was seen fleeing the house following the bombing. This fictionalized narrative is juxtaposed with Wideman's address to his own son, who was sentenced to life in prison at eighteen years of age for kill-

ing another young man while on a camping trip. In *Fatheralong: A Meditation on Fathers and Sons, Race and Society* (1994), Wideman again juxtaposes his own personal life with universal concerns. In this volume, he examines his strained relationship with his father and his difficulties with his own son, and then places them within a context of all father-son relationships and America's history of racism. Wideman combines elements of history, religion, and race to form the story in his novel *The Cattle Killing* (1996); the narrator's memories of his childhood in Philadelphia are woven together with the plight of blacks in the city in the late eighteenth century and the story of the South African Xhosa tribe.

Critical Reception

Wideman's unique combination of fact, fiction, myth, and history has allied him with the modernist tradition and solidified his reputation as a leading American author. Novelist Charles Johnson called him "easily the most acclaimed black male writer of the last decade," and renowned critic Robert Bone, author of *The Negro Novel in America,* called Wideman "perhaps the most gifted black novelist of his generation." Commentary on Wideman's strengths as an author often focuses on the lyrical quality he manages to maintain in his prose while at the same time forging intricate layers of theme and plot and blending fact with fiction. It is Wideman's ability—in both his fiction and nonfiction works—to provide insight into broad, societal issues and personal concerns while retaining a literary mastery over his material that has earned him widespread acclaim and admiration. In assessing his short stories, numerous critics have compared Wideman to William Faulkner; Michael Gorra asserted that such a comparison is legitimate "because both are concerned with the life of a community over time. It is appropriate because they both have a feel for the anecdotal folklore through which a community defines itself, because they both often choose to present their characters in the act of telling stories, and because in drawing on oral tradition they both write as their characters speak, in a language whose pith and vigor has not yet been worn into cliché." Gorra concluded that "the more you read John Edgar Wideman, the more impressive he seems."

PRINCIPAL WORKS

A Glance Away (novel) 1967
Hurry Home (novel) 1970
The Lynchers (novel) 1973
†*Damballah* (short stories) 1981
†*Hiding Place* (novel) 1981
†*Sent for You Yesterday* (novel) 1983

Brothers and Keepers (memoir) 1984
Reuben (novel) 1987
Fever (short stories) 1989
Philadelphia Fire (novel) 1990
All Stories Are True (short stories) 1992
‡*The Stories of John Edgar Wideman* (short stories) 1992
Fatheralong: A Meditation on Fathers and Sons, Race and Society (memoir) 1994
The Cattle Killing (novel) 1996

*These works were reissued in a collected edition as *A Glance Away, Hurry Home, and The Lynchers: Three Early Novels by John Edgar Wideman* (1994).
†These works were reissued in a collected paperback edition as *The Homewood Trilogy* (1985).
‡This volume combines the story collections *Damballah, Fever,* and *All Stories Are True.*

CRITICISM

James W. Coleman (essay date March 1985)

SOURCE: "Going Back Home: The Literary Development of John Edgar Wideman," in *CLA Journal,* Vol. XXVIII, No. 3, March, 1985, pp. 326-43.

[*Coleman is an American educator. In the following essay, he delineates Wideman's return to the thematic realm of family and community in his works following* The Lynchers.]

In a 1972 interview [reprinted in *Interviews with Black Writers,* edited by John O'Brien, 1973], John Edgar Wideman repeatedly stated that in *Hurry Home* (1969) and *The Lynchers* (1973) he was interested in portraying the world of his black characters' imaginations. The imagination is a hellish, nightmarish place where the characters suffer the fears and horrors of past and present black reality in America. The story of the black past, present, and future that emerges is negative and hopeless.

The four black conspirators in *The Lynchers,* who have a revolutionary plan that is supposed to begin with the symbolic lynching of a white policeman and proceed to full-scale revolution by the black masses, are encumbered by hatred and distrust of each other, and fail for this reason. Each of the four characters reveals the nether region of his imagination at some point in the novel, but even some of the more positive thinking of the characters is revealed through a surreal dream consciousness that points to alienation and sterility more than to sustaining myth and worldview. The nightmarish quality of minds charged with hatred, distrust, and frustration distances and distorts everything.

There is a portrayal of family and community in the novel, but it is largely negative. The characters do not have positive family and community histories to relate, but are for the most part circumscribed by negative family relationships and tenuous community ties. Bernice Wilkerson at one point thinks of the blandness and drudgery of her life with her husband, Orin, and their children in the following terms.

> Standing in the emptiness she liked to call *her* kitchen, where she reigned if nowhere else. Cooking and serving their meals. First two to feed, a neat ritual she could give herself to wholly, chiding him playfully to remember to bless the food, then three, a quiet settling down together, boy a image of his father, so pleased with himself, so grown when his seat hiked by a pile of cushions and phone books was pulled to the table, four, five, finally six, four, three, two again . . . sometimes, but not the same two, not the same sleepiness, the anticipation, the gently fumbling progress through the dishes, the down hill glide of simple chores always easing toward the bed they shared. Not the same two. A steep hill you climb then tumble down. One.

Orin Wilkerson and his male friends use their colorful, descriptive street language to tell humorous anecdotes about their sexual exploits and to define what seem to be strong bonds of camaraderie among each other. But Orin stabs to death Childress, his friend of fifteen years, in a drunken brawl over an insignificant sum of money. In spite of the years of shared experience, Orin and Childress still become knife-slinging "niggers" taking out their frustrations on each other.

The Lynchers established Wideman's credentials as a first-rate novelist, but after *The Lynchers,* Wideman did not publish another book-length work of fiction until 1981. The problems of getting works published (particularly Wideman's brand of works that are not easily accessible to readers) account some for the eight-year hiatus between *The Lynchers* and Wideman's next book-length works of fiction in 1981. But looking at the overall development of Wideman's fictional career, one still has to say that Wideman reached a point where he had to bridge a gap, to make a transition that would give him and his fictional world what they needed for continued development. This vital ingredient for continued growth is a myth that will sustain both Wideman and his characters. That a sustaining myth is what Wideman needed for his characters as well as for himself seems to be substantiated by the fact that, in the three works which he has published since 1981, he searches deeply for a sustaining myth in his fictional world.

As brilliant and well-wrought as **The Lynchers** is, and as fine an example of twentieth-century literary negativism as it is, its world of frustration, death, and sterile human imagination that yields no unifying stories or sustaining myth does not provide the impetus for Wideman's further fictional growth. To find the stories and myth that sustain, Wideman returns to his boyhood community of the Homewood section of Pittsburgh to explore his family history and the history of the community. Wideman says in a recent interview [with Linda Putnam in *Rocky Mountain Magazine,* April 4, 1982]: "Family is the metaphor that describes the whole community of Homewood. . . .It goes back to traditional African notions of family and community. Being and identity are founded in community. A man who doesn't reside with other men is like a butterfly without wings."

Wideman starts in **Hiding Place** (1981) almost as far away from any realization of family and community as he ends in **The Lynchers** eight years earlier. We see the novel through the eyes of three characters, Clement, Bess and Tommy, who all begin as alienated, frustrated people separated from the center of family and community. Much more than in **The Lynchers,** the language of the characters is the vernacular of the Homewood streets, and there is less of the surreal and abstract. But still, Wideman limits the perspective and keeps us closer to the interior of the characters' minds than to the exterior world. The technique, as is often true in **The Lynchers,** is Wideman's own stream-of-consciousness technique. Given the limited perspective of the minds of alienated and frustrated characters, the reader must necessarily be inundated by feelings of alienation and frustration.

At the beginning of the first section of **Hiding Place** in which she appears, Bess hears a story about her youth, told by someone else, and a song out of her past, and remembers a terrible dream, "which wasn't a dream but the edge of a stormy sea, tossing, wailing, shaking her soul like a leaf till she drowned in sleep." In spite of the story she hears, Bess does not believe in anything enough to make her own stories. She has been alienated and isolated too long, living alone at the top of Bruston Hill. At the end of her first section in the novel, she remembers the gallery of family faces that used to occupy her thinking, but now feels that she no longer desires to visualize the "sweet babies" and older people in her family who represent the family connections:

> Used to do a lot of that [thinking about my family]. But I been up here too long now. Too many new faces and I can't see nothing in them. No names, no places. Just faces and I think on them and all I see is Bess, myself behind my eyes and I mize well be blind as Mother Owens [the first black family ancestor in Homewood] cause I been up here on this hill too long.

Bess goes on to reconstruct her family gallery, to hear clearly the music of her past, to distance the dreadful dream that inundates her consciousness, and most importantly, to create and tell the story of family and community that becomes the myth which brings her back to life, which reintegrates her back into family and community. Bess creates the story of her family, one in which all the girls "had that long, good hair," "long straight hair [they] could sit on," that was strong and persevered through hard times. All the girls except her reproduced "as easy as dancin'," and there was even the miracle of the life of Lizabeth, born dead but brought to life when she was plunged into a snow bank by her crazy Aunt May. And there were the times when her husband, Riley, brushed her pretty, long hair and whistled those pretty blues songs. Her sister Aida's husband, Bill, could also play pretty music on his guitar, Corrine. And Bill, Riley, and John French, her niece Freeda's husband, could make some of the most beautiful music ever made. In spite of Bess' personal hardship (she had only one child who was killed in World War II), she tells the story of her family, creates the myth of its history in Homewood, as a strong, beautiful one that overcame poverty and hardship to produce bountifully and forge a good life for itself out of its own resiliency and resourcefulness.

From part of the story that Bess tells, we learn that the family forced her down off the Hill to attend the funeral of Kaleesha, Bess' little relative whose mother brought her to Bess so that her evil-witch powers could cure the girl's illness, and at the funeral Bess remained isolated from the others and swore she would never come down off the Hill again. Bess fortified her isolation by creating a "cellophane-winged angel in a blue-eyed gown" who picked apart a cobweb in the roof of the funeral home. On the last page in the novel, Bess used her powers of imagination and creation to convert the "blue-eyed gown" angel into an image that incorporates the life and death of Kaleesha and the struggle leading to transcendence of personal tragedy and alienation that she must wage to be a part of family and community:

> [T]he angel in the blue-eyed gown works with her to set the house on fire. We gon do it, gal. Yes we are. Thank you you little fuzzy-headed got the prettiest black-eyed lazy Susan eyes in the world thing. Don't matter if they's crossed a little bit, don't matter if they roll round sometimes like they ain't got no strings and go on about they own business. And you [her dead husband]. You get up off that bed, man. Cause it's going too, everything in here going so get your whistling self up off that bed and come on.

It takes an unwanted encounter with her great, great nephew Tommy, who is Kaleesha's uncle and who runs from the police to Bess on Bruston Hill, to force Bess to this transformation. Tommy is a young man with a gift for song and talk, but also a young man who has destroyed his life. He has been in jail before, has deservedly lost his wife and son, and is running now because he was involved in a robbery where his friend killed a man. Part of Tommy's problem is that he is a part of a fragmented world of the '60s and '70s, but like Bess, he is isolated and alienated (and he, too, stands apart from the rest of the family at Kaleesha's funeral) for more personal reasons that he must make some attempt to transcend. There is obviously a break in the connection between Tommy and the rest of his family, particularly the older generations, and he has lost most of the mythic support that centered the older people, the support Bess can still call on to reintegrate herself into family and community. In fact, Tommy has no story or mythic structure to center himself, and he has turned inward, where he only finds emptiness, self-pity, and isolation from everything but his own needs. Tommy often finds refuge in a dream state that is sometimes horrible but still provides shelter from the realities of the outside world.

As Tommy looks around Bess' cabin, he sees nothing to connect him to "the time in which he belonged," and he futilely tries to tell a story that will anchor him in time:

> Once upon a time. Once upon a time, he thought, if them stories I been hearing all my life are true, once upon a time they said God's green earth was peaceful and quiet. . . .Aunt Aida talking bout people like they giants. That world was bigger, slower and he'd get jumpy, get lost in it. . . .Once upon a time him and Sarah [his wife] alone in the middle of the night. . . .You're in a story. There's room enough to do what you need to do, what you have to do. . . .

> The stillness unbroken. Sarah rolls closer to him and rises slightly on her elbow so the ring of darker brown around her nipples is visible an instant as the covers fall away from her brown shoulders and he swallows hard because these soft eyes on her chest have a way of seeing through him and taking his breath away. He swallows hard in the stillness because he is seeing another life, a life long gone. Then he is nothing. Smaller than nothing and alone. Stories are lies and Mother Bess pigging down her soup brings him back. Her loud slurping on the soup drowns the noise of his blood, the noise of his heart.

Tommy's use of words suggests that he wants his world to have the romantic quality of a fairy tale, without even going through the fairy tale's grim ritual to reach the romantic and idyllic. Aunt Aida does indeed talk about people "like they giants," but Tommy does not understand that Aunt Aida's stories and experiences also incorporate the hard-

ships and pain of living and participating in family and community. The myth Aunt Aida creates is positive and supporting, but it develops out of a commitment to life that Tommy has been unwilling to make. He cannot hold the positive image of himself and Sarah together because he has not committed himself to Sarah and honestly struggled with the relationship. His romantic image has none of the strong fiber and undergirding structure of positive human participation. He is "smaller than nothing" and his "stories are lies" because he always dwells in the selfish center of himself.

Later in the novel, Bess wakes Tommy from a dream in which he is trying to tell his son "a story [which will] make [him] happy. No fairy tale or nonsense like that. Telling him about life. Real life. . . .When life was full of good things and safe." Again, Tommy's problem is that he wants to get to the good story of real life without actually encountering the life experiences from which one distills the good story and which give that story reality.

Bess' confrontation with Tommy jars her out of her isolation, and interacting with Bess as she makes the connections and reenters family and community also has a positive influence on Tommy. By the end, he at least realizes that a large part of his fear has developed since his granddaddy John French died and "his house fell to pieces," scattering the family members. He knows that he has lost his wife and son and shamed his family, but that he has to conquer his fear and go back to face the consequences of his actions. He knows that he "ain't killed nobody," and says, "I'm ready to live and do the best I can cause I ain't scared."

Part of the ending is ambiguous and alludes to a symbolic action by Tommy that is probably one of the few things in the novel that Wideman does not handle well. It seems implied at the end that Tommy, when running from the police, climbs the mysterious, fairly-tale-like tower on Bruston Hill. This tower has always fascinated him, and he has heard stories about other kids climbing it to discover its mystery, but he has never had the nerve to do it himself. The only way to discover its mysteries for himself is to climb it. His climbing the tower could symbolize an initiation into life and all its possibilities that will allow him to make the connections and tell the good stories he wants to tell. But especially since the ending also leaves open the possibility that the police will kill Tommy, we cannot tell if he, as a member of the present generation, can ever move beyond yearning for lost connection and bold assertion of the self in the face of destiny, which may be fatal, to actual reintegration into family and community. The possibility that Tommy may not actually make the connection makes him similar to John, his brother in *Hiding Place* who "lives out with the white folks" in Wyoming, and Doot, the educated member of the family in *Sent for You Yesterday* (1983) who tries to soak up family and community stories. Both John and Doot are thinly disguised portrayals of Wideman himself.

Clement is the other character whose perceptions shape the narrative structure of the novel. He is a slow-witted orphan who works in Big Bob's barbershop and sleeps in the back. His only community is the barbershop community, which views him as a curious outsider because of his slow wittedness. Clement begins his connection with Bess as a result of a barbershop patron hitting a number after dreaming about Mother Bess. (And it is important to say that dreams do sometimes have a magical quality that is productive, but this is not true of dreams that develop out of the preoccupations of the self in isolation, like the dreams of Tommy, for example). The man sends Clement to Bess with ten dollars for gratitude and for the purpose of appeasing the source of magic. From this point, Clement becomes involved with both Bess and Tommy, and he watches their connection strengthen. At the end, Clement also knows the importance of being connected as opposed to living in isolation. Clement is "going down the hill for *them,* not for her, so he'll have to start all over again. Start with *one* again." The emphasis on the words "them" and "one" says to the reader that "them" and "one" are the same.

Alienation is psychological, and hence we can see how the predominance of the stream-of-consciousness technique in *The Lynchers* and *Hiding Place* is functional. Wideman certainly does not abandon this technique in all the stories in *Damballah* (1981), but does vary his style in some. In these stories, Wideman uses more conventional third-and first-person points of view to remove us a significant distance from the center of the characters' minds, thus providing a more positive setting distanced from the psychological center of alienation.

In *Damballah,* we hear a variety of voices; among them are the voices of the characters, speaking in their own language, the voice of John, the educated relative who lives in Wyoming and is sometimes a first-person narrator, and the voices of the third-person narrator, who is omniscient and sometimes uses the language of the characters and at other times an educated language that the author is capable of using. The point of view sometimes changes within individual stories, and sometimes within a paragraph. But all the voices in the stories combine to tell a story of birth, death, tragedy, struggle, and love, the story of Homewood. In each story except **"Tommy,"** which is told in Tommy's lost, hopeless voice, the voices combine to raise these elements of life high above the flat and mundane, combine to give real human dimension and significance even to death and tragedy. The voices structure Homewood's life events into a triumphant myth.

The title piece **"Damballah,"** the name of which is taken from an ancient African god, presents the account of a native African's heroic attempt to keep alive among American slaves the ways of Africa. The example of Orion, the African, has a profound effect on his community, and the story clearly implies that through a slave boy Orion disseminates his African ways to future generations, giving them many of the qualities of strength, endurance, and transcendence we see in the other stories.

"Daddy Garbage" shows how the rough camaraderie between John French, John and Tommy's grandfather, and his friend Strayhorn is firmly set in values that give them an undeviating moral sense of ritual that belies their poverty. **"Lizabeth: the Caterpillar Story"** is French's daughter and wife's tender, loving reflection on French, the big, loud gambling man who was good as gold in his heart.

"The Songs of Reba Love Jackson" is one of the more interesting pieces in the volume; it focuses on Reba Love—who is not a member of the Hollinger-French family—and her moving gospel songs that are so important to Homewood and that carry so much intense black experience. Reba Love and the other characters in this story often speak in their own voices, and they articulate powerful, centering religious beliefs that overarch the myth of family and community that is so important to Wideman.

The stories of death, tragedy, and suffering usually pull great meaning and human stature from these experiences. In **"The Chinaman,"** John and his mother Lizabeth recount the life and death of John's grandmother Freeda. John concludes from his mother's often-told story about Freeda's confrontation with the Chinaman just before her death that "the Chinaman is a glimpse of [Lizabeth's] God who has a plan and who moves in mysterious ways." **"Solitary"** presents the quiet but powerful confrontation with God that Lizabeth has after her deep foundations of faith are shaken by Tommy's imprisonment. **"Hazel"** is the very painful and tragic story of Hazel's accident that leads to permanent paralysis and her mother Gaybrella's painful death at the end as she accidentally sets herself on fire and burns alive. In spite of the story's searing pain and tragedy, Gaybrella maintains purpose and values in her life, although her daughter's plight certainly twists and cripples her psychologically. And Faun, Hazel's brother who accidentally pushed her down the steps and crippled her, shows, through Lizabeth's account at the end, that he has undergone a long struggle with the reality of his act that has taken him to depths of human compassion that few of us experience.

In **"The Beginning of Homewood,"** the last story, the first-person narrator, a writer, tells the story of Sybella Owen's heroic escape from slavery that led to the beginning of Homewood; part of the story is the connection between Sybella and the present generation of her family, of which the troubled Tommy is a part. At places in the story, the narrator calls on the voice of May to help him tell the story. May is very sympathetic when she views the present generation and draws the connection; the narrator is puzzled but positive and tries to end the volume positively:

> So the struggle doesn't ever end. [Sybella's] story, [Tommy's] story, the connections. But now the story, or the pieces of story are inside this letter [story] and its addressed to you and I'll send it and that seems better than the way it was before. For now, Hold on.

"The Beginning of Homewood" adds to the triumphant myth that grows throughout *Damballah,* but ends the volume on a note where the first-person narrator, a member of Tommy's generation and a character very much like John and Doot in *Sent for You Yesterday,* wrestles with the significance and efficacy of a triumphant myth for him and the present generation. Doot in *Yesterday* carries on this struggle to make the connection and discover the significance of the central myth of family and community for the present generation.

Yesterday focuses on a broader range of Homewood life than Wideman's last two works; the focus is still the Hollinger-French family, but the larger Homewood community is much more prominent here. Orally transmitted stories are central again, and Wideman uses Doot as his surrogate in the process of testing the substance and reality of myth for himself and the present generation. Wideman the author, academic and intellectual, also wants to reach down to a level below the conscious thinking of the characters, and even sometimes below Doot—who is educated but still a character in the novel—to look at the underlying symbols and ideas of the oral myth with the eye of the intellectual and artist. Since the quest here is at least partly a personal quest for Wideman the artist to keep his art alive, to validate the deepest substance of the energizing myth, we can see the need for this level of treatment. Because of this exploration of the region below the surface, Wideman's style in *Yesterday* at places is more difficult than it has been since *The Lynchers.* At stake in *Yesterday* is making the connections and making the myth of family and community a substantive reality for the Homewood product Wideman, who is Doot in the story, and the present Homewood generation, and also making the mythic foundation of family and community one that Wideman the artist and intellectual can truly rely on for support.

In *Damballah,* Lizabeth reflects that "Telling the story right will make it real"; in *Yesterday,* the first-person narrator Doot calls the stories of the street Cassina Way "timeless, intimidating, fragile." Particularly in part two, **"The Courting of Lucy Tate,"** Wideman draws our attention to the pro-

cess through which Doot has acquired the "right" information to make the "timeless, intimidating, [but] fragile" stories "real" for him. In **"The Courting,"** Doot recounts the courting of Lucy Tate by his Uncle Carl, which took place before Doot was born. A part of Doot's story is the story that Lucy told Carl, years ago in the Velvet Slipper, about the shooting of community hero-musician Albert Wilkes by the police in 1934. We see how this story, along with others, was told to Carl by Lucy and, by implication, how Carl must have told Doot, who is now making it part of his story. As time sequences switch back and forth, stories are entangled in stories, past and present, and the process of understanding how Doot gets his version of the courtship becomes difficult. Obviously, here Wideman is concerned with validating and authenticating the process of oral transmission in a way that he is not in *Hiding Place* and *Damballah.* This validation and authentication is not for the benefit of the older generation, which is already immersed in the stories that produce the myth, but for the benefit of Wideman, Doot and the present generation, who are still uncertain about the reality and efficacy of the stories and the myth. Doot never resolves his questions about the rightness of the stories and myth for him, but wants the mythic foundation and accepts the stories of family and community griots, in spite of his questions. Later, a treatment of the ending of *Yesterday* will give further insight into this problem.

The voice that speaks from below the surface is sometimes Doot's, but the voice has a deeper omniscience than we can fully attribute to him. The voice is at least partly that of an omniscient narrator who presents the deepest insights, examines the subjective reality, and portrays the underlying symbolism that concern the artist and intellectual. And the style in many places captures the subjective and symbolic more than the concrete. At this level, there also has to be a way of testing the stories and myth that satisfies Wideman. The myth has to withstand this probing of its misty region where Wideman the artist and intellectual plunges with his deep mind and difficult, sometimes almost expressionistic style. Wideman has to be able to arrange the symbols and subjective reality into some form that is artistically pleasing.

It is not always possible to see clearly when this omniscient voice usurps Doot's voice, but for the shaping of parts of the stories told about each major character, we should clearly be listening for this omniscient voice. In recapturing the stories that the omniscient narrator tells for Albert, Lucy, and Brother, which are similar and merge together into one story, a composite of the black experience, one must interpret the subjective and symbolic and blow out the rich implications of meaning.

Albert Wilkes' piano-playing ability, killing of a white policeman who discovers Albert's affair with his wife, and consequent killing by the police when he returns after seven years are all a part of the Homewood story that the characters know. At the novel's deepest level, Albert Wilkes personifies the heart and soul of black music, and Homewood and its people are central to his life. In Homewood, he can reconfirm contact with his people, and as his foster mother, old Mrs. Tate, tells his story, Albert steps "right dead in the middle of her story and you play awhile [on the piano], measure for measure awhile until the song's yours. Then it's just you there again by yourself again and you begin playing the seven years away." When the police splatter Wilkes' brains and blood over the Tates' house, in a figurative sense they disseminate his musical heart and soul—in which are mingled tragedy and a transcending beauty and sweetness—to the future Homewood generations.

The story the narrator tells for Lucy Tate includes Albert, Brother Tate, Brother's son Junebug, and Samantha, Junebug's mother. Brother Tate, Lucy's brother because they were both adopted by old Mr. and Mrs. Tate, and his son Junebug were both ugly albinos enclosed in their ugly white skins, which at the deepest level are somewhat similar to the folklorist witch's skin which protects a witch and gives her the power of evil. The ugly white skin bodes evil and tragedy for Brother and Junebug, but it also acts as a caul of clairvoyance and insight. At this deep level, Brother and Junebug, like Albert Wilkes, are symbolic of the ugly and tragic aspects of blackness, but they also represent that ability of blacks to pierce through these aspects of their lives to see the meaningful, positive aspects, to see and understand the beautiful, transcendent quality of their music, to see the value in black strength and perseverance.

Junebug tragically died in a fire, and Brother died mysteriously on the train tracks sixteen years after Junebug's death. But silent, scat-singing Brother, who said very few words at any time, and no words at all during the last sixteen years of his life, shockingly duplicated Albert Wilkes' music on night in 1941, and also drew very revealing pictures of Homewood black people with wings, standing for their ability to soar and transcend. And Brother died on the railroad tracks, playing again the dare game with the trains that he and Carl played as kids. His death certainly points out his vulnerability as a black person, but it also points out the black determination to manipulate and not be intimidated by the dangerous, implacable forces that roar through black life on undeviating tracks.

In the last section of the book, entitled "Brother," Wideman takes us to the deepest level of Brother's reality. At this level, Brother, from age twenty-one to his death, finds his life dominated by a horrible train dream in which countless people, including himself, are being flung helplessly about in a pitch-dark train boxcar. The people in the boxcar are like anonymous cattle on the tracks to death. Brother knows that the dream can take him again and again and that it can kill him. In the dream, Brother merges with an becomes Albert Wilkes returning to Homewood after seven years. He becomes Albert Wilkes returning to Homewood to the center of his life, where the police blow him to pieces as he plays his hauntingly beautiful music. Albert Wilkes' life hangs on "him like a skin to be shed, a skin he couldn't shake off, so it was squeezing, choking all his other lives." In the dream and its association with Albert Wilkes, Brother understands a lot that is the essence of the black experience, and in his rattled consciousness at least, he is the one who informs the police on Albert so that Albert's life will stop killing him.

Junebug's death forces Brother to try to articulate to himself some important things about black life. He talks about the long stream of brutality, murder, rape and torture, and tries to talk positively:

> Listen, son. Listen, Junebug. It all starts up again in you. It's all there again. You are in me and I am in you so it never stops. As long as I am, there's you. As long as there's you, I am. It never stops. Nothing stops. We just get tired and can't see no further. Our eyes get cloudy. They close and we can't see no further. But it don't stop.

But Junebug has been burned to death, and Brother wonders if he has lied: "What bright, shining day ever came?" He knows he should tell someone the train dream, but he will never speak again the rest of his life.

At its end, however, Brother's life does maintain positive value. Before he steps up to dare the thundering train, the mate of the dream train, he hears the long-gone voices of Doot's grandfather John French and his wine-drinking buddies "laughing over his shoulder." He tells Junebug: "Ima win this one for you. . . . Watch me play."

Samantha is a physically attractive black woman with a lot of children; she says, "When this old ark [her house] docks be a whole lotta strong niggers clamber out on the Promised Land." But Samantha's life is fraught with tragedy: her involvement with Brother; the experience of Junebug, who is totally rejected by her other children because of his whiteness and ugliness; the deaths of both Brother and Junebug; and her own eventual insanity and institutionalization. Samantha's experience seems more uniformly tragic than that of the other characters, but at the deeper level of reality, she has depth, vision, and understanding, somewhat like Brother, that grow out of her tragic experience. The tragedy of her life is tempered by the memory of the beautiful woman "who used to stride through the Homewood streets like a zulu queen" and by the sacrifice and nationalistic vision she exhibited.

By the end of the "Brother" section, Wideman has used Albert, Brother, Junebug, and Samantha, four characters who are part of the Homewood myth and not a part of the novel's present action, to present an underlying reality that is subjective and symbolic. This territory is misty and foggy, but Wideman uses his tremendous artistic ability to shape and define the contours of thought and form here. Maybe the myth can support the artist and keep the deepest levels of his art alive. But after Wideman has apparently satisfied himself at this level, he must come back to the surface level of the characters' oral stories and myth, where Doot—who again is a surrogate for Wideman the young Homewoodite who searches for foundation and structure in his life—must take some action. At the end Doot is at Lucy's house with Lucy and his Uncle Carl. Doot's fondness for the stories is shown by his desire to hear again about Brother, whose story he has been hearing throughout the book. His uncertainty about the stories and myth is shown by his unwillingness to take action and live with the myth as his centering force: he still wants to listen. But significantly, Lucy pulls him away from listening to stories toward action. She has already told Doot that when he was born she "looked for the old folks [in his eyes]." She feels that the old folks, like Doot's grandfather John French, were tough and persevering, unlike her and Carl, who "got scared and gave up too easy." She reminds him of the time years ago when she got him up to dance to "Sent for You Yesterday, and Here You Come Today." In the last paragraph, Lucy puts on Smokey Robinson's "Tracks of My Tears," and Doot is "on [his] own feet. Learning to stand, to walk, learning to dance." If Wideman can show us how Doot can move from the "learning" stage to scat singing—like the name Brother gave him suggests—and dancing, then the stories will become "real" for Doot, more than sentimentality and nostalgia.

Wideman almost must write a sequel showing Doot, or some similar character, integrating the stories and myths in some way like the Homewood blacks of the older generations. This novel needs a sequel like *Hiding Place* needed *Damballah*, like *Damballah* needed *Sent for You Yesterday*.

In his three most recent works, Wideman again shows us his vast talent and has put together a lot about his family and community and the black experience. Wideman can further use the Homewood material to be prophetic about the black experience, to establish himself as a truly great writer who has been more insightful than most writers.

Jacqueline Berben (essay date Fall 1985)

SOURCE: "'Beyond Discourse': The Unspoken Versus Words in the Fiction of John Edgar Wideman," in *Callaloo*, Vol. 8, No. 3, Fall, 1985, pp. 525-34.

[*Berben is a critic and an educator at the Université de Nice. In the following essay, she examines Wideman's use of both direct and indirect methods of communicating themes and meanings in* Hiding Place.]

Hiding Place, John Edgar Wideman's 1981 novel about a young black's flight from unjust accusation, reveals the ghetto experience as a honeycomb of psychological and verbal subterfuges, all temporary shelters that must eventually give way before the onslaughts of reality. Wideman shifts back and forth between the narrative devices of indirect and direct interior monologue and dialogue to juxtapose the harsh world of poverty with the realm of dreams and fantasies in which the individual can hide from the unpleasant facts of his life. Language itself is rife with "hiding places" which afford a false sense of security to the unwary. Sincerity speaks in non-verbal forms of communication: gestures, songs, telepathic thoughts, heightened sensitivity, and bonds of kinship. Only names have an equivocal value, now a kind of title to dignity and a mark of permanence, now yet another mask to hide behind and change at will. In this network of deceit, of self-deception and pathological lying, the ability to deal with truth becomes the ultimate test of one's success or failure as a human being.

At the heart of this story stands Bruston Hill, replete with all the traditional values of a mountain as "Center" of the world, as the meeting point between heaven and earth, as the land of the dead, as Mircea Eliade's "cosmic navel" or "the point where creation had its beginning." For the top of Bruston Hill is the spot where aged Mother Bess has taken refuge from the world to await long overdue death," . . . the top of this lonely hill where it had all begun and where she was dying." "Where it had all begun" refers to the site on which Bess's family tree had first taken root, planted there by the primogenitor, Mother Sybela Owens, a runaway slave who settled her children in the free state of Pennsylvania. Here the soil was fertile and all seeds scattered upon it germinated; here her children grew and multiplied:

> Always so many kids around it seemed like they came no matter what, landing on top of Bruston Hill like rain and snow, like the change of seasons . . . on top of Bruston Hill where children came thick and regular as flies or mosquitoes and grew like weeds. . . .

Bruston Hill is the beginning, the past, ". . . the place in the stories all my people come from." As Tommy says, the fugitive comes here to elude the police. But it is also the future, thanks to the multitude of children lifting it and carrying it "on those dirty brown feet scurrying around busy all the time." Bruston Hill is fertility and hope, or at least it once was and so it remains in the family myth. It symbolizes the entire family, all the descendants of Mother Owens, who rocks eternally on the porch wrapped in her black cape come summer, come winter, indelibly fixed in everyone's memories and photos. Now, however, Bruston Hill is deserted, the ruins of the Garden of Eden in the Pittsburgh ghetto. It is a land of the dead, a graveyard filled with ghosts and unfulfilled wishes.

Down to the shack in which Bess is living, Bruston Hill is inhabited by ghosts. There in that shack, a fragment of the old homestead destroyed by fire decades earlier, Bess awaits her fate surrounded by the family's collective past. Although the shack is "more like a doghouse," "one of those huts in slave row," Bess has fiercely adopted it as her own. Not only is she "the caretaker of these ruins," she has donned them like a garment, almost a second skin:

> The house is a piece of clothing she has been wearing all these years. . . .The house like a sweater somebody painted on her body so she can't take it off. Not to patch or wash or give it a vacation. The house is painted on, stitched to her skin. . . .

Like Mother Owens with her black cape, Bess in her shack has become the matriarchal figure in the imagination of her people. Whether or not she accepts it, they have all bestowed upon her the name *Mother* Bess. And with the title go the powers of Bruston Hill and its ghosts:

> To be magic, to sing magic, to touch with the power they believed she had because she was old and evil and crazy up there by herself on top of Bruston Hill. Because she lived with the dead. Because she was dead herself.

Bess and Bruston Hill have become one and the same.

In search of the magic, her people make pilgrimages up the steep hill carrying sick babies for her to kiss. They play "Mother Bess" in Big Bob's lottery and win. And Tommy-in-trouble instinctively heads for Bruston Hill as his last chance in life, as towards a magic mountain where he can be regenerated, vivified by the contact with his own roots, protected by some unseen hand securely guiding him back to life.

Time does not exist on Bruston Hill and Tommy desperately needs to gain time, to stop running for a while. He has been here before, "in a dream or once upon a time when he was a kid." Then, as now, the distant city, "white and cold"—the antithesis of welcoming for a black, had both

fascinated and frightened him, but then he had someone to defend him, to support him:

> But his hand had been warm, wrapped in somebody else's and both of them stood staring out over the edge of the world. Somebody had his hand and would protect him from the howling, winged creatures who swooped through the black skies.

Given this outside help and little time, Tommy feels he can tackle anything and succeed. With a few days' rest from pursuit by the police, he will be able to get himself together and go back and face his problem. Now as in the dream or memory, Tommy needs to hide from the fearsome creatures of the night, to crawl in somewhere and curl up, and when the right moment arrives, to come out in triumph: "And he had believed he could rise on the wind and fly away where the city sparkled. Only a matter of time."

Vainly, Tommy has repeatedly sought to stop time, to "freeze" everyone and everything he holds dear while he tries to integrate himself into larger society. Meanwhile, however, his self-confident drive is held in check by chronic insecurity. In order to allow himself to stop running from responsibility, he needs a protective hand to steady his own and to raise a barrier between himself and the hostile forces opposing him. A *temporary* barrier.

Bess's initial inhospitality—her saying "No" to Tommy's request for asylum ("Get on up from there. Go on away from here") when she finds him sleeping in her wood shed after the deadline she had set for his departure, finds him encroaching on "her time"—stands in direct contrast to what he wants to find on Bruston Hill, to all that Bruston Hill signifies to him. Stealing time as he sleeps in Bess's shed, Tommy steals the security he seeks in his dreams. And dreams and fantasies, Freud tells us, are wish-fulfillment. Thus, Tommy returns to the total protection of the womb. The image is so strong that his waking thoughts recreate the birth trauma. Bess is birthing him, *Mother* Bess on fertile Bruston Hill, his own blood and kin ejecting him into the cold world without:

> Have him by the foot and dragging him out the cave where he's been hiding. A deep, dark, warm cave. A cave as black and secret as his blood. Yes. He is hiding deep in the rivers of his blood, in a subterranean chamber where his own blood is gathered in a still, quiet pool. . . .He feels himself sliding, slipping, and he tries to hold on with both his hands but the walls are slick as ice-cream, raw as meat. . . .Splashing his own blood against the walls of the tunnel.

Despite her rejection and coldness, Mother Bess offers to feed him because of the blood ties linking them. Her bowl of soup suffices to lull Tommy's psyche into the cherished illusion of that old dream or "once-upon-a-time-when-he-was-a-kid" memory, to transpose him back to "the best time of his life," living in his grandfather's house and playing with his older "cousins from up on Bruston Hill" until the grandfather died and "it all went to pieces." As Bess precedes him back to her shack, Tommy achieves the sensation of security he has hungered for ever since his childhood. He relives the moment of peace and contentment:

> He felt he was being led, felt as he had that night many years before when he stood under the tall trees at the back of his cousins' house, his hand clasped firmly within someone else's, someone who understood his fear, his sudden urges of daring, someone who stood silent and watchful but would not meddle.

Bruston Hill's significance for Tommy surpasses the immediate situation and provides the key that unlocks his entire character: only here in this strange, magical place rife with symbols of birth and death can Tommy himself be born anew, can be find the guidance, security, and comprehension denied him in the world outside.

Bess, like Tommy, has come to Bruston Hill for its protective powers, to hide from a world that has become too cruel to bear and especially to talk about. Words only bring inexpressible pain. She will not listen to Tommy's troubles because she has heard it all before; she knows trouble and suffering far too intimately for someone else to describe it to her. The tragedy of Bess's life and the source of her resentment against the appellation *Mother* Bess stem from her ironic inability to share in the general fertility of Bruston Hill. Her sterility was all the harder to bear in face of the ease with which all her sisters conceived and gave birth. Easy as dancing. But Bess could not dance, either. She had a man she loved, a man whose touch turned her to "silk and honey" almost like the Biblical promised land where the desert would bear fruit. And their love grew, but no child. Bess who was so good at growing things, who had spent all her life digging in the ground "on her hands and knees or flopped down flat on her belly if nobody was watching," Bess who had long been confident that "anything she planted would grow," who had "cradled" so much "in the black earth," Bess gave her man no son. Then, after they had given up all hope, when they were old "like Abraham and Sarah in the Bible," they had Eugene. But Eugene was killed on Guam, though Bess never accepted the word of the telegram that her man had carried up Bruston Hill. Then it was her man's turn. Twenty years her senior, he passed on and left her alone. So Bess had come back to Bruston Hill to live with her ghosts and await her time to join them in the grave. While she waits, she walls herself in from communication with the outside world that only brings

more pain: no mail, no telephone, no radio, and *no* visitors. All hope has been denied her. Since her womb brought forth death, not life, her image of her own "subterranean chamber" deep inside herself is not Tommy's warm cave of life through which run the rivers of his own blood, but a death hole, a grave:

> Her veins draw the chill, carry the deadness from her limbs to the center of her body, to the place she never knew she had until her son borning took it away with him. There the flow converges, stops there in a lake or a pool that is blacker and deeper than night. There she feels nothing but the guttering in and the depth of the hole into which the icy waters spill.

She recognizes the hole of death in her waking consciousness when she pictures her man slipping away from her, when she sees Shirl's dead baby in her white satin coffin, her beautiful "black-eyed Susan black eyes" staring into space. All Bess can find to say about the injustice of it all are the empty words, "Oh Jesus! Oh God Almighty!" Empty words in her mouth because Bess is no longer a Christian and has not been one ever since she lost the illusion of a guiding, protecting paternal hand in her favorite spiritual, "Father, Father along. "But the real words were *farther, farther* along and so Bess lost her God. Words are hypocritical; words can kill a son or even God himself. One must not listen to words or ever trust in them.

Better than words because truer and more sure is the communication between receptive souls. In spite of all her feigned self-sufficiency, Bess still needs some groceries now and then and a jug of Harry Bow's moonshine to cut the nasty taste of Bruston Hill water. The kindred soul who heeds the old woman's unspoken message is the simple-minded orphan boy, Clement:

> He hears Miss Bess waiting at the top of Bruston Hill. Everything in him blind except the part hearing her silent call.

Clement, like Bess when she was young, is a listener. His sensitive inner ear tends to select out the meaningless words and retain only the essential affect of the utterance or situation. Just as the functions of seeing and listening are mingled in his perception of Bess's summons, they interweave in his daily experience. At Big Bob's barbershop, the morning lies the customers tell each other seem "slow and lazy as worms" to Clement who watches them "squirm and wiggle across the floor." When the young boy approaches Bess's shack and catches Tommy there unaware, he needn't actually see the man to hear him inside, hear him being more quiet now than a minute ago, feel him "shouting at him, *I'm not here, goddamnit*" (italics in text). Lies and fancy talk are wasted on Clement. Bess's unidentified relative, grateful for the good luck playing "Mother Bess" in the lottery brought him, need not pretend to Clement that he's sending her a hundred dollars and leaving Clement a ten dollar tip; he need not wink because he knows Clement can count. And Clement does not bother to repeat Miss Violet's empty threats against Big Bob, her old flame, even though he knows nothing of the language of love—according to Big Bob. Like Bess, Clement can hear and see what he wants to. It is useless for the stranger at the Brass Rail bar to whisper in Carl's ear because Clement can read every word in Carl's agitations:

> . . . Carl twisting this way and that like the stool getting hot up under his buns.
>
> Then Carl start to working his knees. Big thighs flapping like butterfly wings. Getting faster and faster like they pumping something to his mouth.

And Clement knows that they are talking about Tommy Lawson, the ghost he saw through the walls of Miss Bess's shack on Bruston Hill. Only he does not say so. Clement says very little, especially if it is something important, like the secret name for his mother that no one can touch and sully as long as he keeps it secret. So Clement keeps quiet, listens, and counts—hair balls of black wool from the barbershop floor for a pillow "like Violet's titties when she leans on the bar and squeezes her blouse between her arms so they sit there like a pillow," Carl's beers at the bar, or how many times he had climbed Bruston Hill for Bess. Counting is something sure, and numbers do not lie when you are an expert in "numerology and trick ology," as Bess tells him she is, after breaking the bank in Big Bob's numbers game on her first and only try. And Clement makes his rounds, collecting tips for running errands, counting all the while to himself.

The reluctance and mistrust which both Clement and Bess demonstrate towards speech or even the written word are in counterpoint to Tommy's philosophy and the general climate that reigns in the streets of the ghetto. Tommy prides himself on his gift for talk, his ability to warm people up, make them smile and forgive him, yield to his powerful seduction. He knows he is lying, of course, and so do they, but he gets away with it. Tommy is a master of jive, of nonstop flattery or nonsense delivered with a machine-gun-like beat, never stopping for breath or a comeback:

> Hey man, what's to it? Ain't nothing to it man you got it baby hey now where's it at you got it you got it ain't nothing to it something to it I wouldn't be out here in all this sun you looking good you into something go on man you got it all. . . .

Only with Bess does his machine fail, for his gift of talk is a real asset in his world, an exterior sign of wealth at poverty's core.

There is a lie here for every purpose. Big Bob's early-morning customers are in the habit of starting their day with a soft, warm lie to cushion the chilly contact with daytime reality:

> Everybody still too evil to laugh and joke so somebody would mutter something under his breath like he was just talking to himself but if you listened you'd know he was lying and wanted somebody to hear it.

Many raise their self-esteem through "signifying," pretending to have knowledge they do not, pretending to be "hip," trifling with serious matters. Similar to signifying is "talking heavy," loading language down with double-entendre to show off in front of someone, as Carl does with his educated nephew. There are lies to dupe the naive: straightforward Bess has never forgotten that when she was a child and believed that anything she planted would grow, her brothers had tricked her into planting a hambone to grow a new ham. Lying is the basic fact of existence for everyone in the ghetto. Bess will not be fooled about it:

> Anybody got the sense they born with know what kind of world it is down there. But they still down there calling up *down,* and in *out,* and day *night,* and it don't make no difference. White or black or lying or telling the truth ain't nothing down there.

Consequently, Bess rejects as untrue everything that comes from below Bruston Hill, including the mail one must go down to fetch. Hence, even "Letters lie and nobody but a fool believes what letters say." There is no certainty, no security in the land "down there," except for the false assurance gained through duplicitous talk.

If Clement and Bess are wise enough to spurn the trap of verbal deceit, they are nonetheless subject to duping themselves with another kind of lie. Even they are vulnerable and, in one way or another, they must turn away from the truth to survive. For Bess, her weakness manifests itself at the baby's funeral:

> This child staring forever, never blinking, beholding the darkness an old woman cannot bear for more than an instant before she turns away to lies.

Dream lies, escape into fantasies or fond memories of a distant past, entertain Bess and provide her refuge from the unkind world of reality, while Clement transforms his present world into instant gratification of his wishes through dream-like images and serious make-believe. Bess sees herself as a child, happily digging in the earth of Bruston Hill: she hears someone she cannot see telling a story about her when she was young and it was spring, when she and everything in the world were beautiful and promising abundance, and the birds she sees high above the trees become "a handful of dark seeds scattered by an invisible hand" in prophecy of all the children she will one day bear; she feels her man nuzzling her ear, whispering to her that she is "silk and honey" and then nibbling her toes. At Benson's funeral parlor, she transforms the pitiful, tiny baby into a "cellophane-winged angel in a blue-eyed gown" picking apart the sun-catching cobwebs, winding them into balls, and tucking them "into her blue-eyed gown without snapping one thread," the same angel who at the end of the novel appears to inspire Bess to destroy her shack and leave the past. The angel in the blue-eyed gown works with her to set the house on fire:

> . . . Thank you you little blue-gowned, black-eyed thing. Thank you you little fuzzy-headed got the prettiest black-eyed lazy Susan eyes in the whole world thing.

Her angel has the dead baby's hair and eyes, the eyes she cannot forget. Bess trusts in her angel because "Angels don't hurt things. Don't tear apart what other creatures have spent their precious time doing." The angel can be dream, vision, or fantasy. In any of these cases, her presence enables the old woman to face reality once again, albeit on the arm of a beautiful fiction.

Insofar as the simpleminded orphan boy Clement is concerned, the little fictions that render his life tolerable are perfectly childlike in their simplicity of image and their playfulness. Not only do lies become visible worms writhing on the floor, but hands sprout eyes that can see, wink at themselves, and watch everything around them. Wideman escalates the unreal condition, "If hands had eyes," into fact due to necessity: "hands needed eyes to do something behind your back when you're not looking." From there, he develops animation into personification:

> . . . Clement tried to catch them looking at themselves in the mirror. Winking maybe at theyself cause they got the bow so nice and even.

Ultimately, the proposition that started out contrary to fact accentuates its reality through proliferation:

> Big Bob's hand is studded with eyes. They are hidden in the folds of his dumpling-colored palm. If he opened his hand wide Clement knew they'd be there staring up at him.

In parallel manner, synecdoche leaves the rhetorical domain in Clement's childish imagination and wishful thinking projects itself into reality. Thus the broom which symbolizes the boy's principal task, sweeping the floor, becomes the boy himself:

> Clement sees the floor covered with kinky, matted hair. Then he is a broom whisking it into a pile in the corner away from the door.

He can be both the broom and himself, "dreaming while the broom goes on about its business" until Big Bob calls out for him to get his "butt up off that chair, boy." Like Bess and Tommy, Clement can dwell in the comforting world of his illusion, fantasies, and dreams until some voice breaks in on his private world and brings him back to the unkind reality by calling his name.

Of all these hiding places, sleep is the best, for dreams are the reality of sleep. The more the character needs to escape the outside world, the more enticing sleep becomes. In sleep, Clement can pursue his obsession—the quest for a mother. Alone at night, when he is almost asleep, he says her secret name in his heart, and, in the daytime, he fantasizes about making himself a gigantic pillow that will be his bed,

> . . . White and soft. Like Violet's titties . . . Clement feels himself sinking. Into the softness. Into the velvet blackness which lives inside the mirror. Lives inside her white blouse. A million Clements like the million shiny glasses stacked on the counter behind the bar and each one asleep, each one peaceful and dreaming like the glasses inside the mirror.

Sleep is the land on the other side of the looking glass, a safe niche in which to disappear into infinity, into a "million Clements," into the Great Mother's bosom. Unlike Clement, Tommy needs no special cushions to drop into—his need to escape is so great that he can sleep in any position, "Standing up, lying down, sitting in a chair," in any place, "Outside, inside," in any condition, "hot or cold." Even Bess who waits at night for sleep's coup de grace to "mercifully sever her head from her body," who grumbles at being roused from her escapist nap during the baby's funeral, is disturbed by Tommy's constant slumber to the point that she asks him if he has "been hit upside the head" or "got the sleeping sickness." Sleep heals the wounds of the spirit because it provides an asylum from waking cares, an asylum the three focal characters in Wideman's novel are constantly seeking.

Yet, if life is to continue, one cannot remain in hiding forever. Tommy must eventually go to the police with his story and Bess must accept her family's repeated offers of hospitality. If language is not to be trusted and even dreams cradle falsehoods, what terms are there to use, what values can be agreed upon, in order to come to a necessary understanding?—Sense. Good sense, the five senses of seeing, smelling, hearing, touching, tasting, and the sixth sense or intuition. Kinship. And names. Bess does not have to ask Tommy who he is: she has seen him before, sees all his ancestors in him, and although she at first refuses to utter his name—or even to say it to herself—she knows that he is her sister Gert's-daughter-Freeda's-daughter-Lizabeth's son, Thomas. There is no need to tell her he is in trouble—she can see the "scared rabbits" in his eyes. After he is supposed to have left Bruston Hill, Bess can still see Tommy's feet sticking out from her shed right through the walls of her shack. When Bess decides to feed Tommy, he can eat his fill of her soup just by smelling its aroma; actually tasting it is absorbing everything on Bruston Hill:

> The failing light hovering in the bottom of the rear window and leaking under the splayed back door, the purple silhouette on the hills on the horizon, the smoke smell inside the shack, the hiss of wood in the stove's belly, the old woman's voice talking to the vegetables she had peeled and sliced and dropped into bubbling, seasoned stock.

No matter how wide the gap between them, Bess and Tommy will come to grips with the basics and establish common ground. Tommy's fear of death and flight from it meets its equivalent in Bess's fear of life and her attempts to seal herself off from it. Their profound consciousness of their ancestry, of their bloodlines, establishes the first point of contact. Then Bess's eyewitness testimony confirms the validity of the old family myths Tommy has grown up on at the knee of Bess's sister Aida. They now share a common heritage. Before long, Tommy is crawling around, digging in the earth, planting seeds under Bess's instruction and watchful eye. A flicker of hope lights the atmosphere. But the climax of truth, the moment of deepest communication and mutual appreciation comes when Tommy pours his soul into whistling the blues, blues like her man whistled while brushing her hair, blues like sister Aida's man played on his guitar and said were "letters from home," blues like she heard whistled in her dreams but that always faded away each time she tried to get closer—until now. It was while Bess talked to him about the blues that Tommy saw through her facade, saw she was scared and hiding out, too. His music makes Bess confess and realize:

> Once was one time too many to watch people sing the blues and die. Once was enough to listen and then have it all go away and have nothing but silence.

This time, it is in her power to prevent its going away. So Bess comes down from Bruston Hill "to tell them what they needed to know," comes down "on her man's arms."

There is no outside narrator's voice to intrude upon the delicate truths, to trespass upon the private ground of personal feelings which furnishes both the setting and the action of *Hiding Place.* Indirect monologue imperceptibly shifts to direct in the three streams of consciousness, Clement's Bess's and Tommy's, which converge on Bruston Hill and rekindle the hope once brought there by a runaway slave.

John Bennion (essay date Spring/Summer 1986)

SOURCE: "The Shape of Memory in John Edgar Wideman's *Sent for You Yesterday*," in *Black American Literature Forum,* Vol. 20, Nos. 1-2, Spring/Summer, 1986, pp. 143-50.

[Bennion is an American educator and critic. In the following essay, he illustrates the role memory plays in shaping the narrative of Sent for You Yesterday.*]*

Wideman's *Sent for You Yesterday* has a nontraditional form; the stories of Cassina Way sit "timeless, intimidating, fragile." The plot structure is nonlinear, with time looping rhythmically and point of view shifting rapidly. Readers know about events before they happen; they experience scenes through one character, then reexperience them through another; time moves forward and backward until the characters' comings and goings merge. In addition, deeply introspective language, repeated metaphors, and symbiotic relationships between living and dead characters keep readers stretching to apprehend the book. Like the soap bubble caught in Freeda's fingers, the novel trembles between the foreign and the familiar, vacillating from the undefined to the defined; from ghosts and telepathic transfer to bricks and glass and blood; from the voiceless, timeless, faceless "In Heaven with Brother Tate" to the opening sentence of the first section—"Brother Tate stopped talking five years after I was born"—which introduces the organizing consciousness of the novel, the narrator Doot.

The narrator's spherical, rhythmic memory gives shape to the book, with its spiritual interlinking of characters, metaphorical descriptions of places and events, and convoluted sense of time. Relatedly, the reader's struggle to apprehend the familiar and foreign elements of the novel approximates the characters' struggle to apprehend their own world through perception, memory, and metaphorical reconstruction of perception and memory.

In a traditional novel character unfolds through speech and thought. Each character in *Sent for You Yesterday* is, additionally, linked through spirit and identity to every other. For Freeda, "Carl and Brother [are] like two peas in a pod."

Brother is Carl's white shadow, his "ace boon coon running pardner." Lucy, the third of the three musketeers, is linked to Carl by love, but Brother is included: ". . . Brother was a part of it. . . . It was the three of them now. No secrets." Brother receives Albert Wilkes's music when he dies; he dreams that he is Wilkes. Son and father, daughter and mother are linked by blood and mannerism, with Carl rolling his shoulders "to get the mannish John French weight in [his] steps" and with Lizabeth "growing more like her mother every day," revealing Freeda to John. Samantha dreams she is Junebug; Brother sings to the dead Junebug, his son.

The mind of the narrator is connected to all the characters through blood and storytelling, but especially to Brother Tate: ". . . I'm linked to Brother Tate by stories, by his memories of a dead son, by my own memories of a silent, scat singing albino man who was my uncle's best friend." These relationships move beyond the normal interchange of characters in a traditional novel; they occur more often and are frequently supported by repeated images—references to shadows or to mirror images, to characters who dream they are someone else. The linking goes beyond the need of the author for artistic unity to the emotional need of the characters for each other. As the novel's epigraph indicates, "Past lives live in us, through us. Each of us harbors the spirits of people who walked the earth before we did, and those spirits depend on us for continuing existence, just as we depend on their presence to live our lives to the fullest." The result is that the reader apprehends the characters as an interlinked group, which is the way in which Doot views them in his own memory.

In addition to people, places and events in *Sent for You Yesterday* are linked nontraditionally through metaphors, primarily those of a train and an ark. A train may take a character away to terror and death; an ark to the promised land, where sky and earth meet. Brother dreams of destruction in the form of a train: "Train gon catch you . . .," he says to Carl. Carl's body-shaking sexual climax is a "train flying like a giant black bullet at his back." A policeman comes huffing and puffing like a train after John French, and the piano at which Albert Wilkes is shot is large and black as a locomotive. Samantha's womb is an ark; her house, another. Each of the bars and the revival tent outside which Brother listens are ark-like containers of humanity. Cassina Way, Homewood, Pittsburgh, and the North are a series of arks within arks.

Other events are linked through rhythmic, refrain-like repetition—Lucy's pushing Brother in the buggy, her climbing to visit Sam, Albert Wilkes's being shot, and so forth. The many metaphorical and rhythmic links cause the reader to view the book symbolically, but more than the linkages provide a means by which the characters see. Samantha thinks of her house as an ark; Brother sees death as a pow-

erful train. The metaphors are internal and grow naturally from the characters' minds and memories.

Time, a third structural element in *Sent for You Yesterday,* is convoluted beyond the flashbacks one would expect to find in a traditional novel. In the first section of the book, after it is established that all the stories reside in the narrator's memory, the scenes cycle rhythmically backward and forward, shifting times and points of view until the hours and the characters blend. First it's morning, and Carl and Freeda look for John French because Albert Wilkes is home; then it's night, and Albert Wilkes is just coming back. The men in the bar look backward at Wilkes's arrival before he arrives. In addition to simple inversion of chronological order, time is blended; the past lives in the present. Freeda's memories of Gert and John, as well as John's memories of Albert and Lizabeth, are less flashbacks than they are the past cast forward. Throughout the first section of the novel, the sound of Albert Wilkes's scratching at the window is a thread stitching time to time. In the middle section, the shooting of Albert Wilkes is repeated with the power of present action. In the last section, Brother's death and his life are integrated. The men Lucy has known hover around her as she bathes; around her rocking chair vibrates the song of her life's events.

Some parts of the novel hang timelessly in Doot's memory, and some sentences have deliberate twists that spin them into impossibility. "I am not born yet," the narrator writes. Wilkes, walking into the Tates' place, remembers having been there before, so he knows what will come next, his memory moving forward in time. In one instance Brother's hearing transcends time and space: "Through some odd circumstance of atmosphere and temperature, a peculiar alignment of planets and mysterious, incorporeal essences, Brother hears the screams of dying Japanese. . . ." The next two sections cycle outward in the same pattern, including yet moving beyond the day Albert Wilkes returned, reverberating from that point in time like a stone dropped into the pool of Doot's memory.

All these connections—whether among people, events, or days—are the raw material of the novel, having much of the characteristic randomness and emotional linking of memory itself. The shape of the novel, built sentence by sentence, is the shape of Doot's memory. The individual correspondences are the substance which the characters, the narrator, and the reader apprehend similarly, using their mental facilities to organize sensory material into frameworks for thinking, into patterns of perception.

Readers understand early that the characters and the narrator are concerned with perception. Carl, for instance, wonders about the connection between mental pictures of a thing and the thing itself:

[He] . . . daydreamed the other places his father could be. With Brother like a shadow behind him Carl could enter the dream, get from one place to another in Homewood just by thinking where he wanted to go and then the streets would slip past as he thought of them . . ., and it wouldn't be a matter of a certain number of steps and turning here and crossing there because the streets were inside him. The streets were Homewood but they were not real till he thought them. Till he glided with his shadow, Brother, up and down and over the streets sleeping inside him.

Carl diverges from the Western mode of thinking, which distinguishes subject and object. Perception, which links Carl to Homewood, has the additional function of preserving objective reality: Carl wonders, "What would happen to his mother and father if one morning . . . he didn't wake up and start the dream of Homewood." Albert Wilkes thinks of vision as an anchor for reality. When disoriented, he might choose some physical detail and "stare as if it was his job to keep it in place and if he faltered, if he lost concentration for one split second, the thing would disappear and all of Homewood with it."

What could take objective reality away from the characters if they were to stop watching? Freeda blames time itself, which she pictures as a voice pulling her vision away from the past, which is clear and magical, like a soap bubble that she might make a wish on. True memory is important, for it keeps the world real, keeps people from losing their grip, as Samantha does.

Truly, seeing and remembering are artistic abilities. John French, thinking that Homewood might have slipped without any of its inhabitants' knowing, counts on Albert Wilkes's being able to notice a change, for he realizes that someone who has been present the whole time might be unable to recognize a difference: "Albert would see how things had changed. . . .Couldn't see it with Albert's eyes unless you been gone those seven years." But he also worries that, "if Homewood slipping, maybe everything slipping, maybe the whole world and Albert Wilkes too, so when you hear him play again [he] won't be no mirror or nothing else." John has Carl's fear that, unless one watches and remembers, the familiar world could disintegrate.

When John counts on Wilkes to be a mirror, he assumes that artists see and express more clearly than do most people, whether the medium be colors, sounds, or words. John French himself has artistic sensitivity to the colors of the sky, but he doubts whether he can describe them. He doesn't think he could put a picture together the way Albert Wilkes does a song. Carl also has trouble seeing and expressing: "Been looking at Lucy nearly fifty years now and still can't even finish her picture." "People," he adds, "ain't

easy to see. . . . I mean if you look, . . . and you keep looking closer and closer, a person subject to go all to pieces and won't be nothing there to see."

Carl and John suggest that the artist is the one who, through true reformulation of perception, keeps reality from disintegrating, and that the true forms of perception exist backward in time and memory. As John begins to ruminate about "the right color of the sky . . . the first color," his attention shifts to a major concern of the novel: how to perceive one's color. Brother, John thinks, looks "like somebody had used a chisel on him. A chisel then sandpaper to get down to the whiteness underneath the nigger. . . . Down to the first color or no color at all. . . . To first colors or first shapes. . . ." The direction is backward in time, inside mythic memory, to the true color.

Brother, an embodiment of a primary expressive form for the book—carefully controlled action—, is an artist of being who moves like a dancer. His hands sing the streets which Carl names; they are rain falling out of a clear sky. He gives artistic form to the simple action of getting from one place to another: "Brother hears the flat smack of his bare feet on the boards. . . . He doesn't know why [he's walking]. He doesn't care. It's a way of getting up and back, up and back, across the black space of the room." On Cassina Way, in Homewood, in Pittsburgh, and in the world, people are just figuring out a way of getting across. Others—like the men sitting in the Bucket of Blood, Miss Pollard watching over Cassina Way, even Junebug keeping busy—by their very existence are holding places in reality, elevating the act of being to occupational, even universal, status.

Learning how to be black is centrally important to learning how to be. Carl, home from the war, is confused, unable to be: "I'd sit myself down and try to get myself together. You know. Say this is your life, Carl French, the only one you gon git. Now what you gon do with it? What you gon be? . . . Finally I started remembering. . . . You a blackass splib." Remembering determines the way in which he will live; his existence is in the context of memory, of the people who are a part of him. ". . . he's waiting for a witness. A voice to say amen. Waiting for one of the long gone old folks to catch his eye and not at him and say *Yes. Yes. You got that right, boy.*"

Samantha has a more positive idea of blackness. She sleeps only with the blackest men. She knows that black people came from royalty: "Even before birth, before the fetus was three months old, the wanderlust of blackness sent melanocytes migrating through the mysterious terrain of the body. Blackness seeking a resting place, a home in the transparent baby. . . . Blackness would come to rest in the eyes; blackness a way of seeing and being seen. . . . And of course blackness would keep on keeping on to the farthest frontiers." Blackness is royal and powerful—a way of being, of getting across.

While many characters are important perceivers and artists, Brother, as a white Negro, colorless, is uniquely qualified to be a great eye, a watcher, a witness who can see truly. He is also a master of artistic form, painting like Carl and playing like Albert Wilkes; he is the supernatural, extratemporal recipient of their perceptive ability. To him all modes of expression are essentially the same, "only different tunes." "Brother picked the way he wanted to live," says Lucy. "And how he wanted to die. Now how many people have you heard of like that? Jesus maybe. And one, two others like the Africans flying and walking cross water and turning sticks to snakes. . . . Brother was special like that. Not some spook or hoodoo, but a man who could be whatever he wanted to be." He is also given the stature of a Christ figure when, after Junebug's death, he bends through the eye of the needle to see God's face and returns alive.

For Brother and every other character, existence is a dance between life and death, the train game, set firmly in tradition, in an interlinked net of remembered people. Doot, the narrator, as soon as he is born, is "inside the weave of voices, a thought, an idea, a way things might be seen and be said."

What then is the specific form of artistic perception, of the slow body dance in the net of memory? Inside the mind of each character, how are Brother's hands and scat sounds stored? Where are the breaking of glass and the scattering of blood kept? What is the time/shape of memory?

For Freeda, time is a voice pulling her away from a clear, soap bubble world; living is "learning to forget." She uses this image not merely as a way of explaining something, but as the controlling metaphor of her life. "If her life had a shape, the shape was not what she could remember, but what kept tearing her away. . . ." Albert Wilkes and Samantha share Freeda's fear of losing time: He thinks the days he was away are like cards shuffled in the hands of a dealer; Sam throws away the pills that would steal time from her.

Lucy's image of time is also spherical, but it moves round and round with the rhythms of song. She compares events to notes falling down on her as if she were inside one of "those little crystal balls you buy at Murphy's Five and Dime." She weaves memories into the song Albert Wilkes played for her before he was shot, one which made things new because it "joined things, blended them so you follow one note and then it splits and shimmers and spills the thousand things it took to make the note whole, the silences within the note, the voices and songs." In part consciously,

in part subconsciously, Lucy, Albert Wilkes, and Freeda keep time and reality by forming them into metaphors.

Other characters modify the spherical image of time, combining past and present in a cyclical metaphor. ". . . that's the way the world turns," says Carl. "Circles and circles and circles inside circles." His image of Doot as a child is just as vivid as his image of Doot in the present: ". . . it don't make no difference. Just a circle going round and round so you getting closer while you getting further away and further while you getting closer." Mrs. Campbell knows in advance that Albert will die because "once another human being's blood on your hands, ain't nothing you can do but go in circles till you come back where you shed it. What goes round, comes round." Wideman's cyclical metaphor for time is clearly non-Western. Were one to view time traditionally, as a measured continuum, rather than looking at it out of the corner of one's eye, as Doot looks at Brother, then one would fail to see truly.

The narrator, who intermittently allows himself to be overwhelmed by his people, revealing their stories as if he, the reader, and the characters were all sitting inside each teller's head, compares this spherical net of time and person to a spider web. Looking through the window of the house on Cassina Way, he imagines Freeda standing there years earlier. For the reader time curls around itself, as if both Doot and Freeda stand simultaneously.

> I'm trying to remember the inside of her house, its shape, the furniture, the way things in it would trap the silence and spin a dusty, beaded web around her so if you peeked in from Cassina you'd see a young woman draped by layers of transparent gauze, a young woman standing up asleep, her eyes open, threads stretched from the top of her head to all the walls, the things in the room, the places of smoky light surrounding her like wash pinned on lines to dry. That's what I see, invisible in the alley, trying to remember.

This metaphor connects each character and each time to every other.

The characters, then, in their effort to "keep on keepin on," hang smells and days and ghosts on the interconnected net of their memories. The narrator has rolled them into his own consciousness, once more relating their stories with undeviating fidelity to the manner in which he received them, so readers apprehend the material in the same way he does, with the same interconnectedness and leaps that memory has. The movement from novel to reader can be described as a series of dialectical motions, the characters' apprehending events being a unit which the narrator apprehends, which unit is in turn apprehended by the reader.

The characters' and the narrator's formulation of the truth of the characters' lives, as well as the reader's reformulation of it, isn't an idle pastime. It involves a structuring of reality which balances past and present, consciousness and subconsciousness, memory and actuality, life and death. Existence is a careful dance between order and chaos; one slip can destroy time, and hence life. The world is like Brother's dream, in which chaotically tumbling bodies must "hold it in," must see and think and move with absolute awareness, or be ripped out of existence like a scream. Brother, Doot, and the others are "learning to stand, to walk, learning to dance." They formulate reality through the same process of artistic apprehension that a reader must use to enter their world.

Gary Dretzka (review date 29 November 1987)

SOURCE: "Haunting Novel of Rage and Love Packs a Punch," in *Chicago Tribune Books*, November 29, 1987, p. 6.

[*Dretzka is an American journalist and critic. In the following review, he offers a favorable assessment of* Reuben.]

I wasn't prepared for this book, the impact it would have on me. Sure, I knew that any novel by John Edgar Wideman would pack a substantial wallop, but the title was misleading.

Reuben, I thought, picking up the galleys, could be about a 5-year-old boy, a racehorse or a sandwich. Indeed, the opening pages didn't reveal much beyond the fact that the book's central character—a wizened, rat-faced old lawyer who lives in a cluttered trailer in Pittsburgh's Homewood ghetto—was eccentric and, perhaps, something of a miracle worker.

But soon the powerful engine within Wideman's vehicle kicked into gear and the full impact of Reuben's story hit me with the force of a runaway truck. This is a profoundly sad work—full of unfulfilled promises, deceptions and rage—but one fueled by high-octane dialogue and explosive characterizations. It left me quaking.

Reuben is a small man—a black dwarf with a humpback—but he casts a long shadow as the father confessor and legal guardian of generations of poverty-stricken Homewood residents.

Wideman, a PEN-Faulkner Award winner who was born in Homewood, introduces us to some of Reuben's clients and their "troubles."

Kwansa is a sometime prostitute whose young son has been snatched from her by his father, a ne'er-do-well junkie. Wally is a former basketball star who's employed as a recruiter for a college athletic program under investigation for corruption. Through them, and a half-dozen other well-drawn characters, we see Homewood as only someone who lives there can.

Kwansa's poverty reduces her mobility, keeping her on the streets or in the taverns; Wally has been given a ticket out of the ghetto, thanks to sports, but can't escape the Homewood in his mind. This is their story, as much as it is Reuben's.

Because most of the action takes place in the minds of his characters, Wideman presents a challenge to the reader. The novel moves quickly from well-scripted lawyer-client discussions to intricate inner dialogues filled with tricky flashbacks and stream-of-consciousness wanderings.

Reuben's advice and recollections follow Wally nearly everywhere he goes, even on the jogging path:

> "Reuben always talking about doubles, twins, other lives he might or might not have lived. Wally wondered about his own doubles, the letters he posted to himself as he ran, the disguise in his suitcase, all the lies he'd told or believed."

Kwansa, who entrusts Reuben with getting her Cudjoe back, has allowed her youth to be stolen from her by the young stud whose lies promised an escape:

> "She knew he was lying. Knew he was just talk. He'd run away first chance he got. Too pretty to work, too pretty to stay with ugly Kwansa, getting fatter every day. . . ."

Wideman's ability to capture the language and turmoil of the street with such precision marks *Reuben* as a very special work of art, although it's not the kind of book one enjoys, exactly. Indeed, some of the moments may prove painfully unforgettable.

For example, in the midst of sorting out Kwansa and Wally's dilemmas, Reuben tells the story of his own humiliation.

During his school days in Philadelphia, Reuben was the mascot of a white fraternity. He occasionally would escort students to a whorehouse in a black neighborhood near campus, but they repaid Reuben's loyalty with scorn. For his birthday, they plotted an intricate practical joke that involved a session with Flora, a beautiful prostitute who would ignore Reuben's deformities and give him love. The joke backfires, resulting in a tragic fire—an inferno fanned by the students' racism and the frustrations of Flora's piano-man lover.

Wideman lays out Reuben's story in a devastating chapter charged with an emotional fury so graphic that it forced me to put down the book to catch my breath.

"All black men have a Philadelphia," Reuben tells Wally, recalling that birthday long ago. "Even if you escape it, you leave something behind, Part of you. A brother trapped there forever. Do you know what I mean, Wally? My Philadelphia's strange because, for all the horror, more of it's about love. Have you had yours?"

Wally has his "Philadelphia," as does Kwansa, and their horrors are shared vividly with the reader. Be warned: *Reuben* is a book that will haunt your memory long after the last page has been turned.

Harold Jaffe (review date March-April 1988)

SOURCE: "Rage," in *American Book Review*, Vol. 10, No. 1, March-April, 1988, pp. 8-14.

[*Jaffe is a noted critic, editor of* Fiction International, *and author of several books, including* Othello Blues *(1996). In the following review, he responds enthusiastically to* Reuben, *noting Wideman's ability to communicate the tremendous depths of rage present within the novel's characters and their surroundings.*]

The stunning anger pulsing like an outside heart in *Reuben* underscores one of the signal questions of our time for the artist: how to forge an oppositional art. Not merely an art that is, or means to be, uncomplicitous with the dominant ideology, but a calculated art specifically designed to infiltrate, rupture, destabilize.

Fredric Jameson, in an essay on the visual artist Hans Haacke, puts it plainly: "It is no longer possible to oppose or contest the logic of the image-world of late capitalism by reinventing an older logic of the referent (or realism). Instead, at least for the moment, the strategy which imposes itself can best be characterized as *homeopathic:* ever greater does of the poison—to choose and affirm the logic of the simulacrum to the point at which the very nature of that logic is itself dialectically transformed."

That is, by pastiching and displacing the institutionalized simulacra, the artist reveals the ideology *within* the simulacra. This is certainly what many of the "language poets" have been attempting, and Jameson has cited them ap-

provingly. Haacke, though, is doing more than defamiliarizing/revealing ideology; he is destabilizing it by interrogating it, cunningly, aggressively, and with a variable technique. Compare Christo with Haacke: Christo defamiliarizes the Icon; Haacke expropriates the expropriators.

A related critical question, which brings us back to Wideman's rich novel, has to do with the application of Jameson's paradigm. "Homeopathy"/destabilization works for Haacke, as it does for other Caucasian "first" world artists, but what about Rigoberta Menchú writing as a Quiché Indian, or the Nicaraguan Claribel Alegría, or the South African Bessie Head, or the "third" world artists constrained to live and work in a "first" world context? Is it in disputable that *their* socialist realism or expressionist realism can no longer "oppose or contest the logic of the image-world of late capitalism"?

Depending on who you are, the tale you have to tell, and your prospective audience, versions of modernism are not only appropriate but compelling. In this connection, I like the visual art critic Hal Foster's recent formulation: Certain "proponents of postmodernism . . . would displace modernism" not by deconstruction but by foreclosure. What is actually needed is "an opening of its supposed closure." It could be that when the fog lifts, postmodernism will turn out to be "less a break with modernism than an advance in a dialectic in which modernism is reformed."

In *The Lynchers,* Wideman's impressive 1973 novel, four poor black men devise a plot to kidnap and lynch a white policeman as a symbolical payback for their long oppression. In *Reuben* the rage against oppression is undiminished, but here Wideman has deliberately decentered it. Reuben's rickety trailer is the apparent locus of the drama, but Reuben is a shifting figure. Elderly, dwarf-like, a kind of jailhouse lawyer who counsels and intercedes for the bedeviled black locals with The Man downtown, Reuben resembles alternately a generic shaman, Thoth's totemic baboon, even (as one reviewer put it) Ho Chi Minh.

Recipient himself of violent racial attacks, as well as confessor to flagrantly oppressed blacks, Reuben blunts his own rage by invoking "history" as the righter of wrongs. Not history as a self-serving series of power-brokered fictions, but the familiar historicist version of an unmediated sequence orchestrated by a species of *élan vital:* "One age, one set of assumptions, wears itself out, but there is simultaneously a concentration of vital force, incandescence, a final focused energy . . . a final life-sustaining flash of spirit." Does Reuben really believe this? Or is it a convenient fantasy employed to keep sane, lest the rage "fuck with your insides . . . choke you to death." The final scene of the novel has Reuben fetching the imprisoned prostitute

Kwansa's son, Cudjoe, thereby aligning the perhaps pan-African future (suggested in the names Kwansa and Cudjoe) with grievous memory. A tender image, conciliatory, but it doesn't really vibrate.

The *rage* vibrates. Called here "abstract hate," it is Wally, the college basketball recruiter and Reuben's adversary/*Doppelgänger* who articulates two images of it. The first, a fantasy, has Wally swinging a bat at bourgeois, balding, white male heads staked on posts stretching "as far as he could see." The other, obsessively repeated, is the murder of an anonymous, prosperous white male in a Chicago public men's room—the victim knocked senseless, then drowned in an antiseptic toilet bowl. Did Wally commit this murder? Was it committed by an embittered black man with American Indian features whom Wally claims to have encountered on a plane? Is it one of Reuben's dream-voyages?

We don't know; it isn't important. The murder happened even if it didn't happen, since nothing short of insurrection could purge Wally's and Kwansa's and Toodles's and Mr. Tucker's and, yes, Reuben's, violent rage. Wideman's method here is precisely to interface consciousnesses, fantasies, facts. It is of course Reuben whose infected consciousness permeates the text, Reuben lugging "abstract hate" on one misshapen shoulder and history-as-anodyne on the other misshapen shoulder: the burden compounded even as it is "equalized."

This tension with Reuben fuels the novel, but it is a deliberately dispersed tension. The text is anti-illusionist, full of discontinuities: images, snatches of dialogue slipping in and out of seams (semes), language shifting from conceptual to expertly cadenced dialect in the frame of a sentence, Wideman-as-author intervening in the course of a characterization.

The setting is Wideman's familiar Homewood, Pennsylvania, which some critics have compared to Yoknapatawpha or Winesburg, and Wideman lays on some virtuosic Faulkner-riffs just to remind us. But here Homewood is incidental, even as the contours of the text are atomized; Wideman has systematically "alienated" us from the dramatic illusion to the unpurged rage and to Reuben's brave, doomed attempts to integrate it into a semblance of humane living.

Wideman's method, then, is a kind of decentered expressionist realism, an interesting marriage of Faulkner, Ellison, García Márquez, and the deconstructive notions of trace, rupture, indeterminateness. The trace or palimpsest that underinscribes virtually every page of ***Reuben*** is rage: frustrated, denied, displaced, but pulsing like a collective heart/blues/time-bomb in fundamental opposition to the technocratic inheritors of the slave trade.

Matthew Wilson (essay date March 1990)

SOURCE: "The Circles of History in John Edgar Wideman's *The Homewood Trilogy*," in *CLA Journal,* Vol. XXXIII, No. 3, March, 1990, pp. 239-59.

[*Wilson is an American educator and critic. In the following essay, he examines how Wideman combines both elements of the history of an individual family and of American society as a whole in* The Homewood Trilogy.]

Haydn White, in his essay, "The Burden of History," has argued that much of the imaginative literature of this century has been not only consciously a historical but also actively anti-historical. History, for many writers, has implied the burden of both form and point-of-view: the form of "outmoded institutions, ideas, and values," and a *"way of looking at the world,"* the oppression of historically conditioned vision. This is why, he asserts, "so much of modern fiction turns upon the attempt to liberate Western man from the tyranny of the historical consciousness. It tells us that it is only by disenthralling human intelligence from the sense of history that men will be able to confront creatively the problems of the present." Without disputing White's conclusions, I would like to argue that there are contemporary novels which exploit the opposite impulse and attempt to saturate one in the historical consciousness. Novelists as different as Philip Roth in his Zuckerman novels, Mary Lee Settle in *The Beulah Quintet,* and John Edgar Wideman in ***The Homewood Trilogy*** share this impulse. This is not to say, however, that these works have the same historical horizons; it is only to observe that these novel sequences insist, albeit in diverse imaginative ways, on the necessity of being enthralled by and in history.

John Edgar Wideman in ***The Homewood Trilogy***—***Damballah*** (1981), ***Hiding Place*** (1981), and ***Sent for you Yesterday*** (1985)—has written a novel sequence which takes as its ostensible subject one black family from the early days of slavery through 1970. In one sense, the trilogy is a traditional family chronicle because this family is not only meant to be representative of the larger Afro-American community, but also because, Wideman insists, *through* family one connects to community. Wideman has said [in an interview with Linda Putman in *Rocky Mountain Magazine,* April, 1982] that "[f]amily is the metaphor that describes the whole community of Homewood. . . .It goes back to traditional African notions of family and community. A man who doesn't reside with other men is like a butterfly without wings." In ***The Homewood Trilogy,*** the way one connects to community and thus to history is through storytelling. It is through the telling and the preserving of family history that people both create and maintain their place in the grand narrative of history. As Paul Ricoeur claims [in "The Narrative Function," *Hermeneu-*

tics and the Human Species, edited and translated by John B. Thompson, 1981], "historically comes to language only so far as we tell stories or tell history."

In another sense, however, the trilogy is not a traditional family chronicle because the narrative sequence creates juxtapositions over time, which makes for a nonlinear sense of history in the novels. Wideman advises the reader in the Preface to the trilogy: "Do not look for straightforward, linear steps from book to book. Think rather of circles within circles within circles, a stone dropped into a still pool, ripples and wave motion." This sense of circularity exists *within* books as well as between them, and history intervenes in the characters' lives in a complicated motion. If this metaphor of circularity implies some unchanging core in Afro-American experience, the characters also experience a sense of decay and decline, one which is counterbalanced by the experience of the narrator, John/Doot, and the books he is writing.

One way of beginning to examine the intersections of the narratives of family history with the larger narrative of American history is to look at the story which opens the trilogy, **"Damballah."** Before the title page of the first novel, however, Wideman glosses the word, **"Damballah,"** by quoting Maya Deren's *Divine Horsemen: The Voodoo Gods of Haiti.* Damballah is "the ancient, the venerable father" who is remote and detached, and "this very detachment . . . comforts, and . . . is evidence . . . of some original primal vigor that has somehow remained inaccessible to whatever history, whatever immediacy might diminish it." Beneath history, and unaffected by it, there is this mythic, patriarchal presence, which belongs "to another period of history," an ur-history. And to invoke Damballah or his cohorts is to have, Deren writes, "a sense of historical extension, of the ancient origins of the race. To invoke them today is to stretch one's hand back to that time and to gather up all history into a solid, contemporary ground beneath one's feet." Furthermore, in the Fon religion (from which aspects of voodoo were derived) Dambada Hwedo is a personification of forgotten ancestors, "those who lived so long ago that their names are no longer known by their descendants." To invoke Damballah, as Wideman does with his title, is to attempt to connect with those forgotten ancestors and to put that ur-history in touch with contemporary history and for both to become a "solid, contemporary ground." This effort at grounding and connecting is what the sequence is about; in George Lukács' terms [in *The Historical Novel,* translated by Hannah and Stanley Mitchell, 1983], Wideman is "bringing . . . the past to life as the prehistory of the present." The novels demonstrate how "the people experience history directly. History is their own upsurge and decline, the chain of their joys and sorrows."

Although the trilogy begins in America, its prehistory is Africa. One of the two main characters of the title story, **"Damballah,"** is a first-generation slave who has not been broken and who refuses to give up tribal ways and memories. The story opens with this slave, Orion, standing in a river, remembering Africa, and being watched by a young boy. It is crucial to the design of the trilogy that it begins with this act of stubborn, subversive memory; Orion refuses to accede to the image of himself that white people want to impose on him. In refusing to relinquish the knowledge of Africa, Orion is also in touch with the deeper kinds of prophetic knowledge Damballah represents. He knows that he is going to be killed and he also knows that the "boy was there again hiding behind the trees. He could be the one. This boy born so far from home. This boy who knew nothing but what the whites told him. This boy could learn the story and tell it again." This story enacts the importance of a theme embedded in the trilogy, that of the necessity of resistance through a kind of counter vision, one that inheres in "the story." As Wideman writes in his Preface, the trilogy is "a continuous investigation . . . of a culture, a way of seeing and being seen." The sequences takes place within that tension, between "seeing" and "being seen," where the "seeing" implies witnessing and testifying, the telling of the stories, but where "seeing" also implies a persistent, subterranean knowledge, one that subverts the history and culture imposed by the dominant white world.

The unnamed boy learns this knowledge, and after Orion has been brutally murdered for assaulting an overseer, the boy takes Orion's severed head, and sitting before it, he invokes Damballah and conjures the stories. He "drew the cross and said the word and settled down and listened to Orion tell the stories again. Orion talked and he listened and couldn't stop listening. . . ." One last time the boy goes through the ritual of the stories until he hears "the rhythm of one last word," and then he throws the head away:

> Late afternoon and the river slept dark at its edges like it did in the mornings. The boy threw the head as far as he could and he knew the fish would hear it and swim to it and welcome it. He knew they had been waiting. He knew the ripples would touch him when he entered.

The mysterious gesture of throwing the head in the river recalls another head thrown into a river—that of Orpheus, and in Orion, the black slave, Wideman is conflating African material with Greek mythology. For instance, in discussing the name of slaves, the narrator makes clear that the 'whites bestowed "cumbersome" and "ironic" names like Orion and Sybela, but the slaves "rechristen[ed] one another in a secret, second language." Orion's other Africa name in this secret language is never revealed, but the text itself conceals another name—that of Orpheus. Although

Orion is not torn apart limb from limb, his avatars later in the novel are scattered, undergo a *sparagmos,* a rending and diffusion that is also an insemination. This head thrown into the water is also a literalization of Wideman's metaphor in the Preface of "a stone dropped into a still pool," and this "wave motion," its dispersal and reverberations will "touch" many of the characters in the trilogy.

The ritual of listening is, in Wideman's account in the Preface, the origin of the sequence, and narratively, the imperative transmission of "the story" and the necessity to "tell is again" become organizing principles of the trilogy. Wideman writes in the Preface that his grandmother's funeral gave him the impetus for and the vision of a kind of fiction he had been unable to write previously, a fusion of "the tension of multiple traditions. European and Afro-American, the Academy and the Street." He had come to the conviction that "the imperative [must be] suffered and passed on, that such rituals [of storytelling], such gatherings must survive if we as a people are to survive." The ritual of telling, Wideman discovers, is the framework of the narrative of Afro-American history, and their history repeats, over the generations, several interlinked stories: that of oppression by the white world, violence toward that world and its representatives, and the consequent act of running.

The family at the center of *The Homewood Trilogy* is one which has its origin in the act of running away from slavery, but the implications of this action are dramatized ambivalently. Although the narrator, John/Doot, says that the theme of the story that he originally wanted to write of Sybela Owens (escapee and the family's common ancestor) was to be "simple," "the urge for freedom, the resolve of the runaway to live free or die," his narrative, informed by the stories of his relatives, cannot be so simple and heroic, because Sybela is *compelled* to escape. She is almost abducted into freedom, by a white man, Charles Bell, the father of her two children, "when he learned the old man [Bell's father] intended to include them in a lot of slaves sold to a speculator." The family, from the beginning, is a racial mixture, one that is typical of Homewood. As one minor character thinks early in *Damballah,* "Homewood people every color in the rainbow and they talking about white people and black people like there's a brick wall tween them and nobody don't know how to get over." *The Homewood Trilogy* subsumes within its historical horizon James Baldwin's observation [in *Notes of a Native Son,* 1955] that what "distinguishes Americans from other people is that no other people has ever been so deeply involved in the lives of black men, and vice versa." This involvement is both sexual and antagonistic; the trilogy begins with the interracial marriage of Sybela Owens and Charlie Bell, and from that point of origin, the relations of the black men and women to the white world are unremittingly bleak.

Despite the "rainbow" of their colors, the members of this family clearly identity themselves and are identified by the white world as black, and this involves them in a seemingly inescapable set of imperatives. One of these imperatives, that of running away, the narrator struggles with in the final story of *Damballah,* **"The Beginning of Homewood."** In it, he juxtaposes the running away from slavery of Sybela Owens with that of his brother, Tommy, who has been an accessory to murder. His brother, unlike Sybela, has been captured, and the narrator writes directly to him:

> What was not simple was the crime of this female runaway set against your crime. What was not simple was my need to tell Sybela's story so it connected with yours. One was root and the other branch but I was too close to you and she was too far way and there was the matter of guilt, of responsibility. I couldn't tell either story without implicating myself.

At the end of *Damballah,* the narrator sees the "crime" and flight of their ancestor, Sybela Owens, as a "prehistory of the present," but the connection, he realizes, is a complicated one. He has extended this "portrayal of prehistory into the portrayal of self-experienced history," and he is fully aware of the "social and historical causes" that connect Sybela and Tommy over the generations, one "root," the other "branch." He is also aware of the troubling differences between a slave fleeing slavery and a contemporary Afro-American running from his involvement with the murder of another black. In spite of these differences, he perceives that a system of oppression is still in place, and although it has camouflaged itself in response to new historical conditions, its essential nature has not been altered. And since the narrator is, of course, himself an Afro-American, he must suspect his own privilege and must explore his implication in the events he relates, a development that continues throughout the sequence.

This prehistory resonates throughout the second novel of the sequence, *Hiding Place,* which concentrates on Tommy on the run, hiding out on a hill in a deserted section of Homewood with an aged relative, the sister of his great-grandmother, Mother Bess. The novel provides a context for the murder Tommy as involved in and which constituted one of the stories in *Damballah,* and it provides multiples perspectives on Tommy: his brother's, Mother Bess's, and his own. The narrator, as was clear in **"The Beginning of Homewood,"** perceives that his brother is a "victim in a way too," but his anguish is closer to the surface in the second novel, and he feels that he sometimes "gets close to hating" Tommy because he has never been able to "take responsibility." For Mother Bess, his great-grandmother's sister, who for reasons of her own is avoiding contact with almost everyone, Tommy's crime and his running is simply evidence of the unchanging nature of Afro-American experience. "Life's hard," she says. "Didn't nobody never hold you up and look in your eyes and tell you you got to die one day little boy and they be plenty days you wish it be sooner stead of later?" Tommy, however, is unwilling to accept that privileging of suffering, because he has been hearing that sort of line from old people all his life: "Like I ain't been suffering and waiting myself. Like I got all the time in the world. Like I got to suffer a little more and wait a little longer and . . . what's supposed to happen after I suffer some more and wait some more? Tired of that bullshit." Tommy, unlike the older generations, is unwilling to wait, and the oppression he lives under offers him, he knows, only the metaphoric freedom of the street.

The long debate between Tommy and Mother Bess comes to a kind of climax when she point out that his brother, the narrator, "made something of hisself. Plenty people down there ain't got squat but they ain't stealing and robbing. They ain't outlaws." Tommy's long impassioned response deserves to be quoted in full:

> Tell me bout it. Tell me about Mr. Barclay work all his life and got a raggedy truck and a piece of house and they call him Deacon in the church and when he dies ain't gon have the money for a new suit to be buried in. Tell me about the plenty. Old people burning up in shacks. Kids ain't even ten years old and puffing weed and into anything they can get their hands on. Tell me about those fools marching off to Nam and coming back cripples and junkies and strungout worse than these niggers in the street. And coming back dead. Plenty. Yeah you tell me bout plenty and I'll tell you bout jail and tell you bout old home week because that's where everybody at. It's like high school reunion in there, everybody I grew up with's in there or on the way or just getting back. I got your plenty. Shit. Plenty fools just sitting there letting all the shit fall on their heads ain't got the sense to move. I tried. I could tell you something bout trying. On yeah. Work and raise a family they say. Then they say sorry ain't no work. Then ain't no family. Then they say you ain't shit. You an outlaw. But that's what you supposed to be in the first place. And that's my life.

In his powerful reiteration of the world "plenty," Tommy is delimiting the choices open to many Afro-Americans, a narrow range of social choice which remains fairly constant throughout the trilogy, and he is also articulating a transformative disillusionment over the Vietnam War, a sense of historical rupture, which, compounded by the break in family continuity that he experiences, leads Tommy at first to drugs and then further outside the law. He participates in a robbery which goes wrong and ends in a murder, which leads him to hide out on Bruston Hill, "the place in the stories all my people come from."

Returning to the place of origin, of the family and of the stories, Tommy is not only on the run from the white world of the police. He is also cut off from his family; he has little to do with his mother and is separated from his wife and son. Mother Bess becomes, perforce, his last connection, and both of them, divorced from their family, are like butterflies "without wings," but Mother Bess, living on the family's ancestral hill, values the clarity of her memories and the family's collective stories, ones Tommy explicitly rejects. When Mother Bess claims, "I know who you are. Just exactly who you are," she recites his genealogy as proof, and when Tommy says that he "heard that story before" and he "[d]idn't believe it," she responds, "Well, I ain't just talking. I'm a witness and I couldn't care what you believe." Tommy's response to her witnessing is dismissive: "All that old time stuff don't make me no never mind." The phrase "old time" comes to resonate in the experience of Tommy's uncle, Carl, in the next novel of the trilogy, but in rejecting these "old time" stories, Tommy is close to dehistoricizing himself, refusing to see the complicated ways in which that "old time" has dictated his social choices and has defined the frame within which he lives.

In Tommy's near rejection of stories and history, he comes as close as anyone in these novels to uncoupling himself completely from the community. It is this near dehistoricization which allows him to experience powerfully a sudden temptation to murder his relative: "World could bust her up. His fist could smash her dark shell into a thousand pieces. . . . It would be easy to knock her down. . . . Could take what she wouldn't give. World was that hard." As incarnation of the hardness of the "world," Tommy can see her shell, how she is armored, but what he can only dimly see is the consequence of his murdering her: "Instead of a clang, instead of the brittle armor of an insect, his fist would pass through her. . . . And the force of his blow, the lunge of his body into the punch would pull him into empty space, through her and falling forever." His violence, he realizes, would uncouple him from the genealogy which he says is meaningless to him and would leave him in a free-fall, something that the sequence imagines as an ultimate horror, almost a kind of suicide. Tommy, in his separation from wife and son, is already too close to being a pariah to sever his last connection to his family and to history.

Although Tommy resists the temptation to sever his family and communal connections, he is the only character in the sequence to see himself as a victim of this ever-present oppression, to see himself as one who has no chance to be anything but an outlaw. Somehow, he has lost his connection to the subversive counter-knowledge of Orion and has let his self-image be dictated by the oppressors. In Tommy, a continuity has been broken, and later in the novel, he admits, "I was scared a long time. Ever since my granddaddy John French died and his house fell to pieces and everybody scattered I been scared. Scared of people, scared of myself. Of how I look and how I talk, of the nigger in me." His acknowledgement of his fright and the beginnings of self-acceptance impel him off the hill and out of hiding, because, he believes, there is "no reason to be scared now cause ain't nothing they can take from me now."

Paradoxically, it is this break in continuity, Tommy's difference from the narrator, which covertly impels the trilogy. Although Wideman says in the Preface that his grandmother's funeral in 1973 was "the beginning of these three books," another event in 1975 also set them in imaginative motion: Wideman's brother, Robbie, to whom the trilogy is dedicated, was involved in a murder. And both in *The Homewood Trilogy* and in Wideman's nonfiction book of the same period, *Brothers and Keepers* (1985), the writer attempts to complete a letter to his brother, a letter that would help make sense of this event. As Wideman says in his dedication to the trilogy, "these stories are letters. Long overdue letters . . .," and **"The Beginning of Homewood"** opens with a reference to such a story-letter. But as the final novel of the sequence, *Sent for You Yesterday,* demonstrates, it is not only the difference between the narrator and his brother that fuels the fiction, but a difference that the narrator perceives between Tommy and their grandfather's generation.

This difference, this juxtaposition, is of murders; two generations earlier, a friend of their grandfather's, Albert Wilkes, killed a white policeman. We know about Wilkes from one of the first stories in *Damballah,* and his name reverberates throughout the first two novels, but it is only after recreating Tommy's story that the narrator, in *Sent for You Yesterday,* tells Wilkes' contrasting story. Seven years after running away from Homewood for killing a white man who was out to kill him for sleeping with his wife, Wilkes returns, and although he has run, he has refused to conceive of himself as a victim. He takes up where he left off, going back to the white woman. His friend, John French, grandfather of the narrator, is worried about Wilkes' chances of survival: "Less seven years changed your mind about white pussy and piano playing they gon find you soon enough." Despite French's cautions, Wilkes walks around Homewood undisguised, and he begins to play piano again. And Wilkes' playing is brilliant; French thinks that it is like a "mirror," and late in the novel, Lucy, the common-law wife of Carl, the narrator's uncle, remembers Wilkes' playing:

> Albert Wilkes's song so familiar because everything she's ever heard is in it, all the songs and voices she's ever heard, but everything is new and fresh because his music joined things, blended them so you follow one note and then it splits and shimmers and spills the thou-

sand things it took to make the note whole, the silences within the note, the voices and songs.

Like Stevens' man with the blue guitar, who plays, the listeners say, "A tune beyond us, yet ourselves . . . / Of things exactly as they are," Wilkes' playing accurately reflects while simultaneously transcending things as they are. Like the trilogy, it includes "all the songs and voices," and as a kind of summing up of "everything she's ever heard," it includes, necessarily, the pain and the suffering, made coherent, not denied.

The young Lucy thinks of his playing as "the sweetest song a dead man ever played for his own funeral," because while she and Brother are listening, the police break down the door and kill Wilkes at the piano. Cleaning up afterwards, Lucy discovers something "white and hot looking. A pearl. A baby tooth. A chip of ivory. A piece of seashell." What she discovered was a talisman, a "piece of his head. Albert Wilkes' skull the police blowed a hole in and scattered over the living room." Although Wilkes has been killed physically, something of him has been "scattered"; "his musical heart and soul" have been disseminated. The seed of his playing has been cast abroad, and this dissemination, this *sparagmos,* has its analogue in the murder of Orion early in the trilogy. Lucy, a witness like the unnamed boy in **"Damballah,"** is able to testify to Wilkes' music, and the memory of that music and of Wilkes' attitude toward his "crime" allows her to take the measure of her own generation.

Lucy, at the end of *Sent for You Yesterday,* embodies a sense of historical continuity which Carl, as well as Tommy, lacks, and in her response to Carl's claim that the problems of Homewood are intractable, there is a judgment on him and, implicitly, on their generation: "Maybe you never had a chance. Maybe it's not your fault. But you gave up too easy. Maybe you were supposed to give up easy . . . but the old Homewood people taught me you don't have to give up. I mean John French, your daddy. And Mrs. French and Albert Wilkes . . . ." Historically, Carl's giving up is linked to his experience during and immediately after World War II. No character from the trilogy served in the First World War, but the narrator's grandmother remembers the parade when black soldiers returned from that war: "Everybody proud of them and them strutting to beat the band." That pride is absent from Carl's experience of the Second World War; all he sees is the bitterness of circularity, of repetition. Carl says that he has "seen enough dead bodies to fill two Homewoods. Brown and Yellow and White and Black. All the same. All stink the same. That was a job niggers got a lot. Cleanup. Just like over here." For Carl, military life reproduces civilian life; few blacks have an opportunity to escape the roles dictated to them by the white world except "the ones they allowed to die fighting. They ones they let die so the rest of us be free to bring the shovels and brooms back home."

Carl sees the death of these men of many races as buttressing an oppressive social order, a conclusion which is only reinforced by his postwar experience when he attends school on the GI Bill. A brutal white teacher tells him that he is wasting his time there because no one employs black artists. Carl drops out and he, Lucy, and Brother, a black albino, all turn to dope. Carl says to the narrator, "Your uncle did what the rest of the jive niggers did. Let hisself be pushed down. Started sticking myself with needles." Carl claims that being a junkie "was better than being nothing. World was a hurting trick and being high was being out of the world. . . .You take the freedom train running through your veins." Carl finds the same kind of circumscribed "freedom" in junk that Tommy does a generation later in his need for "freedom . . . to get out of the house and be free." Both characters very quickly discover the limits of that freedom and know that junk is a vicious, almost inescapable circle: "You had to go back out into the world so you could turn it off. Shoot it down. On a merry-go-round. Like a sick puppy on a merry-go-round. Chasing in circles after your own tail." It is almost as if the heroin intensified all of the negative aspects of the circularity of Afro-American experience to an unbearable point; one's return to the world became, each time, more wrenching and the escape from it all the more ecstatic, all the more illusory. And the problem, as Carl sees it, is that one begins to be illusory to one's self: "Coming through the door you'd see yourself going. Coming and going like you got a ghost."

Late in **Sent for You Yesterday,** Carl is back in the world, on methadone, but in the last scene of the sequence, he and Lucy come to terms with the memory of an explicit repudiation of their past, a repudiation made possible by junk, by their nearly becoming ghosts, divorced from themselves and their history. Throughout the sequence, music has been a leitmotif, one running parallel to that of storytelling; music, like the case of Albert Wilkes, is a way of expressing the inexpressible. Whether that music is gospel, blues, or jazz, it is seen as having a transcendent value, a value symbolized by the record player, a large RCA Victrola that John French had scavenged from a white neighborhood. Once the Victrola was in his house, he started to collect blues records, "[s]tacks and stacks down in the bottom of the record player. You talk about blues. John French had it all. Big thick records but the kind that break if you look at them cross-eyed." Later, Carl and Lucy begin to collect records of the Big Bands, and all of these records, Lucy realizes, have disappeared. Simultaneously, both she and Carl remember that the records didn't disappear but were destroyed, and they, caught tight in the circle of junk, participated in that destruction, that repudiation:

All these jive-ass, old timey motherfuckers got to go.

Rodney Jones talking in his dope sleep and digging into the stack of seventy-eights and sailing them to every corner of the Tates' living room. Over prone junkies and sitting junkies and junkies on all fours and the ones who are leaving and the ones flying out the way and the ones who couldn't care less groaning in their dreams as the records smash and scatter. . . .

The room crisscrossed with music, with flying songs like a net. She thinks she can hear them the songs rushing past. . . .She thinks of broken pieces. Of the mess Rodney Jones is making. She knows someone will have to clean it up. Albert Wilkes sat on the wall and Albert Wilkes had a great fall. And she will have to find every piece. Dig them out of the dirt. Every splinter of shattered egg. The white pieces and black pieces. . . .

In this orgy of stoned destruction in the room where Albert Wilkes was killed, two kinds of history are being destroyed: the record collection of John French and all that it represented for him and his family, and also a more generalized past, seen as *"jive"* and *"old timey"* (a phrase which is an echo of Tommy's use of a variation of it to describe Mother Bess' memories), a time which Lucy, in the lassitude of dope, cannot defend.

After remembering this incident, Lucy cries—for only the second time in her life, Carl observes—lamenting the recovered memory, lamenting the destruction. But this personal recalling also becomes a reascription of value to that repudiated music, a participation in a communal memory, and the story of the records and their destruction becomes, through the narrator's prompting, a part of the family's common store of stories. These broken records are linked in Lucy's memory not only to the music of Albert Wilkes but also to the memory of his murder and her discovery of a piece of his skull, and in her stoned vision the "white pieces" of Albert Wilkes' skull are commingled with the "black pieces" of the shattered records. And if this debris is to symbolize the destruction of value and continuity within the Afro-American community, the symbolism is particularly ambivalent. Albert Wilkes was murdered, after all, by the white world, while the records were destroyed by Carl and Lucy and their junkie friends. As Carl says, "Shame about those records. Got destroyed just like a lot of innocent bystanders got destroyed by junk. Shame about Daddy's records and shame on us all."

At the end of the trilogy, these characters—representatives of the generation prior to the narrator, "us middle people," Lucy says—arrive at a judgment on their own pasts, a process encouraged by the narrator, who has prompted them to tell their stories, and significantly, the final story centers on the narrator and his liberation. In encouraging his relatives to tell their stories, the narrator also learns (not so incidentally) about himself when he was a child and about *his* connections to the community. Carl remembers the first time the narrator danced during World War II in front of all his relatives. He was a "cute puppy," Carl claims, and when Lucy tried to get him to dance with her, he insisted on dancing alone. "She got you moving but she had to turn you loose. I cracked up. Everybody did. Hardly big as a minute and out their dancing by yourself." The operative word here is "cute," but by the time this scene is revisioned in the final paragraphs of the novel, it yields much more for the narrator, and for the reader, than it did in its first version, and it becomes a demonstration of how an apparently superficial story can be revisioned and thereby connected to the larger patterns of the trilogy.

One minor but significant detail about this scene is that Brother is a witness to it, and from the beginning of **Sent for You Yesterday,** we know that Brother is important to the narrator: "I'm linked to Brother Tate by stories, by his memories of a dead son, by my memories of a silent, scatsinging albino man who was my uncle's best friend." What this list does not reveal, however, is the place of Brother in the architectonics of the novel; Brother was present when Albert Wilkes was killed, and, later in the novel, it is revealed that Brother informed on Wilkes, turned him in to the police, and the reason he informed was his susceptibility to Wilkes' piano playing. Seven years after Wilkes' death in 1934, Brother has a complicated dream in which he is Wilkes returning to Homewood, but in which he is also himself as an adult and as a child, listening to Wilkes play:

> In his song like a window Brother could see way down the tracks. To when he is dreaming. To the time when he will speak to a son. To the time he wouldn't speak anymore. To the lives he would live and the lives he would be inside. Albert Wilkes' song like a hand over the troubled waters, and then the water was still and he could see everything. Everthing gone and everything coming ont mixed up together but still, and calm. Albert Wilkes' life was hanging on him like a skin to be shed, a skin he couldn't shake off, so it was squeezing, choking off all his other lives. It would kill him forever if he didn't shrug it off. . . .

What Brother experiences when Wilkes is playing shows that he, like the boy in **"Damballah"** and like Wilkes himself, is in touch with the prophetic counterknowledge of Orion. In fact Wilkes, as an avatar of Orion, is explicitly Orpheus-like in his transcendent playing, and, like Orion, he is associated with water (Orion is first seen by the name-

less boy entering the water, and Orion thinks of the "sacred obi" as "the watery door no living hands could push open, the crossroads where the spirits passed between worlds"). For Brother, Albert Wilkes' playing is such a watery door, and like Orion, Brother's "skin was becoming like that inbetween place." But Brother's responsibility for Wilkes' murder is a dramatization of his status as one of the "middle people"; he cannot be as heroic as the nameless boy in **"Damballah,"** nor can he abide the invasion of a countervision, "a sound outside of him which slowly forced its way inside."

Wilkes' death, however, does not prevent Brother from being taken over; seven years later, Brother begins spontaneously playing the piano. Someone "got happy and shouted, *Play, Albert, Play, Albert Wilkes. Albert's home again. . . .* If you shut your eyes . . . you wouldn't remember who was playing. . . . All you'd know is that you'd heard the music before and that was why it sounded so good, so right." As a kind of returned spirit of Albert Wilkes, Brother plays for only five years; he stops both playing and talking after the death of his albino son, Junebug, but the narrator knows that he, in a way, became a substitute for Junebug: "Brother treated me special because he could see Junebug in me." Personally, Brother was a kind of remote paternal presence for the narrator, but in terms of the novel he is writing, he is trying to trace out another line of descent—from Orion to the nameless boy, from Albert Wilkes to Brother to himself.

Tracing out that line of spiritual descent is the reason why he hopes one day to learn that he listened to Brother play. But even if he never heard Brother, the circular nature of experience has brought him into Brother's position. Carl, in talking with the narrator and Lucy, articulates something about the nature of both social and personal experience in the novels: "Circles and circles and circles inside of circles. . . . Doot don't make me feel old. Don't make me feel you neither. . . . Just a circle going round and round so you getting closer while you getting further away and further while you getting closer." And the eccentric notion of those moving circles has brought Doot, the narrator, physically, into the position of Brother. As Carl says in inviting him to dinner, "It be three of us again just like in the old days." Once at the house, in the room where Albert Wilkes was murdered, the narrator sits in the "wingback chair. Brother's chair when he sat still long enough to need a chair." Symbolically replacing Brother, the narrator, in the last paragraph of the sequence, dances again. Lucy remembers that the song he first danced to was "Sent for You Yesterday, and Here You Come Today," and as they listen to the radio,

> Brother Tate appears in the doorway. He's grinning his colorless grin and pointing at the piano and Albert

Wilkes starts unsnapping the duster and aiming his behind for the piano bench. I know how good it's going to sound so I start moving to the music coming from the radio. I know Albert Wilkes will blow me away so I start loosening up, getting ready. I'm on my feet and Lucy says, *Go boy* and Carl says, *Get it on, Doot.* Everybody joining in now. All the voices. I'm reaching for them and letting them go. Lucy waves. I'm on my own feet. Learning to stand, to walk, learning to dance.

His dance, in the imagined presence of his artistic forebears, Brother and Albert Wilkes, is a symbolic enactment of the whole trilogy. In the dance are "[a]ll the voices," voices that Lucy earlier heard in Albert Wilkes' playing, ones that he is both "reaching for . . . and letting . . . go." As Wideman wrote in the Preface, "the narrator . . . affirms truths about himself and his history by learning to dance." In the dance, in the music, in the storytelling, and in the writing the narrator and Wideman perceive historical continuities, familial and communal, in the "chain of . . . joys and sorrows" of twentieth-century Afro-American life. Inevitably, though, music and dance, while equally expressive as narrative, do not take precedence to it, because narrative conserves in a way that they cannot. It is, as Wideman has written recently, "a means of preservation for the community, the ethnic group, as well as the individual artist." The form of the novel insists that in preserving family history through the ritual of storytelling, historicity is being created, and a connection to history, if at times a tenuous one, is being maintained. Moreover, what the narrator is attempting to do, in linking the stories and discerning the patterns, is to work against the atomization of individuals caused by the pressures of contemporary urban Afro-American life. Very clearly, even to the popular imagination, cycles of violence, persecution, and self-destruction repeat themselves. Against those cycles has been brought one of qualified reaffirmation, a stubborn persistence in holding onto family memory and a persistence of the Orion-like individual—whether storyteller, singer, or writer—as conservator of history.

John Edgar Wideman with Charles H. Rowell (interview date Winter 1990)

SOURCE: An interview with John Edgar Wideman, in *Callaloo*, Vol. 13, No. 1, Winter, 1990, pp. 47-61.

[*Rowell is the editor of* Callaloo *and chairman of the department of English language and literature at the University of Virginia. In the following interview, which was conducted on October 17, 1989, Wideman discusses his life, his writing, and the issues and experiences that inform his work.*]

[*Rowell:*] *John, what brought you to writing and publishing creative texts? When you were a student at the University of Pennsylvania, you were captain of the basketball team. Then later you became a Rhodes Scholar at Oxford University. How did you resist becoming a professional basketball player? In other words, what made you take the risk of becoming a creative writer?*

[Wideman:] Well, for me, I guess, it wasn't really a risk. Writing was something I had done as long as I could remember—and I simply wanted to try it seriously, full-time. I was very obviously young and ignorant, and I thought if you wanted to do things and if they were important to you that you could do them. And so I had that kind of optimism and, I guess, in a way arrogance. But story telling and writing have been a part of my life forever, and I have enjoyed them for a long time.

This goes back, Charles, to when I was in grade school in Homewood in Pittsburgh. There was no auditorium in the grade school that I went to, which, by the way, was the same one that my mother attended in the 1920s—the same building, same location, obviously, and probably the same pencils and paper, I think. But this school had no auditorium, and so any time there was an assembly people simply sat on the steps in the center hallway, and I found myself, on more than one occasion, being called out by teachers to talk to the entire school when we had an assembly, when we had a program. Also, during homeroom I would get a chance to get up and tell stories, and that was my thing. I guess I was pretty good at it, because I could hold people's attention. I was fascinated by that. Even as a kid I recognized this as power and attention—the attention that I could get, the sense of control that I could have for a few moments, and just the whole fun of spinning out a story and making something up and, as I was making it up, engaging other people. So storytelling was a very satisfactory, personal kind of experience for me, going way back.

And then there were great storytellers in my family, and family gatherings—picnics and weddings, church socials, funerals, wakes—were occasions for other people to exercise their storytelling abilities and talents. So I had around me a kind of world, a creative world, an imaginative world, which I could draw from and which I very much wanted to participate in.

Let me bring it a little closer to the time we're talking about. By the time I had graduated from college and had gone to graduate school, I was thoroughly interested in the romantic notion of being a writer. What power the writer could have—and now I'm talking about the literate tradition—the sense of the writer as adventurer, the writer as explorer. That part of it was something that appealed to me greatly.

Well, how do you move from the orality of the past—that is to say, story-telling—to the writing of stories? How does one make that transition? What in your studies at the University of Pennsylvania or Oxford University, or in your private reading, helped you to make the transition from the oral to the written?

The written had been there from the beginning. I was very lucky in school. I went to school at a time when there were teachers who encouraged writing. We were required to write, and our writing was corrected, critiqued. So writing was very natural for me. I learned to do it early and, again, I enjoyed it. I also had little stories and poems published at an early age, and this wasn't because I was particularly precocious or had any sort of unusual ability, but because I did it, I worked at it, and I was in a circumstance where people responded and reinforced that kind of activity. In that sense I was quite lucky. The reading part is again something I came to early. I loved to read. I read all the books I could get my hands on. That was a way I spent an awful lot of my time.

I was very active; I played sports. But then there were times when the sports weren't available to me. When I was about 12 years old, we moved from Homewood, which was essentially a black community in Pittsburgh, to another community that was predominantly white, middle class and upper-middle class. That meant that the very lively world of the playground, which was part of my life in Homewood, had really more or less dried up. So I had a lot of time on my hands, and I couldn't always find games. And reading became something I really enjoyed. That literate world was there from adolescence and continued to be there.

Now I think that the kind of experience, the kind of movement into writing that you asked me about, I can identify clearly the moment that it happened. It was after reading, reading, reading lots of books. I guess I was about 16, 17, 18 years old, somewhere in there, the end of high school, early college. I began to feel that this book writing wasn't that complicated, and I had that feeling because a lot of what I read was trash. I mean I read Westerns, I read adolescence fantasy stories, I read the Tarzan and sci-fi stories of Edgar Rice Burroughs, things that were heavy on adventure and unusual characters. I began to see the formulas, I began to see how these things worked, what the parts were. And it was pretty easy for me to think at that time, "Well, hell, I can do that too." So I guess I learned to read between the lines and began to become fascinated with how things were made. And I thought I could do it. From

that point on, I guess I wrote more and more, but certainly not on the scale of a novel. Yet I had just had a feeling that I possessed the requisite abilities to write a book.

What do you describe as your first significant text—that is, the first following your early practice as a beginning writer? Did one of your high school teachers or college professors tell you, "Well, maybe you ought to try to get this published"? Had you been discouraged you might have gone another route. You might been a basketball coach for the Philadelphia Eagles or the Boston Celtics. [Laughter.]

Well, I guess the reinforcement occurred at the beginning. I took writing classes at the University of Pennsylvania, and I had a teacher named Christopher Davis who was very encouraging. Also, visiting creative writing teachers came to Penn. I remember Richard Eberhart. I remember Archibald MacLeish. They, to me, were people from a distant and very dreamlike world, big names—poets with a capital P, writers with a capital W. And they dropped in for their usual kind of seminars and readings. Both of these people looked at some early writing of mine and were quite encouraging. I sat down with them, and they said this is good, and this makes sense; you seem to have a talent, and you're a smart young man. That kind of symbolic pat on the back and recognition, both from the writing teacher and these visiting dignitaries, was quite important. And then my peers, people I would share the writing with . . . that always helped. When you are a young writer, what you're looking for is the same thing everybody is looking for—that is, approval, people to like you. You are looking for some sort of acceptance. You wear this writing as a kind of a badge or a way of introducing yourself or a way of trying to share with people what's important and who you are, and if folks respond positively to that, the writing becomes part of your persona, part of who you are, what you are. And I think that happened pretty early for me.

You entered the literary scene in 1967 with the publication of **A Glance Away,** *your first novel. That was during the height of the Black Arts Movement. One critic (I think it was Addison Gayle) has described the Movement as "a Northern urban phenomenon." You are Northern and urban. In fact, you spent a great deal of your life in Pittsburgh, but you were born in Washington, D.C. Why were you never part of the Black Arts Movement?* **Hurry Home, The Lynchers,** *and your first novel suggest that you did not at all subscribe to the tenets of the Black Arts Movement. Without provoking any people out there in our age group who were the architects and the advocates of the Movement, will you comment on why you and many Southern writers like Albert Murray, or the younger Ernest Gaines, or the even younger Alice Walker, were not really part of the Black Arts Movement? Then, too,* *there were also the non-Southern Black writers like Michael Harper and Jay Wright who were never part of the Black Arts Movement.*

Well, this is an enormously complex issue and also, at some level, pretty simple. For one thing, I was out of the country. I was away in another country, England. That was between 1963 and 1967, and so at a time when I might have become intimately, physically, literally involved with the Movement I couldn't. I read about it in the newspaper; I was a distant sort of witness. That's part of it. The second part of it might be that I've always been sort of a loner, and very suspicious of groups and organizations and movements, and suspicious and not really at ease in that kind of situation. Maybe because of an ego that's too large or maybe because of some healthy skepticism or whatever. I won't try to figure that out. But, personally, my sense was that I didn't—I still don't have—an affinity for groups. If something is important to me, maybe I'll talk about it to one person, or maybe I'll talk about it to no one. I try to resolve things on a personal level, and I realize that there're some problems there, but I'm just trying to get at, maybe, why I was not attracted to the Black Arts Movement.

But there are many more general issues also that need to be touched on when someone asks why a person is part of the Black Arts Movement and why they're not. First of all, Alice Walker and myself . . . Albert Murray is really a generation ahead of us . . . if you look back now and ask what was produced, what came out of the sixties that remains of some significance to Afro-American literature, then I would hope that people would say that we were part of it, the Black Arts Movement. (As long as you don't put capital letters on "black arts movement.") In other words, there were many, many things happening. It was a multifaceted cultural event, this growth, this consciousness that was arising in the sixties, and the artwork that was being produced in the sixties. During the sixties, some of the activity was recognized and anointed—that is, got the publicity, got the attention, and a lot was missed. Just as the writers who are "significant" at this present moment are significant for a lot of reasons, but not necessarily because they're the best writers. So when we look back at the sixties, with the advantage of hindsight, we see a different configuration than we did then. When we're in the middle of something we always see as through a glass darkly. We mistook, during the sixties, a lot of attitudinizing and posturing for the real thing, for the leading edge. We confused dogma with innovation, adopted ideas that really weren't all that significant or that were only of secondary significance. And so, as we've tried with the Harlem Renaissance, we're reevaluating the sixties. That period is 20 years away from us now. We have a different picture of what went on, because we've seen what has lasted. Black Arts theorists—and we must remember there were many points of view—should not be

dismissed. They deserve study and reconsideration. What was actually happening was complex, irreducible as life always is. It comes down to the individual, the individual artist, who for one reason or another has that strange combination of gifts and luck and perseverance that has made his/her work endure. The current events, ideological and aesthetic preoccupations of a given time, of the sixties for instance, are always the surface below which the significant activity occurs. Very few people understand at the time where the real action is.

It's not a simple question of repudiating certain figures and certain attitudes of the sixties. For instance, the notion that black people had to tell their own stories, that black people needed to investigate the language, that black people are on the edge of a kind of precipice and that, as a people, we might very well disappear if we didn't start to, number one, demand equality in the political sense, if we didn't begin to investigate our past, if we didn't begin to se ourselves as part of a world, a Third World—all these ideological and philosophical breakthroughs were crucial to reorienting us, and they still provide a basis for much of the thinking and the writing that is significant today. But it's one thing to make lists and programs and then write stories or paint pictures that very baldly reproduce ideas. It's another thing to struggle and refine a medium to embody ideas in an artistic way that will last. And so those of us who are still writing now, I hope, really are beneficiaries of what was going on at all levels in the sixties. I hope we've carried forward the ideas that are most significant, profound, important. I see continuities, rather than simply a break with or repudiation of the Black Arts Movement of the sixties.

In spite of what you say in this interview, some of your readers who know you will probably say, "But John Wideman was a professor at the University of Pennsylvania. He participated in the instituting of the Black Studies programs in the University during the same period." How do you respond to that? I have been told that you had a great hand in the origination of Black Studies at the University of Pennsylvania.

Sure, I was involved. When I came back to the United States, I was stunned in lots of ways, and swept up in the currents of the time, and needed to reorient myself. I understood very quickly that I was in a unique position. For one thing, I could get a job at an Ivy League university. How many black people were in that position at that time? Given that unique opportunity, I felt the responsibility to try to do something with it.

At that time also I began to sabotage my "classical" education (you can substitute "European" for "classical"). I began to broaden the base of my knowledge and understanding and read black writers, and read Third World writers and became aware of the Caribbean and aware of Africa and aware that there were entirely new ways to look at the history of the West. Reinterpretations of world history and culture provided terms I needed to reinterpret my own individual, personal Afro-American past. And in the midst of all this there were the day-to-day responsibilities of being at a school like the University of Pennsylvania. Of course I felt privileged to have a job there and lucky to be in a position to partake of the bounty, but then again a destructive kind of guilt came along with the goodies. I was a black face in a white sea, so I wanted to help transform the University; I wanted to help try to raise its consciousness as I was raising my own.

To some degree I had success starting Afro-American studies at Penn. I learned that W. E. B. DuBois had attempted the same thing about 60 years earlier, and that was an inspiration. I worked in all areas, from recruitment of black students, graduate and undergraduate, to setting up an Afro-American studies curriculum and recruiting Afro-American faculty. It was a busy time. In fact, it was so busy, demanding, and frustrating that one of the reasons I left Philadelphia and left the University of Pennsylvania was because it became clear to me that there was so much work to be done and I could spend all my time doing, it, and it would be very satisfying and possibly significant, but I also knew that I had a need and desire to write and there just was not time for everything, and so I very consciously made a choice that I would have to withdraw at some point from the front-line work, and try to pursue what I thought might be another way of contributing to the cause with whatever talent I had for writing.

Did any of the activity you engaged in prepare you for, assist you in, your second stage (or could one call it your new stage?) of writing after you moved to Wyoming?

Oh absolutely, there are scenes in novels, scenes in stories, that are drawn directly from that experience. What I was doing on one level, Charles, was reorienting myself to my life up to that moment. Rethinking, reseeing things, becoming conscious, becoming aware how the person I was, partly and maybe in too large a degree, had been molded and structured by the college education I had received. How I had been changed, what price I had paid to become a college professor in an Ivy League institution. I wanted to stand back and measure what all that had meant, what that had cost me, what it meant in terms of this new consciousness of blackness. So therefore I stood back, took the luxury of leaving Penn and going to a totally different place, a quieter place, a place where I could get some perspective. The time at Wyoming was spent going over and over and over my life before and after the University and trying to put those two pieces back together again—the life of the black kid growing up in a predominately black neighborhood in

Pittsburgh, the life of a middle-class academic in a white world. I was trying to make sense of the conflicts, contradictions and possible resolutions.

My next question relates, in part, to the previous one on the Black Arts Movement, but its focus is what I continue to witness as the audience's demand of or prescription for black writers in the United States. How do you respond—or do you respond at all—to readers, especially black readers in the United States, frequently demanding "critical realism" from black writers? That is to say, readers so frequently desire to have the black writer engage, socially and politically, his or her own fiction. How do you respond to such a demand?

I don't respond well to anybody who tells me what to do. Whether it's in sports or dress, and certainly not in something as personal and intimate as literature. I listen and I try to make sense of criticism, but I listen much better when I'm not commanded to do something, when I don't feel pushed and shoved. So the bullyish tone and one-dimensional demands that characterized certain critics during the sixties, if anything, made me more sure that as a writer I was responsible to something other than somebody else's ideas of what I should write and how I should write. Especially since I was working very hard to escape the strictures, to break out of the mould imposed by my "classic," Europeanized education. I didn't want to be J. Alfred Prufrock, I didn't want to be Hemingway anymore, I wanted to strike out on my own. And so I wasn't looking for anybody to give me another set of parameters or another path that I had to follow or another load or burden or harness on my back. It was important that I exercise independence and find my own voice, my own prerogative, at this time.

I'm fascinated by your expression "intimate as literature." Will you talk about that? How is literature "intimate"? I love that phrase, "intimate as literature."

Writing for me is an expressive activity, so it's as intimate as my handwriting, or the way I dance, or the way I play basketball. And when I do those things they're not simply instrumental; that is, when I write I'm not only writing to give a message; when I play basketball I'm not doing it simply to score points or to win. But in all those activities—and I think this is true of Afro-American art in general—there are ways of being who I am, and so I need to find the space to express what I am, who I am. Writing for me is a way of opening up, a way of sharing, a way of making sense of the world, and writing's very appeal is that it gives me a kind of hands-on way of coping with the very difficult business of living a life. What could be more intimate than that, what has more significance than that? Writing is like breathing, it's like singing, it takes the whole body and mind and experience. It's also anarchistic. I like to write because it allows me to do things my way, to say them my way. So what if everybody else's way is different.

I want to go back to a question I asked earlier about critics' and general readers' demands on black writers. The case of Irving Howe on Richard Wright is one we all know about. Ralph Ellison and James Baldwin responded—each in his own way—to Howe. Some years later Albert Murray responded to James Baldwin in The Omni-Americans. *Do you think this dialogue, or this discourse, is unfinished? Is the black writer now free to proceed to write? I admit, of course, the way I raise the question loads the case. You can tell where I come from aesthetically.*

Number one, Charles, I'm having a hard time hearing you, but for me one of the most important functions for writing—Afro-American writing, Eskimo writing, whatever—is identical with one of the most important functions of any art, and that is to be a medium of expression, a free medium of expression, a way that people can say what they want to say, do what they want to do, play in a way that they want to play. Art should be something that in many senses goes against the grain of the culture. That's one of its values, disruptive as well as integrative. It's the place where there's craziness, where there's unpredictability, where there is freedom of expression. Art should always be something that to some degree shocks and changes people and worries people and contradicts what the king says. Achebe makes the point that the writer or the artist is always the enemy of the king. Writing, art, is subversion, it turns the world on its head, it makes up things. That's its power, that's its joy. Play, illusion. Any constraints on that, any kind of rules or any allegiances that are externally imposed, have to be looked at by the artist with a lot of suspicion, a lot of skepticism. And that's the point of view where I come from. Which is not to say that an artist cannot be socially responsible, but I think the issue here is that the notion of social responsibility is really quite a wide one. The policing of that responsibility will be done or should be done by the audience. If you are on an ego trip, if you are too deeply involved in some kind of idiosyncratic masturbatory activity, well, people will eventually peek your whole card and not care about what you do. Or critics will come down on your case, etc., etc., but we can't police the activity before things are done, we can't direct art, we can't tell people what to write about, we can't ask people to follow rules. Rules are the anathema as well as the bones of art.

Am I correct in assuming that what you have just said is part of what one might describe as your theory of art? And I don't mean to make it so tight as to say that you have given a manifesto for art. That is, are these some of the aesthetic imperatives you have set for yourself as a fiction writer?

Right, in a casual way, I guess I have come to a very distinct set of ideas about writing at this point. But I think I have different ideas at different times in my life, and if you look at one of my books it probably contains an implicit theory of art, a theory of composition. As I grow older and look at the world, I see art as a gift to people, certainly a gift to the artist, though sometimes it's also a curse. Art is an area where the human personality gets to fulfill itself in a way that it doesn't in most other activities. This is not to make the artist a cult hero, or a priest, or anything like that, but simply to say that all human beings have the capacity for wonder, for play, for imagination, and that's the capacity, the faculty that modern civilization, mass civilization, is eroding, crushing, and so the artist has a crucial role. I like to think of everybody, of anybody with a healthy life, as an artist to some extent. What my grandmother did, what my aunts do, what my brothers do when they tell stories, is a form of artistic expression, a form of salvation. Life is tough, and we need the ability to dream, to make things, and that ability is epitomized by the artist. It doesn't mean the artist is sanctified, but the artist is someone with whom we can identify, who causes us to remember that there are sides to the human personality—creative, imaginative sides—that allow us to escape, transcend, remake, transform a life that is too often pretty brutal, nasty and short.

You mention that there might be a shift if you looked back on your texts, specifically **Hurry Home** *and* **The Lynchers.** *Do you see a shift between those texts and* **Damballah** *and* **Sent for You Yesterday,** *for example?*

Oh, I hope there are many shifts and changes, because as a writer I want to grow. But I see both continuities and shifts. All my books are about family, family relationships, and reordering and transformation of family. Also I think in all of them, one of the major subjects is writing and imagination. As I grew as a writer, I very consciously decided to change some of what I was trying to do stylistically in the earlier books. What I mean by *stylistically* is how I connected my books to what I assumed was the Great Tradition, the writers who came before. In my first three books, the ways I tried to assert continuity with tradition and my sense of tradition were quite different than my understanding of these matters in ***Damballah, Hiding Place, Sent For You Yesterday.*** It became clearer and clearer to me as I wrote that the tradition in which I wanted to place myself was much richer than I had first imagined. That is, for my first books, the tradition was mainly European, mainly literate. Because I was a black man and had grown up in a black community I sort of divided my books. Blackness provided the local habitation and names; the scenes, people, conversations, were largely drawn from my early experience, because that's what I knew best. But I was trying to hook that world into what I thought was something that would give those situations and people a kind of literary resonance, legitimize that world by infusing echoes of T. S. Eliot, Henry James, Faulkner, English and Continental masters. I was attempting through the use of metaphors, images and allusion, through structural parallels, to connect with what I thought of as the Great Tradition. For me, at the time, that strategy was valid, and I think some of what works in my early books validates that approach. But as I grew and learned more about writing, I found, or rediscovered I guess, that what Bessie Smith did when she sang, what Clyde McFater did, what John Coltrane did, what Ralph Ellison did, what Richard Wright did, what the anonymous slave composer and the people who spoke in the slave narratives did, what they were doing was drawing from a realm of experience, a common human inheritance, that T. S. Eliot, Faulkner, Tolstoi, and Austen were also drawing from. As a writer I didn't need to go by way of European tradition to get to what really counted, the common, shared universal core. I could take a direct route and get back to that essential mother lode of pain, love, grief, wonder, the basic human emotions that are the stuff of literature. I could get back to that mother lode through my very own mother's voice. Some people might argue, and I'd partly agree, that understanding and reading *The Wasteland*, being totally blown away by that poem as a kid, taught me how to get back to my own mother's voice. Nothing's easy, you can't skip stages. My writing is what it is because it did follow a particular circuitous path. I blundered into dead ends, made mistakes, had infatuations at one point or another, models that I imitated without really understanding what I was imitating. But that kind of trial and error and back and forth is what learning to write is all about, and that's how I visualize progress in art, not linear but circular, mysteriously wrapped up in time's mysterious unfolding. Circles. Layers. What seemed complex becomes simple, and what seems simple becomes complex.

There is, in **Damballah,** *a "Letter From Home." Does that title have anything to do with what you've just talked about?*

Well, I think very much so. **"Letter From Home"** is a phrase from Homewood. I first heard my Aunt Geral use it, and she used it in a humorous way to refer to a watermelon. When you examine that little idiomatic phrase, it's enormously complex. It has a kind of immediate, concrete substantiality, but then it goes off in many different directions and works on many levels, and that's not even counting the levels that you can't get into writing very well, the tonal qualities produced by the speaking voice. So much is comprised in that phrase, a sense of history, a sense of play, a metaphorical conceit—you take something written, words, and change them into food, into substance. The phrase depends on in-group knowledge and understanding, it turns on its head a stereotype of black people as water-

melon eaters; it asserts that even though my aunt and most of my family were born and raised in urban North, "home" was understood as the South. Then along comes a writer who picks that phrase up and puts it into a book about storytelling and letters, in a story which points out the importance of trying to connect, needing to connect through writing and any means possible to members of the family. That's just stuff that comes off the top of my head right now as giving the phrase resonance. I learned that phrases from the oral tradition could accomplish the same kinds of work as the metaphors, symbols, and allusions of twentieth-century written poetry.

I was going to ask you a question about the use of one's private life in one's own creative writing. I know that one's private life is often important to contemporary poetry. Is it important to the contemporary fiction writer? More specifically, is your private life, your family history, important to you as a fiction writer? How does the fiction writer transform that private life in his or her texts?

Well, my work itself is the answer to the question because I write out of who I am, and my identity and my writing identity, my life as transposed into the art that I practice, are becoming more and more of a piece. I don't make distinctions, I think that's one satisfying development; I don't make distinctions in a way that I once did. I don't think of myself as writer only when I'm sitting down in the morning at my desk in my study, scratching on a piece of paper. I use my imagination, I use what I do when I write all the time, and I feel that anything that happens to me is fair game. And more and more the subjects of the fiction are this strange interpenetration of the imagined life and the actual life and the inextricability of the two. That's what my career, if such a word is appropriate, is all about. Finding a means to live in a world and finding that art is a crucial tool for negotiating that life. This cuts in a lot of different directions; I write about the most intimate, the most personal events in my life, but the fun or the privilege of the artist is that through transformation, through the use of a medium, like language, everything becomes coded, and the reader no matter how astute or how familiar with the writer or the writer's life, can't really decode the real life from the fictional life. So that although I tell all, I can tell it the way I want to tell it. Which doesn't exactly make the private public, because I am the one who's filtering it, I am the one controlling what goes forth. I may have a problem about something, about sleep for instance, but I can transform it into something else, a story about waking, a problem about being awake, and no one would ever know what I was dealing with. Fiction/facts are what the artist creates. Good writing is always about things that are important to you, things that are scary to you, things that eat you up. But the writing is a way of not allowing those things to destroy you.

Twice in this interview, you used the expression "a sense of play," in reference to the writing of fiction. What do you mean by "a sense of play"? There is "a sense of play" in Albert Murray's South to a Very Old Place *and* Train Whistle Guitar. *There is "a sense of play" in Melvin Tolson's* Harlem Gallery. *What does "a sense of play" mean to you in reference to writing?*

Well, it means mostly freedom. It means freedom and it means an outlet for imagination. Maybe a metaphor, maybe a parallel. When I play basketball, it's important to win and score points, but how I score, the personal expression that I can accomplish while scoring the points or while winning the game are, in a way, just as important. No matter what job I'm attempting to accomplish, I need that playful perspective which lets me know that, okay, it's a job, and I'm trying to do it, but hell, who is going to know about this job in a 100 years, and if I get my nose too close too the grindstone doing the job then what's the point of it? It's all pretty arbitrary. Job or not job. I mean from someone's else's point of view it may not even be a job, so don't get totally absorbed, don't get totally task-oriented, don't become the task in a sense that it buries your personality, buries your individuality; let something shine forth, let something come through. That side, that playful side, the side, that says yes, I'm doing this but I'm also a little boy, maybe I'd rather be someplace else and yes I have to cross the *t's* and dot the *i's* but maybe every now and again I'll dot a *t* and cross an *i* and when I talk to you in the writing I want to remind you that this is not some sort of sacred act, it's also a silly act; if it's sacred, it's also very profane. I'm doing something for you, I'm also trying to take something away from you. Multiple consciousness and energy, the fluid situation of freedom that multiple consciousness creates, that's what I mean by play.

You've commented on your use of private history in the writing of **Fever** *(1989), a collection of stories. In the title story of that collection and in your forthcoming novel* [**Philadelphia Fire**] *(1990) on the Philadelphia Fire, you introduce us to "public history" as one of your sources. What does this mean for you as a writer? Is this another shift or stage in your writing career?*

It's not exactly new because I took a lynching and made a story about that. And it wasn't based on a specific lynching, but at the beginning of the book there is a litany of actual lynchings and atrocities committed against black people. But there is a difference. I think that certain public events occur and they have lots of significance, they are very important, they define powerful currents, they are events we shouldn't ignore, that we shouldn't forget, that we should try to make sense of. But at the same time because of the speed of the media and because of the activity that goes around us all the time, the accelerated push

of contemporary life, we miss these events. Then there is also the very conscious censorship and infantilization and lying and distortion the media perpetrates. And there's the political reality of the social environment that we live in, where an individual life counts for less and less. We are being pushed into a communal anthill, living willy-nilly whether we like it or not. Blackness is being attacked not simply in the old ways because of difference, difference *vis-à-vis* whiteness, but just because it's different. There's no time for somebody who asks too many questions. No time for people who want to bring up the past, and reconsider the past. There's no time for people whose lives present a different agenda than the agenda that is central— the majority agenda. And so I'm looking at this kind of situation and I see things happening and I see them getting buried. Fever was based on an actual occurrence of yellow fever in Philadelphia, Pennsylvania in the 1790s. Like Antonin Artaud, I think that societies, in some metaphysical sense, create the diseases they need and that those diseases are metaphors for the basic problems of those societies. It's no coincidence that the yellow fever epidemic, described by many at the time as the end of the world, was allegedly brought to the Americas by slaves from the West Indies. We need to stop the wheel and look at things again, try to understand what they mean.

The events in Philadelphia in 1985, the MOVE massacre, really began in 1978 when a bunch of MOVE people were arrested and put in jail forever for allegedly killing a policeman. The concerted, ruthless campaign of a city government—ironically, a city government under the control of a black mayor—to destroy difference is one of the most important public events that I've observed. It was particularly important because it was buried. A whole city is afflicted by amnesia. In the press it got a little play for awhile, but then it was forgotten. And I think that, maybe in the same sense that you can see the universe in a blade of grass, if we look at certain events long enough and hard enough through the lens of fiction, maybe we can learn more of what we need to know. If we don't try, if we don't fight for the little light there is, then we're going to suffer. In **"Fever"** and the stories that go with it, and in *Philadelphia Fire,* I'm trying to make myself stop, look, listen, and think about what's happening to us.

You have referred to **Damballah** *as a novel. I've always thought of it as a coherent collection of interrelated short stories.* **Fever,** *of course, is a collection of short stories in the traditional sense of a collection. Is that correct?*

I sort of thought that too, Charles, but I'm not so sure now. Because a lot of the stories were reworked and reorganized for the volume, and over half were new. And it doesn't have the kind of organic unity that **Damballah** had. But I'd like to think that the stories have unity in this sense. There's something really rotten in the state of Denmark. Something's really screwed. And the stories are ways of coping with the malaise which is in the air. **"Fever,"** which is the final story in the book, attempts to render that essence, that unnameable uneasiness, that quality of decay or threat or collective anguish that permeates many of the other stories. Many of the other stories are about trouble, either people who are in trouble or who've fallen, and people who are working very hard to keep themselves from falling. And so the idea of the book, of the collection, is that this fever is amongst us still. This fever is something that we are subject to. Its ravages are still among us. So watch out folks. The final story in the book attempts to bridge, to synthesize past, present, and future sources of this fever, which to me clearly is the unresolved question of slavery, the unresolved question of racism, the unresolved question of majority rule that leads to majority domination and oppression.

You are not only a fiction writer and an essayist. You are also an excellent literary critic. Do you see the literary critic or literary theorist as having specific functions or roles? If so, is that reflected in your own writing of criticism?

I still think in the old-fashioned sense that the best criticism is a kind of handmaiden to the arts. Good critics through precept and example remind people that writing is fun, that writing is enjoyable, that writing has a serious side, a constructive side, that if you put work into it, it rewards that work. I think of critics also as a sort of conscience, as well as tour guides. Criticism can be a creative activity in which the critic dreams, the critic plays, the critic experiences a work of art and comes back changed or thoughtful or angry. Those emotions are a kind of evidence or witness to the power of fiction. And I think the best criticism makes us remember what it's like to have a powerful experience with this made-up stuff, this imaginary stuff. And so there's an organic relationship between good writing and good criticism. Too often that meeting doesn't occur. So we keep trying. We should keep trying.

I shall never forget seeing a photograph of you in an issue of Sports Illustrated, *where you were standing before a chalkboard. On that board, you had written statements about Albert Murray. You've also written literary criticism about his work. You've also written about Zora Neale Hurston, about Charles Chestnutt, and about Gayle Jones. These writers are Southerners. Do you find something in them, artistically, in a positive way, that you don't find in other African-American writers? I'm thinking now about your interest in voice, in an article you wrote for the* American Poetry Review. *Voice, of course, is of primary importance in the elegant writing in* **Damballah,** *and in the texts which follow it.*

I think there is such a thing as a core to Afro-American culture. There is a core culture. And part of it can be identified. And you can have fun talking about what you think the core is, but there is definitely one there. We'll never be able to define it once and for all, because then we'll probably start slipping into ideology rather than description. But there is a core and it has to do with the South. It has to do with the locus of that "letter from home" phrase you mentioned before. There was an understanding in me of Southern culture although I never ventured further south than Ohio until I was about 20 years old. As a kid I didn't know I was a carrier of Southern culture in Pittsburgh. My parents were not born in the South. You would have to go all the way back to my grandfathers, both of whom were born in the South. But indirect exposure to that core culture generated by the African background is enough to stamp us. It's what we all share. Knowing the deep structures of African-American culture can tell you more about people than knowing the part of the country that they come from.

Your work obviously indicates that you have studied different literary traditions. In fact, you talked about those traditions earlier in this interview. In terms of what you have set for yourself as a writer, as an artist, how do you view yourself in relation to other American writers, specifically African-American and European-American writers?

I like the idea of a writing community. And I'd like to feel myself a part of one. I'd like to feel that we are all in the same ballgame. I like that sense of respect, mutual respect, that you get when you go to the playground. When you go to the playground to play basketball there are no referees. And the game can't be played unless there is a certain degree of mutual respect and understanding about the rules. And I think it would be wonderful if we had that kind of community and that kind of mutual respect and understanding in this country, rather than cutthroat, commercialized competition and competitiveness. If the rewards were more evenly distributed, if we weren't all fighting the blockbuster syndrome, in which a piece of writing either goes to the top or gets no attention at all. If we had more good bookstores. If the literary establishment had a wider sense of what's valuable. If there weren't so many goddamned unexamined assumptions about what's good. If we taught writing and language more rationally, more humanely in schools, maybe this ideal sense of a literary heritage and a literary community would be a reality. Of course it isn't, and I guess I'm simply describing what it might be at its best and what I'd like to relate to and feel myself part of.

Obviously European-American musicians have learned a whole lot from African-American music. You can say that they've been to school in African-American musical traditions. Do you find anything in African-American lit-

*erary tradition that European-American writers can ben-
efit from? Have you seen evidence of their using the tradition? If I wanted to load the case, I would say that,
obviously, Mark Twain learned something from the slave
narrative. It is obvious too that Tennessee Williams and
William Faulkner were aware of the poetic beauty of African-American speech. Faulkner apparently knew the
African-American folk-sermon.*

I think your examples are well-chosen. You can't really
separate the strands out very easily. And what's incumbent
upon critics and writers and all of us is to understand the
interpenetration that's always existed from the very beginning. The tension that existed between the literate and oral
traditions is epitomized always in the black tradition. And
all writers learned from that. It is no coincidence that some
of the earliest appearances of Afro-American dialect or
vernacular occurred in eighteenth-century American drama,
that from the very beginning our fellow Americans, Euro-
pean-Americans, were listening to what we said and how
we said it, and it entered into their artistic creations at the
very moment those artistic creations began. And that's just
a kind of a simplified identifiable influence. You begin
there and it just proliferates. You can't scratch very deeply
below the surface before you discover evidence of cross-
cultural borrowing, revision, etc. All American art has these
kinds of multicultural strands, these layered influences that
you can identify and point to, and then if you want to go
further than that, the unconscious life of the arts which of
course is very important, the unconscious life any American has as part of its armature, as part of its furniture, the
sense of a captive population, of oppression, of invisible
people and people who were forced into a certain caste. The
American imagination, in its subconscious and unconscious,
is permeated by the facts of our history, the facts of our
lives. So you can't talk about Americans and not talk about
Afro-Americans.

We—the Callaloo *staff and I—are about to sponsor a symposium (November 8-11, 1989) which I'm calling "Economic Censorship and Canon Formation." In that title
I'm referring to poverty and, hence, black Americans' lack
of autonomy. Will you talk about the implications of this
problem for black writers in the United States, and about
how economic censorship has played a major role in canon
formation in and outside African-American literature?*

You will have a lot to talk about in your seminar. And the
problem breaks down into many, many different aspects.
For instance, in my experience, as a kid, the people around
me, the black people, were of crucial importance to my life.
These were my folks, these were the people from whom
I'd learned to walk, talk, dance, and love, and that was my
world. So of course these people weren't marginal in any
sense of the word. Nor were they a minority, because they

were mostly the majority of people I saw. But from somebody else's point of view they were marginal, and we were
a minority. And as I grew up that message was passed along
to me: that my people were marginal and that I was a minority, and that we really didn't count for much. Part of the
reason why that message penetrated my consciousness was
because of economic conditions. It was clear that we didn't
have power, we didn't have big houses, we didn't have fancy
cars, and those that did were sort of criminal people, sort
of outlaws, so this economic marginality reinforced my
sense of the fact that we were outside the mainstream, and
for the longest time to me that meant that maybe my life
was not that important. And that maybe if you wanted to
write about something important, surely you wouldn't pick
these people off here in this little quadrant, in this little
camp over here. You want to write about the big life, Europe, Sartre and all that shit. So at the very beginning there's
an invidious effect, a drastic loss of self-worth caused by
economic marginalization and class consciousness and all
that. That's one answer.

And maybe at the other end is the materialism of this particular American experiment in civilization. It's a society
in which, black or white, what you possess, what you can
show, what you can pile up, is an index to how important
you are and how successful you are, and that materialism
pervades every institution and every value, and it's a hell
of a rock to get past, it's a hell of a hard nut to crack. It's
almost impossible for a writer, and getting more and more
difficult for any artist, to have a decent career in this country. And by decent career I mean not making a mint, but being able to support yourself with writing of quality. Once
that impossibility happens—and it has happened, it's true
today—then art begins to occupy less and less of a significant place in the society. And for the minority writer, the
effects of that kind of economic exclusion are exacerbated
because if only a few are going to be chosen, you know
damn well we are going to be a very few of those few, if
any. And if the literary society or the literary culture is going to be made up of people who are featured in *Time* magazine and featured in *USA Today* and who are profiled in
People and stuff like that, then the chances for us to penetrate these upper levels are very, very small indeed. You
get the sense among younger writers that if they don't get
up to that level then they've failed, that their ticket to the
lottery didn't come up. What's lost is the notion that art
has something to do with honesty. It has something to do
with self-expression, self-respect and inner satisfaction, it
has something to do with fighting for a voice and achieving that voice and sharing it with a group of readers who
care about what you do. Those values get lost in the shuffle.

Jacqueline Berben (essay date April-June 1991)

SOURCE: "Promised Land and Wasteland in John Edgar Wideman's Recent Fiction," in *Revue Francaise D'Etudes*, Vol. XVI, No. 48-49, April-June, 1991, pp. 259-70.

[*Berben is writer and educator at the Université de Nice. In the following essay, she uses examples from Toni Morrison's novel,* Sula, *to illustrate her explication of the significance of land in Wideman's fiction.*]

In America, an ex-colony recolonized from within, as everyone knows, the abundance of land itself gave birth to the doctrine of Manifest Destiny and its corollary myth that wealth and power were available virtually for the taking. Within tacit limits. The black slaves and their descendants, many of whom still constitute an underclass blocked in a subservient position, are seldom included among those who control the land factor. Initially, the African relationship with the land of their ancestors had not been one of individual ownership, nor commercial exploitation in the white sense. Land was part and parcel of religion and ritual rather than being an alienable commodity. Hence the logic behind the popular argument that the differences in fundamental values that Glazer and Moynihan, among others, blame for preventing black Americans from melting in and adapting to the mold of mainstream society, springs from blacks' having been virtually cut off from the frontier experience of land conquest that Frederick Jackson Turner posited as the cornerstone to his theory of the origins of the national character.

At first glance, then, studying the relationship between Afro-Americans and Land seems futile. Nonetheless, from the dawn of the Reconstruction period, descendants of African slaves were quick to acclimate themselves to the Euro-American desire to own land. This land necessarily had to be purchased from whites at first. Why these whites sold to blacks is open to conjecture. George McDaniel in *Hearth and Home* suggests paternalism, the need for handy labor, estate settlement, or even control of who acceded to proprietorship. In any of these circumstances, whatever land was available to blacks must be assimilated to the other minimal goods that the satiated white man was ready to pass on to the hungry black man, as the lament goes in the slap-talk song, "Pattin' Jibba."

A salient example of land as scraps from the white man's table, devalued property suitable for black use, is the "Bottom land" at the top of a hill that Toni Morrison evokes in the opening pages of her novel *Sula,* land that constitutes another white castoff conceded to placate a persistent slave who had been promised better. Although the "Bottom" merits the reader's attention just when it is passing back into white hands, as the black neighborhood that had sprung up on that site is being razed to become the Medallion City Golf Course, the point is that there had been a neighbor-

hood there, a black quarter on black-owned soil in which black pride had been vested. This was the "frontier" pride of creating something from nothing, carving a city from the wilderness, that pride which confers a sense of community identity. Thus, in the forging of Afro-American identity, land, albeit "second-hand", was and continues to be a vital element. Without land, and indispensable American rite of passage—reenacting and reinterpreting the classic founding myth of pioneer settlement and expansion—is denied to part of the citizenship, further raising the barriers between the excluded and mainstream society.

Land, then, lies at the heart of Morrison's universe; it provides the substance into which her characters sink their roots. At the same time, she clings to the tradition of white exploitation of blacks in the nature of the tract given over to black ownership. She orchestrates the double irony of the "nigger joke"—bottom land at the top of a hill, saying the direct opposite of what is meant—to strike several chords at once. These chords range from the emblematic relationship of continuing white exploitation to the Mother Wit humor in the black man's bittersweet reversal of the initial situation, the Fates having turned the Bottom land into a desirable commodity which inevitably returns to its original owners. As overture to the novel, the "Bottom" section might be construed as either an elaborate mise-en-scène or a digression. Morrison implies its functions to be that of a backdrop to black people's being "mightily preoccupied with earthly things", not interracial strife, but day-to-day living together on this site, surviving thanks to an unseen maternal hand that may be an extension of the land itself as her characters live out their lives, "tucked up there in the Bottom" like children snug in their beds.

I use Toni Morrison's *Sula* to introduce my discussion on John Wideman for three reasons. First, Morrison is a more popular writer on the international circuit and the passage is likely to be more familiar. Second, her positioning the section on "the Bottom" at the beginning of her novel immediately makes the relationship between her fictional land and characters explicit. While similar relationships exist in Wideman's **Homewood Trilogy** and **Reuben,** they form a conspicuous thread woven into the fabric of his opus rather than a frontispiece declaration. Wideman's history of Homewood in **Damballah** and again in scattered passages in **Sent for you Yesterday** sounds many of the same notes as Morrison's saga, but in a more complex manner. In *Sula,* the fact that the Bottom is buried beneath the fair lanes of an institution for the idle rich, henceforth inaccessible to the former owners, distances the action, and puts an effective stop to it. Third, John Wideman's creative psyche, like Toni Morrison's, thrives on the quest for ancestral land.

Significant differences, however, set the two writers apart

in their treatment of the theme. Whereas Morrison waxes nostalgic over the lost neighborhood, Wideman struggles to preserve the fragile contract between the blacks and their land. Wideman's representation of land is memory constantly revived, dreams dreamed anew daily, as in the child Carl's conjuring up of Homewood streets each waking morning (*Sent for You Yesterday*). Homewood is the product of an ongoing act of the will. It is land girded with steel rails and armored with cobblestones in Carl's universe. It is arks in which to weather the deluge, like Cassina Way in Doot's memory, "a narrow, cobbled alley teeming with life. Like a wooden-walled ship in the middle of the city, like the ark on which Noah packed two of everything and prayed to land." It is the heady sense of power and possession born with the new day for Albert Wilkes. And, paradoxically, it is the "promised land" of the Long-John-the-Conqueror boast that Carl repeats to Lucy after their first sexual embrace. Homewood *belongs* to its inhabitants, no matter how impoverished, no matter how transient.

A profound sense of permanent, family proprietorship over the town land from which the narrator's ancestors had been expelled, land that great-great grandmother Sybella Owens put a curse on and that her white husband Charlie Bell verbally posted as off-limits to the whites that had ostracized the racially mixed couple, abides in these passages. In the family saga, this town lot is a dry Red Sea which marks a point both of passage and of retribution. Where the family passed through, all those who would follow are engulfed by the forces of destruction.

The second phase in pioneer land ownership comes with the pride of founding a new community, as other blacks flocked to Bruston Hill where Sybela and Charlie had fled for security. What is more, the land seems to hold the key to life and death. Symbols of fertility swarm about the site as flights of birds and throngs of children simultaneously consecrate their vitality to the land from which their seeds sprang. So intense is the attachment to Bruston Hill land that great-great grandmother Owens dies within a week when her children bring her down from the hill, implying that she lost her powers, natural and supernatural, upon severing contact with the sacred, vivifying land.

The ritual aspect of these last points leads into another failing of the frontier exclusion theory in that it neglects the hypnotic fascination of the familiarity of pattern in the variations. It overlooks the universality of the founding legend in societies newly conscious of their identity. Afro-Americans seem to have undergone a series of molts in their consciousness of who they are, what role they play in American society as a whole, and, both literally and figuratively speaking, what ground is theirs to hold. Only in retrospect do clear answers appear. Perhaps that delayed realization also explains why Wideman waited until the

1980s to adopt a new style of writing, one that let him tap the lyricism of his family heritage without sacrificing realism or fantasy. Not until the Homewood trilogy did Wideman stop to recall and pay tribute to that "second-line" frontier experience and to those ancestors who were the first to settle the Homewood section of Pittsburgh as the "pioneer" generation of his family, the builders, the creators, the progenitors. This land they claimed for their own serves as the touchstone of Freedom, the "Promised Land", nourishing Wideman's private homestead myth. Whereas for Orion, the captured African in *Damballah,* salvation and the miraculous realm of his youth lie beyond the sea, for Sybela Owens, the runaway slave, both are to be found on Bruston Hill, the equivalent of "the Bottom" in Morrison's *Sula,* yet infinitely more.

For Bruston Hill and Homewood land, on the narrative level, afford the author a focal point from which to orchestrate his fictional universe. The analytic perspective provided by the land thus allows us as readers to determine the nature of the various environments in which Wideman's characters revolve, nurturing or hostile, "City of God" or Wasteland. This determination allows those character to come to terms with their circumstances and rise above them or succumb to the malevolent forces. A paragon of the former is the mother figure in the story **"Solitary"**: "Her trips to see her son were not so much a matter of covering a certain distance as they were of learning the hostile nature of the space separating her from him." (*Damballah*) While "space" is not an exact synonym for "land", in the story context, space equals territory that is and is not held and thus controlled. This alien, hostile space can encroach upon the secure zone, contaminate and destroy external and internal paradises like halcyon Westinghouse Park and the mother's cherished faith in her God. The Wasteland is not fixed by topological boundaries, but determined by inner submission to or domination of one's surroundings.

An analogy can be made between the prison space in *Damballah* and Mayview, the insane asylum where Sam is confined in *Sent for You Yesterday.* Lucy makes the pilgrimage to Mayview like the mother to the prison, trying to hold on to someone precious to her. Both helplessly witness the alienation of the person locked away, the son from his filial devotion, Sam "from the edge" of reality. Like the mother, after the expedition, Lucy needs the security of the Tate house, another ark that sheltered many children, to survive spiritually intact.

Wideman also uses land to symbolize those who dwell there-upon. Thus land can expose hidden motivations, travails, and illusions, externalizing true values and false alike. Stylistically, there is a progressive impoverishment of the verbal metaphors that define the complex relationship between the characters and land elements and measure its intensity; this linguistic enervation constitutes a syllogism on the decline of a people that loses its values. Apocalyptic imagery binds land to air, water, and fire elements. In *Damballah,* rich poetry flows with the water Orion scoops to his chest as "river" in what Christine Brooke-Rose would call a zero-degree replacement metaphor for water. As such, "river" is elevated to the status of a class of nature like Man or Beast, accentuating the ritual value of Orion's ablutions. This sacramental water constitutes a doorway to the other world, the sacred obi of the African priests whom Orion in his mind's eye watches, "drawing the watery door no living hands could push open, the crossroads where the spirits passed between worlds." (*Damballah*)

Land and water seem to be interchangeable elements for Wideman, as a few lines later, Orion sees himself as a kind of portal, his skin the skin of the earth, "becoming like that in between place the priest scratched in the dust." The parallel drawn between human skin and the earth's crust foreshadows metaphors to come in Wideman's opus and underscores the mental association. For Orion, the air allies itself with the enemy land, assuming its properties. Verbal metaphors attribute a palpable quality to the air which Orion perceived as *wearing out his skin, rubbing* it thinner and thinner" as he "walked the cane rows and the dirt paths of the plantation." Hence "the air of this strange land" assumes the abrasive property of the soil, eroding away the body of the foreign slave by its contact.

By direct opposition to the antagonistic capacity of the soil Orion trods, *Hiding Place*'s Bruston Hill land has a nurturing function that fulfills the prophecy of the Promised Land. It, too, penetrates the corporal being, but in harmonious fashion with its positive connotations, thereby imbuing the folk with its virtues. A salient example is offered by a replacement copula which serves us notice that Bess in her youth "was silk and honey", like the "milk and honey" of the Bible associated with the land that was to become Israel (*Hiding Place*). Although ironic in Bess' case, fertile abundance was her promise, also. She had surprised even herself with "how much she had *cradled* in the black earth", "flopped down flat on her belly if nobody was watching" in an intimate embrace. The image suggests the symbolism of the Egyptian myth of creation with the female principle, Nut, covering the male earth, Geb. Closer to classic Roman myth, it also recalls a scene from Bernardo Bertolucci's *1900*. With humorously tender overtones of sexual awakening, the scene in which the preadolescent peasant boy, Olmo, literally plants his seed in the earth before the uncomprehending eyes of his more naïve, bourgeois playmate, reifies the nature of the peasant's bond to the soil he tills. A more intimate, living relationship with the land than this copulation defies imagination. Even the inverted themes of death, destruction, and despair associated with the land image is powerfully emotional and inti-

mate, as we see Earth Mother Sam, after June Bug's death, in Lucy's memories of cleaning up after her loved ones, snatching a half-buried toy from the dirt which leaves behind a hole:

> And the hole is a black pit opening at her feet. She wants to bury her face, her weary body in it. The earth rises and spins. She needs to stay on her knees or drop down farther, flatten her belly on the hard-packed belly of the dirt. Let it take her. (*Sent for You Yesterday*)

With Tommy's arrival at Bess' shack, the poetic gives way to the prosaic as he finds himself "scrabbling around in the dirt", denigrated by connotation. For all this "cutting and digging" he does, preparing the ground to "plant a seed or two," the modesty of the enterprise suggests the diminished ambitions and expectations of the young generation, newly weaned from the worship of false idols in the Wasteland of the white man's city. Where Orion commingled with the earth elements and Bess consorted, Tommy vainly scratches at its unfamiliar crust. His realm, until it provide illusory, had been the street. Like a litany to the Virgin, he recites the names of the ghetto streets, conjuring up their memory and commanding them to wait for him. Only upon his return from prison, when he loses his way in the labyrinth coming home from his grandfather's funeral, does he grasp the unwritten lesson that his chosen universe is as mortal as the old man they have just buried:

> Away less than a year and the streets had changed. Streets dying, streets blocked, streets made into One Ways, streets gouged out in the middle, streets where the trolley tracks were being ripped from their cobbled beds. Streets going in circles and streets where no cars were allowed. In jail, he had depended upon a dream of those streets, a dream in which they never changed their shape, the life in them remaining the same till he returned. Kept a picture of the streets in his mind. Tioga Dumferline Susquehanna Homewood Hamilton Frankstown Finance a picture frozen like before a commercial on TV.

Tommy's turf is an ironic complement to Orion's plantation land, which prefigures it. The verbs here raise the streets to animate level and Tommy relates to them like a beloved pet whom its indulgent owner forgives for occasionally biting his hand. Orion perpetuates the myth of a lost land while recognizing the hostility of the one he lives in; Tommy worships the inhospitable ghetto streets and escalates their image to the same mythic value as Orion attributes to his African homeland. In the darkness of his cell, Tommy, a self-ordained priest of the street cult, draws a profane *obi* or sacred door of frozen images in a vain attempt to pass through to utopia beyond, fool's paradise though the scriptor makes us recognize it to be. Focalizing upon and through Tommy, Wideman uses the young man's thoughts to reveal his consciousness of the price exacted from him for his fidelity: "Little bloody pieces of himself." The torn flesh links Tommy to the sacrificed African, Orion. It also furnishes an intertextual reference to Wideman's more recent novel, **Reuben,** by associating Tommy with the deified Egyptian, Osiris, whose legend preoccupies the old dwarf hero, and seems to constitute part of his occult methods in service of justice. Unlike Osiris and Orion, whose bloody sacrifices restore the fertility to the barren land in the tradition of Sir James Frazer's *Golden Bough,* Tommy witnesses the futility of his own gesture. His attempt at symbiosis with the city streets corresponds to the same pattern, but is wasted on unsuitable soil.

Less repulsive than the burned out, garbage-stacked slum neighborhood that nourishes Tommy's belief in a promised land, his other dream of golden, sandy beaches is also an illusory paradise that has nothing to do with the nurturing land of his ancestors and that will ultimately disappoint him. The unstated message seems to be that family homestead land represents real values. Losing contact with that land exposes the black man's roots, which can cause them to wither, depriving him of his powers, and leaving him vulnerable to the forces which oppose him.

A word of caution lest the city be seen in a one-to-one correspondence with the wasteland. Not only is the truth mitigated, but, as in T.S. Eliot's poem, the latter corresponds more to the human condition or a state of mind than to a synonym for desert. In the context of the cityscape, land is more akin to a testing ground. For some, it represents the no-man's land of heroic adventure frought with life-threatening dangers, but rich in hidden treasure for the valiant to carry off. Such was Tommy's evaluation of his world before his flight to Bruston Hill. Jive talk and a "bad" reputation had served as talismans for this street hero whose treasures were fine clothes, fine women, fine cars, and the ability to pay the price. Notice this false paradise quickly disintegrated. Grasping for life, Tommy instinctively heads back to the ancestral land on Bruston Hill, the *axis mundi* where Man's outstretched hand can graze the fingertips of the Divine.

For other Wideman characters, city land is the instrument by which they sift and winnow their fellows, judging who are fit for association and who are not. Effectively, Homewood ground must not be considered mere real estate, that is to say, an ensemble of more and less attractive locations. By virtue of its street boundaries, Homewood includes and excludes. Just as Constance Perin sets out to prove in *Belonging in America: Reading between the Lines,* knowing whom to exclude from the fold is an essential element of community identity. The Bum's Forest,

appropriately located on the other side of the railroad tracks, is a wasteland in the eyes of Lizabeth and Freeda, bound to the lower-middle-class values as they are; to John French, as to Tommy in the ghetto, the Bum's Forest is his kingdom where few dare challenge his sovereignty. In sum, the street or the neighborhood that one normally inhabits or regularly frequents subdivides the existing economic and social categories.

Similarly, proper Sunday behavior in Westinghouse Park erects barriers between the "heathen" and the uprighteous in Lizabeth's girlhood memories in **Damballah.** This temple of nature with its symbol-laden green space, blue skies, bird population, and Sunday reminiscences substitutes for the less accessible *axis* mundi of Bruston Hill when the need to reestablish contact with one's origins and the source of life makes itself felt. Here, as with Bruston Hill, there is a sense of relationship and belonging, of taking poetic and psychological root in the leaves of grass one tugs at.

Movement into and out of Westinghouse Park parallels movement to and fro between Bruston Hill and the town. From the textural viewpoint, the alternation creates a systolic and diastolic rhythm that quickens both the novel **Hiding Place** and the short story **"Solitary."** As homestead and outside world are associated with contrasting value systems, juxtaposing the two develops a non-verbal dialectic. Anxiety before an ambiguous, hostile universe faces off with nostalgia for an innocent, idealized past as the scene shifts from the cityscape to the landscape, from rented quarters where the protagonists are buffeted by the winds of fortune to homestead land where, though poor, they exert some control over the situation and their own fate.

Temporal considerations in regard to land complement topological ones, as Homewood is the constant link between past, present, and future which coexist in Wideman's work. Wherever something grows, a timeless quality infiltrates the site, coupling the impermanent to the eternal cycle of nature. Thus, if no one disturbs Reuben's trailer, illegally parked in a vacant lot overrun by weeds, you might offhandedly conclude, as Kwansa first does, that "it's too old to bother with." Or, on second thought, you could echo Kwansa's further observation that "it look like it's just growing out of the ground like the rest of the weeds over there." Whether merely implied or overtly stated, the trailer belongs to Nature. As part of a higher natural order, the trailer cannot be held subject to temporal, man-made laws. The trailer is second-nature to the lot. It is also a sign which can extend its signified to the one who dons it. A pattern emerges: Bess wears her old shack as if it were a second skin, the magic coat of the Numidian lion; the shack Bess "wears" is part of the family saga and is the symbol of her office as matriarchal figure. Such was the case with

Sybela Owen's omnipresent black cape. Reuben, in turn, "wears" his trailer, an insignia recognizable to all the inhabitants of the ghetto. Shack and trailer ratify the covenant Bess and Reuben have made with the land that provides a measure of refuge from the forces that assail them while they, in exchange, minister to the ghosts and gods of the past. Perhaps more obviously in Bess' case than in Reuben's the contact with the property they have both appropriated to their own needs has also left an invisible imprint on the land, a frightening, magic essence that unsettles Clement and Kwansa on their visits, but does not keep them away. Ironically, these apparent deserts are truly havens for the oppressed.

All in all, Wideman's protagonists might need hostile landscapes to stimulate themselves into making an imaginative effort culminating in reasserting the black man's contact with and hence control over the land. Such is the case with Shore Road, the upscale, rural, picturesque, sea coast path Wally jogs along in **Reuben.** There, he alchemizes each accident of the terrain into a surrealistic landscape: Wally's course is jutted with corpses real and imagined and marked by the trails of prehistoric, fantasy reptiles 200 yards long. The metaphoric skin of Shore Road, which Wally compares to the skin of his grandmother's face, has an intimate history he reads and craves to learn like some family saga, deep with revelations about his own identity and destiny. Seeing the road as a living organ, the skin of the earth, temporarily rehumanizes Wally, who functions in the city like a robot bereft of emotions. Survival for the spiritual descendants of Orion in the strange land depends upon their ability to neutralize its destructive forces by binding themselves directly to its surface. Land thus nourishes the manchild at its breast even as it takes on a spatio-temporal function of "witness" to the people and events behind everyone's stories. In short, it is the literal and the literary, fact and fiction, tract and text.

The examination of these pivotal sites in **Damballah, Hiding Place, Sent for You Yesterday,** and **Reuben** reveals that Wideman transforms such inanimate agents into what Greimas terms "actants" who "interact" with his characters by grace of the symbolic, structural, textural, and thematic functions they have been invested with. As we have seen, Bruston Hill is an *axis mundi* and a cradle of civilization, a fertile, life-giving ancestral homeland whose powers spell survival for the clan and destruction for its enemies. Westinghouse Park offers retreat and retribution. The now burned-out heart of the ghetto that young men like Tommy ruled as their turf provides a concrete image of community disintegration, the fire an ambiguous coup de grace to the intangible Paradise already lost. Lastly, Reuben's vacant lot provides the battleground between the profane forces of the dominant, white society and the supernatural forces of pagan gods known and unknown who rule earth and sky.

From wasteland to promised land and back again, from temple of nature to modern cityscape, land remains a vital factor in the never-ending pursuit of the myriad frontiers that tantalize the multi-ethnic American psyche and in the unbroken bond with the multiple gods that invest earth, wind, fire, and water.

Ashraf H. A. Rushdy (essay date Fall 1991)

SOURCE: "Fraternal Blues: John Edgar Wideman's *Homewood Trilogy,*" in *Contemporary Literature,* Vol. XXXII, No. 3, Fall, 1991, pp. 312-45.

[*Rushdy is an educator and the author of* The Empty Garden: The Subject of Late Milton *(1992). In the following essay, he discusses the significance of the narrator gaining his "blues voice" in the Homewood trilogy.*]

> What can purge my heart
> Of the song
> And the sadness?
> What can purge my heart
> But the song
> Of the sadness?
> What can purge my heart
> Of the sadness
> Of the song?
>
> —Langston Hughes, "Song for Billie Holiday"

In **Brothers and Keepers,** John Edgar Wideman contemplates the difficulty of representing the Other without reducing the representation to just another form of solipsism. One way to do so, he thought, would be for him to attempt self-reflexively to perceive his desire for access to what might potentially be an occult area of intelligence, while at the same time acknowledging the limitations that make for an irreducible ignorance about the Other. He takes his grandfather's favorite saying—"Give 'em the benefit of the doubt"—and makes of it a perceptual scheme for understanding Otherness: "You attempted to remove your ego, acknowledge the limitations of your individual view of things. You consulted as far as you were equipped by temperament and intelligence a broader, more abiding set of relationships and connections. . . .You sought the other, better person in yourself who might talk you into relinquishing for a moment your selfish interest in whatever was at stake" (**Brothers**). Much of Wideman's career since the publication of his first three novels has been an attempt to acknowledge those factors limiting him from a better understanding of a whole Other community, in fact the one in which he grew up—Homewood. He had lost touch with the Other, he felt, because he had lost, as he says, his "Homewood ear." And it is precisely that organ of listening that he needed to regain in order to relinquish his ego: "I had to root my fiction-writing self out of our exchanges [between himself and his brother]. I had to teach myself to listen."

When he did not abide by his grandfather's heterological dictum, Wideman found that his very art became nothing less than a co-opting of the Others in his life: "Wasn't writing about people a way of exploiting them?" In the end, what he finds he has to do in order to understand himself better, his brother at all, and his community more profoundly is to listen to the tale of his brother from his brother: "I had to depend on my brother's instincts, his generosity. I had to listen, to listen." By listening carefully to his brother, Wideman is able to find the Other is himself: "I listen to my brother Robby. He unravels my voice." It is a new experience for Wideman—finding himself in his story *through* his brother's voice: "When I caught on, there I was, my listening, waiting self part of the story, listening, waiting for me."

Wideman has generated from this understanding—of how his brother is related to his life in ways that help him better to delve into his own sense of selfhood—a poetics for his writing career. The same tension that exists in Wideman exists in his fictional characters. The successful individuation of any of Wideman's characters can be measured by that character's ability to discover the multiple filiations of Other's lives in his or her own. And in the Homewood trilogy what marks the successful mediation of the life of the Other and one's own life is the ability of the narrator, John Lawson, to negotiate three pertinent modes of narrating—letters, stories, and the "blues." John Lawson's individuation, marked by his ability to perceive how there are Others in his community on whose knowledge he must depend for a better understanding of his own self, is established when he finds a blues voice, which is granted only after he has learned the art of listening.

As a measure of individuation, the blues, according to Houston Baker, act as both the sign and the meaning in those moments in African-American discourse when "personae, protagonists, autobiographical narrators, or literary critics" negotiate their way through an "economics of slavery" to achieve a "resonant, improvisational, expressive dignity" [*Blues, Ideology, and Afro-American Literature,* 1984]. The blues, then as both medium and message, achieve for the singer what Baker calls a "profoundly dignified blues voice" by articulating conditions of the dismal economic system which they are in a sense, according to Ralph Ellison, attempting to "transcend" in that very articulation. Moreover, the blues are intent on appreciating the ways that previous generations' sufferings are imbricated in this generation's experiences. The blues negotiate the economic system at their basis as a way of demonstrating the self's place in history as well as community.

I hope here to demonstrate the process by which Wideman's narrator in the Homewood trilogy achieves a blues voice by understanding how subjectivity is a construct of what the blues mediate—a "phylogenetic recapitulation . . . of species experience" (Baker)—and the ways in which that subjectivity is a manifold construction of interconnections within the community, the family, and the individual. The most important relationship, however, is that between the brothers, John and Tommy Lawson. Thus we may begin our examination of what I'll be calling Wideman's "fraternal blues" by looking briefly at James Baldwin's short story "Sonny's Blues."

At the end of "Sonny's Blues," Creole hands Sonny the space to change lament into delight, to change the sadness into the song. As Sonny's brother comments,

> Sonny's fingers filled the air with life, his life. But that life contained so many others. And Sonny went all the way back, he really began with the spare, flat statement of the opening phrase of the song. Then he began to make it his. It was very beautiful because it wasn't hurried and it was no longer a lament. I seemed to hear with what burning he had made it his, with what burning we had yet to make it ours, how we could cease lamenting.

Sonny's brother listens to Sonny's blues singing of tradition and the culture's ancestors—"that long line"—and begins to understand how another's life may contain his own: "that life contained so many others." Instead of solipsistically assuming that Sonny's life is tangential to his, or that it simply plays a minor role in his, as he had hitherto done, Sonny's brother (who is unnamed) recognizes how his life is represented in that of the Other. This act of selflessness—of appreciating how another's life may contain his in its unfolding, rather than his prior assumption that the other was merely fulfilling a supplementary role in his life's narration—makes the story not only Sonny's blues, but also Sonny's brother's blues. He too achieves what Baker defines as blues subjectivity: "a filled subject, but an anonymous (nameless) voice issuing from the black (w)hole." Finally, because Sonny's brother relinquishes his ego in order to confront the pain in his brother's life, he finds liberation: "Freedom lurked around us and I understood, at last, that he could help us to be free if we would listen, that he would never be free until we did."

Both Sonny's brother and Wideman himself discover that they have to *listen* to their brothers before they can understand their relationships to themselves and to their communities. Listening is preeminently the act of sympathy in achieving what may be called the "blues mind." For the blues are not only a form of music; they also act as an epistemic structure. The blues perform a function akin to that played by what Mary Douglas calls "culture" and Jerome Bruner "narrative." They, too, as Baker points out, "offer interpretations of the experiencing of experience." Working to form structures allowing experience to be mediated in a way comprehensible to the human mind, like narrative and culture, the blues "comprise a mediational site where familiar antinomies are resolved (or dissolved) in the office of adequate cultural understanding." For the blues artist to become competent in her or his interpretive craft, she or he must undergo what Baker sublimely calls "training"—the process of not just being schooled in, but of becoming a (train) traveler through, black America. For the blues, like all back music, according to James Cone, "must be *lived*" before they can be understood [*The Spirituals and the Blues: An Interpretation,* 1972]. Before turning to Wideman's Homewood trilogy and examining the ways that the narrator undergoes a blues training in order to arrive at a blues mind, we might examine some of the constituent factors of that mindset.

When we speak of the training of the blues artist, according to Ralph Ellison, we do not speak of a conservatory, but rather of "apprenticeship, ordeals, initiation ceremonies, of rebirth" [*Shadow and Act,* 1964]. What the artist achieves, once he or she has confronted the "best of the past" and added to that a "personal vision," is a "self-determined identity." But identity for a blues artist is always in a state of tense evolution—always in a state, according to Langston Hughes, of the "yet to come—and always *yet*" [*The Langston Hughes Reader,* 1958]. Likening jazz to "a montage of a dream deferred," Hughes recognizes the essential problem for the individual who wishes to dream an identity in a land refusing to recognize that identity. Difference, here, is what truly causes deferral.

According to Baker, the "crisis of black identity" in a white society is precipitated by the recognition that in the "perceptual schemes of the white dominant culture," he or she represents nothing, what Carolyn F. Gerald calls a "zero image" ["The Black Writer and His Role," *The Black Aesthetic,* 1971] and what Baker calls a self "under erasure." The rite of passage, following on the heels of this recognition, falls into three distinct stages. First of all, the black person withdraws from white society. The second stage, in which the individual is situated in the liminal "betwixt and between" of any social status system, allows that person to accumulate a store of "ancestral wisdom." Thirdly, the individual is now reintegrated, with a new status, into the society from which she or he fled.

This black rite of passage is to some degree analogous to the Jungian model of individuation. "Real liberation," writes [Carl] Jung, comes not "from glossing over or repressing painful states of feeling, but only from experiencing them to the full" [*The Archetypes and the Collective Unconscious. The Collected Works of C. G. Jung,* 20 vols., 1953-73]. The ability to undergo such an experience requires a personality capable of "relinquishing the ego." The danger involved in this self-effacement is potential madness—wherein the relinquished ego's role is taken over by the unconscious which, because it is comprised of "decentralized congeries of psychic processes," endangers the sense of what Jung calls "individuation." It is, however, only from the collaborative play of ego and unconscious that an "indestructible whole, an "individual" is able to emerge. The decentering of self, then, is a prelude to a possibly more integrated self—possessing the tools to tap into both the anima and the animus, both the conscious and unconscious. That self's sense of integrity requires a conscious appraisal of the past. The person who is "unconscious of the historical context and lets slip [the] link with the past is in constant danger of succumbing to the crazes and delusions engendered by all novelties" [*The Development of Personality. The Collected Works of C. G. Jung*]. Maintaining that link with the past requires an act of "anamnesis"—the construction of an etiological narrative of one's selfhood gathered from the discrete scenes of one's personal life (*Archetypes*). The individual is able to return to society and confront its dizzying technological advances because he or she has achieved wholeness, a sort of Taoist state of complete reconciliation between conscious and unconscious states of being.

Such is what we may call a European model of the liberated mind. In American culture, psychic liberation derives from the more complex model I am calling the "blues mind." This model shares with Jung's the necessity of confronting painful states of being in order to be freed from their residual affects, the ability to relinquish one's ego in order to achieve a degree of individuation, and the necessity of engaging with the past as both cause of and analogy for present situations. This model differs from Jung's, first, in that the liberation from painful experience finds its expression not only in a mental state but also in a musical construct—in Hughes's phrase, transforming sadness into song. Secondly, the relinquishing of one's ego—the decentering of one's self—is not necessarily a prerequisite to achieving a stronger *individual* self, but may lead to a stronger sense of a *collective* self. Thirdly, while the Jungian model proposes a confrontation with a *personal* past, however mediated by collective (archetypal) icons, the blues mind model is premised on an engagement with a collective (historical) and communal past that helps explain a personal present. As the blues artist John Lee Hooker has said, the blues are about "not only what happened to you" but also about "what happened to your foreparents and other people" [quoted in *Conversation with the Blues,* by Paul Oliver, 1965]. Finally, whereas Jung's model is premised on an integrated consciousness, the blues mind model is premised on the assumption of a "double consciousness" [W. E. B. Du Bois, *The Souls of Black Folk,* 1903]. First of all, this assumption problematizes the Jungian model's implicit acceptance of the self as the site of identify formation because, as the rite of passage model elucidated by Baker shows, black identity in America is a product of a socialized ambivalence—the need to look at oneself with two sets of eyes. Secondly, and more to the point, the idea of double consciousness allows us to propose a decentered self that is, by virtue of that decentering, a stronger self— what W. E. B. Du Bois might have had in mind when he called the double self a "better and truer self." It is this decentered self that I'll be calling the "blues mind."

The "blues mind," as I define it here, is a composite structure based on impulses borrowed from three pertinent modes of black music—the blues, jazz, and gospel—which should be kept distinct *as forms of music,* despite their points of overlap. Ellison makes the distinctions for us. The blues, he writes, are involved in "an impulse to keep the painful details and episodes of a brutal experience alive in one's aching consciousness, to finger its jagged grain, and to transcend it, not by the consolation of philosophy but by squeezing from it a near-tragle, near-comic lyricism." The blues "at once express both the agony of life and the possibility of conquering it through sheer toughness of spirit" (*Shadow*). Jazz, on the other hand, is more concerned with the possibilities for self-definition within both a historical tradition and a collective ensemble; as Ellison writes, "true jazz is an art of individual assertion within and against the group." This assertion involves the individual as both "member of the collectivity and as a link in the chain of tradition." Gospel, according to Ellison, at least when it is sung by "certain women singers," involves a "technique of 'presence'" that promotes the feeling within a congregation of "a shared community of experience."

Theorists have suggested significant points of intersection among these three forms of music. Craig Werner, for instance, has noted that if "the blues assume their deepest significance when they elicit the recognition of individuals within the community (the listener-participants), jazz challenges the potential limitations inherent in the blues process." But the jazz impulse itself, as Werner notes, extends the "integrity wrested from the blues process" in its promotion of the possibilities of "expanding consciousness" and of "realizing the relational possibilities of the self" ["James Baldwin: Politics and the Gospel Impulse," *New Politics,* Vol. 2, No. 2, 1989]. Despite their different impulses, the blues and jazz may best be situated on a continuum. For Werner, the overarching form of music in this

continuum is the "gospel impulse" which informs both blues and jazz. As Werner writes, gospel constitutes a "communal improvisation on the theme of the blues" and also "demands a consciousness transcending the divisions of intellect, emotion and body, of self and other." It would seem that gospel borrows its theme from the blues and its insistence on expanding consciousness from jazz. Ellison also aligns the blues and jazz when he discusses the "jazz beat and blues mood" that pervaded Minton's in the golden age of jazz, as well as the commingling of the "spirit of jazz" and the "spirit of the blues" in Jimmy Rushing's early Oklahoma days (*Shadow*). The term Ellison uses to combine the two impulses is "the blues idiom." Eileen Southern has noted that it is not always possible to draw any firm dividing line between the "blues and some kinds of spirituals," nor between the blues and jazz; the latter two, she suggests, share a spirit of "individualism" and a "call-and-response style" [*The Music of Black Americans: A History,* 2nd edition, 1983]. What I am calling the "blues mind" is finally a structure premised on the blues sense of lyrical attempts at transcending the various oppressions that are its subject matter, the jazz sense of intersubjective possibilities between self and other, and the gospel sense of the shared community of experience and a political agenda, in Werner's charged words, of a "complex sense of presence as interrelationship."

The example of such a blues mind that I'll be proposing is the character of John Lawson, the narrator of Wideman's Homewood trilogy. At the end of *Sent for You Yesterday,* the third volume of the trilogy, John begins to dance as all the voices in that novel converge in and through him. The conflation of dance and voice is no accident. Indeed, in this novel about conflations of personalities, the collapsing of temporal difference, and the discovery of voice in dreaming, dancing represents the moment when sadness becomes song, when individuality gives way to community. Part of the transformation of sadness to song requires John's expanding sense of selfhood—so that the boundary between self and Other is problematized to the extent that an uneasy integration between those two entities becomes possible. This integration of self and Other is part of the magic of *Sent for You Yesterday,* but the way of achieving it in storytelling is also part of the whole project that is the Homewood trilogy.

The movement from sadness to song is the action of what Baker calls "translation" in the blues—"transforming experiences of a durative (unceasingly oppressive) landscape into the energies of rhythmic song." Blues translation is, then, an act of understanding how historical and economic backgrounds inform personal development. In the act of translating, of understanding, the singer assumes a blues voice and becomes a blues subject—a subject, according to Baker, defined as anonymous and yet wholly representative of a certain historical landscape.

Wideman's trilogy demonstrates how John, like Sonny's brother, assumes a blues voice by taking on Others' voices, transposing himself in Others' dreams, and engaging himself in Others' music. The finest expression of the process of the finding of voice in this trilogy comes from the description of someone's playing the "honky-tonk and gut bucket and low-down dirty blues." I say "someone" because the playing occurs in a dream where the dreamer has assumed two personalities simultaneously (I'll discuss the process and significance of this conflation in the final section). The dreamer is the indefinably named "Brother," who is both colorless and voiceless; the player can be named only as the combination of Albert Wilkes-Brother Tate-John Lawson:

> Play. And then he goes on about his business. He plays his piano song sad as train wheels when they standing still. . . .Mrs. Tate rocks up and back in slow time to something in the music nobody else can hear. Her song is his song. Like Brother hears his. Like Lucy beside him rocks on one foot then the other hearing what she needs to hear [*Sent for You Yesterday*]

The blues here are not only played by an indefinable composite personality but also express an indefinable composite message—articulating what Baker calls an "energizing intersubjectivity." Because the player is a composite being, and therefore the song is representative of a larger entity than any individual, the music speaks to each listener in a different way.

That intersubjectivity is what the third volume of Wideman's trilogy represents. The title is taken from a Jimmy Rushing blues song. It is one of a series of songs which, as Ellison has pointed out, not only make us "aware of the meanings which shimmer just beyond the limits of the lyrics" but also "tell us who and where we are" (*Shadow*). Like all forms of black music, the blues posit that self-identity is impossible to confirm or maintain outside of a cultural community. As Cone writes, "Black music is unifying because it confronts the individual with the truth of black existence and affirms that black being is possible only in a communal context." The blues, as Angela Davis says of "Ma" Rainey's singing, established "the basis in song for the sharing of experiences and the forging of a community capable of persevering through private tribulations and even of articulating new hopes and aspirations" ["Black Women and Music: A Historical Legacy of Struggle," in *Wild Women in the Whirlwind: Afra-American Culture and the Contemporary Literary Renaissance*, edited by Joanne M. Braxton and Andrée Nicola McLaughlin, 1990]; that is, in Ellison's phrasing, the "who" and the "where" are impossible to differentiate. Homewood is both the ghetto in Pittsburgh where all the characters discover themselves and the community that is made possible by their mutual discoveries. As Lucy says in *Sent for You Yesterday,* "Homewood wasn't bricks and boards. Homewood was them singing and loving and getting where they needed to get." Wideman presents in three volumes how this community was forged by a series of communal generations and familial ties—starting with that between an escaped slave and her granddaughter and ending with that between the two brothers John and Tommy Lawson. Wideman's, as much as Sonny's, is a blues vision, connecting the past to the present, changing sadness into song, constructing manifold selves in each individual.

Ellison says that the essential tension in jazz is that moment of the individual artist's "definition of his identity: as individual, as member of the collectivity, and as a link in the chain of tradition." The tension exists not only among the individual artists in the combo but also within each artist: "because jazz finds its very life in an endless improvisation upon traditional materials, the jazzman must lose his identity even as he finds it" (*Shadow*). What Ellison says about jazz is a component of the "blues mind." The "blues mind" in the Homewood trilogy belongs to the narrator John, and through the three volumes I trace how he loses himself in narrating the lives of the Others who help make him the multiply defined self he is—from his slave ancestor to his brother. I will also attempt to trace how he discovers himself through the various modes of relation he employs to narrate those interconnected lives—from "letters" in *Damballah* to the "story" in *Hiding Place* to "the blues" in *Sent for You Yesterday.*

The Fraternal Address: "Damballah"

The letter writer, according to Walter Ong, pretends that her or his reader is present, although the marks of oral address are usually absent. In that way, the letter writer constructs a fictional audience and confects a mood for that audience [*Interfaces of the Word: Studies in the Evolution of Consciousness and Culture,* 1977]. As such, of course, the letter is no different from the novel or the poem. It is different in that the unintended reader of the letter feels some degree of impropriety, some degree of invading the intended reader's privacy. Samuel Richardson knew this well enough when he chose the epistolary form as the most appropriate mode for relating stories about attempted and successful rapes. The poignancy exists in that the letter writer seems to be present, and therefore vulnerable, in a way that a narrator usually is not. The letter writer, we may say, gives the illusion of presence.

Of course the letter can be employed to express a degree of absence and selflessness. In one of [Jacques] Derrida's letters in [*The Post Card: From Socrates to Freud and Beyond,* 1987] for instance, we find this pre-emptive admission of abnegation should the letter be turned to public perusal: "Obviously when beneath my public signature they read these words they will have won out (over just what?) but they will be right: it's not at all like that that it comes to pass, you know well, at this moment my intonation is entirely other[.] I can always say 'it's not me.'" It's worth noting that the pre-emptive absence the writer will assert is only a prophylactic against and in case of public exposure. The writer does not seem to emphasize the absence of selfhood obtaining to writing as a system (at least not here).

The first volume of the Homewood trilogy contains a series of short stories in roughly chronological order, giving us the history of the Lawson family from the slave matriarch Sybela Owens to the brothers John and Tommy Lawson. Through their telling, John Lawson, the narrator, comes to a fuller understanding of his racial identity. In the dedicatory letter **"To Robby"** with which *Damballah* begins, we find a conflation of identity and medium. Initially, we are told that the "stories are letters." Even though the letters/stories are addressed to Robby—"Long overdue letters from me to you"—Wideman is more concerned with establishing the mindset of the unintended reader: "Stories are letters. Letters sent to anybody or everybody. But the best kind are meant to be read by a specific somebody. When you read that kind you know you are eavesdropping. You know a real person somewhere will read the same words you are reading and the story is that person's business and you are a ghost listening in." Wideman makes it ambiguous whether the "you" refers to Robby or to us. In either case, the rest of the opening letter expresses how the narrator has struggled with the classic African-American double consciousness so beautifully defined by Du Bois:

> I never liked watermelon as a kid. I think I remember you did. You weren't afraid of becoming instant nigger, of sitting barefoot and goggle-eyed and Day-Glo black and drippy-lipped on massa's fence if you took one bit of the forbidden fruit. I was too scared to enjoy watermelon. Too self-conscious. I let people rob me of a simple pleasure. Watermelon's still tainted for me. But I know better now. I can play with the idea even if I can't get down and have a natural ball eating a real one.

What the narrator is living out here is a classic African-American double bind. Expressing one form of it, the comedian Godfrey Cambridge tells the joke about the self-conscious middle-class Negro who points to a watermelon and says to the grocer, "That big squash over there. Wrap it up" [quoted in Lawrence W. Levine, *Black Culture and Black Consciousness: Afro-American Folk Thought from Slavery to Freedom,* 1977]. This is one possible response to the double bind of double consciousness—fool-

ing oneself by attempting to avoid living a life that conforms to a caricature constructed by a white society and grafted onto the white perspective of the doubly conscious black. The other response is celebration—a festive act of proclaiming oneself free of the second consciousness. The classical example of this type of construction is Ellison's "invisible man." As he walks the streets of the city, he buys a yam and relishes the public exhibition of eating it—an act that establishes a degree of his overcoming the double consciousness of allowing his acts to be judged by extrinsic standards. "What a group of people we were, I thought. Why, you could cause us the greatest humiliation simply by confronting us with something we liked." In each case, the character attempts to avoid being caught being black; it is only in the second instance that the character gives up the attempt and celebrates the foods and rituals involved in his being black. For the narrator John, moreover, the act of being caught is cast in terms of an antebellum discourse—the judge he fears most is "massa." What John learns through the course of telling these stories is what his Aunt Geraldine tells him: "the melon is a letter addressed to us. A story for us from down home." And "home" is the historical experience of African-Americans: "Down Home being everywhere we've never been, the rural South, the old days, slavery, Africa." In effect, then, John begins narrating the act of his own self-discovery, through writing letters which are both his stories and histories and learning to be able to eat those other letters from down home—"a history we could taste and chew."

The next page contains a passage from Maya Deren's *Divine Horsemen: The Voodoo Gods of Haiti,* describing the god Damballah as one who is "at once the ancient past and the assurance of the future." Invoking Damballah, writes Deren, is an act of gathering up "all history into a solid, contemporary ground beneath one's feet." "Damballah" will become, in the first story, the word that the slave from Africa, Orion, gives to the unnamed slave boy. "Damballah" is for the boy a place he can enter, "a familiar sound he began to anticipate, a sound outside of him which slowly forced its way inside, a sound measuring his heartbeat then one with the pumping surge of his blood." This internalization of a word—making its way from outside to inside—is the legacy the boy receives from Orion, the African who is in fact losing his own resistance to keeping the external at bay by being enslaved in America: "he could feel the air / of this strange land wearing out his skin, rubbing it thinner and thinner until one day his skin would not be thick enough to separate what was inside from everything outside." To counteract this loss of his African inner soul to an American institution, Orion gives the boy a way of internalizing a heritage, a "place he could enter." Orion finally dies after a severe whipping, and after his death he tells the boy stories about flying back to Africa: "The boy wiped his wet hands on his knees and drew the cross and said the word and settled down and listened to Orion tell the stories again. Orion talked and he listened and couldn't stop listening till he saw Orion's eyes rise up through the back of the severed skull and lips rise up through the skull and the wings of the ghost measure out the rhythm of one last word." This act of postmortem narration allows Orion to free his soul at the same time as it gives the boy the capacity to be an African even though his Aunt Lissy, who rebukes him for using "heathen talk," tells him to "talk Merican." Whatever relation this unnamed boy might have to the Owens-French-Lawson family tree, his act is one that regulates each generation of that tree.

In another story, we discover that narration is not only liberating to the soul but is required to make living things real. "Lizabeth needs her mother's voice to make things real. (Years later when she will have grandchildren of her own and her mother and father both long dead Lizabeth will still be trying to understand why sometimes it takes someone's voice to make things real. . . .Telling the story right will make it real)." Lizabeth is John Lawson's mother. In another story, Freeda, John's grandmother, finds that self-knowledge is to be gained only in narration: "To believe who she is Freeda must go backward, must retreat, her voice slowly unwinding, slowly dismantling itself, her voice going backward with her, alone with her as the inevitable silence envelops. Talking to herself. Telling stories. Telling herself." Interestingly, this is the story in which John first makes an appearance and is initiated into the role of family griot: "After the kids were asleep I began to talk about my grandmother. I wished for May's voice and the voices of my people in a circle amening and laughing and filling in what I didn't know or couldn't remember, but it was just me whispering in the dark motel room, afraid to wake my sons." It is in this story, also, that John begins first to glimpse what it will take the Homewood trilogy *in toto* to understand: "the silence of death and the past and lives other than mine." For now, he is alone and lacking the community of internal voices and external hearers that would make his voice the "voices" of his people.

Having then understood how to begin to think about previous generations, how to invoke Damballah, that is, John enters the next story through an act of free indirect discourse. As Aunt May is telling a story, John incorporates it into his voice. Appropriately, the story Aunt May is telling concerns watermelons:

> And May's story of the lost arm reminded her of another story about watermelons. About once there was a very old man Isaac married to an old woman Rebecca. Was in slavery days. Way, way back. Don't nobody care nothing about those times. Don't nobody remember them but old fools like me cause I was there

when Grandpa told it and I ain't never been able to forget much, least much of what I wanted to forget.

According to Henry Louis Gates [in *The Signifying Monkey: A Theory of African-American Literary Criticism,* 1988], the use of free indirect discourse is a feature of what he calls the "speakerly text." Such free indirect discourse in **Damballah,** as much as in Zora Neale Hurston's *Their Eyes Were Watching God,* allows for a form of rhetorical play and the representation of the "protagonist's growth in self-consciousness." The signifier watermelon, we remember, had caused John to feel alienated from "home," from his culture. Now he has reached the point where at least he feels able to incorporate May's story about watermelons into his voice.

The next stage of John's evolving voice is his ability to "experience" the stories his Aunt May tells him. When Janie finishes telling Pheoby her story in Hurston's novel, she concludes, "It's uh known fact, Pheoby, you got tuh *go* there tuh *know* there." Pheoby becomes the mediator between Janie and the Eatonville community, because Pheoby has been there through Janie's story. As he listens to Aunt May, John learns the same lesson:

> That was in Africa. Way, way back like I said. . . .This old lady got sense just good as any you. Like they say. You got to *Go there to Know there.* And ain't I been sitting on Grandpa's knee hearing him tell about slavery days and niggers talking to trees and stones and niggers flying like birds. And he was there. He knows. So in a manner of speaking I was there too.

If experience (going there) is required for knowledge (knowing there), then hearing a story acts as one form of experience. From Aunt May, John learns the lesson the boy learned from Orion—that Damballah was a place he could enter, a story he had to tell.

The next two stories in the collection begin to assume that telling is basic to all acts of narration, and they develop the distinction between two forms of using the voice: writing and singing. When he tries to write the stories, John finds himself appropriating the events he is recording: "I have written it before because I hear my mother now, like a person in a book or a story instructing me. I wrote it that way but it didn't happen that way." What happens when he writes is that the voices get lost: "When I wrote this before there was dialogue." Meanwhile the story of the gospel singer Reba Love Jackson teaches us how song transforms story into life in a way that writing is incapable of doing: "Couldn't speak about some things. She could only sing them. Put her stories in the songs she had heard all her life so the songs became her stories." It is the empathy involved in "listening" that allows Reba Love Jackson's songs to be both part of her life and yet nonetheless representative of those lives about whom she sings. It is, in the end, her ability to listen that gives her songs their poignancy. At the beginning of the story, the narrator answers a phone call for Reba Love. Listening to a man tell of his troubles, the narrator feels somewhat embarrassed. He puts down the receiver and gets Reba Love on the phone. "I stood beside her while she listened. Seems like I could understand better. Watching how Reba Love listened. How the face of that saint got sad-eyed while she shook her head from side to side. I'm hearing the man and understanding him better than when I was holding the phone my own self." Even though she is not singing, Reba Love, simply by listening, is able to express more effectively the blues of someone else's life.

Listening is, for Reba Love, an act of identification. In an essay entitled "Living with Music," Ellison describes living in an apartment underneath a blues singer and having to hear her constant music: "in listening I soon became involved to the point of identification" (*Shadow*). According to the historian of consciousness Julian Jaynes, listening represents the act of what we may call a metavisceral identification: "Consider what it is to listen and understand someone speaking to us. In a certain sense we have to become the other person; or rather, we let him become part of us for a brief second. We suspend our own identities, after which we come back to ourselves and accept or reject what he has said. But that brief second of dawdling identity is the nature of understanding language." In a sense, Reba Love makes the songs of other people's lives hers by assuming selflessness, by relinquishing her ego in an act of listening. It is what John must learn—how to understand language and how to listen.

By the final story of the collection, John learns. He had heard May's story, and Freeda's story, and Lizabeth's story, but he had found that writing transformed those stories by taking the voices out of them. In his final story, the one most explicitly epistolary (addressed directly to his brother Tommy, whose story preceded it), John reflects on the beginnings of Homewood—the escape of the slave Sybela Owens: "Her stories exist because of their parts and each part is a story worth telling, worth examining to find the stories it contains. What seems to ramble begins to cohere when the listener understands the process, understands that the voice seeks to recover everything, that the voice proclaims *nothing is lost,* that the listener is not passive but lives like everything else within the story." It is by learning to understand how voices exist and are transmitted that John finally learns how to be an active listener. The truly told story becomes that in which a listener inhabits the text. His letters, that is, find their ideal listener. Indeed, as he continues, John discovers himself occupying the place of

griot, and this time he has an active audience: "Somebody shouts *Tell the truth.* You shout too. May is preaching and dances out between the shiny, butt-rubbed, wooden pews doing what she's been doing since the first morning somebody said *Freedom.* Freedom." Both May and "you" (and we must remember the way that pronoun was made ambiguous in the dedicatory letter) are quite literally part of an *audience.*

By the end of the first volume of the trilogy, John has developed a sensibility reaching, we might say, beyond the letter. That sensibility allows John to begin mediating configurations of how the past not only lives in us but also transforms our understanding of how we are living. So when John attempts to tell the story of Sybela Owens, the escaped slave at the root of the Lawson family tree, he also finds that he must tell his brother Tommy's story: "So the struggle doesn't ever end. Her story, your story, the connections." Moreover, the mediator in this triangle, the storyteller, finds himself in the story too: "I couldn't tell either story without implicating myself." The reason he is implicated is not only the tie of fraternity but also the recognition of how other lives are registers for our own potential lives: "I ask myself again *why not me.*" And, like Sonny's brother in Baldwin's short story, John does not attempt to make Tommy's story a subtext of his own but rather to make it conterminous with his own.

The first story in the collection demonstrated how the slave boy could internalize Africa in his American self by invoking Damballah, the word and concept that Orion taught him. May tells the story about how Sybela Owens gives her the same gift: "Grandmother Owens touched me and I felt it. Felt all the life running out me and something new filling me up at the same time. Just as clear as a bell I heard her say my name. And say so many other things there ain't no words for but they all rushing in so fast felt my whole self moving out the way to make room" (201). John acquires from Sybela Owens, through Aunt May, the role of witness because he has, like Reba Love, learned to listen: "Sybela's story could end here but it doesn't. I still hear May's voice." And hearing it, he transforms it into a letter: "But now the story, or pieces of story are inside this letter and it's addressed to you and I'll send it and that seems better than the way it was before. For now. Hold on."

As "letters," though, the stories composing *Damballah* have only a limited access to the selflessness of the blues mind. As John tells Tommy, the letter makes things better, but only "For now." There is, one imagines, a better medium for expressing the story. By the end of the collection, John has altered the written letter to the spoken. As he says, "the story came before the letter" (193). The letter, it turns out, is just one way of telling the story—a way that allows John better to appreciate his cultural identity.

The terms of the rites of passage for black identity delineated by Baker do not quite work for this story. John begins as an alien from his own culture, and the stories are about how he regains a place and a voice in that culture. The watermelon he had been ashamed to eat in the beginning turns out to be not so noxious to his sense of self halfway through the collection. The letters allow him to understand his origin in the founding of his family line and his community—in effect, in understanding the history of his people. But the letter can only go so far. Even the philosopher who has taught us to be skeptical of such valorization of voice over letter will admit to that:

> The entire history of postal *tekhne* tends to rivet the destination to identity. To arrive, to happen would be to a subject, to happen to "me." Now a mark, whatever it may be, is coded in order to make an imprint, even if it is a perfume. Henceforth it divides itself, *it is valid several times in one time:* no more unique addressee. This is why, by virtue of this divisibility (the origin of reason, the mad origin of reason and of the principle of identity), *tekhne* does not happen to language—which is why and what I sing to you. [Derrida, *The Post Card*].

If *Of Grammatology* had been interested in expressing that "writing is before the letter," then this missive teaches us that beyond the letter is the song. In terms of Wideman's trilogy, though, between the letter and the song is what is also before the letter and the song: the story.

The Fraternal Story: "Hiding Place"

In Wideman's most recent novel, **Reuben,** the main character Reuben carries with him an icon representing his jailed brother. Reuben's brother is a "stern reflection of himself." Indeed, his brother is what he requires to complete both himself and his brother's self and make thereby "a Reuben larger than both of them." John Lawson began the Homewood trilogy by attempting to find a voice with which to tell the story of his brother. The process of finding that voice took him through a series of letters recounting the history of his family and his community. Having gained that voice, John proceeds to tell the story of his brother. He is inevitably implicated in the telling, as he realized at the end of **Damballah,** but for the most part he is only implicitly involved in **Hiding Place.** The story is told in three voices and through three perspectives, those of Bess, the matriarch living a hermetic existence on Bruston Hill; Tommy, the fugitive hiding out at Bess's house; and Clement, the simple boy who makes deliveries to Bess's house. Only at one point in the novel does John appear, when his Uncle Carl introduces him to Violet at the Brass Rail bar. The person who sees him is Clement, the Benjy Compson-like character. And when Clement sees John Lawson's

eyes, he thinks immediately of Tommy who is at Bess's house (104). That, though, is the only connection between the brothers in this novel. It is otherwise a story about Tommy in which John is implicated only tangentially. Having achieved a lesson about the workings of historical continuity and the ways of establishing selflessness in **Damballah,** John begins to tell the selfless story of another historical connection in **Hiding Place.** The story centers on Bess, who lost a son to the war and thereafter set herself up as a hermit on top of Bruston Hill, and Tommy, who is fleeing the police for a murder charge of which he is not guilty. Part of the story is a continuation of John's meditation on how the past informs the present.

Because her house has no modern amenities, Tommy thinks Bess lives like a slave: "He looks for a light bulb or a lamp, any sign of electricity, any object which would bring him back to the world, to the time in which he belonged. Could be one of those huts in slave row, one of those niggertown shacks clustered around Massa's big white house." Moreover, when confronted with this relic of the past, Tommy begins to play a prescribed role. Complimenting Bess on her soup, he finds himself speaking in a voice that belongs to an atavistic type of "jive, Jack-leg preacher" sitting in front of a platter of fried chicken. Even so, Tommy is intent on denying how the past lives in the present. He tells Bess, "All that old time stuff don't make me no nevermind. Wasn't even born yet." He is tired of the talk that asserts that the "only hurt is the hurt" of the past. But rather than paying "no nevermind" to the stories of past sufferings by his family members, Tommy must learn to attend to how the contingencies of history have placed him where he finds himself. So he must learn to appreciate how Homewood was founded: "They catch Mother Owens keep her down in slavery wouldn't be not Bruston Hill." He must accept how the past is both a continuous process—informing his own life by its being—and a contingent one. As Bess tells him in answer to his assertion that the past is unimportant because he wasn't born yet, "Wasn't for that crazy May wouldn't be no Lizabeth and you wouldn't be sitting here neither." As much as his very existence depended on May's saving the baby Lizabeth's life (so that Lizabeth could then grow up and give birth to Tommy), so too can his sitting where he is (as a fugitive) be informed by acknowledging the community's past. If **Damballah** allowed John to understand the ways that the past is the foundation for the present, then **Hiding Place** allows Tommy to recognize how the past lives in and through him.

When Tommy learns this lesson, it, too, is learned through a process of displacement of self, a relinquishing of ego. It happens in a dream. He dreams about walking on a beach with his son when life was good: "And the story ain't just words. More like it is in them old songs. What made the story so good was that other me listening too. Watching over me and my son. The other me like some kind of god floating in the air so I could listen and make everything true. So I could make it happen." The story—transcending words and approaching the realm of song—is real because it is listened to. As much as Freeda's story gained its reality for her by its being repeated, Tommy's story becomes "good" because he hears it. Not only must Tommy learn to hear his own story and understand it in terms of the past; Bess must learn to hear his story with a like degree of detachment. When he first tells her this dream, she dismisses him: "Don't want to hear your troubles." For as much as Tommy hinders his necessary education by believing that the past doesn't influence the present, so too Bess maintains her selfishness by not attending to how the present helps to explain the past. Tommy, that is, must learn how the present is contingent on the past, and Bess how it is a continuation of it.

Tommy learns first how to tell his story to himself so that he may understand it. He manages to do so only after he learns the lesson of history's contingency—after he begins to appreciate how the accidents of the past led to this particular present. Bess takes longer to learn that she too must listen to understand what those accidents led to. At one point in the narrative, Tommy asks Bess what makes her think she can understand him without hearing his story: "How you know so much about people you never give them a chance to open they mouth? How you know so much?" The novel ends by demonstrating that Bess had indeed been listening, and that her mandate is to tell others to listen. She leaves the house on Bruston Hill to return to Homewood, because

> Somebody has to go down there and tell the truth. Lizabeth's body didn't kill nobody. He wasn't scared. All he needed was another chance and somebody needs to go down there and tell them. And she was going to do just that. Burn down that last bit of shack on Bruston Hill and tell them what they needed to know. That he ain't killed nobody. That he needed one more chance. That he staked his life on one more chance. They should know all that down there. She'll tell them. She'll make sure they hear. Yes indeed. . . .She's coming to tell them he ain't scared no more and they better listen and they better make sure it don't happen so easy ever again.

No longer would Bess co-opt the voices of those she assumed she understood because they were part of a later historical epoch. No longer would Bess be a hermit, isolated in a figurative and literal past. The house on Bruston Hill, which Tommy had thought akin to slave quarters, burns as she heads to town to tell another story.

Stories, though, can go only so far in articulating a

community's desires, its values, its historical relationships. The trajectory of shifts in narrative modalities in the Homewood trilogy suggests that only song is, in the end, capable of expressing that elusive blues "intersubjectivity." It is interesting that Tommy's dream could best be expressed as a song. It is worth noting that as Bess is heading down Bruston Hill, she thinks of her dead husband whistling "Burn Down the House Blues."

The Fraternal Blues: "Sent for You Yesterday"

In **Damballah,** the story of Reba Love Jackson ends with the promise of a song: "Could tell you plenty about Homewood in those days but you'll come to hear singing not talking and that's what I'm going to do now. Sing this last one for Homewood." Before that song begins, however, the rest of the letters about origins have to be completed. About a third of the way through **Hiding Place,** Bess remembers how Bill Campbell could play a guitar he called Corrinne—a guitar, he said, "full of letters from home." He "would read them when he played and you'd listen and know just what he was talking about even though you never been South yourself." By listening to those letters turned songs, the auditor would get "a home you never been to or never saw except in that music."

The blues, writes Langston Hughes, is what you hear no matter where you're from: "I'm not a Southerner. I never worked on a levee. I hardly ever saw a cotton field except from the highway." Despite this distance from the "Blues-originating-land," Hughes has no trouble gaining an appreciation for the music: "One communicates to the other, brother." For singers, like all great interpretive artists, writes Ellison, make us identify with something beyond our realm of experience: "when they sing we have some notion of our better selves" (*Shadow*). Their singing is able to give us the ability to listen more attentively to who we are because they themselves are teaching us the art of listening. As we saw, the narrator of Reba Love Jackson's story understands better by listening to Reba listen than he does by listening himself to the problems of the individual on the phone. The possibility of identifying with what Hughes calls the "other, brother" is best mediated through the singer. **Damballah** contains a series of letters that allow the narrator to understand his origins and his brother's origins; **Hiding Place** tells the story of the brother and the contingencies of history that made them brothers and yet also individuals worlds apart. Along the way it alerts us to how letters are best told in song. The final volume of the Homewood trilogy is a song. Its title, as I said earlier, is taken from the Jimmy Rushing blues song; its story is about how a brother awakens to the blues. It is the story about how John finally learns to listen.

Sent for You Yesterday falls into four sections. The first, only three pages long, is called "In Heaven with Brother Tate." The second, "The Return of Albert Wilkes," relates how Albert returns after seven years of being a fugitive wanted for murder only to be murdered by the police as he sits playing the piano. The third, "The Courting of Lucy Tate," relates the intricate relationship among Lucy Tate, Carl Lawson, and Brother Tate, the next generation following Albert Wilkes's. The final section, "Brother," is a series of four dated visions showing how John Lawson is able to empathize with Brother (who is the Other) to the degree of identification.

The first section contains a vignette of two unnamed characters, one of whom we assume is Brother Tate, in an indefinable place, which we assume is heaven. Each of the characters tells the other about a dream he has. The first character tells a dream about a train bearing a remarkable resemblance to a ship on the Middle Passage. The second character tells a dream about how after he escapes spiders, a whole army of police, marines, and FBI agents, he enters his yard only to find a "big greasy-assed elephant chewing his cud." In a moment of dialogue in which it is hard to differentiate the two participants, the dreams become conflated: "That's my dream, fool. I just told it to you. You spozed to be talking bout your own dream." The rest of the novel plays variations on this theme: how can people inhabit the same dream? How is it that different narratives may embody the same principle of emotion—how an elephant and a train may evoke exactly the same kind of fear? What is principally the issue in the novel is how individuals may share their lives, their sounds, their dreams. In the final variation on this theme, *Sent for You Yesterday* demonstrates how listening allows the narrator John to achieve what Baker calls the "energizing intersubjectivity" that is the hallmark of the blues mind.

An example of this "energizing intersubjectivity" of the blues is to be found in the ways that stories are related between characters in the novel. To begin, we may turn to the Lucy Tate section and examine the structuring of the story Carl tells John in the Velvet Slipper. For in the way that storytellers lose themselves in the telling we may find a way of understanding the structure of a blues mind.

The story begins with Carl reflecting on his relationship with his nephew: "Yesterday. My, my. That's all it seems sometimes. Just yesterday and you was a baby and we was all over there on Cassina Way. Brother named you Doot while we was still on Cassina." To tell the story of Brother to John, Carl must begin by stating the relationship obtaining between the subject of the story and its immediate auditor—about how Brother named John (Doot). Carl then establishes the scene that will act as a register for John's evolving selflessness: the first time he learned to dance. John was hardly a year old, Carl remembers, when he first

took to the floor, dancing to "Basie with Jimmy Rushing on vocal." It was Lucy who tried to teach John to dance, and it is Lucy who is the other auditor of Carl's story. The scene of John's first attempting to dance, then, acts not only as a register for his evolving blues mind but also to situate an earlier scene in which all the elements of the story were involved: subject (Brother), teller (Carl), and audience (John and Lucy). But Lucy is more than an auditor. She begins by being part of the call and response rhythm of Carl's story—"Help him say what she didn't want to hear." Her reluctance to participate as an antiphonal response to Carl's story leads her to tell her own version of the story, and to tell it to herself.

While Carl is telling the story about Brother, his wife Samantha, and their child Junebug, Lucy begins reflecting on John's relationship to Brother: "Brother named him Doot. Now he wants to name Brother. She'll leave Carl's story alone. He doesn't need her helping words, her amens, her reminders of dates, of names. She's telling it to herself." As soon as she tries to tell Brother's story, she realizes that she must assume another's place in order to tell that story: "You had to be Samantha to understand. Sometimes Lucy thought that's what the visits were about. Being Samantha." She goes on to assume Samantha's place in order to tell the story, and by doing so she displaces herself: "If you are Samantha you're waiting for Lucy."

Telling the story from Samantha's place requires Lucy to take yet one more step out of herself. She must dream Samantha's dream, in which Samantha displaces herself in order to take the place of June-bug: "in the dream I'm him. I'm little Junebug." This, then, is the zenith of the storyteller's selflessness. Carl is telling a story, while Lucy is remembering it, through the eyes of Samantha, who is dreaming she is Junebug. This is the furthest selflessness can go in this relation; from four levels removed from the scene of Carl's telling of his story, we find the heart of the tale: the dream narrative of Junebug's death.

Having reached the heart of the story, we begin to return to its peripheries. At the end of her dream of how Junebug felt as he burned to death, Samantha returns to herself: "So when the scream comes I know it's me. I know I'm not Junebug anymore." Lucy eventually leaves the persona of Samantha to return to herself, and then she resumes hearing Carl tell John the story. Within the general framework of Carl's narrative, within Lucy's remembered version of it, within Samantha's telling of that version of it resides the essence of the piece: Samantha's dream of the death of her son Junebug, which can only be told through his mother's perspective, and only in her dream: "If you tell Junebug's story you have to be Samantha." This, then is the epitome of achieving a blues mind—being able to assume an Other's dream in order to understand the most painful thing of that

Other's life. In that assumption, the singer loses her self and understands her life only as it is supplementary to the place from which she sings. Lucy sees her life only as it relates to Samantha's. She has earned the right to sing Samantha's blues only because she has listened to Samantha with an intensity that has allowed her to become Samantha: "Lucy. Lucy Tate. You hear me, girl?"

When we return to the largest frame of this particular story—Carl in the Velvet Slipper—we find that his story, too, has, in parts, been an act of listening: "His eyes turn inward and he's listening rather than telling his story." It is the same act of blues empathy we found Reba Love to have—the ability to listen to the Other and thereby transform that sadness into her song. At the end of the story, Carl realizes that he is implicated in the telling: "I know I'm supposed to be telling you his story. But how Ima tell his without telling mine. And Lucy's. Cause yeah. We was the three musketeers, all right." And to end the Lucy Tate section, Carl invites John to take Brother's place: "You ready, Doot? You come over to the Tates' and it be three of us again just like the old days."

Telling a certain story about the Other requires assuming a certain relationship to the subject of that story. As Lucy realizes, to tell Junebug's story one has to assume the place of Samantha. Junebug, moreover, is the link between John and Brother. As the narrator says earlier, "Brother treated me special because he could see Junebug in me. In Brother's eyes I grew up living not only my own life, but the one snatched from Junebug." John, then, at the end of the Lucy Tate section, has learned about Junebug's life and death, has placed himself in relation to the story, and, finally, has been invited to take the place of Brother. The last section of the novel, "Brother," relates the process of John's assuming a blues mind, of the integration of his self with Brother's.

The Lucy Tate section begins by relating how Brother at age twenty-one had suddenly begun to play the piano although he had received no training on it. That Saturday, at the Elks Club, as Brother plays for the first time, someone calls out, "*Play, Albert. Play, Albert Wilkes. Albert's home again.*" While it is true that "good piano playing and Albert Wilkes were just about the same word in Homewood," it is also true that Brother has taken the place of Albert, who was murdered by the police as he sat playing the piano some seven years earlier. John does not know if he ever heard Brother play the piano—he was born six months before that evening in 1941—but he is sure that in somebody's story sometime he will discover that he was there:

> One day in one of the stories I'm sure someone will
> tell me, I did hear Brother play. On such and such a

day while the sun was shining and the wind died down and them trenches dug in the street so's you could get around I remember Carl getting you ready and your mama saying *No,* saying it's too bad outside, saying it while Carl is wrapping you in sweaters and a snowsuit so you looked like a bowling ball and Cold could have run over you with a truck and you wouldna felt a thing . . . One day I'll be in the Tates' living room listening. I'll hear Brother. I'll hear Albert Wilkes.

This reflection occurs at the beginning of the Lucy Tate section. By the end of it, as we have seen, John has been invited to take Brother's place just as Brother had taken Albert's when he first began playing the piano. The final section, the Brother section, demonstrates how this conflation of personalities occurs. It can only be related, however, once John allows himself to assume a blues mind. Understanding how Junebug's death affected Brother and how he has assumed the place of Junebug in Brother's mind helps him toward assuming that selflessness—that doubleness that is the blues mind.

The Brother section falls into four subsections dated "1941," "1946," "1962," and "1970." The first relates how Brother's train dreams began when he turned twenty-one. The train dream is a more explicit version of the one recounted in the first section (10). Even more explicit is the pain of not having all his parts to himself, of not being whole: "He couldn't disentangle what belonged to him from the mass of bodies struggling in the black pit" (159). In the same image found in Toni Morrison's *Beloved,* gathering one's body together is an act, literally, of *re-membering* one's self and therefore one's racial history: Africa, Middle Passage, slavery, the South. As Brother wakes from the train dream, he "counts the parts of his body. He is remembering." But if remembering is an act of individuation, literally and symbolically, then, just as in Morrison's fiction, it is an act that requires a relinquishing of a stable ego.

When Brother dreams, he dreams that he is not himself but rather Albert Wilkes: "Slowly the dream was turning into nothing as he remembered what it was about. In the dream he had been Albert Wilkes, long dead Albert Wilkes coming back to Homewood again." Moreover, because he is able to dream through Albert's consciousness, Brother is able to assume a blues mind:

> What sings and dances in the hurry of the train starts
> to get to him. He has been sitting a long time, . . . hear-
> ing nothing but the wheels saying I'm tired and still got
> a long way to go. He wouldn't listen because there was
> no play in the sound, nothing but a flat, lonely, almost
> moan like somebody telling the same sad story over
> and over again in the same tired voice and the wheels
> couldn't do nothing but keep on telling the tale. Now

he hears a beat, a gallop. The steel wheels rising and set down one at a time so it's boogity, bop, boogity boopin a little different each measure.

In that sublime moment, Brother's train dream—which had been of the Middle Passage—is transformed twice. Initially the train loses its horrible shiplike quality and becomes a train, and in doing so gains a blues rhythm: "nothing but the wheels saying I'm tired and still got a long way to go." Secondly, the train's rhythm, to employ Hughes's formulation once more, transforms sadness into song—from the "same sad story over and over again" to "boogity, bop, boogity boopin."

Having dreamed another self, Brother returns first to being himself—"and he's Brother again"—and then to being an integration of self and Other: "He is Albert Wilkes all right, and he's caught somewhere in the middle. Maybe he is the window glass. Hot on one side. Cold on the other. Because he is Brother, too. Shuffling his feet and listening to Wilkes playing because Lucy said he's back." This moment when the train is the locus of an epistemic transformation as well as a means of literal transportation is what Baker has called "the training" of the blues artist. It is after this that we find the scene I cited earlier of Wilkes's/Brother's/John's playing of the blues song that allows each auditor to hear what she or he "needs to hear" because the blues artist has assumed a composite self: "Her song in his song."

From that place, where Brother has now assumed Albert's life as an integral part of his own, Brother's life becomes a song: "In his song like a window Brother could see way down the tracks. To now when he is dreaming. To the time when he will speak to a son. To the time he wouldn't speak to anyone anymore. To the lives he would live and the lives he would be inside." What is interesting about the relation of subsection "1941" is that it is told entirely from the site of John's third-person narration. The story of how Brother dreams he is Albert is told *by* John. In the next subsection, "1946," John will not just relate Brother's dream but allow Brother to dream it *through* him. The next subsection, that is, shows John's evolving sense of a composite selfhood.

It begins with the return of Brother's dream train. This time, the train's sadness, which is described in antimusical terms—"the splat, splat rhythmless march"—does not become a song until John surrenders his narratorial place to Brother. For the whole of the italicized section, Brother tells his dream, which contains within it a song.

That's when I sang to Junebug. Sang to him to save his life. Because he was just a baby. Because he didn't know a thing about leaving or coming back

again. So I had to tell him what I knew. Where I had been. . . . I sang to him about crossing oceans. . . .That I had been through it before. That nothing stopped. That I had crossed the ocean in a minute. That I had drowned in rivers and dangled like rotten fruit from trees. . . . That I had seen my mother whipped and my woman raped and my daddy stretched on a cross. That I had even lost my color and lost my tongue but all of that too was only a minute.

I sang to him. I let him know I didn't understand any more than he did. Except I had been a witness. I had been there so I could tell about it.

Giving Junebug a history of the collective sufferings that have accrued throughout what Wideman in the preface to **Damballah** calls "Down Home"—"being everywhere we've never been"—Brother attests to his being a witness and gives his son the testimony of how to transform that suffering into song. Not only does Junebug get the story in the form of a song, but he finds its sorrow transmuted into rhythm: all that suffering is as a minute, and eventually there will be a day when he "would see the curtain pulled away and the great star reveal itself. Its shine a kind of singing."

Brother's dream voice ends with a direct address to his dead son, telling him to "listen" because only in that act can he find the type of intersubjectivity that will make the day of singing possible: "Listen, son. Listen, Junebug. It all starts up again in you. It's all there again. You are in me and I am in you so it never stops. As long as I am, there's you. As long as there's you, I am. It never stops." The double address in this passage is interesting. Brother could just as well be addressing John as Junebug. John, we remember, is living Junebug's life in Brother's eyes. Immediately after this moment, John's narratorial voice returns. Who has learned the lesson of how one needs to be the Other before one can sing? The answer has to be John as much as Junebug.

The final subsection of the Brother section takes place in 1970, returning us to Lucy in the Tates' house waiting for Carl and John to arrive from the Velvet Slipper. It returns us, then, to the beginning of the Lucy Tate section of the novel. As Lucy awaits the arrival of John and Carl, she invokes the spirit of Albert Wilkes:

Play. She commands Albert Wilkes again. Play. She hums his song. A song so full of Albert Wilkes the pieces of him falling around her, drifting lazy and soft like huge, wet snowflakes and she can see the shape of each one. Falling like snow or rain or the names in the stories Carl tells Doot [John].

Albert Wilkes's song so familiar because everything she's ever heard is in it, all the songs and voices she's ever heard, but everything is new and fresh because his music joined things, blended them so you follow one note and then it splits and shimmers and spills the thousand things it took to make the note whole, the silences within the note, the voices and songs.

Albert Wilkes enters the Tates' house in a song that is made up to thousands of notes, with each note being made up of thousands of things. The composite nature of this form of music allows it to speak to each listener and teaches that person how to listen so that the total composition itself is potentially audible.

When John asks Lucy for a story, she finds herself "collapsing one time into another." She is trying to set the state for her story in the same way Carl had set the stage for his. She is also trying to remember the time when John first learned to dance, when she first tried to teach him to dance in 1941. Not only does she remember the vocalist and the band, as Carl had done, but she also remembers the title of the song: *"Sent for you yesterday, and here you come today."* It is a primal moment in the lives of all the characters: Carl, John, Lucy, Brother. She thinks she ought to relate another story, because John has already heard this one: "But you've heard that before." But John has learned how to listen in different ways and to different versions of the same story. He responds, "Never from you." It is a signal moment of his blues training. He wishes to know the story of his life in all its filiations, in all its supplementariness to the lives of many Others. His life is like the song Albert Wilkes plays—made up of notes made up of things. John has learned that one has to listen to the individual things to understand the composite; that he has to let his life be something that, like a song, joins and blends the discrete into the blues. At the end of her story, Lucy names the song that initiated John's dancing life: "Then we are back in the Tates' living room and Lucy finishes the story and says, the song you danced to was 'Sent for you yesterday, and here you come today.'" She turns on the radio to a station playing "Black music," and the moment John anticipated being told about he finds himself living—"one of the stories I'm sure someone will tell me. . . .One day I'll be in the Tates' living room listening. I'll hear Brother. I'll hear Albert Wilkes."

As soon as Lucy names the song, and as soon as the music comes from the radio,

> Brother Tate appears in the doorway. He's grinning his colorless grin and pointing at the piano and Albert Wilkes starts unsnapping the duster and aiming his behind for the piano bench. I know how good it's going to sound so I start moving to the music coming from

the radio. I know Albert Wilkes will blow me away so I start loosening up, getting ready. I'm on my feet and Lucy says, *Go boy* and Carl says, *Get it on, Doot.* Everybody joining in now. All the voices. I'm reaching for them and letting them go. Lucy waves. I'm on my own feet. Learning to stand, to walk, learning to dance.

He has learned all these skills—standing, walking, dancing—because he has learned the one crucial skill the blues teach: how to listen. "All the voices. I'm reaching for them and letting them go." As important as listening to the stories of Others is the ability to let them be the stories of Others. Letting them go means not making them a supplement to his own life's story. And because he has learned how to listen, and listen without reducing the Other's relation to his own, John manages to understand how the past lives in him—how it is that he is as much Brother Tate as Brother Tate was Albert Wilkes.

John's story ends with himself as a character in it, in the Tates' living room "listening." When Wideman learned not to reduce his brother's story into something tangential to his, but to listen to his brother selflessly, he too found himself a character in an Other's story: "When I caught on, there I was, my listening, waiting self part of the story, listening, waiting for me" [**Brothers and Keepers**]. When John Lawson learns to listen to the stories May tells him about the founding of Homewood, he learns to find himself as a listening character in those stories: "the listener is not passive but lives like everything else within the story" (**Damballah**). It is important to note that he finds this listener who inhabits a "story" in a story told in the form of a "letter." Moving from the epistolary **Damballah** to the narrative **Hiding Place,** we find Tommy learning to discover his listening character in his own dream: "And the story ain't just words. More like it is in them old songs. What made the story so good was that other me listening too." Again, it is significant that this discovery of a listener who inhabits a "song" is told in the form of a "story." The shift in the mode of perception, then, goes from letter to story to song, from **Damballah** to **Hiding Place** to **Sent for You Yesterday.** But first and foremost, each mode of relation is concerned with establishing the importance of listening. Listening is the supreme act of empathy, constituting the essential training of the blues mind, the ability to allow the Other to be sufficient unto itself and also a part of the self's life. Reba Love knew how to sing because she knew how to listen. The Homewood trilogy is John's training in the art. **Sent for You Yesterday**—both song and novel—is the production of that training.

It might seem odd, finally, to speak of the blues as a communal form of structuring thought. They are a form of music, after all, in which the individual performer's persona wholly dominates the song; they are, in fact, a form of music, according to Abbe Niles, that expresses a "pure *self*" [quoted in Levine]. But the pure self, as Lawrence W. Levine contends, is in itself communal. For not only does the singer evoke shared experiences common to the group listening, but those who listen are in fact involved because listening is experiencing: "black musical performances properly speaking had no audience, just participants." The blues tell us "you got to go there to know there" at the same time as they take us there. In the end, perhaps Langston Hughes expresses best how the blues take us home and help in that difficult communion we have to go through once we get there: "One communicates to the other, brother."

Jan Clausen (essay date Spring 1992)

SOURCE: "Native Fathers," in *Kenyon Review,* Vol. XIV, No. 2, Spring, 1992, pp. 44-55.

[*In the following essay, Clausen compares and contrasts John Updike's works—including his 1990 novel* Rabbit at Rest—*and Wideman's works, particularly* Philadelphia Fire.]

Two American boys, both named John, born less than a decade apart ('32 and '41), grow up in different regions of Pennsylvania. Brilliant students (one summa cum laude at Harvard, the other an Oxford Rhodes scholar), they become prolific authors, mining childhood memories to create fictional communities through which they portray American (Euro-and African-) life and values. By the time they reach middle age, their book jackets glitter with mention of prizes and honors and those obligatory, weirdly competitive clichés culled from old reviews: "Most gifted writer of his generation—the *New York Times*"; "Perhaps the most gifted black novelist of his generation—the *Nation.*"

In 1990, each publishes a major novel featuring a bitterly flawed male protagonist with whom the author appears to identify intensely, and whose troubles he uses to exemplify and probe the social ills of his native land. It is not an epoch supposed to be particularly hospitable to the social element in fiction, yet between them these two books receive three of said native land's top literary prizes. John Updike's *Rabbit at Rest* wins both the National Book Critics Circle Award and the Pulitzer Prize, John Edgar Wideman's *Philadelphia Fire* the PEN/Faulkner Award.

The inner city of Wideman's anguished, apocalyptic novel is just fifty miles from Updike's fictional Brewer (based on Reading, Pennsylvania), hometown of the famous Harry "Rabbit" Angstrom. Yet what a difference those few miles make. Updike's affluent characters shuttle between semi-

rural Pennsylvania and condo-studded Florida, but shun Philadelphia like HIV; Wideman's find themselves either physically trapped in the suppurating metropolis or mentally tethered to it. Updike's is a conventionally realistic, hero-centered work, bloated with brand names and socio-economic detail, heavily dependent on the author's virtuoso manipulation of visual effects to evoke a corpulent, numbed nation dying of material excess. Its central image of disaster is the rain of doomed bodies cast into icy space from the bland comforts of the passenger plane that blew up over Lockerbie, Scotland. Wideman, on the other hand, deliberately disrupts what starts out as a monophonic third-person narrative. He employs first-person authorial reflection and surreal scenarios of urban hell to confront the implications of *his* central image, also a real event: the infamous 1985 firebombing of the African-American communal group MOVE at the behest of a Philadelphia city administration headed by a Black mayor.

Updike's and Wideman's protagonists are in some respects as dissimilar as the social worlds and narrative frameworks they inhabit. Those who've followed Harry Angstrom through the previous Rabbit novels will not be surprised to find that he remains as good at dodging responsibility as he was at playing basketball during his glory days in high school. In *Rabbit, Run* he was content to settle on God and his wife Janice the burden of his infant daughter's needless death; now his fondness for a recent president seems perfectly in character. "Under Reagan, you know, it was like anesthesia," he remarks wistfully to a liberal golf partner, who warns, "When you come out of anesthesia, it hurts like hell." Wideman's Cudjoe, a blocked writer who has taken his share of evasive action—"drinking and hiding and running," observing from a distance "the funny stuff you Negroes over here got into, sitting in, occupying buildings, Mau-Mauing the Man" —is nevertheless haunted by grave personal mistakes, as well as by a mysteriously intense feeling of involvement with the Philadelphia fire which he returns from Europe to write about.

And yet, and yet. Harry and Cudjoe are both rotten husbands, obsessive womanizers, failed fathers who cut themselves off from real sons only to lavish energy on symbolic offspring. Both are basketball has-beens, returning to the game for some sense of mastery and camaraderie that otherwise eludes them:

> After the winning basket they gathered under the hoop still shuddering from Sky's humongous dunk. Their eyes met, their fists met for a second in the core of a circle, then just as quickly broke apart, each going his own way. [*Philadelphia Fire*]

Both seem fatally isolated, not only within the patterns of emotionally disconnected lives but within the conventions of novels focused on a single protagonist (a departure for Wideman, who usually organizes his fiction around an interplay of experiences and perspectives). And both occupy an imaginative space in which the story worth telling is always *history*.

When I first read the two novels shortly after they were published, I was intrigued that each in its very different way seemed so deeply concerned with connections between our private, feeling lives and an increasingly unmanageable public world. This clearly set them apart from most contemporary mainstream fiction. Both attempted to grasp something essential about "America" itself, and I judged their success particularly striking, given the divergence of their visions.

I saw Updike's America as some version of where I come from: complacently Caucasian, conventionally Protestant, of modest origins yet inexorably rising, in worldview pragmatic verging on anti-intellectual. I was fascinated that his narrative of decay—exploding airplanes, lethal junk food, drugged states, epidemics, dying bodies cocooned by alienating technology—could manage to strike such an elegiac note. In his fiction as in the Iran-Contra investigation, exoneration seemed to follow hard on the heels of indictment—indeed, in some mysterious manner to be indictment's consequence.

In Wideman's world, on the other hand, I saw my contemporary New York life during the years of George Bush and David Dinkins. Though **Philadelphia Fire** sags lamentably in spots, I valued its bumpy achievements far above Updike's impeccable production job. I needed Wideman's willingness to tackle such unusual subjects for fiction as structural racism, the lives of homeless men and street kids (viewed from inside, if only in glimpses), the historically charged dynamics of love and sex between Black men and white women, and the new scourge of Black officialdom's frank collusion in Black emmiseration. I needed the grief-stricken passion of the authorial voice breaking into Cudjoe's story from a reality too desperate for literary treatment:

> Who am I? One of you. With you in the ashes of this city we share. Or if you're not in this city, another one like it. If not now, soon. Soon enough to make it worthwhile for you to imagine this one, where I am.

At first I did not fully grasp the uncanny convergences between Harry's and Cudjoe's stories; I only thought it noteworthy that I, a feminist reader, could be so captivated by these patriarchal fictions. When the books received prestigious prizes, it occurred to me that this said something not only about what it was possible to imagine of America in the nineties, but about what America was willing to imag-

ine of itself. I resolved to reread them as *political* novels, which for me meant scrutinizing race and gender implications alongside their revelations of public life impinging on the private, empires on neighborhoods.

RABBIT IS WHITE

Is it making too much of minor details to observe that in the opening paragraphs of the first Rabbit book, Updike already seems at pains to establish Harry's racial credentials? Our first glimpse of the guy is of "the breadth of white face, the pallor of his blue irises . . . one widespread white hand on top of the ball" (*Rabbit, Run*).

The world of the Rabbit novels is overwhelmingly white—which is to say furtively, almost pruriently obsessed with race. Harry's interactions with African-Americans are dominated by his fantasies and stereotypical projections. This is surely psychologically accurate; the problem comes, however, in Updike's failure to present any alternative reference points. In *Rabbit Redux,* Harry takes in as a houseguest a Black Vietnam veteran named Skeeter, a creepy yet charismatic chap who abuses his host and another guest, a disturbed white teenager named Jill, with their enthusiastic cooperation. (Characteristically, Harry emerges from the experiment virtually unscathed—indeed, "redux"—while Jill, his symbolic daughter and literal bedmate, loses her life.) There is wit and some originality in quasi-allegorical scenes of the provincial Harry being subjected to nightly readings from *The Life and Times of Frederick Douglass,* but it soon becomes apparent that Updike is sporting with history of which he has an extremely shallow understanding.

Even as allegory (and even if the "dialect" is supposed to be parody), the passage in which Skeeter orchestrates a sexual scenario for enactment by himself and his white companions is hideously painful in a way the author completely fails to notice:

> "You is a big black man sittin' right there. You is chained to that chair. And I, I is white as snow . . . And this little girl here . . . an ebony virgin torn from the valley of the river Niger."

(Though Wideman's sense of the tragic dimensions of his subject is miles removed from such flippancy, it's noteworthy that Updike's reversed-identity staging of his tiresome drama of sexual competition between white and Black men—culminating in the seduction/rape of "daughter" Jill by Skeeter—is precisely mirrored by a section of [**Philadelphia Fire**], discussed later, in which Cudjoe rewrites *The Tempest.*)

How much has Updike's vision changed in the two decades

since *Rabbit Redux* appeared? *Rest* opens with Frederick Douglass once again, in an epigraph from his autobiography which reads, "Food to the indolent is poison, not sustenance." I read this as the Great White Author's sly self-positioning above the racial fray, for it is he who allows the African-American sage to pronounce the death sentence upon his white Everyman—and thereby, symbolically, upon the "distended" nation with which Harry is physically identified in such scenes as the one where he dresses up as Uncle Sam for a Fourth of July parade. Harry in fact does die of too much food and indolence—and of his insistence on competing with a young Black stranger, shooting baskets in a final burst of virility as improbable as (and evidently even more important than) his penultimate feat of bedding his beautiful daughter-in-law.

People of color (along with gay men and Jews) are everywhere in *Rest,* waiting to take over; there is, for instance, the Toyota executive, his conversation an unbelievably tasteless variant on the old "filed lice" joke. Harry's response is his usual ambiguous passivity; just as his reaction to Skeeter's sexual appropriation of Jill was an edgy voyeurism, so now he avoids taking a position one way or the other, and is even relieved when Mr. Shimada takes away the Toyota dealership that had been the family's livelihood. He's never had to exert himself for the privileges he enjoys, and he's not about to start now—but perhaps his death should be interpreted as just another form of running, "getting out," before change is forced upon him.

For Wideman's characters, of course, there can be none of Harry's nostalgia for a simpler time—unless it's the fleeting longing for an era like the sixties when positive change seemed imminent. "Things spozed to get better, ain't they?" (14) is one of [*Philadelphia Fire*]'s refrains, along with a line that Harry might echo, from his very different point of view: "Who's in charge?"

The protagonists of Wideman's previous novels have been not individuals but matrices of relationship; the focus has been inward, upon African-American cultural and emotional life, with racism not the subject but the understood condition, the permeating weather of people's lives. In [*Philadelphia Fire*], however, the story of Cudjoe's relationships to several white figures (his wife, his editor) as well as his refashioning of *The Tempest* into an allegory of the Fall from a nonracial paradise into a state of exploitation makes the novel "about" racism in a rather different sense. It is perhaps significant that in a narrative cut loose from communal roots and largely structured around the actions of a conventional artist-hero, a book that takes on the tainted legacies of Western imperialism and Western literature, Wideman appears increasingly preoccupied with Updike's cherished themes of personal alienation, sexist acting out, and failed fatherhood.

FIRE AND ICE

Updike's relentless verisimilitude is both a social symptom and a political strategy. His obsessive transcription of brand names, prices of candy bars and houses, newspaper headlines, golf strokes, car dealers' conversations—all this has grown on him, like Harry's junk food habit. Above all, he relies on a *visual* realism that, like the media it mimics, feeds America's ever-growing appetite for pictures of itself. This appetite is insatiable precisely because ocular confirmations of the "real," especially those involved in television's weird blurring of news and fantasy, are projected in a space in which seeing is no longer the occasion for believing, but rather the convenient excuse for suspending disbelief. (Harry admires the way Reagan "floated above the facts".)

Part of Updike's startling achievement in *Rest* consists in making us feel the profound anxiety lurking just beneath the surface of these obsessive self confirmations, the dangerous instability of flickering images. Yet the surface itself is so addictive, and the political implications of the anxiety so obscured, that the effect is as much confirmatory as critical. No wonder the Great White Author is so popular! As a Wideman character would say, "Who's zooming who?"

Though Updike's technique has evolved over decades, with the first Rabbit novel he had already determined to rely heavily on visual effects (which, as he notes, have temporal implications):

> I saw the present tense in the book as corresponding to the present tense in which we experience the cinema. There is no real past in the movies; things happen, one after the other, right there in front of us. The present tense, in the late 50's, was not at all a common device in American fiction.

Not common then, but destined to be so in a culture increasingly conditioned by movies and video. Updike would use this presciently chosen tense to describe an essentially pastless America, a society in which history seems scarcely thicker than personal memory. In late middle age, Harry does begin to read about antecedents, but thinks of the project in strikingly alienated terms: "It has always vaguely interested him, that sinister mulch of facts our little lives grow out of before joining the mulch themselves."

Harry's interest is vague because he can afford to have it so. History has done nothing to him (nothing he can recognize, at any rate) that would merit his scrutiny. His shallow anchorage in family and place (which evidently suits him, since he never gets away despite all his running) provides him with no saving or damning mythology, no passionate connections. He seems hermetically sealed within his human environment, like the astronauts in their space suits during the moon landing that Updike so brilliantly deploys as foil to the terrestrial action of *Rabbit Redux.*

For Wideman, time itself becomes a medium, and it is *thick* time, palpable time, not the slippery cinematic present. In his classic Homewood trilogy (*Damballah, Hiding Place,* and *Sent for You Yesterday*), his temporal sense is intimately related to his narrative focus on communal wholes:

> Past lives live in us, through us. Each of us harbors the spirits of people who walked the earth before we did, and those spirits depend on us for continuing existence, just as we depend on their presence to live our lives to the fullest. (*Sent for You Yesterday*)

He handles time like a master weaver, expanding the crude technique of flashback and translating oral forms so as to shuttle seemingly at will among the decades of Homewood's history. In several of the novels he includes a family tree that traces the community's origins all the way back to an ex-slave named Sybela Owens (while of Harry Angstrom's ancestry we learn almost nothing beyond who his parents were).

But though [*Philadelphia Fire*]'s Cudjoe shares his name with an eighteenth-century Jamaican Maroon leader, he seems even more cut off than Harry from a usable past. The book opens with his memories of years spent in Greece, putative birth-place of Western Civ. Of his family of origin, we hear only a few paragraphs about his grandmother. We're never even told who raised him. He is not (at first) important because of his connection to anyone else, as the Homewood people always are, but simply because he's clearly the main character, and a struggling artist to boot. As we follow him through his initial efforts to learn the whereabouts of Simba, the young boy who seems to have been the sole survivor of the West Philadelphia holocaust, it appears that Wideman has planned a more formally conventional (though perhaps politically more confrontational) novel than any of the Homewood books.

In fact, [*Philadelphia Fire*] is at once more and less conventional in form than these earlier efforts; the "more," I believe, accounts largely for its problems, the "less" for its eerie impact. A series of strategic disruptions beginning about halfway through pries the narrative open, creating a layering of voices that represents not an organic community, rooted in the past, but a community of strangers, transfixed by a common despair and outrage, native sons (for all are male) of an America whose face is turned toward a desperate and unthinkable future. Among them, the authorial voice gropes to convey the real-life horror of

Wideman's loss of a son to madness and incarceration, part of the tragedy of which consists in the shattering of human continuity:

> . . . it's like undoing that picture of four generations, or the one yet to be taken of five. Having it but then watching it burn, or be erased, or unwinding. . . . This emptiness, this not having is so palpable you can pass it around a room.

In *Rabbit at Rest,* America is also in a bad way, but taking it rather calmly. Like Harry popping heart pills in the Fourth of July parade, Uncle Sam knows his occluded arteries are likely to kill him; he just hopes it will be painless. (Harry eventually ends up on a deathbed of "happy unfeeling.") Reality may be grim, the horror of our mortality underlies all life, but at least it needn't be faced except in split seconds:

> *Smack, splat,* bodies bursting across the golf courses and heathery lanes of Lockerbie drenched in night. What met them was no more than what awaits him. Reality broke upon those passengers as they sat carving their airline chicken with the unwrapped silver or dozing with tubes piping Barry Manilow into their ears and that same icy black reality has broken upon him; death is not a domesticated pet of life but a beast. . . .

Unlike this icy black hell, Wideman's fiery white one is life's whole reality, at least for some people. And this implicates all the rest:

> I could smell the smoke five thousand miles away. Hear kids screaming. We are all trapped in the terrible jaws of something shaking the life out of us.

Part of what is so engaging in Harry Angstrom's character is precisely his selfishness and inauthenticity. We are, after all, all sinners, all frequently guilty of thinking first of ourselves, doing what is pleasant and easy, avoiding the pain of reality. Harry only sins with more candor than most, with a peculiar guilelessness his creator clearly revels in depicting. What is missing from the picture is any sharply focused sense of the pain he inflicts on others. Gary Wills, in a scathing review of *Rest,* accurately points out the recurrence of domestic violence throughout the Rabbit books, but overlooks the most interesting thing about these episodes: Harry is never shown really *hurting* Janice, just as he doesn't *literally* cause the deaths of Jill or his daughter Rebecca, even though his irresponsible behavior surely contributes to their destruction.

Finally, Harry's passivity makes him a peculiarly useful symbol of his nation—for those who want to have their critique and eat their patriotism too. At first glance, his love of inaction seems a subversive strategy. In *Rabbit, Run,* he rebels against the straitjacketing fifties ideal of "maturity" by "preferring not to," and in *Rest* he lies low, secretly holding onto the pleasurable core of self that is sex, memory, forbidden sweets and fats, youthful athletic prowess, the gossipy flow of his everyday consciousness meandering among its social likes and dislikes. Yet passivity risks little of his comfortable existence; as June Jordan's poem "What Would I Do White?" attests, for the privileged doing "nothing" is enough. In Harry's case, doing nothing aligns him with vast and crushing power, power whose consequences (the Philadelphia fire, for instance) we never glimpse within Updike's fictional frame.

In the Fourth of July parade, the spectators Harry passes "wave ironically, calling 'Yaaaay' at the idea of Uncle Sam, this walking flag, this incorrigible taxer and frisky international mischief-maker." The novel's equation of harmless Harry with a bumbling but basically friendly empire accords very well with a familiar majoritarian fantasy of American innocence. ("But it is not permissible that the authors of devastation should also be innocent. It is the innocence which constitutes the crime.") For this reason, I read its "ironic wave" at America's parlous state as less an authentically critical fiction than what might best be termed a legitimating critique.

MAMA'S BABY ... DADDY'S MAYBE

"What was he looking for in women's bodies?" Cudjoe asks himself, referring to his habit of voyeurism and the compulsive conquests that preceded and followed the breakup of his marriage. Uncircumcised Harry thinks of his foreskin as an eyelid, and if he "had been less responsive he might have been a more dependable person, not so crazy to have his eye down there opened." Both men see themselves as sexually irresistible, feel put-upon by wives who won't put out at the proper moment, and include symbolic daughters among their conquests (real or fantasized). Cudjoe spies on his editor's nude teenage daughter in an episode linked to Wideman's reflections on uneasy, half-conscious fantasies about a friend's much younger girl. In *Rabbit Redux* Harry sexually exploits the teenage Jill, and in *Rest* not only fornicates with his daughter-in-law but jealously speculates on his eight-year-old granddaughter's sexual future: "Some man someday will use that tongue."

As the epigraphs to this essay indicate, both authors imply strong connections between their heroes' troubles with women and their failures with their children. (In the passage from *Rabbit, Run,* Harry is about to walk out on wife Janice in rage at her refusal to satisfy him sexually; Janice, desperate and drunk, will then accidentally drown their newborn daughter.) An indication that women present a problem to Updike and Wideman themselves, not merely to

Harry and Cudjoe, lies in the absence of whole female actors, their place too often taken by fetishized parts, the "dark crease . . . spray of curly hairs . . . dark hinge between her legs . . . delicate pinks, soft fleece" [*Philadelphia Fire*] . . . "Spread shots and pink labia and boosted tits and buttocks . . . sad little anatomy like some oyster" (*Rest*). That the fetishizing is somewhat ironically presented does not compensate for the dearth of three-dimensional women characters.

Updike's misogyny is hardly news. In *Rest* he does make a halfhearted effort to show Janice coming into her own, in a thematic parallel to the encroachments of Blacks and Japanese, but his perfunctory excursions into her thoughts sound more satirical than sympathetic. (I regard as duplicitous, by the way, this trick of venturing occasionally into points of view besides Harry's—bit of trompe l'oeil designed to demonstrate that other perspectives do count for Updike, really really they do—and thereby sneakily to reinforce our identification with Harry's dominating consciousness.) Women are reviled as "dumb mutts" or sentimentalized, accordingly as Harry feels "crowded" or aroused; the obvious danger of monotony in this scheme is averted somewhat by his ambivalence, which allows for interesting combinations of the two basic attitudes. In reporting some of his hero's Archie Bunker-like thoughts, Updike also indulges in periodic winks at the reader over Harry's head.

Wideman's fiction, though patriarchally slanted, is rarely misogynistic. In the Homewood books he creates memorable women who exist mostly in relationship to beloved, threatened males: the legendary John French's long-suffering wife Freeda; thorny Aunt Bess nursing memories of "her man" and a son killed in World War II; Lizabeth sorrowing over her imprisoned son Tommy; Lucy Tate, lover of Carl and foster sister to Brother Tate, the albino who fathers Samantha's son Junebug; Samantha, who goes insane when Junebug dies. Yet in "Little Brother" (included in the recent collection *Fever*), as in the depiction of Kwansa and her lesbian lover Toodles in *Reuben,* he seems fully capable of imagining autonomous female characters. One wonders why he doesn't do more of it. I speculate that his talent is at odds with deep-seated convictions; like a rationalist inconveniently gifted with second sight, he perhaps feels embarrassed at the inconsistency.

The pattern repeats in [*Philadelphia Fire*], where he tantalizes us with the pithy, bitter voice and riveting story of Margaret Jones, the woman Cudjoe approaches for information about Simba:

> Those dogs carried out my brothers and sisters in bags.
> And got the nerve to strap those bags on stretchers.
> Woman next to me screamed and fainted when the

cops start parading out with them bags. . . . Where was respect when they was shooting and burning and flooding water on the house? Why'd they have to kill them two times, three times, four times? Bullets, bombs, water, fire, Shot, blowed up, burnt, drowned. Nothing in those sacks but ash and guilty conscience.

After this, it's hard to go back to Cudjoe's self-pitying tale of Europe and writer's block and the pursuit of "dark creases." Yet Wideman drops Margaret Jones, inexplicably—unless perhaps the explanation lies in Cudjoe's (the author's?) uneasy sense that she (and "all her sisters") have his number: "his betrayal was double, about blackness and about being a man."

The omission of African-American women from the novel is most startling in Cudjoe's rewrite of *The Tempest* (which, we're informed, "sits dead center . . . the bounty and hub of all else written about the fire") for production by his inner-city students. Perhaps modeled in part on Aime Cesaire's *Une Tempête,* the drama reimagines the Prospero-Caliban encounter as a tale of "colonialism, imperialism, recidivism, the royal fucking over of weak by strong, colored by white, many by few."

In Cudjoe's version, the "abhorrèd slave" speech is reassigned to "Miss Ann Miranda," a confused young woman who is, Cudjoe mockingly assures us, "trying her best to be her own person," though she is really her father's daughter through and through. She prudishly ignores Caliban's none-too-subtle come-ons ("C'mere fine bitch. Make this talk"). Prospero and Caliban "will fight over her forever. Not really over her. But she is their excuse." Incredibly, Cudjoe proposes to assign Miranda's role to a talented *Black* girl, but never considers whose perspective is absent from his version of the Fall. (What in the world would Margaret Jones have to say? Not to mention Sybela Owens, whose former master's son fathered her twenty children, the original founders of Homewood.)

The Cudjoe narrative is full of inexplicable gaps and unanswered questions. Why does Cudjoe never finish his novel? Why does he seem to desire only European women? Why does he refuse any contact with his sons following his divorce? Does he really believe that Margaret Jones is correct in her assessment of his "betrayal"? Given his author's explicit identification with him ("this airy other" Wideman calls him), what if any connection is there between his suggestion that fathering "half-white sons" constitutes a racial sin and the fact that Wideman's own schizophrenic son has a white mother? (That Wideman's marriage is interracial, though not mentioned here, is discussed in his memoir **Brothers and Keepers.**) Finally, why has a writer so eloquent about his efforts *not* to abandon a son under the most

traumatic circumstances chosen as alter ego an abandoning father?

One can only imagine the difficulties under which the novel was composed. In an authorial intervention, Wideman himself notes that sadness and anxiety have begun to take their toll on his narrative powers. Perhaps the problem with Cudjoe is that Wideman gets carried away with other layers of story (because he is too distraught to control the book's structure? because these layers are simply more interesting? because he wishes deliberately to subvert the reader's expectations?) and so fails to fulfill the demands of a hero-centered narrative, which ought to include some complex exploration of the problems of character that are left dangling here. Whatever the reason, it seems significant that the most problematic lapses should be located precisely where issues of race, gender, and fatherhood converge.

The horror of losing children saturates [*Philadelphia Fire.*] Besides Simba, besides Cudjoe's sons, besides the fragmentary account of Wideman's ordeal of fatherhood, there is the death of the troubled Cassy, Cudjoe's white editor's daughter. And there are hordes of lost (male) youngsters in the streets, chanting rap lyrics that chillingly equate childhood with chattel slavery:

> They tried to shoot us, bomb us
> Drown us burn us
> They brought us here, but they can't return us.

Wideman's vision of their revenge—the zap-and-run crime sprees, the graffiti "KKK" for Kaliban's Kiddie Korps and "MPT" for the Money Power Things they covet —is both surreal and as familiar as the 10 o'clock news in any major metropolitan area.

The loss of Harry's bratty-though-aging son Nelson to cocaine addiction is a major plot element in *Rest* (as the death of daughter Rebecca was in *Rabbit, Run,* the death of "daughter"/lover Jill was in *Rabbit Redux,* and the search for an abandoned illegitimate daughter was in *Rabbit Is Rich*). However, Harry withdrew emotionally from Nelson so long ago that the effect is far from tragic. Besides, the same safety net that stretches beneath the father's small rebellions predictably shields the son from the disaster that overtakes Wideman's inner-city users. ("How's Darnell? He's in the slam, man. Five years now. Damn. Dope, man.") Having cycled through rehab and religious conversion, Nelson is around to hang over his father's deathbed and receive the following report from the edge:

> "Well, Nelson," he says, "all I can tell you is, it isn't so bad." Rabbit thinks he should maybe say more, the kid looks wildly expectant, but enough. Maybe. Enough.

This probably inaudible fragment of parental guidance closes Harry's life, and the tetralogy, on a note of ambiguous reconciliation.

Cudjoe's legacy to his symbolic son Simba is the shaky but heartfelt promise in the words *never again* that enter his mind as he leaves a poorly attended rally commemorating the Philadelphia fire victims. This step out of alienation is charged with both personal and political meaning. It is preceded by Wideman's advice to his own son never to give up because "The picture changes, if only because you've lived through one more day of hell."

Finally, Wideman's refusal to allow either Cudjoe or himself to lie down and die on Harry Angstrom's "bed of happy unfeeling" provides a note of credibly muted hope amid a dazzling catalog of desperations. Yet I set the book aside wondering how either author or "airy other" will be able to help their sons in the absence of a clearer understanding of their relationship to daughters and mothers. I long for a fictional sifting of "the ashes of this city we share" that doesn't leave women out. I marvel at the ways in which an African-American literary master capable of sustaining for the length of a novel the equivalent of James Baldwin's harrowing and still unanswered cry *"What will happen to all that beauty?"* remains a brother under the skin to the Great White Author of our times.

Michael Gorra (review date June 14 1992)

SOURCE: "The Choral Voice of Homewood," in *New York Times Book Review,* Vol. 97, June 14, 1992, p. 13.

[*Gorra is an American educator and critic. In the following review he draws comparisons between Wideman and William Faulkner, and applauds Wideman's characterizations and narrative skills in* The Stories of John Edgar Wideman.]

Any American fiction writer who sets the bulk of his work in the same place, or who draws repeatedly on the same characters, inevitably faces comparison with William Faulkner. With John Edgar Wideman's inner city Pittsburgh neighborhood of Homewood that comparison is particularly apt, though not for those simple reasons alone.

It is appropriate because the stretched-to-the-breaking-point syntax with which Mr. Wideman captures his characters' inner lives seems at times an echo of Faulknerese. It is appropriate because both are concerned with the life of a community over time. It is appropriate because they both have a feel for the anecdotal folklore through which a community defines itself, because they both often choose to present their characters in the act to telling stories, and because in drawing on that oral tradition they both write as their characters speak, in a language whose pith and vigor has not yet been worn into cliché. A basketball in Mr. Wideman's **"Doc's Story"** drops through a hoop Clean as new money"; in child in his **"Everybody knew Bubba Riff"** gets asked if he has "got teeth in them feet boy chewing out the toes of your shoes."

The comparison seems appropriate, too, because Mr. Wideman, like Faulkner, is better at creating a whole imagined world than at creating individual pieces of fiction. *The Stories of John Edgar Wideman* contains two earlier collections, *Fever* (1908) and *Damballah* (1981), along with 10 new pieces grouped under the title *All Stories Are True.* *Damballah* was the first of Mr. Wideman's Homewood books, a group that includes his novel *Sent for You Yesterday* (1993), his memoir *Brothers and Keepers* (1934) and most of his short fiction. It contains a set of linked stories about the family of John French (the name of Mr. Wideman's material grandfather), and it is stronger as a whole than in any of its individual pieces. But these stories do stand as separate works—I can imagine reading them one by one in magazines end coming away satisfied.

That is not true of Mr. Wideman's newer and more explicitly autobiographic work. The richest pieces in *All Stories Are True* seem like jugged fragments ripped from a whole—deliberately rough-edged, in terms of both their material and their finish. **"Backseat"** starts with Mr. Wideman's memories of a former girlfriend whom he sees when he returns to Homewood for his grandmother's funeral. But it then slices back into his family's past his grandmother cooking in the white folks' kitchen; her four husbands, two of them preachers; an uncle lost in World War II; a brother "in the joint" who has become a Muslim. But what binds that history to Mr. Wideman's memories of teen-age love in the back seat of the rusty car parked in his grandmother's backyard? The only thing holding the pieces of the story together is the associational power of memory. Page by page the story provides a superb rendering of moment-by-moment experience. As you read, that seems enough; finish it and you want something more.

Or do you? Put **"Backseat"** next to another visit to Homewood, recorded in the title piece of *All Stories Are True,* next to Mr. Wideman's mother talking on the front porch, remembering an old preacher at Homewood A.M.E. Zion, "black as coal and that's the color of everything he preached. Like his voice tar-brushed the Bible." And as you read you begin to collate the two stories with each other, and both of them with other stories in this volume. They reinforce one another, slowly building up an image of a place, of a world—street corners, playground basketball, churches, bars and stores and street vendors and ever-branching family trees.

The more you read John Edgar Wideman, the more impressive he seems. And I suspect that as he has accumulated this body of work—and especially since *Brothers and Keepers* revealed how heavily he has drawn on his own family's past—he has come increasingly to loosen the structure of individual pieces, allowing himself a kind of open-ended irresolution, as if to suggest that nothing is ever really finished. That is risky, and it makes me suspect that new readers will at first find Mr. Wideman's work confusing, in much the same way as one's first taste of Faulkner can seem bewildering. But to my mind the rewards of his work more than repay the initial effort.

As a kind of odd corollary, the least impressive of Mr. Wideman's recent stories are those meant to stand on their own, bravura set pieces like **"Newborn Thrown in Trash and Dies,"** or **"Signs,"** about a young teacher's experience with anonymous racist hate mail. They are vivid enough, but they seem thin, tight, written to make a point. An exception is **"Everybody Knows Bubba Riff,"** a story done in a single unpunctuated sentence, a melody tossed from instrument to instrument, voice to voice, as mourners file past the casket of a young street hustler: "Bubba go down just like anybody else you beat a cup in his chest no man the word on the set in nobody knows who did it. . . ." It is the choral voice of Homewood.

Mr. Wideman has arranged his work in reverse chronological order, and so in reading one seems to go back in time, back into a more innocent past. Part of that is historical. The earlier stories read to deal with Mr. Wideman's parents and grandparents; the distance from their time to the present can be suggested by comparing the disbelief with which the characters in **"Damballah"** react to finding a baby in a trash can with the world beyond the end of outrage in **"Newborn Thrown in Trash and Dies."**

But the increasing anguish of Mr. Wideman's landscape seems to grow from a steadily darkening personal vision as well. *The Stories of John Edgar Wideman* is a rich collection. And as I write that, I am aware of the irony in my saying so, for much of what makes this collection so rich is its account of the pain and despair of the dead-end streets of America's cities. But it is also rich in language and the imaginative resourcefulness that can give one the strength to bear that pain.

Sven Birkerts (review date 13 and 20 July 1992)

SOURCE: "The Art of Memory," in *New Republic,* Vol. 207, Nos. 4,043 and 4,044, July 13 and 20, 1992, pp. 42-44.

[*Birkerts is a noted critic and author of several books, including* The Gutenberg Elegies: The Fate of Reading in an Electronic Age *(1995). In the following review, he praises* The Stories of John Edgar Wideman *and* The Homewood Books, *calling Wideman "one of our very finest writers."*]

Success comes in different ways to different writers. Some may crash their way through with a big first book, and then spend years, even decades, trying to fulfill the promise. Others appear, disappear, and later come stumbling back. Then there are those who stoke a slow and steady fire, waiting for readers and critics to catch up with them. This has been John Edgar Wideman's way—though of course these things don't happen by design. To a large degree they just happen. The writer writes, publishes, and hopes that readers will buy what he has to sell.

Wideman, the author now of seven novels, three collections of stories and *Brothers and Keepers* (1984) a personal documentary that is probably his best-known work, has been rewarded mostly with honors and reputation-building accolades. Alongside the fireworks of writers like Toni Morrison and Alice Walker, his public reception has been downright humble. There are reasons for this. Wideman's prose is more demanding and his subject matter is less sexy. And black women writers have a much larger constituency of readers than their male counterparts.

But Wideman's train has been running on its own schedule, and it is pulling into the station. This is not so much because his newest work marks any special departure or culmination, but because the happy circumstance of two major gatherings, in *The Homewood Books* and *The Stories of John Edgar Wideman,* suddenly discloses the heft and value of what he has been doing all these years. The career has attained critical mass. Wideman is finally ready to fill the gaping hole marked "leading African-American male writer."

I understand that when I invoke Morrison and Walker as yard-stick figures for gauging Wideman's public reception, I consciously perpetuate what might be called the "segregationist" principle, according to which African-American writers are discussed alongside and in terms of one another. This, I realize, promotes the two culture split. But in truth there are two cultures, even though the greater part of, say, Morrison's or Walker's readership is probably white. The racial distinction is important. The explosion of African-American writing over the past few decades is forging a public literary culture where almost none existed before. At long last a comprehensive picture is emerging of what it is like and has been like to be black in this country. Each act of witness and exposure makes it easier for the next writer to step forward.

Interestingly, few of these works deal overtly with the encounter of black and white. They are, far more, testaments about black life within a fundamentally divided society. It is as if the excavation of the home turf must precede the interracial depictions (and indictments) that are sure to follow. And so long as this is the case, and so long as white writers concern themselves overwhelmingly with white characters in *their* fiction, the two-tier situation is likely to persist. At present it seems a necessary, if not a good, thing.

The core of Wideman's output has now been laid out conveniently before us. *The Homewood Books* comprise *Damballah* (1981), *Hiding Place* (1981), and *Sent For You Yesterday* (1984). The last two are novels, while *Damballah,* not so very different in texture or presentation, is billed as a story collection. All three, at Wideman's own instigation, were published as paperback originally— this marks their hardcover baptism. *The Stories of John Edgar Wideman,* meanwhile, offers new work in *All Stories Are True,* and also includes the author's two other books of stories, *Fever* (1989) and *Damballah.*

Damballah is the linking element here. It is also, as it happens, the best place to begin reading the Wideman archive. For in these loosely linked narratives we not only meet the presiding figures of the author's imagination, but we also encounter in their first formulation the anecdotes and legends that will surface —fleshed out or told from other vantages—in the other books. Wideman is not an inventor. He has little of the fabulist in him and could never spin the kinds of webs that Morrison spins. He is, rather, a writer of very specific witness. He writes what he knows, and what he knows—the world bounded in his nutshell—is the family and kinship network of Pittsburgh's Homewood section. Homewood is a small place, a few dozen raggedy streets, but when seen with the historian's, or genealogist's, optic and inhabited by a spirit of high empathic susceptibility, it is place enough. Through his laminations of detail and his cunning manipulation of echoes, Wideman accomplishes for his Pittsburgh what William Kennedy has for his Albany; he fixes his place to the page as a permanent, and in many ways a universal, habitation.

"Damballah" is an ancient African divinity, and as part of the epigraph citation (from Maya Deren's *Divine Horsemen: The Voodoo Gods of Haiti*) has it: "One song invoking Damballah requests that the 'Gather up the Family.'" Which is, in a sense, just what Wideman does, not only in this work but in his entire oeuvre. The complex family tree that he places, before the test leaves no doubt that these

are his own people, and that the stories, while allowing, a few liberties, are true. What makes this work fiction is the author's way of burrowing into the identities of his various characters.

For Wideman, gathering the family does not mean setting out its extended tale in any chronological fashion. Quite the reverse: Wideman pursues the logic of intimate narration. That is, he stitches together the anecdotes from the family hoard, but does so as an insider would, dispensing with explanatory transitions and cutting back and forth through time in a way that almost assumes familiarity with the big picture. If there is a density about Wideman's page, it has less to do with stylistic complexity—though he does write a packed and muscular prose—than with the reader's need to keep scrambling for a new space-time foothold.

Damballah is the source book, even though many of the characters and incidents will only take on their full significance later, as passages in other books reinscribe their centrality. Here we first read about John French and Freeda Hollinger, Wideman's grandparents, who married and in the early 1900s had four children, one of whom, Lizabeth, is the author's mother. **"Lizabeth, The Caterpillar Story"** recounts a key episode. Freeda sits rocking a young Lizabeth, on her lap, telling her a story about a caterpillar, when she suddenly sees her husband coming along the alley. She also sees that the man behind him has pulled a gun. Freeda promptly crashes her fist through the windowpane, alerting John French to danger, and thereby earning the scar that becomes a kind of bead on the family rosary. While nothing overtly tragic has happened, the moment captures something essential about the family's life: the nimbus of danger that John French wears, the resourcefulness and domestic protectiveness that Freeda embodies. The afternoon takes its place as one of the essential tales in the family repertoire.

Lizabeth, as a girl, loves to sit in Freeda's lap, and loves to listen to her reminisce about early days in Homewood, the times when "Cassina Way nothing but dirt. Crab apple trees and pear trees grew where you see all them shacks." And Wideman in his turn loves to dizzy the reader with unexpected time switches, as in this parenthetical aside:

> Lizabeth needs her mother's voice to make things real. (Years later when she will have grandchildren of her own and her mother and father both long dead Lizabeth will still be trying to understand why sometimes it takes someone's voice to make things real. She will be sitting in a room and the room full of her children and grandchildren and everybody eating and talking and laughing but she will be staring down a dark tunnel and that dark, empty tunnel is her life . . .)

The cadences map the circlings and repetitions of intimate discourse; they gradually connect us with the indescribable potency that lies at the core of all family life.

If the focus of the early stories falls on John French and Freeda and Lizabeth, the later pieces bring a more distressing present into view. It is a tragedy in the life of the real Wideman family that Robby, the author's younger brother, was arrested in 1976 for his part in a robbery, a crime that left one man dead at the scene. Wideman gave the event full-length treatment in his *Brothers and Keepers,* but it has obviously haunted his fiction-writing imagination as well. Indeed, as Wideman wrote in that book:

> At about the time I was beginning to teach Afro-American literature at the University of Pennsylvania, back home on the streets of Pittsburgh Robby was living through the changes in black culture and consciousness I was reading about and discussing with my students in the quiet of the classroom. . . . I was trying to discover words to explain what was happening to black people. That my brother might have something to say about these matters never occurred to me.

By the time he wrote *Damballah,* however, he had discovered the words. In the story **"Tommy,"** Wideman plants himself for the first time in his brother's shoes, summoning up the rage and confusion that spawned the crime and accompanied the terrified escape attempt. He pushes in past the Black Power slogans of the day, to expose the looks and feel of a changed world. What was once a rough but cohesive community is now, at least in Tommy's eyes, a ravaged place from which hope has been barred. Drugs and violence, familiar specters of our own day, tyrannize the streets. It is the most dizzying time switch of all, the bisection of the molten flow of memory by the jagged tremors of a new urban reality. Tommy has not been able to escape as his brother did. Homewood comes to us filtered through his sense of entrapment:

> It was a bitch in the world. Stone bitch, Feeling like Mister Tooth Decay crawling all sweaty out of the gray sheets. Mom could wash them every day, they still be gray. Like his underclothes. Like every mother fucking thing they had and would ever have. Doo Wah Diddy. The rake jerked three or four times through his bush. Left there as a decoration and weapon. You could fuck up a cat with those steel teeth. You could get the points sharp as needles. And draw it swift as Billy the Kid.

"Tommy" lays the ground for *Hiding Place,* the novel that was published the same year as *Damballah. Hiding Place* unfolds in a fairly simple contrapuntal narration. One line belongs to Bess, an old woman identified on the family tree as having been born in the 1880s (she is old enough to re-member Sybela Owens, who escaped from slavery and made her way to Pittsburgh, where she and a man named Charlie Bell had twenty children and founded the Homewood dynasty). Bess lives alone in a derelict shack high up on Bruston Hill, the original family site, where she potters about and continues to mourn Eugene, her one son who died in the last days of the Pacific war.

The other line belongs to Tommy, who has taken refuge from the law in Bess's woodshed. The two are as unlike as can be—the wizened old survivor and the gangly young man with his towering Afro and the "fat nobby-toed shoes with heels as high as a woman's." But behind the harshness of their interchanges we can locate the slightest filament of family tenderness. As Bess mutters to herself in one telling passage (Tommy has fallen asleep in her kitchen): "Crazy as a bedbug but that don't make no nevermind cause I know all about you. Seen them rabbits in your eyes and grave-dust on them long feet. Where else you gon be but out there in my shed?" Wideman merely suggests the connection between Tommy and Bess's long-dead son; we feel it as the lightest prickling on the skin.

Sent For You Yesterday takes yet another vantage on the place and time of Homewood. Here Wideman, speaking as "Doot" (one of his many family nicknames), introduces his uncle Carl (Lizabeth's older brother), recreating scenes from Carl's boyhood friendship with Brother Tate, a piano-playing albino black, and Lucy, the hardluck woman who has become his companion. Carl is a one-time drug user now reformed into a drinker, but the book is not about his habits or vices. Rather, we follow the slow, sad trolling of his memory and the jumbled processional of the many eras of his life. Doot is there to observe and record:

> At certain moments Carl pauses. His eyes turn inward and he's listening rather than telling his story. The words stop. Nothing moves but his vacant eyes searching somewhere for something that will help him continue his tale, complete the frozen gesture. He's telling his own story, he knows his story better than anybody else, but in the long pauses as he sits motionless on a barstool in the Velvet Slipper, he's waiting for a witness. A voice to say amen. waiting for one of the long gone old folks to catch his eye nod to him and say *Yes. Yes. You got that right, boy.*

And on it goes, the drift of time, the sudden flaring forth of the bygone. Out of the back-and-forth shuttling, out of the constant traffic with the sensuous particulars of the then and the now, Homewood rises as if seen through a stereopticon. The sheer abundance of its moods and vistas prohibits any simple tallying of themes. The books are, hackneyed as this may sound, about life: about making do in adversity, about the myriad ways in which people love, fight, celebrate, sin, repent. . . . Men and women are seen into with equal acuity and presented with compassion. Wideman's whole enterprise of recollecting and reanimating the past arises from a deep, one might even say scourging, love.

Since the completion of the Homewood cycle, Wideman has been working with new modes and approaches. With *Brothers and Keepers* he shifted his narrative vantage a few degrees to write the nonfiction account of his brother's crime, sifting the documentary portions together with his own anguished musings about the divergence of fates within one family. In 1989 he published *Fever,* another collection of stories. And the very next year came *Philadelphia Fire,* a bewilderingly fragmented but lyrically intense novel about one man's search, in the wake of the MOVE bombings, for clues about his own and his city's compromised past. Wideman was reaching for new material, trying to break the spell of his history with more urgent bulletins from the present. It was as if he had decided that however inexhaustible his store of material, he could not keep filling in his Homewood portrait for the rest of his writing life.

The Stories of John Edgar Wideman, unlike *The Homewood Books,* is arranged in reverse chronological order. The newest work, the previously unpublished *All Stories Are True,* is positioned first, followed by *Fever; Damballah* anchors the gathering. As it happens, the most powerful stories are the ones that carry the Homewood echo: Wideman is at his best when he culls directly from his experience. The tour de force of *All Stories Are True* is **"Backseat,"** an extended work that braids together vignettes about the life of his dying grandmother with memories of his own sexual initiation. His return to the grandmother's house sparks up memories of his first lover, a girl named Wanda who was the daughter of his grandmother's tenant. The prose is dazzling. Wideman telescopes the whole world of Homewood into his sweeping sentences; he runs the keyboard past to present and back with true stylistic dash, culminating in a burst of sexual surprise regained:

> What I wasn't ready for was the way things speeded up and tangled up, her body with mine, mine with hers, legs, hair, fingers, touching and moaning, little increments of mixed-up back-and forth sallies, then a landslide, stuff I'd only imagined or read in stolen paperbacks, or tried on myself locked in the bathroom or day-dreamed under the covers when I thought my younger brother Otis had finally stopped flopping and farting for the night and was snoring himself to oblivion on his side of the bed. Her smells and wetness, squeezing, opening. Starting slowly inch by inch, amazed at what I was seeing, at how simple it was once you got started, and trying to prolong, imprint, and hurry at the same time everything new and incredible and scaring the shit out of me while I enjoyed it to death.

The past-obsession of **"Backseat"** is an exception. By and large the stories that draw on the author's life have a present-day edge. The title piece is a heartbreaking account of visits by Wideman and his mother to the prison where Wideman's brother is serving his term. And **"Signs"** narrates the chilling stages in the persecution of a young graduate student by a phantom figure who leaves notes and signs for her to find, with messages like *Nig bitch go home.* Another story, **"What He Saw,"** restages a terrifying interlude during a visit to South Africa. We find Wideman vigorously contesting the gravity that kept pulling him back into the realm of family legend.

While the stories feel a bit thinner than the earlier material—they lack the sepia lyricism that the past confers—they are redeemed by the relevance of their racial insights. Squarely, and without histrionics, Wideman communicates the gradations of fear and hopelessness felt by his characters. Racism exists and will not soon disappear. As Kendra, the student in **"Signs,"** realizes after finding a *Whites Only* notice affixed to the bathroom in the grad dorm:

> You couldn't just breeze by it. No more than you could breeze by an old lover in the cafeteria in the morning having coffee with another woman. You were entangled. Like her toes in the faucet. Whatever you did, you were affecting the temperature of the water. Toes twisting or toes frozen, you implicated.

Blacks and whites alike are caught in this tense and baffled entanglement. The segregationist ethos no longer works. For Kendra the dissonance becomes overwhelming—denial erupts and she ends by convincing herself that the incidents never happened. In another story, **"A Voice Foretold,"** the black narrator accompanies a white photographer into a tenement and tries to overcome his hatred of him, later conceding: "I share his hurt, his compassion, curiosity, the weight of memory he wears around his neck on a strap." There are no easy stances, and few simplifying bromides. A keen sense of sorrow and a will to understand the alien perspective mitigate what might in other hands emerge as a chronicle of hopelessness.

Alas, it must be said that some of the other stories, in this grouping as well as in *Fever,* have at times a strained, *literary* feel. We find ourselves in the hands of a virtuoso stylist with an idea, one who is prone (Wideman was an all-Ivy League basketball star) to dribble behind the back when no one is covering him. **"Everybody Knew Bubba Riff,"** for instance, spins a ten-page story out of a single hemorrhaging sentence: "Voices are a river you step in once and again never the same Bubba here you are dead boy dead dead

dead nigger with spooky Boris Karloff powder caked on your face boy . . ." And **"Surfiction,"** in *Fever,* fashions a collage from a professor's extratextual meanderings and a post-structuralist dissection of a work by Charles Chestnutt. There are some intriguing fillips, but the piece hardly stands up alongside the author's more straightforward offerings.

As *Damballah* reminds us, Wideman may not be a master of the classic short story, but he is a sublime storyteller. When he works in extended sequences, free from the demands of formal plot architecture, he is unexcelled. And this collection, my cavils aside, shows the writer working at full muscle, tunneling through the past to connect with the ore rifts of generational experience, but also exposing rifts of the other kind—the societal rifts that have defined so much about black culture in this country and elsewhere. Reading Wideman's collections presents us with a graph of atmospheric changes in black cultural life. Our job is to chalk on the overlay graph, the one that shows the political and economic depredations by the powers that be. As Homewood has gone, so has the nation.

As I suggested at the outset, there has been for some years a vacancy at the table of African-American *letters.* In one sense, of course, it is nonsensical to speak in terms of "leading" this and "foremost" that. But we do it anyway. And while any number of black women writers have staked a claim to the distaff title, the males have not generated a similar excitement. We have had no Ellisons, Wrights, or Baldwins in recent memory. Writers, like Ishmael Reed, John A. Williams, Charles Johnson, David Bradley, and Al Young have all done vital work in fiction, but none has manifested that cumulative solidity—not yet—to make them inheritors of the mantle.

On the basis of the gathered evidence, I would say that John Edgar Wideman has. Though he has not sought the public spokesman's role, he has certainly been having his say. His depictions have evolved into an ever more comprehensive picture of black American life in our time, and they have done so sanely and empathically. The work is balanced— humanly balanced—with extreme scenarios taking their place alongside the evocations of more prosaic domesticity. Through it all there is a feeling of life pushing on with unstemmed momentum.

Wideman may not be a writer bent upon positions and polemics. He feels too strongly the novelist's traditional piety before the workings of fate in individual lives. This does not mean, however, that he cannot get angered and righteous about the miasma of our racial relations. (*Philadelphia Fire* crackles with its narrator's rage at the hypocrisy and corruption of the white power structure.) But Wideman's vision charges him to make constant provision for love and goodness, too. The urge is toward inclusiveness, not accommodation. He is building a picture of the world the hard way—person by person, life by life. He is now our leading black male writer and (casting the nonsense of these divisions aside) one of our very finest writers, period.

John Edgar Wideman with Jessica L. Lustig (interview date Fall 1992)

SOURCE: "Home: An Interview with John Edgar Wideman," in *African American Review,* Vol. 26, No. 3, Fall, 1992, pp. 453-57.

[*In the following interview, Wideman discusses the "fictional, constructed landscapes" he created in his works.*]

I went to Amherst, Massachusetts, on April 23, 1992, to talk with John Edgar Wideman on the U Mass campus, where he teaches a graduate course in creative writing. Wideman's literary mapping and charting of Homewood's neighborhood streets and people indicate the complexities and paradoxes of contemporary American urban literature. In discussing his portraits of Homewood in *Damballah, Hiding Place, Sent for You Yesterday,* and *Reuben,* we explored the ways in which fictional, constructed landscapes can be read.

[*Lustig:*] *You moved from Homewood when you were twelve, yet it's the place that you keep circling back to. I find it interesting that, despite all those years away, it's the primary place in your work, that you keep going back to it as defining* home. *Maybe you could talk a little about that.*

[Wideman:] Okay, but let me start with a distinction. There is a neighborhood in Pittsburgh called Homewood. It was there before I was born, and probably when I'm dead it will still be called that. It's considered a number of streets, houses, population changes—people get old and die. It's real place in that sense. Now, for many of the years between birth and about twelve, I lived in Homewood. Other times I've lived in Shadyside, which is a completely different neighborhood. That's the level of fact. The distinction I want to make is that, once I started to write, I was creating a place based partly on memories of the actual place I lived in, and partly on the exigencies or needs of the fiction I was creating. Once I began to write, to create, I felt no compunction to stay within the bounds of Homewood. Now how that fictional place relates to the actual Homewood is very problematic. And, depending on the questions you ask, that relationship will be important or irrelevant, superfluous.

If I were to tell the story of your life in my fiction, I might talk about your height, and keep you tall, but I also might make your hair dark, because I want a heroine who has dark hair. And I might know your parents well, or know just a tiny bit about them, but I could make one a sailor, and the other a college teacher, just because that's what I need in my fiction. People could then go back and say, well now, what did Wideman know about this young woman named Jessica, and how long did he know her, and how tall is she really, and what do her parents do? But all that might or might not have anything to do with the particular book in which you appear. So although I have lived in other places, the Homewood which I make in my books has continued to grow and be confident. It has its own laws of accretion and growth and reality.

What I think is really interesting about the way this Homewood, in your books, is figured is that the post-1970 landscape has been in a lot of ways devastated. Your characters—and you, for that matter—talk about Homewood Avenue as it is now, as opposed to what it was in the '50s, or the '40s. And yet the way in which the people relate to each other makes it feel almost like a rural place, like a small town. I think that a neighborhood is an urban construct, so I'm very interested in the way that these people seem to interrelate as a small-town community.

I go in the other direction. I think it's the people who make the neighborhood. That's the difference between learning about Homewood through my writing and learning about Homewood from sociologists. There have been interesting books written about Homewood, but the people make the place. They literally *make* it. Yes, Homewood Avenue is devastated, but when the character in **"Solitary"** walks down that street, she sees the street at various times in its history. So it's populated by the fish store, by five-and-tens. She remembers places that were there when she was a little girl. Characters do that all the time. They walk through the landscape which, from the point of view of some person who's either following them with a camera or looking at them from a distance, is just vacant lots, but the person in the story sees something else. What counts most is what the person inside the story sees. That's where the life proceeds; that's where Homewood has a definition.

In other places in my writing I talk about how the old people *made,* created the town. But they created it not so much with bricks and boards; a lot of them simply moved into houses where other people had lived. They created it through their sense of values and the way they treated one another, and the way they treated the place. That's *crucial* to the strength of Homewood, and it's something very basic about African American culture. Africans couldn't bring African buildings, ecology, languages wholesale, in the material sense, to the New World. But they brought the invis-

ible dimensions of their society, of our culture, to this land. That's what you have to recognize: This world that's carried around in people's heads overlays and transcends and transforms whatever the people happen to be. So it's not anything that people in Homewood invented. To make something from nothing is almost a tradition.

Home, what could be called territory or turf, in your books, is often shaped by streets. You know, some of your characters will sort of read a litany of streets. I know that's so in **Hiding Place.** *That seems to me like the equivalent of boundaries or property lines in rural or suburban areas, like a sense of possession, or of defining your place, your landscape.*

Absolutely, and I'd take your point a step further. That litany, or *incantation,* is a way of *possessing* the turf. You name it, you claim it. There isn't that much physical description, I don't think, of Homewood. It's mostly the inner geography, and then street names as the most concrete manifestation of that geography. The street names are there, I think, because they have a magic. They have an evocative quality, and that's something that can be shared when you speak. There are streets, and when I say them to you and you walk down them, that's the opening. It's no coincidence that some of the great catalogues that occur in classical literature have to do with the names of the ships, the names of places. For sailors or voyagers or travelers, naming is a way, literally, of grounding themselves.

Talking about streets, or a neighborhood, in connection with this whole idea of memory and memory links, and evocation, and incantation . . . what I find so striking is what you do with time, and how much of your work starts or is set in the present and then goes back, and back, and back. And a lot of the time the look of the present is very different from that of the past, especially since urban renewal. You often refer to the effects of urban renewal as having devastated whole blocks or houses that you used to live in or live next to. I think that could be an interesting argument against urban renewal, because of the idea of memory, those memory links, the tangible memory links or the physical memory links, to the past.

I don't know that it's so much an argument against urban renewal, because urban renewal is a big political decision, and lots of factors go into it—and some of the reasons for doing it are very good indeed. I mean, if you take that preservationist argument to its logical conclusion, then there's a good reason for keeping the slave barracks in the South behind the big house. You don't want to lock yourself into some ghettoized existence.

There's nothing essential about things; it's how people see them, how people treat them. You could have the same attachment to a shiny new house, if you really felt it was yours, if you felt you had experience in it. For instance, the house that the Tates live in in **Sent For Your Yesterday,** that's a big house, a roomy house. And there are obviously well-put-together staircases and stuff like that. It might even be a house that *had* been urban-renewed, at least remodeled, et cetera. And it's a perfectly good situation, although it's kind of haunted and scary, too.

Well, I'm thinking more of urban renewal as it was conceived of in the late '50s and during the '60s, as it involved the razing of blocks and sometimes of entire neighborhoods.

The impetus behind that kind of urban renewal was a simple-minded remaking of people by changing their external circumstances.

Or slum clearance, as it was sometimes called.

What that really was about was turning black people into white people, without a critique of what was wrong with white people, what was wrong with the world that blacks were being asked to become part of. That's the whole integration-into-a-burning-building kind of thing. That's why it didn't make any sense, and why it was devastating. Nobody asked what was important, what was valuable about the black community that shouldn't go, that should resist the bulldozers. There was just a wholesale exchange. We'll give you these external circumstances because we think they're good, because our lives are prospering. We'll plunk this down on you, and it'll become your world. When you examine it that way, then the real problems behind urban renewal become clearer.

You say, I think it's in **Brothers and Keepers,** *that your grandmother's house on Finance was your link to Homewood at the stage when that book was being written, the early '80s, and you were remembering the railroad tracks going overhead. I know this isn't a fictional work, but that image sticks out for me because it's very evocative, because I understand the sense of this place that is yours, that you're linked into through your grandmother, because I have that with two neighborhoods in Brooklyn that were home to me. I'd like to hear more about why it's Homewood, and not parts of Philadelphia, not parts of Laramie, that you write about. You've been in many places that you could write about as, figure as, home—many places in which you could absorb the stories. A lot of times it seems that your places are alive because of the stories that people tell about the places, continually, to keep them alive.*

Well, there's something simple going on here. Those elements of Philadelphia that I came to appreciate and enjoy,

and the same with Laramie, I plug into Homewood. They're in there, although they're kind of disguised. If I met somebody yesterday who had some quality that I felt was fascinating, and it either reminded me of my grandfather or suddenly opened up some mystery that I had in my mind, well, I might stick that in. It's not like there's this well of Homewood experiences that I keep drawing from; it's stuff in the future that I'm also locating there. It has to happen that way, or else the work would become static, a moldy thing, nostalgic. The neighborhood, the place, is an artistic contrivance for capturing *all* kinds of experience, and it works to the degree that it is permeable, that things that happen outside Homewood continue to grow up.

That makes sense. The idea of plugging in the different parts is an elegant way of putting the writing process, or the writerly process. But if we're talking about the neighborhood as sort of this artistic crucible for you, I'm interested in the environment that you create in your books; that is, Homewood. Am I correct in understanding that the environment forces some of your characters into situations? I read Tommy, in **Hiding Place,** *as having been forced into his situation through an accumulation of circumstances.*

I think it's safer, and it's always more productive and useful, to look at the individual case. That's, again, the break in the fictional from the sociological. The play of environment versus character, versus the individual, to me is pretty meaningless when translated into the statistical terms that you use for gas molecules. You know, where and how they separate, how many will end up in this corner. That's sort of silly when you only have one life and your life pushes you in the way that it does. It's also kind of dangerous to generalize from one life. I want to examine the interplay of environment and character at the level at which it's meaningful, and that is the individual life. What part does biology play, what part does nature, as opposed to nurture, play? You can only answer that, and even then in a very tentative way, by looking at the individual life. I'm not making any case, except the case of the person.

And so this play of the place, and the individual, is going to create different stories for each of the persons in that place?

Exactly. I mean, it's not because Robby gave in, because something in the shape of Robby's life was the shape it was. I had other brothers; there were lots of other kids like Robby who turned out a different way.

I understand. Let me ask you another question about **Hiding Place.** *The last line of that book is, "They better make sure it doesn't happen so easy ever again." It's Mother Bess, you know, talking about Tommy's situation.*

I think that can be really interesting in conjunction with what you said about incantation, and litany. That line, for me, embodies what I see you doing with different memory links as stories passed between people, and between generations, because I think one of the most important things about this place that you create in this book is that it's generational. It's an established neighborhood that's generational, that continues to exist with links between generations. As a reader you wonder, what's going to happen in this place? What is happening with the new generation? I'm not asking you to say, here's what's happening, here's the news, you know, but that kind of line, coming from a representative of the older generation, not the younger one . . . as readers, can we infer that you are saying that, for these people, a memory link has got to be established, and strong, or else the nature of Homewood will be lost, as a place, as a home?

I think that's fair enough, if I understand what you're saying. The learning goes in both directions: Older people teach younger people, and younger people also teach their elders. I wanted Bess's last words to reverberate. I wanted almost to make hers a kind of avenging, or a threatening, voice. The community has learned something, she has learned something, and now it's in the air, it's out there, that idea *should* be out there. And if that idea *is* out there, an idea that has a certain amount of anger, because of what's happened to this relative of hers and, knowing something about his life circumstances, the rotten deal he got, the love she has for him . . . these are things that are very powerful. They can only be allowed to fester, or be ignored, at one's peril. She's arming the community with a knowledge of itself which will hopefully open the door to a healthier future. The singer, or the storyteller, if he or she is functioning the way he or she should, traditionally, should arm, should enlighten, should tell you what's *happening*, tell you what you need to do, what your choices are. That's the stage I wanted to take Bess to, in that book—and, with her, the reader and the community. Bess inhabits the same world the little fairy who helps to burn things down in **Hiding Place** inhabits. Here is a *blood* knowledge, it's very palpable, but it's also a world of the spirit.

It's what you can call upon.

Yeah.

James Robert Saunders (essay date December 1992)

SOURCE: "Exorcizing the Demons: John Edgar Wideman's Literary Response," in *Hollins Critic*, Vol. XXIX, No. 5, December, 1992, pp. 1-10.

[*Saunders is a professor of English at Purdue University and critic. In the following essay, he surveys Wideman's works, delineating the author's response to the inherent dualities of sociology, psychology, and image faced by African Americans.*]

In his socio-literary classic *The Souls of Black Folk* (1903), W. E. B. Du Bois characterized African-Americans as being in possession of a double-consciousness in which "one ever feels his twoness—an American, a Negro; two souls, two thoughts, two unreconciled strivings; two warring ideals in one dark body." The notion is a persistent one in the annals of African-American literature. James Weldon Johnson through his narrator in *The Autobiography of an Ex-Coloured Man* (1912), makes the further observation that this psychological condition reflects a "dual personality" exacerbated in the psyche of a black man "in proportion to his intellectuality." According to that analysis, the condition assumes an even greater significance in direct proportion to an individual's capacity to comprehend his predicament.

If the narrator in Johnson's novel is correct, then we should be especially concerned about what life has consisted of for a person such as John Edgar Wideman. Raised in the predominantly black, inner-city community of Homewood in Pittsburgh, Pennsylvania, Wideman would later win a scholarship to attend the University of Pennsylvania where he would become an All-Ivy League basketball player in addition to being Phi Beta Kappa. But it was the winning of another important distinction that catapulted him into the international spotlight. In 1963, he became only the second African-American to win the prestigious Rhodes Scholarship. Prior to that year, the only African-American ever to have received the award was Alain Locke in 1907.

When Wideman won the scholarship, *Look* magazine covered the story in an article, "The Astonishing John Wideman," where the awardee was credited with having stipulated that as far as he was concerned, "being Negro is only a physical fact." He elaborated:

> "If there were something I wanted very badly that being Negro prevented me from doing, then I might have the confrontation of a racial problem, and I would be driven to do something about it. . . . But so far, the things that I've wanted to do haven't been held back from me because of my being a Negro. So the problem is not my own problem, not something I feel I have to cope with or resolve."

He was saying, in so many words, that race was not an issue for him. And perhaps, during his college years, he was someone who could afford this luxury. Many on the UPenn faculty considered him a genius; fellow students likewise regarded him highly. Maybe he was just one of those rare individuals who would have succeeded in spite of any obstacle.

Then there is another way to interpret Wideman's statement as Chip Brown, in a 1989 *Esquire* article, suggests when he says that "to page through the paean is to study a time capsule on race relations circa 1963: the monochrome white students with their pre-skinhead haircuts, the unquestioned assumption that assimilation is a one-way street and black shall bend to white." How does a young black man respond to his place in a college setting that is overwhelmingly white? How does he respond when he is the star athlete, Pharisee (treasurer of the senior men's honor society), and recipient of a scholarship to Oxford University. *People* magazine, in 1985, quotes Wideman as having said, "I believed in the whole Horatio Alger thing." And why shouldn't he have believed in it? He had come from inauspicious beginnings; his father at various times had been a waiter and a trash collector. The son applied himself, strove to be something better. Why shouldn't he believe in the dream? Why couldn't he be, first and foremost, and American?

Interestingly enough, just one year after the *People* article, Wideman agreed to an interview with Kay Bonetti which appeared in *The Missouri Review*. In this latter interview he expressed a different position than what he had said earlier with regard to how he perceived himself within the Horatio Alger framework. Now he was contradictorily maintaining, "I was never simply somebody who bought the American dream, the Horatio Alger myth. I was always somebody who had ghosts, who had demons." Which John Wideman should be believed? And what exactly was the nature of those demons? Excessive guilt? A sense that he was running from his roots in the Homewood community?

In the *People* article, Wideman's wife, Judy, offered additional insight into her husband's dilemma. She declared:

> "In the '60s, there was a gradual willingness on John's part to look at himself and his background. It was painful, difficult for him to do. In order to achieve the things he'd done, he'd had to look away. The difference between where he was and where his family was was very difficult for him to reconcile."

Upon his return to the United States, Wideman accepted a professorship at his alma mater and set about the task of becoming a writer.

It has become fashionable among some critics to conclude that located within the context of the author's first three novels (*A Glance Away,* 1967; *Hurry Home,* 1969; and *The Lynchers,* 1973) is evidence that he was trying to adjust

his work to meet the standards of a mainstream white literary tradition. In *Glance,* we certainly do see elements of James Joyce and T. S. Eliot. Wideman's Robert Thurley, for example, is just another version of Eliot's J. Alfred Prufrock who mourns "I grow old . . . I grow old . . . / I shall wear the bottoms of my trousers rolled." Thurley is an elderly professor whose limited hopes hinge on the prospect "that life would continue to be played out in half-light, in pleasant bodily fatigue" even as he waits for the musical sounds and "knew the oboe was the sound of death."

Home is the continuation of a modernist style of writing consisting of stream of consciousness technique and Joycean-type reliance on dashes to distinguish between different speakers. In one memorable scene our protagonist, Cecil Braithwaite, accedes to a shoeshine boy who wants to shine Braithwaite's shoes without receiving any payment. But once Braithwaite's shoes are shined, the boy appeals to a nearby crowd of blacks and insists that Braithwaite is attempting to exploit him. The collective voice of the crowd, referring to Braithwaite as magistrate, demands:

> —Pay the boy, magistrate. . .
> —How much do you want.
> —We want you, magistrate. . . .
> —I've done nothing wrong.

Someone punches Braithwaite in the face as he stumbles along, with the mob crowding in on him to exact further punishment. The episode is reminiscent of Kafka's Joseph K. who, in *The Trial* (1925), is awakened by two strangers who drag him off and accuse him of having committed a crime of which he is unaware.

While *Lynchers* is generally regarded as the last novel written in Wideman's early phase, it has also been suggested that it marks the beginning of a major shift in emphasis on the part of the author. James W. Coleman remarks, "The world that he creates is less dominated by white literary vision than that in *A Glance Away,* and he focuses on life in the black community much more here than in *Hurry Home.*" Indeed *Lynchers* is quite different from either of Wideman's earlier works. One is taken aback by the chronological listing of lynchings, beatings, and various other types of assaults by whites against blacks. That list enumerates 116 incidents that took place in the relatively short period between 1867 and 1871. But the message Wideman means to deliver has to do with the building up of animosities over a much longer period of time to the point where four young black men have resolved to turn the tables, so to speak, and conduct a lynching of their own. It will be a modern-day lynching, and the victim will be a white policeman.

Willie Hall, the leader of the conspiracy, explains how the

killing will make an important statement to society's privileged classes. The lynching will serve as a refutation of the complacency that had allowed those upper classes to believe they could exist quietly, insulated from the horrors of inner city life. The lynching will be a warning: "No, the flunkies you pay to keep us within bounds are not enough. We must show how the cops are symbolic. . . . We will lynch one man but in fact we will be denying a total vision of reality." The improper vision of reality that Hall alludes to is the one portraying America as a place where all is well while in actuality society is on the verge of upheaval. Killing the policeman will itself cause upheaval, but this way, there is a good chance that a large amount of control will be in the hands of Hall and those who are like him. Hall urges:

> Do you believe what we're seeing this morning? . . . Do you see the next step? How vulnerable the lies are that hold this mess together as it stands, Do you realize how we have all the evidence we need to expose the lies, to shatter the arbitrary balance and order. Nothing but an alley between two alien forms of life. The whites are just a few paces away living in a manner which makes a mockery of our suffering. Two people in a fifty thousand dollar town house. . . . And babies on this street sleeping in drawers, on the floor. . . . It's an alley we can cross, we can cross in numbers. Nothing in the world can stop us if we decide the barrier is not there anymore. If we all die at least the lie will die with us.

In these times of governmental budgetary crises and private industry layoffs, many whites have also been made to suffer. There is the urge—especially when executives are nonetheless thriving economically—to say that the issue has more to do with class distinctions than with matters of race. Actually, both class and race are important factors. But as one listens to statistics, the racial factor assumes a frightening dimension—infant mortality twice as high among blacks, unemployment twice as high, and a prison population so filled with black men that it has almost become euphemistic to acknowledge that there are more young black men, between the ages of 18 and 25, in jail than there are attending college.

Wideman has always been deeply concerned, in his writing, with those very issues. In a 1988 interview, he made it clear "there was no game plan at the beginning which was scuttled for another game plan somewhere in the middle. There is always back and forward and testing." He pursued creative writing, in large part, due to opportunities he saw for experimentation. In *Lynchers,* even with its racial themes, one still sees the Joycean use of dashes as a means of distinguishing between speakers. Furthermore, stream of consciousness technique continues to be employed to con-

vey an ambiguity that pervades racial issues the author is intent on examining.

A close analysis of *Home*'s Cecil Braithwaite reveals Wideman's alter ego, Braithwaite was the "first of his race to do, to be, etc." Wideman is giving us a glimpse of his years at UPenn. Since, by 1973, many more black undergraduates were attending historically white institutions than was the case during his undergraduate years between 1959 and 1963, the author has updated the social phenomenon and made the institution a historically white law school where, even in the early 1970s, the percentage of black enrollment was still painfully low. A surrealistic chorus of blacks taunts Braithwaite:

> Real is Cecil, real were those fine white men your classmates and what they do and what you will do as practitioner of the law. Nothing good comes without sacrifice. Christ paid for our sins. Let *them* pay for their own. Don't you know *they'll* only drag you down, eat you up, Cecil. Being one of *them* is as impossible, frankly, as is being one of us. That's fact, it's written. I kid you not. Just look at the realities of the situation.

Much of *Home* is devoted to the protagonist's psychological journey in search of himself while the author is simultaneously engaged in a probing intellectual search of his own.

Wideman's search runs him head-on into the circumstances of his younger brother, Robby. In a *60 Minutes* interview conducted in 1985, the younger brother recapitulated events surrounding the first time he ran afoul of the law. John was summoned in from Philadelphia to "take him upstairs and . . . talk to him." The brothers went to Robby's room, but nothing was resolved. "We couldn't talk," explained Robby, "because our worlds were so different."

What had happened between the time when John had grown up in Homewood and the time, 10 years later, when Robby came along? Describing how the community was when he was a boy, John, in that *60 Minutes* interview, made the following assessment:

> "The community itself was much more closely knit. It was much more like a small Southern town. . . . if I went out on the street, somebody on some porch, Mrs. Ellis, would be checking me out. If I went too far, or did something I wasn't supposed to do, she certainly would tell my mother. The crime was petty-ante stuff, and usually not directed with any kind of brutality or viciousness inside of the community."

The community had changed. Adult support mechanisms were no longer as strong as they had been in the past.

However, it should also be considered to what extent sibling rivalry was a factor. In the collection of reminiscences entitled **Brothers and Keepers** (1984), Robby confides, "Wasn't nothing I could do in school or sports that youns hadn't done already. People said, Here comes another Wideman. He's gon be a good student like his brothers and sister. . . . I was another Wideman, the last one, the baby, and everybody knew how I was spozed to act." Robby had a choice: He could go along with the program of high achievement or strike out in a different direction.

John would later come to understand his brother's agony. Sprinkled throughout **Glance** are episodes that convey what it must have been like having an older brother who excelled in everything. Eddie Lawson—as much a major protagonist as Robert Thurley—recalls being teased and thinking, "My brother was the worst . . . because he was my brother and different because he was bigger, stronger and was loved." Perhaps those impressions are not justified. But in the younger brother's mind, the impressions become the reality.

Eddie is fixated on his older brother who "grew fast and rank, a strong hardhanded boy whose shoes had to be left outside at night. Huge, smelly things Martha would carry dangling like fish from their strings, holding her nose but laughing and loving the ritual." The shoes signify communal effort. The brother, Eugene, is John Wideman who shoveled snow off the courts so that he could practice basketball through the winter. The sister's role was to make sure that his shoes were left outside overnight so they would be aired out and ready for use the next day. She facilitated John's efforts as did his parents in struggling to provide a home for the developing star. All that might have been left for other family members to do was simply watch and perhaps contemplate as Tommy (Robby) does in **Hiding Place** (1981) when he ponders how he "could have played the game. Tall and loose. Hands bigger than his brother's. Could palm a ball when he was eleven." But it would have been difficult to have been better than John. Difficult, in fact, to have been half as good as the older brother.

So Robby sought avenues by which he might make his mark in music. But he failed, once again, at what for anyone would have been a difficult proposition. "If that cat hadn't fucked us over with the record," Tommy rationalizes in **Hiding,** "We might have made the big time." It becomes clearer what sort of pressure the younger brother was responding to, a pressure that had been building for quite some time. Robby, in **Brothers,** expounds on his need to fantasize:

> When I was a very little child, oh, about six or seven,
> I had a habit of walking down Walnut and Copeland

streets. . . . As I walked I would look at the cars and in my mind I would buy them, but they only cost nickels or dimes. Big ones a dime, little ones a nickel, some that I liked a whole lot would cost a quarter. So as I got older this became a habit. For years I bought cars with the change that was in my pocket, which in those times wasn't very much.

The danger here is evident, for those cars represent the unattainable. A child's game developed, as Robby goes on to say in **Brothers,** into "a way of looking at things—an unrealistic way—it's like I wanted things to be easy, and misguidedly tried to make everything that way, blinded then to the fact that nothing good or worthwhile comes without serious effort." This realization came late for Robby. School, for him, ceased to be a viable means to achievement, and instead he turned to the streets for his answers, answers that included fast money, drugs, and the prospect of meeting with a too-early death.

While still in Philadelphia, as UPenn's first black tenured professor, John wrote an essay for *The American Scholar* entitled **"Fear in the Streets"** (1971). In this essay he remarks on the dehumanizing consequences of having to live in a decaying inner city. Referring to such an existence as being in a "metaphysical cage," he further reflects that its "filth, violence and brutality—the streets lined with uncollected garbage, the bloody emergency wards, the derelicts and addicts—are an epiphany validating the worst things the black man has heard about himself. "The answer for Wideman was to leave and exchange Philadelphia for the University of Wyoming in Laramie. "I'd come west," the author confesses in **Brothers,** "to escape the demons Robby personified."

Meanwhile, Robby was becoming more and more immersed in a life of crime to the point where one fateful day in November, 1975, he and two friends robbed a used car dealer who also was known to moonlight as a "fence" for stolen goods. What Robby describes in **Brothers** takes on the dimensions of a turbulent blur: An agreement that the fence will buy a truckload of stolen televisions from Robby and his two friends. Only, there are no televisions. The stipulated televisions become a ploy to get the fence to bring money. On the night when the deal is supposed to be consummated, the fence tenders cash, saying, "Okay. Here's the money. Where's the TVS?" Sudden chaos ensues. The robbers demand, "Throw down your money on the ground." A wind blows the cash everywhere. Robby is frantically chasing it. One of the robbers, Michael Dukes, fires a warning shot. The fence is not hit but falls down and then scuffles "to get up again. . . . looked like he was digging in his clothes for something." Dukes fires again, this time fatally wounding the fence. Robby never fired a shot, but he nevertheless was involved in the perpetration of a crime in which a man's life was taken. So he was sentenced to life in prison without the possibility of parole.

Even as he "escaped" to Wyoming, John Wideman was aware of the precariousness of his unique situation. Just how far removed could he allow himself to be from his brother's tormenting situation? True, John had come along during the patient, more tranquil 1950s, whereas Robby grew up 10 years later. There was that all-important difference. Yet, in the *60 Minutes* interview, Robby's words became ominous as he talked about black males who "wanted to be able to believe in our country and believe in the things that we were being told, but the contradictions were there and the majority of all the guys that I grew up with are now either in jail, they're dead, they're in the streets strung out on drugs and, you know, that—that says it there, that very few of us made it through. Very few of us made it through." When a 34-year-old man looks around only to discover that the majority of young men he grew up with are either dead, in jail, or on drugs, then something is terribly wrong. One wonders if there has come into existence a new type of slavery that, though different in many respects, is just as overwhelming and brutal.

This is what the author must have been pondering during the eight-year lull between *Lynchers* in 1973, and the next two books, *Hiding Place* and *Damballah*, both of which first appeared in 1981. The latter two works are his first installments of what has come to be known as *The Homewood Trilogy* (the third installment, *Sent for You Yesterday*, would appear two years later) in which he sought to determine what had made previous generations of blacks so much stronger. Using the rich heritage of his own family, he offers us models such as the elderly Aunt Bess who, in *Hiding*, berates the fugitive Tommy and proclaims, "Life's hard. Didn't, nobody never tell you? Didn't nobody never hold you up and look in your eyes and tell you you got to die one day little boy and they be plenty days you wish it be sooner stead of later?" She wants him to be aware that times were rough for blacks long before he was born, yet they managed somehow to survive and occasionally prosper. They kept hope alive for future generations in spite of the presumed insurmountable odds.

In **"Lizabeth: The Caterpillar Story,"** one of twelve stories in *Damballah*, we are presented with John French, Wideman's maternal grandfather, encountering his little daughter who has just eaten a piece of a bug. The daughter, Lizabeth, is Wideman's mother when she was a child. Freeda French, John French's wife, was supposed to have been watching the girl. "What did she eat?" the grandfather demands. "What you saying she ate? You supposed to be watching this child, woman." Freeda gives her husband what is left of the caterpillar and he "measures the spiraled length of caterpillar . . . strokes its fur . . . seems to be lis-

tening or speaking to it as he passes it close to his face." He is calculating what he must do. Then he swallows the caterpillar and reasons, "I got the most of it then. And if I don't die, she ain't gonna die neither." We are witness to a powerful love.

Wideman broadens the theme of family love when, in *Yesterday*, he shows us Albert Wilkes, who was adopted by the socially conscious Mr. and Mrs. Tate. Wilkes grows up to be an extraordinary piano player, specializing in the blues, but then one day he shoots a white man. The chain of events is ambiguous, best conveyed nonetheless in a conversation between Freeda and John French as they discuss the profound implications of the fugitive Wilkes' return. Calling him "a doomed man," Freeda expostulates:

> I know he shot a white police, and they gon hunt him down till they get him.
>
> Wasn't no policeman. Was a white man coming after Wilkes cause Wilkes been messing with the white man's white woman.
>
> Found him dead in his uniform.
>
> Wilkes knew what that white man after. Uniform didn't make no nevermind.
>
> Lord saith vengeance is mine.
>
> Ain't no vengeance to it. Man come to kill Albert Wilkes. Albert Wilkes got his shot in first. Lord didn't say nothing about standing still and dying just cause some peckerwood decide he needs you dead.

It should be noted, at this point, that the author is no longer using Joycean dashes to distinguish between speakers. Moreover, stream of consciousness technique has given way somewhat to clearer commentary and a clearer dialogue. But Wideman does not altogether eliminate the stream of consciousness technique that had been so much a part of his earlier works. In fact, as Freeda and John French discuss Wilkes' situation, their conversation becomes one voice telling the story of the whole black experience.

A similar function is served through Ralph Ellison's portrayal of Jim Trueblood in the novel *Invisible Man* (1952). Trueblood commits incest with his daughter. At the point of penetration he realizes he was trapped in the impossible position of "having to move *without* movin'." And yet, in the telling of his story, he urges, "When you think right hard you see that that's the way things is always been with me. That's just about been my life." As we ponder the extreme poverty of the Trueblood family—a grinding poverty that forced the two parents and their daughter into the same bed to stay warm—we are made to reconsider the extent to which Trueblood may or may not be morally culpable. When we learn that penetration occurred while Trueblood was in the midst of a dream about an unattainable white woman, we ponder his life even more. It is easy to argue that Trueblood has committed a heinous crime. Yet, it is equally possible to view Trueblood's plight as symbolic of how black Americans as a whole have had to find a way to make the most out of extraordinarily difficult circumstances.

Trueblood actually earns a living better than he had ever been able to do before, now telling his story for money. He becomes a vital cog in the survivalist culture of which the blues is a key ingredient. *Invisible* has been called a blues novel, and in an essay entitled "Richard Wright's Blues" (1945), Ellison defines blues as "an impulse to keep the painful details and episodes of a brutal experience alive in one's aching consciousness, to finger its jagged grain, and to transcend it . . . by squeezing from it a near-tragic, near-comic lyricism." Just as we had been able to do in the case of Trueblood, we must consider, when it comes to Wilkes, all the mediating factors. Did the white woman love Wilkes? Were she and the policeman married? Did the policeman approach Wilkes as an officer of the law or did he approach Wilkes as a jilted lover in the heat of passion? Such details would have helped greatly in our evaluation of Wilkes as he shot the white man. But in such a case, what are the odds of achieving legal justice? Wilkes must flee; the year is 1927. He is a black version of the ballad character, Tom Dooley, who must hang down his head and cry because he, not knowing the Civil War was over, had shot a Union soldier. Dooley flees but then finally is compelled to come home where he, as will be the case with Wilkes, must be killed as a consequence. Flight had preserved a certain victory, and with the hero's death, the onus is upon the community to capture victory through the words of a song.

Yesterday is just one of many such "songs" that in a way vindicate Robby Wideman, for Wilkes personifies a black essence of which Robby can partake. *Reuben* (1987), John Wideman's next novel, serves to vindicate the author himself. In *Home,* Braithwaite had graduated from law school and was so uncertain of who he was that he could only thrash about in life, doing odd jobs. But *Reuben* provides us with a different kind of lawyer who can reconcile his white mainstream education with the all-black community from which he was spawned. He lives and works in an "old wreck of a trailer" where he functions as a one-man legal services operation.

Nobody else in Homewood would do what Reuben would do for the little bit of money he charged. . . . Peace bond, bail bond; divorce, drunk and disorderly, something some-

body stole from you, somebody catching you stealing from them, child support, a will . . . for as long as anybody could remember Reuben had been performing these tricks for the poor and worse than poor in Homewood.

Thus Wideman resolves the dilemma of the black intellectual. He must, in some form or fashion, return to the black community and aid in the quest for survival.

One would have thought that fate had been unkind enough through the process of events that led to Robby's imprisonment. However, that was before the author's youngest son stabbed his roommate in a hotel in Flagstaff, Arizona. The two boys, Jacob Wideman and Eric Kane, were part of a small group who camped regularly in Maine. It was August, 1986, school was out, and the group decided to travel back west, inadvertently ending up in Flagstaff. By the time they made it to University Inn in that town, they were frustrated and exhausted. Three of the boys checked into one room; Jacob and Eric checked into another. Time passed and in the wee hours of the morning, Jacob plunged a knife into Eric's heart, killing him, and leaving a world to ask why?

There is a haunting passage in **Brothers** where the author ponders what the seeds were that led to Robby going wrong. The paradoxical conclusion drawn is that "the more you delve and backtrack and think, the more clear it becomes that nothing has a discrete, independent history; people and events take shape not in orderly, chronological sequence but in relation to other forces and events, tangled skeins of necessity and interdependence and chance that after all could have produced only one result: what is." One might interpret that as meaning certain events are unavoidable. But it also seems to be saying there are some things still within our control.

Jacob was three years old when the family moved to Wyoming. Never in his life did he have to undergo the hardships that, for example, a child of the ghetto has to endure constantly. The author saw to that as he planned for his children to have the optimal in security. What the author did not anticipate was how having a famous father can, in some cases, be just as devastating as being poor, living in an inner city. John Wideman was his high school's valedictorian, captain of the basketball team, and destined to have an equally astonishing career at UPenn. Then he goes on to become a great writer. What will be the expectations of such a father for his child? What pressures will be brought to bear?

Wideman's latest novel, *Philadelphia Fire* (1990), has many autobiographical elements. It is about a father so engrossed in his flourishing career that he becomes estranged from his own son and realizes "I've always known next to nothing about him." However, Wideman does not stop there.

He raises the question of how society in general regards children. Taking on the persona of Cudjoe who "copped the education and ran" to a distant island, he returns to the mainland in search of the boy who escaped the city-authorized bombing of MOVE's (The Movement) headquarters in Philadelphia in 1985. Jacob and the boy become one and the same as the author uses them to symbolize a wide variety of abuses, "atrocities that prove adults don't give a fuck about kids. The lousy school system, abortion, lack of legal rights . . . kiddie porn, kids' bodies used to sell shit on TV, kids on death row, high infant mortality." Susan Sontag, in her book *Against Interpretation* (1966), offers this definition of a writer: "As a man he suffers; as a writer, he transforms his suffering into art." *Fire* is certainly a commendable work of art, a tool the author uses to exorcize his own pain. But it also must serve as a warning for society either to wage war against its various formidable demons or concede that they will consume all of us.

Mel Watkins (review date 13 November 1994)

SOURCE: "A Son's Notes," in *New York Times Book Review,* Vol. 99, November 13, 1994, p. 11.

[*In the following review, Watkins provides a laudatory assessment of* Fatheralong.]

John Edgar Wideman's latest book, *Fatheralong,* is a hybrid. It is at once a memoir and a meditation on fatherhood, race, metaphysics, time and the afterlife. Mr. Wideman has laid claim to a vast landscape, which he traverses boldly, although occasionally with uneven steps.

As a memoir it is superb. The author brings all of his considerable skills (demonstrated in the novels of his Homewood trilogy and in his short fiction) into play in a quest to understand the simultaneous estrangement and physical connection he felt toward his father.

The book's title is derived from the gospel song "Father Along," a song that for Mr. Wideman suggests the value of "resignation, learning to wait and trust and endure." These are the qualities, he writes, that not only lead to spiritual redemption but also enable a son in to bridge the gulf between himself and his father—"to learn (earn) the Father's name." Coming to terms with that struggle is the central theme of *Fatheralong.*

To that end, Mr. Wideman provides a string of vignettes and rich details from his early life in Pittsburgh that contrast his father's distance and coldness ("A familiar stranger. Unpredictable, vaguely threatening") with his mother's in-

timacy and love ("She was always there. With me. If she had disappeared, no there would exist").

The safety of home in the company of his mother, her sisters and their mother, and the rare moments when his father broke through his wall of coldness and demonstrated affection (hoisting the young John onto his shoulders at a parade, for instance), are set against the danger of the elder Wideman's world outside the home ("the disreputable, darker streets of Homewood") and the risks and challenges America's racist legacy still presents to African-Americans—black men in particular.

Illuminated by Mr. Wideman's keen eye and evocative prose, these early scenes, as well as characters like K. Leroy Irvis (a lawyer and the first black speaker of the Pennsylvania of Representatives) or his father's cousin James Karris, known as Littleman, and descriptions of a visit to his grandfather's house in Promised Land, the Mack community outside Greenwood, S.C., or of the tawdry train station in Springfield, Mass., at which he meets his father on the occasion of his own son's marriage, are vividly recounted.

These people and events are the foundation of *Fatheralong,* the substantive core that inspires the ruminations and ideas that resonate throughout the book. Mr. Wideman seems to depict his own technique when he describes the cadence of Littleman's speech: "You take your time, give memories an opportunity to sashay in and out, echo and instruct or fuse with other words, other visions."

Accordingly, the narrative is laced with impressionistic asides and musings on subjects as diverse as America's fascination with racing distinctions or the ambivalent attraction-repulsion the author (as a married college professor) felt when watching dancers at a sleazy topless club. These imaginative junkets are sometimes contradictory, as when Mr. Wideman first annihilates all scientific justification for "the paradigm of race" and then envisions himself as a victim because of race. Sometimes they are intrusive, veering toward sociological jargon. More often, however, they provide a fascinating journey into Mr. Wideman's mind. Observations, fragments of anecdotes, phrases like "my skin recalls sensations I can't name yet," prompt rich allusive riffs that engage ever-broadening questions about time, death and our familial and cultural kinship.

There are musicians—sometimes heralded but often obscure—who are known among their peers as "musicians' musicians" because of their affection for their work, as well as their virtuosity and their subtle manipulation of the elements of their craft. John Edgar Wideman is one of a select group of writers who can claim a similar distinction. With such artists, turning to the work is often a more revealing means of defining it than attempting to apply external criteria. And indeed, embedded in the narrative of **Fatheralong** is perhaps the most telling description of Mr. Wideman's work:

> "He swims with the current of words. Listens to himself, not out of self-consciousness but because the language can feel kind of good rolling off your tongue if you let it, ease up and let it carry you, you and not you, recalling your story told by yourself or heard before in another person's telling, a back porch or parlor as you remember how your story began once, consider where it might go this time."

Read with that in mind, **Fatheralong** is an impressive work.

Mark Shechner (review date March/April 1995)

SOURCE: "Men Will Be Men," in *Tikkun*, Vol. 10, No. 2, March/April, 1995, pp. 80-82.

[*Shechner is an American educator, author, and critic. In the following review, he offers a favorable assessment of* Fatheralong.]

I recall the lectures well, lectures verging upon scoldings, about how "the family" or rather that peculiar constellation of two parents living in the same household with their children, was a "bourgeois" or "late capitalist" institution that had little to say for itself in a post-bourgeois, postmodern age. "The two-parent family could be, and in places had been, superseded by an equivalent, even historically antecedent, constellation the "extended kinship group." It performed all the nursing and rearing functions of the nuclear family and was, if anything, more functional for some ethnic and/or economic groups. No one who was subjected, perhaps a decade ago, to this doxology will forget the intransigent self-assurance with which it was delivered or the armory of footnotes with which it was fortified.

The usual target of the arguments was the father, whom contemporary social developments, already well advanced in certain sectors of the population, had consigned to the museum of outmoded social forms. Paternity was a legal fiction, like usury or vagrancy, and, like them, a victim of changing social practice. "Who is the father of any son that any son should love him or he any son?" asks the hero of a famous modern novel, as if in anticipation of our own age (Joyce's *Ulysses*, in which that sentence appears, is set in 1904).

Who indeed? Stephen Dedalus's question has exploded into a social emergency of staggering proportions in an age of wholesale divorce, abandonment, death by violence, single motherhood, and teen pregnancy. The very concept of fatherhood has been called into question, not just by feminists avid to cashier the father or by critical theorists clustered in university English departments, for whom something called "The Patriarchal Order" is an evil on the scale of The Plantation, but by men themselves. The census statistics confirm what we all know: American children are growing up fatherless in unprecedented numbers.

We still hear the sound of one hand clapping for this state of affairs, as we will when any middle class social institution is being dismantled. But now the self-assurance is missing, as postmodern life overflows with nasty consequences and the repercussions of society without fathers are growing more obvious every day. Writers and artists have been taking notice. A few years ago, the poet Robert Bly took a lot of grief for claiming, in his book *Iron John*, that sons need fathers if they are to become men, and other writers—Paul Auster in *The Invention of Solitude* (1982) and Philip Roth in *Patrimony* (1991)—have written movingly of efforts to bond to prickly or remote fathers.

However, it has been in that part of America that has suffered most grievously from the decline of the family, African-American society, that writers and artists have taken up the question most seriously. If they haven't uniformly issued calls for the resurrection of the nuclear family, they have been putting fatherhood under the magnifying glass and reporting back on their findings. Filmmakers, feeling a special burden of responsibility to do the right thing, have been out front in pleading the case for fatherhood, John Singleton's *Boyz N the Hood* being the bluntest of their films. More obliquely and self-consciously, Matty Rich's *Straight Out of Brooklyn* suggests that even a wastrel, alcoholic, chess-playing father can have a tonic effect upon a son's moral character.

Writers, working in a more flexible and capacious medium, have made more complex contributions to the image of fathers and sons. Nathan McCall, an ex-convict now a reporter for *The Washington Post*, recalls, in his memoir, *Makes Me Wanna Holler: A Young Black Man in America*, that as a youth he did not view his stepfather, a retired Army officer turned gardener, with admiration. Watching his stepfather at work in affluent white homes in Sterling Point, Virginia, the young Nathan would think he "looked too much like the pictures of downtrodden sharecroppers and field slaves." McCall recalls the defining moment when he realized, "There were two distinct worlds in America, and a different set of rules for each: the white one was full of the possibilities of life. The dark was just that—dark and limited." It took him a long time to understand his stepfather's quiet tenacity: "I understand now, as an adult, that my old man was more of a man than I ever could be."

Of course, the paternal coin has a flip side, one described by Brent Staples, an editorial writer for *The New York Times,* in his *Parallel Time: Growing Up in Black and White.* Staples, who grew up with a drunk and violent father, once drew a knife and cut his mother, Staples's brother Blake, a drug dealer, would succumb to the chaos in the family and the temptations of the street and be killed by a rival. Unlike film, which trades in flat types, these books do not serve up idealized figures.

The latest contribution to the reevaluation of the father, and the most penetrating, is novelist John Edgar Wideman's *Fatheralong: A Meditation on Fathers and Sons, Race and Society.* Wideman, author of thirteen books of fiction and memoir, is a more practiced social critic and self-observer than first time MEMOIRIST McCall and Staples, and his contribution possesses a sensitivity to nuance that comes from Wideman's experiences on the one side and his immersion in literature on the other, *Fatheralong,* a memoir cum diatribe on race, is a reminder of how much Wideman can tell us when he is focused for he is a master digression and how seriously we need to take him on the subjects he understands best: male bonding, fathers and sons, and what American life does to Black men. Wideman writes with the authority of his own previous losses, having both a brother and a son in prison on murder convictions. Much of his writing, especially an earlier book about his brother Robbie, *Brothers and Keepers* (1985), has been devoted to understanding how that happened and why.

When Wideman, just entering his fifties, joined his father in 1992 on a trip to the latter's hometown of Promised Land, South Carolina, it was one of the rare occasions that father and son had ever spent time together. Leaving the Charlotte airport, Wideman reflected, "Unless he'd watched me for longer than that when I was a baby, I'd never spent this much time alone with my father, seven hours and counting."

Wideman saw the trip as an occasion to raise baseline questions: about the chill between them, about the father's absences from home, about the remoteness punctuated by flashes of rage, about the street and bar life that the father, Edgar Wideman, preferred to home life, about the musk of masculinity that pervaded a room long after he was out of it.

Edgar Wideman's wasn't a simple case of abandonment so much as an emotional withdrawal from the heartbeat of the family, making him all the more remote for being so inscrutably there, present yet apart. The father's mystique was bound up with his manhood. "Perhaps the secret had something to do with my father's smell, seeping off his body while he slept, in his clothes, the sheets and blankets when he wasn't in the room . . . Not exactly stink but a threat of

nastiness in the scent he marked things with. Pungent nastiness I envied and feared. . .." How different that was from Wideman's mother and her arms "around her children, her grandis, his sisters and brothers, nephews and nieces, and inside that circle of family, smaller circles, two bodies clinging, five or six in a tight huddle, circles concentric, overlapping, intertwined, generations, long gone and yet to be born connected indivisibly."

Buoyed by the feel and smell and taste of the world, even as he fights against riptides of despair and fury within himself, Wideman luxuriates in these sensuous flashbacks. The past, magical and bleak, pumps life into Wideman's prose, fueling its wild fluctuations of voice, now muscular, now languorous, poised, between a father who is always "alone, alone, alone" and women in "warm, scented rooms . . . casual in their bodies." Growing into manhood, Wideman would take neither path. "Neither Father's son nor Mother's son, betraying them both as I became myself. My mother's open arms. My father's arms crossed on his chest."

Arms open and arms closed animate those voices that seem so different from each other. One voice is as forbidding as the photo of Wideman himself on the dust cover, leather-jacketed, scowling, his own arms crossed truculently over his chest. The other voice, rapturous and poetic, can pause tenderly over a son's ecstacy in watching his father shave. The book is a lumpy weave of distinct meditations: on fathers and sons and on race and society, which seem to emerge from disconnected chambers of Wideman's mind: the father-son story being charged with desire, knowledge, and mourning, the race and society story being a sermon on the mount about the "paradigm of race [which] authors one sad story, repeated far too often, that would reduce the complexity of our cultural heritage. Race preempts our right to situate our story where we choose. It casts us as minor characters in somebody else's self-elevating melodrama."

One utters a qualified amen to that sermon: amen for the obvious, bitter wisdom in it, qualified for the exceptions and escape clauses that clamor to be added. *Fatheralong* is laced with such exhortations that fall midway between Jeremiads and bumper stickers and fall short of what Wideman does best: show us the bottom line through human encounters that bypass the commonplace. When a retired history professor guides Wideman through an archive in Abbeville, South Carolina, in search of records concerning Wideman's ancestors, Wideman's gratitude is unexpectedly splashed with rage. "I was grateful, even fond of this elderly man who shared himself, his insights and craft, so unreservedly with a stranger, and that's why I was surprised, shocked even, by the ice cold wave of anger, the fury compressed into one of those if looks could kill looks I found myself flashing down at the back of his thin, freckled bald skull."

Without warning, we have slipped beyond platitudes to someplace more dangerous: the unpredictable world in which race converts to violence. Edgar Wideman, his son thinks, "was about the same age as Bowie Lomas, as smart, as curious and engaging. Yet, because of his color, my father had been denied the prospects, the possibilities that had enriched the career and life of the white man below me." The paradigm of race veers off at an angle to show us more in this snapshot than we could learn in a week of lectures.

John Edgar Wideman straddles broad social and cultural terrain. A novelist and social critic of impressive powers and a professor at the University of Massachusetts at Amherst, he is also intimate with the street and its rhythms and terrors. In some ways, he sounds like Philip Roth: knowing, talky, obsessed, his head filled with local and precisely inflected voices. Wideman's writing is sharp, urban, masculine, sexual, and very aggressive, Wideman claims to know violence from within, to identify with it, to claim a piece of it. There are passages in his *Philadelphia Fire* and *Brothers and Keepers* much as in this book, that are downright menacing, as Wideman intends them to be. But there are open arms for men too, and Wideman writes with vivid force about men and his connections to them. The earlier memoir, *Brothers and Keepers,* is the more potent of the two, for the brother Robbie, who holds center stage in it with his pungent street argot. About the son, Jacob, Wideman has been more diffident, though the coda of *Fatheralong,* an open letter to him, is as heart-breaking a cry of personal grief as you are going to read. A brother lost, a son lost, a father found with Wideman, literature takes root in the hard and rocky soil of family tragedy.

Sanford Pinsker (review date Spring 1995)

SOURCE: "The Moose on the Family Dinner Table," in *Virginia Quarterly Review,* Vol. 71, No. 2, Spring, 1995, pp. 369-72.

[*In the following review, Pinsker responds negatively to* Fatheralong.]

Race in America has been compared to a moose on the dining room table: nobody wants to call attention to the carcass despite the fact that antlers are sticking in the potatoes, hooves drip onto people's laps, and the smell keeps getting worse. Rather than acknowledge the obvious, people crane their necks around the rotting slab of flesh and ask those across the table to pass the salt.

John Edgar Wideman is a writer we've learned to trust when it comes to calling a moose a moose—that is, until

Fatheralong. Ballyhooed as a meditation on "fathers and sons, race and society," Wideman watchers had good reasons to expect the same personal candor and sensitive trenchant social analysis he brought to *Brothers and Keepers,* his 1984 account of a brother jailed on a murder charge. How could the same family circumstances and Pittsburgh ghetto that produced *him*—a University of Pennsylvania graduate and Rhodes scholar: well spoken, ambitious, successful—also give rise to a brother who becomes a street punk and then one more sad statistic in the justice system? What propelled one brother toward restraint and standard English while the other gave way to jive talk and increasingly dangerous hustles; and what does this all say about the distancing, and the debts, a black writer owes to the black community?

I remember thinking that Wideman had sold himself a bit too short—and his brother a bit too long—in *Brothers and Keepers,* that even love is not enough to justify the unswerving defense he mounted on behalf of why so many young black men go bad. At the same time, I was moved by the painful honesty seared onto every page. So, when I learned that Wideman's own son was facing a murder charge, I wondered how the environmental arguments would play out when the situation seemed to radically altered. Unlike his brother, Wideman's son Jake was hardly the product of poverty and the inner city's meaner streets; he grew up in a successful academic's home, and in Laramie, Wyoming to boot.

Long before Murray and Herrnstein's *The Bell Curve* raised an already tense racial climate to new levels of accusation and hurt, Wideman must have ruminated about questions that can only crack the heart. Is racist America the sole reason why so many young black men murder, and are murdered—or are there other more complicated, more wrenching reasons? Given the sheer number of murderers in Wideman's family circle—including a nephew—one is tempted to think that genetic factors must be playing a role, as they do in families with a history of alcoholics. Granted, predisposition is only that—a predisposition—but it cannot be entirely ignored. Nor can the lessons, admittedly less scientific, from the histories of families seemingly fated to doom: the house of Atreus, the Kennedy clan, and now, the Widemans.

What I have been pointing to is nothing more nor less than the moose on the Wideman family dinner table, and the ways that *Fatheralong* skillfully avoids mentioning it until the book's last pages. It is one thing when *Philadelphia Fire* (1990) studiously avoids taking a position about MOVE and the conflagration that provided the novel's title (postmodernist narrative will do that) or when *Reuben* (1987) wraps coded messages about his son Jake in the folds of fiction and quite another when a book of non-fiction purports to talk about fathers, sons, and race and virtually leaves his son—now serving a life sentence—out.

Fatheralong is the mistaken way a very young John Edgar Wideman heard the gospel song "Father Along," but it is also a talisman, a Rosetta stone, for the identity he still quests, and for the cold, distant father who remains an inexorable part of the equation:

> Till I was grown I heard "fatheralong" and thought Fatheralong was God's name in this hymn, the mysterious God who dwelled in Homewood A.M.E.Z. church, a God I'd meet up with some day and He'd understand and say Well done. Also, I thought of my father, Edgar Wideman, his doubleness, his two-personalities, a man who lived in our house, who in a way ruled it, yet also lived somewhere else, distant unknown.

Whatever the confusions, the song, Wideman argues, ultimately speaks the lessons "of resignation, learning to wait and trust and endure." In Wideman's case, father often seemed harsher, more remote than God; nor did the father-son relationship improve markedly during his adult-hood. Things closest to the heart continued to be postponed, to remain unsaid. One mistake, Wideman now admits, was treating his father "as if a father always required a capital F." He then goes on to write this extraordinary passage:

> As long as I carried a deity, a natural force in my mind, I wouldn't see the man on the seat beside me. Why had it been impossible all these years to believe in this man's actual life, him with a suitcase in his hand, excited, anxious to get the hell away from the everyday tedium of growing old, alone and poor.

It took equal measures of courage and integrity to pen these lines; but these are precisely the benchmarks against which our best writers are judged. *Fatheralong* has more than its share of similar moments—when, for example, he visits with Wideman relatives at his grandfather's home in Greenwood, South Carolina, or when he meets his father at the train station near his Massachusetts home on the occasion of his son Danny's wedding. Family history, despite everything, exerts a palpable—and deeply poetic—force.

Families, in a word, *sustain,* just as music and stories do. Granted, each art form (and surely families are just as much a composition as are songs and folktales) is elusive, problematic, troubled, and troubling; but, taken together, they make us what we are. As Wideman puts it, in a passage about Art & Life worth quoting in its entirety:

> Stories are onions. You peel one skin and another grins up at you. And peeling onions can make grown men cry. Which raises other questions. Why does one trans-parent skin on top of another transparent skin, layer after layer you can see through if each is held up to the light, why are they opaque when bound one on top of the other to form an onion or story? Like a sentence with seven clear simple words and you understand each word but the meaning of the sentence totally eludes you. You might suggest there is no light source at the core of the onion, nothing similar to a lamp that can be switched on so you can see from outside in. Or you might say an onion is the light and the truth, or at least as much truth and light as you're ever going to receive on this earth, source and finished product all rounded into one and that's the beauty of solid objects you can hold in your hand. Each skin, each layer a different story, connected to the particular, actual onion you once held whole in your hand as the onion is connected to stars, dinosaurs, bicycles, a loon's cry, to the seed it sprouted from, the earth where the seed rotted and died and slept until it began dreaming of being an onion again, dreamed the steps it would have to climb, the skins it would have to shed and grow to let its light shine again in the world.

Wideman is, of course, describing the curious way that the memories of *Fatheralong* interconnect; but at the same time he is suggesting, however unconsciously, how some stories remain stubbornly hidden beneath the layers. Thus far I have talked about the moose on the Wideman family dinner table as if it were restricted to Jake, the son both absent in fact and in story. But there is yet another moose on this table, for if *Fatheralong* ends with a poignant letter to that son ("I remember walking down towards the lake to be alone [on the day Wideman first heard that his son was missing and the boy sharing his room was dead] because I felt myself coming apart, the mask I'd been wearing, as much for myself as for the benefit of other people, was beginning to splinter. . . . I found myself on my knees, praying to a tree."), it begins with an impassioned plea for a raceless America, one in which color no "preempts our right to situate our story where we choose." Our power, Wideman argues, lies in the "capacity to imagine ourselves as other than what we are." Race, in short, is yet another hard reality Wideman prefers to ignore by wishing it away. Meanwhile, the moose on the table continues to stink.

I am hardly the only Wideman watcher who figured that *Fatheralong* would turn out to be at least as much about Wideman the father as it is about Wideman the son—not, I hope, for prurient interests or hundreds of other wrong reasons, but because I felt he could lead me past newspaper platitudes (senseless, sad, and the all-purpose "tragic") to a deeper understanding of the dark truths underlying much human behavior. I wondered, too, if he would play the race card, and if so, which one; or if he would offer up an explanation I cannot even imagine, but that a genuine writer can. Perhaps Wideman is simply not ready to write such a book, at least not yet. In that case, he should have written about something else because his meditation about fathers and sons, race and society, turns out to be yet another look past the moose on the table. All of us, black and white, have had far too many of those.

Paul West (review date 29 September 1996)

SOURCE: "Too Great a Sacrifice," in *Washington Post Book World,* Vol. XXVI, No. 39, September 29, 1996, p. 5.

[*West is an author and critic. The following is his highly favorable review of* The Cattle Killing.]

One of the men within John Edgar Wideman believes that over the centuries irreparable harm has been done to the black race, and he agonizes over this in his eight novels. Another Wideman, the thinker and scholar, is the Phi Beta Kappa graduate, Rhodes Scholar and two-time winner of the PEN/Faulkner Award. A third Wideman is the lyrical novelist, a stylist dedicated to reverie and musing, little concerned with plot or continuity, almost a symbolist. His novels fuse these simultaneous selves in varying ways and by now compose a shimmering collection. Few American novelists offer a mix this complex or satisfying, and Wideman's new novel gives us more of the same.

Let me explain. At the center of *The Cattle Killing* is an itinerant 18th-century black preacher in Philadelphia, a Tiresias figure who speaks from the dead center of the racial mess, sweeping the horizon with a glass that takes in not only America but South Africa and Europe. If slavery is an index to the inevitable decline and fall of Western civilization, this guy is its Spengler, but he has help is telling that story from both Wideman the savant and Wideman the aesthete. George Stubbs, the English painter of flayed horses, supplies Wideman with a central metaphor for the peeling away of nature's layers until, presto, you have the core: Misery is either the product of original sin or of *deus absconditus* ("the hidden god," the god of deists).

Wideman's clerical man tries to peel away the successive layers of racism, wondering all the time, while he preaches authoritatively to others, where and why humanity went wrong. This fellow's physical and mental meandering comes to us in a disjointed, allusive, tangential voice—more like one part in a Bach cantata than the all-knowing voice of a traditional narrator.

This is Wideman's way, almost a kind of impulsive prose cubism you have to get used to even while he is describing sex, landscape or weather, all of which he does with a fresh, passionate eye.

Since the heart of this book is mystical, it is worth pointing out that Wideman deftly solves the old problem of the mystic: If you dilute an experience to make it accessible, it will not seem special. If you don't, it will be beyond everyone. This is a book pitched between an image—the Xhosa people, who ritually destroyed their cattle so as to defy European domination—and an idea right out of Andre Malraux's *The Walnut Trees of Altenburg:* "What is a man?" A man, in this case, both destroys his herd and narrates this story, assigning the one back to God and offering the other to his father.

There are some engaging sections here about snow, Josiah Wedgewood, Hottentots, levitation, black women in childbirth, "Ebo melancholy," sperm in bathwater, the "soft, dumb weight" of the scrotum—about wanting "every word of a new book to be a warning, to be saturated with the image of a devastated landscape." Wideman has an ample, well-stocked mind crowded with saliences, included here sometimes without benefit of definite or indefinite article or even verb, to be left as they are, foreshortened or developed in the reader's mind ad lib.

Addressed to Clio, the muse of history, *The Cattle Killing* is an intensely personal work that encourages us to fill in the blanks as we go. John Edgar Wideman writes from a vulnerable heart with an educated, worldly compassion that is bound to leave a scar.

Gene Seymour (review date 28 October 1996)

SOURCE: "Dream Surgeon," in *Nation,* Vol. 263, No. 13, October 28, 1996, pp. 58-60.

[*Seymour is an American journalist, editor, and author of such works as* Jazz: The Great American Art. *In the following review, he reflects on the absence of imagination in modern society and responds favorably to Wideman's treatment of the subject in* The Cattle Killing.]

Dream is dead. I should have known about it sooner, but I rarely bought the *Sandman* comic book in separate installments, preferring the bigger, glossier compilations. So it was only when I read *The Kindly Ones* (DC Comics Vertigo), which appears to be the final collection of stories from Neil Gaiman's extraordinary graphic fantasy series, that I found out that Dream—*a k a* Sandman, Lord Morpheus—had ceased to be. Worse, there isn't much left of Morpheus's kingdom except the corpses of his loyal followers and a tender-hearted raven named Matthew, his lone surviving acolyte, Meanwhile, Dream's godlike siblings roam the Superhighway of the Subconscious. Gaiman, after all, calls them the Endless. Among their number are Desire, Destruction, Delirium and, sexiest and sweetest of all, Death herself.

Whatever Gaiman's reasons for finishing off his pale, sad hero, it seems both appropriate and redundant for Dream to have checked out at Millennium Minus Four and Counting. The very notion of artful dreaming has wandered into a dead zone. The movies no longer try to be subtle about ransacking and recycling their past for the quick buck. Music appropriates used riffs and discarded motifs and tags the result "sampling" or "postmodern." The television networks don't know whether they're cloning *Friends* or *The X-Files.* Scheherazade's ability to make stuff up out of thin air seems just beyond the reach of premillennial storytellers. If imagination isn't as dead as Gaiman's Dream Lord, it's been gravely ill for some time now.

Don't take my word for it. Ask John Edgar Wideman. Through style and content, Wideman has made it his calling—really his burden—to chart deficiencies in imagination, both collective and individual. Because Wideman is an engaged, highly visible black writer in twentieth-century America, readers assume that racism, not imagination sickness, drives his work. But what is racism, after all, but a breakdown of the imagination? If you can't imagine properly, you can't empathize and if you can't empathize, you can't see whomever you choose to disdain/dismiss/hate as being connected with your own fate. In a piece written for *Esquire* about the riots that followed acquittal of the police officers who beat Rodney King, Wideman deems this inability to connect "the peculiar and perhaps fatal American violence." This sounds like a simple assessment from a mind as complex as Wideman's. But if it's so simple, why can't the nation figure out anything else to do with its terminal disfigurement of the imagination except cloak it with cosmetics or (for those times when it thinks such deformity is dashing), wear it like a battle scar? Radical surgery? Wouldn't hear of it. Sounds like it would hurt too much. Rest assured, replies Dr. Wideman, the surgeon of dreams, the longer you wait, the more it will hurt.

As a public figure, Wideman offers credulity one of its more formidable challenges. Even the publication of thirteen books in thirty years can't diminish the sheer wonder of his presence. It makes your eyes grow big to think that this product of Pittsburgh's mean streets could hit the books as hard as he nailed jump shots for the University of Pennsylvania and so was able to secure all—Ivy League status and a Rhodes scholarship. And then there's the body of work, breathtaking in its thematic sweep and stylistic reach, haunting in its penchant for richly detailed memory music and nerves rubbed raw by injustice. His memoirs,

Brothers and Keepers (1984) and *Fatheralong* (1994), offer eloquent testimony to the personal travails he had to overcome while tending to his literary calling: first a brother behind bars, then a son. How can anyone stay focused—much less patient or decent—in the face of such calamity?

In chronicling America's failure to connect, Wideman himself has struggled to connect with a mainstream African-American reading audience. But, as is the case with fellow Modernist dream masters like Faulkner, Toni Morrison, Ornette Coleman and any Abstract Expressionist you can name, Wideman demands that his readers work with him in making connections, drawing conclusions, following the map of his characters' souls. The odds against him are grim. One of the worst symptoms of the prevailing imagination-illness is the reader/listener/watcher's refusal to be anything but a passive receptacle for predigested information. Still, Wideman keeps on keeping on. *The Cattle Killing* is the latest and, quite possibly, greatest testament to his heroic struggle against imagination sickness.

The success of Wideman's Homewood trilogy—*Damballah* (1981), *Hiding Place* (1981) and *Sent for You Yesterday* (1983)—tempts the critic to group the rest of his novels into cycles and shared themes. In the case of *The Cattle Killing,* you have to go back to *A Glance Away* (1967) to find a primordial link. In that first novel, Wideman navigates the distance separating the tormented consciences of a young black recovering drug addict and a middle-aged white college professor. While Wideman's manipulation of these two lost souls toward a climactic barroom encounter doesn't quite convince, his eye and ear were already receiving magical signals that he then transmitted through a lush, allusive style. Wideman's erudition got the best of him in his second novel, *Hurry Home* (1970), however bravely the book confronted the division between its black lawyer protagonist's working-class roots and his leisure-class aspirations. The Penn sharpshooter was better off developing his empathic footwork instead of dribbling dualities; *The Lynchers* (1972), a tale of young black activists seeking vengeance on a white policeman, was the strongest demonstration thus far of his ability to immerse himself in dreams and nightmares different from his own.

The Homewood trilogy offered Wideman a chance to kick back with a trip home to the legends, mysteries and myths of his Pittsburgh neighborhood. The journey galvanized his narrative powers, broadened his expressive range, allowed him to internalize to a greater degree the healing power of telling stories. It seemed also to give him the psychic foundation to confront the myriad personal and public demons unearthed in *Philadelphia Fire* (1990), an impressionistic novel that uses the 1985 MOVE bombing as a basis to continue the enquiry of values begun with *A Glance Away* and continued through *The Lynchers*—and, for that matter, the two memoirs. In each of these books, Wideman melds his consciousness with those of disparate blacks and whites as if the act of dreaming their dreams would somehow inoculate his readers against cowardice and dread of each other.

The Cattle Killing is set in Philadelphia where, it seems, Wideman's muse is most agitated by society's disfigurement. It begins inside the head of a black novelist who processes images of the city as is now and as it was when he was growing up. The writer's reveries of his mother warning him of dangers lurking in his old neighborhood are crushed by the weight of present-day shootings of teenagers:

> *Shoot. Chute. Black boys shoot each other. Murder themselves, Shoot. Chute. Panicked cattle funneled down the killing chute, nose pressed in the drippy ass of the one ahead. Shitting and pissing all over themselves because finally, too late, they understand. Understand whose skull is split by the ax at the end of the tunnel.*

Like one of the Dream Lord's emissaries, the novelist is directed toward a corollary nightmare of self-destruction: the long-ago while of the South African Xhosa people who ritually destroyed their precious cattle because some jive prophecy told them it would drive the marauding Europeans from their land. Having thus established that dreams can deceive as surely as they can heal, Wideman makes his novelist dream his way back to 1793. A plague is sweeping through the City of Brotherly Love, giving its white citizens feverish delusions that the pestilence is the sinister work of the blacks in their midst, who are themselves immune. Bearing witness to this madness is a young itinerant minister of mixed racial origins who, with his now lost-and-presumed-dead-at-sea brother, freed his mother from slavery. He wanders about, working at odd jobs, preaching the Gospel. His faith, however sturdy, cannot protect him from the perils of a landscape agitated by disease and race hate. Even the preacher's fine mind betrays him with sudden, spectacular seizures that leave him reeling from shining horrific visions of fire and tumult before giving way to "a starting clarity of vision" and inner peace.

One hot afternoon, the preacher sees—what? "Perhaps a trick of the sun. . . . Perhaps a mote of dust in my eye or a drop of sweat glued to my lashes." The apparition assumes the voluptuous shape of an African woman cradling a package. She appears to the wanderer in fragments. He can't stop staring at her foot:

> A delicate foot, poorly served by rough, rural paths.
> An indoor foot, a foot for silk slippers or soft leather boots with raised heels and many buttons. A foot weeping now. Soot-streaked, bloody tears, and I wished for a basin of cool water in my sack. I wanted to kneel beside her, bathe away the misery, listen to her recite the tale of her misfortune.

A little later, he's certain the feet are made of wood. He is also certain that the bundle she carries is a dead white child she insists on bathing. He can't help himself. He must follow them, offer them charitable, assuring words that, to his horror, cannot stop them from being swallowed by a lake. What is this? One of his apocalyptic visions, only this one in slow motion? He remembers seeing the woman once before; her image is associated with his visits to a community of black worshipers and to the home of an older interracial couple, posing as mistress and slave. The minister witnesses their slaughter by white mobs afflicted with the plague-related racist delusion, but not before he hears their stories, the dreams they use to immunize themselves against the visions that trap others.

Ghosts, Ritual sacrifice. Nightmares of racist retribution. It does appear as if Wideman is playing with chord changes set down by Morrison's *Beloved*. His narrative bends and curves in the same willfully elliptical manner. You're pressed to keep up with the shifting points of view, the morphing of dream and reality, past and present. Wideman also leaves many questions in his path, among the biggest being the exact nature of his tale. Is this a story of a heroic quest? Is it a detective story with multiple solutions? You're better off recognizing that you inhabit a dreamscape where belief itself—in God, in science, even in imagination—is constantly challenged. Real-life eighteenth-century luminaries like the British painter George Stubbs, the American physician Benjamin Thrush and, most vividly, the African-American religious leader Richard Allen appear in the novel, their Enlightenment-forged certainties upset by such random insanities as recreational dissections of human corpses, bloodletting and always, the tyrannical absurdity of racism itself.

What keeps this phantasmagoria under control is Wideman's style. As always, he leads with his learning, empathy and elegance. But there's something different here: a more focused energy, language that is lean, taut and alive. You smell the rooms, the terrain, the blood, sweat and dread of his characters. That his story asks more questions than it answers should not be confused with evasiveness or showing off. If anything, there's more urgency in Wideman's questions than there is in anyone else's answers. And how good are answers anyway if they resemble the prophecy that doomed the Xhosa's cattle? Or made Philadelphians strike back at the innocent of color? Or, for that matter, make otherwise rational people believe that you can save poor children by obliterating their safety net?

Like melancholy Morpheus, now dead and gone, Wideman knows where dreaming can go wrong. Yet when his book winds back to the contemporary novelist's head, there is a moment of oblique serendipity that redeems imagination's power. The conclusion offers a faint shimmer of hope. Or is hope itself just another bogus vision luring us into deep, unruly waters?

By the way, did I mention that there was a child in the last chapter of *The Kindly Ones* who may or may not be Morpheus reborn? Maybe it's not important. . . .

Sven Birkerts (review date 3 November 1996)

SOURCE: "The Fever Days," in *New York Times Book Review*, November 3, 1996, p. 20.

[*Birkerts is a noted critic and author of several books, including* The Gutenberg Elegies: The Fate of Reading in an Electronic Age *(1995). In the following review, he offers a negative appraisal of* The Cattle Killing.]

In August 1793, an epidemic of yellow fever broke out in Philadelphia. Chaos prevailed. Doctors (including Benjamin Rush, a signer of the Declaration of Independence) struggled for cure and containment. The rich either barricaded themselves in their houses or fled, while the less fortunate shifted for themselves. There was widespread looting. What better test for the City of Brotherly Love?

The novelist and short-story writer John Edgar Wideman has had a longstanding interest both in Philadelphia and in this particular historical moment. His previous novel, *Philadelphia Fire,* applied a collage technique to various events leading toward and away from the 1985 Move bombings, laying down severe indictments on both sides of the color line. And the title story of his 1989 collection. *Fever,* offered up a fragmented documentary account of the 18th-century epidemic. Now, with his latest novel, Mr. Wideman looks to give that historical material a more symphonic treatment. But symphonic in the modern, not classical, style—structurally intricate, with jagged rushes of episodic prose, abrupt tonal shifts and few of the harmonic comforts most readers expect.

The Cattle Killing recounts in quasivisionary style the fraught wanderings of the unnamed narrator (though other voices also intrude), who is a young black preacher determined to help his people. These are the fever days, and he is either abroad in the countryside outside Philadelphia or else in the cauldron itself, serving as emissary between the prominent black bishop Richard Allen and Dr. Rush (here called Dr. Thrush). A good part of the narrative comes to use in the form of stories the preacher tells to an unnamed woman (possibly Thrush's black maid, Kathryn, who lies abed, pregnant, and appears to be afflicted with the fever). Other portions are given in diary from by Thrush's wife, a cultivated blind woman who must dictate her thoughts to Kathryn.

Plot is not the point. Stories, memories and visions bleed together in the narrator's stricken soul. An epileptic, he finds himself torn asunder by apocalyptic, then beatific, visitations. At one moment, early on, he is in St. Matthew's, a predominantly white church, sitting in the back pews with the few black congregation members; in the next, he feels "a hideous dragon, red-eyed, scaly, lumbering toward the church." Mr. Wideman sets the following passage in the third person: "St. Matthew's wooden walls turn down like Jericho's walls of stone, like pages of a book, opening upon a fantastical landscape. He could see as far as the ends of the earth in every direction . . . The miracle was that near and far had become interchangeable. Things close at hand, things separated from him by a continent, were blended. One. He roamed everywhere at once. At any moment exactly where he needed to be."

But this is a vision—and the language and imagery of a vision. What the narrator encounters is confusion and delirium: rich whites sending their servants out to die for them or using them (Dr. Thrush coming to Kathryn's cot in the night); villagers burning down the house of the preacher's employers, a mixed-race couple, for their sin of miscegenation. The reader, hurtled along by Mr. Wideman's impressionistic sequences, often feels a craving for clarity. Do the flashes of events, the strange chunks of tales recounted, matter in themselves? Or are they just grist for the grinding stones of metaphor?

Mr. Wideman presides over his narrative materials like a jazzed-up Ovid. Everything is in flux, becoming—or echoing—something else. Early in his wanderings, for example, the narrator has a hallucinatory encounter with a mysterious black woman who is walking along a road carrying a bundled baby on her hip, African style. It turns out that the child—white-skinned, golden-haired—is dead. Is it hers? Her master's? We don't know.

The narrator follows the woman to the shore of a lake and watches, powerless to act, as she discards her clothing and walks steadily in: "Water rises to her thighs, her waist, covers her breasts, the baby in her arms, water finally closing over the dark glisten of her skull." He waits and waits for her to reappear, but of course she doesn't.

Except, that is, in other guises—in later tales, and in the narrator's own excited speculations. He hears about an incident in which the corpse of a beautiful pregnant African woman was auctioned to the highest bidder. After a seizure, he sees an unknown woman watching him. And then there is the shadowy Kathryn, carrying what may be Dr. Thrush's child. These things tie together, but how? Mr. Wideman is not about to gloss his imagery for us.

No less provocative is the legend of the cattle killing from which the novel takes its title. A voice, we learn, spoke to the Xhosa people long ago in Africa, commanding them to destroy their cattle herds and thus, though sacrifice, insure the coming of a new and better world. Meanwhile, the narrator hears the counsel of his own dream voice: "Beware. Do not kill your cattle. Do not speak with your enemy's tongue. Do not fall asleep in your enemy's dream."

The legend and the narrator's reply set up a powerful metaphorical tension. But how to apply this to the circumstances at hand? Are we to superimpose Africa upon America, cattle killing on epidemic—or 18th-century Philadelphia on the present? At different points in the novel, different messages—the despairing, the visionary—seem equally true. Could *that* be the point?

Mr. Wideman may have ventured beyond his readers this time out. Whereas figurative elements traditionally serve narrative interests, here things are the other way around. Filaments of story, of precious sense, are woven like bits of rag into a rug of shimmering but also perplexing suggestiveness.

I have not yet mentioned the novel's framing conceits: the opening passage, in which a writer, presumably Mr. Wideman himself, climbs a hill to visit his aging father and read to him from his new work; and the conclusion, in which a son, Dan, writes to his father about his father's manuscript, "Cattle Killing." The reader can contend with only so many textual strata. If there were a statute of restriction on narrative proliferation. John Edgar Wideman would be—flagrantly, brilliantly—in violation.

Joyce Carol Oates (review date 27 March 1997)

SOURCE: "Troubles I've Seen," in *New York Review of Books,* Vol. XLIV, No. 5, March 27, 1997, pp. 39-40.

[*Oates is a noted author, educator, and critic; her works include* We Were the Mulvaneys. *In the following review, she offers a favorable assessment of* The Cattle Killing.]

In a probate-office storage vault in Abbeville, South Carolina, an elderly white ex-history professor is showing a black writer from Massachusetts, whose slave ancestors lived in the Abbeville region, itemized documents relating to the sale and possession of slaves. The black writer is grateful for the historian's generous assistance (though the historian has never met the writer before, he has volunteered to spend several days with him), and so it comes as a considerable shock to the writer that, as he gazes down at the back of the historian's head, he feels an "ice-cold wave of anger [at him]. . . . at the back of his thin, freckled bald skull," and an impulse to do injury.

> It was Professor Lomax's skull I had envisioned shattering, spilling all its learning, its intimate knowledge of these deeds that transferred in the same "livestock" column as cows, horses, and mules, the bodies of my ancestors from one white owner to another. Hadn't the historian's career been one more mode of appropriation and exploitation of my father's bones. . . . Didn't mastery of Abbeville's history, the power and privilege to tell my father's story, follow from the original sin of slavery that stole, then silenced, my father's voice.

> . . . I knew in that moment my anger flashed we had not severed ourselves from a version of history that had made the lives of my black father and this white man so separate, so distant, yet so intimately intertwined.

This isn't fiction, as we might wish, but a vividly delineated scene from John Edgar Wideman's painfully candid memoir of 1994, which records the author's search for a point of connection between himself and his emotionally remote, elusive father. ("The first rule of my father's world is that you stand alone. Alone, alone, alone. . . . My mother's first rule was love. She refused to believe she was alone.") *Fatheralong* is a sustained brooding upon the mysteries of identity and kinship; the title itself reflects Wideman's childhood mistaking of words in a hymn, "Farther along we'll know more about you. . . ." for "Fatheralong." Though the memoir includes in its penultimate chapter a celebratory rite of passage, a wedding attended by both black and white family members (Wideman is married to a white woman), its predominant tone is one of rage just barely contained by the purity of its honed language. Addressed to Wideman's incarcerated son, who was sentenced to life in prison for the murder of a camp roommate when he was a young adolescent—information only alluded to in the memoir—it takes as its departure point Wideman's melancholy realization, as he gazes at his newborn son in a hospital, of "the chill of the cloud passing ... between you and your boy. The cloud of *race*."

Seen in this way, the documents shown to Wideman by Professor Lomax, who means only to be helpful, and who may well have perceived his own generosity as a token of reparation for his ancestors' crimes against Wideman's ancestors, are an obscenity, confirming "how much the present, my father's life, mine, yours [his son's], are still being determined by the presumption of white over black inscribed in them."

Unsparing in its candor, **Fatheralong** is a fiercely powerful document few readers are likely to forget; a sequel of sorts to Wideman's 1984 **Brothers and Keepers,** a memoir of the author's younger brother, Robby, who is serving a life sentence in Pennsylvania for felony murder. Both autobiographical works can be set beside such masterpieces of American memoir as Richard Wright's *Black Boy* (*American Hunger*) (1945). James Baldwin's *The Fire Next Time* (1963), and *The Autobiography of Malcolm X* (1964).

Just as John Edgar Wideman's memoirs frequently read like urgently dramatized fiction, so do his most characteristic works of fiction, frequently read like memoirs. A transparently autobiographical "I"—variously named, or anonymous, or, as in Wideman's new novel, **The Cattle Killing,** "Eye" ("Eye. Why are you called Eye. Eye short for something else someone named you. Who named you Isaiah.")—sifts through a fine-meshed, virtually Proustian consciousness the same issues of race, identity, and kinship with which the memoirs deal. Since the boldly mythical title story of the collection **Damballah** (1981), and most ambitiously in the title story of the collection **Fever** (1989) and the novel **Philadelphia Fire** (1990), Wideman has been breaking down conventional narrative barriers between characters, places, and times. In Wideman's cosmology, it is quite natural for an African ancestor to inhabit the narrative space of, for instance, a young streetwise Philadelphia black. As one of the narrative voices says in **The Cattle Killing,** "Was it a lie, a cover-up to say they've all looked into the same sky, walked the same earth and thus share a world, a condition?"

While his frequent dissolution of language suggests an impatience with the formal constraints of grammar, Wideman's strategy is to restrict his range of associations to the single haunting and obsessive theme of race. A virtuoso of mimicry, Wideman is capable of leaping without warning from the measured cadences of an idealized eighteenth-century black speech ("Curled in the black hold of the ship he wonders why his life on solid green earth had to end, why the gods had chosen this new habitation for him, chained to other captives, no air, no light, the wooden walls shuddering, battered, as if some madman is determined to destroy even this last pitiful refuge . . . and Esu casts his fate, constant motion, tethered to an iron ring") to the voice of a contemporary Philadelphia black man working as a hospital attendant in a nightmare nursing home ("Yeah, I nurse these old funky motherfuckers, all right. White people, specially old white people, lemme tell you, boy, them peckerwoods stink. Stone dead fishy wet stink.")

Finally, amid the dithyrambic lyricism of voices that tell the minutely interwoven tales of **The Cattle Killing,** there abruptly emerges, at the novel's end, a distinctly contemporary American black voice, a vatic, incantatory voice warning of apocalypse arising from the nightly news tragedies of Pittsburgh and Chicago and Los Angeles and Detroit and New York and Dallas and Cleveland and Oakland and Miami:

> I must warn you there are always machines hovering in the air, giant insects with the power to swoop down spattering death, clean out the square in a matter of instants, All our flesh, millions of arms and legs, powerless, bodies crushed, trampled, ripped apart by a rain of fire from machines driven by men not unlike the ones sprawled below in the square, the dead left behind by the multitude the machines have stampeded away.

> . . . From the ashes of your sacrifice a new world of peace and plenty will arise, they say. The prophets of ghost dance, the prophets of the cattle killing, prophets of Kool-Aid, prophets of bend over and take it in your ear, your behind, prophets of off with your head, prophets of chains and prisons and love thy neighbor if and only if he's you, prophets of one skin more equal than others and if the skin fits, wear it and if it doesn't, strip it layer by layer down to the bone and then the prophets sayeth a new and better day will dawn.

This voice both is, and is not, that of John Edgar Wideman: it is the omniscient "Eye."

Though set for the most part in the eighteenth century in Philadelphia and its vicinity, and in an earlier, mythopoetic black Africa. **The Cattle Killing** is purposefully framed by contemporary American black voices. It begins with a prologue in which the mysterious "Eye" slips away from a literary conference apparently devoted in part to his own work ("You step out the hotel door and into another skin . . . Is it *Eye* or *I* or *Ay* or *Aye* or *Aie*"), and travels to another part of the city to visit his aging father, and to read to him from a work-in-progress clearly resembling **The Cattle Killing.** It ends with an epilogue in which a young man named Dan, evidently Eye's son, has just completed reading the manuscript: "*Dear Dad.* Just finished *Cattle Killing*. Congrats. A fine book. Look forward to talking about it with you soon." A jarringly unlyrical voice, after the artfully constructed language that has preceded it, yet it's crucial for Wideman to link generations of fathers and sons and to collapse the gulf of time between them, and between the present and the past from which the present has evolved.

It happens coincidentally that the young Dan has been doing his own research into the slave trade, and **The Cattle Killing** ends with a letter Dan has photocopied from the

British Museum's African archives, written by a nameless black African to his brother: "This note, the others I intend to write, may never reach you, yet I am sure a time will come when we shall be together again." As Wideman's "Eye" insists, the tales in *The Cattle Killing* are "different stories over and over again that are one story"—the exploitation of people of color by Caucasians, and their tragic, if inadvertent, complicity in their exploitation.

Wideman has described his long, ambitious, hallucinatory story **"Fever"** as a meditation upon history, inspired by the *Narrative* of 1974 of Absalom Jones and Bishop Richard Allen, a contemporary account of the Philadelphia yellow-fever epidemic of 1792-1793, as well as by two recent books, Gary B. Nash's *Forging Freedom* (1988), a history of Philadelphia's blacks, and J.H. Powell's *Bring Out Your Dead* (1949). In the yet more ambitious and hallucinatory *The Cattle Killing*, Wideman's most complex novel to date, the nightmare of the yellow-fever epidemic is re-imagined, with many more subplots, settings, characters, both invented and historical.

In the story **"Fever,"** the Negroes are not only blamed by influential white men, like the bigoted Temperance leader Dr. Benjamin Rush, for bringing "Barbados fever" to Philadelphia; they are accused, against all evidence, of being immune to the disease themselves. ("... A not so subtle device for wresting us from our homes, our loved ones, the afflicted among us, and sending us to aid strangers ... A dark skin was seen not only as a badge of shame for its wearer. Now we were evil incarnate, the mask of long agony and violent death.") But in the novel, Dr. Rush is reimagined as one "Benjamin Thrush," and credited as never having subscribed to the theory that Negroes from the West Indies brought the plague with them; still, like the historic Rush, he is "part of the chorus insisting upon the Negroes' immunity, thereby denying them assistance until he witnessed with his own eyes how the deadly tide of fever had swept through [the] neighborhood ... where the poorest folk, Negroes the poorest of these, are trapped."

The strategy of *The Cattle Killing* is set out explicitly for us at the start of the novel:

> Certain passionate African spirits—kin to the ogbanji who hide in a bewitched woman's womb, dooming her infants one after another to an early death unless the curse is lifted—are so strong and willful they refuse to die. They are not gods but achieve a kind of immortality through serial inhabitation of mortal bodies, passing from one to another, using them up, discarding them, finding a new host. Occasionally, as one of these powerful spirits roams the earth, bodiless, seeking a new home, an unlucky soul will encounter the spirit, fall in love with it, follow the spirit forever, finding it, losing it

in the dance of the spirit's trail through other people's lives.

Souls transmigrate from body to body; the African ritual of cattle killing among the Xhosa people, a desperate and futile attempt to ward off European domination, is evoked as a metaphor for the condition of contemporary American blacks: "The cattle are the people. The people are the cattle."

The Cattle Killing juxtaposes lyrical, parable-like tales with presumably authentic historic accounts and testimonies of the yellow-fever epidemic taken from the *Narrative* of Absalom Jones and Richard Allen. Boldly, the author indicates little distinction between voices, times, or settings. The result is a novel frequently difficult of access, reminiscent of Virginia Woolf's almost too determinedly lyric *The Waves*.

In the foreground is a fairly straightforward story about a former slave who has become an itinerant Christian preacher, and who is haunted by the memory of a Haitian woman he has glimpsed only once carrying a pale, apparently dead infant in her arms. In search of this woman, the preacher arrives in Philadelphia during the mysterious yellow-fever epidemic, and goes to work for the historical Bishop Allen, the head of the African Church, the dedicated leader of Philadelphia's blacks. The preacher meets the powerful Dr. Thrush, "a brilliant, brash, handsome man who they say is impatient with fools, full of himself, perhaps to the point of arrogance, yet a fair and decent sort at bottom, so the stories go." Yet Thrush is also the repeated rapist of the young black woman in his household who has been caring for his blind wife.

As the yellow fever rages throughout the city, apocalyptic terrors and beliefs emerge among both blacks and whites, tempting the superstitious to interpret it in divine punitive terms: "God sent the fever to purge us. To cleanse. To humble us. . . ." The novel then shifts back to an earlier troubled time, in Africa, when the Xhosa people have fallen under the spell of a charismatic psychopath-prophet who has convinced them that only the ritual destruction of their precious herds of cattle will save them from European rule: "Though the prophecy promises paradise, a terrible future lived in the words. They were a mouth eating the people. When we slaughtered our herds, we doomed our children." Perhaps there is no historical explanation for what appears to have been a schism in the Xhosa people between the apocalyptic-visionary prophet and the more levelheaded of the tribal elders, who understand that "to kill our cattle ... would be to kill ourselves."

As *The Cattle Killing* moves to a muted conclusion, it shifts back to Philadelphia. The black preacher has lost his

Christian faith. He is revolted by the injustices toward his people and horrified by Dr. Thrush's rape of the young black woman, Kathryn, who has become pregnant. He is dismayed by Bishop Allen's righteous piety: "I couldn't imagine how he could compose himself to address the crowd gathering to mourn the children . . . How could Allen face the people, how could he speak as emissary of such a god." He loses the ability to speak without stuttering "in this language that's cost me far too much to learn"—the white man's Christian tongue with its doctrine of acquiescence in the face of tragedy (a doctrine preached to the politically powerless, that is: the political history of Christianity is hardly distinguished by its passivity).

The narrative shifts forward again, to the present, in which "Eye" has become a preacher of sorts himself on the subject of contemporary America and Africa: "One day I will tell you about Ramona Africa in her cell and Mandela in his cell and the names of the dead we lit candles for in Philadelphia, in Capetown, in Pittsburgh." He sees, in his long apocalyptic vision, that the curse of cattle killing is still with us.

It should be clear that the experience of reading John Edgar Wideman's prose is radically different from whatever any paraphrase of its subject and theme can suggest. With "Eye" as witness and omniscient narrator, we are constantly aware of the fiction being constructed, though Wideman himself is less intrusive as a character in *The Cattle Killing* than in his earlier work. Still, no contemporary writer, with the possible exception of John Barth, is more riskily self-referential. The dangers of such a preoccupation with self are obvious, yet there are rewards as well, for the gradual accretion of biographical fact establishes the reader as an intimate of the writer's, familiar with both the life and the work.* Or, at any rate, the "life" of Wideman as mediated by the work. In Wideman's meta-fictional imagination, it would seem that "life" and "work" are indistinguishable, so to interrupt a narrative to speak as himself or as the omniscient "Eye" is simply to be honest, authentic; to acknowledge the artificial nature of all language simultaneously with the acknowledgement of the driven personal quest that underlies it.

Though *The Cattle Killing* is a novel, it might be most helpfully read as a kind of music, an obsessive beat in the author's head, a nightmare from which he yearns, like Stephen Dedalus in a similar historic context, to be awakened. It is a work of operatic polyphony that strains to break free of linguistic constraints into theatrical spectacle (in the heightened, surreal mode of, for instance, Suzan-Lori Parks's *Venus,* a recent play by a gifted young black playwright on the Victorian phenomenon of the Hottentot Venus). Despite his tragic subject matter, John Edgar

Wideman is also, and frequently, a celebrant of passion and of intense subjectivity. The "Eye" speaks as the novel ends:

> Tell me, finally, what is a man. What is a woman. Aren't we lovers first, spirits sharing an uncharted space, a space our stories tell, a space chanted, written upon again and again, yet one story never quite erased by the next, each story saving the space, saving itself, saving us. If someone is listening.

Tempered with hesitation and even irony as these words are, they seem to us beautiful, tempting us to believe in the redemptive power of storytelling itself.

Michael Wood (review date 27 November 1997)

SOURCE: "Living in the Enemy's Dream," in *London Review of Books,* Vol. 19, No. 23, November 27, 1997, pp. 25-6.

[*In the following review, Wood delineates Wideman's handling of the various themes, characters, and subjects in* The Cattle Killing *and* Brothers and Keepers.]

'Maybe this is a detective story,' a character thinks in John Edgar Wideman's novel *Philadelphia Fire* (1990). It's a reasonable suspicion, and would be for anyone in any of Wideman's books that I've read. But they are not detective stories. Often structured around a quest, for a missing child, a vanished woman, a former self, a meaning, an answer, they finally take the form of a flight, as If from a horror too great to bear or name, a shock one can only circle again and again, and at last abandon. 'Do I write to escape, to make a fiction of my life?' Wideman asks in his memoir *Brothers and Keepers* (1984). 'Wasn't there something fundamental in my writing, in my capacity to function, that depended on flight, escape?' But Wideman is not avoiding the shocks and horrors, he is allowing himself to be haunted by them, evoking their aftermath in a series of deft and ingenious pictures, taken from all kinds of angles by a restless imagination. The aftermath, though, is as close as he gets, and the need to flee even from that is a measure of the force of the original blast.

What blast? Was there just one? A writer in *Philadelphia Fire* feels the need to explain 'that he must always write about many places at once.' Many times, too. Sometimes this imperative produces a fairly loose universalising of local experiences ('She was the body of woman. No beginning, middle, end to her life. All women. Any women'), but more often, and particularly in Wideman's most recent novel *The Cattle Killing* (1996, now published in the United Kingdom for the first time), it reflects a convincing theory of repetition. Certain acts, lynchings, burnings, rebellions, betrayals, must recur because the conditions and assumptions that cause them have not changed. 'Philadelphia was a prophecy of other cities to come,' we read of the plague time in the 18th century, and the prophecy includes not only future Philadelphias, but Cape Town and Pittsburgh, 20th-century cities to which the narrative leaps in its last pages.

The shock of *Philadelphia Fire* is the shock named in the title, the burning and bombing, on the orders of a black mayor, of a black community in a house on Osage Avenue. The event is briefly recalled in *The Cattle Killing.* There the shock takes several other forms as well; what we might call the invention of race by 18th-century white American Christians, who one day decided to segregate their formerly unsegregated churches; racial slurs and allegations flung about during the plague; the murder of a mixed-race couple in the Pennsylvania countryside; and across the sea in South Africa, the animal massacre which gives the book its title. Heeding a false prophecy given to a girl in a dream, the Xhosa kill their cattle in the belief that this sacrifice will bring about a new world. Instead it hastens their end. Wideman offers various readings of the moral of this story. Not just: 'Do not kill your enemy's tongue. Do not fall asleep in your enemy's dream.' Later he suggests that the Xhosa are 'bewitched by a prophecy that steals them from themselves'.

What is striking about these horrors is their mixture of simplicity and complexity. Raw, mindless prejudice stands side by side with convoluted self-deception, and a willingness to do the enemy's work for him. There seems to be a point, too, where the horrors are not only public or historical; where the political tips over into the personal. At the beginning of *The Cattle Killing,* an unnamed writer is about to read his manuscript, presumably the bulk of the book we have in our hands, to his father. 'Setting out for his father's house he leaves everything behind' is the forceful opening sentence. At the end, a book called *The Cattle Killing* is read and commented on by the writer's son. 'A fine book,' the son says in a letter, but he also thinks: 'As most of his father's books, this one also seemed inspired by something unsaid, unshared, hidden. Silent at the core.' We don't know what the writer's father thinks, but we do see the writer's hankering for a continuity across the generations, something that is always broken by the violent events Wideman keeps returning to. A casual seeming line in *Philadelphia Fire* speaks volumes of silence: 'Playing father, son and holocaust to the kids running wild in streets and vacant lots.' What are we to make of this joke, terrible in every sense?

The plot-line of the manuscript written and read by fathers and sons concerns a young wandering preacher in 18th-cen-

tury Pennsylvania. He announces the gospel in the woods, has epileptic fits and visions, is almost killed in a snow-storm and then cared for by a kindly couple; tries to save the life of a young black servant made pregnant by her philanthropic and negro-friendly master-in her case more than friendly. Wideman gives us all kinds of voices, including those of the philanthropist's blind wife, the servant, an African employed as factotum by the painter George Stubbs. Some of these impersonations are more appealing than others, and there is a dispiriting amount of antiquing going on, as in 'My garments, goodlady,' and 'I was a poor servant girl, possessed nothing but the curse of youthful beauty,' and 'The old fellow has essayed too much this time.' This doesn't stop the old fellow wearing a parka, so you wonder how Wideman is seeing these scenes. But the variety of the voices is more important than any notional authenticity, and Wideman, shrewdly if self-consciously, shares his worries with us.

> He was not the African youngster, never was, never would be . . . What he shared with the 18th-century African boy whose story he wanted to tell . . . would be testimony witnessing what surrounds them both this very moment, an encompassing silence forgetting them both, silence untouched by their passing, by the countless passings of so many others like them, a world distant and abiding and memoryless. The terror of its forgetfulness, its utter lack of concern would be unbearable unless be imagined something else.

There is a further horror here, to add to the ones I've mentioned: that memory itself discriminates, and that forgetting your own past because others choose to forget it is also a way of killing your cattle.

Brothers and Keepers is an intricate, painful account of Wideman's response to his youngest brother Robby's crime and life sentence, and a detailed re-creation, as close as Wideman can make it, of Robby's own perception of what happened and was still happening to him. When the book closes Robby has taken an engineering degree in jail, but he is still in the Western Penitentiary in Pittsburgh, and conditions are getting worse. This edition has no up-date to tell us any more of the story.

The narrative opens in Laramie, Wyoming, where Wideman, an established and well-regarded writer, is teaching literature and creative writing at the university. The time is late 1975, and Wideman gets a phone call from his mother in Pittsburgh. Robby is on the run, wanted for armed robbery and murder. Some three months later Robby shows up in Laramie with two companions, spends the night, moves on. The next day he is arrested, taken back east for trial, and after two years in gaol, he is sentenced. An appeal to the Supreme Court of Pennsylvania was denied in 1981.

We learn that Robby, the youngest of four black children growing up in the Shadyside district of Pittsburgh, was always a little 'wild'. Shadyside was a predominantly white area, and 'black was like the forbidden fruit,' Robby tells his brother. He soon found the fruit in the nearby neighbourhoods, and spent much of his young life on the street, drinking, doing dope, having parties, and dreaming of the big time, a sort of gangster pop star fantasy involving huge cars and slinky girls, and a large cheque presented to Mom so she could buy a house. This at least is how Robby tells it with retrospective irony, but the irony only marks his distance from the dream, the gap between the old imagined life and the reality of the prison, doesn't undercut the power the dream had at the time. The way Robby is going to make it big is through drug money, buying heroin in Detroit and selling it in Pittsburgh, but then everything goes wrong. Robby is arrested for small-time dealing before he can get to the big time. When he is released, the heroin that he and his friends have bought turns bad before they can sell it. And finally, a supposedly simple con job—taking money from a fence for a load of television sets Robby and friends haven't got—becomes a disaster when one of the friends shoots the fence and the fence dies.

A murkiness enters the story around here, both in Wideman's re-creation of his brother's version and in Wideman's own commentary. Both brothers rightly reject the notion that Robby, or any other criminal, is categorically different from other humans, or perhaps not human at all—many of Wideman's most eloquent pages in this book concern the functioning of the prison system as precisely an instrument of this mythology, a locking away of miscreant others as if they had nothing to do with us. A prison is 'a two-sided, unbreakable mirror,' Wideman says. 'When we look at you we see ourselves. We see order and justice. Your uniforms, your rules reflect human discipline . . . When prisoners gaze into the reverse side of the mirror they should see the deformed aberrations they've become. 'Should see, and do see, unless they have reserves of strength and self-worth rarely to be found in the outside world, and Wideman's climactic perception is that 'the character traits that landed Robby in prison are the same ones that have allowed him to survive with dignity, and pain and a sense of himself as infinitely better than the soulless drone prison demands he become.'

The alternative view of Robby's circumstances seems to be that crime is a chain of bad luck, a matter of poor timing or getting caught. If you don't get caught, it's just business. This is a fine satirical argument about a money-making society, and many movies and novels thrive on it, but satire is no way to come to terms with your own past. When Robby in jail thinks of the drug-lord life he might have had, he doesn't think it's wrong, he just thinks it's dangerous: that he might be dead now instead of alive in prison. I'm

not suggesting that Robby needs to moralise more or repent fulsomely, or that either brother needs to start thinking like protected white folks, only that a whole moral dimension is missing here, a sense of what was wrong apart from the accidents. The odd moments when Robby does repent or analyse his faults are the least convincing things in the book. He always wanted things to come easy, he says, now he knows that the hard things are the ones that count. He wanted not money or power but glamour, the sense of being someone that only the dressy, glitzy, risky life could give. Fine, but who doesn't want these things, and why was Robby prepared to go for them in this way? And isn't there something defeated about these particular claims to glamour, a sense of limping bad luck inherent in them, as if all they could do was fail?

Wideman the writer is fully aware of these problems, and leaves plenty of spaces in his book for the unsaid and unsayable. And there are two regions where the otherwise missing moral dimension, without filling up those spaces or providing all the answers, puts in a striking appearance. One is the relation of both men, in and out of jail, to their mother. For Robby, she is the real victim of his crime. He is 'damned sorry' a man got killed, but not sorry for robbing white people or for having a good time. He can scarcely bring himself to think about his mother's suffering.

> I tried to write Mom a letter. Not too long ago . . . I wanted Mom to know I knew what I'd done . . . After all she did for me I turned around and made her life miserable. That's the wrongest thing I've done and I wanted to say I was sorry but I kept seeing her face while I was writing the letter. I'd see her face and it would get older while I was looking. She'd get this old woman's face all lined and wrinkled and tired about the eyes. Wasn't nothing I could do but watch.

For Wideman, the mother is the person who knew about Robby's trouble when everyone else managed not to see it, who was as helpless as the rest but not as ignorant, and whose example teaches him the true meaning of the word 'unbearable'. She is talking about the summer heat in Pittsburgh, but Wideman expects us to see how the real heat can become a wide-ranging metaphor.

> 'Unbearable' is my mother's word. She uses it often but never lightly. In her language it means the heat is something you can't escape . . . Unbearable doesn't mean a weight that gets things over with, that crushes you once and for all, but a burden that exerts relentless pressure . . . Unbearable is not that which can't be borne, but what must be endured for ever.

The mother is also the tolerant black person who is horrified by the sheer repetition of oppressive patterns in American society, and this takes us to the second region where the moral dimension reappears, a territory somewhere between sociology and politics. If we can't fully understand Robby's individual case, and Wideman doesn't pretend to, we can certainly see-can't fail to see unless we willfully avert our eyes-the larger world of ruined or banished opportunities which is the inheritance of far too many American blacks. It's not that the misery of the ghetto excuses crime, we don't need a weepy story of that kind. It's that the very conception of crime changes if justice itself seems to deal in segregation. Is American justice really in such bad shape? One hopes not, and I believe not. But it is perceived to be so by a large proportion of the population, and we can't ignore this perception. More important, we can't just want militant blacks to learn to think the way liberal whites already do. Many of them used to think that way before the world they lived in made them militant. Wideman's patient and open-minded mother was 'radicalised', he says, not by 'demonstrations, protest marches and slogans', but by the neglect of a sick friend of Robby's, whom no clinic will treat, and who finally dies because he was not treated earlier. 'They let him walk the streets till he was dead. It was wrong. Worse than wrong how they did him.' Wideman is shocked by her tone.

> No slack, no margin of doubt was being granted to the forces that destroyed Garth and still pursued her son. She had exhausted her long reserves of understanding and compassion. The long view supplied the same ugly picture as the short.

But hospitals and prisons are quite different institutions, and neither is an instrument of demonised 'forces' intent on destruction. Do we think Mrs Wideman doesn't know that? Sins of omission can be discriminatory, too, and you don't need a conspiracy to achieve a conspiracy's effects.

The other story in this book, the one hinted at in the title, is Wideman's own. Robby, he fears, is the person he might have been, the delegate, even now, of the Pittsburgh he ran away from, via a basketball scholarship, foreign travel and a life as a writer. Wideman needs now to deny his denial of his past and that place, but is sensitive enough to know he can't just use his brother's plight to do this. He comes close to this form of exploitation, registers the risk, makes that, too, part of his book. He is very hard on himself ('I figured which side I wanted to be on when the Saints came marching in . . . To succeed in the man's world you must become like the man and the mans sure didn't claim no bunch of nigger relatives in Pittsburgh'), but as with Robby, and as in Wideman's novels, you feel something is escaping him, some truth which is not necessarily tougher or uglier than the ones he tells but certainly for some reason harder to face.

When God in Genesis asks Cain where his brother is, Cain's famous answers seems to mean his brother is an independent creature, not Cain's ward. It also means: How should I know? But then Cain has already killed Abel by this time, and can scarcely hope to fool God. 'Am I my brother's keeper' means I'll pretend as long as I can that I haven't killed him. If you are not your brother's keeper are you his murderer? The question gets an additional edge from the fact that 'keeper' is the American term for a warder in a prison. The answer is no, but then what are the other options? ***Brothers and Keepers*** is a harrowing exploration of this second question, a flight that takes us back to those old prophecies, life in the enemy's dream.

FURTHER READING

Criticism

Finney, Ron. "To Repair the Two Relations." *Los Angeles Times Book Review* (23 December 1984): 6.
    Outlines the narrative of *Brothers and Keepers.*

Review of *Fatheralong: A Meditation on Fathers and Sons, Race and Society,* by John Edgar Wideman. *Harvard Educational Review* 65, No. 4 (1995): 683-84.
    Favorable review of *Fatheralong,* in which the critic declares that Wideman "presents a timely, critical, and cogent discussion on the paradigm of race and its injurious impact on Black people."

Mullen, Bill. "Looking Back." *Partisan Review* 61, No. 3 (1994): 528-31.
    A laudatory survey of Wideman's works, including *Philadelphia Fire, The Stories of John Edgar Wideman,* and *The Homewood Books.*

Pinckney, Darryl. "Aristocrats." *New York Review of Books* 42, No 8 (11 May 1995): 27-34.
    Offers mixed commentary on *Fatheralong.* Pinckney also discusses two works by other authors who treat racial and familial issues.

——."Cos I'm a So-o-oul Man: The Back-Country Blues of John Edgar Wideman." *Times Literary Supplement* 4612 (August 23, 1991): 19-20.
    A mixed assessment of *Philadelphia Fire* and *Fever.*

Smith, Shawn Michael. "Like Steam from a City Grate." *The Christian Science Monitor* 82, No. 229, (October 23, 1990): 15.
    A review in which Smith provides a laudatory assessment of *Philadelphia Fire.*

Additional information on Wideman's life and works is contained in the following sources published by Gale: *Black Literature Criticism; Black Writers*, Vol. 2; *Contemporary Authors*, Vols. 85-88; *Contemporary Authors New Revision Series*, Vols. 14, 42, and 67; *Dictionary of Literary Biography*, Vols. 33, 143; and *DISCovering Authors Modules: Multicultural.*

☐ Contemporary Literary Criticism

Indexes

Literary Criticism Series
Cumulative Author Index
Cumulative Topic Index
Cumulative Nationality Index
Title Index, Volume 122

How to Use This Index

The main references

Camus, Albert
  1913-1960 . . . . . . .CLC 1, 2, 4, 9, 11,
    14, 32, 69; DA; DAB; DAC; DAM
    DRAM, MST, NOV; DC2; SSC 9;
    WLC

list all author entries in the following Gale Literary Criticism series:

BLC = *Black Literature Criticism*
BLCS = *Black Literature Criticism Supplement*
CLC = *Contemporary Literary Criticism*
CLR = *Children's Literature Review*
CMLC = *Classical and Medieval Literature Criticism*
DA = *DISCovering Authors*
DAB = *DISCovering Authors: British*
DAC = *DISCovering Authors: Canadian*
DAM = *DISCovering Authors Modules*
  DRAM = *dramatists;* *MST* = *most-studied*
  authors; *MULT* = *multicultural authors;* *NOV* =
  novelists; *POET* = *poets;* *POP* = *popular/genre*
  writers; *DC* = *Drama Criticism*
HLC = *Hispanic Literature Criticism*
LC = *Literature Criticism from 1400 to 1800*
NCLC = *Nineteenth-Century Literature Criticism*
PC = *Poetry Criticism*
SSC = *Short Story Criticism*
TCLC = *Twentieth-Century Literary Criticism*
WLC = *World Literature Criticism, 1500 to the Present*
WLCS = *World Literature Criticism Supplement*

The cross-references

See also CA 89-92; DLB 72; MTCW

list all author entries in the following Gale biographical and literary sources:

AAYA = *Authors & Artists for Young Adults*
AITN = *Authors in the News*
BEST = *Bestsellers*
BW = *Black Writers*
CA = *Contemporary Authors*
CAAS = *Contemporary Authors Autobiography Series*
CABS = *Contemporary Authors Bibliographical Series*
CANR = *Contemporary Authors New Revision Series*
CAP = *Contemporary Authors Permanent Series*
CDALB = *Concise Dictionary of American Literary Biography*
CDBLB = *Concise Dictionary of British Literary Biography*

DLB = *Dictionary of Literary Biography*
DLBD = *Dictionary of Literary Biography Documentary Series*
DLBY = *Dictionary of Literary Biography Yearbook*
HW = *Hispanic Writers*
JRDA = *Junior DISCovering Authors*
MAICYA = *Major Authors and Illustrators for Children and Young Adults*
MTCW = *Major 20th-Century Writers*
NNAL = *Native North American Literature*
SAAS = *Something about the Author Autobiography Series*
SATA = *Something about the Author*
YABC = *Yesterday's Authors of Books for Children*

Literary Criticism Series
Cumulative Author Index

See also DLB 1

Alcott, Louisa May 1832-1888 . **NCLC 6, 58; DA; DAB; DAC; DAM MST, NOV; SSC 27; WLC**
See also AAYA 20; CDALB 1865-1917; CLR 1, 38; DLB 1, 42, 79; DLBD 14; JRDA; MAICYA; SATA 100; YABC 1

Aldanov, M. À.
See Aldanov, Mark (Alexandrovich)

Aldanov, Mark (Alexandrovich) 1886(?)-1957 **TCLC 23**
See also CA 118

Aldington, Richard 1892-1962 .... **CLC 49**
See also CA 85-88; CANR 45; DLB 20, 36, 100, 149

Aldiss, Brian W(ilson) 1925- . **CLC 5, 14, 40; DAM NOV; SSC 36**
See also CA 5-8R; CAAS 2; CANR 5, 28, 64; DLB 14; MTCW 1, 2; SATA 34

Alegria, Claribel 1924-**CLC 75; DAM MULT; HLCS 1; PC 26**
See also CA 131; CAAS 15; CANR 66; DLB 145; HW 1; MTCW 1

Alegria, Fernando 1918- .... **CLC 57**
See also CA 9-12R; CANR 5, 32, 72; HW 1, 2

Aleichem, Sholom .... **TCLC 1, 35; SSC 33**
See also Rabinovitch, Sholem

Aleixandre, Vicente 1898-1984
See also CANR 81; HLCS 1; HW 2

Alepoudelis, Odysseus
See Elytis, Odysseus

Aleshkovsky, Joseph 1929-
See Aleshkovsky, Yuz
See also CA 121; 128

Aleshkovsky, Yuz .... **CLC 44**
See also Aleshkovsky, Joseph

Alexander, Lloyd (Chudley) 1924- ... **CLC 35**
See also AAYA 1, 27; CA 1-4R; CANR 1, 24, 38, 55; CLR 1, 5, 48; DLB 52; JRDA; MAICYA; MTCW 1; SAAS 19; SATA 3, 49, 81

Alexander, Meena 1951- .... **CLC 121**
See also CA 115; CANR 38, 70

Alexander, Samuel 1859-1938 .... **TCLC 77**

Alexie, Sherman (Joseph, Jr.) 1966-**CLC 96; DAM MULT**
See also AAYA 28; CA 138; CANR 65; DLB 175, 206; MTCW 1; NNAL

Alfau, Felipe 1902- .... **CLC 66**
See also CA 137

Alger, Horatio, Jr. 1832-1899 .... **NCLC 8**
See also DLB 42; SATA 16

Algren, Nelson 1909-1981**CLC 4, 10, 33; SSC 33**
See also CA 13-16R; 103; CANR 20, 61; CDALB 1941-1968; DLB 9; DLBY 81, 82; MTCW 1, 2

Ali, Ahmed 1910- .... **CLC 69**
See also CA 25-28R; CANR 15, 34

Alighieri, Dante
See Dante

Allan, John B.
See Westlake, Donald E(dwin)

Allan, Sidney
See Hartmann, Sadakichi

Allan, Sydney
See Hartmann, Sadakichi

Allen, Edward 1948- .... **CLC 59**

Allen, Fred 1894-1956 .... **TCLC 87**

Allen, Paula Gunn 1939- .... **CLC 84; DAM MULT**
See also CA 112; 143; CANR 63; DLB 175; MTCW 1; NNAL

Allen, Roland
See Ayckbourn, Alan

Allen, Sarah A.
See Hopkins, Pauline Elizabeth

Allen, Sidney H.
See Hartmann, Sadakichi

Allen, Woody 1935- **CLC 16, 52; DAM POP**
See also AAYA 10; CA 33-36R; CANR 27, 38, 63; DLB 44; MTCW 1

Allende, Isabel 1942- . **CLC 39, 57, 97; DAM MULT, NOV; HLC 1; WLCS**
See also AAYA 18; CA 125; 130; CANR 51, 74; DLB 145; HW 1, 2; INT 130; MTCW 1, 2

Alleyn, Ellen
See Rossetti, Christina (Georgina)

Allingham, Margery (Louise) 1904-1966**CLC 19**
See also CA 5-8R; 25-28R; CANR 4, 58; DLB 77; MTCW 1, 2

Allingham, William 1824-1889 ...... **NCLC 25**
See also DLB 35

Allison, Dorothy E. 1949- .... **CLC 78**
See also CA 140; CANR 66; MTCW 1

Allston, Washington 1779-1843 .... **NCLC 2**
See also DLB 1

Almedingen, E. M. .... **CLC 12**
See also Almedingen, Martha Edith von
See also SATA 3

Almedingen, Martha Edith von 1898-1971
See Almedingen, E. M.
See also CA 1-4R; CANR 1

Almodovar, Pedro 1949(?)-**CLC 114; HLCS 1**
See also CA 133; CANR 72; HW 2

Almqvist, Carl Jonas Love 1793-1866 **NCLC 42**

Alonso, Damaso 1898-1990 .... **CLC 14**
See also CA 110; 131; 130; CANR 72; DLB 108; HW 1, 2

Alov
See Gogol, Nikolai (Vasilyevich)

Alta 1942- .... **CLC 19**
See also CA 57-60

Alter, Robert B(ernard) 1935- .... **CLC 34**
See also CA 49-52; CANR 1, 47

Alther, Lisa 1944- ....**CLC 7, 41**
See also CA 65-68; CAAS 30; CANR 12, 30, 51; MTCW 1

Althusser, L.
See Althusser, Louis

Althusser, Louis 1918-1990 .... **CLC 106**
See also CA 131; 132

Altman, Robert 1925- .... **CLC 16, 116**
See also CA 73-76; CANR 43

Alurista 1949-
See Urista, Alberto H.
See also DLB 82; HLCS 1

Alvarez, A(lfred) 1929- .... **CLC 5, 13**
See also CA 1-4R; CANR 3, 33, 63; DLB 14, 40

Alvarez, Alejandro Rodriguez 1903-1965
See Casona, Alejandro
See also CA 131; 93-96; HW 1

Alvarez, Julia 1950- .... **CLC 93; HLCS 1**
See also AAYA 25; CA 147; CANR 69; MTCW 1

Alvaro, Corrado 1896-1956 .... **TCLC 60**
See also CA 163

Amado, Jorge 1912- **CLC 13, 40, 106; DAM MULT, NOV; HLC 1**
See also CA 77-80; CANR 35, 74; DLB 113; HW 2; MTCW 1, 2

Ambler, Eric 1909-1998 .... **CLC 4, 6, 9**

See also CA 9-12R; 171; CANR 7, 38, 74; DLB 77; MTCW 1, 2

Amichai, Yehuda 1924- ... **CLC 9, 22, 57, 116**
See also CA 85-88; CANR 46, 60; MTCW 1

Amichai, Yehudah
See Amichai, Yehuda

Amiel, Henri Frederic 1821-1881 .... **NCLC 4**

Amis, Kingsley (William) 1922-1995**CLC 1, 2, 3, 5, 8, 13, 40, 44; DA; DAB; DAC; DAM MST, NOV**
See also AITN 2; CA 9-12R; 150; CANR 8, 28, 54; CDBLB 1945-1960; DLB 15, 27, 100, 139; DLBY 96; INT CANR-8; MTCW 1, 2

Amis, Martin (Louis) 1949-**CLC 4, 9, 38, 62, 101**
See also BEST 90:3; CA 65-68; CANR 8, 27, 54, 73; DLB 14, 194; INT CANR-27; MTCW 1

Ammons, A(rchie) R(andolph) 1926-**CLC 2, 3, 5, 8, 9, 25, 57, 108; DAM POET; PC 16**
See also AITN 1; CA 9-12R; CANR 6, 36, 51, 73; DLB 5, 165; MTCW 1, 2

Amo, Tauraatua i
See Adams, Henry (Brooks)

Amory, Thomas 1691(?)-1788 .... **LC 48**

Anand, Mulk Raj 1905- .. **CLC 23, 93; DAM NOV**
See also CA 65-68; CANR 32, 64; MTCW 1, 2

Anatol
See Schnitzler, Arthur

Anaximander c. 610B.C.-c. 546B.C.**CMLC 22**

Anaya, Rudolfo A(lfonso) 1937- ..... **CLC 23; DAM MULT, NOV; HLC 1**
See also AAYA 20; CA 45-48; CAAS 4; CANR 1, 32, 51; DLB 82, 206; HW 1; MTCW 1, 2

Andersen, Hans Christian 1805-1875**NCLC 7, 79; DA; DAB; DAC; DAM MST, POP; SSC 6; WLC**
See also CLR 6; MAICYA; SATA 100; YABC 1

Anderson, C. Farley
See Mencken, H(enry) L(ouis); Nathan, George Jean

Anderson, Jessica (Margaret) Queale 1916-**CLC 37**
See also CA 9-12R; CANR 4, 62

Anderson, Jon (Victor) 1940- .. **CLC 9; DAM POET**
See also CA 25-28R; CANR 20

Anderson, Lindsay (Gordon) 1923-1994**CLC 20**
See also CA 125; 128; 146; CANR 77

Anderson, Maxwell 1888-1959**TCLC 2; DAM DRAM** '
See also CA 105; 152; DLB 7; MTCW 2

Anderson, Poul (William) 1926- .... **CLC 15**
See also AAYA 5; CA 1-4R; CAAS 2; CANR 2, 15, 34, 64; CLR 58; DLB 8; INT CANR-15; MTCW 1, 2; SATA 90; SATA-Brief 39; SATA-Essay 106

Anderson, Robert (Woodruff) 1917-**CLC 23; DAM DRAM**
See also AITN 1; CA 21-24R; CANR 32; DLB 7

Anderson, Sherwood 1876-1941**TCLC 1, 10, 24; DA; DAB; DAC; DAM MST, NOV; SSC 1; WLC**
See also AAYA 30; CA 104; 121; CANR 61; CDALB 1917-1929; DLB 4, 9, 86; DLBD 1; MTCW 1, 2

Andier, Pierre
See Desnos, Robert

Andouard

See Giraudoux, (Hippolyte) Jean

Andrade, Carlos Drummond de .... **CLC 18**
See also Drummond de Andrade, Carlos

Andrade, Mario de 1893-1945 ...... **TCLC 43**

Andreae, Johann V(alentin) 1586-1654 **LC 32**
See also DLB 164

Andreas-Salome, Lou 1861-1937 ... **TCLC 56**
See also CA 178; DLB 66

Andress, Lesley
See Sanders, Lawrence

Andrewes, Lancelot 1555-1626 .... **LC 5**
See also DLB 151, 172

Andrews, Cicily Fairfield
See West, Rebecca

Andrews, Elton V.
See Pohl, Frederik

Andreyev, Leonid (Nikolaevich) 1871-1919
TCLC 3
See also CA 104

Andric, Ivo 1892-1975 .... **CLC 8; SSC 36**
See also CA 81-84; 57-60; CANR 43, 60; DLB
147; MTCW 1

Androvar
See Prado (Calvo), Pedro

Angelique, Pierre
See Bataille, Georges

Angell, Roger 1920- .... **CLC 26**
See also CA 57-60; CANR 13, 44, 70; DLB 171,
185

Angelou, Maya 1928- **CLC 12, 35, 64, 77; BLC**
1; DA; DAB; DAC; DAM MST, MULT,
POET, POP; WLCS
See also AAYA 7, 20; BW 2, 3; CA 65-68;
CANR 19, 42, 65; CDALBS; CLR 53; DLB
38; MTCW 1, 2; SATA 49

Anna Comnena 1083-1153 .... **CMLC 25**

Annensky, Innokenty (Fyodorovich) 1856-1909
TCLC 14
See also CA 110; 155

Annunzio, Gabriele d'
See D'Annunzio, Gabriele

Anodos
See Coleridge, Mary E(lizabeth)

Anon, Charles Robert
See Pessoa, Fernando (Antonio Nogueira)

Anouilh, Jean (Marie Lucien Pierre) 1910-1987
CLC 1, 3, 8, 13, 40, 50; DAM DRAM; DC
8
See also CA 17-20R; 123; CANR 32; MTCW
1, 2

Anthony, Florence
See Ai

Anthony, John
See Ciardi, John (Anthony)

Anthony, Peter
See Shaffer, Anthony (Joshua); Shaffer, Peter
(Levin)

Anthony, Piers 1934- .... **CLC 35; DAM POP**
See also AAYA 11; CA 21-24R; CANR 28, 56,
73; DLB 8; MTCW 1, 2; SAAS 22; SATA 84

Anthony, Susan B(rownell) 1916-1991 **T C L C**
84
See also CA 89-92; 134

Antoine, Marc
See Proust, (Valentin-Louis-George-Eugene-)
Marcel

Antoninus, Brother
See Everson, William (Oliver)

Antonioni, Michelangelo 1912- .... **CLC 20**
See also CA 73-76; CANR 45, 77

Antschel, Paul 1920-1970
See Celan, Paul
See also CA 85-88; CANR 33, 61; MTCW 1

Anwar, Chairil 1922-1949 .... **TCLC 22**
See also CA 121

Anzaldua, Gloria 1942-
See also CA 175; DLB 122; HLCS 1

Apess, William 1798-1839(?) **NCLC 73; DAM**
MULT
See also DLB 175; NNAL

Apollinaire, Guillaume 1880-1918 **TCLC 3, 8,**
51; DAM POET; PC 7
See also Kostrowitzki, Wilhelm Apollinaris de
See also CA 152; MTCW 1

Appelfeld, Aharon 1932- .... **CLC 23, 47**
See also CA 112; 133

Apple, Max (Isaac) 1941- .... **CLC 9, 33**
See also CA 81-84; CANR 19, 54; DLB 130

Appleman, Philip (Dean) 1926- .... **CLC 51**
See also CA 13-16R; CAAS 18; CANR 6, 29,
56

Appleton, Lawrence
See Lovecraft, H(oward) P(hillips)

Apteryx
See Eliot, T(homas) S(tearns)

Apuleius, (Lucius Madaurensis) 125(?)-175(?)
CMLC 1
See also DLB 211

Aquin, Hubert 1929-1977 .... **CLC 15**
See also CA 105; DLB 53

Aquinas, Thomas 1224(?)-1274 ..... **CMLC 33**
See also DLB 115

Aragon, Louis 1897-1982 .. **CLC 3, 22; DAM**
NOV, POET
See also CA 69-72; 108; CANR 28, 71; DLB
72; MTCW 1, 2

Arany, Janos 1817-1882 .... **NCLC 34**

Aranyos, Kakay
See Mikszath, Kalman

Arbuthnot, John 1667-1735 .... **LC 1**
See also DLB 101

Archer, Herbert Winslow
See Mencken, H(enry) L(ouis)

Archer, Jeffrey (Howard) 1940- ..... **CLC 28;**
DAM POP
See also AAYA 16; BEST 89:3; CA 77-80;
CANR 22, 52; INT CANR-22

Archer, Jules 1915- .... **CLC 12**
See also CA 9-12R; CANR 6, 69; SAAS 5;
SATA 4, 85

Archer, Lee
See Ellison, Harlan (Jay)

Arden, John 1930- **CLC 6, 13, 15; DAM DRAM**
See also CA 13-16R; CAAS 4; CANR 31, 65,
67; DLB 13; MTCW 1

Arenas, Reinaldo 1943-1990 . **CLC 41; DAM**
MULT; HLC 1
See also CA 124; 128; 133; CANR 73; DLB
145; HW 1; MTCW 1

Arendt, Hannah 1906-1975 .... **CLC 66, 98**
See also CA 17-20R; 61-64; CANR 26, 60;
MTCW 1, 2

Aretino, Pietro 1492-1556 .... **LC 12**

Arghezi, Tudor 1880-1967 .... **CLC 80**
See also Theodorescu, Ion N.
See also CA 167

Arguedas, Jose Maria 1911-1969 **CLC 10, 18;**
HLCS 1
See also CA 89-92; CANR 73; DLB 113; HW 1

Argueta, Manlio 1936- .... **CLC 31**
See also CA 131; CANR 73; DLB 145; HW 1

Arias, Ron(ald Francis) 1941-
See also CA 131; CANR 81; DAM MULT; DLB
82; HLC 1; HW 1, 2; MTCW 2

Ariosto, Ludovico 1474-1533 .... **LC 6**

Aristides

See Epstein, Joseph

Aristophanes 450B.C.-385B.C. **CMLC 4; DA;**
DAB; DAC; DAM DRAM, MST; DC 2;
WLCS
See also DLB 176

Aristotle 384B.C.-322B.C. ... **CMLC 31; DA;**
DAB; DAC; DAM MST; WLCS
See also DLB 176

Arlt, Roberto (Godofredo Christophersen)
1900-1942 **TCLC 29; DAM MULT; HLC 1**
See also CA 123; 131; CANR 67; HW 1, 2

Armah, Ayi Kwei 1939- . **CLC 5, 33; BLC 1;**
DAM MULT, POET
See also BW 1; CA 61-64; CANR 21, 64; DLB
117; MTCW 1

Armatrading, Joan 1950- .... **CLC 17**
See also CA 114

Arnette, Robert
See Silverberg, Robert

Arnim, Achim von (Ludwig Joachim von
Arnim) 1781-1831 ...... **NCLC 5; SSC 29**
See also DLB 90

Arnim, Bettina von 1785-1859 .... **NCLC 38**
See also DLB 90

Arnold, Matthew 1822-1888 **NCLC 6, 29; DA;**
DAB; DAC; DAM MST, POET; PC 5;
WLC
See also CDBLB 1832-1890; DLB 32, 57

Arnold, Thomas 1795-1842 .... **NCLC 18**
See also DLB 55

Arnow, Harriette (Louisa) Simpson 1908-1986
CLC 2, 7, 18
See also CA 9-12R; 118; CANR 14; DLB 6;
MTCW 1, 2; SATA 42; SATA-Obit 47

Arouet, Francois-Marie
See Voltaire

Arp, Hans
See Arp, Jean

Arp, Jean 1887-1966 .... **CLC 5**
See also CA 81-84; 25-28R; CANR 42, 77

Arrabal
See Arrabal, Fernando

Arrabal, Fernando 1932-.... **CLC 2, 9, 18, 58**
See also CA 9-12R; CANR 15

Arreola, Juan Jose 1918-
See also CA 113; 131; CANR 81; DAM MULT;
DLB 113; HLC 1; HW 1, 2

Arrick, Fran .... **CLC 30**
See also Gaberman, Judie Angell

Artaud, Antonin (Marie Joseph) 1896-1948
TCLC 3, 36; DAM DRAM
See also CA 104; 149; MTCW 1

Arthur, Ruth M(abel) 1905-1979 ...... **CLC 12**
See also CA 9-12R; 85-88; CANR 4; SATA 7,
26

Artsybashev, Mikhail (Petrovich) 1878-1927
TCLC 31
See also CA 170

Arundel, Honor (Morfydd) 1919-1973 **CLC 17**
See also CA 21-22; 41-44R; CAP 2; CLR 35;
SATA 4; SATA-Obit 24

Arzner, Dorothy 1897-1979 .... **CLC 98**

Asch, Sholem 1880-1957 .... **TCLC 3**
See also CA 105

Ash, Shalom
See Asch, Sholem

Ashbery, John (Lawrence) 1927- **CLC 2, 3, 4,**
6, 9, 13, 15, 25, 41, 77; DAM POET; PC 26
See also CA 5-8R; CANR 9, 37, 66; DLB 5,
165; DLBY 81; INT CANR-9; MTCW 1, 2

Ashdown, Clifford
See Freeman, R(ichard) Austin

Ashe, Gordon

See Mikszath, Kalman

Balzac, Honore de 1799-1850**NCLC 5, 35, 53;
DA; DAB; DAC; DAM MST, NOV; SSC
5; WLC**
See also DLB 119

Bambara, Toni Cade 1939-1995 **CLC 19, 88;
BLC 1; DA; DAC; DAM MST, MULT;
SSC 35; WLCS**
See also AAYA 5; BW 2, 3; CA 29-32R; 150;
CANR 24, 49, 81; CDALBS; DLB 38;
MTCW 1, 2

Bamdad, A.
See Shamlu, Ahmad

Banat, D. R.
See Bradbury, Ray (Douglas)

Bancroft, Laura
See Baum, L(yman) Frank

Banim, John 1798-1842 .... **NCLC 13**
See also DLB 116, 158, 159

Banim, Michael 1796-1874 .... **NCLC 13**
See also DLB 158, 159

Banjo, The
See Paterson, A(ndrew) B(arton)

Banks, Iain
See Banks, Iain M(enzies)

Banks, Iain M(enzies) 1954- .... **CLC 34**
See also CA 123; 128; CANR 61; DLB 194;
INT 128

Banks, Lynne Reid .... **CLC 23**
See also Reid Banks, Lynne
See also AAYA 6

Banks, Russell 1940- .... **CLC 37, 72**
See also CA 65-68; CAAS 15; CANR 19, 52,
73; DLB 130

Banville, John 1945- .... **CLC 46, 118**
See also CA 117; 128; DLB 14; INT 128

Banville, Theodore (Faullain) de 1832-1891
NCLC 9

Baraka, Amiri 1934-**CLC 1, 2, 3, 5, 10, 14, 33,
115; BLC 1; DA; DAC; DAM MST, MULT,
POET, POP; DC 6; PC 4; WLCS**
See also Jones, LeRoi
See also BW 2, 3; CA 21-24R; CABS 3; CANR
27, 38, 61; CDALB 1941-1968; DLB 5, 7,
16, 38; DLBD 8; MTCW 1, 2

Barbauld, Anna Laetitia 1743-1825**NCLC 50**
See also DLB 107, 109, 142, 158

Barbellion, W. N. P. .... **TCLC 24**
See also Cummings, Bruce F(rederick)

Barbera, Jack (Vincent) 1945- .... **CLC 44**
See also CA 110; CANR 45

Barbey d'Aurevilly, Jules Amedee 1808-1889
NCLC 1; SSC 17
See also DLB 119

Barbour, John c. 1316-1395 .... **CMLC 33**
See also DLB 146

Barbusse, Henri 1873-1935 .... **TCLC 5**
See also CA 105; 154; DLB 65

Barclay, Bill
See Moorcock, Michael (John)

Barclay, William Ewert
See Moorcock, Michael (John)

Barea, Arturo 1897-1957 .... **TCLC 14**
See also CA 111

Barfoot, Joan 1946- .... **CLC 18**
See also CA 105

Barham, Richard Harris 1788-1845**NCLC 77**
See also DLB 159

Baring, Maurice 1874-1945 .... **TCLC 8**
See also CA 105; 168; DLB 34

Baring-Gould, Sabine 1834-1924 .. **TCLC 88**
See also DLB 156, 190

Barker, Clive 1952- .... **CLC 52; DAM POP**

See also AAYA 10; BEST 90:3; CA 121; 129;
CANR 71; INT 129; MTCW 1, 2

Barker, George Granville 1913-1991 **CLC 8,
48; DAM POET**
See also CA 9-12R; 135; CANR 7, 38; DLB
20; MTCW 1

Barker, Harley Granville
See Granville-Barker, Harley
See also DLB 10

Barker, Howard 1946- .... **CLC 37**
See also CA 102; DLB 13

Barker, Jane 1652-1732 .... **LC 42**

Barker, Pat(ricia) 1943- .... **CLC 32, 94**
See also CA 117; 122; CANR 50; INT 122

Barlach, Ernst 1870-1938 .... **TCLC 84**
See also CA 178; DLB 56, 118

Barlow, Joel 1754-1812 .... **NCLC 23**
See also DLB 37

Barnard, Mary (Ethel) 1909- .... **CLC 48**
See also CA 21-22; CAP 2

Barnes, Djuna 1892-1982**CLC 3, 4, 8, 11, 29;
SSC 3**
See also CA 9-12R; 107; CANR 16, 55; DLB
4, 9, 45; MTCW 1, 2

Barnes, Julian (Patrick) 1946-**CLC 42; DAB**
See also CA 102; CANR 19, 54; DLB 194;
DLBY 93; MTCW 1

Barnes, Peter 1931- .... **CLC 5, 56**
See also CA 65-68; CAAS 12; CANR 33, 34,
64; DLB 13; MTCW 1

Barnes, William 1801-1886 .... **NCLC 75**
See also DLB 32

Baroja (y Nessi), Pio 1872-1956**TCLC 8; HLC
1**
See also CA 104

Baron, David
See Pinter, Harold

Baron Corvo
See Rolfe, Frederick (William Serafino Austin
Lewis Mary)

Barondess, Sue K(aufman) 1926-1977 **CLC 8**
See also Kaufman, Sue
See also CA 1-4R; 69-72; CANR 1

Baron de Teive
See Pessoa, Fernando (Antonio Nogueira)

Baroness Von S.
See Zangwill, Israel

Barres, (Auguste-) Maurice 1862-1923**T C L C
47**
See also CA 164; DLB 123

Barreto, Afonso Henrique de Lima
See Lima Barreto, Afonso Henrique de

Barrett, (Roger) Syd 1946- .... **CLC 35**

Barrett, William (Christopher) 1913-1992
CLC 27
See also CA 13-16R; 139; CANR 11, 67; INT
CANR-11

Barrie, J(ames) M(atthew) 1860-1937 **T C L C
2; DAB; DAM DRAM**
See also CA 104; 136; CANR 77; CDBLB
1890-1914; CLR 16; DLB 10, 141, 156;
MAICYA; MTCW 1; SATA 100; YABC 1

Barrington, Michael
See Moorcock, Michael (John)

Barrol, Grady
See Bograd, Larry

Barry, Mike
See Malzberg, Barry N(athaniel)

Barry, Philip 1896-1949 .... **TCLC 11**
See also CA 109; DLB 7

Bart, Andre Schwarz
See Schwarz-Bart, Andre

Barth, John (Simmons) 1930-**CLC 1, 2, 3, 5, 7,**

9, 10, 14, 27, 51, 89; DAM NOV; SSC 10
See also AITN 1, 2; CA 1-4R; CABS 1; CANR
5, 23, 49, 64; DLB 2; MTCW 1

Barthelme, Donald 1931-1989**CLC 1, 2, 3, 5, 6,
8, 13, 23, 46, 59, 115; DAM NOV; SSC 2**
See also CA 21-24R; 129; CANR 20, 58; DLB
2; DLBY 80, 89; MTCW 1, 2; SATA 7;
SATA-Obit 62

Barthelme, Frederick 1943- ...... **CLC 36, 117**
See also CA 114; 122; CANR 77; DLBY 85;
INT 122

Barthes, Roland (Gerard) 1915-1980**CLC 24,
83**
See also CA 130; 97-100; CANR 66; MTCW
1, 2

Barzun, Jacques (Martin) 1907- .... **CLC 51**
See also CA 61-64; CANR 22

Bashevis, Isaac
See Singer, Isaac Bashevis

Bashkirtseff, Marie 1859-1884 ...... **NCLC 27**

Basho
See Matsuo Basho

Basil of Caesaria c. 330-379 .... **CMLC 35**

Bass, Kingsley B., Jr.
See Bullins, Ed

Bass, Rick 1958- .... **CLC 79**
See also CA 126; CANR 53; DLB 212

Bassani, Giorgio 1916- .... **CLC 9**
See also CA 65-68; CANR 33; DLB 128, 177;
MTCW 1

Bastos, Augusto (Antonio) Roa
See Roa Bastos, Augusto (Antonio)

Bataille, Georges 1897-1962 .... **CLC 29**
See also CA 101; 89-92

Bates, H(erbert) E(rnest) 1905-1974**CLC 46;
DAB; DAM POP; SSC 10**
See also CA 93-96; 45-48; CANR 34; DLB 162,
191; MTCW 1, 2

Bauchart
See Camus, Albert

Baudelaire, Charles 1821-1867 .**NCLC 6, 29,
55; DA; DAB; DAC; DAM MST, POET;
PC 1; SSC 18; WLC**

Baudrillard, Jean 1929- .... **CLC 60**

Baum, L(yman) Frank 1856-1919 ... **TCLC 7**
See also CA 108; 133; CLR 15; DLB 22; JRDA;
MAICYA; MTCW 1, 2; SATA 18, 100

Baum, Louis F.
See Baum, L(yman) Frank

Baumbach, Jonathan 1933- ....**CLC 6, 23**
See also CA 13-16R; CAAS 5; CANR 12, 66;
DLBY 80; INT CANR-12; MTCW 1

Bausch, Richard (Carl) 1945- .... **CLC 51**
See also CA 101; CAAS 14; CANR 43, 61; DLB
130

Baxter, Charles (Morley) 1947- **CLC 45, 78;
DAM POP**
See also CA 57-60; CANR 40, 64; DLB 130;
MTCW 2

Baxter, George Owen
See Faust, Frederick (Schiller)

Baxter, James K(eir) 1926-1972 .... **CLC 14**
See also CA 77-80

Baxter, John
See Hunt, E(verette) Howard, (Jr.)

Bayer, Sylvia
See Glassco, John

Baynton, Barbara 1857-1929 .... **TCLC 57**

Beagle, Peter S(oyer) 1939- .... **CLC 7, 104**
See also CA 9-12R; CANR 4, 51, 73; DLBY
80; INT CANR-4; MTCW 1; SATA 60

Bean, Normal
See Burroughs, Edgar Rice

Beard, Charles A(ustin) 1874-1948 **TCLC 15**
See also CA 115; DLB 17; SATA 18

Beardsley, Aubrey 1872-1898 .... **NCLC 6**

Beattie, Ann 1947-**CLC 8, 13, 18, 40, 63; DAM NOV, POP; SSC 11**
See also BEST 90:2; CA 81-84; CANR 53, 73; DLBY 82; MTCW 1, 2

Beattie, James 1735-1803 .... **NCLC 25**
See also DLB 109

Beauchamp, Kathleen Mansfield 1888-1923
See Mansfield, Katherine
See also CA 104; 134; DA; DAC; DAM MST; MTCW 2

Beaumarchais, Pierre-Augustin Caron de 1732-1799 .... **DC 4**
See also DAM DRAM

Beaumont, Francis 1584(?)-1616**LC 33; DC 6**
See also CDBLB Before 1660; DLB 58, 121

Beauvoir, Simone (Lucie Ernestine Marie Bertrand) de 1908-1986 **CLC 1, 2, 4, 8, 14, 31, 44, 50, 71; DA; DAB; DAC; DAM MST, NOV; SSC 35; WLC**
See also CA 9-12R; 118; CANR 28, 61; DLB 72; DLBY 86; MTCW 1, 2

Becker, Carl (Lotus) 1873-1945 ..... **TCLC 63**
See also CA 157; DLB 17

Becker, Jurek 1937-1997 .... **CLC 7, 19**
See also CA 85-88; 157; CANR 60; DLB 75

Becker, Walter 1950- .... **CLC 26**

Beckett, Samuel (Barclay) 1906-1989**CLC 1, 2, 3, 4, 6, 9, 10, 11, 14, 18, 29, 57, 59, 83; DA; DAB; DAC; DAM DRAM, MST, NOV; SSC 16; WLC**
See also CA 5-8R; 130; CANR 33, 61; CDBLB 1945-1960; DLB 13, 15; DLBY 90; MTCW 1, 2

Beckford, William 1760-1844 .... **NCLC 16**
See also DLB 39

Beckman, Gunnel 1910- .... **CLC 26**
See also CA 33-36R; CANR 15; CLR 25; MAICYA; SAAS 9; SATA 6

Becque, Henri 1837-1899 .... **NCLC 3**
See also DLB 192

Becquer, Gustavo Adolfo 1836-1870
See also DAM MULT; HLCS 1

Beddoes, Thomas Lovell 1803-1849 **NCLC 3**
See also DLB 96

Bede c. 673-735 .... **CMLC 20**
See also DLB 146

Bedford, Donald F.
See Fearing, Kenneth (Flexner)

Beecher, Catharine Esther 1800-1878 **N C L C 30**
See also DLB 1

Beecher, John 1904-1980 .... **CLC 6**
See also AITN 1; CA 5-8R; 105; CANR 8

Beer, Johann 1655-1700 .... **LC 5**
See also DLB 168

Beer, Patricia 1924- .... **CLC 58**
See also CA 61-64; CANR 13, 46; DLB 40

Beerbohm, Max
See Beerbohm, (Henry) Max(imilian)

Beerbohm, (Henry) Max(imilian) 1872-1956 **TCLC 1, 24**
See also CA 104; 154; CANR 79; DLB 34, 100

Beer-Hofmann, Richard 1866-1945**TCLC 60**
See also CA 160; DLB 81

Begiebing, Robert J(ohn) 1946- .... **CLC 70**
See also CA 122; CANR 40

Behan, Brendan 1923-1964 **CLC 1, 8, 11, 15, 79; DAM DRAM**
See also CA 73-76; CANR 33; CDBLB 1945-1960; DLB 13; MTCW 1, 2

Behn, Aphra 1640(?)-1689 **LC 1, 30, 42; DA; DAB; DAC; DAM DRAM, MST, NOV, POET; DC 4; PC 13; WLC**
See also DLB 39, 80, 131

Behrman, S(amuel) N(athaniel) 1893-1973 **CLC 40**
See also CA 13-16; 45-48; CAP 1; DLB 7, 44

Belasco, David 1853-1931 .... **TCLC 3**
See also CA 104; 168; DLB 7

Belcheva, Elisaveta 1893- .... **CLC 10**
See also Bagryana, Elisaveta

Beldone, Phil "Cheech"
See Ellison, Harlan (Jay)

Beleno
See Azuela, Mariano

Belinski, Vissarion Grigoryevich 1811-1848 **NCLC 5**
See also DLB 198

Belitt, Ben 1911- .... **CLC 22**
See also CA 13-16R; CAAS 4; CANR 7, 77; DLB 5

Bell, Gertrude (Margaret Lowthian) 1868-1926 **TCLC 67**
See also CA 167; DLB 174

Bell, J. Freeman
See Zangwill, Israel

Bell, James Madison 1826-1902 ...**TCLC 43; BLC 1; DAM MULT**
See also BW 1; CA 122; 124; DLB 50

Bell, Madison Smartt 1957- ..... **CLC 41, 102**
See also CA 111; CANR 28, 54, 73; MTCW 1

Bell, Marvin (Hartley) 1937-**CLC 8, 31; DAM POET**
See also CA 21-24R; CAAS 14; CANR 59; DLB 5; MTCW 1

Bell, W. L. D.
See Mencken, H(enry) L(ouis)

Bellamy, Atwood C.
See Mencken, H(enry) L(ouis)

Bellamy, Edward 1850-1898 .... **NCLC 4**
See also DLB 12

Belli, Gioconda 1949-
See also CA 152; HLCS 1

Bellin, Edward J.
See Kuttner, Henry

Belloc, (Joseph) Hilaire (Pierre Sebastien Rene Swanton) 1870-1953 **TCLC 7, 18; DAM POET; PC 24**
See also CA 106; 152; DLB 19, 100, 141, 174; MTCW 1; YABC 1

Belloc, Joseph Peter Rene Hilaire
See Belloc, (Joseph) Hilaire (Pierre Sebastien Rene Swanton)

Belloc, Joseph Pierre Hilaire
See Belloc, (Joseph) Hilaire (Pierre Sebastien Rene Swanton) .

Belloc, M. A.
See Lowndes, Marie Adelaide (Belloc)

Bellow, Saul 1915-**CLC 1, 2, 3, 6, 8, 10, 13, 15, 25, 33, 34, 63, 79; DA; DAB; DAC; DAM MST, NOV, POP; SSC 14; WLC**
See also AITN 2; BEST 89:3; CA 5-8R; CABS 1; CANR 29, 53; CDALB 1941-1968; DLB 2, 28; DLBD 3; DLBY 82; MTCW 1, 2

Belser, Reimond Karel Maria de 1929-
See Ruyslinck, Ward
See also CA 152

Bely, Andrey .... **TCLC 7; PC 11**
See also Bugayev, Boris Nikolayevich
See also MTCW 1

Belyi, Andrei
See Bugayev, Boris Nikolayevich

Benary, Margot
See Benary-Isbert, Margot

Benary-Isbert, Margot 1889-1979 .... **CLC 12**
See also CA 5-8R; 89-92; CANR 4, 72; CLR 12; MAICYA; SATA 2; SATA-Obit 21

Benavente (y Martinez), Jacinto 1866-1954 **TCLC 3; DAM DRAM, MULT; HLCS 1**
See also CA 106; 131; CANR 81; HW 1, 2; MTCW 1, 2

Benchley, Peter (Bradford) 1940- **CLC 4, 8; DAM NOV, POP**
See also AAYA 14; AITN 2; CA 17-20R; CANR 12, 35, 66; MTCW 1, 2; SATA 3, 89

Benchley, Robert (Charles) 1889-1945**T C L C 1, 55**
See also CA 105; 153; DLB 11

Benda, Julien 1867-1956 .... **TCLC 60**
See also CA 120; 154

Benedict, Ruth (Fulton) 1887-1948 **TCLC 60**
See also CA 158

Benedict, Saint c. 480-c. 547 .... **CMLC 29**

Benedikt, Michael 1935- .... **CLC 4, 14**
See also CA 13-16R; CANR 7; DLB 5

Benet, Juan 1927- .... **CLC 28**
See also CA 143

Benet, Stephen Vincent 1898-1943 . **TCLC 7; DAM POET; SSC 10**
See also CA 104; 152; DLB 4, 48, 102; DLBY 97; MTCW 1; YABC 1

Benet, William Rose 1886-1950 .... **TCLC 28; DAM POET**
See also CA 118; 152; DLB 45

Benford, Gregory (Albert) 1941- ..... **CLC 52**
See also CA 69-72, 175; CAAE 175; CAAS 27; CANR 12, 24, 49; DLBY 82

Bengtsson, Frans (Gunnar) 1894-1954**T C L C 48**
See also CA 170

Benjamin, David
See Slavitt, David R(ytman)

Benjamin, Lois
See Gould, Lois

Benjamin, Walter 1892-1940 .... **TCLC 39**
See also CA 164

Benn, Gottfried 1886-1956 .... **TCLC 3**
See also CA 106; 153; DLB 56

Bennett, Alan 1934-**CLC 45, 77; DAB; DAM MST**
See also CA 103; CANR 35, 55; MTCW 1, 2

Bennett, (Enoch) Arnold 1867-1931**TCLC 5, 20**
See also CA 106; 155; CDBLB 1890-1914; DLB 10, 34, 98, 135; MTCW 2

Bennett, Elizabeth
See Mitchell, Margaret (Munnerlyn)

Bennett, George Harold 1930-
See Bennett, Hal
See also BW 1; CA 97-100

Bennett, Hal .... **CLC 5**
See also Bennett, George Harold
See also DLB 33

Bennett, Jay 1912- .... **CLC 35**
See also AAYA 10; CA 69-72; CANR 11, 42, 79; JRDA; SAAS 4; SATA 41, 87; SATA-Brief 27

Bennett, Louise (Simone) 1919-**CLC 28; BLC 1; DAM MULT**
See also BW 2, 3; CA 151; DLB 117

Benson, E(dward) F(rederic) 1867-1940 **TCLC 27**
See also CA 114; 157; DLB 135, 153

Benson, Jackson J. 1930- .... **CLC 34**
See also CA 25-28R; DLB 111

Benson, Sally 1900-1972 .... **CLC 17**

See also CA 19-20; 37-40R; CAP 1; SATA 1, 35; SATA-Obit 27

Benson, Stella 1892-1933 .... **TCLC 17**
See also CA 117; 155; DLB 36, 162

Bentham, Jeremy 1748-1832 .... **NCLC 38**
See also DLB 107, 158

Bentley, E(dmund) C(lerihew) 1875-1956
TCLC 12
See also CA 108; DLB 70

Bentley, Eric (Russell) 1916- .... **CLC 24**
See also CA 5-8R; CANR 6, 67; INT CANR-6

Beranger, Pierre Jean de 1780-1857**NCLC 34**

Berdyaev, Nicolas
See Berdyaev, Nikolai (Aleksandrovich)

Berdyaev, Nikolai (Aleksandrovich) 1874-1948
TCLC 67
See also CA 120; 157

Berdyayev, Nikolai (Aleksandrovich)
See Berdyaev, Nikolai (Aleksandrovich)

Berendt, John (Lawrence) 1939- ...... **CLC 86**
See also CA 146; CANR 75; MTCW 1

Beresford, J(ohn) D(avys) 1873-1947 **T C L C 81**
See also CA 112; 155; DLB 162, 178, 197

Bergelson, David 1884-1952 .... **TCLC 81**

Berger, Colonel
See Malraux, (Georges-)Andre

Berger, John (Peter) 1926- ....**CLC 2, 19**
See also CA 81-84; CANR 51, 78; DLB 14, 207

Berger, Melvin H. 1927-......................**CLC 12**
See also CA 5-8R; CANR 4; CLR 32; SAAS 2; SATA 5, 88

Berger, Thomas (Louis) 1924-**CLC 3, 5, 8, 11, 18, 38; DAM NOV**
See also CA 1-4R; CANR 5, 28, 51; DLB 2; DLBY 80; INT CANR-28; MTCW 1, 2

Bergman, (Ernst) Ingmar 1918- **CLC 16, 72**
See also CA 81-84; CANR 33, 70; MTCW 2

Bergson, Henri(-Louis) 1859-1941 **TCLC 32**
See also CA 164

Bergstein, Eleanor 1938- .... **CLC 4**
See also CA 53-56; CANR 5

Berkoff, Steven 1937- .... **CLC 56**
See also CA 104; CANR 72

Bermant, Chaim (Icyk) 1929- .... **CLC 40**
See also CA 57-60; CANR 6, 31, 57

Bern, Victoria
See Fisher, M(ary) F(rances) K(ennedy)

Bernanos, (Paul Louis) Georges 1888-1948
TCLC 3
See also CA 104; 130; DLB 72

Bernard, April 1956-........................**CLC 59**
See also CA 131

Berne, Victoria
See Fisher, M(ary) F(rances) K(ennedy)

Bernhard, Thomas 1931-1989 **CLC 3, 32, 61**
See also CA 85-88; 127; CANR 32, 57; DLB 85, 124; MTCW 1

Bernhardt, Sarah (Henriette Rosine) 1844-1923
TCLC 75
See also CA 157

Berriault, Gina 1926- . **CLC 54, 109; SSC 30**
See also CA 116; 129; CANR 66; DLB 130

Berrigan, Daniel 1921-........................**CLC 4**
See also CA 33-36R; CAAS 1; CANR 11, 43, 78; DLB 5

Berrigan, Edmund Joseph Michael, Jr. 1934-1983
See Berrigan, Ted
See also CA 61-64; 110; CANR 14

Berrigan, Ted ....**CLC 37**
See also Berrigan, Edmund Joseph Michael, Jr.
See also DLB 5, 169

Berry, Charles Edward Anderson 1931-
See Berry, Chuck
See also CA 115

Berry, Chuck ....**CLC 17**
See also Berry, Charles Edward Anderson

Berry, Jonas
See Ashbery, John (Lawrence)

Berry, Wendell (Erdman) 1934- **CLC 4, 6, 8, 27, 46; DAM POET; PC 28**
See also AITN 1; CA 73-76; CANR 50, 73; DLB 5, 6; MTCW 1

Berryman, John 1914-1972**CLC 1, 2, 3, 4, 6, 8, 10, 13, 25, 62; DAM POET**
See also CA 13-16; 33-36R; CABS 2; CANR 35; CAP 1; CDALB 1941-1968; DLB 48; MTCW 1, 2

Bertolucci, Bernardo 1940- .... **CLC 16**
See also CA 106

Berton, Pierre (Francis Demarigny) 1920-
CLC 104
See also CA 1-4R; CANR 2, 56; DLB 68; SATA 99

Bertrand, Aloysius 1807-1841 .... **NCLC 31**

Bertran de Born c. 1140-1215 .... **CMLC 5**

Besant, Annie (Wood) 1847-1933 .... **TCLC 9**
See also CA 105

Bessie, Alvah 1904-1985 .... **CLC 23**
See also CA 5-8R; 116; CANR 2, 80; DLB 26

Bethlen, T. D.
See Silverberg, Robert

Beti, Mongo ... **CLC 27; BLC 1; DAM MULT**
See also Biyidi, Alexandre
See also CANR 79

Betjeman, John 1906-1984 **CLC 2, 6, 10, 34, 43; DAB; DAM MST, POET**
See also CA 9-12R; 112; CANR 33, 56; CDBLB 1945-1960; DLB 20; DLBY 84; MTCW 1, 2

Bettelheim, Bruno 1903-1990............ **CLC 79**
See also CA 81-84; 131; CANR 23, 61; MTCW 1, 2

Betti, Ugo 1892-1953 .... **TCLC 5**
See also CA 104; 155

Betts, Doris (Waugh) 1932- ...... **CLC 3, 6, 28**
See also CA 13-16R; CANR 9, 66, 77; DLBY 82; INT CANR-9

Bevan, Alistair
See Roberts, Keith (John Kingston)

Bey, Pilaff
See Douglas, (George) Norman

Bialik, Chaim Nachman 1873-1934**TCLC 25**
See also CA 170

Bickerstaff, Isaac
See Swift, Jonathan

Bidart, Frank 1939-........................... **CLC 33**
See also CA 140

Bienek, Horst 1930- .... **CLC 7, 11**
See also CA 73-76; DLB 75

Bierce, Ambrose (Gwinett) 1842-1914(?)
TCLC 1, 7, 44; DA; DAC; DAM MST; SSC 9; WLC
See also CA 104; 139; CANR 78; CDALB 1865-1917; DLB 11, 12, 23, 71, 74, 186

Biggers, Earl Derr 1884-1933 .... **TCLC 65**
See also CA 108; 153

Billings, Josh
See Shaw, Henry Wheeler

Billington, (Lady) Rachel (Mary) 1942- **C L C 43**
See also AITN 2; CA 33-36R; CANR 44

Binyon, T(imothy) J(ohn) 1936- .... **CLC 34**
See also CA 111; CANR 28

Bioy Casares, Adolfo 1914-1999**CLC 4, 8, 13, 88; DAM MULT; HLC 1; SSC 17**
See also CA 29-32R; 177; CANR 19, 43, 66; DLB 113; HW 1, 2; MTCW 1, 2

Bird, Cordwainer
See Ellison, Harlan (Jay)

Bird, Robert Montgomery 1806-1854**NCLC 1**
See also DLB 202

Birkerts, Sven 1951- .... **CLC 116**
See also CA 128; 133; 176; CAAE 176; CAAS 29; INT 133

Birney, (Alfred) Earle 1904-1995**CLC 1, 4, 6, 11; DAC; DAM MST, POET**
See also CA 1-4R; CANR 5, 20; DLB 88; MTCW 1

Biruni, al 973-1048(?) .... **CMLC 28**

Bishop, Elizabeth 1911-1979 **CLC 1, 4, 9, 13, 15, 32; DA; DAC; DAM MST, POET; PC 3**
See also CA 5-8R; 89-92; CABS 2; CANR 26, 61; CDALB 1968-1988; DLB 5, 169; MTCW 1, 2; SATA-Obit 24

Bishop, John 1935-............................. **CLC 10**
See also CA 105

Bissett, Bill 1939- .... **CLC 18; PC 14**
See also CA 69-72; CAAS 19; CANR 15; DLB 53; MTCW 1

Bissoondath, Neil (Devindra) 1955-**CLC 120; DAC**
See also CA 136

Bitov, Andrei (Georgievich) 1937- ... **CLC 57**
See also CA 142

Biyidi, Alexandre 1932-
See Beti, Mongo
See also BW 1, 3; CA 114; 124; CANR 81; MTCW 1, 2

Bjarme, Brynjolf
See Ibsen, Henrik (Johan)

Bjoernson, Bjoernstjerne (Martinius) 1832-1910 .... **TCLC 7, 37**
See also CA 104

Black, Robert
See Holdstock, Robert P.

Blackburn, Paul 1926-1971 ....**CLC 9, 43**
See also CA 81-84; 33-36R; CANR 34; DLB 16; DLBY 81

Black Elk 1863-1950**TCLC 33; DAM MULT**
See also CA 144; MTCW 1; NNAL

Black Hobart
See Sanders, (James) Ed(ward)

Blacklin, Malcolm
See Chambers, Aidan

Blackmore, R(ichard) D(oddridge) 1825-1900
TCLC 27
See also CA 120; DLB 18

Blackmur, R(ichard) P(almer) 1904-1965
CLC 2, 24
See also CA 11-12; 25-28R; CANR 71; CAP 1; DLB 63

Black Tarantula
See Acker, Kathy

Blackwood, Algernon (Henry) 1869-1951
TCLC 5
See also CA 105; 150; DLB 153, 156, 178

Blackwood, Caroline 1931-1996**CLC 6, 9, 100**
See also CA 85-88; 151; CANR 32, 61, 65; DLB 14, 207; MTCW 1

Blade, Alexander
See Hamilton, Edmond; Silverberg, Robert

Blaga, Lucian 1895-1961 .... **CLC 75**
See also CA 157

Blair, Eric (Arthur) 1903-1950
See Orwell, George
See also CA 104; 132; DA; DAB; DAC; DAM

MST, NOV; MTCW 1, 2; SATA 29

Blair, Hugh 1718-1800 .... **NCLC 75**

Blais, Marie-Claire 1939-**CLC 2, 4, 6, 13, 22;
DAC; DAM MST**
See also CA 21-24R; CAAS 4; CANR 38, 75;
DLB 53; MTCW 1, 2

Blaise, Clark 1940- .... **CLC 29**
See also AITN 2; CA 53-56; CAAS 3; CANR
5, 66; DLB 53

Blake, Fairley
See De Voto, Bernard (Augustine)

Blake, Nicholas
See Day Lewis, C(ecil)
See also DLB 77

Blake, William 1757-1827 . **NCLC 13, 37, 57;
DA; DAB; DAC; DAM MST, POET; PC
12; WLC**
See also CDBLB 1789-1832; CLR 52; DLB 93,
163; MAICYA; SATA 30

Blasco Ibanez, Vicente 1867-1928 **TCLC 12;
DAM NOV**
See also CA 110; 131; CANR 81; HW 1, 2;
MTCW 1

Blatty, William Peter 1928-**CLC 2; DAM POP**
See also CA 5-8R; CANR 9

Bleeck, Oliver
See Thomas, Ross (Elmore)

Blessing, Lee 1949- .... **CLC 54**

Blish, James (Benjamin) 1921-1975 . **CLC 14**
See also CA 1-4R; 57-60; CANR 3; DLB 8;
MTCW 1; SATA 66

Bliss, Reginald
See Wells, H(erbert) G(eorge)

Blixen, Karen (Christentze Dinesen) 1885-1962
See Dinesen, Isak
See also CA 25-28; CANR 22, 50; CAP 2;
MTCW 1, 2; SATA 44

Bloch, Robert (Albert) 1917-1994 .... **CLC 33**
See also Fiske, Tarleton; Folke, Will; Hindin,
Nathan; Jarvis, E. K.; Kane, Wilson; Sheldon,
John; Young, Collier
See also AAYA 29; CA 5-8R; 179; 146; CAAE
179; CAAS 20; CANR 5, 78; DLB 44; INT
CANR-5; MTCW 1; SATA 12; SATA-Obit
82

Blok, Alexander (Alexandrovich) 1880-1921
TCLC 5; PC 21
See also CA 104

Blom, Jan
See Breytenbach, Breyten

Bloom, Harold 1930- .... **CLC 24, 103**
See also CA 13-16R; CANR 39, 75; DLB 67;
MTCW 1

Bloomfield, Aurelius
See Bourne, Randolph S(illiman)

Blount, Roy (Alton), Jr. 1941- .... **CLC 38**
See also CA 53-56; CANR 10, 28, 61; INT
CANR-28; MTCW 1, 2

Bloy, Leon 1846-1917 .... **TCLC 22**
See also CA 121; DLB 123

Blume, Judy (Sussman) 1938- ... **CLC 12, 30;
DAM NOV, POP**
See also AAYA 3, 26; CA 29-32R; CANR 13,
37, 66; CLR 2, 15; DLB 52; JRDA;
MAICYA; MTCW 1, 2; SATA 2, 31, 79

Blunden, Edmund (Charles) 1896-1974 **C L C
2, 56**
See also CA 17-18; 45-48; CANR 54; CAP 2;
DLB 20, 100, 155; MTCW 1

Bly, Robert (Elwood) 1926-**CLC 1, 2, 5, 10, 15,
38; DAM POET**
See also CA 5-8R; CANR 41, 73; DLB 5;
MTCW 1, 2

Boas, Franz 1858-1942 .... **TCLC 56**
See also CA 115

Bobette
See Simenon, Georges (Jacques Christian)

Boccaccio, Giovanni 1313-1375 ... **CMLC 13;
SSC 10**

Bochco, Steven 1943- .... **CLC 35**
See also AAYA 11; CA 124; 138

Bodel, Jean 1167(?)-1210 .... **CMLC 28**

Bodenheim, Maxwell 1892-1954 .... **TCLC 44**
See also CA 110; DLB 9, 45

Bodker, Cecil 1927- .... **CLC 21**
See also CA 73-76; CANR 13, 44; CLR 23;
MAICYA; SATA 14

Boell, Heinrich (Theodor) 1917-1985 **CLC 2,
3, 6, 9, 11, 15, 27, 32, 72; DA; DAB; DAC;
DAM MST, NOV; SSC 23; WLC**
See also CA 21-24R; 116; CANR 24; DLB 69;
DLBY 85; MTCW 1, 2

Boerne, Alfred
See Doeblin, Alfred

Boethius 480(?)-524(?) .... **CMLC 15**
See also DLB 115

Boff, Leonardo (Genezio Darci) 1938-
See also CA 150; DAM MULT; HLC 1; HW 2

Bogan, Louise 1897-1970 . **CLC 4, 39, 46, 93;
DAM POET; PC 12**
See also CA 73-76; 25-28R; CANR 33, 82; DLB
45, 169; MTCW 1, 2

Bogarde, Dirk 1921-1999 .... **CLC 19**
See also Van Den Bogarde, Derek Jules Gaspard
Ulric Niven
See also CA 179; DLB 14

Bogosian, Eric 1953- .... **CLC 45**
See also CA 138

Bograd, Larry 1953- .... **CLC 35**
See also CA 93-96; CANR 57; SAAS 21; SATA
33, 89

Boiardo, Matteo Maria 1441-1494 .... **LC 6**

Boileau-Despreaux, Nicolas 1636-1711 . **LC 3**

Bojer, Johan 1872-1959 .... **TCLC 64**

Boland, Eavan (Aisling) 1944- .. **CLC 40, 67,
113; DAM POET**
See also CA 143; CANR 61; DLB 40; MTCW
2

Boll, Heinrich
See Boell, Heinrich (Theodor)

Bolt, Lee
See Faust, Frederick (Schiller)

Bolt, Robert (Oxton) 1924-1995**CLC 14; DAM
DRAM**
See also CA 17-20R; 147; CANR 35, 67; DLB
13; MTCW 1

Bombal, Maria Luisa 1910-1980
See also CA 127; CANR 72; HLCS 1; HW 1

Bombet, Louis-Alexandre-Cesar
See Stendhal

Bomkauf
See Kaufman, Bob (Garnell)

Bonaventura .... **NCLC 35**
See also DLB 90

Bond, Edward 1934- **CLC 4, 6, 13, 23; DAM
DRAM**
See also CA 25-28R; CANR 38, 67; DLB 13;
MTCW 1

Bonham, Frank 1914-1989 .... **CLC 12**
See also AAYA 1; CA 9-12R; CANR 4, 36;
JRDA; MAICYA; SAAS 3; SATA 1, 49;
SATA-Obit 62

Bonnefoy, Yves 1923- ... **CLC 9, 15, 58; DAM
MST, POET**
See also CA 85-88; CANR 33, 75; MTCW 1, 2

Bontemps, Arna(ud Wendell) 1902-1973**C L C
1, 18; BLC 1; DAM MULT, NOV, POET**
See also BW 1; CA 1-4R; 41-44R; CANR 4,
35; CLR 6; DLB 48, 51; JRDA; MAICYA;
MTCW 1, 2; SATA 2, 44; SATA-Obit 24

Booth, Martin 1944- .... **CLC 13**
See also CA 93-96; CAAS 2

Booth, Philip 1925- .... **CLC 23**
See also CA 5-8R; CANR 5; DLBY 82

Booth, Wayne C(layson) 1921- .... **CLC 24**
See also CA 1-4R; CAAS 5; CANR 3, 43; DLB
67

Borchert, Wolfgang 1921-1947 .... **TCLC 5**
See also CA 104; DLB 69, 124

Borel, Petrus 1809-1859 .... **NCLC 41**

Borges, Jorge Luis 1899-1986**CLC 1, 2, 3, 4, 6,
8, 9, 10, 13, 19, 44, 48, 83; DA; DAB; DAC;
DAM MST, MULT; HLC 1; PC 22; SSC
4; WLC**
See also AAYA 26; CA 21-24R; CANR 19, 33,
75; DLB 113; DLBY 86; HW 1, 2; MTCW
1, 2

Borowski, Tadeusz 1922-1951 .... **TCLC 9**
See also CA 106; 154

Borrow, George (Henry) 1803-1881 **NCLC 9**
See also DLB 21, 55, 166

Bosch (Gavino), Juan 1909-
See also CA 151; DAM MST, MULT; DLB 145;
HLCS 1; HW 1, 2

Bosman, Herman Charles 1905-1951 **T C L C
49**
See also Malan, Herman
See also CA 160

Bosschere, Jean de 1878(?)-1953 ... **TCLC 19**
See also CA 115

Boswell, James 1740-1795**LC 4, 50; DA; DAB;
DAC; DAM MST; WLC**
See also CDBLB 1660-1789; DLB 104, 142

Bottoms, David 1949- .... **CLC 53**
See also CA 105; CANR 22; DLB 120; DLBY
83

Boucicault, Dion 1820-1890 .... **NCLC 41**

Boucolon, Maryse 1937(?)-
See Conde, Maryse
See also BW 3; CA 110; CANR 30, 53, 76

Bourget, Paul (Charles Joseph) 1852-1935
TCLC 12
See also CA 107; DLB 123

Bourjaily, Vance (Nye) 1922- .... **CLC 8, 62**
See also CA 1-4R; CAAS 1; CANR 2, 72; DLB
2, 143

Bourne, Randolph S(illiman) 1886-1918
TCLC 16
See also CA 117; 155; DLB 63

Bova, Ben(jamin William) 1932- ...... **CLC 45**
See also AAYA 16; CA 5-8R; CAAS 18; CANR
11, 56; CLR 3; DLBY 81; INT CANR-11;
MAICYA; MTCW 1; SATA 6, 68

Bowen, Elizabeth (Dorothea Cole) 1899-1973
**CLC 1, 3, 6, 11, 15, 22, 118; DAM NOV;
SSC 3, 28**
See also CA 17-18; 41-44R; CANR 35; CAP 2;
CDBLB 1945-1960; DLB 15, 162; MTCW
1, 2

Bowering, George 1935- .... **CLC 15, 47**
See also CA 21-24R; CAAS 16; CANR 10; DLB
53

Bowering, Marilyn R(uthe) 1949- .... **CLC 32**
See also CA 101; CANR 49

Bowers, Edgar 1924- .... **CLC 9**
See also CA 5-8R; CANR 24; DLB 5

Bowie, David .... **CLC 17**
See also Jones, David Robert

Bowles, Jane (Sydney) 1917-1973 **CLC 3, 68**

See also CA 19-20; 41-44R; CAP 2

Bowles, Paul (Frederick) 1910- **CLC 1, 2, 19, 53; SSC 3**
See also CA 1-4R; CAAS 1; CANR 1, 19, 50, 75; DLB 5, 6; MTCW 1, 2

Box, Edgar
See Vidal, Gore

Boyd, Nancy
See Millay, Edna St. Vincent

Boyd, William 1952-............ **CLC 28, 53, 70**
See also CA 114; 120; CANR 51, 71

Boyle, Kay 1902-1992 **CLC 1, 5, 19, 58, 121; SSC 5**
See also CA 13-16R; 140; CAAS 1; CANR 29, 61; DLB 4, 9, 48, 86; DLBY 93; MTCW 1, 2

Boyle, Mark
See Kienzle, William X(avier)

Boyle, Patrick 1905-1982 .... **CLC 19**
See also CA 127

Boyle, T. C. 1948-
See Boyle, T(homas) Coraghessan

Boyle, T(homas) Coraghessan 1948-**CLC 36, 55, 90; DAM POP; SSC 16**
See also BEST 90:4; CA 120; CANR 44, 76; DLBY 86; MTCW 2

Boz
See Dickens, Charles (John Huffam)

Brackenridge, Hugh Henry 1748-1816**NCLC 7**
See also DLB 11, 37

Bradbury, Edward P.
See Moorcock, Michael (John)
See also MTCW 2

Bradbury, Malcolm (Stanley) 1932- **CLC 32, 61; DAM NOV**
See also CA 1-4R; CANR 1, 33; DLB 14, 207; MTCW 1, 2

Bradbury, Ray (Douglas) 1920-**CLC 1, 3, 10, 15, 42, 98; DA; DAB; DAC; DAM MST, NOV, POP; SSC 29; WLC**
See also AAYA 15; AITN 1, 2; CA 1-4R; CANR 2, 30, 75; CDALB 1968-1988; DLB 2, 8; MTCW 1, 2; SATA 11, 64

Bradford, Gamaliel 1863-1932 ...... **TCLC 36**
See also CA 160; DLB 17

Bradley, David (Henry), Jr. 1950- ...**CLC 23, 118; BLC 1; DAM MULT**
See also BW 1, 3; CA 104; CANR 26, 81; DLB 33

Bradley, John Ed(mund, Jr.) 1958- .. **CLC 55**
See also CA 139

Bradley, Marion Zimmer 1930-**CLC 30; DAM POP**
See also AAYA 9; CA 57-60; CAAS 10; CANR 7, 31, 51, 75; DLB 8; MTCW 1, 2; SATA 90

Bradstreet, Anne 1612(?)-1672**LC 4, 30; DA; DAC; DAM MST, POET; PC 10**
See also CDALB 1640-1865; DLB 24

Brady, Joan 1939-............................. **CLC 86**
See also CA 141

Bragg, Melvyn 1939-......................... **CLC 10**
See also BEST 89:3; CA 57-60; CANR 10, 48; DLB 14

Brahe, Tycho 1546-1601 .... **LC 45**

Braine, John (Gerard) 1922-1986**CLC 1, 3, 41**
See also CA 1-4R; 120; CANR 1, 33; CDBLB 1945-1960; DLB 15; DLBY 86; MTCW 1

Bramah, Ernest 1868-1942 .... **TCLC 72**
See also CA 156; DLB 70

Brammer, William 1930(?)-1978 .... **CLC 31**
See also CA 77-80

Brancati, Vitaliano 1907-1954 .... **TCLC 12**

See also CA 109

Brancato, Robin F(idler) 1936- ....**CLC 35**
See also AAYA 9; CA 69-72; CANR 11, 45; CLR 32; JRDA; SAAS 9; SATA 97

Brand, Max
See Faust, Frederick (Schiller)

Brand, Millen 1906-1980 .... **CLC 7**
See also CA 21-24R; 97-100; CANR 72

Branden, Barbara .... **CLC 44**
See also CA 148

Brandes, Georg (Morris Cohen) 1842-1927 **TCLC 10**
See also CA 105

Brandys, Kazimierz 1916- .... **CLC 62**

Branley, Franklyn M(ansfield) 1915-**CLC 21**
See also CA 33-36R; CANR 14, 39; CLR 13; MAICYA; SAAS 16; SATA 4, 68

Brathwaite, Edward (Kamau) 1930-**CLC 11; BLCS; DAM POET**
See also BW 2, 3; CA 25-28R; CANR 11, 26, 47; DLB 125

Brautigan, Richard (Gary) 1935-1984**CLC 1, 3, 5, 9, 12, 34, 42; DAM NOV**
See also CA 53-56; 113; CANR 34; DLB 2, 5, 206; DLBY 80, 84; MTCW 1; SATA 56

Brave Bird, Mary 1953-
See Crow Dog, Mary (Ellen)
See also NNAL

Braverman, Kate 1950-..................... **CLC 67**
See also CA 89-92

Brecht, (Eugen) Bertolt (Friedrich) 1898-1956 **TCLC 1, 6, 13, 35; DA; DAB; DAC; DAM DRAM, MST; DC 3; WLC**
See also CA 104; 133; CANR 62; DLB 56, 124; MTCW 1, 2

Brecht, Eugen Berthold Friedrich
See Brecht, (Eugen) Bertolt (Friedrich)

Bremer, Fredrika 1801-1865 .... **NCLC 11**

Brennan, Christopher John 1870-1932**TCLC 17**
See also CA 117

Brennan, Maeve 1917-1993 .... **CLC 5**
See also CA 81-84; CANR 72

Brent, Linda
See Jacobs, Harriet A(nn)

Brentano, Clemens (Maria) 1778-1842**NCLC 1**
See also DLB 90

Brent of Bin Bin
See Franklin, (Stella Maria Sarah) Miles (Lampe)

Brenton, Howard 1942- .... **CLC 31**
See also CA 69-72; CANR 33, 67; DLB 13; MTCW 1

Breslin, James 1930-1996
See Breslin, Jimmy
See also CA 73-76; CANR 31, 75; DAM NOV; MTCW 1, 2

Breslin, Jimmy .... **CLC 4, 43**
See also Breslin, James
See also AITN 1; DLB 185; MTCW 2

Bresson, Robert 1901- .... **CLC 16**
See also CA 110; CANR 49

Breton, Andre 1896-1966**CLC 2, 9, 15, 54; PC 15**
See also CA 19-20; 25-28R; CANR 40, 60; CAP 2; DLB 65; MTCW 1, 2

Breytenbach, Breyten 1939(?)- . **CLC 23, 37; DAM POET**
See also CA 113; 129; CANR 61

Bridgers, Sue Ellen 1942- .... **CLC 26**
See also AAYA 8; CA 65-68; CANR 11, 36; CLR 18; DLB 52; JRDA; MAICYA; SAAS

1; SATA 22, 90; SATA-Essay 109

Bridges, Robert (Seymour) 1844-1930**TCLC 1; DAM POET; PC 28**
See also CA 104; 152; CDBLB 1890-1914; DLB 19, 98

Bridie, James .... **TCLC 3**
See also Mavor, Osborne Henry
See also DLB 10

Brin, David 1950-............................. **CLC 34**
See also AAYA 21; CA 102; CANR 24, 70; INT CANR-24; SATA 65

Brink, Andre (Philippus) 1935- **CLC 18, 36, 106**
See also CA 104; CANR 39, 62; INT 103; MTCW 1, 2

Brinsmead, H(esba) F(ay) 1922- .... **CLC 21**
See also CA 21-24R; CANR 10; CLR 47; MAICYA; SAAS 5; SATA 18, 78

Brittain, Vera (Mary) 1893(?)-1970 . **CLC 23**
See also CA 13-16; 25-28R; CANR 58; CAP 1; DLB 191; MTCW 1, 2

Broch, Hermann 1886-1951 .... **TCLC 20**
See also CA 117; DLB 85, 124

Brock, Rose
See Hansen, Joseph

Brodkey, Harold (Roy) 1930-1996 .... **CLC 56**
See also CA 111; 151; CANR 71; DLB 130

Brodskii, Iosif
See Brodsky, Joseph

Brodsky, Iosif Alexandrovich 1940-1996
See Brodsky, Joseph
See also AITN 1; CA 41-44R; 151; CANR 37; DAM POET; MTCW 1, 2

Brodsky, Joseph 1940-1996 **CLC 4, 6, 13, 36, 100; PC 9**
See also Brodskii, Iosif; Brodsky, Iosif Alexandrovich
See also MTCW 1

Brodsky, Michael (Mark) 1948-........ **CLC 19**
See also CA 102; CANR 18, 41, 58

Bromell, Henry 1947-......................... **CLC 5**
See also CA 53-56; CANR 9

Bromfield, Louis (Brucker) 1896-1956**TCLC 11**
See also CA 107; 155; DLB 4, 9, 86

Broner, E(sther) M(asserman) 1930- **CLC 19**
See also CA 17-20R; CANR 8, 25, 72; DLB 28

Bronk, William (M.) 1918-1999 .... **CLC 10**
See also CA 89-92; 177; CANR 23; DLB 165

Bronstein, Lev Davidovich
See Trotsky, Leon

Bronte, Anne 1820-1849 .... **NCLC 71**
See also DLB 21, 199

Bronte, Charlotte 1816-1855 **NCLC 3, 8, 33, 58; DA; DAB; DAC; DAM MST, NOV; WLC**
See also AAYA 17; CDBLB 1832-1890; DLB 21, 159, 199

Bronte, Emily (Jane) 1818-1848**NCLC 16, 35; DA; DAB; DAC; DAM MST, NOV, POET; PC 8; WLC**
See also AAYA 17; CDBLB 1832-1890; DLB 21, 32, 199

Brooke, Frances 1724-1789 .... **LC 6, 48**
See also DLB 39, 99

Brooke, Henry 1703(?)-1783 .... **LC 1**
See also DLB 39

Brooke, Rupert (Chawner) 1887-1915 **TCLC 2, 7; DA; DAB; DAC; DAM MST, POET; PC 24; WLC**
See also CA 104; 132; CANR 61; CDBLB 1914-1945; DLB 19; MTCW 1, 2

Brooke-Haven, P.

See Wodehouse, P(elham) G(renville)

Brooke-Rose, Christine 1926(?)- .... **CLC 40**
See also CA 13-16R; CANR 58; DLB 14

Brookner, Anita 1928- **CLC 32, 34, 51; DAB; DAM POP**
See also CA 114; 120; CANR 37, 56; DLB 194; DLBY 87; MTCW 1, 2

Brooks, Cleanth 1906-1994 **CLC 24, 86, 110**
See also CA 17-20R; 145; CANR 33, 35; DLB 63; DLBY 94; INT CANR-35; MTCW 1, 2

Brooks, George
See Baum, L(yman) Frank

Brooks, Gwendolyn 1917- **CLC 1, 2, 4, 5, 15, 49; BLC 1; DA; DAC; DAM MST, MULT, POET; PC 7; WLC**
See also AAYA 20; AITN 1; BW 2, 3; CA 1-4R; CANR 1, 27, 52, 75; CDALB 1941-1968; CLR 27; DLB 5, 76, 165; MTCW 1, 2; SATA 6

Brooks, Mel .... **CLC 12**
See also Kaminsky, Melvin
See also AAYA 13; DLB 26

Brooks, Peter 1938- .... **CLC 34**
See also CA 45-48; CANR 1

Brooks, Van Wyck 1886-1963 .... **CLC 29**
See also CA 1-4R; CANR 6; DLB 45, 63, 103

Brophy, Brigid (Antonia) 1929-1995 **CLC 6, 11, 29, 105**
See also CA 5-8R; 149; CAAS 4; CANR 25, 53; DLB 14; MTCW 1, 2

Brosman, Catharine Savage 1934- ..... **CLC 9**
See also CA 61-64; CANR 21, 46

Brossard, Nicole 1943- .... **CLC 115**
See also CA 122; CAAS 16; DLB 53

Brother Antoninus
See Everson, William (Oliver)

The Brothers Quay
See Quay, Stephen; Quay, Timothy

Broughton, T(homas) Alan 1936- ..... **CLC 19**
See also CA 45-48; CANR 2, 23, 48

Broumas, Olga 1949- .... **CLC 10, 73**
See also CA 85-88; CANR 20, 69

Brown, Alan 1950- .... **CLC 99**
See also CA 156

Brown, Charles Brockden 1771-1810 **NCLC 22, 74**
See also CDALB 1640-1865; DLB 37, 59, 73

Brown, Christy 1932-1981 .... **CLC 63**
See also CA 105; 104; CANR 72; DLB 14

Brown, Claude 1937- **CLC 30; BLC 1; DAM MULT**
See also AAYA 7; BW 1, 3; CA 73-76; CANR 81

Brown, Dee (Alexander) 1908- .. **CLC 18, 47; DAM POP**
See also AAYA 30; CA 13-16R; CAAS 6; CANR 11, 45, 60; DLBY 80; MTCW 1, 2; SATA 5

Brown, George
See Wertmueller, Lina

Brown, George Douglas 1869-1902 **TCLC 28**
See also CA 162

Brown, George Mackay 1921-1996 **CLC 5, 48, 100**
See also CA 21-24R; 151; CAAS 6; CANR 12, 37, 67; DLB 14, 27, 139; MTCW 1; SATA 35

Brown, (William) Larry 1951- .... **CLC 73**
See also CA 130; 134; INT 133

Brown, Moses
See Barrett, William (Christopher)

Brown, Rita Mae 1944- **CLC 18, 43, 79; DAM NOV, POP**

See also CA 45-48; CANR 2, 11, 35, 62; INT CANR-11; MTCW 1, 2

Brown, Roderick (Langmere) Haig-
See Haig-Brown, Roderick (Langmere)

Brown, Rosellen 1939- .... **CLC 32**
See also CA 77-80; CAAS 10; CANR 14, 44

Brown, Sterling Allen 1901-1989 **CLC 1, 23, 59; BLC 1; DAM MULT, POET**
See also BW 1, 3; CA 85-88; 127; CANR 26; DLB 48, 51, 63; MTCW 1, 2

Brown, Will
See Ainsworth, William Harrison

Brown, William Wells 1813-1884 ... **NCLC 2; BLC 1; DAM MULT; DC 1**
See also DLB 3, 50

Browne, (Clyde) Jackson 1948(?)- .... **CLC 21**
See also CA 120

Browning, Elizabeth Barrett 1806-1861 **NCLC 1, 16, 61, 66; DA; DAB; DAC; DAM MST, POET; PC 6; WLC**
See also CDBLB 1832-1890; DLB 32, 199

Browning, Robert 1812-1889 . **NCLC 19, 79; DA; DAB; DAC; DAM MST, POET; PC 2; WLCS**
See also CDBLB 1832-1890; DLB 32, 163; YABC 1

Browning, Tod 1882-1962 .... **CLC 16**
See also CA 141; 117

Brownson, Orestes Augustus 1803-1876 **NCLC 50**
See also DLB 1, 59, 73

Bruccoli, Matthew J(oseph) 1931- ... **CLC 34**
See also CA 9-12R; CANR 7; DLB 103

Bruce, Lenny .... **CLC 21**
See also Schneider, Leonard Alfred

Bruin, John
See Brutus, Dennis

Brulard, Henri
See Stendhal

Brulls, Christian
See Simenon, Georges (Jacques Christian)

Brunner, John (Kilian Houston) 1934-1995 **CLC 8, 10; DAM POP**
See also CA 1-4R; 149; CAAS 8; CANR 2, 37; MTCW 1, 2

Bruno, Giordano 1548-1600 .... **LC 27**

Brutus, Dennis 1924- **CLC 43; BLC 1; DAM MULT, POET; PC 24**
See also BW 2, 3; CA 49-52; CAAS 14; CANR 2, 27, 42, 81; DLB 117

Bryan, C(ourtlandt) D(ixon) B(arnes) 1936- **CLC 29**
See also CA 73-76; CANR 13, 68; DLB 185; INT CANR-13

Bryan, Michael
See Moore, Brian

Bryant, William Cullen 1794-1878 . **NCLC 6, 46; DA; DAB; DAC; DAM MST, POET; PC 20**
See also CDALB 1640-1865; DLB 3, 43, 59, 189

Bryusov, Valery Yakovlevich 1873-1924 **TCLC 10**
See also CA 107; 155

Buchan, John 1875-1940 ..... **TCLC 41; DAB; DAM POP**
See also CA 108; 145; DLB 34, 70, 156; MTCW 1; YABC 2

Buchanan, George 1506-1582 .... **LC 4**
See also DLB 152

Buchheim, Lothar-Guenther 1918- .... **CLC 6**
See also CA 85-88

Buchner, (Karl) Georg 1813-1837 . **NCLC 26**

Buchwald, Art(hur) 1925- .... **CLC 33**
See also AITN 1; CA 5-8R; CANR 21, 67; MTCW 1, 2; SATA 10

Buck, Pearl S(ydenstricker) 1892-1973 **CLC 7, 11, 18; DA; DAB; DAC; DAM MST, NOV**
See also AITN 1; CA 1-4R; 41-44R; CANR 1, 34; CDALBS; DLB 9, 102; MTCW 1, 2; SATA 1, 25

Buckler, Ernest 1908-1984 .... **CLC 13; DAC; DAM MST**
See also CA 11-12; 114; CAP 1; DLB 68; SATA 47

Buckley, Vincent (Thomas) 1925-1988 **CLC 57**
See also CA 101

Buckley, William F(rank), Jr. 1925- **CLC 7, 18, 37; DAM POP**
See also AITN 1; CA 1-4R; CANR 1, 24, 53; DLB 137; DLBY 80; INT CANR-24; MTCW 1, 2

Buechner, (Carl) Frederick 1926- **CLC 2, 4, 6, 9; DAM NOV**
See also CA 13-16R; CANR 11, 39, 64; DLBY 80; INT CANR-11; MTCW 1, 2

Buell, John (Edward) 1927- .... **CLC 10**
See also CA 1-4R; CANR 71; DLB 53

Buero Vallejo, Antonio 1916- ..... **CLC 15, 46**
See also CA 106; CANR 24, 49, 75; HW 1; MTCW 1, 2

Bufalino, Gesualdo 1920(?)- .... **CLC 74**
See also DLB 196

Bugayev, Boris Nikolayevich 1880-1934 **TCLC 7; PC 11**
See Bely, Andrey
See also CA 104; 165; MTCW 1

Bukowski, Charles 1920-1994 **CLC 2, 5, 9, 41, 82, 108; DAM NOV, POET; PC 18**
See also CA 17-20R; 144; CANR 40, 62; DLB 5, 130, 169; MTCW 1, 2

Bulgakov, Mikhail (Afanas'evich) 1891-1940 **TCLC 2, 16; DAM DRAM, NOV; SSC 18**
See also CA 105; 152

Bulgya, Alexander Alexandrovich 1901-1956 **TCLC 53**
See also Fadeyev, Alexander
See also CA 117

Bullins, Ed 1935- **CLC 1, 5, 7; BLC 1; DAM DRAM, MULT; DC 6**
See also BW 2, 3; CA 49-52; CAAS 16; CANR 24, 46, 73; DLB 7, 38; MTCW 1, 2

Bulwer-Lytton, Edward (George Earle Lytton) 1803-1873 .... **NCLC 1, 45**
See also DLB 21

Bunin, Ivan Alexeyevich 1870-1953 **TCLC 6; SSC 5**
See also CA 104

Bunting, Basil 1900-1985 ..... **CLC 10, 39, 47; DAM POET**
See also CA 53-56; 115; CANR 7; DLB 20

Bunuel, Luis 1900-1983 .. **CLC 16, 80; DAM MULT; HLC 1**
See also CA 101; 110; CANR 32, 77; HW 1

Bunyan, John 1628-1688 ... **LC 4; DA; DAB; DAC; DAM MST; WLC**
See also CDBLB 1660-1789; DLB 39

Burckhardt, Jacob (Christoph) 1818-1897 **NCLC 49**

Burford, Eleanor
See Hibbert, Eleanor Alice Burford

Burgess, Anthony **CLC 1, 2, 4, 5, 8, 10, 13, 15, 22, 40, 62, 81, 94; DAB**
See also Wilson, John (Anthony) Burgess
See also AAYA 25; AITN 1; CDBLB 1960 to Present; DLB 14, 194; DLBY 98; MTCW 1

Burke, Edmund 1729(?)-1797 **LC 7, 36; DA; DAB; DAC; DAM MST; WLC**
See also DLB 104

Burke, Kenneth (Duva) 1897-1993 **CLC 2, 24**
See also CA 5-8R; 143; CANR 39, 74; DLB 45, 63; MTCW 1, 2

Burke, Leda
See Garnett, David

Burke, Ralph
See Silverberg, Robert

Burke, Thomas 1886-1945 .... **TCLC 63**
See also CA 113; 155; DLB 197

Burney, Fanny 1752-1840 .... **NCLC 12, 54**
See also DLB 39

Burns, Robert 1759-1796 . **LC 3, 29, 40; DA; DAB; DAC; DAM MST, POET; PC 6; WLC**
See also CDBLB 1789-1832; DLB 109

Burns, Tex
See L'Amour, Louis (Dearborn)

Burnshaw, Stanley 1906- .... **CLC 3, 13, 44**
See also CA 9-12R; DLB 48; DLBY 97

Burr, Anne 1937- .... **CLC 6**
See also CA 25-28R

Burroughs, Edgar Rice 1875-1950 . **TCLC 2, 32; DAM NOV**
See also AAYA 11; CA 104; 132; DLB 8; MTCW 1, 2; SATA 41

Burroughs, William S(eward) 1914-1997 **CLC 1, 2, 5, 15, 22, 42, 75, 109; DA; DAB; DAC; DAM MST, NOV, POP; WLC**
See also AITN 2; CA 9-12R; 160; CANR 20, 52; DLB 2, 8, 16, 152; DLBY 81, 97; MTCW 1, 2

Burton, Sir Richard F(rancis) 1821-1890 **NCLC 42**
See also DLB 55, 166, 184

Busch, Frederick 1941- ..... **CLC 7, 10, 18, 47**
See also CA 33-36R; CAAS 1; CANR 45, 73; DLB 6

Bush, Ronald 1946- .... **CLC 34**
See also CA 136

Bustos, F(rancisco)
See Borges, Jorge Luis

Bustos Domecq, H(onorio)
See Bioy Casares, Adolfo; Borges, Jorge Luis

Butler, Octavia E(stelle) 1947- **CLC 38, 121; BLCS; DAM MULT, POP**
See also AAYA 18; BW 2, 3; CA 73-76; CANR 12, 24, 38, 73; DLB 33; MTCW 1, 2; SATA 84

Butler, Robert Olen (Jr.) 1945- **CLC 81; DAM POP**
See also CA 112; CANR 66; DLB 173; INT 112; MTCW 1

Butler, Samuel 1612-1680 .... **LC 16, 43**
See also DLB 101, 126

Butler, Samuel 1835-1902 . **TCLC 1, 33; DA; DAB; DAC; DAM MST, NOV; WLC**
See also CA 143; CDBLB 1890-1914; DLB 18, 57, 174

Butler, Walter C.
See Faust, Frederick (Schiller)

Butor, Michel (Marie Francois) 1926- **CLC 1, 3, 8, 11, 15**
See also CA 9-12R; CANR 33, 66; DLB 83; MTCW 1, 2

Butts, Mary 1892(?)-1937 .... **TCLC 77**
See also CA 148

Buzo, Alexander (John) 1944- .... **CLC 61**
See also CA 97-100; CANR 17, 39, 69

Buzzati, Dino 1906-1972 .... **CLC 36**
See also CA 160; 33-36R; DLB 177

Byars, Betsy (Cromer) 1928- .... **CLC 35**
See also AAYA 19; CA 33-36R; CANR 18, 36, 57; CLR 1, 16; DLB 52; INT CANR-18; JRDA; MAICYA; MTCW 1; SAAS 1; SATA 4, 46, 80; SATA-Essay 108

Byatt, A(ntonia) S(usan Drabble) 1936- **C L C 19, 65; DAM NOV, POP**
See also CA 13-16R; CANR 13, 33, 50, 75; DLB 14, 194; MTCW 1, 2

Byrne, David 1952- .... **CLC 26**
See also CA 127

Byrne, John Keyes 1926-
See Leonard, Hugh
See also CA 102; CANR 78; INT 102

Byron, George Gordon (Noel) 1788-1824 **NCLC 2, 12; DA; DAB; DAC; DAM MST, POET; PC 16; WLC**
See also CDBLB 1789-1832; DLB 96, 110

Byron, Robert 1905-1941 .... **TCLC 67**
See also CA 160; DLB 195

C. 3. 3.
See Wilde, Oscar

Caballero, Fernan 1796-1877 .... **NCLC 10**

Cabell, Branch
See Cabell, James Branch

Cabell, James Branch 1879-1958 .... **TCLC 6**
See also CA 105; 152; DLB 9, 78; MTCW 1

Cable, George Washington 1844-1925 **T C L C 4; SSC 4**
See also CA 104; 155; DLB 12, 74; DLBD 13

Cabral de Melo Neto, Joao 1920- ... **CLC 76; DAM MULT**
See also CA 151

Cabrera Infante, G(uillermo) 1929- **CLC 5, 25, 45, 120; DAM MULT; HLC 1**
See also CA 85-88; CANR 29, 65; DLB 113; HW 1, 2; MTCW 1, 2

Cade, Toni
See Bambara, Toni Cade

Cadmus and Harmonia
See Buchan, John

Caedmon fl. 658-680 .... **CMLC 7**
See also DLB 146

Caeiro, Alberto
See Pessoa, Fernando (Antonio Nogueira)

Cage, John (Milton, Jr.) 1912-1992 .. **CLC 41**
See also CA 13-16R; 169; CANR 9, 78; DLB 193; INT CANR-9

Cahan, Abraham 1860-1951 .... **TCLC 71**
See also CA 108; 154; DLB 9, 25, 28

Cain, G.
See Cabrera Infante, G(uillermo)

Cain, Guillermo
See Cabrera Infante, G(uillermo)

Cain, James M(allahan) 1892-1977 **CLC 3, 11, 28**
See also AITN 1; CA 17-20R; 73-76; CANR 8, 34, 61; MTCW 1

Caine, Mark
See Raphael, Frederic (Michael)

Calasso, Roberto 1941- .... **CLC 81**
See also CA 143

Calderon de la Barca, Pedro 1600-1681 .. **L C 23; DC 3; HLCS 1**

Caldwell, Erskine (Preston) 1903-1987 **CLC 1, 8, 14, 50, 60; DAM NOV; SSC 19**
See also AITN 1; CA 1-4R; 121; CAAS 1; CANR 2, 33; DLB 9, 86; MTCW 1, 2

Caldwell, (Janet Miriam) Taylor (Holland) 1900-1985 **CLC 2, 28, 39; DAM NOV, POP**
See also CA 5-8R; 116; CANR 5; DLBD 17

Calhoun, John Caldwell 1782-1850 **NCLC 15**
See also DLB 3

Calisher, Hortense 1911- **CLC 2, 4, 8, 38; DAM NOV; SSC 15**
See also CA 1-4R; CANR 1, 22, 67; DLB 2; INT CANR-22; MTCW 1, 2

Callaghan, Morley Edward 1903-1990 **CLC 3, 14, 41, 65; DAC; DAM MST**
See also CA 9-12R; 132; CANR 33, 73; DLB 68; MTCW 1, 2

Callimachus c. 305B.C.-c. 240B.C. **CMLC 18**
See also DLB 176

Calvin, John 1509-1564 .... **LC 37**

Calvino, Italo 1923-1985 **CLC 5, 8, 11, 22, 33, 39, 73; DAM NOV; SSC 3**
See also CA 85-88; 116; CANR 23, 61; DLB 196; MTCW 1, 2

Cameron, Carey 1952- .... **CLC 59**
See also CA 135

Cameron, Peter 1959- .... **CLC 44**
See also CA 125; CANR 50

Camoens, Luis Vaz de 1524(?)-1580
See also HLCS 1

Camoes, Luis de 1524(?)-1580
See also HLCS 1

Campana, Dino 1885-1932 .... **TCLC 20**
See also CA 117; DLB 114

Campanella, Tommaso 1568-1639 .... **LC 32**

Campbell, John W(ood, Jr.) 1910-1971 **C L C 32**
See also CA 21-22; 29-32R; CANR 34; CAP 2; DLB 8; MTCW 1

Campbell, Joseph 1904-1987 .... **CLC 69**
See also AAYA 3; BEST 89:2; CA 1-4R; 124; CANR 3, 28, 61; MTCW 1, 2

Campbell, Maria 1940- .... **CLC 85; DAC**
See also CA 102; CANR 54; NNAL

Campbell, (John) Ramsey 1946- **CLC 42; SSC 19**
See also CA 57-60; CANR 7; INT CANR-7

Campbell, (Ignatius) Roy (Dunnachie) 1901-1957 .... **TCLC 5**
See also CA 104; 155; DLB 20; MTCW 2

Campbell, Thomas 1777-1844 .... **NCLC 19**
See also DLB 93; 144

Campbell, Wilfred .... **TCLC 9**
See also Campbell, William

Campbell, William 1858(?)-1918
See Campbell, Wilfred
See also CA 106; DLB 92

Campion, Jane .... **CLC 95**
See also CA 138

Campos, Alvaro de
See Pessoa, Fernando (Antonio Nogueira)

Camus, Albert 1913-1960 **CLC 1, 2, 4, 9, 11, 14, 32, 63, 69; DA; DAB; DAC; DAM DRAM, MST, NOV; DC 2; SSC 9; WLC**
See also CA 89-92; DLB 72; MTCW 1, 2

Canby, Vincent 1924- .... **CLC 13**
See also CA 81-84

Cancale
See Desnos, Robert

Canetti, Elias 1905-1994 **CLC 3, 14, 25, 75, 86**
See also CA 21-24R; 146; CANR 23, 61, 79; DLB 85, 124; MTCW 1, 2

Canfield, Dorothea F.
See Fisher, Dorothy (Frances) Canfield

Canfield, Dorothea Frances
See Fisher, Dorothy (Frances) Canfield

Canfield, Dorothy
See Fisher, Dorothy (Frances) Canfield

Canin, Ethan 1960- .... **CLC 55**
See also CA 131; 135

Cannon, Curt
See Hunter, Evan

See also CA 104; 122; DAC; DAM MST, NOV

Chretien de Troyes c. 12th cent. - . **CMLC 10**
See also DLB 208

Christie
See Ichikawa, Kon

Christie, Agatha (Mary Clarissa) 1890-1976
**CLC 1, 6, 8, 12, 39, 48, 110; DAB; DAC;
DAM NOV**
See also AAYA 9; AITN 1, 2; CA 17-20R; 61-
64; CANR 10, 37; CDBLB 1914-1945; DLB
13, 77; MTCW 1, 2; SATA 36

Christie, (Ann) Philippa
See Pearce, Philippa
See also CA 5-8R; CANR 4

Christine de Pizan 1365(?)-1431(?) .... **LC 9**
See also DLB 208

Chubb, Elmer
See Masters, Edgar Lee

Chulkov, Mikhail Dmitrievich 1743-1792**LC 2**
See also DLB 150

Churchill, Caryl 1938- ..... **CLC 31, 55; DC 5**
See also CA 102; CANR 22, 46; DLB 13;
MTCW 1

Churchill, Charles 1731-1764 .... **LC 3**
See also DLB 109

Chute, Carolyn 1947- .... **CLC 39**
See also CA 123

Ciardi, John (Anthony) 1916-1986 . **CLC 10,
40, 44; DAM POET**
See also CA 5-8R; 118; CAAS 2; CANR 5, 33;
CLR 19; DLB 5; DLBY 86; INT CANR-5;
MAICYA; MTCW 1, 2; SAAS 26; SATA 1,
65; SATA-Obit 46

Cicero, Marcus Tullius 106B.C.-43B.C.
CMLC 3
See also DLB 211

Cimino, Michael 1943- .... **CLC 16**
See also CA 105

Cioran, E(mil) M. 1911-1995 .... **CLC 64**
See also CA 25-28R; 149

Cisneros, Sandra 1954- . **CLC 69, 118; DAM
MULT; HLC 1; SSC 32**
See also AAYA 9; CA 131; CANR 64; DLB 122,
152; HW 1, 2; MTCW 2

Cixous, Helene 1937- .... **CLC 92**
See also CA 126; CANR 55; DLB 83; MTCW
1, 2

Clair, Rene .... **CLC 20**
See also Chomette, Rene Lucien

Clampitt, Amy 1920-1994 ..... **CLC 32; PC 19**
See also CA 110; 146; CANR 29, 79; DLB 105

Clancy, Thomas L., Jr. 1947-
See Clancy, Tom
See also CA 125; 131; CANR 62; INT 131;
MTCW 1, 2

Clancy, Tom .. **CLC 45, 112; DAM NOV, POP**
See also Clancy, Thomas L., Jr.
See also AAYA 9; BEST 89:1, 90:1; MTCW 2

Clare, John 1793-1864 **NCLC 9; DAB; DAM
POET; PC 23**
See also DLB 55, 96

Clarin
See Alas (y Urena), Leopoldo (Enrique Garcia)

Clark, Al C.
See Goines, Donald

Clark, (Robert) Brian 1932- .... **CLC 29**
See also CA 41-44R; CANR 67

Clark, Curt
See Westlake, Donald E(dwin)

Clark, Eleanor 1913-1996 .... **CLC 5, 19**
See also CA 9-12R; 151; CANR 41; DLB 6

Clark, J. P.
See Clark, John Pepper

See also DLB 117

Clark, John Pepper 1935-.. **CLC 38; BLC 1;
DAM DRAM, MULT; DC 5**
See also Clark, J. P.
See also BW 1; CA 65-68; CANR 16, 72;
MTCW 1

Clark, M. R.
See Clark, Mavis Thorpe

Clark, Mavis Thorpe 1909- .... **CLC 12**
See also CA 57-60; CANR 8, 37; CLR 30;
MAICYA; SAAS 5; SATA 8, 74

Clark, Walter Van Tilburg 1909-1971**CLC 28**
See also CA 9-12R; 33-36R; CANR 63; DLB
9, 206; SATA 8

Clark Bekederemo, J(ohnson) P(epper)
See Clark, John Pepper

Clarke, Arthur C(harles) 1917-**CLC 1, 4, 13,
18, 35; DAM POP; SSC 3**
See also AAYA 4; CA 1-4R; CANR 2, 28, 55,
74; JRDA; MAICYA; MTCW 1, 2; SATA 13,
70

Clarke, Austin 1896-1974 .... **CLC 6, 9; DAM
POET**
See also CA 29-32; 49-52; CAP 2; DLB 10, 20

Clarke, Austin C(hesterfield) 1934-**CLC 8, 53;
BLC 1; DAC; DAM MULT**
See also BW 1; CA 25-28R; CAAS 16; CANR
14, 32, 68; DLB 53, 125

Clarke, Gillian 1937- .... **CLC 61**
See also CA 106; DLB 40

Clarke, Marcus (Andrew Hislop) 1846-1881
NCLC 19

Clarke, Shirley 1925- .... **CLC 16**

Clash, The
See Headon, (Nicky) Topper; Jones, Mick;
Simonon, Paul; Strummer, Joe

Claudel, Paul (Louis Charles Marie) 1868-1955
TCLC 2, 10
See also CA 104; 165; DLB 192

Claudius, Matthias 1740-1815 .... **NCLC 75**
See also DLB 97

Clavell, James (duMaresq) 1925-1994**CLC 6,
25, 87; DAM NOV, POP**
See also CA 25-28R; 146; CANR 26, 48;
MTCW 1, 2

Cleaver, (Leroy) Eldridge 1935-1998**CLC 30,
119; BLC 1; DAM MULT**
See also BW 1, 3; CA 21-24R; 167; CANR 16,
75; MTCW 2

Cleese, John (Marwood) 1939- .... **CLC 21**
See also Monty Python
See also CA 112; 116; CANR 35; MTCW 1

Cleishbotham, Jebediah
See Scott, Walter

Cleland, John 1710-1789 .... **LC 2, 48**
See also DLB 39

Clemens, Samuel Langhorne 1835-1910
See Twain, Mark
See also CA 104; 135; CDALB 1865-1917; DA;
DAB; DAC; DAM MST, NOV; DLB 11, 12,
23, 64, 74, 186, 189; JRDA; MAICYA; SATA
100; YABC 2

Cleophil
See Congreve, William

Clerihew, E.
See Bentley, E(dmund) C(lerihew)

Clerk, N. W.
See Lewis, C(live) S(taples)

Cliff, Jimmy .... **CLC 21**
See also Chambers, James

Cliff, Michelle 1946- .... **CLC 120; BLCS**
See also BW 2; CA 116; CANR 39, 72; DLB
157

Clifton, (Thelma) Lucille 1936- **CLC 19, 66;
BLC 1; DAM MULT, POET; PC 17**
See also BW 2, 3; CA 49-52; CANR 2, 24, 42,
76; CLR 5; DLB 5, 41; MAICYA; MTCW 1,
2; SATA 20, 69

Clinton, Dirk
See Silverberg, Robert

Clough, Arthur Hugh 1819-1861 ... **NCLC 27**
See also DLB 32

Clutha, Janet Paterson Frame 1924-
See Frame, Janet
See also CA 1-4R; CANR 2, 36, 76; MTCW 1,
2

Clyne, Terence
See Blatty, William Peter

Cobalt, Martin
See Mayne, William (James Carter)

Cobb, Irvin S(hrewsbury) 1876-1944 **T C L C
77**
See also CA 175; DLB 11, 25, 86

Cobbett, William 1763-1835 .... **NCLC 49**
See also DLB 43, 107, 158

Coburn, D(onald) L(ee) 1938- .... **CLC 10**
See also CA 89-92

Cocteau, Jean (Maurice Eugene Clement) 1889-
1963**CLC 1, 8, 15, 16, 43; DA; DAB; DAC;
DAM DRAM, MST, NOV; WLC**
See also CA 25-28; CANR 40; CAP 2; DLB
65; MTCW 1, 2

Codrescu, Andrei 1946- **CLC 46, 121; DAM
POET**
See also CA 33-36R; CAAS 19; CANR 13, 34,
53, 76; MTCW 2

Coe, Max
See Bourne, Randolph S(illiman)

Coe, Tucker
See Westlake, Donald E(dwin)

Coen, Ethan 1958- .... **CLC 108**
See also CA 126

Coen, Joel 1955- .... **CLC 108**
See also CA 126

The Coen Brothers
See Coen, Ethan; Coen, Joel

Coetzee, J(ohn) M(ichael) 1940- **CLC 23, 33,
66, 117; DAM NOV**
See also CA 77-80; CANR 41, 54, 74; MTCW
1, 2

Coffey, Brian
See Koontz, Dean R(ay)

Coffin, Robert P(eter) Tristram 1892-1955
TCLC 95
See also CA 123; 169; DLB 45

Cohan, George M(ichael) 1878-1942**TCLC 60**
See also CA 157

Cohen, Arthur A(llen) 1928-1986 . **CLC 7, 31**
See also CA 1-4R; 120; CANR 1, 17, 42; DLB
28

Cohen, Leonard (Norman) 1934- **CLC 3, 38;
DAC; DAM MST**
See also CA 21-24R; CANR 14, 69; DLB 53;
MTCW 1

Cohen, Matt 1942- .... **CLC 19; DAC**
See also CA 61-64; CAAS 18; CANR 40; DLB
53

Cohen-Solal, Annie 19(?)- .... **CLC 50**

Colegate, Isabel 1931- .... **CLC 36**
See also CA 17-20R; CANR 8, 22, 74; DLB
14; INT CANR-22; MTCW 1

Coleman, Emmett
See Reed, Ishmael

Coleridge, M. E.
See Coleridge, Mary E(lizabeth)

Coleridge, Mary E(lizabeth) 1861-1907**TCLC**

Cunninghame
See also CA 119; DLB 98
Currie, Ellen 19(?)- .... **CLC 44**
Curtin, Philip
See Lowndes, Marie Adelaide (Belloc)
Curtis, Price
See Ellison, Harlan (Jay)
Cutrate, Joe
See Spiegelman, Art
Cynewulf c. 770-c. 840 .... **CMLC 23**
Czaczkes, Shmuel Yosef
See Agnon, S(hmuel) Y(osef Halevi)
Dabrowska, Maria (Szumska) 1889-1965**CLC 15**
See also CA 106
Dabydeen, David 1955- .... **CLC 34**
See also BW 1; CA 125; CANR 56
Dacey, Philip 1939- .... **CLC 51**
See also CA 37-40R; CAAS 17; CANR 14, 32, 64; DLB 105
Dagerman, Stig (Halvard) 1923-1954 **T C L C 17**
See also CA 117; 155
Dahl, Roald 1916-1990**CLC 1, 6, 18, 79; DAB; DAC; DAM MST, NOV, POP**
See also AAYA 15; CA 1-4R; 133; CANR 6, 32, 37, 62; CLR 1, 7, 41; DLB 139; JRDA; MAICYA; MTCW 1, 2; SATA 1, 26, 73; SATA-Obit 65
Dahlberg, Edward 1900-1977 .. **CLC 1, 7, 14**
See also CA 9-12R; 69-72; CANR 31, 62; DLB 48; MTCW 1
Daitch, Susan 1954- .... **CLC 103**
See also CA 161
Dale, Colin .... **TCLC 18**
See also Lawrence, T(homas) E(dward)
Dale, George E.
See Asimov, Isaac
Dalton, Roque 1935-1975
See also HLCS 1; HW 2
Daly, Elizabeth 1878-1967 .... **CLC 52**
See also CA 23-24; 25-28R; CANR 60; CAP 2
Daly, Maureen 1921- .... **CLC 17**
See also AAYA 5; CANR 37; JRDA; MAICYA; SAAS 1; SATA 2
Damas, Leon-Gontran 1912-1978 .... **CLC 84**
See also BW 1; CA 125; 73-76
Dana, Richard Henry Sr. 1787-1879**NCLC 53**
Daniel, Samuel 1562(?)-1619 .... **LC 24**
See also DLB 62
Daniels, Brett
See Adler, Renata
Dannay, Frederic 1905-1982 . **CLC 11; DAM POP**
See also Queen, Ellery
See also CA 1-4R; 107; CANR 1, 39; DLB 137; MTCW 1
D'Annunzio, Gabriele 1863-1938**TCLC 6, 40**
See also CA 104; 155
Danois, N. le
See Gourmont, Remy (-Marie-Charles) de
Dante 1265-1321 .... **CMLC 3, 18; DA; DAB; DAC; DAM MST, POET; PC 21; WLCS**
d'Antibes, Germain
See Simenon, Georges (Jacques Christian)
Danticat, Edwidge 1969-..................... **CLC 94**
See also AAYA 29; CA 152; CANR 73; MTCW 1
Danvers, Dennis 1947- .... **CLC 70**
Danziger, Paula 1944- .... **CLC 21**
See also AAYA 4; CA 112; 115; CANR 37; CLR 20; JRDA; MAICYA; SATA 36, 63, 102; SATA-Brief 30

Da Ponte, Lorenzo 1749-1838 .... **NCLC 50**
Dario, Ruben 1867-1916 .... **TCLC 4; DAM MULT; HLC 1; PC 15**
See also CA 131; CANR 81; HW 1, 2; MTCW 1, 2
Darley, George 1795-1846 .... **NCLC 2**
See also DLB 96
Darrow, Clarence (Seward) 1857-1938**T C L C 81**
See also CA 164
Darwin, Charles 1809-1882 .... **NCLC 57**
See also DLB 57, 166
Daryush, Elizabeth 1887-1977 ...... **CLC 6, 19**
See also CA 49-52; CANR 3, 81; DLB 20
Dasgupta, Surendranath 1887-1952**TCLC 81**
See also CA 157
Dashwood, Edmee Elizabeth Monica de la Pasture 1890-1943
See Delafield, E. M.
See also CA 119; 154
Daudet, (Louis Marie) Alphonse 1840-1897 **NCLC 1**
See also DLB 123
Daumal, Rene 1908-1944 .... **TCLC 14**
See also CA 114
Davenant, William 1606-1668 .... **LC 13**
See also DLB 58, 126
Davenport, Guy (Mattison, Jr.) 1927-**CLC 6, 14, 38; SSC 16**
See also CA 33-36R; CANR 23, 73; DLB 130
Davidson, Avram (James) 1923-1993
See Queen, Ellery
See also CA 101; 171; CANR 26; DLB 8
Davidson, Donald (Grady) 1893-1968**CLC 2, 13, 19**
See also CA 5-8R; 25-28R; CANR 4; DLB 45
Davidson, Hugh
See Hamilton, Edmond
Davidson, John 1857-1909 .... **TCLC 24**
See also CA 118; DLB 19
Davidson, Sara 1943- .... **CLC 9**
See also CA 81-84; CANR 44, 68; DLB 185
Davie, Donald (Alfred) 1922-1995.**CLC 5, 8, 10, 31**
See also CA 1-4R; 149; CAAS 3; CANR 1, 44; DLB 27; MTCW 1
Davies, Ray(mond Douglas) 1944- ... **CLC 21**
See also CA 116; 146
Davies, Rhys 1901-1978 .... **CLC 23**
See also CA 9-12R; 81-84; CANR 4; DLB 139, 191
Davies, (William) Robertson 1913-1995 **C L C 2, 7, 13, 25, 42, 75, 91; DA; DAB; DAC; DAM MST, NOV, POP; WLC**
See also BEST 89:2; CA 33-36R; 150; CANR 17, 42; DLB 68; INT CANR-17; MTCW 1, 2
Davies, William Henry 1871-1940 ... **TCLC 5**
See also CA 104; 179; DLB 19, 174
Davies, Walter C.
See Kornbluth, C(yril) M.
Davis, Angela (Yvonne) 1944- **CLC 77; DAM MULT**
See also BW 2, 3; CA 57-60; CANR 10, 81
Davis, B. Lynch
See Bioy Casares, Adolfo; Borges, Jorge Luis
Davis, B. Lynch
See Bioy Casares, Adolfo
Davis, Harold Lenoir 1894-1960 ...... **CLC 49**
See also CA 178; 89-92; DLB 9, 206
Davis, Rebecca (Blaine) Harding 1831-1910 **TCLC 6**
See also CA 104; 179; DLB 74

Davis, Richard Harding 1864-1916 **TCLC 24**
See also CA 114; 179; DLB 12, 23, 78, 79, 189; DLBD 13
Davison, Frank Dalby 1893-1970 ..... **CLC 15**
See also CA 116
Davison, Lawrence H.
See Lawrence, D(avid) H(erbert Richards)
Davison, Peter (Hubert) 1928- .... **CLC 28**
See also CA 9-12R; CAAS 4; CANR 3, 43; DLB 5
Davys, Mary 1674-1732 .... **LC 1, 46**
See also DLB 39
Dawson, Fielding 1930-...................... **CLC 6**
See also CA 85-88; DLB 130
Dawson, Peter
See Faust, Frederick (Schiller)
Day, Clarence (Shepard, Jr.) 1874-1935 **TCLC 25**
See also CA 108; DLB 11
Day, Thomas 1748-1789 .... **LC 1**
See also DLB 39; YABC 1
Day Lewis, C(ecil) 1904-1972 . **CLC 1, 6, 10; DAM POET; PC 11**
See also Blake, Nicholas
See also CA 13-16; 33-36R; CANR 34; CAP 1; DLB 15, 20; MTCW 1, 2
Dazai Osamu 1909-1948 .... **TCLC 11**
See also Tsushima, Shuji
See also CA 164; DLB 182
de Andrade, Carlos Drummond 1892-1945
See Drummond de Andrade, Carlos
Deane, Norman
See Creasey, John
Deane, Seamus (Francis) 1940- .... **CLC 122**
See also CA 118; CANR 42
de Beauvoir, Simone (Lucie Ernestine Marie Bertrand)
See Beauvoir, Simone (Lucie Ernestine Marie Bertrand) de
de Beer, P.
See Bosman, Herman Charles
de Brissac, Malcolm
See Dickinson, Peter (Malcolm)
de Chardin, Pierre Teilhard
See Teilhard de Chardin, (Marie Joseph) Pierre
Dee, John 1527-1608 .... **LC 20**
Deer, Sandra 1940- .... **CLC 45**
De Ferrari, Gabriella 1941- .... **CLC 65**
See also CA 146
Defoe, Daniel 1660(?)-1731..... **LC 1, 42; DA; DAB; DAC; DAM MST, NOV; WLC**
See also AAYA 27; CDBLB 1660-1789; DLB 39, 95, 101; JRDA; MAICYA; SATA 22
de Gourmont, Remy(-Marie-Charles)
See Gourmont, Remy (-Marie-Charles) de
de Hartog, Jan 1914-......................... **CLC 19**
See also CA 1-4R; CANR 1
de Hostos, E. M.
See Hostos (y Bonilla), Eugenio Maria de
de Hostos, Eugenio M.
See Hostos (y Bonilla), Eugenio Maria de
Deighton, Len .... **CLC 4, 7, 22, 46**
See also Deighton, Leonard Cyril
See also AAYA 6; BEST 89:2; CDBLB 1960 to Present; DLB 87
Deighton, Leonard Cyril 1929-
See Deighton, Len
See also CA 9-12R; CANR 19, 33, 68; DAM NOV, POP; MTCW 1, 2
Dekker, Thomas 1572(?)-1632 ..**LC 22; DAM DRAM**
See also CDBLB Before 1660; DLB 62, 172
Delafield, E. M. 1890-1943 .... **TCLC 61**

Feinberg, David B. 1956-1994 .... **CLC 59**
See also CA 135; 147

Feinstein, Elaine 1930- .... **CLC 36**
See also CA 69-72; CAAS 1; CANR 31, 68;
DLB 14, 40; MTCW 1

Feldman, Irving (Mordecai) 1928- ..... **CLC 7**
See also CA 1-4R; CANR 1; DLB 169

Felix-Tchicaya, Gerald
See Tchicaya, Gerald Felix

Fellini, Federico 1920-1993 .... **CLC 16, 85**
See also CA 65-68; 143; CANR 33

Felsen, Henry Gregor 1916- .... **CLC 17**
See also CA 1-4R; CANR 1; SAAS 2; SATA 1

Fenno, Jack
See Calisher, Hortense

Fenollosa, Ernest (Francisco) 1853-1908
TCLC 91

Fenton, James Martin 1949- .... **CLC 32**
See also CA 102; DLB 40

Ferber, Edna 1887-1968 .... **CLC 18, 93**
See also AITN 1; CA 5-8R; 25-28R; CANR 68;
DLB 9, 28, 86; MTCW 1, 2; SATA 7

Ferguson, Helen
See Kavan, Anna

Ferguson, Samuel 1810-1886 .... **NCLC 33**
See also DLB 32

Fergusson, Robert 1750-1774 .... **LC 29**
See also DLB 109

Ferling, Lawrence
See Ferlinghetti, Lawrence (Monsanto)

Ferlinghetti, Lawrence (Monsanto) 1919(?)-
CLC 2, 6, 10, 27, 111; DAM POET; PC 1
See also CA 5-8R; CANR 3, 41, 73; CDALB
1941-1968; DLB 5, 16; MTCW 1, 2

Fernandez, Vicente Garcia Huidobro
See Huidobro Fernandez, Vicente Garcia

Ferre, Rosario 1942- .... **SSC 36; HLCS 1**
See also CA 131; CANR 55, 81; DLB 145; HW
1, 2; MTCW 1

Ferrer, Gabriel (Francisco Victor) Miro
See Miro (Ferrer), Gabriel (Francisco Victor)

Ferrier, Susan (Edmonstone) 1782-1854
NCLC 8
See also DLB 116

Ferrigno, Robert 1948(?)- .... **CLC 65**
See also CA 140

Ferron, Jacques 1921-1985 .... **CLC 94; DAC**
See also CA 117; 129; DLB 60

Feuchtwanger, Lion 1884-1958 .... **TCLC 3**
See also CA 104; DLB 66

Feuillet, Octave 1821-1890 .... **NCLC 45**
See also DLB 192

Feydeau, Georges (Leon Jules Marie) 1862-
1921 .... **TCLC 22; DAM DRAM**
See also CA 113; 152; DLB 192

Fichte, Johann Gottlieb 1762-1814 **NCLC 62**
See also DLB 90

Ficino, Marsilio 1433-1499 .... **LC 12**

Fiedeler, Hans
See Doeblin, Alfred

Fiedler, Leslie A(aron) 1917- . **CLC 4, 13, 24**
See also CA 9-12R; CANR 7, 63; DLB 28, 67;
MTCW 1, 2

Field, Andrew 1938- .... **CLC 44**
See also CA 97-100; CANR 25

Field, Eugene 1850-1895 .... **NCLC 3**
See also DLB 23, 42, 140; DLBD 13; MAICYA;
SATA 16

Field, Gans T.
See Wellman, Manly Wade

Field, Michael 1915-1971 .... **TCLC 43**
See also CA 29-32R

Field, Peter

See Hobson, Laura Z(ametkin)

Fielding, Henry 1707-1754 ..... **LC 1, 46; DA;
DAB; DAC; DAM DRAM, MST, NOV;
WLC**
See also CDBLB 1660-1789; DLB 39, 84, 101

Fielding, Sarah 1710-1768 .... **LC 1, 44**
See also DLB 39

Fields, W. C. 1880-1946 .... **TCLC 80**
See also DLB 44

Fierstein, Harvey (Forbes) 1954- ... **CLC 33;
DAM DRAM, POP**
See also CA 123; 129

Figes, Eva 1932- .... **CLC 31**
See also CA 53-56; CANR 4, 44; DLB 14

Finch, Anne 1661-1720 .... **LC 3; PC 21**
See also DLB 95

Finch, Robert (Duer Claydon) 1900- **CLC 18**
See also CA 57-60; CANR 9, 24, 49; DLB 88

Findley, Timothy 1930- . **CLC 27, 102; DAC;
DAM MST**
See also CA 25-28R; CANR 12, 42, 69; DLB
53

Fink, William
See Mencken, H(enry) L(ouis)

Firbank, Louis 1942-
See Reed, Lou
See also CA 117

Firbank, (Arthur Annesley) Ronald 1886-1926
TCLC 1
See also CA 104; 177; DLB 36

Fisher, Dorothy (Frances) Canfield 1879-1958
TCLC 87
See also CA 114; 136; CANR 80; DLB 9, 102;
MAICYA; YABC 1

Fisher, M(ary) F(rances) K(ennedy) 1908-1992
CLC 76, 87
See also CA 77-80; 138; CANR 44; MTCW 1

Fisher, Roy 1930- .... **CLC 25**
See also CA 81-84; CAAS 10; CANR 16; DLB
40

Fisher, Rudolph 1897-1934 **TCLC 11; BLC 2;
DAM MULT; SSC 25**
See also BW 1, 3; CA 107; 124; CANR 80; DLB
51, 102

Fisher, Vardis (Alvero) 1895-1968 ...... **CLC 7**
See also CA 5-8R; 25-28R; CANR 68; DLB 9,
206

Fiske, Tarleton 1917-1994
See Bloch, Robert (Albert)
See also CA 179; CAAE 179

Fitch, Clarke
See Sinclair, Upton (Beall)

Fitch, John IV
See Cormier, Robert (Edmund)

Fitzgerald, Captain Hugh
See Baum, L(yman) Frank

FitzGerald, Edward 1809-1883 .... **NCLC 9**
See also DLB 32

Fitzgerald, F(rancis) Scott (Key) 1896-1940
**TCLC 1, 6, 14, 28, 55; DA; DAB; DAC;
DAM MST, NOV; SSC 6, 31; WLC**
See also AAYA 24; AITN 1; CA 110; 123;
CDALB 1917-1929; DLB 4, 9, 86; DLBD 1,
15, 16; DLBY 81, 96; MTCW 1, 2

Fitzgerald, Penelope 1916- ... **CLC 19, 51, 61**
See also CA 85-88; CAAS 10; CANR 56; DLB
14, 194; MTCW 2

Fitzgerald, Robert (Stuart) 1910-1985 **CLC 39**
See also CA 1-4R; 114; CANR 1; DLBY 80

FitzGerald, Robert D(avid) 1902-1987 **CLC 19**
See also CA 17-20R

Fitzgerald, Zelda (Sayre) 1900-1948 **TCLC 52**
See also CA 117; 126; DLBY 84

Flanagan, Thomas (James Bonner) 1923-
CLC 25, 52
See also CA 108; CANR 55; DLBY 80; INT
108; MTCW 1

Flaubert, Gustave 1821-1880 **NCLC 2, 10, 19,
62, 66; DA; DAB; DAC; DAM MST, NOV;
SSC 11; WLC**
See also DLB 119

Flecker, Herman Elroy
See Flecker, (Herman) James Elroy

Flecker, (Herman) James Elroy 1884-1915
TCLC 43
See also CA 109; 150; DLB 10, 19

Fleming, Ian (Lancaster) 1908-1964 . **CLC 3,
30; DAM POP**
See also AAYA 26; CA 5-8R; CANR 59;
CDBLB 1945-1960; DLB 87, 201; MTCW
1, 2; SATA 9

Fleming, Thomas (James) 1927- .... **CLC 37**
See also CA 5-8R; CANR 10; INT CANR-10;
SATA 8

Fletcher, John 1579-1625 .... **LC 33; DC 6**
See also CDBLB Before 1660; DLB 58

Fletcher, John Gould 1886-1950 .... **TCLC 35**
See also CA 107; 167; DLB 4, 45

Fleur, Paul
See Pohl, Frederik

Flooglebuckle, Al
See Spiegelman, Art

Flying Officer X
See Bates, H(erbert) E(rnest)

Fo, Dario 1926- **CLC 32, 109; DAM DRAM;
DC 10**
See also CA 116; 128; CANR 68; DLBY 97;
MTCW 1, 2

Fogarty, Jonathan Titulescu Esq.
See Farrell, James T(homas)

Folke, Will 1917-1994
See Bloch, Robert (Albert); Bloch, Robert
(Albert)
See also CA 179; CAAE 179

Follett, Ken(neth Martin) 1949- ..... **CLC 18;
DAM NOV, POP**
See also AAYA 6; BEST 89:4; CA 81-84; CANR
13, 33, 54; DLB 87; DLBY 81; INT CANR-
33; MTCW 1

Fontane, Theodor 1819-1898 .... **NCLC 26**
See also DLB 129

Foote, Horton 1916- **CLC 51, 91; DAM DRAM**
See also CA 73-76; CANR 34, 51; DLB 26; INT
CANR-34

Foote, Shelby 1916- **CLC 75; DAM NOV, POP**
See also CA 5-8R; CANR 3, 45, 74; DLB 2,
17; MTCW 2

Forbes, Esther 1891-1967 .... **CLC 12**
See also AAYA 17; CA 13-14; 25-28R; CAP 1;
CLR 27; DLB 22; JRDA; MAICYA; SATA
2, 100

Forche, Carolyn (Louise) 1950- **CLC 25, 83,
86; DAM POET; PC 10**
See also CA 109; 117; CANR 50, 74; DLB 5,
193; INT 117; MTCW 1

Ford, Elbur
See Hibbert, Eleanor Alice Burford

Ford, Ford Madox 1873-1939 **TCLC 1, 15, 39,
57; DAM NOV**
See also CA 104; 132; CANR 74; CDBLB
1914-1945; DLB 162; MTCW 1, 2

Ford, Henry 1863-1947 .... **TCLC 73**
See also CA 115; 148

Ford, John 1586-(?) .... **DC 8**
See also CDBLB Before 1660; DAM DRAM;
DLB 58

See also AAYA 17; CA 85-88; CANR 32, 54; MTCW 1

Fugard, Sheila 1932- .... **CLC 48**
See also CA 125

Fuller, Charles (H., Jr.) 1939-**CLC 25; BLC 2; DAM DRAM, MULT; DC 1**
See also BW 2; CA 108; 112; DLB 38; INT 112; MTCW 1

Fuller, John (Leopold) 1937- .... **CLC 62**
See also CA 21-24R; CANR 9, 44; DLB 40

Fuller, Margaret .... **NCLC 5, 50**
See also Ossoli, Sarah Margaret (Fuller marchesa d´)

Fuller, Roy (Broadbent) 1912-1991**CLC 4, 28**
See also CA 5-8R; 135; CAAS 10; CANR 53; DLB 15, 20; SATA 87

Fulton, Alice 1952- .... **CLC 52**
See also CA 116; CANR 57; DLB 193

Furphy, Joseph 1843-1912 .... **TCLC 25**
See also CA 163

Fussell, Paul 1924- .... **CLC 74**
See also BEST 90:1; CA 17-20R; CANR 8, 21, 35, 69; INT CANR-21; MTCW 1, 2

Futabatei, Shimei 1864-1909 .... **TCLC 44**
See also CA 162; DLB 180

Futrelle, Jacques 1875-1912 .... **TCLC 19**
See also CA 113; 155

Gaboriau, Emile 1835-1873 .... **NCLC 14**

Gadda, Carlo Emilio 1893-1973 .... **CLC 11**
See also CA 89-92; DLB 177

Gaddis, William 1922-1998**CLC 1, 3, 6, 8, 10, 19, 43, 86**
See also CA 17-20R; 172; CANR 21, 48; DLB 2; MTCW 1, 2

Gage, Walter
See Inge, William (Motter)

Gaines, Ernest J(ames) 1933- **CLC 3, 11, 18, 86; BLC 2; DAM MULT**
See also AAYA 18; AITN 1; BW 2, 3; CA 9-12R; CANR 6, 24, 42, 75; CDALB 1968-1988; DLB 2, 33, 152; DLBY 80; MTCW 1, 2; SATA 86

Gaitskill, Mary 1954- .... **CLC 69**
See also CA 128; CANR 61

Galdos, Benito Perez
See Perez Galdos, Benito

Gale, Zona 1874-1938**TCLC 7; DAM DRAM**
See also CA 105; 153; DLB 9, 78

Galeano, Eduardo (Hughes) 1940- . **CLC 72; HLCS 1**
See also CA 29-32R; CANR 13, 32; HW 1

Galiano, Juan Valera y Alcala
See Valera y Alcala-Galiano, Juan

Galilei, Galileo 1546-1642 .... **LC 45**

Gallagher, Tess 1943- ...... **CLC 18, 63; DAM POET; PC 9**
See also CA 106; DLB 212

Gallant, Mavis 1922- ... **CLC 7, 18, 38; DAC; DAM MST; SSC 5**
See also CA 69-72; CANR 29, 69; DLB 53; MTCW 1, 2

Gallant, Roy A(rthur) 1924- .... **CLC 17**
See also CA 5-8R; CANR 4, 29, 54; CLR 30; MAICYA; SATA 4, 68

Gallico, Paul (William) 1897-1976 ..... **CLC 2**
See also AITN 1; CA 5-8R; 69-72; CANR 23; DLB 9, 171; MAICYA; SATA 13

Gallo, Max Louis 1932- .... **CLC 95**
See also CA 85-88

Gallois, Lucien
See Desnos, Robert

Gallup, Ralph
See Whitemore, Hugh (John)

Galsworthy, John 1867-1933**TCLC 1, 45; DA; DAB; DAC; DAM DRAM, MST, NOV; SSC 22; WLC**
See also CA 104; 141; CANR 75; CDBLB 1890-1914; DLB 10, 34, 98, 162; DLBD 16; MTCW 1

Galt, John 1779-1839 .... **NCLC 1**
See also DLB 99, 116, 159

Galvin, James 1951- .... **CLC 38**
See also CA 108; CANR 26

Gamboa, Federico 1864-1939 .... **TCLC 36**
See also CA 167; HW 2

Gandhi, M. K.
See Gandhi, Mohandas Karamchand

Gandhi, Mahatma
See Gandhi, Mohandas Karamchand

Gandhi, Mohandas Karamchand 1869-1948 **TCLC 59; DAM MULT**
See also CA 121; 132; MTCW 1, 2

Gann, Ernest Kellogg 1910-1991 ...... **CLC 23**
See also AITN 1; CA 1-4R; 136; CANR 1

Garcia, Cristina 1958- .... **CLC 76**
See also CA 141; CANR 73; HW 2

Garcia Lorca, Federico 1898-1936**TCLC 1, 7, 49; DA; DAB; DAC; DAM DRAM, MST, MULT, POET; DC 2; HLC 2; PC 3; WLC**
See also CA 104; 131; CANR 81; DLB 108; HW 1, 2; MTCW 1, 2

Garcia Marquez, Gabriel (Jose) 1928-**CLC 2, 3, 8, 10, 15, 27, 47, 55, 68;DA; DAB; DAC; DAM MST, MULT, NOV, POP; HLC 1; SSC 8; WLC**
See also AAYA 3; BEST 89:1, 90:4; CA 33-36R; CANR 10, 28, 50, 75, 82; DLB 113; HW 1, 2; MTCW 1, 2

Garcilaso de la Vega, El Inca 1503-1536
See also HLCS 1

Gard, Janice
See Latham, Jean Lee

Gard, Roger Martin du
See Martin du Gard, Roger

Gardam, Jane 1928- .... **CLC 43**
See also CA 49-52; CANR 2, 18, 33, 54; CLR 12; DLB 14, 161; MAICYA; MTCW 1; SAAS 9; SATA 39, 76; SATA-Brief 28

Gardner, Herb(ert) 1934- .... **CLC 44**
See also CA 149

Gardner, John (Champlin), Jr. 1933-1982 **CLC 2, 3, 5, 7, 8, 10, 18, 28, 34; DAM NOV, POP; SSC 7**
See also AITN 1; CA 65-68; 107; CANR 33, 73; CDALBS; DLB 2; DLBY 82; MTCW 1; SATA 40; SATA-Obit 31

Gardner, John (Edmund) 1926-**CLC 30; DAM POP**
See also CA 103; CANR 15, 69; MTCW 1

Gardner, Miriam
See Bradley, Marion Zimmer

Gardner, Noel
See Kuttner, Henry

Gardons, S. S.
See Snodgrass, W(illiam) D(e Witt)

Garfield, Leon 1921-1996 .... **CLC 12**
See also AAYA 8; CA 17-20R; 152; CANR 38, 41, 78; CLR 21; DLB 161; JRDA; MAICYA; SATA 1, 32, 76; SATA-Obit 90

Garland, (Hannibal) Hamlin 1860-1940 **TCLC 3; SSC 18**
See also CA 104; DLB 12, 71, 78, 186

Garneau, (Hector de) Saint-Denys 1912-1943 **TCLC 13**
See also CA 111; DLB 88

Garner, Alan 1934-**CLC 17; DAB; DAM POP**

See also AAYA 18; CA 73-76, 178; CAAE 178; CANR 15, 64; CLR 20; DLB 161; MAICYA; MTCW 1, 2; SATA 18, 69; SATA-Essay 108

Garner, Hugh 1913-1979 .... **CLC 13**
See also CA 69-72; CANR 31; DLB 68

Garnett, David 1892-1981 .... **CLC 3**
See also CA 5-8R; 103; CANR 17, 79; DLB 34; MTCW 2

Garos, Stephanie
See Katz, Steve

Garrett, George (Palmer) 1929-**CLC 3, 11, 51; SSC 30**
See also CA 1-4R; CAAS 5; CANR 1, 42, 67; DLB 2, 5, 130, 152; DLBY 83

Garrick, David 1717-1779 ....**LC 15; DAM DRAM**
See also DLB 84

Garrigue, Jean 1914-1972 .... **CLC 2, 8**
See also CA 5-8R; 37-40R; CANR 20

Garrison, Frederick
See Sinclair, Upton (Beall)

Garro, Elena 1920(?)-1998
See also CA 131; 169; DLB 145; HLCS 1; HW 1

Garth, Will
See Hamilton, Edmond; Kuttner, Henry

Garvey, Marcus (Moziah, Jr.) 1887-1940 **TCLC 41; BLC 2; DAM MULT**
See also BW 1; CA 120; 124; CANR 79

Gary, Romain .... **CLC 25**
See also Kacew, Romain
See also DLB 83

Gascar, Pierre .... **CLC 11**
See also Fournier, Pierre

Gascoyne, David (Emery) 1916- .... **CLC 45**
See also CA 65-68; CANR 10, 28, 54; DLB 20; MTCW 1

Gaskell, Elizabeth Cleghorn 1810-1865**NCLC 70; DAB; DAM MST; SSC 25**
See also CDBLB 1832-1890; DLB 21, 144, 159

Gass, William H(oward) 1924-**CLC 1, 2, 8, 11, 15, 39; SSC 12**
See also CA 17-20R; CANR 30, 71; DLB 2; MTCW 1, 2

Gasset, Jose Ortega y
See Ortega y Gasset, Jose

Gates, Henry Louis, Jr. 1950-**CLC 65; BLCS; DAM MULT**
See also BW 2, 3; CA 109; CANR 25, 53, 75; DLB 67; MTCW 1

Gautier, Theophile 1811-1872 .. **NCLC 1, 59; DAM POET; PC 18; SSC 20**
See also DLB 119

Gawsworth, John
See Bates, H(erbert) E(rnest)

Gay, John 1685-1732 ... **LC 49; DAM DRAM**
See also DLB 84, 95

Gay, Oliver
See Gogarty, Oliver St. John

Gaye, Marvin (Penze) 1939-1984 ..... **CLC 26**
See also CA 112

Gebler, Carlo (Ernest) 1954- .... **CLC 39**
See also CA 119; 133

Gee, Maggie (Mary) 1948- .... **CLC 57**
See also CA 130; DLB 207

Gee, Maurice (Gough) 1931- .... **CLC 29**
See also CA 97-100; CANR 67; CLR 56; SATA 46, 101

Gelbart, Larry (Simon) 1923- .... **CLC 21, 61**
See also CA 73-76; CANR 45

Gelber, Jack 1932- .... **CLC 1, 6, 14, 79**
See also CA 1-4R; CANR 2; DLB 7

Gellhorn, Martha (Ellis) 1908-1998 **CLC 14,**

See also AITN 1; BW 1, 3; CA 124; 114; CANR
82; DLB 33
Gold, Herbert 1924- .... **CLC 4, 7, 14, 42**
See also CA 9-12R; CANR 17, 45; DLB 2;
DLBY 81
Goldbarth, Albert 1948- .... **CLC 5, 38**
See also CA 53-56; CANR 6, 40; DLB 120
Goldberg, Anatol 1910-1982 .... **CLC 34**
See also CA 131; 117
Goldemberg, Isaac 1945- .... **CLC 52**
See also CA 69-72; CAAS 12; CANR 11, 32;
HW 1
Golding, William (Gerald) 1911-1993**CLC 1,
2, 3, 8, 10, 17, 27, 58, 81; DA; DAB; DAC;
DAM MST, NOV; WLC**
See also AAYA 5; CA 5-8R; 141; CANR 13,
33, 54; CDBLB 1945-1960; DLB 15, 100;
MTCW 1, 2
Goldman, Emma 1869-1940 .... **TCLC 13**
See also CA 110; 150
Goldman, Francisco 1954- .... **CLC 76**
See also CA 162
Goldman, William (W.) 1931- .... **CLC 1, 48**
See also CA 9-12R; CANR 29, 69; DLB 44
Goldmann, Lucien 1913-1970 .... **CLC 24**
See also CA 25-28; CAP 2
Goldoni, Carlo 1707-1793**LC 4; DAM DRAM**
Goldsberry, Steven 1949- .... **CLC 34**
See also CA 131
Goldsmith, Oliver 1728-1774 . **LC 2, 48; DA;
DAB; DAC; DAM DRAM, MST, NOV,
POET; DC 8; WLC**
See also CDBLB 1660-1789; DLB 39, 89, 104,
109, 142; SATA 26
Goldsmith, Peter
See Priestley, J(ohn) B(oynton)
Gombrowicz, Witold 1904-1969**CLC 4, 7, 11,
49; DAM DRAM**
See also CA 19-20; 25-28R; CAP 2
Gomez de la Serna, Ramon 1888-1963**CLC 9**
See also CA 153; 116; CANR 79; HW 1, 2
Goncharov, Ivan Alexandrovich 1812-1891
NCLC 1, 63
Goncourt, Edmond (Louis Antoine Huot) de
1822-1896 .... **NCLC 7**
See also DLB 123
Goncourt, Jules (Alfred Huot) de 1830-1870
NCLC 7
See also DLB 123
Gontier, Fernande 19(?)- .... **CLC 50**
Gonzalez Martinez, Enrique 1871-1952
TCLC 72
See also CA 166; CANR 81; HW 1, 2
Goodman, Paul 1911-1972...... **CLC 1, 2, 4, 7**
See also CA 19-20; 37-40R; CANR 34; CAP 2;
DLB 130; MTCW 1
Gordimer, Nadine 1923-**CLC 3, 5, 7, 10, 18, 33,
51, 70; DA; DAB; DAC; DAM MST, NOV;
SSC 17; WLCS**
See also CA 5-8R; CANR 3, 28, 56; INT CANR-
28; MTCW 1, 2
Gordon, Adam Lindsay 1833-1870 **NCLC 21**
Gordon, Caroline 1895-1981**CLC 6, 13, 29, 83;
SSC 15**
See also CA 11-12; 103; CANR 36; CAP 1;
DLB 4, 9, 102; DLBD 17; DLBY 81; MTCW
1, 2
Gordon, Charles William 1860-1937
See Connor, Ralph
See also CA 109
Gordon, Mary (Catherine) 1949-**CLC 13, 22**
See also CA 102; CANR 44; DLB 6; DLBY
81; INT 102; MTCW 1

Gordon, N. J.
See Bosman, Herman Charles
Gordon, Sol 1923- .... **CLC 26**
See also CA 53-56; CANR 4; SATA 11
Gordone, Charles 1925-1995**CLC 1, 4; DAM
DRAM; DC 8**
See also BW 1, 3; CA 93-96; 150; CANR 55;
DLB 7; INT 93-96; MTCW 1
Gore, Catherine 1800-1861 .... **NCLC 65**
See also DLB 116
Gorenko, Anna Andreevna
See Akhmatova, Anna
Gorky, Maxim 1868-1936**TCLC 8; DAB; SSC
28; WLC**
See also Peshkov, Alexei Maximovich
See also MTCW 2
Goryan, Sirak
See Saroyan, William
Gosse, Edmund (William) 1849-1928**TCLC 28**
See also CA 117; DLB 57, 144, 184
Gotlieb, Phyllis Fay (Bloom) 1926- ..**CLC 18**
See also CA 13-16R; CANR 7; DLB 88
Gottesman, S. D.
See Kornbluth, C(yril) M.; Pohl, Frederik
Gottfried von Strassburg fl. c. 1210- **CMLC
10**
See also DLB 138
Gould, Lois ....**CLC 4, 10**
See also CA 77-80; CANR 29; MTCW 1
Gourmont, Remy (-Marie-Charles) de 1858-
1915 .... **TCLC 17**
See also CA 109; 150; MTCW 2
Govier, Katherine 1948- .... **CLC 51**
See also CA 101; CANR 18, 40
Goyen, (Charles) William 1915-1983**CLC 5, 8,
14, 40**
See also AITN 2; CA 5-8R; 110; CANR 6, 71;
DLB 2; DLBY 83; INT CANR-6
Goytisolo, Juan 1931- . **CLC 5, 10, 23; DAM
MULT; HLC 1**
See also CA 85-88; CANR 32, 61; HW 1, 2;
MTCW 1, 2
Gozzano, Guido 1883-1916 .... **PC 10**
See also CA 154; DLB 114
Gozzi, (Conte) Carlo 1720-1806 .... **NCLC 23**
Grabbe, Christian Dietrich 1801-1836**NCLC
2**
See also DLB 133
Grace, Patricia Frances 1937- .... **CLC 56**
See also CA 176
Gracian y Morales, Baltasar 1601-1658**LC 15**
Gracq, Julien .... **CLC 11, 48**
See also Poirier, Louis
See also DLB 83
Grade, Chaim 1910-1982 .... **CLC 10**
See also CA 93-96; 107
Graduate of Oxford, A
See Ruskin, John
Grafton, Garth
See Duncan, Sara Jeannette
Graham, John
See Phillips, David Graham
Graham, Jorie 1951- .... **CLC 48, 118**
See also CA 111; CANR 63; DLB 120
Graham, R(obert) B(ontine) Cunninghame
See Cunninghame Graham, R(obert) B(ontine)
See also DLB 98, 135, 174
Graham, Robert 1943-
See Haldeman, Joe (William)
See also CA 179; CAAE 179
Graham, Tom
See Lewis, (Harry) Sinclair
Graham, W(illiam) S(ydney) 1918-1986**CLC**

29
See also CA 73-76; 118; DLB 20
Graham, Winston (Mawdsley) 1910-**CLC 23**
See also CA 49-52; CANR 2, 22, 45, 66; DLB
77
Grahame, Kenneth 1859-1932**TCLC 64; DAB**
See also CA 108; 136; CANR 80; CLR 5; DLB
34, 141, 178; MAICYA; MTCW 2; SATA
100; YABC 1
Granovsky, Timofei Nikolaevich 1813-1855
NCLC 75
See also DLB 198
Grant, Skeeter
See Spiegelman, Art
Granville-Barker, Harley 1877-1946**TCLC 2;
DAM DRAM**
See also Barker, Harley Granville
See also CA 104
Grass, Guenter (Wilhelm) 1927-**CLC 1, 2, 4, 6,
11, 15, 22, 32, 49, 88; DA; DAB; DAC;
DAM MST, NOV; WLC**
See also CA 13-16R; CANR 20, 75; DLB 75,
124; MTCW 1, 2
Gratton, Thomas
See Hulme, T(homas) E(rnest)
Grau, Shirley Ann 1929- . **CLC 4, 9; SSC 15**
See also CA 89-92; CANR 22, 69; DLB 2; INT
CANR-22; MTCW 1
Gravel, Fern
See Hall, James Norman
Graver, Elizabeth 1964- .... **CLC 70**
See also CA 135; CANR 71
Graves, Richard Perceval 1945- .... **CLC 44**
See also CA 65-68; CANR 9, 26, 51
Graves, Robert (von Ranke) 1895-1985 **CLC
1, 2, 6, 11, 39, 44, 45; DAB; DAC; DAM
MST, POET; PC 6**
See also CA 5-8R; 117; CANR 5, 36; CDBLB
1914-1945; DLB 20, 100, 191; DLBD 18;
DLBY 85; MTCW 1, 2; SATA 45
Graves, Valerie
See Bradley, Marion Zimmer
Gray, Alasdair (James) 1934- .... **CLC 41**
See also CA 126; CANR 47, 69; DLB 194; INT
126; MTCW 1, 2
Gray, Amlin 1946- .... **CLC 29**
See also CA 138
Gray, Francine du Plessix 1930- ..... **CLC 22;
DAM NOV**
See also BEST 90:3; CA 61-64; CAAS 2;
CANR 11, 33, 75, 81; INT CANR-11;
MTCW 1, 2
Gray, John (Henry) 1866-1934 ...... **TCLC 19**
See also CA 119; 162
Gray, Simon (James Holliday) 1936-**CLC 9,
14, 36**
See also AITN 1; CA 21-24R; CAAS 3; CANR
32, 69; DLB 13; MTCW 1
Gray, Spalding 1941-**CLC 49, 112; DAM POP;
DC 7**
See also CA 128; CANR 74; MTCW 2
Gray, Thomas 1716-1771**LC 4, 40; DA; DAB;
DAC; DAM MST; PC 2; WLC**
See also CDBLB 1660-1789; DLB 109
Grayson, David
See Baker, Ray Stannard
Grayson, Richard (A.) 1951- .... **CLC 38**
See also CA 85-88; CANR 14, 31, 57
Greeley, Andrew M(oran) 1928- ..... **CLC 28;
DAM POP**
See also CA 5-8R; CAAS 7; CANR 7, 43, 69;
MTCW 1, 2
Green, Anna Katharine 1846-1935 **TCLC 63**

See also CA 112; 159; DLB 202

Green, Brian
See Card, Orson Scott

Green, Hannah
See Greenberg, Joanne (Goldenberg)

Green, Hannah 1927(?)-1996 .... **CLC 3**
See also CA 73-76; CANR 59

Green, Henry 1905-1973 .... **CLC 2, 13, 97**
See also Yorke, Henry Vincent
See also CA 175; DLB 15

Green, Julian (Hartridge) 1900-1998
See Green, Julien
See also CA 21-24R; 169; CANR 33; DLB 4,
72; MTCW 1

Green, Julien .... **CLC 3, 11, 77**
See also Green, Julian (Hartridge)
See also MTCW 2

Green, Paul (Eliot) 1894-1981 **CLC 25; DAM
DRAM**
See also AITN 1; CA 5-8R; 103; CANR 3; DLB
7, 9; DLBY 81

Greenberg, Ivan 1908-1973
See Rahv, Philip
See also CA 85-88

Greenberg, Joanne (Goldenberg) 1932- **C L C
7, 30**
See also AAYA 12; CA 5-8R; CANR 14, 32,
69; SATA 25

Greenberg, Richard 1959(?)- .... **CLC 57**
See also CA 138

Greene, Bette 1934- .... **CLC 30**
See also AAYA 7; CA 53-56; CANR 4; CLR 2;
JRDA; MAICYA; SAAS 16; SATA 8, 102

Greene, Gael .... **CLC 8**
See also CA 13-16R; CANR 10

Greene, Graham (Henry) 1904-1991 **CLC 1, 3,
6, 9, 14, 18, 27, 37, 70, 72; DA; DAB; DAC;
DAM MST, NOV; SSC 29; WLC**
See also AITN 2; CA 13-16R; 133; CANR 35,
61; CDBLB 1945-1960; DLB 13, 15, 77,
100, 162, 201, 204; DLBY 91; MTCW 1, 2;
SATA 20

Greene, Robert 1558-1592 .... **LC 41**
See also DLB 62, 167

Greer, Richard
See Silverberg, Robert

Gregor, Arthur 1923- .... **CLC 9**
See also CA 25-28R; CAAS 10; CANR 11;
SATA 36

Gregor, Lee
See Pohl, Frederik

Gregory, Isabella Augusta (Persse) 1852-1932
TCLC 1
See also CA 104; DLB 10

Gregory, J. Dennis
See Williams, John A(lfred)

Grendon, Stephen
See Derleth, August (William)

Grenville, Kate 1950- .... **CLC 61**
See also CA 118; CANR 53

Grenville, Pelham
See Wodehouse, P(elham) G(renville)

Greve, Felix Paul (Berthold Friedrich) 1879-
1948
See Grove, Frederick Philip
See also CA 104; 141, 175; CANR 79; DAC;
DAM MST

Grey, Zane 1872-1939 .. **TCLC 6; DAM POP**
See also CA 104; 132; DLB 212; MTCW 1, 2

Grieg, (Johan) Nordahl (Brun) 1902-1943
TCLC 10
See also CA 107

Grieve, C(hristopher) M(urray) 1892-1978

CLC 11, 19; DAM POET
See also MacDiarmid, Hugh; Pteleon
See also CA 5-8R; 85-88; CANR 33; MTCW 1

Griffin, Gerald 1803-1840 .... **NCLC 7**
See also DLB 159

Griffin, John Howard 1920-1980 ..... **CLC 68**
See also AITN 1; CA 1-4R; 101; CANR 2

Griffin, Peter 1942- .... **CLC 39**
See also CA 136

Griffith, D(avid Lewelyn) W(ark) 1875(?)-1948
TCLC 68
See also CA 119; 150; CANR 80

Griffith, Lawrence
See Griffith, D(avid Lewelyn) W(ark)

Griffiths, Trevor 1935- .... **CLC 13, 52**
See also CA 97-100; CANR 45; DLB 13

Griggs, Sutton Elbert 1872-1930(?) **TCLC 77**
See also CA 123; DLB 50

Grigson, Geoffrey (Edward Harvey) 1905-1985
CLC 7, 39
See also CA 25-28R; 118; CANR 20, 33; DLB
27; MTCW 1, 2

Grillparzer, Franz 1791-1872 .... **NCLC 1**
See also DLB 133

Grimble, Reverend Charles James
See Eliot, T(homas) S(tearns)

Grimke, Charlotte L(ottie) Forten 1837(?)-1914
See Forten, Charlotte L.
See also BW 1; CA 117; 124; DAM MULT,
POET

Grimm, Jacob Ludwig Karl 1785-1863 **NCLC
3, 77; SSC 36**
See also DLB 90; MAICYA; SATA 22

Grimm, Wilhelm Karl 1786-1859 **NCLC 3, 77;
SSC 36**
See also DLB 90; MAICYA; SATA 22

Grimmelshausen, Johann Jakob Christoffel von
1621-1676 .... **LC 6**
See also DLB 168

Grindel, Eugene 1895-1952
See Eluard, Paul
See also CA 104

Grisham, John 1955-..... **CLC 84; DAM POP**
See also AAYA 14; CA 138; CANR 47, 69;
MTCW 2

Grossman, David 1954- .... **CLC 67**
See also CA 138

Grossman, Vasily (Semenovich) 1905-1964
CLC 41
See also CA 124; 130; MTCW 1

Grove, Frederick Philip .... **TCLC 4**
See also Greve, Felix Paul (Berthold Friedrich)
See also DLB 92

Grubb
See Crumb, R(obert)

Grumbach, Doris (Isaac) 1918- **CLC 13, 22, 64**
See also CA 5-8R; CAAS 2; CANR 9, 42, 70;
INT CANR-9; MTCW 2

Grundtvig, Nicolai Frederik Severin 1783-1872
NCLC 1

Grunge
See Crumb, R(obert)

Grunwald, Lisa 1959- .... **CLC 44**
See also CA 120

Guare, John 1938- . **CLC 8, 14, 29, 67; DAM
DRAM**
See also CA 73-76; CANR 21, 69; DLB 7;
MTCW 1, 2

Gudjonsson, Halldor Kiljan 1902-1998
See Laxness, Halldor
See also CA 103; 164

Guenter, Erich
See Eich, Guenter

Guest, Barbara 1920- .... **CLC 34**
See also CA 25-28R; CANR 11, 44; DLB 5,
193

Guest, Edgar A(lbert) 1881-1959 .. **TCLC 95**
See also CA 112; 168

Guest, Judith (Ann) 1936- **CLC 8, 30; DAM
NOV, POP**
See also AAYA 7; CA 77-80; CANR 15, 75;
INT CANR-15; MTCW 1, 2

Guevara, Che .... **CLC 87; HLC 1**
See also Guevara (Serna), Ernesto

Guevara (Serna), Ernesto 1928-1967 **CLC 87;
DAM MULT; HLC 1**
See also Guevara, Che
See also CA 127; 111; CANR 56; HW 1

Guicciardini, Francesco 1483-1540 .... **LC 49**

Guild, Nicholas M. 1944- .... **CLC 33**
See also CA 93-96

Guillemin, Jacques
See Sartre, Jean-Paul

Guillen, Jorge 1893-1984 .... **CLC 11; DAM
MULT, POET; HLCS 1**
See also CA 89-92; 112; DLB 108; HW 1

Guillen, Nicolas (Cristobal) 1902-1989 **C L C
48, 79; BLC 2; DAM MST, MULT, POET;
HLC 1; PC 23**
See also BW 2; CA 116; 125; 129; HW 1

Guillevic, (Eugene) 1907- .... **CLC 33**
See also CA 93-96

Guillois
See Desnos, Robert

Guillois, Valentin
See Desnos, Robert

Guimaraes Rosa, Joao 1908-1967
See also CA 175; HLCS 2

Guiney, Louise Imogen 1861-1920 **TCLC 41**
See also CA 160; DLB 54

Guiraldes, Ricardo (Guillermo) 1886-1927
TCLC 39
See also CA 131; HW 1; MTCW 1

Gumilev, Nikolai (Stepanovich) 1886-1921
TCLC 60
See also CA 165

Gunesekera, Romesh 1954- .... **CLC 91**
See also CA 159

Gunn, Bill .... **CLC 5**
See also Gunn, William Harrison
See also DLB 38

Gunn, Thom(son William) 1929- **CLC 3, 6, 18,
32, 81; DAM POET; PC 26**
See also CA 17-20R; CANR 9, 33; CDBLB
1960 to Present; DLB 27; INT CANR-33;
MTCW 1

Gunn, William Harrison 1934(?)-1989
See Gunn, Bill
See also AITN 1; BW 1, 3; CA 13-16R; 128;
CANR 12, 25, 76

Gunnars, Kristjana 1948- .... **CLC 69**
See also CA 113; DLB 60

Gurdjieff, G(eorgei) I(vanovich) 1877(?)-1949
TCLC 71
See also CA 157

Gurganus, Allan 1947- . **CLC 70; DAM POP**
See also BEST 90:1; CA 135

Gurney, A(lbert) R(amsdell), Jr. 1930- . **C L C
32, 50, 54; DAM DRAM**
See also CA 77-80; CANR 32, 64

Gurney, Ivor (Bertie) 1890-1937 ... **TCLC 33**
See also CA 167

Gurney, Peter
See Gurney, A(lbert) R(amsdell), Jr.

Guro, Elena 1877-1913 .... **TCLC 56**

Gustafson, James M(oody) 1925- ... **CLC 100**

See also CA 25-28R; CANR 37

Gustafson, Ralph (Barker) 1909- ..... **CLC 36**
See also CA 21-24R; CANR 8, 45; DLB 88

Gut, Gom
See Simenon, Georges (Jacques Christian)

Guterson, David 1956- .... **CLC 91**
See also CA 132; CANR 73; MTCW 2

Guthrie, A(lfred) B(ertram), Jr. 1901-1991
CLC 23
See also CA 57-60; 134; CANR 24; DLB 212;
SATA 62; SATA-Obit 67

Guthrie, Isobel
See Grieve, C(hristopher) M(urray)

Guthrie, Woodrow Wilson 1912-1967
See Guthrie, Woody
See also CA 113; 93-96

Guthrie, Woody .... **CLC 35**
See also Guthrie, Woodrow Wilson

Gutierrez Najera, Manuel 1859-1895
See also HLCS 2

Guy, Rosa (Cuthbert) 1928- .... **CLC 26**
See also AAYA 4; BW 2; CA 17-20R; CANR
14, 34; CLR 13; DLB 33; JRDA; MAICYA;
SATA 14, 62

Gwendolyn
See Bennett, (Enoch) Arnold

H. D. .... **CLC 3, 8, 14, 31, 34, 73; PC 5**
See also Doolittle, Hilda

H. de V.
See Buchan, John

Haavikko, Paavo Juhani 1931- .. **CLC 18, 34**
See also CA 106

Habbema, Koos
See Heijermans, Herman

Habermas, Juergen 1929- .... **CLC 104**
See also CA 109

Habermas, Jurgen
See Habermas, Juergen

Hacker, Marilyn 1942- **CLC 5, 9, 23, 72, 91;**
DAM POET
See also CA 77-80; CANR 68; DLB 120

Haeckel, Ernst Heinrich (Philipp August) 1834-
1919 .... **TCLC 83**
See also CA 157

Hafiz c. 1326-1389 .... **CMLC 34**

Hafiz c. 1326-1389(?) .... **CMLC 34**

Haggard, H(enry) Rider 1856-1925 **TCLC 11**
See also CA 108; 148; DLB 70, 156, 174, 178;
MTCW 2; SATA 16

Hagiosy, L.
See Larbaud, Valery (Nicolas)

Hagiwara Sakutaro 1886-1942 **TCLC 60; PC**
18

Haig, Fenil
See Ford, Ford Madox

Haig-Brown, Roderick (Langmere) 1908-1976
CLC 21
See also CA 5-8R; 69-72; CANR 4, 38; CLR
31; DLB 88; MAICYA; SATA 12

Hailey, Arthur 1920- **CLC 5; DAM NOV, POP**
See also AITN 2; BEST 90:3; CA 1-4R; CANR
2, 36, 75; DLB 88; DLBY 82; MTCW 1, 2

Hailey, Elizabeth Forsythe 1938- ..... **CLC 40**
See also CA 93-96; CAAS 1; CANR 15, 48;
INT CANR-15

Haines, John (Meade) 1924- .... **CLC 58**
See also CA 17-20R; CANR 13, 34; DLB 212

Hakluyt, Richard 1552-1616 .... **LC 31**

Haldeman, Joe (William) 1943- .... **CLC 61**
See also Graham, Robert
See also CA 53-56, 179; CAAE 179; CAAS 25;
CANR 6, 70, 72; DLB 8; INT CANR-6

Hale, Sarah Josepha (Buell) 1788-1879 **NCLC**
75
See also DLB 1, 42, 73

Haley, Alex(ander Murray Palmer) 1921-1992
CLC 8, 12, 76; BLC 2; DA; DAB; DAC;
DAM MST, MULT, POP
See also AAYA 26; BW 2, 3; CA 77-80; 136;
CANR 61; CDALBS; DLB 38; MTCW 1, 2

Haliburton, Thomas Chandler 1796-1865
NCLC 15
See also DLB 11, 99

Hall, Donald (Andrew, Jr.) 1928- **CLC 1, 13,**
37, 59; DAM POET
See also CA 5-8R; CAAS 7; CANR 2, 44, 64;
DLB 5; MTCW 1; SATA 23, 97

Hall, Frederic Sauser
See Sauser-Hall, Frederic

Hall, James
See Kuttner, Henry

Hall, James Norman 1887-1951 ..... **TCLC 23**
See also CA 123; 173; SATA 21

Hall, Radclyffe
See Hall, (Marguerite) Radclyffe
See also MTCW 2

Hall, (Marguerite) Radclyffe 1886-1943
TCLC 12
See also CA 110; 150; DLB 191

Hall, Rodney 1935- .... **CLC 51**
See also CA 109; CANR 69

Halleck, Fitz-Greene 1790-1867 .... **NCLC 47**
See also DLB 3

Halliday, Michael
See Creasey, John

Halpern, Daniel 1945- .... **CLC 14**
See also CA 33-36R

Hamburger, Michael (Peter Leopold) 1924-
CLC 5, 14
See also CA 5-8R; CAAS 4; CANR 2, 47; DLB
27

Hamill, Pete 1935- .... **CLC 10**
See also CA 25-28R; CANR 18, 71

Hamilton, Alexander 1755(?)-1804 **NCLC 49**
See also DLB 37

Hamilton, Clive
See Lewis, C(live) S(taples)

Hamilton, Edmond 1904-1977 .... **CLC 1**
See also CA 1-4R; CANR 3; DLB 8

Hamilton, Eugene (Jacob) Lee
See Lee-Hamilton, Eugene (Jacob)

Hamilton, Franklin
See Silverberg, Robert

Hamilton, Gail
See Corcoran, Barbara

Hamilton, Mollie
See Kaye, M(ary) M(argaret)

Hamilton, (Anthony Walter) Patrick 1904-1962
CLC 51
See also CA 176; 113; DLB 191

Hamilton, Virginia 1936- .... **CLC 26; DAM**
MULT
See also AAYA 2, 21; BW 2, 3; CA 25-28R;
CANR 20, 37, 73; CLR 1, 11, 40; DLB 33,
52; INT CANR-20; JRDA; MAICYA;
MTCW 1, 2; SATA 4, 56, 79

Hammett, (Samuel) Dashiell 1894-1961 **C L C**
3, 5, 10, 19, 47; SSC 17
See also AITN 1; CA 81-84; CANR 42; CDALB
1929-1941; DLBD 6; DLBY 96; MTCW 1,
2

Hammon, Jupiter 1711(?)-1800(?) ..**NCLC 5;**
BLC 2; DAM MULT, POET; PC 16
See also DLB 31, 50

Hammond, Keith
See Kuttner, Henry

Hamner, Earl (Henry), Jr. 1923- ...... **CLC 12**
See also AITN 2; CA 73-76; DLB 6

Hampton, Christopher (James) 1946- **CLC 4**
See also CA 25-28R; DLB 13; MTCW 1

Hamsun, Knut .... **TCLC 2, 14, 49**
See also Pedersen, Knut

Handke, Peter 1942- **CLC 5, 8, 10, 15, 38; DAM**
DRAM, NOV
See also CA 77-80; CANR 33, 75; DLB 85, 124;
MTCW 1, 2

Hanley, James 1901-1985 ..... **CLC 3, 5, 8, 13**
See also CA 73-76; 117; CANR 36; DLB 191;
MTCW 1

Hannah, Barry 1942- .... **CLC 23, 38, 90**
See also CA 108; 110; CANR 43, 68; DLB 6;
INT 110; MTCW 1

Hannon, Ezra
See Hunter, Evan

Hansberry, Lorraine (Vivian) 1930-1965 **CLC**
17, 62; BLC 2; DA; DAB; DAC; DAM
DRAM, MST, MULT; DC 2
See also AAYA 25; BW 1, 3; CA 109; 25-28R;
CABS 3; CANR 58; CDALB 1941-1968;
DLB 7, 38; MTCW 1, 2

Hansen, Joseph 1923- .... **CLC 38**
See also CA 29-32R; CAAS 17; CANR 16, 44,
66; INT CANR-16

Hansen, Martin A(lfred) 1909-1955 **TCLC 32**
See also CA 167

Hanson, Kenneth O(stlin) 1922- .... **CLC 13**
See also CA 53-56; CANR 7

Hardwick, Elizabeth (Bruce) 1916- **CLC 13;**
DAM NOV
See also CA 5-8R; CANR 3, 32, 70; DLB 6;
MTCW 1, 2

Hardy, Thomas 1840-1928 **TCLC 4, 10, 18, 32,**
48, 53, 72; DA; DAB; DAC; DAM MST,
NOV, POET; PC 8; SSC 2; WLC
See also CA 104; 123; CDBLB 1890-1914;
DLB 18, 19, 135; MTCW 1, 2

Hare, David 1947- .... **CLC 29, 58**
See also CA 97-100; CANR 39; DLB 13;
MTCW 1

Harewood, John
See Van Druten, John (William)

Harford, Henry
See Hudson, W(illiam) H(enry)

Hargrave, Leonie
See Disch, Thomas M(ichael)

Harjo, Joy 1951- **CLC 83; DAM MULT; PC 27**
See also CA 114; CANR 35, 67; DLB 120, 175;
MTCW 2; NNAL

Harlan, Louis R(udolph) 1922- .... **CLC 34**
See also CA 21-24R; CANR 25, 55, 80

Harling, Robert 1951(?)- .... **CLC 53**
See also CA 147

Harmon, William (Ruth) 1938- .... **CLC 38**
See also CA 33-36R; CANR 14, 32, 35; SATA
65

Harper, F. E. W.
See Harper, Frances Ellen Watkins

Harper, Frances E. W.
See Harper, Frances Ellen Watkins

Harper, Frances E. Watkins
See Harper, Frances Ellen Watkins

Harper, Frances Ellen
See Harper, Frances Ellen Watkins

Harper, Frances Ellen Watkins 1825-1911
TCLC 14; BLC 2; DAM MULT, POET;
PC 21
See also BW 1, 3; CA 111; 125; CANR 79; DLB
50

Harper, Michael S(teven) 1938- .... **CLC 7, 22**

Heller, Joseph 1923-CLC 1, 3, 5, 8, 11, 36, 63; DA; DAB; DAC; DAM MST, NOV, POP; WLC
  See also AAYA 24; AITN 1; CA 5-8R; CABS 1; CANR 8, 42, 66; DLB 2, 28; DLBY 80; INT CANR-8; MTCW 1, 2

Hellman, Lillian (Florence) 1906-1984CLC 2, 4, 8, 14, 18, 34, 44, 52; DAM DRAM; DC 1
  See also AITN 1, 2; CA 13-16R; 112; CANR 33; DLB 7; DLBY 84; MTCW 1, 2

Helprin, Mark 1947-CLC 7, 10, 22, 32; DAM NOV, POP
  See also CA 81-84; CANR 47, 64; CDALBS; DLBY 85; MTCW 1, 2

Helvetius, Claude-Adrien 1715-1771 .. LC 26

Helyar, Jane Penelope Josephine 1933-
  See Poole, Josephine
  See also CA 21-24R; CANR 10, 26; SATA 82

Hemans, Felicia 1793-1835 .... NCLC 71
  See also DLB 96

Hemingway, Ernest (Miller) 1899-1961 C L C 1, 3, 6, 8, 10, 13, 19, 30, 34, 39, 41, 44, 50, 61, 80; DA; DAB; DAC; DAM MST, NOV; SSC 1, 25, 36; WLC
  See also AAYA 19; CA 77-80; CANR 34; CDALB 1917-1929; DLB 4, 9, 102,210; DLBD 1, 15, 16; DLBY 81, 87, 96, 98; MTCW 1, 2

Hempel, Amy 1951- .... CLC 39
  See also CA 118; 137; CANR 70; MTCW 2

Henderson, F. C.
  See Mencken, H(enry) L(ouis)

Henderson, Sylvia
  See Ashton-Warner, Sylvia (Constance)

Henderson, Zenna (Chlarson) 1917-1983S S C 29
  See also CA 1-4R; 133; CANR 1; DLB 8; SATA 5

Henkin, Joshua .... CLC 119
  See also CA 161

Henley, Beth .... CLC 23; DC 6
  See also Henley, Elizabeth Becker
  See also CABS 3; DLBY 86

Henley, Elizabeth Becker 1952-
  See Henley, Beth
  See also CA 107; CANR 32, 73; DAM DRAM, MST; MTCW 1, 2

Henley, William Ernest 1849-1903 .. TCLC 8
  See also CA 105; DLB 19

Hennissart, Martha
  See Lathen, Emma
  See also CA 85-88; CANR 64

Henry, O. .... TCLC 1, 19; SSC 5; WLC
  See also Porter, William Sydney

Henry, Patrick 1736-1799 .... LC 25

Henryson, Robert 1430(?)-1506(?) ...... LC 20
  See also DLB 146

Henry VIII 1491-1547 .... LC 10
  See also DLB 132

Henschke, Alfred
  See Klabund

Hentoff, Nat(han Irving) 1925- .... CLC 26
  See also AAYA 4; CA 1-4R; CAAS 6; CANR 5, 25, 77; CLR 1, 52; INT CANR-25; JRDA; MAICYA; SATA 42, 69; SATA-Brief 27

Heppenstall, (John) Rayner 1911-1981 C L C 10
  See also CA 1-4R; 103; CANR 29

Heraclitus c. 540B.C.-c. 450B.C. .. CMLC 22
  See also DLB 176

Herbert, Frank (Patrick) 1920-1986 CLC 12, 23, 35, 44, 85; DAM POP
  See also AAYA 21; CA 53-56; 118; CANR 5,

43; CDALBS; DLB 8; INT CANR-5; MTCW 1, 2; SATA 9, 37; SATA-Obit 47

Herbert, George 1593-1633 ..... LC 24; DAB; DAM POET; PC 4
  See also CDBLB Before 1660; DLB 126

Herbert, Zbigniew 1924-1998 ..... CLC 9, 43; DAM POET
  See also CA 89-92; 169; CANR 36, 74; MTCW 1

Herbst, Josephine (Frey) 1897-1969 CLC 34
  See also CA 5-8R; 25-28R; DLB 9

Heredia, Jose Maria 1803-1839
  See also HLCS 2

Hergesheimer, Joseph 1880-1954 .. TCLC 11
  See also CA 109; DLB 102, 9

Herlihy, James Leo 1927-1993 .... CLC 6
  See also CA 1-4R; 143; CANR 2

Hermogenes fl. c. 175- .... CMLC 6

Hernandez, Jose 1834-1886 .... NCLC 17

Herodotus c. 484B.C.-429B.C. .... CMLC 17
  See also DLB 176

Herrick, Robert 1591-1674LC 13; DA; DAB; DAC; DAM MST, POP; PC 9
  See also DLB 126

Herring, Guilles
  See Somerville, Edith

Herriot, James 1916-1995CLC 12; DAM POP
  See also Wight, James Alfred
  See also AAYA 1; CA 148; CANR 40; MTCW 2; SATA 86

Herrmann, Dorothy 1941- .... CLC 44
  See also CA 107

Herrmann, Taffy
  See Herrmann, Dorothy

Hersey, John (Richard) 1914-1993CLC 1, 2, 7, 9, 40, 81, 97; DAM POP
  See also AAYA 29; CA 17-20R; 140; CANR 33; CDALBS; DLB 6, 185; MTCW 1, 2; SATA 25; SATA-Obit 76

Herzen, Aleksandr Ivanovich 1812-1870 NCLC 10, 61

Herzl, Theodor 1860-1904 .... TCLC 36
  See also CA 168

Herzog, Werner 1942- .... CLC 16
  See also CA 89-92

Hesiod c. 8th cent. B.C.- .... CMLC 5
  See also DLB 176

Hesse, Hermann 1877-1962CLC 1, 2, 3, 6, 11, 17, 25, 69; DA; DAB; DAC; DAM MST, NOV; SSC 9; WLC
  See also CA 17-18; CAP 2; DLB 66; MTCW 1, 2; SATA 50

Hewes, Cady
  See De Voto, Bernard (Augustine)

Heyen, William 1940- .... CLC 13, 18
  See also CA 33-36R; CAAS 9; DLB 5

Heyerdahl, Thor 1914- .... CLC 26
  See also CA 5-8R; CANR 5, 22, 66, 73; MTCW 1, 2; SATA 2, 52

Heym, Georg (Theodor Franz Arthur) 1887-1912 .... TCLC 9
  See also CA 106

Heym, Stefan 1913- .... CLC 41
  See also CA 9-12R; CANR 4; DLB 69

Heyse, Paul (Johann Ludwig von) 1830-1914 TCLC 8
  See also CA 104; DLB 129

Heyward, (Edwin) DuBose 1885-1940 T C L C 59
  See also CA 108; 157; DLB 7, 9, 45; SATA 21

Hibbert, Eleanor Alice Burford 1906-1993 CLC 7; DAM POP
  See also BEST 90:4; CA 17-20R; 140; CANR

9, 28, 59; MTCW 2; SATA 2; SATA-Obit 74

Hichens, Robert (Smythe) 1864-1950 T C L C 64
  See also CA 162; DLB 153

Higgins, George V(incent) 1939-CLC 4, 7, 10, 18
  See also CA 77-80; CAAS 5; CANR 17, 51; DLB 2; DLBY 81, 98; INT CANR-17; MTCW 1

Higginson, Thomas Wentworth 1823-1911 TCLC 36
  See also CA 162; DLB 1, 64

Highet, Helen
  See MacInnes, Helen (Clark)

Highsmith, (Mary) Patricia 1921-1995CLC 2, 4, 14, 42, 102; DAM NOV, POP
  See also CA 1-4R; 147; CANR 1, 20, 48, 62; MTCW 1, 2

Highwater, Jamake (Mamake) 1942(?)- C L C 12
  See also AAYA 7; CA 65-68; CAAS 7; CANR 10, 34; CLR 17; DLB 52; DLBY 85; JRDA; MAICYA; SATA 32, 69; SATA-Brief 30

Highway, Tomson 1951-CLC 92; DAC; DAM MULT
  See also CA 151; CANR 75; MTCW 2; NNAL

Higuchi, Ichiyo 1872-1896 .... NCLC 49

Hijuelos, Oscar 1951- CLC 65; DAM MULT, POP; HLC 1
  See also AAYA 25; BEST 90:1; CA 123; CANR 50, 75; DLB 145; HW 1, 2; MTCW 2

Hikmet, Nazim 1902(?)-1963 .... CLC 40
  See also CA 141; 93-96

Hildegard von Bingen 1098-1179 . CMLC 20
  See also DLB 148

Hildesheimer, Wolfgang 1916-1991 .. CLC 49
  See also CA 101; 135; DLB 69, 124

Hill, Geoffrey (William) 1932- CLC 5, 8, 18, 45; DAM POET
  See also CA 81-84; CANR 21; CDBLB 1960 to Present; DLB 40; MTCW 1

Hill, George Roy 1921- .... CLC 26
  See also CA 110; 122

Hill, John
  See Koontz, Dean R(ay)

Hill, Susan (Elizabeth) 1942- .... CLC 4, 113; DAB; DAM MST, NOV
  See also CA 33-36R; CANR 29, 69; DLB 14, 139; MTCW 1

Hillerman, Tony 1925- . CLC 62; DAM POP
  See also AAYA 6; BEST 89:1; CA 29-32R; CANR 21, 42, 65; DLB 206; SATA 6

Hillesum, Etty 1914-1943 .... TCLC 49
  See also CA 137

Hilliard, Noel (Harvey) 1929- .... CLC 15
  See also CA 9-12R; CANR 7, 69

Hillis, Rick 1956- .... CLC 66
  See also CA 134

Hilton, James 1900-1954 .... TCLC 21
  See also CA 108; 169; DLB 34, 77; SATA 34

Himes, Chester (Bomar) 1909-1984CLC 2, 4, 7, 18, 58, 108; BLC 2; DAM MULT
  See also BW 2; CA 25-28R; 114; CANR 22; DLB 2, 76, 143; MTCW 1, 2

Hinde, Thomas .... CLC 6, 11
  See also Chitty, Thomas Willes

Hindin, Nathan 1917-1994
  See Bloch, Robert (Albert)
  See also CA 179; CAAE 179

Hine, (William) Daryl 1936- .... CLC 15
  See also CA 1-4R; CAAS 15; CANR 1, 20; DLB 60

Hinkson, Katharine Tynan

See Tynan, Katharine
Hinojosa(-Smith), Rolando (R.) 1929-
See Hinojosa-Smith, Rolando
See also CA 131; CAAS 16; CANR 62; DAM MULT; DLB 82; HLC 1; HW 1, 2; MTCW 2
Hinojosa-Smith, Rolando 1929-
See Hinojosa(-Smith), Rolando (R.)
See also CAAS 16; HLC 1; MTCW 2
Hinton, S(usan) E(loise) 1950- **CLC 30, 111; DA; DAB; DAC; DAM MST, NOV**
See also AAYA 2; CA 81-84; CANR 32, 62; CDALBS; CLR 3, 23; JRDA; MAICYA; MTCW 1, 2; SATA 19, 58
Hippius, Zinaida .... **TCLC 9**
See also Gippius, Zinaida (Nikolayevna)
Hiraoka, Kimitake 1925-1970
See Mishima, Yukio
See also CA 97-100; 29-32R; DAM DRAM; MTCW 1, 2
Hirsch, E(ric) D(onald), Jr. 1928- .... **CLC 79**
See also CA 25-28R; CANR 27, 51; DLB 67; INT CANR-27; MTCW 1
Hirsch, Edward 1950- .... **CLC 31, 50**
See also CA 104; CANR 20, 42; DLB 120
Hitchcock, Alfred (Joseph) 1899-1980 **CLC 16**
See also AAYA 22; CA 159; 97-100; SATA 27; SATA-Obit 24
Hitler, Adolf 1889-1945 .... **TCLC 53**
See also CA 117; 147
Hoagland, Edward 1932- .... **CLC 28**
See also CA 1-4R; CANR 2, 31, 57; DLB 6; SATA 51
Hoban, Russell (Conwell) 1925- . **CLC 7, 25; DAM NOV**
See also CA 5-8R; CANR 23, 37, 66; CLR 3; DLB 52; MAICYA; MTCW 1, 2; SATA 1, 40, 78
Hobbes, Thomas 1588-1679 .... **LC 36**
See also DLB 151
Hobbs, Perry
See Blackmur, R(ichard) P(almer)
Hobson, Laura Z(ametkin) 1900-1986 **CLC 7, 25**
See also CA 17-20R; 118; CANR 55; DLB 28; SATA 52
Hochhuth, Rolf 1931- .. **CLC 4, 11, 18; DAM DRAM**
See also CA 5-8R; CANR 33, 75; DLB 124; MTCW 1, 2
Hochman, Sandra 1936- .... **CLC 3, 8**
See also CA 5-8R; DLB 5
Hochwaelder, Fritz 1911-1986 **CLC 36; DAM DRAM**
See also CA 29-32R; 120; CANR 42; MTCW 1
Hochwalder, Fritz
See Hochwaelder, Fritz
Hocking, Mary (Eunice) 1921- .... **CLC 13**
See also CA 101; CANR 18, 40
Hodgins, Jack 1938- .... **CLC 23**
See also CA 93-96; DLB 60
Hodgson, William Hope 1877(?)-1918 **TCLC 13**
See also CA 111; 164; DLB 70, 153, 156, 178; MTCW 2
Hoeg, Peter 1957- .... **CLC 95**
See also CA 151; CANR 75; MTCW 2
Hoffman, Alice 1952- ... **CLC 51; DAM NOV**
See also CA 77-80; CANR 34, 66; MTCW 1, 2
Hoffman, Daniel (Gerard) 1923- **CLC 6, 13, 23**
See also CA 1-4R; CANR 4; DLB 5
Hoffman, Stanley 1944- .... **CLC 5**
See also CA 77-80
Hoffman, William M(oses) 1939- ...... **CLC 40**

See also CA 57-60; CANR 11, 71
Hoffmann, E(rnst) T(heodor) A(madeus) 1776-1822 .... **NCLC 2; SSC 13**
See also DLB 90; SATA 27
Hofmann, Gert 1931- .... **CLC 54**
See also CA 128
Hofmannsthal, Hugo von 1874-1929 **TCLC 11; DAM DRAM; DC 4**
See also CA 106; 153; DLB 81, 118
Hogan, Linda 1947- ... **CLC 73; DAM MULT**
See also CA 120; CANR 45, 73; DLB 175; NNAL
Hogarth, Charles
See Creasey, John
Hogarth, Emmett
See Polonsky, Abraham (Lincoln)
Hogg, James 1770-1835 .... **NCLC 4**
See also DLB 93, 116, 159
Holbach, Paul Henri Thiry Baron 1723-1789 **LC 14**
Holberg, Ludvig 1684-1754 .... **LC 6**
Holden, Ursula 1921- .... **CLC 18**
See also CA 101; CAAS 8; CANR 22
Holderlin, (Johann Christian) Friedrich 1770-1843 .... **NCLC 16; PC 4**
Holdstock, Robert
See Holdstock, Robert P.
Holdstock, Robert P. 1948- .... **CLC 39**
See also CA 131; CANR 81
Holland, Isabelle 1920- .... **CLC 21**
See also AAYA 11; CA 21-24R; CANR 10, 25, 47; CLR 57; JRDA; MAICYA; SATA 8, 70; SATA-Essay 103
Holland, Marcus
See Caldwell, (Janet Miriam) Taylor (Holland)
Hollander, John 1929- .... **CLC 2, 5, 8, 14**
See also CA 1-4R; CANR 1, 52; DLB 5; SATA 13
Hollander, Paul
See Silverberg, Robert
Holleran, Andrew 1943(?)- .... **CLC 38**
See also CA 144
Hollinghurst, Alan 1954- .... **CLC 55, 91**
See also CA 114; DLB 207
Hollis, Jim
See Summers, Hollis (Spurgeon, Jr.)
Holly, Buddy 1936-1959 .... **TCLC 65**
Holmes, Gordon
See Shiel, M(atthew) P(hipps)
Holmes, John
See Souster, (Holmes) Raymond
Holmes, John Clellon 1926-1988 ...... **CLC 56**
See also CA 9-12R; 125; CANR 4; DLB 16
Holmes, Oliver Wendell, Jr. 1841-1935 **TCLC 77**
See also CA 114
Holmes, Oliver Wendell 1809-1894 **NCLC 14**
See also CDALB 1640-1865; DLB 1, 189; SATA 34
Holmes, Raymond
See Souster, (Holmes) Raymond
Holt, Victoria
See Hibbert, Eleanor Alice Burford
Holub, Miroslav 1923-1998 .... **CLC 4**
See also CA 21-24R; 169; CANR 10
Homer c. 8th cent. B.C.- ... **CMLC 1, 16; DA; DAB; DAC; DAM MST, POET; PC 23; WLCS**
See also DLB 176
Hongo, Garrett Kaoru 1951- .... **PC 23**
See also CA 133; CAAS 22; DLB 120
Honig, Edwin 1919- .... **CLC 33**
See also CA 5-8R; CAAS 8; CANR 4, 45; DLB

5
Hood, Hugh (John Blagdon) 1928- **CLC 15, 28**
See also CA 49-52; CAAS 17; CANR 1, 33; DLB 53
Hood, Thomas 1799-1845 .... **NCLC 16**
See also DLB 96
Hooker, (Peter) Jeremy 1941- .... **CLC 43**
See also CA 77-80; CANR 22; DLB 40
hooks, bell .... **CLC 94; BLCS**
See also Watkins, Gloria
See also MTCW 2
Hope, A(lec) D(erwent) 1907- .... **CLC 3, 51**
See also CA 21-24R; CANR 33, 74; MTCW 1, 2
Hope, Anthony 1863-1933 .... **TCLC 83**
See also CA 157; DLB 153, 156
Hope, Brian
See Creasey, John
Hope, Christopher (David Tully) 1944- **C L C 52**
See also CA 106; CANR 47; SATA 62
Hopkins, Gerard Manley 1844-1889 .. **N C L C 17; DA; DAB; DAC; DAM MST, POET; PC 15; WLC**
See also CDBLB 1890-1914; DLB 35, 57
Hopkins, John (Richard) 1931-1998 .. **CLC 4**
See also CA 85-88; 169
Hopkins, Pauline Elizabeth 1859-1930 **T C L C 28; BLC 2; DAM MULT**
See also BW 2, 3; CA 141; CANR 82; DLB 50
Hopkinson, Francis 1737-1791 .... **LC 25**
See also DLB 31
Hopley-Woolrich, Cornell George 1903-1968
See Woolrich, Cornell
See also CA 13-14; CANR 58; CAP 1; MTCW 2
Horatio
See Proust, (Valentin-Louis-George-Eugene-) Marcel
Horgan, Paul (George Vincent O'Shaughnessy) 1903-1995 .... **CLC 9, 53; DAM NOV**
See also CA 13-16R; 147; CANR 9, 35; DLB 212; DLBY 85; INT CANR-9; MTCW 1, 2; SATA 13; SATA-Obit 84
Horn, Peter
See Kuttner, Henry
Hornem, Horace Esq.
See Byron, George Gordon (Noel)
Horney, Karen (Clementine Theodore Danielsen) 1885-1952 .... **TCLC 71**
See also CA 114; 165
Hornung, E(rnest) W(illiam) 1866-1921 **TCLC 59**
See also CA 108; 160; DLB 70
Horovitz, Israel (Arthur) 1939- **CLC 56; DAM DRAM**
See also CA 33-36R; CANR 46, 59; DLB 7
Horvath, Odon von
See Horvath, Oedoen von
See also DLB 85, 124
Horvath, Oedoen von 1901-1938 ... **TCLC 45**
See also Horvath, Odon von
See also CA 118
Horwitz, Julius 1920-1986 .... **CLC 14**
See also CA 9-12R; 119; CANR 12
Hospital, Janette Turner 1942- .... **CLC 42**
See also CA 108; CANR 48
Hostos, E. M. de
See Hostos (y Bonilla), Eugenio Maria de
Hostos, Eugenio M. de
See Hostos (y Bonilla), Eugenio Maria de
Hostos, Eugenio Maria
See Hostos (y Bonilla), Eugenio Maria de

Jensen, Laura (Linnea) 1948- .... **CLC 37**
See also CA 103

Jerome, Jerome K(lapka) 1859-1927**TCLC 23**
See also CA 119; 177; DLB 10, 34, 135

Jerrold, Douglas William 1803-1857**NCLC 2**
See also DLB 158, 159

Jewett, (Theodora) Sarah Orne 1849-1909
TCLC 1, 22; SSC 6
See also CA 108; 127; CANR 71; DLB 12, 74;
SATA 15

Jewsbury, Geraldine (Endsor) 1812-1880
NCLC 22
See also DLB 21

Jhabvala, Ruth Prawer 1927-**CLC 4, 8, 29, 94;**
DAB; DAM NOV
See also CA 1-4R; CANR 2, 29, 51, 74; DLB
139, 194; INT CANR-29; MTCW 1, 2

Jibran, Kahlil
See Gibran, Kahlil

Jibran, Khalil
See Gibran, Kahlil

Jiles, Paulette 1943- .... **CLC 13, 58**
See also CA 101; CANR 70

Jimenez (Mantecon), Juan Ramon 1881-1958
TCLC 4; DAM MULT, POET; HLC 1; PC
7
See also CA 104; 131; CANR 74; DLB 134;
HW 1; MTCW 1, 2

Jimenez, Ramon
See Jimenez (Mantecon), Juan Ramon

Jimenez Mantecon, Juan
See Jimenez (Mantecon), Juan Ramon

Jin, Ha 1956- .... **CLC 109**
See also CA 152

Joel, Billy .... **CLC 26**
See also Joel, William Martin

Joel, William Martin 1949-
See Joel, Billy
See also CA 108

John, Saint 7th cent. - .... **CMLC 27**

John of the Cross, St. 1542-1591 .... **LC 18**

Johnson, B(ryan) S(tanley William) 1933-1973
CLC 6, 9
See also CA 9-12R; 53-56; CANR 9; DLB 14,
40

Johnson, Benj. F. of Boo
See Riley, James Whitcomb

Johnson, Benjamin F. of Boo
See Riley, James Whitcomb

Johnson, Charles (Richard) 1948-**CLC 7, 51,**
65; BLC 2; DAM MULT
See also BW 2, 3; CA 116; CAAS 18; CANR
42, 66, 82; DLB 33; MTCW 2

Johnson, Denis 1949- .... **CLC 52**
See also CA 117; 121; CANR 71; DLB 120

Johnson, Diane 1934- .... **CLC 5, 13, 48**
See also CA 41-44R; CANR 17, 40, 62; DLBY
80; INT CANR-17; MTCW 1

Johnson, Eyvind (Olof Verner) 1900-1976
CLC 14
See also CA 73-76; 69-72; CANR 34

Johnson, J. R.
See James, C(yril) L(ionel) R(obert)

Johnson, James Weldon 1871-1938 **TCLC 3,**
19; BLC 2; DAM MULT, POET; PC 24
See also BW 1, 3; CA 104; 125; CANR 82;
CDALB 1917-1929; CLR 32; DLB 51;
MTCW 1, 2; SATA 31

Johnson, Joyce 1935- .... **CLC 58**
See also CA 125; 129

Johnson, Judith (Emlyn) 1936- ..... **CLC 7, 15**
See also CA 25-28R, 153; CANR 34

Johnson, Lionel (Pigot) 1867-1902 **TCLC 19**
See also CA 117; DLB 19

Johnson, Marguerite (Annie)
See Angelou, Maya

Johnson, Mel
See Malzberg, Barry N(athaniel)

Johnson, Pamela Hansford 1912-1981**CLC 1,**
7, 27
See also CA 1-4R; 104; CANR 2, 28; DLB 15;
MTCW 1, 2

Johnson, Robert 1911(?)-1938 .... **TCLC 69**
See also BW 3; CA 174

Johnson, Samuel 1709-1784 . **LC 15, 52; DA;**
DAB; DAC; DAM MST; WLC
See also CDBLB 1660-1789; DLB 39, 95, 104,
142

Johnson, Uwe 1934-1984 .. **CLC 5, 10, 15, 40**
See also CA 1-4R; 112; CANR 1, 39; DLB 75;
MTCW 1

Johnston, George (Benson) 1913- ..... **CLC 51**
See also CA 1-4R; CANR 5, 20; DLB 88

Johnston, Jennifer 1930- .... **CLC 7**
See also CA 85-88; DLB 14

Jolley, (Monica) Elizabeth 1923-**CLC 46; SSC**
19
See also CA 127; CAAS 13; CANR 59

Jones, Arthur Llewellyn 1863-1947
See Machen, Arthur
See also CA 104; 179

Jones, D(ouglas) G(ordon) 1929- ...... **CLC 10**
See also CA 29-32R; CANR 13; DLB 53

Jones, David (Michael) 1895-1974**CLC 2, 4, 7,**
13, 42
See also CA 9-12R; 53-56; CANR 28; CDBLB
1945-1960; DLB 20, 100; MTCW 1

Jones, David Robert 1947-
See Bowie, David
See also CA 103

Jones, Diana Wynne 1934- .... **CLC 26**
See also AAYA 12; CA 49-52; CANR 4, 26,
56; CLR 23; DLB 161; JRDA; MAICYA;
SAAS 7; SATA 9, 70, 108

Jones, Edward P. 1950- .... **CLC 76**
See also BW 2, 3; CA 142; CANR 79

Jones, Gayl 1949- .... **CLC 6, 9; BLC 2; DAM**
MULT
See also BW 2, 3; CA 77-80; CANR 27, 66;
DLB 33; MTCW 1, 2

Jones, James 1921-1977 ...... **CLC 1, 3, 10, 39**
See also AITN 1, 2; CA 1-4R; 69-72; CANR 6;
DLB 2, 143; DLBD 17; DLBY 98; MTCW 1

Jones, John J.
See Lovecraft, H(oward) P(hillips)

Jones, LeRoi .... **CLC 1, 2, 3, 5, 10, 14**
See also Baraka, Amiri
See also MTCW 2

Jones, Louis B. 1953- .... **CLC 65**
See also CA 141; CANR 73

Jones, Madison (Percy, Jr.) 1925- .... **CLC 4**
See also CA 13-16R; CAAS 11; CANR 7, 54;
DLB 152

Jones, Mervyn 1922- .... **CLC 10, 52**
See also CA 45-48; CAAS 5; CANR 1; MTCW
1

Jones, Mick 1956(?)- .... **CLC 30**

Jones, Nettie (Pearl) 1941- .... **CLC 34**
See also BW 2; CA 137; CAAS 20

Jones, Preston 1936-1979 .... **CLC 10**
See also CA 73-76; 89-92; DLB 7

Jones, Robert F(rancis) 1934- .... **CLC 7**
See also CA 49-52; CANR 2, 61

Jones, Rod 1953- .... **CLC 50**
See also CA 128

Jones, Terence Graham Parry 1942- **CLC 21**
See also Jones, Terry; Monty Python
See also CA 112; 116; CANR 35; INT 116

Jones, Terry
See Jones, Terence Graham Parry
See also SATA 67; SATA-Brief 51

Jones, Thom 1945(?)- .... **CLC 81**
See also CA 157

Jong, Erica 1942- . **CLC 4, 6, 8, 18, 83; DAM**
NOV, POP
See also AITN 1; BEST 90:2; CA 73-76; CANR
26, 52, 75; DLB 2, 5, 28, 152; INT CANR-
26; MTCW 1, 2

Jonson, Ben(jamin) 1572(?)-1637 .. **LC 6, 33;**
DA; DAB; DAC; DAM DRAM, MST,
POET; DC 4; PC 17; WLC
See also CDBLB Before 1660; DLB 62, 121

Jordan, June 1936-**CLC 5, 11, 23, 114; BLCS;**
DAM MULT, POET
See also AAYA 2; BW 2, 3; CA 33-36R; CANR
25, 70; CLR 10; DLB 38; MAICYA; MTCW
1; SATA 4

Jordan, Neil (Patrick) 1950- .... **CLC 110**
See also CA 124; 130; CANR 54; INT 130

Jordan, Pat(rick M.) 1941- .... **CLC 37**
See also CA 33-36R

Jorgensen, Ivar
See Ellison, Harlan (Jay)

Jorgenson, Ivar
See Silverberg, Robert

Josephus, Flavius c. 37-100 .... **CMLC 13**

Josipovici, Gabriel 1940- .... **CLC 6, 43**
See also CA 37-40R; CAAS 8; CANR 47; DLB
14

Joubert, Joseph 1754-1824 .... **NCLC 9**

Jouve, Pierre Jean 1887-1976 .... **CLC 47**
See also CA 65-68

Jovine, Francesco 1902-1950 .... **TCLC 79**

Joyce, James (Augustine Aloysius) 1882-1941
TCLC 3, 8, 16, 35, 52; DA; DAB; DAC;
DAM MST, NOV, POET; PC 22; SSC 3,
26; WLC
See also CA 104; 126; CDBLB 1914-1945;
DLB 10, 19, 36, 162; MTCW 1, 2

Jozsef, Attila 1905-1937 .... **TCLC 22**
See also CA 116

Juana Ines de la Cruz 1651(?)-1695 .... **LC 5;**
HLCS 1; PC 24

Judd, Cyril
See Kornbluth, C(yril) M.; Pohl, Frederik

Julian of Norwich 1342(?)-1416(?) . **LC 6, 52**
See also DLB 146

Junger, Sebastian 1962- .... **CLC 109**
See also AAYA 28; CA 165

Juniper, Alex
See Hospital, Janette Turner

Junius
See Luxemburg, Rosa

Just, Ward (Swift) 1935- ....**CLC 4, 27**
See also CA 25-28R; CANR 32; INT CANR-
32

Justice, Donald (Rodney) 1925- .. **CLC 6, 19,**
102; DAM POET
See also CA 5-8R; CANR 26, 54, 74; DLBY
83; INT CANR-26; MTCW 2

Juvenal c. 60-c. 13 .... **CMLC 8**
See also Juvenalis, Decimus Junius
See also DLB 211

Juvenalis, Decimus Junius 55(?)-c. 127(?)
See Juvenal

Juvenis
See Bourne, Randolph S(illiman)

Kacew, Romain 1914-1980
See Gary, Romain

Lampman, Archibald 1861-1899 ... **NCLC 25**
See also DLB 92

Lancaster, Bruce 1896-1963 .... **CLC 36**
See also CA 9-10; CANR 70; CAP 1; SATA 9

Lanchester, John .... **CLC 99**

Landau, Mark Alexandrovich
See Aldanov, Mark (Alexandrovich)

Landau-Aldanov, Mark Alexandrovich
See Aldanov, Mark (Alexandrovich)

Landis, Jerry
See Simon, Paul (Frederick)

Landis, John 1950- .... **CLC 26**
See also CA 112; 122

Landolfi, Tommaso 1908-1979 .... **CLC 11, 49**
See also CA 127; 117; DLB 177

Landon, Letitia Elizabeth 1802-1838 **N C L C 15**
See also DLB 96

Landor, Walter Savage 1775-1864 **NCLC 14**
See also DLB 93, 107

Landwirth, Heinz 1927-
See Lind, Jakov
See also CA 9-12R; CANR 7

Lane, Patrick 1939- ... **CLC 25; DAM POET**
See also CA 97-100; CANR 54; DLB 53; INT 97-100

Lang, Andrew 1844-1912 .... **TCLC 16**
See also CA 114; 137; DLB 98, 141, 184; MAICYA; SATA 16

Lang, Fritz 1890-1976 .... **CLC 20, 103**
See also CA 77-80; 69-72; CANR 30

Lange, John
See Crichton, (John) Michael

Langer, Elinor 1939- .... **CLC 34**
See also CA 121

Langland, William 1330(?)-1400(?) ... **LC 19; DA; DAB; DAC; DAM MST, POET**
See also DLB 146

Langstaff, Launcelot
See Irving, Washington

Lanier, Sidney 1842-1881 ..... **NCLC 6; DAM POET**
See also DLB 64; DLBD 13; MAICYA; SATA 18

Lanyer, Aemilia 1569-1645 .... **LC 10, 30**
See also DLB 121

Lao-Tzu
See Lao Tzu

Lao Tzu fl. 6th cent. B.C.- .... **CMLC 7**

Lapine, James (Elliot) 1949- .... **CLC 39**
See also CA 123; 130; CANR 54; INT 130

Larbaud, Valery (Nicolas) 1881-1957 **TCLC 9**
See also CA 106; 152

Lardner, Ring
See Lardner, Ring(gold) W(ilmer)

Lardner, Ring W., Jr.
See Lardner, Ring(gold) W(ilmer)

Lardner, Ring(gold) W(ilmer) 1885-1933 **TCLC 2, 14; SSC 32**
See also CA 104; 131; CDALB 1917-1929; DLB 11, 25, 86; DLBD 16; MTCW 1, 2

Laredo, Betty
See Codrescu, Andrei

Larkin, Maia
See Wojciechowska, Maia (Teresa)

Larkin, Philip (Arthur) 1922-1985 **CLC 3, 5, 8, 9, 13, 18, 33, 39, 64; DAB; DAM MST, POET; PC 21**
See also CA 5-8R; 117; CANR 24, 62; CDBLB 1960 to Present; DLB 27; MTCW 1, 2

Larra (y Sanchez de Castro), Mariano Jose de 1809-1837 .... **NCLC 17**

Larsen, Eric 1941- .... **CLC 55**

See also CA 132

Larsen, Nella 1891-1964 .... **CLC 37; BLC 2; DAM MULT**
See also BW 1; CA 125; DLB 51

Larson, Charles R(aymond) 1938- ... **CLC 31**
See also CA 53-56; CANR 4

Larson, Jonathan 1961-1996 .... **CLC 99**
See also AAYA 28; CA 156

Las Casas, Bartolome de 1474-1566 ... **LC 31**

Lasch, Christopher 1932-1994 .... **CLC 102**
See also CA 73-76; 144; CANR 25; MTCW 1, 2

Lasker-Schueler, Else 1869-1945 ... **TCLC 57**
See also DLB 66, 124

Laski, Harold 1893-1950 .... **TCLC 79**

Latham, Jean Lee 1902-1995 .... **CLC 12**
See also AITN 1; CA 5-8R; CANR 7; CLR 50; MAICYA; SATA 2, 68

Latham, Mavis
See Clark, Mavis Thorpe

Lathen, Emma .... **CLC 2**
See also Hennissart, Martha; Latsis, Mary J(ane)

Lathrop, Francis
See Leiber, Fritz (Reuter, Jr.)

Latsis, Mary J(ane) 1927(?)-1997
See Lathen, Emma
See also CA 85-88; 162

Lattimore, Richmond (Alexander) 1906-1984 **CLC 3**
See also CA 1-4R; 112; CANR 1

Laughlin, James 1914-1997 .... **CLC 49**
See also CA 21-24R; 162; CAAS 22; CANR 9, 47; DLB 48; DLBY 96, 97

Laurence, (Jean) Margaret (Wemyss) 1926-1987 .. **CLC 3, 6, 13, 50, 62; DAC; DAM MST; SSC 7**
See also CA 5-8R; 121; CANR 33; DLB 53; MTCW 1, 2; SATA-Obit 50

Laurent, Antoine 1952- .... **CLC 50**

Lauscher, Hermann
See Hesse, Hermann

Lautreamont, Comte de 1846-1870 **NCLC 12; SSC 14**

Laverty, Donald
See Blish, James (Benjamin)

Lavin, Mary 1912-1996 **CLC 4, 18, 99; SSC 4**
See also CA 9-12R; 151; CANR 33; DLB 15; MTCW 1

Lavond, Paul Dennis
See Kornbluth, C(yril) M.; Pohl, Frederik

Lawler, Raymond Evenor 1922- .... **CLC 58**
See also CA 103

Lawrence, D(avid) H(erbert Richards) 1885-1930 . **TCLC 2, 9, 16, 33, 48, 61, 93; DA; DAB; DAC; DAM MST, NOV, POET; SSC 4, 19; WLC**
See also CA 104; 121; CDBLB 1914-1945; DLB 10, 19, 36, 98, 162, 195; MTCW 1, 2

Lawrence, T(homas) E(dward) 1888-1935 **TCLC 18**
See also Dale, Colin
See also CA 115; 167; DLB 195

Lawrence of Arabia
See Lawrence, T(homas) E(dward)

Lawson, Henry (Archibald Hertzberg) 1867-1922 .... **TCLC 27; SSC 18**
See also CA 120

Lawton, Dennis
See Faust, Frederick (Schiller)

Laxness, Halldor .... **CLC 25**
See also Gudjonsson, Halldor Kiljan

Layamon fl. c. 1200- .... **CMLC 10**
See also DLB 146

Laye, Camara 1928-1980 **CLC 4, 38; BLC 2; DAM MULT**
See also BW 1; CA 85-88; 97-100; CANR 25; MTCW 1, 2

Layton, Irving (Peter) 1912- **CLC 2, 15; DAC; DAM MST, POET**
See also CA 1-4R; CANR 2, 33, 43, 66; DLB 88; MTCW 1, 2

Lazarus, Emma 1849-1887 .... **NCLC 8**

Lazarus, Felix
See Cable, George Washington

Lazarus, Henry
See Slavitt, David R(ytman)

Lea, Joan
See Neufeld, John (Arthur)

Leacock, Stephen (Butler) 1869-1944 **TCLC 2; DAC; DAM MST**
See also CA 104; 141; CANR 80; DLB 92; MTCW 2

Lear, Edward 1812-1888 .... **NCLC 3**
See also CLR 1; DLB 32, 163, 166; MAICYA; SATA 18, 100

Lear, Norman (Milton) 1922- .... **CLC 12**
See also CA 73-76

Leautaud, Paul 1872-1956 .... **TCLC 83**
See also DLB 65

Leavis, F(rank) R(aymond) 1895-1978 **CLC 24**
See also CA 21-24R; 77-80; CANR 44; MTCW 1, 2

Leavitt, David 1961- ..... **CLC 34; DAM POP**
See also CA 116; 122; CANR 50, 62; DLB 130; INT 122; MTCW 2

Leblanc, Maurice (Marie Emile) 1864-1941 **TCLC 49**
See also CA 110

Lebowitz, Fran(ces Ann) 1951(?)- **CLC 11, 36**
See also CA 81-84; CANR 14, 60, 70; INT CANR-14; MTCW 1

Lebrecht, Peter
See Tieck, (Johann) Ludwig

le Carre, John .... **CLC 3, 5, 9, 15, 28**
See also Cornwell, David (John Moore)
See also BEST 89:4; CDBLB 1960 to Present; DLB 87; MTCW 2

Le Clezio, J(ean) M(arie) G(ustave) 1940- **CLC 31**
See also CA 116; 128; DLB 83

Leconte de Lisle, Charles-Marie-Rene 1818-1894 .... **NCLC 29**

Le Coq, Monsieur
See Simenon, Georges (Jacques Christian)

Leduc, Violette 1907-1972 .... **CLC 22**
See also CA 13-14; 33-36R; CANR 69; CAP 1

Ledwidge, Francis 1887(?)-1917 .... **TCLC 23**
See also CA 123; DLB 20

Lee, Andrea 1953- .... **CLC 36; BLC 2; DAM MULT**
See also BW 1, 3; CA 125; CANR 82

Lee, Andrew
See Auchincloss, Louis (Stanton)

Lee, Chang-rae 1965- .... **CLC 91**
See also CA 148

Lee, Don L. .... **CLC 2**
See also Madhubuti, Haki R.

Lee, George W(ashington) 1894-1976 **CLC 52; BLC 2; DAM MULT**
See also BW 1; CA 125; DLB 51

Lee, (Nelle) Harper 1926- .. **CLC 12, 60; DA; DAB; DAC; DAM MST, NOV; WLC**
See also AAYA 13; CA 13-16R; CANR 51; CDALB 1941-1968; DLB 6; MTCW 1, 2; SATA 11

Lee, Helen Elaine 1959(?)- .... **CLC 86**

DLB 9, 102; DLBD 1; MTCW 1, 2

Lewis, (Percy) Wyndham 1882(?)-1957 **TCLC 2, 9; SSC 34**
See also CA 104; 157; DLB 15; MTCW 2

Lewisohn, Ludwig 1883-1955 .... **TCLC 19**
See also CA 107; DLB 4, 9, 28, 102

Lewton, Val 1904-1951 .... **TCLC 76**

Leyner, Mark 1956- .... **CLC 92**
See also CA 110; CANR 28, 53; MTCW 2

Lezama Lima, Jose 1910-1976**CLC 4, 10, 101; DAM MULT; HLCS 2**
See also CA 77-80; CANR 71; DLB 113; HW 1, 2

L'Heureux, John (Clarke) 1934- .... **CLC 52**
See also CA 13-16R; CANR 23, 45

Liddell, C. H.
See Kuttner, Henry

Lie, Jonas (Lauritz Idemil) 1833-1908(?)
TCLC 5
See also CA 115

Lieber, Joel 1937-1971 .... **CLC 6**
See also CA 73-76; 29-32R

Lieber, Stanley Martin
See Lee, Stan

Lieberman, Laurence (James) 1935- **CLC 4, 36**
See also CA 17-20R; CANR 8, 36

Lieh Tzu fl. 7th cent. B.C.-5th cent. B.C.
CMLC 27

Lieksman, Anders
See Haavikko, Paavo Juhani

Li Fei-kan 1904-
See Pa Chin
See also CA 105

Lifton, Robert Jay 1926- .... **CLC 67**
See also CA 17-20R; CANR 27, 78; INT CANR-27; SATA 66

Lightfoot, Gordon 1938- .... **CLC 26**
See also CA 109

Lightman, Alan P(aige) 1948- .... **CLC 81**
See also CA 141; CANR 63

Ligotti, Thomas (Robert) 1953-**CLC 44; SSC 16**
See also CA 123; CANR 49

Li Ho 791-817 .... **PC 13**

Liliencron, (Friedrich Adolf Axel) Detlev von 1844-1909 .... **TCLC 18**
See also CA 117

Lilly, William 1602-1681 .... **LC 27**

Lima, Jose Lezama
See Lezama Lima, Jose

Lima Barreto, Afonso Henrique de 1881-1922
TCLC 23
See also CA 117

Limonov, Edward 1944- .... **CLC 67**
See also CA 137

Lin, Frank
See Atherton, Gertrude (Franklin Horn)

Lincoln, Abraham 1809-1865 .... **NCLC 18**

Lind, Jakov .... **CLC 1, 2, 4, 27, 82**
See Landwirth, Heinz
See also CAAS 4

Lindbergh, Anne (Spencer) Morrow 1906-
CLC 82; DAM NOV
See also CA 17-20R; CANR 16, 73; MTCW 1, 2; SATA 33

Lindsay, David 1878-1945 .... **TCLC 15**
See also CA 113

Lindsay, (Nicholas) Vachel 1879-1931 **TCLC 17; DA; DAC; DAM MST, POET; PC 23; WLC**
See also CA 114; 135; CANR 79; CDALB 1865-1917; DLB 54; SATA 40

Linke-Poot
See Doeblin, Alfred

Linney, Romulus 1930- .... **CLC 51**
See also CA 1-4R; CANR 40, 44, 79

Linton, Eliza Lynn 1822-1898 .... **NCLC 41**
See also DLB 18

Li Po 701-763 .... **CMLC 2**

Lipsius, Justus 1547-1606 .... **LC 16**

Lipsyte, Robert (Michael) 1938-**CLC 21; DA; DAC; DAM MST, NOV**
See also AAYA 7; CA 17-20R; CANR 8, 57; CLR 23; JRDA; MAICYA; SATA 5, 68

Lish, Gordon (Jay) 1934- ... **CLC 45; SSC 18**
See also CA 113; 117; CANR 79; DLB 130; INT 117

Lispector, Clarice 1925(?)-1977 ...... **CLC 43; HLCS 2; SSC 34**
See also CA 139; 116; CANR 71; DLB 113; HW 2

Littell, Robert 1935(?)- .... **CLC 42**
See also CA 109; 112; CANR 64

Little, Malcolm 1925-1965
See Malcolm X
See also BW 1, 3; CA 125; 111; CANR 82; DA; DAB; DAC; DAM MST, MULT; MTCW 1, 2

Littlewit, Humphrey Gent.
See Lovecraft, H(oward) P(hillips)

Litwos
See Sienkiewicz, Henryk (Adam Alexander Pius)

Liu, E 1857-1909 .... **TCLC 15**
See also CA 115

Lively, Penelope (Margaret) 1933- ..**CLC 32, 50; DAM NOV**
See also CA 41-44R; CANR 29, 67, 79; CLR 7; DLB 14, 161, 207; JRDA; MAICYA; MTCW 1, 2; SATA 7, 60, 101

Livesay, Dorothy (Kathleen) 1909-**CLC 4, 15, 79; DAC; DAM MST, POET**
See also AITN 2; CA 25-28R; CAAS 8; CANR 36, 67; DLB 68; MTCW 1

Livy c. 59B.C.-c. 17 .... **CMLC 11**
See also DLB 211

Lizardi, Jose Joaquin Fernandez de 1776-1827
NCLC 30

Llewellyn, Richard
See Llewellyn Lloyd, Richard Dafydd Vivian
See also DLB 15

Llewellyn Lloyd, Richard Dafydd Vivian 1906-1983 .... **CLC 7, 80**
See also Llewellyn, Richard
See also CA 53-56; 111; CANR 7, 71; SATA 11; SATA-Obit 37

Llosa, (Jorge) Mario (Pedro) Vargas
See Vargas Llosa, (Jorge) Mario (Pedro)

Lloyd, Manda
See Mander, (Mary) Jane

Lloyd Webber, Andrew 1948-
See Webber, Andrew Lloyd
See also AAYA 1; CA 116; 149; DAM DRAM; SATA 56

Llull, Ramon c. 1235-c. 1316 .... **CMLC 12**

Lobb, Ebenezer
See Upward, Allen

Locke, Alain (Le Roy) 1886-1954 . **TCLC 43; BLCS**
See also BW 1, 3; CA 106; 124; CANR 79; DLB 51

Locke, John 1632-1704 .... **LC 7, 35**
See also DLB 101

Locke-Elliott, Sumner
See Elliott, Sumner Locke

Lockhart, John Gibson 1794-1854 .. **NCLC 6**
See also DLB 110, 116, 144

Lodge, David (John) 1935- .... **CLC 36; DAM POP**
See also BEST 90:1; CA 17-20R; CANR 19, 53; DLB 14, 194; INT CANR-19; MTCW 1, 2

Lodge, Thomas 1558-1625 .... **LC 41**

Lodge, Thomas 1558-1625 .... **LC 41**
See also DLB 172

Loennbohm, Armas Eino Leopold 1878-1926
See Leino, Eino
See also CA 123

Loewinsohn, Ron(ald William) 1937-**CLC 52**
See also CA 25-28R; CANR 71

Logan, Jake
See Smith, Martin Cruz

Logan, John (Burton) 1923-1987 .... **CLC 5**
See also CA 77-80; 124; CANR 45; DLB 5

Lo Kuan-chung 1330(?)-1400(?) .... **LC 12**

Lombard, Nap
See Johnson, Pamela Hansford

London, Jack . **TCLC 9, 15, 39; SSC 4; WLC**
See also London, John Griffith
See also AAYA 13; AITN 2; CDALB 1865-1917; DLB 8, 12, 78, 212; SATA 18

London, John Griffith 1876-1916
See London, Jack
See also CA 110; 119; CANR 73; DA; DAB; DAC; DAM MST, NOV; JRDA; MAICYA; MTCW 1, 2

Long, Emmett
See Leonard, Elmore (John, Jr.)

Longbaugh, Harry
See Goldman, William (W.)

Longfellow, Henry Wadsworth 1807-1882
NCLC 2, 45; DA; DAB; DAC; DAM MST, POET; WLCS
See also CDALB 1640-1865; DLB 1, 59; SATA 19

Longinus c. 1st cent. - .... **CMLC 27**
See also DLB 176

Longley, Michael 1939- .... **CLC 29**
See also CA 102; DLB 40

Longus fl. c. 2nd cent. - .... **CMLC 7**

Longway, A. Hugh
See Lang, Andrew

Lonnrot, Elias 1802-1884 .... **NCLC 53**

Lopate, Phillip 1943- .... **CLC 29**
See also CA 97-100; DLBY 80; INT 97-100

Lopez Portillo (y Pacheco), Jose 1920- . **CLC 46**
See also CA 129; HW 1

Lopez y Fuentes, Gregorio 1897(?)-1966**CLC 32**
See also CA 131; HW 1

Lorca, Federico Garcia
See Garcia Lorca, Federico

Lord, Bette Bao 1938- .... **CLC 23**
See also BEST 90:3; CA 107; CANR 41, 79; INT 107; SATA 58

Lord Auch
See Bataille, Georges

Lord Byron
See Byron, George Gordon (Noel)

Lorde, Audre (Geraldine) 1934-1992**CLC 18, 71; BLC 2; DAM MULT, POET; PC 12**
See also BW 1, 3; CA 25-28R; 142; CANR 16, 26, 46, 82; DLB 41; MTCW 1, 2

Lord Houghton
See Milnes, Richard Monckton

Lord Jeffrey
See Jeffrey, Francis

Melies, Georges 1861-1938 .... **TCLC 81**
Melikow, Loris
    See Hofmannsthal, Hugo von
Melmoth, Sebastian
    See Wilde, Oscar
Meltzer, Milton 1915- .... **CLC 26**
    See also AAYA 8; CA 13-16R; CANR 38; CLR
        13; DLB 61; JRDA; MAICYA; SAAS 1;
        SATA 1, 50, 80
Melville, Herman 1819-1891**NCLC 3, 12, 29,
    45, 49; DA; DAB; DAC; DAM MST, NOV;
    SSC 1, 17; WLC**
    See also AAYA 25; CDALB 1640-1865; DLB
        3, 74; SATA 59
Menander c. 342B.C.-c. 292B.C. .... **CMLC 9;
    DAM DRAM; DC 3**
    See also DLB 176
Menchu, Rigoberta 1959-
    See also HLCS 2
Menchu, Rigoberta 1959-
    See also CA 175; HLCS 2
Mencken, H(enry) L(ouis) 1880-1956 **T C L C
    13**
    See also CA 105; 125; CDALB 1917-1929;
        DLB 11, 29, 63, 137; MTCW 1, 2
Mendelsohn, Jane 1965(?)- .... **CLC 99**
    See also CA 154
Mercer, David 1928-1980**CLC 5; DAM DRAM**
    See also CA 9-12R; 102; CANR 23; DLB 13;
        MTCW 1
Merchant, Paul
    See Ellison, Harlan (Jay)
Meredith, George 1828-1909 . **TCLC 17, 43;
    DAM POET**
    See also CA 117; 153; CANR 80; CDBLB 1832-
        1890; DLB 18, 35, 57, 159
Meredith, William (Morris) 1919-**CLC 4, 13,
    22, 55; DAM POET; PC 28**
    See also CA 9-12R; CAAS 14; CANR 6, 40;
        DLB 5
Merezhkovsky, Dmitry Sergeyevich 1865-1941
    TCLC 29
    See also CA 169
Merimee, Prosper 1803-1870**NCLC 6, 65; SSC
    7**
    See also DLB 119, 192
Merkin, Daphne 1954- .... **CLC 44**
    See also CA 123
Merlin, Arthur
    See Blish, James (Benjamin)
Merrill, James (Ingram) 1926-1995**CLC 2, 3,
    6, 8, 13, 18, 34, 91; DAM POET; PC 28**
    See also CA 13-16R; 147; CANR 10, 49, 63;
        DLB 5, 165; DLBY 85; INT CANR-10;
        MTCW 1, 2
Merriman, Alex
    See Silverberg, Robert
Merriman, Brian 1747-1805 .... **NCLC 70**
Merritt, E. B.
    See Waddington, Miriam
Merton, Thomas 1915-1968**CLC 1, 3, 11, 34,
    83; PC 10**
    See also CA 5-8R; 25-28R; CANR 22, 53; DLB
        48; DLBY 81; MTCW 1, 2
Merwin, W(illiam) S(tanley) 1927- **CLC 1, 2,
    3, 5, 8, 13, 18, 45, 88; DAM POET**
    See also CA 13-16R; CANR 15, 51; DLB 5,
        169; INT CANR-15; MTCW 1, 2
Metcalf, John 1938- .... **CLC 37**
    See also CA 113; DLB 60
Metcalf, Suzanne
    See Baum, L(yman) Frank
Mew, Charlotte (Mary) 1870-1928 .. **TCLC 8**

See also CA 105; DLB 19, 135
Mewshaw, Michael 1943- .... **CLC 9**
    See also CA 53-56; CANR 7, 47; DLBY 80
Meyer, June
    See Jordan, June
Meyer, Lynn
    See Slavitt, David R(ytman)
Meyer-Meyrink, Gustav 1868-1932
    See Meyrink, Gustav
    See also CA 117
Meyers, Jeffrey 1939- .... **CLC 39**
    See also CA 73-76; CANR 54; DLB 111
Meynell, Alice (Christina Gertrude Thompson)
    1847-1922 .... **TCLC 6**
    See also CA 104; 177; DLB 19, 98
Meyrink, Gustav .... **TCLC 21**
    See also Meyer-Meyrink, Gustav
    See also DLB 81
Michaels, Leonard 1933- **CLC 6, 25; SSC 16**
    See also CA 61-64; CANR 21, 62; DLB 130;
        MTCW 1
Michaux, Henri 1899-1984 .... **CLC 8, 19**
    See also CA 85-88; 114
Micheaux, Oscar (Devereaux) 1884-1951
    TCLC 76
    See also BW 3; CA 174; DLB 50
Michelangelo 1475-1564 .... **LC 12**
Michelet, Jules 1798-1874 .... **NCLC 31**
Michels, Robert 1876-1936 .... **TCLC 88**
Michener, James A(lbert) 1907(?)-1997 **C L C
    1, 5, 11, 29, 60, 109; DAM NOV, POP**
    See also AAYA 27; AITN 1; BEST 90:1; CA 5-
        8R; 161; CANR 21, 45, 68; DLB 6; MTCW
        1, 2
Mickiewicz, Adam 1798-1855 .... **NCLC 3**
Middleton, Christopher 1926- .... **CLC 13**
    See also CA 13-16R; CANR 29, 54; DLB 40
Middleton, Richard (Barham) 1882-1911
    TCLC 56
    See also DLB 156
Middleton, Stanley 1919- .... **CLC 7, 38**
    See also CA 25-28R; CAAS 23; CANR 21, 46,
        81; DLB 14
Middleton, Thomas 1580-1627 **LC 33; DAM
    DRAM, MST; DC 5**
    See also DLB 58
Migueis, Jose Rodrigues 1901- .... **CLC 10**
Mikszath, Kalman 1847-1910 .... **TCLC 31**
    See also CA 170
Miles, Jack .... **CLC 100**
Miles, Josephine (Louise) 1911-1985**CLC 1, 2,
    14, 34, 39; DAM POET**
    See also CA 1-4R; 116; CANR 2, 55; DLB 48
Militant
    See Sandburg, Carl (August)
Mill, John Stuart 1806-1873 .... **NCLC 11, 58**
    See also CDBLB 1832-1890; DLB 55, 190
Millar, Kenneth 1915-1983 .... **CLC 14; DAM
    POP**
    See also Macdonald, Ross
    See also CA 9-12R; 110; CANR 16, 63; DLB
        2; DLBD 6; DLBY 83; MTCW 1, 2
Millay, E. Vincent
    See Millay, Edna St. Vincent
Millay, Edna St. Vincent 1892-1950 **TCLC 4,
    49; DA; DAB; DAC; DAM MST, POET;
    PC 6; WLCS**
    See also CA 104; 130; CDALB 1917-1929;
        DLB 45; MTCW 1, 2
Miller, Arthur 1915-**CLC 1, 2, 6, 10, 15, 26, 47,
    78; DA; DAB; DAC; DAM DRAM, MST;
    DC 1; WLC**
    See also AAYA 15; AITN 1; CA 1-4R; CABS

3; CANR 2, 30, 54, 76; CDALB 1941-1968;
    DLB 7; MTCW 1, 2
Miller, Henry (Valentine) 1891-1980**CLC 1, 2,
    4, 9, 14, 43, 84; DA; DAB; DAC; DAM
    MST, NOV; WLC**
    See also CA 9-12R; 97-100; CANR 33, 64;
        CDALB 1929-1941; DLB 4, 9; DLBY 80;
        MTCW 1, 2
Miller, Jason 1939(?)- .... **CLC 2**
    See also AITN 1; CA 73-76; DLB 7
Miller, Sue 1943- .... **CLC 44; DAM POP**
    See also BEST 90:3; CA 139; CANR 59; DLB
        143
Miller, Walter M(ichael, Jr.) 1923-**CLC 4, 30**
    See also CA 85-88; DLB 8
Millett, Kate 1934- .... **CLC 67**
    See also AITN 1; CA 73-76; CANR 32, 53, 76;
        MTCW 1, 2
Millhauser, Steven (Lewis) 1943-**CLC 21, 54,
    109**
    See also CA 110; 111; CANR 63; DLB 2; INT
        111; MTCW 2
Millin, Sarah Gertrude 1889-1968 ... **CLC 49**
    See also CA 102; 93-96
Milne, A(lan) A(lexander) 1882-1956**TCLC 6,
    88; DAB; DAC; DAM MST**
    See also CA 104; 133; CLR 1, 26; DLB 10, 77,
        100, 160; MAICYA; MTCW 1, 2; SATA 100;
        YABC 1
Milner, Ron(ald) 1938-**CLC 56; BLC 3; DAM
    MULT**
    See also AITN 1; BW 1; CA 73-76; CANR 24,
        81; DLB 38; MTCW 1
Milnes, Richard Monckton 1809-1885**N C L C
    61**
    See also DLB 32, 184
Milosz, Czeslaw 1911- **CLC 5, 11, 22, 31, 56,
    82; DAM MST, POET; PC 8; WLCS**
    See also CA 81-84; CANR 23, 51; MTCW 1, 2
Milton, John 1608-1674 **LC 9, 43; DA; DAB;
    DAC; DAM MST, POET; PC 19; WLC**
    See also CDBLB 1660-1789; DLB 131, 151
Min, Anchee 1957- .... **CLC 86**
    See also CA 146
Minehaha, Cornelius
    See Wedekind, (Benjamin) Frank(lin)
Miner, Valerie 1947- .... **CLC 40**
    See also CA 97-100; CANR 59
Minimo, Duca
    See D'Annunzio, Gabriele
Minot, Susan 1956- .... **CLC 44**
    See also CA 134
Minus, Ed 1938- .... **CLC 39**
Miranda, Javier
    See Bioy Casares, Adolfo
Miranda, Javier
    See Bioy Casares, Adolfo
Mirbeau, Octave 1848-1917 .... **TCLC 55**
    See also DLB 123, 192
Miro (Ferrer), Gabriel (Francisco Victor) 1879-
    1930 .... **TCLC 5**
    See also CA 104
Mishima, Yukio 1925-1970**CLC 2, 4, 6, 9, 27;
    DC 1; SSC 4**
    See also Hiraoka, Kimitake
    See also DLB 182; MTCW 2
Mistral, Frederic 1830-1914 .... **TCLC 51**
    See also CA 122
Mistral, Gabriela .... **TCLC 2; HLC 2**
    See also Godoy Alcayaga, Lucila
    See also MTCW 2
Mistry, Rohinton 1952- .... **CLC 71; DAC**
    See also CA 141

Mitchell, Clyde
See Ellison, Harlan (Jay); Silverberg, Robert
Mitchell, James Leslie 1901-1935
See Gibbon, Lewis Grassic
See also CA 104; DLB 15
Mitchell, Joni 1943- .... **CLC 12**
See also CA 112
Mitchell, Joseph (Quincy) 1908-1996 **CLC 98**
See also CA 77-80; 152; CANR 69; DLB 185;
DLBY 96
Mitchell, Margaret (Munnerlyn) 1900-1949
TCLC 11; DAM NOV, POP
See also AAYA 23; CA 109; 125; CANR 55;
CDALBS; DLB 9; MTCW 1, 2
Mitchell, Peggy
See Mitchell, Margaret (Munnerlyn)
Mitchell, S(ilas) Weir 1829-1914 ... **TCLC 36**
See also CA 165; DLB 202
Mitchell, W(illiam) O(rmond) 1914-1998 **CLC 25; DAC; DAM MST**
See also CA 77-80; 165; CANR 15, 43; DLB 88
Mitchell, William 1879-1936 .... **TCLC 81**
Mitford, Mary Russell 1787-1855 ... **NCLC 4**
See also DLB 110, 116
Mitford, Nancy 1904-1973 .... **CLC 44**
See also CA 9-12R; DLB 191
Miyamoto, (Chujo) Yuriko 1899-1951 **T C L C 37**
See also CA 170, 174; DLB 180
Miyazawa, Kenji 1896-1933 .... **TCLC 76**
See also CA 157
Mizoguchi, Kenji 1898-1956 .... **TCLC 72**
See also CA 167
Mo, Timothy (Peter) 1950(?)- .... **CLC 46**
See also CA 117; DLB 194; MTCW 1
Modarressi, Taghi (M.) 1931- .... **CLC 44**
See also CA 121; 134; INT 134
Modiano, Patrick (Jean) 1945- .... **CLC 18**
See also CA 85-88; CANR 17, 40; DLB 83
Moerck, Paal
See Roelvaag, O(le) E(dvart)
Mofolo, Thomas (Mokopu) 1875(?)-1948
TCLC 22; BLC 3; DAM MULT
See also CA 121; 153; MTCW 2
Mohr, Nicholasa 1938- **CLC 12; DAM MULT; HLC 2**
See also AAYA 8; CA 49-52; CANR 1, 32, 64;
CLR 22; DLB 145; HW 1, 2; JRDA; SAAS
8; SATA 8, 97
Mojtabai, A(nn) G(race) 1938- **CLC 5, 9, 15, 29**
See also CA 85-88
Moliere 1622-1673 **LC 10, 28; DA; DAB; DAC; DAM DRAM, MST; WLC**
Molin, Charles
See Mayne, William (James Carter)
Molnar, Ferenc 1878-1952 .. **TCLC 20; DAM DRAM**
See also CA 109; 153
Momaday, N(avarre) Scott 1934- **CLC 2, 19, 85, 95; DA; DAB; DAC; DAM MST, MULT, NOV, POP; PC 25; WLCS**
See also AAYA 11; CA 25-28R; CANR 14, 34,
68; CDALBS; DLB 143, 175; INT CANR-
14; MTCW 1, 2; NNAL; SATA 48; SATA-
Brief 30
Monette, Paul 1945-1995 .... **CLC 82**
See also CA 139; 147
Monroe, Harriet 1860-1936 .... **TCLC 12**
See also CA 109; DLB 54, 91
Monroe, Lyle
See Heinlein, Robert A(nson)

Montagu, Elizabeth 1720-1800 .... **NCLC 7**
Montagu, Mary (Pierrepont) Wortley 1689-
1762 ....**LC 9; PC 16**
See also DLB 95, 101
Montagu, W. H.
See Coleridge, Samuel Taylor
Montague, John (Patrick) 1929- **CLC 13, 46**
See also CA 9-12R; CANR 9, 69; DLB 40;
MTCW 1
Montaigne, Michel (Eyquem) de 1533-1592
LC 8; DA; DAB; DAC; DAM MST; WLC
Montale, Eugenio 1896-1981 **CLC 7, 9, 18; PC 13**
See also CA 17-20R; 104; CANR 30; DLB 114;
MTCW 1
Montesquieu, Charles-Louis de Secondat 1689-
1755 .... **LC 7**
Montgomery, (Robert) Bruce 1921-1978
See Crispin, Edmund
See also CA 179; 104
Montgomery, L(ucy) M(aud) 1874-1942
TCLC 51; DAC; DAM MST
See also AAYA 12; CA 108; 137; CLR 8; DLB
92; DLBD 14; JRDA; MAICYA; MTCW 2;
SATA 100; YABC 1
Montgomery, Marion H., Jr. 1925- .... **CLC 7**
See also AITN 1; CA 1-4R; CANR 3, 48; DLB
6
Montgomery, Max
See Davenport, Guy (Mattison, Jr.)
Montherlant, Henry (Milon) de 1896-1972
CLC 8, 19; DAM DRAM
See also CA 85-88; 37-40R; DLB 72; MTCW
1
Monty Python
See Chapman, Graham; Cleese, John
(Marwood); Gilliam, Terry (Vance); Idle,
Eric; Jones, Terence Graham Parry; Palin,
Michael (Edward)
See also AAYA 7
Moodie, Susanna (Strickland) 1803-1885
NCLC 14
See also DLB 99
Mooney, Edward 1951-
See Mooney, Ted
See also CA 130
Mooney, Ted .... **CLC 25**
See also Mooney, Edward
Moorcock, Michael (John) 1939- **CLC 5, 27, 58**
See also Bradbury, Edward P.
See also AAYA 26; CA 45-48; CAAS 5; CANR
2, 17, 38, 64; DLB 14; MTCW 1, 2; SATA
93
Moore, Brian 1921-1999 **CLC 1, 3, 5, 7, 8, 19, 32, 90; DAB; DAC; DAM MST**
See also CA 1-4R; 174; CANR 1, 25, 42, 63;
MTCW 1, 2
Moore, Edward
See Muir, Edwin
Moore, G. E. 1873-1958 .... **TCLC 89**
Moore, George Augustus 1852-1933 **TCLC 7; SSC 19**
See also CA 104; 177; DLB 10, 18, 57, 135
Moore, Lorrie .... **CLC 39, 45, 68**
See also Moore, Marie Lorena
Moore, Marianne (Craig) 1887-1972 **CLC 1, 2, 4, 8, 10, 13, 19, 47; DA; DAB; DAC; DAM MST, POET; PC 4; WLCS**
See also CA 1-4R; 33-36R; CANR 3, 61;
CDALB 1929-1941; DLB 45; DLBD 7;
MTCW 1, 2; SATA 20
Moore, Marie Lorena 1957-
See Moore, Lorrie

See also CA 116; CANR 39
Moore, Thomas 1779-1852 .... **NCLC 6**
See also DLB 96, 144
Mora, Pat(ricia) 1942-
See also CA 129; CANR 57, 81; CLR 58; DAM
MULT; DLB 209; HLC 2; HW 1, 2; SATA
92
Morand, Paul 1888-1976 .... **CLC 41; SSC 22**
See also CA 69-72; DLB 65
Morante, Elsa 1918-1985 .... **CLC 8, 47**
See also CA 85-88; 117; CANR 35; DLB 177;
MTCW 1, 2
Moravia, Alberto 1907-1990 **CLC 2, 7, 11, 27, 46; SSC 26**
See also Pincherle, Alberto
See also DLB 177; MTCW 2
More, Hannah 1745-1833 .... **NCLC 27**
See also DLB 107, 109, 116, 158
More, Henry 1614-1687 .... **LC 9**
See also DLB 126
More, Sir Thomas 1478-1535 .... **LC 10, 32**
Moreas, Jean .... **TCLC 18**
See also Papadiamantopoulos, Johannes
Morgan, Berry 1919- .... **CLC 6**
See also CA 49-52; DLB 6
Morgan, Claire
See Highsmith, (Mary) Patricia
Morgan, Edwin (George) 1920- .... **CLC 31**
See also CA 5-8R; CANR 3, 43; DLB 27
Morgan, (George) Frederick 1922- .. **CLC 23**
See also CA 17-20R; CANR 21
Morgan, Harriet
See Mencken, H(enry) L(ouis)
Morgan, Jane
See Cooper, James Fenimore
Morgan, Janet 1945- .... **CLC 39**
See also CA 65-68
Morgan, Lady 1776(?)-1859 .... **NCLC 29**
See also DLB 116, 158
Morgan, Robin (Evonne) 1941- .... **CLC 2**
See also CA 69-72; CANR 29, 68; MTCW 1;
SATA 80
Morgan, Scott
See Kuttner, Henry
Morgan, Seth 1949(?)-1990 .... **CLC 65**
See also CA 132
Morgenstern, Christian 1871-1914 . **TCLC 8**
See also CA 105
Morgenstern, S.
See Goldman, William (W.)
Moricz, Zsigmond 1879-1942 .... **TCLC 33**
See also CA 165
Morike, Eduard (Friedrich) 1804-1875 **NCLC 10**
See also DLB 133
Moritz, Karl Philipp 1756-1793 .... **LC 2**
See also DLB 94
Morland, Peter Henry
See Faust, Frederick (Schiller)
Morley, Christopher (Darlington) 1890-1957
TCLC 87
See also CA 112; DLB 9
Morren, Theophil
See Hofmannsthal, Hugo von
Morris, Bill 1952- .... **CLC 76**
Morris, Julian
See West, Morris L(anglo)
Morris, Steveland Judkins 1950(?)-
See Wonder, Stevie
See also CA 111
Morris, William 1834-1896 .... **NCLC 4**
See also CDBLB 1832-1890; DLB 18, 35, 57,
156, 178, 184

1810-1850
See Fuller, Margaret
See also SATA 25

Ostrovsky, Alexander 1823-1886NCLC 30, 57

Otero, Blas de 1916-1979 .... CLC 11
See also CA 89-92; DLB 134

Otto, Rudolf 1869-1937 .... TCLC 85

Otto, Whitney 1955- .... CLC 70
See also CA 140

Ouida .... TCLC 43
See also De La Ramee, (Marie) Louise
See also DLB 18, 156

Ousmane, Sembene 1923- .... CLC 66; BLC 3
See also BW 1, 3; CA 117; 125; CANR 81;
MTCW 1

Ovid 43B.C.-17 CMLC 7; DAM POET; PC 2
See also DLB 211

Owen, Hugh
See Faust, Frederick (Schiller)

Owen, Wilfred (Edward Salter) 1893-1918
TCLC 5, 27; DA; DAB; DAC; DAM MST,
POET; PC 19; WLC
See also CA 104; 141; CDBLB 1914-1945;
DLB 20; MTCW 2

Owens, Rochelle 1936- .... CLC 8
See also CA 17-20R; CAAS 2; CANR 39

Oz, Amos 1939-CLC 5, 8, 11, 27, 33, 54; DAM
NOV
See also CA 53-56; CANR 27, 47, 65; MTCW
1, 2

Ozick, Cynthia 1928- CLC 3, 7, 28, 62; DAM
NOV, POP; SSC 15
See also BEST 90:1; CA 17-20R; CANR 23,
58; DLB 28, 152; DLBY 82; INT CANR-
23; MTCW 1, 2

Ozu, Yasujiro 1903-1963 .... CLC 16
See also CA 112

Pacheco, C.
See Pessoa, Fernando (Antonio Nogueira)

Pacheco, Jose Emilio 1939-
See also CA 111; 131; CANR 65; DAM MULT;
HLC 2; HW 1, 2

Pa Chin .... CLC 18
See also Li Fei-kan

Pack, Robert 1929- .... CLC 13
See also CA 1-4R; CANR 3, 44, 82; DLB 5

Padgett, Lewis
See Kuttner, Henry

Padilla (Lorenzo), Heberto 1932-..... CLC 38
See also AITN 1; CA 123; 131; HW 1

Page, Jimmy 1944-.............................. CLC 12

Page, Louise 1955- .... CLC 40
See also CA 140; CANR 76

Page, P(atricia) K(athleen) 1916- CLC 7, 18;
DAC; DAM MST; PC 12
See also CA 53-56; CANR 4, 22, 65; DLB 68;
MTCW 1

Page, Thomas Nelson 1853-1922 .... SSC 23
See also CA 118; 177; DLB 12, 78; DLBD 13

Pagels, Elaine Hiesey 1943-.............. CLC 104
See also CA 45-48; CANR 2, 24, 51

Paget, Violet 1856-1935
See Lee, Vernon
See also CA 104; 166

Paget-Lowe, Henry
See Lovecraft, H(oward) P(hillips)

Paglia, Camille (Anna) 1947- .... CLC 68
See also CA 140; CANR 72; MTCW 2

Paige, Richard
See Koontz, Dean R(ay)

Paine, Thomas 1737-1809 .... NCLC 62
See also CDALB 1640-1865; DLB 31, 43, 73,
158

Pakenham, Antonia
See Fraser, (Lady) Antonia (Pakenham)

Palamas, Kostes 1859-1943 .... TCLC 5
See also CA 105

Palazzeschi, Aldo 1885-1974 .... CLC 11
See also CA 89-92; 53-56; DLB 114

Pales Matos, Luis 1898-1959
See also HLCS 2; HW 1

Paley, Grace 1922-CLC 4, 6, 37; DAM POP;
SSC 8
See also CA 25-28R; CANR 13, 46, 74; DLB
28; INT CANR-13; MTCW 1, 2

Palin, Michael (Edward) 1943-......... CLC 21
See also Monty Python
See also CA 107; CANR 35; SATA 67

Palliser, Charles 1947- .... CLC 65
See also CA 136; CANR 76

Palma, Ricardo 1833-1919 .... TCLC 29
See also CA 168

Pancake, Breece Dexter 1952-1979
See Pancake, Breece D'J
See also CA 123; 109

Pancake, Breece D'J .... CLC 29
See also Pancake, Breece Dexter
See also DLB 130

Panko, Rudy
See Gogol, Nikolai (Vasilyevich)

Papadiamantis, Alexandros 1851-1911T C L C
29
See also CA 168

Papadiamantopoulos, Johannes 1856-1910
See Moreas, Jean
See also CA 117

Papini, Giovanni 1881-1956 .... TCLC 22
See also CA 121

Paracelsus 1493-1541 .... LC 14
See also DLB 179

Parasol, Peter
See Stevens, Wallace

Pardo Bazan, Emilia 1851-1921 .... SSC 30

Pareto, Vilfredo 1848-1923 .... TCLC 69
See also CA 175

Parfenie, Maria
See Codrescu, Andrei

Parini, Jay (Lee) 1948- .... CLC 54
See also CA 97-100; CAAS 16; CANR 32

Park, Jordan
See Kornbluth, C(yril) M.; Pohl, Frederik

Park, Robert E(zra) 1864-1944 ...... TCLC 73
See also CA 122; 165

Parker, Bert
See Ellison, Harlan (Jay)

Parker, Dorothy (Rothschild) 1893-1967C L C
15, 68; DAM POET; PC 28; SSC 2
See also CA 19-20; 25-28R; CAP 2; DLB 11,
45, 86; MTCW 1, 2

Parker, Robert B(rown) 1932-CLC 27; DAM
NOV, POP
See also AAYA 28; BEST 89:4; CA 49-52;
CANR 1, 26, 52; INT CANR-26; MTCW 1

Parkin, Frank 1940- .... CLC 43
See also CA 147

Parkman, Francis, Jr. 1823-1893 ..NCLC 12
See also DLB 1, 30, 186

Parks, Gordon (Alexander Buchanan) 1912-
CLC 1, 16; BLC 3; DAM MULT
See also AITN 2; BW 2, 3; CA 41-44R; CANR
26, 66; DLB 33; MTCW 2; SATA 8, 108

Parmenides c. 515B.C.-c. 450B.C. CMLC 22
See also DLB 176

Parnell, Thomas 1679-1718 .... LC 3
See also DLB 94

Parra, Nicanor 1914- ...... CLC 2, 102; DAM
MULT; HLC 2
See also CA 85-88; CANR 32; HW 1; MTCW
1

Parra Sanojo, Ana Teresa de la 1890-1936
See also HLCS 2

Parrish, Mary Frances
See Fisher, M(ary) F(rances) K(ennedy)

Parson
See Coleridge, Samuel Taylor

Parson Lot
See Kingsley, Charles

Partridge, Anthony
See Oppenheim, E(dward) Phillips

Pascal, Blaise 1623-1662 .... LC 35

Pascoli, Giovanni 1855-1912 .... TCLC 45
See also CA 170

Pasolini, Pier Paolo 1922-1975 . CLC 20, 37,
106; PC 17
See also CA 93-96; 61-64; CANR 63; DLB 128,
177; MTCW 1

Pasquini
See Silone, Ignazio

Pastan, Linda (Olenik) 1932- CLC 27; DAM
POET
See also CA 61-64; CANR 18, 40, 61; DLB 5

Pasternak, Boris (Leonidovich) 1890-1960
CLC 7, 10, 18, 63; DA; DAB; DAC; DAM
MST, NOV, POET; PC 6; SSC 31; WLC
See also CA 127; 116; MTCW 1, 2

Patchen, Kenneth 1911-1972 ... CLC 1, 2, 18;
DAM POET
See also CA 1-4R; 33-36R; CANR 3, 35; DLB
16, 48; MTCW 1

Pater, Walter (Horatio) 1839-1894 .. NCLC 7
See also CDBLB 1832-1890; DLB 57, 156

Paterson, A(ndrew) B(arton) 1864-1941
TCLC 32
See also CA 155; SATA 97

Paterson, Katherine (Womeldorf) 1932-C L C
12, 30
See also AAYA 1; CA 21-24R; CANR 28, 59;
CLR 7, 50; DLB 52; JRDA; MAICYA;
MTCW 1; SATA 13, 53, 92

Patmore, Coventry Kersey Dighton 1823-1896
NCLC 9
See also DLB 35, 98

Paton, Alan (Stewart) 1903-1988 CLC 4, 10,
25, 55, 106; DA; DAB; DAC; DAM MST,
NOV; WLC
See also AAYA 26; CA 13-16; 125; CANR 22;
CAP 1; DLBD 17; MTCW 1, 2; SATA 11;
SATA-Obit 56

Paton Walsh, Gillian 1937-
See Walsh, Jill Paton
See also CANR 38; JRDA; MAICYA; SAAS 3;
SATA 4, 72, 109

Patton, George S. 1885-1945 .... TCLC 79

Paulding, James Kirke 1778-1860 ... NCLC 2
See also DLB 3, 59, 74

Paulin, Thomas Neilson 1949-
See Paulin, Tom
See also CA 123; 128

Paulin, Tom .... CLC 37
See also Paulin, Thomas Neilson
See also DLB 40

Paustovsky, Konstantin (Georgievich) 1892-
1968 .... CLC 40
See also CA 93-96; 25-28R

Pavese, Cesare 1908-1950 ... TCLC 3; PC 13;
SSC 19
See also CA 104; 169; DLB 128, 177

Pavic, Milorad 1929- .... CLC 60
See also CA 136; DLB 181

See also CA 29-32R; CAAS 4; CANR 58; DLBY 82, 98; MTCW 2

Pinta, Harold
  See Pinter, Harold

Pinter, Harold 1930-**CLC 1, 3, 6, 9, 11, 15, 27, 58, 73; DA; DAB; DAC; DAM DRAM, MST; WLC**
  See also CA 5-8R; CANR 33, 65; CDBLB 1960 to Present; DLB 13; MTCW 1, 2

Piozzi, Hester Lynch (Thrale) 1741-1821 **NCLC 57**
  See also DLB 104, 142

Pirandello, Luigi 1867-1936**TCLC 4, 29; DA; DAB; DAC; DAM DRAM, MST; DC 5; SSC 22; WLC**
  See also CA 104; 153; MTCW 2

Pirsig, Robert M(aynard) 1928-**CLC 4, 6, 73; DAM POP**
  See also CA 53-56; CANR 42, 74; MTCW 1, 2; SATA 39

Pisarev, Dmitry Ivanovich 1840-1868 **N C L C 25**

Pix, Mary (Griffith) 1666-1709 .... **LC 8**
  See also DLB 80

Pixerecourt, (Rene Charles) Guilbert de 1773-1844 .... **NCLC 39**
  See also DLB 192

Plaatje, Sol(omon) T(shekisho) 1876-1932 **TCLC 73; BLCS**
  See also BW 2, 3; CA 141; CANR 79

Plaidy, Jean
  See Hibbert, Eleanor Alice Burford

Planche, James Robinson 1796-1880**NCLC 42**

Plant, Robert 1948- .... **CLC 12**

Plante, David (Robert) 1940- **CLC 7, 23, 38; DAM NOV**
  See also CA 37-40R; CANR 12, 36, 58, 82; DLBY 83; INT CANR-12; MTCW 1

Plath, Sylvia 1932-1963 **CLC 1, 2, 3, 5, 9, 11, 14, 17, 50, 51, 62, 111; DA; DAB; DAC; DAM MST, POET; PC 1; WLC**
  See also AAYA 13; CA 19-20; CANR 34; CAP 2; CDALB 1941-1968; DLB 5, 6, 152; MTCW 1, 2; SATA 96

Plato 428(?)B.C.-348(?)B.C. .... **CMLC 8; DA; DAB; DAC; DAM MST; WLCS**
  See also DLB 176

Platonov, Andrei .... **TCLC 14**
  See also Klimentov, Andrei Platonovich

Platt, Kin 1911- .... **CLC 26**
  See also AAYA 11; CA 17-20R; CANR 11; JRDA; SAAS 17; SATA 21, 86

Plautus c. 251B.C.-184B.C. .**CMLC 24; DC 6**
  See also DLB 211

Plick et Plock
  See Simenon, Georges (Jacques Christian)

Plimpton, George (Ames) 1927- .... **CLC 36**
  See also AITN 1; CA 21-24R; CANR 32, 70; DLB 185; MTCW 1; SATA 10

Pliny the Elder c. 23-79 .... **CMLC 23**
  See also DLB 211

Plomer, William Charles Franklin 1903-1973 **CLC 4, 8**
  See also CA 21-22; CANR 34; CAP 2; DLB 20, 162, 191; MTCW 1; SATA 24

Plowman, Piers
  See Kavanagh, Patrick (Joseph)

Plum, J.
  See Wodehouse, P(elham) G(renville)

Plumly, Stanley (Ross) 1939- .... **CLC 33**
  See also CA 108; 110; DLB 5, 193; INT 110

Plumpe, Friedrich Wilhelm 1888-1931**T C L C 53**

See also CA 112

Po Chu-i 772-846 .... **CMLC 24**

Poe, Edgar Allan 1809-1849 **NCLC 1, 16, 55, 78; DA; DAB; DAC; DAM MST, POET; PC 1; SSC 34; WLC**
  See also AAYA 14; CDALB 1640-1865; DLB 3, 59, 73, 74; SATA 23

Poet of Titchfield Street, The
  See Pound, Ezra (Weston Loomis)

Pohl, Frederik 1919- .... **CLC 18; SSC 25**
  See also AAYA 24; CA 61-64; CAAS 1; CANR 11, 37, 81; DLB 8; INT CANR-11; MTCW 1, 2; SATA 24

Poirier, Louis 1910-
  See Gracq, Julien
  See also CA 122; 126

Poitier, Sidney 1927- .... **CLC 26**
  See also BW 1; CA 117

Polanski, Roman 1933- .... **CLC 16**
  See also CA 77-80

Poliakoff, Stephen 1952- .... **CLC 38**
  See also CA 106; DLB 13

Police, The
  See Copeland, Stewart (Armstrong); Summers, Andrew James; Sumner, Gordon Matthew

Polidori, John William 1795-1821 . **NCLC 51**
  See also DLB 116

Pollitt, Katha 1949- .... **CLC 28, 122**
  See also CA 120; 122; CANR 66; MTCW 1, 2

Pollock, (Mary) Sharon 1936-**CLC 50; DAC; DAM DRAM, MST**
  See also CA 141; DLB 60

Polo, Marco 1254-1324 .... **CMLC 15**

Polonsky, Abraham (Lincoln) 1910- **CLC 92**
  See also CA 104; DLB 26; INT 104

Polybius c. 200B.C.-c. 118B.C. .... **CMLC 17**
  See also DLB 176

Pomerance, Bernard 1940- .... **CLC 13; DAM DRAM**
  See also CA 101; CANR 49

Ponge, Francis (Jean Gaston Alfred) 1899-1988 **CLC 6, 18; DAM POET**
  See also CA 85-88; 126; CANR 40

Poniatowska, Elena 1933-
  See also CA 101; CANR 32, 66; DAM MULT; DLB 113; HLC 2; HW 1, 2

Pontoppidan, Henrik 1857-1943 .... **TCLC 29**
  See also CA 170

Poole, Josephine .... **CLC 17**
  See also Helyar, Jane Penelope Josephine
  See also SAAS 2; SATA 5

Popa, Vasko 1922-1991 .... **CLC 19**
  See also CA 112; 148; DLB 181

Pope, Alexander 1688-1744 **LC 3; DA; DAB; DAC; DAM MST, POET; PC 26; WLC**
  See also CDBLB 1660-1789; DLB 95, 101

Porter, Connie (Rose) 1959(?)- .... **CLC 70**
  See also BW 2, 3; CA 142; SATA 81

Porter, Gene(va Grace) Stratton 1863(?)-1924 **TCLC 21**
  See also CA 112

Porter, Katherine Anne 1890-1980**CLC 1, 3, 7, 10, 13, 15, 27, 101; DA; DAB; DAC; DAM MST, NOV; SSC 4, 31**
  See also AITN 2; CA 1-4R; 101; CANR 1, 65; CDALBS; DLB 4, 9, 102; DLBD 12; DLBY 80; MTCW 1, 2; SATA 39; SATA-Obit 23

Porter, Peter (Neville Frederick) 1929-**CLC 5, 13, 33**
  See also CA 85-88; DLB 40

Porter, William Sydney 1862-1910
  See Henry, O.
  See also CA 104; 131; CDALB 1865-1917; DA;

DAB; DAC; DAM MST; DLB 12, 78, 79; MTCW 1, 2; YABC 2

Portillo (y Pacheco), Jose Lopez
  See Lopez Portillo (y Pacheco), Jose

Portillo Trambley, Estela 1927-1998
  See also CANR 32; DAM MULT; DLB 209; HLC 2; HW 1

Post, Melville Davisson 1869-1930 **TCLC 39**
  See also CA 110

Potok, Chaim 1929- ... **CLC 2, 7, 14, 26, 112; DAM NOV**
  See also AAYA 15; AITN 1, 2; CA 17-20R; CANR 19, 35, 64; DLB 28, 152; INT CANR-19; MTCW 1, 2; SATA 33, 106

Potter, (Helen) Beatrix 1866-1943
  See Webb, (Martha) Beatrice (Potter)
  See also MAICYA; MTCW 2

Potter, Dennis (Christopher George) 1935-1994 **CLC 58, 86**
  See also CA 107; 145; CANR 33, 61; MTCW 1

Pound, Ezra (Weston Loomis) 1885-1972 **CLC 1, 2, 3, 4, 5, 7, 10, 13, 18, 34, 48, 50, 112; DA; DAB; DAC; DAM MST, POET; PC 4; WLC**
  See also CA 5-8R; 37-40R; CANR 40; CDALB 1917-1929; DLB 4, 45, 63; DLBD 15; MTCW 1, 2

Povod, Reinaldo 1959-1994 .... **CLC 44**
  See also CA 136; 146

Powell, Adam Clayton, Jr. 1908-1972**CLC 89; BLC 3; DAM MULT**
  See also BW 1, 3; CA 102; 33-36R

Powell, Anthony (Dymoke) 1905-**CLC 1, 3, 7, 9, 10, 31**
  See also CA 1-4R; CANR 1, 32, 62; CDBLB 1945-1960; DLB 15; MTCW 1, 2

Powell, Dawn 1897-1965 .... **CLC 66**
  See also CA 5-8R; DLBY 97

Powell, Padgett 1952- .... **CLC 34**
  See also CA 126; CANR 63

Power, Susan 1961- .... **CLC 91**

Powers, J(ames) F(arl) 1917-**CLC 1, 4, 8, 57; SSC 4**
  See also CA 1-4R; CANR 2, 61; DLB 130; MTCW 1

Powers, John J(ames) 1945-
  See Powers, John R.
  See also CA 69-72

Powers, John R. .... **CLC 66**
  See also Powers, John J(ames)

Powers, Richard (S.) 1957- .... **CLC 93**
  See also CA 148; CANR 80

Pownall, David 1938- .... **CLC 10**
  See also CA 89-92; CAAS 18; CANR 49; DLB 14

Powys, John Cowper 1872-1963**CLC 7, 9, 15, 46**
  See also CA 85-88; DLB 15; MTCW 1, 2

Powys, T(heodore) F(rancis) 1875-1953 **TCLC 9**
  See also CA 106; DLB 36, 162

Prado (Calvo), Pedro 1886-1952 ... **TCLC 75**
  See also CA 131; HW 1

Prager, Emily 1952- .... **CLC 56**

Pratt, E(dwin) J(ohn) 1883(?)-1964 **CLC 19; DAC; DAM POET**
  See also CA 141; 93-96; CANR 77; DLB 92

Premchand .... **TCLC 21**
  See also Srivastava, Dhanpat Rai

Preussler, Otfried 1923- .... **CLC 17**
  See also CA 77-80; SATA 24

Prevert, Jacques (Henri Marie) 1900-1977 **CLC 15**

See also CDBLB Before 1660; DLB 172

Rallentando, H. P.
See Sayers, Dorothy L(eigh)

Ramal, Walter
See de la Mare, Walter (John)

Ramana Maharshi 1879-1950 .... **TCLC 84**

Ramoacn y Cajal, Santiago 1852-1934**T C L C 93**

Ramon, Juan
See Jimenez (Mantecon), Juan Ramon

Ramos, Graciliano 1892-1953 .... **TCLC 32**
See also CA 167; HW 2

Rampersad, Arnold 1941- .... **CLC 44**
See also BW 2, 3; CA 127; 133; CANR 81; DLB 111; INT 133

Rampling, Anne
See Rice, Anne

Ramsay, Allan 1684(?)-1758 .... **LC 29**
See also DLB 95

Ramuz, Charles-Ferdinand 1878-1947**T C L C 33**
See also CA 165

Rand, Ayn 1905-1982 **CLC 3, 30, 44, 79; DA; DAC; DAM MST, NOV, POP; WLC**
See also AAYA 10; CA 13-16R; 105; CANR 27, 73; CDALBS; MTCW 1, 2

Randall, Dudley (Felker) 1914-**CLC 1; BLC 3; DAM MULT**
See also BW 1, 3; CA 25-28R; CANR 23, 82; DLB 41

Randall, Robert
See Silverberg, Robert

Ranger, Ken
See Creasey, John

Ransom, John Crowe 1888-1974**CLC 2, 4, 5, 11, 24; DAM POET**
See also CA 5-8R; 49-52; CANR 6, 34; CDALBS; DLB 45, 63; MTCW 1, 2

Rao, Raja 1909- ..... **CLC 25, 56; DAM NOV**
See also CA 73-76; CANR 51; MTCW 1, 2

Raphael, Frederic (Michael) 1931-**CLC 2, 14**
See also CA 1-4R; CANR 1; DLB 14

Ratcliffe, James P.
See Mencken, H(enry) L(ouis)

Rathbone, Julian 1935- .... **CLC 41**
See also CA 101; CANR 34, 73

Rattigan, Terence (Mervyn) 1911-1977**CLC 7; DAM DRAM**
See also CA 85-88; 73-76; CDBLB 1945-1960; DLB 13; MTCW 1, 2

Ratushinskaya, Irina 1954- .... **CLC 54**
See also CA 129; CANR 68

Raven, Simon (Arthur Noel) 1927- .. **CLC 14**
See also CA 81-84

Ravenna, Michael
See Welty, Eudora

Rawley, Callman 1903-
See Rakosi, Carl
See also CA 21-24R; CANR 12, 32

Rawlings, Marjorie Kinnan 1896-1953**T C L C 4**
See also AAYA 20; CA 104; 137; CANR 74; DLB 9, 22, 102; DLBD 17; JRDA; MAICYA; MTCW 2; SATA 100; YABC 1

Ray, Satyajit 1921-1992 .. **CLC 16, 76; DAM MULT**
See also CA 114; 137

Read, Herbert Edward 1893-1968 ..... **CLC 4**
See also CA 85-88; 25-28R; DLB 20, 149

Read, Piers Paul 1941- .... **CLC 4, 10, 25**
See also CA 21-24R; CANR 38; DLB 14; SATA 21

Reade, Charles 1814-1884 .... **NCLC 2, 74**

See also DLB 21

Reade, Hamish
See Gray, Simon (James Holliday)

Reading, Peter 1946- .... **CLC 47**
See also CA 103; CANR 46; DLB 40

Reaney, James 1926- .. **CLC 13; DAC; DAM MST**
See also CA 41-44R; CAAS 15; CANR 42; DLB 68; SATA 43

Rebreanu, Liviu 1885-1944 .... **TCLC 28**
See also CA 165

Rechy, John (Francisco) 1934- **CLC 1, 7, 14, 18, 107; DAM MULT; HLC 2**
See also CA 5-8R; CAAS 4; CANR 6, 32, 64; DLB 122; DLBY 82; HW 1, 2; INT CANR-6

Redcam, Tom 1870-1933 .... **TCLC 25**

Reddin, Keith .... **CLC 67**

Redgrove, Peter (William) 1932- ..**CLC 6, 41**
See also CA 1-4R; CANR 3, 39, 77; DLB 40

Redmon, Anne .... **CLC 22**
See also Nightingale, Anne Redmon
See also DLBY 86

Reed, Eliot
See Ambler, Eric

Reed, Ishmael 1938-**CLC 2, 3, 5, 6, 13, 32, 60; BLC 3; DAM MULT**
See also BW 2, 3; CA 21-24R; CANR 25, 48, 74; DLB 2, 5, 33, 169; DLBD 8; MTCW 1, 2

Reed, John (Silas) 1887-1920 .... **TCLC 9**
See also CA 106

Reed, Lou .... **CLC 21**
See also Firbank, Louis

Reeve, Clara 1729-1807 .... **NCLC 19**
See also DLB 39

Reich, Wilhelm 1897-1957 .... **TCLC 57**

Reid, Christopher (John) 1949- .... **CLC 33**
See also CA 140; DLB 40

Reid, Desmond
See Moorcock, Michael (John)

Reid Banks, Lynne 1929-
See Banks, Lynne Reid
See also CA 1-4R; CANR 6, 22, 38; CLR 24; JRDA; MAICYA; SATA 22, 75

Reilly, William K.
See Creasey, John

Reiner, Max
See Caldwell, (Janet Miriam) Taylor (Holland)

Reis, Ricardo
See Pessoa, Fernando (Antonio Nogueira)

Remarque, Erich Maria 1898-1970 **CLC 21; DA; DAB; DAC; DAM MST, NOV**
See also AAYA 27; CA 77-80; 29-32R; DLB 56; MTCW 1, 2

Remington, Frederic 1861-1909 .... **TCLC 89**
See also CA 108; 169; DLB 12, 186, 188; SATA 41

Remizov, A.
See Remizov, Aleksei (Mikhailovich)

Remizov, A. M.
See Remizov, Aleksei (Mikhailovich)

Remizov, Aleksei (Mikhailovich) 1877-1957 **TCLC 27**
See also CA 125; 133

Renan, Joseph Ernest 1823-1892 ..**NCLC 26**

Renard, Jules 1864-1910 .... **TCLC 17**
See also CA 117

Renault, Mary .... **CLC 3, 11, 17**
See also Challans, Mary
See also DLBY 83; MTCW 2

Rendell, Ruth (Barbara) 1930- . **CLC 28, 48; DAM POP**

See also Vine, Barbara
See also CA 109; CANR 32, 52, 74; DLB 87; INT CANR-32; MTCW 1, 2

Renoir, Jean 1894-1979 .... **CLC 20**
See also CA 129; 85-88

Resnais, Alain 1922- .... **CLC 16**

Reverdy, Pierre 1889-1960 .... **CLC 53**
See also CA 97-100; 89-92

Rexroth, Kenneth 1905-1982**CLC 1, 2, 6, 11, 22, 49; 112; DAM POET; PC 20**
See also CA 5-8R; 107; CANR 14, 34, 63; CDALB 1941-1968; DLB 16, 48, 165,212; DLBY 82; INT CANR-14; MTCW 1, 2

Reyes, Alfonso 1889-1959**TCLC 33; HLCS 2**
See also CA 131; HW 1

Reyes y Basoalto, Ricardo Eliecer Neftali
See Neruda, Pablo

Reymont, Wladyslaw (Stanislaw) 1868(?)-1925 **TCLC 5**
See also CA 104

Reynolds, Jonathan 1942- .... **CLC 6, 38**
See also CA 65-68; CANR 28

Reynolds, Joshua 1723-1792 .... **LC 15**
See also DLB 104

Reynolds, Michael Shane 1937- .... **CLC 44**
See also CA 65-68; CANR 9

Reznikoff, Charles 1894-1976 .... **CLC 9**
See also CA 33-36; 61-64; CAP 2; DLB 28, 45

Rezzori (d'Arezzo), Gregor von 1914-1998 **CLC 25**
See also CA 122; 136; 167

Rhine, Richard
See Silverstein, Alvin

Rhodes, Eugene Manlove 1869-1934**TCLC 53**

Rhodius, Apollonius c. 3rd cent. B.C.- **C M L C 28**
See also DLB 176

R'hoone
See Balzac, Honore de

Rhys, Jean 1890(?)-1979 **CLC 2, 4, 6, 14, 19, 51; DAM NOV; SSC 21**
See also CA 25-28R; 85-88; CANR 35, 62; CDBLB 1945-1960; DLB 36, 117, 162; MTCW 1, 2

Ribeiro, Darcy 1922-1997 .... **CLC 34**
See also CA 33-36R; 156

Ribeiro, Joao Ubaldo (Osorio Pimentel) 1941- **CLC 10, 67**
See also CA 81-84

Ribman, Ronald (Burt) 1932- .... **CLC 7**
See also CA 21-24R; CANR 46, 80

Ricci, Nino 1959- .... **CLC 70**
See also CA 137

Rice, Anne 1941- .... **CLC 41; DAM POP**
See also AAYA 9; BEST 89:2; CA 65-68; CANR 12, 36, 53, 74; MTCW 2

Rice, Elmer (Leopold) 1892-1967 **CLC 7, 49; DAM DRAM**
See also CA 21-22; 25-28R; CAP 2; DLB 4, 7; MTCW 1, 2

Rice, Tim(othy Miles Bindon) 1944- **CLC 21**
See also CA 103; CANR 46

Rich, Adrienne (Cecile) 1929-**CLC 3, 6, 7, 11, 18, 36, 73, 76; DAM POET; PC 5**
See also CA 9-12R; CANR 20, 53, 74; CDALBS; DLB 5, 67; MTCW 1, 2

Rich, Barbara
See Graves, Robert (von Ranke)

Rich, Robert
See Trumbo, Dalton

Richard, Keith .... **CLC 17**
See also Richards, Keith

Richards, David Adams 1950- **CLC 59; DAC**

See also DLB 146

Rolvaag, O(le) E(dvart)
See Roelvaag, O(le) E(dvart)

Romain Arnaud, Saint
See Aragon, Louis

Romains, Jules 1885-1972 .... **CLC 7**
See also CA 85-88; CANR 34; DLB 65; MTCW 1

Romero, Jose Ruben 1890-1952 .... **TCLC 14**
See also CA 114; 131; HW 1

Ronsard, Pierre de 1524-1585 .. **LC 6; PC 11**

Rooke, Leon 1934- .. **CLC 25, 34; DAM POP**
See also CA 25-28R; CANR 23, 53

Roosevelt, Franklin Delano 1882-1945 **T C L C 93**
See also CA 116; 173

Roosevelt, Theodore 1858-1919 ..... **TCLC 69**
See also CA 115; 170; DLB 47, 186

Roper, William 1498-1578 .... **LC 10**

Roquelaure, A. N.
See Rice, Anne

Rosa, Joao Guimaraes 1908-1967 .. **CLC 23; HLCS 1**
See also CA 89-92; DLB 113

Rose, Wendy 1948- **CLC 85; DAM MULT; PC 13**
See also CA 53-56; CANR 5, 51; DLB 175; NNAL; SATA 12

Rosen, R. D.
See Rosen, Richard (Dean)

Rosen, Richard (Dean) 1949- .... **CLC 39**
See also CA 77-80; CANR 62; INT CANR-30

Rosenberg, Isaac 1890-1918 .... **TCLC 12**
See also CA 107; DLB 20

Rosenblatt, Joe .... **CLC 15**
See also Rosenblatt, Joseph

Rosenblatt, Joseph 1933-
See Rosenblatt, Joe
See also CA 89-92; INT 89-92

Rosenfeld, Samuel
See Tzara, Tristan

Rosenstock, Sami
See Tzara, Tristan

Rosenstock, Samuel
See Tzara, Tristan

Rosenthal, M(acha) L(ouis) 1917-1996 . **C L C 28**
See also CA 1-4R; 152; CAAS 6; CANR 4, 51; DLB 5; SATA 59

Ross, Barnaby
See Dannay, Frederic

Ross, Bernard L.
See Follett, Ken(neth Martin)

Ross, J. H.
See Lawrence, T(homas) E(dward)

Ross, John Hume
See Lawrence, T(homas) E(dward)

Ross, Martin
See Martin, Violet Florence
See also DLB 135

Ross, (James) Sinclair 1908-1996 ... **CLC 13; DAC; DAM MST; SSC 24**
See also CA 73-76; CANR 81; DLB 88

Rossetti, Christina (Georgina) 1830-1894 **NCLC 2, 50, 66; DA; DAB; DAC; DAM MST, POET; PC 7; WLC**
See also DLB 35, 163; MAICYA; SATA 20

Rossetti, Dante Gabriel 1828-1882 . **NCLC 4, 77; DA; DAB; DAC; DAM MST, POET; WLC**
See also CDBLB 1832-1890; DLB 35

Rossner, Judith (Perelman) 1935- **CLC 6, 9, 29**
See also AITN 2; BEST 90:3; CA 17-20R;

CANR 18, 51, 73; DLB 6; INT CANR-18; MTCW 1, 2

Rostand, Edmond (Eugene Alexis) 1868-1918 **TCLC 6, 37; DA; DAB; DAC; DAM DRAM, MST; DC 10**
See also CA 104; 126; DLB 192; MTCW 1

Roth, Henry 1906-1995 ..... **CLC 2, 6, 11, 104**
See also CA 11-12; 149; CANR 38, 63; CAP 1; DLB 28; MTCW 1, 2

Roth, Philip (Milton) 1933- **CLC 1, 2, 3, 4, 6, 9, 15, 22, 31, 47, 66, 86, 119; DA; DAB; DAC; DAM MST, NOV, POP; SSC 26; WLC**
See also BEST 90:3; CA 1-4R; CANR 1, 22, 36, 55; CDALB 1968-1988; DLB 2, 28, 173; DLBY 82; MTCW 1, 2

Rothenberg, Jerome 1931- .... **CLC 6, 57**
See also CA 45-48; CANR 1; DLB 5, 193

Roumain, Jacques (Jean Baptiste) 1907-1944 **TCLC 19; BLC 3; DAM MULT**
See also BW 1; CA 117; 125

Rourke, Constance (Mayfield) 1885-1941 **TCLC 12**
See also CA 107; YABC 1

Rousseau, Jean-Baptiste 1671-1741 ...... **LC 9**

Rousseau, Jean-Jacques 1712-1778 **LC 14, 36; DA; DAB; DAC; DAM MST; WLC**

Roussel, Raymond 1877-1933 .... **TCLC 20**
See also CA 117

Rovit, Earl (Herbert) 1927- .... **CLC 7**
See also CA 5-8R; CANR 12

Rowe, Elizabeth Singer 1674-1737 ...... **LC 44**
See also DLB 39, 95

Rowe, Nicholas 1674-1718 .... **LC 8**
See also DLB 84

Rowley, Ames Dorrance
See Lovecraft, H(oward) P(hillips)

Rowson, Susanna Haswell 1762(?)-1824 **NCLC 5, 69**
See also DLB 37, 200

Roy, Arundhati 1960(?)- .... **CLC 109**
See also CA 163; DLBY 97

Roy, Gabrielle 1909-1983 **CLC 10, 14; DAB; DAC; DAM MST**
See also CA 53-56; 110; CANR 5, 61; DLB 68; MTCW 1; SATA 104

Royko, Mike 1932-1997 .... **CLC 109**
See also CA 89-92; 157; CANR 26

Rozewicz, Tadeusz 1921- .. **CLC 9, 23; DAM POET**
See also CA 108; CANR 36, 66; MTCW 1, 2

Ruark, Gibbons 1941- .... **CLC 3**
See also CA 33-36R; CAAS 23; CANR 14, 31, 57; DLB 120

Rubens, Bernice (Ruth) 1923- .... **CLC 19, 31**
See also CA 25-28R; CANR 33, 65; DLB 14, 207; MTCW 1

Rubin, Harold
See Robbins, Harold

Rudkin, (James) David 1936- .... **CLC 14**
See also CA 89-92; DLB 13

Rudnik, Raphael 1933- .... **CLC 7**
See also CA 29-32R

Ruffian, M.
See Hasek, Jaroslav (Matej Frantisek)

Ruiz, Jose Martinez .... **CLC 11**
See also Martinez Ruiz, Jose

Rukeyser, Muriel 1913-1980 **CLC 6, 10, 15, 27; DAM POET; PC 12**
See also CA 5-8R; 93-96; CANR 26, 60; DLB 48; MTCW 1, 2; SATA-Obit 22

Rule, Jane (Vance) 1931- .... **CLC 27**
See also CA 25-28R; CAAS 18; CANR 12; DLB 60

Rulfo, Juan 1918-1986 ...... **CLC 8, 80; DAM MULT; HLC 2; SSC 25**
See also CA 85-88; 118; CANR 26; DLB 113; HW 1, 2; MTCW 1, 2

Rumi, Jalal al-Din 1297-1373 .... **CMLC 20**

Runeberg, Johan 1804-1877 .... **NCLC 41**

Runyon, (Alfred) Damon 1884(?)-1946 **T C L C 10**
See also CA 107; 165; DLB 11, 86, 171; MTCW 2

Rush, Norman 1933- .... **CLC 44**
See also CA 121; 126; INT 126

Rushdie, (Ahmed) Salman 1947- **CLC 23, 31, 55, 100; DAB; DAC; DAM MST, NOV, POP; WLCS**
See also BEST 89:3; CA 108; 111; CANR 33, 56; DLB 194; INT 111; MTCW 1, 2

Rushforth, Peter (Scott) 1945- .... **CLC 19**
See also CA 101

Ruskin, John 1819-1900 .... **TCLC 63**
See also CA 114; 129; CDBLB 1832-1890; DLB 55, 163, 190; SATA 24

Russ, Joanna 1937- .... **CLC 15**
See also CANR 11, 31, 65; DLB 8; MTCW 1

Russell, George William 1867-1935
See Baker, Jean H.
See also CA 104; 153; CDBLB 1890-1914; DAM POET

Russell, (Henry) Ken(neth Alfred) 1927- **C L C 16**
See also CA 105

Russell, William Martin 1947- .... **CLC 60**
See also CA 164

Rutherford, Mark .... **TCLC 25**
See also White, William Hale
See also DLB 18

Ruyslinck, Ward 1929- .... **CLC 14**
See also Belser, Reimond Karel Maria de

Ryan, Cornelius (John) 1920-1974 ..... **CLC 7**
See also CA 69-72; 53-56; CANR 38

Ryan, Michael 1946- .... **CLC 65**
See also CA 49-52; DLBY 82

Ryan, Tim
See Dent, Lester

Rybakov, Anatoli (Naumovich) 1911-1998 **CLC 23, 53**
See also CA 126; 135; 172; SATA 79; SATA-Obit 108

Ryder, Jonathan
See Ludlum, Robert

Ryga, George 1932-1987 **CLC 14; DAC; DAM MST**
See also CA 101; 124; CANR 43; DLB 60

S. H.
See Hartmann, Sadakichi

S. S.
See Sassoon, Siegfried (Lorraine)

Saba, Umberto 1883-1957 .... **TCLC 33**
See also CA 144; CANR 79; DLB 114

Sabatini, Rafael 1875-1950 .... **TCLC 47**
See also CA 162

Sabato, Ernesto (R.) 1911- **CLC 10, 23; DAM MULT; HLC 2**
See also CA 97-100; CANR 32, 65; DLB 145; HW 1, 2; MTCW 1, 2

Sa-Carniero, Mario de 1890-1916 . **TCLC 83**

Sacastru, Martin
See Bioy Casares, Adolfo

Sacastru, Martin
See Bioy Casares, Adolfo

Sacher-Masoch, Leopold von 1836(?)-1895 **NCLC 31**

Sachs, Marilyn (Stickle) 1927- .... **CLC 35**

See also AAYA 2; CA 17-20R; CANR 13, 47;
CLR 2; JRDA; MAICYA; SAAS 2; SATA 3,
68

Sachs, Nelly 1891-1970 .... **CLC 14, 98**
See also CA 17-18; 25-28R; CAP 2; MTCW 2

Sackler, Howard (Oliver) 1929-1982 **CLC 14**
See also CA 61-64; 108; CANR 30; DLB 7

Sacks, Oliver (Wolf) 1933- .... **CLC 67**
See also CA 53-56; CANR 28, 50, 76; INT
CANR-28; MTCW 1, 2

Sadakichi
See Hartmann, Sadakichi

Sade, Donatien Alphonse Francois, Comte de
1740-1814 .... **NCLC 47**

Sadoff, Ira 1945- .... **CLC 9**
See also CA 53-56; CANR 5, 21; DLB 120

Saetone
See Camus, Albert

Safire, William 1929- .... **CLC 10**
See also CA 17-20R; CANR 31, 54

Sagan, Carl (Edward) 1934-1996 **CLC 30, 112**
See also AAYA 2; CA 25-28R; 155; CANR 11,
36, 74; MTCW 1, 2; SATA 58; SATA-Obit
94

Sagan, Francoise .... **CLC 3, 6, 9, 17, 36**
See also Quoirez, Francoise
See also DLB 83; MTCW 2

Sahgal, Nayantara (Pandit) 1927- .... **CLC 41**
See also CA 9-12R; CANR 11

Saint, H(arry) F. 1941- .... **CLC 50**
See also CA 127

St. Aubin de Teran, Lisa 1953-
See Teran, Lisa St. Aubin de
See also CA 118; 126; INT 126

Saint Birgitta of Sweden c. 1303-1373 **CMLC
24**

Sainte-Beuve, Charles Augustin 1804-1869
NCLC 5

**Saint-Exupery, Antoine (Jean Baptiste Marie
Roger) de** 1900-1944 **TCLC 2, 56; DAM
NOV; WLC**
See also CA 108; 132; CLR 10; DLB 72;
MAICYA; MTCW 1, 2; SATA 20

St. John, David
See Hunt, E(verette) Howard, (Jr.)

Saint-John Perse
See Leger, (Marie-Rene Auguste) Alexis Saint-
Leger

Saintsbury, George (Edward Bateman) 1845-
1933 .... **TCLC 31**
See also CA 160; DLB 57, 149

Sait Faik .... **TCLC 23**
See also Abasiyanik, Sait Faik

Saki .... **TCLC 3; SSC 12**
See also Munro, H(ector) H(ugh)
See also MTCW 2

Sala, George Augustus .... **NCLC 46**

Salama, Hannu 1936- .... **CLC 18**

Salamanca, J(ack) R(ichard) 1922- **CLC 4, 15**
See also CA 25-28R

Salas, Floyd Francis 1931-
See also CA 119; CAAS 27; CANR 44, 75;
DAM MULT; DLB 82; HLC 2; HW 1, 2;
MTCW 2

Sale, J. Kirkpatrick
See Sale, Kirkpatrick

Sale, Kirkpatrick 1937- .... **CLC 68**
See also CA 13-16R; CANR 10

Salinas, Luis Omar 1937- ...... **CLC 90; DAM
MULT; HLC 2**
See also CA 131; CANR 81; DLB 82; HW 1, 2

Salinas (y Serrano), Pedro 1891(?)-1951
TCLC 17

See also CA 117; DLB 134

Salinger, J(erome) D(avid) 1919- **CLC 1, 3, 8,
12, 55, 56; DA; DAB; DAC; DAM MST,
NOV; POP; SSC 2, 28; WLC**
See also AAYA 2; CA 5-8R; CANR 39; CDALB
1941-1968; CLR 18; DLB 2, 102, 173;
MAICYA; MTCW 1, 2; SATA 67

Salisbury, John
See Caute, (John) David

Salter, James 1925- .... **CLC 7, 52, 59**
See also CA 73-76; DLB 130

Saltus, Edgar (Everton) 1855-1921 . **TCLC 8**
See also CA 105; DLB 202

Saltykov, Mikhail Evgrafovich 1826-1889
NCLC 16

Samarakis, Antonis 1919- .... **CLC 5**
See also CA 25-28R; CAAS 16; CANR 36

Sanchez, Florencio 1875-1910 .... **TCLC 37**
See also CA 153; HW 1

Sanchez, Luis Rafael 1936- .... **CLC 23**
See also CA 128; DLB 145; HW 1

Sanchez, Sonia 1934- .... **CLC 5, 116; BLC 3;
DAM MULT; PC 9**
See also BW 2, 3; CA 33-36R; CANR 24, 49,
74; CLR 18; DLB 41; DLBD 8; MAICYA;
MTCW 1, 2; SATA 22

Sand, George 1804-1876 **NCLC 2, 42, 57; DA;
DAB; DAC; DAM MST, NOV; WLC**
See also DLB 119, 192

Sandburg, Carl (August) 1878-1967 **CLC 1, 4,
10, 15, 35; DA; DAB; DAC; DAM MST,
POET; PC 2; WLC**
See also AAYA 24; CA 5-8R; 25-28R; CANR
35; CDALB 1865-1917; DLB 17, 54;
MAICYA; MTCW 1, 2; SATA 8

Sandburg, Charles
See Sandburg, Carl (August)

Sandburg, Charles A.
See Sandburg, Carl (August)

Sanders, (James) Ed(ward) 1939- .. **CLC 53;
DAM POET**
See also CA 13-16R; CAAS 21; CANR 13, 44,
78; DLB 16

Sanders, Lawrence 1920-1998 **CLC 41; DAM
POP**
See also BEST 89:4; CA 81-84; 165; CANR
33, 62; MTCW 1

Sanders, Noah
See Blount, Roy (Alton), Jr.

Sanders, Winston P.
See Anderson, Poul (William)

Sandoz, Mari(e Susette) 1896-1966 .. **CLC 28**
See also CA 1-4R; 25-28R; CANR 17, 64; DLB
9, 212; MTCW 1, 2; SATA 5

Saner, Reg(inald Anthony) 1931- .... **CLC 9**
See also CA 65-68

Sankara 788-820 .... **CMLC 32**

Sannazaro, Jacopo 1456(?)-1530 .... **LC 8**

Sansom, William 1912-1976 **CLC 2, 6; DAM
NOV; SSC 21**
See also CA 5-8R; 65-68; CANR 42; DLB 139;
MTCW 1

Santayana, George 1863-1952 .... **TCLC 40**
See also CA 115; DLB 54, 71; DLBD 13

Santiago, Danny .... **CLC 33**
See also James, Daniel (Lewis)
See also DLB 122

Santmyer, Helen Hoover 1895-1986 . **CLC 33**
See also CA 1-4R; 118; CANR 15, 33; DLBY
84; MTCW 1

Santoka, Taneda 1882-1940 .... **TCLC 72**

Santos, Bienvenido N(uqui) 1911-1996 . **C L C
22; DAM MULT**

See also CA 101; 151; CANR 19, 46

Sapper .... **TCLC 44**
See also McNeile, Herman Cyril

Sapphire
See Sapphire, Brenda

Sapphire, Brenda 1950- .... **CLC 99**

Sappho fl. 6th cent. B.C.- ...... **CMLC 3; DAM
POET; PC 5**
See also DLB 176

Saramago, Jose 1922- ...... **CLC 119; HLCS 1**
See also CA 153

Sarduy, Severo 1937-1993 **CLC 6, 97; HLCS 1**
See also CA 89-92; 142; CANR 58, 81; DLB
113; HW 1, 2

Sargeson, Frank 1903-1982 .... **CLC 31**
See also CA 25-28R; 106; CANR 38, 79

Sarmiento, Domingo Faustino 1811-1888
See also HLCS 2

Sarmiento, Felix Ruben Garcia
See Dario, Ruben

Saro-Wiwa, Ken(ule Beeson) 1941-1995 **C L C
114**
See also BW 2; CA 142; 150; CANR 60; DLB
157

Saroyan, William 1908-1981 **CLC 1, 8, 10, 29,
34, 56; DA; DAB; DAC; DAM DRAM,
MST, NOV; SSC 21; WLC**
See also CA 5-8R; 103; CANR 30; CDALBS;
DLB 7, 9, 86; DLBY 81; MTCW 1, 2; SATA
23; SATA-Obit 24

Sarraute, Nathalie 1900- **CLC 1, 2, 4, 8, 10, 31,
80**
See also CA 9-12R; CANR 23, 66; DLB 83;
MTCW 1, 2

Sarton, (Eleanor) May 1912-1995 **CLC 4, 14,
49, 91; DAM POET**
See also CA 1-4R; 149; CANR 1, 34, 55; DLB
48; DLBY 81; INT CANR-34; MTCW 1, 2;
SATA 36; SATA-Obit 86

Sartre, Jean-Paul 1905-1980 **CLC 1, 4, 7, 9, 13,
18, 24, 44, 50, 52; DA; DAB; DAC; DAM
DRAM, MST, NOV; DC 3; SSC 32; WLC**
See also CA 9-12R; 97-100; CANR 21; DLB
72; MTCW 1, 2

Sassoon, Siegfried (Lorraine) 1886-1967 **C L C
36; DAB; DAM MST, NOV, POET; PC 12**
See also CA 104; 25-28R; CANR 36; DLB 20,
191; DLBD 18; MTCW 1, 2

Satterfield, Charles
See Pohl, Frederik

Saul, John (W. III) 1942- **CLC 46; DAM NOV,
POP**
See also AAYA 10; BEST 90:4; CA 81-84;
CANR 16, 40, 81; SATA 98

Saunders, Caleb
See Heinlein, Robert A(nson)

Saura (Atares), Carlos 1932- .... **CLC 20**
See also CA 114; 131; CANR 79; HW 1

Sauser-Hall, Frederic 1887-1961 ...... **CLC 18**
See also Cendrars, Blaise
See also CA 102; 93-96; CANR 36, 62; MTCW
1

Saussure, Ferdinand de 1857-1913 **TCLC 49**

Savage, Catharine
See Brosman, Catharine Savage

Savage, Thomas 1915- .... **CLC 40**
See also CA 126; 132; CAAS 15; INT 132

Savan, Glenn 19(?)- .... **CLC 50**

Sayers, Dorothy L(eigh) 1893-1957 **TCLC 2,
15; DAM POP**
See also CA 104; 119; CANR 60; CDBLB 1914-
1945; DLB 10, 36, 77, 100; MTCW 1, 2

Sayers, Valerie 1952- .... **CLC 50, 122**

Sierra, Gregorio Martinez
See Martinez Sierra, Gregorio
Sierra, Maria (de la O'LeJarraga) Martinez
See Martinez Sierra, Maria (de la O'LeJarraga)
Sigal, Clancy 1926- .... **CLC 7**
See also CA 1-4R
Sigourney, Lydia Howard (Huntley) 1791-1865
NCLC 21
See also DLB 1, 42, 73
Siguenza y Gongora, Carlos de 1645-1700**L C
8; HLCS 2**
Sigurjonsson, Johann 1880-1919 ... **TCLC 27**
See also CA 170
Sikelianos, Angelos 1884-1951 .... **TCLC 39**
Silkin, Jon 1930- .... **CLC 2, 6, 43**
See also CA 5-8R; CAAS 5; DLB 27
Silko, Leslie (Marmon) 1948-**CLC 23, 74, 114;
DA; DAC; DAM MST, MULT, POP;
WLCS**
See also AAYA 14; CA 115; 122; CANR 45,
65; DLB 143, 175; MTCW 2; NNAL
Sillanpaa, Frans Eemil 1888-1964 ... **CLC 19**
See also CA 129; 93-96; MTCW 1
Sillitoe, Alan 1928- ... **CLC 1, 3, 6, 10, 19, 57**
See also AITN 1; CA 9-12R; CAAS 2; CANR
8, 26, 55; CDBLB 1960 to Present; DLB 14,
139; MTCW 1, 2; SATA 61
Silone, Ignazio 1900-1978 .... **CLC 4**
See also CA 25-28; 81-84; CANR 34; CAP 2;
MTCW 1
Silver, Joan Micklin 1935- .... **CLC 20**
See also CA 114; 121; INT 121
Silver, Nicholas
See Faust, Frederick (Schiller)
Silverberg, Robert 1935- **CLC 7; DAM POP**
See also Jarvis, E. K.
See also AAYA 24; CA 1-4R; CAAS 3; CANR
1, 20, 36; CLR 59; DLB 8; INTCANR-20;
MAICYA; MTCW 1, 2; SATA 13, 91; SATA-
Essay 104
Silverstein, Alvin 1933- .... **CLC 17**
See also CA 49-52; CANR 2; CLR 25; JRDA;
MAICYA; SATA 8, 69
Silverstein, Virginia B(arbara Opshelor) 1937-
CLC 17
See also CA 49-52; CANR 2; CLR 25; JRDA;
MAICYA; SATA 8, 69
Sim, Georges
See Simenon, Georges (Jacques Christian)
Simak, Clifford D(onald) 1904-1988**CLC 1, 55**
See also CA 1-4R; 125; CANR 1, 35; DLB 8;
MTCW 1; SATA-Obit 56
Simenon, Georges (Jacques Christian) 1903-
1989 .. **CLC 1, 2, 3, 8, 18, 47; DAM POP**
See also CA 85-88; 129; CANR 35; DLB 72;
DLBY 89; MTCW 1, 2
Simic, Charles 1938- .... **CLC 6, 9, 22, 49, 68;
DAM POET**
See also CA 29-32R; CAAS 4; CANR 12, 33,
52, 61; DLB 105; MTCW 2
Simmel, Georg 1858-1918 .... **TCLC 64**
See also CA 157
Simmons, Charles (Paul) 1924- .... **CLC 57**
See also CA 89-92; INT 89-92
Simmons, Dan 1948- ..... **CLC 44; DAM POP**
See also AAYA 16; CA 138; CANR 53, 81
Simmons, James (Stewart Alexander) 1933-
CLC 43
See also CA 105; CAAS 21; DLB 40
Simms, William Gilmore 1806-1870 **NCLC 3**
See also DLB 3, 30, 59, 73
Simon, Carly 1945- .... **CLC 26**
See also CA 105

Simon, Claude 1913-1984 .. **CLC 4, 9, 15, 39;
DAM NOV**
See also CA 89-92; CANR 33; DLB 83; MTCW
1
Simon, (Marvin) Neil 1927-**CLC 6, 11, 31, 39,
70; DAM DRAM**
See also AITN 1; CA 21-24R; CANR 26, 54;
DLB 7; MTCW 1, 2
Simon, Paul (Frederick) 1941(?)- ..... **CLC 17**
See also CA 116; 153
Simonon, Paul 1956(?)- .... **CLC 30**
Simpson, Harriette
See Arnow, Harriette (Louisa) Simpson
Simpson, Louis (Aston Marantz) 1923-**CLC 4,
7, 9, 32; DAM POET**
See also CA 1-4R; CAAS 4; CANR 1, 61; DLB
5; MTCW 1, 2
Simpson, Mona (Elizabeth) 1957- .... **CLC 44**
See also CA 122; 135; CANR 68
Simpson, N(orman) F(rederick) 1919-**CLC 29**
See also CA 13-16R; DLB 13
Sinclair, Andrew (Annandale) 1935-. **CLC 2,
14**
See also CA 9-12R; CAAS 5; CANR 14, 38;
DLB 14; MTCW 1
Sinclair, Emil
See Hesse, Hermann
Sinclair, Iain 1943- .... **CLC 76**
See also CA 132; CANR 81
Sinclair, Iain MacGregor
See Sinclair, Iain
Sinclair, Irene
See Griffith, D(avid Lewelyn) W(ark)
Sinclair, Mary Amelia St. Clair 1865(?)-1946
See Sinclair, May
See also CA 104
Sinclair, May 1863-1946 .... **TCLC 3, 11**
See also Sinclair, Mary Amelia St. Clair
See also CA 166; DLB 36, 135
Sinclair, Roy
See Griffith, D(avid Lewelyn) W(ark)
Sinclair, Upton (Beall) 1878-1968 **CLC 1, 11,
15, 63; DA; DAB; DAC; DAM MST, NOV;
WLC**
See also CA 5-8R; 25-28R; CANR 7; CDALB
1929-1941; DLB 9; INT CANR-7; MTCW
1, 2; SATA 9
Singer, Isaac
See Singer, Isaac Bashevis
Singer, Isaac Bashevis 1904-1991**CLC 1, 3, 6,
9, 11, 15, 23, 38, 69, 111; DA; DAB; DAC;
DAM MST, NOV; SSC 3; WLC**
See also AITN 1, 2; CA 1-4R; 134; CANR 1,
39; CDALB 1941-1968; CLR 1; DLB 6, 28,
52; DLBY 91; JRDA; MAICYA; MTCW 1,
2; SATA 3, 27; SATA-Obit 68
Singer, Israel Joshua 1893-1944 .... **TCLC 33**
See also CA 169
Singh, Khushwant 1915- .... **CLC 11**
See also CA 9-12R; CAAS 9; CANR 6
Singleton, Ann
See Benedict, Ruth (Fulton)
Sinjohn, John
See Galsworthy, John
Sinyavsky, Andrei (Donatevich) 1925-1997
CLC 8
See also CA 85-88; 159
Sirin, V.
See Nabokov, Vladimir (Vladimirovich)
Sissman, L(ouis) E(dward) 1928-1976**CLC 9,
18**
See also CA 21-24R; 65-68; CANR 13; DLB 5
Sisson, C(harles) H(ubert) 1914- .... **CLC 8**

See also CA 1-4R; CAAS 3; CANR 3, 48; DLB
27
Sitwell, Dame Edith 1887-1964 **CLC 2, 9, 67;
DAM POET; PC 3**
See also CA 9-12R; CANR 35; CDBLB 1945-
1960; DLB 20; MTCW 1, 2
Siwaarmill, H. P.
See Sharp, William
Sjoewall, Maj 1935- .... **CLC 7**
See also CA 65-68; CANR 73
Sjowall, Maj
See Sjoewall, Maj
Skelton, John 1463-1529 .... **PC 25**
Skelton, Robin 1925-1997 .... **CLC 13**
See also AITN 2; CA 5-8R; 160; CAAS 5;
CANR 28; DLB 27, 53
Skolimowski, Jerzy 1938- .... **CLC 20**
See also CA 128
Skram, Amalie (Bertha) 1847-1905**TCLC 25**
See also CA 165
Skvorecky, Josef (Vaclav) 1924- **CLC 15, 39,
69; DAC; DAM NOV**
See also CA 61-64; CAAS 1; CANR 10, 34,
63; MTCW 1, 2
Slade, Bernard .... **CLC 11, 46**
See also Newbound, Bernard Slade
See also CAAS 9; DLB 53
Slaughter, Carolyn 1946- .... **CLC 56**
See also CA 85-88
Slaughter, Frank G(ill) 1908- .... **CLC 29**
See also AITN 2; CA 5-8R; CANR 5; INT
CANR-5
Slavitt, David R(ytman) 1935- ...... **CLC 5, 14**
See also CA 21-24R; CAAS 3; CANR 41; DLB
5, 6
Slesinger, Tess 1905-1945 .... **TCLC 10**
See also CA 107; DLB 102
Slessor, Kenneth 1901-1971 .... **CLC 14**
See also CA 102; 89-92
Slowacki, Juliusz 1809-1849 .... **NCLC 15**
Smart, Christopher 1722-1771 .. **LC 3; DAM
POET; PC 13**
See also DLB 109
Smart, Elizabeth 1913-1986 .... **CLC 54**
See also CA 81-84; 118; DLB 88
Smiley, Jane (Graves) 1949-**CLC 53, 76; DAM
POP**
See also CA 104; CANR 30, 50, 74; INT CANR-
30
Smith, A(rthur) J(ames) M(arshall) 1902-1980
CLC 15; DAC
See also CA 1-4R; 102; CANR 4; DLB 88
Smith, Adam 1723-1790 .... **LC 36**
See also DLB 104
Smith, Alexander 1829-1867 .... **NCLC 59**
See also DLB 32, 55
Smith, Anna Deavere 1950- .... **CLC 86**
See also CA 133
Smith, Betty (Wehner) 1896-1972 .... **CLC 19**
See also CA 5-8R; 33-36R; DLBY 82; SATA 6
Smith, Charlotte (Turner) 1749-1806 **N C L C
23**
See also DLB 39, 109
Smith, Clark Ashton 1893-1961 .... **CLC 43**
See also CA 143; CANR 81; MTCW 2
Smith, Dave .... **CLC 22, 42**
See also Smith, David (Jeddie)
See also CAAS 7; DLB 5
Smith, David (Jeddie) 1942-
See Smith, Dave
See also CA 49-52; CANR 1, 59; DAM POET
Smith, Florence Margaret 1902-1971
See Smith, Stevie

See also CA 17-18; 29-32R; CANR 35; CAP 2; DAM POET; MTCW 1, 2

Smith, Iain Crichton 1928-1998 .... **CLC 64**
See also CA 21-24R; 171; DLB 40, 139

Smith, John 1580(?)-1631 .... **LC 9**
See also DLB 24, 30

Smith, Johnston
See Crane, Stephen (Townley)

Smith, Joseph, Jr. 1805-1844 .... **NCLC 53**

Smith, Lee 1944- .... **CLC 25, 73**
See also CA 114; 119; CANR 46; DLB 143; DLBY 83; INT 119

Smith, Martin
See Smith, Martin Cruz

Smith, Martin Cruz 1942- ..... **CLC 25; DAM MULT, POP**
See also BEST 89:4; CA 85-88; CANR 6, 23, 43, 65; INT CANR-23; MTCW 2; NNAL

Smith, Mary-Ann Tirone 1944- .... **CLC 39**
See also CA 118; 136

Smith, Patti 1946- .... **CLC 12**
See also CA 93-96; CANR 63

Smith, Pauline (Urmson) 1882-1959**TCLC 25**

Smith, Rosamond
See Oates, Joyce Carol

Smith, Sheila Kaye
See Kaye-Smith, Sheila

Smith, Stevie .... **CLC 3, 8, 25, 44; PC 12**
See also Smith, Florence Margaret
See also DLB 20; MTCW 2

Smith, Wilbur (Addison) 1933- .... **CLC 33**
See also CA 13-16R; CANR 7, 46, 66; MTCW 1, 2

Smith, William Jay 1918- .... **CLC 6**
See also CA 5-8R; CANR 44; DLB 5; MAICYA; SAAS 22; SATA 2, 68

Smith, Woodrow Wilson
See Kuttner, Henry

Smolenskin, Peretz 1842-1885 .... **NCLC 30**

Smollett, Tobias (George) 1721-1771**LC 2, 46**
See also CDBLB 1660-1789; DLB 39, 104

Snodgrass, W(illiam) D(e Witt) 1926-**CLC 2, 6, 10, 18, 68; DAM POET**
See also CA 1-4R; CANR 6, 36, 65; DLB 5; MTCW 1, 2

Snow, C(harles) P(ercy) 1905-1980**CLC 1, 4, 6, 9, 13, 19; DAM NOV**
See also CA 5-8R; 101; CANR 28; CDBLB 1945-1960; DLB 15, 77; DLBD 17; MTCW 1, 2

Snow, Frances Compton
See Adams, Henry (Brooks)

Snyder, Gary (Sherman) 1930-**CLC 1, 2, 5, 9, 32, 120; DAM POET; PC 21**
See also CA 17-20R; CANR 30, 60; DLB 5, 16, 165, 212; MTCW 2

Snyder, Zilpha Keatley 1927- .... **CLC 17**
See also AAYA 15; CA 9-12R; CANR 38; CLR 31; JRDA; MAICYA; SAAS 2; SATA 1, 28, 75

Soares, Bernardo
See Pessoa, Fernando (Antonio Nogueira)

Sobh, A.
See Shamlu, Ahmad

Sobol, Joshua .... **CLC 60**

Socrates 469B.C.-399B.C. .... **CMLC 27**

Soderberg, Hjalmar 1869-1941 ..... **TCLC 39**

Sodergran, Edith (Irene)
See Soedergran, Edith (Irene)

Soedergran, Edith (Irene) 1892-1923 **T C L C 31**

Softly, Edgar
See Lovecraft, H(oward) P(hillips)

Softly, Edward
See Lovecraft, H(oward) P(hillips)

Sokolov, Raymond 1941- .... **CLC 7**
See also CA 85-88

Solo, Jay
See Ellison, Harlan (Jay)

Sologub, Fyodor .... **TCLC 9**
See also Teternikov, Fyodor Kuzmich

Solomons, Ikey Esquir
See Thackeray, William Makepeace

Solomos, Dionysios 1798-1857 .... **NCLC 15**

Solwoska, Mara
See French, Marilyn

Solzhenitsyn, Aleksandr I(sayevich) 1918-**CLC 1, 2, 4, 7, 9, 10, 18, 26, 34, 78; DA; DAB; DAC; DAM MST, NOV; SSC 32; WLC**
See also AITN 1; CA 69-72; CANR 40, 65; MTCW 1, 2

Somers, Jane
See Lessing, Doris (May)

Somerville, Edith 1858-1949 .... **TCLC 51**
See also DLB 135

Somerville & Ross
See Martin, Violet Florence; Somerville, Edith

Sommer, Scott 1951- .... **CLC 25**
See also CA 106

Sondheim, Stephen (Joshua) 1930- .**CLC 30, 39; DAM DRAM**
See also AAYA 11; CA 103; CANR 47, 68

Song, Cathy 1955- .... **PC 21**
See also CA 154; DLB 169

Sontag, Susan 1933-**CLC 1, 2, 10, 13, 31, 105; DAM POP**
See also CA 17-20R; CANR 25, 51, 74; DLB 2, 67; MTCW 1, 2

Sophocles 496(?)B.C.-406(?)B.C. ... **CMLC 2; DA; DAB; DAC; DAM DRAM, MST; DC 1; WLCS**
See also DLB 176

Sordello 1189-1269 .... **CMLC 15**

Sorel, Georges 1847-1922 .... **TCLC 91**
See also CA 118

Sorel, Julia
See Drexler, Rosalyn

Sorrentino, Gilbert 1929-**CLC 3, 7, 14, 22, 40**
See also CA 77-80; CANR 14, 33; DLB 5, 173; DLBY 80; INT CANR-14

Soto, Gary 1952- **CLC 32, 80; DAM MULT; HLC 2; PC 28**
See also AAYA 10; CA 119; 125; CANR 50, 74; CLR 38; DLB 82; HW 1, 2; INT 125; JRDA; MTCW 2; SATA 80

Soupault, Philippe 1897-1990 .... **CLC 68**
See also CA 116; 147; 131

Souster, (Holmes) Raymond 1921-**CLC 5, 14; DAC; DAM POET**
See also CA 13-16R; CAAS 14; CANR 13, 29, 53; DLB 88; SATA 63

Southern, Terry 1924(?)-1995 .... **CLC 7**
See also CA 1-4R; 150; CANR 1, 55; DLB 2

Southey, Robert 1774-1843 .... **NCLC 8**
See also DLB 93, 107, 142; SATA 54

Southworth, Emma Dorothy Eliza Nevitte 1819-1899 .... **NCLC 26**

Souza, Ernest
See Scott, Evelyn

Soyinka, Wole 1934-**CLC 3, 5, 14, 36, 44; BLC 3; DA; DAB; DAC; DAM DRAM, MST, MULT; DC 2; WLC**
See also BW 2, 3; CA 13-16R; CANR 27, 39, 82; DLB 125; MTCW 1, 2

Spackman, W(illiam) M(ode) 1905-1990**C L C 46**
See also CA 81-84; 132

Spacks, Barry (Bernard) 1931- .... **CLC 14**
See also CA 154; CANR 33; DLB 105

Spanidou, Irini 1946- .... **CLC 44**

Spark, Muriel (Sarah) 1918-**CLC 2, 3, 5, 8, 13, 18, 40, 94; DAB; DAC; DAM MST, NOV; SSC 10**
See also CA 5-8R; CANR 12, 36, 76; CDBLB 1945-1960; DLB 15, 139; INTCANR-12; MTCW 1, 2

Spaulding, Douglas
See Bradbury, Ray (Douglas)

Spaulding, Leonard
See Bradbury, Ray (Douglas)

Spence, J. A. D.
See Eliot, T(homas) S(tearns)

Spencer, Elizabeth 1921- .... **CLC 22**
See also CA 13-16R; CANR 32, 65; DLB 6; MTCW 1; SATA 14

Spencer, Leonard G.
See Silverberg, Robert

Spencer, Scott 1945- .... **CLC 30**
See also CA 113; CANR 51; DLBY 86

Spender, Stephen (Harold) 1909-1995**CLC 1, 2, 5, 10, 41, 91; DAM POET**
See also CA 9-12R; 149; CANR 31, 54; CDBLB 1945-1960; DLB 20; MTCW 1, 2

Spengler, Oswald (Arnold Gottfried) 1880-1936 **TCLC 25**
See also CA 118

Spenser, Edmund 1552(?)-1599**LC 5, 39; DA; DAB; DAC; DAM MST, POET; PC 8; WLC**
See also CDBLB Before 1660; DLB 167

Spicer, Jack 1925-1965 **CLC 8, 18, 72; DAM POET**
See also CA 85-88; DLB 5, 16, 193

Spiegelman, Art 1948- .... **CLC 76**
See also AAYA 10; CA 125; CANR 41, 55, 74; MTCW 2; SATA 109

Spielberg, Peter 1929- .... **CLC 6**
See also CA 5-8R; CANR 4, 48; DLBY 81

Spielberg, Steven 1947- .... **CLC 20**
See also AAYA 8, 24; CA 77-80; CANR 32; SATA 32

Spillane, Frank Morrison 1918-
See Spillane, Mickey
See also CA 25-28R; CANR 28, 63; MTCW 1, 2; SATA 66

Spillane, Mickey .... **CLC 3, 13**
See also Spillane, Frank Morrison
See also MTCW 2

Spinoza, Benedictus de 1632-1677 .... **LC 9**

Spinrad, Norman (Richard) 1940- ... **CLC 46**
See also CA 37-40R; CAAS 19; CANR 20; DLB 8; INT CANR-20

Spitteler, Carl (Friedrich Georg) 1845-1924 **TCLC 12**
See also CA 109; DLB 129

Spivack, Kathleen (Romola Drucker) 1938-**CLC 6**
See also CA 49-52

Spoto, Donald 1941- .... **CLC 39**
See also CA 65-68; CANR 11, 57

Springsteen, Bruce (F.) 1949- .... **CLC 17**
See also CA 111

Spurling, Hilary 1940- .... **CLC 34**
See also CA 104; CANR 25, 52

Spyker, John Howland
See Elman, Richard (Martin)

Squires, (James) Radcliffe 1917-1993**CLC 51**
See also CA 1-4R; 140; CANR 6, 21

Srivastava, Dhanpat Rai 1880(?)-1936
See Premchand
See also CA 118
Stacy, Donald
See Pohl, Frederik
Stael, Germaine de 1766-1817
See Stael-Holstein, Anne Louise Germaine Necker Baronn
See also DLB 119
Stael-Holstein, Anne Louise Germaine Necker Baronn 1766-1817 .... **NCLC 3**
See also Stael, Germaine de
See also DLB 192
Stafford, Jean 1915-1979 **CLC 4, 7, 19, 68; SSC 26**
See also CA 1-4R; 85-88; CANR 3, 65; DLB 2, 173; MTCW 1, 2; SATA-Obit 22
Stafford, William (Edgar) 1914-1993 **CLC 4, 7, 29; DAM POET**
See also CA 5-8R; 142; CAAS 3; CANR 5, 22; DLB 5, 206; INT CANR-22
Stagnelius, Eric Johan 1793-1823 . **NCLC 61**
Staines, Trevor
See Brunner, John (Kilian Houston)
Stairs, Gordon
See Austin, Mary (Hunter)
Stairs, Gordon
See Austin, Mary (Hunter)
Stalin, Joseph 1879-1953 .... **TCLC 92**
Stannard, Martin 1947- .... **CLC 44**
See also CA 142; DLB 155
Stanton, Elizabeth Cady 1815-1902 **TCLC 73**
See also CA 171; DLB 79
Stanton, Maura 1946- .... **CLC 9**
See also CA 89-92; CANR 15; DLB 120
Stanton, Schuyler
See Baum, L(yman) Frank
Stapledon, (William) Olaf 1886-1950 **T C L C 22**
See also CA 111; 162; DLB 15
Starbuck, George (Edwin) 1931-1996 **CLC 53; DAM POET**
See also CA 21-24R; 153; CANR 23
Stark, Richard
See Westlake, Donald E(dwin)
Staunton, Schuyler
See Baum, L(yman) Frank
Stead, Christina (Ellen) 1902-1983 **CLC 2, 5, 8; 32, 80**
See also CA 13-16R; 109; CANR 33, 40; MTCW 1, 2
Stead, William Thomas 1849-1912 **TCLC 48**
See also CA 167
Steele, Richard 1672-1729 .... **LC 18**
See also CDBLB 1660-1789; DLB 84, 101
Steele, Timothy (Reid) 1948- .... **CLC 45**
See also CA 93-96; CANR 16, 50; DLB 120
Steffens, (Joseph) Lincoln 1866-1936 **T C L C 20**
See also CA 117
Stegner, Wallace (Earle) 1909-1993 **CLC 9, 49, 81; DAM NOV; SSC 27**
See also AITN 1; BEST 90:3; CA 1-4R; 141; CAAS 9; CANR 1, 21, 46; DLB 9, 206; DLBY 93; MTCW 1, 2
Stein, Gertrude 1874-1946 **TCLC 1, 6, 28, 48; DA; DAB; DAC; DAM MST, NOV, POET; PC 18; WLC**
See also CA 104; 132; CDALB 1917-1929; DLB 4, 54, 86; DLBD 15; MTCW 1, 2
Steinbeck, John (Ernst) 1902-1968 **CLC 1, 5, 9, 13, 21, 34, 45, 75; DA; DAB; DAC; DAM DRAM, MST, NOV; SSC 11; WLC**

See also AAYA 12; CA 1-4R; 25-28R; CANR 1, 35; CDALB 1929-1941; DLB 7, 9, 212; DLBD 2; MTCW 1, 2; SATA 9
Steinem, Gloria 1934- .... **CLC 63**
See also CA 53-56; CANR 28, 51; MTCW 1, 2
Steiner, George 1929- ... **CLC 24; DAM NOV**
See also CA 73-76; CANR 31, 67; DLB 67; MTCW 1, 2; SATA 62
Steiner, K. Leslie
See Delany, Samuel R(ay, Jr.)
Steiner, Rudolf 1861-1925 .... **TCLC 13**
See also CA 107
Stendhal 1783-1842 **NCLC 23, 46; DA; DAB; DAC; DAM MST, NOV; SSC 27; WLC**
See also DLB 119
Stephen, Adeline Virginia
See Woolf, (Adeline) Virginia
Stephen, Sir Leslie 1832-1904 .... **TCLC 23**
See also CA 123; DLB 57, 144, 190
Stephen, Sir Leslie
See Stephen, Sir Leslie
Stephen, Virginia
See Woolf, (Adeline) Virginia
Stephens, James 1882(?)-1950 .... **TCLC 4**
See also CA 104; DLB 19, 153, 162
Stephens, Reed
See Donaldson, Stephen R.
Steptoe, Lydia
See Barnes, Djuna
Sterchi, Beat 1949- .... **CLC 65**
Sterling, Brett
See Bradbury, Ray (Douglas); Hamilton, Edmond
Sterling, Bruce 1954- .... **CLC 72**
See also CA 119; CANR 44
Sterling, George 1869-1926 .... **TCLC 20**
See also CA 117; 165; DLB 54
Stern, Gerald 1925- .... **CLC 40, 100**
See also CA 81-84; CANR 28; DLB 105
Stern, Richard (Gustave) 1928- .... **CLC 4, 39**
See also CA 1-4R; CANR 1, 25, 52; DLBY 87; INT CANR-25
Sternberg, Josef von 1894-1969 .... **CLC 20**
See also CA 81-84
Sterne, Laurence 1713-1768 ... **LC 2, 48; DA; DAB; DAC; DAM MST, NOV; WLC**
See also CDBLB 1660-1789; DLB 39
Sternheim, (William Adolf) Carl 1878-1942 **TCLC 8**
See also CA 105; DLB 56, 118
Stevens, Mark 1951- .... **CLC 34**
See also CA 122
Stevens, Wallace 1879-1955 **TCLC 3, 12, 45; DA; DAB; DAC; DAM MST, POET; PC 6; WLC**
See also CA 104; 124; CDALB 1929-1941; DLB 54; MTCW 1, 2
Stevenson, Anne (Katharine) 1933- **CLC 7, 33**
See also CA 17-20R; CAAS 9; CANR 9, 33; DLB 40; MTCW 1
Stevenson, Robert Louis (Balfour) 1850-1894 **NCLC 5, 14, 63; DA; DAB; DAC; DAM MST, NOV; SSC 11; WLC**
See also AAYA 24; CDBLB 1890-1914; CLR 10, 11; DLB 18, 57, 141, 156, 174; DLBD 13; JRDA; MAICYA; SATA 100; YABC 2
Stewart, J(ohn) I(nnes) M(ackintosh) 1906-1994 .... **CLC 7, 14, 32**
See also CA 85-88; 147; CAAS 3; CANR 47; MTCW 1, 2
Stewart, Mary (Florence Elinor) 1916- **CLC 7, 35, 117; DAB**
See also AAYA 29; CA 1-4R; CANR 1, 59;

SATA 12
Stewart, Mary Rainbow
See Stewart, Mary (Florence Elinor)
Stifle, June
See Campbell, Maria
Stifter, Adalbert 1805-1868 **NCLC 41; SSC 28**
See also DLB 133
Still, James 1906- .... **CLC 49**
See also CA 65-68; CAAS 17; CANR 10, 26; DLB 9; SATA 29
Sting 1951-
See Sumner, Gordon Matthew
See also CA 167
Stirling, Arthur
See Sinclair, Upton (Beall)
Stitt, Milan 1941- .... **CLC 29**
See also CA 69-72
Stockton, Francis Richard 1834-1902
See Stockton, Frank R.
See also CA 108; 137; MAICYA; SATA 44
Stockton, Frank R. .... **TCLC 47**
See also Stockton, Francis Richard
See also DLB 42, 74; DLBD 13; SATA-Brief 32
Stoddard, Charles
See Kuttner, Henry
Stoker, Abraham 1847-1912
See Stoker, Bram
See also CA 105; 150; DA; DAC; DAM MST, NOV; SATA 29
Stoker, Bram 1847-1912 **TCLC 8; DAB; WLC**
See also Stoker, Abraham
See also AAYA 23; CDBLB 1890-1914; DLB 36, 70, 178
Stolz, Mary (Slattery) 1920- .... **CLC 12**
See also AAYA 8; AITN 1; CA 5-8R; CANR 13, 41; JRDA; MAICYA; SAAS 3; SATA 10, 71
Stone, Irving 1903-1989 .. **CLC 7; DAM POP**
See also AITN 1; CA 1-4R; 129; CAAS 3; CANR 1, 23; INT CANR-23; MTCW 1, 2; SATA 3; SATA-Obit 64
Stone, Oliver (William) 1946- .... **CLC 73**
See also AAYA 15; CA 110; CANR 55
Stone, Robert (Anthony) 1937- **CLC 5, 23, 42**
See also CA 85-88; CANR 23, 66; DLB 152; INT CANR-23; MTCW 1
Stone, Zachary
See Follett, Ken(neth Martin)
Stoppard, Tom 1937- **CLC 1, 3, 4, 5, 8, 15, 29, 34, 63, 91; DA; DAB; DAC; DAM DRAM, MST, DC 6; WLC**
See also CA 81-84; CANR 39, 67; CDBLB 1960 to Present; DLB 13; DLBY 85; MTCW 1, 2
Storey, David (Malcolm) 1933- **CLC 2, 4, 5, 8; DAM DRAM**
See also CA 81-84; CANR 36; DLB 13, 14, 207; MTCW 1
Storm, Hyemeyohsts 1935- ...... **CLC 3; DAM MULT**
See also CA 81-84; CANR 45; NNAL
Storm, Theodor 1817-1888 .... **SSC 27**
Storm, (Hans) Theodor (Woldsen) 1817-1888 **NCLC 1; SSC 27**
See also DLB 129
Storni, Alfonsina 1892-1938 . **TCLC 5; DAM MULT; HLC 2**
See also CA 104; 131; HW 1
Stoughton, William 1631-1701 .... **LC 38**
See also DLB 24
Stout, Rex (Todhunter) 1886-1975 ..... **CLC 3**
See also AITN 2; CA 61-64; CANR 71

Wells, H(erbert) G(eorge) 1866-1946**TCLC 6, 12, 19; DA; DAB; DAC; DAM MST, NOV; SSC 6; WLC**
See also AAYA 18; CA 110; 121; CDBLB 1914-1945; DLB 34, 70, 156, 178; MTCW 1, 2; SATA 20

Wells, Rosemary 1943- .... **CLC 12**
See also AAYA 13; CA 85-88; CANR 48; CLR 16; MAICYA; SAAS 1; SATA 18, 69

Welty, Eudora 1909- **CLC 1, 2, 5, 14, 22, 33, 105; DA; DAB; DAC; DAM MST, NOV; SSC 1, 27; WLC**
See also CA 9-12R; CABS 1; CANR 32, 65; CDALB 1941-1968; DLB 2, 102, 143; DLBD 12; DLBY 87; MTCW 1, 2

Wen I-to 1899-1946 .... **TCLC 28**

Wentworth, Robert
See Hamilton, Edmond

Werfel, Franz (Viktor) 1890-1945 ... **TCLC 8**
See also CA 104; 161; DLB 81, 124

Wergeland, Henrik Arnold 1808-1845**N C L C 5**

Wersba, Barbara 1932- .... **CLC 30**
See also AAYA 2, 30; CA 29-32R; CANR 16, 38; CLR 3; DLB 52; JRDA; MAICYA; SAAS 2; SATA 1, 58; SATA-Essay 103

Wertmueller, Lina 1928- .... **CLC 16**
See also CA 97-100; CANR 39, 78

Wescott, Glenway 1901-1987**CLC 13; SSC 35**
See also CA 13-16R; 121; CANR 23, 70; DLB 4, 9, 102

Wesker, Arnold 1932- .... **CLC 3, 5, 42; DAB; DAM DRAM**
See also CA 1-4R; CAAS 7; CANR 1, 33; CDBLB 1960 to Present; DLB 13; MTCW 1

Wesley, Richard (Errol) 1945- .... **CLC 7**
See also BW 1; CA 57-60; CANR 27; DLB 38

Wessel, Johan Herman 1742-1785......... **LC 7**

West, Anthony (Panther) 1914-1987 **CLC 50**
See also CA 45-48; 124; CANR 3, 19; DLB 15

West, C. P.
See Wodehouse, P(elham) G(renville)

West, (Mary) Jessamyn 1902-1984**CLC 7, 17**
See also CA 9-12R; 112; CANR 27; DLB 6; DLBY 84; MTCW 1, 2; SATA-Obit 37

West, Morris L(anglo) 1916- .... **CLC 6, 33**
See also CA 5-8R; CANR 24, 49, 64; MTCW 1, 2

West, Nathanael 1903-1940 **TCLC 1, 14, 44; SSC 16**
See also CA 104; 125; CDALB 1929-1941; DLB 4, 9, 28; MTCW 1, 2

West, Owen
See Koontz, Dean R(ay)

West, Paul 1930- .... **CLC 7, 14, 96**
See also CA 13-16R; CAAS 7; CANR 22, 53, 76; DLB 14; INT CANR-22; MTCW 2

West, Rebecca 1892-1983 ... **CLC 7, 9, 31, 50**
See also CA 5-8R; 109; CANR 19; DLB 36; DLBY 83; MTCW 1, 2

Westall, Robert (Atkinson) 1929-1993**CLC 17**
See also AAYA 12; CA 69-72; 141; CANR 18, 68; CLR 13; JRDA; MAICYA; SAAS 2; SATA 23, 69; SATA-Obit 75

Westermarck, Edward 1862-1939 . **TCLC 87**

Westlake, Donald E(dwin) 1933- **CLC 7, 33; DAM POP**
See also CA 17-20R; CAAS 13; CANR 16, 44, 65; INT CANR-16; MTCW 2

Westmacott, Mary
See Christie, Agatha (Mary Clarissa)

Weston, Allen
See Norton, Andre

Wetcheek, J. L.
See Feuchtwanger, Lion

Wetering, Janwillem van de
See van de Wetering, Janwillem

Wetherald, Agnes Ethelwyn 1857-1940**T C L C 81**
See also DLB 99

Wetherell, Elizabeth
See Warner, Susan (Bogert)

Whale, James 1889-1957 .... **TCLC 63**

Whalen, Philip 1923- .... **CLC 6, 29**
See also CA 9-12R; CANR 5, 39; DLB 16

Wharton, Edith (Newbold Jones) 1862-1937 **TCLC 3, 9, 27, 53; DA; DAB; DAC; DAM MST, NOV; SSC 6; WLC**
See also AAYA 25; CA 104; 132; CDALB 1865-1917; DLB 4, 9, 12, 78, 189; DLBD 13; MTCW 1, 2

Wharton, James
See Mencken, H(enry) L(ouis)

Wharton, William (a pseudonym)CLC 18, 37
See also CA 93-96; DLBY 80; INT 93-96

Wheatley (Peters), Phillis 1754(?)-1784**LC 3, 50; BLC 3; DA; DAC; DAM MST, MULT, POET; PC 3; WLC**
See also CDALB 1640-1865; DLB 31, 50

Wheelock, John Hall 1886-1978 .... **CLC 14**
See also CA 13-16R; 77-80; CANR 14; DLB 45

White, E(lwyn) B(rooks) 1899-1985 **CLC 10, 34, 39; DAM POP**
See also AITN 2; CA 13-16R; 116; CANR 16, 37; CDALBS; CLR 1, 21; DLB 11, 22; MAICYA; MTCW 1, 2; SATA 2, 29, 100; SATA-Obit 44

White, Edmund (Valentine III) 1940-**CLC 27, 110; DAM POP**
See also AAYA 7; CA 45-48; CANR 3, 19, 36, 62; MTCW 1, 2

White, Patrick (Victor Martindale) 1912-1990 **CLC 3, 4, 5, 7, 9, 18, 65, 69**
See also CA 81-84; 132; CANR 43; MTCW 1

White, Phyllis Dorothy James 1920-
See James, P. D.
See also CA 21-24R; CANR 17, 43, 65; DAM POP; MTCW 1, 2

White, T(erence) H(anbury) 1906-1964 **C L C 30**
See also AAYA 22; CA 73-76; CANR 37; DLB 160; JRDA; MAICYA; SATA 12

White, Terence de Vere 1912-1994 ... **CLC 49**
See also CA 49-52; 145; CANR 3

White, Walter
See White, Walter F(rancis)
See also BLC; DAM MULT

White, Walter F(rancis) 1893-1955 **TCLC 15**
See also White, Walter
See also BW 1; CA 115; 124; DLB 51

White, William Hale 1831-1913
See Rutherford, Mark
See also CA 121

Whitehead, E(dward) A(nthony) 1933-**CLC 5**
See also CA 65-68; CANR 58

Whitemore, Hugh (John) 1936- .... **CLC 37**
See also CA 132; CANR 77; INT 132

Whitman, Sarah Helen (Power) 1803-1878 **NCLC 19**
See also DLB 1

Whitman, Walt(er) 1819-1892 . **NCLC 4, 31; DA; DAB; DAC; DAM MST, POET; PC 3; WLC**
See also CDALB 1640-1865; DLB 3, 64; SATA 20

Whitney, Phyllis A(yame) 1903- ..... **CLC 42; DAM POP**
See also AITN 2; BEST 90:3; CA 1-4R; CANR 3, 25, 38, 60; CLR 59; JRDA; MAICYA; MTCW 2; SATA 1, 30

Whittemore, (Edward) Reed (Jr.) 1919-**CLC 4**
See also CA 9-12R; CAAS 8; CANR 4; DLB 5

Whittier, John Greenleaf 1807-1892**NCLC 8, 59**
See also DLB 1

Whittlebot, Hernia
See Coward, Noel (Peirce)

Wicker, Thomas Grey 1926-
See Wicker, Tom
See also CA 65-68; CANR 21, 46

Wicker, Tom .... **CLC 7**
See also Wicker, Thomas Grey

Wideman, John Edgar 1941-**CLC 5, 34, 36, 67, 122; BLC 3; DAM MULT**
See also BW 2, 3; CA 85-88; CANR 14, 42, 67; DLB 33, 143; MTCW 2

Wiebe, Rudy (Henry) 1934- .. **CLC 6, 11, 14; DAC; DAM MST**
See also CA 37-40R; CANR 42, 67; DLB 60

Wieland, Christoph Martin 1733-1813**N C L C 17**
See also DLB 97

Wiene, Robert 1881-1938 .... **TCLC 56**

Wieners, John 1934- .... **CLC 7**
See also CA 13-16R; DLB 16

Wiesel, Elie(zer) 1928- **CLC 3, 5, 11, 37; DA; DAB; DAC; DAM MST, NOV; WLCS**
See also AAYA 7; AITN 1; CA 5-8R; CAAS 4; CANR 8, 40, 65; CDALBS; DLB 83; DLBY 87; INT CANR-8; MTCW 1, 2; SATA 56

Wiggins, Marianne 1947- .... **CLC 57**
See also BEST 89:3; CA 130; CANR 60

Wight, James Alfred 1916-1995
See Herriot, James
See also CA 77-80; SATA 55; SATA-Brief 44

Wilbur, Richard (Purdy) 1921-**CLC 3, 6, 9, 14, 53, 110; DA; DAB; DAC; DAM MST, POET**
See also CA 1-4R; CABS 2; CANR 2, 29, 76; CDALBS; DLB 5, 169; INT CANR-29; MTCW 1, 2; SATA 9, 108

Wild, Peter 1940- ....**CLC 14**
See also CA 37-40R; DLB 5

Wilde, Oscar 1854(?)-1900**TCLC 1, 8, 23, 41; DA; DAB; DAC; DAM DRAM, MST, NOV; SSC 11; WLC**
See also CA 104; 119; CDBLB 1890-1914; DLB 10, 19, 34, 57, 141, 156, 190; SATA 24

Wilder, Billy .... **CLC 20**
See also Wilder, Samuel
See also DLB 26

Wilder, Samuel 1906-
See Wilder, Billy
See also CA 89-92

Wilder, Thornton (Niven) 1897-1975**CLC 1, 5, 6, 10, 15, 35, 82; DA; DAB; DAC; DAM DRAM, MST, NOV; DC 1; WLC**
See also AAYA 29; AITN 2; CA 13-16R; 61-64; CANR 40; CDALBS; DLB 4, 7,9; DLBY 97; MTCW 1, 2

Wilding, Michael 1942- .... **CLC 73**
See also CA 104; CANR 24, 49

Wiley, Richard 1944- .... **CLC 44**
See also CA 121; 129; CANR 71

Wilhelm, Kate .... **CLC 7**
See also Wilhelm, Katie Gertrude
See also AAYA 20; CAAS 5; DLB 8; INT CANR-17

Zelazny, Roger (Joseph) 1937-1995 . **CLC 21**
See also AAYA 7; CA 21-24R; 148; CANR 26,
60; DLB 8; MTCW 1, 2; SATA 57; SATA-
Brief 39

Zhdanov, Andrei Alexandrovich 1896-1948
TCLC 18
See also CA 117; 167

Zhukovsky, Vasily (Andreevich) 1783-1852
NCLC 35
See also DLB 205

Ziegenhagen, Eric .... **CLC 55**

Zimmer, Jill Schary
See Robinson, Jill

Zimmerman, Robert
See Dylan, Bob

Zindel, Paul 1936-**CLC 6, 26; DA; DAB; DAC;**
DAM DRAM, MST, NOV; DC 5
See also AAYA 2; CA 73-76; CANR 31, 65;
CDALBS; CLR 3, 45; DLB 7, 52; JRDA;
MAICYA; MTCW 1, 2; SATA 16, 58, 102

Zinov'Ev, A. A.
See Zinoviev, Alexander (Aleksandrovich)

Zinoviev, Alexander (Aleksandrovich) 1922-
CLC 19
See also CA 116; 133; CAAS 10

Zoilus
See Lovecraft, H(oward) P(hillips)

Zola, Emile (Edouard Charles Antoine) 1840-
1902**TCLC 1, 6, 21, 41; DA; DAB; DAC;**
DAM MST, NOV; WLC
See also CA 104; 138; DLB 123

Zoline, Pamela 1941- .... **CLC 62**
See also CA 161

Zorrilla y Moral, Jose 1817-1893 .... **NCLC 6**

Zoshchenko, Mikhail (Mikhailovich) 1895-1958
TCLC 15; SSC 15
See also CA 115; 160

Zuckmayer, Carl 1896-1977 .... **CLC 18**
See also CA 69-72; DLB 56, 124

Zuk, Georges
See Skelton, Robin

Zukofsky, Louis 1904-1978**CLC 1, 2, 4, 7, 11,**
18; DAM POET; PC 11
See also CA 9-12R; 77-80; CANR 39; DLB 5,
165; MTCW 1

Zweig, Paul 1935-1984 .... **CLC 34, 42**
See also CA 85-88; 113

Zweig, Stefan 1881-1942 .... **TCLC 17**
See also CA 112; 170; DLB 81, 118

Zwingli, Huldreich 1484-1531 .... **LC 37**
See also DLB 179

Literary Criticism Series
Cumulative Topic Index

This index lists all topic entries in Gale's *Classical and Medieval Literature Criticism, Contemporary Literary Criticism, Literature Criticism from 1400 to 1800, Nineteenth-Century Literature Criticism,* and *Twentieth-Century Literary Criticism.*

Topic Index

Topic Index

Topic Index

Contemporary Literary Criticism
Cumulative Nationality Index

Nationality Index

Nationality Index

Nationality Index

Nationality Index

Nationality Index

Nationality Index

CLC-122 Title Index

ISBN 0-7876-3197-3

90000

9 780787 631970